Consumer Interest in Direct Marketing by Product Category

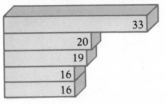

Most Popular Product Categories	Percentage of Consumers Who Prefer Buying Via Direct Marketing
Books, records, tapes	33
Casual clothing	20
Underwear, intimate apparel	19
Sports equipment	16
Small kitchen appliances	16

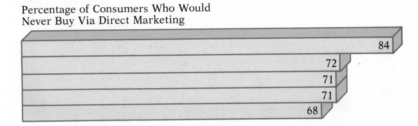

Least Popular Product Categories	Percentage of Consumers Who Would Never Buy Via Direct Marketing
Expensive jewelry	84
Expensive dresses	72
Major appliances	71
Woman's/man's suits	71
Shoes	68

Source: *Direct Marketing in the Year 2000* (New York: Yankelovich, Skelly and White/Clancy Shulman, Inc., 1987), p. 43.

Benefits of Point-of-Sales (POS) Systems to Discounters/ Mass Merchandisers, Department Stores, and Specialty Stores

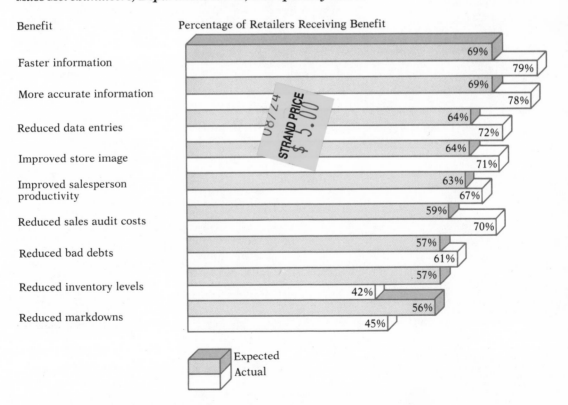

Benefit	Percentage of Retailers Receiving Benefit
Faster information	Expected 69% / Actual 79%
More accurate information	Expected 69% / Actual 78%
Reduced data entries	Expected 64% / Actual 72%
Improved store image	Expected 64% / Actual 71%
Improved salesperson productivity	Expected 63% / Actual 67%
Reduced sales audit costs	Expected 59% / Actual 70%
Reduced bad debts	Expected 57% / Actual 61%
Reduced inventory levels	Expected 57% / Actual 42%
Reduced markdowns	Expected 56% / Actual 45%

Expected
Actual

Source: Adapted by the authors from "NRMA's New POS Study," *Stores* (April 1987), p. 68.

Retail Management

A Strategic Approach

Retail 4th edition
Management

A Strategic Approach

Barry Berman □ Joel R. Evans
HOFSTRA UNIVERSITY   HOFSTRA UNIVERSITY

Macmillan Publishing Company

NEW YORK

Collier MacMillan Publishers

LONDON

Macmillan Publishing Company
866 Third Avenue, New York, New York 10022

Collier Macmillan Canada, Inc.

Library of Congress Cataloging in Publication Data
Berman, Barry.
    Retail management: a strategic approach / Barry Berman, Joel R.
  Evans.—4th ed.
      p.   cm.
    Includes indexes.
    ISBN 0-02-308641-6
    1. Retail trade—Management. I. Evans, Joel R. II. Title.
HF5429.B45 1989
658.8'7—dc19   88-18935
                                                                                                    CIP

Printing: 4 5 6 7 8   Year: 1 2 3 4 5 6 7 8

To Linda, Glenna, and Lisa
To Linda, Jennifer, and Stacey

Thank you for your continuing patience and understanding.

Preface

We are gratified by the continuing responses to this text, as evidenced by adoptions at over 400 colleges and universities. In this fourth edition, we have set out to retain the material and features most desired by professors and students, add new material and features requested by professors and students, keep the book as current as possible, and maintain the length of prior editions.

As in earlier editions, the concepts of a strategic approach and a retail strategy form the foundation of *Retail Management: A Strategic Approach,* 4th Edition. With a strategic approach, "the underlying principle is that a retail firm needs to plan for and adapt to a complex, changing environment. Both opportunities and threats must be considered." A retail strategy is "the overall plan that guides the firm. Such a strategy has an influence on the retailer's business activities and its response to market forces." The major objectives of our text are to enable the reader to become a good retail planner and decision maker and to help focus on change and adaptation to change.

The book is designed as a one-semester text for a beginning student of retailing. In many cases, such a student will have already been introduced to marketing principles. We strongly believe that retailing should be viewed as one form of marketing and not distinct from it.

These significant features have been retained from earlier editions of *Retail Management: A Strategic Approach:*

❑ Full coverage of all major retailing topics—including consumer behavior, marketing research, store location, service retailing, the retail audit, retail institutions, franchising, human resource management, computerization in retailing, and retailing in a changing environment.

❑ A decision-making orientation, with many flowcharts, figures, tables, and photos.

❑ A real-world approach that focuses on both small and large retail firms. Among the well-known retailers discussed in the text are Lands' End, McDonald's, 7-Eleven, Bloomingdale's, Toys "R" Us, Sears, The Limited, and Wal-Mart.

vii

❏ Thirty-four end-of-chapter cases involving a wide range of retailers and retail practices.

❏ Up-to-date information from such sources as *Advertising Age, Business Week, Chain Store Age Executive, Direct Marketing, Discount Store News, Forbes, Fortune, Journal of Retailing, National Retail Merchants Association, Progressive Grocer, Stores,* and *Wall Street Journal.*

❏ A convenient, one-semester format.

❏ Numerous questions at the end of each chapter·in the text.

❏ "How to Solve a Case Study," following Chapter 1 in the text.

❏ An appendix on franchising, following Chapter 3.

❏ A career orientation, with actual career ladders and a thorough discussion of ownership and employment alternatives.

❏ Three end-of-text appendixes: careers in retailing, firms with retailing positions for college graduates, and a glossary.

These new features have been added for *Retail Management: A Strategic Approach,* 4th Edition:

❏ A new, more visually attractive text design. The use of figures and photos has been greatly expanded. Color photos appear in numerous places throughout the text.

❏ A new organizational format. The text is now divided into eight parts, with part openers that provide overviews of the chapters in every section. Each part contains two to three related chapters; and the eight parts flow in a smooth strategically oriented manner. Some chapters have been repositioned to improve their placement in the text.

❏ A new chapter on operations management (Chapter 10).

❏ A new end-of-chapter appendix on direct marketing (following Chapter 4).

❏ Two "Retailing in Action" boxes in each chapter. These boxes further illustrate the concepts presented in the text by focusing on such real companies as Ben & Jerry's, Food Lion, Neiman-Marcus, Dunkin' Donuts, Service Merchandise, Auto Shack, Zayre's, Compact Disc Warehouse, and Piggly Wiggly.

❏ All new chapter-opening vignettes, based on real retail firms and situations.

❏ New or expanded coverage of such topics as channel of distribution relationships, competitive advantage, the hypermarket, consumer demographics, perceived risk by consumers, the data collection role of retailers, retail information systems, Huff's law of shopper attraction, Theory Z in personnel management, asset management, the strategic profit model, budgeting, cash flow, resource allocation, opportunity costs, productivity, store maintenance, inventory management, store security, insurance, crisis management, the battle of the brands, the profit-and-loss statement, direct product profitability (DPP), pricing alternatives for service retailers, and international retailing.

❏ All new or substantially revised chapter-ending cases.

❏ Eight comprehensive cases, one at the end of each part in the text. All of these cases are new to the fourth edition or substantially revised.

❏ More data on retailing opportunities and an assortment of career ladders in the text-ending Appendix A.

As mentioned, *Retail Management: A Strategic Approach* is divided into eight parts. Part One introduces the field of retailing, the basic principles of strategic planning, and the decisions to be made in owning/managing a retail business.

In Part Two, retail institutions are examined on the basis of ownership types as well as store-based, nonstore-based, and service versus goods strategy mixes. The wheel of retailing, scrambled merchandising, and the retail life cycle are also covered. Part Three focuses on selecting a target market and information-gathering methods, including discussions of the consumer decision process and the retailing information system. Part Four presents a four-step approach to location planning: trading area analysis, choosing the most desirable type of location, selecting a general locale, and deciding on a specific site.

Part Five discusses the elements involved in managing a retail business: the retail organization structure, human resource management, and operations management. Part Six concentrates on merchandise management (both the buying and handling of merchandise and the financial aspects of merchandising) and pricing, including the key internal and external factors in decision making. In Part Seven, various methods of communicating with customers are analyzed, with special attention to store image, atmosphere, and promotion techniques. Part Eight details three aspects of retailing that are crucial in anticipating, planning for, and responding to the future: integrating and controlling a retail strategy, service retailing, and the changing environment within which retailers operate.

At the end of the text, Appendix A describes various careers in retailing, Appendix B presents a listing of almost 170 potential retail-related employers, and Appendix C offers a 460-item glossary.

Two student supplements are available to accompany *Retail Management: A Strategic Approach*, 4th Edition:

❑ A comprehensive companion text (*Applying Retail Management: A Strategic Approach*, 4th Edition) that contains chapter objectives, key terms and concepts, readings and exercises on real-life companies and situations, chapter questions, and a complete appendix on retail mathematics (with 80 problems to be solved).

❑ A new computer diskette, containing retail management exercises that are keyed to each part of the text, is available to schools adopting the text. This user-friendly diskette brings more excitement to student learning of key retailing concepts and is personal computer-based.

A well-rounded teaching package is available for instructors. It includes a detailed instructor's manual, transparency masters, a large test bank, and the semi-annual *Retailing Update* newsletter. In addition, new to this edition full-color videos are available to adopters. These videos cover a broad spectrum of retailers and retailing practices. All of the instructional materials have been developed and written by the authors (except for the videos, which we personally selected).

Please feel free to send us comments regarding any aspect of *Retail Management* or its package: Barry Berman or Joel R. Evans, Department of Marketing and International Business, Hofstra University, Hempstead, N.Y., 11550. We promise to reply to any correspondence we receive.

B.B.
J.R.E.

Acknowledgments

Many people have assisted us in the preparation of this book, and to them we extend our warmest appreciation.

We thank these colleagues for contributing cases:

John I. Coppett, University of Houston—Clear Lake
Jack Gifford, Miami University of Ohio
Pat Gifford, Miami University of Ohio
Marvin A. Jolson, University of Maryland
John Roman, Rochester Institute of Technology
Franklin Rubenstein, Retail Management Consultant
Steven J. Shaw, University of South Carolina
Elaine Sherman, Hofstra University
William A. Staples, University of Houston—Clear Lake

We thank the following reviewers, who have reacted to this or earlier editions of the text. Each of these reviewers provided us with perceptive reviews that helped us crystallize our thoughts:

Larry Audler, University of New Orleans
Ramon Avila, Ball State University
Charlane Bomrad, Onondaga Community College
Stephen Batory, Bloomsburg University
Joseph Belonax, Western Michigan University
Ronald Bernard, Diablo Valley College
John J. Buckley, Orange County Community College
Joseph A. Davidson, Cuyahoga Community College
Peter T. Doukas, Westchester Community College
Jack D. Eure, Jr., Southwest Texas State University
Letty Fisher, Westchester Community College
Myron Gable, Shippensburg University
Linda L. Golden, University of Texas at Austin
Mary Higby, Eastern Michigan University
Marvin A. Jolson, University of Maryland

Ruth Keyes, SUNY College of Technology
J. Ford Laumer, Jr., Auburn University
Richard C. Leventhal, Metropolitan State College
John Lloyd, Monroe Community College
James O. McCann, Henry Ford Community College
Frank McDaniels, Delaware County Community College
Ronald Michman, Shippensburg University
Roy B. Payne, Purdue University
Curtis Reierson, Baylor University
Steven J. Shaw, University of South Carolina
Gladys S. Sherdell, Montgomery College
John E. Swan, University of Alabama in Birmingham
Lillian Werner, University of Minnesota
Kaylene Williams, University of Delaware
Terrell G. Williams, Utah State University

Special thanks and acknowledgment are due to Bill Oldsey and Dave Shafer, our fine Macmillan editors. We are also indebted to Edward Neve, Ann Berlin, Bob Doran, Leo Malek, Carrie O'Donnell, Bob Pirrung, and Andy Zutis of Macmillan; John C. Galloway, Jr., for his computer work; Sandra Cramer, our research assistant; and Linda Berman for compiling the index.

Barry Berman
Joel R. Evans
Hofstra University

Brief Contents

xiii

Contents

xv

**Part Two:
Situation
Analysis 63**

**Part Three:
Selecting a Target
Market and
Gathering
Information   141**

9   *Retail Organization and Human Resource
Management*

**Part Five:
Managing a
Retail
Business   275**

276

Part Six:
Merchandise
Management
and Pricing   345

PART ONE

An Overview of Strategic Retail Management

❑ *In Part One, the field of retailing, the basic principles of strategic planning, and the decisions made in owning/managing a retail business are introduced.*

❑ *Chapter 1 describes the framework of retailing, shows why retailing is an important field to study, and examines several of its special characteristics. The steps in strategic planning are noted and applied to three diverse firms. The elements of the retailing concept are presented. The focus and format of the text are detailed. At the end of the chapter, hints for solving case studies are offered.*

❑ *Chapter 2 shows the value of strategic planning for all kinds of retailers. Each aspect of the planning process is examined in depth: situation analysis, objectives, identifying consumers, overall strategy, specific activities, control, and feedback. The controllable and uncontrollable components of a retail strategy are highlighted. Strategic planning is viewed as a series of interrelated steps that are continuously reviewed.*

Chapter 1

An Introduction to Retailing

❑ **Chapter Objectives** ❑

1 To define retailing, demonstrate its importance, and note its special characteristics

2 To introduce the concept of strategic planning and apply it to retailing through several examples

3 To relate the marketing concept to retailing

4 To indicate the focus and format of the text

In 1938, William Dillard, then in his early twenties, borrowed $8,000 from his parents and opened a retail store in Nashville, Arkansas. Ten years later, Dillard sold that first store and bought a larger one in Texarcana, Arkansas. During 1960, he purchased the biggest store in Tyler, Texas. Today, Dillard's is a widely admired chain of 150 department stores located mostly in Sunbelt and Midwest states that generate $2.2 billion in annual sales.

The success and growth of Dillard's are based on the sound retailing practices that Bill Dillard still follows. He has a "passion for details" and a "vision for growth." On a regular basis, Dillard visits stores throughout the chain and talks with employees and customers. This enables him to monitor performance, communicate company policies, and anticipate future trends and potential prob-

lems. Dillard is a greater believer in planning and is willing to try out new ideas; suggestions are encouraged, not stifled.

Rather than going head-on with other major retailers, Dillard's usually locates stores in small- and medium-sized cities "that lack myriad competitors." It also buys out competitors that are not faring well (such as Macy's Midwest division and Stix, Baer & Fuller, a St. Louis, Missouri, chain) and refurbishes and reinvigorates them.

Dillard's has been an innovator with regard to computerization and automation. For example, it has invested $20 million in a centralized computer inventory system to link all its stores. This system reduces costs, coordinates shipments, improves relations with vendors (by providing them with better information), and monitors inventory turnover.

As a result, Dillard's has more money to spend on advertising and sales personnel (who can offer extra customer service).

Bill Dillard has a business philosophy that could be applied by every retailer and prospective retailer: "We believe that if you do the right thing, there's enough business for everyone."[1]

The Framework of Retailing

Retailing consists of those business activities involved in the sale of goods and services to consumers for their personal, family, or household use. It is the final stage in the distribution process.

Students are sometimes apt to think of retailing as including only the sale of tangible (physical) goods. However, it is important to realize that retailing also encompasses the sale of services. A service may be the shopper's primary purchase (insurance, airline ticket); or it may be part of the shopper's purchase of a good (delivery, warranty, credit).

Retailing does not have to involve the use of a store. Mail and telephone orders, direct selling to consumers in their homes, and vending machines all fit within the scope of retailing.

Lastly, retailing does not have to include a "retailer." Manufacturers, importers, nonprofit firms, and wholesalers are acting as retailers when they sell goods and/or services to final consumers. On the other hand, purchases made by manufacturers, wholesalers, and other organizations for their use in the organization or further resale are not part of retailing.

The color photo portfolios following page 8, and throughout the text, illustrate the stimulating and diverse nature of retailing and its associated activities.

Reasons for Studying Retailing

Among the reasons for studying the field of retailing are its impact on the economy, its functions in distribution, and its relationship with firms that sell goods and services to retailers for their resale or use. These factors are discussed in this section. A fourth, and quite important, element for students of retailing is the broad range of career opportunities, which are described separately in Appendix A at the end of the text.

The Impact of Retailing on the Economy

Retailing is a significant aspect of the U.S. economy. Both retail sales and employment are substantial contributors to total U.S. sales and employment. And trends in retail sales often mirror trends in the overall economy.

According to the U.S. Department of Commerce, 1986 retail store sales (including some mail-order sales by store retailers) were almost $1.5 trillion, double those in 1977. During 1986, telephone and mail-order sales by nonstore retailers, vending machines, and direct-to-home selling generated an additional $200 billion in revenues. Furthermore, personal consumption expenditures on financial, medical, legal, education, and other services account for another several hundred billion dollars in annual retail revenues.

Retailing is a major source of employment. According to the U.S. Department of Labor, about 18 million people were employed by traditional retailers in the United States during 1987. This figure understates the actual number of people working in retailing because it does not include several million persons employed by various service firms, seasonal employees, proprietors, or unreported employees in a family business or partnership. Leading retail employers are eating and drinking places, food stores, general merchandise stores, apparel and accessory stores, and furniture and home furnishings stores.

3

FIGURE 1-1
**The High Costs and Low Profits of
Retailing—Where the Typical $10
Spent in a Specialty Store Goes**

From another perspective—costs—retailing is a significant field of study. On the average, over 40 cents of every dollar spent in department or specialty stores and over 20 cents of every dollar spent in supermarkets go to the retailers as payment for the operating costs they incur and the activities they perform. These include store rent, point-of-sale displays, personnel compensation, advertising, and store maintenance. Only a small portion of each sales dollar is actually profit for the retailer. In 1986, the fifty largest U.S. retailers earned average after-tax profits amounting to 2.3 per cent of sales.[2] See Figure 1-1. A change in retail efficiency would therefore have a great impact on consumers and the economy. Price levels and product assortment are also affected by retailer competence.

Retail store sales from 1977 to 1986 are presented in Table 1-1. Overall retail store sales more than doubled between 1977 and 1986. Although this increase was impressive, it was only 10 per cent above the rate of inflation for the period. The sales of durable goods stores increased at a rate much higher than that for nondurable goods and service stores. For example, major purchases were particularly strong from 1983 to 1986 because of the favorable U.S. economy. Gasoline service stations had declining sales from 1981 to 1986 as a result of a drop in petroleum prices. Variety and liquor store sales rose slowly because of changing consumer shopping patterns and life-styles. For the same reason, shoe store sales rose a lot. Some other nondurable goods stores had limited growth because of intense competition and the resultant price cuts.

TABLE 1-1
Retail Store Sales by Kind of Business, 1977–1986
(Millions of Dollars)

Type of Retailing	1977	1978	1979	1980	1981	1982	1983	1984	1985	1986	Av. Yrly. Percentage Increase
All retail stores	725,220	807,426	900,558	962,816	1,047,573	1,075,679	1,174,298	1,293,062	1,379,621	1,454,411	8.1
Durable good stores, total	248,692	278,617	302,357	292,811	316,020	320,868	396,493	465,798	517,981	568,057	9.9
Automotive group	149,952	166,139	174,662	158,276	173,922	182,390	232,750	278,534	311,859	335,822	9.8
Furniture and appliance group	33,176	36,928	42,789	44,939	46,462	46,513	54,689	61,843	69,584	78,487	10.2
Lumber, building materials, and hardware group	33,214	38,592	44,320	43,683	44,800	42,544	59,669	69,488	75,556	88,093	12.1
Nondurable goods/services stores, total	476,528	528,809	598,201	670,005	731,553	754,811	777,805	827,264	861,640	886,354	7.2
General merchandise group	90,686	103,321	110,282	115,733	127,948	131,282	139,386	152,913	149,952	155,262	6.2
Department stores*	73,647	84,112	89,152	93,345	103,672	107,030	116,562	129,054	135,528	142,503	7.7
Variety stores	7,095	7,370	8,062	8,180	8,705	8,735	8,624	9,095	8,854	8,449	2.4
Apparel group	35,565	40,489	43,422	46,188	50,270	51,991	60,304	65,103	74,321	80,775	9.6
Men's and boys' wear stores	6,943	7,498	7,819	7,813	8,152	8,110	7,962	8,327	8,826	9,564	3.7
Women's apparel, accessory stores	13,458	15,740	16,707	17,184	18,553	19,288	24,484	27,094	30,901	33,899	10.4
Family and other apparel stores	8,055	8,311	8,785	9,796	10,682	10,830	15,435	16,597	16,781	17,836	9.8
Shoe stores	5,650	6,618	7,688	8,307	9,279	9,854	9,794	10,335	14,010	14,927	15.9
Gasoline service stations	56,468	60,648	75,325	97,434	108,231	104,633	98,862	99,464	101,266	86,618	5.7
Eating and drinking places	63,276	71,869	82,270	90,367	98,585	107,357	114,684	124,541	133,457	144,966	9.7
Food group	157,941	175,700	199,210	222,687	241,102	252,802	254,878	270,430	283,987	296,040	7.3
Drug and proprietary stores	23,196	25,378	28,173	30,613	33,593	35,849	40,050	43,174	46,191	49,316	8.8
Liquor stores	12,967	13,767	15,551	17,507	18,631	19,031	19,014	18,157	19,491	19,792	4.9

*Beginning in 1979, mail-order data are included in department store sales.

Source: Bureau of the Census, U.S. Department of Commerce; and authors' calculations.

TABLE 1-2
The Twenty-Five Largest Retailing Companies, 1986

1986 Rank	Company	Sales (thousands)	Net Income (thousands)*	Employees
1	Sears Roebuck	$ 44,281,500	$1,351,300	485,500
2	K mart	24,246,000	582,000	320,000
3	Safeway Stores	20,311,480	−14,260	172,412
4	Kroger	18,383,408	51,493	173,900
5	J.C. Penney	14,740,000	478,000	176,000
6	American Stores	14,021,484	144,000	129,000
7	Wal-Mart	11,909,076	450,086	141,000
8	Southland	11,081,835	200,445	67,200
9	Federated Department Stores	10,512,425	287,600	133,000
10	May Department Stores	10,376,000	381,000	151,700
11	Dayton Hudson	9,773,800	310,000	126,000
12	Lucky Stores	8,775,871	225,940	44,000
13	Winn-Dixie Stores	8,225,244	116,391	76,900
14	Great Atlantic & Pacific (A&P)	6,615,422	88,290	60,000
15	F.W. Woolworth	6,501,000	214,000	120,500
16	Supermarkets General	5,560,130	60,865	53,000
17	Albertson's	5,379,643	100,152	40,000
18	Zayre	5,350,638	88,974	63,500
19	Marriott	5,266,500	191,700	194,600
20	Melville	5,262,364	238,332	80,394
21	Allied Stores	5,025,000	−58,000	61,800
22	Montgomery Ward	4,383,000	110,000	56,300
23	McDonald's[†]	4,143,508	479,725	159,000
24	Carter Hawley Hale	4,089,794	4,214	46,000
25	Stop & Shop	4,033,843	38,400	46,000
		$268,248,965	$6,120,647	3,177,706

*After taxes.
[†]From company-owned outlets and real-estate holdings only.

Source: "The 50 Largest Retailing Companies," *Fortune* (June 8, 1987), pp. 210–211. Reprinted from the FORTUNE Directory by permission; © 1987 Time Inc. All rights reserved.

Table 1-2 shows the twenty-five largest retailers in the United States during 1986. These retailers accounted for over $268 billion in annual sales (about 18 per cent of total U.S. retail store sales) and employed almost 3.2 million workers. Their net income after taxes ranged from 11.6 per cent for McDonald's to −1.2 per cent for Allied Stores. Department stores and discount department stores (e.g., Sears, K mart, J.C. Penney), supermarkets (e.g., Safeway, Kroger), variety stores (e.g., Woolworth), and fast-food chains (e.g., McDonald's) are among the wide range of retail types represented in the table.

Retail Functions in Distribution

Retailing is the last stage in a **channel of distribution,** which comprises all of the businesses and people involved in the physical movement and transfer of ownership of goods and services from producer to consumer. A typical distribution channel is shown in Figure 1-2.

In a distribution channel, retailing plays an important role as an intermediary between manufacturers, wholesalers, and other suppliers and final consumers. The retailer collects an assortment of goods and services from various suppliers and offers them to customers. This procedure is called the **sorting process.**[3] To

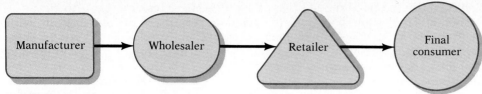

FIGURE 1-2
A Typical Channel of Distribution

maximize efficiency, many manufacturers (suppliers) would like to make one basic type of item and sell the entire inventory to as few buyers as possible. Yet, many customers want to choose from a variety of goods and services and purchase a limited quantity. Through the sorting process, the retailer bridges the gap between manufacturers (suppliers) and final consumers. See Figure 1-3.

A retailer satisfies manufacturers (suppliers) by buying their limited range of products in large quantities. In this way, each manufacturer (supplier) becomes more efficient. A retailer satisfies customers by offering an assortment of goods and services, collected from a number of suppliers, and by selling them in small quantities. Wide retail assortments enable customers to undertake one-stop shopping; and consumers are able to choose and buy the product version and quantity that they desire. The word *retailing* is actually based on this breaking-bulk func-

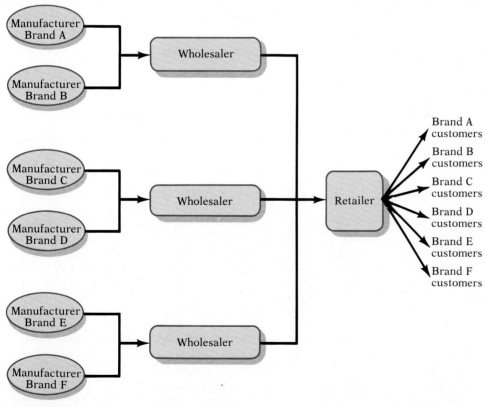

FIGURE 1-3
The Retailer's Role in the Sorting Process

tion. It is derived from the old French word *retailler*, which means "to cut up."

Another distribution function that retailers perform is to communicate with their customers and with their manufacturers and wholesalers. Via ads, sales personnel, and store displays, customers are informed about the availability and characteristics of goods and services, store hours, special sales, and so on. Manufacturers, wholesalers, and others are informed about sales forecasts, delays in shipping, customer complaints, defective products, inventory turnover (by style, color, and size) and so on. Many goods and services have been modified as a result of retailer feedback to suppliers.

For small manufacturers and wholesalers, retailers can provide valuable assistance by shipping, storing, marking, advertising, and prepaying for merchandise. On the other hand, small retailers need the same type of help from their suppliers. The number of functions performed by a retailer has a direct bearing on the percentage of each sales dollar that it receives.

Retailers also complete transactions with their customers. This means trying to promptly and accurately fill orders, and it often involves processing customer credit through the retailer's or another charge plan. In addition, retailers frequently provide customer services such as gift wrapping, delivery, and installation.

For these reasons, in most cases, goods and services are sold via retail outlets not owned by a manufacturer. This enables the manufacturer to reach more customers, reduce expenditures, improve cash flow, increase sales more rapidly, and concentrate on its area of expertise.

In some instances, firms such as Sherwin-Williams and Goodyear operate their own retailing facilities. These manufacturers need to understand and complete the full range of retailing functions in order to compete with traditional retailers. They must consider how many final consumers will buy their products, how

---

RETAILING IN ACTION

Can a Chocolate Manufacturer Be a Retailer Too?

After experimenting with a retail chocolate store at Disneyland, Nestlé decided to open shops in Atlanta, Chicago, Cleveland, Los Angeles, Nashville, and Orlando during 1987 and 1988. Why would one of the world's great chocolatiers make the decision to also be a retailer?

First, Nestlé believed that the image it was projecting through traditional retail outlets did not appeal to upscale consumers; by having its own stores (and calling them the Chocolate Collection of Henri Nestlé), the firm could "reposition itself as a purveyor of upscale chocolates." Gourmet chocolate is one of the fastest-growing segments of the confectionary market. Second, other chocolatiers, such as Godiva and Kron, were actively expanding their retail store opera-

tions; Nestlé did not want to fall behind them. Third, Nestlé had begun a mail-order catalog business several years earlier, and it was doing well. The firm believed that the catalog and store businesses would complement each other.

Will this new venture succeed? It depends on several factors. Will Nestlé be able to handle all retailing functions effectively and efficiently? What investment will be required if it wants its retailing efforts to grow (in 1988, Godiva had about sixty stores)? Will consumers shop at a store carrying a limited assortment of candy and only one chocolate brand? How will traditional retailers feel about Nestlé's competing with them? How will competitors such as Hershey react?

Source: Based on material in Judith Graham, "Nestlé Plans Retail Chocolate Shops," *Advertising Age* (November 9, 1987), p. 28.

Retailing comprises all of the business activities involved in the sale of goods and services to consumers for personal, family, or household use. In many cases, retailers have small average sales, deal with consumers who make impulse purchases, and rely on store locations. A retail strategy is the overall plan that guides the firm.

Most successful retailers, such as the Stew Leonard's food store depicted here, have a clear retail strategy and adhere to the retailing concept. They have a customer orientation, coordinate their efforts, and have a goal orientation. They also recognize that they can make shopping a "fun" experience for their customers.

Photos courtesy of Stew Leonard's.

Retail institutions can be classified on the basis of ownership and retail strategy mix. For example, the Southland Corporation operates 7-Eleven outlets that are both company-owned and franchisee-owned. 7-Eleven stores feature convenience-oriented food and household products, and offer Citgo gasoline in many locations.

Photo courtesy of Southland Corporation.

One of the most important decisions a retailer makes involves the choice of a store location. A store-based retailer may situate in an isolated site, an unplanned business district, or a planned shopping center. Shown here is the inside entrance to a Sears' store in the Montclair Plaza shopping center in California.

Photo courtesy of Sears. Abby Sadin photographer.

Human resource management is a key ingredient in a good retail strategy. Qualified, motivated employees must be recruited, selected, trained, compensated, and supervised. At Ames Department Stores, a Corporate Training Department administers a wide variety of programs to properly teach employees.

Photo courtesy of Ames Department Stores, Inc.

The merchandise buying and handling process involves a series of interrelated steps from establishing a buying organization to determining merchandise sources to handling merchandise to re-evaluating on a regular basis. Toys "R" Us operates large warehouse/distribution centers so that stores can maintain strong in-stock positions.

Photo courtesy of Toys "R" Us.

There are many ways in which retailers can communicate with their customers. Atmosphere involves the physical characteristics that a retailer uses to develop an image and to draw customers. Advertising, publicity, personal selling, and sales promotion are the four basic promotion tools available to retailers. Through an exciting display for its juniors clothing department, J.C. Penney is able to project a dynamic image to its customers.

Photo courtesy of J.C. Penney.

In the future, retailers will be placing greater emphasis on computer technology to hold down their costs, coordinate and fine-tune their strategies, and better respond to customer needs. At Big Bear, a supermarket chain, a new computer system is the culmination of efforts by data processing, management, merchandising, and purchasing professionals. As a result, considerable information is now available on a daily basis.

Photo courtesy of Big Bear.

geographically dispersed these consumers are, what resources are needed to fulfill retailing functions, what service will be required by consumers, and a number of other factors. Sometimes, even successful manufacturers fail as retailers. As an illustration, a few years ago, IBM opened several company-owned IBM Product Centers to sell PCs, typewriters, and accessories. But IBM encountered many problems: a limited assortment, an inadequate number of stores, unattractive decors, improper staffing, and a poor record-keeping system. In 1986, after a few disappointing years in the marketplace, IBM sold its stores and exited from retailing.[4]

The Relationships Among Retailers and Their Suppliers

It is essential that the complex relationships among retailers and their suppliers be understood. On the one hand, retailers are part of a distribution channel; and manufacturers and wholesalers must be concerned about coverage of the consumer market, adequate product displays, consumer services, store hours, and retailer reliability. On the other hand, retailers are major customers of goods and services such as items for resale, store fixtures, data-processing equipment, management consulting, and insurance.

Frequently, retailers and their suppliers have divergent viewpoints, which need to be reconciled. Control over the distribution channel, the allocation of profits, the number of competing retailers handling the suppliers' goods and services, in-store display space and locations, advertising support, payment terms, and flexibility in operations are just a few of the issues over which retailers and suppliers have their own different priorities and goals. And because of the growing number of regional and national retail chains, retailers have more power in the distribution channel than ever before.

Channel relations are generally smoothest when exclusive distribution is involved. With **exclusive distribution,** suppliers enter into agreements with one or a few retailers that designate the latter as the only companies in specified geographic areas that are allowed to carry certain brands and/or product lines. This arrangement stimulates both parties to work together in maintaining an image, assigning shelf space, allotting profits and costs, advertising, and so on. However, it also usually requires that the retailer limit its assortment of goods/services in the product categories covered by the agreement; this means a retailer might have to pass up handling other suppliers' items. From a manufacturer's perspective, exclusive distribution may limit its long-run total sales potential.

Channel relations tend to be most volatile when intensive distribution is used. With **intensive distribution,** suppliers sell through as many retailers as possible. This arrangement usually maximizes suppliers' sales; and it enables retailers to offer many different brands and product versions. As a result, competition among retailers selling the same items is high. In response, retailers may use tactics not beneficial to individual suppliers, as they are more interested in overall store sales than in the sales of any one brand. The retailer may allocate shelf space, set prices, and advertise in a way that adversely affects individual brands (by giving them poor shelf space, using them as sale items, and not advertising them).

Selective distribution is an approach that combines aspects of both exclusive and intensive distribution. With **selective distribution,** suppliers sell through a moderate number of retailers. This allows suppliers to have higher sales than possible in exclusive distribution and lets retailers carry some competing brands. It encourages suppliers to provide advertising and other support, and encourages retailers to provide adequate shelf space. Yet, this middle-ground approach generally has neither the level of channel cooperation found in exclusive distribution nor the sales potential of intensive distribution. See Figure 1-4.

Unless suppliers are aware of the characteristics and needs of their retailers, they cannot develop good rapport with them; and as long as a choice of suppliers

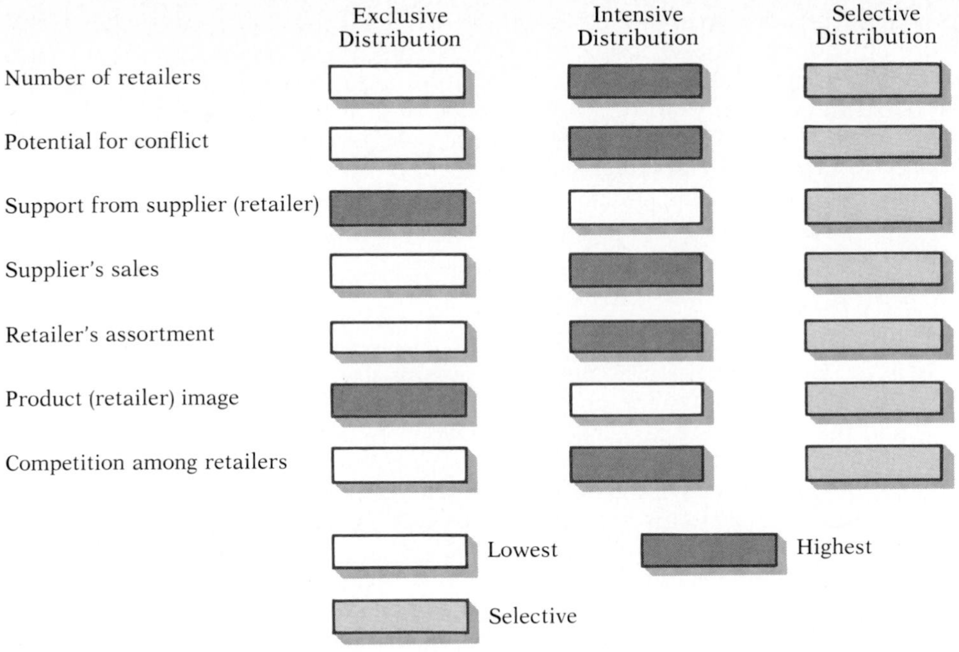

	Exclusive Distribution	Intensive Distribution	Selective Distribution
Number of retailers	☐	■	▨
Potential for conflict	☐	■	▨
Support from supplier (retailer)	■	☐	▨
Supplier's sales	☐	■	▨
Retailer's assortment	☐	■	▨
Product (retailer) image	■	☐	▨
Competition among retailers	☐	■	▨

☐ Lowest ■ Highest

▨ Selective

FIGURE 1-4
Comparing Exclusive, Intensive, and Selective Distribution

exists, retailers will select those that understand and react to their needs. The following illustrate several key issues in retailer–supplier relationships:

❑ Competition in the marketplace—When PepsiCo acquired Kentucky Fried Chicken (it already owned Pizza Hut and Taco Bell), Wendy's started serving Coca-Cola products instead of Pepsi. It took out full-page ads saying that PepsiCo was "in direct competition with Wendy's" and "PepsiCo's interests are in direct conflict with ours."[5]

❑ Product image—Cadillac has introduced the two-seat $55,000+ Allante sports model in order to reposition the Cadillac brand to younger, more upscale customers. However, dealers have developed their own television ads geared toward traditional, and older, customers. One dealer ad showed that the Fleetwood Brougham is the largest car in the United States.[6]

❑ The role of manufacturers' representatives—Wal-Mart, the seventh largest retailer in the United States, recently enacted a policy aimed at eliminating independent manufacturers' sales representatives from the distribution process. Wal-Mart wanted to buy directly from their manufacturers and sought to receive lower prices because the representatives' 2–6 per cent commissions would be eliminated. Small manufacturers were upset by this because the use of representatives enabled them to expand their geographic market coverage without hiring their own sales forces.[7]

❑ Purchase terms—A number of retailers, particularly supermarkets, now require fees from manufacturers for premium shelf space (e.g., end-of-aisle) or to carry new items at all. And manufacturers are not very happy about this: "With our brands as hostages, we pay the ransom, for the risk of noncompliance is ultimately death. A slow and painful process, their demise comes at the hands of the retailers who can deny brands exposure in their stores."[8]

❑ Distribution access—As a result of problems with earlier Atari video games and computers and its past image as a toy manufacturer, many retailers decided not to carry the firm's new line of powerful personal computers. To increase distribution, Atari had to purchase a consumer electronics retailer with outlets in California, Texas, Arizona, and Kansas. Although the retailer was losing money at the time Atari acquired it, Atari paid $67 million for the chain.[9]

Manufacturers of goods used by retailers must also have a knowledge of retailing. For example, a store fixture manufacturer has to understand the requirements of the retailer. Store layout, linear feet of shelf space, self-service merchandising, routing of customer traffic, and storage specifications are some of the criteria used in the selection of store fixtures. Knowledge of basic retailing principles, as well as the special factors relative to a given type of retailer, are necessary for the fixture manufacturer to succeed.

Firms that sell services, such as store insurance, to retailers benefit from an understanding of retailing. Inventory valuation, construction costs of facilities, crime rates, and depreciation are some of the factors that must be examined. For example, how should merchandise that has been marked down in price be appraised if there is a fire? Or how much will fire insurance premiums be reduced if sprinklers are installed in a store?

Special Characteristics of Retailing

Several special characteristics distinguish retailing from other types of business. See Figure 1-5. The average size of a sales transaction for retailers is much less than for manufacturers. Final consumers make many unplanned purchases; those who buy for resale or for use in manufacturing products or running a business are more systematic and plan ahead. Most retail customers must be drawn to a store location; salespeople generally visit manufacturers, wholesalers, and other firms to initiate and consummate transactions. Each of these factors imposes unique requirements on retail firms.

Average sales transactions are about $30 for department stores, $3 for convenience stores (not counting gasoline), and $15 for chain supermarkets.[10] These low average sales create a need to tightly control the costs associated with each transaction (such as credit verification, delivery, and bagging); to maximize the number of customers drawn to the store, which may place an emphasis on advertising and special promotions; and to increase impulse sales by more aggres-

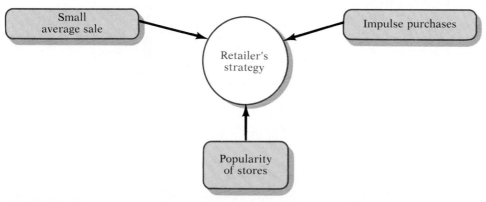

FIGURE 1-5
Special Characteristics Affecting Retailers

sive in-store selling. However, low average sales and high costs cannot always be controlled by the retailer. For example, in 1979, the average transaction in a specialty store was $28.77; in 1985, it had only risen to $28.81. And despite their high costs, over 63 per cent of department store sales are on credit.[11]

Because of many small sales transactions to a large number of different customers, inventory management is often difficult for retailers. As an illustration, whereas the average chain supermarket had yearly sales of $8.8 million in 1986, it also had nearly 11,000 weekly transactions.[12] This makes it harder for retailers to determine the levels of existing stock and the popularity of various brands, sizes, and prices of merchandise. For that reason, retailers are expanding their use of computerized inventory systems.

Often, retail sales involve unplanned or impulse purchases. For example, surveys indicate that 75 per cent of grocery consumers ignore newspaper ads before shopping, 69 per cent do not prepare shopping lists in advance, and 53 per cent of grocery purchases are completely unplanned.[13] This signifies the importance of point-of-purchase displays, attractive store layouts, well-organized stores, and store windows. Candy, cosmetics, snack foods, magazines, and other items can be sold as impulse goods if they are placed in visible, high-traffic locations in the store. Because consumers buy so many goods and services in an unplanned manner, the retailer's ability to forecast, budget, order merchandise, and have the proper number of personnel on the selling floor is lessened.

Retail customers normally visit a store, even though mail and telephone sales have increased dramatically in recent years. The large number of final consumers; the interest of many consumers in shopping in person and in comparison shopping among different brands, models, and so on; the small average sale size; the unplanned nature of purchases; and consumers' desire for privacy from in-home selling—these are just some of the reasons for the popularity of retail stores. And because consumers must be attracted to a particular store, the retailer needs to consider such factors as location, transportation facilities, store hours, proximity of competitors, merchandise assortment, parking, and advertising.

Developing and Applying Retail Strategies

A **retail strategy** is the overall plan that guides the firm. Such a strategy has an influence on the retailer's business activities and its response to market forces, such as competition or the economy. Any retailer, regardless of size or type, can and should utilize these six steps in strategic planning:

1. The type of business is defined in terms of the goods or service category and the specific orientation of the firm (such as full-service or "no frills").
2. Long-run and short-run objectives are set with regard to sales and profit, market share, image, and so on.
3. The customer market to which to appeal is defined on the basis of its characteristics (such as gender and income level) and needs (such as product and brand preferences).
4. An overall, long-run plan is developed and gives general direction to the firm and its employees.
5. An integrated strategy, which combines such factors as store location, product assortment, pricing, and advertising and displays, is implemented to achieve objectives.
6. Performance is regularly evaluated, and weaknesses or problems are corrected as they are observed.

This section will examine portions of the retail strategies of Stew Leonard's, Lands' End, and Jane's Camera Shop. These firms have been selected because they represent diversity in retailing. They differ in size and structure and use different strategies.

In 1967, the state of Connecticut decided to construct a highway that would run through the Leonard family's dairy plant. At that time, thirty-seven-year-old Stew Leonard, who was working for the family as a milkman covering a local delivery route, visited dairies of all types and sizes throughout the United States and conferred with customers on his route. Based on this research, in 1969, Leonard opened a retail dairy store that featured only eight basic items (such as milk and eggs) and low prices. The store had a life-sized plastic cow in front and large windows, so that customers could see fresh milk being bottled. The first week the dairy was open, it did $17,000 in business, an unheard-of amount for a small dairy store.

Since opening, Stew Leonard's store in Norwalk, Connecticut, has expanded twenty-six times. Today, Stew Leonard's is no longer just a dairy store, but a large food retailer. The Norwalk store occupies 110,000 square feet (about six to seven times the size of a conventional supermarket) and generates $100 million in annual sales (almost twelve times the amount in an average chain-supermarket outlet). Customers are attracted from as far away as Rhode Island, New York, and Massachusetts. Stew Leonard has been praised in the best-selling book *A Passion for Excellence* and in the video *In Search of Excellence*. And his store has been called the "Disney World" of food retailing. As there are over ninety other food stores within fifteen miles of Stew Leonard's, the store's success is even more remarkable.

Stew Leonard's strategy includes these key elements:

❏ Clear objectives—Stew Leonard's has set up a number of goals to which it tries to adhere. For example, "We try to make sure prices are at least 10 per cent lower than stores within a five-mile radius," and "We have to sell at least 1,000 units of an item a week to include it in inventory."

❏ Customer consciousness—Stew Leonard reads the suggestion box daily. By mid-morning, he wants to see problem areas corrected. If checkout lanes are more than three deep, customers on line are given cookies or ice cream to make their visit more tolerable. On a three-ton granite block in front of the store (next to the full-sized plastic cow) is Stew Leonard's basic philosophy, "Rule 1: The customer is always right! Rule 2: If the customer is ever wrong, reread Rule 1." Each year, 3.5 million customers shop at Stew Leonard's.

❏ Merchandising—The store carries only 750 items versus 8,000 to 12,000 in an average supermarket. Stew Leonard selects fast-moving items, buys on special deals, uses the store brand name on many products, and is very concerned about freshness. The store stocks just four kinds of cereal, two brands of yogurt, one brand of peanut butter, and one brand of chicken. And some items normally found in supermarkets, such as flour, sugar, and household cleansers, are not carried at all. In a typical week, Stew Leonard's sells 5 tons of chocolate cookies, 100,000 pounds of Perdue chicken, 40,000 croissants, 190,000 quarts of milk, and almost 20,000 ice cream cones.

❏ Concern about quality—Stew Leonard is a stickler for quality. The restrooms have fresh flowers and are cleaned often. To ensure product freshness, Perdue chickens arrive three times per week, and fish is delivered daily. Leonard will visit suppliers and chastise them if merchandise is of inferior quality or not fresh enough.

❏ Atmosphere—Stew Leonard's is an exciting and fun place in which to shop. Through the use of one horseshoe-shaped aisle, all customers must pass by each product display. To entertain patrons and their children, an employee dresses in a cow suit and dances with them. And the store has a petting zoo, two robot dogs, a robot cow, and a farmer singing nursery rhymes.

Pizza is baked in front of customers. Free samples of lemonade, horseradish cheese, cupcakes, gazpacho, and other goodies are plentiful. As one patron noted, "You come in here just for milk and you walk out with a shopping cart full of food." See Figure 1-6.

❑ Competitive intelligence—A customized fifteen-person van is used to make regular visits to interesting stores, even if they are in another business or up to four hundred miles away. After every visit, each employee on the trip is asked to come up with one idea that can be implemented immediately.

❑ Employees—Stew Leonard's has 650 employees and encourages them to perform to their potential. They are expected to adhere to the principles of S.T.E.W.: satisfy the customer, teamwork, excellence, and wow. It pays for employees to take Dale Carnegie courses to improve their skills. Recognition for superior performance is plentiful. Prominently displayed pictures acknowledge star employees of the month, top performers of the year, and so on; and plaques, gift certificates, and $100 dinners are awarded.

❑ Community involvement—Stew Leonard's is an active member of its community. For example, tours of the store are offered for school, after-school, and adult groups.

Overall, Stew Leonard's has done an excellent job of applying strategic planning principles. The initial focus of Stew Leonard's has been altered from a dairy store to a large food store to take advantage of growth opportunities, goals have

Reprinted by permission.

FIGURE 1-6
The Exciting Atmosphere of Stew Leonard's

been set, an emphasis on consumer satisfaction has been enacted well, and an innovative merchandising philosophy (and its accompanying atmosphere) has been carefully devised and carried out in an integrated manner. Yet, despite its success, Stew Leonard's regularly monitors performance through a suggestion box, visits to other stores, and so on.

Lands' End: From Outlet Store to Mail-Order Leadership[15]

Gary Comer worked for the Young & Rubicam advertising agency for ten years; but his true vocation was sailing. So, in 1963, Gary left the ad agency and with his sailing partner, Dick Stearns, opened a catalog outlet store in Chicago that specialized in sailing equipment and fittings. This enabled him to combine business and pleasure.

After five years, and only moderate success, Gary Comer bought out his partner and started tinkering with the catalog. He added clothing, accessories, and luggage that were aimed at full-time and weekend sailors. In 1976, Comer decided to no longer carry sailing equipment; competition was too intense. Lands' End began to focus on recreational and informal clothing, accessories, shoes, and soft-sided luggage and broadened its customer market.

Today, annual sales (almost all of which are through mail-order and toll-free telephone transactions) have reached more than $250 million; and over three million customers buy from a Lands' End catalog in a three-year period. The company's headquarters, warehousing facilities, and customer-service operations are located in the quiet Wisconsin farming community of Dodgeville.

Lands' End's strategy includes these major elements:

❑ Growth-oriented objectives—Lands' End is directed toward long-run growth. For this reason, in 1986, the company offered 1.4 million shares of stock to the general public in order to fund further expansion. Land's End is interested in generating higher sales volume from existing customers and in getting some of the three million customers in its data base who have not purchased in the last three years to do so.

❑ Appeal to a prime consumer market—Lands' End is very strong with thirty-five- to forty-nine-year-old customers, 60 per cent of whom have incomes of $35,000 and up, 90 per cent of whom have attended college, and 70 per cent of whom are professionals: "We evolved into a higher socioeconomic market segment. We offer products that a certain market wants."

❑ Outstanding customer service—Lands' End's long-standing "principles of business," shown in Figure 1-7, indicate the emphasis that it places on customer service. These two observations bear this out further: (1) A mail-order industry consultant said that Lands' End has "devoted an extraordinary amount of attention to customer service, delivery, and warehouse operations, anything that would enrich its relationship with customers. It's much better than the industry as a whole." (2) Based on a poll of its readership, *Consumer Reports* stated that Lands' End had a merchandise satisfaction rating of 94 per cent.

❑ Personalized company image—Unlike traditional mail-order retailers, which only show pictures of their products, present brief descriptions of them, and cite their prices, Lands' End adds a personal touch. A typical catalog may contain an eight-page story on the history of wool and "chatty news" about each item carried in the catalog. Lands' End's full and unconditional guarantee is clearly displayed in the catalog, as is its toll-free 800 number. Customers who call Lands' End are likely to reach one of its full-time, year-round operators, who provide information, answer questions, and process orders (which are usually received by customers within two weeks).

Principles of Doing Business.

Principle 1.

We do everything we can to make our products better. We improve material, and add back features and construction details that others have taken out over the years. We never reduce the quality of a product to make it cheaper.

Principle 2.

We price our products fairly and honestly. We do not, have not, and will not participate in the common retailing practice of inflating markups to set up a future phony "Sale."

Principle 3.

We accept any return, for any reason, at any time. Our products are guaranteed. No fine print. No arguments. We mean exactly what we say: GUARANTEED. PERIOD.

Principle 4.

We ship faster than anyone we know of. We ship items in stock the day after we receive the order. At the height of the last Christmas season the longest time an order was in the house was 36 hours, excepting monograms which took another 12 hours.

Principle 5.

We believe that what is best for our customer is best for all of us. Everyone here understands that concept. Our sales and service people are trained to know our products, and to be friendly and helpful. They are urged to take all the time necessary to take care of you. We even pay for your call, for whatever reason you call.

Gary Comer

Gary Comer, President

Principle 6.

We are able to sell at lower prices because we have eliminated middlemen; because we don't buy branded merchandise with high protected markups and because we have placed our contracts with manufacturers who have proved that they are cost conscious and efficient.

Principle 7.

We are able to sell at lower prices because we operate efficiently. Our people are hard working, intelligent and share in the success of the company.

Principle 8.

We are able to sell at lower prices because we support no fancy emporiums with their high overhead. Our main location is in the middle of a 40-acre cornfield in rural Wisconsin. We still operate our first location in Chicago's Near North tannery district.

Reprinted by permission.

FIGURE 1-7
Lands' End

❑ Consistent promotion program—Lands' End mails out a new catalog every four weeks. It also runs ads in appropriate publications, such as *Fortune, Inc.,* the *New York Times Sunday Magazine,* the *Wall Street Journal,* and *USA Today.* All ads "convey to our readers and customers the humanity of our company. First and foremost, Lands' End is a study in personal relations."

❑ Efficient operations—Ordering, warehousing, and other operations are highly automated and computerized. The firm runs outlet stores in Chicago and in Madison, Wisconsin. These stores are used to sell returned merchandise or items that have been overordered and must be cleared out.

It is clear that Lands' End is committed to its customers and to an ongoing, integrated strategic retailing plan. The company has a distinct product offering, solid objectives, a large and loyal customer base, and sound operating principles, as well as a system for implementing and improving its strategy.

Jane Riddell has owned and operated Jane's Camera Shop for eleven years. The store is a full-service, independent camera shop that offers a good selection of cameras, slide projectors, VCRs, video cameras, film, film processing, and photographic accessories. Jane's Camera Shop is located in a suburban shopping center about twenty miles from a major downtown shopping district known for its discount retailers (which also engage in heavy mail-order sales).

Over the years, Riddell has done well, in large part because of a comprehensive and integrated strategy:

❑ Concentrated product offering—Jane's Camera Shop is just that, a camera shop. It does not sell stereos, televisions, microwave ovens, or personal computers (all items that competitors carry). This enables the store to project a specialist image and maintain a high level of expertise.

❑ Realistic goals—Jane does not plan to open additional outlets but wants to make the current store as efficient and profitable as possible. A steady yearly sales growth of 7–8 per cent, with a net pre-tax profit of 8–10 per cent on sales, is sought. Currently, Jane's annual sales are just over $650,000; and pre-tax profit for the most recent year was $60,000.

❑ Individual customer attention—Either Jane or one of her salespeople is always available to demonstrate cameras or provide advice on picture taking. According to Riddell, "We will never sell a camera or equipment unless the customer is sure it is the right model for him or her and understands how to use it. Customer satisfaction is crucial for us."

❑ Use of a one-price policy—Prices are clearly marked on all items, and customer bargaining is neither encouraged nor permitted. Although Jane's prices are 10–20 per cent higher than those charged by downtown discounters, the store's prices are honest and represent its full-service orientation. Jane's does not surprise customers with hidden charges (such as pricing separately for the bulb and tray in a slide projector); and discounters are reluctant to demonstrate cameras or to compare different models.

❑ Stocking only items purchased from manufacturers' authorized U.S. distributors—Many competitors purchase imported items from unauthorized distributors overseas. The "gray market" products carried by competitors are priced very low, sometimes below an authorized distributor's wholesale price; however, instructions may be in a foreign language, and they may not have a standard U.S. warranty (which precludes repairs being carried out by authorized distributors). Jane's and its distributors honor all U.S. warranties; and Jane's offers an extra one-year store warranty at no charge on all products priced at $100 and over.

❑ Good store location—Jane's Camera Shop is situated in a medium-sized shopping center anchored by a branch outlet of a leading department store chain. The shopping center is off a heavily traveled highway in a middle-class residential community. Special events, such as photography exhibits, add to the attractiveness of the center. Parking is plentiful.

❑ Regular evaluation of performance—Each three months, Jane Riddell does a complete analysis of sales and costs by product category. Redesigned displays, special sales, and changes in ordering patterns are based on Jane's analysis.

Over the last year and a half, Riddell has made two major changes in her strategy. First, Jane's added one-hour film processing; more recently, it began carrying video cameras and VCRs.

One-hour film processing was introduced because Riddell was concerned that film and film-processing sales were not rising satisfactorily. This was disconcerting for several reasons. Film and film processing represent about 10 per cent of total store sales and 15 per cent of profits. Film and film-processing sales help generate consumer traffic into the store; once inside, customers frequently buy batteries, camera cases, extra lenses, and so on and see displays for new models. Customer names on film-processing receipts can be used in mailing lists for advertisements and promotions, and to determine the extent of Jane's trading area.

Jane's acquired a state-of-the-art Kis S.A. one-hour film-processing machine for $32,900. This machine requires only twenty-five square feet of space and is one-tenth the size of a traditional machine. It can process fifty to sixty rolls of film per day. So far, one-hour film processing has turned out well for Jane's. Film processing is up 25 per cent, and film sales have increased by 15 per cent.

About six months ago, Jane Riddell determined that video cameras would fit in well with her product mix and that they had a strong long-term potential. Jane's now stocks four brands of full-sized video cameras, three brands of compact video cameras, and one brand of 8mm video camera. A full line of accessories is also stocked.

At that time, Riddell planned to continue her policy of not carrying VCRs, feeling that they were more appropriate for the discount retailers than for her store. But after several video camera customers expressed disappointment in being unable to purchase VCRs to go with their new cameras, Jane agreed to carry four models of full-feature VCRs. Today, the video camera and VCR business is thriving.

By examining the policies followed by Jane's Camera Shop, it can be seen that strategic planning in retailing is applicable to small firms and to those selling services (in this case, film processing) as well as goods (film and cameras). Jane Riddell knows her business and where it is headed, has a systematic plan, and is flexible enough to modify the strategy when it is desirable to do so.

The Marketing Concept Applied to Retailing

All of the firms described here have demonstrated a sincere long-term desire to please their customers. Stew Leonard's combines an entertaining family atmosphere with low prices. Lands' End advertises that "if you are not completely satisfied with any item you buy from us, at any time during your use of it, return it and we will refund your full purchase price." Jane's Camera Store has a patient and knowledgeable sales force and uses honest pricing.

In addition to a customer orientation, it has been shown that each of the three firms utilizes a coordinated, companywide approach to strategy development and implementation and expresses a clear goal orientation. Together, these principles form the marketing concept, a notion first introduced by General Electric (a leading U.S. manufacturer).

The marketing concept can be transformed into the retailing concept and should be understood and used by all retailers. See Figure 1-8. The **retailing concept** has these elements:

1. Customer orientation—A retailer must determine the characteristics and needs of its customers and must endeavor to satisfy customer needs to the fullest.

2. Coordinated effort—A retailer must integrate all plans and activities to maximize efficiency.

3. Goal orientation—A retailer must set goals and then use its strategy to attain them.

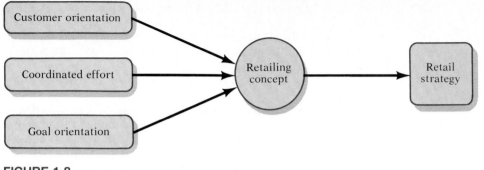

FIGURE 1-8
Applying the Retailing Concept

Unfortunately, the retailing concept is not understood and used by every retailer. Some are indifferent to customer needs, plan haphazardly, and have unclear goals. Too often, retailers are not receptive to change or new ideas, or they blindly follow strategy changes implemented by competitors. Some retailers do not research their customers or get feedback from them; they rely on the reports of their suppliers or their own past sales trends.

Nonetheless, the retailing concept is fairly easy to adopt. It just requires communicating with consumers and considering their desires as critical to the retailer's success, developing and enacting a consistent strategy (such as having designer brands, plentiful sales personnel, attractive displays, and above-average

RETAILING IN ACTION

What Companies Are Best Following the Retailing Concept?

Recently, *Fortune* magazine evaluated firms in a number of retailing and nonretailing industries on the basis of their customer orientation, stating that "As competition intensifies and companies invade each other's markets, cost and quality differences among all sorts of goods and services are shrinking. The company that coddles customers best has a competitive advantage."

These are the retailers in their respective industries that were recognized by *Fortune* for best adhering to the retailing concept:

❑ Automobile dealers—Honda Acura and Mercedes-Benz.
❑ Hotel chains—Embassy Suites, Stouffer, Marriott, and Westin.

❑ Supermarket chains—Wegmans, Publix, and Fred Meyer.
❑ Mail-order firms—L.L. Bean, Lands' End, J.C. Penney, Brookstone, and Omaha Steaks.
❑ Domestic airlines—American and Delta.

The preceding recognition is due to careful planning and hard work by the firms involved. For example, when it launched a new car division, American Honda awarded Acura dealerships only to the top 25 per cent of the dealers that were already selling Hondas. And as the president of another outstanding firm noted, "My attitude is, if you could put Frank Borman on the moon and bring him back alive, we ought to be able to solve any customer's problems."

Source: Based on material in Bro Uttal, "Companies That Serve You Best," *Fortune* (December 7, 1987), pp. 98–116.

prices in an upscale clothing boutique), and working to achieve meaningful, specific, and reachable goals.

The retailing concept is a guide to company strategy. It does not deal with a firm's internal capabilities or competitive advantages but offers a broad framework for planning.

The Focus and Format of the Text

There are various approaches to the study of retailing: an institutional approach, which describes the various types of retailing and their development; a functional approach, which concentrates on the activities retailers must perform (such as buying, pricing, and personnel practices); and a strategic approach, which involves defining the retail business, setting long- and short-term objectives, appealing to an appropriate customer market, developing an overall plan, implementing an integrated strategy, and regularly reviewing operations.

We will study retail management from each of these perspectives, but we will focus on the **strategic approach.** The underlying principle is that a retail firm needs to plan for and adapt to a complex, changing environment. Both opportunities and constraints must be considered. Strategic retail management constantly encourages a retailer to evaluate competitors, economic factors, changes in consumers, marketplace trends, legal restrictions, and so on. A retailer will prosper when its competitive strengths are matched with the opportunities presented in the environment, weaknesses are eliminated or minimized, and plans look to the future as well as the past.

This text is divided into eight parts. The balance of Part One presents the strategic planning process in retailing. Each of the steps in the process is covered in detail.

Part Two classifies and characterizes retailing institutions on the basis of ownership, store strategy mix, nonstore retailing, and service retailing. Part Three deals with consumer behavior and marketing research in retailing.

Parts Four to Seven discuss the specific elements of a retailing strategy: store location planning; human resource management and retail operations; merchandise planning, handling, and pricing; and communicating with the customer.

Part Eight shows how a retailing strategy may be integrated and controlled. It also looks at the special characteristics of service retailing and the changing environment of retailing.

SUMMARY

Retailing encompasses the business activities involved in the sale of goods and services to consumers for their personal, family, or household use. It includes tangible and intangible items, does not have to utilize a store, and can be conducted by manufacturers and others as well as by retail firms.

Retail store sales in 1986 were almost $1.5 trillion. In addition, telephone and mail-order retailers, vending machines, direct-to-home selling, and a variety of personal service providers account for hundreds of billions of dollars in revenues annually. About 18 million people in the United States are employed by traditional retailers, a number that greatly understates the number of people actually employed in some retailing capacity. Retailers such as department and specialty stores receive 40 cents of every sales dollar as compensation for their operating costs and the functions they perform. Trends in retailing often mirror those of the overall U.S. economy.

Retailing is the last stage in a channel of distribution, which contains all of the businesses and people involved in the physical movement and transfer of ownership of goods and services from producer to consumer. In such a channel, retailers perform many valuable functions as the intermediaries between manufacturers, wholesalers, and other suppliers and final consumers. Through the sorting process, retailers collect an assortment of goods and services from various suppliers and offer them to customers. Retailers communicate with customers and with other channel members, such as manufacturers and wholesalers. Retailers may ship, store, mark, advertise, and prepay for merchandise. They complete transactions with customers and frequently provide customer services.

Retailers and their suppliers have complex relationships because the retailers serve two roles. They are part of a distribution channel aimed at the final consumer; and they are also major customers for their suppliers. As a result, divergent viewpoints may occur, and they must be reconciled. Channel relations are smoothest with exclusive distribution; they are most volatile with intensive distribution. Selective distribution combines aspects of both in an attempt to balance sales goals and channel member cooperation.

Retailing has several special characteristics. The average size of a sales transaction is small. Final consumers make many unplanned purchases. Most retail customers must be drawn to a store location.

A retail strategy is the overall plan that guides the firm. It contains six basic steps: defining the business, setting objectives, defining the customer market, developing an overall plan, implementing an integrated strategy, and evaluating performance and making necessary modifications. The strategies of Stew Leonard's, Lands' End, and Jane's Camera Shop have been particularly well designed and carried out.

The retailing concept should be understood and used by all retailers. It consists of a customer orientation, a coordinated effort, and a goal orientation. Unfortunately, despite its ease of use, many firms do not adhere to one or more elements of the retailing concept.

Retailing may be studied by using an institutional approach, a functional approach, and a strategic approach. Although all three of these approaches are utilized in this text, the focus will be on the strategic approach. The underlying principle is that a retail firm needs to plan for and adapt to a complex, changing environment.

QUESTIONS FOR DISCUSSION

1. Which of these involve retailing? Explain your answers.
   a. Travel agency dealing with corporate accounts
   b. Gift shop in a museum
   c. House painter
   d. College restaurant
2. According to Table 1-1, sales by women's apparel and accessory stores are 3.5 times of those of men's and boys' apparel and accessory stores. As a prospective retailer, what would this mean to you?
3. Describe the sorting process from the manufacturer's perspective. From the retailer's perspective.
4. What kinds of information do retailers communicate to customers? To suppliers?
5. Evaluate Wendy's decision to drop Pepsi and switch to Coke when PepsiCo bought Kentucky Fried Chicken and added it to its restaurant division.
6. What are the pros and cons of Atari's acquiring a consumer electronics retailer?

7. Which aspects of retailing would it be important for an advertising agency that specializes in retailers' ads to know? Why?
8. Describe how the special characteristics of retailing offer unique opportunities and problems for retailers.
9. What is a retail strategy? Could it be utilized by a small neighborhood bakery? Why or why not?
10. What are the common factors in the strategies of Stew Leonard's, Lands' End, and Jane's Camera Shop?
11. Give several suggestions for Stew Leonard's or Lands' End to increase business in the future.
12. Comment on Jane Riddell's decision to carry VCRs.
13. Explain the retailing concept. Apply it to an ice-cream store chain.
14. Differentiate among these approaches to the study of retailing:
    a. Institutional
    b. Functional
    c. Strategic

NOTES

1. Isadore Barmash, "New Moves from Two Grand Old Men of Retailing," *New York Times* (January 24, 1988), Section 3, p. 7; "Dillard: Steady as a Rock," *Chain Store Age Executive* (August 1986), pp. 25–26; and Michael Totty, "Expansion-Minded Dillard Is Catching Some Attention," *Wall Street Journal* (March 16, 1988), p. 8.

2. David P. Schulz, " '86: Better FOR Some," *Stores* (November 1987), p. 92; "54th Annual Report of the Gro-

cery Industry," *Progressive Grocer* (April 1987), pp. 19, 35; and "The 50 Largest Retailing Companies," *Fortune* (June 8, 1987), pp. 210–211.

3. This concept was formally introduced by Wroe Alderson, *Marketing Behavior and Executive Action* (Homewood, Ill.: Richard D. Irwin, 1957), pp. 199–211.

4. Peter Petre, "IBM: Misadventures in the Retail Jungle," *Fortune* (July 23, 1984), p. 80; and "IBM's 84 Retail Stores Are Acquired by Nynex," *New York Times* (April 23, 1986), pp. D1, D2.

5. Wendy's advertisement, *Wall Street Journal* (October 16, 1986), p. 25.

6. Raymond Serafin, "Cadillac, Dealers Project Opposites," *Advertising Age* (May 4, 1987), p. 12.

7. Arthur Bragg, "Wal-Mart's War on Reps," *Sales & Marketing Management* (March 1987), pp. 41–43.

8. Rebecca Fannin, "Bring a Bag of Money," *Marketing & Media Decisions* (June 1987), pp. 38–45; Laurie Freeman and Janet Meyers, "Grocer 'Fee' Hampers New-Product Launches," *Advertising Age* (August 3, 1987), pp. 1, 60; and Judann Dagnoli and Laurie Freeman, "Marketers Seek Slotting-Fee Truce," *Advertising Age* (February 22, 1988), pp. 12, 68.

9. Ken Wells, "Atari, Seeking Outlets for Its Computers, Will Buy Federated Group, a Retailer," *Wall Street Journal* (August 25, 1987), p. 10.

10. Schulz, " '86: Better FOR Some," p. 92; "54th Annual Report of the Grocery Industry," p. 20; and authors' estimates.

11. Schulz, "'86: Better FOR Some," p. 92.

12. "54th Annual Report of the Grocery Industry," pp. 8, 21.

13. Judann Dagnoli, "Impulse Governs Shoppers," *Advertising Age* (October 5, 1987), p. 93.

14. Much of the material has been drawn from Katharine Davis Fishman, "The Disney World of Supermarkets," *New York* (March 18, 1985), pp. 46–52; Stew Leonard, "Love That Customer," *Management Review* (October 1987), pp. 36–39; and Joanne Kaufman, "In the Moo: Shopping at Stew Leonard's," *Wall Street Journal* (September 17, 1987), p. 32.

15. Much of the material has been drawn from Laurie Freeman, "Lands' End a Beacon for Mail-Order Market," *Advertising Age* (December 8, 1986), pp. 4, 69, 74; and "Mail-Order Companies," *Consumer Reports* (October 1987), pp. 610–611, 614.

16. Jane's Camera Shop is a composite camera retailer based on the authors' research.

How to Solve a Case Study

The information contained in this section is intended to give the reader some insights into the analysis of case studies. A case study is a collection of facts and data based on a real or hypothetical problem-oriented business situation.

The objective of a case study is to develop one's ability to solve complex business problems, using a logical framework. The problems within a case are generally not unique to a specific individual, company, or industry, and they frequently deal with more than one element of a retail strategy. Sometimes the material presented within a case can be in conflict. For example, two managers can disagree about a strategy; statistics can be contradictory; or there can be several interpretations of the same information.

In all case studies, the reader must analyze the material presented and state which specific actions best resolve the major issues or problems present. These actions must reflect the information contained in the case and the environment facing the firm.

Retailing case studies revolve around the identification of key issues and the presentation and evaluation of proposed courses of action. Any analysis of a case study should include the following sequential steps:

Steps in Solving a Case Study

1. Presentation of the facts surrounding the case.
2. Identification of the key issues.
3. Listing of alternative courses of action that could be taken.
4. Evaluation of alternative courses of action.
5. Recommendation of the best course of action.

Presentation of the Facts Surrounding the Case

It is helpful to read the case several times until one is familiar with the information contained therein. Rereadings often aid the reader to understand facts, possible strategies, or questions that need clarification that were not apparent earlier. It is important to pay particular attention to exhibits, tables, charts, and diagrams. Often data can reveal vital information when translated into percentages or compared with prior years.

In analyzing the case, the reader should assume that he or she is a retailing consultant hired by the company. Although facts and figures should be accepted as true, statements, judgments, and decisions made by the individuals in the case should be questioned, especially when not supported by facts or figures—or when one individual disagrees with another.

During the first and subsequent readings of the case, the reader should

❑ Underline important facts.

❑ Interpret all figures and charts.

❑ Question comments made by individuals.

❑ Judge the rationality of past and current decisions.

❑ Develop a list of questions whose answers would be useful in addressing the retailer's key issue(s).

Identification of the Key Issue(s)

Many times, the facts surrounding a case point out the key issue(s) facing a retailer, such as new opportunities, a changing environment, a decline in market share, poor profitability, and/or excess inventories. As a retailing consultant, you must identify the characteristics and ramifications of the issue(s) and examine them using the material contained in the case and in the text. In some instances, you must delve deeply because the key issue(s) and their characteristics may not be immediately obvious.

Listing of Alternative Courses of Action That Could Be Taken

Next, alternative courses of action pertaining to the key issue(s) in the case, identified in the previous step, are listed. These courses of action are considered on the basis of their appropriateness to the company and the situation. Thus, the advertising strategy for a small neighborhood stationery store would not be appropriate for a large gift store located in a major shopping center.

Proposed courses of action should take into account factors such as:

❑ Business category.

❑ Objectives.

❑ Customer market.

❑ Overall strategy.

❑ Product assortment.

❑ Competition.

❑ Legal restrictions.

❑ Economic trends.

❑ Marketplace trends.

❑ Financial capabilities.

❑ Personnel capabilities.

❑ Sources of supply.

Evaluation of Alternative Courses of Action

Each potential course of action must be evaluated, according to the facts surrounding the case, the key issue(s), and the environment of the firm. Specific criteria should be used, and each alternative should be analyzed on the basis of these criteria. The ramifications and risks associated with each course of action should also be considered. Important information and statistics not included in the case should be mentioned.

Recommendation of the Best Course of Action

Be sure that your case analysis is not just a summary of the case. The analysis will be critiqued by your professor on the basis of how well you identify the key issues or problems, outline and assess the alternative courses of action, and reach realistic conclusions (that take the retailer's size, competition, image, and so on into consideration). It is most important that you show a good understanding of the dynamics of the case.

Be precise about which alternative is more desirable for the retailer in its current context. Remember that the objective of case study analysis is the learning of a logical reasoning process applied to retailing. A written report must demonstrate this process.

Note: The cases in this text have questions to guide you in your analysis. However, your analysis should not be limited by them.

Chapter 2

Strategic Planning in Retailing: Owning or Managing a Business

❏ **Chapter Objectives** ❏

1 To show the value of strategic planning for all types of retailers

2 To explain the steps in strategic planning for retailers: situation analysis, objectives, identification of consumers, overall strategy, specific activities, control, and feedback

3 To examine the controllable and uncontrollable elements of a retail strategy

4 To present strategic planning as a series of integrated steps

Lens Crafters is a fast-growing six-year-old retail chain of optical stores that follows a sound strategic plan. It has clearly outlined its business philosophy and goals, appeals to a specific consumer market, and provides an integrated retail offering. Its key competitive advantage is one-hour service for most eyeglass orders. Each store has one or more optometrists, an assortment of four thousand frames, and an on-premises lens-grinding facility. A typical Lens Crafters outlet has annual sales of almost $2 million; the average customer purchase amount per transaction is $150; and sales per square foot are double those in a clothing store.

In the words of Dean Butler, Lens Crafters' founder, these are the firm's guiding principles:

This industry was ripe for something new. It hadn't changed for years. You know why? Optometrists con-

trolled it. They wrote state regulations aimed at protecting solo practitioner optometrists. So there wasn't much outside competition. No new retailing ideas, either. Optometrists examined your eyes and sold you frames from a relatively small selection. Two weeks later you got your glasses. But why should a customer have to wait two weeks? Grinding glasses is mostly machine-shop work. It can be done very fast.

Most optometrists say we're "commercializing" the eye business. So what? We're giving customers what they want—convenient service. We're in shopping malls, and we keep retail hours. Optometrists like professional buildings and close at five. We "sell" glasses to "customers." Optometrists don't like those words. They "dispense" glasses to "patients."

Lens Crafters' ability to operate as it does is due in part to a shifting legal environment in the United States. Today, optometric firms are permitted to advertise, and optometrists are required to give their patients prescriptions for eyeglasses, so that people may go to stores such as Lens Craf-ters if they so desire (rather than having no choice as to where their glasses can be bought).[1]

Overview

As noted in Chapter 1, a **retail strategy** is an overall plan or framework of action that guides a retailer. Ideally this plan will be at least one year in duration and will outline the philosophy, objectives, consumer market, overall and specific activities, and control mechanisms of the retailer over the length of the plan. Without a predefined and well-integrated strategy, the firm may flounder and be unable to cope with the environment that surrounds it.

A retail strategy has several attractive features. First, it provides a thorough analysis of the requirements of different types of retailing. Second, it outlines the objectives of the retailer. Third, a firm is shown how it can differentiate itself from competitors and develop an offering that appeals to a group of customers. Fourth, the retailer is forced to study the legal, economic, and competitive environments. Fifth, the total efforts of the company are coordinated. Sixth, crises are anticipated and often avoided.

Strategic planning can be conducted by the owner of the firm, by professional management, or by a combination of the two. When one moves up a retail career ladder, a key measure of performance and advancement potential is whether increased planning responsibility is undertaken and how well it is completed.

It is important to note that the steps in a retail strategy are interdependent, and often a firm will start off with a general plan that becomes more specific as alternatives, payoffs, and so on become clearer. In this chapter, we concentrate on the development of a comprehensive, integrated retail strategy, as shown in Figure 2-1.[2]

Situation Analysis

Situation analysis is the objective evaluation of the opportunities and potential problems facing a prospective or existing retailer. It seeks to answer two general questions: What position or status is the retailer in now? And in which direction should it be heading? For a retailer, situation analysis means defining and adhering to a philosophy of business, evaluating ownership and management alternatives, and outlining (in broad terms) the goods/service category to be sold.

Philosophy of Business

A **philosophy of business** is a retailer's understanding of its role in the business system; it is reflected in the firm's attitudes toward consumers, employees, competitors, government, and others. A philosophy of business enables a retailer to create a consumer following and distinguish itself from competitors.

For example, McDonald's philosophy of business is based on providing budget-conscious individuals and families with high-quality food, quick service, clean surroundings, and a wholesome environment. Sears' philosophy is reflected in its slogan: "There's more for your life at Sears." As the world's largest retailer, Sears attracts middle-class consumers to its extensive offerings of goods and services, and it is establishing several hundred "stores of the future." For many years, in recognition of its second-place standing in the car rental market, Avis coined a slogan summarizing its philosophy: "We try harder."

A firm's philosophy is a long-term commitment to a type of business and a place in the market. One key decision a retailer must make is whether to organize the business around the goods and services sold or around consumer needs. For example, a retailer entering the lumber business must decide if a line of bathroom vanities should be stocked in addition to raw lumber products. Probably,

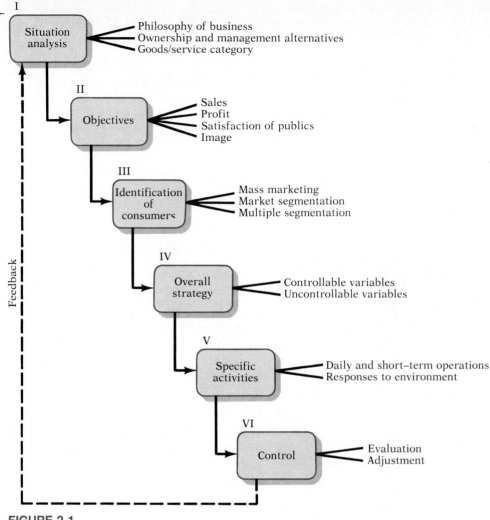

FIGURE 2-1
Elements of a Retail Strategy

the retailer would decide not to carry the vanities because they seem unconnected to its perceived business. However, a retailer who views the lumberyard as a do-it-yourself home-improvement center would see the bathroom vanities as a logical part of the product mix.

In the first case, the retailer has a traditional product-oriented philosophy of business. The retailer in the second instance has a philosophy of satisfying a certain type of customer (the do-it-yourselfer). This store will carry any merchandise that the consumer, not the storekeeper, desires. See Figure 2-2. A retailer must consider its philosophy and its reasons for entering the business and examine the alternative approaches available.

Although the development of a philosophy of business is the first step in a retailer's planning process, the philosophy should be continually reviewed and adjusted to reflect changing company objectives and a dynamic retail environment.

FIGURE 2-2
Lowe's Customer-Oriented Philosophy of Business
Lowe's chain of home centers offers a broad range of products for do-it-yourselfers. Within each
product line, customers are given a variety of products from which to choose, such as the "good,"
"better," and "best" lumber shown here. Reprinted by permission.

Ownership and Management Alternatives

A very essential part of situation analysis is the assessment of ownership and management alternatives. Ownership decisions include whether to operate as a sole proprietorship, a partnership, or a corporation as well as whether to start a new business, to buy an existing business, or to become a franchisee. Management alternatives include owner-manager versus professional manager and centralized versus decentralized structures.

A **sole proprietorship** is an unincorporated retail firm owned by one person. All benefits, profits, risks, and costs accrue to the single owner. A sole proprietorship is simple to form, fully controlled by the owner, operationally flexible, easy to dissolve, and subject to single taxation by the government. It does make the owner personally liable with regard to legal claims from suppliers, creditors, and others; and it may result in limited capital and limited expertise.

A **partnership** is an unincorporated retail firm owned by two or more persons, each of whom has a financial interest. Partners share benefits, profits, risks, and costs. A partnership allows responsibility and expertise to be divided among two or more owners, provides a greater capability of raising capital than a sole proprietorship, is simpler to form than a corporation, and is subject to single taxation by the government. It, too, makes owners personally liable regarding legal claims from suppliers, creditors, and others; may be dissolved upon the death of a partner or because of a disagreement; binds all partners to actions made by any individual partner acting on behalf of the company; and usually has less ability to raise capital than a corporation. As one observer has noted, "Partners who fail to resolve deep disagreements put their businesses and the quality of their personal lives at risk."[3]

A **corporation** is a retail firm that is formally incorporated under state law. It is a legal entity apart from its individual stockholders. A corporation allows capital to be raised through the sale of company stock, does not allow legal claims against individuals, makes ownership transfer relatively easy, is assured of long-term existence (even if a founder leaves, retires, or dies), has the most use of professional managers, and sets clear operating authority via corporate officers. It is subject to double taxation (company earnings and stockholder dividends), faces more government rules than other ownership forms, requires a complex and costly process when established, may be viewed as impersonal, and may separate ownership from management.

Starting a new business offers a retailer flexibility in location, operations, product lines, customer markets, and so on; and it allows the strategy to be fully tailored to the owner's desires and strengths. It may also mean having construction or renovation costs, having a time lag until the business is ready to open and then until profits are earned, beginning with an unknown name and image, and having to establish supplier relationships and develop an inventory of goods. Figure 2-3 presents several factors to be considered when starting a new business.

Buying an existing business allows a retailer to acquire an established company name, a customer following, a good location, trained personnel, and standing facilities; to operate immediately; to generate ongoing sales and profits; and possibly to obtain good lease terms and/or financing (at favorable interest rates) from the seller. It also means that fixtures may be older, there is less flexibility in developing and enacting a strategy tailored to the new owner's desires and strengths, and the growth potential of the business may be limited. Figure 2-4 provides a checklist of questions to consider when purchasing an existing retail business.

Becoming a franchisee allows a retailer to combine independent ownership with franchisor management assistance, thorough strategy planning, a well-known company name and a loyal customer following, cooperative advertising and buying, and a regional or national (rather than local) image. It also means that a contractual agreement may specify rigid operations standards, limit the product lines to be sold, and restrict the choice of suppliers; the franchisor usually receives continuous payments in the form of royalties; advertising fees may be required; and there is a possibility of termination by the franchisor if the agreement is not followed satisfactorily.

Strategically, the management format chosen has an additional impact on decision making. With an owner-manager system, planning tends to be less formal and more intuitive, and many functions tend to be reserved for the owner-manager (such as employee supervision). With a professional manager system, planning tends to be more formal and systematic. However, the professional manager is usually more constrained in his or her authority than the owner-manager. In a centralized structure, decision-making authority is limited to top

NAME OF BUSINESS _____

A. SELF–ASSESSMENT AND BUSINESS CHOICE

1. Evaluate your strengths and weaknesses.
2. Commitment paragraph: Why should you be in business for yourself? Why open a new business rather than acquire an existing one or become a member of a franchise chain?
3. Describe the type of retail business that best fits your strengths and desires. What will make it unique? What will the business offer for customers? How will you capitalize on the weaknesses of competitors?

B. OVERALL RETAIL PLAN

1. State your philosophy of business.
2. Choose an ownership form (sole proprietorship, partnership, or corporation).
3. State your long– and short–run goals.
4. Analyze your customers from their point of view.
5. Research your market size and store location.
6. Quantify the total retail sales of your goods/service category in your trading area.
7. Analyze your competition.
8. Quantify your potential market share.
9. Develop your retail strategy: store location and operations, merchandising, pricing, and store image and promotion.

C. FINANCIAL PLAN

1. What level of funds will you need to get started and to get through the first year? Where will they come from?
2. Determine the first year profit, return on investment, and salary that you need/want.
3. Project monthly cash flow and profit–and–loss statements for the first two years.
4. What sales will be needed to break–even during the first year? What will you do if these sales are not reached?

D. ORGANIZATIONAL DETAILS PLAN (ADMINISTRATIVE MANAGEMENT)

1. Describe your personnel plan (hats to wear), organizational plan, and policies.
2. List the jobs you like and want to do and those you dislike, cannot do, or do not want to do.
3. Outline your accounting and inventory systems.
4. Note your insurance plans.
5. Specify how day–to–day operations would be conducted for each aspect of your strategy.
6. Review the risks you face and how you plan to cope with them.

Source: Adapted by the authors from *Small Business Management Training Instructor's Guide: No. 109* (Washington, D.C.: U.S. Small Business Administration).

FIGURE 2-3
Selected Factors to Consider When Starting a New Retail Business

management or ownership; in a decentralized structure, managers in individual departments have major input into decisions. Regardless of management format, a retailer is best able to develop and enact a successful strategy only if there is ample information and communication.

A comprehensive discussion of independent retailers, chains, franchises, leased departments, vertical marketing systems, and consumer cooperatives appears in Chapter 3.

Goods/Service Category

Before a prospective retail firm is able to design a well-defined plan, it must determine the general goods/service category in which to operate. Figure 2-5 shows the diversity of goods/service categories from which a retailer may choose.

These questions should be considered when purchasing an existing retail business:

1. Why is the seller placing the business up for sale?

2. How much are you paying for goodwill (the cost of the business above its tangible asset value)?

3. Have sales, inventory levels, and profit figures been confirmed by your accountant?

4. Will the seller introduce you to his/her customers and stay on during the transition period?

5. Will the seller sign a statement that he/she will not open a directly-competing business in the same trading area for a reasonable time period?

6. If sales are seasonal, are you purchasing the business at the right time of year?

7. In the purchase of the business, are you assuming existing debts of the seller?

8. Who receives proceeds from transactions made prior to the sale of the business but not yet paid by creditors?

9. What is the length of the lease if property is rented?

10. If property is to be purchased along with the business, has it been inspected by a professional engineer?

11. How modern are the storefront and store fixtures?

12. Is inventory fresh? Does it contain a full merchandise assortment?

13. Are advertising policy, customer service policy, and pricing policy of the past owner similar to yours? Can you continue old policies?

14. If the business is to be part of a chain, is the new unit compatible with existing units? How much trading area overlap is there with existing stores?

15. Has a lawyer examined the proposed contract?

16. What effect will owning this business have on your life-style and on your family relationships?

FIGURE 2-4
A Checklist for Purchasing an Existing Retail Business

Chapter 4 examines the characteristics of food-based and general merchandise store retailers, nonstore retailers, and the differences between goods and service retailing in detail. Chapter 17 looks at the special strategic features of service retailing.

When selecting the goods/service category, the potential retailer should select a type of business that will allow him or her to match personal abilities, financial resources, and time availability with those required by the kind of business.

Personal Abilities

Personal abilities depend on an individual's aptitudes—the preference for a type of business and the potential to do well; education—formal learning about retail practices and policies; and experience—practical learning about retail practices and policies.

A retailer must have an aptitude for the business he or she chooses to enter. For example, the retailer who wants to run his or her own store, who likes to use initiative, and who has the ability to react quickly to competitive developments will be suited to a different type of situation from the retailer who depends

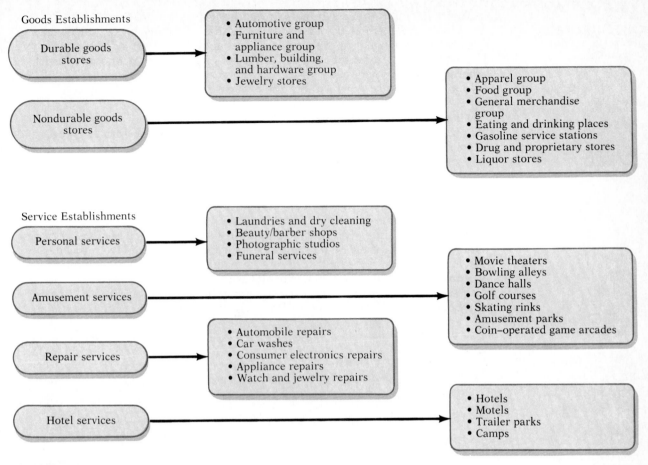

FIGURE 2-5
Selected Kinds of Retail Goods and Services Establishments

on others for advice and does not like to make decisions. The first retailer could enter business as an independent operator, in a dynamic business such as fashion; the second retailer should look for partners or a franchise and a business that is relatively static, like a car wash. In addition, some retailers enjoy close personal interaction with their customers; these would dislike the impersonality of a pure discount or self-service operation. Still others enjoy the impersonality of mail-order retailing. These illustrations show the importance of aptitude in the selection of a type of business.

Education and experience requirements are clearly specified in certain fields and are enforced by federal or state laws. Insurance brokers, stockbrokers, real-estate brokers, barbers, beauticians, certified public accountants, pharmacists, and opticians represent a good cross section of the kinds of retailers who must satisfy minimum educational and/or experience standards. Professional competency must be demonstrated. For instance, a real-estate broker must be licensed. This licensing involves an analysis of the individual's ethical character, as well as an examination of the person's knowledge of real-estate practice and law. (However, designation as a broker does not depend on the ability to sell, keep good financial records, or negotiate with buyers and sellers.)

Some skills can be learned through education and/or experience; other skills are inborn. Potential retailers must be able to examine their personal skills and match them with the requirements of a business. This is a difficult process that involves insight into oneself and careful, honest reflection. Strengths and weaknesses must be assessed and evaluated in this matching process. Partnerships may arise when two or more parties possess complementary skills. A person with extensive selling experience and ability will often join someone possessing the operational skills necessary to open a store. Each partner has valuable skills but cannot operate the store without the expertise of the other.

Financial Resources

A second major consideration in the selection of a goods/service category for a retail business is the level of **financial resources** required. Many enterprises, especially new, independent ones, fail because the owners do not correctly estimate the financial resources needed to succeed. Figure 2-6 outlines some of the financial investments for a new retail venture.

New retailers frequently underestimate the need for a drawing account, cited in Figure 2-6. This drawing account is used for the personal needs of the retailer and his or her family during the early, unprofitable stage of a business. Housing, clothing, food, medical, and other personal expenses are paid from this account. Because very few new retail stores are immediately profitable, the budget for the venture must include personal expenditures.

The costs of renovating an existing facility are also often underestimated by the new retailer. It is common for undercapitalized (low-on-funds) retailers to

Use of Funds	Source of Funds
Land and building (lease or purchase)	Personal savings, bank loan, commercial finance company
Inventory	Personal savings, manufacturer credit, commercial finance company, sales revenues
Fixtures (including: display cases, storage facilities, signs, lighting, carpeting, etc.)	Personal savings, manufacturer credit, bank loan, commercial finance company
Equipment (including: cash register, marking machine, office equipment, computers, etc.)	Personal savings, manufacturer credit, bank loan, commercial finance company
Personnel (including: salespersons, cashiers, stockpersons, etc.)	Personal savings, bank loan, sales revenues
Promotion	Personal savings, sales revenues
Personal drawing account	Personal savings, life insurance loan
Miscellaneous: Equipment repair Credit sales (bad debts) Professional services Repayment of loans	Personal savings, manufacturer and wholesaler credit, bank credit plan, bank loan, commercial finance company

Note: Collateral for a bank loan may be a retailer's building, fixtures, land, inventory, and/or personal residence.

FIGURE 2-6
Financial Investments for a New Retail Venture

invest initially in only essential renovations. Other improvements are made when the firm is prospering, and the costs of these alterations are paid out of profits. Although this practice does reduce the initial investment, it can give the store a poor image.

Merchandise width and depth of assortment, as well as the types of goods and services sold, have an impact on the financial outlay required of a new retailer. The use of a partnership or a franchise agreement will also have an effect on the initial investment.

Table 2-1 provides a description of the financial resources and requirements of a hypothetical used-car dealer. Table 2-2 shows inventory costs and revenues for this retailer.[4]

TABLE 2-1
Financial Requirements for a Used-Car Dealer

Total investments (first year)	
Lease (10 years, $40,000 per year)	$ 40,000
Beginning inventory (fifty cars, average cost of $4,750)	237,500
Replacement inventory (fifty cars, average cost of $4,750)*	237,500
Fixtures and equipment (includes painting, paneling, carpeting, lighting, signs, heating and air-conditioning system, electronic cash register, service bay)	40,000
Replacement parts	20,000
Personnel (one mechanic)	27,000
Promotion (brochures and newspaper advertising)	15,000
Drawing account (to cover owner's personal expenses for one year; all selling and operating functions except mechanical ones performed by the owner)	30,000
Accountant	6,000
Miscellaneous (including loan payments)	35,000
Profit (projected)	20,000
	$708,000
Source of funds	
Personal savings	$133,000
Bank loan	200,000
Sales revenues (based on expected sales of fifty cars, average price of $7,500)	375,000
	$708,000

*Assumes that fifty cars are sold during the year. As each type of car is sold, a replacement is bought by the dealer and placed in inventory. At the end of the year, inventory on hand remains at fifty units.

TABLE 2-2
Analysis of Beginning Inventory Costs and Expected First Year Sales Revenues by Type of Car for a Used-Car Dealer

Type of Car	Number of Cars in Beginning Inventory	Average Cost	Average Selling Price	Total Cost of Beginning Inventory	Annual Total Revenue*
Subcompact	10	$3,500	$ 5,200	$ 35,000	$ 52,000
Compact	14	4,250	6,750	59,500	94,500
Intermediate	15	5,000	8,000	75,000	120,000
Full-size/luxury	6	6,667	11,000	40,000	66,000
Station wagon/van	5	5,600	8,500	28,000	42,500
	50	$4,750	$ 7,500	$237,500	$375,000

*Fifty cars are sold during the year. As each type of car is sold, a replacement is bought by the dealer and placed in inventory. At the end of the year, inventory on hand remains at fifty units.

The initial personal savings investment of $133,000 required to enter this type of business would force many potential retailers to rethink the choice of product category as well as the intended format of the retail organization. First, the plans for a fifty-car inventory reflect the entrepreneur's desire to have a balanced product line. However, if the dealer described in Tables 2-1 and 2-2 concentrates on subcompact, compact, and intermediate cars, he or she can become more specialized and can reduce significantly the size of the inventory. This would lead to lower investment costs. Second, the entering used-car dealer can also reduce the initial investment by seeking a location that has facilities that do not have to be modified, for example, the site of another used-car dealer. Third, fewer financial resources are needed if the dealer enters into a partnership, which would allow the costs (as well as the profits) to be shared.

Time Demands

The **time demands** on retail owners (or managers) differ significantly by goods or service category. The time requirements are influenced both by consumer demand and needs and by the owners' or managers' ability to automate operations or delegate activities to others.

A firm such as a major appliance store must be open during weekends and evening hours, and even on holidays because appliance purchases are usually made jointly by the husband and the wife (those times are especially convenient for these types of customers). A mom-and-pop grocery store or a convenience food store sells its greatest volume when supermarkets are closed; therefore evening and weekend hours must be maintained. Gift shops, sporting goods stores, house painters, and others have extreme seasonal shifts in business and are forced to keep long hours during the prime seasons. On the other hand, mail-order firms (which can process orders during any part of the day) have much more flexible hours.

The ability or inability of a retailer to automate operations or delegate duties also affects the number of hours worked. Some types of businesses require relatively low involvement by the owner. These include gasoline stations that offer no repair or maintenance services, coin-operated laundromats, movie theaters, and motels. The emphasis on automation, self-service, standardized goods and services, and extensive financial controls allows these retailers to minimize their time investments. Other types of businesses require the active involvement of the owners. Beauty parlors, television repair stores, butcher shops, luncheonettes, and jewelry stores are examples of time-consuming businesses.

Intensive owner participation can be caused by several factors. First, the owner may be the major worker, and consumers may be attracted by his or her skills (the major competitive advantage of the retailer). In this case, the delegation of work to others will diminish consumer loyalty. Associated with this aspect is the personal service and expertise that only an owner can give to certain customers. Second, some types of retailing, such as personal services, are not easy to automate. In these cases, the time involvement of the retailer is needed to provide the services. Third, many smaller retailers are undercapitalized. Therefore, the owner and his or her family must operate all aspects of the business because there are insufficient funds to hire employees. Fourth, a business that operates on a cash basis and has weak financial controls requires the owner to be on the premises to avoid being cheated. In a small store with poor inventory procedures, it may be difficult to match sales with inventory levels. So it may be easy for employees to pocket cash sales if not watched by the owner.

A common error is to assume that the retailer works only when a store is open. For many retailers, off-hours activities are necessary. A butcher must go to the meat wholesaler at least once a week to make purchases. (Meat wholesalers are busiest between 3 and 6 A.M.) In a luncheonette, foods must be prepared before the store opens. A jeweler specializing in diamonds must go to the city's diamond exchange to examine and negotiate for merchandise. An antique dealer often spends nonstore hours hunting for goods. A small storekeeper sweeps, stocks shelves, and does the books during the hours the store is closed.

The prospective retailer should also examine his or her own time preferences in terms of stability versus seasonality (some would rather work 40 hours per week for 48 weeks a year; others would rather work 80 hours per week for 24 weeks a year and relax the balance of the year); ideal working hours (days and times); and the level of personal involvement (absentee ownership or on-site management).

Objectives

After situation analysis, the objectives of a firm are developed. **Objectives** are the goals, long-run and short-run, that a retailer hopes to attain. The statement of clear objectives helps to mold a strategy and translate the company philosophy into action. A retailer may be concerned with one or more of the following objectives: sales (including growth, stability, and market share); profit (including level, return on investment, and efficiency); satisfaction of publics (including stockholders and consumers); and image (including customer and industry perceptions). Each of these objectives is sought by many retailers. Some retailers attempt to achieve all of the objectives; others select a few and attempt to achieve these well.

Sales

Sales objectives are those concerned with the sales volume of a retailer. Growth, stability, and/or market share are the sales objectives most often sought by retailers.

Some retailers set sales growth as a top priority. Under this objective, a firm is interested in expanding operations and increasing sales. There is less emphasis on short-run profits. The assumption is that investments in the present will yield profits in the future. A small or large retailer that does well often becomes interested in opening new units and increasing sales volume. However, too active a pursuit of expansion can result in problems. Many retailers who are successful in their current business fail when they open new units. Management skills and the "personal touch" are sometimes lost with improper expansion. Sales growth is a legitimate goal for large and small retailers, but growth should not be too fast or exclude the consideration of other objectives.

Stability in annual sales and profits is the objective of a wide range of retailers. These companies place their emphasis on maintaining their sales volume, market share, price lines, and so on. Small retailers are often interested in stable sales that will enable them to make a satisfactory living every year, without the pressure of downswings or upsurges. Other retailers develop a loyal following of consumers and are intent not on expanding but on maintaining the services that have attracted the original consumers.

Another objective of many retailers is proper market share. Market share is the percentage of total retail-category sales contributed by one company. In retailing, market share is usually an objective only for large retailers or retail chains.[5] The small retailer is more concerned with competition across the street or down the block than with total sales in a metropolitan area.

Sales objectives may be expressed in dollars and units. To achieve its dollar objectives, a retailer can employ a discount strategy (low prices and high unit sales), a moderate strategy (medium prices and medium unit sales), or a prestige strategy (high prices and low unit sales). In the long run, the use of sales units as an indicator of performance is important. Dollar sales over a two- to three-year period may be difficult to compare because of changing retail prices and the rate of inflation. However, sales in units are relatively easy to compare from year to year. A company with dollar sales of $350,000 in 1980 and $500,000 in 1988 might assume that it is doing very well, until unit figures are computed: 10,000 in 1980 and 8,000 in 1988.

Profit

Profitability means that the retailer wants to attain at least a minimum level of profits during a designated time period, usually a year. Profits may be expressed in dollars or as a percentage of sales. For a retailer having yearly sales of $5 million and total yearly costs of $4.2 million, profits in dollars are $800,000, and profits as a percentage of sales are 16 per cent. If the profit objectives of the firm are equal to or less than $800,000, or 16 per cent, the retailer is satisfied. If the profit objectives are greater than $800,000, or 16 per cent, the retailer has not attained the minimum desired level of profits and is therefore dissatisfied.

Retailers who invest large capital expenditures in land, buildings, equipment, and so on often have return on investment (ROI) as a company objective. Return on investment is the relationship between company profits and investment in capital items. This statistic is used in the same manner as the profit statistic. A satisfactory rate of return is predefined by the company, and this rate is compared with the actual rate of return at the end of the year or other designated time period. If a company has annual sales of $5 million and expenditures (including the long-term payment of capital items) of $4 million, the yearly profit is $1 million. Assume that the cost of land, buildings, and equipment is $10 million. Then ROI equals $1 million/$10 million, or 10 per cent per year. The company's ROI objective would have to be 10 per cent or less per year for it to be satisfied.

Increased efficiency in operations is an objective of many retailers. Efficiency may be expressed as $1 - $ (selling expenses/company sales). The larger this figure, the more efficient the firm. A retailer with sales of $2 million and selling expenses of $1 million has an efficiency rating of 50 per cent ([$1 - ($1 million/$2 million)]). Fifty cents of every sales dollar are contributed to nonselling costs such as merchandise purchases and to profits, and fifty cents go for selling expenses. The retailer might set as an objective for next year an increase in selling efficiency to 60 per cent. On sales of $2 million, selling expenses would have to be reduced to $800,000 ([$1 - ($800,000/$2 million)]). In this instance, 60 cents of every sales dollar are contributed to nonselling costs and profits; only 40 cents go for selling expenses. The increase in efficiency will lead to an overall increase in the retailer's profits. Nonetheless, a retailer must be careful with this objective. If expenses are cut too much, customer service may decline; and this would probably lead to a sales drop and a resulting profit decrease.

Satisfaction of Publics

A retailer is often concerned with **satisfying its publics,** including stockholders, consumers, suppliers, employees, and government. Stockholder satisfaction is a vital objective for any retail establishment that is publicly owned. It is up to store management to set and attain goals that are consistent with the wishes of stockholders. Many companies have policies that lead to small annual increases in sales and profits (because these goals can be sustained over the long run and indicate good management), rather than policies of introducing innovative ideas that might lead to peaks and valleys in company sales and profits (indicating poor management). Stable earnings for the firm lead to stable dividends for stockholders.

Consumer satisfaction with the total retail offering is an objective that most firms are practicing today, although some have acknowledged this only recently.

It is crucial for the company to satisfy the consumer and not to adopt a policy of caveat emptor ("Let the buyer beware"). Retailers must be willing to take criticism and adapt to the desires of the consumer. They can easily accomplish this by gearing a company's philosophy and objectives to the consumer. If the consumer is satisfied, the other objectives are more likely to be accomplished. Despite the inclusion of consumer satisfaction as a stated objective of today's retailers, the importance of this objective ranks too low for many, large and small alike. The other objectives cited rate higher in the list of priorities.

Good supplier relations are important. A retailer must understand and work with suppliers, such as manufacturers and wholesalers, if favorable prices, new products, good return policies, prompt shipments, and cooperation are to be received. Because suppliers perform many functions for small retailers, good relations are particularly important for them.

Favorable employee relations are crucial to the performance of a retailer, whether the firm is small or large. Positive employee morale leads to less absenteeism, better performance, and lower turnover. Employee relations can be improved through effective selection, training, and motivation.

Because federal, state, and local governments all impose restrictions on retailers, it is important to understand and react to these policies. In some cases, retailers are able to influence government regulations by acting singly or as members of large groups, such as trade associations or chambers of commerce.

Image (Store Positioning)

Image refers to how a retailer is perceived by consumers and others. A firm may be viewed as innovative or conservative, distinctive or "me too," well-stocked or understocked, caring of consumers or indifferent, economical or high priced, and so on. Virtually all retailers are concerned with how they are viewed and set as an objective the creation and maintenance of the image that they want consumers to have. The key to a successful image is that consumers view retailers in the manner the latter intend. See Figure 2-7.

Store positioning enables a retailer to determine how consumers perceive the company (its image) relative to its retail category and its competitors. For example, a retailer selling women's clothing could be generally positioned as an upscale specialty store, a mid-priced specialty store, a department store, a discount department store, or a discount specialty store, and it could be specifically positioned in relation to any nearby retailers selling women's clothing.

This is illustrated by Mandy's Women's Shop, a store located in a regional shopping center that is two miles from a discount shopping district. As shown in Figure 2-8, Mandy's is positioned as an upscale specialty store. This is a small retail category, but it has loyal customers and high profit margins. Mandy's is well positioned for its category, having a very good fashion/price mix. Of Mandy's nearby competitors, one is an upscale specialty store, five are mid-priced specialty stores, two are department stores, two are discount department stores, and four are discount specialty stores.

For some retailers, such as McDonald's, Hertz, or the market-leading drugstore chain in your region, industry leadership (which may be local) is an important objective. This leadership often results in two major benefits for a firm. First, company image may be improved because consumers are apt to place the leader on a higher plateau than its competitors. Second, other retailers may follow pricing and other strategies of the leader rather than developing their own innovative approaches; this form of imitation is the best kind of flattery. Another subsidiary benefit is the internal satisfaction that accompanies being "number one," and this encourages all to work harder.

Identity Problem: Abercrombie & Fitch, a specialty sporting goods retailer, needed a strong brand identity for an exclusive line of safari clothing and accessories. Management wanted an upscale private label identity that suited A&F's distinctive image of elegance and adventure.

Selame Solution: To capture the A&F tradition, a mark depicting the prized black rhinoceros was developed. The "charging rhino" is underscored by A&F's unique typestyle and corporate colors. The symbol, combined with the slogan, "The Adventure Goes On," effectively targets the upscale sportsperson.

Identity Problem: Jamesway's steady growth as a Mid-Atlantic discount chain retailer led to store interiors lacking a uniform prototype and color scheme. Local restrictions caused variations in signage size and design. With ten new stores opening in ten months, management wanted an easily adapted identity system to communicate quality, not high prices.

Selame Solution: Bridging the fine line between a promotional and fashion image, the turquoise and orange typestyle accentuates the Jamesway name and allows the retailer to project a more coordinated visual image on exterior signs and interior decor.

Identity Problem: Twenty years ago, Bradlees came to Selame in need of an updated symbol that would communicate its new direction in hard and soft goods. The Bradlees "B" was developed as a signaling device for instant highway recognition.

Selame Solution: Ten years later, Bradlees had established a market in other areas—personal products and fashion clothing. Retaining years of equity, Selame combined the "B" into a single, more fashion-oriented signature, simplifying private labeling and reducing signage square footage to meet new signing codes.

Identity Problem: Richman Gordman's success as a retailer of popularly priced clothing to middle America was due to their promotional department store strategy. An updated identity was needed to keep pace with new prototype stores. The long company name needed a "signal" device for instant recognition.

Selame Solution: RG, as the store was often called, became the signal device. Designed at a 45° angle to project a contemporary mood, the mark reflects a progressive marketing strategy. It also helps to visually unify exterior signage, interiors, packaging, and advertising.

FIGURE 2-7
The Importance of a Retail Image
The retailers represented here all used Selame Design to devise updated store identities that would project the retailers' desired images to customers. Reprinted by permission of Selame Design.

Selection of Objectives

The objective(s) that a retailer selects will have a great influence on the development of an overall strategy. A retailer that clearly defines objectives and develops a strategy to achieve them improves its chances of success.

An example of a retailer that has well-defined objectives and an appropriate strategy to attain them is Wherehouse Entertainment, a chain with more than 350 outlets in California, Arizona, Nevada, and Washington. The company has sales and profit growth, employee satisfaction, and unique store positioning among its goals. In 1985 and 1986, Wherehouse Entertainment was recognized by both *Business Week* and *Forbes* as one of the best small companies in America, based on a combination of sales and profit growth and return on investment. Today, the firm is not so small.

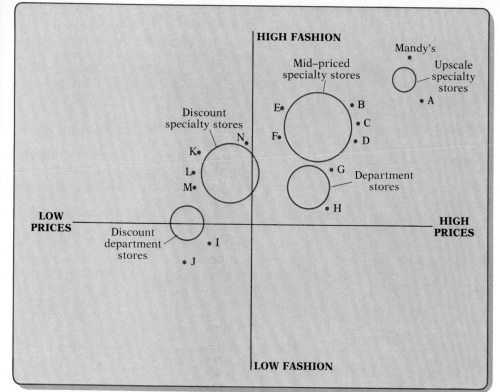

Consumers' perception of store positioning for a retail category. The size
of the circle refers to the relative sales of the category for the women's
clothing lines carried by Mandy's.

• Consumers' perception of Mandy's and 14 of its competitors (A–N).

FIGURE 2-8
A Store Positioning Map for Mandy's Women's Shop

To sustain growth, Wherehouse Entertainment is adding thirty new outlets per year; annual sales are now well over $250 million. It realizes that short-run profits will be lower to pay for this expansion; but much higher long-run profits are expected. To maximize employee satisfaction, Wherehouse Entertainment requires all workers to be stockholders to share in the firm's success; and it has set up Wherehouse University to improve managerial and selling skills. The retailer has a distinctive positioning strategy as an "entertainment software company." It carries a large assortment of records, tapes, compact discs, movie videos, personal computer programs, and other "software." It does not stock stereos, CD players, or other "hardware"; instead, the software products complement the hardware sold by consumer electronics stores.[6]

Next, the retailer or prospective retailer must identify the characteristics and needs of its consumers. The customer group that a retailer tries to satisfy is called the **target market.** In selecting its target market, a retailer may use one of three techniques: selling goods and services to a broad spectrum of consumers, the **mass market;** zeroing in on one specific group, a **market segment;** or aiming at two or more distinct consumer groups, **multiple segments,** with different retailing approaches for each group.

**Identification
of Consumer
Characteristics
and Needs**

Conventional supermarkets and drugstores and traditional shoe stores (such as Thom McAn) are examples of retailers that define their target markets broadly. These stores have a wide assortment of medium-quality items that are sold at popular prices. In contrast, a small upscale men's shoe store or a fruit-and-vegetable store exemplifies the retailer that selects a well-defined and specific consumer group and offers a narrow, deep product assortment at above-average prices (or in other cases, below-average prices). A retailer aiming at one segment does not try to appeal to everyone.

Department stores are among the retailers that seek multiple market segments. They cater to several groups of customers and provide unique goods and services for each. As an example, women's clothing may be sold in a number of distinctive boutiques scattered throughout the store. Also, large retail chains frequently have divisions that appeal to different market segments. Dayton Hudson Corporation operates Hudson's and Dayton's department stores for customers interested in full service and Target and Mervyn's discount stores for customers interested in low prices.

As shown in Figure 2-9, the selection and clear statement of a target market give direction to a retailer's choice of a location, a goods and services mix, promotion efforts, and prices. They further enable a firm to stress its competitive advantages and to allocate financial resources. Although each of these factors is important, the concept of **competitive advantage**—the distinct competency of a retailer relative to its competitors—is too often overlooked. The choice of a target

Strategic Implications	Target Market Selected		
	Mass Market	**Market Segment**	**Multiple Segments**
Retailer's Location	Near a large population base	Near a small or medium population base	Near a large population base
Goods and Services Mix	Wide assortment of medium–quality items	Deep assortment of high–quality or low–quality items	Distinct goods/ services aimed at each market segment
Promotion Efforts	Mass advertising	Direct mail, subscription	Different media and messages for each segment
Price Orientation	"Popular prices"	High or low	High, medium, and low— depending on market segment
Strategy Emphasis	One general, "middle–of–the road" strategy directed at a large homogeneous (similar) group of consumers	One specific strategy directed at a specific, limited group of customers	Several specific strategies, each directed at different (hetero-geneous) groups of consumers

FIGURE 2-9
Methods for Selecting a Target Market

market and its satisfaction by a unique retail offering are necessary for retailers to achieve their goals. Some examples will demonstrate this.

Saks Fifth Avenue defines its target market as upper-class, status-conscious consumers. Saks situates stores in prestigious shopping areas, offers exclusive brands of high-quality merchandise, uses finely drawn ads in newspapers, has extensive customer service, and charges relatively high prices. K mart describes its target market as middle-class, value-conscious consumers. K mart locates stores in mid-range shopping centers and districts, offers national brands and K mart brands of medium-quality merchandise, features "good values" in its ads, maintains some customer service, and charges below-average to average prices. Off-price stores appeal to extremely price-conscious consumers. They locate in discount strip shopping centers or districts, offer national brands (sometimes manufacturers' overruns or merchandise not sold by other retailers) of average to below-average quality merchandise, emphasize low prices in ads, offer no customer service, and set very low prices. The key to the success of each of these retailers is their ability to define their customers and cater to their needs in a distinctive manner.

A retailer is better able to select a target market and satisfy customer needs if it has a good understanding of consumer behavior. This topic is discussed in Chapter 5.

Overall Strategy

After completing a situation analysis, setting objectives, and selecting a target market, the retailer is ready to develop an in-depth overall strategy. This strategy involves two components: those aspects of business that the retailer can directly affect (such as store hours and sales personnel) and those to which the retailer must adapt (such as laws, the economy, and competition). The former are called **controllable variables,** and the latter are called **uncontrollable variables.** See Figure 2-10.

Retailers must develop their strategies with both of these kinds of variables in mind. And the ability of firms to understand and predict the effects of controllable and uncontrollable variables is aided by the use of marketing research. In Chapter 6, marketing research in retailing is described.

Controllable Variables

The controllable parts of a retail strategy are broken down into the basic categories shown in Figure 2-10: store location and operations, merchandising, pricing, and store image and promotion. A good strategy integrates all four of these

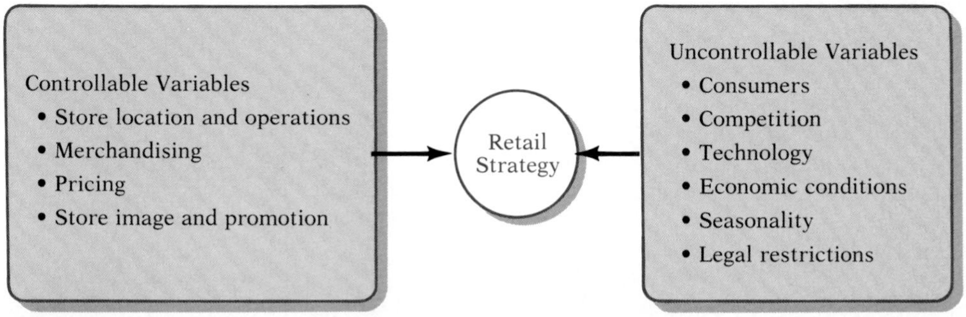

Controllable Variables
- Store location and operations
- Merchandising
- Pricing
- Store image and promotion

Retail Strategy

Uncontrollable Variables
- Consumers
- Competition
- Technology
- Economic conditions
- Seasonality
- Legal restrictions

FIGURE 2-10
Developing an Overall Retail Strategy

areas so that a consistent, unified plan is developed and followed. These elements are comprehensively covered in Chapters 7 through 17.

Store Location and Operations

A retailer has several store location and operations decisions to make. The first decision involves whether to utilize a store or a nonstore (e.g., mail-order) format. Next, for store-based retailers, a general location and a specific site must be determined. Competitors, transportation access, population density, type of neighborhood, nearness to suppliers, and so on are the factors to be considered when picking a store location. The terms of tenancy (such as rent, flexibility, and length of contract) must be evaluated; and a build, buy, or rent decision must be made. The store size, the type of building, and the fixtures need to be chosen. The location of multiple outlets, an increasing phenomenon in today's retailing environment, must be considered if expansion is an objective of the firm. Each of these aspects of location can cause problems if not adequately defined in the strategy phase.

Operations decisions involve a number of elements. Personnel management and policies pertain to employee hiring, training, compensating, supervising, and so on. Job descriptions and functions should be detailed and communicated, along with the authority and responsibility of all personnel and the chain of command. The financial dynamics of operations involve asset management, budgeting, and resource allocation. Other specific aspects of operations management include store format, size, and space allocation; personnel utilization;

RETAILING IN ACTION

How Does the Leading Toy Store Chain Stay on Top?

In 1984, Toys "R" Us accounted for 11 per cent of all U.S toy sales. By 1987, its market share had risen to over 20 per cent; and the firm's sales were almost four times those of the next biggest toy store chain, Child World. The goal of Toys "R" Us is to attain a 25 per cent market share by the year 2000. How has Toys "R" Us been able to sustain its leadership position, when competition from toy stores, department stores, discounters, and others is higher than ever?

Toys "R" Us has a distinctive and progressive retail strategy; and it is not complacent. These are a few of the features of the strategy of Toys "R" Us:

❑ It maintains a large year-round inventory of toys. 18,000 to 20,000 items are carried in a typical outlet. This gives people ample choice and encourages patronage on the part of undecided customers (who can make a decision in the store).

❑ By purchasing toys in the off season, the company gets extra discounts and can test new brands or concepts early in the year.

❑ Everyday low pricing is employed, with sales featured as necessary.

❑ There is a large budget for newspaper and television advertising.

❑ When adding new stores (and Toys "R" Us enters about two new markets every year), a regional approach is followed to maximize efficiency. Several outlets and a warehouse distribution center are placed in each new market.

❑ An advanced computer system is used to track sales by product and store. This provides valuable information.

❑ Complementary Kids "R" Us clothing stores are being opened adjacent to many toy outlets.

Source: Based on material in Isadore Barmash, "Toys 'R' Us Prospers as Holiday Sales Rise," *New York Times* (December 21, 1987), p. D3; "Most Toy Chains Increase Volume: TRU Cracks $2 Bil.," *Discount Store News* (July 20, 1987), pp. 39–76; and Subrata Chakraverty, "Will Toys 'B' Great?" *Forbes* (February 22, 1988), pp. 37–39.

store maintenance; inventory management; store security; insurance; credit management; computerization; and crisis management.

Merchandising

The second aspect of strategic planning deals with merchandising, which requires a number of choices. The general quality of the goods and/or services offered must be determined. Decisions are necessary about the width of assortment (the number of different goods and service categories that a retailer carries) and the depth of assortment (the variety of goods or services carried within a given category).

Policies are needed with regard to how innovative the retailer is going to be in the introduction of new goods or services. Criteria for buying decisions (how often, what terms, which suppliers, and so on) need to be set. Forecasting, budgeting, and retail accounting procedures must be outlined. The level of inventory (average stock on hand) has to be outlined for each type of merchandise that is carried. Finally, the retailer should devise procedures to assess the success or failure of each good or service sold.

Pricing

The third area of retail strategy involves pricing decisions. A retailer would choose from among several pricing techniques (such as leading, following, cost-plus, and demand-oriented). It would decide what level of prices to charge: low, medium, or high. Which of these levels is consistent with the retailer's image and the quality of the goods and services offered? The number of prices within each goods or service category would be determined. For example, how many prices of candy should a retailer carry? This concept is called price lining. Psychological pricing may also be used; this requires a thorough understanding of the consumer and his or her willingness to pay high prices for certain items, such as cosmetics.

The method of payment, such as cash only or cash plus credit, must be planned. Most retailers allow credit purchases today. A major exception is the supermarket industry, because of the already low profit margins of supermarkets. Even small delicatessens and cleaning stores allow credit on an informal, personal basis. Billing terms must also be determined: the length of deferred payments and the resulting interest charges, the use of COD, discounts for cash or early payments, and so on.

Store Image and Promotion

The fourth broad area of strategic planning encompasses the establishment of a store image and the utilization of promotion techniques. As mentioned earlier in this chapter, image is critical for retailers. If the target market does not perceive the retailer in the manner intended, then the retailer usually cannot succeed. Therefore, a distinctive and desirable (by the target market) image must be sought. This image can be created and sustained through the use of several techniques.

The physical attributes, or atmosphere, of a store and its surrounding area greatly influence the consumer's perception of a retailer. The impact of the storefront (the building's exterior) on a firm's atmosphere and image should not be undervalued, as it is the first part of the store seen by the customer. Inside the store, layouts and displays (the arrangement and positioning of merchandise), wall and floor colors, styles of lighting used, scents, music, and the kind of sales personnel also contribute to a store's image. A prestige retailer creates and upholds its image through fancy outside display windows, plush carpeting, wide aisles, attractive in-store displays, and hidden price tags. A discounter creates and upholds its image through no-frills outside display windows, bare floors, crowded in-store displays, clearly visible price tags, and self-service.

Customer services and community relations can generate a favorable image for the retailer. Customer services are such offerings as parking, gift wrapping, a liberal return policy, extended store hours during special seasons, layaway plans, alterations, credit, and telephone and mail sales. Community relations are enhanced by participation in civic activities, donations to charity, and so on.

The proper use of promotion techniques can enhance a retailer's sales performance. The techniques can range from inexpensive door-to-door flyers for a supermarket or take-out restaurant to an expensive national advertising campaign for a franchise chain. Three forms of paid promotion are available to retailers. Mass advertising—via television, radio, magazines, billboards, direct mail, and most often, newspapers—allows a retailer to direct a message at a large number of customers. Personal selling enables a retailer to have one-to-one relationships with customers. Sales promotion provides added persuasion through coupons, contests, shopping bags, and other tools. In addition to paid promotion, a retailer can obtain free publicity when stories about the firm are written, televised, or broadcast.

The preceding discussion has outlined the four basic controllable portions of a retail strategy. However, the retailer must also keep the uncontrollable environmental factors in mind when setting up a strategy. A discussion of these uncontrollable variables follows.

Uncontrollable Variables

The uncontrollable parts of a retailing strategy can be divided into the categories shown in Figure 2-10: consumers, competition, technology, economic conditions, seasonality, and legal restrictions. Retailers need to monitor the external environment and adapt the controllable parts of their strategies to take into account the elements beyond their immediate control. The uncontrollable nature of these variables is explained next.

Once a retailer has picked a target market, its strategy must be set accordingly. A good retailer recognizes that it cannot alter demographic trends, change lifestyle patterns, impose tastes, or "force" goods and services on customers. Rather, the retailer needs to learn about its target market and develop an offering consistent with consumer trends and desires. Selecting a target market is within the control of a retailer, but the firm will be unable to sell goods or services that are beyond the price range of its customers, that are not wanted, or that are not displayed or advertised in the proper manner. The total retail effort must be geared toward satisfying the target market.

After the type of business is selected and a store location is chosen, there is little that most retailers can do to limit the entry of competitors. In fact, the success of a retailer may encourage the entry of new firms or cause established companies to modify their strategies to capitalize on the popularity of that retailer's offerings. An increase in competition should lead the retailer to re-examine its overall strategy, including the definition of its target market and its merchandising focus, to ensure that a competitive advantage is maintained. An error that too many retailers make is assuming that being first in a location is a sufficient competitive advantage in fighting off new entrants. However, a continued willingness to satisfy the target market better than any other retailer is fundamental.

In today's world of retailing, technology is rapidly advancing. Complex computer systems are now available for inventory control and checkout operations. Electronic surveillence may be used to reduce shoplifting. The Universal Product Code, in growing use at the present time, is revolutionizing merchandise handling and inventory control. More efficient warehousing and transporting of merchandise have been developed. Toll-free 800 numbers are more popular than ever before for consumer ordering. Nonetheless, some of these improvements are expensive and may be beyond the reach of small retailers. For instance, although small firms may be able to use computerized checkouts, they will probably be unable to use automated inventory systems or toll-free 800 numbers. As a result, the efficiency of small firms will be less than that of their larger competitors. They must adapt to this situation by providing more personalized service (because prices will be above average to reflect operating costs).

Economic conditions are beyond the control of any retailer, no matter how large. Inflation, unemployment, interest rates, tax levels, and the annual Gross National Product (GNP) are just some aspects of the economy with which a retailer must cope and which it cannot change. In delineating the controllable aspects of its strategy, the retailer needs to consider and adapt to forecasts about international, national, state, and local economies.

Another constraint on certain types of retailers is the seasonality of goods and services and the possibility that unpredictable weather changes will play havoc with sales forecasts. For example, retailers involved with sports equipment, clothing, fresh food, travel services, amusement parks, and car rentals cannot control the seasonality of consumer demand or bad weather. A solution to this uncontrollable part of strategic planning may be for retailers to diversify their offerings. A goods/service mix containing items that are popular in each season of the year could be developed. For instance, a sporting-goods retailer can emphasize ski equipment and snowmobiles in the winter, baseball and golf equipment in the spring, scuba equipment and fishing gear in the summer, and basketball and football supplies in the fall. In this way, the effects of seasonality and weather are minimized by adapting the controllable part of the retail strategy.

Finally, all retailers should be familiar with the federal, state, and local legal restrictions placed on them. Table 2-3 shows how each of the four controllable aspects of a retail strategy are affected by the legal environment. A brief discussion of legislation at the different levels of government follows.[7]

RETAILING IN ACTION

What Deceptive Selling Practices Should New-Car Dealers Avoid?

It is in the retailer's best interest to comply voluntarily with fair selling practices, rather than being forced to adhere to state and local laws. Recently, the state attorney general in Maryland made this quite clear to new-car dealers in that state.

The attorney general sent letters to all the licensed new-car dealers in Maryland encouraging them to make the state "a model of fair and informative dealer advertising practices." Although no immediate legal action was threatened, "the stick is there and hopefully it will be perceived that way."

In the letter, seventeen potential violations of Maryland law were cited; and dealers were asked not to engage in those practices. Here are some examples:

❑ Selling a car for more than its advertised price to a customer who is unaware of the advertised price.

❑ Advertising a guaranteed minimum value for a trade-in without disclosing that the sales price of the new car might be raised to cover the inflated amount given for the trade-in.

❑ Claiming to sell cars at or a little above dealer's cost when that is not occurring (because of manufacturer rebates to the dealer).

❑ Advertising vehicles that are not available.

❑ Advertising "no money down" if taxes, license plates, or transportation charges must be paid at the time a car is purchased.

Source: Based on material in "Maryland Attorney General to Car Dealers: End Deceptive Practices," *Marketing News* (October 23, 1987), p. 15.

❑

TABLE 2-3
The Impact of the Legal Environment on Retailing*

Controllable Factor Affected	Selected Legal Constraints on Retailers
Store Location and Operations	Zoning laws—Restrict the potential choices for a location and the type of facilities that may be constructed.
	Blue laws—Restrict the days and hours during which retailers may operate.
	Licensing provisions—Mandate minimum education and/or experience requirements for personnel in certain retail businesses.
	Local ordinances—Involve licensing, fire, smoking, outside lighting, capacity, and other regulations.
	Personnel laws—Involve the nondiscriminatory hiring, promoting, and firing of employees.
	Antitrust laws—Limit mergers and expansion.
	Franchise agreements—Require parties to abide by legal precedents with regard to purchase terms, customer service levels, etc.
	Business taxes—Include real-estate and income taxes.
	Recycling laws—Mandate that retailers participate in the recycling process for various containers and packaging materials.
	Leases and mortgages—Require parties to abide by the stipulations in tenancy documents.
Merchandising	Trademarks—Provide retailers with exclusive rights to the brand names they develop.
	Licensing agreements—Allow retailers to sell goods and services created by others in return for royalties.
	Merchandise restrictions—Forbid some retailers from carrying or selling specified goods or services.
	Product safety laws—Prohibit retailers from selling items that have been inadequately tested or that have been declared unsafe.
	Product liability—Allows retailers to be sued if they sell defective products.
	Warranties and guarantees—Must adhere to federal standards.
	Delivery laws—Penalties for late deliveries are imposed in some states.
	Inventory laws—Mandate that retailers must have sufficient stock when running sales.
	Labeling laws—Require merchandise to be correctly labeled and displayed.
	Lemon laws—Specify consumer rights if new products, usually autos, require continuing repairs.

At the federal level, legislation began in 1890 with the Sherman Act, which was designed to reduce monopolies and restraints of trade. The Clayton Act (1914) was enacted to strengthen the Sherman Act. Also in 1914, the Federal Trade Commission was established to deal with unfair trade practices and consumer complaints. In the 1930s, the Robinson-Patman Act (1936) and the Miller-Tydings Act (1937) were passed. Both of these laws were aimed at protecting small retailers after the Depression. The Robinson-Patman Act was enacted because of the discounts A&P was getting in the purchase of its products. The Miller-Tydings Act (fair trade) attempted to limit discounting on the part of large retailers by forcing all retailers to sell fair-traded items at the same prices. The fair trade law has now been removed in all states.

The Anti-Merger Act was passed in 1950 to limit mergers between large firms. The 1960s and 1970s saw a number of consumer protection acts in such areas as door-to-door sales, product labeling, product safety, product packaging, consumer credit, and product warranty and guarantee. Although these acts are mostly oriented toward manufacturers, they affect retailers that use deceptive selling practices and/or sell private-label merchandise. The 1980s have been a period of federal deregulation and self-regulation, allowing retailers some greater freedom in their strategies and operations.

At the state and local levels, there are many restrictions placed on retailers. Zoning laws prohibit retailers from operating at certain locations and require building specifications to be met. Construction, fire, elevator, smoking, and other codes are imposed on retailers by the state and city. Minimum resale laws sometimes require that specified items cannot be sold for less than a floor price. Blue laws limit the days or hours during which retailers can conduct business. Other

48

TABLE 2-3 (Continued)
The Impact of the Legal Environment on Retailing*

Controllable Factor Affected	Selected Legal Constraints on Retailers
Pricing	Sales taxes—In many states, consumers are required to pay state and/or local taxes on items in addition to the prices set by retailers.
	Unit-pricing laws—Require price per unit to be displayed (most often applied to supermarkets).
	Correct marking—Specifies that discounted and sale items must be marked properly.
	Dual pricing—Occurs when the same item has different prices on different containers (to reflect the higher prices of new goods). In some areas, this is not permitted.
	Collusion—Retailers are not allowed to discuss selling prices with competitors under any circumstances.
	Sale prices—Defined as a reduction from the retailer's normal selling prices. Anything else called a sale is illegal.
	Minimum-price and loss-leader laws—Require that certain items not be sold for less than their cost plus a markup to cover retail overhead costs.
	Price discrimination—Suppliers are generally not allowed to offer unjustified discounts to large retailers that are unavailable to smaller ones.
	Item-price-removal laws—Mandate that prices be marked on each item as well as on store shelves.
Store Image and Promotion	Truth-in-advertising and -selling laws—Require retailers to be honest and not to omit key facts in ads or sales presentations.
	Truth-in-credit laws—Require that consumers be fully informed of all terms when buying on credit.
	Comparative advertising—Retailers are expected to provide complete documentation when making claims about their offerings versus those of their competitors (e.g., lower prices).
	Bait-and-switch laws—Make it illegal to lure shoppers into a store to buy low-priced items and to then aggressively try to switch them to higher-priced ones.
	Door-to-door (direct-to-home) selling—Are subject to many legal restrictions regarding hours of business and consumer privacy.
	Cooling-off laws—Allow customers to cancel completed orders, often made via in-home sales, within three days of a contract date.
	Other restrictions—Prohibit some goods and services from being advertised in certain media (e.g., no liquor ads on radio or television).

*This table is broad in nature and purposely omits a law-by-law description. Many laws are state or locally oriented and apply only to certain areas; the laws in each locale differ widely. The intent is to give the reader some understanding of the current legal environment as it affects retail management. For more specifics, contact the sources named in the chapter.

ordinances, called Green River laws, restrict direct-to-home sales practices. In addition, various licenses necessary for operation are under the jurisdiction of the state or city. Also, many states and municipalities are involved in consumer protection, and they police retailers from this vantage point.

A retailer that voluntarily adheres to the spirit and the letter of the law is one that will maintain a consumer following and is less likely to attract government attention. A retailing strategy must be established in a manner that satisfies all three levels of government. For further information, the reader should contact the Federal Trade Commission, state and local regulatory agencies, the National Retail Merchants Association (NRMA), or the local Better Business Bureau.

Integrating Overall Strategy

At this point, the retailer has completed the development of an overall strategy. It has chosen a philosophy of business, an ownership and management style, and its goods/service category. The most important long-run and short-run goals have been set. A consumer market has been designated, and its characteristics and needs have been studied. General decisions have been made about store location and operations, merchandising, pricing, and store image and promotion.

All of these elements must be coordinated to have a consistent, integrated, unified retail strategy. And the uncontrollable variables affecting the retailer (consumers, competition, technology, economic conditions, seasonality, and legal restrictions) must be systematically accounted for in the strategy and its components.

Now the retailer is ready to undertake the specific activities necessary to carry out its strategy productively.

Specific Activities

Short-run decisions have to be made and implemented for each controllable part of the retail strategy outlined in the preceding section and in Figure 2-10. These actions are called **tactics** and encompass the daily and short-term operations of a retailer. They must be responsive to the uncontrollable environment. Here are some of the tactical decisions that the retailer needs to make and carry out:

❑ Store location and operations—Lease terms and provisions must be negotiated and fulfilled. A chain must carefully decide on the sites of new outlets. Facilities must actually be built or modified and must be maintained. Personnel must be hired, trained, and supervised. The budget must be spent properly (and throughout the year). Store hours should be modified when necessary. Inventory must be properly marked, stored, and matched with sales.

❑ Merchandising—The expansion or contraction of goods or service departments, the assortments within these departments, and the amount of space allotted to each department require constant tactical decision making. Innovative retailers must always be on the lookout for new merchandise and be willing to clear out slow-moving items. Purchase terms may have to be constantly negotiated, and new suppliers sought.

❑ Pricing—The retailer must be sure that the prices of all items always reflect its image and target market. Within merchandise categories, price alternatives can be used to offer consumers some choice. Actions may be needed to stimulate the sale of slow-moving merchandise, to respond to higher prices by suppliers, and to react to competitors' raising or lowering their prices. In some stores, such as supermarkets, hundreds or thousands of prices may have to be set weekly.

❑ Store image and promotion—The exterior storefront and display windows, interior store layout, and interior merchandise displays need constant attention. These elements can help the retailer gain consumer enthusiasm, present a fresh look, introduce new merchandise categories, or reflect changing seasons. Specific advertisements must be developed and then placed during the proper time and in the appropriate medium. The use of sales personnel varies by merchandise category and season.

Consumer demand, competitor actions, economic conditions, seasonality, and legal restrictions especially need to be considered in a retailer's tactical decisions. The essence of good retailing is building a sound strategy and "fine-tuning" it as the environment changes. A retailer that stands still is often moving backward. Tactical decision making is discussed in much greater detail in Chapters 7 through 17.

Control

As already noted, retail strategy and tactics should be evaluated and revised continuously. A semiannual or annual review of the company should take place (Step VI in Figure 2-1), with the strategy and tactics (Steps IV and V) that have been developed and implemented being evaluated against the business philosophy, objectives, and target market (Steps I, II, and III) of the firm. This procedure is called a **retail audit,** a systematic process for analyzing the performance of a retailer. The retail audit is covered in Chapter 16.

After the performance of a retailer is assessed, the strengths and weaknesses of the company are revealed. The aspects of the retail strategy that have gone well should be left alone; and the aspects that have gone poorly should be revised, consistent with the firm's philosophy, objectives, and target market. If possible, minor adjustments should be made, because major changes in a retailer's operations may only confuse and intimidate customers. The adjustments that are made should be evaluated in the next retail audit.

Feedback

During each stage in the development of a retail strategy, management receives signals or cues as to the success of that part of the strategy. These signals or cues are known as **feedback**. See Figure 2-1. Some forms of positive feedback are high sales, no problems with the government, and low employee turnover. Some forms of negative feedback are low sales, government interference, and high employee turnover.

The retailer should look for both positive and negative signals or cues, so that it can determine their causes and immediately capitalize on opportunities or rectify problems. The changing retail environment is examined in Chapter 18.

SUMMARY

A retail strategy is the overall plan or framework of action that guides a firm. It contains a situation analysis, objectives, the identification of a customer market, a broad strategy, specific activities, control, and feedback.

Situation analysis is the objective evaluation of the opportunities and potential problems facing a retailer. It seeks to determine a retailer's current position and where it should be heading. This analysis consists of defining and adhering to a philosophy of business, evaluating ownership and management alternatives, and outlining the goods/service category to be sold. A philosophy of business is a long-term commitment to a type of business and a place in the market. Ownership and management alternatives are selected from a sole proprietorship, partnership, or corporation; starting a new business, buying an existing one, or being a franchisee; being run by an owner-manager or a professional manager; and being centralized or decentralized. The goods/service category chosen depends on personal abilities, financial resources, and time resources.

Objectives are the long- and short-run goals of a retailer. A company may be interested in one or more of these objectives: sales (growth, stability, and market share), profit (level, return on investment, and efficiency), satisfaction of publics (stockholders, consumers, and others), and image (customer and industry perceptions).

Next, consumer characteristics and needs are determined, and a retailer selects a target market. A retailer can sell to a broad spectrum of consumers (the mass market); zero in on one customer group (a market segment); or aim at two or more distinct groups of consumers (multiple segments), with separate retailing approaches for each.

Then, a broad retail strategy is formed. This strategy involves controllable variables (those aspects of business that the retailer can directly affect) and uncontrollable variables (those factors that the retailer cannot control and to which it must adapt). The major controllable variables are store location and operations, merchandising, pricing, and store image and promotion. The key uncontrollable variables are consumers, competition, technology, economic conditions, seasonality, and legal restrictions. All of those elements must be coordinated and taken into consideration in order to have a consistent, integrated, unified strategy.

After the general strategy has been set, a retailer has to make and implement short-run decisions (tactics) for each controllable part of that strategy. These actions must be forward-looking and respond to the external environment.

Through a control process, retail strategy and tactics should be evaluated and revised continuously. A retail audit systematically reviews a strategy and its execution on a regular basis. Strengths need to be emphasized and weaknesses minimized or eliminated.

The retailer must also be constantly alert for signals or cues, known as feedback, that indicate the level of performance at each step in the strategy.

QUESTIONS FOR DISCUSSION

1. Why is it necessary to develop a thorough, well-integrated retail strategy? What could happen if a company did not develop such a strategy?
2. How would situation analysis differ for a new retailer and an existing retailer?
3. In which situation is each of these the preferred ownership form for a retailer: sole proprietorship, partnership, and corporation?
4. Develop a checklist that would help a prospective retailer to choose the proper goods/service category in which to operate. Include personal abilities, financial resources, and time demands in this checklist.
5. Why do retailers frequently underestimate the financial and time requirements of a business?
6. Comment on these objectives: "Dayton Hudson Corporation is a growth company focusing exclusively on retailing. It aims to provide exceptional value to the American consumer through multiple retail formats."
7. Draw and explain a store-positioning chart showing the kinds of retailers selling jewelry.
8. Discuss local examples of a retailer appealing to a mass market, a retailer appealing to a market segment, and a retailer appealing to multiple segments.
9. Jack Watson is a thirty-five-year-old former shoe salesman. Jack has saved $75,000 and wants to open his own retail shoe store. Develop an overall strategy for Jack, including store location and operations, merchandising, pricing, and store atmosphere and promotion.
10. A competing retailer has a better store location than you do. It is in a modern shopping center with a lot of customer traffic. Your store is located in an older neighborhood and requires customers to travel a great distance to reach you. How would you develop a merchandising, pricing, and store image and promotion strategy to overcome your disadvantageous location?
11. How could each of these minimize the effects of seasonality?
    a. Toy retailer
    b. Travel agency
    c. College bookstore
12. Describe how a retailer would use fine tuning.
13. How are the control and feedback phases of a retail strategy interrelated?
14. Should a small retailer plan a strategy differently from a large retailer? Why or why not?

NOTES

1. John Merwin, "New, Improved Eyewear," *Forbes* (October 6, 1986), pp. 152, 156.
2. For interesting articles on strategic planning, see Bert Rosenbloom, "Strategic Planning in Retailing: Prospects and Problems," *Journal of Retailing*, Vol. 56 (Spring 1980), pp. 107–120; Robert F. Lusch and Michael G. Harvey, "A Framework for Retail Planning," *Business*, Vol. 33 (October–December 1983), pp. 20–26; Isadore Barmash, "How They Plan," *Stores* (September 1983), pp. 7–15; Norman M. Scarborough and Thomas W. Zimmerer, "Strategic Planning for the Small Business," *Business*, Vol. 37 (April–June 1987), pp. 11–19; and Jim Kobs, "Marketing Strategies for Maximum Growth," *Direct Marketing* (May 1987), pp. 32–39, 155.
3. Philip H. Thurston, "When Partners Fall Out," *Harvard Business Review*, Vol. 64 (November–December 1986), pp. 24–34.
4. For an in-depth look at how used-car dealers apply retail strategies, see Francis C. Brown III, "Independent Used-Car Dealers Are Trying New Ways to Respond to Stiff Competition," *Wall Street Journal* (August 14, 1984), p. 33.

5. See Lewis A. Spalding, "Strategies for Share-Boosting," *Stores* (June 1986), pp. 11–14.
6. Rhonda Razzano, "The Philosophy of the Ant and the Elephant," *Chain Store Age Executive* (September 1987), pp. 13–15.
7. For additional information, see Norma Ganim Barnes, "Small Stores See Sunday Profits as 'Blue Laws' Fade," *Marketing News* (June 19, 1987), p. 5; Martha Brannigan, "Pharmacists Will Soon Prescribe Drugs in Florida, to the Chagrin of Physicians," *Wall Street Journal* (April 3, 1986), p. 29; Alice Z. Cuneo, "Calif. Begins Taxing Direct Marketers," *Advertising Age* (July 13, 1987), p. 89; Maria Lombardi Bullen, Roger H. Hermanson, and Ronald T. Mott, "Small Business Meets Tax Reform '86," *Business*, Vol. 37 (January–March 1987), pp. 13–24; Robert Reinhold, "Recycling Law Hints Breakthrough," *New York Times* (October 10, 1987), p. 12; Jules Abend, "New Trucking Game," *Stores* (May 1986), pp. 54–65; Steven A. Meyerowitz, "Beware of Price-Discrimination Pitfalls," *Business Marketing* (June 1986), pp. 136–140; and "Comparative Advertising Legislation on Rise Among States," *Discount Store News* (December 14, 1987), p. 205.

Otto's Super Wash: Evaluating a Retailing Opportunity

Case 1

Bill Janis, a recent college graduate, is seeking to purchase a business with the financial assistance of his father. Bill has always been an entrepreneurial type, is fascinated by retailing, and has a high energy level. He is keeping in mind these criteria in the search for an appropriate opportunity:

❑ Bill does not want to become a franchisee. He does not want to pay franchising fees, contribute to a national advertising program, or have his ability to manage a business restricted.

❑ Bill wants to purchase an established business that has not met its full potential. In this way, the risks of failing will be reduced. He will consider a moderately successful firm that has absentee management or a complacent owner; this will allow him to apply his talents.

❑ Bill wants a service-based business, as service retailers are growing at a faster rate than goods-based retailers. A service firm also requires less inventory investment.

❑ Bill wants a business with some barriers to entry. He does not want to look at upholstery and carpet-cleaning firms or sixty-minute film-processing studios, as they require low capital investments and little training. He wants to avoid oversaturation and price competition.

❑ Bill wants to own the real estate on which his firm is located. This will allow him to use depreciation as an expense, to control maintenance, and to be free from concerns about lease renewal.

For the past year, Bill has examined the car wash industry and several individual firms within a thirty-mile radius of his house. In particular, Bill likes several aspects of this business. One, the average sale is between $4 and $10, and many customers pay extra for car buffing, premium wax, motor steaming, and other services. Two, zoning restrictions and the limited availability of large, prime locations often limit competitors' entry. Three, little technical expertise, except for equipment repair, is required. Four, absentee ownership is prevalent; this represents good potential for Bill.

About three weeks ago, Bill saw this ad in his daily newspaper: "Car Wash. Exterior/interior. One owner for 25 years. Excellent location, includes land and building. $100,000 down. Call Otto's Super Wash. 555-1155." The next day, he visited the car wash and jotted down detailed notes based on a conversation with the owner, Otto Franke. Bill was also provided with Otto's most recent financial statement, which was verified by Bill's accountant. See Tables 1, 2, and 3.

The total purchase price for the car wash is $400,000, which seems reasonable to Bill. Otto is willing to provide him with a $300,000 loan at a 10 per cent interest rate. Yearly payments for principal and interest would be about $36,000 for a loan that would be fully repaid in fifteen years.

TABLE 1
The Characteristics of Otto's Super Wash (as Noted by Bill Janis)

1. This is an older car wash; it is not brushless. Such a car wash can cause scuff marks on autos and may break car antennas or damage loose molding. Some equipment (e.g., the drying machine) does not function well. As the equipment is not state-of-the-art, car buffing, undercarriage washing, and other services cannot be offered.
2. The car wash handles about 700 cars in an average week. It is open Monday through Saturday, 8 A.M. to 6 P.M. There are three full-time employees.
3. Prices are low: $3 for exterior only; $4 for full service (interior vacuuming, windows cleaned, ashtrays emptied); $1 extra for hot wax. These prices may be difficult to raise.
4. Business is heaviest on Fridays and Saturdays and two to three days after major snowfalls.
5. The car wash is located on a heavily traveled road. It is highly visible and easy to reach by passing vehicles.
6. Otto will provide financing. A $100,000 down payment is required. A $300,000 fifteen-year loan will have to be taken.

TABLE 1 (continued)
The Characteristics of Otto's Super Wash (as Noted by Bill Janis)

7. A real-estate appraiser values the car wash's property at $200,000. This does not include the value of the car wash itself.
8. If a renovation is undertaken, the car wash would have to be closed for a month. The renovation would cost $35,000 to $75,000, depending on the modifications. However, this would enable the car wash to offer other services (such as undercarriage cleaning) and to raise prices.

TABLE 2
The Characteristics of Otto's Competitors (as Noted by Bill Janis)

Location	Comments
A	Situated on a side street six miles from Otto's. Poor locale with little road visibility. Car-drying area is limited, which results in congestion on busy days. New state-of-the-art equipment; all cars are hand-dried. Car wash prices range from $4.95 to $9.95. Company aggressively uses $2-off coupons in local newspapers. Excellent-quality car wash.
B	Situated on a main road seven miles from Otto's. Excellent location with new equipment. For years, this firm had poor equipment and very low prices. New equipment and new ownership necessitated a price increase from $3.00 to $4.50 for exterior only, and from $4.00 to $5.50 for full service. Good-quality car wash.
C	Situated on a main road four miles from Otto's. Excellent location with modern, but no-frills, equipment. Tied into a gas station; exterior wash only. Consumers get a car wash for $2.50 with the purchase of eight gallons of gas. Poor to average quality.
D	Situated on a main road five miles from Otto's. Excellent location with modern equipment. There is a very large car-drying area. All cars are hand-dried. Car wash prices range from $5.95 to $10.95. Selective use of discount coupons. Has reputation as the best car wash in the area.

TABLE 3
Selected Financial Data on Otto's Super Wash, Latest Year

Revenues:		
Exterior-only washes	$60,000	
Full-service washes	65,000	
Wax applications	29,000	
		$154,000
Expenses:		
Wages/fringes	$45,000	
Equipment repair	18,000	
Wax/water treatment chemicals	12,000	
Property taxes	8,000	
Property repairs	6,000	
Electricity	7,000	
Property and liability insurance	4,000	
		$100,000
Net profit before taxes		$ 54,000

1. Comment on Bill's criteria for selecting a retail opportunity.
2. What other kinds of information should Bill acquire before making a decision?

3. Evaluate the information contained in Tables 1, 2, and 3. On the basis of the facts presented in this case, should Bill make an offer for the car wash? Explain your answer.

4. Develop an appropriate retail strategy for Bill in terms of objectives, the name of the car wash, renovation plans, service options, pricing, and promotion. In answering this question, assume that Bill will buy the car wash.

Bicycles Unlimited, Inc.: Situation Analysis by an Ongoing Retailer*

Case 2

Haley Allison and Darlene Gray are faced with a major strategy question that will affect the future direction of their retail bicycle store: Should they broaden their goods/service category to include mopeds and dirt bikes? Before reaching a conclusion, the two co-owners have decided to assess the past and present performance of their business.

Allison and Gray opened their bicycle outlet in March 1984 in Jackson, Tennessee. Prior to that, the two women had been classmates at the University of Tennessee, and they were avid bicyclists. They agreed that the store would sell bicycles and accessories for both children and adults. After a review of names used by other retailers located in Tennessee, the two friends incorporated their business as Bicycles Unlimited, Inc., to highlight the products their store would carry.

As a result of the store's success during 1984 and because of customer requests, Haley and Darlene added clothing and accessories in 1985 for those bicycle riders who rode for competition as well as exercise and pleasure. Helmets, gloves, knee pads, water bottles, and air pumps were a few of the accessories added to the original product line. These products did reasonably well after a brief introductory period.

Because of the number of young families with children in their primary market area, Allison and Gray decided to add scooters, skateboards, and roller skates in mid-1986. Although different products appealed to various market segments, a number of their customers also purchased items from more than one product category. In just a few short years, their business had grown dramatically. Indicators in terms of market share, inventory turnover, and financial liquidity were all positive. Table 1 shows the percentage of sales accounted for by each major product category from 1984 through 1987.

TABLE 1
Percentage of Sales by Product Category

	1984	1985	1986	1987
Bicycles				
Children	65	60	55	50
Adult	35	30	20	15
Clothing and Accessories		10	5	5
Scooters			10	15
Skateboards			5	8
Roller Skates			5	7
	100	100	100	100

*This case was prepared and written by Professor William A. Staples and Professor John I. Coppett, University of Houston—Clear Lake, Houston, Texas.

Now, another product line expansion opportunity has presented itself: mopeds and dirt bikes. Although these are much higher in price than their existing products, Allison and Gray believe that there is high sales and profit potential due to the life-styles and incomes of their customers. However, they also realize that existing moped and dirt bike retailers have extensive service and repair facilities; their store would have to add such facilities.

Whereas Haley is leaning toward adding mopeds and dirt bikes, Darlene believes this would be too risky for their young business. The partners realize that they must determine what kind of retail business they want to operate in the future. In conducting a situation analysis, they have identified some issues that must be considered before any future actions are taken:

❑ In reviewing the plan that they developed prior to opening their store, Haley and Darlene have noticed that the goods/service category description was "bicycles for children and adults for their use in recreation, fun, and exercise." They realize that the business has significantly changed in the past four years.

❑ They are unsure how the image of their store will change, particularly because the safety aspects of some types of dirt bikes have been questioned.

❑ It is already somewhat confusing to advertise the store using the name Bicycles Unlimited, Inc. Many customers are surprised to discover that such a wide variety of products is offered. The partners are contemplating changing the name to Wheels Unlimited, Inc., or Bikes Unlimited, Inc., to get away from the possible identity of selling only bicycles.

❑ Allison and Gray want to find out why people shop at their store rather than at their competitors' outlets.

Haley Allison and Darlene Gray are uncertain as to what they should do. They know that the competitiveness of the marketplace calls for a decision in a relatively short period of time.

QUESTIONS

1. Evaluate the goods/service category description that Haley Allison and Darlene Gray used in their original plan.
2. Evaluate the data in Table 1.
3. Develop a goods/service category description for Bicycles Unlimited, Inc., based on its current product offerings. Would your answer differ if mopeds and dirt bikes are included? Why or why not?

4. What are the pros and cons of changing the store's name to Wheels Unlimited, Inc., or Bikes Unlimited, Inc?
5. Would you recommend that the co-owners add the proposed line of mopeds and dirt bikes? Explain your answer.

Part One Comprehensive Case

Federated Department Stores: A Retail Strategy in Transition*

Introduction

On April 1, 1988, after weeks of spirited bidding, the Campeau Corporation of Canada acquired Federated Department Stores for $6.6 billion, the largest acquisition in U.S. retailing history. Prior to the acquisition, Federated's senior management had been criticized as "inheriting the premier department-store chain in the country and turning it into an also-ran. To some extent, Federated was a victim of changing shopping habits and demographics. But the decisive leadership needed to respond to those changes was not in place." This case examines the strategy of Federated before it was acquired by Campeau and some of the implications of the acquisition.

Federated Department Stores was a diversified retail firm with department stores, mass-merchandising stores, supermarkets, and other retail divisions. It had fifteen operating units, which had 631 stores in thirty-six states in 1986. During that year, total company revenues were about $10.5 billion and net income was $287.6 million (2.7 per cent of sales).

Table 1 lists 1986 sales data for each of Federated's operating units, organized on the basis of their major retail business. Because Federated was a decentralized company, each of its operating units had the ability to satisfy its target market through specific merchandise offerings, services, and store atmosphere. Most of the units were headed by their own two-person senior management team, consisting of a chairman and a president. Each team had responsibility for day-to-day operations in all the stores in its unit. At the corporate level, every division was supervised by either Federated's chairman or vice-chairman.

As Table 2 shows, department and mass-merchandising stores accounted for about 75 per cent of Federated's overall sales and almost 93 per cent of gross profit (gross margin in dollars). Federated operated two types of department stores: headquarters and upscale. Headquarters stores were broad-lined outlets targeted at moderate to upper-moderate shoppers. These included Abraham & Straus, Burdines, Rich's, Foley's, and Sanger Harris. Upscale stores were more selective in their merchandise offerings and were targeted at fashion-conscious shoppers. These included Bloomingdale's, Bullock's/Bullocks Wilshire, and I. Magnin.

Federated's recent financial performance was weak. While sales increased at over 10 per cent per year from 1982 to 1984, sales growth slowed markedly from 1984 to 1986. And between 1982 and 1986, net income declined in three of the five years and increased by only 0.3 per cent in another year. See Table 3.

R.H. Macy came to be viewed by many analysts as the leading department store innovator, a position previously occupied by Federated. For example, Macy's converted its basement area into a fashionable boutique many years before Federated followed. Federated's MainStreet stores, first opened in late 1984, were a close copy of Dayton Hudson's Mervyn's (which was started many years earlier).

In addition, department store chains such as Federated had to deal with heightened competition. Off-price chains competed for the same target market but could outprice department stores. Specialty stores took much of the market in cameras, electronics, designer apparel, home-improvement items, and sporting goods. As a result, department stores had to be more aggressive in dealing with vendors and in promoting merchandise offerings.

Corporate Strategic Planning Emphasis

Howard Goldfeder, Federated's chairman of the board for the seven years before the acquisition, was the first person outside the Lazarus family to run the firm (after thirty-five years of control by the founding Lazarus family). Goldfeder introduced Federated to corporate strategic planning.

Each operating unit developed detailed five-year plans. These plans were based on research into every facet of the unit (such as markdown levels, private-label policies, and customer service levels) and were used as the basis of capital expenditure budgeting. The planning process ended the notion that each unit could assume that it automatically had access to its "fair share" of capital expenditures.

---

*The material in this case is drawn from "Accessory Place: Price Points Plus Panache," *Chain Store Age Executive* (August 1987), pp. 90–91; *Federated Department Stores Inc., 1986 Annual Report;* Holly Klokis, "Retailing's Grande Dame: Cloaked in New Strategies," *Chain Store Age Executive* (March 1985), pp. 18–20; Jolie Solomon, "Federated Aims to Restore Some Faded Luster," *Wall Street Journal* (December 27, 1985), p. 4; Carol Hymowitz, "Federated Chief Draws Blame for Attracting Attention of Raiders," *Wall Street Journal* (February 19, 1988), pp. 1, 14; Isadore Barmash, "Canadian Bidder Beats Macy in Fight for Federated Stores," *New York Times* (April 2, 1988), pp. 1, 33; Kurt Eichenwald, "Expansion Awaits Federated Stores," *New York Times* (April 4, 1988), pp. A1, D4; Bryan Burrough, Jacquie McNish, and Carol Hymowitz, "Campeau at Last Gets Federated—Now Can He Make a Go of It?" *Wall Street Journal* (April 4, 1988), pp. 1, 10; and Jacquelyn Bivens, "Campeau in Control at Federated," *Chain Store Age Executive* (May 1988), pp. 39–42.

TABLE 1
Sales Data for Federated Department Stores' Business Segments, As of January 31, 1987

Operating Unit		1986 Net Sales (millions)	Gross Space (thousands of square feet)	Number of Stores		Annual Sales per Square Foot
Department Stores						
Abraham & Straus		$ 778.6	5,578	15		$139.58
Bloomingdale's		1,050.0	4,269	26		245.96
Bullock's/Bullocks Wilshire		751.8	4,805	28		156.46
Burdines		809.7	5,069	29		159.74
Filene's		390.8	2,117	16		184.60
Foley's		1,107.0	8,003	37		138.32
Goldsmith's		174.0	1,338	6		130.04
Lazarus		904.7	7,385	32		122.50
I. Magnin		317.1	1,828	26		173.47
Rich's		690.6	4,878	20		141.57
	Total	$ 6,974.3	45,270	235	Average	$154.06
Mass Merchandising						
Gold Circle		$ 969.2	8,239	76		$117.64
Supermarkets						
Ralphs		$ 2,045.7	5,324	127		$384.24
Other Retail Divisions						
The Children's Place		$ 161.8	880	166		$183.86
Filene's Basement		252.1	801	22		314.73
MainStreet		109.3	1,088	15		100.46
	Total	$ 523.2	2,769	203	Average	$188.95
Overall Total		$10,512.4	61,602	631	Average	$170.65

Source: Federated Department Stores Inc., 1986 Annual Report.

TABLE 2
Federated Department Stores' Performance Data for Business Segments, 1986

		Performance	Percentage of Total
Net Sales (millions)			
Department stores		$ 6,974.4	66.3
Mass-merchandising stores		969.2	9.2
Supermarkets		2,045.7	19.5
Other retail divisions		523.2	5.0
	Total	$10,512.5	100.0
Operating Profit* (millions)			
Department stores		$628.7	88.2
Mass-merchandising stores		31.8	4.5
Supermarkets		59.2	8.3
Other retail divisions		(6.9)	(1.0)
	Total	$712.8	100.0

*Does not include central office costs, interest expense, unusual items, or income tax.

Source: Federated Department Stores Inc., 1986 Annual Report.

TABLE 3
Selected Financial Data for Federated Department Stores, 1982–1986

	1986	1985	1984	1983	1982
Revenues ($ bil)	10.5	10.0	9.7	8.7	7.7
Operating profit* ($ mil)	712.8	710.1	692.7	731.1	564.4
Net income ($ mil)	287.6	286.6	329.3	338.3	232.8
Number of stores	631	604	589	551	508
Gross square feet (millions)	61.6	59.1	60.5	58.7	58.4
Net income (as a % of sales)	2.7	2.9	3.4	3.9	3.0
Average annual sales per square foot ($)	170.65	169.20	160.33	148.21	131.85
Change in sales over prior year (%)	+5.0	+3.1	+11.5	+13.0	+10.0
Change in net income over prior year (%)	+0.3	−13.0	−3.7	+45.3	−10.9

*Does not include central office costs, interest expense, unusual items, or income tax.

Source: Federated Department Stores Inc., 1986 Annual Report.

Because of its planning process, Federated's capital allocations were keyed to each unit's prospects and needs, the competitive environment, and an analysis of business opportunities and risks rather than past performance. The firm made significant capital investments in remodeling and expanding existing stores. See Table 4. Situation analysis revealed that Federated had the best retail locations in many key market areas, but that its store presentation needed improvement.

In the strategic planning process, every operating unit was asked to identify its target market and to review its services, merchandise, presentation strategies, and tactics. The decentralized nature of the planning process allowed each division to have its own identity, and to more carefully differentiate its offerings from those of competitors and other Federated divisions. Some marketing, consumer re-

search, real-estate, and store-planning functions were transferred from the corporate to the unit level. This gave the units more control over these areas. For example, Bullock's (Federated's Los Angeles department store chain) decided to drop furniture and electronics and add more sportswear and fancy housewares, after long-range planning revealed that this product mix was more appropriate for its upscale consumers.

As a result of planning, Federated divested its major ownership interests in shopping centers and consolidated several operating units. Foley's and Sanger Harris (its two Texas-based department store chains) were merged into Foley's; Shillito's, Rike's, and Lazarus (its three Ohio-based department store chains) were merged into Lazarus; and Richway and Gold Circle (its two mass-merchandising chains) were merged into Gold Circle. The consolidations

TABLE 4
Federated Department Stores' Investment Data for Business Segments, 1986

	Investment	Percentage of Total
Capital Expenditures* (millions)		
Department stores	$266.3	52.4
Mass-merchandising stores	12.5	2.5
Supermarkets	158.6	31.3
Other retail divisions	66.4	13.1
Central office	3.6	0.7
Total	$507.4	100.0
Total Assets as of January 31, 1987 (millions)		
Department stores	$4,287.5	75.4
Mass-merchandising stores	379.3	6.7
Supermarkets	548.0	9.6
Other retail divisions	353.6	6.2
Central office	119.3	2.1
Total	$5,687.7	100.0

*Includes buildings, fixtures, and equipment.

Source: Federated Department Stores Inc., 1986 Annual Report.

were intended to reduce Federated's costs, to allow activities (such as purchasing and data processing) to be more centralized, to result in a sharper image for each new operating unit, and to provide Federated with greater coordination among units.

Federated tried to change "from a series of independent, even rivalrous, fiefdoms into a nation-state," according to Goldfeder. In previous years, Federated units such as Burdines (Florida), Foley's (Houston), and Filene's (Boston) were viewed as independent, and it would have been unthinkable to have two separate units in the same city. Then, Federated even placed Sanger Harris and Bloomingdale's in the same Dallas shopping center.

Prior to 1983, Bloomingdale's had been limited to a few Eastern states (New York, New Jersey, Connecticut, Massachusetts, Pennsylvania, and Maryland). At that point, it was decided that Bloomingdale's would be the first full-line national fashion department store chain. The expansion was to help Federated increase its overall market share in cities such as Dallas (where Federated had Sanger Harris units), Miami (where it had Burdines units), Chicago (where it had MainStreet stores), and Los Angeles (where Bullock's was situated).

The company recognized the need to focus on target customers and to revise strategies regarding supplier selection, store services, store design, merchandise offerings, and personnel to reflect the target customers' needs. In particular, Federated's department stores began to put greater emphasis on professional women, aged twenty-five to fifty-four, as a prime market segment. Federated's interest in this segment was based on several factors:

❑ Many professional women were from two-income households. These households had incomes that were 40 per cent greater than those of the average U.S. household.
❑ They were attracted to one-stop shopping.
❑ They spent 3.5 times as much for apparel as their nonworking counterparts.
❑ The group was expected to expand in the future.

Consumer research conducted for Federated found several reasons why shoppers patronized conventional department stores in general and Federated stores in particular. Among the attractions of department stores were their role in determining fashion trends and fashion acceptability, their ability to demonstrate how and under what circumstances current fashion should be worn or used in the house, their pleasant shopping environments (store atmosphere), and the distinctive character of department stores. Federated's specific strengths were high consumer loyalty and prime locations.

Those in the firm who praised the planning process stated that it broadened the perspective of many executives who in the past too often focused on product-related developments. Others reported that Goldfeder's policy of intensely questioning executives about their plans made them more careful planners as well as better businesspeople.

However, the manner in which the planning process was implemented did concern some Federated division executives and some retail analysts. These executives felt "buried

in paperwork"; found creativity limited ("You couldn't bet your job"); or believed that they could no longer react quickly. Although senior Federated executives insisted that all units retained their traditional autonomy in the strategic planning process, in fact, the better run units had more autonomy. Ralphs, for example, had more independence than some units because it was viewed as a "very well run business."

Store Strategies

Federated decided to use one broad overall strategy for headquarters stores, because customer preferences were relatively similar. In contrast, upscale department store customer preferences were less similar; each of these operating units required separate plans.

The headquarters store strategy sought to build market share and return on investment by

❑ Efficiently allocating floor space. Federated eliminated all its budget departments, despite the fact that they contained 1.5 per cent of total department store merchandise. This freed space for adding other product lines appealing to professional women.
❑ Expanding buying offices in New York. Federated developed its own brand names, such as Allen Solly, to exert more channel control and to reduce competition from off-price chains on traditional male and female apparel. At the same time, Federated planned to increase business in branded fashion merchandise and to increase its cooperation with vendors.
❑ Remodeling and expanding existing department stores to enhance their position. Between 1983 and 1986, Federated committed nearly $300 million in capital expenditures to department store renovations and expansions. This involved about 22 per cent of Federated's total department store selling space.
❑ Launching a major review of various product categories within the stores.
❑ Emphasizing personal selling as a means of differentiating headquarters stores from their competitors.

These were some of the strategies employed by Federated for its nonheadquarters stores:

❑ Regarding upscale stores, Federated planned to increase Bloomingdale's locations in south Florida and Chicago. That unit's sales surpassed $1 billion in sales in 1986. It also intended to expand Bloomingdale's By Mail. Upscale mail-order sales totaled more than $100 million in 1987. I. Magnin placed greater emphasis on apparel assortments and private-label merchandise. In 1987, Bullocks Wilshire opened a new store in Palm Desert, California.
❑ Gold Circle had new store designs that focused on current fashions and everyday low prices.
❑ Ralphs supermarkets added new Ralphs Giant stores. Each of these stores averaged 70,000 square feet and featured quality produce, bakery, deli, seafood, and meat departments. Grocery items were displayed in warehouse-style racks. Ralphs Giant store expansion

was part of a program meant to replace smaller, older outlets with new, larger ones. In 1986, Ralphs' overall sales exceeded $2 billion for the first time, and profits also set a record.

❑ The Children's Place (with value-oriented merchandise for young families), Filene's Basement (with moderate- to better-quality merchandise for price-conscious upscale consumers), and MainStreet (with affordably priced apparel for the entire family) were rapidly growing units. Among these three units, fifteen new stores were opened in 1987.

❑ In late 1983, Filene's Basement was set up as a separate operating unit from Filene's department stores. Filene's Basement appealed to shoppers who were both value- and fashion-conscious. It was expected to compete vigorously against other off-price chains, but not against traditional stores. Filene's Basement stores did not always have complete selections, and items may not have been in-season. As in Filene's department stores, Filene's Basement stores utilized an automatic markdown policy, whereby unsold goods were systematically reduced in price (based on the number of days the goods were on the selling floor) and given to charity if not sold in thirty days.

❑ MainStreet, Federated's Chicago-based chain, sought to carve out a niche between the medium- to low-priced mass merchandiser and the higher-priced traditional department store. MainStreet relied on brand-name merchandise and had 40 per cent more personnel per square foot than the average mass merchandiser. MainStreet was targeted at families headed by 25- to 40-year-old adults with annual incomes of $20,000 to $40,000. Children's clothing and related products were featured; carpets, furniture, and major appliances were not carried by MainStreet.

❑ In late 1986, Federated opened its first Accessory Place outlet, which sold fashion accessories and related items with low to medium price points. Merchandise included jewelry, handbags, sunglasses, hosiery, hair goods, hats, and gloves. The store targeted young women aged sixteen to thirty-four. This unit was too new for inclusion in Table 1.

A Time of Transition

Prior to its Federated purchase in April 1988, Campeau Corporation was a major Canadian real-estate developer that had entered U.S. retailing in 1986 when it acquired Allied Stores. Through the Allied acquisition, Campeau owned Ann Taylor and Brooks Brothers fashion stores (both based in New York) and these department store chains: Jordan Marsh (based in Boston), Maas Brothers (based in Florida), Stern's (based in New Jersey), and the Bon (based in Seattle).

To finance its purchase of Federated Department Stores, Campeau made these arrangements before consummating that acquisition:

❑ It agreed to sell Brooks Brothers fashion stores to Marks & Spencer, a British-based firm.
❑ It agreed to sell Filene's and Foley's to May Department Stores.
❑ It agreed to sell Bullock's/Bullocks Wilshire and I. Magnin to R.H. Macy.

Although Campeau had ambitious plans to expand Bloomingdale's after the Federated acquisition was finalized, its other plans were less certain. It had to decide which other operating units to sell (if any), how to integrate divisions smoothly, how to best utilize existing managers and employees, which strategic concepts to leave in place and which to modify, and how to restore Federated to its earlier status as the "premier" department store chain in the United States.

QUESTIONS

1. Did Federated adhere to the retailing concept? Explain your answer.
2. Analyze Federated's overall strategy before its acquisition by Campeau. Refer to Figure 2-1 in your answer.
3. Interpret the data in Tables 1 through 4.
4. Evaluate Federated's planning process and store strategies prior to its acquisition by Campeau.
5. Assume that it is April 1988. Develop a retail strategy for the expanded Campeau Corporation. Include all the steps in Figure 2-1 in your answer.
6. Go to the library and determine which operating divisions are currently owned by Campeau. Comment on this from a strategic planning perspective. What should Campeau do next?
7. What uncontrollable factors should Campeau study in planning for the future? Why?

PART TWO

Situation Analysis

❑ *In Part Two, the philosophy of business, ownership and management alternatives, goods/service categories, and objectives of a broad range of retail institutions are presented. By understanding the unique attributes of these institutions, prospective and ongoing retailers are better able to develop and adapt their own strategies.*

❑ *Chapter 3 examines the characteristics of retail institutions on the basis of ownership type: independent, chain, franchise, leased, vertical marketing, and consumer cooperative. The methods used by manufacturers, wholesalers, and retailers to obtain control in a distribution channel are also discussed. An end-of-chapter appendix offers additional information on franchising.*

❑ *Chapter 4 describes retail institutions on the basis of strategy mix. Three key concepts are introduced: the wheel of retailing, scrambled merchandising, and the retail life cycle. Then, a variety of store-based, nonstore-based, and service versus goods strategy mixes are examined in depth. An end-of-chapter appendix provides further information on direct marketing.*

Chapter 3

Retail Institutions by Ownership

☐ **Chapter Objectives** ☐

1 To present the ways in which retail institutions can be classified
2 To study retailers on the basis of ownership type and examine the characteristics of each
3 To explore the methods used by manufacturers, wholesalers, and retailers to obtain control in the distribution channel

In the United States, the growing do-it-yourself retail industry accounts for $90 billion in annual sales of items such as hardware, building and home improvement materials, wallcoverings, and tools. As a result, major chains, including Lowe's, Builders Square (K mart), Builders Emporium (Wickes), and Payless Cashways, have opened huge stores and aggressively captured a large share of the market.

Accordingly, some industry experts have predicted the downfall of small mom-and-pop stores. Compared to these stores, the big chains have huge assortments (up to 40,000 or more different items in some outlets), do a much better job of appealing to consumer desires for one-stop shopping, spend great amounts on advertising, and offer low prices. Nonetheless, a number of small stores have been able to counteract their much larger competitors. These stores are playing up their major advantage (service) and enacting a broad range of defensive tactics to retain competitiveness.

This is particularly true of small hardware stores. Personnel often greet customers by name and are able to answer all sorts of questions. Many consumers view the atmosphere as cozy: "People would be very sad to see the demise of the old-fashioned hardware store."

Through cooperative affiliations, independent hardware stores are able to secure better prices from suppliers and can share advertising expenses (or else, they could not afford to advertise). They also get good marketing research data, enabling them to "order smarter." There are about a dozen hardware-buying cooperatives in the United States, representing most of the 24,000 independents now operating. True Value and Ace are two of the bigger cooperatives, and they provide a full range of services for members.[1]

As this situation illustrates, independent retailers can compete with chains if they are creative in their approach.

The term **retail institution** refers to the basic format or structure of a business. In the United States, about 1.6 million different firms are defined as retailers by the Bureau of the Census; and these firms operate 2 million establishments.

An institutional study of retailers shows the relative sizes and diversity of different kinds of retailing; enables firms to better develop and enact their own strategies; and indicates how various types of retailers are affected by the external environment. In particular, institutional analysis is important in these phases of strategic retail planning: selecting a philosophy of business, choosing an ownership alternative, defining the goods/service category, and setting objectives.

In this chapter and the next, retail institutions are examined from these perspectives: ownership (Chapter 3), store-based retail strategy mix (Chapter 4), nonstore-based retail strategy mix (Chapter 4), and service versus goods retail strategy mix (Chapter 4). Figure 3-1 contains a breakdown of each category. These classifications are not mutually exclusive; that is, a retail institution may be correctly placed in more than one category. For example, a department store unit may be part of a chain, will have a specific store-based retail strategy mix, may accept mail-order sales, and may sell services as well as goods.

It is essential that the data presented in Chapters 3 and 4 be interpreted carefully. Because the institutional categories may not be mutually exclusive, care should be taken in combining statistics to obtain aggregate data or else double counting may occur. And although the data used are as current as possible, not all information corresponds to a common date and the last complete published government census on retailing is the *1982 Census of Retail Trade.*

A number of retail institutions appear within the ownership category. Retail businesses may be independently owned, chain-owned, franchisee-operated, leased, owned by manufacturers or wholesalers, or consumer-owned.

Although retailers are primarily small (almost 80 per cent of all retail stores are operated by firms owning only one outlet and about half of all companies have two or fewer paid employees), there are also very large retailers. According to *Fortune*, the five leading U.S. retailers averaged 265,000 employees and over $24 billion in annual sales in 1986.

Independent

An **independent** retailer owns only one retail unit. In the United States, there are more than 1.5 million small, owner-operated independents. The high number of them is associated with the ease of entry into the marketplace. Because of low capital requirements and no, or relatively simple, licensing provisions, entry for many kinds of small retailers is easy. The investment per worker in retailing is usually much lower than that for manufacturers. Retailer licensing, although more stringent in recent years, is still pretty routine. In 1986, about 73,000 new retail businesses, most independents, opened in the United States.[2]

The ease of entry into retailing is reflected in the low market shares of the leading firms in virtually all retail goods/service categories as a percentage of total category sales. For example, the five largest drugstore retailers and the five leading food retailers account for only about 25 and 28 per cent of sales in their respective categories.[3]

A great degree of competition is generated because of the relative ease of entry into retailing. As a result, it is also undoubtedly an important factor in the high rate of retail business failures among newer firms. The Small Business Administration estimates that one-third of new retailers do not survive their first year, and that two-thirds of new retailers do not continue beyond their third year.[4] Most of these failures involve independents. Since recent years have been good

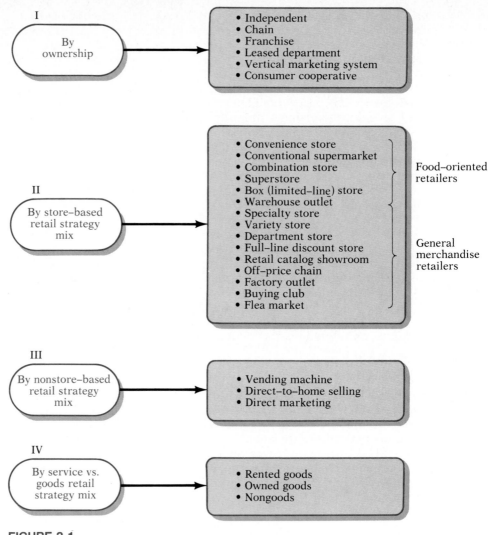

FIGURE 3-1
A Classification Method for Retail Institutions

economically for the United States, these figures are comparatively low. The failure rate is particularly high when the economy slows down.

Competitive Advantages and Disadvantages of Independents

Independent retailers have a variety of advantages and disadvantages facing them. Among the advantages are flexibility, low investments, specialized offerings, direct control of strategy, image, uniformity, independence, and entrepreneurial drive.

Independent retailers have a great deal of flexibility when choosing store locations and developing strategy. Because only one store location is involved, a detailed list of specifications can be derived for the best location and a thorough search undertaken. Uniform location standards are not developed, as they are for chain stores, and the independent does not have to worry about being too close to other company stores.

In setting strategy, independents have great latitude in selecting customer markets. Because many independents have modest goals, small portions of the overall customer market may be selected rather than the mass market. Product assortments, prices, store hours, and so on are then set consistently with the market.

Because independents run only one store, investment costs for leases, fixtures, employees, and merchandise can be held down. In addition, there is no duplication of stock or personnel functions. Responsibilities are also clearly delineated within the store.

Many independents are able to operate as specialists and so develop skills in a niche of a particular goods/service category. These firms can then be more efficient and can attract customers interested in specialized retailers.

Independent retailers can exert strong control over their strategies because only one store must be managed, and the owner-operator is usually on the premises. Decision making is usually centralized, and the layers of management personnel are minimized.

There is a certain image attached to independents, particularly small ones, that chains would have difficulty in capturing. This is the image of a friendly, personalized retailer that provides a comfortable atmosphere in which to shop.

Independents are able to sustain uniformity because only one geographic market is served and only one strategy (store hours, product assortment, prices, sales personnel, promotion, and so on) is carried out. For example, there cannot be problems because two branch stores are selling identical items at different prices.

An independent retailer has "independence." The owner-operator is generally in full control and does not have to worry about stockholders, meetings of the board of directors, and labor unrest. For example, independents are often free from union work rules and seniority regulations. This can materially affect labor productivity.[5]

As a last major advantage, independents usually have a strong entrepreneurial drive. They have a personal investment in a business, success or failure has substantial implications, and there is a high degree of ego involvement.

Among the disadvantages of independent retailing are limits in bargaining power, few economies of scale, intensiveness of labor, reduced access to media, overdependence on the boss, and little time and few resources for planning.

When bargaining with suppliers, independents do not have much power because they often buy in small quantities. Therefore, in some instances, independents may be bypassed by manufacturers or wholesalers or may be limited in the selection of merchandise made available to them. Reordering may also be difficult for independents; and minimum order requirements may be too high for small retailers to qualify. To overcome this problem, a growing number of independents, such as hardware stores, are forming buying groups to increase their power in dealing with suppliers.

Independents are usually unable to establish economies of scale (low per unit costs due to the handling of many units at one time) in buying and maintaining inventory. Because of demand and financial constraints, small assortments of items are purchased several times per year rather than large orders once or twice per year. This means that transportation, ordering, and handling costs per unit are high.

Operations for many independents are very labor-intensive. There is often little computerization. Ordering, taking inventory, marking merchandise, ringing up sales, and bookkeeping are generally done manually. Manual operations are time-consuming and less efficient than computer tabulations (which are expensive in terms of initial investment).

Because of the costs of television ads and the large geographic coverage of magazines (too large for independents), independent retailers are limited in their access to advertising media and sometimes pay abnormally high fees per ad compared to regular users. However, a creative independent has a number of promotion tools available (see Chapter 15).

A key problem for independents—particularly small, family-run businesses— is an overdependence on the owner. In too many cases, all decisions are made by this person, and no continuity of management is stipulated for the time the owner-boss is ill or on vacation or retires. Long-run success and employee morale can be affected by overdependence on the owner.

Another critical problem for independent retailers is the limited amount of time and resources allocated to long-run planning. Because the owner is intimately involved in the day-to-day running of the store, adaptation to new legislation, new goods or services, and/or new competitors often suffers.

Chain

A **chain** can be defined as multiple retail units under common ownership; it usually engages in some level of centralized (or coordinated) purchasing and decision making. In the United States, there are now 60,000 to 70,000 retail chains that own about 500,000 establishments.

Table 3-1 provides data on the number of establishments, their sales volume, and their payroll as a percentage of the U.S. total for firms with differing numbers of units during 1972, 1977, and 1982 (the most recent data available). It is clear from the table that the relative strength of chains is great, and that their popularity has been rising. In 1982, multiunit firms operated 21 per cent of all estab-

---

RETAILING IN ACTION

What Does It Take to Start a Retail Business?

Today, annual ice-cream sales are approaching $10 billion, and there are about 20,000 ice-cream shops throughout the United States (up from 10,000 in 1980). So, what does it take to start a profitable retail ice-cream business? The answer, if Ben & Jerry's is the guide, is creativity, persistence, and an awareness of one's limitations.

In 1977, Ben Cohen and Jerry Greenfield decided they wanted to open an ice-cream parlor and spent $5 on a Penn State correspondence course titled "Ice Cream." They then amassed $8,000 and purchased an abandoned gasoline station in Burlington, Vermont (a city where the temperature is below freezing 161 days a year). At first, they sold homemade ice cream, soup, and crepes. But they quickly stopped selling the soup and crepes. Ben & Jerry's focused on its now-famous exotic superpremium ice cream featuring such ingredients as chocolate chunks, almonds,

and other treats. It also sought out and received a large amount of media attention.

During the first year of business, Ben & Jerry's had sales of $200,000. By 1982, the company was prospering; however, Cohen and Greenfield were not happy. They did not feel comfortable running a growing business: "It got to the point where we were becoming businessmen instead of ice cream makers. We didn't want that, so we hired Chico so we could have fun." Fred (Chico) Lager, with a Southern California MBA, has run Ben & Jerry's since then, while the partners have spent their time developing new flavors and promotions. The partners work in jeans and Ben & Jerry's T-shirts and let the staff that has been hired have significant operating autonomy.

Currently, Ben & Jerry's has yearly sales of $30 million. And it sells ice cream through traditional retailers as well as via its own outlets.

Source: Based on material in Erik Larson, "The Best-Laid Plans," *Inc.* (February 1987), p. 61; and Kevin Maney, "Ice Cream Sellers Scoop Up Business," *USA Today* (July 17, 1987), pp. 1–2.

TABLE 3-1
Independent Versus Chain Retailing

	Number of Retailers	Establishments as Percentage of Total*			Sales as Percentage of Total*			Payroll as Percentage of Total*		
	1982	1982	1977	1972	1982	1977	1972	1982	1977	1972
U.S. total	1,572,792	100.0	100.0	100.0	100.0	100.0	100.0	100.0	100.0	100.0
Total independents	1,521,846	79.1	82.1	84.7	47.7	52.0	54.9	47.0	49.2	51.4
Total chain retailers	50,946	20.9	17.9	15.2	52.3	48.0	45.1	53.0	50.8	48.6
2 to 4 units	41,612	5.2	4.6	4.4	8.1	7.3	7.0	9.1	8.5	8.4
5 to 9 units	5,505	1.8	1.8	1.4	3.6	3.3	3.0	3.8	3.7	3.4
10 to 24 units	2,422	1.8	1.7	1.3	4.0	3.6	3.5	4.0	3.9	3.6
25 to 99 units	1,031	2.5	2.2	1.8	7.1	6.7	6.3	6.7	6.5	6.4
100 or more units	376	9.5	7.7	6.1	29.5	26.9	25.3	29.3	28.3	26.8

*Rounding errors appear in some of the percentages.

Source: 1982 Census of Retail Trade; and authors' estimates.

lishments, up from 15 per cent in 1972; but they accounted for 52 per cent of total sales, up from 45 per cent in 1972, and 53 per cent of total payroll, up from 49 per cent in 1982.

Although 82 per cent of all retail chains had 4 or fewer outlets in 1982, the 376 retailers having 100 or more units were responsible for 30 per cent of total U.S. retail store sales. Today, chains with 100 or more establishments undoubtedly account for more than a third of retail store sales. Furthermore, there are now about twenty retailers owning at least 1,000 outlets each; F.W. Woolworth, through its various divisions, has around 7,000 stores.[6]

The prevalence of chains varies greatly by the type of retailer. For example, in these categories, chains generate 75 per cent or more of total retail sales: department store, variety store, and grocery store. On the other hand, stationery, beauty salon, furniture, and liquor store chains generate far less than 50 per cent of total retail sales in their categories. See Figure 3-2. Chains owning 100 or more establishments are most likely in these categories: grocery store, gasoline service station, variety store, drugstore, shoe store, and auto accessory store.

Competitive Advantages and Disadvantages of Chains

There are many competitive advantages for chain retailers: bargaining power, wholesale function efficiencies, multiple-store efficiencies, computerization, access to media, well-defined management, and long-range planning.[7]

Many chains have bargaining power when dealing with their suppliers because of the amount of their annual purchases. As a result, these chains can receive new items as soon as they are introduced, have reorders promptly filled, get good service and selling support from suppliers, and obtain the best prices possible. In addition, large chains may gain exclusive rights to selling certain items and may have suppliers make goods under the retailers' brands. For example, Sears has exclusive selling rights for certain Disney products and buys appliances carrying its own Kenmore brand.

A chain retailer can achieve cost efficiencies by performing wholesaling functions itself. Buying directly from suppliers and in large quantities; shipping and storing goods; and attending trade shows sponsored by suppliers to learn about new offerings—these are just some of the wholesaling activities that can be performed by the retailer. By doing so, they can sometimes bypass wholesalers, and the result is lower supplier prices to the retailer. For this reason, the prices paid by chains are often less than those paid by independents, without violation of the Robinson-Patman Act.

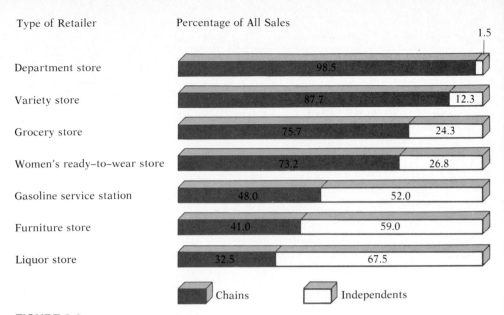

Type of Retailer · Percentage of All Sales

Type of Retailer	Chains	Independents
Department store	98.5	1.5
Variety store	87.7	12.3
Grocery store	75.7	24.3
Women's ready–to–wear store	73.2	26.8
Gasoline service station	48.0	52.0
Furniture store	41.0	59.0
Liquor store	32.5	67.5

Chains   Independents

FIGURE 3-2
The Popularity of Chains for Selected Types of Retailer
Source: *1982 Census of Retail Trade.*

Efficiency in multiple-store operations can be gained as a result of shared warehousing facilities; volume purchases of standardized store fixtures, employee uniforms, and so on; centralized purchasing and decision making; and other factors. It is typical for a chain retailer to give headquarters executives broad authority for overall personnel policies as well as buying, pricing, and advertising decisions.

Chain retailers, because of their resources and number of transactions, are able to use computers in ordering merchandise, taking inventory, forecasting, ringing up sales, and bookkeeping. This use of computers increases efficiency and reduces overall costs.

Chains, particularly national or regional ones, can take advantage of a variety of media, from television to magazines to traditional newspapers. Large sales volume and geographic coverage of the market allow chains to utilize all forms of media.

Most chains have well-defined management philosophies, whether centralized or decentralized. Overall strategies are clearly delineated, and the responsibilities of employees are clearly outlined. In addition, continuity is ensured when managerial personnel are absent or retire.

Finally, many chain retailers expend considerable time and resources in long-run planning. Frequently, specific personnel are assigned to long-term planning on a permanent basis. Opportunities and constraints are also carefully monitored.

Chain retailers do have a number of disadvantages: inflexibility, high investments, lack of control, and limited independence.

Once a chain retailer is well established, its flexibility is limited. Adequate, nonoverlapping store locations may be difficult to find. A consistent strategy must be maintained throughout all of the branches; prices, promotions, and product assortments must be similar for each store. For chains that use centralized decision making, there may be difficulty in adapting to local needs, such as taking into account differences in life-styles among city, suburban, and rural customers.

For chains, investment costs may be high. Multiple-store leases, fixtures, product assortments, and employees are involved. The purchase of any merchandise may be costly because a number of store branches must be stocked.

Managerial control can present a problem for chains, especially for those having geographically dispersed branches. Top management cannot maintain the control over each branch that an independent owner has over his or her single outlet. Lack of communication and time delays in making and enacting decisions are two particular problems.

Personnel in large chains have limited independence. In many cases, there are several layers of management, unionized employees, stockholders, and boards of directors.

Franchising

Franchising is defined as a contractual arrangement between a franchisor (which may be a manufacturer, a wholesaler, or a service sponsor) and a retail franchisee, which allows the franchisee to conduct a given form of business under an established name and according to a given pattern of business. In a typical franchise arrangement, the franchisee pays an initial fee and a monthly percentage of gross sales in exchange for the exclusive rights to sell goods and services in a specified geographic area. Franchising represents a retail organizational form in which small businesspeople can benefit by being part of a large, multiunit chain-type retail institution.

There are two broad types of franchising arrangements: product/trademark franchising and business format franchising.[8] In a product/trademark franchising arrangement, franchised dealers acquire the identity of their suppliers by agreeing to sell the latter's products and/or to operate under the suppliers' names. These franchised dealers operate relatively autonomously from the suppliers. Although they must adhere to certain operating rules, they set store hours, choose locations, determine store facilities and displays, and otherwise run their stores. Product/trademark franchising represents about 70 per cent of all retail franchising. Examples are auto dealers and many gasoline service stations.

In business format franchising, there is a more active relationship between the franchisor and the franchisee. The franchisee receives assistance on site location, quality control, accounting systems, startup practices, management training, and responding to problems—in addition to the right to sell goods and services. The use of prototype stores, standardized merchandise lines, and cooperative advertising enable business format franchises to achieve a level of coordination previously found only in chains. Over the past three decades, the major growth in franchising has involved business format arrangements. These arrangements are common for restaurants and other food outlets, real estate, and service retailing. See Figure 3-3.

Although many variations in franchising exist, McDonald's is a good example of a business format franchise arrangement. The company provides each new franchisee with an intensive training program at its "Hamburger U," a detailed operations manual (complete down to the most minute facets of running machinery), regular visits by field service managers, and repeat trips to Hamburger U for brush-up training courses. In return for these rights and privileges, the McDonald's Corporation receives up to $450,000 and more for a long-term agreement to operate a franchise. A large down payment is required, and a McDonald's franchisee pays a royalty fee, based on gross sales, to the franchisor.

Size and Structural Arrangements

Retail franchising began in the United States in 1851 when the Singer Sewing Machine Company first franchised its dealers. However, retail franchising did not become popular until undercapitalized automobile manufacturers started utilizing franchising to expand their distribution systems in the early 1900s.[9]

FIGURE 3-3
Business Format Franchising
McDonald's and Wendy's are two of the leading business format franchise chains in the world. Reprinted by permission.

Although auto and truck dealers still account for about 55 per cent of all franchise sales, there are few retail industry groups that have not been affected by franchising's growth. In 1987, 435,000 franchise outlets in the United States were expected to account for more than $550 billion in retail sales, over one-third of total U.S. retail store sales. Table 3-2 shows 1987 retail franchise sales by goods/service category.

Overall, 85 per cent of franchising sales and 75 per cent of franchised outlets are from franchisee-owned units; the balance are from franchisor-owned outlets. When franchisees operate only one outlet, they are classified as independents by

TABLE 3-2
1987 Retail Franchise Sales*

Type of Retailer	Sales (billions)	Percentage of Total Sales
Auto and truck dealers	$305.6	55.0
Gasoline service stations	94.9	17.1
Restaurants (all types)	58.0	10.4
General merchandise stores	25.2	4.5
Hotels and motels	16.7	3.0
Automotive goods and services stores	12.9	2.4
Convenience stores	12.8	2.3
Other food stores	11.6	2.1
Rental services	7.4	1.3
Personal and household services	6.2	1.1
Recreation, entertainment, and travel businesses	3.2	0.6
Miscellaneous	1.0	0.2
Total	$555.5	100.0

*Because the U.S. Department of Commerce does not break down all the types of firms listed in this table into retail and nonretail categories, a small amount of nonretail sales may be included in some cases.

Source: Andrew Kostecka, *Franchising in the Economy: 1985–1987* (Washington, D.C.: U.S. Department of Commerce, 1987), p. 27.

the U.S. Department of Commerce; franchisees that operate two or more outlets and franchisor-owned stores are classed as chains. Today, a large and growing number of franchisees operate as chains.

Three types of structural arrangements dominate retail franchising:

❑ Manufacturer-retailer—A manufacturer gives an independent businessperson the right to sell goods and related services (subject to conditions) through a licensing agreement.

❑ Wholesaler-retailer
   a. Voluntary—A wholesaler organizes a franchise system and grants franchises to individual retailers.
   b. Cooperative—A group of retailers sets up a franchise system and shares the ownership and operations of a wholesaling organization.

❑ Service sponsor-retailer—A service firm licenses individual retailers to allow them to provide specific service packages (subject to conditions) to consumers.

Figure 3-4 presents examples of each of these structural arrangements.

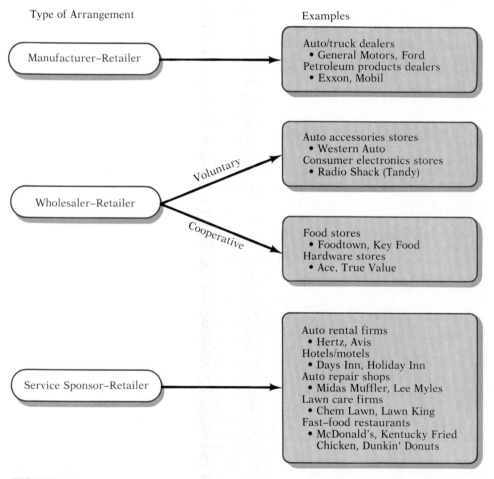

FIGURE 3-4
Structural Arrangements in Retail Franchising

Competitive Advantages and Disadvantages of Franchising

The franchisee receives several benefits by investing in a successful franchise operation. First, an individual businessperson can own and operate a retail enterprise with a relatively small capital investment. Second, the franchisee acquires a well-known name and goods/service line. Third, standard operating procedures and management skills are taught to the franchisee. Fourth, a cooperative marketing program is usually employed (e.g., national advertising) that could not otherwise be afforded. Fifth, the franchisee obtains exclusive selling rights for a specified geographical territory. Sixth, purchases may be made more cheaply because of volume.

Some potential problems exist for franchisees. First, oversaturation occurs when too many franchisees are located in one geographic area; therefore, the sales and profits of each unit are adversely affected. Second, because of the overzealous selling of franchises, the income potential and required managerial ability, initiative, and investment of a franchise unit may be incorrectly stated.[10] Third, a franchisee may be locked into a contract provision whereby purchases must be made through the franchisor or certain approved vendors. Fourth, cancellation provisions may give the franchisor the right to cancel a franchise if any provision of the franchise agreement is not met.[11] Fifth, in some industries, franchise agreements are of short duration. Sixth, under most franchise contracts, royalties are a percentage of gross sales, regardless of the franchisees' profits. These six factors result in **constrained decision making,** whereby the franchisor can exclude franchisees from or limit their involvement in the strategic planning process.

In an effort to curb unfair franchisor sales practices, the Federal Trade Commission has a rule entitled "Disclosure Requirements and Business Opportunities." This rule applies to all franchisors in the United States and is intended

RETAILING IN ACTION

How Can Franchising Opportunities Motivate Store Managers?

"Motivating and retaining store managers is a challenge every retailer faces. Finding qualified people to buy franchised outlets is a problem peculiar to the franchising industry." A Denver-based tire store franchisor, Big O Tires Inc., has a unique strategy for addressing both issues.

Big O realizes that store managers who work on a straight-salary basis have little or no incentive to improve their outlets' productivity or sales. It further recognizes that there are few potential franchisees for tire stores who have the proper background in the industry. To remedy this, Big O has implemented a system whereby store managers can become owners of franchised outlets in return for generating store profits.

Under the Big O system, a percentage of a store's profit goes into the manager's account,

which is used to build up that person's equity in the store. After a period of years, the manager would own a substantial part of the outlet: "For a young guy with no money and a lot of energy, there's nothing that beats it." Over one-quarter of Big O's 260 + outlets have been purchased in that manner.

As an example, Jeffrey Wandel (age twenty-seven) is in the process of purchasing a Big O store in Sonoma, California. His half interest will eventually cost $143,000. But none of this amount will come out of Jeff's salary. Over a ten-year period, his profit-sharing will be applied toward the purchase amount. Said Wandel's sponsors, "You want him to have an incentive to do as good a job as you would do yourself."

Source: Based on material in Steven P. Galante, "Tire Franchiser Offers Equity to Rev Up Store Managers," *Wall Street Journal* (October 19, 1987), p. 33.

to provide potential franchisees with adequate information prior to making an investment. In addition, a number of states have enacted fair practice laws stipulating that franchisors may not terminate, cancel, or fail to renew a franchise without sufficient cause. Arizona, California, Indiana, New Jersey, Virginia, Washington, and Wisconsin are among the states with fair practice laws. Furthermore, many states require that franchise offerings be registered.[12]

The franchisor accrues many benefits by selling individual franchises. First, a national presence can be developed more quickly and with a smaller investment on the part of the franchisor. Second, qualifications for franchise ownership can be set and enforced. Third, money is obtained when goods are delivered rather than when they are sold. Fourth, agreements can be drawn up that require franchisees to abide by stringent regulations set by the franchisor. Fifth, because franchisees are owners and not employees, they have a greater incentive to work hard. Sixth, after a franchisee has paid for the franchise, the franchisor also receives royalties or sells products to the individual proprietors.

A franchisor may also face potential problems. First, individual franchisees can ruin the overall image and reputation of the franchise if they do not maintain company standards. Second, lack of uniformity adversely affects customer loyalty. Third, intrafranchise competition is not desirable. Fourth, the resale value of individual units is injured if franchisees perform poorly. Fifth, an ineffective franchise unit directly injures the franchisor's profitability from the sales of services, materials, or products to franchisees, or from royalty fees. Sixth, franchisees, in greater numbers, are seeking independence from franchisor rules and regulations.

Additional information on franchising is contained in the appendix that follows the cases at the end of this chapter.

Leased Department

A **leased department** is a department in a retail store—usually a department, discount, or specialty store—that is rented to an outside party. The proprietor of a leased department is usually responsible for all aspects of its operations (including fixtures) and normally pays the store a percentage of sales as rent. The store imposes various requirements on the leased department to ensure overall consistency and coordination.

In most situations, leased departments have been used by existing retailers to broaden merchandise or service offerings into product categories requiring highly specialized skills or knowledge not possessed by the retailers themselves. Consequently, leased departments operate in categories that tend to be on the fringe of the store's major product lines. Leased departments are most common for in-store beauty salons, photographic studios, and millinery, shoe, jewelry, watch repair, shoe repair, and sewing-machine departments. They account for about $11 billion in annual sales in department stores. See Figure 3-5. Unfortunately, data on current overall leased department sales are not available.

Competitive Advantages and Disadvantages of Leased Departments

From the store's perspective, using leased departments has a number of benefits. Store personnel might otherwise lack the merchandising ability to handle and sell certain goods and services. The leased-department operator pays for inventory and personnel expenses, thus reducing store costs. The market can be enlarged by providing one-stop shopping for customers. Personnel management, merchandise displays, the reordering of items, and so on are undertaken by the lessee. A percentage of revenues is received on a regular basis.

There are also some potential disadvantages from the store's perspective. The leased department may use operating procedures that conflict with those of the

(1)

(2)

(3)

FIGURE 3-5
Footwear Retailing: Leased Departments
Wohl, a division of the Brown Group, is the largest operator of leased shoe departments in U.S. department stores. Among the stores in which it operates are D.H. Holmes (1), Winkelman's (2), and Pizitz (3). Reprinted by permission.

store. The lessee may adversely affect the store's image. Customers may blame problems on the store rather than the lessee.

For the leased department operator, there are these advantages: Existing stores are usually well known, have a large number of steady customers, and generate immediate sales for leased departments. Some expenses are reduced because of shared facilities, such as security equipment and outside display windows. There are economies of scale (volume savings) in pooled advertising. The lessee's image is aided by its relationship with a popular store.

Lessees face these potential problems: There may be inflexibility with regard to hours open and operating style. The goods/service lines offered will usually be restricted. If the lessee is successful, the store may raise the rent or may not renew a lease when it expires. The in-store location may not generate the sales expected.

A leased department may be viewed from two perspectives: as an element in a shopping center and as a part of a franchise system. In the shopping-center context, the leased department is renting an area with a given traffic flow to conduct its business. The leased-department operator must examine the character of the traffic and its relationship to the chosen consumer market. The lessor must examine the extent to which the department will either create additional traffic or be a parasite and live off the traffic generated by other parts of the store. The franchise analogy relates to the leased department's ability to blend with the merchandise philosophy of another retailer and the need to set a broad policy for all departments, so that an entire store's reputation is not injured by one operator.

An example of a successful long-term lease arrangement is one utilized by the CPI Corporation and Sears. For more than 25 years, CPI has operated photographic studios in Sears stores. In exchange for the use of 300 square feet of space in each of hundreds of Sears stores, CPI pays Sears 15 per cent of its gross sales. CPI regularly has annual sales per square foot that are 50 per cent higher than Sears' overall average. CPI's agreement with Sears can be terminated by Sears on sixty days' notice.[13]

Vertical Marketing System

A **vertical marketing system** consists of all the levels of independently owned businesses along a channel of distribution. Goods and services are normally distributed through one of these types of vertical marketing systems: independent, partially integrated, and fully integrated. See Figure 3-6.

In an **independent vertical marketing system,** there are three levels of independently owned businesses: manufacturers, wholesalers, and retailers. Such a system is most often used if manufacturers and/or retailers are small, intensive distribution is sought, customers are widely dispersed, unit sales are high, company resources are low, channel members want to share costs and risks, and task specialization is desirable. Independent vertical marketing systems are used by many stationery stores, gift shops, hardware stores, food stores, drugstores, and a number of others. They are the leading form of vertical marketing system.

With a **partially integrated vertical marketing system,** two independently owned businesses along a channel perform all production and distribution functions without the aid of the third. The most common form of this system occurs when a manufacturer and a retailer complete transactions and shipping, storing, and other distribution functions in the absence of an independently owned wholesaler. A partially integrated system is most likely if manufacturers and/or retailers are large, selective or exclusive distribution is sought, unit sales are moderate, company resources are high, greater channel control is desired, and existing wholesalers are too expensive or unavailable. Partially integrated systems are often used by furniture stores, appliance stores, restaurants, computer retailers, and mail-order firms.

Through a **fully integrated vertical marketing system,** a single firm performs all production and distribution functions without the aid of any other firms. In the past, this type of system was usually employed by manufacturers, such as Avon, Premark (Tupperware), Hartmarx, and Firestone. But today, more retailers are using fully integrated systems for at least some of their products. For example, Kroger and Southland (7-Eleven) manufacture dairy products, baked goods, ice cream, and other items; and Sears has ownership shares in an appliance maker, a paint and detergent maker, an apparel maker, and others.

A fully integrated vertical marketing system enables a firm to have total control over its strategy, have direct contact with final consumers, lower per-unit costs by eliminating channel members, be self-sufficient and not rely on others, have exclusivity over the goods and services offered, and keep all profits within the

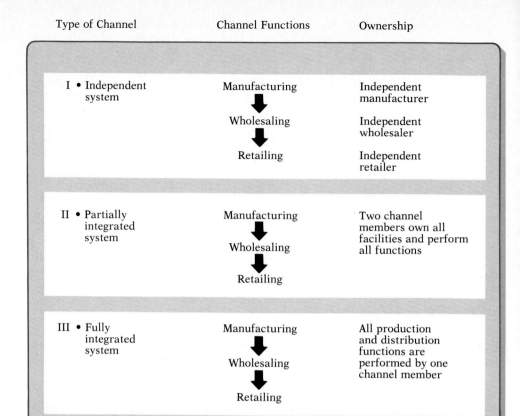

Type of Channel	Channel Functions	Ownership
I • Independent system	Manufacturing ↓ Wholesaling ↓ Retailing	Independent manufacturer Independent wholesaler Independent retailer
II • Partially integrated system	Manufacturing ↓ Wholesaling ↓ Retailing	Two channel members own all facilities and perform all functions
III • Fully integrated system	Manufacturing ↓ Wholesaling ↓ Retailing	All production and distribution functions are performed by one channel member

FIGURE 3-6
Vertical Marketing Systems: Functions and Ownership

company. For example, by making most of the products sold in its Radio Shack stores, Tandy maximizes product visibility, trains and supervises store personnel, has exclusivity over its brands, controls retail prices, and so on. However, there may be some difficulties associated with a fully integrated system, including high investment costs and a lack of expertise in both manufacturing and retailing. As an illustration, after an evaluation of its candy-making operations, Kroger's chief executive reached this conclusion: "We can make candy as *good* as anyone. We just can't make it as efficiently."[14]

Some firms use a **dual vertical marketing system,** whereby they are involved in more than one type of system. For example, Avon has a fully integrated system for its Avon line and has its own sales force making in-home sales. Avon also sells its Giorgio and Deneuve perfumes and cosmetics through department and specialty stores via a partially integrated system. Thus, Avon can appeal to different consumers, increase sales volume, share some of its costs, and maintain a good degree of control over its strategy.[15] See Figure 3-7.

In addition to partially or fully integrating a vertical marketing system, a firm can exert power in a distribution channel because of its economic, legal, or political strength; superior knowledge and abilities; customer loyalty; or other factors. **Channel control** occurs when one member of a distribution channel is able to dominate the decisions made in that channel through the power it pos-

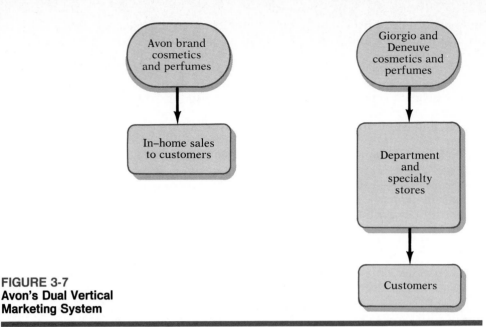

FIGURE 3-7
Avon's Dual Vertical
Marketing System

sesses. Manufacturers, wholesalers, and retailers each have a combination of tools available in interacting with one another.

Manufacturers can exert control through franchising, whereby the franchisee's marketing program comes under close scrutiny; developing strong brand loyalty, wherein retailers are forced to stock merchandise because of consumer pressure; preticketing merchandise, thereby designating suggested list or selling prices; and exclusive distribution, whereby the retailer voluntarily agrees to adhere to given standards in exchange for sole distribution rights in a geographic area.

Wholesalers have the ability to exert control over manufacturers and retailers. If the wholesaler is large, its business is important and it can put pressure on suppliers and buyers. Wholesalers can introduce their own private brands and circumvent manufacturers. A franchise system and/or brand loyalty can also be developed to control the distribution system. The wholesaler can become the most efficient member in the channel for the functions it performs, such as shipping and processing reorders.

Retailers are able to exert control over other channel members in the following instances: a large proportion of a manufacturer's output is sold to one retailer, private branding is employed, or economic power (large gross sales) exists.

When one retailer represents a large percentage of a manufacturer's sales volume, channel control may be applied. For example, there are a number of independent companies from which Sears purchases a large proportion of its output. One such company is Armstrong Rubber (manufacturer of tires and tubes), which makes a large amount of its sales through Sears. As a result, Sears has a very strong bargaining position.

Store brands or private labels enable a retailer to possess channel control, improve competitive positioning, and raise profit margins. Eighty-five per cent of the merchandise purchased by J.C. Penney is specifically made for the company. At Sakowitz, Macy's, Dayton's, Nordstrom, and Lord & Taylor department stores, from 20 to 40 per cent of apparel purchases involve private labels. Even at K mart, which stresses manufacturer brands, 25 per cent of merchandise is privately branded.[16]

Through private labeling, retailers gain significant power over wholesalers and manufacturers by attaining brand loyalty for their goods, converting it to store loyalty, and causing merchandise to be made to specifications. Private labeling thus enables retailers to switch vendors (sellers) with no impact on their customer loyalty as long as the same product specifications are followed. The threat of switching vendors (with no offsetting impact on the private brand sales) is often adequate action to get a manufacturer into line on a retailer's price, delivery, or terms request.

It is important to note that in many cases, channel control has significant advantages for the controlled party, as well as the leader. Long-term relationships allow for scheduling efficiencies and enable vendors to obtain bank loans (because of presold inventories). Some economies result because many activities are eliminated, simplified, or repositioned. Advertising, financing, and billing are drastically simplified, and many functions, such as merchandise marking, can be performed by the manufacturer.

Consumer Cooperative

A **consumer cooperative** is a retail firm that is owned by its customers. In a cooperative arrangement, a group of consumers invests in the company, receives stock certificates, elects officers, manages operations, and shares the profits or savings that accrue. In the United States, there are about 30,000 consumer cooperatives, ranging from small buying clubs to Recreational Equipment Inc. (REI) with $175 million in annual sales. Overall, consumer cooperatives account for less than three-tenths of one per cent of retail store sales.

Consumer cooperatives exist for these fundamental reasons: Some consumers believe they can operate retail stores as well as or better than traditional retailers. They also feel that existing retailers are inadequately fulfilling customer needs with regard to healthful, environmentally safe products. They further believe that existing retailers often make excessive profits.

This is how one small and one large consumer cooperative operate:

❑ Cincinnati Food Co-op has 800 members and $500,000 in annual sales. There are three full-time and four part-time paid employees. Each member is required to work 1.5 hours per month for the co-op without compensation. The initial fee to join the co-op is $115 for a single person or $150 for a family; the yearly membership fee is $15. Prices average 25 per cent less than competitors'.[17]

❑ REI sells outdoor recreational equipment, such as backpacks and bicycles, to its 1.9 million members. It has more than 1,100 employees in about twenty stores. There is a one-time membership fee of $10, which entitles customers to shop at REI, elect the twelve-person board of directors, and share in profits (based on the amount spent by each member). The profits distributed to members amount to about a 12 per cent discount from REI's already low prices.[18]

Cooperatives have not grown beyond their current level because they involve a lot of consumer initiative and drive; consumers are usually not expert in buying, handling, and selling goods and services; cost savings and low selling prices have not been as expected in many cases; and consumer boredom frequently sets in. Traditional retailers are also now doing a better a job of appealing to consumer niches in categories such as health foods.

SUMMARY

There are about 1.6 million different retail firms in the United States operating 2 million establishments. These retailers can be classified on the basis of ownership, store-based retail strategy mix, non-store-based retail strategy mix, and service versus goods retail strategy mix. These categories are not mutually exclusive; that is, many retailers can be placed in more than one category. This chapter deals with retail ownership. Chapter 4 examines the other classifications.

Almost 80 per cent of all U.S. retailers are independent and own only one outlet or store. The large number of independents is largely due to the ease of entry into retailing. Among the competitive advantages of independents are their flexibility, low investments, specialized offerings, direct control of strategy, image, uniformity, independence, and entrepreneurial spirit. Disadvantages include limited bargaining power, few economies of scale, labor-intensiveness, reduced media access, overdependence on the boss, and limited planning.

Retail chains are comprised of multiple retail units under common ownership, which usually engage in some amount of centralized purchasing and decision making. Chains make up one-fifth of all retail firms but generate over one-half of total U.S. retail sales. Chains have these advantages: bargaining power, wholesale function efficiencies, multiple-store efficiencies, computerization, access to media, well-defined management, and long-range planning. They face these potential problems: inflexibility, high investments, lack of control, and limited independence.

Franchising involves contractual arrangements between franchisors (which may be manufacturers, wholesalers, or service sponsors) and retail franchisees. These arrangements allow franchisees to conduct a given form of business under an established name and according to a given pattern of business. The 435,000 franchise outlets account for more than one-third of total U.S. retail store sales. Franchisees receive these benefits: small capital investment, well-known company name, standardized operating procedures and training, cooperative marketing efforts, exclusive selling rights, and volume purchases. They may also face constrained decision making via oversaturation, lower-than-promised profits, strict contract provisions, cancellation clauses, short-term contracts, and continuing royalty payments. Franchisors benefit by more quickly and cheaply developing a large business, setting franchisee qualifications, improving cash flow, outlining strict operating procedures, high franchisee motivation, and receiving ongoing royalties. They may suffer if individual franchisees hurt the company image, do not operate uniformly, compete with one another, lower resale values, and seek greater independence.

Leased departments are in-store locations that are rented to outside parties. These departments usually operate in categories that are on the fringe of their stores' major product lines. The store gains these advantages: expertise from the leased-department operator, reduced inventory and personnel costs, greater store traffic, merchandising support, and a percentage of revenues. Potential disadvantages are conflicts with the lessee and adverse effects on store image. Benefits for the lessee are a well-known store name, steady customers, immediate sales, reduced expenses and economies of scale, and an image associated with the store. Potential problems are inflexibility, restrictions on the goods/services sold, lease nonrenewal, and poorer results than expected.

Vertical marketing systems consist of all the levels of independently owned businesses along a channel of distribution. In independent vertical marketing systems, there are independently owned manufacturers, wholesalers, and retailers. With partially integrated vertical marketing systems, two independently owned firms along a channel, usually manufacturers and retailers, perform all production and distribution functions without the aid of the third. Through fully integrated vertical marketing systems, single firms perform all production and distribution functions. Some firms use dual vertical marketing systems, whereby they are involved in more than one type of system. Even without an integrated system, channel control can be exerted by the most powerful firm(s) in the channel. Manufacturers, wholesalers, and retailers each have methods for increasing their ability to exert control.

Consumer cooperatives are retail firms owned by their customers, who invest, receive company stock, elect officers, manage operations, and share in savings or profits. In total, there are about 30,000 cooperatives in the United States, and they account for less than three-tenths of one per cent of retail store sales. Cooperatives are formed when consumers believe they can perform retailing functions, goods/services offerings of traditional retailers are inadequate, and traditional retailers' profits are too high. Consumer cooperatives have not grown further because they require a lot of consumer initiative, expertise may be lacking, expectations have frequently not been met, and boredom sets in.

QUESTIONS FOR DISCUSSION

1. What are the characteristics of each of the ownership forms discussed in this chapter?
2. May a retailer be categorized by more than one ownership form? Explain your answer.
3. Independents represent almost 80 per cent of all retailers. Yet, they generate less than half of all sales. Comment on this.
4. How can an independent retailer overcome the problem of overdependence on the owner?
5. What difficulties might an independent encounter if it tries to expand into a chain?
6. Do you expect retail chains with 100 or more outlets to continue their recent growth pattern? Explain your answer.
7. What are the similarities and differences between chains and franchising?
8. For a prospective franchisee, under what circumstances would product/trademark franchising be advantageous? When would business format franchising be better?
9. "Overall, 85 per cent of franchising sales and 75 per cent of franchised outlets are from franchisee-owned units; the balance are from franchisor-owned outlets." Comment on this.
10. Why would a department store want to lease space to an outside operator rather than run a business, such as a beauty salon, itself? What would be its risks in this approach?
11. What are the pros and cons of Avon's using a dual vertical marketing system?
12. At the County Seat, a 300-outlet retail apparel chain, store brands account for more than 50 per cent of sales. Evaluate this strategy from a channel control perspective.
13. How could a small independent stationery store increase its channel control?
14. Why have consumer cooperatives not expanded much in recent years? What would you recommend to change this?

NOTES

1. Jo Ellen Davis, "Hardware Wars: The Big Boys Might Lose This One," *Business Week* (October 14, 1985), pp. 84–90; *Lowe's 1986 Annual Report;* and *Hechinger Company 1987 Annual Report.*

2. Dun & Bradstreet, "Business Starts," *Wall Street Journal* (May 15, 1986), p. 31. See also David L. Birch, "The Truth About Start-Ups," *Inc.* (January 1988), pp. 14–15.

3. *Standard & Poor's Industry Surveys: Retailing* (January 22, 1987), pp. 87–88; "The 50 Largest Retailing Companies," *Fortune* (June 8, 1987), pp. 210–211; and "54th Annual Report of the Grocery Industry," *Progressive Grocer* (April 1987), p. 8.

4. Jacquelyn Bivens, "Franchising Boom Makes Headway," *Chain Store Age Executive* (October 1986), p. 19. See also *Business Failure Record* (New York: Dun & Bradstreet, 1987).

5. See John Merwin, "A Piece of the Action," *Forbes* (September 24, 1984), pp. 146–148 ff.

6. "Exec 100," *Chain Age Store Executive* (August 1987), p. 11.

7. See Richard T. Hise, J. Patrick Kelly, Myron Gable, and James B. McDonald, "Factors Affecting the Performance of Individual Chain Store Units: An Empirical Analysis," *Journal of Retailing*, Vol. 59 (Summer 1983), pp. 22–39.

8. Andrew Kostecka, *Franchising in the Economy: 1985–1987* (Washington, D.C.: U.S. Department of Commerce, 1987), pp. 1–5.

9. Brenton R. Schlender, "Working on the Chain Gang," *Wall Street Journal* (May 19, 1986), p. 14D.

10. See John R. Nevin, Shelby D. Hunt, and Michael Levas, "Legal Remedies for Deceptive and Unfair Practices in Franchising," *Journal of Macromarketing*, Vol. 1 (Spring 1981), pp. 23–34.

11. See Paul N. Bloom, Richard Heinzelmann, and Frank B. Alt, "An Evaluation of Franchisee-Protection Legislation in the Petroleum Industry," *Journal of Public Policy & Marketing*, Vol. 5 (1986), pp. 105–122.

12. Thomas O'Donnell, "Franchising: No Entrepreneurs Need Apply," *Forbes* (December 3, 1984), p. 130; Philip S. Gutis, "The Stunning Franchise Explosion," *New York Times* (January 20, 1985), Section 3, p. 4; and David Diamond, "The Dark Side of Franchising," *New York Times* (January 12, 1986), Section 3, p. 4.

13. Updated by the authors from John A. Byrne, "Profit from Portraits," *Forbes* (June 6, 1983), pp. 107–108.

14. Bill Saporito, "Kroger: The New King of Supermarketing," *Fortune* (February 21, 1983), pp. 75–76.

15. Amy Dunkin, "Big Names Are Opening Doors for Avon," *Business Week* (June 1, 1987), pp. 96–97.

16. *J.C. Penney Merchandise*, p. 3; Ann Morrison, "The Upshot of Off-Price," *Fortune* (June 13, 1983), p. 129; Steve Weiner, "Caught in a Cross-Fire, Brand-Apparel Makers Design Their Defenses," *Wall Street Journal* (January 24, 1984), pp. 1, 17; and Isadore Barmash, "Private Label: Flux," *Stores* (April 1987), pp. 17–23.

17. Don Veraska, "Co-Ops Pay Attention to Marketing," *Advertising Age* (April 18, 1985), p. 48.

18. Ken Wells, "REI Plans to Double Sales in 5 Years," *Wall Street Journal* (August 21, 1985), p. 6; and "REI, Eddie Bauer Expand," *Chain Store Age Executive* (August 1987), pp. 46–47.

Andy Nichols: Opening an Independently Owned Store

Andy Nichols worked as a salesman for Hoover Vacuum Cleaner for over twenty years. Although Andy always wanted to be his own boss, he did not have enough savings to start a business until this year.

Now Andy plans to open a store specializing in the sale and service of a complete line of Hoover vacuum cleaners. Nichols feels that this store is a natural for him:

❑ He knows Hoover products better than any sales clerk in a retail store and can ascertain which model will best satisfy a customer's needs.

❑ Because he has sold vacuum cleaners to many department, discount, and appliance stores, he knows the actual prices paid for Hoover cleaners by each store type, how to display the cleaners effectively, and the characteristics of competition.

❑ His contacts at Hoover will enable him to make special buys of discontinued models, trade show samples, and manufacturer's remakes (defective machines returned by

TABLE 1
Comparison of Selected Product Lines of Stores Selling Vacuum Cleaners

Points of Comparison	Proposed Nichols Product Line	Current Department Store Product Line	Current Discount Store Product Line
Brands carried	Hoover only	Hoover, Eureka, Whirlpool	Hoover, Eureka
Total number of different models carried and the retail list price ranges of these models:			
Canister	4 models $110–$180	3 models $110–$160	2 models $100–$130
Upright	4 models $130–$330	3 models $130–$250	2 models $115–$150
Power canister	3 models $280–$460	2 models $280–$320	1 model $240
Electric broom	3 models $40–$70	2 models $40–$50	2 models $30–$45
Hand-held vacuum	2 models $35–$60	None	None
Different models of Hoover carried and the retail list price ranges of these models:			
Canister	Same as above	2 models $110–$135	1 model $100
Upright	Same as above	2 models $130–$200	1 model $115
Power canister	Same as above	1 model $280	1 model $240
Electric broom	Same as above	1 model $40	None
Hand-held vacuum	Same as above	None	None
In-store demonstration	Yes	No	No
Retail sales price	List	List	10%–20% off list
Return privilege	10 days	7 days (but very liberal, as long as machine is in original container)	7 days

department stores and rebuilt by the manufacturer). These special buys will allow Andy to compete with department store and discount store prices.

❑ Andy has the ability to service machines, and service is important for a vacuum cleaner store. It acquaints customers with the store. The repair of in-warranty machines is paid for by the manufacturer and is provided free to store customers. Accessory products, like vacuum cleaner bags, are profitable. Customer loyalty is maintained through services such as a loaner vacuum (provided while the customer's machine is under repair).

Nichols' marketing plan is to open a store in a suburb of Boise, Idaho (about ten minutes from his home). The proposed location is a fifteen-minute drive to the nearest department store and four miles from a full-line discount house. These two stores are the most successful Hoover dealers in the area.

Unlike his competitors, Andy intends to sell only Hoover vacuums. This will enable him to properly service all machines he sells, utilize his superior product knowledge, and stock a full line of cleaners. A consumer shopping for a vacuum cleaner will know that Nichols stocks all models, not just the fast-selling, popular ones carried by department and discount stores.

Nichols also plans to have demonstrator models of each machine displayed in the store and to have a fact tag on each model. The fact tag will outline the machine's technical specifications: horsepower, suction ability, weight, cord length, whether the cord is retractable, filter bag capacity, and features.

Andy has drawn up a comparison of his proposed store and the leading competitors. He is currently working on this comparison. See Table 1.

QUESTIONS

1. What additional information does Nichols need before making the decision to open the store?
2. As an independent retailer, will Nichols have any operational advantages or disadvantages in competing with the department store and the discount store (both of which are members of large chains)?
3. How can Nichols prevent customers from using his store to acquire information and then buying elsewhere?
4. Should Andy open the store? Explain your answer.

Case 2

Joshua Slocum: Utilizing a Vertically Integrated Retailing Strategy*

Joshua Slocum is a 32-store apparel chain that operates under the Spaars and Post Horn names. The firm began in 1985 when it acquired a small factory outlet store chain from apparel manufacturer J.G. Hook. In 1987, its sales volume was $16 million. Joshua Slocum's long-term goal is to expand into a national company with annual sales of $100 million.

Spaars is an upscale apparel chain aiming its products at both career-oriented women and teenagers. Its stores are located in better malls in secondary markets in the Northeast. This unit sells classic-styled women's clothing at prices from $40 to $200. Most of the garments are sold under the Spaars private label. Post Horn consists of discount outlets for Spaars' merchandise. Its stores are located primarily in "value-oriented" centers in upscale areas. Post Horn apparel is generally sold at prices that are 25 per cent lower than Spaars'.

Slocum is careful to avoid major metropolitan markets, where competition for good store sites and for customers is high. Thus, Spaars locates in such areas as Princeton, New Jersey, and Nashville, Tennessee. Post Horn stores are located in New Bedford, Massachusetts; Saratoga, New York; and Freeport, Maine. Whereas competitors in larger cities pay rents as high as $35 per square foot, Spaars averages $22 and Post Horn pays $10 per square foot. The firm keeps its rental costs below 10 per cent of sales.

*The material in this case is drawn from "Joshua Slocum's Horizon Is Vertical," *Chain Store Age Executive* (August 1987), pp. 75–76.

The key to Slocum's retailing strategy is its reliance on an almost fully integrated vertical marketing system, an approach similar to that used by the much larger Benetton, The Gap, and The Limited. The company uses virtually no independent channel members. It designs most of its own fabrics and fashions, has apparel made to its specifications by garment manufacturers, and buys directly from these manufacturers.

By vertically integrating, Slocum can underprice competing retailers. For example, a garment that costs $25 to manufacture typically sells for $50 to a retailer and $100 to a final consumer (assuming the manufacturer and retailer each receive 50 per cent markups based on their selling prices). Because Joshua Slocum participates in the manufacturing process, it is able to buy the same-quality garment for its retail stores for $25 and sell it to its final consumers for $65. Thus, Slocum would obtain a 62 per cent markup based on the retail price, and the customer would be able to save $35 on the garment. Vertical integration also allows Slocum to control merchandise displays and personal selling efforts, closely monitor sales of fast-moving apparel, determine retail selling prices, set the number of outlets in a given area, and gain exclusive selling rights for the Spaars brand name.

The chain is particularly strong in knitwear apparel. Half of its knitwear is made entirely by hand; half is machine-knitted. By eliminating several layers of channel members and by having strong bargaining power with its offshore vendors, Slocum claims that it can sell consumers handmade sweaters for $110 each. These sweaters retail elsewhere for as much as $350 apiece.

Decisions at Joshua Slocum are made by a committee, which is comprised of the company president and three designers. The committee decides on fabrics, colors, and silhouettes; what items should be prints or solids; and what pieces are needed to round out an ensemble. It then evaluates the designs made by pattern makers. During a typical knitwear-selection process, the committee chooses 15 to 18 items from among 100 samples.

There are some disadvantages to Slocum's vertical integration strategy:

❑ This approach requires a high level of investment, which may restrict growth potential. For example, Slocum must fund three designers, a dress buyer, a trim buyer, a specification writer, a sample department, and a production manager, as well as facilities normally maintained by wholesalers and retailers. Slocum has generated capital through stock offerings instead of debt.

❑ A small vertically integrated firm has less of a fashion selection for consumers than a retailer that purchases from multiple sources. Even though Benetton, The Gap, and The Limited are vertically integrated, they have substantial financial resources and large product assortments. In addition, Benetton financed its growth via retail franchising.

❑ Slocum cannot cancel its purchase orders for slow-selling merchandise or prevail upon wholesalers to provide new apparel styles. It also does not benefit from cooperative advertising allowances from manufacturers or from the image of designer labels or national brands.

QUESTIONS

1. Evaluate Joshua Slocum's vertical integration strategy in terms of its advantages and disadvantages for a relatively small and young firm.
2. Comment on the firm's decision to open stores in secondary markets rather than in larger cities.
3. Should Slocum add franchised stores to its retail chain? Explain your answer.
4. Should Slocum's stores carry well-known manufacturers' and designers' brands? Why or why not?

Appendix on Franchising

This appendix is presented because of the substantial growth of franchising and the interest in it. The appendix goes beyond the discussion of franchising in Chapter 3 and provides information on managerial issues in franchising and on the relationships between franchisors and franchisees.

Since 1980, annual retail franchising sales have almost doubled. Today, the 435,000 franchise establishments in the United States are affiliated with about 2,200 franchisors and employ 6 million full- and part-time workers (including the proprietors). The 53 largest franchisors all have at least 1,000 outlets; together, they are affiliated with 150,000 outlets and have systemwide yearly sales of $70 billion. Thirteen of these firms are in the restaurant industry; nine others sell auto goods and services.[1] The U.S. Department of Commerce predicts that one-half of total U.S. retail sales will come from franchising by the year 2000.

Managerial Issues in Franchising

Franchising appeals to many owners and potential owners of small businesses for a variety of reasons. Most franchises have easy-to-learn standardized operating methods that have been perfected over the years. This means that a new business operator will not have to learn via his or her own trial-and-error method, which is often costly and time-consuming. Franchisors often have training facilities where franchisees are taught how to operate equipment, manage employees, maintain records, and improve customer relations; they usually follow up with field visits by a service staff.

A new outlet of a nationally advertised franchise (such as Midas Muffler, Avis, and Chem Lawn) can develop a large customer following rather quickly and easily because of the reputation of the firm. And not only does franchising result in good initial sales and profits, it also reduces the franchisee's risk of failure. According to the Department of Commerce, less than 4 per cent of franchisees fail; and many times, their stores are sold or taken back by franchisors. In 1985, franchise failures accounted for only 0.4 per cent of total U.S. franchising sales.[2]

The investment and start-up costs for a franchise outlet can be as low as a few thousand dollars for a personal service business and as high as several million dollars for a large hotel. In return for its expenditures, a franchisee typically gets exclusive selling rights for a geographic area, training, store equipment and fixtures, and assistance in picking out a store site, negotiating with suppliers, advertising, and so on.

What kind of person is most interested in becoming a franchisee? This is what two franchisors believe:

It used to be that the potential franchisees would be someone looking for a second income, or a husband and wife wanting to work together. But today the person coming to us is definitely more sophisticated. He or she has often worked in the corporate world and senses the nonsense and craziness and decides that he doesn't need the aggravation any more.

When someone buys a franchise, he has a safety net—if there's a problem there's someone to catch you. If someone wants to start a new company in a business that he already knows, then he doesn't really need to become a franchisee. But if someone wants to start a business in which he has no experience, it is better to buy a franchise. The ideal franchisee is intelligent, hard-working, has the necessary capital, is good with people, and wants to succeed.[3]

As a cautionary note, one franchising consultant states, "People with a lot of ideas, who like risk and think they can do it better than anyone, will not be successful franchisees."[4]

An illustration of how inexpensive franchising can be is Express Lube, a Colorado firm that has franchisees visit customers by appointment and change automobile oil filters, lubricate the chassis, check fluid levels, wash windows, and vacuum interiors. There is no store location or upkeep. Each franchisee pays about $25,000 to Express Lube to cover the franchise fee, training, equipment, and a van.[5]

Table 1 shows the costs paid by new franchisees affiliated with the ten fastest-

TABLE 1
1987 New Franchisee Costs for the Fastest-Growing Retail Franchise Businesses in the United States

Franchisor	New Outlets per Year (1986–1987)	Total Start-up Costs*	Royalty Fee[†]	Other Fees[††]
Domino's Pizza	577	$79,700–$134,500	5.5%	3%
McDonald's	390	$325,000–$451,000	12.0%[†††]	4%
Burger King	262	$341,100–$471,200	3.5%	4%
Jazzercise	253	$2,200–$8,400	30.0%	None
Fantastic Sam's (hair)	248	$50,200–$67,500	$131/week	$61/week
Wendy's	237	$734,000–$1,400,000	4.0%	4%
Ice Cream Churn	225	$6,700–$15,800	$1/gallon	None
Rainbow International Carpet Dyeing & Cleaning	225	$20,600	7.0%	None
Hardee's	211	$421,600–$793,800	4.0%	$180/month
Thrifty Rent-A-Car	211	Not available	3.0%	2%

*Start-up costs usually include real estate, equipment, and inventory.

[†]Royalty fee and other fees are a percentage of gross sales unless otherwise specified.

[††]Other fees are mostly for advertising.

[†††]Includes rent.

Source: "The Fastest-Growing Franchises," *Wall Street Journal* (May 15, 1987), p. 15D; and authors' estimates. Reprinted by permission. © Dow Jones & Company, Inc., 1987. All rights reserved.

growing franchises (in number of outlets) in the United States during 1986–1987. Table 2 shows the median investments and start-up cash required by new franchisees in several goods/service categories in 1985.

In addition to monetary payments, a franchisor may sell goods and services to its franchisees. Sometimes, this is required; more often, for legal reasons, such purchases are at the discretion of the franchisee (subject to franchisor specifications). In 1987, franchisors sold $10.3 billion of items to franchisees (69 per cent from nonfood merchandise for resale, 20 per cent from food ingredients, 5 per cent from supplies, and 6 per cent from other items).[6]

The franchisor can enforce detailed standards covering every aspect of business, such as signs, product freshness, merchandise selection, the level of involvement expected of the franchisee, and employee uniforms. These standards must be adhered to by franchisees. As a result, the franchisor's concern about systemwide consistency and the franchisee's desire to conduct his or her own business sometimes lead to conflicts.

Franchise outlets can be purchased directly from the franchisor, from a master franchisee, or from a current franchisee. The franchisor sells either new locations or company-owned outlets (some of which may have been taken back from unsuccessful franchisees). In some cases, the franchisor sells the right to develop outlets in an entire area or county to a master franchisee, who then deals with individual franchisees. A current franchisee generally has the right to sell his or her unit, if it is first offered to the franchisor; if the potential purchaser meets all of the franchisor's financial and other criteria; and/or if the purchaser undergoes a comprehensive training program. Table 3 shows the percentages of outlets and sales that are from franchisor-owned outlets and franchisee-owned outlets by goods/service category.

Figure 1 contains a checklist by which potential franchisees can evaluate opportunities. When using this checklist, the franchisee should obtain a full prospectus and a financial status report from the franchisor and should survey existing franchise operators and customers.

TABLE 2
1985 Investment and Start-Up Costs for New Franchisees by Goods/Service Category*

Goods/Service Category	Median Investment	Median Start-Up Cash Needed	Total Median Initial Costs
Hotels and motels	$1,500,000	$250,000	$1,750,000
Restaurants (all types)	$240,000	$75,000	$315,000
Rental services	$100,000–$150,000	$50,000–$65,000	$150,000–$215,000
General merchandise stores	$100,000	$50,000	$150,000
Other food stores	$100,000	$45,000	$145,000
Recreation, entertainment, and travel businesses	$100,000	$35,000	$135,000
Convenience stores	$100,000	$32,000	$132,000
Automotive goods and services stores	$90,000	$40,000	$130,000
Personal and household services	$40,000–$115,000	$15,000–$35,000	$55,000–$150,000

*Data are not available for auto and truck dealers and gasoline service stations.

Source: Andrew Kostecka, *Franchising in the Economy: 1985–1987* (Washington, D.C.: U.S. Department of Commerce, 1987), p. 50.

TABLE 3
Outlets and Sales of Franchisor-Owned and Franchisee-Owned
Retail Businesses by Goods/Service Category

Goods/Service Category	Number of Franchisor-Owned Outlets as Percentage of Total	Number of Franchisee-Owned Outlets as Percentage of Total	Percentage of Annual Sales from Franchisor-Owned Outlets	Percentage of Annual Sales from Franchisee-Owned Outlets
Auto and truck dealers	0	100	0	100
Gasoline service stations	18	82	18	82
Restaurants (all types)	30	70	35	65
General merchandise stores	23	77	31	69
Hotels and motels	14	86	42	58
Automotive goods and services stores	13	87	35	65
Convenience stores	58	42	60	40
Other food stores	16	84	27	73
Rental services	21	79	55	45
Personal and household services	7	93	26	74
Recreation, entertainment, and travel businesses	6	94	28	72

Source: Computed by the authors from Andrew Kostecka, *Franchising in the Economy: 1985–1987* (Washington, D.C.: U.S. Department of Commerce, 1987), p. 27.

Franchisor–Franchisee Relationships

Many franchisors and franchisees have good relationships because they share goals regarding store image, the way the business is operated and managed, the goods/service offering, cooperative advertising, and sales and profit growth. As one observer noted, "There is a symbiotic relationship between the franchisor and the franchisee. If the franchisor wins and the franchisee doesn't, it's no good for either one."[7]

This symbiotic relationship is illustrated by the philosophy of Bathtique, a bath and gift products franchisor:

> The advantage for us in franchising is that we know we have committed people in the stores. That's particularly important to us because our business is very, very service- and customer-oriented. We negotiate a location for retailers at a rent they can pay and still make money. We also have their stores built for them, write their opening orders, and guarantee open dating for them. Through the buying system we have developed, the franchisees can also reorder merchandise at lower prices—and Bathtique provides full market coverage through attendance at all of the major bath and giftware shows.[8]

However, for several reasons, tensions do exist between a large number of franchisors and their franchisees. These are just some of the reasons:

❑ The franchisor–franchisee relationship is not one of employer to employee. Franchisor controls are often viewed as rigid.

❑ Many franchise agreements are considered too short in duration by franchisees. In the United States, 20 per cent of all agreements are five years in duration or less, usually at the franchisor's request.

❑ For the many franchisees that lease their outlets' property from their franchisors, the loss of a franchise license generally means eviction; and the franchisee receives nothing for "goodwill."

❑ Some franchisees believe their franchisors want to buy back their units because of higher profit potential.

1. What are the required franchisor fees: initial fee, advertising appropriations, and royalties?

2. What degree of technical knowledge is required of the franchisee?

3. What is the required investment in time by the franchisee? Does the franchisee have to be actively involved in the day–to–day operations of the franchise?

4. What is the extent of control of a franchise by a franchisor in terms of materials purchased, sales quotas, space requirements, pricing, the range of goods to be sold, required inventory levels, and so on?

5. Can the franchisee accept the regimentation and rules of the franchisor?

6. Are the costs of required supplies and materials purchased from the franchisor at market value, above market value, or below market value?

7. What degree of brand recognition do consumers have of the franchise? Does the franchisor have a national advertising program?

8. What reputation does the franchise have among consumers, and among current franchisees?

9. What are the level and quality of services provided by the franchisor to franchisees: site selection, training, bookkeeping, human relations, equipment maintenance, and trouble–shooting?

10. What is the franchisor policy in terminating franchisees? What are the conditions of franchise termination? What is the rate of franchise termination and nonrenewal?

11. What is the franchisor's legal history?

12. What is the length of the franchise agreement?

13. What is the failure rate of existing franchises?

14. What is the franchisor's policy with regard to company–owned and franchisee–owned outlets?

15. What policy does the franchisor have in allowing franchisees to sell their business?

16. What is the franchisor's policy with regard to territorial protection for existing franchisees with regard to new franchisees and new company–owned establishments?

17. What is the earning potential of the franchise during the first year? The first five years?

FIGURE 1
A Checklist for Prospective Franchisees to Evaluate Franchise Opportunities

❑ Franchisors may not give adequate territorial protection to franchisees and may open new outlets near to existing ones.

❑ Franchisees may refuse to participate in cooperative advertising programs.

❑ Franchisees may disregard operating standards and adversely affect the overall company image.

❑ Some franchisors use minor contract infractions to oust franchisees.

❑ Franchisee outlets that are put up for sale must usually be offered first to franchisors, which also have approval of sales to third parties.

❑ Some franchisees believe franchisor support is low.

❑ Franchisees may be prohibited from operating competing businesses.

❑ Restrictions on purchases and suppliers may cause franchisees to pay higher prices and/or to have limited product assortments.

❑ Franchisees may band together to force changes in franchisor policies.

❑ Sales and profit expectations may not be realized.

Tensions can lead to disagreements, conflicts, and even litigation. Potential negative franchisor actions include terminating the franchise agreement; reducing promotional and sales support; and creating unnecessary red tape for orders, information requests, and warranty work. Potential negative franchisee actions include terminating the franchise agreement, adding competitors' product lines, refusing to promote goods and services, and not complying with franchisor information requests. In 1985, 1,174 franchise agreements were not renewed, 7,450 agreements were terminated before their expiration dates, and 3,400 franchisees sold their outlets. These actions were taken at the initiative of both franchisors and franchisees.[9]

Although franchising has historically been characterized by the franchisor's possessing more power than the franchisee, this inequality has been reduced. First, a number of franchisees have joined together to increase their power. For example, the Midas Dealers' Association represents about 80 per cent of the franchisees running Midas muffler repair outlets. The association recently negotiated a plan to protect existing units, when Midas began a large expansion program.[10] Second, a number of umbrella organizations representing franchisees, such as the California Franchise Council and the National Franchise Association Coalition, have been formed. Third, many franchisees now operate more than one outlet, so that they have greater clout. The major oil producers fear that multiunit gasoline stations can amass enough power to purchase gas from independent suppliers. Fourth, there has been a substantial rise in litigation between franchisors and their franchisees.

Improved communication and better cooperation will be necessary to resolve these issues.

NOTES

1. Andrew Kostecka, "Restaurant Franchising in the Economy," *Restaurant Business* (March 20, 1987), p. 182.

2. Thomas Petzinger, Jr., "So You Want to Get Rich?" *Wall Street Journal* (May 15, 1987), p. 15D; and Andrew Kostecka, *Franchising in the Economy: 1985–1987* (Washington, D.C.: U.S. Department of Commerce, 1987), p. 12.

3. Jacquelyn Bivins, "Franchising Boom Makes Headway," *Chain Store Age Executive* (October 1986), pp. 19–20.

4. Petzinger, "So You Want to Get Rich?" p. 15D.

5. Steven P. Galante, "Auto-Related Franchises Join the Ranks of Home Services," *Wall Street Journal* (May 18, 1987), p. 29.

6. Kostecka, *Franchising in the Economy: 1985–1987*, p. 42.

7. Brenton R. Schlender, "Working on the Chain Gang," *Wall Street Journal* (May 19, 1986), p. 14D.

8. Bivins, "Franchising Boom Makes Headway," pp. 19, 22.

9. Kostecka, *Franchising in the Economy: 1985–1987*, p. 13.

10. Teri Agins, "Owning Has Pluses, but Wealth Isn't Guaranteed," *Wall Street Journal* (October 22, 1984), p. 33.

Chapter 4

Retail Institutions by Strategy Mix

Fred Meyer is a full-line discount store chain with about 100 outlets and annual sales of more than $1 billion. It is strongest in Oregon, Washington, Alaska, Montana, Utah, and Idaho. Whereas the chain's existing stores occupy an average of less than 100,000 square feet of space, its newer units range from 160,000 to more than 200,000 square feet. The bigger outlets offer "an entire shopping center under the roof of a single store" and have up to eleven distinct departments, including food, home improvement materials, apparel, consumer electronics, fine jewelry, shoes, and a pharmacy. There is also a full-scale restaurant.

Meyer has a unique management style. Rather than have a single store manager for each outlet, there are separate department managers who are responsible for the operations of their departments:

> By having our managers focus on the specific departments we are better able to match up our offerings to what the customer wants. We think that if the departments themselves are strong, the store as a whole will be strong.

Because Meyer views itself as a series of discount specialty shops in one store setting, its strategy mix is very responsive to competition from supermarkets, specialty clothing stores, department stores, retail catalog showrooms, and fellow full-line discounters. For example, it has been revamping and expanding its grocery department, adding more well-known brands of clothing and other merchandise, and increasing advertising expenditures (to almost $40 million per year).

The chain is very tuned in to its customers. It recently redesigned the checkout areas, because this was the aspect of its stores that was receiving the greatest number of complaints. And the interior decor and displays have been upgraded to enhance store atmosphere. The company prides itself on being distinctive: "If people from this area move away, one of the first things they discover is that there is no store like Fred Meyer."[1]

Full-line discounting is just one of the many strategy mixes available to retailers.

Overview

In Chapter 3, retail institutions were described by type of ownership. In this chapter, we view retail institutions from three strategic perspectives: store-based, nonstore-based, and service versus goods retailing.

Considerations in Planning a Retail Strategy Mix

A retailer can be classified by its **strategy mix**, which is its combination of store location, operating procedures, goods/services offered, pricing tactics, and promotion methods. Store location refers to the use of a store or nonstore format, placement in a geographic area, and the kind of location (such as a shopping center versus an isolated store). Operating procedures involve the kinds of personnel employed, management style, store hours, and other factors. The goods/services offered may encompass several product categories or just one; and quality may be low, medium, or high. Pricing refers to the retailer's comparative strategy: prestige pricing (creating a quality image through high prices); competitive pricing (setting prices at the level of one's rivals); or penetration pricing (underpricing other retailers to attract value-conscious consumers). Promotion involves the retailer's activities in such areas as advertising, displays, personal selling, and sales promotion. By combining these elements, a retailer can develop a unique strategy.

Before we examine specific retail strategy mixes, three important concepts that help explain the performance and evolution of these mixes should be understood: the wheel of retailing, scrambled merchandising, and the retail life cycle. These concepts are particularly useful in describing the performance of existing retailers, predicting new retail institutions, determining the impact of new institutions on existing retailers, and forecasting how existing retailers are likely to respond to change.[2] See the color photo portfolio following page 104.

The Wheel of Retailing

According to the **wheel-of-retailing** theory, retail innovators often first appear as low-price operators with a low-cost structure and low profit-margin requirements. Over time, the innovators upgrade the products they carry and improve store facilities and customer services (by adding better-quality items, situating in higher-rent locations, accepting exchanges and allowing refunds, providing credit and delivery, and so on), and prices rise accordingly. As these innovators mature, they become vulnerable to new discount retailers with lower cost structures; hence, the wheel of retailing.[3] See Figure 4-1.

The wheel of retailing is based on four basic hypotheses:

1. There are many price-sensitive shoppers willing to trade customer services, wide selections, and convenient locations for lower prices.

2. Price-sensitive shoppers are often not store-loyal and are willing to switch to retailers offering lower prices. Other, prestige-sensitive customers like to shop at stores with high-end strategies.

3. New institutions are frequently able to implement lower operating costs than existing institutions.

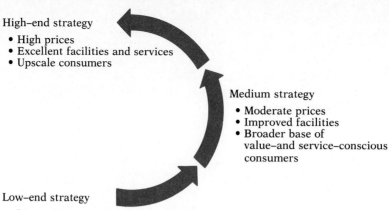

High–end strategy
- High prices
- Excellent facilities and services
- Upscale consumers

Medium strategy
- Moderate prices
- Improved facilities
- Broader base of value–and service–conscious consumers

Low–end strategy
- Low prices
- Limited facilities and services
- Price–sensitive consumers

As a low–end retailer upgrades its strategy, to increase sales and profit margins, a new form of discounter takes its place.

FIGURE 4-1
The Wheel of Retailing

4. Retailers typically move up the wheel to increase sales, broaden the target market, and improve store image.

During the 1950s and again in the 1970s, prices in department stores rose to levels that encouraged the growth of two institutional forms: the full-line discount store and the retail catalog showroom. These retailers were able to emphasize low prices because of such cost-cutting techniques as a small sales force, poor location, inexpensive fixtures, high stock turnover, and only cash or check payments for goods.

As discount stores and retail catalog showrooms succeeded, they looked to develop into more traditional types of stores. This meant enlarging the sales force, improving the location, upgrading fixtures, carrying lower-turnover merchandise, and granting credit. These improvements led to higher costs, which, in turn, led to higher prices. In the 1980s, the wheel of retailing has again been functioning as newer types of discounters, such as off-price chains, factory outlets, and flea markets, have expanded to satisfy the needs of the price-conscious consumer.

Figure 4-2 shows the opposing alternatives a retailer faces when considering a strategy mix. Through this dichotomy, one can differentiate between the two extreme cases of strategic emphasis: low-end and high-end. The wheel of retailing suggests that established retailers should be cautious in adding services or in converting their strategy from low-end to high-end. Because price-conscious shoppers are not usually store-loyal, they are likely to switch to lower-priced firms. Furthermore, retailers may be eliminating the competitive advantages that have led to profitability.

Scrambled Merchandising

Whereas the wheel of retailing focuses on strategy changes based on product quality, prices, and customer service, scrambled merchandising involves a retailer's increasing its width of assortment (the number of different product lines carried). **Scrambled merchandising** occurs when a retailer adds goods and services that are unrelated to each other and to the firm's original business. See Figure 4-3.

94

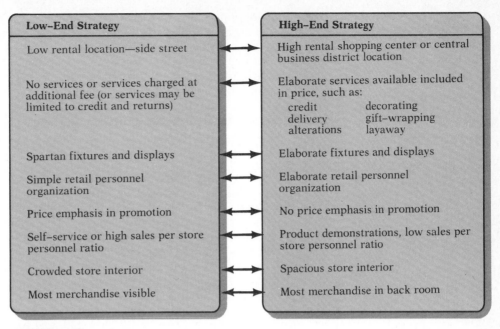

FIGURE 4-2
Retail Strategy Alternatives

Low–End Strategy	High–End Strategy
Low rental location—side street	High rental shopping center or central business district location
No services or services charged at additional fee (or services may be limited to credit and returns)	Elaborate services available included in price, such as: credit decorating / delivery gift–wrapping / alterations layaway
Spartan fixtures and displays	Elaborate fixtures and displays
Simple retail personnel organization	Elaborate retail personnel organization
Price emphasis in promotion	No price emphasis in promotion
Self–service or high sales per store personnel ratio	Product demonstrations, low sales per store personnel ratio
Crowded store interior	Spacious store interior
Most merchandise visible	Most merchandise in back room

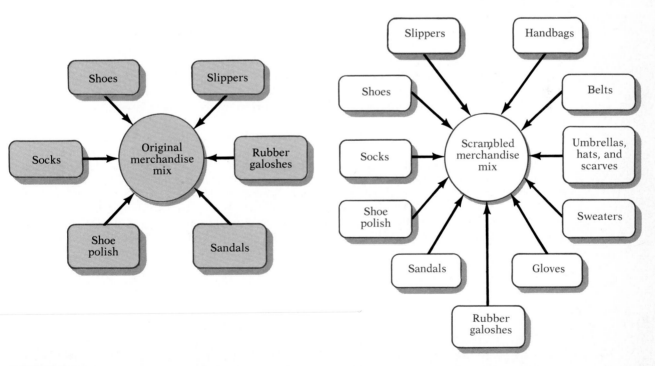

FIGURE 4-3
Scrambled Merchandising by a Shoe Store

The great popularity of scrambled merchandising in recent years is due to a number of factors: retailers are interested in increasing overall sales volume; goods and services that are fast-selling and have high profit margins are usually the ones added; consumers may make more impulse purchases; consumers are attracted to one-stop shopping; different target markets may be reached; and the effects of seasonality and competition may be reduced.

It is important to note the contagious nature of scrambled merchandising. For example, drugstores, bookstores, florists, and photo-developing firms are all affected by scrambled merchandising on the part of supermarkets. About 10 per cent of total U.S. supermarket sales is from general merchandise, health and beauty aids, and other nongrocery items, such as pharmacy products, books and magazines, flowers, and film developing.[4] In response, these retailers are compelled to use scrambled merchandising to fill the void in their sales being caused by the supermarkets. They have added unrelated items, such as toys and gift items, greeting cards, batteries, and cameras. This then creates a void for other retailers, which are also forced to scramble.

The growth in scrambled merchandising means that competition among different types of retailers is increasing and that distribution costs for manufacturers are rising as sales are dispersed over more retailers. There are other limitations to scrambled merchandising, such as the lack of retailer expertise in buying, selling, and servicing items with which they are unfamiliar; the costs associated with a broader product assortment (including lower inventory turnover); and the potential damage to a retailer's image if it performs poorly.

The Retail Life Cycle

A third useful concept in understanding the performance and evolution of different retail strategy mixes is the **retail life cycle.** This theory assumes that retail institutions, like goods and services, pass through an identifiable life cycle that has four stages: innovation, accelerated development, maturity, and decline.[5] The direction and speed of institutional changes can be interpreted from this theory.

During the first stage of the life cycle (innovation), there is a strong departure from the retail strategy mix of existing retail institutions. A firm in this stage significantly alters at least one element of the retail strategy mix from that of traditional competitors. During innovation, sales and then profits rise for the first retailers in the category.

An example of an institution in the innovation stage is the videodisc kiosk, a free-standing interactive terminal that displays products and related information on a video screen, enables the consumer to place an order, and then completes the transaction (usually with a credit card) and arranges for the product to be shipped. Viodeodisc kiosks can be situated virtually anywhere, from the lobby of a college dormitory to an airport. By 1990, there are expected to be 20,000 kiosks generating $350 million in sales throughout the United States.[6]

In the second stage (accelerated development), both the sales and profits of a retail institution exhibit rapid growth. Progressive firms expand their geographic bases of operations, and newer companies of the same type enter the marketplace. Toward the end of accelerated development, cost pressures (to cover a larger staff, a more complex inventory system, and extensive controls) begin to affect profits.

Consumer electronics discount superstores represent a retail institution that is in the growth stage of the retail life cycle. These stores occupy up to 50,000 square feet of floor space, about eight to ten times the size of a traditional consumer electronics store. The superstores have a huge selection of merchandise, wall-to-wall displays, excellent inventory control, and bargaining power with suppliers. They also advertise extensively. They account for about $5 billion in annual sales today, up from virtually nothing less than a decade ago.[7]

The third stage (maturity) is characterized by a slowdown in sales growth for the institutional type. This is brought on by management skills inadequate to direct larger companies, saturation of the market, and competition from newer forms of retailers.

The off-price apparel chain is a retail institution that is now in the maturity stage of the life cycle. Such chains appeal to price-conscious consumers and usually have minimal services (such as limited or no alterations and plain community-style dressing rooms). They sell national brands and are heavily dependent on manufacturers' overruns and closeouts. After climbing from $3 billion in 1979 to $9.5 billion in 1984, total off-price apparel chain sales rose to only $9.9 billion in 1987. The slowdown has been due to overexpansion, competition from other retailers, saturation of the market niche, and an inability to ensure continuous merchandise availability.[8]

The final stage in the retail life cycle is decline. In some cases, a decline is difficult or almost impossible to reverse. In others, the decline can be avoided or postponed by repositioning the institution.

TABLE 4-1
The Retail Life Cycle

		Stage in the Life Cycle			
	Area or Subject of Concern	**Innovation**	**Accelerated Development**	**Maturity**	**Decline**
Market characteristics	Number of competitors	Very few	Moderate	Many direct competitors; moderate indirect competition	Moderate direct competition; many indirect competitors
	Rate of sales growth	Very rapid	Rapid	Moderate to slow	Slow or negative
	Level of profitability	Low to moderate	High	Moderate	Very low
	Duration of new innovations	3–5 years	5–8 years	Indefinite	Indefinite
Appropriate retailer actions	Investment/growth/ risk decisions	Investment minimization, high risks accepted	High level of investment to sustain growth	Tightly controlled growth in untapped markets	Marginal capital expenditures and only when essential
	Central management concerns	Concept refinement through adjustment and experimentation	Establishing a preemptive market position	Excess capacity and "overstoring," prolonging maturity and revising the retail concept	Engaging in a "run-out" strategy
	Use of management control techniques	Minimal	Moderate	Extensive	Moderate
	Most successful management style	Entrepreneurial	Centralized	"Professional"	Caretaker

Source: Adapted from an exhibit in William R. Davidson, Albert D. Bates, and Stephen J. Bass, "The Retail Life Cycle," *Harvard Business Review*, Vol. 54 (November–December 1976), p. 92. Reprinted with permission of the *Harvard Business Review*. Copyright © 1976 by the President and Fellows of Harvard College; all rights reserved.

TABLE 4-2
Store-Based Retail Strategy Mixes

Type of Retailer	Location	Merchandise	Prices	Customer Services	Promotion
Food-Oriented					
Convenience store	Neighborhood	Medium width and narrow depth of assortment; average quality	Average to above-average	Average	Moderate
Conventional supermarket	Neighborhood	Extensive width and depth of assortment; average quality; national, private, and generic brands	Competitive	Average	Heavy use of newspapers, flyers, and coupons; self-service
Combination store	Community shopping center or isolated site	Full selection of supermarket and drugstore products or drugstore and general merchandise; average quality	Competitive	Average	Heavy use of newspapers and flyers; self-service
Superstore	Community shopping center or isolated site	Full assortment of supermarket items, plus health and beauty aids and general merchandise	Competitive	Average	Heavy use of newspapers and flyers; self-service
Box (limited-line) store	Neighborhood	Narrow width and depth of assortment; no perishables; few national brands	Very low	Low	Little or none
Warehouse store	Secondary site, often in industrial area	Narrow width and depth; emphasis on national brands purchased at discounts	Very low	Low	Little or none

For example, retail catalog showroom sales reached a peak of almost $11 billion in 1984; by 1987, annual sales had fallen to less then $7 billion. And the future does not look promising. Catalog showrooms are limited in the kinds of merchandise they sell, are required to print prices far in advance, and have struggled against newer discounters (and the consumer electronics superstores) that have been able to underprice them.[9]

On the other hand, conventional supermarkets have been able to slow their decline by locating new units in shopping centers and suburbs, redesigning interiors, lengthening store hours, maintaining low prices, closing unprofitable smaller units, expanding their use of scrambled merchandising, and/or converting to larger outlets.

Overall, the retail life-cycle concept is helpful in indicating how retailers should respond as their institutions evolve. Expansion should be the focus in the initial stages, administrative skills and operations become critical in maturity, and

TABLE 4-2
(Continued)

Type of Retailer	Location	Merchandise	Prices	Customer Services	Promotion
General Merchandise					
Specialty store	Central business district or shopping center	Very narrow width of assortment; extensive depth of assortment; average to good quality	Above-average or competitive	High level and quality	Heavy use of displays; extensive sales force
Variety store	Central business district, shopping center, or isolated store	Good width and depth of assortment; below-average to average quality	Average	Limited	Heavy use of newspapers; self-service
Department store	Central business district, shopping center, or isolated store	Extensive width and depth of assortment; average to good quality	Average to above-average	Good to excellent	Heavy use of ads; catalogs; direct mail; personal selling
Full-line discount store	Central business district, shopping center, or isolated store	Very good width and depth of assortment; average to good quality	Competitive	Below-average to average	Heavy use of newspapers; price-oriented; limited sales force
Retail catalog showroom	Central business district, shopping center, or isolated store	Good width and depth of assortment; average to good quality	Competitive	Little or low	Heavy use of catalogs; little advertising; self-service
Off-price chain	Suburban shopping strip or isolated store	Moderate width, but poor depth of assortment; average to good quality; low continuity	Low	Little	Use of newspapers; brands not advertised; limited sales force
Factory outlet	Out-of-the-way site or discount mall	Moderate width, but poor depth of assortment; some irregular merchandise; low continuity	Very low	Very low	Little; self-service
Buying club	Isolated store or secondary site (industrial park)	Moderate width, but poor depth of assortment; low continuity	Very low	Very low	Little; some direct mail; limited sales force
Flea market	Isolated site, racetrack, arena, or parking lot	Extensive width, but poor depth of assortment; variable quality; low continuity	Very low	Very low	Limited; self-service

adaptation is essential at the end of the cycle. Table 4-1 summarizes the retail life cycle.

Retail Institutions Categorized by Store-Based Strategy Mix

The strategy mixes of fifteen store-based retailers are presented in this section and highlighted in Table 4-2. The strategy mixes are divided into food-oriented and general merchandise groupings. Although not all-inclusive, the fifteen strategy mixes do provide a fairly comprehensive overview of store-based retailing strategies.

Food-Oriented Retailers

Six basic strategy mixes are used by food-oriented retailers: convenience store, conventional supermarket, combination store, superstore, box (limited-line) store, and warehouse store. Each of these is discussed in the following subsections.

Convenience Store

A **convenience store** is usually a food-oriented retailer that is well located, is open long hours, and carries a moderate number of items. This type of retailer is small (about one-fifth the size of a conventional supermarket), has average to above-average prices, and average customer services. The ease of shopping and the impersonal nature of many large supermarkets make convenience stores particularly appealing to their customers, over half of whom are male.

Thirty years ago, there were only 500 convenience stores with annual sales of less than $200 million. By 1986, there were 65,000 convenience stores with annual sales of $60 billion. Today, convenience stores account for 8 per cent of retail grocery sales, 5 per cent of fast-food sales, and 20 per cent of gasoline sales in the United States.[10]

Whereas items such as milk, eggs, and bread once represented the major portion of a convenience store's sales, sandwiches, tobacco products, soft drinks, beer, and videocassette rentals are now also key items. In addition, gasoline generates between one-quarter and one-third of total convenience store sales; in 1970, virtually no convenience stores carried gasoline. Several convenience stores have recently installed automatic teller machines and expanded their offerings to remain attractive to shoppers.

7-Eleven (owned by the Southland Corporation) is the largest convenience store chain in the United States with about 8,000 outlets and annual sales of $8 billion. 7-Eleven derives its sales from these product categories:[11]

❑ Gasoline	22.1%	❑ Nonfoods	6.4
❑ Tobacco products	15.8	❑ Dairy products	5.2
❑ Beer/wine	11.7	❑ Candy	4.0
❑ Soft drinks	10.9	❑ Baked goods	3.5
❑ Groceries	8.6	❑ Health/beauty aids	2.6
❑ Food service	8.1	❑ Customer services	1.1

Seventy per cent of 7-Eleven's customers are male.

The convenience store's natural market advantages are its usefulness for fill-in merchandise when a shopper does not want to encounter long lines, the ability of customers to buy gasoline and fill-in merchandise at the same time, the use of drive-through windows, and the long hours maintained. Over half the items sold by a convenience store are consumed within thirty minutes of their purchase. And 25 per cent of the U.S. population shops at a convenience store at least two or three times a week. The average sale is about $3 (excluding gasoline).

FIGURE 4-4
Convenience Store Retailing Comes to Gasoline Stations
To increase sales and operate more efficiently, a number of gasoline stations now also offer food and
related products. Reprinted by permission of Selame Design.

Because of limited shelf space, convenience stores receive about seventy deliveries each week, and their prices reflect the low average sales and high handling
costs. However, convenience store customers are less price-sensitive than those
shopping at other food-oriented retailers; that is why their gross margins are 50
per cent higher than those of conventional supermarkets.[12]

Among the leading convenience store chains are 7-Eleven, Circle K, and Convenient Food Mart. In addition, Amoco, Phillips, Unocal, Conoco, and Chevron
are among the many petroleum firms that have converted traditional gasoline
stations into convenience stores. See Figure 4-4.

Conventional Supermarket

The Food Marketing Institute defines a **supermarket** as a self-service food store
with grocery, meat, and produce departments and minimum annual sales of $2
million.* Included in this definition are conventional supermarkets, combination
stores, superstores, box (limited-line) stores, and warehouse stores.

A **conventional supermarket** is a departmentalized food store that emphasizes
a wide range of food and related products; sales of general merchandise are
limited. It started as a retail institution in the 1930s. At this time, it was realized
that only a large-scale operation would enable a retailer to combine volume sales,
self-service, and low prices. The self-service concept allowed supermarkets to cut
costs as well as to increase volume. Personnel costs were reduced, and impulse
buying increased. The automobile and the refrigerator contributed to the supermarket's success by lowering travel costs and adding to the life span of perishable

---

*Prior to 1981, supermarkets included food stores with annual sales of at least $1 million. This
should be noted when comparing data before and after 1981.

items. Easy parking and lower prices (for consumers buying in bulk) were marketing strategies used by the supermarket to exploit these inventions.

Since 1962, overall supermarket sales have stabilized at about 72–75 per cent of total U.S. grocery sales, with conventional supermarkets now responsible for 52 per cent of total supermarket sales. In 1986, conventional supermarkets operated almost 22,000 stores and had sales of $115 billion.[13] Chains account for the majority of sales. Leading chains are Safeway, Kroger, American Stores, Winn-Dixie, and A&P. Most independent supermarkets are affiliated with cooperative or voluntary organizations, such as IGA, Red and White, Super Valu, and Clover Farm.

Conventional supermarkets have generally relied on high inventory turnover (volume sales). Their profit margins are very low. In general, average gross margins (selling prices less merchandise costs) are 20 per cent of sales and net operating profits are 1–2 per cent of sales.

Conventional supermarkets are facing intense competition from other types of food stores: convenience stores offer greater customer convenience; combination stores and superstores have more assortment and variety (and better gross margins); and box and warehouse stores have lower operating costs and prices. Since 1980, more than 7,000 conventional supermarkets have closed; a number of others have changed their retail strategy mix to another format. The emerging variations of the conventional supermarket are discussed next.[14]

RETAILING IN ACTION

How Can Conventional Supermarkets Compete in the Marketplace?

Food Lion, a chain based in Salisbury, South Carolina, is living proof that conventional supermarkets (although Food Lion is far from conventional) can prosper in the face of intense competition from combination stores, superstores, and warehouse stores. Since 1981, annual sales have increased by an average of 29 per cent; and the company's net profit margin is twice that of the typical grocery retailer.

This is how Food Lion does it. A no-frills, low-price strategy keeps costs down and generates a steady stream of customer traffic. In general, a Food Lion store is somewhat larger and more spartan than a conventional supermarket. And it stocks fewer brands and varieties of merchandise to keep inventory turnover high. The firm is constantly on the lookout for wholesalers' specials. When it comes to pricing, Food Lion has a low everyday policy, and it even sells some items (that draw consumers into the store) such as cereal and pet food at cost.

The firm has its own warehouses, which service all the stores in a 200-mile radius. It believes in only a moderate amount of scrambled merchandising; for example, there are no flower shops or seafood counters. Some displays consist of recycled banana crates. Food by-products, such as ground meat bones, are sold for fertilizer (and yield $1 million in yearly revenues). Employees are not unionized; so wages are below the industry norm.

Food Lion's ads are usually produced in-house; the company's chief executive officer appears as a company spokesperson in half of its television commercials; and small newspaper ads are used. As a result, advertising costs are 0.5 per cent of sales, compared with a supermarket industry average of 2 per cent.

The company's philosophy is "1,000 things 1% better."

Source: Based on material in Richard W. Anderson, "That Roar You Hear Is Food Lion," *Business Week* (August 24, 1987), pp. 65–66.

Combination Store

A **combination store** combines supermarket and general merchandise sales in one facility, with general merchandise accounting for 30–40 per cent of total store sales. The introduction of food-based combination stores can be traced to the late 1960s and early 1970s, when common checkout areas were developed for independently owned supermarkets and drugstores or supermarkets and general merchandise stores. A natural offshoot of this was to fully integrate the two operations under one management. As of 1986, over 900 combination stores (including hypermarkets, which are described next) had entered the marketplace; and 1986 sales reached $13 billion.[15]

Combination stores are popular for these reasons. They are very large, from 30,000 up to 100,000 or more square feet. This results in operating efficiencies and cost savings. Consumers like one-stop shopping and will travel a longer distance to get to the store. Impulse sales are high. Many general merchandise items have better gross margins than traditional supermarket items. Supermarkets and drugstores have many commonalities in the customers served and the kinds of low-price high-turnover items sold. Drugstore and general merchandise customers are drawn to the store more frequently than they would be otherwise.

A **hypermarket** is a special type of combination store that integrates an economy supermarket with a discount department store. It was first introduced in Europe and has recently come to the United States, where there are now about fifty outlets. These stores are at least 60,000 square feet in size (Wal-Mart has a 200,000 square-foot store in Garland, Texas), and they stock even more than the 30,000 items carried by other combination stores.[16]

Among the firms operating combination stores are Jewel, Albertson's, Tom Thumb-Page, and Bigg's.

Superstore

A **superstore** is a food-based retailer that is larger and more diversified than a conventional supermarket but usually smaller and less diversified than a combination store. This format originated in the 1970s as supermarkets sought to erode sales declines by expanding store size and the level of nonfood items carried. Although some supermarkets merged with drugstores or general merchandise stores, more of them grew into superstores. There were 4,750 superstores in the United States, with sales of $65 billion, in 1986.[17]

The typical superstore occupies 25,000 to 50,000 square feet of space and obtains 20–30 per cent of total sales from general merchandise items, such as garden supplies, wine, flowers, small household appliances, and film developing. It caters to consumers' complete grocery needs and offers them the ability to buy fill-in general merchandise.

Like combination stores, superstores are efficient, offer consumers a degree of one-stop shopping, stimulate impulse purchases, and feature high-profit general merchandise. But they also offer these advantages: It is easier and less costly to redesign and convert supermarkets into superstores than into combination stores. Many consumers feel more comfortable shopping in true food stores than in huge combination stores. Management expertise is better focused in superstores.

Box (Limited-Line) Store

The **box (limited-line) store** is a food-based discounter that focuses on a small selection of items, restricted hours of operation, few services, and limited national brands. There are usually fewer than 1,500 items, no refrigerated perishables, and one size and brand per item. Price marking is on the shelf or on overhead signs. Items are displayed in cut cases. Customers do their own bagging. Checks are not accepted. Box stores depend on aggressively priced private-label or controlled brands. They aim to price merchandise 20–30 per cent below supermarkets.

The box store concept originated in Europe around 1970 and was exported to the United States in 1975–1976. The growth of these stores has not been as high as anticipated. Other food stores, in many cases, have matched box store prices. Some customers are loyal to national brands. And box stores cannot fulfill one-stop shopping needs.

There were about two hundred box stores in the United States in 1986 with sales of $600 million.[18] Among the leading box operators are Texas T and Aldi.

Warehouse Store

A **warehouse store** is a discounter that offers a moderate number of food items in a no-frills setting. Unlike box stores, warehouse stores appeal to one-stop food shoppers. These stores concentrate on special purchases of national brands. They use cut-case displays, provide little service, post prices on shelves, and are situated in secondary locations (such as industrial districts).

Warehouse stores began in the late 1970s. As of 1986, there were three thousand stores with $30 billion in sales.[19] There are three warehouse store formats in terms of size: from 15,000 to 25,000 square feet, from 25,000 to 35,000 square feet, and from 50,000 to 65,000 square feet.

The largest store is known as a super warehouse. There are 135 of them in the United States. They have average annual sales of $20 million each and contain a variety of departments, including produce. High ceilings are used to accommodate pallet loads of groceries. See Figure 4-5. Shipments are made directly to the store. Customers pack their own groceries. Super warehouses can be profitable at 14 per cent gross margins versus 20 per cent for conventional supermarkets.[20] Major super warehouse chains are Food 4 Less (Fleming Companies), Sun Food Market (A&P), and Cub Foods (Super Valu).

A potential problem, which may limit the growth of warehouse stores, is the lack of brand continuity. Because products are purchased by the stores when special deals are available, brands may be temporarily or permanently out of stock. In addition, many consumers do not like shopping in warehouse settings.

Table 4-3 provides operating data for convenience stores, conventional supermarkets, combination stores, superstores, box stores, and warehouse stores.

FIGURE 4-5
The Interior of a Typical
Warehouse Store
Reprinted by permission of Winn-Dixie.

When planning a retail strategy mix, the wheel of retailing, scrambled merchandising, and the retail life cycle should be considered. The wheel of retailing occurs when low-price operators upgrade their offerings and raise their prices, thus leaving an opportunity for new low-price firms to enter the industry. Scrambled merchandising, represented in these photos of Winn-Dixie (above) and Laneco (right) supermarkets, takes place when retailers add goods and services unrelated to each other and to the firms' original business. The retail life cycle explains how retail institutions evolve over time.

Photos courtesy of Winn-Dixie and Wetterau.

Retail institutions may be examined from three strategic perspectives: store-based, nonstore-based, and service versus goods retailing. As shown here, nonstore retailers are quite innovative and aggressive in their efforts to expand their share of retail sales. Vending machines are convenient, provide around-the-clock service, and can be clustered to offer complementary products. To increase its sales, Avon now has sales representatives demonstrating and selling products at the workplace, as well as through traditional in-home contacts.

Photos courtesy of ARA Services and Avon.

TABLE 4-3
Selected Operating Data for Food-Oriented Retailers, 1986

Factor	Convenience Store	Conventional Supermarket	Combination Store	Superstore	Box (Limited-Line) Store	Warehouse Store
Number of stores	65,000	22,000	925	4,750	200	3,000
Total annual sales	$60 billion	$115 billion	$13 billion	$65 billion	$600 million	$30 billion
Average annual sales per store	$925,000	$5.3 million	$14.1 million	$13.7 million	$3 million	$10 million
Average store selling area (sq. feet)	3,500	15,000–20,000	30,000+	25,000+	5,000–9,000	15,000+
Number of checkouts per store	1–3	6–10	10+	10+	3–5	7+
Gross margin	25%–30%	18%–22%	25%	20%–25%	10%–12%	12%–15%
Number of items stocked per store	3,000–4,000	8,000–12,000	20,000+	20,000+	Under 1,500	4,000+
Major emphasis	Daily fill-in needs; dairy, bakery, tobacco, gas, magazines	Food; only 5% of sales from general merchandise	One-stop shopping; general merchandise is 30%–40% of sales	Positioned between supermarket and combo store; 20%–30% of sales from general merchandise	Low prices; few or no perishables	Low prices; variable assortments; may or may not stock perishables

Sources: "54th Annual Report of the Grocery Industry," *Progressive Grocer* (April 1987); H. R. Janes, "Retail Formats Are Changing," *Nielsen Researcher* (Number 3, 1985), pp. 2–5; *Circle K Corporation 1987 Annual Report;* "Grocery Marketing," *Advertising Age* (May 4, 1987), pp. S-1–S-24; Walter H. Heller, "A New Look at Store Formats," *Progressive Grocer* (December 1986), pp. 29–34; and authors' estimates.

General Merchandise Retailers

There are nine store-based general merchandise retail strategy mixes shown in Table 4-2; each is discussed in the following subsections: specialty store, variety store, department store, full-line discount store, retail catalog showroom, off-price chain, factory outlet, buying club, and flea market.

Specialty Store

A **specialty store** concentrates on selling one goods or service line, such as apparel and its accessories, toys, furniture, or muffler repair. In contrast to a mass-marketing approach, specialty stores usually carry a narrow, but deep, assortment of goods or services in their specific goods/service category and tailor their strategy to selective market segments. This enables specialty stores to maintain better selections and sales expertise than competitors, which are often department stores. It also allows them to control their investments and exercise a certain amount of flexibility.

Consumers shop at specialty stores because of the knowledgeable sales personnel, the variety of choices within the goods/service category, the intimate store size and atmosphere, customer service policies, the lack of crowds, and the absence of aisles of merchandise unrelated to their purchase intentions (they will not have to search through several departments for the desired merchandise).

Can a Specialty Store Make It Selling Just Socks?

Specialty stores appeal to customers because of their emphasis on one product category. But at what point does a store become too specialized? For example, can a store succeed by just selling hosiery? Thus far, the Sock Shop is demonstrating that consumers will patronize a store that is so narrowly focused.

Sophie Mirman opened the first Sock Shop in Great Britain in 1983 with the goal of operating a chain of six stores if all went well. By the end of 1987, the company had sixty-three stores (including three in New York City) and was considered "one of the fastest-growing specialty businesses in Europe." Sophie became a multimillionaire.

Initially, many experts felt the Sock Shop concept was "silly." After all, the hosiery market was saturated, and department stores accounted for most of sales. This is why the Sock Shop has boomed:

❑ Stores are located in areas with a lot of pedestrian traffic, such as downtown shopping districts, train stations, and commercial business districts.

❑ Many customers want to purchase hosiery without having to walk through department stores. Mirman compares her outlets to newsstands: "People should be able to buy socks and stockings as easily as they buy newspapers."

❑ The open entranceways of stores allow passers-by to look inside; thus, impulse purchases are stimulated. Rock music adds to the ambience.

❑ Hundreds of styles of socks and stockings are displayed. Many have bright colors and bold designs. New designs are introduced regularly. And 85 per cent of sales involve women's hosiery.

Despite Sock Shop's success to date, two questions remain: Will this concept work in the United States? Is the chain a fad or a new permanent specialty store type?

Source: Based on material in Steve Lohr, "The Sock Shop Makes Way to U.S.," *New York Times* (November 23, 1987), pp. D1, D5.

Although some specialty stores have elaborate fixtures and upscale merchandise for affluent consumers, others have a discount orientation and aim at price-conscious consumers.

Total specialty store sales are difficult to estimate because they sell almost all kinds of goods and services, and aggregate specialty store data are not compiled by the U.S. Department of Commerce. Nonetheless, these selective statistics demonstrate the significance of specialty retailers. In 1986, the top 100 specialty store chains had sales of $47 billion and operated 42,000 outlets. Of the top 100, 40 were involved with apparel, 15 with consumer electronics, 11 with shoes, 10 with furniture, 4 with toys, and 4 with books.[21] The 10 leaders were:

❑ The Limited (apparel)
❑ Mervyn's (apparel)
❑ Radio Shack (consumer electronics)
❑ Toys "R" Us (toys)
❑ Marshall's (clothing)
❑ Petrie Stores (apparel)
❑ Circuit City (consumer electronics)
❑ T.J. Maxx (apparel)
❑ Zale (jewelry)
❑ Volume Shoe (shoe)

A specialty store can be adversely affected by seasonality or a decline in the popularity of its product category, because its offering is so concentrated. This type of store may also fail to attract consumers interested in one-stop shopping.

Table 4-4 contains selected 1986 operating data for specialty stores with annual sales over $1 million.

TABLE 4-4
Selected Operating Results for Specialty Stores with Annual Sales over $1 Million, 1986

Average gross sale	about $30.00
Terms of sale (%)	
Cash	48.6
In-house credit	28.7
Outside cards	22.7
Cumulative markon (%)	52.0
Markdowns (%)	15.0
Stock shortages (%)	2.1
Gross margins (owned retail departments—%)	41.3
Total company gross margin (%)	40.6
Sales per square foot	$206.89
Sales promotion (%)	10.0
Stock turns (times)	3.0
Pre-tax earnings (%)	2.5
Net operating expenses (%)	39.0

Source: " '86: Better FOR Some," *Stores* (November 1987), pp. 92–94; and authors' estimates. Copyright National Retail Merchants Association 1987. Reprinted by permission.

Variety Store

A **variety store** handles a wide assortment of inexpensive and popularly priced goods and services, such as stationery, gift items, women's accessories, toiletry articles, light hardware, toys, housewares, confectionary items, and shoe repair. Sales are usually on a cash basis. There are open displays and few sales personnel. Variety stores do not carry complete lines of merchandise, are not usually departmentalized, and do not deliver merchandise.

In 1986, variety store sales were almost $8.5 billion, about 0.6 per cent of total U.S. retail store sales. F.W. Woolworth, with 1,200 outlets and $2 billion in sales in 1986, and McCrory, with 800 outlets and $1.5 billion in sales in 1986, dominate this store category. At Woolworth's, the best-selling items are health and beauty aids, housewares, stationery, greeting cards, toys, books, and candy.[22]

Since 1977, variety stores have shown the least growth of any retail store category, and 1986 sales were at their lowest level since 1980. This trend is due to the heavy competition from specialty stores and discounters, the older facilities of many stores, the low profit margins associated with some of the items carried, and the decision of firms such as Woolworth to diversify (less than one-third of its 1986 sales were from variety stores).

Department Store

A **department store** is a large retail business unit that handles an extensive assortment (width and depth) of goods and services and is organized into separate departments for purposes of buying, promotion, customer service, and control. To be defined as a department store by the U.S. Bureau of the Census, a store has to meet three criteria. First, at least twenty-five people must be employed. Second, the merchandise assortment must include some items in each of these lines: dry goods and household items; family wearing apparel; and furniture, home furnishings, appliances, and TV sets. Third, if annual store sales are less than $10 million, no more than 80 per cent of the sales can come from any one of the lines. If sales are at least $10 million, there is no limitation on the percentage of sales from any one line, as long as the combined sales of the smallest two lines are at least $1 million.

Two types of retailers satisfy the Bureau of Census definition: the traditional department store (which was introduced by Macy's, Wanamaker, and others in the 1860s) and the full-line discount store (which was introduced by K mart, Target, Wal-Mart, and Korvettes in 1962). Together, they accounted for almost $143 billion in sales in 1986, about 10 per cent of U.S. retail store revenues. The traditional department store is discussed here; the full-line discount store is examined in the following subsection.

At traditional department stores, merchandise quality ranges from average to quite good. Pricing is moderate to above-average. Customer service ranges from medium levels of sales help, credit, delivery, and so on to high levels of each. For example, Macy's strategy is aimed at middle-class shoppers interested in a wide assortment and moderate prices, whereas Bloomingdale's aims at upscale consumers through more trendy merchandise and higher prices. Some department stores (such as Sears, Dayton's, and Rich's) sell dry goods, family wearing apparel, and furniture and appliances. Others (such as Nordstrom, Lord & Taylor, and Saks Fifth Avenue) place greater emphasis on apparel and do not carry major appliances.

A typical department store has the greatest assortment of any general merchandise retailer, often serves as the anchor store in a shopping center or district, has strong credit-card penetration, and is usually part of a chain. Over the years, this form of retailer has been responsible for many innovations, such as advertising prices, implementing a one-price policy (whereby all consumers pay the same price for the same good or service), developing computerized checkout facilities, offering money-back guarantees, adding branch stores, decentralizing management, and moving into suburban shopping centers.

However, overall sales of traditional department stores have stagnated in recent years and long-time chains such as Gimbels have gone out of business, leading one observer to ask "will the department store survive?" These are some reasons for the department store's difficulties:[23]

❑ Department stores no longer have brand exclusivity for many of the items they sell; manufacturers' brands are available at specialty and discount stores.

❑ Many of them have been too passive with private-label goods. Instead of creating their own brands, they have signed exclusive licensing agreements with fashion designers to use the latters' names. This perpetuates customer loyalty to the designer and not the store.

❑ The increased popularity of shopping malls has aided specialty stores, since consumers can now accomplish one-stop shopping via several specialty stores in the same mall or shopping center. Previously, department stores were viewed as the major institution for one-stop shopping.

❑ The number of large specialty chains has steadily increased, so that they have strong supplier relations and extensive advertising campaigns. Therefore, department stores do not dominate the smaller stores around them the way they did in the past.

❑ Many discount institutions, which did not previously, now accept credit-card sales.

❑ There are more price-conscious consumers than ever before, and they are attracted to discount retailers.

❑ Department store service has deteriorated; and store personnel are not as loyal, helpful, or knowledgeable as before.

❑ Many department stores are too large. They have too much unproductive selling space and low-turnover merchandise.

❑ The scrambled merchandising of food retailers has drawn sales away from department stores.

❑ Unlike specialty stores, many department stores have a weak focus on customer market segments and a fuzzy image. Too often, departments are organized by supplier brand name rather than according to customer needs. This requires shoppers to walk through several departments to buy related items.

❑ In many cases, the management of a department store chain has been too decentralized, so that there are different merchandising strategies in branch stores (which blur the firm's overall image).

❑ Department stores are not as innovative in their merchandise decisions as they were; they react to suppliers rather than making suggestions to them.

❑ Often, specialty stores have better assortments than department stores in the product categories they carry. For example, no department store has the toy selection of Toys "R" Us or the sporting-goods assortment of Herman's.

To overcome these difficulties, department stores need to clarify their niche in the marketplace (store positioning); place greater emphasis on customer service and quality sales personnel; present more exciting, better organized store interiors and displays—and change them frequently; better utilize space by downsizing stores and eliminating slow-selling, space-consuming items (such as J.C. Penney recently dropping consumer electronics products); and open outlets in smaller, underdeveloped towns and cities (as Sears has been doing). They can also centralize more buying and promotion functions, do better research, and reach customers more efficiently (via tools such as targeted mailing pieces).[24]

Table 4-5 contains selected 1986 operating results for department stores with annual sales over $5 million. The data in this table can be compared with those in Table 4-4 (operating results for specialty stores). For example, department stores made more sales through in-house credit, had a higher percentage of markdowns, spent more on sales promotion, and had lower operating expenses and higher profits. Specialty store sales per square foot were almost 20 per cent higher.

TABLE 4-5
Selected Operating Results for Department Stores with Annual Sales over $5 Million, 1986

Average gross sale	about $30.00
Terms of sale (%)	
Cash	36.6
In-house credit	51.2
Outside cards	12.2
Cumulative markon (%)	49.6
Markdowns (%)	19.3
Stock shortages (%)	1.9
Gross margins (owned retail departments—%)	40.2
Total company gross margin (%)	39.5
Sales per square foot	$174.37
Sales promotion (%)	12.0
Stock turns (times)	2.8
Pre-tax earnings (%)	6.8
Net operating expenses (%)	34.2

Source: " '86: Better FOR SOME," *Stores* (November 1987), pp. 92–94. Copyright National Retail Merchants Association 1987. Reprinted by permission.

Full-Line Discount Store

A **full-line discount store** is a type of department store that is characterized by these features:

❑ A broad merchandise assortment, which in scope (but not in price) resembles that of a traditional department store. Less fashion-sensitive merchandise is carried.

❑ Relatively low operating costs as a percentage of sales. On average, these costs are 10–15 per cent lower than for traditional department stores and specialty stores.

❑ Credit sales amounting to less than 25 per cent of all sales, compared with 50–60 per cent in traditional department stores and specialty stores.

❑ Relatively inexpensive buildings, equipment, and fixtures.

❑ Low-rent locations.

❑ Emphasis on self-service.

❑ Heavy promotion of national-brand merchandise.

❑ Frequent use of leased departments.

❑ Everyday low prices.

In 1986, 8,100 full-line discount stores had sales of $83 billion, almost 60 per cent of all department store sales and triple their 1972 volume. Four chains (K mart, Wal-Mart, Target, and Zayre) had $40 billion in sales and 4,000 full-line discount stores during that year.[25]

The success of discount department stores is due to a combination of factors. They have a clear focus on their customers: middle-class and lower-middle-class shoppers looking for good values. The stores feature popular brands of average-to good-quality merchandise at competitive prices. They have been aggressive in adding new goods and service categories and are beginning to have their own (well-advertised) brands. The stores have worked hard to improve their image and have made more customer services available. The average outlet is well under 100,000 square feet in size, less than half that of a traditional department store; this improves productivity. Sales per square foot are much higher than those in traditional department stores and about equal to those in specialty stores. A number of full-line discount stores are located in small towns, where competition is reduced. The chains have been very well managed, with standardized branch outlets and good employee relations. And because full-line discounting is less than thirty years old, their facilities are much newer than those of many traditional department stores.[26]

The greatest challenges facing full-line discounters are the competition from other retailers, too rapid expansion of some chains, and the saturation of prime locations.

Table 4-6 shows selected 1986 operating results for full-line discount stores by product category. Note the high overall sales from apparel and housewares, as well as the high sales per square foot from photo, consumer electronics, and jewelry products.

Retail Catalog Showroom

A **retail catalog showroom** is an operation in which the consumer selects merchandise from a catalog and shops at a warehouse-style store. In some instances, the shopper not only selects the merchandise by number but also writes up the sales order. Usually, all the goods are stored out of the shoppers' reach; the closed inventory rooms may encompass up to two-thirds of the outlet's space.

Retail catalog showrooms need to make actual merchandise decisions months in advance of sale due to catalog-preparation lead time. They attempt to make

TABLE 4-6
Selected Operating Results for Full-Line Discount Stores, 1986

Product Category	Total Sales (billions)	Average Annual Sales per Store	Average Annual Sales per Square Foot	Average Annual Stock Turns	Percentage Initial Markup	Percentage Gross Margin
Ladies' wear	$15.8	$1,948,000	$195	4.5	47.4	31.3
Housewares	11.4	1,405,000	189	3.5	35.0	24.8
Men's/boys' wear	9.1	1,122,000	144	3.7	44.5	34.2
Hardware and paint	6.7	825,000	188	2.5	41.8	32.7
Consumer electronics	6.3	776,000	338	3.3	30.0	17.2
Health and beauty aids	5.9	727,000	227	5.0	25.0	19.3
Automotives	5.5	678,000	283	2.8	33.8	25.2
Toys	4.6	567,000	221	2.9	37.0	27.2
Sporting goods	4.0	493,000	197	2.0	37.2	28.5
Domestics	3.7	456,000	145	2.5	44.2	35.0
Photo	3.3	406,000	603	3.1	25.3	18.0
Stationery	2.4	295,000	158	3.5	47.0	41.6
Jewelry	1.7	209,000	322	2.1	49.2	40.5

Source: "Full-Line Discount Store Productivity," *Discount Store News* (July 20, 1987), p. 22. Reprinted by permission. © Copyright Lebhar-Friedman, Inc., 425 Park Avenue, N.Y., N.Y., 10022.

long-term price and delivery arrangements with many suppliers to reduce the impact of inflation, to minimize changes in catalog selling prices, and to ensure adequate stocks of merchandise.

The sales mix is an important part of a retail catalog showroom's overall strategy. Five categories (jewelry, electronics, housewares, gifts, and watches) account for close to 70 per cent of overall sales, with jewelry usually yielding 25 per cent or more of sales. Although the gross profit margins on product categories such as personal care, photography, housewares, electronics, hardware, and tools are generally 10 to 20 per cent of sales, the profit margins on jewelry are close to 50 per cent. Retail catalog showrooms do not normally stock soft goods such as apparel.

The strategy of the catalog showroom is based on its ability to cut costs below those of other types of retailers:

❑ Losses from shoplifting are low because goods are kept in a stockroom.

❑ Payroll expenses are low. There are few salespeople; products are not demonstrated; customers write up orders; and products are not assembled or delivered.

❑ Store decoration costs are low because 60 per cent of floor space is in the warehouse area.

❑ By avoiding clothes and other high-fashion items, showrooms eliminate the worry of style changes and size complexities, so that reordering is easier.

❑ Because most customers preshop in catalogs at home, there is less need for displays and sales assistance.

❑ Catalogs generally cost the showroom about $2 to $5 each to print and distribute. Catalogs and flyers are the major advertising expense.

In the United States, 1,450 retail catalog showrooms had sales of $6.9 billion during 1987, down from 2,000 outlets and sales of $10.7 billion in 1984. The ten leading catalog chains account for 85 per cent of industry sales and operate about 750 stores. The largest firms are Service Merchandise, Best Products, and Consumers Distributing.[27]

The decline of the retail catalog showroom has occurred for a number of reasons: A variety of other retailers are aggressively cutting costs and prices;

showrooms are no longer low-price leaders. Catalog showrooms have a difficult time reacting both to inflation and to price cuts by competitors, because catalogs must be printed so far in advance. Many consumer electronics stores will "beat any advertised price," so consumers take their catalogs to these stores to receive better prices. Because of the need to reach more consumers, advertising expenses have increased. Too many of the items sold are slow-sellers and/or have low profit margins. Some consumers find catalog showrooms to be too crowded and dislike writing up orders; and the lack of displays reduces browsing time. The lack of apparel goods has also held down sales volume.[28]

Off-Price Chain

An **off-price chain** features brand-name (sometimes designer label) apparel, footwear (primarily women's and family), linens, fabrics, and/or housewares and sells them at low prices in an austere, limited-service environment. It frequently utilizes community dressing rooms, centralized checkout counters, no gift wrapping, extra charges for alterations, and no delivery. Merchandise is bought opportunistically, when special deals occur. Other retailers' canceled orders, manufacturers' irregulars and overruns, and end-of-season merchandise are often purchased for one-fifth to one-fourth of their original wholesale prices.[29]

Off-price chains usually compete for the same type of shoppers as department stores: married suburban females, aged thirty to thirty-nine, with children and household incomes of $35,000. Off-price stores are geared to upscale customers who know brands and price levels. And a number of off-price shopping centers now appeal to these consumers' interest in one-stop shopping.

The most important part of the strategy of off-price chains involves the buying of merchandise and establishing long-term relationships with suppliers. To succeed, the chains must secure large quantities of merchandise at reduced wholesale prices and must have a regular flow of goods into the stores. Their stock turnover is three times that of department stores.

In some cases, the manufacturer seeks out the off-price chain in order to sell samples and products that have not done well (this generally occurs three to four weeks after the beginning of a season) and/or merchandise remaining on hand near the end of a season. In this way, the manufacturer has access to quick cash, obtains a market for closeouts and discontinued items, and encourages a relationship with a retailer that promises not to mention brand names or prices in ads (so as not to alienate a department store or specialty store client). Also, off-price chains are usually less demanding than department stores in terms of the credit and advertising allowances requested from suppliers. According to an executive at T.J. Maxx, a major off-price chain:

> A vendor looks forward to a T.J. Maxx coming in, buying a ton of merchandise, not caring about the colors and sizes, not threatening to return it, paying on time, and wanting it sent to one location, not all over the country. It's kind of tough for vendors to walk away from that.[30]

In other cases, off-price chains employ a more active buying strategy. Instead of waiting for closeouts and canceled orders, they convince manufacturers to make garments during off-seasons and pay cash for items before they are produced (or delivered).

In 1987, sales were $9.9 billion. The ten leading off-price chains had sales of $5.2 billion and operated 2,300 stores. Among these chains are Marshalls, T.J. Maxx, Ross, and Burlington Coat.[31]

The slowdown in the growth of off-price chains is due to the competition from other firms, the discontinuity of their merchandise, poor management at some firms, insufficient customer service for some upscale shoppers, and the shakeout of some underfinanced companies.

Factory Outlet

A **factory outlet** is a manufacturer-owned store that sells the manufacturer's closeouts, canceled orders, discontinued merchandise, and irregulars. Manufacturers' interest in outlet stores has increased for three basic reasons. First, a manufacturer can control where discounted merchandise is sold. By placing outlets in out-of-the-way locations, in depressed areas, or in areas with low sales penetration of the firm's brands, factory outlet sales are unlikely to affect a manufacturer's key customers (which may be specialty and department stores). Second, these outlets can be profitable despite prices up to 50 per cent less than customary retail prices. This occurs because of low operating costs, such as few services, low rent, limited displays, and plain store fixtures. In addition, the manufacturer does not have to compensate wholesalers and/or retailers. Third, through factory outlets, manufacturers can control the visibility of the stores, establish promotional policies, remove labels, and be sure that discontinued items and irregulars are disposed of properly. As the president of Phillips–Van Heusen noted, factory outlets represent "the only way in which a brand can keep clean" and not be sold through discounters competing with traditional stores.[32]

Recently, factory outlets have begun to locate in clusters or in outlet malls to expand customer traffic and utilize cooperative advertising. There are currently 400 factory outlet malls in Tennessee, Georgia, New York, Connecticut, Florida, and other states.[33] It is estimated that annual factory outlet sales are $2 to $3 billion. Examples of manufacturers operating factory outlets are Warnaco (maker of Hathaway shirts, White Stag sportswear, and Warner's lingerie), Phillips–Van Heusen, Palm Beach (maker of Evan Picone and Gant sportswear), U.S. Shoe Corp. (with its Bannister Shoe stores), and Hamilton Clock.

When determining whether to enter into or expand factory outlets, manufacturers need to be cautious. They must evaluate their expertise in retailing, the dollar investment costs, the impact on existing retailers who buy from them, and the response of final customers. Certainly, manufacturers will not want to jeopardize their products' sales at full retail prices.

Buying Club

A **buying club,** also known as a warehouse membership club, appeals to price-conscious consumers, who are required to be members in order to be able to shop there. It straddles the line between wholesaling and retailing. About 12 per cent of a typical club's members are small businesses that pay an annual fee of $25 to $35 each and buy merchandise at wholesale prices; these customers represent 60 per cent of total club sales. The bulk of members are individual consumers who purchase for their own use; they represent 40 per cent of overall club sales. Final consumers usually pay no membership fee, but they must belong to a union, be municipal employees, work for educational institutions, or belong to other specified groups in order to become members (in reality, eligibility is often defined so broadly as to exclude few consumers). They are charged prices that are 5 per cent above those paid by business customers.

The buying club is a derivative of the membership-based discount retailer that was popular in the 1950s and 1960s in the United States and the giant European warehouse outlet that caters to small food and drugstore retailers. The operating strategy of the current buying club began in the mid-1970s and centers on large store facilities (up to 100,000 square feet), inexpensive isolated or industrial-park locations, opportunistic buying (with no continuity of merchandise), one-fifth the number of items stocked by full-line discount stores, little or no advertising, plain fixtures, wide aisles (to allow forklift trucks to have access to shelves), concrete floors, no delivery, little or no credit, merchandise sent directly from manufacturers to stores, and very low prices.

A buying club generally sells three kinds of goods: general merchandise, such as appliances, housewares, tires, and apparel (40–60 per cent of sales); food (20–30 per cent of sales); and sundries, such as health and beauty aids, tobacco, liquor, and candy (15–30 per cent of sales). It has a stock turnover rate that is five to six times that of a traditional department store.[34]

In 1987, the retail aspect of buying clubs had sales of almost $5 billion, up from $2.5 billion in 1985. The ten leading firms owned about three hundred outlets and accounted for 90 per cent of industry sales. Among the leaders are Price, Sam's, Costco, PACE, and BJ's.[35]

The major retailing challenges faced by buying clubs are the limited size of their final consumer market segment, the allocation of efforts between business and final consumer accounts (without antagonizing one group or the other, and without presenting a blurred store image), the intense competition and concentration among the industry leaders, and the potential for overexpansion.

Flea Market

A **flea market** has many retail vendors that offer a range of goods at discount prices in plain surroundings. It is rooted in the centuries-old tradition of street selling—shoppers touch, sample, and haggle over the prices of items. Once, flea markets sold only antiques, bric-a-brac, and assorted used merchandise. Today, they also frequently sell new goods, such as clothing, cosmetics, watches, consumer electronics, housewares, and gift items. Many flea markets are located in nontraditional sites not normally associated with retailing: racetracks, stadiums, arenas, and drive-in movie parking lots. Others are at sites abandoned by supermarkets and department stores. They may be indoor or outdoor.

At a flea market, individual retailers rent space on a daily, weekly, or seasonal basis. For example, a large flea market might rent twenty-foot by forty-foot spaces for $30 to $50 or more per day, depending on the location. Some flea markets impose a parking fee or admission charge on consumers shopping there.

There are about 250 major flea markets in the United States, but sales data are not available. Inflation, the rising interest in Sunday shopping, the broadened product mix, consumer interest in bargaining, the availability of some brand-name merchandise, and the improved credibility of a number of flea markets (which have been operating for a long time and are open throughout the year) have all contributed to the growth of this retail institution. The largest flea markets in the United States are at Roosevelt Raceway in Long Island, New York (which has 1,600 merchants and draws as many as 35,000 people a day to its 15,000 car parking lot) and the Rose Bowl Flea Market in Pasadena, California (which attracts up to 40,000 people a day).[36]

Other retailers are not happy about flea markets. They believe that flea markets represent an unfair method of competition because the quality of private-label merchandise and seconds may be misrepresented, consumers may purchase items at flea markets and then return them to traditional retailers for refunds that are higher than the prices paid, suppliers are often unaware that their merchandise is sold there, state and federal taxes can be easily avoided, and operating costs are extremely low. Furthermore, flea markets may cause excessive traffic congestion.

The high total sales volume generated by off-price chains, factory outlets, buying clubs, and flea markets can be explained by the wheel of retailing. All these institutions are low-cost retailers that appeal to price-sensitive consumers who are not satisfied with retailers that have upgraded their merchandise and customer services, raised prices, and moved along the wheel.

Firms are engaged in **nonstore retailing** when they use strategy mixes that are not store-based to reach consumers and complete transactions. Nonstore retailing is conducted through vending machines, direct-to-home selling, and direct marketing. Some retailers, such as Sears and L.L. Bean, combine both store and nonstore activities to expand their customer markets and sales potential. Others, such as Mary Kay and Encyclopaedia Britannica, concentrate on nonstore retailing to better target their market segments and keep down operating costs. In 1987, overall nonstore retailing sales were greater than $200 billion. A discussion of each of the three nonstore-based strategy mixes is next.

Vending Machine

A **vending machine** is a retailing format that involves the coin- or card-operated dispensing of goods (such as beverages) and services (such as life insurance sales at airports). It eliminates the use of sales personnel and allows for around-the-clock sales. Machines can be placed wherever they are most convenient for consumers, for example, inside or outside a store, in a motel corridor, at a train station, or on a street corner.

Although many attempts have been made to "vend" clothing, magazines, and other general merchandise, 97 per cent of the more than $19 billion of goods and services sold through vending machines in 1987 consisted of hot and cold beverages, food items, and cigarettes. With the heavy concentration of vending-machine sales in beverages and foods, the greatest sales volume is achieved in factory, office, and school lunchrooms and refreshment areas; public places such as service stations are also popular sites for machines. Newspapers on street corners and sidewalks, various machines in hotels and motels, and cigarette machines in restaurants and at train stations are highly visible aspects of vending, but they account for less than 30 per cent of total U.S. vending-machine sales.[37] Two of the leading vending-machine operators are Canteen Corporation and ARA Services.

Items priced above $1.50 have not sold well in vending machines because too many coins are required for each transaction. Furthermore, many consumers have been reluctant to purchase more expensive items that they cannot see displayed, demonstrated, or explained. However, consumers' expanded access to and use of credit cards and debit cards (whereby customer bank balances are immediately reduced to reflect purchases) are expected to have a major impact on resolving the payment issue; and the new video kiosk type of vending machine lets people see merchandise displays and obtain detailed information (and then place a credit-card order). Well-known brands and standardized nonfood items are best suited to increased sales via vending machines.

To improve productivity and customer relations, vending-machine operators are applying a variety of innovations. For instance, machine malfunctions have been reduced by the application of electronic mechanisms to coin-handling and dispensing controls. Microprocessors are being utilized to track consumer preferences, trace malfunctions, and record receipts. Some machines even have voice synthesizers that are programmed to say "Thank you, come again" or "Your change is fifteen cents."

Operators must still deal with these issues: theft, vandalism, stockouts, above-average prices, and the perceptions of a great many consumers that vending machines should be patronized only for fill-in convenience items.

Direct-to-Home Selling

Direct-to-home selling includes both personal contact with consumers in their homes and telephone solicitations that are initiated by the seller. Cosmetics, household goods and services (such as carpet cleaning and lawn care), vacuum cleaners, encyclopedias, dairy products, and magazines are among the items that are sometimes sold in this manner. In 1987, direct-to-home selling accounted for about $7 to $9 billion in sales and employed four to five million people.

The strategy mix for direct-to-home selling emphasizes convenience and a personal touch. In many cases, complete demonstrations can be made. Consumers are often more relaxed in their homes than in stores. They are also likely to be attentive and are not exposed to competing brands (as they are in stores). For some shoppers, such as older consumers and parents with young children, in-store shopping is difficult to undertake because of limited mobility. For the retailer, direct-to-home selling has lower overhead costs because store locations and fixtures are not necessary.

Nonetheless, direct-to-home sales have stagnated or fallen over the last few years. These are some reasons why:

❏ More women are now working; therefore, they may not be interested in or available for in-home purchases.

❏ Improved job opportunities in other fields and an upswing in the economy have reduced the number of people interested in jobs as direct-to-home salespersons.

❏ A firm's geographic coverage is limited by the size of its sales force. Many companies are able to reach fewer than one-half of their potential customers.

❏ Sales productivity is low because the average transaction is small and most consumers are unreceptive to this type of selling. Many people are suspicious and will not open their doors to salespeople or talk to telephone sales representatives.

❏ Selling costs are high because of travel requirements and the very high turnover of the sales force. The bulk of employees are poorly supervised part-timers.

❏ To stimulate sales personnel, compensation is usually 35–50 per cent of the sales they generate. This means average to above-average prices.

❏ Many legal restrictions are in effect because of deceptive or high-pressure sales tactics.

❏ A poor image is associated with the term *door-to-door*; hence, the industry preference for the term *direct-to-home selling*.

Firms are responding to these issues in various ways. For example, Mary Kay and Tupperware use community residents as sales personnel and have a party atmosphere rather than a strict door-to-door cold-canvassing approach; this requires networks of family, friends, and neighbors. As Fuller Brush salespeople reach about 65 per cent of U.S. households, it is using mail-order catalogs to reach the other 35 per cent. It is also advertising for sales positions in the catalogs. Avon—the largest firm, with over 400,000 salespersons—is now offering free training (it used to charge a fee) and rewarding the best workers with better territories.[38]

Among the leaders in direct-to-home selling are Avon and Mary Kay (cosmetics), Amway (household supplies), Shaklee (vitamins and health foods), Encyclopaedia Britannica, Fuller Brush (small household products), and Tupperware (plastic food containers). Large department stores, such as J.C. Penney, also use direct-to-home selling. At Penney, trained decorator consultants sell a complete line of furnishings, not available in its stores, to consumers in their homes.

Direct Marketing

Direct marketing is a form of retailing in which a customer is first exposed to a good or service through a nonpersonal medium (such as direct mail, conventional or cable television, radio, magazine, or newspaper) and then orders by mail or telephone (usually through a toll-free 800 number). Annual U.S. sales are about $175 billion, and at least one-half of all households make one or more direct-marketing purchases during a typical year. The products bought most frequently include gift items, apparel, magazine subscriptions, books and records, and home accessories.[39]

Direct marketing has a number of strategic advantages:

❑ Costs are reduced: initial investments are low; a business may be operated out of a garage or basement; reduced inventory levels can be maintained; no fixtures or displays are needed; a prime location is unnecessary; regular store hours do not have to be kept; and a personal sales force is not needed.

❑ It is possible for a firm to offer lower prices (due to reduced costs) than store retailers selling the same items. A very large geographic area can be covered inexpensively and efficiently.

❑ The customer is given a convenient method of shopping; there are no crowds, parking congestion, or lines at cash registers.

❑ Specific consumer segments can be pinpointed through mailings.

❑ Often, a consumer can legally avoid paying sales tax by purchasing items from direct marketers that do not operate retail facilities in the consumer's state (some states, such as California, are beginning to eliminate this loophole).

❑ A store-based retailer can use direct marketing to supplement its regular business and expand its geographic trading area (even becoming a national retailer) without adding outlets.

There are some limitations to direct marketing, but they are not as critical as the problems that face direct-to-home sellers. First, merchandise cannot be examined prior to its purchase by a consumer. Thus, the range of items sold via direct marketing is usually more limited than that sold in stores. Also, direct marketers need liberal return policies to attract and maintain customers. Second, prospective retailers may underestimate entry costs. Catalogs are costly: printing and mailing costs are easily $2 to $3 or more per catalog. A computer system may be required to track shipments, monitor purchases and returns, and keep mailing lists current. A twenty-four-hour telephone staff may be necessary.

Third, since most catalogs are delivered by third-class mail, the profitability of direct marketers is highly sensitive to postal rates and to the costs of paper stock. Fourth, even the most successful catalogs draw purchases from less than 10 per cent of recipients. The high costs and relatively low response rates have caused some merchants to charge for their catalogs (with the fee usually reimbursed after the first order is placed) or to limit catalogs to customers previously meeting minimum purchase amounts. Fifth, direct marketing clutter exists. In 1986, almost 12 billion catalogs were mailed—nearly 140 apiece for every U.S. household.[40] Sixth, some unscrupulous direct marketers have given the industry a poor image because of delays in delivery and the shipment of damaged goods. Seventh, because catalogs are prepared six months to a year in advance, prices and styles may be difficult to plan.

The "30-day rule" is a federal regulation that greatly affects direct marketers. This regulation requires that mail-order merchants ship orders within 30 days after their receipt or notify customers of delays. If an order cannot be shipped within 60 days, the customer must be given a specific delivery date and offered the option of canceling the order and obtaining a refund or continuing to wait for the order to be filled.

Direct marketers can be divided into two broad categories: general merchandise and specialty merchandise. General-merchandise firms offer a full line of products and sell everything from clothing to housewares. Sears, Spiegel, and J.C. Penney are examples of general-merchandise direct marketers. Specialty-merchandise firms concentrate on a narrow product line, like their specialty store counterparts. Book-of-the-Month Club, Spencer Gifts, L. L. Bean, Franklin Mint, and Time, Inc., are just a few of the several thousand specialty-merchandise direct marketers operating in the United States.

Long-run growth for direct marketing is projected for several reasons. Consumer interest in convenience and the difficulty in setting aside time for shopping are expected to continue. More direct marketers will be operating twenty-four-hour service for mail orders. The standardization of products and the recognition of manufacturer brands will reduce the consumer's perception of risk when buying on the basis of a catalog description. Direct marketers are rapidly improving their skills and efficiency; they are becoming much more effective than ever before. Technological breakthroughs, such as in-home computerized ordering systems, are expected to encourage more consumer sales.

Because direct marketing represents such a large, expanding, and dynamic aspect of retailing, further information is provided in the appendix at the end of the chapter, after the cases.

Retail Institutions Categorized by Service Versus Goods Strategy Mix

Service retailing involves market transactions between companies or individuals and final consumers where the goal is "other than the transfer of ownership of a tangible commodity."[41] **Goods retailing** focuses on the sale of tangible (physical) products. Some retailers are engaged in either service retailing (such as travel agencies) or goods retailing (such as hardware stores); others offer some combination of the two (such as car rental firms that also sell used vehicles). As noted in Chapter 1, total U.S. service-retailing sales are several hundred billion dollars annually. For example, 1986 sales for hotels and motels, personal services, auto repair and rental, amusement parks, and miscellaneous repair services amounted to nearly $200 billion.[42]

There are three kinds of service retailing: **rented-goods services,** in which consumers lease and use goods for specified periods of time; **owned-goods services,** in which goods owned by consumers are repaired, improved, or maintained; and **nongoods services,** in which intangible personal services (rather than goods) are offered to consumers as "experiential possessions."[43]

Some examples of rented-goods service retailing are Hertz car rentals, carpet cleaner rentals from a supermarket, and videocassette rentals at a 7-Eleven. In each case, a tangible good is leased for a fee for a fixed time duration. The consumer may enjoy the use of the item, but ownership is not obtained and the good must be returned when the rental period is up.

Owned-goods service retailing illustrations include the repair of a watch mainspring, lawn care to eliminate weeds, and an annual air-conditioner tune-up to maintain performance. In this category, the retailer providing the service never owns the good involved.

In nongoods service retailing, the retailer offers personal services requiring the use of his or her or an employee's time in return for a fee; no tangible goods are involved. Some examples are baby-sitters, stock brokers, tutors, travel guides, beauticians, and real-estate brokers. In every instance, the seller offers his or her personal expertise for a specified time period.

The marketing characteristics of services differ significantly from those of goods, as shown by the following list:

❏ Services are sometimes expressed via rates, fees, admissions, charges, tuition, and so on, and not in terms of price.

❏ The buyer of a service is often called a *client* and not a *customer.*

❏ Service firms are highly differentiated in their approaches to marketing.

❑ Surpluses cannot be inventoried; therefore, services are highly perishable.

❑ Some services are nonprofit in nature.

❑ Many services are marketed in a professional or formal manner.

❑ Standards are not precise, because many services cannot be mass produced.

❑ Price-setting practices vary greatly.

❑ It is difficult to apply the economic concepts of supply and demand, and costs are also difficult to apply because of the intangible nature of services.

❑ Few service chains have existed (but this is now changing rapidly—examples are Century 21 Real Estate and H&R Block Tax Service), and concentration in the service sector is relatively small.

❑ Many service retailers do not understand that their services must be marketed; being available does not guarantee business.

❑ Symbolism derives from how well a service is performed rather than from the ownership of a good.

❑ In some cases, consumers may decide to bypass retailers and complete services themselves.

It should be noted that although some services have not been commonly considered a part of retailing (such as medical, dental, legal, and educational services), they should be when they entail a transaction with a final consumer.

Chapter 17 presents a detailed discussion of strategic planning concepts as they apply to service retailing.

SUMMARY

In Chapter 3, retail institutions were examined by type of ownership. This chapter views retailers from three strategy perspectives: store-based, nonstore-based, and service versus goods retailing. A retail strategy mix is the combination of store location, operating procedures, goods/services offered, pricing tactics, and promotion methods.

Three important concepts help explain the performance and evolution of various retail strategy mixes. According to the wheel of retailing, retail innovators often first appear as low-price operators with a low-cost structure and low profit-margin requirements. Over time, these firms upgrade their offerings and customer services and raise prices accordingly. They then become vulnerable to new discounters with low-cost structures who take their place along the wheel. Scrambled merchandising occurs when a retailer adds goods and services that are unrelated to each other and the firm's original business in order to increase overall sales and profit margins. Scrambled merchandising is contagious, and retailers often use it in self-defense. The retail life cycle assumes that retail institutions pass through identifiable stages of innovation, development, maturity, and decline. Retailers' characteristics and strategies change as their type of institution matures.

Retail institutions may be categorized by store-based strategy mix and divided into food-oriented and general merchandise groupings. In all, fifteen store-based strategy mixes are covered in the chapter.

These are the food-oriented store-based retailers. A convenience store is well located, is open long hours, and offers a moderate number of fill-in items at average to above-average prices. A conventional supermarket is a departmentalized store that carries a wide range of food and related items; little general merchandise is stocked and prices are competitive. A combination store combines supermarket and general merchandise sales in one large facility and charges competitive prices; the hypermarket is a special type of combination store. A superstore is larger and more diversified than a conventional supermarket but smaller and less diversified than a combination store. The box (limited-line) store is a discounter that focuses on a small product selection, restricted hours, few services, and limited national brands. A warehouse store is a discounter that offers a moderate number of food items in a no-frills setting that can be quite large (for a super warehouse).

These are the general merchandise store-based retailers. A specialty store concentrates on one goods or service line; it has a tailored strategy. A variety store has an assortment of inexpensive and popularly priced items in a simple setting. A department store is a large retailer that carries an extensive assortment of goods and services; a traditional store has a range of customer services and charges average to above-average prices. A full-line discount store is a type of department store that has a low-cost, low-price strategy. A retail catalog showroom is a discounter at which customers select merchandise from catalogs and shop in a warehouse-style store. An off-price chain features brand-name items and sells them at low prices in an austere environment. A factory outlet is manufacturer-owned and sells that firm's closeouts, discontinued merchandise, and irregulars at very low prices. A buying club appeals to price-conscious shoppers, who are required to be members to be eligible to shop there. A flea market has many retail vendors that offer a range of goods at discount prices in nontraditional store settings.

Firms are engaged in nonstore retailing when they use strategy mixes that are not store-based to reach customers and complete transactions. A vending machine is a format that involves the coin- or card-operated dispensing of goods and services; it may be placed at any site that is convenient for consumers. Direct-to-home selling includes both personal contact with consumers in their homes and telephone solicitations by the seller. In direct marketing, a consumer is first exposed to a good or service through a nonpersonal medium and then orders by mail or telephone.

Service marketing involves transactions between companies or individuals and final consumers where the goal is other than the transfer of ownership of a tangible commodity. Goods retailing focuses on the sale of tangible (physical) products. A retailer may engage in one format or the other, or it may combine the two. There are three kinds of service retailing: rented-goods services, owned-goods services, and nongoods services. Strategic planning for service retailers is examined in Chapter 17.

QUESTIONS FOR DISCUSSION

1. Explain the wheel of retailing. Is this theory applicable today? Why or why not?
2. Develop a low-end retail strategy mix for a gift shop. Include location, operating procedures, goods/services offered, pricing tactics, and promotion methods.
3. The gift shop in Question 2 wants to upgrade to a high-end strategy. Outline the changes that must be made in the firm's strategy mix. What are the risks facing the retailer?
4. How could these retailers best apply scrambled merchandising? Explain your answers.
   a. Hardware store
   b. Lawn-care service company
   c. Restaurant
   d. Florist
5. Could a retailer prosper today without some level of scrambled merchandising? Why or why not?
6. Contrast the strategy emphasis that should be followed by institutions in the innovation and growth stages of the retail life cycle with the emphasis by institutions in the maturity stage.
7. What alternative approaches are there for institutions that are in the decline phase of the retail life cycle?
8. Contrast the strategy mixes of convenience stores, conventional supermarkets, superstores, and warehouse stores. Is there room for each in the marketplace? Explain your answer.
9. The sales of combination stores are expected to continue rising, while box store sales are leveling off. Comment on this.
10. Contrast the strategy mixes of specialty stores, traditional department stores, and full-line discount stores.
11. What must the retail catalog showroom do to succeed in the future?
12. Do you agree that nonstore retailing will continue to grow? Explain your answer.
13. Differentiate between direct-to-home selling and direct marketing. What are the strengths and weaknesses of each?
14. One retailer sells televisions and other major appliances; another firm rents these items to consumers. Develop a strategy mix for each, and compare these mixes.

1. Rhonda Razzano, "Fred Meyer: Power Player in the Northwest," *Chain Store Age Executive* (January 1988), pp. 21–28.

2. See Malcolm P. McNair and Eleanor G. May, *The Evolution of Retail Institutions in the U.S.* (Cambridge, Mass.: Marketing Science Institute, 1976); Rom J. Markin and Calvin P. Duncan, "The Transformation of Retail Institutions: Beyond the Wheel of Retailing and Life Cycle Theories," *Journal of Macromarketing*, Vol. 1 (Spring 1981), pp. 58–66; E. Terry Deiderick and H. Robert Dodge, "The Wheel of Retailing Rotates and Moves," in John Summey et al. (Editors), *Marketing: Theories and Concepts for an Era of Change* (Carbondale, Ill.: Southern Marketing Association, 1983), pp. 149–152; and Sylvia Kaufman, "Coping with Rapid Retail Evolution," *Journal of Consumer Marketing*, Vol. 2 (Winter 1985), pp. 17–27.

3. The pioneering works on the wheel of retailing are Malcolm P. McNair, "Significant Trends and Developments in the Postwar Period," in A. B. Smith (Editor), *Competitive Distribution in a Free High Level Economy and Its Implications for the University* (Pittsburgh: University of Pittsburgh Press, 1958), pp. 17–18; and Stanley Hollander, "The Wheel of Retailing," *Journal of Marketing*, Vol. 25 (July 1960), pp. 37–42.

4. "Supermarket Sales by Category," *Progressive Grocer* (July 1987), p. 46.

5. The description of the retail life cycle and its stages is drawn from William R. Davidson, Albert D. Bates, and Stephen J. Bass, "The Retail Life Cycle," *Harvard Business Review*, Vol. 54 (November–December 1976), pp. 89–96.

6. Rifka Rosenwein, "Whir, Click, Thanks: Merchandisers Turn to Electronic Salesmen in 24-Hour Kiosks," *Wall Street Journal* (June 23, 1986), p. 23; and "New-Age Shopping: The Video Kiosk," *Consumer Reports* (October 1987), p. 593.

7. Holly Klokis, "Superstores Plug into CE Power," *Chain Store Age Executive* (September 1986), pp. 28–33.

8. Leslie Schulz, "Taking on the Off-Pricers," *Inc.* (January 1985), p. 25; "Discount Industry Segment Sales," *Discount Store News* (July 20, 1987), p. 21; and "Off-Price Centers: Offbeat or Off-Stride?" *Chain Store Age Executive* (May 1986), pp. 94–102.

9. Katherine Strauss Burger and Roberta Janasz, "Industry's Volume Should Pass $10 Billion Mark in '84," *Catalog Showroom Business* (September 1984), p. 3; and "Discount Industry Segment Sales," p. 21.

10. *Circle K Corporation 1986 Annual Report*, p. 5; Lisa Gubernick, "Stores for Our Times," *Forbes* (November 3, 1986), pp. 40–42; Karen Blumenthal, "Convenience Stores Try Cutting Prices and Adding Products to Attract Women," *Wall Street Journal* (July 3, 1987), p. 15; and Teresa Carson and Todd Vogel, "Karl Eller's Big Thirst for Convenience Stores," *Business Week* (June 13, 1988), pp. 86, 88.

11. John Holusha, "7-Eleven Sells Convenience," *New York Times* (July 13, 1987), pp. D1, D6.

12. *1982 Major Market Study* (Dallas: 7-Eleven Research Department, 1982); Francis C. Brown III, "Convenience Stores Moving to Diversify," *Wall Street Journal* (September 12, 1984), p. 35; "51st Annual Report of the Grocery Industry," *Progressive Grocer* (April 1984), p. 96; and *Circle K Corporation 1986 Annual Report*, p. 6.

13. "54th Annual Report of the Grocery Industry," *Progressive Grocer* (April 1987), p. 8.

14. See Walter H. Heller, "A Look at New Store Formats," *Progressive Grocer* (December 1986), pp. 29–34.

15. Estimated by the authors from "54th Annual Report of the Grocery Industry," p. 8.

16. "Wal-Mart's Hypermarket Nears Completion in Tex.," *Discount Store News* (October 26, 1987), pp. 1, 30; and "Hypermarkets: Successful at Last?" *Chain Store Age Executive* (January 1988), pp. 15–18.

17. Estimated by the authors from "54th Annual Report of the Grocery Industry," p. 8.

18. Ibid.

19. Ibid.

20. Jacquelyn Bivins, "Is It a Store? Is It a Grocery? It's a Super Warehouse!" *Chain Store Age Executive* (August 1983), p. 18; and "Super Warehouses 'Chomp' into the Food Business," *Business Week* (April 16, 1984), p. 72.

21. Computed by the authors from David P. Schulz, "The Top 100 Specialty Stores," *Stores* (August 1987), pp. 26–29.

22. Amy Dunkin, "Making Woolworth a Star on the Dow," *Business Week* (September 8, 1986), pp. 44–45; *F. W. Woolworth Co. 1986 Annual Report*; and Holly Klokis, "McCrory: Refining the 5 & 10," *Chain Store Age Executive* (July 1987), pp. 15–17.

23. Arthur Bragg, "Will the Department Store Survive?" *Sales & Marketing Management* (April 1986), pp. 60–64; Walter K. Levy, "Department Stores, The Next Generation: Form and Rationale," *Retailing Issues Letter* (1987); and "Loeb: Department Stores Handcuff Future by Shunning Risk," *Discount Store News* (July 21, 1986), p. 4.

24. Anthony Ramirez, "Department Stores Shape Up," *Fortune* (September 1, 1986), pp. 50–52; and "Return to Traditionalism, Local Ownership Result in Seattle Department Store's Revival," *Marketing News* (April 24, 1987), pp. 16–17.

25. "Annual Industry Report," *Discount Store News* (July 20, 1987), pp. 21–22, 28.

26. Isadore Barmash, "The Big Squeeze in Retailing," *New York Times* (June 20, 1986), pp. D1, D5; and "25 Years of Discounting," *Discount Store News* (September 14, 1987), pp. 35–82.

27. "Annual Industry Report," pp. 21, 75.

28. Kimberley Carpenter, "Catalog Showrooms Revamp to Keep Their Identity," *Business Week* (June 10, 1985), pp. 117, 120; and Mary Kuntz, "Catalog of Woes," *Forbes* (May 4, 1987), pp. 75, 78.

29. "Off-Pricers Grab Growing Retail Market Share," *Marketing News* (March 13, 1987), pp. 9, 14.

30. Ann M. Morrison, "The Upshot of Off-Price," *Fortune* (June 13, 1983), p. 124.

31. "Annual Industry Report," pp. 21, 40, 77.

32. Claudia Ricci, "Discount Business Booms, Pleasing Buyers, Irking Department Stores," *Wall Street Journal* (May 3, 1983), p. 35.

33. Lois Therrien and Amy Dunkin, "The Wholesale Success of Factory Outlet Malls," *Business Week* (February 3, 1986), pp. 92–94; and Joe Agnew, "Regional Centers Combine Off-Prices, Mall Amenities," *Marketing News* (March 13, 1987), p. 14.

34. Jack G. Kaikati, "The Boom in Warehouse Clubs," *Business Horizons*, Vol. 30 (March–April 1987), pp. 68–73; "Food Dominates Wholesale Club," *Food Merchandising for Discount Retailers* (February 1986), pp. 11–14; and "Membership Warehouse Game Adds Players," *Chain Store Age Executive* (November 1986), pp. 69–72.

35. Estimated by the authors from "Top Warehouse Clubs Dominate Industry in Sales, Units," *Discount Store News* (July 20, 1987), p. 35.

36. Isadore Barmash, "Flea Markets: New Retail Force," *New York Times* (November 24, 1980), p. D1; and Rita Reif, "Flea Markets in Season All Over Region," *New York Times* (June 12, 1981), pp. C1, C15. See also Elaine Sherman, Kevin F. McCrohan, and James D. Smith, "Informal Retailing: An Analysis of Products, Attitudes, and Expectations," in Elizabeth Hirschman and Morris Holbrook (Editors), *Advances in Consumer Research*, Vol. 12 (Provo, Utah: Association for Consumer Research, 1985), pp. 204–208.

37. *Vending Times Census, 1987;* and National Automatic Merchandising Association.

38. See Kate Ballen, "Get Ready for Shopping at Work," *Fortune* (February 15, 1988), pp. 95–98; Amy Dunkin, "Big Names Are Opening Doors for Avon," *Business Week* (June 1, 1987), pp. 96–97; and Len Strazewski, "Tupperware Locks in New Strategy," *Advertising Age* (February 8, 1988), p. 30.

39. Estimated by the authors from "Direct Marketing Sales Far Outpace Estimates," *Marketing News* (November 23, 1984), pp. 1, 8. For a good overview of direct marketing, see Denny E. McCorkle, "The Effects of General Source and Task Definition on Relative Attribute Importance When In-Home Catalog Shopping," unpublished D.B.A. dissertation, Memphis State University, 1987.

40. Janice Steinberg, "Cacophony of Catalogs Fill All Niches," *Advertising Age* (October 26, 1987), pp. S-1–S-8.

41. Robert C. Judd, "The Structure and Classification of the Service Market," unpublished Ph.D. dissertation, University of Wisconsin, 1962, p. 21; and Robert C. Judd, "The Case for Redefining Services," *Journal of Marketing*, Vol. 28 (January 1964), p. 59.

42. U.S. Department of Commerce, *Current Business Reports: 1986 Service Annual Survey.*

43. Judd, "The Structure and Classification of the Service Market," p. 21; and Judd, "The Case for Redefining Services," p. 59.

Case 1

The Limited, Inc.: Is Its Specialty Store Strategy Nearing Saturation?*

According to *Stores* magazine's "Top 100 Specialty Stores" study, The Limited, Inc., was the leading specialty retailer in the United States, with $3.14 billion in sales in 1986. If the firm's divisions were listed separately, five of them would have been cited in the top 100 list: The Limited stores, with sales of nearly $1 billion; Lerner Shops, with sales of more than $600 million; Lane Bryant stores, with sales of $500 million; Limited Express stores, with sales of $250 million; and Sizes Unlimited stores, with sales of $150 million.

Leslie H. Wexner, the founder and chairman of the board of The Limited, Inc., started the chain about twenty-five years ago with an investment of $5,000. Mr. Wexner currently owns 30 per cent of the corporation's stock, has a personal fortune worth over $2 billion, and is one of the richest people in the United States.

According to *Forbes'* "1986 Annual Report on American Industry," The Limited, Inc., ranked first among the specialty retailers studied in terms of asset appreciation, return on equity, earnings per share, and sales growth. Between 1981 and 1986, sales rose an average of 54 per cent annually, net income rose an average of 59 per cent annually, and shareholders' equity rose an average of 57 per cent annually. Part of the growth was due to the acquisition of such chains as Lerner (a fashion-forward retailer of popular- and budget-priced women's apparel), Lane Bryant (the nation's leading retailer of women's large-size apparel), and Victoria's Secret (a women's lingerie chain and mail-order retailer). It has also grown by generating additional volume from existing stores. For example, The Limited, Inc.'s sales grew by 32 per cent between 1985 and 1986, when the number of stores operated increased by 14 per cent.

*The material in this case is drawn from Carol Hymowitz and Francine Schwadel, "In Specialty Clothing, a Sameness Threatens a Shakeout," *Wall Street Journal* (October 7, 1987), pp. 1, 29; David P. Schulz, "The Top 100 Specialty Stores," *Stores* (August 1987), pp. 24–31; Steven B. Weiner, "The Unlimited," *Forbes* (April 6, 1987), pp. 76–80; and The Limited, Inc., 1986 Annual Report.

Each of The Limited, Inc.'s divisions has a clearly focused target market. The Limited stores sell high-fashion, moderately priced, merchandise to twenty- to forty-year-old women. The Limited Express focuses on trendy apparel for fifteen- to twenty-five-year-old women. Lerner appeals to budget-conscious women. Lane Bryant and Sizes Unlimited sell fashionable clothing to women in sizes 14 and up; the latter is an off-price chain. Victoria's Secret specializes in designer intimate apparel. Henri Bendel sells high-styled clothing in an exclusive New York City location. The company also operates Brylane, the nation's largest catalog retailer of special-sized apparel and shoes, and Mast Industries, which coordinates merchandise production and delivery. It has begun testing a retail concept for male apparel: The Express Man.

Although each store division appeals to a particular market, the stores also have many common elements in their strategies:

❏ Stores feature complementary groups of easy-to-match clothing rather than apparel separates. This approach maximizes sales by encouraging a consumer to purchase an outfit, not a single item. The practice facilitates one-stop shopping for the consumer and lets a clothing budget be stretched (for example, consumers can create new outfits by buying different colors of blouses to go with the same skirt).

❏ Buying staffs are creative copiers. They are always on the lookout for successful fashions and are able to quickly imitate styles that they view as having the potential to be fast-selling. Their copies are generally moderate in price.

❏ Private labels, which are very popular with customers, are stressed. Many of The Limited, Inc.'s brands have distinct images. For instance, Forenza is marketed as a prominent Italian designer's label, and Outback Red has an Australian or safari image.

❏ Only the most successful styles are maintained in stock. Buyer mistakes are quickly sold to off-price retailers. This makes the stores exciting and the inventory turnover high.

Despite its past growth rate, a number of analysts are beginning to question the appropriateness of The Limited, Inc.'s strategy for the future. Much of the criticism centers on the firm's growing too fast, its foreign-based production arrangements, and the "sameness" of its merchandise.

The large size of The Limited, Inc., has strained the company by making it harder to fill all the needed senior- and middle-level executive positions and to staff 3,000 stores (up from 430 at the beginning of 1982). Many executives have suffered from burnout caused by long hours and a pressure-filled environment. The facilities of suppliers have also been strained to meet the firm's increased manufacturing requirements. As a result, it had to add eleven hundred suppliers between 1986 and 1987.

Over 50 per cent of The Limited, Inc.'s merchandise is made overseas (in contrast, less than 20 per cent of Sears' apparel is imported). This strategy is risky because the firm's profit margins suffer when the U.S. dollar is weak, and apparel import restrictions may limit the amount of merchandise it can obtain from any one country. To combat such problems, the company often has suppliers in as many as five different countries for the same garment. As a result, the quality of the finished garments varies, depending on the source.

Some observers feel that a sense of sameness exists in the apparel industry and at The Limited, Inc. Garments such as denim skirts, cotton and ramie pullover sweaters, oversized cotton sweatshirts, and rugby shirts have become commodities. Comparable products are now available at multiple retailers; this reduces store loyalty. Moreover, The Limited, Inc.'s different units have blurred their distinct identities by selling similar merchandise and using common displays.

QUESTIONS

1. Evaluate the overall strengths and weaknesses of The Limited, Inc.'s specialty store strategy.
2. Should each of The Limited, Inc.'s store divisions have similar elements in their overall retail strategy? Explain your answer.
3. As a department store chain, how would you compete against The Limited, Inc.?
4. The Limited, Inc.'s goal is to double its 1986 an-

nual sales by the end of 1989 without further acquisitions of other chains. This growth is to be achieved by opening 500 new stores per year, introducing its own credit cards for some of its stores, creating a mail-order catalog for The Limited and Limited Express, and opening menswear outlets. Evaluate this strategy.

Avon: A Direct-to-Home Retailer Revises Its Strategy*

Avon is the world's largest cosmetics manufacturer, with net sales of $2.9 billion in 1986. Although Avon sells products other than cosmetics, its beauty group accounts for 80 per cent of the company's sales and 85 per cent of its pre-tax earnings. For almost one hundred years, it sold products exclusively on a direct-to-home basis. During that time, emphasis was placed on expanding the size of the sales force and reducing each representative's territory size. This approach enabled each salesperson to call on preferred accounts more often and to intensively work the territory, and it led to steadily higher company sales. In the past, Avon had not tried to reach consumers at work for fear that this would alienate its direct-to-home sales force.

However, two factors caused Avon to re-examine its distribution strategy. The increase in the number of working women led to fewer answered doorbells as well as to fewer sales representatives. In early 1986, the firm had fewer than 400,000 representatives, 5 per cent below the number in 1984. Avon also realized that 80 per cent of all beauty products were purchased in retail stores and that it had no store distribution.

After evaluating its direct-to-home strategy, Avon decided that it should also sell its products in department and specialty stores. Forty-two per cent of all U.S. cosmetics are sold in department stores alone. The firm set this long-term goal: to "have 3 solid legs in cosmetics—direct sales, upscale retail, and mass retail." It developed the Catherine Deneuve brand internally, acquired Giorgio (the top-selling fragrance in the United States), and purchased Parfums Stern (which markets the Oscar de la Renta and Valentino brands). Giorgio and Parfums Stern have combined annual sales of $300 million.

The acquisitions gave Avon immediate access to department and specialty stores as retail channels of distribution. For example, at the time it was bought by Avon, Giorgio was being sold in 710 prestige stores. In addition, the Giorgio name can also be used on a fuller cosmetics line and on licensed products such as sunglasses. Giorgio also gives Avon entry into the upscale fragrance and cosmetics market, which is growing at a faster rate than Avon's traditional market.

At the same time, Avon decided to improve its direct-to-home distribution. It has refocused on productivity rather than just sales. Now, sales representatives are given more training in how to sell products; on average, these salespeople are 15 per cent more productive and remain with Avon 35 per cent longer than those without appropriate training. A $6 service charge to sales representatives for small orders has been eliminated, a move that has improved morale. Sales commissions have been raised. For example, currently, the 20 per cent of Avon's salespeople who sell at least $8,000 worth of products in a year earn 40–50 per cent commissions. Salespeople are ranked in terms of their potential (based upon past performance and a questionnaire they fill out), and high-potential sellers are given the territories with the best sales histories. Areas with the greatest possibilities are given special emphasis. As a result of these tactics, the sales force rose to 403,000 persons in 1987, the first increase since 1982.

Recently, Avon has also given more attention to markets in which it has low degrees of penetration. Sales representatives can now reach and serve customers wherever and however they want to buy: at work or at home, in person or by phone. Sales personnel are being trained to sell at the workplace without alienating employers. Today, nonterritory selling, primarily at the workplace, accounts for between 20 and 25 per cent of Avon's total cosmetics sales. In addition, telephone contact is increasingly being used; this medium accounts for about 20–25 per cent of Avon's cosmetics sales. Last, the firm has identified about ten million "stranded" customers, who would buy Avon products but are not reached by its direct-to-home sales personnel. Avon plans to contact these customers via mail catalogs and direct-response television-based advertising.

*The material in this case is drawn from Teri Agins, "Minding the Dollars and Scents at Avon," *Wall Street Journal* (December 9, 1987), p. 44; Hank Gilman, "As the Avon Lady Recaptures Spotlight, Company Predicts a Jump in Earnings," *Wall Street Journal* (December 14, 1987), p. 28; Amy Dunkin, "Big Names are Opening Doors for Avon," *Business Week* (June 1, 1987), pp. 96–97; and Pat Sloan, "Avon Plans Mass-Retail Expansions," *Advertising Age* (October 26, 1987), p. 2.

Although most observers view Avon's revamped distribution strategy positively, there are potential problems:

❑ The competition for counter space at department and specialty stores is intense. For example, Neiman-Marcus, a leading upscale chain, acknowledges that it generally drops about six slow-moving cosmetics or fragrance lines each year.

❑ Avon has had little experience in marketing to upscale customers. Its typical direct-to-home customer is from Middle America's small towns and rural communities, aged eighteen to forty-nine, and married with children; 60 per cent have household incomes below $35,000. There is little overlap between these and department/specialty-store customers' demographic profiles. Avon's prior exposure to affluent customers, through the purchase of Tiffany's (since divested), was unsuccessful.

❑ Although direct-to-home selling is culturally accepted in Japan and other countries, some analysts argue that this distribution system is antiquated in the United States. They cite such factors as the continued rise in the number of working women and the increased difficulty of getting people to let sales representatives into their homes.

❑ Direct-to-home sales personnel may become upset by Avon's new orientation toward store distribution. These personnel may see the strategy as competing with their efforts, not as selling to new and previously untapped market segments.

QUESTIONS

1. Evaluate Avon's current overall distribution strategy.
2. Comment on the differences between store-based and nonstore-based retailing strategy mixes as they relate to Avon.
3. Should Avon sell its products at discount retail outlets as well as at department and specialty stores? Why or why not?
4. Assess the potential problem areas facing Avon. How can they be minimized?

Appendix on Direct Marketing

Although direct marketing is one of the largest and fastest-growing retail institutions in the United States, it is also one of the most misunderstood. A recent study of direct marketing thought-leaders found that 66 per cent of those surveyed did not consider it well-defined: "Direct marketing will increasingly lose its identity—because it does not have a clear one—and will be treated more and more as an invisible part of advertising and marketing in general."[1] Nonetheless, direct marketing is extremely different from store-based retailing. As an expert commented, "In the retail store business, you buy an inventory and sell it off. In the direct-marketing business, you create a demand and fill it."[2]

Therefore, an appendix on direct marketing can give the reader further insights into this important, evolving, and challenging retail institution. We will discuss the domain of direct marketing, emerging trends, the steps in a direct-marketing strategy, and key issues facing direct marketers.

What Is Direct Marketing?

As defined in Chapter 4, direct marketing is a type of retailing in which a consumer is exposed to a good or service through a nonpersonal medium and then orders by mail or telephone. It may also be viewed in this manner:

> Direct marketing is an interactive system of retailing which uses one or more advertising media to effect a measurable response and/or transaction at any location. It requires the existence and maintenance of a data base to record names of customers, expires,* and prospects; to provide a vehicle for storing, then measuring, results of advertising, usually direct response advertising; to provide a vehicle for storing, then measuring, purchasing performance; and to provide a vehicle for continuing direct communication.[3]

> In talking about direct marketing, direct marketers speak of it in terms of a way of doing business, a methodology or approach as opposed to a collection of specific pursuits. Just as general retailing encompasses a wide range of techniques in its pursuit of reaching the customer, so, too, direct marketing is seen as a specific way of thinking about retailing.[4]

*Expires are those prospects who have been or shortly will be dropped from a data base.

126

Accordingly, we *do* include the following as forms of direct marketing: any catalog; mail, television, radio, magazine, newspaper, telephone directory, or other advertisement; or other nonpersonal medium that stimulates customers to place orders via the mail or the telephone.

We *do not* include these retail institutions as forms of direct marketing:

❑ Traditional vending machines—Consumers are exposed to nonpersonal media but do not generally complete transactions via mail or telephone. These shoppers do not really interact with the firm, and a data base cannot be generated and maintained.

❑ Direct-to-home selling—Consumers are solicited through in-home personal selling efforts or seller-originated telephone calls. In both instances, the company uses personal, rather than nonpersonal, communication to initiate contact with consumers.

Direct marketing *is* involved in many videodisc kiosk transactions; when items are mailed to consumers, there is interaction between the firm and the customer, and a data base can be formed. And it is involved when consumers originate telephone calls, based on catalogs or ads they have seen.

Several emerging trends are relevant to direct marketing: changing consumer life-styles, the increased competition among firms, the greater use of dual distribution channels, newer roles for catalogs, and technological advances.

Emerging Trends

Changing Consumer Life-Styles

From a direct marketing perspective, the life-styles of American consumers have shifted dramatically over the last two decades, mostly because of the large number of women who are now in the labor force and the longer commuting time to and from work for suburban residents. Currently, many consumers do not have the time and/or the inclination to shop at retail stores. They are attracted by the convenience and ease of purchases through direct marketing.

Since consumers are now more satisfied with their direct marketing experiences than in the past (owing to improved company performance), sales should continue to be strong. These are some of the factors consumers consider when selecting a direct marketing firm with which to deal:

❑ Company reputation (image).
❑ Types of goods/services offered.
❑ Assortment.
❑ Brand names carried.
❑ Availability of a toll-free telephone number for ordering.
❑ Credit-card acceptance.
❑ Promised delivery time.
❑ Comparable store prices.
❑ Satisfaction with past purchases.

Increased Competition Among Firms

As direct marketing sales have increased, so have the number of firms in the industry. Although there are a number of large direct marketers, such as Sears and Spiegel, there are also thousands of small companies. For example, in 1986, about 5,000 companies sent 8,500 different catalogs through the mail.[5]

The high level of competition has occurred because entry into direct marketing is far easier and less costly than entry into store retailing. A direct marketer does not need a store location, can function with a limited staff, and can place inexpensive one-inch ads in the back of leading magazines or send out brochures to targeted customer groups. It can keep minimal inventory on hand and place orders with suppliers after customers have paid for items (as long as the direct marketer abides by the 30-day rule of the Federal Trade Commission).

The classified advertising section of *Runner's World* magazine (with 425,000 subscribers) can be used to further illustrate the ease of entry into direct marketing. In 1988, it cost $140 for each ad of twenty-five words or less and $5.65 for every additional word. Among the mail-order items advertised in that section in a typical issue were a runner's pulsemeter, an air purifier, discount eyewear and vitamins, and computer software to enhance running performance.[6]

Because direct marketing lures many small firms whose owners may inadequately define their market niche, offer nondistinctive goods and services, have limited experience, underestimate the effort required, have trouble keeping supplier continuity, and receive a large share of consumer complaints, about one out of every two new direct-marketing companies fails.[7]

Greater Use of Dual Distribution Channels

Another contributor to the intense competition among direct marketers is the expanding use of dual distribution channels by store-based retailers. In the past, most store retailers used advertising to draw customers to their stores. But today, many of them are supplementing in-store revenues by utilizing ads, brochures, and catalogs to generate mail-order and telephone sales. They recognize that direct marketing is efficient, can focus on specific consumer segments, appeals to customers who might not otherwise patronize them, and requires a lower investment to reach new geographic markets than opening branch outlets.

Bloomingdale's and Marshall Field are examples of two store-based retailers that have entered into direct marketing relatively recently. Bloomingdale's by Mail was established in 1982 and has seen sales grow by 30–40 per cent annually since then. In 1987, it issued thirty catalogs and had sales of $100 million (about 8–9 per cent of total Bloomingdale's revenues). Marshall Field's Expressed was started in 1984; by 1987, it was sending out twenty-four catalogs per year and generating rapidly increasing sales of several million dollars annually.[8]

These comments sum up the appeal of direct marketing to store-based retailers:

> The two sales mediums are clearly complementary to each other, rather than competitive. The synergy of store-based retailing and direct marketing is a way to expand in two very competitive markets.
>
> I don't know anyone who buys everything by mail. People who buy by mail and phone also buy a lot in our stores.
>
> In terms of growth potential, we can grow faster than the three years it takes to build a new store.
>
> Anytime we go into a new area and open a store, we already have a whole set of customers there from the catalog.[9]

Newer Roles for Catalogs

Direct marketers are recasting the ways in which they use their catalogs in three basic areas. First, many firms are now printing "specialogs" in addition to (or instead of) the annual catalog that features all of a company's offerings. For example, in 1987, Spiegel sent out 68 catalogs in all, including separate specialogs for petite women, stationery, gifts, shoes, intimate apparel, and other goods. By using specialogs, firms can cater to the specific needs of customer segments, emphasize a limited number of items, and reduce their catalog production and postage costs (as a specialog may be twenty-five to fifty pages in length compared to several hundred pages for a general catalog).[10]

Second, to help defray catalog costs, some companies are now accepting advertising from noncompeting firms that are compatible with the direct marketers' images. For instance, since 1985, Bloomingdale's by Mail has had ads for cognac, Lincoln Continental, and Club Med. And at Sears, beginning in 1988, full-page ads for fast-food, automobiles, and other products have been sought for eight of the twenty catalogs it prints, through a program called the "Sears Advantage." Overall, catalog ads provided $10 million in revenues for direct marketers during 1987.[11]

Third, both to stimulate sales and to defray costs, some catalogs are now being sold in bookstores, supermarkets, airports, and so on. In 1987, over 75,000 store outlets carried an assortment of the 250 catalogs that were made available to them. The 1,000 WaldenBooks' stores alone sold an average of 100,000 catalogs per month; and the percentage of consumers buying a catalog who actually made a product purchase was about five to seven times higher than that obtained by catalogs sent through the mail.[12]

Technological Advances

Direct marketing is in the midst of a technological revolution that is improving operating efficiency and offering enhanced sales opportunities. These are just a few of the advances taking place:

❑ Companies can inexpensively use computers to enter customer orders when they are received by mail or telephone, arrange for merchandise shipments, monitor inventory on hand, and maintain data bases of prospective consumers.

❑ Customers can dial toll-free 800 telephone numbers to place orders and get information. The cost per call for the direct marketer is quite low.

❑ Videodisc kiosks are a convenient and interactive method for consumers to purchase goods and services.

❑ Videocassette catalogs enable consumers to view detailed, animated descriptions of merchandise in the privacy of their own homes.

❑ Special cable-television programming allows consumers to view twenty-four-hour shopping channels and place telephone or mail orders.

❑ In-home computerized shopping transactions can be completed by consumers who have personal computers and modems (to interface with the seller).

Technological advances in retailing are discussed in more depth in Chapter 18.

The Steps in a Direct Marketing Strategy

A direct marketing strategy consists of eight stages: business definition, generating customers, media selection, presenting the message, customer contact, customer response, order fulfillment, and measuring results and maintaining the data base. See Figure 1.

Business Definition

First, a firm must make these two decisions regarding its business definition:

❑ Is the company going to be a pure direct marketer or is it going to engage in a dual distribution channel (involving both store-based and direct mar-

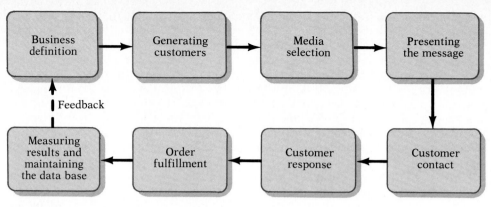

FIGURE 1
Executing a Direct Marketing Strategy

keting)? If the company chooses the latter, it must clarify the role of direct marketing in its overall retail strategy.

❑ Is the company going to be a general merchandiser and carry a broad assortment of merchandise, or is it going to specialize in one goods/service category? In either case, a broad merchandising strategy needs to be outlined.

Generating Customers

Next, a mechanism for generating customers must be employed. Several options are available. A direct marketer can

❑ Purchase a mailing list from an established list broker. For a single mailing, such a list usually costs from $50 to $100 or more per 1,000 consumer names and addresses; it is supplied in mailing-label format. In 1986, mailing-list suppliers rented or sold 27.5 billion consumer names and/or addresses to direct marketers.[13] The firm can buy a general list or one broken down by gender, location, occupation, and so on. When purchasing a mailing list, the direct marketer should be assured of its currency.

❑ Send out a blind mailing to all the residents in a particular area. This method can be expensive and may receive a very low response rate.

❑ Advertise in a newspaper, magazine, or other medium and ask customers to order by mail or call a telephone number.

❑ Contact consumers who have previously purchased from the firm or requested information. This is the most efficient means, but it takes a while to develop this data base. And if a company wants to grow, it cannot rely solely on these consumers.

Media Selection

Several media are available to direct marketers. They include

❑ Printed catalogs.

❑ Direct-mail ads and brochures.

❑ Inserts with monthly credit-card and other bills ("statement stuffers").

❑ Free-standing displays with coupons, brochures, or catalogs (such as magazine subscription cards at the supermarket checkout counter).

❑ Ads or programs in the mass media: newspapers, magazines, radio, television.

❑ Videodisc kiosks.

❑ On-line computer services.

❑ Video catalogs.

When choosing among these alternatives, the direct marketer would consider costs, ease of distribution, lead time required, and other factors.

Presenting the Message

At this point, the firm needs to develop and present its message in a manner that engenders consumer interest, creates (or maintains) the appropriate image, points out compelling reasons for a purchase, and provides information about the goods or services offered (such as prices, sizes, colors, and so on). The message must also contain complete ordering instructions, including the method of payment, how to designate the items purchased, shipping charges, and the address/telephone number of the firm.

The direct marketer should plan its message and the medium in which it is presented in the same manner that a traditional retailer plans its store. The latter uses a storefront, lighting, carpeting, the interior store layout, displays, and facilities to foster a particular store atmosphere and image. In direct marketing, the headlines, message content, use of color, paper quality, personalization of letters to customers, space devoted to each item, and order in which items are presented are among the elements that affect the shopping atmosphere and image of the firm.[14]

Customer Contact

Direct marketers must decide whether to contact all the customers in their data bases or seek out specific market segments (with different messages and/or media aimed at each). They can classify prospective customers as regulars (those who have bought from the firm on a continuous basis); nonregulars (those who have bought from the firm on an infrequent basis); new contacts (those who have never been sought before by the firm); and nonrespondents (those who have been contacted before but have never made a purchase).

Regulars and nonregulars are the most likely to respond to any future offerings of the company. Furthermore, a direct marketer can better target its efforts to these customers because it has purchase histories on them. For example, customers who have bought clothing in the past are prime prospects for specialized apparel catalogs.

New contacts probably know little about the firm. Messages to them must create interest, accurately portray the firm, and present meaningful reasons for consumers to purchase. This group is critical if growth is sought.

Nonrespondents who have been contacted repeatedly by the firm without making any purchases are highly unlikely to buy in the future. Unless a firm can present its message in a vastly different format, it will be inefficient to continue seeking this group. Nonetheless, companies such as Publishers' Clearinghouse annually send out millions of mailings to people who have never made a purchase; in their case, this is appropriate since they are selling inexpensive impulse items and need only a small response rate to succeed.

Customer Response

Customers can respond to direct marketers in one of three ways: they can make a purchase by mail or telephone; they can request further information, such as a catalog; or they can ignore the message. In general, purchases are made by no more than 2–3 per cent of the consumers contacted. This rate is higher for specialogs, mail-order clubs (e.g., for books or music), and firms that concentrate on repeat customers.

Table 1 shows the items that consumers have the greatest and least interest in purchasing via direct marketing.

Order Fulfillment

The firm needs a system to process orders. If they are received by mail, the company must sort them, determine if payment is enclosed, check whether the requested merchandise is in stock, mail the appropriate announcement to customers if items cannot be sent on time, coordinate shipments, and replenish inventory. If orders are placed by telephone, the company must have a trained sales staff available during the hours in which customers may call. The sales staff answer questions, make suggestions, enter the orders, note the method of payment, check whether the items are in stock, coordinate shipments, and replenish inventory. In both cases, customer names, addresses, and purchase information are added to the data base for future reference.

During peak seasons, additional warehouse, shipping, and sales personnel will be necessary to supplement regular employees. Direct marketers that are highly regarded by consumers fill orders promptly (usually within two to three weeks), have knowledgeable and courteous personnel, do not misrepresent merchandise quality, and provide liberal return policies.

Measuring Results and Maintaining the Data Base

The last step in a direct marketing strategy is to analyze results and maintain the data base. Most forms of direct marketing yield clearly measurable results, such as these:

❑ Overall response rate—It can be determined what number and/or percentage of the people reached by a particular brochure, catalog, and so on actually make a purchase.

❑ Average purchase amount—This can be examined by customer location, gender, and so on.

❑ Sales volume by product category—Sales can be related to the space allocated to each product in brochures, catalogs, and so on.

❑ Value of list brokers—The revenues generated by various mailing lists can be compared.

After measuring results, the direct marketer reviews its customer data base and makes sure that new shoppers are entered, that address changes have been noted for existing customers, that purchase and customer background information is current and available in various segmentation categories, and that nonrespondents are purged from the data base (when feasible).

This stage provides valuable feedback for the direct marketer each time it plans a new campaign.

Key Issues Facing Direct Marketers

In planning and implementing their strategies, direct marketers need to keep these key issues in mind.[15]

A large number of American households still dislike some aspect of direct marketing. The greatest levels of consumer dissatisfaction deal with late or nondelivery, deceptive claims about merchandise characteristics, items broken or damaged in transit, the wrong items being delivered, and the lack of information

TABLE 1

133

Retail Institutions
by Strategy Mix

Consumer Interest in Direct Marketing by Product Category

Product Category	Percentage Who Prefer Buying Via Direct Marketing	Percentage Who Would Never Buy Via Direct Marketing
Books, records, tapes	33	29
Casual clothing	20	46
Underwear, intimate apparel	19	48
Sports equipment	16	45
Small kitchen appliances	16	48
Home tools	15	45
Children's clothing	12	48
Cosmetics	11	55
Costume jewelry	11	60
Cameras	10	62
Shoes	7	68
Gourmet food	6	65
Woman's/man's suits	6	71
Major appliances	6	71
Expensive dresses	5	72
Children's shoes	4	62
Expensive jewelry	3	84

Source: Direct Marketing in the Year 2000 (New York: Yankelovich, Skelly and White/ Clancy, Shulman, Inc. 1987), p. 43. Reprinted by permission.

provided. However, in most cases, the leading direct marketers are highly rated by consumers.

Sixty-seven per cent of American households report that they open all direct mail; but forty-two per cent would like to receive less of it. Since the average American adult and child is sent fifty catalogs a year, in addition to hundreds of other direct-mail pieces, direct marketers must be very concerned about the glut or clutter in the marketplace. It is hard to be distinctive in this kind of environment and to increase customer response rates.

Some consumers are concerned that their names and background information are being sold by list brokers; they believe the practice is an invasion of privacy. To counteract this, the industry will remove names of consumers from mailing-list circulation if they make a request to the Direct Marketing Association.

Dual distribution retailers need to sustain a consistent image for their store-based and direct-marketing efforts. They must also recognize both the similarities and the differences in the strategies for each approach. As one dual distribution retailer has stated, "Store-based retailing and direct marketing are different specializations. Just because someone knows how to run a good catalog doesn't mean that he or she will be a good store retailer and vice versa. You've got to know both."[16]

Finally, direct marketers must carefully monitor the legal environment. In particular, they must be aware that over the next several years, a number of states will probably require their residents to pay sales tax on out-of-state direct marketing purchases; the companies would have to remit these tax payments to the affected state. And postal rates are regularly subject to U.S. Postal Service review; every time the rates go up, direct marketers' costs rise.

1. *Direct Marketing in the Year 2000* (New York: Yankelovich, Skelly and White/Clancy, Shulman Inc., 1987), p. 13.

2. Holly Klokis, "Catalog Options: Mail-Order or Store Traffic?" *Chain Store Age Executive* (May 1985), p. 31.

3. Adapted by the authors from "Direct Marketing—What Is It?" *Direct Marketing*. The definition appears in every issue of this monthly magazine.

4. Adapted by the authors from *Direct Marketing in the Year 2000*, p. 14.

5. Ann Hagedorn, " 'Tis Already the Season for Catalog Firms," *Wall Street Journal* (November 24, 1987), p. 6.

6. "Classified Advertising," *Runner's World* (February 1988), p. 92.

7. Hagedorn, " 'Tis Already the Season for Catalog Firms," p. 6.

8. Cara S. Trager, "Retailers, Catalogers Cross Channels," *Advertising Age* (October 26, 1987), pp. S-9–S-10.

9. Ibid.

10. Janice Steinberg, "Generalists Divvy Up the Segments," *Advertising Age* (October 26, 1987), pp. S-2, S-4–S-5.

11. Pat Sloan, "Bloomies' Book Adds Ads; Will Editorial Come Next?" *Advertising Age* (July 29, 1985), pp. 3, 63; and "Sears Welcomes Other Marketers into Its Catalogs," *Advertising Age* (December 14, 1987), p. 82.

12. Hagedorn, " 'Tis Already the Season for Catalog Firms," p. 6; and Janice Steinberg, "Cacophony of Catalogs Fill All Niches," *Advertising Age* (October 26, 1987), p. S-5.

13. Gloria Savini, "Guide to List Suppliers," *Direct Marketing* (August 1987), p. 41; David J. Scholes, "What You Should Know About List Brokers," *Direct Marketing* (February 1987), pp. 60–64; and Walter Wolf, "Net Name Arrangements Interact with Segmentation Techniques," *Direct Marketing* (October 1987), pp. 48–55, 102.

14. See Freeman Gosden, Jr., "What My Mail Box Taught Me in 1987," *Direct Marketing* (February 1988), pp. 36–42; Joe Morrone, "Time-Tested Tactics for the Outer Envelope," *Direct Marketing* (August 1987), pp. 83–87; Dave Wilkison, "The Letter & the Personalized Letter," *Direct Marketing* (April 1987), pp. 74, 79; Dave Wilkison, "The Brochure," *Direct Marketing* (May 1987), pp. 62–63, 123; Dave Wilkison, "Peripherals," *Direct Marketing* (June 1987), p. 68; and Dave Wilkison, "Sweepstakes Mailings—A Basic Primer," *Direct Marketing* (September 1987), pp. 47–48.

15. *Simmons Direct Marketing Study* (New York: Simmons Market Research Bureau, 1985); "Mail-Order Companies," *Consumer Reports* (October 1987), pp. 607–614; and *Direct Marketing in the Year 2000*, p. 46.

16. Trager, "Retailers, Catalogers Cross Channels," p. S-10.

Part Two Comprehensive Case

The Granzins: Deciding Whether to Purchase a McDonald's, Burger King, or Wendy's Franchise*

Introduction

Alice and John Granzin met while they were MBA students at a large university, and they were married just after they graduated about eight years ago. Since that time, Alice has worked as an account executive for an advertising agency, specializing in the advertising campaigns of noncompeting local retailers. John has worked for a medium-sized management consulting firm, concentrating on human resource management. At present, Alice and John are considering career and life-style changes and are seriously interested in the purchase of a fast-food franchise.

They understand the long hours and financial investment involved but feel that the chances of success, the personal satisfaction associated with ownership, and the opportunity to eventually operate multiple outlets far outweigh any disadvantages. The decision as to which franchise with which to affiliate is especially important: the dollar investment for a franchise unit varies widely; a noncompeting clause may forbid a franchisee from operating outlets in another chain (meaning that the franchisee must select the best franchising agreement and live with it); and growth and profit potential differ significantly.

The Granzins have narrowed their choices down to the three largest hamburger-based fast-food franchises: McDonald's, Burger King, and Wendy's. They have assembled data on franchising in the restaurant industry and on the individual companies. In addition, they have secured franchising requirements information directly from each of the firms.

Franchising in the Restaurant Industry

The restaurant franchise industry had total systemwide sales of $58 billion in 1987. The largest segment of the industry comprised firms emphasizing hamburgers, franks, and/or roast beef. This segment accounted for 49 per cent of total restaurant franchise sales, as shown in Table 1. The next largest segment, steak and full-menu restaurant franchises, represented 16 per cent of sales.

Sales for hamburger, frank, and roast beef establishments rose by 22 per cent between 1985 and 1987, average for all restaurant franchises. The fastest-growing franchise categories were sandwich restaurants (which had a 62 per cent sales increase during this period) and pizza restaurants (which had a 30 per cent increase). Franchise categories with low growth were full-menu steak restaurants (10 per cent increase) and pancake/waffle restaurants (16 per cent increase).

Tables 2 and 3 show the sales and number of units accounted for by company-owned and franchisee-owned hamburger, frank, and roast beef franchises from 1985 to 1987. Both the percentage of sales and the percentage of outlets operated by franchisees remained relatively constant during this time. However, average sales were slightly higher for company-owned outlets, which comprised 25.7 per cent of sales with 22.7 per cent of outlets in 1987.

---

*The material in this case is drawn from Marilyn Alva, "BK 'Best Food' Campaign Leads with Breakfast Promo 'to Go,' " *Nation's Restaurant News* (March 16, 1987), p. 3; Dan Cook, "Wendy's Tries Warming Up the Basic Burger," *Business Week* (May 18, 1987), p. 51; Rona Gindin, "Franchising Report: Hamburgers," *Restaurant Business* (March 20, 1987), pp. 116–119; Don Jeffrey, "Wendy's Joins Baskin-Robbins in Second Venture," *Nation's Restaurant News* (February 2, 1987), p. 3; Robert Johnson, "McDonald's Franchisee Shakes Things Up," *Wall Street Journal* (August 25, 1987), p. 44; Robert Johnson, "Three States Charge McDonald's Ads on Its Foods' Nutrition Are Deceptive," *Wall Street Journal* (April 27, 1987), p. 14; Andrew Kostecka, "Restaurant Franchising in the Economy," *Restaurant Business* (March 20, 1987), pp. 182 ff.; Robert Johnson, "Fast-Food Leader," *Wall Street Journal* (December 18, 1987), pp. 1, 12; *McDonald's Corporation 1986 Annual Report;* "Patrons Seeing Green at All McDonald's," *Restaurants & Institutions* (August 19, 1987), pp. 86–87; *The Pillsbury Company 1987 Annual Report;* Mary J. Pitzer, "Can BK's Man Spice Up Pillsbury's Eateries," *Business Week* (May 18, 1987), pp. 50–51; *Wendy's International, Inc., 1986 Annual Report;* Richard Gibson, "Despite Critics, McDonald's Sees Nothing to Beef About," *Wall Street Journal* (April 1, 1988), p. 4; Patricia Strnad, "K mart, Wendy's Drop Eatery Test," *Advertising Age* (March 28, 1988), p. 59; J. Ernest Beazley, "Wendy's Returns to Profitability, Citing Refocus on Burgers, Buffet," *Wall Street Journal* (April 28, 1988), p. 34; and Penny Moser, "The McDonald's Mystique," *Fortune* (July 4, 1988), pp. 112–116.

135

TABLE 1
Restaurant Franchising Sales, 1985–1987

		1985		1986*		1987*	
Major Emphasis	Number of Firms	Sales (thousands)	Market Share (%)	Sales (thousands)	Market Share (%)	Sales (thousands)	Market Share (%)
Chicken	30	$ 4,118,947	8.6	$ 4,488,168	8.7	$ 4,994,913	8.6
Hamburgers, franks, roast beef	105	23,407,433	49.1	25,609,781	49.7	28,591,880	49.4
Pizza	102	6,193,899	13.0	6,939,483	13.5	8,067,688	13.9
Mexican (taco, etc.)	36	2,400,009	5.0	2,571,079	5.0	2,881,165	5.0
Seafood	14	1,212,951	2.6	1,355,337	2.6	1,526,190	2.6
Pancakes, waffles	13	1,101,858	2.3	1,169,664	2.3	1,285,229	2.2
Steak, full menu	117	8,562,410	18.0	8,541,838	16.6	9,500,179	16.4
Sandwich and other	53	680,854	1.4	812,792	1.6	1,103,888	1.9
Total	470	$47,678,361	100.0	$51,488,142	100.0	$57,951,132	100.0

*Estimated.

Source: "Restaurant Franchising in the Economy," *Restaurant Business* (March 20, 1987), pp. 184–185. Reprinted by permission of *Restaurant Business* magazine.

TABLE 2
Retail Sales for Hamburger, Frank, and Roast Beef Franchises by Type of Ownership, 1985–1987

		Sales (thousands)	Percentage of Sales
1985	Sales by company-owned units	$ 5,862,555	25.0
	Sales by franchisee-owned units	17,544,878	75.0
	Total sales	$23,407,433	100.0
1986*	Sales by company-owned units	$ 6,607,980	25.8
	Sales by franchisee-owned units	19,001,801	74.2
	Total sales	$25,609,781	100.0
1987*	Sales by company-owned units	$ 7,357,159	25.7
	Sales by franchisee-owned units	21,234,721	74.3
	Total sales	$28,591,880	100.0

*Estimated.

Source: "Restaurant Franchising in the Economy," *Restaurant Business* (March 20, 1987), pp. 184–185. Reprinted by permission of *Restaurant Business* magazine.

A review of trade publications by the Granzins also yielded these findings:

❑ Good sites are becoming increasingly difficult to find. And with land and construction costs rising, new sites need a high sales volume to pay for leasing costs. More franchise outlets are locating at nontraditional sites, such as on college campuses, at industrial plants, and at U.S. Army exchanges.

❑ The burger market is becoming increasingly segmented. The Granzins feel that the niches in the market are rather small and that each niche will be able to support one or two medium-sized chains. As an illustration, "gourmet" hamburger franchises such as Flakey Jake's and Fuddruckers feature butcher shops and ground beef on the premises. At Flakey Jake's, customers can choose from a topping bar consisting of twenty items.

❑ For several reasons, hamburger chains are developing new products. First, new products are needed for defensive purposes; hamburger chains do not want to lose customers to other kinds of fast-food outlets. Second, new products are needed to attract breakfast customers and additional dinner patrons. It is also more efficient to have a steady stream of people throughout the day. Third, different market segments like different products. Females are more likely to desire chicken, diet-conscious people prefer salads, etc.

TABLE 3

Ownership of Hamburger, Frank, and Roast Beef Franchised Outlets, 1985–1987

		Number of Units	Percentage of Units
1985	Company-owned units	6,666	21.8
	Franchisee-owned units	23,897	78.2
	Total units	30,563	100.0
1986*	Company-owned units	7,250	22.6
	Franchisee-owned units	24,789	77.4
	Total units	32,039	100.0
1987*	Company-owned units	7,848	22.7
	Franchisee-owned units	26,689	77.3
	Total units	34,537	100.0

*Estimated.

Source: "Restaurant Franchising in the Economy," *Restaurant Business* (March 20, 1987), pp. 184–185. Reprinted by permission of *Restaurant Business* magazine.

☐ Consumers are becoming more interested in the nutritional and caloric value of foods. As a result, McDonald's has reduced the sodium in its menu by about 15 per cent since 1983 and has begun using vegetable shortening to fry its chicken and fish. Wendy's offers baked potatoes as a healthy alternative to french fries. Burger King and Wendy's have salad bars; McDonald's offers prepackaged salads.

☐ Some restaurant franchise executives concede that they may have added new outlets too quickly. As a result, there is now a greater emphasis on price discounting (and coupons) and a larger number of marginal or unprofitable franchise outlets than in previous years.

☐ Many franchises report problems in attracting and retaining part-time workers. For example, at Burger King, the average part-time employee stays only four months, and it costs about $500 to hire and train each new worker. Teenagers make up 85 per cent of the fast-food work force, and in the United States, the number of teenagers has declined by 2.3 million since 1981; this trend will continue into the 1990s.

☐ A significant amount of comparative advertising exists in the fast-food industry. Burger King, for example, sponsored a $30-million "Chicken Tenders" campaign promoting their quality versus McDonald's Chicken McNuggets. Kentucky Fried Chicken and Taco Bell (both units of PepsiCo) have used ads that mock McDonald's packaging and food preparation.

Background Information on Individual Fast-Food Franchises

The Granzins have assembled basic sales and outlet information for McDonald's, Burger King, and Wendy's, as shown in Tables 4 and 5. They have used these tables to compute average sales per franchisee-owned outlet in 1986: McDonald's, $1,312,000; Burger King, $901,000;

and Wendy's, $715,000. A thorough review of trade and company materials then yielded the following additional background information on the three firms.

McDonald's

McDonald's serves about one of every three hamburgers consumed in U.S. restaurants and more than one-quarter of all french fries. In studies of consumer awareness of fast-food eating places, McDonald's is mentioned by consumers more often than the next six most frequently named chains combined.

It opens new restaurants at the rate of one every seventeen hours; yet, less than 0.5 per cent of the new units fail. McDonald's franchisees are prohibited from operating other kinds of restaurants or from being absentee owners.

McDonald's continually revises its menu offerings. For example, after just a few years on the market, the McD.L.T. (in which the hot hamburger is placed in one part of the container and the cold lettuce, tomato, and other condiments are placed in the other part) currently generates about 15 per cent of McDonald's total nonbreakfast sales. The firm has been testing Chicken L.T., a nonbreaded chicken breast that is grilled and served with lettuce and tomato. This product uses the same packaging technique as McD.L.T. Chicken L.T. contains only 270 calories; this should attract women and calorie-conscious consumers. Chicken L.T. is McDonald's first chicken sandwich since McChicken was pulled from test markets in 1984. Both Burger King and Wendy's offer a chicken sandwich product.

Since 1987, McDonald's has introduced prepackaged salads into almost half its domestic restaurants, where they are capturing between 5 and 15 per cent of total sales. Although McDonald's offers six prepackaged salad varieties (chicken oriental, pasta, garden, chef's, shrimp, and spinach), not all varieties are offered in each market. The use of prepackaged salads rather than salad bars gives McDonald's significant advantages. Prepackaged salads can be sold at drive-through windows, do not have portion control difficulties, involve less of a health risk, do not create a

137

TABLE 4
**1985–1986 U.S. and Foreign Systemwide Sales for
McDonald's, Burger King, and Wendy's**

		McDonald's* (millions)	Burger King[t] (millions)	Wendy's* (millions)
1985	Sales by company-owned units	$ 2,770	$ 599[tt]	$1,032
	Sales by franchisee-owned units	8,231	3,392[tt]	1,663
	Total sales	$11,001	$3,991	$2,695
1986	Sales by company-owned units	$ 3,106	$ 765[tt]	$1,037
	Sales by franchisee-owned units	9,326	3,735[tt]	1,710
	Total sales	$12,432	$4,500	$2,747

*Calendar-year results.

[t]Fiscal-year-end results.

[tt]Estimate by *Restaurant Business*.

Source: "Restaurant Franchising in the Economy," *Restaurant Business* (March 20, 1987), p. 200. Reprinted by permission of *Restaurant Business* magazine.

TABLE 5
**1985–1986 U.S. and Foreign Franchise Unit Ownership for
McDonald's, Burger King, and Wendy's**

		McDonald's*	Burger King[t]	Wendy's*
1985	Company-owned units	2,225	635	1,257
	Franchisee-owned units	6,676	3,590	2,175
	Total units	8,901	4,225	3,442
1986	Company-owned units	2,301	829	1,335
	Franchisee-owned units	7,109	4,146	2,392
	Total units	9,410	4,975	3,727

*Calendar-year-end results.

[t]Fiscal-year-end results.

Source: "Restaurant Franchising in the Economy," *Restaurant Business* (March 20, 1987), p. 200. Reprinted by permission of *Restaurant Business* magazine.

messy store interior, and save labor. Salads are also used to show McDonald's interest in health and nutrition.

McDonald's spends more on advertising and promotion than the four largest competitors combined. One-third of its customers are children; a significant amount of its advertising and promotion is oriented to them. In 1987, McDonald's spent an estimated $20 million on ads showing the "positive nutritional value" of its food. The print campaign focused on McDonald's use of ingredients from manufacturers such as Kraft, Heinz, Sara Lee, and Gorton's: "the same premium brand names customers trust when shopping for their families."

McDonald's has an excellent community relations program. It has opened and maintains 107 Ronald McDonald houses, which provide low-cost room and board to families visiting their seriously ill children in hospitals. It donates more than $50 million to various charities annually and sponsors numerous amateur athletic competitions.

Burger King

Burger King is affiliated with Pillsbury, which operates the company-owned outlets and sets franchise policies. To compete with McDonald's, Burger King is more adult-oriented in its advertising, stresses that its Whoppers are flame-broiled, and carries Pepsi soda products.

The company has had some problems since the late 1970s as a result of management changes, strategy modifications, ineffective advertising campaigns, and unsuccessful new product introductions (such as pizza and veal parmigiana sandwiches). Even a Burger King executive acknowledged that "McDonald's is still the best operated fast-food hamburger establishment." As a result, Burger King's share of the hamburger chain market has declined in recent years; and it has been rumored that Pillsbury might sell Burger King.

Burger King's 1984–1985 $40-million "Herb" advertising campaign illustrates the firm's difficulties. That campaign was based on a fictitious character who had never visited a Burger King outlet and did not know what he was missing. It was overwhelmed by McDonald's McD.L.T. campaign, which had a $100-million advertising budget. The Herb promotion, which offered prizes for spotting Herb on his cross-country tour of Burger King stores, was also not as creative as Wendy's use of Clara Peller in its "Where's the beef?" ads. Then, after the Herb campaign, Burger King used three different themes in a one-year period. This had a negative impact on consumer advertising recall and showed the company's lack of focus.

Despite its problems, Burger King has been working hard to improve results. Its annual advertising and promotion budget is about $200 million. In 1986, Burger King launched a $30-million advertising campaign in support of Chicken Tenders, its new white-meat-chicken finger food. This was Burger King's first legitimate new product since the breakfast croissant several years earlier. Chicken Tenders are expected to generate as much as 15 per cent of the chain's total sales, with an overall sales gain of as much as 5 per cent. Unlike McDonald's McNuggets (which are made from processed chicken parts), Chicken Tenders are cut from fillets of chicken breast, breaded in whole wheat flour, and then fried in 100 per cent vegetable (cholesterol-free) oil. Because Chicken Tenders are made from chicken breasts and are not processed, Burger King has had some difficulties maintaining a constant size and shape.

It has also started an aggressive campaign for the breakfast business, emphasizing croissant-based products. The firm has been testing "Egglet," a finger-food item that resembles a small omelet.

Burger King is utilizing some creative distribution strategies. More than 45 per cent of sales are now made at drive-through windows. Twenty-one Burger King Express vans travel to special locations, such as fairs, beaches, college campuses, and downtown urban areas. Home delivery is currently being tested. This may make Burger King's sales less weather-sensitive and allow it to compete better with pizza-based restaurants.

Wendy's

Wendy's is positioned as a quality, adult-oriented fast-food hamburger chain; however, only 40 per cent of sales are beef-based. It uses fresh meat and prepares all meals to customer specifications, unlike McDonald's and Burger King. The firm's motto is "Quality Is Our Recipe." Wendy's has the most diverse menu of the three chains and the largest proportion of female customers.

It was the first fast-food chain to introduce a salad bar, and its baked-potato products remain unique. Wendy's baked potatoes are topped with ingredients such as broccoli and cheese, sour cream and cheese, bacon and cheese, and chili and cheese. It also offers chicken sandwiches, chicken nuggets, bacon cheeseburgers, and taco salad.

Wendy's used to sell only territorial franchise rights, under which franchisees agreed to open a specified number of outlets in an area. Today, individual franchise units are sold in territories where commitments have not been met or at sites falling between territorial areas. It is also testing dual concept outlets, in which a Wendy's restaurant is paired with another business under one roof. For example, Wendy's has outlets in Days Inn hotels, and it is testing Baskin-Robbins facilities inside Wendy's restaurants. Nonetheless, Wendy's is still underrepresented in some large markets, such as California and New York. This means that Wendy's customers must be willing to travel to its outlets.

Like Burger King, Wendy's has had some difficulties in recent years, and in 1986, it reported its first annual loss ($4.9 million). Although the loss was due to Wendy's decision to sell or close 164 marginal or unprofitable company-owned outlets, its performance has lagged in several areas.

Wendy's experiment with breakfast items was reported to be a disaster. Four made-to-order-omelet menu options took too long to prepare; this was more coffee-shop than fast-food service in orientation. Only 30 per cent of its breakfast sales were take-out; fast-food competitors had 60 per cent to 70 per cent of breakfast sales on a take-out basis. Wendy's customers complained that they could not drive and eat an omelet at the same time.

Since its highly successful "Where's the beef?" campaign ended, Wendy's ads have been criticized by franchisees and industry analysts as unfocused. For example, because of expenditures on breakfast ads in 1985 and 1986, Wendy's de-emphasized burger advertising. And none of the ad themes in the last few years have done a good job in pulling in new customers.

Two major new product introductions (the quarter-pound Big Classic and Crispy Chicken Nuggets) are "me-too" menu items. The Big Classic is only a minor change from the firm's standard burger (the Classic has set condiments: mayonnaise, ketchup, pickels, and onion). Wendy's was the last of the three major hamburger chains to introduce chicken nuggets.

Wendy's is taking several positive steps to improve its situation. It is seeking to building strength in the children's market by testing hot dogs and two-ounce hamburgers. It now has separate executives in charge of each menu segment: hamburger, chicken, and salad. Menus are being studied and streamlined to speed cooking and waiting times. New advertising agencies have been hired.

Franchising Requirements

The Granzins have requested and received franchise application materials from McDonald's, Burger King, and Wendy's. The franchising requirements of each firm have a number of similarities. The franchisors want applicants to devote full time to their franchise outlets, have a net worth of $200,000 or more (not counting home, auto, and personal belongings), initially invest over $150,000 in the franchise, and be willing to relocate. Application forms ask about business experience, education, personal references, personal finances, areas of geographic preference, and past business ventures.

Table 6 outlines the total required franchising fees for McDonald's, Burger King, and Wendy's. The amounts above the initial investment are to be paid out over a period of several years.

TABLE 6

Required Franchising Fees for a Single McDonald's, Burger King, or Wendy's Outlet

	McDonald's	Burger King	Wendy's
Technical assistance fee	—	$5,000	$25,000
Land	—	—	$150,000–$450,000*
Building	—	—	$190,000–$280,000*
Site improvement, equipment, and miscellaneous (initial inventory, working capital, taxes, insurance, pre-opening expenses, etc.)	$428,500[†]	$296,100–$426,200[††]	$344,000–$620,000
Franchise fee	$22,500	$40,000	$25,000
Total investment	$451,000	$341,100–$471,200	$734,000–$1,400,000
Ongoing fees	12% rent and services, 4% advertising allowance	3.5% rent and services, 4% advertising allowance	4% services, 4% advertising allowance
Time period of agreement	20 years	20 years	20 years
Minimum initial investment	$180,000	$160,000	$200,000

*Franchisee owns land and building.

[†]Includes playground but does not include sound system, security system, or projector system.

[††]Includes $15,000 refundable security deposit.

QUESTIONS

1. What are the pros and cons of the Granzins' operating a franchise outlet rather than opening their own independent fast-food restaurant? Develop a checklist of factors they should consider in deciding whether franchising is right for them.

2. Evaluate the data in Tables 1–3. Do you agree with the Granzins' decision to concentrate on a hamburger fast-food outlet? Explain your answer.

3. Relate these concepts to fast-food retailing: the wheel of retailing, scrambled merchandising, and the retail life cycle.

4. Describe the basic differences in the strategies of McDonald's, Burger King, and Wendy's. Be sure to include an analysis of Tables 4–6 in your answer.

5. What are the benefits of choosing one franchisor over another? The disadvantages?

6. What additional information should the Granzins acquire before making a decision? Provide several sources that they can use to gain this information.

PART THREE

Targeting Customers and Gathering Information

❑ *In Part Three, various techniques for identifying and understanding consumers, and selecting a target market, are presented. Then, information-gathering methods—which may be used in selecting a target market as well as in developing and implementing an overall strategy—are described.*

❑ *Chapter 5 discusses why it is necessary for a retailer to properly describe and respond to its target market, the customer group that the firm tries to satisfy. Consumer demographics, life-styles, and decision making are all examined and related to retailing. Throughout the chapter, relevant research findings are noted.*

❑ *Chapter 6 deals with marketing research in retailing. First, the difficulties that may arise from basing a retail strategy on nonsystematic research are considered. Then, the marketing research process is outlined, with particular emphasis on the characteristics and alternative kinds of secondary data and primary data. The chapter concludes with a look at the retail information system, its components, and recent advances in information systems.*

Chapter 5

Identifying and Understanding Consumers

Today, despite the number of men and women in the work force and the resulting tight time constraints, the average American adult spends a total of six hours per week shopping. More than two-thirds of adults go to a regional shopping center at least once a week, and grocery shopping generally involves two trips per week. About one-third of mall shoppers are now men (compared with one-quarter in 1981). Even teenage boys are spending an average of two hours per week in some form of shopping.

Although some shopping trips may be viewed as "drudgery," a significant proportion of them are made for other reasons. Here are several:

☐ To alleviate loneliness—"When I don't have anything to do and don't have anybody to talk to, I go to the mall and look at the people."

☐ To dispel boredom—"If you look in my closet, you'll say I don't need anything. But I get sick of things after a couple of months."

☐ Shopping as a sport—"I spend a lot of time eyeballing, and I love to find something cheaper at another store."

- Shopping as an escape—"It's a little vacation from your daily tasks. It's absolutely mindless behavior."

- To fulfill a fantasy—"I usually come to get something to eat, and then I look for what I can get—what I'd like to have in the future, what I can look forward to. It gives me a goal, something to save my money for."

- To relieve tension—"Just the thought of going shopping makes me feel better. I think about the clothes, the colors. I may not feel better in the long run, but it takes my mind off my problems."[1]

If they recognize why their consumers spend time shopping, retailers can plan their strategy mixes better.

Overview

A retailer's ability to develop and apply a sound strategy depends on how well that retailer identifies and understands its customers. This involves determining which type of target market to reach (mass market, market segment, or multiple segments), identifying the characteristics and needs of the retailer's specific target market, and understanding how consumers make decisions:

> Retailers have long depended on their ability to size up their customers when they walk in the door. Customers give themselves away by their clothing, speech, mannerisms, and body language. While gut instinct still works for some retailers, the era of successful scrutiny has passed. You can no longer pigeonhole at a glance because the increasing diversity of consumers has made such stereotyping futile. Today you need a more systematic way to understand your customers.[2]

As defined in Chapter 2, the target market is the customer group that a retailer tries to satisfy. With a mass-market approach, a company such as a supermarket or a drugstore sells goods and services to a broad spectrum of consumers; it does not really focus efforts on any one kind of customer. With a market-segment approach, a retailer tailors its strategy to the needs of one distinct consumer group, such as working women; it does not attempt to satisfy people outside that segment. With a multiple-segment approach, a retailer aims at two or more distinct consumer groups, such as men and boys, with a different strategy mix for each segment; a firm can do this by operating more than one kind of outlet (such as separate men's and boys' clothing stores) or by having distinct departments grouped by market segment within a single store (as a department store might do). When deciding on the type of target market to reach, a firm would consider its goods/service category, its goals, what competitors are doing, the size of various consumer segments, the relative efficiency of each target-market alternative for the particular company, the resources required, and other factors. See Figure 5-1.

After the retailer chooses a target-market method, it identifies the characteristics and needs of those customers to whom it wants to appeal and endeavors to understand how they make purchase decisions. Consumer characteristics include demographic and life-style factors. Consumer needs relate to a firm's store location, goods/service assortment, prices, and so on. Purchase decisions can be made impulsively or may encompass a detailed thought process.

In this chapter, we examine consumer characteristics and needs and the way purchase decisions are made. See the color photo portfolio following page 168.

Identifying Consumer Characteristics and Needs

Consumer characteristics and needs can be identified by studying a variety of demographic and life-style factors. Then, the retailer can develop a profile of its target market by combining two or more of the factors. **Demographics** are easily identifiable and measurable population statistics. **Life-styles** are the ways in which individual consumers and families (households) live and spend time and money.

(1)

(2)

(3)

FIGURE 5-1
Multiple Segmentation by Hartmarx
Hartmarx appeals to a number of distinct consumer groups through the different retail stores it operates, including Old Mill, a ladies sportswear factory outlet chain (1); Kuppenheimer, a men's clothier (2); and Barrie Place, Ltd., which features clothing for women executives (3). Reprinted by permission.

Consumer Demographics

Consumers can be identified in terms of these demographic variables: population size, number of households, place of residence, mobility, gender, employment status, age, occupation, ethnic/racial background, marital and family status, education level, income, and physical traits.

First, a retailer should have some basic knowledge of the overall demographics of the U.S. population. Next, it would determine the demographic attributes of its own target market.

A Demographic Snapshot of the United States[3]

Here is a demographic overview of the United States:

There are almost 250 million people living in 90 million households. The population is growing at a rate of less than 1 per cent annually. About 22 million adults live alone, more than ever before.

Over 75 per cent of the people reside in urban or suburban areas; the fastest-growing cities and states are in the South Atlantic, Southwest, Mountain, and Pacific regions. See Figure 5-2. About 15–17 per cent of the population changes residences each year; 60 per cent of all moves are in the same county.

There are 6 million more females than males, and 54 per cent of adult females are in the labor force (most full time). The population is aging; the average age is now thirty-two and will rise to thirty-six by the year 2000. On average, females live seven years longer than males (seventy-eight years to seventy-one years).

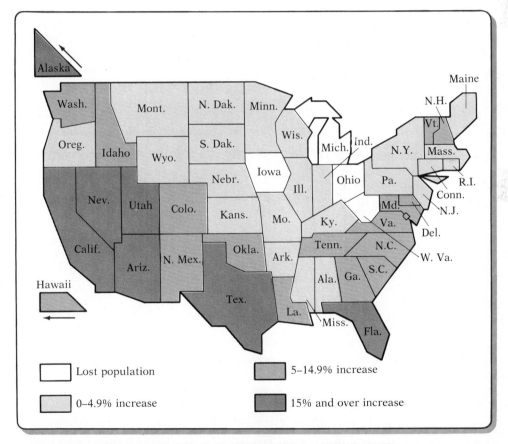

FIGURE 5-2   Population Growth in the United States, 1980 to 1987
Source: Bureau of the Census; and authors' estimates.

Most employment is in the service sector. There are now more professionals and white-collar workers than previously and far fewer blue-collar and agricultural workers.

The population comprises a number of different ethnic and racial groups. For example, in the United States, there are 17 million Hispanics and 30 million blacks; these groups represent large potential target markets.

About two-thirds of the adult population is married, but one of every two marriages ends in divorce. Adults are waiting longer to marry (the average age at first marriage is twenty-six for men and twenty-three for women) and to have children; the current birth rate is much lower than that in the 1960s. However, one-half of all families have one or more children under age eighteen; over 40 per cent of annual births involve firstborns. Over 70 per cent of all U.S. households consist of families, whereby two or more related persons live together.

More adults have attended some level of college than ever before. About one-quarter of adults aged twenty-five to thirty-four have graduated from college. Males and females are now graduating from college in roughly equal numbers.

The typical American family has an annual income of about $30,000. The top one-quarter of U.S. families have yearly incomes of $50,000 or more; however, the lowest one-quarter earn under $15,000 per year. When earnings are high, consumers have discretionary income (money left over after paying taxes and buying necessities).

Relating Demographics to the Target Market

Although the preceding gives a good picture of the United States as a whole, consumer demographics vary widely by geographic area. For example, some areas have larger populations and more affluent, older, and better-educated resi-

RETAILING IN ACTION

How Well Off Are Today's U.S. Consumers?

Retailers must be careful in comparing how well off today's consumers are versus those in the past. For example, in actual dollar terms, an average American family currently has a yearly income six times that of an average family thirty years ago. But if income is adjusted for inflation (which accounts for the rising prices of goods and services), today's family income is only 50 per cent higher than that thirty years ago. This means that consumers may not have as much discretionary income now as some retailers may believe.

A good way of determining how well off today's U.S. consumers really are is to contrast the amount of work time that is now required to earn various goods and services with the work time needed in the past. Recently, *Fortune* magazine did just that and compared the work effort required in 1986 with the effort required in 1956:

Work Time Needed to Buy	1956	1986	% Change
A chicken for dinner	15 min.	6 min.	−64
Dry cleaning for one dress	15 min.	6 min.	−64
A movie ticket	27 min.	29 min.	+7
A six-pack of beer	39 min.	21 min.	−46
A man's haircut	46 min.	39 min.	−11
A visit to the doctor	2.3 hr.	3 hr.	+30
A gallon of paint	3.6 hr.	2.4 hr.	−33
A car tune-up	10.4 hr.	9.2 hr.	−11
Auto insurance	33.6 hr.	50.3 hr.	+50
A man's suit	67 hr.	30 hr.	−55
A kitchen range	125.1 hr.	41.4 hr.	−67

This is useful information for retailers as they study their customers and try to anticipate and satisfy their needs.

Source: Based on material in Sylvia Nasar, "Do We Live as Well as We Used To?" *Fortune* (September 14, 1987), pp. 32–46. Table reprinted by permission. © 1987 Time Inc. All rights reserved.

dents than others. Because most retailers are local or regional, they must compile information about the people living in their particular trading areas and/or those most likely to patronize them. A firm would use this information to develop a demographic profile of its specific target market.

A retailer could identify its target market in terms of some combination of the following demographic factors:

❑ Market size—How many consumers are in the target market?

❑ Where people live—How large is the trading area from which customers can realistically be drawn?

❑ Mobility—What percentage of the target market moves each year (into and out of the trading area)?

❑ Gender—Is the target market predominantly male or female, or are they equal in proportion?

❑ Employment status—Does the target market contain working women, retirees, and so on?

❑ Age—What are the prime age groups to which the firm appeals?

❑ Occupation—In what industries and occupations are customers working? Are they professionals, office workers, or of some other designation?

❑ Ethnic/racial background—Does the target market consist of a distinctive racial or ethnic subgroup?

❑ Marital and family status—Are consumers single or married? Do families have children?

❑ Education—Are customers college-educated?

❑ Income—Is the target market lower-income, middle-income, or upper-income? Is discretionary income available for luxury purchases?

❑ Physical traits—Does the target market have unusual physical attributes (such as tallness or largeness)?

Consumer Life-Styles

Consumer life-styles are based on a combination of social and psychological factors. They are greatly affected by people's demographic backgrounds.

As with demographics, a retailer should first have some basic knowledge of various consumer life-style concepts. Then, the retailer would determine the life-style attributes of its own target market.

Social Factors

These social factors are key components in identifying consumer life-styles: culture, social class, reference groups, performance, family life cycle, and time utilization.

A **culture** is a group of people sharing a distinctive heritage. It influences the importance of family, work, education, and other concepts by passing on a series of beliefs, norms, and customs. In the United States, there is an overall culture, which stresses individuality, success, education, and material comfort, as well as many different subcultures (such as Hispanic and Oriental) because of the many countries from which residents have come.

A **social class** system is an informal ranking of people in a culture based on income, occupation, education, dwelling, and so on. In each social class category, there are people with similar values and life-styles. See Figure 5-3.

Reference groups influence people's thoughts and/or behavior. They may be categorized as aspirational, membership, and dissociative. An aspirational group is one to which a person does not belong but wishes to join, such as a higher

Class	Size	Characteristics
Upper–Upper	Less than 1%	Social elite. Inherited wealth. Exclusive neighborhood. Summer home. Children attend best schools. Money not important in purchases. Secure in status.
Lower–Upper	Combined with Upper–Upper equals 3%	Highest income level. Earned wealth. Often professionals. Social mobility. "Nouveaux riche." College educated, not at the best schools. Seek the best for children. Active in social affairs. Value material possessions. Not secure in position. "Conspicuous consumption." Money not important in purchases.
Upper–Middle	12%	Career–oriented. Successful professionals and business–people. Earnings over $30,000. Status based on occupation and earnings. Education important. Most educated in society. Not from prestige schools. Demanding of children. Quality products purchased. Careful but conspicuous. Attractive home. Nice clothing. "Gracious living."
Lower–Middle a. Prosperous b. Core c. Poor but honorable	35%	"Typical American." Respectable. Conscientious. Obedient. Church–going. Conservative. Home ownership is sought. Do–it–yourselfers. Neat. Work at shopping. Price sensitive. Variety of low–level white–collar occupations. Incomes from $15,000 to $30,000. Purchases related to income and occupation. College for children.
Upper–Lower	40%	Routine existence. Blue–collar occupations. Limited education. Seek job security. Income can overlap with lower–middle. Life of wife monotonous. Child–oriented. Impulsive for new purchases. Brand loyal for regular items. "National brands." Little social contact. Not status–oriented. Protective against lower–lower.
Lower–Lower	10%	Present–oriented. Impulsive. Overpay. Use credit. Poor education. Limited information. Unemployed or most menial jobs. Large market for foods. Poor housing.

FIGURE 5-3 Social Classes in the United States

Sources: This table is derived from James F. Engel, Roger D. Blackwell, and Paul W. Miniard, *Consumer Behavior*, Fifth Edition (Hinsdale, Ill.: Dryden Press, 1985), pp. 346–347; and Terrell G. Williams, *Consumer Behavior: Fundamentals and Strategies* (St. Paul: West Publishing, 1982), pp. 194–196.

social class, a professional club, or a fraternity. A membership group is one to which the person does belong, such as the current social class, his or her family, or a union. A dissociative group is one to which the person does not want to belong, such as a lower social class or an unpopular club. Those reference groups that are face-to-face, such as families, have the greatest impact on people. In addition, within reference groups, there are opinion leaders whose views are respected and sought.

Social performance refers to how well a person carries out his or her roles as worker, citizen, parent, consumer, and so on. A person's performance determines acceptance by peers and influences the types of goods and services bought. For example, a poor performer can emulate peers in an attempt to win their approval, withdraw and become a loner, or buy expensive goods to "show off."

The **family life cycle**, shown in Figure 5-4, describes how a typical family evolves from bachelorhood to children to solitary retirement. At each stage in the cycle, a family's needs, purchases, and income change. In addition to plan-

Stage in Cycle	Characteristics	Relevance for Retailing
Bachelor	Independent. Young. Early stage of career. Low earnings. Low discretionary income.	Clothing. Automobile. Stereo. Travel. Restaurants. Entertainment. Appeal to status.
Newly Married	Two incomes. Relative independence. Present– and future–oriented.	Furnishing apartment. Travel. Clothing. Durables. Appeal to enjoyment and togetherness.
Full Nest I	Youngest child under 6. One income. Limited independence. Future–oriented.	Goods and services geared to child. Family use items. Practicality of items. Durability. Safety. Drugs. Appeal to economy.
Full Nest II	Youngest child over 6, but dependent. One–and–a–half incomes. Husband established in career. Limited independence. Future–oriented.	Savings. Home. Education. Family vacations. Child–oriented products. Some interest in luxuries. Appeal to comfort and long–range enjoyment.
Full Nest III	Youngest child living at home, but independent. Highest income level. Independent. Thoughts of retirement.	Education. Expensive durables for children. Replacement and improvement of parents' durables. Appeal to comfort and luxury.
Empty Nest I	No children at home. Independent. Good income. Thoughts of self and retirement.	Retirement home. Travel. Clothing. Entertainment. Luxuries. Appeal to self-gratification.
Empty Nest II	Retirement. Limited income and expenses. Present–oriented.	Travel. Recreation. Living in new home. Drugs and health items. Little interest in luxuries. Appeal to comfort at a low price.
Sole Survivor I	Only one spouse alive. Actively employed. Present–oriented. Good income.	Immersion in job and friends leads to opportunities in travel, clothing, health, and recreation areas. Appeal to productive citizen.
Sole Survivor II	Only one spouse alive. Retired. Feeling of futility. Poor income.	Travel. Recreation. Drugs. Security. Appeal to economy and social activity.

FIGURE 5-4
Applying the Traditional Family Life Cycle to Retailing

ning for the traditional family life cycle, retailers need to be responsive to the increasing number of adults who never marry, divorced and widowed adults, single-parent families, and childless couples.[4]

Time utilization refers to the types of activities in which a person is involved and the amount of time allocated to them. Some of the broad categories of time utilization are work, transportation, eating, recreation, entertainment, parenting, sleeping, and (retailers hope) shopping. In today's environment, many consumers allocate much less time to shopping activities than in the past.

Psychological Factors

These psychological factors are key components in identifying consumer life-styles: personality, class consciousness, attitudes, perceived risk, and the importance of the purchase.

A **personality** is the sum total of an individual's traits, which make that individual unique. Personality traits include a person's levels of self-confidence, aggressiveness, innovativeness, autonomy, sociability, emotional stability, and so on. Together, these attributes have a great impact on a consumer's life-style.

Class consciousness is the extent to which social status is desired and pursued. It helps determine a consumer's use of reference groups and the importance of prestige purchases. A person who is class conscious is concerned about the social status associated with goods, services, and particular retailers. A person who is not class conscious is more interested in pleasing himself or herself; actual goods/ service/retailer quality, not their status, is essential.

Attitudes (opinions) are the positive, neutral, or negative feelings a person has about the economy, politics, goods, services, institutions, and so on. They are also the feeling consumers have toward an individual retailer, its location, its personnel, the goods and services offered, the prices charged, and the displays and ads used. Of particular concern to a retailer is whether the consumer believes its strategy is desirable, unique, and fairly priced.

Perceived risk is the level of risk a consumer believes exists regarding the purchase of a specific good or service from a specific retailer, whether or not that belief is factually correct. There are six types of perceived risk: functional (Will the good or service perform as expected?); physical (Can the good or service hurt me?); financial (Can I really afford the purchase?); social (What will my peers think of my shopping with this retailer?); psychological (Am I doing the right thing?); and time (How much effort must I exert to make a purchase?).[5] Perceived risk will be highest when the retailer and/or the brands it carries are new, the consumer is on a tight budget, the consumer has little past experience, there are many alternatives from which to choose, the purchase is socially visible, and so on. See Figure 5-5. Retailers must work to reduce perceived risk by providing ample information to consumers.

The **importance of the purchase** to the consumer affects the amount of time which that person will spend in making a decision and the range of alternatives considered. When a purchase is viewed as important, perceived risk tends to be higher than when it is viewed as unimportant; and the retailer must act accordingly.

Relating Life-Style Concepts to the Target Market

A retailer could develop a life-style profile of its target market by analyzing these concepts:

- ❑ Culture—What cultural values, norms, and customs are most important to the target market?
- ❑ Social class—Are consumers lower-, middle-, or upper-class? Are they socially mobile?
- ❑ Reference groups—Whom do consumers look to for purchasing advice? Does this differ by good or service category? How can the retailer appeal to opinion leaders?
- ❑ Social performance—Are customers high or low performers? How do they react to this status?

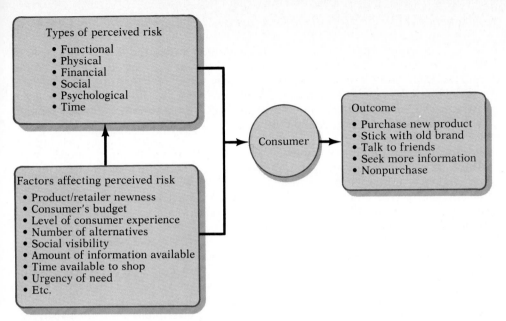

FIGURE 5-5
The Impact of Perceived Risk on Consumers

❑ Family life cycle—In what stage(s) of the cycle are the bulk of the customers?

❑ Time utilization—How do consumers spend their time? How do they view the time spent shopping?

❑ Personality—Do customers have identifiable personality traits?

❑ Class consciousness—Are consumers status conscious?

❑ Attitudes—How does the target market feel about the retailer and its offerings in terms of specific strategy components?

❑ Perceived risk—Do customers feel risk in connection with the retailer? Which goods and services have the greatest perceived risk?

❑ Importance of the purchase—How important are the goods/services offered by the retailer to the target market?

Selected Retail Research Findings

Retail research studies have identified consumer characteristics in diverse settings. It should be pointed out that the results of the studies described in this and later sections may be limited to the specific product categories/retailer types that were investigated. Following are examples of the findings.

Shopper Profiles

Considerable research has been aimed at describing overall consumer shopping profiles as well as more specific shopper profiles with regard to mall patronage, department stores, clothing stores, and grocery stores.

The most comprehensive research project surveyed 6,800 people in twelve Northwest, Midwest, Southeast, Northern Plains, and Central states. Seven major overall shopper profiles (market segments) were identified: inactive shoppers, active shoppers, service shoppers, traditional shoppers, dedicated fringe shoppers, price shoppers, and transitional shoppers. Seventy-eight per cent of all consumers could be placed in these categories.[6] The profiles are highlighted in Figure 5-6.

A study on mall-prone and mall-avoiding consumers found that shoppers who enjoy patronizing malls are younger and live in a smaller community than mall avoiders. Mall-prone consumers are also more interested in store variety, mall facilities, innovative retailers, and credit usage.[7]

Another study found that frequent department-store shoppers can be defined on the basis of demographics, activities, interests, opinions, and media usage. Overall, frequent shoppers are younger and better educated and have a higher income than less frequent shoppers. They are active in vacationing, interested in fashion, and believe in a modern family structure. They are also frequent magazine readers and enjoy other media.[8]

A comparison of consumers who described themselves as clothing fashion leaders and fashion followers revealed that more leaders are aged eighteen to twenty-four, are single, enjoy shopping, are not cost conscious, and are not practical. Fashion leaders rate themselves as more sophisticated, modern, individualistic, willing to take chances, creative, and sociable than fashion followers.[9]

An analysis of grocery shoppers showed that they could be classified into involved, apathetic, convenience, and price groups. Involved shoppers have positive images of their favorite stores; believe prices are low, advertising is good, and convenience and quality are high at these stores; are oldest and most likely to be married; and are the least store loyal. Apathetic shoppers have negative attitudes, are skeptical about value and advertising, are the youngest, and are store loyal. Convenience shoppers represent the largest category, trade off price for convenience, are the most store loyal, and are the most likely to shop at high-priced stores. Price shoppers trade convenience and some quality for low prices, rely on newspaper advertisements, and have a low degree of store loyalty.[10]

In-Home Shopping

Studies done on in-home shoppers reveal some interesting results. The in-home shopper is not always a captive audience. Shopping is often discretionary, not necessary. Convenience in ordering one item, without traveling for it, is important. In-home shoppers are also active store shoppers, and they are affluent and well educated.[11] Many in-home shoppers are self-confident, younger, and venturesome. They like in-store shopping but have low opinions of local shopping conditions. For many catalog shoppers, time is not an important shopping variable.[12] In households with young children, in-home shopping is more likely if the female is employed part time or not at all than if she works full time.[13]

When appealing to in-home shoppers, the retailer should recognize the differences between in-home and store purchases. In particular, in-home shoppers have a limited ability to comparison shop; cannot touch, feel, handle, or examine products firsthand; are concerned about service; usually do not have a salesperson from whom information can be acquired; and may have difficulty in making sense of a product's physical dimensions.[14] Also, the retailer needs to understand how consumer behavior is affected by electronic in-home shopping rather than by catalog. For example, more comparative shopping is done via catalog than by an electronic system.[15]

Outshopping

Outshopping (out-of-hometown shopping) is important for both local and surrounding retailers. The former want to minimize this behavior, whereas the latter want to maximize it. Outshoppers are often male, young, members of a large family, and new to the community.[16] Income and education vary by situation. This is important information for suburban shopping centers.

Outshoppers differ in their life-styles from those who patronize neighborhood or hometown stores. Outshoppers enjoy fine foods, like to travel out-of-town, are

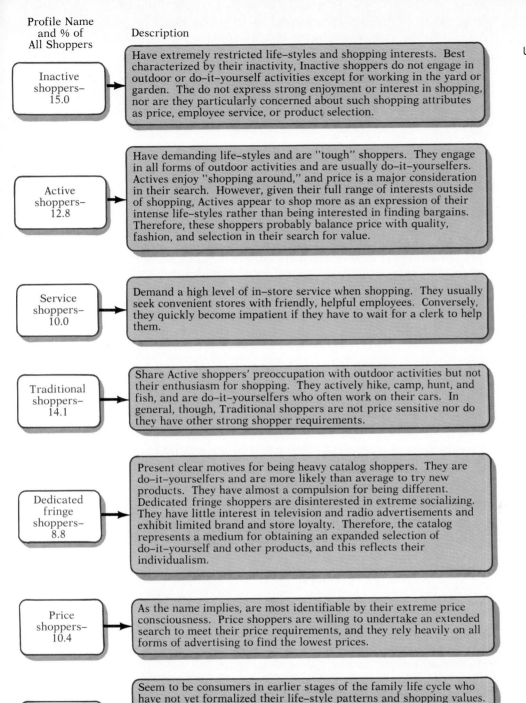

Profile Name and % of All Shoppers	Description
Inactive shoppers– 15.0	Have extremely restricted life–styles and shopping interests. Best characterized by their inactivity, Inactive shoppers do not engage in outdoor or do–it–yourself activities except for working in the yard or garden. The do not express strong enjoyment or interest in shopping, nor are they particularly concerned about such shopping attributes as price, employee service, or product selection.
Active shoppers– 12.8	Have demanding life–styles and are "tough" shoppers. They engage in all forms of outdoor activities and are usually do–it–yourselfers. Actives enjoy "shopping around," and price is a major consideration in their search. However, given their full range of interests outside of shopping, Actives appear to shop more as an expression of their intense life–styles rather than being interested in finding bargains. Therefore, these shoppers probably balance price with quality, fashion, and selection in their search for value.
Service shoppers– 10.0	Demand a high level of in–store service when shopping. They usually seek convenient stores with friendly, helpful employees. Conversely, they quickly become impatient if they have to wait for a clerk to help them.
Traditional shoppers– 14.1	Share Active shoppers' preoccupation with outdoor activities but not their enthusiasm for shopping. They actively hike, camp, hunt, and fish, and are do–it–yourselfers who often work on their cars. In general, though, Traditional shoppers are not price sensitive nor do they have other strong shopper requirements.
Dedicated fringe shoppers– 8.8	Present clear motives for being heavy catalog shoppers. They are do–it–yourselfers and are more likely than average to try new products. They have almost a compulsion for being different. Dedicated fringe shoppers are disinterested in extreme socializing. They have little interest in television and radio advertisements and exhibit limited brand and store loyalty. Therefore, the catalog represents a medium for obtaining an expanded selection of do–it–yourself and other products, and this reflects their individualism.
Price shoppers– 10.4	As the name implies, are most identifiable by their extreme price consciousness. Price shoppers are willing to undertake an extended search to meet their price requirements, and they rely heavily on all forms of advertising to find the lowest prices.
Transitional shoppers– 6.9	Seem to be consumers in earlier stages of the family life cycle who have not yet formalized their life–style patterns and shopping values. They take an active interest in repairing and personalizing cars. Most participate in a variety of outdoor activities. They are more likely than average to try new products. Transitional shoppers exhibit little interest in shopping around for low prices. They are probably "eclectic shoppers" because they appear to make up their minds quickly to buy products once they become interested.

FIGURE 5-6 Seven Overall Shopper Profiles
Source: Jack A. Lesser and Marie Adele Hughes, "The Generalizability of Psychographic Market Segments Across Geographic Locations," *Journal of Marketing,* Vol. 50 (January 1986), p. 23. Reprinted by permission.

active, like to change stores, and read out-of-town newspapers more than home-town shoppers. They also downplay hometown stores and compliment out-of-town stores.[17]

Outshoppers have the same basic reasons for patronizing out-of-town shopping areas whether they reside in small or large communities. Among these reasons are easy access, liberal credit terms, store diversity, product assortments, prices, the presence of large chain outlets, entertainment facilities, customer services, and product quality.[18]

Manufacturer, Dealer, and Generic Brands

During recent years, some retailers have increased the sales of dealer (private) brands and generic brands at the expense of manufacturers' (national) brands. At Sears and J.C. Penney, where dealer brands are being de-emphasized, these brands still account for the major portion of sales. Generic brands have had their greatest success with pharmaceutical and supermarket products. In total, dealer brands and generic brands account for about 25 per cent of supermarket sales.

Studies of supermarket customers buying generics show these shoppers to be younger, upscale, employed in good jobs, from larger families (children), and well educated. They shop frequently, have a high product usage rate, generally purchase lower-priced items, and have a high level of store loyalty. These consumers believe they will be better off financially in the future, are willing to try unknown brands, and are confident about their performance.[19]

Addressing Consumer Needs

While developing an in-depth profile of its target market, the retailer should also identify the most important consumer needs. These are just a few of the questions that could be considered:

- ❏ How far will customers travel to get to the retailer?
- ❏ How important is convenience?
- ❏ What store hours are desired? Are evening and weekend hours required?
- ❏ What level of customer services is preferred?
- ❏ How extensive a goods/service assortment is desired?
- ❏ What level of goods/service quality is preferred?
- ❏ How important is price?
- ❏ What actions are necessary to reduce perceived risk?
- ❏ Do different market segments have special needs? If so, what are they?

When the retailer gears its strategy toward satisfying consumer needs, it is appealing to their **motives,** the reasons for their behavior. The better the firm addresses the most desired needs of its target market, the more motivated (likely to purchase) the customers will be. See Figure 5-7.

For example, consumers 65 and older are most concerned about the ease of returning unsatisfactory products, product quality, attractive prices, the availability of sizes and styles suitable for older people, and access to convenient parking. To succeed with this segment, a retailer must do a good job in satisfying these needs. On the other hand, older consumers do not place nearly as much emphasis on home delivery, dealing with salespeople similar to them in age, being able to place phone orders, having a retailer provide transportation to its store, having a store offer a limited variety so that items may be easily found, and having in-store rest areas.[20] A retailer should think carefully before including these elements in its strategy.

FIGURE 5-7
Motivating Consumers to Shop
Target Stores recognizes that consumers can be motivated to spend time shopping if the retailer
provides the proper atmosphere and makes it easy for them to find merchandise categories.
Reprinted by permission of *Discount Store News*.

Following are three illustrations of how retailers are addressing the needs of various target markets:

❑ Working women—Tiffany, Cartier, and Black Starr & Frost are among the jewelry retailers now placing greater emphasis on the working-woman market. They have expanded their lines of "quietly handsome jewelry that has the tailored look women executives prefer." Ads portray jewelry as the working woman's symbol of achievement. Mail-order catalogs are used to make shopping easier.[21]

❑ Children—To attract more young customers, WaldenBooks has opened a chain of WaldenKids stores (Creative Centers for Children). These outlets sell books and educational games and toys, have playgroundlike entrances, and encourage children to play with an assortment of toys and games almost anywhere inside the stores. As one thirteen-year-old customer observed, "They don't fuss at you if you touch things, like they do at other stores."[22]

❑ Hispanics—Many retailers are acting to meet the unique needs of Hispanic consumers. Firms such as McDonald's and Domino's use Spanish in ads in areas with significant numbers of Hispanics ("Domino's Pizza delivers" becomes "Domino's Pizza entrega"). J.C. Penney has an English/Spanish store

What Do We Know About Supermarket Shopping Behavior?

Thanks to *Progressive Grocer's Annual Report of the Grocery Industry,* a lot is known about supermarket shopping behavior. Here are selected findings from its recent research:

❑ In four-fifths of households, females do the primary grocery shopping.

❑ The fewest shopping trips are made on Sunday and Monday. Customers who work full time are four times as likely to shop in the evening as those who do not work.

❑ Three-quarters of consumers have shopped at their current supermarket for more than two years. When stores are switched, it is because the consumer has moved, a new outlet has opened, or the existing store is perceived as having high prices.

❑ These practices turn off customers the most:

long lines at checkout counters, uninformed employees, untidiness or lack of cleanliness, constant rearrangement of the store, poor quality of produce and meat, running out of products, and unfriendly employees.

Industry observers add these comments: "Retailers should recognize that shoppers' time is the most valuable commodity in the store"; "Supermarkets should stop the games and giveaways and concentrate on quality and service"; "If food samples were available throughout the store during the postwork rush hour, customers might (1) relax more and buy more, (2) feel welcome, and (3) be positively reinforced about shopping in that store"; and "I'm seeing a lot of 'If we don't have what you want, ask and we'll get it.' This is a constructive step."

Source: Based on information in "54th Annual Report of the Grocery Industry," *Progressive Grocer* (April 1987), pp. 40–45; and Robert E. O'Neill, "What Will Turn Your Customers On—and Off?" *Progressive Grocer* (January 1986), pp. 31–41.

directory in its Miami, Florida, branch. At Centeno's Super Markets in San Antonio, Texas, stores carry tamales, tortillas, chile ancho and chile cascabel, papaya, and jicama—although, 90 per cent of sales come from items found in any typical supermarket.[23]

Understanding How Consumers Make Decisions

In addition to identifying the characteristics of its target market, a retailer should have an understanding of how its customers make decisions. This requires some knowledge of **consumer behavior,** which is "the process whereby individuals decide whether, what, when, where, how, and from whom to purchase goods and services."[24] Such behavior is influenced by a person's background and traits.

The Consumer Decision Process

The **consumer decision process** consists of two parts: the process itself and the factors affecting the process. The decision process has six basic steps: stimulus, problem awareness, information search, evaluation of alternatives, purchase, and postpurchase behavior. Factors that affect the process are a consumer's demographics and life-style. The complete consumer decision process is shown in Figure 5-8.

Each time a person buys a good or service, he or she goes through a decision process. In some situations, all six steps in the process are utilized; in others, only a few of the steps are employed. For example, a consumer who has previously and satisfactorily purchased luggage at a local luggage store may not use the same extensive decision process as a customer who has never bought luggage before.

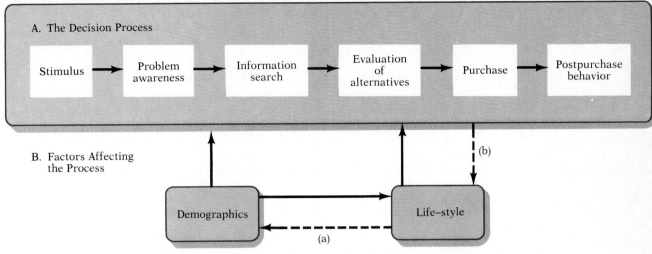

A. The Decision Process

Stimulus → Problem awareness → Information search → Evaluation of alternatives → Purchase → Postpurchase behavior

B. Factors Affecting the Process

Demographics → Life–style (a) (b)

Note: Solid arrows connect all the elements in the decision process and show the impact of demographics and life–style upon the process. Dashed arrows show feedback. (a) shows the impact of life–style on certain demographics, such as family size, location, and marital status. (b) shows the impact of a purchase on elements of life–style, such as social class, reference groups, and social performance.

FIGURE 5-8
The Consumer Decision Process

The decision process outlined in Figure 5-8 assumes that the end result is a purchase of a good or service by the consumer. It is important to realize that at any point in the process, a potential customer may decide not to buy, and the process then stops at this point. The good or service may be unnecessary, unsatisfactory, or too expensive.

Before we consider the different ways in which the consumer uses the decision process, the entire process depicted in Figure 5-8 is explained.

Stimulus

A **stimulus** is a cue (social or commercial) or a drive (physical) meant to motivate or arouse a person to act. When one talks with friends, fellow employees, professors, and so on, **social cues** are received. These cues may activate behavior. Some examples of social cues are:

"Gee Ed, I hear that the Tivoli Theater has a good movie. Let's go."

"We haven't been to a football game in a long time, and the Super Bowl is next month. Let's get tickets tomorrow."

"It's Thursday. Please meet me at the supermarket."

"Alice, I found an excellent new hair salon. You should really try it."

Each of these cues is a hint at arousing some action, which the individual on the receiving end may ignore, treat as unimportant, or follow through on. The distinguishing attribute of a social cue is that it comes from an interpersonal, noncommercial source.

A second type of stimulus is a **commercial cue.** This is a message that is sponsored by a retailer, a manufacturer, a wholesaler, or some other seller. The objective of a commercial cue is to interest a consumer in a particular store, good, or service. Advertisements, sales pitches, and point-of-purchase displays are commercial stimuli. Some examples of commercial cues are:

"Our store is going out of business. If you are thinking about a winter coat, *now* is the time for a bargain."

157

"When was the last time you treated yourself to a night on the town? At the Palace, we will wine and dine you with service fit for royalty."

"Holiday Health Spas. A younger, healthier, more attractive you. You'll love the new you. *They'll* love the new you."

"*My Fair Lady.* Last 7 performances of this revival."

These cues have the same objective as social stimuli: the creation of excitement about an object, a person, an idea, and so on as the first step in a decision process. However, commercial cues may not be regarded as highly as social ones by consumers because the messages are seller-controlled. A consumer may receive a cue differently when a friend rather than a salesperson makes a suggestion.

A third type of stimulus is a **physical drive.** This occurs when a person's physical senses are affected. Pain, hunger, thirst, cold, heat, and fear lead to physical reactions. If the stimulus is weak, it may be ignored. A strong physical drive, however, normally impels some type of action. Examples of physical drives are:

"My eyes really hurt when I woke up last Thursday morning. I knew that I had to think about making an appointment with an eye doctor."

"It's five after one. My stomach is awfully noisy. Another homework problem and I'll break for lunch."

"We've been driving for five hours, and I am really thirsty. We better stop for a soda before my tongue falls out."

"When I went out yesterday, it was 80 degrees. Today, it's 45. I'm freezing. And I don't even have a winter coat."

"This summer has been a real scorcher. Last night, I tossed and turned. I couldn't sleep at all."

"My car broke down. I was afraid that I would be late for my job interview."

In each of these cases, the person's physical senses are affected, and a desire to act is created. However, the remaining steps in the decision process help determine whether a person will actually act or just think about acting.

A potential consumer may be exposed to any or all three stimuli for any good or service. If a person is aroused, he or she will go on to the next step in the decision process. If a person is not sufficiently aroused, he or she will ignore the stimulus. This terminates the decision process for the given good or service.

Problem Awareness

At the **problem awareness** stage in the decision process, the consumer not only has been aroused by social, commercial, and/or physical stimuli but also recognizes that the good or service under consideration may solve a problem of shortage or unfulfilled desire.

A consumer moves from the stimulus to the problem awareness stage because of a motivation or desire for a good (service). It is sometimes difficult to determine why a consumer is motivated, especially because many consumers buy the same product for different reasons (price, image, quality, durability, and so on); a consumer may not know his or her own motivation (it may be subconscious); and consumers may not tell a retailer their real reasons for buying a good or service.

Recognition of shortage occurs when a consumer discovers that a good or service needs to be repurchased. Goods may wear down beyond repair (automobile, refrigerator, watch, clothing), or the consumer may run out of items (milk, bread, tissues, cigarettes). Services are required when goods can be repaired (automobile, refrigerator, watch) or services wear out (hair cutting, lawn mowing, car washing). In each instance, the consumer sees a need to replenish a good or service. Examples of stimuli interacting with problem awareness (recognition of shortage) are:

> "The sun is strong today. I'll need protection for my eyes *(stimulus)*, but my old sunglasses are broken *(recognition of shortage)*."

> "Why did I have to get a flat tire *(stimulus)*? I don't even have a spare *(recognition of shortage)*."

> "Debbie said that she didn't like the way my hair looked *(stimulus)*. Maybe it is too long *(recognition of shortage)*."

> "I really want a cough drop *(stimulus)*. But I gave my last one to Herb *(recognition of shortage)*."

If the people in the preceding examples feel that their problems are important enough for further action, they will continue to the next step in the decision process. Should these people think about their shortages and then shrug them off, the decision process will end and no purchase will be made.

Recognition of unfulfilled desire occurs when a consumer becomes aware of a good or service that has not been purchased before. The good or service may improve the person's looks, self-image, status, and so on in a way that the person has not tried before (hair transplant, cosmetic surgery, charm school, health spa, European vacation), or it may offer new, unheard-of performance characteristics (self-cleaning oven, pot-cleaning dishwasher, pocket computer). In this situation, the consumer is aroused by the desire to improve himself or herself and considers the necessity of fulfilling these dreams. Examples of stimuli interacting with problem awareness (recognition of unfulfilled desires) are:

> HENRY: "We've been married thirty-one years and have never been on a real vacation *(stimulus)*."

> BARBARA: "Why can't we go on a trip where it's sunny and the sand is beautiful *(recognition of unfulfilled desire)*?"

> "I don't like the way I look. My hair, my face—I just don't like anything *(stimulus)*. Why don't I find a good plastic surgeon and have cosmetic surgery. Then I'll be the life of the party *(recognition of unfulfilled desire)*."

> "One of the reasons I hate to cook is that I dislike washing pots *(stimulus)*. General Electric just came out with a line of dishwashers that do a great job of cleaning pots as well as dishes *(recognition of unfulfilled desire)*."

> "All my friends eat at good restaurants and have fine meals at least once a week, but I eat at fast-food houses *(stimulus)*. Just once, I'd like to go into a restaurant, have a maitre d' show me to a table, drink a bottle of fine wine, and enjoy a delicious meal *(recognition of unfulfilled desire)*."

Most consumers are more hesitant to react to unfulfilled desires than to shortages. There are more risks and the benefits are more indeterminate. This is especially true when the consumer has had substantial satisfactory experience with the good or service to be replaced. When a consumer feels that he or she would consider satisfying an unfulfilled desire, the remaining steps in the purchase process are undertaken.

Whether the consumer is aware of a problem of shortage or a problem of unfulfilled desire, he or she will act only if it is perceived as a problem worth solving. An unworthy problem will not be acted on, and the decision process will terminate. A strong stimulus does not mean the presence of a worthy problem. For instance:

> "The sun is strong today. I'll need protection for my eyes. My old sunglasses are broken, but I can tape the frame together."

"Debbie said that she didn't like the way my hair looked, but she would criticize Robert Redford."

"I really want a cigarette, but it's dangerous to my health. Maybe I'll give up smoking."

HENRY: "We've been married thirty-one years and have never been on a real vacation."

BARBARA: "You're just dreaming again. You know that you enjoy working in your garden more than travel."

Information Search

After the consumer decides that the shortage or unfulfilled desire is worth further consideration, information is sought. The **information search** involves two parts: (1) determining the alternative goods or services that will solve the problem at hand and (2) determining the characteristics of each alternative.

First, the consumer compiles a list of various goods or services that address the problem stated in the previous step of the decision process. This list does not have to be very formal nor even in written form. It may be a group of items that the consumer thinks about. The key is that the consumer amasses a list of the relevant solutions to his or her problem. This aspect of information search may be internal or external.

A consumer with a lot of purchasing experience (in the specific area) will normally utilize an internal search of his or her memory to determine the goods or services that would be satisfactory for the solution of the given problem. A typical thought process of this type is:

"It's raining *(stimulus)*. My old raincoat is torn; I really need a new one *(problem awareness)*. The question is: Will I buy a London Fog, a Botany, or a Harbor Master raincoat *(internal search for listing alternatives)*?"

A consumer with little purchasing experience will usually use an external search to develop a list of goods or services that would solve the given problem. This external search can involve commercial sources (mass media, salespeople), noncommercial sources (*Consumer Reports*, government publications), and social sources (family, friends, colleagues). In this instance, the consumer seeks information outside his or her memory. Examples of commercial, noncommercial, and social sources of information used in the listing of alternatives are:

"Our roof is leaking *(stimulus)*. This house is getting on my nerves. Let's look for a new one *(problem awareness)*. Sunday's edition of the *Gazette* will have a listing of all the new houses in our area. We should use it to develop a list of possibilities *(commercial source for listing alternatives)*."

"It just cost me $400 for a new transmission. I am worried that the car will cause me more problems *(stimulus)*. Now is the time to look for a new car before this one breaks down again *(problem awareness)*. *Consumer Reports* lists the new-model cars in its next issue. Let's get that issue and see what's going to be available this year *(noncommercial source for listing alternatives)*."

ALICE: "We haven't eaten out in a long time. I'm in the mood to have a good meal tonight *(stimulus)*."

DEAN: "You're right, I didn't realize how long it has been since we have gone out *(problem awareness)*. Where should we go?"

ALICE: "We can go to the Mandarin Inn, the Elm Tree restaurant, the Swan Club, or the Homestead *(social source for listing alternatives)*."

The second type of information that a consumer gathers concerns the characteristics of each alternative. Once the various good or service alternatives are known, the consumer must determine the attributes of each. This kind of information may be obtained internally (memory) or externally (commercial, noncommercial, social), in much the same manner as the list of alternatives is generated.

An experienced consumer will search his or her memory for the attributes (pros and cons) of each good or service alternative:

"It's raining *(stimulus).* I need a new raincoat because my old one is torn *(problem awareness).* I want to choose from among London Fog, Botany, and Harbor Master *(list of alternatives).* London Fog makes a fine product, but it's rather expensive. Botany makes a fine product, but I can't get it in my area. Harbor Master makes an equally fine product, but I have trouble with the fit *(internal search for characteristics of alternatives)."*

The consumer with little experience or a lot of uncertainty will search externally for information about each alternative under consideration. Commercial, noncommercial, and social sources are available for the collection of information about good or service attributes:

"My wife and I want to go to Europe this summer for a vacation *(stimulus* and *problem recognition).* Your ad mentioned six different packages *(list of alternatives).* Please explain the details and costs of each one *(commercial source for characteristics of alternatives)."*

"As I am interested in a new refrigerator *(stimulus* and *problem recognition),* I want to read *Consumer Reports.* Not only are all models listed, but every one is described in depth *(noncommercial source for list* and *characteristics of alternatives)."*

"OK, I agree that we should go to the Mandarin Inn, the Elm Tree Restaurant, the Swan Club, or the Homestead *(stimulus, problem awareness,* and *list of alternatives).* But let's consider the quality of food, service, and prices before we make a decision *(social source for characteristics of alternatives.)"*

The extent to which a consumer searches for information depends, in part, on the consumer's perception of the risk attached to the purchase of a specific good or service. Risk varies among individuals and by situation. For some, it is inconsequential; for others, it is quite important.

The retailer's role in a search process is to provide the consumer with enough information to evaluate alternative products, thereby reducing the consumer's perceived risk. Point-of-purchase advertising, product displays, and knowledgeable sales personnel provide consumers with the information they need to make decisions.

Once the consumer's search for information is completed, he or she must determine if the shortage or unfulfilled desire can be satisfied by any of the alternatives. When one or more goods or services are found satisfactory, the consumer moves to the next step in the decision process. However, the consumer will discontinue the process should no satisfactory goods or services be found. For example, when all restaurants are viewed as too expensive or all vacations are unappealing, the consumer will not continue the purchase process.

Evaluation of Alternatives

At this point, the consumer has enough information to select one good or service alternative from the list of choices. Sometimes this is quite easy, if one alternative is clearly superior to the others across all attributes. A product that is of excellent quality and has a low price will be the easy choice over more expensive, average-quality items.

Often the selection is not that simple, and the consumer must carefully **eval-**

uate the alternatives before making a decision. When two or more alternatives seem attractive, the consumer will determine what criteria (attributes) to evaluate and the relative importance of the criteria (attributes). Then the alternatives will be ranked, and a choice will be made.

The criteria for a decision are those good or service attributes that the consumer finds to be relevant. These criteria may include price, quality, fit, color, durability, and warranty. The consumer sets standards for these characteristics and evaluates each alternative according to its ability to meet the standards. The importance of each criterion is also determined by the consumer. And the attributes of a good or service are usually of different importance to each consumer. As an example, for some consumers, the initial price may be more important than the operating costs (as measured by electrical consumption) of a new air conditioner. In selecting a brand of air conditioner, this type of consumer will choose a less expensive product that consumes a lot of energy over a more expensive, more efficient product.

Next, the consumer ranks the alternatives (from favorite to least favorite) and selects one good or service from among the list of alternatives. The following illustration will show the entire process of evaluating alternatives:

> Judy and Larry had talked about visiting California for several years. This year they finally decided they would leave Vermont for the first time and go to California. They talked with friends, read newspapers, and consulted a travel agent. Three alternatives were available: a fourteen-day Amtrak trip, a seventeen-day car trip, or a ten-day plane trip. Judy and Larry agreed that their choice of a trip would depend on cost, time available for sightseeing, and sightseeing. Cost was important, but the time available for sightseeing and the sightseeing itself were more important. The Amtrak trip was the cheapest; the plane trip was the most expensive. The car trip left the least time for sightseeing; the plane trip provided the most. The car trip was the best for sightseeing because it was so flexible; the Amtrak trip provided the worst sightseeing because it included a fixed itinerary. Judy and Larry decided that, on the basis of their criteria and the order of these criteria, the plane trip was the best available alternative. The Amtrak trip was the worst.

For some goods or services, it is difficult to evaluate the characteristics of the available alternatives because the items are technical, poorly labeled, new, and so on. In this instance, consumers often use price, brand name, or store name as an indicator of a product's overall quality, and they choose a good or service based on this criterion.

Once a consumer examines the attributes of the alternatives and ranks them, the good or service that is most satisfactory is then chosen. In situations where no alternative proves to be adequate, a decision not to purchase is made.

Purchase

Following the choice of the best good or service from the list of alternatives, the consumer is ready for the **purchase act**—an exchange of money or a promise to pay for the ownership or use of a good or service. Decision making still goes on during this step in the process. From a retailing perspective, the purchase act may be the most crucial aspect of the decision process because the consumer is mainly concerned with three factors: place of purchase, terms, and availability. See Figure 5-9.

The consumer must determine where to buy the good or service. The place of purchase may be a store or a nonstore location. Many more items are bought at store locations (department, drug, furniture, and so on) than at nonstore locations (home, work, school, and so on). The place of purchase is evaluated in the same manner as the good or the service itself. The alternative places of purchase are listed, their characteristics are defined, and a ranking is computed. The most desirable place of purchase is then used.

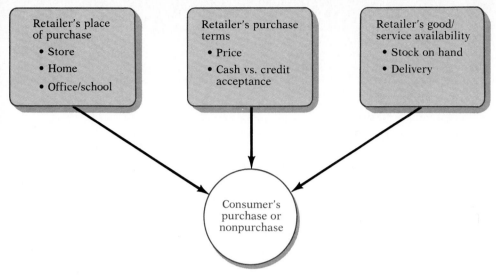

FIGURE 5-9
Key Factors in the Purchase Act

Criteria for store selection include store location, store layout, customer service, sales help, store image, and level of prices. Criteria for the selection of a nonstore retailer include image, level of prices, hours, and convenience. A consumer will shop with the store or nonstore retailer that offers the best combination of criteria, as defined by that consumer.

The consumer is also interested in the terms of purchase and the availability of the good or service. The terms of purchase are the price and method of payment. Price is the dollar amount of a good or service that the consumer must pay to achieve ownership or use. Method of payment is the way the price may be paid (cash, short-term credit, long-term credit). Availability relates to stock-on-hand and delivery. Stock-on-hand is the amount of an item that the place of purchase has in its inventory. Delivery is the time span between the order and the receipt of an item and the ease with which an item is transported to its place of use.

When the consumer is satisfied with these three components of the purchase act, the good or service will be bought. When there is dissatisfaction with the place of purchase, the terms of purchase, and/or availability, the consumer may not buy the good or service even though there is contentment with the item itself. The following are examples of each situation:

Jenny was interested in buying a new sofa to complete her living-room set. She already had two chairs and a coffee table, but until now, Jenny could not afford a new sofa. She knew exactly what she wanted, a Sealy convertible (Model 155). The questions were where to buy the sofa, how to pay for it, how soon it could be delivered, and how it would be delivered. Jenny selected the Living Room Store from among four possible stores and bought the sofa. She never considered buying by telephone or mail because she didn't trust nonpersonal shopping. The Living Room Store provided Jenny with what she wanted. She received good service at a convenient location. A special discount was given for a cash payment. Because the sofa was in stock, it was delivered within one week. Delivery was included in the sofa's price.

Ken wanted to buy a stereo system. He knew what system to get and had saved $100 for a down payment. But after a month of trying to buy the stereo, Ken gave up in disgust. He explained why: "The system I wanted was sold in only three stores in my neighborhood and through a mail-order house. Two of the stores overpriced the stereo by about $75. The third store had a really good price, $399; but the owner insisted that I pay in cash. In addition, I would have had to drive to their warehouse fifty miles away and pick up the system myself. The mail-order company had a really good deal—low price, credit, and delivery. But they ran out of the model I was interested in and told me the wait would be four months. After I heard that, I just gave up. My portable cassette player will have to suffice."

Postpurchase Behavior

Following the purchase of a good or service, the consumer is often involved in **postpurchase behavior.** Such behavior falls into either of two categories: further purchases or re-evaluation. In many situations, buying one good or service leads to further purchases. For instance, the purchase of an automobile leads to buying insurance. The purchase of a new suit may be accompanied by the purchase of a new shirt and tie. Buying a stereo system will require records or tapes to play on it. Therefore, it can be stated that some purchases provide the impetus for others, and the decision process continues until the last purchase is made. The characteristics of the supplementary items are noted and the alternatives ranked, just as in the decision process for the original item. A retailer who utilizes scrambled merchandising by stocking nonrelated items may also stimulate a shopper to further purchases once the primary good or service is bought.

A warning: the retailer should carefully evaluate his or her expansion of product lines (related or nonrelated). The skills necessary to obtain a supplemental purchase may not be similar to those required for the major good or service category. For example, real-estate transactions and property insurance sales involve different skills; television sales and service contracts require different retailer activities; and muffler repairs and transmission overhauls are quite dissimilar.

The consumer may also re-evaluate the purchase of a good or service. Does it perform as promised? Do the actual attributes of the good or service match the expectations the consumer had of these attributes? Satisfaction may lead to customer contentment, a repurchase when the good or service wears out, and favorable conversations with friends interested in the same item. Dissatisfaction may lead to unhappiness, brand or store switching when the good or service wears out, and unfavorable conversations with friends interested in the same item.

The latter situation (dissatisfaction) may result from **cognitive dissonance,** that is, doubt that the correct decision has been made. The consumer may regret that the purchase was made at all or may wish that another alternative from the list had been chosen. To overcome cognitive dissonance and dissatisfaction, the retailer must realize that the consumer decision process does not end with the purchase. Aftercare of the consumer (via a telephone call, a service call, or an advertisement) may be as important as anything the retailer can do to complete the sale. When items are expensive and/or important to the consumer, aftercare takes on added significance because the person really wants to be right. In addition, the more alternatives from which to choose, the greater the doubt after the decision is made and the more the importance of aftercare.

Many retailers recognize that consumers often have doubts and second thoughts about recent purchases. Wanamaker and others pioneered the concept of a money-back guarantee, so that customers could return merchandise if doubts or second thoughts became too great.

Realistic sales presentations and advertising campaigns can minimize dissatisfaction because consumers' expectations will not exceed reality. If overly high expectations are created, a consumer is more likely to become unhappy because the good or service does not perform at the level promised. The coupling of an honest sales presentation with good aftercare of the consumer should reduce or eliminate cognitive dissonance and dissatisfaction.

As noted earlier, every time a consumer purchases a good or service, he or she uses a form of the decision process described in the preceding subsections. Often, the process is used subconsciously, and a person is not even aware of its use. Also, as indicated in Figure 5-8, the decision process is affected by the characteristics of the consumer.

For example, older consumers may not spend as much time as younger ones in making purchase decisions because of their experience. Well-educated consumers may search out many information sources before making a decision. Upper-income consumers may spend little time making a decision because they can afford to buy again if the item purchased is unsatisfactory. In a family with children, each member may have an input into a decision, thus lengthening the process. Class-conscious consumers may be more interested in social sources than in commercial or noncommercial ones. Consumers with low self-esteem and/or high perceived risk may use each step in the decision process in detail. And people who are under time pressure may skip steps in the process to save time.

The decision process is used differently in different situations. One situation (such as the purchase of a new home) may require the thorough use of each step in the process; perceived risk will probably be high regardless of the consumer's background. Another situation (such as the purchase of a magazine) may enable the consumer to skip certain steps in the process; perceived risk will probably be low regardless of the person's background.

There are three types of decision processes: extended decision making, limited decision making, and routine decision making. These are explained next.

Extended Decision Making

Extended decision making occurs when a consumer makes full use of the decision process shown in Figure 5-8. A considerable amount of time is spent gathering information and evaluating alternatives before a purchase is made. After a purchase is completed, the potential for cognitive dissonance is great. In this category are expensive, complex goods and services with which the consumer has had little or no experience. Perceived risk of all kinds is high. Examples of goods and services requiring extended decision making are a house, a first car, and a college education.

At any point in the purchase process, a consumer can stop, and for expensive, complex items, this occurs quite often. Consumer characteristics (such as age, education, income, marital status, time utilization, and class consciousness) have their greatest impact in extended decision making.

Because their customers use extended decision making, retailers such as real-estate brokers and automobile dealers should emphasize personal selling, store displays, and other methods of communication to provide as much information as possible. A low-key approach should be employed, so that shoppers feel comfortable and not threatened. In this way, the consumer's perceived risk can be minimized.

Limited Decision Making

Limited decision making occurs when a consumer uses each of the steps in the purchase process but does not need to spend a great deal of time on each of the steps. This type of decision making requires less time than extended decision making because the consumer probably has some experience. In this category are items that the consumer has purchased before, but not regularly. Risk is moderate, and the consumer is willing to spend some time shopping. The thoroughness with which the decision process is used depends mostly on the prior experience of the consumer. Priority would probably be placed on evaluating known alternatives according to consumer desires and standards, although the information search is also important for some. Examples of goods and services requiring limited decision making are a second car, clothing, a vacation, and gifts.

Consumer characteristics have an impact on decision making, but the effect becomes less as risk decreases and experience increases. Income, the importance of the purchase, and motives play very strong roles in the uses of limited decision making.

This form of consumer decision making is most relevant to retailers such as department stores and specialty stores that cater to in-store shopping behavior and carry goods and services that customers have bought before. The internal environment and assortment of the store are very important. Sales personnel should be available to answer questions and to differentiate between brands or models.

Routine Decision Making

Routine decision making takes place when the consumer buys out of habit and skips steps in the purchase process. The person is willing to spend little or no time shopping, and the same brands are usually repurchased. In this category are items that are purchased regularly. These goods and services have little risk for the consumer because of experience. The key step for this type of decision making is problem awareness. When the consumer realizes that a good or service is needed, a repurchase is made. Information search, evaluation of alternatives, and postpurchase behavior are less likely than in limited or extended decision making. These steps will not be undertaken as long as the consumer is satisfied. Examples of goods and services usually requiring routine decision making are weekly groceries, newspapers, and haircuts.

Consumer characteristics have little impact on purchases in routine decision making. Problem awareness almost inevitably leads to a purchase.

This type of consumer decision making is most relevant to retailers such as supermarkets, dry cleaners, and fast-food restaurants. For them, these strategic elements are most critical: good location, long hours of operation, clear in-store displays, and, most important, product availability. Advertising should be reminder-oriented. The major task for sales personnel would be completing the transaction quickly and precisely.

Selected Retail Research Findings

Both the individual components of the consumer decision process and the level of decision making have been investigated in many different retail settings. Following are examples of the findings.

Problem Awareness

A study on apparel shoppers differentiated between consumers on the basis of problem-awareness style. One segment includes people whose awareness is usually activated when a product wears out or breaks down (recognition of shortage); the other consists of people interested in change or novelty (recognition of unfulfilled desire). The latter would agree with the statement, "It's not unusual for me to buy new clothes simply because I want something new." They are also more likely to consider themselves innovators, to like shopping, to be confident, to shop often, and to consult many information sources.[25]

Information Search

Research in this area has focused on the impact of social class, perceived risk, and consumer categories on the kind and amount of information sought.

One survey examined the impact of two factors (social class and perceived risk) on the information search behavior of working women. It found that lower-class women are much more likely to seek information from friends and relatives on products such as clothing, sheets, and towels than are upper-class women. For major items such as automobiles, upper-class women more frequently consult with consumer guidebooks than lower-class women. With regard to perceived risk, the findings were that working women are often apt to avoid any level of information search for low-risk products such as food. As perceived risk increases, they not only gather more information but also place greater emphasis on consumer guidebooks, friends, sales personnel, and relatives; newspaper ads become less important.[26]

A study of urban cosmetics shoppers discovered that the information sought depends on the consumer category:

❑ A special shopper (who looks for discounts) emphasizes samples, print ads, and home-oriented magazines.

❑ A brand-loyal consumer relies on newspaper and magazine ads, and on salespeople. Information on competing brands is not sought.

❑ A store-loyal consumer seeks information from salespeople but not friends or neighbors. The brands carried by a store are important.

❑ A problem-solving consumer utilizes television, friends, and salespeople. All kinds of information are sought.

❑ A psychosocializing consumer relies on friends and neighbors and also looks at television and print ads.

❑ A name-conscious consumer is interested in well-known stores, uses print ads and salespeople, and looks to fashion, news, and business media.[27]

Evaluation of Alternatives

An important aspect in the consumer's evaluation of alternatives are the criteria set by that person. A study of the selection of food stores determined that consumers rate low prices, pleasant shopping experience/helpful personnel/good service, one-stop shopping, the clear marking of prices on individual items, and the variety of store brands and lower-priced products as the most important criteria. A comparison of supermarket shoppers and warehouse store shoppers reveals that the former are less interested in low prices and much more interested in the marking of prices on individual items and the variety of store brands.[28]

A survey of women beauty salon customers found that frequent patrons are most interested in the quality of work, cleanliness, flexibility in scheduling appointments, cost, and adherence to the schedule. On the other hand, less frequent patrons are most concerned about the quality of work, cost, operator's knowledge of style trends, cleanliness, and friendliness of the operator.[29]

In-Store Behavior

A consumer's in-store shopping behavior is affected by factors such as sales personnel, displays, and stockouts. Retailers need to develop their strategies to take these factors into account.

Studies on retail sales personnel show that customers react more favorably if salespeople are perceived as being like themselves. This is particularly true of the racial similarity of the customer and the salesperson.[30] As product complexity increases, consumers place greater emphasis on the salesperson's product expertise, empathy, trustworthiness, personal appearance, credibility, and professionalism.[31]

A study on in-store displays in supermarkets found that the value of these displays varies widely by product category. However, for all but one of the twelve products examined, in-store displays increased sales. In-store displays have the greatest impact for hand and body lotions, shampoo, salad dressings, canned fruit drinks, and trash bags. They are least effective for toilet tissue, carbonated beverages, headache remedies, heavy-duty detergents, and ready-to-eat cereals (all products that are extensively advertised).[32]

In-store behavior is also affected by stockouts of merchandise. One investigation determined that stockouts cause consumers to have a lower store image, less satisfaction with purchase behavior, and reduced purchase intentions for particular product categories. Sale shoppers are much less sensitive to stockouts than nonsale shoppers. Stockout behavior does vary by product category.[33]

Consumer Satisfaction/Dissatisfaction

Retailers are extremely interested in the causes of consumer satisfaction and dissatisfaction because they want to optimize their strategies. A study of department store consumers found that satisfaction with the shopping experience is most influenced by store salespersons, special store sales, the goods/services purchased at the store, the store environment, and the value–price relationships offered by the store.[34]

A study of electric food-mixer consumers discovered that shoppers usually select the brand providing the most information. Those consumers buying brands for which there is little information tend to be more dissatisfied with their purchases than those buying brands for which there is ample information. Consumers assume that undisclosed information is less favorable than that which is disclosed.[35]

According to a third study, there are several significant differences between complainers (those who have actively complained once or more during the past year) and noncomplainers. Complainers are more likely to be male, actively engage in comparison shopping, believe that many products break or go wrong soon after purchase, and feel that most companies do not handle complaints properly. Nonetheless, more complainers also believe that consumers are better treated by business today than in the past.[36]

Level of Consumer Decision Making

Three concepts have been investigated with regard to the level of consumer decision making involved: shopping and travel time, impulse purchases, and store loyalty.

When a consumer utilizes extended or limited decision making, he or she is more willing to spend time shopping and traveling to a retailer than if routine decision making is involved. The type of decision making used depends on the consumer segment, as these research findings indicate: Service-oriented bank customers spend more time selecting and driving to a bank than do convenience-oriented customers. The former are interested in securing the best interest and loan rates; the latter want to minimize the time involved and bank where they shop.[37] Television customers spend more time in the purchase process if they feel they "would obtain a better deal on this item by shopping around and comparing prices."[38] In supermarket shopping, females are more likely than males to make shopping lists, check supermarket ads, and look for coupons. Males make a lot of quick in-store decisions and usually spend more.[39] Apparel shoppers under time pressure place greater importance on store familiarity, immediate salesperson attention, and product assortment than those not under such pressure.[40]

In general, retailers need to emphasize a unique and broad product selection, good sales personnel, competitive prices, a pleasant shopping atmosphere, and goods/service guarantees to encourage consumers to spend more time in a store and to travel a greater distance to shop.[41] Consumers are apt to patronize nearby stores unless there are compelling reasons to do otherwise. **Mapping** is a good

At several of its traditional toy store locations, Toys "R" Us operates adjacent Kids "R" Us outlets. Kids "R" Us features all types of clothing, from baby apparel to items for older girls and boys. In this way, Toys "R" Us appeals to and satisfies the needs of its diverse target market.

Photos courtesy of Toys "R" Us.

Because of today's busy consumer lifestyles, many retailers are stressing convenience in their strategy mixes. They are making it easier for consumers to undertake purchase decisions and buy goods and services. Everything for the couple's dinner (shown above) — the precooked Cornish game hen, the fresh salad, the wine, and the floral arrangement — was purchased on the way home from work at a single Kroger food store. To attract people who are unable or unwilling to visit a regular Burger King restaurant facility, the company is experimenting with a new fleet of express vans, "Burger King mobile restaurants."

Photos courtesy of Kroger and Burger King.

technique for a retailer to use in evaluating the trading area of a store. With it, a firm determines the distances consumers are likely to travel to get to a store, the population density of the geographic area surrounding the store, and the travel patterns and times from various locations. Then a map is drawn showing these factors.

Impulse purchases occur when consumers purchase products and/or brands that they had not planned on buying before entering a store or reading a mail-order catalog. With impulse purchases, at least part of consumer decision making is influenced by the retailer. There are three kinds of impulse shopping:

❑ Completely unplanned—A consumer has no intention of making a purchase in a product category before he or she comes into contact with a retailer.

❑ Partially unplanned—A consumer intends to make a purchase in a product category but has not chosen a brand before he or she comes into contact with a retailer.

❑ Unplanned substitution—A consumer intends to buy a specific brand of a product but changes his or her mind about the brand after coming into contact with a retailer.[42]

With partially unplanned and substitution kinds of impulse purchases, some decision making takes place before a person interacts with a retailer. In these cases, the consumer may be involved with any type of process (extended, limited, or routine). However, completely unplanned shopping is usually related to routine decision making or limited decision making; there is little or no time spent shopping, and the key step is problem awareness. Impulse purchases are more susceptible to in-store displays than preplanned purchases.[43]

According to a major study, in supermarkets, about 53 per cent of purchases are completely unplanned (on a given shopping trip); 10 per cent are partially unplanned; and 3 per cent are unplanned substitutions. Over 80 per cent of the purchases of these products involve some level of impulse behavior: candy, gum, snacks, pasta, cookies, crackers, and condiments.[44]

Other research on impulse shopping has yielded these findings: Discount-store customers are more likely to make impulse purchases, but department store customers are apt to make more costly impulse purchases; and situation variables (store environment and product- and trip-specific factors) have a greater impact on impulse purchases than customer characteristics.[45] Impulse purchases in a department store vary by product category. They are high for costume jewelry, bakery products, women's sportswear, curtains/draperies, women's/girls' footwear, and meals and snacks. They are much lower for women's lingerie, cosmetics and toiletries, men's clothing, and books and stationery.[46]

When **store loyalty** exists, a consumer regularly patronizes a retailer that he or she knows, likes, and trusts. Such loyalty enables a person to reduce decision making because he or she does not have to invest time in learning about and choosing the retailer from which to make purchases.

Research shows that store-loyal consumers tend to be time-conscious, to use entertainment media, to enjoy shopping locally, to be fashion leaders, not to rely on credit, and not to be engaged in outshopping.[47] Retailers can plan by defining the customers whose loyalty is sought, determining the benefits desired by these people, and formulating an appropriate strategy.[48] In a service setting, such as an automobile repair shop, customer satisfaction with service quality often leads to store loyalty; price has little bearing on decisions.[49]

SUMMARY

In order to properly develop and apply a strategy, a retailer must identify and understand its customers. This involves determining which type of target market to reach, identifying the characteristics and needs of the chosen target market, and understanding how consumers make decisions.

Consumer characteristics and needs can be identified by studying demographic and life-style factors. Demographics are easily identifiable and measurable population statistics; life-styles are the ways in which consumers live and spend time and money.

Consumers can be described in terms of these demographic factors: population size, number of households, place of residence, mobility, gender, employment status, age, occupation, ethnic/racial background, marital and family status, education level, income, and physical traits. This chapter presents a demographic overview of the United States, based on these factors, and relates demographics to the retailer's identification of its target market.

Consumer life-styles are comprised of social and psychological elements and are greatly affected by demographics. Social factors include culture, social class, reference groups, performance, the family life cycle, and time utilization. Psychological factors include personality, class consciousness, attitudes, perceived risk, and the importance of the purchase. As with demographics, a retailer can generate a life-style profile of its target market by analyzing these concepts.

When a retailer gears its strategy toward satisfying consumer needs, that retailer is appealing to their motives—the reasons for their behavior. The better a company addresses the needs of its customers, the more likely they are to make a purchase.

Retailers also require some knowledge of consumer behavior, the process whereby individuals decide whether, what, when, where, how, and from whom to purchase goods and services. The consumer decision process has six basic steps: stimulus, problem awareness, information search, evaluation of alternatives, purchase, and postpurchase behavior. The process is influenced by a person's background and traits.

A stimulus may be a social or commercial cue or a physical drive meant to motivate a person to act. At problem awareness, the consumer not only has been aroused by a stimulus but further recognizes that the good or service under consideration may solve a problem of shortage or unfulfilled desire. Next, an information search determines the available alternatives and the characteristics of each. Then, the alternatives are evaluated and ranked. During the purchase act, a consumer considers the place of purchase, the terms, and availability. After a purchase is made, there may be postpurchase behavior in the form of additional purchases or re-evaluation. The consumer may have cognitive dissonance if there is doubt that the correct decision has been made.

Every time a consumer makes a purchase, he or she uses a form of the decision process. However, the process may be used subconsciously, and it is affected by the consumer's characteristics. Extended decision making occurs when a person makes full use of the six steps in the decision process. In limited decision making, each of the steps in the process is used, but not in great depth. Routine decision making takes place when a person buys out of habit and skips steps in the purchase process.

Retail research findings provide insights into various aspects of consumer demographics, life-styles, and decision making, such as shopper profiles, in-home shopping, outshopping, information search, impulse purchases, and store loyalty.

QUESTIONS FOR DISCUSSION

1. Comment on this statement: "Retailers have long depended on their ability to size up their customers when they walk in the door. Today you need a more systematic way to understand your customers."
2. Contrast the mass-market approach used by many supermarkets with the market-segment approach used by gourmet butcher shops. How could a retailer combine these two approaches?
3. Describe how a national clothing store chain could use the demographic information presented in the chapter.
4. Develop demographic profiles for two different market segments to which a restaurant could appeal.
5. Why is the family life cycle a useful concept for drugstores?
6. Explain how a retailer selling do-it-yourself bookcases (with precut wood) could reduce the six types of perceived risk.

7. Distinguish between in-home shopping and out-shopping. In each case, what should be the strategic emphasis of retailers?
8. What couldd a retailer learn from studying the consumer decision process?
9. Describe how the consumer decision process would operate for the following purchases:
    a. A new magazine
    b. Tickets to a movie
    c. A used car
    d. A microwave oven
10. For each of the items cited in Question 9, which elements of the decision process are most important to retailers? Develop appropriate strategies.
11. What criteria could a consumer use in deciding which hardware store to patronize? How would these criteria differ by market segment?
12. Why should a real-estate broker care whether or not its customers have cognitive dissonance, since the seller moves after the transaction and the buyer will not be in the market for another house again until a great many years have elapsed?
13. Differentiate among the three types of impulse purchases. Give an example of each.
14. How does store loyalty benefit both the retailer and the consumer?

NOTES

1. Betsy Morris, "As a Favored Pastime, Shopping Ranks High with Most Americans," *Wall Street Journal* (July 30, 1987), pp. 1, 13; and Ellen Graham, "The Pleasure Dome," *Wall Street Journal* (May 13, 1988), p. 5R.

2. Marvin Nesbit and Arthur Weinstein, "How to Size Up Your Customers," *American Demographics* (July 1986), p. 34.

3. The data presented in this section are all from the U.S. Bureau of the Census, *Current Population Reports*.

4. See, for example, Patrick E. Murphy and William A. Staples, "A Modernized Family Life Cycle," *Journal of Consumer Research*, Vol. 6 (June 1979), pp. 12–22; and James M. Sinkula, "A Look at Some Shopping Orientations in Single Parent Households," in Russell W. Belk et al. (Editors), *1984 AMA Educators' Proceedings* (Chicago: American Marketing Association, 1984), pp. 22–25.

5. Leon G. Schiffman and Leslie Lazar Kanuk, *Consumer Behavior*, Third Edition (Englewood Cliffs, N.J.: Prentice-Hall, 1987), pp. 214–215.

6. Jack A. Lesser and Marie Adele Hughes, "The Generalizability of Psychographic Market Segments Across Geographic Locations," *Journal of Marketing*, Vol. 50 (January 1986), pp. 18–27; and Jack A. Lesser and Marie Adele Hughes, "Towards a Typology of Shoppers," *Business Horizons*, Vol. 29 (November–December 1986), pp. 56–62.

7. Jon M. Hawes, David E. Jordan, Jr., and James R. Lumpkin, "An Exploratory Study of the Mall-Prone Shopper," in John Summey et al. (Editors), *Marketing: Theories and Concepts for an Era of Change* (Carbondale, Ill.: Southern Marketing Association, 1983), pp. 135–138.

8. Melvin R. Crask and Fred D. Reynolds, "An Indepth Profile of the Department Store Shopper," *Journal of Retailing*, Vol. 54 (Summer 1978), pp. 23–32.

9. Jonathan Gutman and Michael K. Mills, "Fashion Life Style, Self-Concept, Shopping Orientation, and Store Patronage: An Integrative Analysis," *Journal of Retailing*, Vol. 58 (Summer 1982), pp. 64–86.

10. Robert H. Williams, John J. Painter, and Herbert R. Nicholas, "A Policy-Oriented Typology of Grocery Shoppers," *Journal of Retailing*, Vol. 54 (Spring 1978), pp. 27–42.

11. Peter L. Gillett, "A Profile of In-Home Shoppers," *Journal of Marketing*, Vol. 34 (July 1970), pp. 40–45; and Peter L. Gillett, "In-Home Shoppers—An Overview," *Journal of Marketing*, Vol. 40 (October 1976), pp, 81–88.

12. Fred D. Reynolds, "An Analysis of Catalog Buying Behavior," *Journal of Marketing*, Vol. 38 (July 1974), pp. 47–51.

13. Jean C. Darian, "In-Home Shopping: Are There Consumer Segments?" *Journal of Retailing*, Vol. 63 (Summer 1987), pp. 163–186.

14. Shirley Mitchell, "Eager Marketers May Overlook Consumers Not So Eager for 'Shopless Shopping,'" *Marketing News* (December 12, 1980), p. 20.

15. Subhash Sharma, William O. Bearden, and Jesse E. Teel, "Differential Effects of In-Home Shopping Methods," *Journal of Retailing*, Vol. 59 (Winter 1983), pp. 29–51.

16. A. Coskun Samli and Ernest B. Uhr, "The Outshopping Spectrum: Key for Analyzing Intermarket Leakages," *Journal of Retailing*, Vol. 50 (Summer 1974), pp. 70–78 ff.

17. Fred D. Reynolds and William R. Darden, "Intermarket Patronage: A Psychographic Study of Consumer Outshoppers," *Journal of Marketing*, Vol. 36 (October 1972), pp. 50–54; N. G. Papadopoulos, "Consumer Outshopping Research: Review and Extension," *Journal of Retailing*, Vol. 56 (Winter 1980), pp. 41–58; and James R. Lumpkin, Jon M. Hawes, and William R. Darden, "Shopping Patterns of the Rural Consumer: Exploring the Relationship Between Shopping Orientations and Outshopping," *Journal of Business Research*, Vol. 14 (1986), pp. 63–81.

18. A. Coskun Samli, Glen Riecken, and Ugur Yavas, "Intermarket Shopping Behavior and the Small Community: Problems and Prospects of a Widespread Phenomenon," *Journal of the Academy of Marketing Science*, Vol. 11 (Winter 1983), pp. 1–14; and R. Eric Reidenbach, M. Bixby Cooper, and Mary Carolyn Harrison, "A Factor Analytic Comparison of Outshopping Behavior in Larger Re-

tail Trade Areas," *Journal of the Academy of Marketing Science*, Vol. 12 (Spring 1984), pp. 145–158.

19. Kenneth R. Evans and Richard F. Beltramini, "An Integrative Assessment of Consumers of Generic Products: Retail Marketing Strategy Considerations," in Patrick E. Murphy et al. (Editors), *1983 AMA Educators' Proceedings* (Chicago: American Marketing Association, 1983), pp. 257–261; Martha R. McEnally and Jon M. Hawes, "The Market for Generic Brand Grocery Products: A Review and Extension," *Journal of Marketing*, Vol. 48 (Winter 1984), pp. 75–83; and Ken Kono, "Psychographic Profile of Generics Buyers," in Patrick E. Murphy et al. (Editors), *1983 AMA Educators' Proceedings* (Chicago: American Marketing Association, 1983), pp. 11–15.

20. James R. Lumpkin, Barnett A. Greenberg, and Jac L. Goldstucker, "Marketplace Needs of the Elderly," *Journal of Retailing*, Vol. 61 (Summer 1985), pp. 75–105.

21. Susan Caminiti, "Jewelers Woo the Working Woman," *Fortune* (June 8, 1987), pp. 71–73.

22. Russell Mitchell and Kevin Kelly, "WaldenBooks Tries Hooking Young Bookworms," *Business Week* (May 11, 1987), p. 48.

23. Raymond Serafin, "Domino's Plans Hispanic Push," *Advertising Age* (June 15, 1987), p. 29; Julie Ritzer, "Chains Reach Out to Hispanic Consumers," *Chain Store Age Executive* (October 1986), pp. 52–56; and Michael Sansolo, "Are You Speaking Their Language?" *Progressive Grocer* (February 1986), pp. 20–28.

24. C. Glenn Walters, *Consumer Behavior: Theory and Practice*, Third Edition (Homewood, Ill.: Richard D. Irwin, 1978), p. 7.

25. Gordon C. Bruner II, "Problem Recognition Styles and Search Patterns: An Empirical Investigation," *Journal of Retailing*, Vol. 62 (Fall 1986), pp. 281–297.

26. Paul Hugstadt, James W. Taylor, and Grady D. Bruce, "The Effects of Social Class and Perceived Risk on Consumer Information Search," *Journal of Consumer Marketing*, Vol. 4 (Spring 1987), pp. 41–45.

27. George P. Moschis, "Shopping Orientations and Consumer Use of Information," *Journal of Retailing*, Vol. 52 (Summer 1976), pp. 61–70 ff. See also, Ralph W. Jackson and Jeffrey K. Sager, "An Inventory of Shopper Typologies: Research Directions and Strategic Implications," in John C. Crawford and James R. Lumpkin (Editors), *1983 Proceedings of the Southwestern Marketing Association*, pp. 206–209.

28. "What's Important in Choosing a Store," *Progressive Grocer* (October 1983), pp. 36–37, 52.

29. Hazel F. Ezell and Phillip J. Ward, "Differentiating Between Frequent and Less-Frequent Patrons of Beauty Salons: A Focus on Working Women," in John Summey et al. (Editors). *Marketing: Theories and Concepts for an Era of Change* (Carbondale, Ill.: Southern Marketing Association, 1983), pp. 68–71.

30. Ishmael P. Akaah, "Dyadic Similarity and Its Influence on Customer Preferences: An Experimental Study," in Richard P. Bagozzi et al. (Editors), *Marketing in the 80's* (Chicago: American Marketing Association, 1980), pp. 114–117.

31. Ronald E. Michaels, "Differences in Customer Expectations Concerning Salesperson Characteristics Across

Products of Varying Complexity," in Kenneth Bernhardt et al. (Editors), *The Changing Marketing Environment: New Theories and Applications* (Chicago: American Marketing Association, 1981), pp. 131–134.

32. "Display Effectiveness: An Evaluation," *Nielsen Researcher* (Number 2, 1983), pp. 2–8.

33. Paul H. Zinzer and Jack A. Lesser, "An Empirical Evaluation of the Role of Stock-Out on Shopper Patronage Processes," in Richard P. Bagozzi et al. (Editors), *Marketing in the 80's*, (Chicago: American Marketing Association, 1980), pp. 221–224.

34. Robert A. Westbrook, "Sources of Consumer Satisfaction with Retail Outlets," *Journal of Retailing*, Vol. 57 (Fall 1981), pp. 68–85.

35. W. E. Patton III, "Brand Choice and Varying Quantity of Information," *Journal of Business Research*, Vol. 12 (1984), pp. 75–85.

36. Mel S. Moyer, "Characteristics of Consumer Complainants: Implications for Marketing and Public Policy," *Journal of Public Policy and Marketing*, Vol. 3 (1984), pp. 67–84.

37. W. Thomas Anderson, Jr., Eli P. Cox III, and David G. Fulcher, "Bank Selection Decisions and Market Segmentation," *Journal of Marketing*, Vol. 40 (January 1976), pp. 40–45.

38. Sharon E. Beatty and Scott M. Smith, "External Search Effort: An Investigation Across Several Product Categories," *Journal of Consumer Research*, Vol. 14 (June 1987), pp. 83–95.

39. Mary Johnson, "Consumer Watch: Cooking, Cleaning, Shopping—The Manly Things to Do," *Progressive Grocer* (July 1983), p. 19.

40. Bruce E. Mattison, "Situational Influences on Store Choice," *Journal of Retailing*, Vol. 58 (Fall 1982), pp. 46–58.

41. "Keying in on Convenience," *Chain Store Age Executive* (February 1986), pp. 11–15.

42. Judann Dagnoli, "Impulse Governs Shoppers," *Advertising Age* (October 5, 1987), p. 93.

43. See Cathy J. Cobb and Wayne D. Hoyer, "Planned Versus Impulse Purchase Behavior," *Journal of Retailing*, Vol. 62 (Winter 1986), pp. 384–409.

44. Dagnoli, "Impulse Governs Shoppers," p. 93.

45. V. Kanti Prasad, "Unplanned Buying in Two Retail Settings," *Journal of Retailing*, Vol. 51 (Fall 1975), pp. 3–12.

46. Danny H. Bellenger, Dan H. Robertson, and Elizabeth C. Hirschman, "Impulse Buying Varies by Product," *Journal of Advertising Research*, Vol. 18 (December 1978), pp. 15–18.

47. Fred D. Reynolds, William R. Darden, and Warren S. Martin, "Developing an Image of the Store-Loyal Customer," *Journal of Retailing*, Vol. 50 (Winter 1974–75), pp. 73–84.

48. Kenneth E. Miller and Kent L. Granzin, "Simultaneous Loyalty and Benefit Segmentation of Retail Store Customers," *Journal of Retailing*, Vol. 55 (Spring 1979), pp. 47–60.

49. Gabriel J. Biehal, "Consumers' Prior Experiences and Perceptions in Auto Repair Choice," *Journal of Marketing*, Vol. 47 (Summer 1983), pp. 82–91.

Wawa: A Convenience Store Seeks to Broaden Its Customer Base*

Wawa is a convenience store chain with headquarters in Pennsylvania. It is a privately held company that had sales of about $360 million in 1986. Wawa operates convenience stores averaging 3,000 square feet in New Jersey, Pennsylvania, Delaware, Maryland, and Virginia.

Like many convenience store chains, Wawa knows that its traditional customers have been mostly 18- to 35-year-old males who are high school graduates with household incomes of $20,000 or more. It is actively seeking to expand business by attracting more women (particularly those who are working).

Wawa's interest in appealing to working women is due to two main factors: the large size of that market segment and the level of shopping convenience desired by working women. Already, well over half of all adult women in the United States are employed, and this figure is expected to rise in the future. This is important for convenience stores because working women are likely to do less cooking at home and to purchase prepared foods. Wawa feels its offerings are very appealing to working women. It provides convenient locations near homes, easy parking, short checkout lines, and a good selection of staple grocery products and snack foods. In general, the convenience store industry welcomes the opportunity to serve new market segments, since the average annual sales growth for a typical outlet has been only 2–3 per cent over the last few years.

Unfortunately, convenience stores have had a negative image to many female shoppers. Stores have been perceived as dirty, high-priced, hangouts for kids in the evening, and selling foods that are unhealthy (too "junk-food" oriented). Many women view the core customer of the convenience store as a male blue-collar worker, and a lot of them would not shop at an outlet with that kind of image.

In a positive vein, industry experts feel that Wawa is doing an excellent job in trying to satisfy the needs of the working-woman market. In comparison to the typical convenience store chain, Wawa outlets carry a greater selection of groceries, meat, and produce (most convenience stores do not sell produce at all). The firm is very conscious of its image. As a result, Wawa does not sell beer, cigarettes are placed behind smoked-glass panels, and it has a lavish assortment of deli products. Following are some of the other tactics used by Wawa to attract female consumers.

It aims to get shoppers in and out of a store quickly. Therefore, outlets have no aisle or countertop displays. While many convenience stores use these displays to increase impulse sales, Wawa realizes that working women want to complete their shopping quickly. It has also separated the checkout area from the sandwich/deli area. This is more costly from a labor perspective, but it means that a consumer wanting to pay for a purchase does not have to wait until a prior customer's sandwich is prepared. Over 60 per cent of Wawa's advertising stresses that consumers can find what they need at Wawa and that they can get out of a store fast.

Wawa also tries to communicate this message to potential women customers: "Studies show that in our stores we have over 85 per cent of what is available in the average supermarket, and approximately 70 per cent of this is selling for comparable prices. Sure, the consumer goes to a supermarket to do her weekly shopping; but, during the week, she can still pick up what she needs fresh."

Products that appeal to working women have been added. There is now a greater emphasis on poultry in the deli area, lower-sodium foods, and foods lower in fat content. In addition, single-serving fruit juices are stocked. Wawa developed Lite Bite salads in 1985; this was its first product directly targeted to the working woman. The salads are made in the store and prepared from Wawa's own produce. Although consumers were originally skeptical about a salad that had been prepackaged (they assumed it had been made several days before, even though it had been made the same day), the product has done well since being advertised on television.

Because of Wawa's efforts, women are changing their attitudes toward convenience stores. In 1985, a sample of females was asked by Wawa researchers, "When you need

*The material in this case is drawn from "Wawa Sets Sites on Female Market Segment," *Chain Store Age Executive* (July 1987), pp. 18–22; and Jeremy Schlosberg, "The Demographics of Convenience," *American Demographics* (October 1986), pp. 36–42.

just a few things, where do you prefer to shop?" Of the respondents, 54.4 per cent said that they preferred a supermarket, and 42.9 per cent preferred a convenience store. When Wawa repeated the study in 1986, 41.3 per cent of the female respondents said that they preferred supermarkets, and 55.2 per cent preferred a convenience store.

QUESTIONS

1. Why do you think that the traditional convenience store customer has been an 18- to 35-year-old male?
2. What are the pros and cons of Wawa's emphasis on working-women customers?
3. Which other market segments (besides 18- to 35-year-old males and working women) should Wawa consider trying to reach? For each segment, what tactics should Wawa employ to attract consumer interest?
4. Relate the consumer decision process to convenience store purchases. What are the implications for Wawa?

Case 2 — Peters' Antiques: Regaining Lost Customers

Warren Peters has owned and operated an antique business in southern Florida for twelve years. Until recently, Warren has been quite successful. In 1986, sales totaled $300,000, and profits were $30,000 (Peters and his wife also drew salaries of $15,000 each). However, annual sales have fallen to $280,000, despite increases in inventory costs. As a result, no profits are currently being earned.

When Peters opened 12 years ago, he carried only antique clocks and furniture. As business improved, he added rifles, china, silverware, millinery, and art. His shop is located on a shopping strip near a major highway. Tourists and local residents alike patronize the store, which is noted for its low prices. The store window and interior displays are all handwritten, -drawn, or -painted and provide an authentic atmosphere. Peters, his wife, and two college salespeople dress as American pioneers. They alternate between pilgrim and frontier costumes.

Most of Peters' antiques are pre-Civil War. Few are dated after World War I. There is a special display of a pilgrim's and a frontiersman's wardrobe (not for sale) to attract tourists. Free apple cider is ladled out to thirsty browsers.

The average prices of the antiques are between $150 and $250. Items are available for as little as $2 (rifle shell) and as much as $8,000 (complete set of china). Peters never runs a sale. Rather, uniqueness and value are stressed.

The best-selling product is a pot-bellied stove. At least four a week are sold, usually to tourists. For local patrons, rifles are the main attraction, and Peters has an extensive collection. Antique clocks are also popular for both the tourists and the local customers.

Peters advertises in local newspapers and national magazines. He offers low prices, prompt delivery, and a willingness to try to find any object requested by a sincere customer. Antiques have been ordered from as far away as the Philippines and Japan. Peters and his wife have been all over the world searching for antiques, although they have cut down their shopping trips in recent years.

Over the years, the environment around Peters has changed, and he has altered his retailing strategy. Twelve years ago, there were no competitors in the area. Today three other antique dealers exist. Each is larger than Peters, doing an estimated annual business of $500,000 to $750,000.

Originally 70 per cent of Peters' sales were to local people. Only 30 per cent were to tourists. Now 80 per cent of the sales are to tourists and 20 per cent to local customers. This change has not occurred for the other antique dealers. A profile of local patrons and tourists is shown in Table 1.

Often customers go to Peters' Antiques, look inside, and leave without making a purchase. Shopper comments indicate why:

❑ Too many items are tourist traps, not good buys.

❑ Displays and attire of sales personnel are gimmick-oriented and do not provide information.
❑ The assortment of products is wide but shallow.
❑ Credit transactions are not allowed; payments must be made in cash or by check. Peters does allow a layaway plan.
❑ No returns are allowed.
❑ Despite low-price claims, competitors' prices are not higher.
❑ The store is crowded. There is little room for walking around.
❑ Peters has not joined the local chapter of antique dealers; this has hurt his image.
❑ College sales personnel can quote prices but are weak on the history of the antiques. And some customers are uncomfortable bargaining with them.
❑ Too many items are foreign, not American.
❑ Delivery charges are added to the purchase price.
❑ Few magazines on antiques are carried.

Peters is distressed over the nonpurchases and the loss of customers, especially because he has instituted many consumer-oriented strategies. The store displays and the sales personnel's attire have received favorable newspaper publicity. The free cider has drawn many compliments. Layaway purchases, increased store hours, and wider product lines are responses to consumer demand. Delivery charges and the no-return policy have been caused by tremendous increases in inventory and labor costs.

Warren Peters is concerned. His business is declining while competitors do well.

TABLE 1
Description of Antique Customers

Characteristic	Local Patron	Tourist
Age	Average is 52.	Average is 42.
Education	Average is 12.7 years.	Average is 14.6 years.
Family size	Average is 3.	Average is 4.
Family income	Average is $22,000 per year.	Average is $33,000 per year.
Occupation	Average is retired or a white-collar worker.	Average is a white-collar worker.
Possessions	Average owns an apartment, a television, and a washer and dryer.	Average owns a home, a VCR, a good 35mm camera, and a stereo.
Item purchased	Rifle, furniture	Pot-bellied stove, silverware.
Average dollar purchase	$125.	$200.

QUESTIONS

1. Comment on the demographic profiles of the antique customers shown in Table 1. What other information about his customers would be useful to Peters?

2. How can Peters reduce his customers' perceived risk? Be sure to comment on each type of perceived risk in your answer.

3. Does Peters understand the consumer decision process for antiques? Explain your answer.

4. Make several suggestions for Peters to improve his business.

Chapter 6

Marketing Research in Retailing

❑ **Chapter Objectives** ❑

1 To show why retailers should systematically collect and analyze information when developing and modifying their strategies

2 To describe the marketing research process: problem definition, secondary data search, generating primary data (if needed), data analysis, recommendations, and implementing findings

3 To discuss the characteristics and types of secondary data and primary data

4 To examine the role of the retail information system, its components, and the recent advances in such systems

In researching their customers, companies realize that what people say is not necessarily what they actually believe or do. When asked about their attitudes or behavior, respondents may be unable to answer, may not want to provide certain information, may "shade" the truth, or may have a poor memory.

Sometimes, "what people report isn't even close to reality. People tend to recall familiar brands or stores, not what they actually looked at or bought." For this reason, observing consumers in action is being used more frequently as a supplement to surveys in conducting marketing research.

As an illustration, since so many items are sold in a typical store (such as 8,000 to 12,000 items in a supermarket), retailers are quite interested in learning which product package designs, shapes, and colors will catch the consumer's eye, encour-

age impulse purchases, and make in-store displays more attractive. Surveying consumers about packaging and store displays may not yield sufficient information; observation may be a more appropriate way to determine the attractiveness of different product packages and store displays.

One mechanical technique for observing consumer responses to package design and store displays uses an eye-tracking machine. With such a technique, a consumer is shown a color slide depicting a store shelf with many packages on it. Then, "an invisible beam of infrared light is bounced off the consumer's corneas and received by a device that indicates on the slide where the eyes are focused." In this way, the actual effectiveness of a package and a display may be determined.

Critics of eye-tracking techniques, such as the

one just described, point out that are there limitations to observation, just as there are with surveys: consumer attitudes are not obtained, the situation may be artificial ("It's easy to make a package stand out on an eye-tracking test by using a loud, obtrusive color palette that isn't appropriate for that product. A green bread package, for instance, might be distinctive, but it could suggest mold"), and store atmosphere is not taken into consideration.[1]

That is why retailers should consider combining two or more different research techniques in order to gather a full range of information, particularly if crucial strategic decisions on the part of the firm are involved.

Overview

Marketing research in retailing is the systematic collection and analysis of information relating to any part of a retailing strategy. Whether one is developing a new strategy or modifying an existing one, marketing research can be valuable.

Various aspects of retailing can be researched, such as store location, store management and operations, goods and service offerings, pricing, and store image and promotion. Examples of research in these and other areas are provided throughout the chapter.

Research is useful because it reduces a retailer's risk. Without research, risk is higher, because an incorrect strategy decision may occur based on little information or on information gathered nonsystematically. The extent of research activity should, to a large degree, be determined by the level of risk involved in a decision. For instance, there is considerable risk for a department store considering a new branch-store location. There is much less risk when a retailer is deciding whether a store should carry a new line of slacks. For the branch-store location problem, several thousand dollars for research and many months of study may be necessary. In the case of ordering new slacks, limited research is probably sufficient.

Marketing research should be a continuous process, yielding information for planning and control. Unless research is done on a continuous basis, it often becomes concerned with day-to-day problems (crises) as opposed to the long-range strategy-planning needs of the retailer.

Retail Strategies Based on Nonsystematic Research

Retailers are often tempted to rely on nonsystematic measures in developing and evaluating strategies because of time constraints, cost constraints, or lack of research capabilities. Examples of nonsystematic attempts at research include the following:

❑ The use of intuition (e.g., "My gut reaction is to order 100 dozen quartz watches and sell them for $50 each as Christmas gifts.")

❑ A continuation of what was done before (e.g., "I have never sold jewelry on credit. Why should I do so now?")

❑ The copying of a successful competitor's strategy (e.g., "Bloomingdale's has had great success with the sale of gourmet foods. We should stock and promote these products.")

❑ The development of a strategy from speaking to a few individuals about their perceptions (e.g., "My friends Bill and Mary feel that my prices are too high. I ought to lower them to improve sales and profits.")

❑ The assumption that past trends will continue into the future (e.g., "The wholesale prices of compact disc players have fallen off 25 per cent in the last year. I will wait another six months to make a purchase and get a really low price. I can then underprice my competitors, who are buying now.")

177

In this section, several decisions made by retailers who have not used systematic research are described, and their strategic errors are analyzed.

A movie theater charges $5 for tickets throughout the entire week. The manager cannot understand why attendance is poor during weekday afternoons. The theater manager thinks that because all patrons are seeing the same movie, the prices should be the same for a Monday matinee as for a Saturday evening show. However, a research study would indicate that people prefer Saturday evening performances and would pay more to see a movie at this time. Weekday customers have to be attracted, and a lower price is one means of doing so.

A toy store orders conservatively for the holiday season because the previous year's sales were poor. The store sells out a month before the peak of the season, and additional merchandise cannot be delivered to the store in time for holiday sale. The toy store uses a technique familiar to many companies: incremental budgeting. Under this policy, a percentage is added or subtracted from the previous year's budget to arrive at the present year's budget. In this instance, the store owner assumed that the previous year's poor sales would occur again. However, a survey of consumers would have revealed a new degree of optimism and an increased desire to give gifts. A research-based retailer would have planned its inventory accordingly.

A chain bookstore decides to open a new branch unit seventy miles away from its closest store. The decision is based on the growing population in the area and the current absence of an outlet by the chain. After a year, the new store is attaining only 40 per cent of its expected business. A subsequent study by the chain reveals that the store name (and image) was relatively unknown in the area and that the choice of advertising media was incorrect. In planning the new branch, these two important factors were not researched.

A mail-order retailer is doing well selling small appliances, portable televisions, and moderately priced cameras. However, recent expansion into furniture and stereo systems has yielded poor results. This retailer has developed a good reputation in its traditional product lines and has attracted loyal customers. It feels that the time is ripe for expansion into other product lines to capitalize on its name and customer goodwill. But the retailer has not conducted research on the consumer behavior of mail-order customers. People will buy standard, branded merchandise through the mail; they will not buy most furniture and stereos (both of which must be seen and handled) via the mail. These items must be experienced or tried out before a purchase.

A florist cuts the price of two-day-old flowers from $3.00 to $0.75. They don't sell. The florist cuts the prices of older flowers because they have a short life expectancy. It assumes that bargain-hunting consumers will buy these flowers as gifts or for floral arrangements. What the florist does not realize (because of no research) is that consumers perceive the older flowers to be of inferior quality, color, and smell. The reduced price is actually too low and turns off customers!

The conclusion to be drawn from these examples is that nonsystematic means of collecting and/or analyzing data can cause a retailer to develop and/or implement an inappropriate strategy.

The Marketing Research Process

Marketing research in retailing involves a series of activities: defining the problem to be researched, examining secondary data (previously collected), generating primary data (if necessary), analyzing data, making recommendations, and implementing findings. It is not a single act. The use of this process will enable the retailer to collect and evaluate data systematically to better resolve strategy decisions.

Figure 6-1 outlines the research process. Note that each of the activities is conducted sequentially. For instance, secondary data cannot be examined until after the problem is defined. The dashed line around the primary data suggests

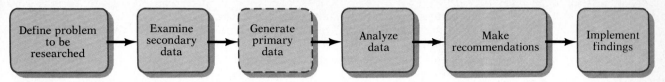

FIGURE 6-1
The Marketing Research Process in Retailing

that primary data need to be generated only when the secondary data search does not yield enough information to make a strategy decision. The components of the research project are described next.

Problem definition involves a clear statement of the topic to be examined. What information does the retailer want to obtain in order to make a decision? Without a clear understanding of the topic to be researched, potentially irrelevant and confusing data could be collected. Some examples of problem definition for a downtown shoe retailer are:

1. "Of three potential new store locations, which should we choose?"
2. "What store hours should we keep?"
3. "How can we improve the sales of our men's shoes?"
4. "Why is our competitor doing well? How can we draw customers away from that store?"

It is important to note from these examples that research problems differ in their nature. Whereas the first problem relates to evaluating three alternative locations and is fairly structured, the third problem is much less structured.

After the research problem has been defined, **secondary data** sources are examined. Secondary data are those that have already been gathered for purposes other than solving the problem currently under investigation. Secondary data may be internal (company records) or external (government reports, trade publications). Secondary data sources are described in the following section.

Primary data are those collected to solve the specific problem under investigation. This type of data may be developed through surveys, experiments, observations, and simulation. Primary data are discussed more fully later in the chapter.

By generating secondary and/or primary data, these kinds of information can be compiled for the shoe store problems defined previously:

Problem Definition	Information Needed to Solve Problem
1. Which store location?	1. Data on access to transportation, traffic, consumer profiles, rent, store size, and types of competition are collected from government reports, trade publications, and observation by the owner for each of the three potential store locations.
2. What store hours?	2. Local ordinances for store hours are reviewed, as are the hours of neighboring and competing stores. Consumer attitudes are determined.
3. How to improve sales of shoes?	3. Store sales records for the past five years by product category are gathered. A consumer survey in a nearby mall is conducted.
4. How to draw consumers away from a competitor's store?	4. Extensive information about the competitor's strategy is gathered through observation. Consumers leaving the competitor's store are questioned.

179

In some instances, primary data are collected; in others, secondary data are relied upon. Sometimes, both are used. Three points are noteworthy. First, the diversity of data collection (types and costs) is great. Second, only data that are relevant to the problem under investigation should be amassed. Third, primary data are usually acquired only if the secondary data search yields insufficient information (hence, the dashed box in Figure 6-1).

After the secondary and/or primary data are gathered, **data analysis** must be performed that relates the information to the defined problem. The alternative solutions should be clearly outlined. For example:

Problem Definition	Alternative Solutions
1. Which store location?	1. Each store location is ranked for all of the criteria (access to transportation, traffic, consumer profiles, rent, store size, and types of competition).
2. What store hours?	2. The advantages and disadvantages of different store hours are compared (in terms of increased sales and increased costs).
3. How to improve sales of shoes?	3. Alternative strategies to boost shoe sales are analyzed and ranked.
4. How to draw consumers away from a competitor's store?	4. The reasons for the competitor's success are studied, and possible reactions are listed.

Then the advantages and disadvantages of each alternative are enumerated. See Table 6-1.

At this point, **recommendations** are made. What strategy should the retailer use to best solve its problem? (From the alternatives, which is best?) Table 6-1 shows the recommendations for the problems discussed throughout this section.

Last, but not least in importance, is the **implementation** of the recommended strategy. If research is to replace intuition in developing and enacting a retail strategy, a retail manager must follow the recommendations of marketing research even if they appear to contradict his or her ideas.

Secondary Data

Advantages and Disadvantages

Secondary data (information previously gathered for other purposes) have several advantages over primary data. The assembly of data is inexpensive. Company records, trade journals, government publications, and so on are all inexpensive to use. No data-collection forms, interviewers, and tabulations are needed.

Secondary data can be collected quickly. Company or library records can be analyzed immediately, whereas the generation of primary data may take up to several months.

For many retailing problems, several sources of secondary data are available. These allow a company to receive many perspectives and large quantities of data. With a primary study, limited data and only one perspective are obtained.

A secondary source may possess information that the retailer would otherwise be unable to get. For example, government publications often have statistics that no private company could acquire on its own. Furthermore, the data contained in government literature may be more honest and accurate than those a private company could collect.

When secondary data are assembled by a source such as *Progressive Grocer*,

TABLE 6-1
Research-Based Recommendations

Problem	Alternative	Pros and Cons of Alternatives	Recommendation
1. Which store location?	Site A.	Best transportation, traffic, and consumer profiles. Highest rent. Smallest store space. Extensive competition.	Site A: the many advantages far outweigh the disadvantages.
	Site B.	Poorest transportation, traffic, and consumer profiles. Lowest rent. Largest store space. No competition.	
	Site C.	Intermediate on all criteria.	
2. What store hours?	9 A.M.–8 P.M.	Hours maintained by neighboring stores. Not early enough for customers. No legal violations.	7 A.M.–6 P.M.: satisfy customers and show results of informal survey to other merchants.
	7 A.M.–6 P.M.	Hours desired by customers. Violation of voluntary retail dealers' agreement. No legal violations.	
3. How to improve sales of shoes?	Increased assortment.	Will attract and satisfy many more customers. High costs. High level of inventory. Reduces turnover for many items.	Lower prices and add advertisements: additional customers offset higher costs and lower margins; combination best expands business.
	Drop some lines and specialize.	Will attract and satisfy a specific consumer market. Excludes many segments. Costs and inventory reduced.	
	Slightly reduce prices.	Unit sales increase. Markup and profit per item decline.	
	Advertise.	Will increase traffic and new customers. High costs.	
4. How to draw consumers away from a competitor's store?	Sharply reduce prices, increase inventories, add salespeople.	Similar to successful strategy of competitor. Will increase costs and appeal to a different consumer market (old customers may be lost). Imitation.	Modernize facilities and improve image: competitive advantages are retained and improved; poor strategy to imitate competitor and lose present customers.
	Modernize facilities and advertise high-quality image.	Maintains old customers and attracts new ones with a distinctive image. Expensive and time-consuming.	

A.C. Nielsen, *Business Week,* or the federal government, the results are believable. Each of these sources has a high level of credibility and a reputation for thoroughness.

Often a retailer may have only a rough idea of the topics that it wants to investigate. In this instance, a search of secondary data may help the firm to define the problem more specifically. In addition, background information about a problem can be gathered from secondary sources before the primary study is undertaken.

Although the use of secondary data has many advantages, there are several disadvantages. Available data may not suit the purposes of the current study because they have been collected for other purposes. As an illustration, the units of measurement may be different. A retailer normally needs local demographic and other types of information. However, neighborhood statistics are rarely found in secondary sources (which usually contain federal, state, and city statistics). Data may also be categorized in an unusable fashion. For example, a gasoline station owner would be interested in the number of local citizens having automobiles. He or she would want this information broken down by year, model, and mileage driven, so that he or she can stock parts. The motor vehicle bureau can provide statistics on the models but not the mileage driven.

Secondary data may be dated. Because the information has already been assembled for another purpose, it may have outlived its usefulness. The conclusions reached five or even two years ago may not be valid today. As an example, the *Census of Population* is conducted every ten years. The last one was done in 1980, and the statistics contained in this census are rapidly becoming outdated. In addition, there is often a long time delay between the completion of the census and the release of data.

The accuracy of secondary data must be evaluated. The retailer must determine whether the data have been compiled in an unbiased, objective manner. The objectives of the original study, the data collection techniques, and the method of analysis should each be examined for bias. Determination of bias is especially important when the research has been undertaken by a company that has a stake in the study's findings. The supporting evidence (raw data) should be read, as well as summary reports. In addition, some secondary data sources have low levels of accuracy.

The source of secondary data can be a disadvantage as well as an advantage. A partisan, profit-making company usually does not provide competitors with information that will hurt it. Generalities and omissions should be noted by the retailer. Also some sources are known for their poor data collection techniques, and these should be avoided. When conflicting data are found, it is important to distinguish among sources and select the one with the best reputation for accuracy. Conflicting results presented by equally accurate sources may lead a retailer into primary research (the collection of its own data).

Finally, the reliability of secondary data is not always known. Reliability is the ability to replicate a study and get the same outcome. In retailing, many research projects are not retested; therefore, the user of secondary data is hoping that the results from one narrow study are applicable to his or her problem.

A retailer that desires information to solve a problem has many criteria to consider when contemplating the use of secondary data. Low costs, speed, and access to materials are weighed against improper fit, out-of-date statistics, and accuracy of data.

Whether secondary data solve the retailer's problem or not, their low cost and immediate availability require that primary data not be collected until after a thorough search of secondary data. If secondary sources prove unsatisfactory or incomplete, then primary data should be collected.

In the following section, a variety of secondary data sources for retailers are detailed.

Sources

There are different types of secondary data. The major distinctions are between internal and external retail data. Internal secondary data are obtainable within the company. External secondary data must be collected from sources outside the firm.

Internal Secondary Data

Before spending time and money searching for external secondary data or primary data, the retailer should look at the information that is available inside the company. Table 6-2 shows some of the major sources of internal data.

At the beginning of the year, most retailers develop budgets for the next twelve months of the year. These budgets, based on sales forecasts, outline planned expenditures during the coming year. The retail budget and a store's performance in the attainment of budgetary goals (adherence to the outlined plan of expenditures) are good sources for secondary data.

Retailers often use sales figures as indicators of success. For many retailers, these figures are accurately and rapidly available through point-of-sale cash registers. By examining the sales of each store, department, item, and salesperson and comparing these sales with prior time periods, a retailer gets a feeling of growth or contraction. But this feeling, and an overdependence on sales data, may be misleading. Increased sales do not always lead to increased profits.

Budgets
Sales figures
Profit-and-loss statements
Customer billings
Inventory records
Prior company research reports
Written reports on company performance

To be valuable, sales data should be used in conjunction with profit-and-loss statistics.

A retailer's profit-and-loss statements reveal a great deal of information. If profit goals have been set, actual achievements can be measured against these goals. Trends in company success can be determined over time. Profits can be analyzed by store, department, item, and salesperson. A detailed breakdown of profits and losses can show strengths and weaknesses in retail operations and management and can lead to improvements.

Customer billings provide a host of information. A retailer is able to learn about inventory movement, sales made by different personnel, peak selling times, and sales volume. For credit customers, the retailer is able to examine sales by geographic area, outstanding debts, length of repayment time, types of purchases made, and demographic data. Company invoices show the retailer its own past purchase history and allow the retailer to evaluate this performance against budgetary or other goals.

Inventory records show the levels of merchandise carried by a retailer throughout the year and the movement of this merchandise. Knowledge of the lead time necessary to place and receive orders from suppliers and of the amounts of safety stock (excess merchandise kept on hand to prevent running out) held at different times during the year aid in inventory planning. These are valuable sources of secondary data.

If the retailer conducts market research, the research report should be retained for future use. When the report is used initially, it is primary data. However, later reference to the report is secondary in nature (because the report is no longer being employed for its "primary" purpose). A thorough report should have some validity in the future unless conditions change drastically, although the datedness of the report must be noted.

Written reports on company performance are another source of internal secondary data. The reports may be composed by management, buyers, sales personnel, stockroom workers, and so on. For example, the turnover of sales personnel and the responses of customers to in-store displays are the kinds of information available through written reports. With proper direction, all phases of retail management can be improved through formal report procedures.

External Secondary Data

After checking internal sources, a retailer should consult external secondary data sources if the available information is not sufficient for a decision to be made regarding the defined problem (topic). External secondary data sources are broken down into government and nongovernment categories.

In order to use either form of external secondary data properly, a retailer should be familiar with the available reference guides. A reference guide contains a listing of written materials on a subject (e.g., *Business Periodicals Index* lists important business references) or a wide range of subjects (e.g., *Monthly Catalog of United States Government Publications* lists all federal government publica-

TABLE 6-3
Selected Reference Guides to External Secondary Data

ABI/INFORM (data base). Covers 550 journals in business/management. In 300 core journals, all major articles are indexed and abstracted.

Business Index. Monthly. Covers 180 periodicals, including newspapers.

Business Periodicals Index. Monthly, except for July. Cumulations quarterly, semiannually, and annually. Subject index of approximately 120 U.S. and British periodicals.

Catalog of U.S. Census Publications. Monthly, with an annual cumulation.

Lorna M. Daniells, *Business Information Sources* (Boston: Baker Library, 1979); and "Note on Sources of External Marketing Data" (Boston: Harvard Business School, 1980), 9-580-107 (revised 1985).

Encyclopedia of Associations (Detroit: Gale Research Co., 1988).

Encyclopedia of Business Information Sources (Detroit: Gale Research Co., 1986).

Journal of Marketing. Quarterly. Provides an annotated bibliography arranged by subject.

Management Contents (data base). Indexes and abstracts articles in over 700 business/ management periodicals.

Measuring Markets: A Guide to the Use of Federal and State Statistical Data (Washington, D.C.: U.S. Industry and Trade Administration, 1979).

Monthly Catalog of United States Government Publications. Monthly, with subject index. Lists publications of all branches of government.

New York Times Index. Semimonthly, with subject index and annual cumulation.

Predicasts F&S Index. Weekly, with monthly, quarterly, and annual cumulations. Covers industries and companies.

Public Affairs Information Service Index. Weekly, with cumulations five times a year and annually. Index more than 1,000 periodicals.

Reader's Guide to Periodical Literature. Semimonthly and annual. Indexes over 125 publications.

Martha Farnsworth Riche, "Directory of Demographic Products and Services," *American Demographics* (July 1985), pp. 34–41.

Wall Street Journal Index. Monthly, with annual cumulation.

tions) for a specified time period. Listings within the guides are usually by subject or topic heading. Table 6-3 contains selected reference guides, chosen because of their importance to retailers. These guides include government and nongovernment sources and encompass thousands of publications. They are available in any business library or large library.

The government distributes a wide range of statistics and written materials. Table 6-4 shows some selected government publications. The items detailed in this table should be in any business library or medium-sized library. In their totality, these publications provide a wealth of information on retail trade, consumer profiles, transportation, and so on.

Government agencies, such as the Federal Trade Commission, also provide a variety of pamphlets and booklets on topics like franchising, unit pricing, deceptive advertising, and credit policies. The Small Business Administration helps smaller retailers, providing literature and managerial advice. The pamphlets or booklets are either distributed free of charge or sold for a nominal fee. The *Monthly Catalog of United States Government Publications* contains a listing of these materials.

Nongovernment secondary data come from a variety of sources, many of which are listed in reference guides. Four sources of nongovernment data are noted: regular periodicals; books, monographs, and other nonregular publications; other channel members; and commercial research houses. Table 6-5 contains a listing of these sources.

The regular periodicals are available in business libraries or via personal sub-

Census of Business, Retail Trade (Every five years ending in 2 and 7). Statistics for almost 100 store classifications by metropolitan region. Data include multiple ownership, employment, goods/service categories, and sales.

Census of Housing (Every ten years ending in 0). Statistics on types of structures, appliances, rent paid, race of occupants, size of dwelling, etc., by city block for larger cities.

Census of Population (Every ten years ending in 0). Population statistics by state, county, city, metropolitan area, and census tract (a highly urban area of 4,000 within a large city). Data include age, income, sex, education, job, etc.

Census of Service Industries (Every five years ending in 2 and 7). Similar to *Census of Business, Retail Trade* but covers 200 service industries. Data include form of organization, size, geographic area, and reports on specific service industries.

Consumer Expenditure Survey. Annual survey of consumer expenditures used in revising the consumer price index.

County and City Data Book (Washington, D.C.: Superintendent of Documents, Government Printing Office, 1982). Statistics on population, income, education, etc., for every city and county over 25,000.

Monthly Labor Review. Monthly data from the Bureau of Labor Statistics, including employment, salaries, consumer price index, wholesale price index, etc.

State and Metropolitan Area Data Book (Washington, D.C.: Superintendent of Documents, Government Printing Office, 1986). Statistics of the United States, each state, and each Metropolitan Statistical Area.

Statistical Abstract (Washington, D.C.: Superintendent of Documents, Government Printing Office, annual). The standard annual summary of U.S. statistics.

Survey of Current Business. Monthly, with weekly supplements. On all aspects of business, as reported by the Department of Commerce.

Other. Registration data (births, deaths, automobile registrations, etc.). Available through a variety of federal, state, and local agencies.

scriptions. Some of the periodicals are quite broad in scope *(Business Week, Fortune, Journal of Marketing)* and discuss a great number of different business topics. Other periodicals are more specialized in their coverage *(Chain Store Age, Journal of Retailing, Stores)* and deal only with topics of concern to retailers. Solutions to a retail problem may be found in both the broad and the narrow publications. However, it is important that readers of periodicals understand the differences in orientation and quality among various publications.

Regular periodicals contain articles on all aspects of retailing and provide insights for strategy development and implementation. Following are some examples of the kinds of information that may be found in this literature. These examples are intended to provide an overview of the diversity of information available and are not exhaustive:

❑ Store location—Articles have appeared on computer-based models for site selection, the drawing power of stores, the use of demographic reports in location analysis, store saturation, and pedestrian malls.[2]

❑ Operations—Articles have appeared on the use of strategic management techniques in retailing, cost control, innovative training techniques, personnel productivity, employee turnover, the attributes of good store managers, and shoplifting.[3]

❑ Merchandising—Articles have appeared on the attractiveness of different goods/service categories, criteria for selecting items, the proper product mix, judgment strategies of retail buyers, inventory management, and stockouts.[4]

TABLE 6-5
Selected Sources of External Secondary Data: Nongovernment

Regular Periodicals

Advertising Age. Weekly magazine of advertising, with applications to retailing.

Business Week. Weekly magazine, with articles on all phases of business.

Chain Store Age Executive. Monthly, catering to chain store information.

CSM Upscale Discounting. Monthly, on trends in catalog showrooms.

Dealerscope Merchandising. Monthly, with articles on appliance and electronics retailing.

Direct Marketing. Monthly, articles on direct marketing, direct mail, and promotion.

Discount Store News. Biweekly, with articles on discount store developments.

Drug Store News. Biweekly, with articles on current trends, health and beauty aids, productivity statistics.

Fortune. Semimonthly magazine, with articles on all phases of business.

Harvard Business Review. Bimonthly, with articles on all aspects of business.

Journal of the Academy of Marketing Science. Quarterly, developments in all areas of marketing.

Journal of Advertising Research. Bimonthly, includes articles on advertising in retailing.

Journal of Marketing. Quarterly, developments in all areas of marketing.

Journal of Marketing Research. Quarterly, research developments in all areas of marketing.

Journal of Retailing. Quarterly, developments in all aspects of retailing.

Marketing News. Biweekly, covers all aspects of marketing.

Progressive Grocer. Monthly, emphasis on trends in food retailing.

Restaurant Business. Eighteen times per year, developments in restaurant field.

Retail Control. Monthly, with focus on credit, store security, and inventory management.

Sales & Marketing Management. Monthly, of interest to retailers: annual survey of buying power by county (based on income, retail sales, and population in each county).

Stores. Monthly, with emphasis on department stores, specialty stores, and off-price retailing.

Supermarket Business. Monthly, with articles on supermarket retailing.

Supermarket News. Weekly, includes articles on market share, changes in markets, financial data on supermarket industry.

Wall Street Journal. Five times per week, articles on all aspects of business.

Women's Wear Daily. Five times per week, emphasis on fashion information.

Other periodicals. Regular publications for retailers in areas such as hardware, supermarket, franchising, furniture, and department stores.

❑ Pricing—Articles have appeared on the importance of retail prices to consumers, the implications of the Robinson-Patman Act, price differentials between department stores and off-price stores, the impact of sale prices, and price wars.[5]

❑ Store image and promotion—Articles have appeared on how store image is developed, point-of-sale displays, promotion mix planning, the role of advertising, cooperative advertising, salesperson performance, and coupon redemption.[6]

❑ Evaluating the strategy—Articles have appeared on company mergers, overall efficiency, different measures of success, advertising effectiveness, sales and profits by product category, and the redesign of strategies.[7]

A number of organizations publish books, monographs, and other nonregular literature on retailing. Some are traditional publishing companies (such as Macmillan) that concentrate on textbooks and practitioner-oriented books. Others, such as the organizations listed in Table 6-5, have distinct goals in publishing their materials.

One type of organization (such as the American Management Association and the American Marketing Association) distributes information in the hope of increasing the awareness and level of knowledge of its readers with regard to various topics. A second type (such as the Better Business Bureau and the Cham-

TABLE 6-5
(Continued)

187

Marketing Research in
Retailing

Books, Monographs, and Other Nonregular Publications*

The following publish a variety of information pertaining to retailing:

Academy of Marketing Science.
American Collegiate Retailing Association.
American Management Association.
American Marketing Association.
Better Business Bureau.
Chamber of Commerce.
Conference Board.
Direct Marketing Association.
Food Marketing Institute.
International Association of Chain Stores.
International Council of Shopping Centers.
International Franchise Association.
International Mass Retail Association.
Marketing Science Institute.
National Retail Furniture Association.
National Retail Hardware Association.
National Retail Merchants Association.
Point-of-Purchase Advertising Institute.
Radio Advertising Bureau.
Super Market Institute.

Other Channel Members

Advertising agencies.
Franchise operators.
Manufacturers.
Wholesalers.

Commercial Data†

More specialized information can be obtained from these research companies:

Audits and Surveys. Provides a physical audit of merchandise in stores.
Information Resources Inc. Gathers information via in-store scanning equipment and consumer household panels.
Market Research Corporation of America. Examines purchasing behavior via a large consumer panel. Consumer and store data computed.
A.C. Nielsen. Conducts a Retail Index service. Continuous data on food, drug, cosmetic, tobacco, toiletry, and other products sold in food stores and drugstores.
R.L. Polk. Provides mailing lists and automobile registrations.
Selling Area—Marketing, Inc. (SAMI). Gathers information on the flow of products to retail outlets.
Standard Rate and Data Service. Collects information on advertising rates for various media. Consumer data include income, retail sales. etc.

*Many other sources may be found in any business library.

†This is a sampling of commercial researchers. Others may be found in the classified section of local telephone directories.

ber of Commerce) is interested in improving the public's image of business and expanding the role of industry self-regulation. These associations provide literature to familiarize companies with efficient and legal practices. A third category (such as the National Retail Merchants Association and the Direct Marketing Association) describes current industry practices and emerging trends, and also functions as a retail spokesperson and lobbyist in advocating the best interests of retailers. All three types of organizations publish and send out materials for nominal fees or free of charge (to members). In addition to the associations cited

How Does the FMI Serve as an External Secondary Data Source?

The Food Marketing Institute (FMI) is a large trade association with headquarters in Washington, D.C. The FMI serves three basic functions: it provides information to member firms, communicates with the media, and lobbies for legislation on behalf of the food industry. Its role as an external secondary data source is extensive: "The business is getting more and more complex. We try to be a credible and responsive source."

The FMI maintains a sizable library and answers all types of questions that are mailed or phoned in. It publishes a regular newsletter to keep members apprised of key developments in or affecting the food industry. It publishes pamphlets on topics involving all sorts of food retailing issues and conducts industrywide research projects.

Recently, the FMI has expanded its use of seminars/workshops and videotapes. In addition to its annual national conference, the association now runs a regular series of regional seminars geared to independent food retailers. These sessions are held in locales such as La Crosse, Wisconsin; Springfield, Massachusetts; Minneapolis, Minnesota; Oakland, California; and Denver, Colorado. It also offers videotapes (for $50 each) on topics ranging from the proper techniques for bagging groceries to methods of improving productivity.

Among the questions that the FMI can answer for a food retailer is this one: How much sales must a store generate to make up for the loss of a single $125 shopping cart? (About $8,000, because of the industry's low profit margins.)

Source: Based on material in Michael Sansolo, "A Supermarket of Information," *Progressive Grocer* (May 1986), pp. 80–87.

in Table 6-5, one can uncover others by contacting the National Retail Merchants Association.

Often, retailers can obtain information from their channel members: advertising agencies, franchise operators, manufacturers, and wholesalers. Whenever any of these firms undertakes research for its own purposes (such as determining what type of consumer is most likely to buy a particular product, the kind of retailer that the consumer will patronize in making a purchase, or the advertising message that is most effective) and then presents some or all of the findings to its retailers, external secondary data are involved. The channel members will pass along their findings in order to enhance sales and relations with retailers. They generally do not charge the retailers for the information.

The last external secondary data source is the commercial research house that conducts ongoing studies and makes the results of these studies available to many clients for a fee. The fee can be quite low, or it can range into the thousands of dollars, depending on the complexity of the problem. This type of research is secondary when the retailer acts as a subscriber and does not request specific studies pertaining only to its company.

Several of the large commercial houses that specialize in secondary data for retailers are shown in Table 6-5. The companies provide a host of subscription services at much lower costs (and probably with greater expertise) than the retailer would incur if the data were collected only for its primary use.

Primary Data

Advantages and Disadvantages

After a retailer has exhausted the available secondary data, its defined problem may still not be solved. In this instance, primary data (those collected for the solution of the specific problem at hand) are necessary. In cases where secondary data research is sufficient, primary data are not collected.

There are several advantages of primary data. They are collected to fit the specific purposes of the retailer. The units of measure and the data categories are also designed to satisfy the problem under investigation. The data are current. In addition, the retailer either personally collects the data or hires an outside party for the study. Therefore, the source is known and controlled, and the methodology is constructed for the specific study. There are no conflicting data from different sources, and the reliability of the research can be determined, if desired. When secondary data do not solve the problem, the collection and analysis of primary data are the only alternative.

There are several disadvantages of primary data. They are more expensive to obtain than secondary data. The collection is more time consuming. Some types of information cannot be acquired by an individual retailer. If only primary data are collected, the perspective may be limited. In some cases, irrelevant information is collected when the retailer does not state the problem specifically enough.

A retailer that desires information for solving a problem has many criteria to consider when evaluating the use of primary data. Specificity, currentness, and reliability are weighed against high costs, time, and limited access to materials. The benefits of research must be weighed against the costs.

In the following subsection, a diversity of primary data sources for retailers is explained.

Sources

The first decision to be made in the collection of primary data is who will undertake it. A retailer can gather the data itself (internal) or hire a research company (external). Internal data collection is usually quicker and cheaper. External data collection is usually more objective and formalized.

Second, a sampling methodology would be specified. Instead of gathering data from all stores, all products, all customers, and so on, a retailer can obtain accurate information by studying a sample of stores, products, or customers. Sampling saves time and money.

There are two broad sampling approaches: probability and nonprobability. In a probability (random) sample, every store, product, or customer has an equal or known probability of being chosen for study. In a nonprobability sample, the stores, products, or customers are chosen by the researcher based on judgment or convenience. A probability sample is more accurate but is also more costly and difficult to undertake. A further discussion of sampling is beyond the scope of this book.

Third, the retailer must choose among four basic types of primary data collection: survey, observation, experiment, and simulation. All of these methods are capable of generating data for each of the elements of a retail strategy.

Survey

The **survey** is a research technique with which information is systematically gathered from respondents by communicating with them. A survey may be conducted in person, over the telephone, or via the mail. In almost all cases, a questionnaire is used.

A personal survey is face-to-face, flexible, and able to elicit lengthy responses. In addition, any ambiguity in the questionnaire can be explained. It is expensive, and interviewer bias is possible (the interviewer may affect the results by inadvertently suggesting ideas to the respondent). A telephone survey is fast and relatively inexpensive. Responses are usually short, and nonresponse may be a problem. It must be verified that the desired respondent is contacted. A mail survey can reach a wide range of respondents, has no interviewer bias, and is relatively inexpensive. Slowness of return, high nonresponse rates, and participation by incorrect respondents are the major problems. The technique that is chosen depends upon the objectives and the needs of the research project.

The retailer must also decide whether the survey is to be nondisguised or disguised. In a **nondisguised survey,** the respondent is told the real purpose of the study. In a **disguised survey,** the respondent is not told the real purpose of the study. For example, it may be inappropriate to divulge the intent of the study or its sponsor if a retailer is interested in the consumer's perception of its image. Otherwise, the respondent may answer what he or she thinks the interviewer wants to hear.

Survey techniques are used in a variety of retail settings, as the following illustrations show. Figures 6-2 and 6-3 show two nondisguised surveys. A movie theater owner uses the questions in Figure 6-2 to determine the market's behavior and attitudes. The questions in Figure 6-3 are used to ascertain the attitudes of shoppers toward Macy's. In both surveys, the respondents (those answering the questions) are told the real purposes of the studies, and questionnaire forms are used to enter responses.

Disguised surveys are used to gather information about consumer attitudes or personalities without revealing the true intent of the research. These surveys may utilize word associations, sentence completions, cartoon analysis, and/or questions. Figure 6-4 contains an example of a picture analysis study. The respondent is asked to describe the woman and the restaurant represented in the picture. The respondent is not told that the answer actually describes herself.[8]

The **semantic differential** (a list of bipolar adjective scales) is a survey technique that may be disguised or nondisguised, depending on whether the respondent is told the true purpose of the study. In the semantic differential, a respondent is asked to rate one or more retailers on several criteria. Each criterion is evaluated along a bipolar adjective scale, such as good–bad or clean–dirty. By computing the average rating of all respondents for each criterion, an overall store profile can be developed.

An example of a semantic differential appears in Figure 6-5. Store A is a prestige, high-quality furniture store, and Store B is a medium-quality, family-run furniture store. The semantic differential reveals the overall images of each furniture retailer and graphically portrays them.

Another survey research tool that is becoming popular is **multidimensional scaling.** In this type of research, attitudinal data are collected for several attributes in a manner that allows a single overall rating of a retailer to be developed (rather than a profile of several individual characteristics). A statistical description of this technique is beyond the scope of the text,[9] but Figure 6-6 shows how multidimensional scaling can be used to construct single overall ratings. In this example, service level, product assortment, and price level are the major criteria used in establishing profiles for four competing drugstores. These ratings define the consumer's perceptions of each store, show the strengths and weaknesses of each store, and aid in strategy development and modification.

From Figure 6-6, these conclusions can be reached: Drugstore A is rated as good on all three criteria; it is the best-liked store. Drugstore B is equal to A in terms of service level and product assortment; it is viewed as having high (bad) prices. Drugstore C is equal to A in terms of product assortment and price level; it is viewed as providing bad service. Drugstore D is equal to A in terms of service level and price level; it is viewed as having a bad product assortment. Drugstores B, C, and D need to improve their strategies to compete with A.

Other types of survey techniques also can be utilized, but those described here should provide the reader with a sense of the usefulness of this primary data procedure.

1. Did you ever go to a theater   ☐ Yes
   to see a movie over the
   past year?   ☐ No

   IF NO, PLEASE DO NOT ANSWER ANY MORE QUESTIONS.

2. During an average year, about how many movies do you see at a theater?_____

3. What type of movie theater do you patronize most often? Please rank these types
   from 1, least often, to 4, most often. Answer 0 if you never attend that type.
   ☐ Drive–In
   ☐ Multiscreen Theater
   ☐ Single–Screen Downtown Theater
   ☐ Single–Screen Neighborhood Theater

4. Please describe why you go to see a movie.
   _____
   _____
   _____
   _____

5. Please rank the factors you consider in the selection of a movie theater. Let 1 be
   the most important factor and 7 the least important.
   ☐ Cleanliness of Theater   ☐ Refreshments
   ☐ Location of Theater   ☐ Ticket Prices
   ☐ The Movie Playing at the Theater   ☐ Time Schedule of the Theater
   ☐ Parking

6. Are there any reasons why you do not go to see more movies?

                    ☐ Yes
                    ☐ No

   IF YES, PLEASE EXPLAIN.
   _____
   _____
   _____

FIGURE 6-2
A Survey on Behavior and Attitudes Toward Movie Theaters

Observation

Observation is a form of research in which present behavior or the results of past behavior are observed and recorded. People are not questioned. Observation does not require the cooperation of respondents, and interviewer or question biases are minimized. In many instances, observation is used in actual situations, eliminating the influences of artificial environments. The major disadvantage of using observation (by itself) is that attitudes cannot be obtained.

Examples of the use of observation by retailers include determining the quality of sales personnel presentations (through use of a mystery shopper), measuring related-item buying by consumers, determining store activity (by time of day and

Please indicate how you feel about each of the following statements describing Macy's department store. For each statement, indicate your level of agreement or disagreement by checking the appropriate space. We are interested in your honest opinions about Macy's.

	Strongly agree	Agree	Neither agree nor disagree	Disagree	Strongly disagree
1. Macy's has a wide assortment of items.	___	___	___	___	___
2. The products carried are of high quality.	___	___	___	___	___
3. Macy's is very dependable.	___	___	___	___	___
4. The employees are quite helpful.	___	___	___	___	___
5. Prices are high.	___	___	___	___	___
6. Macy's is old–fashioned.	___	___	___	___	___
7. Delivery service is prompt and reliable.	___	___	___	___	___
8. The displays in the store are confusing.	___	___	___	___	___
9. Macy's is a friendly store.	___	___	___	___	___
10. When Macy's runs a sale, real bargains can be found.	___	___	___	___	___

FIGURE 6-3
An Attitudinal Survey for a Department Store

day of week), making traffic counts (to measure new locations), and determining the proportion of shopping-center patrons using public transportation.

When a retailer utilizes observation, several decisions are necessary: natural or contrived, disguised or nondisguised, structured or unstructured, direct or indirect, and human or mechanical.

Natural observation occurs when a person is viewed entering, shopping in, and leaving a store. Contrived observation takes place when observers pose as customers to determine a salesperson's "pitch" or a special display is set up for the observation of shoppers' reactions.

In disguised observation, the shopper is not aware that he or she is being watched. A two-way mirror or hidden camera provides disguised observation. In nondisguised observation, the participant knows that he or she is being observed. An example would be a department manager's observing the sales behavior of an employee.

Structured observation requires the observer to watch for and note specific behavior. Unstructured observation demands that the observer watch and note all actions performed by the person under study. An example of unstructured observation is an apparel store researcher's watching the total purchasing behavior of customers to determine the actions they take and the items they buy.

The observer watches the present behavior of people in direct observation. The observer examines evidence of past behavior in indirect observation. Litter in garbage dumps and food cans in consumer pantries are examples of items that would be analyzed via indirect observation.

Human observation is carried out by people and is flexible. It may be disguised; but the observer may enter biased notations or interpretations and may miss behavior. Mechanical observation eliminates viewer bias and does not miss any

"Describe the woman you see here and the restaurant shown in the background."

FIGURE 6-4
Picture Analysis for a Restaurant

Please check the blanks that best indicate your feelings about Stores A and B.

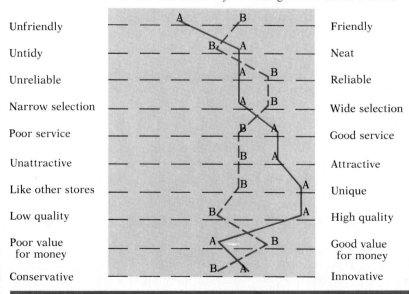

Unfriendly		Friendly
Untidy		Neat
Unreliable		Reliable
Narrow selection		Wide selection
Poor service		Good service
Unattractive		Attractive
Like other stores		Unique
Low quality		High quality
Poor value for money		Good value for money
Conservative		Innovative

FIGURE 6-5
A Semantic Differential for Two Furniture Stores

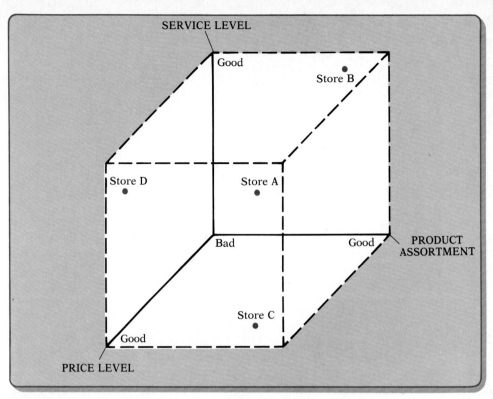

FIGURE 6-6
Multidimensional Scaling Applied to Drugstores

behavior. A movie camera that films in-store behavior is an example of mechanical observation.

Experiment

An **experiment** is a type of research in which one or more factors are manipulated under controlled conditions. A factor may be price, store layout, a shelf display, or store hours. In an experiment, just the factor under investigation is manipulated; all other factors remain constant. For example, if a retailer is interested in finding out the effects of a price change on a brand's unit sales, only the price factor is varied (e.g., making this week's price $0.99, next week's $1.19, then comparing unit sales for each week). The other elements of the retail strategy remain the same. This way, only the effect of the price change is measured.

An experiment may utilize survey or observation techniques to record information. In a survey, questions are asked about the experiment: How does Product A differ from Product B? Did you buy Brand Z because of its new shelf display? Are you buying extra ice cream because it's on sale? In an observation, behavior is observed during the experiment: the sales of Brand Z increase by 20 per cent when a new display is used; ice cream sales go up by 25 per cent during a special sale.

Survey and observation techniques are experimental if they take place under controlled conditions. When a survey asks broad attitudinal questions or observation of unstructured behavior occurs, an experimental procedure is not being utilized. In a retail setting, an experiment is difficult to undertake because many factors beyond the control of the retailer (such as weather, competition, and the economy) may influence the results. On the other hand, a well-controlled experiment is quite accurate.

The major advantage of an experiment is its ability to show cause and effect (e.g., a lower price equals higher sales). It is also systematically structured and implemented. The major disadvantages are high costs, contrived settings, and uncontrollable factors.

Simulation

Simulation is a type of experiment defined as "the act of creating a complex model to resemble a real process or system, and running and experimenting with the model in the hope of learning something about the real system."[10] To phrase this in simple terms, simulation is a computer-based technique that manipulates retailing factors on paper rather than in a real setting. A model of the controllable and uncontrollable factors (and their interactions) facing the retailer is constructed. These factors are then manipulated via a computer so that their effects on the overall retail strategy are determined. Simulation will become more popular for retailers as their level of mathematical and computer sophistication increases.

Further discussion of this research tool is beyond the scope of this text. We have introduced the concept to show its availability and utility. It is somewhat difficult to use. However, no consumer cooperation is needed, and many different factors and combinations of factors can be manipulated.

The Data Collection Role of Retailers in a Distribution Channel

Retailers often have a key role in the collection of primary data because of their position at the final stage in a distribution channel. Of all the companies in a channel, it is usually only the retailer that has direct contact with and easy access to consumers.

These are some of the ways in which retailers can assist other channel members in collecting primary data. They can

❑ Provide informal feedback on a supplier's prices, ads, and so on, based on their past experience.

❑ Allow data to be gathered on their premises. For example, many marketing-research companies conduct interviews at shopping centers because a large and broad base of people is available.

❑ Gather specific information requested by a supplier, such as how shoppers are reacting to a prescribed in-store display.

❑ Pass along information on the characteristics of consumers purchasing particular brands, models, and so on. Since for many retailers, credit transactions account for a significant portion of sales, they can link purchases with consumer age, income, occupation, and other factors.

❑ Participate in single-source data collection by allowing their stores to have specially equipped computerized checkouts. In single-source data collection, a research company (such as Information Resources Inc. or A.C. Nielsen) develops a sample of consumer households, determines the demographic and life-style backgrounds of these households through surveys, observes television viewing behavior via in-home cable hookups to the firm's microcomputers, and monitors shopping behavior by having participants make food purchases in designated stores. At these stores, consumers present an identification card similar to a credit card; then, all items bought are recorded by computerized scanning equipment. This system is more accurate than multisource data collection (whereby the consumers surveyed are different from those whose behavior is observed). It is a relatively new and expensive way of amassing data, and has thus far been mostly limited to food purchases in supermarkets.[11]

The Retail Information System

As stated earlier in the chapter, retailers should not approach marketing research as a one-shot solution to a single problem. Rather, the collection of useful information should be viewed as an ongoing, well-integrated process or system. A **retail information system** anticipates the information needs of retail managers; collects, organizes, and stores relevant data on a continuous basis; and directs the flow of information to the proper retail decision makers.

Developing and Using a Retail Information System

Figure 6-7 presents a retail information system. In this system, a retailer begins by clearly stating its business philosophy and objectives. The philosophy and objectives are influenced by the environment (such as competitors, economy, and government).

The retailer's philosophy and objectives provide very broad guidelines, which direct management planning. Some management plans are repetitive (routine) and, in the long run, may require little re-evaluation. Other plans are nonrepetitive (nonroutine) and will require careful evaluation each time they arise.

Once the retail strategy is outlined, the data needed to implement it are collected, analyzed, and interpreted. If the data are already available, they are retrieved from storage in the company's files. Exact instructions, orders, and specifications are then determined and put into operation.

After the retailer starts operating, performance results are fed back into the information control center and evaluated against preset standards. Data are retrieved from files, or further data are collected. Routine adjustments are implemented immediately. Summary reports and exception reports (explanations of deviations from expected performance) are sent to the appropriate managers. When necessary, the retailer adapts to performance results in a way that affects its overall philosophy or objectives (such as changing a store's image). An innovative reaction may also require a change in philosophy or objectives (such as sacrificing short-run profits to introduce a new, computerized checkout counter). See Figure 6-8.

All types of information should be stored in the control center for future and ongoing use; and the control center should be integrated into the short-run and long-run planning and operations of the company. Information should not be gathered sporadically and haphazardly. It should be gathered systematically, consistent with management objectives, plans, and operations.

Having a retail information system offers several advantages. First, information collection is organized and broad in perspective. Second, data are continuously collected and stored. Therefore, opportunities are foreseen and crises avoided. Third, the elements of retail strategy can be coordinated. Fourth, new strategies are developed more quickly. Fifth, quantitative results are obtainable, and cost–benefit analysis can be conducted. However, developing a retail information system may not be easy. It may require high initial time and labor investments. Complex decision making may be necessary.

Recent studies of retailers with annual sales of $1 million or more reveal these characteristics about retail information systems:

❑ Many information systems fall under the jurisdiction of the financial area of the retailer.

❑ A formal, written annual plan is often produced for information systems departments.

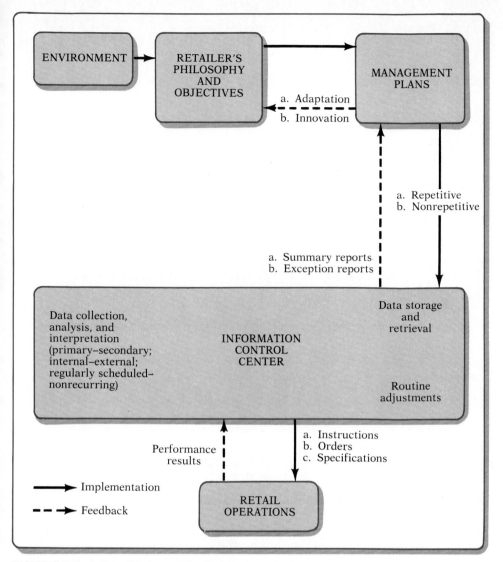

FIGURE 6-7 A Retail Information System
Source: Adapted by the authors from Fremont E. Kast and James E. Rosenzweig, *Organization and Management: A Systems and Contingency Approach*, Third Edition (New York: McGraw-Hill, 1979), p. 356. Reprinted by permission.

❑ Microcomputers are used by most companies using information systems analysis.

❑ Retailers spend between 0.5 and 1.5 per cent of sales on their information systems efforts.

❑ Substantial growth in the use of retail information systems is expected.

❑ There are many differences among retailers, on the basis of sales and type of stores operated.[12]

As computer technology has become both more sophisticated and less expensive, greater numbers of retailers (of all types) have developed comprehensive information systems. For example, in 1978, only about 200 supermarkets used computerized scanning systems; a decade later, about 15,000 supermarkets (representing 65 per cent of total grocery store sales) had installed such systems.[13] In the mid-1970s, the computerized systems were used only to reduce clerical

Step 1: Raw data flow from stores and warehouses to a mainframe computer, usually at chain headquarters. Included are sales records from checkout stands, data on product delivery schedules, employee work schedules, energy use, and the amount of time products spend in chain warehouses before they're shipped to stores.

Step 2: The numbers are crunched to help make better decisions about what products to sell, how to display them, and how to make their storage and delivery more efficient. Headquarters can determine which brands of soap make the most money, for example, and cut back on the least profitable ones. Or it can use computer–projected cost estimates to gauge how profitable a new brand of soap might be. The numbers might also suggest whether products should be delivered directly to stores or go to a central warehouse first.

Step 3: Headquarters sends its recommendations back to the store and to warehouse managers and their assistants. Sometimes called "Plan–a–Grams," these instructions include detailed schematics of every shelf, showing the store manager where to display each of the thousands of products sold in the supermarkets. The plan may even recommend prices for these goods.

Step 4: Headquarters also gives or sells the numbers generated in Step 1 to manufacturers, which may subsequently modify their products. For instance, the numbers may tell a soap maker that its products would sell better if they were packaged differently.

FIGURE 6-8
How a Retail Information System Can Make Supermarkets More Efficient
Source: "Using Information to Make Supermarkets More Efficient," *Business Week* (August 11, 1986), p. 64. Reprinted by special permission. © McGraw-Hill, Inc.

cashier errors and improve inventory control. Today, computers often form the foundation for a retail information system and are involved in consumer surveys, ordering, transfers of merchandise between stores, and other diverse activities. Figure 6-9 shows just some of the capabilities of a computerized retail information system.

These are illustrations of how retailers are placing greater emphasis on computerizing their information systems. At Mervyn's, a leading discount chain, storewide computerized scanning has been introduced via NCR point-of-sale (POS) registers. Mervyn's is "aggressively going with scanning and bar coding. We [in information systems] feel we're a vital part of the strategy and where Mervyn's is going . . . it's a real tool to our success."[14]

K mart is spending over $1 billion on its information system. Half the expenditures are for capital investments in new point-of-sale equipment and a satellite communications linkup among its stores, and half are for labor costs, in-house software, and computer-processing support. The major goals of the new system are to improve customer service, to better detect trends and buying behavior, and to make better decisions on prices, inventory levels, and assortments.[15]

Rite Aid drugstores did not have a comprehensive computerized information system until 1982: "The chain had no POS network and clerks were checking out customers on electronic cash registers; the only data being collected were sales

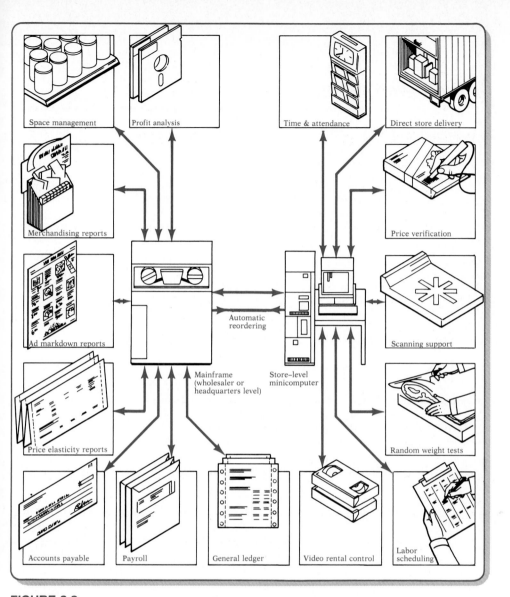

FIGURE 6-9
Selected Capabilities of a Computerized Retail Information System
Source: "The Capability of Computerization," *Progressive Grocer* (January 1987), p. 41. Reprinted by permission.

and department totals. Store personnel would manually record sales information on scanning documents that were mailed to the Harrisburg headquarters where they were read by an optical scanner and fed into the mainframe. It was a paperwork jungle." Today, Rite Aid has a sophisticated SASI point-of-sale system that provides detailed data on all phases of company operations.[16]

The Wholesale Club is a retail/wholesale buying club with headquarters in Indianapolis. It has point-of-sale terminals in each store connected to an NCR mainframe computer at headquarters. Through its system, the Wholesale Club can automatically look up prices (since they are not marked on individual items), compute selling prices for each transaction based on membership category (e.g., 5 per cent more for retail customers), authorize customer payments by check,

How Can Electronic Data Interchange Improve Retail Efficiency?

Through electronic data interchange (EDI), retailers and their suppliers hope to improve the efficiency of each party via quicker and more accurate responses to the marketplace:

This involves a cooperative effort aimed at reducing the retailer's inventory while at the same time providing for a supply of merchandise that more closely meets the actual buying patterns of consumers.

On the retailer's side, it calls for monitoring sales down to the item level with the purpose of spotting trends as they occur, and then relating this information in the most expedient way possible [EDI] to the supplier. The supplier responds by manufacturing, or pulling from its inventory, smaller batches of merchandise that more closely reflect consumer de-

mand. The retailer's opening order is smaller, and ensuing orders are shipped more frequently.

As a result, the retailer has a lower inventory on hand and can place orders closer to the date it expects to sell the merchandise. Such a system relies on the retailer's computer "talking" to its suppliers' computers; in this way, the information flow is maximized.

Retailers experimenting with EDI have had good results. For example, Wal-Mart, J.C. Penney, and Dillard's have each been pilot-testing their own EDI system. In each case, sales have increased, inventory levels are lower, and inventory turnover rates have risen.

Source: Based on material in "EDI and QR: A Lot More Than Alphabet Soup," *Chain Store Age Executive* (January 1988), pp. 89–90.

---

customize displays and receipts, generate and distribute reports on a regular basis, maintain information by member, and schedule employees.[17]

Gathering Product Information Through the UPC and OCR-A

Two different computer-based technologies have been developed for retailers to record and process product-related information at the point of sale: the **Universal Product Code (UPC)** and **Optical Character Recognition (OCR-A)**. Both of these technologies enable retailers to record information instantaneously on a product's model number, size, color, and so on when an item is sold, and to transmit the data to a computer that monitors unit sales, inventory levels, and other factors. The retailer's goals are to generate better merchandising information, improve inventory management and control, speed transaction time, increase productivity, reduce clerical errors in processing transactions, and coordinate the flow of information.

With the Universal Product Code, products (or tags attached to them) are marked with a series of thick and thin vertical lines, which represent each item's identification code. These lines are "read" by optical scanning equipment at the checkout counter; and the cashier does not have to enter a transaction manually. Because the UPC is not readable by humans, the retailer must attach a ticket or label to every product that specifies its price and, sometimes, contains other information (such as size or exact color).

In an Optical Character Recognition system, product information and a computer strip are placed on the price tags attached to the products. The information is readable by humans and by computers. As with the UPC, the cashier does not have to enter a transaction manually; scanning equipment "reads" the strip on a price tag.

When these alternate technologies were introduced, the UPC was widely adopted by food retailers, which found this method easy to implement and able to process transactions quickly. OCR-A was accepted by general merchandise retailers, such as Sears and J.C. Penney, which were more concerned about the image projected by the tags attached to their products and the greater information possible through OCR-A—and less interested in transaction speed.

However, for a number of reasons, by 1986, the UPC had emerged as the

FIGURE 6-10
How UPC Price Tags Have Improved
Today's technology enables UPC price tags to contain information that is controlled by the retailer (as well as the manufacturer) and that is human readable (in addition to the vertical line codes that can only be read by computer). Reprinted by permission of Monarch Marking, Inc., a subsidiary of Pitney Bowes, Inc.

dominant technology and it was predicted that OCR-A would soon fall into disuse:[18]

❑ Many more manufacturers have adhered UPC designations to their products, so that the retailer is relieved of this task.

❑ The UPC is much more standardized than OCR-A, so that industrywide standards can be applied.

❑ Many OCR-A tags have contained only human-readable data and not the computerized strip, thus eliminating some of the intended retail-information-system benefits. In these instances, product code numbers must be entered manually (or special keys must be pressed on an electronic cash register), so that data entry is hard or time consuming. As a result, some cashiers have chosen to manually enter only essential transaction data and ignore information entry.

❑ Over the years, the UPC system has substantially improved, while the OCR-A system has stagnated. See Figure 6-10.

❑ The amount of nonfood items sold in grocery stores has increased dramatically, and these retailers want UPC codes on merchandise.

❑ Both retailers and manufacturers see the need for a single technology. As the National Retail Merchants Association stated, "The NRMA has previously endorsed a voluntary vendor source marking standard of OCR-A. But, the NRMA has determined that changes in industry conditions, needs, and technological direction indicate that the Universal Product Code structure as administered by the Uniform Code Council is the preferable industry standard."

In a recent survey, 73 per cent of discount stores, 60 per cent of hard-goods specialty stores, 57 per cent of department stores, and 38 per cent of soft-goods specialty stores indicated that they planned to use UPC technology in their retail information systems by 1991. Among all general merchandise retailers, 86 per cent of those with annual sales over $350 million planned to use the UPC, compared with 32 per cent of those with annual sales under $50 million.[19] The UPC is discussed further in Chapter 12 ("Financial Merchandise Management").

SUMMARY

Whether developing a new retail strategy or modifying an existing one, good information is necessary. And the use of sound marketing research techniques (the systematic collection and analysis of data relating to any part of a strategy) enables a retailer to generate the proper information. Retailers that rely only on intuition increase their probabilities of failure.

Marketing research in retailing consists of a series of activities: defining the problem to be researched, examining secondary data, gathering primary data (if needed), analyzing the data, making recommendations, and implementing findings. It is not a single act.

Secondary data (information previously gathered for other purposes) offer several advantages: they are inexpensive, can be collected quickly, may have several sources, and may provide otherwise unattainable information. Some sources are quite credible. And when the problem is ill defined, a secondary data search can clarify it. There are also a number of disadvantages to secondary data: they may not suit the purposes of the study; the units of measurement and the categories of data may not be specific enough; information may be dated and/or inaccurate; a source may be disreputable, and different sources may present conflicting results; and the data may not be reliable.

Secondary data should always be consulted before primary data are obtained. Internal secondary data come from within the firm. External secondary data come from sources outside the company. They are available from government and nongovernment sources. Reference guides, regular periodicals, nonregular publications, channel members, and commercial research firms all provide external secondary data.

Primary data (those gathered for the solution of the specific problem at hand) have several advantages: they are precise and current; the data are collected and categorized with the measures desired; the methodology is known; there are no conflicting results; and the level of reliability can be determined. When secondary data do not exist, primary data are the only alternative. The disadvantages of primary data are costs, time, limited access, narrow perspective, and the amassing of irrelevant information.

Primary research may be done internally or externally. Four types of primary data collection are available: survey (personal, telephone, or mail), observation (natural-contrived, human-mechanical), experiment, and simulation. Each technique has its own advantages and disadvantages.

Retailers often have a key role in collecting primary data because of their position at the final stage in a distribution channel. Retailers can provide informal feedback to suppliers, allow data to be gathered on their premises, assist suppliers in monitoring consumer behavior, pass along information on consumer characteristics, and participate in single-source data collection.

Obtaining useful information should be viewed as an ongoing, well-integrated process. A retail information system anticipates the information needs of retail managers; continuously collects, organizes, and stores relevant data; and directs the flow of information to the proper retail decision makers.

In recent years, retailers have greatly increased their use of computerized retail information systems, and the Universal Product Code (UPC) has become the dominant technology for recording and processing product-related information. Optical Character Recognition (OCR-A) is declining in usage and importance.

QUESTIONS FOR DISCUSSION

1. At the beginning of this chapter, several unsuccessful strategies were described. What types of research would you recommend for each of the retailers?
   a. Movie theater
   b. Toy store
   c. Chain bookstore
   d. Mail-order retailer
   e. Florist
2. What are the steps in the marketing research process? May any of these steps be skipped? Why or why not?
3. Cite the major advantages and disadvantages of secondary data.
4. How could a sporting-goods store use secondary data to analyze sales by product category?
5. As a card store owner, what kinds of secondary data would you want to obtain from Hallmark or American Greeting Cards?
6. Under which circumstances should a retailer collect primary data?
7. Describe the major advantage of each method of gathering primary data: survey, observation, experiment, and simulation.

8. What are the benefits and risks of using non-disguised consumer surveys?
9. Develop a ten-item semantic differential for Baskin-Robbins to judge its image. Who should be surveyed? Why?
10. Under which circumstances should the following kinds of observation be used?
    a. Contrived
    b. Disguised
    c. Unstructured
    d. Indirect
11. Discuss some of the potential problems a retailer could face in conducting a pricing experiment.
12. How do the terms *marketing research in retailing* and *retail information system* differ?
13. How could a small retailer devise a retail information system?
14. Why is the Universal Product Code replacing Optical Character Recognition as the desired technology used in the information systems of general merchandise retailers?

NOTES

1. "Eye-Stopping Design in the Supermarket," *Wall Street Journal* (January 22, 1988), p. 29.
2. "Site Selection: A Computerized Approach," *Chain Store Age Executive* (August 1987), pp. 48–50; Glen E. Weisbrod, Robert J. Parcells, and Clifford Kern, "A Disaggregate Model for Predicting Shopping Area Market At-

traction," *Journal of Retailing*, Vol. 60 (Spring 1984), pp. 65–83; James A. Paris, "How to Read a Demographic Report," *American Demographics* (April 1986), pp. 22–25, 50–52; Jeremy Main, "Merchants' Woe: Too Many Stores," *Fortune* (May 13, 1985), pp. 62–72; and Laurie M. Grossman, "City Pedestrian Malls Fail to Fulfill Promise of Revitalizing Downtown," *Wall Street Journal* (June 17, 1987), p. 29.

3. Glen S. Omura and M. Bixby Cooper, "Three Strategic Planning Techniques for Retailers," *Business*, Vol. 33 (January–March 1983), pp. 2–8; Steve Weinstein, "Costs: Trying to Hold the Line," *Progressive Grocer* (January 1987), pp. 23–28; "Trainees Build Skills in Risk-Free Contest," *Chain Store Age Executive* (June 1987), pp. 56–58; David W. Cunningham, "Change Old-Time Attitudes to Improve People Productivity," *Discount Store News* (December 14, 1987), pp. 203, 205; William R. Darden, Ronald D. Hampton, and Earl W. Boatwright, "Investigating Retail Employee Turnover: An Application of Survival Analysis," *Journal of Retailing*, Vol. 63 (Spring 1987), pp. 69–88; Michael Sansolo, "The Right Stuff," *Progressive Grocer* (May 1986), pp. 47–50; and James R. Norman, "Gremlins Are Eating Up the Profits at Ames," *Business Week* (October 19, 1987), pp. 132–133.

4. Adam Finn, "Characterizing the Attractiveness of Retail Markets," *Journal of Retailing*, Vol. 63 (Summer 1987), pp. 129–162; Robert E. O'Neill, "New Criteria for New Items," *Progressive Grocer* (February 1986), pp. 35–40; "The Recipe for Profit," *Progressive Grocer* (October 1986), pp. 35–37; Richard Ettenson and Janet Wagner, "Retail Buyers' Saleability Judgments: A Comparison of Information Use Across Three Levels of Experience," *Journal of Retailing*, Vol. 62 (Spring 1986), pp. 41–63; William E. Moss and Daniel C. Seeley, "Inventory Management Crucial to Good Customer Service," *Discount Store News* (November 9, 1987), pp. 51, 57; and William H. Motes and Stephen B. Castleberry, "A Longitudinal Field Test of Stockout Effects on Multi-Brand Inventories," *Journal of the Academy of Marketing Science*, Vol. 13 (Fall 1985), pp. 54–68.

5. "Price Is Leading Attribute Sought by Shoppers: Study," *Marketing News* (March 13, 1987), p. 17; James C. Johnson and Kenneth C. Schneider, "The Robinson-Patman Act: Potential Pitfalls for Retailers," *Business*, Vol. 34 (January–March 1984), pp. 34–42; Gail Hutchinson Kirby and Rachel Dardis, "Research Note: A Pricing Study of Women's Apparel in Off-Price and Department Stores," *Journal of Retailing*, Vol. 62 (Fall 1986), pp. 321–330; Rockney G. Walters and Heikki J. Rinne, "An Empirical Investigation into the Impact of Price Promotions on Retail Store Performance," *Journal of Retailing*, Vol. 62 (Fall 1986), pp. 237–266; and Leonard L. Berry, "Multidimensional Strategies Can Combat Price Wars," *Marketing News* (January 31, 1986), pp. 10, 17.

6. David Mazursky and Jacob Jacoby, "Exploring the Development of Store Images," *Journal of Retailing*, Vol. 62 (Summer 1986), pp. 145–165; Joe Agnew, "P-O-P Displays Are Becoming a Matter of Consumer Convenience," *Marketing News* (October 9, 1987), pp. 14, 16; Arthur Allaway, J. Barry Mason, and Gene Brown, "An Optimal Decision Support Model for Department-Level Promotion Mix Planning," *Journal of Retailing*, Vol. 63 (Fall 1987), pp. 215–242; Richard De Santa, "Advertising: A Balancing Act," *Progressive Grocer* (June 1987), pp. 89–96; Martin Lader, "Vendor Dollars Provide the Lever," *Sales & Marketing Management* (May 1986), pp. 111–113; Alan J. Dubinsky and Steven W. Hartley, "Antecedents of Retail Salesperson Performance: A Path-Analytic Perspective," *Journal of Business Research*, Vol. 14 (June 1987), pp. 253–268; and Steve Kingsbury, "Study Provides Overview of Who's Redeeming Coupons—and Why," *Marketing News* (January 2, 1987), p. 56.

7. Dan Cook, Edith Terry, and Amy Dunkin, "Is Campeau in over His Head at Allied Stores?" *Business Week* (February 9, 1987), pp. 52–53; Robert E. O'Neill, "Is This America's Most Efficient Supermarket?" *Progressive Grocer* (March 1986), pp. 109–116; "Different Ballparks, Different Winners," *Chain Store Age Executive* (August 1987), p. 14; "Ad Effectiveness: Can It Be Calculated?" *Chain Store Age Executive* (September 1987), pp. 64–68; "Supermarket Sales by Category," *Progressive Grocer* (July 1987), p. 46; and "Flat Sales, Earnings Spur New Strategies," *Chain Store Age Executive* (August 1986), pp. 21–28.

8. Adapted from Burton H. Marcus, "Image Variation and the Multi-unit Establishment," *Journal of Retailing*, Vol. 48 (Summer 1972), pp. 29–43.

9. For good discussions on multidimensional scaling in retailing, see Ricardo Singson, "Multidimensional Scaling Analysis of Store Image and Shopping Behavior," *Journal of Retailing*, Vol. 51 (Summer 1975), pp 38–52 ff.; Raj Arora, "Consumer Involvement in Retail Store Positioning," *Journal of the Academy of Marketing Science*, Vol. 10 (Spring 1982), pp. 109–124; and Pradeep K. Korgaonkar and Kamal El Sheshai, "Assessing Retail Competition with Multidimensional Scaling," *Business*, Vol. 32 (April–June 1982), pp. 30–33.

10. Philip Kotler and Randall L. Schultz, "Marketing Simulations: Review and Prospect," *Journal of Business*, Vol. 43 (July 1970), p. 238.

11. See Felix Kessler, "High-Tech Shocks in Ad Research," *Fortune* (July 6, 1986), pp. 58–62; Robert N. Bock, "Scan Data Quality: The Nielsen Approach," *Nielsen Researcher* (Spring 1987), pp. 2–9; Joanne Lipman, "Single-Source Ad Research Heralds Detailed Look at Household Habits," *Wall Street Journal* (February 16, 1988), p. 39; and Stephen P. Phelps, "Single Source: Proceed with Caution," *Journal of Advertising Research*, Vol. 27 (October–November 1987), pp. RC-8–RC-9.

12. "POS Applications: Retail Checklist," *Stores* (June 1984), pp. 82, 84; "NRMA's New POS Study," *Stores* (April 1987), pp. 67–73; and Randy Allen and Daniel McCarthy, "Survey Reveals Computerization Improves Bottom Line Profits," *Discount Store News* (June 8, 1987), pp. 52, 55.

13. Estimated by the authors from "54th Annual Report of the Grocery Industry," *Progressive Grocer* (April 1987), pp. 8, 21–23.

14. "Mervyn's Installs Storewide Scanning: Tests Satellite System," *Discount Store News* (November 23, 1987), p. 3.

15. Patricia Strnad, "K mart Moving to Scanners," *Advertising Age* (June 8, 1987), p. 36.

16. "Hands Off, System On," *Chain Store Age Executive* (January 1986), pp. 94, 98.

17. "The Wholesale Club: Solving MIS Problems," *Chain Store Age Executive* (April 1987), pp. 77–78; and "Programmable POS System Fulfills Unique Club Needs," *Discount Store News* (May 11, 1987), pp. 125–126.

18. David Schulz, "Is UPC in Your Future?" *Stores* (September 1986), pp. 36–42; Jules Abend, "Update on the UPC," *Stores* (March 1987), pp. 48–57; and Judith Graham, "Bar Codes Becoming Universal," *Advertising Age* (April 18, 1988), p. 36.

19. "NRMA's New POS Study," pp. 70–73.

Olive Garden: Utilizing Marketing Research to Develop a New Restaurant Chain*

Case 1

Olive Garden is part of General Mills' restaurant group, along with Red Lobster (a full-service dinnerhouse chain featuring fresh fish and pasta), York's (a shopping-mall-based contemporary chain that has expanded its menu in evolving from a steakhouse), and Leean Chin's (which offers premium-quality Chinese cuisine). In 1987, the restaurant group had total sales of $1.25 billion.

The Olive Garden menu offers a selection of northern and southern Italian dishes at moderate prices. Its goal is to become America's leading Italian dinnerhouse restaurant chain and to eventually operate five hundred restaurants. After several years of testing, the chain grew from 4 to 14 units in 1986; by the end of 1987, it had 58 outlets. The typical Olive Garden restaurant has annual sales of more than $2.5 million and annual pre-tax earnings of $300,000. Most new outlets become profitable within six months. Olive Garden's sales and profit performance is particularly impressive, considering that about 50 per cent of all new restaurants fail within their first year, according to data compiled by the National Restaurant Association.

There were two major reasons that General Mills originally decided to invest $100 million to start the Olive Garden chain. First, restaurants' share of overall U.S. food sales rose from 25 per cent in the mid-1950s to 40 per cent in the mid-1980s, indicating the potential for innovative restaurant concepts. Second, although Italian cuisine was ranked as the most popular ethnic food by adults, Italian restaurants were in short supply. As of 1987, there were 17,000 Oriental restaurants and 14,000 Mexican restaurants in the United States, but only 4,800 Italian restaurants (other than pizza parlors).

The two executives put in charge of the Olive Garden startup had no experience in running a restaurant. One was a marketing researcher, whose prior employment had been at Pillsbury, redesigning supermarket display racks. The other, now the restaurant division's vice-president for new-concept development, had previously been a Cape Canaveral space engineer and then a General Mills financial analyst. Although neither executive had a particular fondness for Italian food, they both saw Olive Garden as a significant opportunity for their personal advancement and for corporate profitability. They were extremely motivated to succeed, were great believers in the value of research in developing the Olive Garden concept, and were quite open-minded in their approach. Following is a description of some of the marketing-research efforts used with Olive Garden.

Prior to opening any Olive Garden outlets, over twenty interviewers were hired to question consumers. And the two executives responsible for the new venture sometimes ordered as many as thirteen different meals a day in restaurants to try a wide variety of Italian dishes. The research showed that consumers had only vague impressions of Italy and that there were limits on the types of foods and seasonings they would accept. The research also led to three concepts for General Mills to consider: a restaurant with a large bar that would appeal to single professionals; a cozy inn with a fireplace; and a restaurant with plants, windows, and a lobby area where patrons could view pasta being made. The third option became Olive Garden.

After an analysis of the results of preliminary consumer interviews, Olive Garden was developed with "an ambience and cuisine that are sort of Italian—the restaurants do serve

*The material in this case is drawn from *General Mills 1986 Annual Report;* and Robert Johnson, "General Mills Risks Millions Starting Chain of Italian Restaurants," *Wall Street Journal* (September 21, 1987), pp. 1, 12.

spaghetti—but not so Italian as to put off the American mass market. Americans may think they like real Italian food, but General Mills knows better." For example, Olive Garden serves non-Italian items such as a chicken teriyaki dish (which is Oriental) and a chocolate mousse dessert (which is French). Both of these items are preferred by consumers over traditional Italian dishes.

In preparing Olive Garden's menu, General Mills also relied heavily on taste testing. It canvassed more than 1,000 restaurants for recipes, surveyed 5,000 consumers, and ultimately discarded more than eighty pots of spaghetti sauce before settling on a final version. As a supplement to consumer interviews, employees at nearby hotels and at competing restaurants were offered free meals and then asked for their comments and recommendations.

Because research showed that consumers think that Italian food has too much basil and garlic, these ingredients are used sparingly. Chefs at Olive Garden outlets are not allowed to deviate from strictly developed recipes. This ensures consistency within each Olive Garden restaurant over time and among different Olive Garden locales. Eye appeal was also deemed important, and much time was devoted to creating a tomato sauce that would cling to the pasta and not run to the edge of the plate. And the lyrics for singing waiters were written by the General Mills marketing department: "From the pasta we make to lasagna we bake, we're cooking fresh Italiano."

Even with a substantial research effort, the first experimental Olive Garden restaurant needed fine tuning. For example, consumers did not want an "authentic" Italian breakfast consisting of a spicy omelet; instead, they wanted pancakes. Many patrons also did not like the background music, which, like the initial breakfast menu, was quickly changed.

Olive Garden is now expanding in southern, north-central, and western U.S. markets. And in response to its popularity, competitive restaurant chains, such as TGI Friday's and Bennigan's, have added Italian entrees to their menus. Other competitors are also weighing whether or not to develop their own nationwide chains of Italian restaurants.

QUESTIONS

1. Evaluate General Mills' research efforts in developing Olive Garden.
2. How should traditional Italian restaurants react to the information in this case?
3. Design a questionnaire that would measure customer satisfaction with Olive Garden.

4. What kinds of information could Olive Garden generate through computerized cash registers? How could it use these data?

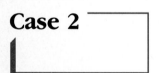

Ukrop's Supermarkets: Using Electronic Couponing in a Retail Information System*

Ukrop's Supermarkets is a privately held chain of eighteen stores based in Richmond, Virginia. The firm has recently been testing an electronic couponing program, developed by a subsidiary of Citicorp, that has enabled Ukrop to collect data on every purchase made by the over 9,000 customers who are enrolled in the program. At the one outlet that is involved in the test, sales have increased by 10 per cent.

This is the way the electronic couponing program works:

❑ Each participating customer is issued a bar-coded card (resembling a credit card) that identifies him or her as a member of the Valued Customer Program. Ukrop's records every person's name and address, and maintains a data base of these shoppers.

❑ Members of the program are given store accounts into which coupons are electronically deposited, subject to a maximum value of about $500 per year. Monthly, members

*The material in this case is drawn from Holly Klokis, "Ukrop's Tests Data Base Marketing Program," *Chain Store Age Executive* (September 1987), pp. 73–75.

receive a statement showing that about fifty new coupons with an average value of 25 cents apiece have been deposited in their account; they receive an automatic price reduction whenever they buy an item covered by a coupon. The statement also summarizes how much the person has actually saved as a result of his or her membership.

❑ A member presents his or her identification card at the start of the supermarket checkout transaction. The computer-based information system then deducts the electronically deposited coupon when the appropriate item is scanned. As a result, the electronic coupons require no effort on the customer's part. Members can also receive credit for traditional paper-based coupons, which must be clipped out and presented to the cashier.

❑ During the test, manufacturers were charged $50 for each coupon offering they placed in Ukrop's system. Since there were 9,000 consumers in the test, it cost a manufacturer only one-half a cent per member for a coupon offering. Manufacturers are promised exclusivity within a product category; for example, only one brand of frozen pizza can be listed at a time.

❑ Items with electronic coupon offers have labels on their display shelves indicating the amount of the reduction.

❑ All member purchases, as well as electronic coupon-redemption data, are recorded via computer. These data are reported to Ukrop on a weekly basis by Citicorp, which has a specific person helping Ukrop maximize its use of the information (Ukrop's own computer facilities monitor prices, inventory movement, employee hours, and so on). When this program is expanded, Citicorp plans to continue offering staff assistance to retailers and to sell the data to the makers of products sold in supermarkets.

An important advantage of the electronic couponing program to Ukrop (besides increased sales and store loyalty) is the enhancement of its retail information system. Ukrop can use the data to improve its performance; previously, it did not have good information on consumers and could not link purchases to specific customers. For example, through the Citicorp program, Ukrop can identify customers who have not shopped in its store within the past month and offer them special incentives. It can compare the effectiveness of 25- and 50-cent store coupons for the same brand. It is able to target coupons to customers based on their product usage category, such as giving heavy users of shampoo a $1 electronic coupon to stimulate their trial of a store brand.

In the Citicorp program, the data obtained by Ukrop are store-specific, unlike the external secondary data that can be purchased from commercial research houses such as Information Resources Inc. (IRI). IRI's BehaviorScan data are collected on 10,000 households in ten diverse cities and towns. Thus, Ukrop will be able to alter its strategy to reflect differences in shopper behavior at its specific store locales. The electronic-couponing consumer data may also be preferrable to BehaviorScan data because members receive valuable incentives in the form of discounts. These incentives should provide large sample sizes, a high proportion of shoppers joining, and fewer members' dropping out of the plan.

Consumer members in an electronic couponing program gain valuable benefits. They will not have to cut out coupons and categorize them by product type and aisle location, and they will receive more coupons for products they actually use. The ease of use and the targeted nature of electronic couponing are important because only 4 per cent of traditional paper-based coupons are redeemed by consumers.

QUESTIONS

1. What kinds of customer information available via secondary data should Ukrop regularly monitor and store in its retail information system? Explain your answer.

2. What kinds of customer information should Ukrop obtain through primary data collection? Explain your answer.

3. Describe the potential pitfalls that Ukrop must avoid if it expands electronic couponing into all of its stores.

4. Contrast how Ukrop and manufacturers such as Procter & Gamble would use electronic couponing data. Do you think electronic couponing will increase or decrease the tensions between retailers and their suppliers?

Part Three Comprehensive Case

Spiegel: Considering the Implications of a Consumer Behavior Study*

Company Background

Spiegel, Inc., the third largest mail-order retailer in the United States, was founded in 1865 by Joseph Spiegel (a German settler). The company began as a quality furniture store in downtown Chicago; it catered to affluent residents. However, by the early 1900s, Spiegel had expanded its merchandise selection and began issuing catalogs to appeal to the large number of lower-income immigrants who were attracted to Chicago. The firm was a pioneer in the concept of no-money-down credit plans, and it continued to be successful through the Great Depression. Sales growth was strong until the mid-1970s, and Spiegel became almost exclusively a direct marketer.

In 1973, sales reached $319 million, but they fell to $266 million in 1976. According to Ted Spiegel, vice-president of marketing and a great grandson of the founder:

> Our market share was shrinking, and we were losing the low-end business to big discount chains and catalog giants like Sears and Ward that were better known and backed with actual stores.

Spiegel's me-too approach in merchandising did not allow it to have any competitive advantage, except in the area of credit. It had become "a last resort to a low-income group that was shrinking every day." Spiegel appealed to budget-conscious, low-income consumers who were concentrated in small rural communities in the South and the Midwest. Spiegel accepted monthly installment payments as low as $7 per month. The "easy" credit terms became very expensive for Spiegel during this period.

At that point, Spiegel's parent company, Beneficial Finance (which had owned the retailer since 1965), hired a consulting firm to evaluate Spiegel's strategy and performance. The firm recommended that a new, more upscale target market be sought and a revised strategy implemented. To accomplish this, Henry Johnson (then the head of Avon Direct Products) was hired.

Immediately, Johnson sought to attract higher-income customers, many of whom came from two-income families and had little time to shop. A new marketing effort was aimed at women "who look for quality and value rather than the lowest price tag, and who want convenience." Spiegel wanted to become "a department store in print" for people who put a premium on time, as well as the "fashion catalog of the country."

The transition has been a difficult one for Spiegel for a variety of reasons. First, it was hard to get existing employees and managers to think in terms of quality and value—not just price. Many executives disagreed with the transformation strategy and either left Spiegel or were fired. Second, the initial customer mailing list dropped by 500,000 households, as lower-income customers were deleted. Yet it was hard to woo affluent consumers. Third, the closing of two hundred order stores reduced sales because some customers liked to view samples and place orders in a store environment. Fourth, some manufacturers that sold goods to department stores were not favorably disposed to Spiegel, due to its former image and customer base.

In 1982, Spiegel was purchased by Otto Versand, Europe's second largest catalog firm. The purchase price was a reported $49 million.

Spiegel's Current Strategy

Spiegel's current strategy can be described in terms of its target market, uses of marketing research, mailing-list generation, products available for sale, services provided, and catalog production.

Target Market

Today, Spiegel defines its target market as fashion-conscious working women in their late thirties with annual household incomes of about $40,000. About one-third of U.S. households fit into this category. Had Spiegel continued its old ways, its typical shopper would have been from a larger, less-educated blue-collar household with an annual income of $20,000 to $25,000. The company estimates that 91 per cent of its total sales are made to women. Spiegel

*The material in this case is drawn from Charlotte Ahern, "Spiegel Rolls with Punches," *Advertising Age* (December 14, 1987), pp. 85 ff.; Winston Williams, "The Metamorphosis of Spiegel," *New York Times* (July 15, 1984), Section 3, pp. 8–9; "Behavior and Attitudes of Telephone Shoppers: 800 Number Consumer Survey," *Direct Marketing* (October 1987), pp. 66 ff.; "Behavior and Attitudes of Telephone Shoppers: Inbound Telemarketing Series," *Direct Marketing* (September 1987), pp. 50–51 ff.; Arnold Fishman, "1986 Mail Order Guide," *Direct Marketing* (July 1987), pp. 40–42 ff.; Laurie Freeman, "Spiegel, Sears Try New Ideas," *Advertising Age* (August 3, 1987), p. 32; Ann Hagedorn, " 'Tis Already the Season for Catalog Firms," *Wall Street Journal* (November 24, 1987), p. 6; Lisa Redd, "Catalog Firms: Season's Bright," *Newsday* (December 17, 1987), p. 55; "Spiegel's Catalog to Spotlight Italy," *Women's Wear Daily* (June 23, 1986), p. 10; "Shopping by Catalog," *Wall Street Journal* (January 7, 1988), p. 21; Judith Graham, "Spiegel Expands Retail Base," *Advertising Age* (April 11, 1988), p. 32; and Bob Garfield, "Spiegel Catalog Strips Its Mass-Market Image," *Advertising Age* (April 11, 1988), p. 84.

assumes that working women are pressed for time and use mail-order catalogs for themselves and for important people in their lives.

Unlike many of its competitors (such as Sears, J.C. Penney, Bloomingdale's, and Neiman Marcus), Spiegel's major emphasis is on its catalog business. Over 90 per cent of Spiegel's annual sales are from mail-order transactions.

To broaden its business beyond catalog sales, Spiegel is now experimenting with its own retail stores.* Two "For You" stores have been opened in suburban Chicago. These stores feature moderate-priced fashions for larger women, sizes 30 to 46. Designers such as Bill Blass, Carol Bird, and I. B. Diffusion are featured. Merchandise carried at these stores is also available through Spiegel's "For You" specialty catalog. Spiegel also recently acquired Honeybee, a small upscale women's apparel chain, and Eddie Bauer, an outdoor clothing and equipment store and mail-order chain (to increase Spiegel's coverage of the male market). In addition, the firm is testing electronic merchandising in the Chicago area, whereby consumers will be able to use their touch-tone telephones to order items that are shown on their television sets.

Uses of Marketing Research

Spiegel actively uses attitudinal research to determine if customer perceptions of the firm are in line with its goals. In particular, Spiegel is interested in building and maintaining a general, continuous awareness of the company and its offerings. It recognizes that every advertisement and direct-mail piece contributes to a consumer's overall impression of Spiegel.

Spiegel is regularly involved in unaided awareness studies of its target market (upscale working women). Unaided awareness is surveyed when consumers are not given any prompting about a company. A typical question would be "Please tell me what you know about Spiegel."

Mailing-List Generation

The majority of Spiegel catalogs are sent to people who have previously ordered merchandise. Spiegel shoppers who place at least two $50 credit-card-based orders every six months automatically receive the next regular catalog. New customers can receive a regular catalog by sending $3 (which is refunded with the first order).

Some new customers are introduced to Spiegel through a "Discover" catalog, which offers special prices on regular merchandise; these catalogs are mailed to several million potential customers. Spiegel sometimes generates mailing lists by renting them from sources with similar target markets. Recently, Spiegel and Bloomingdale's by Mail have begun to rent each other's mailing lists. Other new customers are attracted through catalog request cards found in advertisements. A third group of new customers are those who request company catalogs without any solicitation by Spiegel.

Spiegel publishes a number of specialty catalogs per year, with a combined circulation of several million copies. Specialty catalogs can be purchased for a nominal fee (refundable with the first order). The specialty catalogs are generally keyed to gender (such as "Spiegel Men"), special size needs (such as "For You" large-sized women's apparel and "Proportions" for women five feet four inches tall and under), and age group (such as "Here's Looking at You Kid" for young children and "American Hits" fashions and furnishings for older children). Spiegel also features an "In Home" catalog with traditional home furnishings.

Spiegel advertises the availability of its regular and specialty catalogs in more than twenty magazines. In 1986, its media spending totaled $3.2 million, up 60 per cent from its 1985 level.

During 1986, Spiegel spent almost $8 million to update its mailing lists. This updating reflected household moves, purged duplicate names, noted marriages, and removed names of those not making purchases.

Products Available for Sale

Spiegel's product assortment has changed radically. It no longer stocks tires, curtain rods, pool tables, auto supplies, and a host of similar products. It does handle clothing, jewelry, housewares, furniture, clocks, and other merchandise that appeal to its target market.

These are some highlights of Spiegel's product assortment:

❑ Sheets and towels account for about one-quarter of company sales, compared with 5–7 per cent for an average department store.

❑ Designer merchandise is featured, including goods by Liz Claiborne, Pierre Cardin, Jean-Charles de Castelbajac, Ralph Lauren, and Gloria Vanderbilt. Spiegel is the largest seller of Laura Ashley products, with the exception of the designer's own stores.

❑ A typical general catalog displays $550 black-onyx cuff bracelets, $225 women's tops, $1,799 grandfather clocks, and $5,695 red-fox coats among the thousands of items shown in its approximately 850 pages. A recent catalog was able to sell 1,500 $495 fur-lined raincoats and 800 Jackie Rogers Italian-linen envelope dresses.

❑ Children's wear and tailored men's clothes are selling well.

Spiegel's semiannual catalog is typically divided into two sections: Fashion Collection and Home Collection. Each section has a separate index. The Fashion Collection features designer brands and has a layout that highlights important areas. These areas include Career Dress, Maternity Shop, Fitness Shop, and Men's Wear. The Home Collection has extensive offerings of linens (towels, blankets, comforters, curtains, pillows, and sheets), furniture and accessories, and electronics.

---

*Although Spiegel has had ten stores in the Chicago area for a while, they have been used as closeout outlets for clearing out unsold merchandise from its catalog operations.

Spiegel executives see the catalog as a "department store in print," and Ralph Lauren's eight pages in a catalog as a shop.

Services Provided

Spiegel offers a large variety of services to its catalog customers. These include a toll-free 800 telephone number; order takers on duty twenty-four hours per day, seven days per week (inventory availability and delivery time information are available between 8 A.M. and 10 P.M.); credit-card transactions (Spiegel accepts American Express, MasterCard, Visa, and its own card); and liberal return privileges. Spiegel accepts all returns without question, and it pays all shipping costs for returned goods.

Catalog Production

In order to effectively reach its target market, Spiegel has upgraded the paper, photographs, and merchandise presentation in its catalogs. These catalogs include the work of many of the country's most successful fashion photographers, have uncluttered pages, and use bold and imaginative graphics.

An important issue for Spiegel in producing its catalogs is the early press deadlines that make it difficult for the firm to adequately feature a new fashion trend. For example, the fall catalog, which is mailed out July 1, must be compiled by early February, and fall designer collections are generally not viewed until the last week of March.

Even though Spiegel works hard to be as trendy as possible, at times its catalogs miss important developments. As Spiegel's fashion coordinator commented,

Some designers will add items to their collections closer to the time of presentation. If something develops and a trend receives coverage, we're not able to intensify or act on it early. As a catalog company, we do not have the flexibility the stores have to bring in trendy items at the last minute. We have a press time to meet.

Recent Financial Performance

Spiegel's revamped retailing strategy has led to positive results for the firm. Between 1982 and 1986, Spiegel's sales grew at an average rate of more than 20 per cent per year. In 1987, sales exceeded $900 million and net income rose to $49 million.

Nonetheless, Spiegel is not without problems. For example, industrywide, mail-order firms generally have gross margins [(selling price − cost of merchandise to the firm) ÷ selling price] of between 40 per cent and 60 per cent; in 1986, Spiegel's gross margin was 32 per cent. This means that its profits as a percentage of sales are low and that its merchandise mix is still not emphasizing enough upscale brands and product lines.

Furthermore, despite its Number Three ranking among catalog retailers, Spiegel is much smaller than the two firms positioned above it. Sears' catalog sales are more than four times as high. See Table 1.

TABLE 1
The Largest Catalog Retailers, 1986

Company	1986 Catalog Sales (millions)
Sears	$3,711.4
J.C. Penney	2,332.0
Spiegel	882.2
Brylane[1]	475.0*
L.L. Bean	367.8
Fingerhut[2]	316.0*
Lands' End	265.0
Hanover House[3]	256.0
Avon	216.2
General Mills[4]	200.0*
Foster & Gallagher[5]	185.0*
Inmac	143.0
Sharper Image	59.3
Williams-Sonoma	55.2
CML Group[6]	52.6
Gander Mountain	52.3

*Estimate.

[1]Subsidiary of The Limited.

[2]Division of Primerica.

[3]Division of Horn & Hardart.

[4]Through two catalogs: Eddie Bauer and Talbots; both have since been sold (Eddie Bauer to Spiegel).

[5]Breck's and Spring Hill Nurseries.

[6]Includes Carroll Reed.

Source: Blunt, Ellis & Loewi Inc., " 'Tis Already the Season for Catalog Firms," *Wall Street Journal* (November 24, 1987), p. 6. Reprinted by permission. © Dow Jones & Company, Inc., 1987. All rights reserved.

Consumer Behavior Research

Recently, AT&T commissioned a study to examine the behavior of consumers who make purchases through toll-free 800 telephone numbers and/or who order goods and services via the mail. In this survey, 904 U.S. adults completed and returned a lengthy mail questionnaire. Of these respondents, 632 had used an 800 telephone number to place at least one order during the prior year (they may also have ordered through the mail); 230 had ordered at least once through the mail but had not placed a phone order during the prior year; and 42 had ordered neither by phone nor by mail at least once during the prior year. Although this study was not geared to the consumer patronage of any single direct-marketing firm, the results have great significance for Spiegel and should give the firm crucial insights into direct-marketing customers and how to further improve company performance.

The shopping orientation and attitudes toward nonstore shopping of the respondents are summarized in Figures 1 and 2. Please note that in these figures, users were those who had ordered by phone at least once in the previous year; nonusers were all those who had not placed phone orders during the year (even if they had ordered by mail).

"Please circle one number to the right of each item to indicate how strongly you agree or disagree with each statement based on your habits and experience in shopping for products other than groceries."

Per cent saying "4" or "5" on a five–point scale where 5 = "strongly agree" and 1 = "strongly disagree."

Agree That	All Consumers Base: (904)	Users (632)	Nonusers (272)
Price			
You get what you pay for	73%	72%	74%
I find myself checking the prices of even small items	73%	70%	81%
I shop discount and off–price stores whenever possible	60%	61%	60%
I usually comparison shop only for major purchases	47%	47%	45%
Brand			
A brand name is a good indication of product qualtity	72%	73%	68%
A store's "private label" brand is often as good as regular brands	56%	55%	57%
"No brand" merchandise does not appeal to me	31%	30%	32%
Convenience			
I tend to keep shopping until I find exactly what I want	69%	68%	72%
I like to get my shopping done as quickly as I can	68%	68%	68%
It's hard for me to find the time to shop	44%	45%	38%
I do not mind paying higher prices if a store is conveniently located	36%	37%	34%
Other Factors			
The selection in my local stores is often limited	50%	51%	49%
I really enjoy shopping	49%	48%	50%
I spend a lot of time browsing rather than buying	30%	30%	32%

FIGURE 1
Source: AT&T, "Behavior and Attitudes of Telephone Shoppers," Direct Marketing (October 1987), p. 70. Reprinted by permission.

Following are several specific consumer behavior findings from the AT&T study.

Profiling the Toll-Free 800-Telephone-Number Shopper

These were some of the characteristics of consumers who shopped via toll-free 800 telephone numbers:

☐ The five leading goods/service categories purchased by phone and the percentage of telephone shoppers reporting a purchase of these categories were clothing and accessories, 49 per cent; records and tapes, 17 per cent; housewares and cookware, 14 per cent;

travel reservations, 12 per cent; and books and educational materials, 12 per cent.

☐ Customers were equally likely to place an order in the morning, the afternoon, or the evening. Seventy-nine per cent preferred placing orders on weekdays.

☐ In general, phone shoppers were younger and better-educated, had higher incomes, and were more apt to have children at home than nonphone shoppers.

☐ These consumers were more likely to have made phone orders for clothing and accessories: those who had attended college, resided in the Northeast, had a high income, used credit cards, were female, pre-

Attitudes Toward Nonstore Shopping

"Please circle one number to the right of each item to indicate how strongly you agree or disagree with each statement based on your shopping habits and experience."

Per cent saying "4" or "5" on a five–point scale where 5 = "strongly agree" and 1 = "strongly disagree."

Agree That	All Consumers Base: (904)	Users (632)	Nonusers (272)
Quality/Reputability			
Most mail–order companies will stand behind their products	57%	61%	45%
You take a chance when you order through the mail	54%	52%	60%
I need to see a product before I buy it	49%	45%	62%
Most companies that sell through the mail are reputable	37%	39%	31%
Convenience/Usage			
Ordering products by phone is convenient	86%	90%	71%
Mailing something back to a company requires a lot of effort	66%	64%	74%
Telephone ordering is a convenient way to send gifts to people outside my local area	53%	55%	44%
I sometimes order by phone to save a trip to the store	50%	55%	32%
I frequently shop at home by ordering merchandise from catalogs that companies send me	45%	50%	29%
Other Issues			
I enjoy looking through the catalogs that companies send me	86%	88%	80%
I worry about giving out credit–card information over the phone	60%	56%	72%
Many times the same brand or item is a little less expensive if you order by phone	37%	40%	26%
I prefer to order from a company that is not too far away	19%	19%	21%

FIGURE 2

Source: AT&T, "Behavior and Attitudes of Telephone Shoppers," *Direct Marketing* (October 1987), p. 70. Reprinted by permission.

ferred phone purchases to mail orders, actively engaged in both telephone and mail ordering, and felt comfortable with phone purchases. On average, their most expensive telephone purchase was $100 to $249.

❑ The major stimulus for purchases was catalogs. Of the phone shoppers, 88 per cent made at least one purchase during the year after seeing a good/service in a catalog; one-third made over 50 per cent of their phone purchases after looking at a catalog. The next most popular media were direct mail, magazine advertisements, and television commercials; in each

case, over one-half of phone shoppers made at least one purchase during the year after exposure to one of those media.

❑ Fifty-five per cent paid for their phone purchases with a national credit card.

Profiling the Mail-Order Shopper Who Has Not Purchased Via the Telephone

In the AT&T study, 85 per cent of the respondents who had not purchased by phone over the prior year had placed at least one order through the mail during that time. These were some of the characteristics of mail-order customers who had not shopped via toll-free 800 telephone numbers:

- ❏ The five leading goods/service categories purchased by mail and the percentage of mail-order shoppers reporting a purchase in these categories were clothing and accessories, 50 per cent; books and educational materials, 23 per cent; housewares and cookware, 18 per cent; toys and games, 16 per cent; and magazine subscriptions, 12 per cent.
- ❏ In general, these consumers were more likely to purchase through catalogs: those who were college graduates, homeowners, those with medium and high incomes, females, and those who were not brand-conscious.
- ❏ People with no children in the home were more likely to buy clothing and accessories through the mail than those with children. Unmarried shoppers were more likely to buy records and tapes through the mail than married shoppers.
- ❏ Most consumers (81 per cent) used checks or money orders to pay for at least some mail orders. Only 40 per cent ever used a credit card.
- ❏ The major stimulus for purchases was catalogs; the majority of mail shoppers made a purchase during the year after seeing a good/service in a catalog. The next most popular media were magazine ads, television commercials, and direct mail.
- ❏ Just one-third of the consumers had ever placed an order for $100 or more of merchandise through the mail. Almost 40 per cent had never placed an order for more than $50. Males were more apt to place large mail orders than females.

QUESTIONS

1. Evaluate Spiegel's shift from the "mass" to the "class" market.
2. Analyze the findings of the AT&T study that are presented in the case and highlighted in Figures 1 and 2 from the perspective of Spiegel.
3. Describe the decision process for consumers buying clothing and accessories through the mail. What are the implications for Spiegel?
4. What valuable data does Spiegel have access to by virtue of its being a direct marketer? Explain your answer.
5. How can Spiegel use the results of the AT&T study in its retail information system?
6. What are the limitations of the AT&T study?
7. Assess Spiegel's long-term prospects. What must it do to maximize its chances for success?

PART FOUR

Choosing a Store Location

❑ *After a retailer conducts a situation analysis, sets objectives, and identifies consumer characteristics and needs, it is ready to develop and implement an overall strategy. In Parts Four through Seven, the major elements of such a strategy are examined: store location and operations, merchandising, pricing, and store image and promotion. Part Four concentrates on store location.*

❑ *Chapter 7 discusses the crucial nature of store location for retailers and presents a four-step approach to location planning. Step 1, trading-area analysis, is covered in this chapter. Among the topics studied are the size and shape of trading areas, how to determine the trading areas of existing and new stores, and the major factors to consider in assessing trading areas. Several data sources are described.*

❑ *Chapter 8 deals with the last three steps in location planning: deciding on the most desirable type of location, selecting a general location, and choosing a particular store site within that location. Isolated-store, unplanned-business-district, and planned-shopping-center locations are contrasted. And criteria for evaluating each location are outlined and detailed.*

Chapter 7

Trading-Area Analysis

❏ **Chapter**
Objectives ❏

1 To demonstrate the importance of store location for a retailer
2 To examine the major factors involved in selecting a trading area
3 To discuss various sources of data that can be used in trading-area analysis
4 To describe a number of methods for evaluating trading areas and store saturation

One of the most attractive locations in the United States for retailers and prospective retailers is Phoenix, Arizona. Why? By 1990, Phoenix is expected to be the seventeenth largest metropolitan area in the country, and annual retail sales are forecast to rise from $12 billion in 1987 to $19 billion in 1990 (a gain of more than 58 per cent).

These are some other reasons for the popularity of Phoenix among retailers. The population is upscale, with above-average income. Despite the high number of retirees, the median age is thirty-one, and the fastest-growing age group consists of children who are thirteen and under (representing over one-fifth of all residents). In the winter, "snowbirds" vacation or live in Phoenix; they spend $300 million in annual retail sales.

The business climate and economic base are strong:

The government here is not anti-business. It is inter-

ested in growth. Our economy is not tied directly to any single sector, although we are geared toward service industries. We are luring a lot of young, professional people who welcome the affordable housing available in the area and who recognize that there are a lot of business opportunities here.

The retail facilities are relatively new and quite modern. For the first time, interstate highways are being built around Phoenix; these will be very beneficial to suburban regional shopping centers. And Phoenix is a good market for retailers based in California, which have saturated that area.

Nonetheless, some experts are raising one cautionary note; retail expansion in Phoenix may be moving too rapidly. As an observer recently noted, "At one major intersection, I saw small centers on all four corners come out of the ground at the same time."[1]

216

One of the most crucial strategic decisions a retailer makes involves the selection of a store location. This chapter and Chapter 8 explain why store location is so critical and describe the steps a retailer should take when choosing a location for a store and deciding whether to build, lease, or purchase facilities.

Overview

The Importance of Location to a Retailer

The importance of store location to a retailer should not be underestimated. Decision making is complex, costs are high, there is little flexibility once a location has been chosen, and the attributes of a location have a strong impact on the retailer's strategy. In general, a good location may enable a retailer to succeed even if its strategy mix is relatively mediocre. For example, a hospital gift shop may do very well, although its merchandise assortment is limited, prices are above average, and it does not advertise. On the other hand, a poor location may be such a liability that even the most able retailer will be unable to overcome it. For example, a small mom-and-pop grocery store may not do well if it is situated across the street from a superstore; although the small firm features personal service and long hours, it cannot match the product selection and prices of the superstore. Yet, in a different location, it might do quite well.

The selection of a store location requires extensive decision making by the retailer because of the number of criteria that need to be considered. These include the size and characteristics of the surrounding population, the level of competition, access to transportation, the availability of parking, the attributes of nearby stores, property costs, the length of the agreement, population trends, legal restrictions, and other factors.[2]

Store location usually requires a sizable financial investment and a long-term commitment by the retailer. Even a retailer that seeks to minimize its costs by leasing (rather than owning a building and land) can have an investment of hundreds of thousands of dollars. Besides lease payments that are locked in for the term of an agreement, the retailer must spend money on lighting, fixtures, the storefront, and so on.

Although leases of less than five years are common in less desirable retailing locations, leases in good shopping centers or shopping-district locations are usually five to ten years or more. It is not uncommon for a supermarket site to be leased for fifteen, twenty, or thirty years. Department stores and large specialty stores, which locate on major downtown thoroughfares, have been known to occasionally sign leases longer than thirty years.

Because of its fixed nature, the amount of the investment, and the length of lease agreements, store location is the least flexible element of a retailer's strategy mix. A retailer such as a department store cannot easily move to another site or be converted into another type of retail operation. In contrast, advertising, prices, customer services, and the goods/service assortment can be modified rather quickly if the environment (consumers, competition, economy, and so on) changes. Furthermore, if a retailer breaks a lease, it may be responsible for any financial damages incurred by the property owner. In some instances, a retailer may be prohibited from renting its location to another party during the term of an agreement.

A retailer that owns its building and the land on which it is situated may also find it difficult to change locations. It would have to find an acceptable buyer, which might take several months or longer; and it may have to assist the buyer in financing the property. It may incur a financial loss, should it sell during an economic downturn.

All retailers that move from one location to another face three potential problems. First, some loyal customers and employees may be lost; the greater the distance between the old and the new locations, the greater the loss. Second, a new location may not possess the same characteristics as the original one. Third, existing store fixtures and renovations at an old location often cannot be transferred to a new one; their remaining value is lost if they have not been fully depreciated.

Store location has a strong impact on a retailer's long-run and short-run planning. In the long run, the choice of a location affects the firm's overall strategy. The retailer needs to operate at a store site that will be consistent with its philosophy of business, its objectives, and its target market over an extended period of time. The company also needs to regularly study and monitor the status of its location with regard to population trends, the distances consumers travel to the store, and the entry and exit of competitors, and to adapt long-run plans accordingly.

In the short run, store location influences the specific elements of a retail strategy mix (product assortment, prices, promotion, and so on). For example, a store that locates in a downtown area populated by office buildings may have little pedestrian traffic on weekends. Therefore, it would probably be inappropriate to sell major appliances at this location (because these items are purchased jointly by husbands and wives). The retailer at this downtown site would have to either close on weekends and not stock certain types of merchandise or remain open on weekends and try to attract customers to the area by using extensive promotion and/or aggressive pricing. If the firm closes on weekends, it is adapting its strategy mix to the attributes of the location. If it stays open, it must invest additional resources in advertising to attempt to alter consumer buying habits. A retailer that tries to overcome its location generally faces greater risks than one adapting to its site.

In choosing a store location, retailers should follow these four steps:

1. Evaluate alternate geographic areas in terms of the characteristics of residents and existing retailers.
2. Determine whether to locate as an isolated store, in an unplanned business district, or in a planned shopping center within the geographic area.
3. Select the general isolated store, unplanned business district, or planned shopping-center location.
4. Analyze alternate sites contained in the specified retail location type.

This chapter concentrates on Step 1. Chapter 8 details Steps 2, 3, and 4. The selection of a store location must be viewed as a process involving each of these four steps. The color photo portfolio following page 232 highlights several of the aspects of store-location planning.

Trading-Area Analysis

A **trading area** is "the geographic area from which a store draws its customers."[3] It is also defined as

> A district whose size is usually determined by the boundaries within which it is economical in terms of volume and cost for a marketing unit or group to sell and/or deliver a good or service.[4]

The first step in the choice of a retail store location consists of describing and evaluating alternate trading areas and then deciding on the most desirable one. After a trading area is picked, it should be reviewed regularly.

An analysis of trading areas provides the retailer with several benefits:

❑ The demographic and socioeconomic characteristics of consumers can be detailed. Government and other published data can be utilized to obtain this information. For an existing store, it can be determined if the current retail strategy matches the needs of consumers. The study of proposed trading areas reveals the market opportunities that exist and the retail strategy necessary for success.

❑ The focus of promotional activities can be ascertained. For example, a retailer that finds that 95 per cent of consumers live within a three-mile radius of a store location would have a considerable amount of waste if it advertised in a newspaper with a citywide audience. To avoid wasted circulation, the retailer could assess the media coverage patterns of existing or proposed locations.

❑ It can be determined whether a proposed branch store will service new customers or take away business from existing stores in the chain or franchise. For example, a supermarket chain currently has an outlet in Jackson, Mississippi. This outlet has a trading area of two miles. The chain is considering an additional location, three miles from its Jackson store. Figure 7-1 shows the distinct markets and overlap of the two outlets. The shaded portion represents the **trading-area overlap** between the stores; the same customers are served by both branches.

  The chain needs to find out the overall net increase in sales if it adds the proposed location shown in Figure 7-1 (total revised sales of existing store + total sales of new store − total previous sales of existing store). Management must also recognize that a competitor may open at the new location if expansion does not take place, and lost sales would occur.

❑ The proper number of outlets operated by a chain retailer in a geographic region can be calculated. How many outlets should a bank, a travel agency, and so on situate in a region to provide adequate service for its customers (without raising investment costs too much)?

❑ Geographic weaknesses are highlighted. For instance, a suburban shopping center conducted a trading-area analysis and discovered that a significant number of people residing south of town did not shop there. A more thorough study revealed that there was a dangerous railroad crossing on the

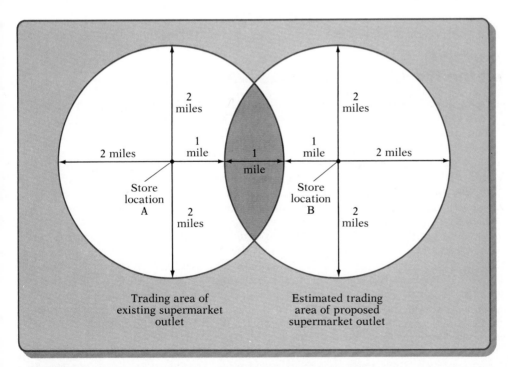

FIGURE 7-1
The Trading Areas of Current and Proposed Supermarket Outlets

southern outskirts of town, and residents were afraid to cross it. The shopping center exerted political pressure to make the crossing safer and was able to increase shopping in the suburb.

❏ Other factors can be described and evaluated. Competition, availability of financial institutions, transportation, availability of labor, location of suppliers, legal restrictions, and projected growth can each be ascertained for the trading area(s) being examined.

The Size and Shape of Trading Areas

Each trading area comprises three parts: primary, secondary, and fringe. The **primary trading area** encompasses 50 to 70 per cent of a store's customers. It is the area closest to the store and possesses the highest density of customers to population and the highest per capita sales. There is a minimum of overlap with other trading areas (intra- and interstore).

The **secondary trading area** contains an additional 20 to 25 per cent of a store's customers. It is located outside the primary area, and customers are more widely dispersed. The **fringe trading area** includes all the remaining customers, and they are the most widely dispersed. For example, a discount-store chain reported that its outlets have a primary trading area of four miles, a secondary trading area of four miles, and a fringe trading area of eight miles.[5]

Figure 7-2 contains an illustration of a trading area. Trading areas do not have to follow this concentric or circular pattern. They adjust to the environment. The size and shape of a trading area are determined by a variety of factors, among

RETAILING IN ACTION

How Does Computerized Trading-Area Mapping Work?

With a computerized trading-area map, the retailer is able to visually evaluate potential store locations in terms of their demographic, geographic, and other characteristics: "One of the most important aspects of mapping is the fact that it gives you the added dimension of geography, which is really the way most people perceive markets in the first place." A number of research firms have developed computerized systems that they sell to retail clients. One such firm is National Decision Systems (NDS), which has developed VISION.

This is how VISION works: NDS purchases census data from the U.S. government and, through its own projections, updates the information. Then, demographic, socioeconomic, and housing characteristics describing the 260,000 neighborhood blocks in the United States are used to identify homogeneous market segments. Each segment "represents consumers with a unique pattern of purchasing, consumption, media, and financial behavior." Finally, VISION users can display maps of the geographic areas of interest to them via their personal computers. These maps can show the market segment and the geographic traits of individual blocks, census tracts, zip code areas, and so on, depending on the needs of the user.

By using computerized maps, retailers can determine the attributes of consumers living in their primary, secondary, and fringe trading areas; decide where to locate new stores; evaluate the trading areas for each store in a chain; and compare their sites with those of competitors.

Source: Based on material in Lisa Del Priore, "Geomapping Tools for Market Analysis," *Marketing Communications* (March 1987), pp. 91–94.

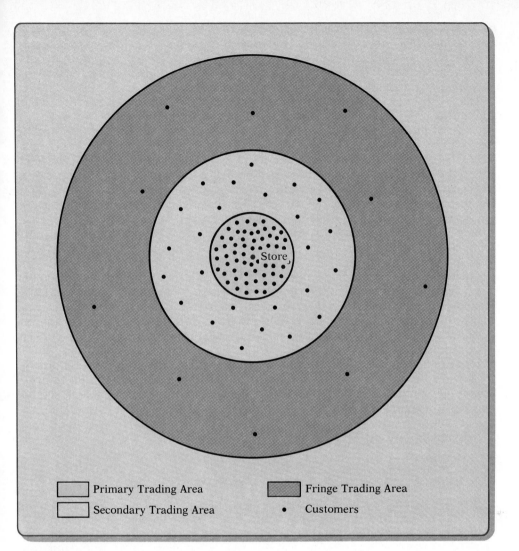

FIGURE 7-2
The Segments of a Trading Area

them: store type, store size, the location of competitors, travel time and traffic barriers (toll bridge or a poor road), and availability of media.

Two types of stores can have different trading areas even though they are both located in the same shopping district or shopping center. A store can offer a wide assortment of merchandise, promote extensively, and create a strong image. This store would have a trading area two to three times that of a weaker competitor. As an illustration, the trading area of a convenience food store is much smaller than that of a supermarket.[6]

One type of store, called a **parasite,** does not create its own traffic and has no trading area of its own. The store depends on customers who are drawn into the area for other reasons. A magazine stand located in a hotel lobby and a snack bar situated in a shopping center are examples of parasites. Their customers are not drawn to the trading area because of them but patronize these stores while they are in the area.

The size of a store's trading area is affected by its own size. As the store gets larger, its trading area usually increases. This relationship exists because the size of a store usually reflects the assortment and variety of goods and services that can be provided for customers. However, trading-area size does not increase proportionally with increasing store size. In a regional shopping center, department stores have the largest trading areas, followed by apparel stores. Gift stores in such a center have comparatively small trading areas.

The location of a retailer's competitors determines their impact on the size of its trading area. Whenever potential customers are situated between two stores, the size of the trading area is reduced for each. The size of each store's trading area will increase as the distance between them increases (then the target markets will not overlap). On the other hand, when stores are located near each other, the size of the trading area would not be reduced, because of competition. The grouping of stores may actually increase the trading area for each store because consumers would be attracted by the variety of goods and services. However, it is important to recognize that each store's market penetration (percentage of total retail sales in the trading area) may be low with this type of competition. Also, the entry of a new store may change the shape and/or create gaps in the trading areas of existing stores.

Travel or driving time has an influence on the size of a trading area that may not be clear from a study of the geographic distribution of the population. Physical barriers (such as toll bridges, tunnels, poor roads, rivers, railroad tracks, and one-way streets) usually reduce trading areas and contribute to their odd shapes. Economic barriers (such as differences in sales taxes between two towns) also affect the size and shape of trading areas. If one town has significantly lower taxes than another, it may entice consumers to travel longer and save more.

The size of a trading area can be expanded with proper promotion. In areas where newspapers and other forms of local advertising are available, a retailer can easily expand the trading area. When local media are not available, the retailer must weigh the cost and waste of advertising against the possibilities of increasing the trading area.

Delineating the Trading Area of an Existing Store

The size, shape, and characteristics of the trading area for an existing store (or shopping district or shopping center) can be delineated quite accurately. Store records (secondary data) and/or a special study (primary data) can be used to measure the trading area. In addition, many specialized firms offer computer-generated data and maps based on census and other data. These data can be tailored to individual retailers' needs.[7]

Store records can reveal the addresses of both credit and cash customers. Addresses of credit customers can be obtained through the store's billing department; addresses of cash customers can be acquired from an analysis of delivery tickets or cash sales slips. Because many large stores have computerized credit-card systems, they can easily estimate their trading areas by studying the addresses of these customers. Primary, secondary, and fringe trading areas can be described on the basis of

❏ The frequency with which customers in a geographic area buy merchandise at a particular store.

❏ The average purchase (in dollars) by a customer within a given geographic area.

❏ The concentration of a store's credit-card holders within a given area.

Although it is usually easy to obtain data on credit-card customers, the conclusions drawn from these data may not be valid if cash customers are excluded from the analysis. The use of credit may vary among different geographic areas, especially if the characteristics of the consumers in each area are different. Therefore, an evaluation of only credit customers may overstate or understate the total number of customers in an area. This bias is eliminated if data are also collected for cash customers.

Other sources of data on the location of credit and cash customers are store contests (sweepstakes) and check-cashing operations. For both of these, the analysis of addresses is inexpensive and quick because the data are collected for other purposes (secondary data).

A retailer can also collect primary data to determine the size of the trading area. It can record the license plate numbers of cars parked near the store, find the addresses of the owners of these vehicles by contacting the state motor vehicle office or the local treasurer's office, and then note them on a map. For less than $2,000, a retailer could have R.L. Polk (a marketing research company) record the license plate numbers and determine the associated owner addresses and demographics of 500 vehicles.[8] In either case, general addresses (zip code and street of residence, but not the exact house number) are used to protect people's privacy. As in the case of credit-card analysis, nondrivers and passengers must not be omitted. Customers who walk to a store, use public transportation, or are driven by others should be included in the research. To collect data on these customers, questions must usually be asked (survey).

Regardless of the type of analysis, the retailer should be aware that a time bias may exist. For example, a downtown business district is patronized by different types of customers during the week than on weekends. Or "grand openings" may attract customers from great distances for only brief periods of time. After the store is open awhile, the size of the trading area may decline. Therefore, an accurate estimate of the size of a store's trading area can be obtained only through complete and continuous investigation.

After any trading area is delineated, a retailer should map out the locations and densities of customers. This may be done in either of two ways. First, a geographic map may be drawn. Different colors of dots or pins are placed on this map to represent densities, incomes, size of purchases, cash and credit customers, and other factors. Second, customer addresses may be placed in zip code order. The primary, secondary, and fringe trading areas are defined by zip codes. Customers can then be reached by promotions aimed at particular zip codes.

Delineating the Trading Area of a New Store*

Alternate trading areas for a new store must often be evaluated by an assessment of market opportunities rather than current traffic (pedestrian and vehicular) patterns. Because the techniques already described for delineating the trading area of an established store are not sufficient, additional tools must be utilized.

Trend analysis and/or surveys can be conducted. Trend analysis (estimating the future based on the past) involves the examination of government data concerning predictions about population location, automobile registrations, new housing starts, mass transportation, highways, zoning, and so on. Consumer surveys can be used to gather information about the time and distance people are willing to travel to various retail locations, the features that would attract people to a new retail store, the addresses of the people most likely to visit a new store, and so on. Either or both of these techniques may provide a basis for delineating alternate new-store trading areas. Other, more specific, methods for defining new trading areas are described next.

---

*A new store opening in an established trading area can use the techniques detailed in the prior section. This section refers to a newer trading area with ill-defined traffic patterns.

Reilly's Law

The traditional means of trading-area delineation was developed by William J. Reilly in 1929,[9] and is called **Reilly's law of retail gravitation.** The law's purpose is to establish a **point of indifference** between two cities or communities, so that the trading area of each can be determined. The point of indifference is the geographic breaking point between two cities (at which consumers would be indifferent to shopping at either). The law may be expressed algebraically as[10]

$$Dab = \frac{d}{1 + \sqrt{\dfrac{Pb}{Pa}}}$$

where

Dab = limit of city A's trading area, measured in miles along the road to city B

d = distance in miles along a major roadway between cities (towns) A and B

Pa = population of city A

Pb = population of city B

Based on this formula, a city with a population of 90,000 (A) would draw people from three times the distance as a city with 10,000 (B). If the cities are 20 miles apart, the point of indifference for the larger city is 15 miles, and for the smaller city, it is 5 miles:

$$Dab = \frac{20}{1 + \sqrt{\dfrac{10,000}{90,000}}} = \frac{20}{1 + \sqrt{\dfrac{1}{9}}} = \frac{20}{1 + \dfrac{1}{3}} = \frac{20}{\dfrac{4}{3}} = 15 \text{ miles}$$

City A	15 miles	5 miles	City B
90,000 population	●←——←——←——←——←——●	●——→——→ ●	10,000 population

Point of indifference

Reilly's law rests on two major assumptions: (1) the two competing areas are equally accessible from the major road; and (2) merchants in the two areas are equally effective. Other factors are held constant or ignored. Consumers are attracted to the larger population center because a greater amount of store facilities (assortment) exists, making the increased travel time worthwhile.

The law of retail gravitation is an important contribution to trading-area analysis because of its ease of calculation and the research that has been conducted on it. Reilly's law is most useful when other data are not available or when the costs of compiling other data are too great. By combining this technique with others, a merchant can determine if the most appropriate trading area is being considered.

Despite its usefulness, Reilly's law does have limitations. First, distance measurement is confined to major thoroughfares and does not involve cross streets; yet people will travel shorter distances along these slower cross streets. A better measure might be travel time. Second, actual distance may not correspond with the consumer's perception of distance. A store that offers few consumer conveniences, few services, and crowded aisles is a greater perceived distance from the customer than a store with a more pleasant environment.

Huff's Law

In the 1960s, David L. Huff isolated several variables (rather than just one, as Reilly had done) and related them to trading-area size. **Huff's law of shopper** attraction outlines trading areas on the basis of the product assortment (of the items desired by the consumer) carried at various shopping locations, travel times from the consumer's home to alternative shopping locations, and the sensitivity of the kind of shopping to travel time. The assortment variable is measured by the square feet of selling space allocated to a product category. Sensitivity to the kind of shopping entails the purpose of a trip (restocking versus shopping) and the type of good/service sought (such as furniture versus clothing versus groceries).[11]

Huff's law is expressed as

$$Pij = \frac{\dfrac{Sj}{(Tij)^\lambda}}{\sum\limits_{j=1}^{n} \dfrac{Sj}{(Tij)^\lambda}}$$

where

Pij = probability of a consumer's traveling from home i to shopping location j

S_j = square footage of selling space in shopping location j devoted to a particular product category

Tij = travel time from consumer's home i to shopping location j

λ = a parameter used to estimate the effect of travel time on different kinds of shopping trips

n = number of different shopping locations

λ must be determined through research or via a computer program.

This formula may be applied as follows: Assume that there are three shopping locations with 200, 300, and 500 square feet of space allocated to men's cologne. A group of potential customers lives 7 minutes from the first location, 10 minutes from the second, and 15 minutes from the third. From previous research, the retailer estimates the effect of travel time to be 2. Therefore, the probability of consumers' shopping at Location 1 is 43.9 per cent; it is 32.2 per cent for Location 2 and 23.9 per cent for Location 3:

$$Pi1 = \frac{(200)/(7)^2}{(200)/(7)^2 + (300)/(10)^2 + (500)/(15)^2} = 43.9\%$$

$$Pi2 = \frac{(300)/(10)^2}{(200)/(7)^2 + (300)/(10)^2 + (500)/(15)^2} = 32.2\%$$

$$Pi3 = \frac{(500)/(15)^2}{(200)/(7)^2 + (300)/(10)^2 + (500)/(15)^2} = 23.9\%$$

As a result, if 200 males live 7 minutes from Location 1, about 88 of them will shop there.

These points should be considered in the use of Huff's law:

❑ To determine the overall trading area for Location 1, the same type of computations would have to be made for consumers living 5, 10, 15, 20 minutes, and so on away. The number of consumers at each distance who would shop there are summed. In this way, the stores in Location 1 would be able to estimate their total market, the size of the trading area, and the primary, secondary, and fringe areas for a particular product category.

❑ The probability of consumers' shopping at a particular location are highly dependent on the effect of travel time for the product category. In the previous example, if the product is changed to a more important item such as men's watches, consumers would be less sensitive to travel time. A λ value of 1 would result in these probabilities: Location 1, 31.1%; Location 2, 32.6%; and Location 3, 36.3%. Location 3 becomes much more attractive for this product category because of its assortment.

❏ All of the variables are somewhat difficult to calculate; and for mapping purposes, travel time needs to be converted to distance in miles. In addition, travel time depends on the form of transportation used.

❏ On different shopping trips, consumers buy different items. That means the trading area would vary from trip to trip.

Other Research

In recent years, a number of other researchers have examined trading-area size in a variety of settings and have introduced additional factors and sophisticated statistical techniques to explain the consumer's choice of shopping location.[12] For example, in his model, Gautschi added to Huff's analysis by including shopping-center descriptors (such as center design and hours of operation) and transportation conditions (such as cost, performance, and safety).[13] Weisbrod, Parcells, and Kern studied the attractiveness of shopping centers on the basis of expected population changes, expected store characteristics, and the evolving transportation network.[14] Ghosh developed a consumer behavior model that takes into consideration multipurpose shopping trips.[15]

In general, expected sales in an area can be calculated through this formula:

Expected annual sales = (number of consumers in the area)
× (percentage of consumers shopping in the area)
× (annual expected purchase per consumer)

Characteristics of Trading Areas

After the size and shape of each trading area, existing or proposed, has been determined, the retailer should examine the characteristics of the areas. Of special interest are the attributes of the residents and how well they match with the retailer's definition of the target market. Thus an automobile repair franchisee may estimate the opportunities available in an area by examining the number of automobile registrations; a hearing-aid retailer may evaluate the percentage of the population sixty-five years of age or older; and a bookstore retailer may be concerned with the educational level of the residents.

Among the trading-area characteristics that should be studied by most retailers are the population size and features, availability of labor, closeness to supply, promotion facilities, economic base, competition, availability of locations, and regulations. The **economic base** refers to an area's industrial and commercial structure, the companies and industries that residents depend on to earn a living. The dominant industry (company) in an area is very important because a drastic decline in the industry may have adverse effects on a large proportion of the area's residents. An area with a diverse economic base, where residents work for a variety of nonrelated industries, is more secure than an area dependent on one major industry.

Figure 7-3 summarizes some of the major factors to be considered in the evaluation of retail trading areas. Much of the information necessary to describe an area can be obtained from the Bureau of the Census, the *Survey of Buying Power, Editor & Publisher Market Guide, Rand McNally Commercial Atlas & Market Guide, American Demographics, Standard Rate & Data Service*, regional planning boards, public utilities, chambers of commerce, shopping-center owners, and renting agents.

Although all of the criteria in Figure 7-3 are not equally important in all retail location decisions, each should be considered (to prevent an oversight). The most important criteria should be viewed as "knockout" factors: if a location does not meet minimum standards on key criteria, it is immediately knocked out.

Population Size and Characteristics		
• Total size and density • Age distribution • Average educational level • Per cent of residents owning homes • Total disposable income • Per capita disposable income • Occupation distribution • Trends		

Availability of Labor

• Management
• Management trainee   > Analysis of:
• Clerical

a. High school and college graduates
b. Outmigration of graduates
c. Average wages in the area vs. average wages in the U.S.

Closeness to Sources of Supply

• Delivery costs
• Timeliness
• Number of manufacturers and wholesalers
• Availability and reliability of product lines

Promotion

• Availability and frequency of media
• Costs
• Waste

Economic Base

• Dominant industry
• Extent of diversification
• Growth projections
• Freedom from economic and seasonal fluctuations
• Availability of credit and financial facilities

Competitive Situation

• Number and size of existing competitors
• Evaluation of strengths and weaknesses for all competitors
• Short–run and long–run outlook
• Level of saturation

Availability of Store Locations

• Number and type of locations
• Access to transportation
• Owning versus leasing opportunities
• Zoning restrictions
• Costs

Regulations

• Taxes
• Licensing
• Operations
• Minimum wages
• Zoning

FIGURE 7-3
Major Factors to Consider in Evaluating Retail Trading Areas

The following are examples of desirable trading-area descriptions, as developed by some fast-food franchisors, off-price chains, and department stores:

Franchisors

❏ The community meets specific population-size requirements.

❏ Property at a good site is already owned or can be acquired.

❏ A good franchisee is available in the community.

❑ An adequate supply of labor is available.

❑ The income level in the community is sufficient for an active market.

❑ There is little competition.[16]

Off-price chains

❑ There are stores with compatible offerings.

❑ Many households have incomes over $30,000.

❑ Good roads exist.

❑ The population base is growing.[17]

Department stores

Each area must have a

❑ Favorable economic forecast.

❑ Favorable population growth for the target market.

❑ Stability of payroll sources.

❑ Community awareness of the parent store's existence.

❑ Minimal transfer of customers from other company-owned stores.

❑ Presence of the proper level of dominant retailers.[18]

The entire process involved in the analysis of a retail area is shown by the flowchart in Figure 7-4. This chart incorporates not only the characteristics of residents but also the characteristics of competition. By studying both of these factors, a retailer can determine how saturated an area is for its type of business.

In the next sections, three factors in trading-area selection are discussed: population characteristics, economic base characteristics, and the nature of competition and the level of saturation.

Characteristics of the Population

A great deal of information on population characteristics is available from secondary data sources. These sources provide information about population size, number of households, income distribution, education levels, and age distributions. Because the *Census of Population,* the *Survey of Buying Power,* and *Editor & Publisher Market Guide* are such valuable sources, each will be briefly described.

Census of Population

The *Census of Population* supplies a wide range of population data for cities and surrounding areas. Data are organized on a geographic basis, starting with blocks (groups of about 200 households) and continuing to census tracts (which average 1,200 households), cities, counties, states, and regions. As a rule, fewer data are available for blocks and census tracts than for larger units because of concerns about individuals' privacy.

After a retailer has defined the trading area, it can use census data by combining the geographic units contained in that area. A major breakthrough for retailers occurred with the 1970 census, when the U.S. Bureau of the Census created a computer file for the storage and retrieval of population data by geographic area. A number of private marketing-research firms have developed computer-based site-evaluation systems, based in part on census data. Some of these firms also project the data to the present year.[19]

The 1980 census added data categories that are useful for retailers interested in market segmentation. These include racial and ethnic data, small-area income data, and commuting patterns. An on-line computer system also makes 1980 census data available.

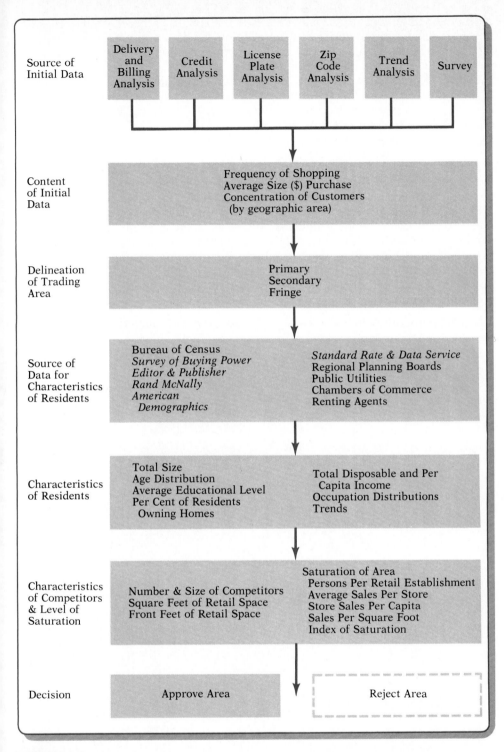

FIGURE 7-4
Analyzing Retail Trading Areas

The major drawback of census data is that they are gathered only once every ten years. Thus, the material can be quite out of date and inaccurate. Supplementary sources, such as municipal building departments or utilities, must be used to update census data during the later years.

The value of census tract data can be demonstrated through an illustration of Long Beach, New York, a city of more than 34,000 residents located thirty miles east of New York City on the south shore of Long Island. Long Beach is composed of six census tracts, numbers 4164, 4165, 4166, 4167.01, 4167.02, and 4168. See Figure 7-5. Although census tract 4163 is contiguous with Long Beach, it represents Atlantic Beach, another community.

Table 7-1 contains a variety of population statistics for each of the census tracts in Long Beach. The characteristics of the residents in each tract differ markedly; a retailer who is successful in one tract may not be successful in another.

For example, a growing bookstore chain is evaluating two potential trading areas. Area A corresponds roughly with census tracts 4165 and 4166. Area B is similar to census tracts 4167.01, 4167.02, and 4168. The population data for these two areas have been extracted from Table 7-1 and are presented in Table 7-2. Some interesting comparisons can be made.

Area A is substantially different from Area B, despite their geographic proximity and similar size:

❏ The population in Area B is 35 per cent larger than the population in Area A.

❏ Area B had some population growth during 1970–1980, whereas the population of Area A declined during this time period.

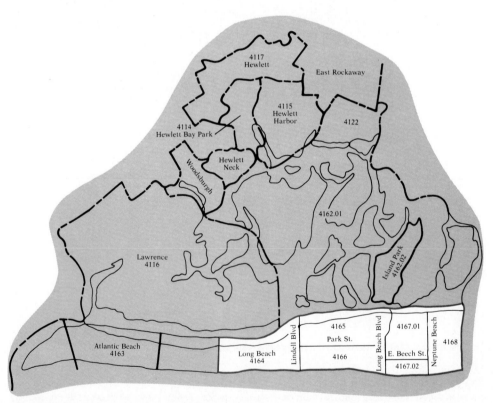

FIGURE 7-5
The Census Tracts of Long Beach, New York

TABLE 7-1

Selected Characteristics of Long Beach, New York, Residents by Census Tract, 1970 and 1980

	Tract Number					
	4164	4165	4166	4167.01	4167.02	4168
Total population:						
1970	6,352	5,229	6,499	4,062	4,769	6,216
1980	6,921	5,480	6,059	4,299	5,008	6,308
1980 population 25 and older	4,442	2,828	4,344	2,900	4,042	4,682
Number of Households:						
1970	1,993	1,709	2,426	1,355	2,210	2,412
1980	2,582	1,791	2,183	1,559	2,526	2,976
Education:						
College graduates (% of population 25 and older, 1980)	13.7	9.9	18.7	22.6	17.2	27.7
Income:						
Median household income, 1970	$ 8,500	$ 8,100	$ 3,100	$ 9,600	$ 5,400	$13,200
Median household income, 1980	$16,651	$14,089	$11,883	$21,955	$12,606	$21,341
Selected occupations:						
Managerial and professional specialty occupations (% of employed persons 16 and older, 1980)	24.0	14.8	26.4	28.7	27.1	35.5

Source: 1980 Census of Population and Housing, Census Tracts Nassau–Suffolk New York Standard Metropolitan Statistical Area (Washington, D.C.: U.S. Department of Commerce, Bureau of the Census); and authors' estimates and computations.

❏ The number of Area B residents aged 25 and older with college degrees is more than two times greater than that of Area A, and median income is over 40 per cent higher.

❏ The percentage of Area B workers who are managers or are in professional specialty occupations is greater in Area B than in Area A.

The management of the bookstore chain would probably select Area B because its residents have the characteristics desired of the target market. Area A would probably be rejected because its residents do not possess the characteristics required by the chain.

TABLE 7-2

Selected Population Statistics for Long Beach Trading Areas A and B

	Area A (Tracts 4165 and 4166)	Area B (Tracts 4167.01, 4167.02, and 4168)
Total population, 1980	11,539	15,615
Population change, 1970–1980	−1.6%	+3.8%
Number college graduates, 25 and older, 1980	1,093	2,646
Median household income, 1980	$12,877	$18,352
Managerial and professional specialty occupations (% of employed persons 16 and older), 1980	21.8	30.9

Survey of Buying Power

The *Survey of Buying Power* is published annually by *Sales & Marketing Management* magazine. This survey reports current data on metropolitan areas, cities, and state bases. It provides some data not available from census tracts, such as retail sales by specific merchandise categories, effective buying income, total retail sales by area, population projections, and retail sales projections.

The most important disadvantage of the *Survey* is its use of broad geographic territories. These territories may not correspond with a store's trading area and cannot be broken down easily.

The value of the *Survey of Buying Power* can be shown by a prospective new-car dealer's applying it to trading-area analysis. This dealer is investigating three counties near Chicago: Du Page, Kane, and Lake. A location for a new store is sought.

Table 7-3 lists important population data for the three Illinois counties under investigation. The statistics are updated annually (Table 7-3 is based on the year that ended on December 31, 1986), and five-year projections are made (1991 projections are noted in Table 7-3).

TABLE 7-3
Selected Data from *Survey of Buying Power* Relating to the Automobile Market in Three Illinois Counties, 1986

	County		
	Du Page	Kane	Lake
December 31, 1986			
Total population	738,200	310,500	478,200
Number of people 18 and over	538,900	221,000	345,300
Percentage of population 18 and over	73.0	71.1	72.2
Number of households	264,300	109,100	158,000
Total effective buying income (EBI)	$13,402,182,000	$4,310,199,000	$7,776,152,000
Median household EBI	$41,739	$31,599	$36,405
Per capita EBI	$18,155	$13,881	$16,261
Percentage of households with $35,000–$49,999 EBI	24.9	22.8	21.5
Percentage of households with $50,000+ EBI	36.5	20.6	30.8
Total retail sales	$6,079,609,000	$1,667,285,000	$3,097,077,000
Buying power index	0.4091	0.1318	0.2327
Percentage of U.S. EBI	0.4494	0.1446	0.2608
Percentage of U.S. retail sales	0.4118	0.1129	0.2098
Percentage of U.S. population	0.3035	0.1277	0.1966
Automobile retail sales, 1986	$1,481,917,000	$327,012,000	$1,161,800,000
Projections for December 31, 1991			
Total population	793,700	331,900	501,700
Percentage of change in population, 1986–1991	7.5	6.9	4.9
Total EBI	$20,771,926,000	$6,525,099,000	$11,672,917,000
Percentage change in total EBI, 1986–1991	55.0	51.4	50.1
Total retail sales	$9,075,873,000	$2,295,075,000	$4,601,473,000
Percentage change in total retail sales, 1986–1991	49.3	37.7	48.6
Buying power index (%)	0.4313	0.1342	0.2397

Source: Adapted from *1987 Survey of Buying Power: Sales & Marketing Management* (July 27, 1987), pp. B-3–B-7, C-58–C-64; and *1987 Survey of Buying Power, Part II: Sales & Marketing Management* (October 26, 1987), p. 65. Reprinted by permission of Sales & Marketing Management Inc. © 1987, S&MM Survey of Buying Power.

When choosing a store location, the characteristics of various trading areas need to be studied and compared. Of particular importance are the size and shape of alternative trading areas. Through computerized trading-area maps, such as those shown here, a retailer can learn about such characteristics as population density, average household income, and future population changes for each trading area under consideration, and then decide on the most appropriate area in which to situate.

Photos courtesy of Urban Decision Systems, Inc., which generated the computerized maps on this page.

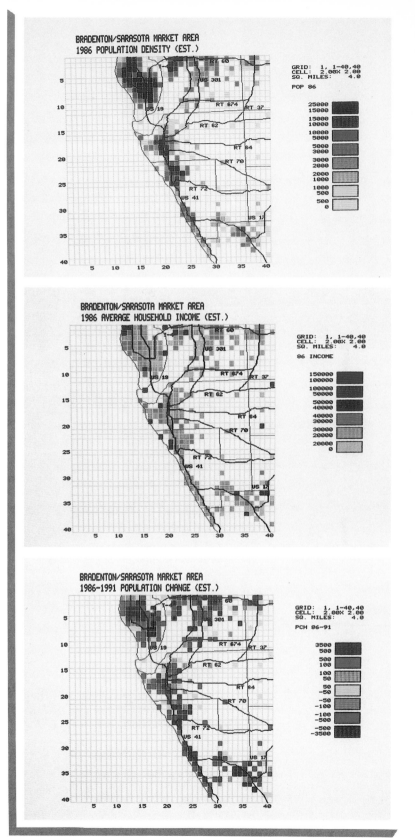

Many retailers locate in unplanned business districts, where two or more stores are situated together or in close proximity to one another with little prior planning as to the composition of the retailers. Large unplanned business districts rely on the customer traffic drawn by office buildings as well as cultural and entertainment facilities. While some unplanned business districts have declined because of traffic congestion, aging buildings, and so on, others have been extensively renovated and are flourishing. The latter include Faneuil Hall, Boston (1); The Gallery at Harborplace, Baltimore (2 and 3); and Union Station, St. Louis (4), all developed by the Rouse Company.

Photos courtesy of Rouse.

Today, planned shopping centers, which are centrally owned or managed, planned as a unit, based on balanced tenancy, and surrounded by parking, are very popular sites for retailers. The largest shopping center in the world is the West Edmonton Mall in Canada, shown above. This mall occupies the same space as 115 football fields and has parking for 20,000 vehicles. It has 58 entrances, a mile-long concourse, 11 department stores, and over 800 other stores. To entertain customers, the West Edmonton Mall has a full-scale indoor amusement park (including rides and animal exhibits), an ice rink, a miniature golf course, and other attractions.

Photos courtesy of Triple Five Corporation Ltd.

In evaluating alternative retail locations, pedestrian and vehicular traffic, parking facilities, transportation, and the image and composition of nearby stores are some of the criteria to be assessed. Black, Starr & Frost, an upscale jewelry chain, is very careful in selecting appropriate shopping centers and luxury hotels in which to place its stores.

Photo courtesy of Kay Jewelers, the owner of Black, Starr & Frost.

In rating specific sites within a retail location, store visibility; the placement in the location; the size, shape, condition, and age of the lot and the building; ownership or leasing terms; operations and maintenance costs; taxes; zoning restrictions; and voluntary restrictions are just some of the factors to consider. At Claypool Court in Indianapolis, retail tenants have excellent interior visibility; attractive mall displays enhance store placement, regardless of the side of the mall in which a store is situated; modern facilities; and competitive leasing terms, costs, taxes, and restrictions.

Photo courtesy of Melvin Simon and Company.

In order for one to analyze Table 7-3, two of the terms used by *Sales & Marketing Management* must be defined.[20] Effective buying income is personal income (wages, salaries, interest, dividends, profits, and property revenues) minus federal, state, and local taxes and nontax payments (such as personal contributions for social security insurance). Effective buying income is commonly known as disposable personal income. The **buying power index (BPI)** is a single weighted measure combining effective buying income, retail sales, and population size into an overall indicator of an area's sales potential, expressed as a percentage of total U.S. sales:

Buying power index = 0.5 (the area's percentage of U.S. effective buying income)
+ 0.3 (the area's percentage of U.S. retail sales)
+ 0.2 (the area's percentage of U.S. population)

Each of the three criteria in the index is assigned a weight, based on its importance.

The buying power indexes for Du Page, Kane, and Lake Counties are computed in Table 7-4. The BPI of Du Page is over three times greater than that of Kane and almost 80 per cent greater than Lake. Du Page has a larger population and more people eighteen and older than either Kane and Lake. These are vital statistics for an auto dealer. In addition, 61.4 per cent of Du Page's residents have effective buying incomes of $35,000 or better compared to 43.4 per cent of Kane's residents and 52.3 per cent of Lake's residents. In 1986, automobile sales were almost $1.5 billion in Du Page, compared to $327 million in Kane and $1.16 billion in Lake.

Therefore, a Cadillac dealer using *Survey of Buying Power* data might select Du Page and a Chevrolet dealer might select Kane. It must be noted that the *Survey* is broad in nature. Several subsections of Kane may be quite superior choices to subsections in Du Page (based on census data) for the Cadillac dealer. And the level of competition in each area must be noted.

Editor & Publisher Market Guide

Editor & Publisher Market Guide provides a variety of city data on a yearly basis, including principal sources of employment, transportation networks, bank deposits, automobile registrations, number of gas and electric meters, newspaper circulations, and major shopping centers. *Editor & Publisher,* like other sources, also contains statistics on population size and total households.

TABLE 7-4
Computations of Buying Power Indexes: Du Page, Kane, and Lake Counties, 1986*

Du Page County
Buying power index = 0.5 (0.4494%) + 0.3 (0.4118%) + 0.2 (0.3035%)
= 0.4091%

Kane County
Buying power index = 0.5 (0.1446%) + 0.3 (0.1129%) + 0.2 (0.1277%)
= 0.1318%

Lake County
Buying power index = 0.5 (0.2608%) + 0.3 (0.2098%) + 0.2 (0.1966%)
= 0.2327%

*BPI = 0.5 (area's % of U.S. effective buying income) + 0.3 (area's % of U.S. retail sales) + 0.2 (area's % of U.S. population). There are rounding errors in the computations in this table.

Like the *Survey of Buying Power, Editor & Publisher Market Guide* has one serious drawback for retailers. The data cover broad geographic areas and are difficult to disaggregate.

The value of *Editor & Publisher* can be described by its application to Sacramento, California. See Figure 7-6. Sacramento is the capital of California. It has

---

SACRAMENTO

1 - LOCATION: Sacramento County (MSA), E&P Map B-4, State Capital and County Seat. State Gov't; U.S. aircraft repair & modification; farming; manufacturing; aerospace; food processing; lumber products; mobile home manufacturing and wholesale center. Army depot and technical training center; electronics; Calif. Expo. 89 mi. E of San Francisco.

2 - TRANSPORTATION: Railroads - Southern Pacific; Santa Fe; Union Pacific; Sacramento Northern; Central California Traction; overnight freight service on Sacramento S.F. Bay and Sacramento; Sea Port (deepwater channel to San Francisco Bay; and Pacific Ocean; River Container Barge System); RT Metro.
Motor Freight Carriers - 16 interstate common carriers with local terminals; 542 total carriers (the majority of which have p.u.c. permits).
Intercity Bus Lines - Greyhound.
Airlines - United, PSA, Air Calif.; American West; Horizon Air; American Eagle; American; Delta; Northwest; Continental; United Express.

3 - POPULATION:
Corp. City 80 Cen. 275,741; E&P 87 Est. 331,950
NDM–ABC: (80) 1,059,461
County 80 Cen. 783,381; E&P 87 Est. 962,274
MSA 80 Cen. 1,099,814; E&P 87 EST. 1,366,294
Demographic Information available from Newspaper. See paragraph 14.

4 - HOUSEHOLDS:
City 80 Cen. 112,859; E&P 87 Est. 142,987
NDM–ABC: (80) 400,151
County 80 Cen. 299,805; E&P 87 Est. 382,739
MSA 80 Cen. 416,356; E&P 87 Est. 537,266

5 - BANKS

	NUMBER	DEPOSITS
Commercial	73	$6,731,513,000
Savings & Loan	45	$5,594,421,000

6 - PASSENGER AUTOS: County 514,404

7 - ELECTRIC METERS: County 400,500

8 - GAS METERS: County 269,680

9 - PRINCIPAL INDUSTRIES: Industry, No. of Wage Earners - Retail Trade 102,100; Whol. Trade 25,100; All Mfg. 37,900; Nondurable Goods 14,800; Durables 23,000; Agric., Forestry & Fishing 7,800; Fed. Gov't 30,200; State & Local Gov't 129,500; Constr. 30,400; Trans. & Public Util. 23,700; Fin., Ins. & R.E. 30,600; Services 107,800.

10 - CLIMATE: Min & Max. Temp. – Spring 48–71; Summer 59–93; Fall 52–77; Winter 39–53.

11 - TAP WATER: Varies, soft to hard, not fluoridated.

12 - RETAILING: Principal Shopping Centers - Sunrise Mall (113 stores) 5900-6100 Sunrise Blvd.; Florin Mall (96 stores) 5901 Florin Road; Country Club Plaza (57 stores) 2300 Watt Ave.; Country Club Centre (46 stores) 3300 El Camino; Arden Fair Mall (86 stores) 1601 Arden Way; Downtown Plaza (60 stores) Downtown; Birdcage Walk (64 stores) 5901-6197 Sunrise Blvd.

Nearby Shopping Centers

Name (No. of stores)	Miles from Downtown	Principal Stores
Arcade Square (18)	NA	Raley's Mkt.
Arden Fair (86)	NA	Woolworth, Sears, Thrifty Drug, Weinstock's
Arden Plaza (17)	NA	Lucky Mkt., Manor Drug
Arden Town (16)	NA	Holiday Mkt.
Birdcage Walk (64)	NA	Long's, Wards, Corti Bros., Macy's
Camellia City (9)	NA	Lucky Mkt., TG&Y
College Greens (8)	NA	Raley's Mkt.
Country Club Center (46)	NA	Wards
Country Club Plaza (57)	NA	Weinstock's, JCPenney
County Fair Mall	NA	Woodland, Rosenberg's, Mervyn's, JCPenney
Cordova (30)	NA	Thrifty
Crestview (27)	NA	Lucky Mkt., Thrifty, Ross
Downtown Plaza (60)	NA	Macy's, Weinstock's, I. Magnin
Florin Plaza	NA	Jumbo Mkt.
Florin Square (23)	NA	
Florin Mall (96)	NA	Weinstock's, Sears, JCPenney, Wards
Fort Sutter (11)	NA	Raley's
Fruitridge (29)	NA	Holiday Mkt., Manor Drug
Grand Oaks (23)	NA	Lucky Mkt., Hancock Fabrics
Grant Plaza (Citrus Heights)	NA	Thrifty, Alpha Beta
Hollywood Plaza (6)	NA	Raley's
Lanai (38)	NA	
Loehmann's Plz.	NA	Lucky's, Loehmann's Dept., Linens 'N Things
Madison Mall (35)	NA	Raley's
Midway (El Camino) (14)	12	Jumbo Mkt.
Mills (18)	NA	Raley's Mkt.
Northridge (17)	NA	Raley's Mkt.
N. Sacramento (4)	NA	Safeway
Pavilions	NA	Laura Ashley, Ann Taylor, Williams Sonoma, Julius
Point West (20)	NA	Mervyn's
River Park (13)	NA	Pantry
Roseville Sq. (37)	NA	Thrifty, Ross, Pay 'n Pak
Southgate (27)	NA	Thrifty Drug, Ross, American Sports Club, Federated
South Hills (31)	NA	Sprouse-Reitz, Jumbo
Sunrise Mall (113)	NA	Weinstock's, Sears, JCPenney, Macy's
Sunrise Oaks (21)	NA	Thrifty
Talliac Vlg. (14)	NA	Vans
Taylor's (23)	NA	Lucky Mkt.
Town & Country (55)	NA	William Glen
University Vlg. (23)	NA	Safeway

Almond Orchard (20)	NA	
Country West (15)	NA	Big R
Elkhorn/Watt (11)	NA	Thrifty, Albertson's, K mart
Manzanita/ Madison (12)	NA	Cloth World, Raley's

Principal Shopping Days - Dept. Stores - Thur., Fri., Sat.; Grocery Stores - Wed. through Sun.
Stores Open Evenings - Dept. Stores - Mon. thru Fri. Food Every night.
Stores Open Sundays - Grocery; Drugs; Discount; Dept; Automotive.

13 - RETAIL OUTLETS: Department Stores - Weinstock's 5; Macy's 3; Sears 3; Montgomery Ward 3; JCPenney 3; Mervyn's 5.
Discount Stores - K mart 10; Best Products 3.
Variety Stores - Woolworth 3; Ben Franklin 2; Sprouse-Reitz 6; TG&Y.
Chain Drug Stores - Payless 17; Manor 3; Raley's 16; Thrifty 24; Long's 12.
Chain Supermarkets - Safeway 18; 7-Eleven 41; Corti Bros. 4; Bel Air 9; Lucky 28; Jumbo 8; Raley's 16; Van's; Albertson's 8; Circle K 59; Comptons/ Holiday 9.

Other Chain Stores - Firestone; Goodyear; Goodrich; See's; Zale's Jewelry; Fuller Paints; Mary Carter Paints; Pittsburgh Paints; Sherwin-Williams Paints; Thom McAn; Gallenkamps; Kirby's; Chandler's; Florsheim; Leeds; Lerner; Sherman Clay; Breuners; Grodins; Kinney Shoes; Price Club; Eddie Bauer; Federated Group; B. Dalton Books; I. Magnin; Singer Co.; Lane Bryant; Baskin Robbins; Levitz Furn.; Oshman's; Waldenbooks; Big 5; Pay N Pak; Athletic Shoe Factory; Knapp Shoes; Fleet Feet; Furnishings 2000; The Gap; Wherehouse Records; Fashion Conspiracy; Lumberjack; Rogers Jewelers; Gran Tree; Mother-to-Be; Merle Norman; Radio Shack; McCurry's; Fotomat; Groths Shoes; Huston Shoes; Hickory Farms; Marlenes; Devon Jewelers; Richman Bros.; Kinder Foto; Marshalls; Toys R Us; Fox Photo; Cost Plus Imports; Pier 1 Imports; Tower Records; Tower Books; Ross; Home Club; Dress Barn; Miller's Outpost; Loehmann's; Pep Boys; The Good Guys; Casual Corner.

14 - NEWSPAPERS: BEE (m) 245,377; (S) 289,083; Mar. 31, 1987 ABC.
Local Contact for Advertising and Merchandising Data: Clifford Chapman, Gen. Adv. Mgr., BEE, 21st & Q Sts.; PO Box 15779, Sacramento, CA 95852; Tel. (916) 321-1476.
National Representative: Cresmer, Woodward, O'Mara & Ormsbee.

UNION (m) 90,888; (S) 89,561; Mar. 31, 1987 ABC.
Local Contact for Advertising and Merchandising Data: Nicolas A. Hyman, Adv. Dir., UNION, 301 Capitol Mall, Sacramento, CA 95812; Tel. (916) 442-7811.
National Representative: Landon Associates.

Source: *Editor & Publisher Market Guide*, 1988 Edition, pp. II39–II40. Reprinted by permission.

FIGURE 7-6
Editor & Publisher's Description of Sacramento, California

a large transportation system involving several railroads, motor freight carriers, intercity bus routes, and airlines. The population of several hundred thousand uses 73 commercial banks, 45 savings and loan associations, 514,404 passenger autos, 670,180 electric and gas meters, and 2 newspapers. Among Sacramento's major industries are U.S. aircraft repair, farming, manufacturing, aerospace, food processing, and lumber products. There are a number of major shopping centers and retail outlets.

The bookstore chain noted earlier may not obtain adequate consumer information from this source, but the information on shopping centers and retailers should be quite helpful. The auto dealer may also find that *Editor & Publisher* offers limited but useful data. The extent of the transportation network and the number of passenger cars are vital information. *Editor & Publisher Market Guide* is best used as a supplement to census and *Sales & Marketing Management* statistics.

It should be realized that different retailers require different kinds of information about the population characteristics of an area. The location decision for a bookstore or an automobile dealer usually requires more data than are needed for a fast-food franchise. For a fast-food franchise location, income and education are not significant factors. The prime criterion in area evaluation is population density. Many fast-food franchises seek communities having a large number of people living or working within a three- or four-mile radius of their stores. On the other hand, bookstore owners and automobile dealers cannot locate merely on the basis of population density. They must consider a more complex combination of population attributes in evaluating areas and should look at the sources of data described in this section.

Economic Base Characteristics

It is important to study the characteristics of each area's economic base. This base indicates the sources of income for a community's residents. A retailer seeking stability will normally prefer an area with a diversified economic base (a large number of nonrelated industries) to one with an economic base consisting of one major industry. The latter area is more affected by a strike, declining demand for one product line, and cyclical fluctuations.

In evaluating a trading area, a retailer should investigate the percentage of the labor force in each industry or trade grouping, the impact of economic fluctuations on the area and particular industries, and the future of individual industries (companies). These data can be obtained from *Editor & Publisher Market Guide*, studies by regional planning commissions, regional industrial development organizations, and chambers of commerce.

The Nature of Competition and the Level of Saturation

The retail opportunity in an area cannot be accurately assessed unless the competitive structure is studied. Although a trading area may have residents who match the retailer's desired market and may have a strong economic base, it may be a poor location for a new store if competition is extensive. Similarly, an area with a small population and a narrow economic base may be a good location if competition is minimal.

When examining competition, several factors should be analyzed: the number of existing stores, the size distribution of existing stores, the rate of new-store openings, the strengths and weaknesses of all stores, short-run and long-run trends, and the level of saturation. These factors should be evaluated in relation to an area's population size and growth, not just in absolute terms.

For example, many retailers have recently opened new stores in southeastern and southwestern states with growing populations. Tiffany, Saks Fifth Avenue,

Gumps, Target, Marshall Field, Lord & Taylor, and Macy's are among the retailers that have recently begun operations in New Orleans, Dallas, and/or Phoenix in order to locate stores in areas with expanding populations.[21] However, there is some concern that locations such as these will become quickly saturated because of the influx of new stores. In fact, although the population in the Northeast is declining relative to the Southeast and the Southwest, one of its major strengths—population density—should not be overlooked by retailers. The states in the Northeast have a population density of nearly 300 persons per square mile compared with a density of less than 100 persons per square mile in some southeastern and southwestern states.[22]

A trading area can be understored, overstored, or saturated. An **understored area** has too few stores selling a specified good or service to satisfy the needs of its population. An **overstored area** has so many stores selling a specified good or service that some retailers are unable to earn an adequate profit. A **saturated area** has just enough retail facilities to satisfy the needs of its population for a specified good or service.

Measuring Trading-Area Saturation

Measures of retail saturation are based on the premise that any trading area can support only a given number of stores or square feet of selling space devoted to a particular goods/service category. The ratios mentioned in this and the next section attempt to quantify retail store saturation. These ratios are meaningful only if norms are established; then the level of saturation in a trading area can be measured against a standard set by the retailer, or it can be compared with that of other trading areas.

Among the ratios most often used to calculate an area's level of retail saturation are the number of persons per retail establishment, average sales per retail store,

---

RETAILING IN ACTION

900 North Michigan: Friend or Foe for Existing Retailers?

In late 1988, 900 North Michigan, a vertical retail shopping center on prestigious North Michigan Avenue in Chicago, made its debut. The new shopping center is anchored by Bloomingdale's and has a 200,000-square-foot atrium, a Four Seasons hotel, about eighty specialty stores, 500,000 square feet of office space, luxury condominiums, and a big parking garage.

With the opening of 900 North Michigan, this is the question other North Michigan Avenue retailers are pondering: Will the new center be a friend or a foe? For example, only two blocks away is Water Tower Place, another upscale vertical retail shopping center. It "might now be the No. 1 shopping facility in the country in terms of sales per square foot." But what impact will 900 North Michigan have on that?

The developer of 900 North Michigan (which also constructed Water Tower Place) believes that the new facility will be a good friend:

> We are positioning 900 North Michigan to take over where Water Tower leaves off [in terms of prices]. We don't really feel the retailers in the two centers will be competing with one another, and we have no intention of duplicating the same tenants. We expect that people coming to town will shop both centers.
>
> Chicago has a sophisticated customer base that controls a tremendous amount of wealth—and there are not a lot of places to spend that wealth. And at the same time, Chicagoans are becoming a lot more conscious of trends and what is happening in fashion.

Source: Based on material in "900 North Michigan Rises on Chicago Skyline," *Chain Store Age Executive* (April 1987), pp. 30–40.

store sales per capita or household, and sales per square foot of selling area. The statistics necessary to compute these and other ratios can be obtained from city and state license and tax records, telephone directories, personal visits, *Dun & Bradstreet* reference books, *Editor & Publisher Market Guide, County Business Patterns,* and other sources. Retail sales by product category can be found in the *Survey of Buying Power.*

In the investigation of an area's level of saturation for a specific good or service, a retailer must interpret the saturation ratios carefully. Sometimes the variations between areas may not be true indicators of differences in saturation. For example, automobile sales per capita will be different for a suburban and for an urban area because suburban residents have a much greater need for automobiles. Therefore, each area's level of saturation should be evaluated against different standards—based on the optimum per capital sales figures in each area.

Table 7-5 compares the level of saturation for full-line discount stores in three metropolitan markets: Atlanta, Houston, and Milwaukee. Although Houston has the greatest total full-line discount store sales, it also has the greatest number of these stores. Of the markets studied, Houston and Milwaukee have a considerably fewer number of both persons per full-line discount store and households per full-line discount store than Atlanta. Full-line discount store sales per household per $1 of median household EBI, average sales per store, and average sales per square foot are very similar for the three areas. Overall, these ratios suggest that Atlanta, Houston, and Milwaukee have comparable levels of saturation for full-line discount stores.

The Index of Retail Saturation

One general ratio has been developed to measure store saturation in an area: the **index of retail saturation.** This index examines the number of customers, the retail expenditures, and the size of retail facilities for a specified good or

TABLE 7-5
Store Saturation Data for Full-Line Discount Stores in Three Metropolitan Markets, 1986 (Estimated)

	Metropolitan Market		
	Atlanta	Houston	Milwaukee
Total full-line discount store sales	$566,000,000	$808,000,000	$354,000,000
Total population	2,460,700	3,211,000	1,401,000
Total number of households	902,700	1,168,800	527,700
Median household effective buying income (EBI)	$27,770	$28,695	$26,847
Number of full-line discount stores	56	80	35
Square footage full-line discount stores	4,206,000	6,008,000	2,629,000
Full-line discount store sales per household	$627.00	$691.31	$670.84
Number of persons per full-line discount store	43,941	40,138	40,029
Number of households per full-line discount store	16,120	14,610	15,077
Full-line discount store sales per household per $1 of median household EBI	$0.023	$0.024	$0.025
Average sales per store	$10,107,143	$10,100,000	$10,114,286
Average sales per square foot	$134.57	$134.49	$134.65

Source: "The Discount Industry by Metro Market," *Discount Store News* (July 21, 1986), p. 30; and authors' computations. Reprinted by permission. Copyright Lebhar-Friedman, Inc., 425 Park Avenue, N.Y., N.Y. 10022.

service category in each trading area under consideration:[23]

$$IRS_i = \frac{C_i \cdot RE_i}{RF_i}$$

where

IRS_i = index of retail saturation for trading area i for the good (service) category

C_i = number of customers in area i for the good (service) category

RE_i = expenditures (dollars) per customer in area i for the good (service) category

RF_i = total square feet in area i allocated to the good (service) category

The use of the index of retail saturation can be illustrated by an analysis of the three trading areas shown in Table 7-6 that are under consideration by a specialty-store retailer. The firm has predetermined that its sales must be at least $160 per square foot of store space for its product category (housewares) to be profitable. The trading area chosen will be the one that yields the best index of retail store saturation. In this case, the retailer selects Area 1, which has an index of saturation of $180.

When calculating the index, the retailer must remember to include the proposed store. If that store is not included, the relative value of each area may be distorted. If the proposed store is excluded in Table 7-6, Area 3 has the best level of sales per square foot ($400); however, this area is not desirable after the prospective store is added to the computation. It should be noted that sales per foot decline the most when new outlets are added to a small area.

The retailer should also examine whether a new store will expand the total consumer market for a specific good (service) category or increase the firm's market share in the area without expanding the total market. This is particularly important when the retailer has either high levels of service or carries an unusually wide assortment of products.[24]

TABLE 7-6
Using the Index of Saturation

	Area		
	1	2	3
Number of customers annually buying housewares	60,000	30,000	10,000
Average annual houseware purchases per customer	$60	$75	$100
Total store footage allocated to housewares	20,000	15,000	7,500
Index of retail saturation	$180	$150	$133
Total store footage allocated to housewares (excluding the proposed store)	15,000	10,000	2,500
Index of retail saturation (excluding the proposed store)	$240	$225	$400

SUMMARY

The choice of a store location is important because of the complex decision making involved, the high costs, the lack of flexibility once a site is chosen, and the impact of a site on a retailer's strategy. A good location may enable a retailer to succeed even if its strategy mix is relatively mediocre.

The selection of a store location consists of four steps: (1) evaluating alternative trading areas; (2) determining the most desirable type of location; (3) picking a general site; and (4) settling on a specific site. This chapter concentrates on Step 1. Chapter 8 details Steps 2, 3, and 4.

A trading area is the geographic area from which a store draws its customers. Each such area has primary, secondary, and fringe components; the further consumers live from a shopping area, the less likely they are to travel there. The size and shape of a trading area depend on store type, store size, the location of competitors, travel time and traffic barriers, and media availability.

The size, shape, and characteristics of the trading area for an existing store or group of stores can be delineated quite accurately. A retailer can gather data by examining store records, sponsoring contests, recording license plate numbers and linking them to customer addresses, and surveying consumers. Time biases must be considered when amassing data. Results should be mapped and customer densities noted.

Alternate trading areas for a new store must often be described in terms of market opportunities rather than current traffic patterns. Trend analysis and consumer surveys may be employed. Two quantitative methods for defining trading-area size are Reilly's law of retail gravitation, which relates the population size of different cities to the size of their trading areas; and Huff's law of shopper attraction, which is based on each area's shopping assortment, the distance of consumers from various retail locales, and the sensitivity of people to travel time.

After the size and shape of each trading area has been determined, its characteristics should be studied in depth. These characteristics include population size and features, availability of labor, closeness to supply, promotion facilities, economic base, competition, availability of locations, and regulations. The *Census of Population, Survey of Buying Power,* and *Editor & Publisher Market Guide* are good sources of data on trading areas. These sources have complementary strengths and weaknesses for retailers.

A trading area may be understored, overstored, or saturated. Store saturation may be measured in several ways, such as the number of persons per retail establishment, the average sales per retail store, the store sales per capita or household, and the sales per square foot of selling space. One general ratio is the index of retail saturation, which is based on the number of customers, their retail expenditures, and the square footage available for a given good/service category in each trading area.

QUESTIONS FOR DISCUSSION

1. If a retailer has a new twenty-year store lease, does this mean that the next time it studies the characteristics of its trading area should be twenty years from now? Explain your answer.
2. What is trading-area overlap? Are there any disadvantages to a chain retailer's having low overlap among its various stores? Why or why not?
3. How could your college or university determine its primary, secondary, and fringe trading areas? Discuss the value of your school's obtaining this information.
4. Why do few trading areas look like concentric circles?
5. How could a parasite store increase the size of its trading area?
6. Explain Reilly's law. What are its advantages and disadvantages?
7. Use Huff's law to compute the probability of consumers' traveling from their homes to each of three shopping areas: square footage of selling space—Location 1, 1,000; Location 2, 2,000; Location 3, 4,000; travel time—to Location 1, 10 minutes; to Location 2, 10 minutes; to Location 3, 20 minutes; effect of travel time on shopping trip—2. Explain your answer.
8. What are the major advantages and disadvantages of *Census of Population* data in delineating trading areas?
9. Describe the kinds of retail information contained in the *Survey of Buying Power.* What is its most critical disadvantage?
10. Define the buying power index. How may it be used?
11. Evaluate the economic base of Sacramento, California. Refer to Figure 7-6.
12. If a retail area is acknowledged to be "satu-

rated," what does this signify for existing retailers? For prospective retailers considering this area?

13. Describe the criteria each of the following retailers should utilize in evaluating the level of competition in an area:
   a. Sporting-goods store
   b. Restaurant
   c. Drugstore

14. Calculate store saturation, given the following data:

Annual sales per customer	$400
Number of customers	117,000
Existing store footage	20,000 square feet
Proposed store footage	8,000 square feet

Explain your answer.

NOTES

1. "Phoenix: Rising in Its Demands for Centers," *Chain Store Age Executive* (November 1987), pp. 78–88; and "Retail Heats Up in the Valley of the Sun," *Chain Store Age Executive* (November 1987), pp. 96–98.

2. See "Why Site Selection," *Chain Store Age Executive* (January 1983), pp. 29–37; Eric C. Peterson, "Site Selection," *Stores* (July 1986), pp. 30–36; and Howard L. Green, "Good Site Analysts Know Where to Put a New Store," *Marketing News* (September 11, 1987), pp. 6–7.

3. Manuel D. Plotkin, "The Use of Credit Accounts and Computers in Determining Store Trading Areas," in Frederick E. Webster, Jr. (Editor), *New Directions in Marketing: Proceedings of the 48th National Conference of the American Marketing Association* (Chicago: American Marketing Association, 1965), p. 271.

4. Ralph S. Alexander (Chairman), *Marketing Definitions: A Glossary of Marketing Terms* (Chicago: American Marketing Association, 1960), p. 22.

5. "Selecting a Store Site, the Computer Way," *Chain Store Age Executive* (March 1981), p. 47.

6. Franklin S. Houston and John Stanton, "Evaluating Retail Trade Areas for Convenience Stores," *Journal of Retailing*, Vol. 60 (Spring 1984), pp. 124–136.

7. See Bernie Whalen, "'Cheap and Friendly' Software Lets 'Little Guys' Have In-House Mapping," *Marketing News* (March 16, 1984), Section 1, pp. 1, 4–5; Martha Farnsworth Riche, "Computer Mapping Takes Center Stage," *American Demographics* (June 1986), pp. 26–31 ff.; and "Site Selection: A Computerized Approach," *Chain Store Age Executive* (August 1987), pp. 48–50.

8. Larry D. Crabtree and James A. Paris, "Survey Car License Plates to Define Retail Trade Area," *Marketing News* (January 4, 1985), p. 12.

9. William J. Reilly, *Method for the Study of Retail Relationships*, Research Monograph No. 4 (Austin: University of Texas Press, 1929), University of Texas Bulletin No. 2944.

10. Richard L. Nelson, *The Selection of Retail Locations* (New York: F.W. Dodge, 1959), p. 149.

11. David L. Huff, "Defining and Estimating a Trading Area," *Journal of Marketing*, Vol. 28 (July 1964), pp. 34–38; and David L. Huff and Larry Blue, *A Programmed Solution for Estimating Retail Sales Potential* (Lawrence: University of Kansas, 1966).

12. A good summary of the research up to the early 1980s is C. Samuel Craig, Avijit Ghosh, and Sara Mc-Lafferty, "Models of the Retail Location Process: A Review," *Journal of Retailing*, Vol. 60 (Spring 1984), pp. 5–36.

13. David A. Gautschi, "Specification of Patronage Models for Retail Center Choice," *Journal of Marketing Research*, Vol. 18 (May 1981), pp. 162–174.

14. Glen E. Weisbrod, Robert J. Parcells, and Clifford Kern, "A Disaggregate Model for Predicting Shopping Area Market Attraction," *Journal of Retailing*, Vol. 60 (Spring 1984), pp. 65–83.

15. Avijit Ghosh, "The Value of a Mall and Other Insights from a Revised Central Place Model," *Journal of Retailing*, Vol. 62 (Spring 1986), pp. 79–97.

16. Ronald F. Bush, Ronald L. Tatham, and Joseph F. Hair, Jr., "Community Location Decisions by Franchisors: A Comparative Analysis," *Journal of Retailing*, Vol. 50 (Fall 1974), pp. 13–22 ff.

17. "Seeking the Elusive Dame," *Chain Store Age Executive* (January 1984), pp. 93–95.

18. Lewis A. Spalding, "New Store Locations," *Stores* (October 1980), pp. 30–35.

19. See James A. Paris, "How to Read a Demographic Report," *American Demographics* (April 1986), pp. 22–25 ff.; Lisa Del Priore, "Geomapping Tools for Market Analysis," *Marketing Communications* (March 1987), pp. 91–94; and John Chapman, "A Critical Eye," *American Demographics* (February 1987), pp. 30–33.

20. "Definitions of Terms Used in the Survey," *1987 Survey of Buying Power: Sales & Marketing Management* (July 27, 1987).

21. Jeffrey A. Trachtenberg, "The Second Battle of New Orleans," *Forbes* (July 2, 1984), pp. 65–66; Isadore Barmash, "Battle of Retailers in Dallas," *New York Times* (September 5, 1983), pp. 31–32; and "Retail Heats Up in the Land of the Sun," *Chain Store Age Executive* (November 1987), pp. 96–98.

22. Eugene Carlson, "Population Density Remains Primary Factor for Retailers," *Wall Street Journal* (November 6, 1984), p. 31; and "Developers Track the Data," *Chain Store Age Executive* (March 1984), pp. 80–81.

23. Adapted from Bernard J. LaLonde, "New Frontiers in Store Location," *Supermarket Merchandising* (February 1963), p. 110.

24. Charles A. Ingene and Robert F. Lusch, "Market Selection Decisions for Department Stores," *Journal of Retailing*, Vol. 56 (Fall 1980), p. 39.

Janet's Jewelry: Conducting a Trading-Area Analysis

Janet's Jewelry is a small local jewelry store that has been in the same location for the past twenty years. Janet Hill, the store's owner, feels that her store's long-standing success is attributable to three factors:

- ❏ Full service—Unlike many other jewelers, Janet's Jewelry can repair watches, size rings, and remodel old jewelry on the premises. This enables the firm to make emergency repairs for favored customers and to have more control over the quality of repairs. The repair business also generates sales for new merchandise, as in the case of watches.

- ❏ Fair pricing—Janet's Jewelry uses a standard 50 per cent markup at retail for most items (e.g., a ring costing $100 is sold for $200). Hill deplores retailers who inflate their initial prices and then run a "phony" 50-per-cent-off sale. Janet's Jewelry's semiannual special sales, which reduce regular prices by 20 per cent, represent real savings for customers.

- ❏ Wide assortments—Hill recognizes the necessity of having ample merchandise in stock. Customer purchases of many jewelry items, especially engagement rings, Valentine's Day presents, and anniversary gifts, are time sensitive. Being out of stock can easily lead to a lost sale.

Although Janet Hill has done well in her current location, she now faces the decision as to whether to renew her store lease. And this decision is not automatic, as several factors concern Janet. First, the new landlord will undoubtedly raise the rent between 30 and 50 per cent. Second, Hill feels that she is increasingly losing neighborhood customers to retail catalog showrooms, flea markets, and department stores. Yet, many of these customers come to Janet's Jewelry to reset, redesign, or repair merchandise purchased at these stores. Janet knows that many of the items are not being purchased at low prices, but customers perceive these merchants as offering better value than she does. Also, some of the items bought are thin, hollow gold, or sold through unauthorized distributors. Janet's Jewelry does not handle these items. Third, Hill realizes that many of the items desired by her traditional working-class customers are commoditylike (such as stamped-out gold bracelets and necklaces, "tank-style" watches, and inexpensive earrings). Janet would rather buy and sell more upscale pieces. Last, Hill recognizes that after twenty years at the same location, she would have to renovate the store at considerable expense in terms of money and time.

In evaluating her current site, Janet Hill has also conducted an informal trading-area analysis. Although she does not have good sales data, Janet feels that she can divide her trading area into primary, secondary, and fringe components on the basis of consumer characteristics. Primary trading-area customers generally purchase small gifts, such as necklaces, inexpensive rings, and earrings. Secondary trading-area customers are more affluent and purchase fine watches, heavier jewelry, and pearl necklaces. Fringe trading-area customers trust Hill and would travel to her regardless of where she is located. These customers typically purchase expensive watches and jewelry. See Table 1.

One new location that Janet Hill is seriously considering is about four miles from her current store. This would enable her to keep many of her primary trading-area customers and to be more accessible to most of her secondary and fringe trading-area patrons. Table 2 outlines the characteristics of the primary trading areas of the two locations.

The current and proposed sites are comparable in quality. Both are located on a main street along with suitable adjacent stores, such as a furrier, a ladies' accessory store, and a ladies' shoe store. They have similar pedestrian traffic and parking facilities.

TABLE 1
Janet's Jewelry's Present Trading Area

	Distance from the Store	Percentage of Customers	Percentage of Sales	Average Sale
Primary trading area	Less than 3 miles	70	30	$ 60
Secondary trading area	3–7 miles	25	35	$ 200
Fringe trading area	Above 7 miles	5	35	$1,000

TABLE 2
Trading-Area Characteristics for the Current and Proposed Locations

Characteristics	Current Location	Proposed Location
Population within 3 miles	11,800	7,500
Median household income	$30,000	$47,000
Number of jewelry stores within 3 miles	2	1
Estimate of Janet's Jewelry's annual sales	$340,000	$340,000

Hill estimates that the new location would be 20 per cent more costly than her present store (after adding in the anticipated rent increase); in either case, about $30,000 in renovations would be necessary.

QUESTIONS

1. Evaluate Tables 1 and 2.
2. What sources can Janet Hill use to further evaluate the current and proposed trading areas?
3. Develop a ten-item checklist for Janet Hill to consider before making a decision.
4. Should Janet Hill stay or move? Explain your answer.

Case 2

Big Man Shops: An Area Selection Decision for a Branch Store

Big Man Shops is a seven-store chain specializing in a full line of clothes for tall and big men. The chain started eighteen years ago, when its owner Jack Gale (a six-foot five-inch, 300-pound former college football star), realized the difficulties large men had in purchasing clothing and decided to open a store that caters to them.

The typical clothing store carries a few items that can fit men taller than six feet three inches and/or who weigh more than 235 pounds. As Gale describes it, "In the event a store stocks any clothes in large sizes, their styles are usually not up-to-date and there is no selection in the different sizes."

Few people realize the difficulties large men have when purchasing clothes. According to Gale, "Even ties have to be made especially for tall men. About the only item a traditional haberdashery store has that a big man can use is a handkerchief."

Even though Big Man Shops' strategy is aimed at a very small percentage of the population, the chain is very successful. This is attributed to three major factors. First, average purchases are high because men buy complete wardrobes when they shop. Because few stores stock items for large men, they satisfy all their clothing needs at Big Man Shops.

Second, the trading areas of Big Man Shops' outlets are quite large. The typical customer is willing to drive up to fifteen miles to a store; some travel as far as thirty miles. The large trading areas are due to the difficulty big men have in obtaining acceptable clothing near their homes, and to their aversion to buying through mail-order catalogs and shopping in department stores and traditional men's clothing stores.

Third, Jack Gale has always maintained a fair price and service policy. Prices are comparable to those in other clothing stores. In addition, free alterations are included in the prices, and adjustments are made if patrons are dissatisfied. Big Man Shops will repeatedly alter, free of charge, any garment purchased from it at full price (in case a customer gains or loses weight). This practice gets patrons back into the store on a regular basis and recognizes the special needs of big men, whose weight often fluctuates a lot.

Gale's strategy over the past eighteen years has been to invest company profits (after his salary) in expansion. This has given Jack great leverage in bargaining with suppliers, allows Big Man to obtain specially made styles, and enables the chain to use mass media (store locations have been arranged so that the market for the local newspaper has been blanketed).

Gale is currently searching for a location to place an eighth outlet. Two areas (Danbury, Massachusetts, and Caesar, Massachusetts) are under consideration. Data on these areas have been found in the *Census of Population,* the *Survey of Buying Power, Editor & Publisher Market Guide,* and other sources. The data are shown in Table 1.

The retailer has also compiled its own sales data for the Danbury and Caesar locations in order to assess trading-area overlap. This was easy to accomplish, since the name and address of each customer is recorded on sales invoices. See Table 2.

Jack Gale wants to select an area and a specific site in the area within the next two months. He wants to open the new branch within one year. The additional outlet is necessary for Gale to pursue his plans of advertising on the local television station.

TABLE 1
Proposed Areas for Locating a New Big Man Shops Outlet

	Danbury, Mass.	Caesar, Mass.
Population	20,000	35,000
Median household effective buying income	$37,000	$31,000
Percentage of employed who are professional, technical, managers, or administrators	45	30
Area's percentage of U.S. effective buying income	0.0103	0.0151
Area's percentage of U.S. retail sales	0.0099	0.0130
Area's percentage of U.S. population	0.0080	0.0143
Projected change in population (1988–1993)	+1.0%	+6.0%
Distance to nearest Big Man Shops store (miles and travel time)	23 miles, 35 minutes	14 miles, 20 minutes
Distance to nearest men's clothing store	4 miles	8 miles
Total square feet of men's clothing stores in trading area	8,000	12,500
Number of private autos	9,000	12,000

TABLE 2
Current Big Man Shops' Sales in Danbury and Caesar

	Danbury, Mass.	Caesar, Mass.
Number of residents who purchased at least one item in an existing Big Man store within the past year	150	525
Total sales in existing Big Man stores to residents within the past year	$38,750	$109,200

QUESTIONS

1. Compute the buying power indexes for Danbury and Caesar.
2. Evaluate the data in Tables 1 and 2.
3. On the basis of the information presented in the case, which area should Big Man Shops select?
4. What additional information should be studied before an area is selected?

Chapter 8

Site Selection

❑ **Chapter Objectives** ❑

1 To examine the types of locations available to a retailer: isolated store, unplanned business district, and planned shopping center

2 To present several criteria for evaluating general retail locations and the specific sites within them

3 To discuss a number of key location concepts, including the one-hundred per cent location and affinity

4 To contrast the alternatives of building, purchasing, and leasing store facilities

Today, Dadeland Mall in Florida is one of the most successful regional shopping centers in the United States. It attracts thirty million shoppers each year. But things were not always so rosy:

When Dadeland Mall opened its doors, 25 years ago, locals called it "Deadland." Executives of Burdines department store had chosen the vast, barren site from a blimp, but on the ground it was hardly inspiring. Land to the west was populated mainly with alligators, and the main east-west access road was known as "the road to nowhere."

Even now, "it doesn't include prize-winning architecture. Dadeland resembles a fallen tree trunk—a long strip, with branches grafted on during six expansions."

Dadeland's success is due to several factors. The population in the trading area has steadily risen. Median family income for nearby residents is 70 per cent greater than the average for the county. The highway system has improved dramatically. Popular stores anchor the mall. In addition to Burdines, there are Jordan Marsh, J.C. Penney, Saks Fifth Avenue, and Lord & Taylor units.

Dadeland began with 35 stores. Now, there are 175 stores, making Dadeland's "broad array of merchandise unmatched in the area." Furthermore, it began as an "open-air Florida-style" shopping center but converted to an enclosed mall to stimulate consumers to stay longer.

The mall's interior is well maintained, and storefronts stand out underneath a skylight and neon lighting. Individual stores are encouraged to renovate. For example, Baron's men's store recently invested $500,000 to upgrade its fixtures and facilities. And as that store's manager commented, "If you can't spend the money to upgrade, when your lease is up you'll be gone."[1]

244

After a retailer investigates alternative trading areas (Step 1), it then determines what type of location is desirable (Step 2), selects the general location (Step 3), and chooses a particular store site (Step 4). Steps 2, 3, and 4 are discussed in this chapter. **Overview**

There are three basic types of locations that a retailer should distinguish among: the isolated store, the unplanned business district, and the planned shopping center. Each of these types of location has its own characteristics relating to the composition of competing stores, parking facilities, nearness to nonretail institutions (such as office buildings), and other factors.

Types of Locations

Step 2 in the location process is a determination of which type of location to use.

The Isolated Store

An **isolated store** is a free-standing retail outlet located on either a highway or a side street. There are no adjacent retailers with which this type of store shares traffic.

The advantages of this type of retail location are many:

❏ There is no competition.
❏ Rental costs are low.
❏ There is flexibility.
   a. No group rules must be abided by in operation.
   b. Larger space may be attained.
   c. Location is by choice.
❏ Isolation is good for stores involved in one-stop or convenience shopping.
❏ Better road and traffic visibility is possible.
❏ Facilities can be adapted to individual specifications.
❏ Easy parking can be arranged.
❏ Cost reductions are possible, leading to lower prices.

There are also various disadvantages to this retail location:

❏ Initial customers may be difficult to attract.
❏ Many people like variety in shopping.
❏ Many consumers will not travel to one store.
❏ Advertising costs may be high.
❏ Operating costs cannot be shared, such as outside lighting, security, maintenance of grounds, and garbage collection.
❏ Zoning laws may restrict access to desirable locations.
❏ In most cases, a store must be built rather than rented.

The difficulty of attracting and holding a target market is the reason that large or convenience-oriented retailers are usually those best suited to isolated locations. Smaller specialty stores may be unable to develop a customer following because customers may be unwilling to travel to or shop at isolated stores that do not have a wide assortment of products (width and/or depth) and a local or national reputation.

Years ago, when discount operations were frowned on by traditional retailers, shopping centers forbade the entry of discounters. This forced the discounters

245

to become isolated stores or to build their own centers, and they have been successful.

Today, various retailers operate in isolated locations as well as at business-district and shopping-center sites. Examples of retailers using this location strategy are K mart, Kinney Shoes, McDonald's, Carvel, and Sears. Some retailers, such as many gasoline stations and convenience stores, continue to operate predominantly in isolated spots.

The Unplanned Business District

An **unplanned business district** is a retail location where two or more stores are situated together or in a close proximity that is not the result of prior planning. Stores situate on the basis of what is best for them, not for the district. Accordingly, four shoe stores may exist in an area that has no pharmacy.

There are four types of unplanned business districts: the central business district, the secondary business district, the neighborhood business district, and the string. A brief description of each of these follows.

Central Business District

The **central business district (CBD)** is the hub of retailing in a city. It is the largest shopping area in a city and is synonymous with the term "downtown." The CBD exists in that part of a town or city that has the greatest concentration of office buildings and retail stores. Vehicular and pedestrian traffic are highly concentrated. The core of the CBD usually does not exceed a square mile. Cultural and entertainment facilities surround it. Consumers are drawn from the whole urban area and include all ethnic groups and all classes of people.

The CBD has at least one major department store and a broad grouping of specialty and convenience stores. The arrangement of these stores follows no format; it depends on history (first come, first located), retail trends, and luck.

The CBD has various strengths and weaknesses. These are some of the strengths that enable CBDs to attract a large number of shoppers and potential shoppers: the excellent goods/service assortment available, access to public transportation, the variety of store images within one area, the variety of prices offered, the variety of customer services, the high level of pedestrian traffic, and the nearness to commercial and social facilities. In addition, chain headquarters are often situated in CBDs. Some of the inherent weaknesses of the CBD are inadequate parking, traffic and delivery congestion, increased travel time for those living in the suburbs, the age of the retail facilities, the declining condition of many central cities, high rents and taxes, and the discontinuity of offerings (e.g., four shoe stores and no pharmacy).

Although the central business district remains a major force in retailing, over the past thirty-five years its share of overall sales has declined substantially relative to those of the planned shopping center. Much of the decline has been the result of the continuing suburbanization of the population. In the first half of the twentieth century, central cities had a well-balanced mix of income, racial, and cultural groups, but gradually, many middle-class and well-to-do people have moved to the suburbs (where they are served by planned shopping centers).

Nonetheless, a number of CBDs are doing well and others are striving to return to their former stature. Many are applying innovations such as closing off streets to vehicular traffic, modernizing storefronts and equipment, developing strong cooperative merchants' associations, planting trees to create "atmosphere," building vertical malls (with several floors of stores), improving transportation, and integrating a commercial and residential environment. There are signs of a turnaround in a number of cities.

One of the best examples of a CBD turnaround involves Minneapolis. Its Downtown Council has worked hard to strengthen the CBD to make it more competitive with suburban shopping centers and to stimulate office construction. The Nicollet Mall, the hub of the Minneapolis downtown renewal area, received an initial $38-million investment (which has been supplemented many times since the revival began). Most of the financing was raised through property assessments on "benefit zones" around the mall. The assessment formula included two kinds of benefit zones (on the mall and off the mall), and each zone was subdivided into sectors so that properties closest to the center would bear the greatest proportion of both construction and maintenance expenses.

The mall is a totally reconstructed area containing more than a dozen city blocks, with redesigned streets shared by pedestrians and public transit. Cars can cross the mall at through streets but are not allowed on the mall itself. Sidewalks are wide. Above-ground "skyways" connect buildings for pedestrians. There are benches for relaxing and resting. Shade trees, flowers, and fountains add to the atmosphere. Frequent activities such as boat shows, symphony orchestra performances, and antique car exhibits sustain a sense of excitement. In late 1987, The Conservatory, a new $75-million specialty-store shopping complex was opened to "re-establish downtown Minneapolis as the regional destination for upscale shopping."[2]

Faneuil Hall in Boston is a different type of successful CBD renovation. When developer James Rouse took over the 6.5-acre site containing three 150-year-old, block-long former food warehouses, the site had been abandoned for almost ten years. Rouse creatively used landscaping, fountains, banners, courts, and graphics to enable Faneuil Hall to capture a "spirit of festival." Faneuil Hall has combined shopping, eating, and watching activities and made them fun. Today, Faneuil Hall attracts around ten million visitors annually, almost as many as Disneyland in California.[3]

Other major CBD projects include Bayside Marketplace (Miami), Ford City (Chicago), The Gallery (Philadelphia), City Center Square (St. Louis), the Silicon Valley Financial Center (San Jose), and Grand Avenue (Milwaukee).[4]

Secondary Business District

The **secondary business district (SBD)** is a shopping area in a city or town that is usually bounded by the intersection of two major streets. Cities generally have several SBDs, each having at least a junior department store, a variety store, and several small service shops. The SBD has grown in importance as cities have increased in population and "sprawled" over larger geographic areas.

The types of goods and services sold in the SBD are similar to those in the central business district. However, the SBD has smaller stores, less width and depth of assortment, and a smaller trading area (consumers will not travel very far) and sells many convenience items.

The strengths and weaknesses of the SBD are similar to those of the CBD. The major strengths are good product assortment, access to public transportation or thoroughfares, less crowding, more personalized service, and location near residential areas. The major weaknesses are discontinuity of offerings, high rent and taxes (not as high as in the CBD), congestion of traffic and deliveries, aging facilities, parking difficulties, and fewer chain stores. In general, these weaknesses have not affected the SBD to the extent that they have affected the CBD, and parking problems, travel time, and congestion are less for the SBD.

Neighborhood Business District

The **neighborhood business district (NBD)** is a shopping area that emerges to satisfy the convenience-shopping needs of a neighborhood. The NBD contains several small stores, with the major retailer being either a supermarket or a variety store, and it is located on the major street(s) of a residential area.

This business district offers consumers a good location, long store hours, good parking, and a less hectic atmosphere than either the CBD or the SBD. On the

Back to the Streets?

After years of situating mostly in planned shopping centers, a number of leading retail chains are now "taking to the streets." These firms include The Gap, Pier I, The Limited, Benetton, and Talbot's. Given all the positive attributes of shopping-center sites and the problems with unplanned locations, why are retailers going back to the streets?

Two experts answer this way:

The reasoning is fairly simple. No. 1 is that they're not building as many regional malls or malls that normal mall-type tenants would look to occupy. No. 2, these chain stores still have to expand. And No. 3, they're finding that occupancy costs in the malls are killing them. Maybe the minimum rent is OK, but they have to pay all sorts of extra fees or charges.

In additon to generally lower rents and related charges, retailers also cite setting their own store hours, longer lease terms, and less stringent construction criteria as some of the advantages of street locations.

The lack of adequate shopping-center space is particularly evident in the Northeast. However, the chain retailers noted above are not necessarily returning to traditional downtown locales. Instead, they are placing stores on streets or village squares in suburban areas such as Shadyside, Pennsylvania (outside Pittsburgh), and Birmingham, Michigan (outside Detroit). Said Talbot's real-estate manager, "We go to our customers' doorsteps. They live in the suburbs where there's a nice village square with a few shops and stores. That's where we go because that's where they are."

Source: Based on material in Holly Klokis, "Retailers Are Taking to the Streets," *Chain Store Age Executive* (September 1987), pp. 19–22.

---

other hand, there is a limited selection of goods and services, and prices (on the average) tend to be higher because competition is less than in the CBD or the SBD.

String

The **string** is composed of a group of retail stores, often with similar or compatible product lines, that have located along a street or highway. A string may start as an isolated store, success then breeding competitors. Car dealers, antique stores, and clothing stores are examples of the types of stores that locate in a string. There is little extension of the shopping area onto streets perpendicular to the string street.

A string location possesses many of the advantages associated with an isolated store site (low rent, flexibility, road visibility, parking, lower operating costs), along with some of its disadvantages (limited variety of products, travel time, high advertising costs, zoning, building of premises). Unlike an isolated store, a string store has competition. This causes more customer traffic and allows for some sharing of common costs. It also leads to less control over prices and lower store loyalty. But the increase in traffic flow may exceed the losses caused by competition. This may explain why four gasoline service stations will locate on opposing corners.

Figure 8-1 shows a map depicting the various forms of unplanned business districts and isolated locations.

The Planned Shopping Center

A **planned shopping center** is centrally owned or managed, is planned as a unit, is based on balanced tenancy (the group of stores complement each other

Legend:
A Central Business District
B Secondary Business District
C Neighborhood Business District
D String
E Isolated Location

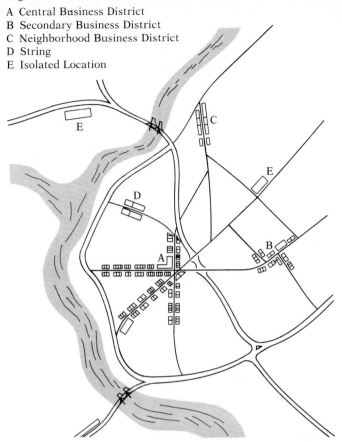

FIGURE 8-1
Unplanned Business Districts and Isolated Locations
Courtesy Kenneth Cooperman.

in the quality and variety of their merchandise offerings), and is surrounded by parking facilities. **Balanced tenancy** means that the type and number of stores within any planned center are related to the overall needs of the surrounding population. To ensure that balance will exist, a planned shopping center often specifies the proportion of total space that can be occupied by each type of retailer. In addition, the center places limits on the merchandise lines that can be stocked by each of the various retailers.

The planned center has one or more anchor, or generator, stores and a variety of smaller stores. In most cases, a unified and cooperative retailing strategy is followed. This locational format has grown to the point where annual sales in the nation's more than 30,000 shopping centers are expected to comprise about half of total retail-store sales by 1990.

There are several reasons for the success of the planned shopping center. Here are some of them:

❏ Well-rounded goods and service offerings because of long-range planning.
❏ Growing suburban population.
❏ Interest in one-stop, family shopping.
❏ Cooperative planning and sharing of common costs.

❑ Creation of a distinctive shopping-center image.
❑ Maximization of pedestrian traffic through the location of the center and individual stores.
❑ Access to highways and availability of parking.
❑ Declining appeal of city shopping.
❑ Lower rent and taxes than central district stores.
❑ Lower theft rates.
❑ Popularity of malls.
  a. Open (shopping area closed to vehicular traffic).
  b. Closed (shopping area closed to vehicular traffic and all stores under one temperature-controlled roof). See Figure 8-2.
❑ Growth of discount malls.

FIGURE 8-2
The Closed Shopping Mall
Many of J.C. Penney's stores are situated in closed shopping malls, such as the one shown here, throughout the United States. Reprinted by permission.

Despite this overwhelming list of reasons for locating in a planned shopping center, there are some potential limitations to this arrangement:

❑ Regulations that reduce each retailer's operating flexibility, such as required store hours.
❑ Rent higher than for an isolated store.
❑ Restrictions as to the goods/services that can be sold by each store.
❑ Competitive environment.
❑ Required payments for items that may be of little or no value to an individual retailer, such as membership in a merchants' association.
❑ Overexpansion.
❑ Domination by large anchor stores.

The importance of planned shopping centers can be seen by an examination of several factors. First, in 1956, there were 940 centers; by 1987, there were over 30,000, including 3,000 closed shopping malls. Second, center customers are active. Of all consumers who patronize shopping centers, about 70 per cent shop at some type of center at least once each week. Third, individual retail chains have large stakes in shopping centers. For example, The Limited, B. Dalton Bookseller, and J.C. Penney are among the vast number of chains that derive substantial sales and profits from outlets in shopping centers.

Fourth, some big retailers have been involved in shopping-center development. Typically, these firms buy a site of their choosing, years in advance, and contact another major retailer (depending on the center's size). They then bring in a developer, who builds, owns, and leases the center and connects it to anchor stores. For instance, Sears has participated in the construction of dozens of shopping centers, and Publix Supermarkets operates centers with hundreds of small-store tenants. Fifth, most of total new retail square footage and about 90 per cent of new department stores currently being constructed are in shopping centers.[5]

To sustain their long-term growth, shopping centers are engaging in a variety of practices:

❑ Several older centers have been or are being renovated, expanded, repositioned, and so on. Mall of the Americas (formerly named the Midway Mall) in Dade County, Florida; Marquette Mall in Michigan City, Indiana; Seminary South in Fort Worth, Texas; and Chesterfield Mall in Richmond, Virginia—these are just a few of the ten- to twenty-five-year-old centers that have recently been revitalized.[6]
❑ The mix of retailers has been broadened at many centers to attract greater customers to one-stop shopping. The centers are now more likely to include banks, stock brokers, dentists, beauty salons, theaters, television repair services, and car-leasing offices.[7]
❑ Some off-price shopping centers are locating in suburban areas. Unlike traditional off-price sites, these centers feature new stores and balanced tenancy. One such off-price center is the Washington Outlet Mall in Dale City, Virginia. It has over 1 million square feet of space, large anchor stores, and 100 smaller stores. It expects to draw customers from as far as 250 miles away, with a regular trading area of 60 to 90 miles.[8]

There are three major types of planned shopping centers: regional, community, and neighborhood. The characteristics of these centers are displayed in Table 8-1, and they are described next.

TABLE 8-1
Characteristics of Neighborhood, Community, and Regional Types of Planned Shopping Centers

Features	Type of Center		
	Regional	Community	Neighborhood
Floor area (sq ft)	400,000 to over 2,000,000	100,000–400,000	30,000–100,000
Average gross floor area (sq ft)	750,000	200,000	40,000
Average site area (acres)	30–100+	10–30	3–10
Minimum number of families and people needed to support center	50,000–300,000 families; over 100,000 people	5,000–10,000 families; 20,000–100,000 people	1,000 families; 3,000–50,000 people
Principal tenant	One, two, or more department stores	Variety or junior department store	Supermarket or drugstore
Number of stores	50–125 or more	15–25	5–15
Types of goods sold	Emphasis on shopping goods, large assortment	Mostly convenience goods, some shopping goods	Emphasis on convenience goods
Trading area in driving time	Up to 30 minutes	Up to 20 minutes	Fewer than 15 minutes
Location	Outside central city, on arterial highway or expressway	Close to populated suburbs	Along a major thoroughfare
Layout	Mall, often enclosed with anchor stores at either end	Strip or L shape	Strip
% of all centers	7	26	67

Regional Shopping Center

The **regional shopping center** is a planned shopping location that sells predominantly shopping goods to a geographically dispersed market. A regional center has at least one or two large department stores and as many as 100 or more small retailers, as illustrated in Figure 8-3. The market for the average regional center is over 100,000 people, who live up to thirty minutes' driving time from the center. (People travel an average of seventeen minutes.) Some large regional shopping centers have as many as six major retailers and 2 million or more square feet of space.

The regional center is the result of a planned effort to re-create the shopping services of a central city in suburbia. Some experts even credit the regional shopping center with becoming the social, cultural, and vocational focal point of an entire community. Frequently, a regional shopping center is used as a town plaza, a community meeting place, and a concert hall. A *U.S. News & World Report* survey found that Americans spend more time in shopping centers than anywhere else outside their home and workplace. And according to *Chain Store Age Executive,* on a typical visit to a regional center, two-thirds of all customers spend two hours or more there.

The first regional shopping center was established in 1950 in Seattle, Washington, anchored by a branch of Bon Marche, a large downtown department store. Southdale Center (outside Minneapolis), built in 1956 for the Dayton Hudson Corporation, was the first fully enclosed, climate-controlled mall.

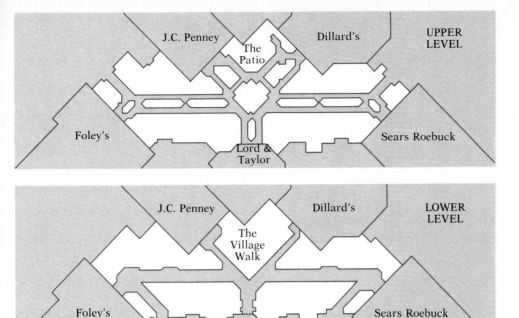

FIGURE 8-3
The Collin Creek Mall, Dallas, Texas
The Collin Creek Mall is anchored by the five department stores shown above. The mall also contains more than 160 other shops and restaurants (which are situated in the white spaces adjacent to the anchor stores). Over 250,000 people live within 10 miles of Collin Creek. Courtesy Collin Creek Mall.

Community Shopping Center

The **community shopping center** is a planned shopping area that sells both convenience and shopping items to city and suburban dwellers. The community shopping center has a variety store and/or a small department store in addition to the outlets found in a neighborhood shopping center. A greater assortment of products is available than in a neighborhood center. From 20,000 to 100,000 people, who live within ten to twenty minutes of the center, are serviced by this type of retail arrangement.

Greater and more long-range planning is used for the community shopping center than for the neighborhood shopping center. For example, balanced tenancy is usually enforced strictly. A barbershop owner would have to sell to someone interested in continuing the business. The store could not be sold to a dry cleaner.

Neighborhood Shopping Center

The **neighborhood shopping center** is a planned shopping area that sells mostly convenience items. The largest store is a supermarket and/or a drugstore. Other retailers in the center may include a hardware store, a barbershop and/or a beauty parlor, a bakery, a laundry–dry cleaner, and a gasoline station. The neighborhood shopping center caters to 3,000 to 50,000 people who live within fifteen minutes' driving time (usually less than ten minutes).

The neighborhood shopping center is usually arranged in a strip. When first developed, it is carefully planned, and tenants are balanced. Over time, the planned aspects of this center diminish as newcomers face fewer restrictions. For example, a barbership could be replaced by a liquor store. In this case, there would be no barbership. The ability of the center to maintain balance depends on its continuing attractiveness to potential tenants.

The difference between the neighborhood shopping center and the string is that the former plans to satisfy a wide range of consumer needs and the latter concentrates on individual store planning and success.

Choice of a General Location

The last part of Step 2 in location planning requires the retailer to choose one of the three types of locations: isolated, unplanned district, or planned center. The choice would depend on the retailer's strategy and a careful evaluation of the advantages and disadvantages of each type of location.

As an illustration, Lamston (a Northeastern variety-store chain) avoids planned shopping centers and concentrates on unplanned business districts:[9]

> One reason why variety stores have not done well in malls is because that's where people go when they have a lot of time to shop. In a mall, unlike a downtown location, a customer is offered a specialty store in every line we carry. If she wants to buy a greeting card, she goes to a greeting card store or whatever.
>
> We need heavily trafficked areas where the customers have to shop in a hurry. [Then customers] want to find that variety of merchandise at one store. We benefit from offering a convenience that stands us in good stead in our locations.

Once the type of location is determined, the retailer must select a broadly defined store site, Step 3. Two decisions are necessary. First, the specific type of isolated store, unplanned business district, or planned shopping center location must be picked. If the retailer wants an isolated store, it must decide whether to locate on a highway or a side street. Should the retailer desire an unplanned business area, it must opt for a location in a CBD, an SBD, an NBD, or a string. The retailer seeking a planned area must choose either a regional, a community, or a neighborhood shopping center.

Second, the retailer must define the general location. For an isolated store, a specific highway or side street is selected. For an unplanned district or planned center, the specific district (e.g., downtown Los Angeles or a Pittsburgh suburb) or center (e.g., Southdale) is designated.

In Step 3, the retailer narrows down the decisions made in the first two steps and selects a general location. Step 4 requires the retailer to select the exact site, including the position on a block (or in a center), the side of the street, and the terms of tenancy. The evaluations of a general location and a specific site within that location are described together in the next section because many strategic decisions are similar for these two steps.

Location and Site Evaluation

The evaluation of each general location and the specific sites contained within them requires extensive analysis. Site selection is as crucial as the choice of a retail area, especially for stores that rely on customer traffic patterns to generate business.

In any area, the optimum site for a particular store is called the **one-hundred per cent location.** Because different kinds of retailers need different kinds of locations, a location classified as 100 per cent for one retailer may be less than optimal for another retailer.

For example, a ladies' specialty shop may seek a location with different strengths from those desired by a convenience store. The specialty shop would benefit from heavy pedestrian traffic, closeness to major department stores, and proximity to other specialty stores. The convenience store would rather locate in an area with ample parking and heavy vehicular traffic. It does not need to be close to other stores.

Figure 8-4 contains a checklist for location and site evaluation. When choosing

Rate each of the following criteria on a scale of 1 to 10, with 1 being excellent and 10 being poor		
Pedestrian Traffic	Number of people	_____
	Type of people	_____
Vehicular Traffic	Number of vehicles	_____
	Type of vehicles	_____
	Traffic congestion	_____
Parking Facilities	Number and quality of parking spots	_____
	Distance to store	_____
	Availability of employee parking	_____
Transportation	Availability of mass transit	_____
	Access from major highways	_____
	Ease of deliveries	_____
Store Composition	Number and size of stores	_____
	Affinity	_____
	Retail balance	_____
Specific Site	Visibility	_____
	Placement in the location	_____
	Size and shape of the lot	_____
	Size and shape of the building	_____
	Condition and age of the lot and building	_____
Terms of Occupancy	Ownership or leasing terms	_____
	Operations and maintenance costs	_____
	Taxes	_____
	Zoning restrictions	_____
	Voluntary regulations	_____
Overall Rating	General location	_____
	Site	_____

FIGURE 8-4
A Location/Site Evaluation Checklist

a location, the retailer would rate each alternative location (and specific site) on all of the criteria and develop an overall rating for each alternative. It should be pointed out again that two stores may rate the same location quite differently, depending on the requirements of the stores. Also, this figure should be used in conjunction with the area data discussed in Chapter 7, not instead of them.

Pedestrian Traffic

Probably the single most important measure of a location's and site's value is the number and type of people passing by it. Other things being equal, the site with the highest pedestrian traffic is often best.

Because everyone passing by a store site is not a good prospect for all types of stores, many retailers employ selective counting procedures, such as counting only males and females carrying shopping bags. Otherwise, pedestrian traffic totals will include too many nonshoppers. As an example, it would be incorrect for an appliance store to count as prospective shoppers all of the people who pass the store on the way to work. In fact, much of the traffic in a downtown location may be people who are in the area for specific nonretailing activities.

A proper pedestrian traffic count should include these four elements:

❑ A separation of the count by age and gender (children under a certain age should not be counted).

❑ A division of the count by time (this allows the study of peaks, low points, and changes in the gender of the people passing by the hour).

❑ Pedestrian interviews (these enable the researchers to verify the proportion of potential shoppers).

❑ Spot analysis of shopping trips (these interviews verify stores visited or planned to be visited).

Vehicular Traffic

The quantity and characteristics of vehicular traffic must be examined, especially by retailers who appeal to driving customers. Stores in regional shopping centers, fast-food franchises, gasoline stations, and convenience food stores are examples of drive-in retailers that depend on heavy vehicular traffic. Automotive traffic studies are particularly important in suburban areas, where pedestrian traffic is often limited.

As in the analysis of pedestrian traffic, some adjustments to the raw count of vehicular traffic should be made. Some retailers count only homeward-bound traffic. Some exclude vehicles passing on the other side of a divided highway. Many retailers omit out-of-state license plates in their counts.

Data pertaining to traffic patterns are usually available from the state highway department, the county engineer, or the regional planning commission.

In addition to traffic counts, the retailer should study the extent and timing of congestion (caused by heavy traffic, detours, narrow and poor roads, and so on). Vehicular customers will normally avoid heavily congested areas and will shop in areas where driving time and driving difficulties are minimized.

Parking Facilities

The importance of good parking facilities must not be overlooked in an evaluation of a location and a specific site within it. The vast majority of all retail stores built in the United States since the end of World War II include some provision for off-street parking. In several central business districts, parking facilities are provided by individual stores, cooperative arrangements among stores, and municipal governments. The number and quality of parking spots, their distances from the store site, and the availability of employee parking should all be evaluated.

It is difficult to generalize about the parking needs of retailers. However, shopping centers normally require about 4 or 5 parking spaces per 1,000 square feet of gross floor area. The needs of different retailers vary significantly, depending on the length of an average shopping trip and the variation of shoppers during a day or season. A supermarket may require 10 to 15 parking spaces per 1,000 square feet of gross floor area, whereas a furniture store needs only 3 or 4 parking spaces per 1,000 square feet. With more compact cars on the road, the Urban Land Institute recommends that retailers restripe their parking lots. This would increase the number of parking spaces by 15–30 per cent.[10]

Sometimes, free parking in shopping locations close to downtown areas creates problems. Commuters and employees of nearby businesses park in these facilities, reducing the number of spaces available for shoppers. This problem can be lessened by the validation of shoppers' parking stubs and requiring payment from nonshoppers.

Another problem occurs when the number of stores in a location expands. The increase in stores can be the result of a growing population in the trading area or a reaction to increased competition from another shopping location. Whatever the reason, parking facilities may suffer because space that was formerly allocated to parking is used for new store sites, and because parking needs rise to accommodate new employees, new shoppers, and longer shopping trips.

Double-deck parking or parking tiers are possible solutions to this problem. In addition to saving land, these types of parking shorten the distance from a parked car to a store. This is important when one recognizes that a customer of a regional shopping center does not like to walk more than five hundred feet from his or her car to the center.

Having too large a parking facility may also create a problem. If the facility is not full, store image may suffer. An illusion of emptiness is created, and customers wonder why. A parking lot may contain 150 cars, but if the capacity of the lot is 500 cars, it appears that the lot is empty and the stores unpopular.

Parking adequacy, as mentioned, is difficult to determine. It depends on factors such as the trading area of the store, the type of store, the portion of shoppers using an automobile, the existence of other parking facilities, the turnover of spaces, parking by nonshoppers, and fluctuations in parking demand.

Transportation

The availability of mass transportation, access from major highways, and ease of deliveries must be examined in the evaluation of a location and a specific site.

In downtown areas, closeness to public transportation is important, particularly to customers who do not own cars or customers who would not drive into an area with heavy traffic congestion and poor parking. The availability of buses, taxicabs, subways, trains, or other kinds of public transportation must be investigated for locations not catering to vehicular traffic. Most downtown shopping areas are at the hub of a transportation network, allowing customers from all over a city to shop there.

Locations depending on vehicular traffic should be rated on the basis of their access to major thoroughfares. As mentioned in the previous chapter, driving time is an important consideration for many customers. In addition, drivers heading eastbound on a highway often do not like to make a U-turn to get to a store on the westbound side of the highway.

The transportation network should also be examined for its ability to convey heavy delivery trucks to and from the store. Many thoroughfares are excellent for customer traffic but ban truck traffic or are unable to bear its weight.

Store Composition

The store composition in the area should be studied. How many stores are there? How large are they? The number and size of stores should be consistent with the kind of location selected. For example, a retailer interested in an isolated site would want no stores nearby; a retailer interested in a neighborhood business district would want to locate in an area with ten or fifteen small stores; and a retailer interested in a regional shopping center would desire a location with more than fifty stores, including at least two large ones.

A store's compatibility with adjacent or nearby retailers should be weighed. **Affinity** occurs when various stores are attracted to the same location in order to complement, blend, and cooperate with one another, and each benefits from the others' presence. If stores located together have a strong level of affinity, the sales of each store are greater, because of the high level of customer traffic, than they would be if the stores were situated apart from each other.

The practice of similar or complementary stores' locating near each other is based on two major premises: (1) customers like to compare the offerings of similar stores as to price, style, selection, and service, and (2) customers like the concept of one-stop shopping. A variety of products are often purchased from different stores (complementary) on the same shopping trip. Thus, affinities can exist among competitive stores as well as among complementary stores; because many more consumers will travel to shopping areas with large selections than to more convenience-oriented ones, the sales of all stores are enhanced.

One measure of compatibility is the degree to which stores exchange customers. The stores within the following categories are very compatible with each other and have a high level of customer interchange:

❑ Drugstore, supermarket, bakery, fruit-and-vegetable store, meat store.
❑ Department store, apparel store, hosiery store, lingerie shop, shoe store, variety store, jewelry store, dry goods store, knitting store.

For example, Publix Supermarkets are frequently located in neighborhood shopping centers with Eckerd drugstores; Publix does not locate in regional centers because of the different nature of the shopping trip and the low turnover of parking spaces. Radio Shack likes its stores to be near hardware or menswear outlets; it views beauty salons negatively. Walgreen rates small centers with laundromats highly: "People in laundromats have nothing to do while waiting for their clothes to go around."[11]

A location's retail balance should also be considered. **Retail balance** refers to the mix of stores within a district or shopping center. Proper balance occurs when the number of store facilities for each merchandise or service classification is equal to the location's market potential; when a wide range of goods and service classifications is provided to ensure one-stop shopping; when there is an adequate assortment within any good or service classification; and when there is a proper mix of store types (tenant balance).

Specific Site

In addition to the criteria already detailed, the specific site should be evaluated on the basis of visibility, placement in the location, size and shape of the lot, size and shape of the building, and condition and age of the lot and building.

Visibility is a site's ability to be seen by pedestrian and vehicular traffic. A site that is on a side street or at the end of a shopping center does not achieve the same visibility as a site on a major road or at the entrance of a shopping center. High visibility makes passersby aware that a store exists and is open. Furthermore, some shoppers feel uncomfortable going down a side street or to the end of a center.

Placement in the location refers to a site's relative position in the district or center. A corner location is often desirable because it is situated at the intersection of two streets and therefore results in "corner influence." A corner site is usually more expensive to own or lease because it offers these advantages: increased show-window display area, greater pedestrian traffic due to converging traffic flows from two streets, and easing of traffic congestion through the use of two or more entrances. Corner influence is greatest in high-volume retail locations. As an example, most of the 7-Eleven stores opened since 1980 occupy corner lots.

Some of the advantages of a corner location are reduced in a shopping center. For instance, traffic on the streets perpendicular to a mall is usually sparse. Accordingly, little additional traffic accrues to a corner store. Also, because many stores have two entrances (one in the mall and one in the parking area), shoppers can go from parking spots to the main mall without using the designated walkways, window display space is greater, and traffic flows are eased.

Placement decisions should be keyed to retailer needs. For example, a convenience-oriented retailer, such as a stationery store, would have needs much different from a shopping-oriented retailer, such as a furniture store. The stationery store would be concerned about the side of the street, the location relative to other stores, nearness to parking, access to a bus stop, and distance from homes. The furniture store would be interested in roominess, the accessibility of its pickup platform to consumers, the ease of deliveries to the store, the use of a corner site to increase window display space, and proximity to wallpaper and other related retailers.

The size and shape of the lot should be evaluated. As an example, a department store requires significantly larger space than a boutique; and a department store may desire a square site, whereas the boutique may seek a rectangular site. Any site should be assessed in terms of the total space needed: parking, walkways, selling, nonselling, and so on.

When a retailer buys or rents an existing building, its size and shape should be examined. In addition, the condition and age of the lot and the building should be investigated. These site characteristics are then measured against the needs of the retailer.

Several retailers have developed computer models to aid in site selection. One firm, Victory Markets (a large supermarket chain operating out of Norwich, New York), has constructed a model to predict the weekly retail sales of a potential site. Safeway has used computerized site-selection models since 1973. A number of department store chains use computer models in selecting regional shopping-center sites.

There are three types of computer site-selection models: analog, regression, and gravity. The **analog model** is the most simple and popular model. Potential sales are estimated on the basis of competition, market shares, and the size and density of the primary trading area. The **regression model** develops a series of mathematical equations that show the association between sales and a variety of independent variables at each location under consideration. As an illustration, Victory Markets analyzes population, number of households, existence of rivers and railroad tracks, and traffic patterns. The **gravity model** is an adaptation of Reilly's law, which is based on the theory that consumers gravitate to stores that are closer and more attractive than competitors'. Variables such as the distance between consumers and competitors, the distance between consumers and the site, and store image are contained in a gravity model.

Computer site-selection models offer several benefits to retailers: they are more objective and systematic than nonquantitative evaluation methods; they offer insights into the weight of each locational attribute; they are useful in the screening of a large number of locations; and they can be used to assess management performance by comparing forecasts with actual results.

Terms of Occupancy

Terms of occupancy must be evaluated. They include ownership versus leasing, the type of lease, operations and maintenance costs, taxes, zoning restrictions, and voluntary regulations.

Ownership Versus Leasing

A retailer with adequate financial resources can either own or lease premises. Ownership is more common in small stores, in small communities, and/or at inexpensive locations. It has several advantages over leasing. There is no risk that an outside property owner will not renew a lease or will double or triple rent when a lease expires. With ownership, monthly mortgage payments are stable. Operations are flexible; the retailer can engage in scrambled merchandising, break down walls, and so on. It is also likely that property value will appreciate over time, giving a retailer a tangible asset if it decides to sell the business. The disadvantages of ownership are the high initial costs, the long-term commitment that is necessary, and the inflexibility in changing sites.

If a retailer chooses to own its store premises, it must decide whether to construct a new facility or purchase an existing building. In weighing these alternatives, a retailer should consider the purchase price and maintenance costs, zoning restrictions, the age and condition of existing facilities, the adaptability of existing facilities to its needs, and the time necessary to erect a new building. To encourage building rehabilitation in small towns (5,000 to 50,000 people), Congress enacted the Main Street program of the National Trust for Historic Preservation in 1981. Retailers have benefited through participation in this program by receiving tax credits and low-interest loans.[12]

Despite the advantages of ownership, most retailers lease store sites. This enables them to minimize initial investment, reduce risk, move to prime locations that could not handle additional stores, gain immediate occupancy and customer traffic, and reduce long-term commitment. Retailers may also feel that they can open more outlets or spend more on other elements of a strategy mix via leasing. These firms accept the disadvantages of leasing: limits on operating flexibility, restrictions on subletting and selling the business, nonrenewal problems, future rent increases, and no benefit from the rising value of real estate.

Some large retailers build their new stores and then sell them to real-estate investors who lease the buildings back to the retailers on a long-term basis. This practice is known as a **sale-leaseback.** Retailers using sale-leasebacks can construct stores to their specifications, have bargaining power in leasing terms, and reduce their capital expenditures.

Recently, tax-exempt industrial revenue bonds have also been used to finance retail facilities. In this arrangement, a state or municipality uses bond proceeds to build stores or warehouses and gives retailers long leases (with the payments used to pay bond principal and interest). The practice reduces location costs for retailers.

Types of Leases

Because most retailers lease facilities, it is important to understand the types of leases being used by building owners: straight lease, percentage lease, graduated lease, maintenance-increase-recoupment lease, and net lease. Property owners no longer rely only on constant rent payments, partly because of the high inflation rate in the early 1980s, and terms can therefore become quite complicated. A typical lease runs from five to twenty years, although some are shorter and others are longer.

The simplest, most straightforward arrangement is the **straight lease.** With this type of agreement, a retailer pays a fixed dollar amount per month over the life of the lease. Rent usually ranges from $1 to $50 annually per square foot, depending on the desirability of the location, store traffic, and so on. In some sites, rents can be much higher (up to $400 per square foot and more). Nationwide, rents in large shopping malls average $12 per square foot, including common-area charges.[13]

A **percentage lease** stipulates that rent is related to the retailer's sales or profits. In contrast, a straight rental lease provides for constant payments each month,

Temporary Tenants: Here Today, Gone Tomorrow?

When the phrase "short-term lease" is used in retailing, it usually refers to a situation in which a tenant rents a store facility for one to three years. But some creative shopping-center operators are now really focusing on the words *short term;* they are allowing some tenants to sign leases for as little as one day or one week. In such arrangements, tenants rent space in small kiosks that are situated throughout the center or for their push-carts.

Temporary tenancy provides benefits for both the developer and the tenant. This is how the developer gains:

The small vendors help to create an exciting atmosphere of a constantly busy, constantly changing marketplace; their presence means the developer can lease out as much floor space as possible, maximiz-

ing profit; and, in some cases, the set-up can serve as a test for future store tenants.

This is how the tenant gains:

They can move in and move out, and go from one center to another; their flexibility is maximized; fixed costs are kept down, since they don't pay rent during nonselling seasons; there is a captive audience of shoppers; and the appeal is to consumer impulse shopping and to fads.

Temporary tenancy also has limitations. The tenants are not available to handle customer complaints or returns. The image of the shopping center may suffer if tenants are not monitored properly. And larger, permanent store tenants may not be happy to lose some of their sales to these vendors.

Source: Based on material in "Temporary Tenants Are Permanent Fixtures," *Chain Store Age Executive* (November 1987), pp. 103–108; and "Here Today, Gone Next Month," *Chain Store Age Executive* (November 1987), pp. 108–112.

regardless of volume. For example, a drugstore may pay 4 per cent of sales, a toy store 6 per cent, and a camera store 12 per cent (these figures are keyed to space occupied and inventory turnover). This type of arrangement allows the property owner to cover inflation or maintenance cost increases, and the tenant finds that the lease is a variable cost, which means that low sales for a new store result in low rental payments. The rate varies by type of shopping district or center as well as by type of store.

Percentage leases have some variations. In one variation, a minimum or maximum rental is noted:

❑ Percentage lease with specified minimum—This recognizes that low sales are partly the retailer's responsibility and that the property owner should receive some minimum payments to pay taxes and maintain the property.

❑ Percentage lease with specified maximum—This recognizes that a very successful retailer should not pay more than a maximum rental charge. Superior merchandising, promotion, and pricing result in rewards to the retailer.

A second variation of the percentage lease is the sliding scale. In this agreement, the ratio of rent to sales changes as sales increase. The sliding-down scale requires the retailer to pay a lower percentage of sales as sales go up; 5 per cent of the first $100,000 in sales and 3 per cent of all sales over $100,000 is an example. The sliding-down scale gives an incentive to the effective retailer, while benefiting the property owner.

A **graduated lease** calls for precise rent increases over a specified period of time. Thus, rent may be $2,000 per month for the first five years, $2,400 per month for the next five years, and $2,800 per month for the last five years of a lease. Rental payments are known in advance by both the retailer and the property owner and are based on anticipated increases in sales and costs. There is no problem in auditing sale figures, as there is for percentage leases. The graduated lease is often used with small retailers, whose financial statements and controls are weak.

A lease with a provision for **maintenance increase recoupment** provides for increases in rent if the property owner's taxes, heating bills, insurance, and expenses go beyond a certain point. This provision is usually associated with a straight rental lease.

A **net lease** mandates that all maintenance expenses, such as heat, insurance, and interior repair, are to be paid by the retailer, who is responsible for the satisfactory quality of these items. A net lease allows a property owner to be freed from management of the facility and enables a retailer to have control over the maintenance of the store.

Other Considerations

After assessing ownership and leasing opportunities, a retailer must determine the costs of operations and maintenance. Mortgage or rental payments are only one part of a site's costs. The age and condition of a facility may cause a retailer to have high total monthly costs, even though the mortgage or rent is low. Furthermore, the costs of extensive renovations should be calculated.

Taxes must be evaluated, especially in an ownership situation. Long-run projections, as well as current taxes, must be examined. Differences in sales taxes (those that customers pay) and business taxes (those that the retailer pays) among alternative sites must be weighed. Business taxes should be broken down into real-estate and income categories.

Zoning restrictions should be analyzed. These are legal prohibitions pertaining to store location, store size, building height, type of merchandise carried, and so on. For example, San Francisco recently passed a law requiring "mandatory sunlight access" onto Union Square. As a result, new building height and size are severely restricted in this district to allow sunshine to reach sidewalks.[14]

Voluntary restrictions should also be examined. These are most prevalent in planned shopping centers and include membership in merchants' groups, uniform store hours, and cooperative security forces. For example, leases within shopping centers have often included restrictive clauses that protect the anchor tenants (large department stores) from too much competition—especially from discounters. These restrictive clauses may involve limits on merchandise lines, restrictions on employee parking, prohibitions of discounting, mandatory membership in a merchants' group, payments for common services, and control of stores' operations. Department stores have been given these protective clauses because developers need their long-term commitments to finance the building of their centers.[15]

Some shopping-center practices have been limited by the Federal Trade Commission (FTC). In a case involving Tyson's Corners in Virginia (one of the largest shopping centers in the United States), the center's developers and their key tenants were prohibited from using leases that allowed them to approve tenants, determine the amount of floor space available to tenants, exclude particular types of tenants, approve the types or brands of merchandise sold by tenants, specify the price range of products, control advertising content, and prohibit price advertising.

Tyson's Corners was permitted to enter into leasing agreements with tenants that maintain a balanced tenancy; prohibit the occupancy of an objectionable tenant (such as an adult bookstore); do not force them to occupy space adjacent to other tenants who create undue noise, litter, or odor; require reasonable appearance standards; and establish a shopping center layout that designates stores, locations, and size and height of buildings.[16]

The last step in the selection of a general location, and a specific site within it, is the computation of an overall rating. First, each location under consideration is given an overall rating based on its performance on all of the criteria displayed in Figure 8-4. The overall ratings of alternative locations are then compared, and the best location is chosen. Second, the same procedure is used to evaluate the alternative sites within the location.

It is often difficult to develop and compare composite evaluations, because some attributes may be positive while others are negative. For example, the general location may be a good shopping center, but the site in the center may be poor; or an area may have excellent potential but take two years to build a store. Therefore, the attributes in Figure 8-4 need to be weighted according to their importance. An overall rating should also include certain knockout factors that would preclude consideration of a site. Possible knockout factors are a short-duration lease (fewer than three years), no evening or weekend pedestrian traffic, and a poor maintenance record by the landlord.

SUMMARY

After a retailer assesses alternative trading areas, it determines what type of location is desirable, selects the general location, and chooses a particular store site. There are three basic types of locations that a retailer should distinguish among: the isolated store, the unplanned business district, and the planned shopping center.

The isolated store is a free-standing retail establishment, not adjacent to other stores. This type of location has several advantages: no competition, low rent, flexibility, road visibility, easy parking, and lower property costs. There are also several disadvantages: difficulty in attracting traffic, no variety for shoppers, no shared costs, and zoning restrictions.

The unplanned business district is a shopping area where two or more stores are located together or in close proximity. Store composition is not based on long-range planning. Unplanned business districts can be broken down into four categories: the central business district, the secondary business district, the neighborhood business district, and the string.

The unplanned business district has several points in its favor: variety of goods, services, and prices; access to public transportation; nearness to commercial and social facilities; and pedestrian traffic. However, the shortcomings of this type of location have led to the growth of the planned shopping center: inadequate parking, older facilities, high rents and taxes, discontinuity of offerings, traffic and delivery congestion, high theft rates, and some declining central cities.

The planned shopping center is a centrally owned or managed, well-balanced shopping area. A center usually has one or more large (anchor) stores and many smaller stores. During the past several years, the growth of the planned shopping center has been great. This growth is the result of the extensive goods and service offerings, growth of the suburbs, shared strategy planning and costs, location, parking, low rent and taxes, low theft rate, popularity of malls, and declining appeal of inner-city shopping. The negative aspects of the planned shopping center include inflexible operations and domination by anchor stores. There are three forms of planned shopping centers: neighborhood, community, and regional.

The evaluation of each general location and the specific sites contained within them requires extensive analysis. In any area, the optimum site for a particular store is called the one-hundred per cent location. These factors should be used in examining locations: pedestrian traffic, vehicular traffic, parking facilities, transportation, store composition, attributes of each specific site, and terms of occupancy. Affinity occurs when various stores are attracted to the same location in order to complement, blend, and cooperate with one another; each benefits from the others' presence.

Terms of occupancy are critical in the choice of a site. The retailer must decide whether to own or lease a site. If it leases, the type of agreement must be negotiated (straight lease, percentage lease, graduated lease, maintenance-increase-recoupment lease, and/or net lease). Operating costs, taxes, zoning restrictions, and voluntary restrictions would also be weighed. Then, an overall rating is computed for each site, and the best one is selected.

QUESTIONS FOR DISCUSSION

1. An apparel retailer has decided to open stores in a combination of isolated locations, unplanned business districts, and planned shopping centers. Comment on this strategy.
2. Why do supermarkets often locate in shopping centers or business districts, whereas convenience stores, such as 7-Eleven, often operate at isolated sites?
3. From the retailer's perspective, compare the advantages of locating in unplanned business districts versus planned shopping centers.
4. Differentiate among the central business district, the secondary business district, the neighborhood business district, and the string.
5. Develop a brief plan to revitalize a neighborhood business district near your campus.
6. Distinguish among the regional shopping center, the community shopping center, and the neighborhood shopping center.
7. Evaluate the regional shopping center nearest your campus.

8. What are some of the problems that planned shopping centers will probably have to address in the future? How should they respond?
9. What criteria should a small retailer use in selecting a type of store location? A large retailer?
10. Explain why a one-hundred per cent location for a fast-food restaurant may not be a one-hundred per cent location for another kind of restaurant.
11. What difficulties are there in using a rating scale such as that shown in Figure 8-4? What are the benefits?
12. How do the parking needs for a supermarket, a furniture store, and a movie theater differ?
13. Under what circumstances would it be more desirable for a retailer to build a new store rather than to buy or lease an existing facility?
14. What are the ramifications of the Tyson's Corners case for other shopping-center developers? For small retailers located in shopping centers?

NOTES

1. Roger Lowenstein, "Dadeland's Formula for Building a Mall: Keep Adding Stores, Push Improvements," *Wall Street Journal* (April 13, 1987), p. 25.
2. Shawn Mitchell, "Downtown Renewal? Minneapolis Really Did It," *Stores* (September 1974), pp. 10–12; "The Internationally Famous Nicollet Mall," Minneapolis Convention and Tourism Commission, n.d.; Robert Guenther, "Minneapolis Seeks Solution to the Aging of a Model Mall," *Wall Street Journal* (September 10, 1986), p. 35; and "The Conservatory Comes to Nicollet Mall," *Chain Store Age Executive* (November 1987), pp. 154–156.
3. Stanley H. Slom, "Boston's Faneuil Hall: A Rouseing Success," *Chain Store Age Executive* (March 1982), pp. 58, 63; and Howard Rudnitsky, "Make Room, Disney World, Federated and Gimbels," *Forbes* (May 9, 1983), pp. 100–104.
4. See "Miami Spice Flavors Bayside Marketplace," *Chain Store Age Executive* (May 1987), pp. 118–122; "There's a New Ford City in Chicago's Future," *Chain Store Age Executive* (November 1987), pp. 160–161; and "Do You Know the Way to Rejuvenate San Jose?" *Chain Store Age Executive* (May 1987), pp. 108–110.
5. See "A Life Raft for Malls When a Tenant Sinks," *Business Week* (August 30, 1982), p. 30; George Sternlieb and James W. Hughes, "Shopping Centers Pull Up the Anchor," *American Demographics* (November 1985), pp.

32–35 ff.; N. R. Kleinfield, "Why Everyone Goes to the Mall," *New York Times* (December 21, 1986), Section 3, pp. 1, 33; and Ellen Graham, "The Pleasure Dome," *Wall Street Journal* (May 13, 1988), pp. 5R–6R.
6. "Out-of-Date Florida Mall Gets an Update," *Chain Store Age Executive* (November 1987), pp. 172–174; "Facelift Rejuvenates Marquette Mall," *Chain Store Age Executive* (August 1986), pp. 42–50; "Seminary South Gets Facelift, New Tenant Mix," *Chain Store Age Executive* (May 1987), pp. 132–136; "Chesterfield Mall Keeps Up with the Joneses," *Chain Store Age Executive* (November 1987), pp. 143–144; and Diane Schneidman, "Buildings Saved from Wrecker's Ball, Enjoy Second Life as a Shopping Mall," *Marketing News* (February 15, 1988), p. 7.
7. Eric Peterson, "New Neighbors," *Stores* (September 1984), pp. 36 ff.; and "New Mixes Cater to Today's Tastes," *Chain Store Age Executive* (April 1987), pp. 25–26.
8. "Washington Outlet Mall: Developing a Capital Idea," *Chain Store Age Executive* (September 1984), pp. 68–74. See also "Whatever the Name, Value Is the Game," *Chain Store Age Executive* (February 1985), pp. 47–48 ff.
9. Jacquelyn Bivins, "F.W. Woolworth: Turning Back the Clock?" *Chain Store Age Executive* (October 1983), p. 32; and Isadore Barmash, "Lamston Still Small and Local," *New York Times* (November 22, 1983), pp. D1, D23.

10. Urban Land Institute, *Shopping Center Development Handbook,* Second Edition (Washington, D.C.: Urban Land Institute, 1985).

11. "A Sixth Sense for Site Selection," *Progressive Grocer* (September 1980), p. 68; and John R. Dorfman, "Sense of Site," *Forbes* (February 14, 1983), pp. 122–123.

12. "Investors Find a New Home: Small-Town Main Streets," *Business Week* (August 6, 1984), pp. 71–72.

13. Eric C. Peterson, "Higher Rents? Downsize!" *Stores* (March 1986), pp. 40–44.

14. Carrie Dolan, "San Francisco Keeps Stores in Sunlight," *Wall Street Journal* (November 16, 1984), p. 33.

15. See Holly Klokis, "Leasing Issues: Developers Speak Out," *Chain Store Age Executive* (November 1987), pp. 37–42.

16. Joseph Barry Mason, "Power and Channel Conflict in Shopping Center Development," *Journal of Marketing,* Vol. 39 (April 1975), pp. 28–35.

Donut Village: Developing Site Selection Criteria for Nontraditional Locations

Case 1

Donut Village is a successful franchisor of doughnut shops throughout the United States. One of the most significant services that the firm provides to franchisees is site selection research. Donut Village recognizes that even the most successful operator would be hindered by a poor location and that a marginal operator would greatly benefit from a superior site. Because the company typically negotiates for twenty-year leases, it also knows the long-term consequences of site selection.

Donut Village applies these site selection criteria to its traditional main-road suburban stores:

❑ The correct side of the street is extremely critical. The firm is aware that many of its potential customers do not like to cross double-lined roads or highways or to make U-turns. Therefore, when it conducts vehicular traffic counts for prospective sites, vehicles traveling on the opposite side of the road are heavily discounted.

❑ The busiest time for doughnut shops is typically before work (6:30 A.M. to 9:30 A.M.). Traffic counts at this time of day are very important.

❑ Site visibility from the road is a major consideration. A site with poor visibility means that potential consumers might pass the shop before they actually see it. This would drastically reduce sales potential.

❑ Doughnut stores need to be close to a large population base to prosper. The most successful stores are often located near office buildings, factories, and colleges and universities.

❑ The company's required ratio of parking spots to store square footage is much less stringent than McDonald's or Burger King's, since the average customer time in a doughnut shop is considerably less than in a hamburger-based franchise (because of the doughnut shop's large take-out business and limited menu).

❑ Factors such as retail balance and the characteristics of the residents in a community (in terms of income, age, or education) are relatively unimportant.

At present, Donut Village is contemplating the use of nontraditional sites for new outlets. Because good traditional sites are increasingly difficult to obtain, it must seek new kinds of locations if it is to maintain the present growth rate. By studying the operations of McDonald's and Burger King, Donut Village executives discovered that they have each been creative in their use of nontraditional locations. For example, McDonald's and Burger King have outlets in U.S. naval installations, high schools, zoos, hospitals, office buildings, and parks, and on turnpikes. Burger King also has mobile units that can be moved to different sites.

Despite the popularity of McDonald's and Burger King's new locales, Donut Village executives understand that the nature of their business is significantly different from hamburger-based franchising: the doughnut business is more snack-oriented, doughnuts have a higher percentage of take-out business, and doughnuts are more frequently purchased in multiple units.

This is how Donut Village executives view a number of nontraditional sites that are under their consideration:

❑ Office buildings—Franchisees can sell products from coffee wagons in buildings that provide very high concentrations of people. The office environment fits well with the breakfast and coffee-break orientation of Donut Village. Special arrangements would have to be worked out with each property owner.

❑ Mobile units—These units can be dispatched to specific sites with high but temporary concentrations of people, such as sporting events, parades, and dog shows. This is a flexible location approach. Separate arrangements would have to be made with each event manager for the right to sell Donut Village products.

❑ Highway locations—Donut Village quick-stop units can be developed. These locations would provide an ideal place for car drivers and their passengers, bus passengers, and truck drivers to take a coffee break. Doughnuts and coffee could be consumed in the customer's car. This operation could be open twenty-four hours a day.

❑ College/university cafeterias—Self-contained operations located alongside schools' conventional cafeterias could be developed in a standardized prototype format. Such operations would provide quick service, portability (students and faculty can take a doughnut and coffee to class), large concentrations of people, and no need for additional parking facilities. There would be evening and weekend business in selling to dorm students, and in catering small parties. Special arrangements would have to be made with each school. In many cases, cafeteria operators have exclusive rights to sell food on a campus.

QUESTIONS

1. What are the pros and cons of each of these options for doughnut shops: isolated store locations, unplanned business district sites, and planned shopping-center sites?

2. Evaluate the criteria used by Donut Village in planning for its traditional sites.

3. Develop a site location checklist for use by Donut Village in assessing nontraditional sites. How would you weigh each criterion?

4. Evaluate the four nontraditional sites proposed by Donut Village. Which kind of site is best? Explain your answer.

Case 2

Richland Fashion Mall: Renovation Plans for a Regional Shopping Center*

Hooker/Barnes, an Australian real-estate developer and the owner of such U.S. retail chains as Bonwit Teller, Parisian, and B. Altman department stores, is now involved in a major regional-shopping-center renovation project at the Richland Mall in Columbia, South Carolina.

Hooker/Barnes' renovation plans call for:

❑ Changing the name from the Richland Mall to the Richland Fashion Mall, in order to emphasize the wide assortment of high-fashion apparel and accessory shops.

❑ Revising the tenant mix. This includes adding a new 80,000-square-foot Bonwit Teller unit as the anchor store for the Retail East section of the mall, and about ninety specialty shops to be located between Bonwit Teller and the 126,000-square-foot, newly refurbished J.B. White department store (situated in the center of the mall). An additional ninety specialty shops will be located between J.B. White and a 100,000-square-foot Retail West anchor store (which has not been determined at this time). See Figure 1.

❑ Enclosing the mall.

*This case was prepared and written by Professor Steven J. Shaw, University of South Carolina, Columbia, South Carolina.

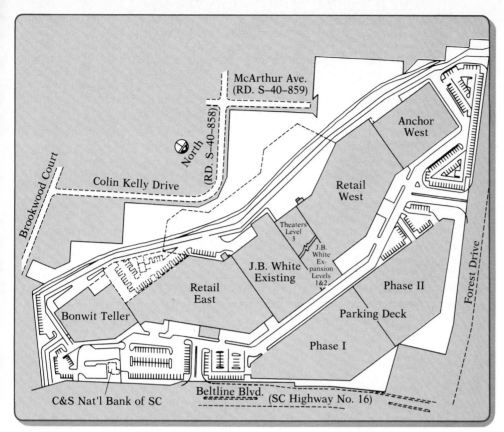

FIGURE 1
Richland Fashion Mall: Project Development Plan
Source: Forest Acres.

❑ Modifying the mall's configuration from a single-level to a two-story structure.
❑ Expanding the overall mall from 288,000 to more than 1 million square feet.
❑ Tripling parking capacity to provide a total of 3,900 spaces in an open lot and a new multilevel parking deck.

Increased competition and the physical condition of the Richland Mall are the major reasons behind the mall's repositioning and renovation. In the last two years, the number of retail shopping centers in metropolitan Columbia, South Carolina, has increased from 38 to 83. Most of these centers are within a 15-mile radius of the Richland Mall and have merchandise and tenant mixes similar to those at Richland before its repositioning. As a result of the growth of centers with an emphasis on low- to medium-priced apparel, Columbia has become overstored for these products. In contrast, Richland's developers believe that the market for upscale, high-fashion apparel is understored. According to a retail consultant, there are few upscale shops in the larger shopping centers and other nearby locales.

Richland is Columbia's oldest shopping center. Before the renovation began, the center was drab and, in many ways, not suitable for repositioning. For example, because the center was not enclosed, weather conditions adversely affected the sales of individual retailers as well as center profitability (because many retailers had percentage-of-sales leases).

Not everyone has been happy with the plans for the upscale Richland Fashion Mall. The owner of a bookstore in the mall was concerned about higher rent, the need for shoppers to use a multilevel parking garage, and the potential customer confusion in finding his store in a much larger center. A hardware store owner, another current tenant, feared that he would not be able to raise prices enough to offset the increased costs. Both of these tenants decided not to operate in the new Richland Fashion Mall.

Furthermore, existing merchants must relocate to the new East Wing because the West Wing is being constructed at their old stores' sites (and the old mall is being torn down). These merchants have to pay for moving expenses and new fixtures, and have to absorb losses due to the disruption of their businesses. Current and prospective tenants are also anxiously awaiting Hooker/Barnes' announcement of the new anchor store for the rebuilt West Wing.

To attract both regional and national retailers to the Richland Fashion Mall, the center's management is stressing these advantages of the area and the site:

❑ Hooker/Barnes has purchased an option on 125 acres located within three miles of the mall. This will protect tenants from increased competition.

❑ The location of the Richland Fashion Mall is convenient to an excellent network of connecting highways, which will enable the new center to attract residents from adjacent counties.

❑ Hooker/Barnes is an experienced merchant. It owns Bonwit Teller, Parisian (an upscale chain of department stores in Florida, Georgia, and Alabama), and B. Altman (a department store chain based in the New York metropolitan area). It is widely speculated that the West Wing anchor will be either Parisian or B. Altman.

❑ Although income in the metropolitan Columbia area is $1,500 less than the national average, it is $1,800 above South Carolina's average. Household income in the metropolitan Columbia area has also increased markedly in the past six years.

❑ Five hundred acres of land within three miles of the center has one-third-acre zoning. This area is suitable for luxury homes.

QUESTIONS

1. Brittons is a high-fashion men's apparel store currently located in Richland Mall. Describe the advantages and disadvantages of this merchant's moving to the Retail East Wing.

2. The unhappy bookstore retailer noted in the case decided to move to a much smaller center about one mile from Richland Fashion Mall. Comment on this strategy.

3. Develop a tenant composition plan for the specialty shops in the East and West Wings. How many of these retail facilities should be upscale? Explain your answer.

4. If you were a gift shop owner, what factors would you consider in selecting a specific site in the Richland Fashion Mall?

Part Four Comprehensive Case

Olson's Health Club: A Location Decision*

Introduction

Olson's Health Club operates two outlets in suburban areas within twenty-five miles of downtown Milwaukee, Wisconsin. The units are situated about eighteen miles from each other and occupy similar amounts of floor space. Both Olson's Health Club facilities offer a variety of stationary cycles, rowing machines, treadmills, a pool, aerobic exercises designed to improve cardiovascular conditioning, and weights and related equipment to tone, strengthen, and build muscles. Each club has modern showers and lockers, a steam room, and a sauna. There are also small on-premises health bars, which serve a variety of juices, fruit, salads, and so on. According to Harry Olson, the owner, "My clubs are physical fitness centers, not social need centers. Members join to get in shape and stay in shape, not to enhance their social lives."

Unfortunately, Harry Olson now realizes that his initial location strategy, which was based, in part, on minimizing trading-area overlap, was a poor one:

❑ The two clubs must rely on separate newspapers for their local advertising. This has led to high ad costs and a lot of wasted circulation. Harry estimates that the overall trading area for each location is about ten miles, and that the greatest concentration of users comes from a three-mile radius.

❑ The distance between the two clubs makes it difficult and costly to coordinate and oversee operations. Managers and repair personnel must frequently travel between locations; it takes between twenty-five minutes and an hour to go from one club to the other, depending on traffic conditions. The distance also means that personnel cannot be easily transferred between locations if one club is overstaffed and the other is understaffed.

❑ Olson believes that more tightly clustered locations would result in greater word-of-mouth communication among patrons and an increased awareness of the clubs throughout the trading area.

Olson also knows that there are significant advantages to increasing the number of units in his chain. First, by adding new outlets, he will be able to open larger full-facility clubs. Olson's current clubs do not have running tracks or tennis or racquetball courts because of size limitations. Present lease commitments and lack of landlord interest will not allow these clubs to be expanded. The lack of some facilities limits the attractiveness of Olson's Health Club and does not enable Olson to adequately differentiate his clubs from the more spartan facilities offered by YMCAs and community centers. As the market for health clubs becomes more saturated, Harry feels that the absence of state-of-the-art facilities will hurt his chances to attract new members and get existing members to renew.

Second, Olson's marketing efforts will be enhanced. By the addition of other outlets, his newspaper advertising will become more efficient, he will be able to hire an ad agency to develop themes, fewer members will leave one of the clubs because of their moving, and there will be greater bargaining power with suppliers.

Because of his dissatisfaction with the present location situation, Olson has established these guidelines for prospective club sites:

1. New clubs should be clustered together. This will correct many of the problems that now exist because the two clubs are 18 miles apart.

2. Each potential site should be large enough to accommodate at least a running track or tennis (racquetball) courts.

3. Each potential site should allow Olson to have the same usable floor space to allow him to develop a prototype club. Many competitors have locations with differing sizes and facilities. This causes confusion among members and potential members (Should they select a closer, more convenient, location or one with more facilities?), overcrowding at the outlets with indoor running tracks in the winter, and a complex pricing structure.

4. Once three new clubs are fully functional, the existing ones will be closed. This is expected to occur within six years.

*The material in this case is drawn from "Chains Flock to Small Centers," *Chain Store Age Executive* (May 1986), pp. 64–74; Holly Klokis, "Retailers Are Taking to the Streets," *Chain Store Age Executive* (September 1987), pp. 19–22; "Shoppers Rediscover Small Centers," *Chain Store Age Executive* (July 1986), pp. 69–72; "Small Centers Grow in Numbers and Strength," *Chain Store Age Executive* (November 1987), pp. 72–74; "The Next Fitness Trend or Boom???," *The Club Marketing & Management Newsletter* (January 1987), pp. 1–2; "Too Big or Not Too Big," *Chain Store Age Executive* (August 1986), pp. 37–40; "Urban Centers: New Retail Options," *Chain Store Age Executive* (June 1986), pp. 23–28; Game Plan, Inc., *Why People Join: A Marketing Research Study for Racquet and Fitness Clubs* (Boston: International Racquet Sports Association, 1985); and "Small Centers: They Are Being Developed in All Shapes and Sizes," *Chain Store Age Executive* (February 1988), Section Two.

Olson understands that both his philosophy of business and his consumer research need to be reflected in location decisions.

Philosophy of Business

Olson's Health Club has a well-conceived philosophy of business. It applies to each of the current club locations and is clearly articulated to all employees. Olson is a stickler for image consistency in his clubs and insists that this continue in the future. Table 1 shows the Olson philosophy.

Consumer Research

Olson has been studying the available secondary data on health and fitness clubs and is now analyzing the findings of a primary study on his own members. Among the information being examined are industrywide member profiles, Olson's member profiles, and trading-area data.

Olson is particularly interested in the results of a 1985 industrywide survey of 3,380 members at 171 fitness clubs across the United States, which was conducted by Game Plan, Inc. (a consulting firm). The clubs participating in the study fall into four categories: racquetball only, tennis only, multiple facilities with a pool, and multiple facilities without a pool. The rationale for conducting that study was provided in this statement:

Increasingly, industry leaders have come to perceive that clubs cannot survive, much less thrive, by focusing primarily on what range of goods and services they can *sell;* rather, club management must do what all successful marketing organizations do—"go to great lengths to examine and measure what their market *wants* and *needs*. They use that information for *everything* they do . . . deciding what goods and services to offer, how they will be packaged, distributed, promoted, and priced." The focus must change from what clubs sell to what—and why—members *buy*.

These are some of the key findings from the industry study:

❑ Demographics—55 per cent of the respondents were male, 53 per cent were married, about one-third had children living at home, three-quarters had an annual household income of more than $25,000, 80 per cent had attended college (57 per cent had earned degrees), and 70 per cent were between the ages of twenty-five and forty-four (14 per cent were eighteen to twenty-four).

❑ Club membership—65 per cent of the respondents had belonged to a club for more than four years (only 4 per cent had joined their first club within the previous year), about half were still members of the first club they had joined, and 35 per cent had joined their first club during the fall of the year they enrolled (only 13 per cent did this over the summer).

❑ Factors in club selection—Almost 40 per cent of the respondents had joined a club on the basis of recommendations of friends; just 6 per cent cited advertising as the primary factor in picking a club. These were among the most cited reasons members gave for joining their current club: interest in getting and staying in shape, the availability of fitness equipment and activities, convenience of the location, social factors, and "feeling better about myself." Only 14 per cent identified price as a major reason for joining their club.

TABLE 1
Olson's Health Club: A Philosophy of Business

❑ Olson's places great value on its reputation among customers and on their satisfaction. A clean, invigorating, low-pressure environment is maintained: "Exercise can be fun. A regular routine, that one can sustain, is the key to a healthful life."

❑ All facilities are properly staffed by trained personnel. An exercise physiologist works with members to develop individual workout programs. Every new member is given demonstrations in the proper use of equipment.

❑ Equipment is adjustable for people of varying size, weight, and physical condition. All equipment can be used by both sexes.

❑ Each club has an adequate amount of equipment, and the equipment is regularly serviced and kept in good condition. Waiting times during different parts of the week (e.g., evenings and weekends) are monitored, and additional equipment is ordered when necessary.

❑ Clubs are physical fitness centers, not executive or social clubs. Massage rooms, hair salons, and tanning booths are not offered to members.

❑ Fair customer practices are followed. Each prospective member is offered a free trial session. No high-pressure sales tactics are used. Membership is placed "on hold" during periods of prolonged absence or illness. Olson's refunds the prorated balance of an unused membership if an individual moves so that he or she lives more than fifteen miles away from an Olson club.

❑ Olson's is truly concerned about the welfare of its members. New members are questioned about their medical history and are guided appropriately. At least one employee per shift is fully trained in first-aid procedures, and a physician is always on call. Emergency alarm devices are installed in various club areas to make it easy to summon assistance.

❑ All basic expenses (such as fresh towels and a large locker) are included in the yearly membership fee, except nursery and baby-sitting services.

- Club usage—70 per cent of the respondents went to their club three or more times per week. The most frequently used equipment and services were weight machines, tennis and racquetball courts, steam/sauna, and aerobic/exercise classes. 21 per cent said they used the pool on a regular basis.
- Satisfaction/dissatisfaction with club—The best-liked club attributes were the range and quality of facilities, the convenience of the location, the atmosphere, the personal staff, and cleanliness. The least-liked attributes were poor parking, costs, and crowding. Moving or changing jobs was the main reason given for leaving a club.

These are the highlights of Olson's survey (which he patterned after the industry study) of his clubs' members:

- Demographics—65 per cent of the members are male, 59 per cent are married, about half have children living at home, two-thirds have an annual household income of more than $25,000, 60 per cent have attended college (42 per cent have earned degrees), and 75 per cent are between the ages of twenty-five and forty-four (8 per cent are eighteen to twenty-four).
- Club membership—80 per cent of the members have belonged to Olson's Health Club for more than four years (only 3 per cent have joined a club within the previous year).
- Factors in club selection—Over 50 per cent of members originally joined on the basis of recommendations of friends; 3 per cent cited advertising as the primary factor in picking a club. These are among the reasons that members have joined an Olson's club: interest in getting and staying in shape, the availability of fitness equipment, and convenience of the location. 20 per cent say price was a major reason for joining a club.
- Club usage—76 per cent of the members go to a club three or more times per week. The most frequently used equipment and services are weight machines, steam/sauna, and aerobic/exercise classes; 35 per cent swim in the pool on a regular basis.
- Satisfaction/dissatisfaction with club—The best-liked club features are the knowledge and friendliness of the personnel, the individualized exercise programs, the quality of the facilities, the convenience of the location, the atmosphere, and the fair prices. The least-liked attributes are the lack of some facilities and the inadequate number of locations. Moving or changing jobs and the lack of facilities are the main reasons for leaving a club.

A review of members' and former members' home addresses indicates that 70 per cent of Olson's Health Club clients live within a three-mile radius of one of the clubs, 25 per cent live between three and seven miles from a club, and 5 per cent reside more than seven miles away. Olson is not sure about the accuracy of his trading-area estimates because many members travel to a club from work and not from home. The high level of competition among health clubs also means that consumers are becoming less likely to travel more than fifteen minutes to get to a club.

New-Club Location Alternatives

Harry Olson's plan is to open a new health club every eighteen months, with the first one to debut a year from now. This rate of expansion will not strain personnel resources and will allow much of the funding to be internally generated. However, Harry realizes that he may have to speed this expansion pace because excellent locations are scarce (such locations often have five- to ten-year leases with lengthy renewal options, so that few sites are available at any point in time), and he is anxious to close his existing clubs.

A friend who is a real-estate broker has shown Olson about thirty prospective sites for his first new club. All but three have already been rejected as inappropriate. Olson's reasons for eliminating most of the locations include high rent, distance from a current Olson club, small size not conducive to offering a full complement of facilities, building not properly maintained by the landlord/managing agent, and weak neighborhood demographics with respect to the target market profile.

The three locations being considered by Olson are all available for immediate rental, within an eight-mile radius of Olson's current locations, and have the correct minimum size dimensions. The trading-area characteristics for each of the three sites are described in Table 2, and Table 3 summarizes the attributes of each site. Harry acquired the information in these tables from observation, state and local offices, and the landlords of each site.

The first site is in the basement area of a new luxury mixed-use urban center, which combines retail, office, and residential space in a preplanned environment. About 30 per cent of the total complex is currently occupied. Advantages of this location include a relatively low rent per square foot; two months' free rent; a long-term lease; a modern, attractive building; locational convenience for office workers and residents; a ready-made market; a high population density; and no competition in the urban center. Disadvantages include paying regular rent before the center is fully occupied, poor site visibility, a high need to advertise to attract outside members, the uneven utilization of center facilities (the highest use is expected before work, during lunch, and after work during weekdays; low use is expected during weekends), poor parking for nonresidents, and many people incorrectly perceiving that membership is restricted to center residents and employees.

The second site is in a suburban string in an upscale area. Advantages include excellent store visibility, good vehicular traffic, a homogeneous population, very little overlap with current outlets' trading areas, and the freedom to set club hours. Disadvantages include a relatively low population density in a three-mile radius, versus the mixed-use project and the planned shopping center; only four years remaining on the current lease, which must be renegotiated; restricted parking in front of the club site; no control over neighboring retail facilities; the need for elaborate security; and no cooperative tenant—center promotions.

The third site is in the back of an established regional shopping center, next door to a large multiscreen movie theater. Advantages of this site include convenience for shoppers and retail personnel, the great number of cus-

TABLE 2
The Trading-Area Characteristics of Three Potential Sites for a New Olson's Health Club Outlet

Mixed-Use Center

Total population within the center—at capacity (includes residents and those working in the building)	1,500
Percentage of population 25–44 years of age	40
Percentage of population with household income of $25,000+	90
Percentage of population with household income of $60,000+	28
Total population within 3 miles	150,000
Percentage of population 25–44 years of age	25
Percentage of population with household income of $25,000+	68
Percentage of population with household income of $60,000+	11

String Location

Total population within 3 miles	35,000
Percentage of population 25–44 years of age	25
Percentage of population with household income of $25,000+	74
Percentage of population with household income of $60,000+	23

Regional Shopping Center

Total population within 3 miles	18,000
Percentage of population 25–44 years of age	25
Percentage of population with household income of $25,000+	59
Percentage of population with household income of $60,000+	8
Total population within 12 miles*	400,000
Percentage of population 25–44 years of age	40
Percentage of population with household income of $25,000+	64
Percentage of population with household income of $60,000+	19

*Estimated trading area of a major department store located in the center.

tomers drawn to the location by the department stores and other retailers (this is significantly greater than a health club could attract by itself), ample free and nonrestricted parking, access to cooperative mall promotions, and mall security. Disadvantages include poor visibility from the mall; less pedestrian traffic than at other sites in the mall; proximity to the movie theater, which has a different target market; and possible traffic congestion, especially before Christmas and Easter, and on other key shopping days.

TABLE 3
The Attributes of Each Potential Site

Attributes	Mixed-Use Center	String Location	Regional Shopping Center
Square footage available for health club	22,000	27,000	18,000
Annual rent per square foot	$22	$20	$27
Lease terms	2 months' free rent; 10-year lease + 10-year renewal option at market value	4 years remaining on existing lease; must be renegotiated	5-year lease + 3- to 5-year renewal options (each at market value)
External site visibility	Poor	Good	Can be seen only from northwest corner of the mall
Pedestrian and vehicular traffic	Pedestrian moderate; vehicular poor	Poor pedestrian; good vehicular	Both good
Parking availability	Residents do not require additional parking; parking for nonresidents is $2 per hour in peak periods.	Metered parking is limited; a small free lot is about 200 yards from the site for the club.	Ample convenient and free parking is available.

272

QUESTIONS

1. Evaluate Harry Olson's original location strategy.
2. How should Olson's philosophy of business and the available consumer research findings affect his locational choice?
3. What limitations in the industry membership study and his own study should Harry be aware of when selecting a new site and developing expanded facilities?
4. Comment on Olson's decision to close his present clubs once the new ones are open.
5. Assess the data in Tables 2 and 3. What additional information should Harry acquire before making a choice?
6. How would you determine Olson's primary, secondary, and fringe trading areas for each of the sites being considered? Be sure to consider customers who go to a club before, during, or right after work; those who drive from home; and those who go in conjunction with a shopping trip.
7. What are the pros and cons of a long lease to Harry? Which other leasing terms should he carefully examine?
8. Based on the information in the case, which location alternative, if any, should Harry pursue? Why?

PART FIVE

Managing a Retail Business

❑   *In Part Five, the elements in managing a retail enterprise are discussed. First, the steps in setting up a retail organization are identified. Then, the special human resource management environment of retailing is presented. Third, operations management is covered.*

❑   *Chapter 9 details how a retailer would use a clear organization structure to assign tasks, policies, resources, authority, responsibilities, and rewards to satisfy the needs of the target market, employees, and management. Examples of organizational patterns for various types of retailers are presented. Human resource management is necessary to have the retail organization work properly. It consists of recruiting, selecting, training, compensating, and supervising personnel in a manner consistent with the retailer's organization structure and strategy mix.*

❑   *Chapter 10 focuses on the role of operations management in implementing a retail strategy. The dynamics of asset management, budgeting, and resource allocation are discussed. Also, several specific operations management concepts are analyzed, including store format and space allocation, personnel utilization, store maintenance, inventory management, store security and insurance, credit management, computerization, and crisis management.*

Chapter 9

Retail Organization and Human Resource Management

❑ **Chapter Objectives** ❑

1 To study the process involved in setting up a retail organization

2 To examine the various organizational arrangements utilized in retailing

3 To describe the principles and practices of human resource management in retailing

Thirty-seven-year-old Linda Koslow has been general manager of Marshall Field's Oak Brook, Illinois, store for more than three years. She is responsible for the operations of that outlet and oversees a staff of 900 (which grows to 1,300 during the five-week Christmas selling season). Koslow's store is the third largest of twenty-five in the Marshall Field chain with annual sales of $90 million and is situated in a regional shopping center. Koslow's annual compensation is about $100,000; and she has full use of a company van.

Koslow started in retailing in 1970 as a jewelry sales clerk at a Famous-Barr department store outlet in St. Louis. After managing a candy department for Famous-Barr, she moved to Chicago as a buyer for Marshall Field. But soon thereafter, Linda switched to store management, a decision she has never regretted.

Linda Koslow's major responsibility involves keeping expenses in line with sales trends. Yet, she has no control over the prices in her store; those

are set by Marshall Field's buyers. Linda fulfills her responsibility by tightly monitoring the number of employees in the store, assigning more workers to the departments with the greatest sales potential, striving to keep employee morale high, making sure that "hot" merchandise gets prime display space, and responding to the tactics of other retailers in her shopping center.

In a typical ten-hour day, Linda walks through each of the four floors in her store several times. She checks on personnel and displays, picks up litter, and helps answer shopper questions. If the store is very busy, Koslow might even work in the administrative office and make change for department managers. She also regularly reviews computer printouts to see how the store is doing in comparison with prior periods and to identify potential opportunities or trouble spots. Koslow often visits competitors' stores to see what and how they are doing.

Despite Linda's enthusiasm and upbeat attitude,

276

the job can be wearying at times, particularly during the Christmas season. As Koslow once noted, she had not been to the grocery store in so long that "my cat and I are sharing meow mix."[1]

Setting up a goal-oriented organization structure and managing human resources are activities that all retailers must undertake.

Overview

There are three basic steps to properly operating a retail business: setting up an organization structure, hiring and managing personnel, and managing operations. In this chapter, the first two steps are covered. Chapter 10 concentrates on operations management.

Setting Up a Retail Organization

Through a **retail organization**, a firm structures and assigns tasks (functions), policies, resources, authority, responsibilities, and rewards in order to efficiently and effectively satisfy the needs of its target market, employees, and management. Figure 9-1 shows a variety of needs that a retailer should take into account when planning and assessing an organization.

As a rule, a retailer cannot survive unless its organization structure satisfies the needs of the target market, regardless of how well employee and/or management needs are met. For example, an organization structure that reduces costs through centralized buying but results in the retailer's insensitivity to geographic differences in customer preferences would be inappropriate.

Even though many retail firms carry out similar tasks or functions (e.g., buying, pricing, displaying, and wrapping merchandise), there are many ways of organizing to perform these functions and focus on the needs of customers, employees, and management. The process of setting up a retail organization is outlined in Figure 9-2 and described in the following subsections.

Specifying Tasks To Be Performed

The general tasks to be performed must be enumerated. Among these tasks are

- ❑ Buying merchandise.
- ❑ Shipping merchandise.
- ❑ Receiving merchandise.
- ❑ Checking incoming shipments.
- ❑ Setting prices.
- ❑ Marking merchandise.
- ❑ Inventory storage and control.
- ❑ Preparation of merchandise and window displays.
- ❑ Facilities maintenance (e.g., keeping the store clean).
- ❑ Customer research.
- ❑ Customer contact (e.g., advertising, personal selling).
- ❑ Facilitating customer shopping (e.g., convenient location, short checkout lines).
- ❑ Customer follow-up and complaint handling.
- ❑ Personnel management.
- ❑ Repairs and alteration of merchandise.

TARGET MARKET NEEDS
Are there a sufficient number of personnel (salespeople, delivery persons, cashiers, etc.) available to provide customer service at the appropriate levels?
Are personnel knowledgeable and courteous?
Are store facilities well maintained?
Are the specific needs of branch store customers met?
Are changing needs promptly addressed?
EMPLOYEE NEEDS
Are positions challenging enough?
Is there an orderly promotion program?
Is the employee able to participate in decision making?
Are the channels of communication clear and open?
Are jobs satisfying?
Is the authority–responsibility relationship clear?
Does the firm promote from within?
Does each employee get treated fairly?
Is good performance rewarded?
MANAGEMENT NEEDS
Is it relatively easy to obtain and retain competent personnel?
Are personnel procedures clearly defined?
Does each worker report to only one supervisor?
Can each manager properly supervise and control the number of workers reporting to him (her)?
Do operating departments have adequate staff support (i.e., computerized reports, market research, and advertising)?
Are the levels of organization properly developed?
Are the organization's plans well integrated?
Are employees motivated?
Is absenteeism low?
Does the organization provide continuity so that personnel can be replaced in an orderly manner?
Is the organization flexible enough to adapt to changes in customer preference and/or regional growth patterns?

FIGURE 9-1
Selected Factors That Must Be Considered in Planning and Assessing a Retail Organization

❑ Billing customers.
❑ Handling receipts and financial records.
❑ Credit operations.
❑ Gift wrapping.
❑ Delivery.
❑ Return of merchandise to vendors.
❑ Sales forecasting and budgeting.
❑ Coordination.

The proper performance of each of these activities is often necessary for efficient retailing to occur, depending on the strategy mix chosen.

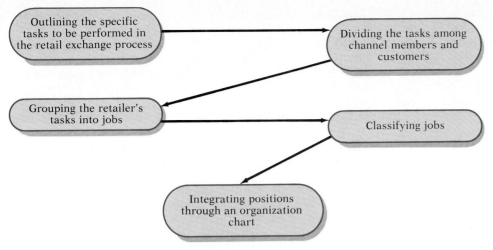

FIGURE 9-2
The Process of Organizing a Retail Firm

Dividing Tasks Among Channel Members and Customers

Although the tasks just cited are performed in retailing, they do not necessarily have to be performed by a retailer. Some can be assumed by a manufacturer, a wholesaler, a specialist, or the consumer. Figure 9-3 shows the types of activities that can be carried out by each party. The following example describes some of the criteria that would be considered in the allocation of retail tasks (with consumer credit used as the basic function).

A retail task should be carried out only if desired by the target market. An appliance dealer could offer cash-only sales if a survey of the target market proves this acceptable, not because of convenience for the store. For some retailers, liberal credit policies may provide significant advantages over competitors. For

Performer	Tasks
Retailer	Can perform all or some of the tasks listed in the preceding section, from buying merchandise to coordination.
Manufacturer or Wholesaler	Can perform few or many functions, such as: shipping, marking merchandise, inventory storage and control, display preparation, research, sales forecasting, etc.
Specialist(s)	Can include the following types: buying office, delivery firm, warehouse, marketing research firm, advertising agency, accountant, credit bureau, computer service firm. Each specializes in the performance of a particular task.
Consumer	Can assume responsibility for delivery, credit (cash–only sales), sales effort (self–service or direct marketing), product alterations (do–it–yourselfers), etc.

FIGURE 9-3
The Division of Retail Tasks

others, a cash-only policy may reduce the firms' overhead and lead to lower prices.

A retail task should be performed by the party that has special competence and/or equipment. Credit collection may require a legal staff and a computer-based bookkeeping system. These are usually affordable only by medium-sized or large retailers. Smaller retailers would rely on bank credit cards to overcome the lack of necessary resources.

The retailer should consider the loss of control over an activity when it is allocated to another party. Delegation of a task involves the loss of some control by the retailer. A credit collection firm, pressing hard to collect on a past-due account, may antagonize a customer to the point of losing future sales for the retailer.

The institutional framework of the retailer can have an impact on the allocation of tasks. A cooperative credit bureau may be possible only in the franchise form of retailing. Independents cannot do this task as readily.

Task allocation should take into consideration cost savings achieved by the sharing or shifting of tasks. The credit function can be better performed by a credit bureau if its personnel are specialized, WATS (long-distance phone lines) calls are used, and lower rent is paid (because of an out-of-the-way location). Many retailers cannot gain these savings themselves.

Grouping Tasks into Jobs

After the retailer decides which functions to perform, tasks are grouped into jobs. These jobs must be clearly defined and structured. Some examples of grouping tasks into jobs are

Tasks	Jobs
Displaying merchandise, customer contact, gift wrapping, customer follow-up	Sales personnel
Billing customers, handling cash receipts, gift wrapping, inventory control	Cashier(s)
Receiving merchandise, checking incoming shipments, marking merchandise, inventory storage and control, returning merchandise to vendors	Inventory personnel
Window dressing, interior display setups, use of mobiles	Display personnel
Billing customers, credit operations, customer research	Credit personnel
Repairs and alterations of merchandise, customer complaints, customer research	Customer service personnel
Cleaning store, replacing old fixtures	Janitorial personnel
Personnel management, sales forecasting, budgeting, pricing, coordination of tasks	Management personnel

When grouping tasks into jobs, the retailer must consider the use of specialization. Under specialization, each employee is responsible for limited functions (as opposed to each employee's performing many or all functions). Specialization has the advantages of clearly defined tasks, greater expertise, reduced training costs and time, and hiring personnel with narrow education and experience. Problems can result through extreme specialization: poor morale (boredom), personnel not being aware of the importance of their jobs, and the need for an increased number of employees.

The proper use of specialization involves assigning specific duties and responsibilities to individuals, so that a position encompasses a relatively homogeneous cluster of work tasks. These work tasks should have an essential and enduring purpose within the retail organization.

JOB TITLE: Store Manager for 34th Street Branch of Pombo's Department Stores

POSITION REPORTS TO: Senior Vice–President

POSITIONS REPORTING TO STORE MANAGER: All personnel working in the
                                        34th Street store

OBJECTIVES: To properly staff and operate the 34th Street store

DUTIES AND RESPONSIBILITIES:

1. Personnel recruitment, selection, training, motivation, and evaluation
2. Merchandise display
3. Inventory storage and control
4. Approving orders for merchandise
5. Transferring merchandise among stores
6. Sales forecasting
7. Budgeting
8. Handling store receipts
9. Preparing bank transactions
10. Locking and unlocking store
11. Reviewing customer complaints
12. Reviewing computer data forms
13. Semiannual review of overall operations
14. Forwarding reports to top management

COMMITTEES AND MEETINGS:

1. Store Managers' Review Committee
2. Attendance at monthly meetings with Senior Vice–President
3. Supervision of weekly meetings with department managers

FIGURE 9-4
A Job Description for a Store Manager

After tasks are grouped to form jobs, job descriptions are constructed. These are detailed outlines of the job titles, objectives, duties, and responsibilities for each position. They are used as a hiring, supervision, and evaluation tool. Figure 9-4 contains a job description for a store manager.

Classifying Jobs

Jobs can then be broadly categorized through a functional, product, geographic, or combination classification system. In a **functional classification**, jobs are divided among functional areas such as sales promotion, buying, and store operations. Expert knowledge is utilized.

Product classification divides jobs on a goods or service basis. For example, a department store can hire personnel for clothing, furniture, giftware, appliances, and so on. Product classification recognizes that differences exist in the personnel requirements for different products. Tighter control and responsibility are also possible.

Geographic classification is useful for multiunit stores operating in different areas. Personnel are adapted to local conditions. Job descriptions and qualifications are under the control of individual branch managers.

For larger retailers, combinations of these three classifications are often used. As an example, a branch unit of a department store may hire and supervise its own selling staff, while buying personnel for each product line are centrally hired and controlled by the headquarters' store. Thus, the functional, product, and geographic forms of organization are combined.

Developing an Organization Chart

When planning its organization structure, a retailer should not look at jobs as individual units but as parts of the whole. Accordingly, the format of a retail organization must be planned in an integrated, coordinated manner. Jobs must be delineated and separated; yet the interrelationships among positions must be clear.

The **hierarchy of authority** outlines the job relationships within a company by describing the reporting relationships among employees (from the lowest level to the store manager or board of directors). Coordination and control are provided through this hierarchy.

The levels in a retail organization are the number of positions separating the top official from the lowest employee. An organization with a large number of subordinates reporting to one supervisor is called a **flat organization**. Some benefits of a flat organization are good communication, quicker handling of problems, and better employee identification with a job. The major problem tends to be too many employees reporting to one manager.

A **tall organization** has several levels of managers. This arrangement leads to close supervision and fewer employees reporting to each manager. The problems include a long channel of communication, an impersonal impression given to employees, and inflexible rules.

With all these factors in mind, a retailer can develop an **organization chart**, which graphically displays the hierarchal relationships within the firm. Figure 9-5 lists the principles to be considered in establishing an organization chart. Figure 9-6 contains examples of functional, product, geographic, and combination organization charts.

Organizational Patterns in Retailing

Retail organization structures differ by institutional type. As an example, an independent retailer has a much simpler organization than a chain retailer. An independent does not have to manage units that may be distant from the main store, the owner-manager usually personally supervises all employees, and workers have ready access to the owner-manager in the event of any personal or work-related problems. In contrast, a chain retailer must specify how tasks are to be delegated, coordinate multiple-store operations, and establish common policies for all employees.

Even though an independent retailer often requires a relatively simple organization, that organization should still be designed so that all functions and employees are coordinated. A discussion of organizational arrangements used by independent retailers, department stores, chain retailers, and diversified retailers follows.

Organizational Arrangements Used by Small Independent Retailers

Small independent retailers generally use simple organizational arrangements, because they contain only two or three levels of personnel (the owner-manager and employees), and the owner-manager personally runs the business and supervises employees. There are few workers. Little departmentalization (specialization) is used. There are no branch units. Yet, while these factors lead to a simple organization structure, this does not mean that fewer activities must be performed.

The small retailer has little specialization of functions because there are many

An organization should be concerned about its employees. Job rotation, promotion from within, participatory management, recognition, job enrichment, etc., improve worker morale.

Employee turnover, lateness, and absenteeism should be monitored, as they may indicate personnel problems.

The line of authority should be traceable from the highest to the lowest positions. In this way, employees know whom to report to and who reports to them (chain of command).

A subordinate should only report to one supervisor. This avoids the problem of workers' receiving conflicting orders (unity of command).

Responsibility should be associated with adequate authority. A person responsible for a given objective needs the power to achieve it.

While a supervisor can delegate authority, he/she retains responsibility for the acts of subordinates. The delegation of authority cannot be an excuse for a manager's failing to achieve a goal. This concept requires that a manager actively evaluate the performance of subordinates while they are working to reach a goal.

There is a limit to the number of employees a manager can directly supervise (span of control).

The firm should strive to limit the number of organization levels. The greater the number of levels, the longer the time for communication to travel and the greater the coordination problems.

An organization has an informal structure aside from the formal organization chart. Informal relationships exercise power in the organization and may bypass formal relationships and procedures.

FIGURE 9-5
Principles for Organizing a Retail Firm

tasks to be performed relative to the number of workers available to perform them. Accordingly, each employee must allocate a portion of his or her time to several activities.

Figure 9-7 illustrates the organization structures used by two small independent stores. In A, a boutique is organized on a functional basis: merchandising versus operations. Merchandising personnel are responsible for buying and selling goods and services, assortments, displays, and advertising. Operations personnel are responsible for store maintenance and operations (e.g., inventory management and financial reports). In B, a furniture store is organized on a product-oriented basis, with the personnel in each category responsible for selected activities. All of the product categories get appropriate attention, and some expertise is developed. This expertise is particularly important because different skills are necessary to buy and sell each type of furniture.

Organizational Arrangements Used by Department Stores

Many medium-sized and large department stores use organizational arrangements that are a modification of the Mazur plan, which was first introduced in 1927. The basic **Mazur plan** divides all retail activities into four functional areas: merchandising, publicity, store management, and accounting and control.[2] These functional areas include the following activities:

1. Merchandising—buying, selling, stock planning and control, planning of promotional events.

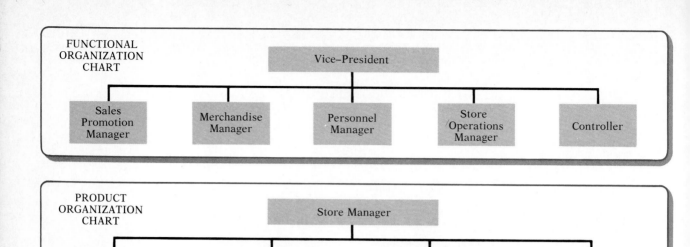

FUNCTIONAL ORGANIZATION CHART

Vice–President

Sales Promotion Manager | Merchandise Manager | Personnel Manager | Store Operations Manager | Controller

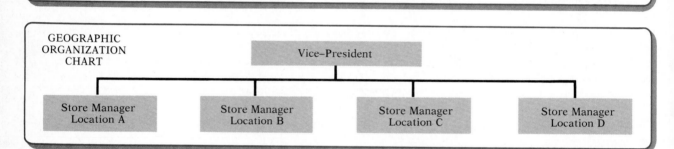

PRODUCT ORGANIZATION CHART

Store Manager

Men's Outerwear Manager | Ladies' Outerwear Manager | Lingerie Manager | Appliance Manager

GEOGRAPHIC ORGANIZATION CHART

Vice–President

Store Manager Location A | Store Manager Location B | Store Manager Location C | Store Manager Location D

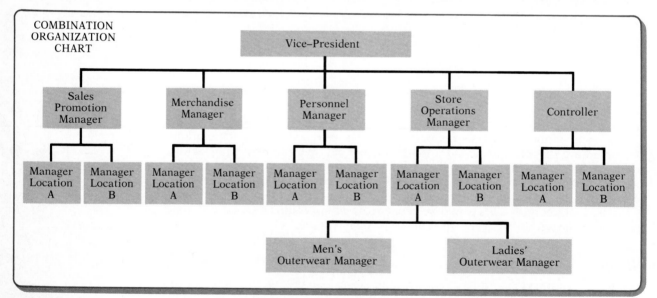

COMBINATION ORGANIZATION CHART

Vice–President

Sales Promotion Manager | Merchandise Manager | Personnel Manager | Store Operations Manager | Controller

Manager Location A | Manager Location B | Manager Location A | Manager Location B | Manager Location A | Manager Location B | Manager Location A | Manager Location B | Manager Location A | Manager Location B

Men's Outerwear Manager | Ladies' Outerwear Manager

FIGURE 9-6
Different Forms of Retail Organization

Mr. Marcus, Can You Give Us Some Management Tips?

Stanley Marcus, the driving force behind Neiman-Marcus (from which he retired about a decade ago), recently was interviewed by *Inc.* magazine on a variety of topics. Here are some excerpts:

Inc.—Suppose you're a successful, ambitious retailer. You want to grow, but you're afraid of getting too big to be able to service customers well. What's your advice?

Marcus—That's a tough question. Even the great merchants, the ones who stay intimately involved in their stores as they grow, reach a limit beyond which they cease to be effective. It's a very tough decision knowing how far you can extend yourself.

Inc.—Are those limits best defined by sales volume? Number of employees? Number of stores?

Marcus—Most likely it's the number of stores that becomes the poison pill. I'm guessing a bit here, but if you can get to each location every three, maybe four weeks, you'll probably catch problems before they get out of hand. Once every six weeks, you may be in trouble. Regional chains are a little easier to manage than national ones, naturally.

Inc.—Doesn't the computer extend your reach by giving you detailed information on what is going on in each store—which items are moving, which are profitable and which are not, which salespeople are doing the best? If you have that kind of information on a daily basis, isn't that what you need to manage?

Marcus—No, because you still haven't spent enough time on the selling floor, meeting customers, understanding the merchandise, watching the salespeople.

Inc.—And yet you'll have to admit that the computer has provided an incredible amount of valuable information that yesterday's retailers rarely had.

Marcus—There's no doubt about it. But the danger is that it's like an addictive drug. You become hooked on numbers to the point that you neglect your products and your people. I've walked into department stores around the country and found buyers sitting in their offices in sweat suits. You know what that tells me? It tells me that they have no intention of spending any time on the selling floor. Their whole life is tied to that computer screen.

Source: Based on material in "Merchant Prince Stanley Marcus," *Inc.* (June 1987), p. 43. Reprinted by permission. Copyright © 1987 by Inc. Publishing Company, 38 Commercial Wharf, Boston, MA, 02110.

2. Publicity—window and interior display, advertising, planning and executing promotional events (in cooperation with the merchandising department), advertising research, public relations.

3. Store management—merchandise care, customer services (such as adjustment bureaus), purchasing store supplies and equipment, store maintenance, operating activities (such as receiving, checking, marking, and delivering merchandise; maintenance of warehouse operations), store and merchandise protection such as insurance and security, personnel (training, compensation, and so on), workroom operations.

4. Accounting and control—credit and collection, expense budgeting and control, inventory planning and control, record keeping.

These four areas are organized with the use of line (direct authority and responsibility) and staff (advisory or support) components. For example, the controller and the publicity manager provide staff services to the merchandising divisions, but within these staff areas, personnel are organized on a line basis. This principle can be more clearly understood from an examination of Figure 9-8, which illustrates the basic Mazur plan.

As can be seen in Figure 9-8, the merchandising division is responsible for buying and selling activities and is headed by a merchandising manager. This executive is often regarded as the most important area executive in the store and is responsible for supervising buyers, developing a financial control system for

285

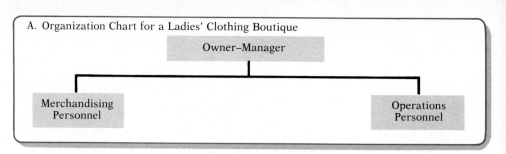

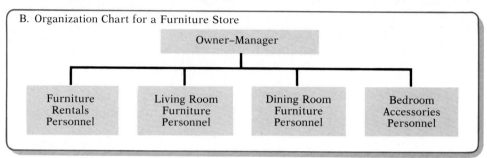

FIGURE 9-7
Organization Structures Used by Small Independents

each department, coordinating department merchandise plans and policies (so that a store has a consistent image among departments), and interpreting economic data and their effect on the store. In stores with many departments (some stores have dozens of departments), divisional merchandise managers are utilized, so that the number of buyers reporting to a single manager does not become unwieldy.

The buyer, under the basic Mazur plan, has complete responsibility for controlling expenses and reaching profit goals within his or her department. The duties of the buyer include preparing preliminary budgets, studying fashion trends, bargaining with vendors over price, planning the number of salespeople needed, and informing sales personnel about merchandise purchased and fashion trends. The grouping of buying and selling activities into one job (buyer) may present a major problem. Because buyers are not constantly on the selling floor, control of personnel (training, scheduling, and discipline) may suffer.

The growth of branch department stores has caused three alternative forms of the original Mazur plan to emerge: the **mother hen with branch store chickens**, whereby the parent organization operates the branches; the **separate store** arrangement, whereby each branch has its own buying responsibilities; and **equal store** arrangements, whereby buying is centralized and branches become sales units with equal organization status.

In the "mother hen" organization, most authority remains with managers at the headquarters store. Merchandise planning and buying activities, advertising, financial controls, store hours, and many other areas are centrally managed. To a great extent, this organization standardizes the performance of the main store and its branches. Branch store managers hire and supervise the employees in their stores and are responsible for making sure that day-to-day operations conform to company policies. This organization works well when there are few branches and the buying preferences of branch customers are similar to those of the main store's customers. However, as the branch stores increase in number, the buyers, the advertising director, the controller, and so on become overworked and give too little attention to the branches. In addition, because the main store's

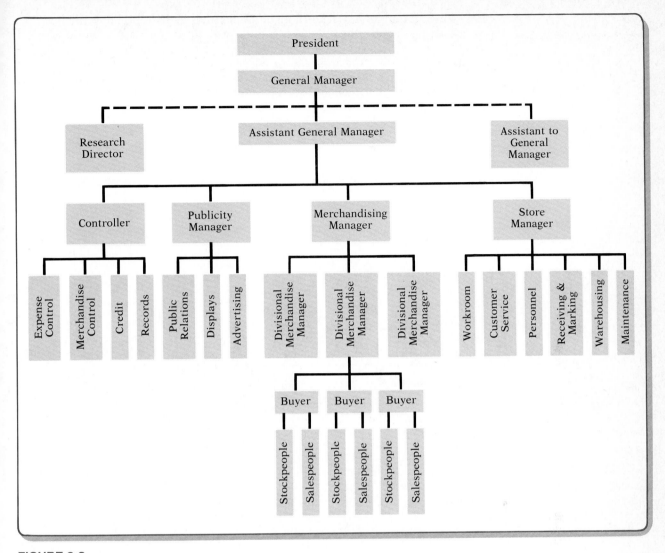

FIGURE 9-8
The Basic Mazur Organization Plan for Department Stores
Source: Adapted from Paul Mazur, *Principles of Organization Applied to Modern Retailing* (New York: Harper & Brothers, 1927), frontispiece. Reprinted with permission.

personnel are physically removed from the branches, differences in customer preferences may easily be overlooked.

The "separate store" organization places merchandise managers directly in branch stores. Each branch outlet has autonomy for merchandising and operations decisions. Customer needs are quickly identified, but duplication by managers in the main store and the branches is possible. Coordination can also be a problem (e.g., maintaining a consistent overall store image). Transferring stock between branches becomes more complex and more costly. This organization is best when individual stores are large, branches are geographically separated, and/or local customer tastes vary widely.

With the "equal store" organization, department stores try to achieve the benefits of both centralization and decentralization. It is probably the most popular arrangement today for multiunit department stores. Buying functions such as

287

forecasting, planning, buying, pricing, merchandise distribution to branches, and promotion are centrally managed. Selling functions such as presenting merchandise, selling, customer services, and store hours are managed in each outlet. All outlets, including the main store, are treated equally; and buyers are freed from supervising personnel in the main store. Data gathering is critical since buyers have less customer and store contact, and responsibility is more widely dispersed (and harder to pin down—buyer versus sales manager).

Organizational Arrangements Used by Chain Retailers

Chain retailers of various types often follow the equal-store organizational format explained in the preceding section and shown in Figure 9-9. Although

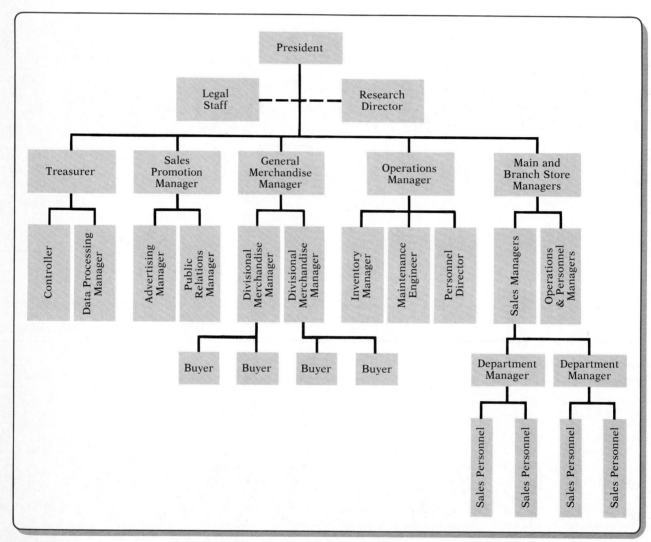

FIGURE 9-9
The Equal-Store Organizational Format Used by Many Chain Stores

chain-store organization structures may differ, they generally have these characteristics:

❑ There are a large number of functional divisions, such as sales promotion, merchandise management, distribution, store operations, real estate, personnel, and information systems.

❑ Authority and responsibility are centralized, with individual store managers responsible for sales.

❑ Operations are standardized (fixtures, store layout, building design, merchandise lines, credit policy, and store service).

❑ An elaborate control system keeps management informed.

❑ A limited amount of decentralization enables branch stores to adapt better to local conditions and increases the store manager's responsibilities. For example, while 80 per cent of K mart's merchandise is standardized on a national basis, store managers are free to fine-tune 10–20 per cent of the mix in an effort to appeal directly to local markets—be they rural or urban, black or Hispanic, high or low income.[3]

Figure 9-10 shows the organizational structure for Lucky Stores (a leading food chain now owned by American Stores). It is an equal-store format organized by function and geographic area.

Organizational Arrangements Used by Diversified Retailers

A **diversified retailer**, also known as a conglomerchant or retail conglomerate, is a multiline merchandising firm under central ownership.[4] Like a chain, a diversified retailer has more than one outlet; however, unlike a typical chain, these outlets cover different types of retail operations. These are some examples of diversified retailers:

❑ F.W. Woolworth operates a variety store chain, women's accessory stores, gift shops, shoe stores, apparel stores, and other retail outlets. See Figure 9-11.

❑ K mart operates a discount department store chain (K mart), a bookstore chain (WaldenBooks), a home-improvement chain (Builders Square), a discount variety store chain (Bargain Harold's), and a drugstore chain (Pay Less).

❑ Melville Corporation operates three shoe-store chains (Thom McAn, Open Country, and Pimento), three clothing chains (Chess King, Wilsons, and Marshalls), an off-price linens chain (Linens 'n Things), two drugstore chains (CVS and Freddy's), a toy/hobby chain (Kay-Bee), a furniture chain (This End Up), a prints and posters chain (Prints Plus), and leased shoe departments in all U.S. K mart stores (Meldisco).

Because of their multiple strategy mixes, diversified retailers face atypical considerations in developing and maintaining an organization structure. First, interdivision control is needed. Operating procedures and clear goals must be communicated among divisions. Second, interdivision competition must be coordinated (e.g., Should a firm's department stores and discount stores carry the same brands?). Third, resources must be allocated among different divisions. Fourth, potential image and advertising conflicts must be avoided. Fifth, management skills must be adapted to radically different operations. Accordingly, a diversified retailer usually has a very complex organization structure.

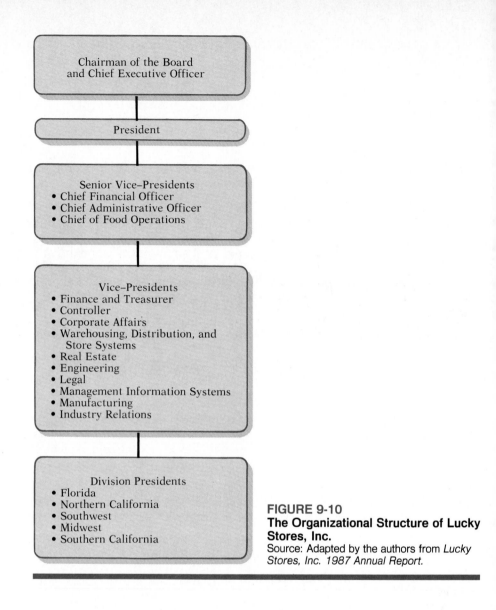

FIGURE 9-10
The Organizational Structure of Lucky Stores, Inc.
Source: Adapted by the authors from *Lucky Stores, Inc. 1987 Annual Report.*

Human Resource Management in Retailing

Human resource management involves the recruitment, selection, training, compensation, and supervision of personnel in a manner consistent with the retailer's organization structure and strategy mix. It is required of all retailers, with policies dependent on their line of business, the number of employees, the location of outlets, and so on.

Since good personnel are needed to develop and carry out retail strategies, and labor costs can amount to 50 per cent or more of some retailers' operating expenses, the importance of effective human resource management is clear. This is further illustrated through the following:

❑ Since retailing employs over eighteen million people, there is a constant need to attract new employees. However, since 1980, the number of U.S. workers aged sixteen to twenty-four has dropped by more than 10 per cent, and this trend will continue well into the 1990s. This makes the recruitment and retention of full- and part-time employees harder. For example, 2.5

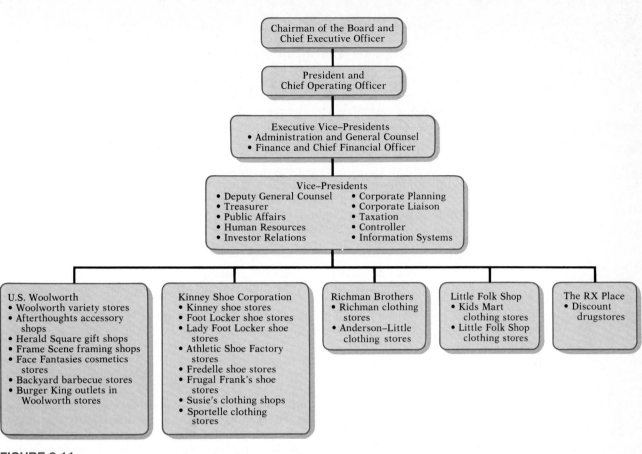

FIGURE 9-11
The Organizational Structure of F.W. Woolworth (United States only)
Source: Adapted by the authors from *F. W. Woolworth Co. 1987 Annual Report.*

million fast-food workers are aged sixteen to twenty, and they must be regularly replaced because they stay in their jobs for only a short time.[5]

❑ K mart has realigned its corporate structure in order to promote younger employees to higher-level positions. This is part of an overall program to expand and upgrade the chain and ensure an "orderly transition during the years immediately ahead."[6]

❑ Shoney coffee shops operate in several mideastern and southeastern states. The chain is very profitable and growing nicely. Experts credit "close restaurant supervision" as a key to this success. For example, each coffee shop has seven managers, two to three more than most competitors.[7]

❑ An Arthur D. Little consulting report predicts that "store managers of the future will be analytical, pinstripe suit types with college degrees." They will supervise outlets with "more customers, higher sales volume, greater product diversity, and more capital investment."[8]

The Special Human Resource Environment of Retailing

Retailers face a special human resource environment, which is characterized by a large number of inexperienced workers, long hours, highly visible employees, many part-time workers, and variations in customer demand. These factors often make the hiring, staffing, and supervision of employees a difficult process.

The greatest personnel difficulty for many retailers is probably the relative inexperience of a lot of their workers. As noted above, there is a need for a large labor force in retailing. Therefore, persons with little or no prior experience are frequently hired. For numerous new workers, a position in retailing represents their first "real" job. People are attracted to retailing because they find jobs near to their homes; and often, retail positions require limited education, training, and skill (e.g., checkout clerks, wrappers, stock clerks, and some types of sales personnel). Also, the low wages paid for some positions necessitate the hiring of inexperienced people. As a result, there are high employee turnover and instances of poor performance, lateness, and absenteeism.

The long working hours generally encountered in retailing, including Saturdays and Sundays in various localities, turn off some prospective employees, and there is a strong trend toward longer store hours, since family shoppers and working-women shoppers look for stores with evening and weekend hours. This means that some retailers must have at least two shifts of full-time employees.

In retailing, employees are highly visible to the customer. Therefore, when a retailer selects and trains personnel, special care must be taken with regard to their manners and appearance. Unfortunately, some small retailers may not recognize the importance of employee appearance (e.g., clean-shaven, appropriately attired, neatly groomed).

Because of the long hours of retail stores, firms often have to hire part-time personnel. For example, in many supermarkets, over half the employees are part-time. Problems can arise accordingly. Part-time workers may be more lackadaisical, late, absent, or likely to quit their jobs than full-time employees (who are more career-oriented). This means that part-time workers must be closely monitored.

Last, variations in customer demand by day, time period, or season may cause personnel planning problems. For example, almost two-thirds of consumers make their major supermarket shopping trips on Thursday, Friday, or Saturday. How many employees should a supermarket have on the premises Sunday (or Monday) through Wednesday, and how many should be used Thursday through Saturday? Demand differences during the day (e.g., morning, afternoon, evening) and by season (e.g., fall, Christmas) also affect personnel planning.

In general, retailers should consider these points:

❑ Employee selection procedures must be able to screen large quantities of applicants efficiently.

❑ Training must be intensive and short in duration because many workers are inexperienced and temporary.

❑ Career paths must be available to employees who look at retailing as a career.

❑ Appearance and work habits must be explained and reviewed.

❑ Morale problems may result from the high rate of employee turnover and the large number of part-time workers.

❑ Full-time and part-time employees may have conflicts, especially when part-time personnel are used to minimize overtime for full-time workers.

The Human Resource Management Process in Retailing

The **human resource management process** in retailing consists of several interrelated personnel activities: recruitment, selection, training, compensation, and supervision. The goals of this process are to obtain, develop, and retain employees. In the following subsections, each of the activities in the process is discussed for retail sales and middle-management positions.

Recruitment of Retail Personnel

Recruitment is the activity whereby a retailer generates a list of job applicants. Sources of potential employees are educational institutions, other channel members (such as wholesalers and manufacturers), competitors, advertisements, employment agencies, and unsolicited applicants. In addition, a retailer may have employees who are looking for promotions (transfers) or who recommend friends. Table 9-1 lists recruiting sources and their characteristics.

For entry-level sales personnel, retailers are likely to rely on educational institutions, advertising, walk-ins (or write-ins), and employee recommendations. For middle-management positions, retailers are apt to use employment agencies, competitors, ads, and current employees.

During recruitment, the retailer's major goal is to develop a large list of potential employees, which will be sharply reduced during selection. However, retailers who list applicants for further consideration only if they meet minimum back-

TABLE 9-1
Recruitment Sources and Their Characteristics

Sources	Characteristics
1. Outside the Company	
Educational institutions	a. High schools, business schools, community colleges, universities, graduate schools b. Good for training positions; ensures minimum educational requirements are fulfilled; especially useful when long-term contacts with instructors are developed
Other channel members, competitors	a. Employees of vendors, wholesalers, manufacturers, advertising agencies, competitors; leads from each of the preceding b. Reduces extent of training; can evaluate performance with prior company (ies); must instruct in company policy; some negative morale if current employees feel bypassed for promotions
Advertisements	a. Newspapers, trade publications, professional journals b. Large quantity of applicants; average applicant quality may not be high; cost/applicant is low; additional responsibility placed on screening; can reduce number of unacceptable applicants by noting job qualifications in the advertisement
Employment agencies	a. Private organizations, professional organizations, government, executive search firms b. Must be carefully selected; must be determined who pays fee; good for screening applicants; specialists in personnel
Unsolicited applicants	a. Walk-ins, write-ins b. Wide variance in quality; must be carefully screened; file should be kept for future positions
2. Within the Company	
Current and former employees	a. Promotion or transfer of existing full-time employees, part-time employees, laid-off employees b. Knowledge of company policies and personnel; good for morale; honest appraisal from in-house supervisor
Employee recommendations	a. Friends, acquaintances, relatives b. Value of recommendation depends upon honesty and judgment of current employee

ground standards (e.g., education, experience) can save a lot of time and money during selection.

Selection of Retail Personnel

Next, the retailer selects its new employees from among those it has recruited. The major objective in a selection procedure is to match the characteristics of potential employees with the requirements of the jobs to be filled. Such a procedure should include job analysis and description, the application blank, interviewing, testing, references, and a physical examination. These steps should be followed in an integrated manner.

Job analysis consists of gathering information about each job's functions and requirements: duties, responsibilities, aptitude, interest, education, experience, and physical condition. It is used for selecting personnel, establishing job performance standards, and salary administration.

Job analysis should lead to written job descriptions. A traditional **job description** contains each position's title, supervisory relationships (superior and subordinate), committee assignments, and the specific functions, tasks, and duties to be performed on an ongoing basis. Figure 9-4 showed a job description for a store manager, and Figure 9-12 is a job description for a salesperson.

However, for several reasons, the traditional job description has been criticized. It may

❑ Limit the scope of a job, as well as its authority, responsibility, and decision-making power.

❑ Be static and not allow a person to grow.

❑ Limit a worker's activities to those listed.

❑ Not discuss position objectives or evaluations.

❑ Not describe how organization levels or positions are coordinated.[9]

As a supplement to the traditional job description, many personnel authorities are now advocating a **goal-oriented job description**, which enumerates basic functions, the relationship of each job to overall goals, the interdependence of

---

JOB TITLE: Salesperson, Women's Jewelry Department,
               34th Street Branch of Pombo's Department Stores

POSITION REPORTS TO: Department Manager

POSITIONS REPORTING TO SALES CLERK: None

OBJECTIVES: To satisfy customer requests and maintain
               well–stocked displays

DUTIES AND RESPONSIBILITIES:

1. Customer contact
2. Stocking displays
3. Setting up displays
4. Handling cash and credit sales
5. Noting understocked merchandise

COMMITTEES AND MEETINGS:

1. No committees
2. Attendance at weekly department meeting

FIGURE 9-12
A Job Description for a Retail Salesperson

positions, and information flows. Figure 9-13 contains a goal-oriented job description.

The **application blank** is usually the first stage in screening applicants. It is short, requires little interpretation, and can be used as the basis for probing during an interview. An application blank provides data on education, experience, health, reasons for leaving previous jobs, organizational memberships, hobbies, and references.

Attributes Required	Ability	Desire	In the Retailing Environment
ANALYTICAL SKILLS: ability to solve problems; strong numerical ability for analysis of facts and data for planning, managing, and controlling.			Retail executives are problem solvers. Knowledge and understanding of past performance and present circumstances form the basis for action and planning.
CREATIVITY: ability to generate and recognize imaginative ideas and solutions; ability to recognize the need for and to be responsive to change.			Retail executives are idea people. Successful buying results from sensitive, aware decisions, while merchandising requires imaginative, innovative techniques.
DECISIVENESS: ability to make quick decisions and render judgments, take action, and commit oneself to completion.			Retail executives are action people. Whether it's new fashion trends or customer desires, decisions must be made quickly and confidently in this ever–changing environment.
FLEXIBILITY: ability to adjust to the ever–changing needs of the situation; ability to adapt to different people, places, and things; willingness to do whatever is necessary to get the task done.			Retail executives are flexible. Surprises in retailing never cease. Plans must be altered quickly to accommodate changes in trends, styles, and attitudes, while numerous ongoing activities cannot be ignored.
INITIATIVE: ability to originate action rather than wait to be told what to do and ability to act based on conviction.			Retail executives are doers. Sales volumes, trends, and buying opportunities mean continual action. Opportunities for action must be seized.
LEADERSHIP: ability to inspire others to trust and respect your judgment; ability to delegate and to guide and persuade others.			Retail executives are managers. Running a business means depending on others to get the work done. One person cannot do it all.
ORGANIZATION: ability to establish priorities and courses of action for self and/or others; skill in planning and following up to achieve results.			Retail executives are jugglers. A variety of issues, functions, and projects are constantly in motion. To reach your goals, priorities must be set, work must be delegated to others.
RISK–TAKING: willingness to take calculated risks based on thorough analysis and sound judgment and to accept responsibility for the results.			Retail executives are courageous. Success in retailing often comes from taking calculated risks and having the confidence to try something new before someone else does.
STRESS TOLERANCE: ability to perform consistently under pressure, to thrive on constant change and challenge.			Retail executives are resilient. As the above description should suggest, retailing is fast–paced and demanding.

FIGURE 9-13

A Goal-Oriented Job Description for a Management Trainee

Source: *Rate Yourself as a Retail Executive* (New York: Abraham & Straus), p. 1. Reprinted with permission.

One refinement of the basic application blank is the **weighted application blank**. Retailers using such a form have analyzed the performance of current and past employees and determined which criteria (education, experience, and so on) are best correlated with job success (which can be measured by longer tenure, higher sales volume, and less absenteeism). Factors that have a high relationship with success are given more weight than others, and a certain number of points are assigned to each factor that is rated. After weighted scores are given to all job applicants (based on the information they provide), a minimum total score can be used as a cutoff point for hiring. An effective weighted application blank would aid a retailer in reducing job turnover, identifying high achievers, and so on.

The application blank should be used in conjunction with the job description. Those who meet the minimum requirements of a job are processed further (interview). Those who do not are immediately rejected. In this way, the application blank provides a quick and inexpensive method of screening.

The interview seeks to obtain information that can be amassed only through personal questioning and observation. It enables the prospective employer to determine the oral ability of the candidate, note his or her appearance, ask questions based on the application blank, and probe into career objectives.

Several decisions about the interviewing process must be made: level of formality, number of interviews, length of each interview, physical location of interviews, the person to do the interviewing, relaxed or tense atmosphere, and the degree to which the interview is structured. These decisions depend on the ability of the interviewer and the requirements of the job.

Many, particularly smaller, retailers hire an applicant if he or she performs well during the interview. Other, usually larger, retailers use an additional selection device: testing. In this case, a candidate who does well during the interview is asked to complete psychological (e.g., personality, intelligence, interest, leadership skills) tests and/or achievement tests (which measure learned knowledge). The Ghiselli Self-Description Inventory is an example of a psychological test that has been used in the evaluation of store managers. It tests intelligence, supervisory ability, initiative, self-assurance, perceived occupational level, decision-making approach, and sociometric popularity.

Among the other psychological tests available to retailers are the Strong Vocational Interest Blank, Minnesota Multiphasic Personality Inventory, Edwards Personal Preference Scale, Wonderlic Personnel Test, and the Kuder Preference Record. These tests should be administered and interpreted by professionals. It is important that standardized examinations not be used unless they are proven as effective predictors of job performance.

Achievement tests deal with specific skills or information, such as industry knowledge, the ability to make a sales presentation, and insights into the principles of retailing. These tests are much easier to administer and interpret than psychological tests, and direct relationships between knowledge and ability can be determined.

In conjunction with interviewing and testing, retailers usually gather references from job applicants. References can be checked either before or after the interview stage. The purposes of contacting references are to determine how enthusiastically others recommend an applicant, to check the honesty of the applicant, to ask a prior employer why the applicant left an earlier job, and to review the types of people who will vouch for the applicant.[10] Mail and telephone reference checks are inexpensive, fast, and easy to do.

If a candidate successfully completes the interview, testing, and reference check steps, many retailers require a physical examination before giving a job. This is especially important because of the physical activity, long hours, and tensions involved in many retailing positions. A clean bill of health would mean that the candidate is offered a job.

Each of the steps in the selection process complements the others, and they give the retailer a total package of information upon which to base personnel decisions. As a rule, retailers should use job descriptions, application blanks, interviews, and reference checks. The use of follow-up interviews, psychological and achievement tests, and physical examinations depends on the nature of the retailer and the open positions.

Inexpensive tools (such as application blanks) should be used in the early screening stages, whereas more expensive, in-depth tools (such as personal interviews) should be used after the number of applicants has been reduced substantially. Federal and state regulations require that only questions that are directly linked to job performance be asked in the selection process. Equal opportunity practices must be followed.

Training Retail Personnel

When a new employee first joins the company, he or she should be exposed to a pretraining session. **Pretraining** is an indoctrination on the history and policies of the retailer and a job orientation on the hours, compensation, chain of command, and job duties. In addition, the new employee should be introduced to his or her co-workers.

Training programs are used to teach new (and old) personnel how best to perform their jobs or how to improve themselves. Training can range from one- or two-day sessions on writing sales checks, operating a cash register, personal selling techniques, or compliance with affirmative action programs to two-year programs for executive trainees on all aspects of the retailer and its operations. Figure 9-14 outlines the initial executive training program at Emporium Capwell, a San Francisco retail chain.

Effective retailers realize that training is an ongoing activity. New equipment, changes in laws, and new product lines, as well as employee promotions, motivating current personnel, and employee turnover, necessitate not only training but retraining as well. For example, Scandinavian Design, a Massachusetts-based furniture retailer, operates a training program for employees at all levels. It has established its own Scandinavian Design University with courses in sales training, time management, leadership skills, product training, and so on. Overall, the firm allots about 1 per cent of sales to employee development annually.[11]

Several training decisions need to be made, as shown in Table 9-2. In setting up a training program, those decisions can be divided into three categories: identifying needs, devising appropriate training methods, and evaluation.

By measuring the gap between current employee skills and desired job skills, a retailer can identify immediate training needs. Furthermore, training should prepare an employee for promotions. A five-year plan for labor development would enable the retailer to identify future needs and train employees accordingly. Both short-run and long-run training needs can be identified via informal observations, communications with upper management, group discussions, employee requests, employee performance, and analysis of reports.

After needs are identified, the best training method(s) for addressing them must be uncovered from among lectures, demonstrations, films, programmed instruction, conferences, sensitivity training, case studies, role playing, behavior modeling, and competency-based instruction.[12] The characteristics of these training methods are shown in Figure 9-15. Often retailers use two or more techniques during the training period to reduce boredom and cover the material better.

For training to be successful, an environment conducive to learning must be created. These are the essential principles for enacting such an environment:

❏ All people can learn if taught properly.

❏ A person learns better when motivated; intelligence alone is not sufficient.

Formal Training

Week 1 — Orientation in the following areas:

      —Company and corporate history   —Basic systems
      —Organizational structure   —Customer service
      —Personnel

Weeks 2,
3, & 4 — Store training assignment—TRAINEE will be exposed to basic merchandising and management responsibilities of a Department Sales Manager including:

      —Scheduling and supervision of sales staff
      —Basic systems (price changes, transfers, advertising reports, etc.)
      —Analysis of departmental business (usage of store reports to develop business)
      —Communication with central merchandising staff and store management
      —Comparison shopping
      —Merchandising of selling floor

Weeks 5
& 6 — Buying office assignment—TRAINEE will be exposed to and actively participate in:

      —Basic reports   —Resource meetings
      —Competitive shopping   —Advertising meetings
      —Service building operations   —Forecasting and planning
      —Store visits

Seminar Training

Seminars are held two times per week during the six weeks of formal training. All sessions are taught by EXECUTIVES in the Company and TRAINEES are expected to prepare for and actively participate in each seminar. Topics covered include:

—Merchandise presentation   —Sales staffing
—Floor merchandising disciplines   —Labor relations
—Merchandise math/gross margin   —Analyzing your business
—Trend and item merchandising   —Supervision of sales performance
—Merchandise traffic and transportation   —Retail selling skills
—Time management   —Advertising

Evaluation

The TRAINER will complete a performance evaluation on the TRAINEE at the end of each on–the–job assignment. Additionally, an exam will follow the six week program to assess the TRAINEES' understanding of basic retailing concepts taught in the seminars. TRAINEES will also be asked to evaluate their training at the conclusion of the six weeks, as well as evaluate their TRAINERS.

Placement

TRAINEES will competitively interview for Department Sales Manager positions.

FIGURE 9-14
Emporium Capwell's Initial Executive Training Program
Source: Emporium Capwell. Reprinted by permission.

❑ Learning should be goal-oriented.

❑ A trainee learns more when he or she participates and is not a passive listener.

❑ The teacher must provide guidance.

❑ Learning should be viewed as a process of steps rather than a one-time occurrence.

TABLE 9-2
Selected Training Decisions

299

Retail Organization and
Human Resource
Management

1. When does training occur? (At the time of hiring or after being at the workplace?)
2. How long should training be?
3. Who should conduct the training? (Supervisor, co-worker, or training department?)
4. Where should training take place? (At the workplace or in a training room?)
5. What material (content) should be learned? How should it be taught?
6. Should audiovisuals be used?
7. How can the effectiveness of training be measured?

❏ Learning should be spread out over a reasonable period of time rather than compressed.

❏ The learner should be encouraged to do homework or otherwise practice.

❏ Different methods of learning should be combined.

❏ Performance standards should be set, and good performance recognized.

❏ The learner should feel a sense of achievement.

❏ The teacher should adapt to the learner and to the situation.

A training program must be systematically evaluated for effectiveness. Comparisons may be made between the performances of those who have received training and those who have not. Comparisons may also be made among em-

RETAILING IN ACTION

Dunkin' Donuts University: Higher Education in Donuts?

Dunkin' Donuts is a franchisor with over 1,700 outlets that make and sell doughnuts, muffins, croissants, cookies, coffee, soup, croissant sandwiches, and related products. New franchisees (who are really owner-managers of their individual stores) must attend and pass a rigorous training program at Dunkin' Donuts University in Braintree, Massachusetts.

Each year, about six-hundred people attend the tuition-free school, which costs Dunkin' Donuts about $1.5 million annually to operate. There are several reasons Dunkin' Donuts makes such an investment. One, it is interested in uniformity in its stores; a customer should get the same quality products in all outlets. Two, since baked goods are made on the premises and must be regularly replenished, baking techniques and kitchen management skills are important; and these must be learned by new owners. Three, the firm wants to control the educational environment and be able to prepare franchisees for any possible situation.

The program has both classroom and experiential segments. In the classroom, "students" study the properties of yeast, learn about kitchen management, and so on. There are videotapes on topics such as croissant making. In the kitchen, students actually make doughnuts, coffee, and other foods. By program's end, each trainee will have made hundreds of dozens of doughnuts as well as the full range of Dunkin' Donuts products. In a mock store, the trainees work behind a simulated Dunkin' Donuts counter.

Franchisees take the program very seriously, spending an average of two hours per night on homework (reading baking manuals and gluten charts). To pass the course, they must satisfactorily complete a rigorous eight-hour exam, which includes making 140 dozen doughnuts properly. Five per cent of the students do not pass the course on the first attempt. They must repeat the course.

Source: Based on material in "At Braintree's Only University, Higher Education in Donuts," *New York Times* (February 21, 1988), p. 44.

Method	Characteristics
Lecture	Factual, uninterrupted presentation of material; can use professional educator and/or expert in the field; no active participation by trainees
Demonstration	Good for showing equipment or sales presentation; shows relevance of training; active participation by trainees
Film	Animated; good for demonstration; can be used many times; no active participation by trainees
Programmed Instruction	Presents information in a structured manner; requires response from trainees; provides performance feedback; adjustable to trainees' pace; high initial investment
Conference	Useful for supervisory training; conference leader must encourage participation; reinforces training
Sensitivity Training	Extensive interaction; good for supervisors as a tool for understanding employees
Case Study	Actual or hypothetical problem presented including circumstances, pertinent information, and questions; learning by doing; exposure to a wide variety of problems
Role Playing	Trainees placed into real–life situations and act out conflicts
Behavior Modeling	Trainees taught to imitate models shown on videotape or in role–playing sessions
Competency–Based Instruction	Trainees given a list of tasks or exercises that are developed in a self–paced format

FIGURE 9-15
The Characteristics of Retail Training Methods

ployees receiving different types of training for the same job. When a retailer measures the success of a training program, evaluations should always be made in relation to stated training goals. In addition, the effects of training should be measured over several time intervals (e.g., immediately, thirty days later, six months later), and appropriate records maintained.

Compensation of Retail Personnel

Compensation includes direct monetary payments (such as salary, commission, and bonus) and indirect payments (such as paid vacations, health and life insurance benefits, and retirement plan). Some retailers also use profit-sharing plans to better motivate employees. Smaller retailers often pay personnel salary, commission, and/or bonus, with little emphasis on fringe benefits. Bigger firms generally pay employees salary, commission, and/or bonus plus fringe benefits. To be effective, total compensation should be fair to both the retailer and the employee.

For many larger retailers, compensation is determined through collective-bargaining contracts. As an example, over half of supermarket chains employ unionized personnel; in contrast, only 16 per cent of independent supermarkets have unionized workers.[13] Union contracts frequently affect nonunion personnel, who ask for similar compensation.

Under a straight-salary plan, an employee is paid a fixed amount per hour, week, month, or year. Earnings are not directly related to productivity. The advantages of a straight-salary plan are retailer control, security for employees, and known expenses. The disadvantages are retailer inflexibility, limited worker incentive to increase productivity, and fixed costs. Lower-level retail personnel (e.g., clerks, cashiers) are almost always paid salaries.

With a straight-commission plan, the earnings of an employee are directly related to productivity (e.g., sales volume). A fixed amount is not paid out. The advantages of straight commission are retailer flexibility, the tie to worker productivity, no fixed costs, and employee incentive. The disadvantages are the retailer's potential lack of control over the tasks employees perform, the risk of low earnings to employees, the instability of retail costs, and the lack of limits placed on worker earnings. Sales personnel for automobiles, real estate, insurance, furniture, jewelry, and other expensive items are sometimes paid on straight commission. Direct-to-home sales personnel are also paid this way.

To combine the attributes of both salary and commission plans, some retailers pay their employees a salary plus commission. Shoe salespeople, major appliance salespeople, and some management personnel are among the employees paid in this manner. Sometimes bonuses are awarded as supplements to salary and/or commission. These are normally given for outstanding company or individual performance.

In some instances, top retail management is paid via a compensation cafeteria, where the executive can choose his or her own combination of salary, bonus, deferred bonus, fringe benefits, life insurance, stock options, and deferred retirement benefits.

Supervision of Retail Personnel

Supervision is the manner of providing a job environment that encourages accomplishment. The objectives of supervision are to oversee personnel, achieve good performance, maintain employee morale and motivation, control expenses, minimize redundancies, communicate company policies, and resolve problems. Supervision is provided through personal contact, meetings, and written reports between managers and their subordinates.

A key element of supervision is the continued motivation of employees. **Motivation** is the drive within people to attain goals. The role of supervision is to motivate employees to achieve company goals, or to harness human energy to the retailer's needs. Several theories of motivation have been developed, three of which are McGregor's Theory X and Theory Y, Herzberg's theory of satisfiers and dissatisfiers, and Theory Z (popularized by the Japanese and now in growing use in the United States).

Theory X is the traditional view of motivation and has been applied to lower-level retail positions:

❑ Management is responsible for organizing money, materials, equipment, and people resources.

❑ Personnel should be directed, motivated, controlled, and modified in accordance with the needs of the organization.

❑ Management must actively intervene with personnel; otherwise, people are passive and resistant to organizational needs.

❑ The average worker lacks ambition, dislikes responsibility, and prefers to be led.

❑ The average worker is self-centered and resistant to change.[14]

Theory Y is a more modern view of motivation and applies to all levels of retail personnel:

❑ Management is responsible for organizing money, materials, equipment, and people resources.

❑ People are not by nature passive or resistant to organizational needs.

❑ Motivation, potential for development, capacity for assuming responsibility, and readiness to achieve company goals are all present in people. Management must make it possible for people to recognize and develop their abilities.

❑ The essential task of management is to arrange the organizational environment so that employees can achieve their own goals by directing their efforts toward company objectives.[15]

Theory X assumes that employees must be closely supervised and controlled. Economic inducements provide motivation. Theory Y assumes that employees can use self-management and can be delegated authority. Motivation is social and psychological. Management is decentralized and participatory.

Herzberg's theory offers another perspective on motivation. According to this theory, the factors involved in producing job satisfaction and motivation (satisfiers) are distinct from the factors that lead to job dissatisfaction (dissatisfiers). Factors that can result in retail job satisfaction are achievement, recognition for achievement, the job itself, responsibility, and growth or advancement. Factors that can result in retail job dissatisfaction are a worker's unhappiness with company policies and their administration, the method of supervision, interpersonal relationships, work conditions, salary, and security.[16]

Theory Z adapts elements from Theory Y and Herzberg's theory. With Theory Z, employees are given a more participatory role in defining their jobs and share some decision making with management. There is mutual loyalty between the firm and its workers, and both parties enthusiastically cooperate for the long-term benefit of the company (and employees).[17] Although Theory Z is most widely used by manufacturing firms in the United States, the applications by retailers are growing. For example, A&P was able to keep open over fifty Philadelphia stores by negotiating employee wage reductions in exchange for active participation in management decisions and a share of gross sales for improving labor productivity. Today, A&P is a much stronger chain.[18]

It is critical that supervision motivate employees in a manner that yields job satisfaction, low turnover, low absenteeism, and high productivity.

SUMMARY

A retail organization is used to structure and assign tasks, policies, resources, authority, responsibilities, and rewards in order to efficiently and effectively satisfy the needs of a firm's target market, employees, and management. Five steps are involved in setting up a retail organization: outlining the specific tasks to be performed in the retail exchange, dividing the tasks among channel members and customers, grouping tasks into jobs, classifying jobs, and integrating positions through an organization chart.

Specific tasks include buying, shipping, receiving, checking, and marking merchandise; setting prices; inventory control; display preparation; facilities maintenance; research; customer contact and follow-up; personnel management; merchandise repairs; finances and credit; gift wrapping; delivery; returns; forecasting; and coordination. These tasks may be divided among retailers, manufacturers, wholesalers, specialists, and customers.

After the retailer determines which tasks to perform, they are grouped into jobs, such as salesperson, cashier, inventory personnel, display personnel, credit personnel, customer service personnel, janitorial personnel, and management. Jobs can be categorized according to functional, product, geographic, or combination classifications. The organization chart graphically displays the hierarchy of authority and the relationship among jobs, and it coordinates the personnel of the store. Small independents, department stores, chain retailers, and diversified retailers each utilize different organizational forms.

Human resource management in retailing is composed of several interrelated activities: recruitment, selection, training, compensation, and supervision.

Special human resource considerations for retailers are inexperienced workers, long hours, visible employees, part-time workers, and variations in customer demand.

Recruitment is the activity of generating job applicants. Sources include educational institutions, channel members, competitors, advertisements, employment agencies, current and former employees, and unsolicited applications.

The selection of retail personnel requires a thorough job analysis, the creation of a job description, the use of an application blank, interview(s), testing (optional), the checking of references, and the completion of a physical examination. After personnel are selected, employees go through pretraining (job orientation) and job training. An effective training program revolves around identifying needs, devising appropriate training methods, and evaluating the results. Training may be necessary for continuing as well as new personnel.

Employees can be compensated via direct monetary payments and indirect payments. The alternative direct compensation plans are straight salary, straight commission, and salary plus commission and/or bonus. Indirect payments involve such items as paid vacations, health benefits, and retirement plans.

Supervision and motivation are necessary to obtain good employee performance. Supervision can be provided through personal contact, meetings, and written reports. Motivation theories include McGregor's Theory X–Theory Y, Herzberg's satisfiers–dissatisfiers, and Theory Z.

QUESTIONS FOR DISCUSSION

1. Cite at least five objectives retailers should take into consideration when setting up their organization structures.
2. Why are target-market needs important in developing a retail organization?
3. Are the steps involved in setting up a retail organization the same for small and large retailers? Explain your answer.
4. Present a five-item checklist that could be used to group retail tasks into jobs.
5. How would the hierarchy of authority in a flat organization differ from that in a tall organization? What are the potential ramifications?
6. What are the strengths and weaknesses of analyzing a retailer on the basis of its organization chart?
7. Describe the greatest similarities and differences among the organization structures of small independents, department stores, chain retailers, and diversified retailers.
8. Distinguish between small and large retailer strategies for each of the following:
   a. Recruitment
   b. Selection
   c. Training
   d. Compensation
   e. Supervision
9. Why are the job analysis and the job description so important in employee selection?
10. What problems can occur during the interviewing and testing of prospective employees?
11. How may training needs be determined for existing employees? Present a plan for training existing employees without making it seem punitive.
12. Describe the goals of a compensation plan in a retail setting.
13. Under what circumstances should Theory X be used? Theory Y?
14. Comment on Herzberg's theory of satisfiers and dissatisfiers, and contrast it with Theory Z.

NOTES

1. Francine Schwadel, "Christmas Sales' Lack of Momentum Tests Store Manager's Mettle," *Wall Street Journal* (December 16, 1987), pp. 1, 10.
2. Paul M. Mazur, *Principles of Organization Applied to Modern Retailing* (New York: Harper & Brothers, 1927).
3. Molly Brauer, "K mart Assumes New Posture," *Chain Store Age Executive* (August 1984), pp. 25–29; and N. R. Kleinfield, "Countdown to Christmas at K mart," *New York Times* (December 20, 1987), Section 3, pp. 1, 7.
4. See Rollie Tillman, "Rise of the Conglomerchant," *Harvard Business Review*, Vol. 49 (November–December 1971), pp. 44–51; and Jacquelyn Bivins, "Diversification: Retailers Reach Out," *Chain Store Age Executive* (March 1984), pp. 25 ff.
5. Aaron Bernstein, Richard W. Anderson, and Wendy Zellner, "Help Wanted," *Business Week* (August 10, 1987), pp. 48–53.
6. "K mart Corp. Realigns Structure, Promotes

Younger Employees," *Wall Street Journal* (December 20, 1984), p. 18.

7. "At Shoney's, Details Count," *New York Times* (June 8, 1984), pp. D1, D5.

8. "Megastores Need Strategic, Not Hands-On, Managers," *Marketing News* (September 14, 1984), p. 45.

9. Dennis J. Sutherland, "Managing by Objectives in Retailing," *Journal of Retailing*, Vol. 47 (Fall 1971), p. 15.

10. See "Certified Resumes Eliminate Hiring Fears," *Chain Store Age Executive* (June 1987), p. 68.

11. Ellen Wojahn, "A Touch of Class," *Inc.* (September 1983), pp. 79–86.

12. For example, see "Computers as Classrooms," *Chain Store Age Executive* (January 1986), p. 128; and "Trainees Build Skills in Risk-Free Contest," *Chain Store Age Executive* (June 1987), pp. 56–58.

13. "54th Annual Report of the Grocery Industry," *Progressive Grocer* (April 1987), p. 35.

14. Douglas McGregor, "The Human Side of Enterprise," in Warren G. Bennis and Edgar Schein (Editors), *Leadership and Motivation: Essays of Douglas McGregor* (Cambridge, Mass.: MIT Press, 1966).

15. Ibid.

16. Frederick Herzberg, "One More Time: How Do You Motivate Employees?" *Harvard Business Review*, Vol. 46 (January–February 1968), pp. 53–62.

17. William Ouchi, *Theory Z* (Reading, Mass.: Addison-Wesley, 1981).

18. John Merwin, "A Piece of the Action," *Forbes* (September 24, 1984), pp. 146–148 ff.; and Christopher S. Eklund, "How A&P Fattens Profits by Sharing Them," *Business Week* (December 22, 1986), p. 44.

Case 1

Home Security Alarms, Inc.: Assessing An Employee Incentive System

Brad Miller is the owner of Home Security Alarms, Inc., a burglar/fire alarm installation and service company catering to residential home owners. Brad sincerely believes in offering merit-based incentives to as many employees as possible. For example, he has divided all installation and repair tasks into work units. Installers and repairpersons are given bonuses based upon their completing more than a given number of work units per day. While salespeople receive a salary, they also have an incentive system based upon sales revenues and profitability. See Table 1.

Miller likes the concept of an employee incentive system for several reasons. One, this system rewards performance on a regular basis. Brad does not feel that rewarding personnel with an end-of-year bonus provides proper motivation throughout the year. He wants his

TABLE 1
Examples of Home Security Alarms' Employee Incentive Programs

---

For Installers and Repairpersons:

The expected workday performance is based on ten work units. Each task has a standard time based on work units. For instance, diagnosing and repairing a short circuit equals two work units. For each work unit completed over seven per day, installers and repairpersons receive a $10 bonus. When a callback arises within forty-eight hours after an installation or a repair has been conducted, the employee involved has his or her work unit accumulation deducted by double the value of the original work.

For Salespeople:

They receive
❑ A three per cent commission on new alarm systems (with installation) priced at 20–30 per cent above standard cost.

❑ A seven per cent commission on new alarm systems (with installation) priced at 31–40 per cent above standard cost.

❑ A ten per cent commission on new alarm systems (with installation) priced at 41–50 per cent above standard cost.

❑ An additional 2 per cent commission on all individual orders priced above $4,000.

❑ A five per cent commission on all upgrades of existing alarm systems priced at $500 or above.

❑ A $25 bonus for selling central station alarm monitoring (at $15 per month).

---

employees to be performance-oriented at all times. Two, unlike an increase in salary, which becomes a fixed, ongoing expense (regardless of performance), the Home Security Alarms' incentive system requires that employees earn their bonuses in each pay period. Three, the bonus system helps Home Security Alarms attract and retain high achievers. The firm does not want people who just "come to work."

Despite the advantages of its employee incentive program, Home Security Alarms has several issues to address:

❑ Installers and repair personnel feel that it is unfair to charge them for callbacks if the equipment (and not the installation or repair) proves to be defective within two days of service. However, it is hard for Home Security to determine if the part or the installation is at fault. Installers and repairpersons also feel that they are not properly compensated for the extra-heavy work schedules on Monday and Saturday. They argue that Home Security builds loyalty by promptly servicing customers' systems but that they receive the same bonus regardless of when the work is done (given that they have reached their work unit standard for the day).

❑ While salesperson incentive compensation varies considerably, the difference in incentive compensation among installers and repairpersons is relatively small. Brad is concerned that there is something fundamentally wrong when 80 per cent of these employees are earning a comparable incentive payment on a yearly basis.

❑ The program rewards performance but not effort for both installers–repairpersons and salespeople. Persons improving significantly, but still not reaching incentive performance minimum levels, receive no extra compensation.

❑ Some salespeople recommend alarm systems on the basis of price (to maximize their commissions) rather than customer needs. In a few communities, neighbors owning virtually identical development-type homes have reported getting different estimates from different Home Security salespeople. The commission-conscious salespeople are pushing more costly systems by telling customers that optional features are really necessary. In contrast, other salespeople are encouraging customers to buy a basic system now and to purchase "optional" components at a later date. Brad has also been told that the price discrepancy for the same alarm systems sold to different customers can be as much as 20 per cent, depending on the salesperson.

❑ While Miller designed the incentive plan to be flexible, in reality all personnel see the incentives as a basic part of their compensation. There is a large, companywide resistance to making any changes in the incentives. This is especially true if the firm attempts to get employees to do more than in previous years for the same incentive payments.

QUESTIONS

1. What tasks should be performed by Home Security Alarms' installers–repairpersons and salespersons? Be complete in your answer.
2. Evaluate Home Security Alarm's incentive program in terms of the tasks you identified in Question 1.
3. Comment on each of the issues raised in this case regarding Home Security Alarms' incentive program.
4. If Home Security Alarms decides to modify its incentive program, how should it present these modifications to its employees? How would you respond to the objections that they may raise?

High Value Supermarkets: Dealing with Personnel Problems

Case 2

High Value Supermarkets operates a ten-store chain of small supermarkets in and around Denver, Colorado. All of the stores are within ten miles of Denver. During the past three years, High Value has experienced difficulties with its part-time personnel. Turnover, especially among stock clerks, has increased significantly. Absenteeism and lateness are quite

1.	Part–time employees are those who work less than twenty hours per week.
2.	Each store manager, on a decentralized basis, makes all personnel decisions relating to recruiting, screening, hiring, training, evaluating, and firing.
3.	The company prefers the use of high school and college students as part–time employees, and likes to hire only students with B or better averages.
4.	All personnel, part– and full–time, are subject to strict dress codes. Males must wear solid, light–colored shirts with ties. Females must wear dresses or skirts and collared blouses; pants suits are not acceptable. Neither male nor female personnel are permitted to wear jeans, sweatshirts, tee shirts, or shorts to work.
5.	Wages for new part–time employees (stock clerks, cashiers, baggers, delivery) are the current minimum wage plus 50¢ per hour. After one year, part–time employees receive 10¢ per hour increments. After two years, part–time employees receive 20¢ per hour increases.
6.	Part–time employees are not eligible for any fringe benefits except those mandated by state and federal statutes (i.e., Social Security, unemployment insurance, disability insurance, and Workmen's Compensation). After three years of continuous service, part–time employees receive two paid sick days, one week of vacation, and five paid holidays. Before three years are completed, none of these benefits are provided.

FIGURE 1
High Value Supermarkets' Policies for Part-Time Employees

common. The part-time employees do not get along well with the full-time workers, particularly when part-timers are used to avoid paying overtime to full-timers.

Stanley Rice, president of the chain, has remarked that he is surprised by these developments: "We have always valued and respected our part-time workers and feel they are integral members of our organization. I mistakenly thought that these employees were happy working for us. It is certainly time for us to re-evaluate our current policies with regard to part-time employees" (see Figure 1).

As a first step toward solving High Value's problems, Rice conducted informal interviews with 20 part-time employees, 20 full-time employees, and 50 customers. The results of these interviews are contained in Table 1.

TABLE 1
Results of Informal Interviews with Part-Time Employees,
Full-Time Employees, and Customers

1. Comments by Part-Time Employees	No. Commenting	% Commenting
(20 interviews)		
a. Full-time college student	12	60
b. Working for High Value less than one year	14	70
c. Dissatisfied with menial tasks and close supervison	12	60
d. Originally interested in retail careers, not any	10	50
longer	18	90
e. Clothing regulations out-of-date	8	40
f. Pay too low	14	70
g. Not enjoyable to work for High Value	6	30
h. Full-timers act superior	12	60
i. No sense of achievement		

2. Comments by Full-Time Employees	No. Commenting	% Commenting
(20 interviews)		
a. Part-timers rude	10	50
b. Part-timers have no sense of responsibility	10	50
c. Part-timers do not know basic information	14	70
d. Part-timers not helpful	6	30
e. Part-timers a cheap source of labor	17	85
f. Too much overlap in part-time and full-time		
functions	12	60
g. Part-timer turnover a major problem	16	80

3. Comments by Customers	No. Commenting	% Commenting
(50 interviews)		
a. Part-timers impolite	14	28
b. Part-timers unknowledgeable	21	42
c. Part-timers lackadaisical	17	34
d. Part-timers sloppy and disheveled	13	26
e. Part-timers "basically good kids"	38	76
f. Behavior of part-timers High Value's doing	40	80

QUESTIONS

1. Evaluate the information contained in Figure 1 and Table 1.
2. Can High Value use an integrated approach to personnel management for all types of personnel? Explain your answer.
3. How should Rice react to McGregor's and Herzberg's theories and Theory Z for his personnel? Does your answer vary by type of employee and type of job?
4. What specific management policy changes should be implemented, based upon the interviews?

Chapter 10

Operations Management

Gromer Supermarket is a highly successful retailer that operates one 50,000 square-foot store in Elgin, Illinois. A great part of its success is due to Gromer's willingness to try new techniques to improve its productivity. For example, in 1977, Gromer was one of the first food stores to install optical scanning equipment at its checkout counters. This has sped up transaction times, provided better inventory information, and reduced cashier errors.

More recently, Gromer has implemented a new computerized time and attendance system to better supervise employees. The system allows it to monitor the hours of 250 employees, 70 per cent of whom are part-timers. Every employee has a plastic card with a magnetic strip that he or she must slide into a time clock whenever beginning and leaving work. The clock will not accept a card

if an employee reports for work too early, and it is programmed to watch for long lunches. But the system goes beyond simply monitoring hours:

> The significant thing is not just tracking employees, but automating the payroll process. The system saves 10 to 12 hours of work each week. It used to take two-and-a-half people from 7 in the morning until noon every Monday to calculate the payroll; this is now done by computer.

Gromer also offers its own computerized check-cashing cards to customers (to reduce bad checks and speed transactions), generates shelf labels from equipment that logs in new merchandise when it arrives, has a computerized shelf-space allocation system, and is installing a system to track videotape rentals and inventory. For the latter, "you need to know what you're renting, who is renting it, and when it is due back."[1]

All retailers, large and small, are interested in being as efficient as possible. As can be seen by observing Gromer Supermarket, a firm does not have to be a giant chain to improve its level of productivity—as long as it is willing to be progressive.

Overview

After a retailer develops an organization structure and establishes a human resource management plan, it concentrates on **operations management**. This involves efficiently and effectively implementing the tasks and policies necessary to satisfy the firm's customers, employees, and management (and stockholders, if a publicly owned company).

Retailers should recognize that the way they operate their businesses has a major impact on sales and profitability. For example, large inventory levels, long store hours, expensive fixtures, extensive customer services, and heavy advertising may encourage consumers to shop and lead to higher sales volume. But at what cost? If a supermarket must pay night-shift salaries that are 50 per cent higher than day-shift salaries, is staying open twenty-four hours per day worthwhile (i.e., do the increased sales and profits justify the increased costs?)?

The first part of this chapter covers the financial dynamics of operations management. The second part examines a number of specific aspects of operations management.

The Financial Dynamics of Operations Management

It is essential that retailers understand the financial ramifications of operations management, since the efficiency and effectiveness of their performance are strongly related to the way assets and costs are deployed. Three concepts are discussed in the following sections: asset management, budgeting, and resource allocation.

Asset Management

Each retailer has various assets that it must manage and liabilities that it must control. **Assets** are any items that a retailer owns that have a monetary value. Current assets consist of cash on hand (or in the bank) and items that are readily converted to cash in the short run, such as inventory on hand (or in transit to the retailer) and accounts receivable (amounts owed to the retailer by its customers). Fixed assets consist of the present value of property, buildings (a retail store, a warehouse, and so on), store fixtures, and equipment such as cash registers and trucks; these are used in operations over a long period of time.

Liabilities are any financial obligations that a retailer incurs in operating a business. Current liabilities comprise payroll expenses payable, taxes payable, accounts payable (amounts owed to suppliers), and short-term loans; these obligations must be paid within the coming year. Fixed liabilities comprise mortgages and long-term loans; these obligations are generally repaid over several years.

A retailer's **net worth** is computed as its assets minus its liabilities. Net worth is also known as owner's equity and represents the value of a retail business after deducting financial obligations.

A **balance sheet** itemizes a retailer's assets, liabilities, and net worth at a specific point in time; it is based on the principle that assets = liabilities + net worth. Table 10-1 shows a balance sheet for Donna's Gift Shop.

TABLE 10-1
A Retail Balance Sheet for Donna's Gift Shop (as of December 31, 1988)

Assets			Liabilities			
Current:			Current:			
Cash on hand	$ 13,300		Payroll expenses payable	$ 4,000		
Inventory	24,100		Taxes payable	9,000		
Accounts receivable	1,100		Accounts payable	21,400		
Total		$ 38,500	Short-term loan	700		
			Total		$ 35,100	
Fixed (present value):						
Property	$125,000		Fixed:			
Building	42,000		Mortgage	$ 65,000		
Store fixtures	9,700		Long-term loan	4,500		
Equipment	1,700		Total		$ 69,500	
Total		$178,400				
			Total liabilities			$104,600
Total assets		$216,900				
			Net Worth			$112,300
			Liabilities + net worth			$216,900

In operations management, the retailer's goal is to use its assets in the manner that provides the best financial results possible. There are two ways of measuring those results: return on assets (ROA) and return on net worth (RONW).

Return on assets is a ratio based on a retailer's net sales, net profit, and total assets:

$$\text{Return on assets} = \frac{\text{Net sales}}{\text{Total assets}} \times \frac{\text{Net profit}}{\text{Net sales}}$$

$$= \frac{\text{Net profit}}{\text{Total assets}}$$

For example, if Donna's Gift Shop had net sales of $220,000 and a net profit of $19,000 during 1988, its ROA would be:

$$\text{Return on assets} = \frac{\$220,000}{\$216,900} \times \frac{\$19,000}{\$220,000}$$

$$= 1.0143 \times .0864 = .0876 = 8.8\%$$

From an operations standpoint, these two key pieces of information may be learned by studying a retailer's ROA. First, the firm can determine the relationship between its sales and assets (asset turnover). In the case of Donna's Gift Shop, asset turnover is 1.0143; this means that the firm averages just over $1.01 in sales per dollar of total assets. To improve its asset turnover ratio, a retailer would have to generate increased sales via the same level of assets or maintain the same sales with a reduced asset base. A company might increase sales by staying open longer hours, accepting mail-order sales, training employees better, stocking more well-known national brands instead of local brands, and so on; none of these tactics requires the asset base to be expanded. Or the company might maintain sales on a lower asset base by moving to a smaller store (less wasted space), simplifying store fixtures (or having suppliers install and own the fixtures), keeping a more basic inventory on hand, and so on.

Second, the firm can examine the relationship between profit and sales (profit margin). In the case of Donna's Gift Shop, the profit margin is a little over 8.6

per cent; for a gift shop, this is a fairly good percentage. To enhance its profit margin, a retailer could seek to reduce its operating expenses as a percentage of sales. It could place greater emphasis on self-service and lower personnel costs, refinance a mortgage when interest rates fall, reduce energy costs (one type of account payable), and so on. In this manner, the retailer's profit margin would rise. However, the firm would have to be careful not to lower customer service to the extent that sales and profit would decline.

Return on net worth is a ratio based on a retailer's net profit, total assets, and net worth:

$$\text{Return on net worth} = \frac{\text{Net profit}}{\text{Total assets}} \times \frac{\text{Total assets}}{\text{Net worth}}$$

$$= \frac{\text{Net profit}}{\text{Net worth}}$$

This is the RONW for Donna's Gift Shop:

$$\text{Return on net worth} = \frac{\$19,000}{\$216,900} \times \frac{\$216,900}{\$112,300}$$

$$= .0876 \times 1.9314 = .1692 = 16.9\%$$

The initial half of this ratio (net profit/total assets) represents the retailer's ROA, which was just explained. The second half (total assets/net worth) adds another vital piece of information: the retailer's financial leverage ratio. In the case of Donna's Gift Shop, the financial leverage ratio is 1.9314; this means that assets are slightly less than double Donna's net worth and that total liabilities and net worth are roughly equal. As a result, Donna's approach could be viewed as rather conservative. Owner's equity is relatively high and could be partially replaced by increasing the amount of the short- and long-term loans and/or the accounts payable. In this way, some of the equity funds could be taken out of the business by the owner (stockholders, if a public company). But a retailer must be careful not to have too high a financial leverage ratio or else its liabilities may be excessive.

When a retailer develops its strategy on the basis of both return on assets (which focuses on asset turnover and profit margin) and return on net worth (which focuses on financial leverage), it is involved with a concept known as the **strategic profit model.** This may be expressed as follows:

$$\text{Strategic profit model} = \frac{\text{Net sales}}{\text{Total assets}} \times \frac{\text{Net profit}}{\text{Net sales}} \times \frac{\text{Total assets}}{\text{Net worth}}$$

$$= \text{Asset turnover} \times \text{Profit margin} \\ \times \text{Financial leverage}$$

$$= \text{Return on net worth}$$

Budgeting

Budgeting outlines a retailer's planned expenditures for a given time period based on its expected performance. In this way, a retailer's costs can be linked to satisfying target market, employee, and management goals. For example, what should planned personnel costs be if the retailer wants to provide a certain level of customer service, such as no shopper waiting in a supermarket checkout line for more than ten minutes? What level of compensation should be planned to motivate sales personnel? What amount of total planned expenses will enable management to generate satisfactory sales revenue and reach profit goals?

There are several reasons that a retailer should systematically develop a detailed budget. By budgeting:

❑ Expenditures are clearly related to expected performance, and costs can be adjusted as goals are revised. This enhances productivity.

❑ Resources can be allocated to the appropriate divisions, product categories, and so on.

❑ Cost standards can be set, such as advertising equals 5 per cent of sales.

❑ Expenditures for various departments, product lines, and so on can be coordinated.

❑ The retailer can prepare for the future rather than react to it.

❑ Management can be stimulated to plan in a structured, integrated manner. The goal of efficiency would thereby be given more prominence.

❑ The retailer can monitor expenditures during a budget cycle. If a firm has allocated $50,000 to purchase new merchandise for a budget cycle, and it has spent $33,000 on such merchandise halfway through that cycle, it has planned expenditures of $17,000 remaining.

❑ The retailer can analyze and explain the differences between its expected and actual costs and performance.

❑ A company's expected and actual costs and performance can be contrasted with industry averages. For instance, how do a specialty store chain's total net operating expenses as a percentage of sales compare to the industry average?

When establishing a budget, the retailer should be aware of the effort and time involved, recognize that expectations may not be fully accurate (because of unexpected consumer demand, competitors' tactics, and so on), and be willing to modify plans as necessary. It should not allow itself to become overly conservative (or inflexible) or simply add a percentage to each current expense category to arrive at next year's budget, such as increasing expenditures by 3 per cent across the board based on anticipated sales growth of 3 per cent.

The budgeting process is shown in Figure 10-1 and described next.

Preliminary Budgeting Decisions

There are six preliminary budgeting decisions that a retailer must make.

First, the person(s) responsible for budgeting decisions would be specified. **Top-down budgeting** places decisions in the hands of upper management; these decisions are then communicated down the line to succeeding levels of managers. **Bottom-up budgeting** requires that lower-level executives develop budget requests for their departments; these requests are then assembled, and an overall companywide budget is designed. With top-down budgeting, senior management centrally directs and controls budgets. With bottom-up budgeting, varied perspectives are included, managers are held accountable for their own decisions, and employee morale is enhanced. For these reasons, many firms combine aspects of the two approaches.

Second, the budgeting time frame would be defined. Most retailers set budgets that have yearly, quarterly, and monthly components. In this way, annual expenditures can be planned and expected versus actual costs, and performance can be reviewed on a regular basis. As a result, a firm can control overall costs, while responding to seasonal or other fluctuations. Sometimes, the time frame can be longer than a year or shorter than a month. For example, when a retailer such as Dayton Hudson decides to open a number of new stores over a five-year period, it would specify its capital expenditures (property, construction, and

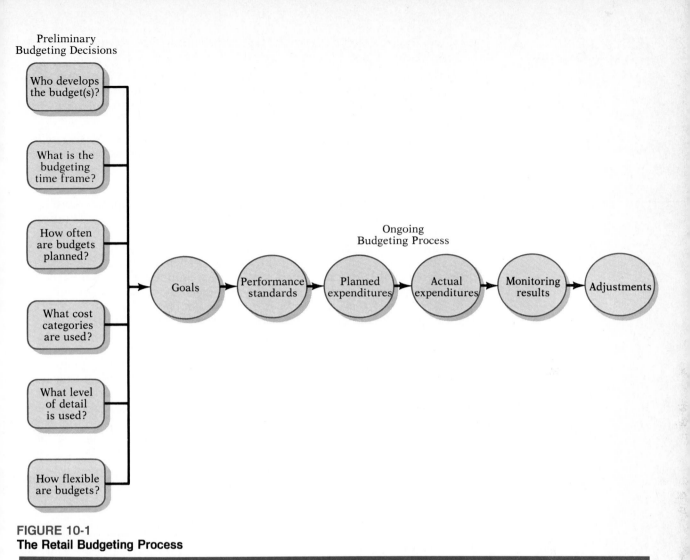

Preliminary Budgeting Decisions

- Who develops the budget(s)?
- What is the budgeting time frame?
- How often are budgets planned?
- What cost categories are used?
- What level of detail is used?
- How flexible are budgets?

Ongoing Budgeting Process

Goals → Performance standards → Planned expenditures → Actual expenditures → Monitoring results → Adjustments

FIGURE 10-1
The Retail Budgeting Process

other investment costs) for the entire five years. When a supermarket chain such as Lucky Stores orders milk, baked goods, and other perishable goods, it would have daily or weekly budgets for each of these items.

Third, the frequency with which budgets are planned would be determined. While many retailers review their budgets on a regular, ongoing basis, the great majority of companies plan their budgets once a year. In some firms, several months may be set aside each year for the budgeting process to be undertaken; this enables all participants to have ample time to gather information and allows retailers to take their budgets through several drafts before giving final approval.

Fourth, cost categories would be established:

❑ Capital expenditures involve major long-term investments in land, buildings, fixtures, and equipment. Operating expenditures include the short-term selling and administrative expenses of running a retail business.

❑ Fixed costs are those that remain relatively constant for the period of a budget, such as store security expenses and real-estate taxes, regardless of the retailer's performance. Variable costs are those that are related to the retailer's performance during the budget period, such as sales commissions. When performance standards are high, these expenses rise.

❑ Direct costs are incurred by specific departments, product lines, and so on, such as the earnings of department-based salespeople and cashiers. Indirect costs are shared by two or more departments, product lines, and so on, such as exterior store displays and centralized cashiers.

❑ Natural account expenses are reported by the names of the costs, such as salaries, and not assigned by their purpose. Functional account expenses are classified on the basis of the purpose or activity for which expenditures are made, such as cashier salaries.

Tables 10-2 and 10-3 show the natural and functional account expense categories outlined by the National Retail Merchants Association. Please note: Individual firms may use different categories from those shown in these tables, and for some retailers, certain categories may not be appropriate (such as executive office and central wrapping and packing expenses for a small retailer).

Fifth, the level of budgeting detail would be ascertained. For example, should planned expenditures be allocated by department (e.g., produce), product category (e.g., fresh fruit), product subcategory (e.g., apples), or product item (e.g., McIntosh apples)? If a retailer has a very detailed budget, it must be sure that every expense subcategory is adequately covered.

Sixth, the amount of flexibility in the budget would be set. On the one hand, the budget should be rigid enough to serve its purpose in guiding planned expenditures and linking costs to goals. On the other hand, a budget that is too inflexible would not allow a retailer to adapt to changing market conditions, to capitalize on unexpected opportunities, and/or to minimize the costs associated with a strategy that is poorly received by the target market. Therefore, many retailers express their budgeting flexibility in quantitative terms. For example, a

TABLE 10-2
Natural Account Expense Categories

01	Payroll
02	Allocated fringe benefits
03	Media costs
04	Taxes
06	Supplies
07	Services purchased
08	Unclassified
09	Travel
10	Communications
11	Pensions
12	Insurance
13	Depreciation
14	Professional services
16	Bad debts
17	Equipment rentals
18	Outside maintenance and equipment service contracts
20	Real property rentals
90	Expense transfers in
91	Expense transfers out
92	Credits and outside revenues

Source: Retail Accounting Manual, Revised (New York: National Retail Merchants Association, Financial Executive Division, 1978).

TABLE 10-3

315

Operations Management

Functional Account Expense Categories*

010 Property and equipment
    020 Real estate, buildings, and building equipment
    030 Furniture, fixtures, and nonbuilding equipment
100 Company management
    110 Executive office
    130 Branch management
    140 Internal audit
    150 Legal and consumer activities
200 Accounting and management information
    210 Control management, general accounting, and statistical
    220 Sales audit
    230 Accounts payable
    240 Payroll and time-keeping department
    280 Data processing
300 Credit and accounts receivable
    310 Credit management
    330 Collection
    340 Accounts receivable and bill adjustment
    350 Cash office
    360 Branch-store/selling-location offices
400 Sales promotion
    410 Sales promotion management
    420 Advertising
    430 Shows, special events, and exhibits
    440 Display
500 Service and operations
    510 Service and operations management
    530 Security
    550 Telephones and communications
    560 Utilities
    570 Housekeeping
    580 Maintenance and repairs
600 Personnel
    610 Personnel management
    620 Employment
    640 Training
    660 Medical and other employee services
    670 Supplementary benefits
700 Merchandise receiving, storage, and distribution
    710 Management of merchandise receiving, storage, and distribution
    720 Receiving and marking
    730 Reserve stock shortage
    750 Shuttle services
800 Selling and supporting services
    810 Selling supervision
    820 Direct selling
    830 Customer services
    840 Selling support services
    860 Central wrapping and packing
    880 Delivery
900 Merchandising
    910 Merchandising management
    920 Buying
    930 Merchandise control

*These are also known as expense centers.

Source: Retail Accounting Manual, Revised (New York: National Retail Merchants Association, Financial Executive Division, 1978).

buyer could be allowed to increase his or her quarterly budget by a certain maximum percentage if customer demand is higher than anticipated.

Ongoing Budgeting Process

After preliminary budgeting decisions are made, the retailer would engage in the ongoing budgeting process shown in Figure 10-1:

❑ Goals are set. These goals are based upon customer, employee, and management needs (as discussed in Chapter 9).

❑ Performance standards to achieve these goals are specified. Such standards include customer service levels, the compensation amounts needed to motivate employees and minimize personnel turnover, and the sales and profit levels needed to satisfy management. Frequently, a budget is related to a retailer's sales forecast, which is a projection of expected company revenues for the next budget period. Forecasts are usually broken down by department or product category.

❑ The retailer plans expenditures in a manner that will allow it to attain performance standards. With **zero-based budgeting,** a firm starts each new budget from scratch and outlines the expenditures that would be necessary to reach the company's goals during that period. All expenses must be justified each time a budget is devised. With **incremental budgeting,** a firm uses current and past budgets as guides and adds or subtracts from these budgets to arrive at the coming period's expenditures. Despite its conservative nature, most retailers apply incremental budgeting since it is easier to use, less time-consuming, and less risky.

❑ Actual expenditures are made. The retailer pays rent and employee salaries, buys merchandise, places advertisements, and so on.

❑ Results are monitored. This involves two types of analysis. One, actual expenditures are compared with planned expenditures for each expense category previously specified by the retailer, and reasons for any deviations are considered. Two, the firm determines whether or not goals and performance standards have been met and tries to explain any deviations.

❑ The budget is adjusted. Major or minor revisions in the original budget would be made, depending on how closely a retailer has come to achieving its goals. The funds allocated to some expense categories may be reduced, while greater funds may be provided to other categories.

Table 10-4 shows the highlights of Donna's Gift Shop's 1988 budget. In this case, actual sales turned out to be higher than expected. As a result, the cost of goods sold was greater than anticipated. However, because of solid cost controls, actual operating expenses were a little lower than expected. Overall, 1988 was a very good year for Donna; her personal salary was $35,000 and the store's before-tax profit was $19,000 (much higher than she had projected).

When planning and implementing a budget, the retailer must carefully consider **cash flow,** which relates the amount and timing of revenues received to the amount and timing of expenditures made during a specific time period. In cash flow management, the retailer's intention is usually to make sure that revenues are received prior to expenditures' being made.[2] Otherwise, short-term loans may have to be taken out or profits tied up in the business to pay off inventory expenses and so on. For seasonal businesses, this may be unavoidable. Table 10-5 provides two examples of cash flow.

Resource Allocation

In allocating financial resources, a retailer should examine two basic factors: the magnitude of various costs and productivity. Each has significance for asset management and budgeting.

TABLE 10-4

317

Operations Management

Donna's Gift Shop, 1988 Budget

	Expected		Actual	
Net sales		$200,000		$220,000
Cost of goods sold		$110,000		$120,000
Gross profit		$ 90,000		$100,000
Operating expenses:				
Salaries	$ 50,000		$ 50,000	
Advertising	3,500		3,300	
Supplies	1,200		1,100	
Shipping	900		1,000	
Insurance	3,000		3,000	
Maintenance	3,400		3,400	
Other	2,000		1,700	
Total	$ 64,000		$ 63,500	
Other costs	$ 17,500		$ 17,500	
Total costs		$ 81,500		$ 81,000
Net profit before taxes		$ 8,500		$ 19,000

The Magnitude of Various Costs

As noted earlier in the chapter, retailers' expenditures can be divided into capital and operating categories. Capital expenditures are long-term investments in fixed assets. Operating expenditures are the short-term costs of running a retail business. Before making decisions, it is imperative that retailers have a sense of the magnitude of various capital and operating costs. The following examples illustrate this point.

In 1987, the following were the average capital expenditures for erecting a single store for a range of retailers. These amounts include the basic building; heating, ventilation, and air-conditioning; lighting; flooring; fixtures; roofing; ceilings; and signage:

❑ Supermarket—$2.05 million.

❑ Department store—$9.3 million.

❑ Full-line discount store—$4.0 million.

❑ Apparel specialty store—$610,000.

❑ Drugstore—$385,000.

❑ Home center—$1.25 million.[3]

Accordingly, a full-line discount-store chain must be prepared to invest $4 million to build and furnish each new outlet it opens. This does not include land and merchandise costs, and the total could be higher if a larger-than-average store is built.

Regarding operating expenses, such costs are usually expressed as a percentage of sales and range from 19 per cent in supermarkets to 24 per cent in full-line discount stores to 34 per cent in department stores to 39 per cent in specialty stores.[4] This means that a conventional supermarket would have annual operating costs of $1 million or more.

Resource allocation must also take opportunity costs into account. **Opportunity costs** involve forgoing the possible benefits that may occur if the retailer makes expenditures in an opportunity other than the one it has chosen. For example, if a supermarket chain decides to renovate ten existing stores at a total cost of $2 million, it would not be able to open a new outlet requiring a $2-

TABLE 10-5
The Effects of Cash Flow

A. A retailer has relatively consistent sales throughout the year. Therefore, its cash flow during any given month is positive. This means no short-term loans are needed, and the owner can withdraw funds from the firm if she so desires:

Linda's Luncheonette,
Cash Flow for January

Cash inflow:		
Net sales		$11,000
Cash outflow:		
Cost of goods sold	$2,500	
Operating expenses	3,500	
Other costs	2,000	
Total		$ 8,000
Positive cash flow		$ 3,000

B. A retailer has highly seasonal sales that peak in December. Yet, to have a good assortment of merchandise on hand during December, it must order merchandise in September and October and pay for it in November. As a result, it has a negative cash flow in November that must be financed by a short-term loan. All debts are paid off in January, after the peak selling season is completed:

Dave's Party Favors,
Cash Flow for November

Cash inflow:		
Net sales		$14,000
Cash outflow:		
Cost of goods sold	$12,500	
Operating expenses	3,000	
Other costs	2,100	
Total		$17,600
Net cash flow		$ (3,600)
Short-term loan		$ 3,600
(to be paid off in January)		

---

million investment (excluding land and merchandise costs). Since financial resources are always limited, retailers are frequently faced with either/or decisions. In the case of the supermarket chain, it expects to earn greater profits from renovating than from building a new store; therefore, the latter becomes a lost opportunity—at least for now.

Productivity

Because of erratic sales, mixed economic growth, rising labor costs, increasing competition, and other factors over the last several years, many retailers are now placing priority on improving **productivity,** the efficiency with which a retail strategy is carried out. The key question is: How can sales and profit goals be reached while keeping control over costs?

Productivity may be described in terms of costs as a percentage of sales, the time it takes a cashier to complete a transaction, the percentage of customers

What Should You Do When Loans of $147 Million Are Due Shortly?

Because of expansion, inadequate cost controls, and less-than-satisfactory profits, Service Merchandise (the largest retail catalog showroom chain in the United States) found itself in a poor cash-flow position during 1987. By March 31, 1988, it had to pay off $147 million in loans owed to eleven banks or find lenders that would refinance the loans or portions of them (at higher interest rates): "We let our expenses grow faster than sales."

To improve its cash-flow situation, Service Merchandise embarked on an austerity program which included the following:

❑ Two thousand of its twenty-four thousand employees were dismissed.

❑ It abolished the corporate position of secretary/treasurer and gave the relevant duties to the chief financial officer.

❑ It reduced the number of planned new store openings from twenty to ten.

❑ It closed the fourteen apparel centers in showrooms that it had obtained when it acquired H.J. Wilson.

❑ It stopped experimenting with drive-up windows.

❑ Twelve stores were remodeled to be more productive.

❑ Excess space in stores would be leased to outside parties.

Commented one Service Merchandise senior executive, "We are looking at everything from a standpoint of, is it necessary? We're taking the posture that every vacancy presents the opportunity to eliminate a job. We're a simple business, and we overcomplicated our lives. Now we're focusing on what we do best and getting our costs under control." The company's cash-flow problems are changing the fundamental ways in which it does business.

Source: Based on material in Richard C. Halverson, "Service's Cash Flow Squeeze Prompts Cost-Cutting Efforts," *Discount Store News* (August 24, 1987), pp. 3, 62.

---

that a salesperson sees during an average day who actually make purchases, profit margins, inventory turnover, and so on. For each of these measures, productivity goals require that the firm implement its strategy as efficiently as possible. Since different retail strategy mixes have distinct resource requirements regarding store location, fixtures, the level of personnel, and other elements, productivity measures must be related to norms for each type of strategy mix (such as department stores versus full-line discount stores).

These are some of the strategies retailers have been using to improve their productivity:

❑ Both K mart and Sears recently closed regional administrative offices to reduce overhead costs.[5]

❑ Dollar General, a discount chain, has added a third distribution center in Georgia to make transporting and warehousing its merchandise more economical. This is necessary because Dollar General has opened over five hundred new outlets since 1983.[6]

❑ Best Products, a retail catalog showroom retailer, is placing greater emphasis on newspaper ads and seasonal minicatalogs that are aimed at specific target audiences and putting less importance on the annual catalog (which has a lot of wasted audience).[7]

❑ Some regional shopping centers are decreasing the amount of free or open space in their malls and expanding selling space (via kiosks and so on).[8]

TABLE 10-6
Selected Methods Being Used to Improve Retail Productivity*

Methods	Discount Stores (% using)	Drugstores (% using)	Supermarkets (% using)	Department Stores (% using)	Home Centers (% using)	Specialty Stores (% using)	Total Stores (% using)
Changing merchandise mix	70	80	53	87	77	70	73
Improving sales training	73	80	67	80	73	60	72
Redesigning stores	80	60	73	63	53	73	67
Adding/improving point-of-sale computers	60	33	73	43	53	50	52
Changing the personnel mix in departments	43	33	47	53	30	30	39
Adding/improving nonpoint-of-sale computers	30	33	40	47	17	40	34
Creating incentives for salespeople	30	30	17	33	33	47	32
Reducing existing selling space	20	13	7	27	7	17	15
Building smaller stores	20	27	3	10	7	20	14
None of the above	3	3	—	—	—	3	2

*This table is based on the results of a survey of executives at 180 retail chains, 30 for each type of store shown.

Source: "Retailers Developing Methods to Gauge Productivity," *Chain Store Age Executive* (September 1984), p. 25. Reprinted by permission. Copyright Lebhar-Friedman, Inc., 425 Park Avenue, N.Y., N.Y., 10022.

❑ Toys "R" Us operates toy stores and clothing stores (Kids "R" Us) side by side in order to share as many costs as possible, such as maintenance, security, parking, and warehousing.[9]

❑ Nankin Express, a Minneapolis-based Chinese fast-food chain, has lowered labor costs from 50 per cent to 5 per cent of operating expenses by enacting a four-step process for food preparation and standardizing labor tasks.[10]

Table 10-6 shows some of the methods a broad cross section of retailers is using to improve their overall productivity.

In general, productivity can be enhanced in two ways. The retailer can expand the output of employees, shelf space, and so on by enhancing training programs, increasing advertising, and other tactics. And/or, it can reduce costs by automating, requiring suppliers to perform certain tasks, taking advantage of quantity discounts, seeking out cheaper suppliers, being flexible in operations, and so on. An example of flexibility would be a retailer that employs a lot of part-time workers during busy times and employs only a small core of full-time workers during slow times.

The remainder of this chapter concentrates on several specific aspects of operations management. To ensure long-run success, these areas need to be managed as productively as possible. For example, at a typical supermarket, a 10 per cent drop in operating expenses could mean the difference between a yearly profit and a yearly loss.

Specific Aspects of Operations Management

Retail executives need to make a wide range of operating decisions in areas such as these:

❑ What is the optimal format and size of a store?

❑ What is the relationship among shelf space, shelf location, and sales for each item in the store? How would total store sales change by varying space allocations and shelf locations?

320

❑ Are personnel matched to customer traffic flows? Would increased staffing improve or reduce productivity?

❑ What impact would the use of self-service versus sales personnel have on the sales of each product category?

❑ Are energy costs controlled properly?

❑ Is inventory managed appropriately?

❑ How could inventory losses due to theft be reduced without disturbing most customers or employees?

❑ What levels of insurance are required?

❑ How can credit transactions be managed most effectively?

❑ What type of computer system is most appropriate?

❑ Is management prepared to handle crises?

In the next several sections, these aspects of operations management are analyzed: store format, size, and space allocation; personnel utilization; store maintenance; inventory management; store security; insurance; credit management; computerization; and crisis management. The color photo portfolio following page 328 focuses on store security and computerization.

Store Format, Size, and Space Allocation

With regard to store format, a retailer should consider whether productivity would be increased by such tactics as locating in an enclosed rather than in an open shopping area, using prefabricated materials rather than customized ones in construction, and implementing certain kinds of store design and display layouts (which are discussed in Chapter 14). As always, the firm's decisions must be related to its retail strategy mix. A crucial store format decision for chain retailers is whether or not to use **prototype stores,** whereby each outlet conforms to relatively uniform construction, layout, and operations standards.

Prototype stores offer many benefits. They make construction and centralized management control easier, reduce construction costs, enable operating methods to be standardized, facilitate the interchange of employees among outlets, allow fixtures and other materials to be purchased in quantity, and enforce a consistent chain image. However, a strict reliance on prototypes may lead to inflexibility, a failure to adapt to and/or capitalize on local customer needs, and a lack of creativity. Radio Shack, K mart, fast-food outlets, Toys "R" Us, and Silo are among the firms using prototype stores. Silo is a 150-outlet consumer electronics chain based in Philadelphia. It uses three distinct prototype store formats that are geared to different markets; the prototypes range from 12,000 to 50,000 square feet in size and have unique interiors and product assortments.[11]

Because of the high rents and store saturation in many major metropolitan U.S. markets, retailers are engaging in two contrasting store-size strategies. On the one hand, large discount-oriented warehouse stores and hypermarkets are opening in secondary sites, where rents are much lower. These stores draw customers from large trading areas. Cub Foods, Wal-Mart, and others are applying this approach.

On the other hand, a number of retailers that are situated in high-rent areas or now realize that large stores are not efficient to serve saturated or small markets are downsizing their stores. For example, 6,000-square-foot Woolworth Express stores are opening in shopping malls; these units concentrate on candy, snacks, party goods, stationery, and cosmetics. Lazarus is opening junior department stores that are about one-quarter to one-third the size of its typical stores in locales such as Heath, Lancaster, and Zanesville, Ohio. In 1987, the average size of new supermarkets, apparel specialty stores, and drugstores declined over prior years.[12]

Also as a result of rising rents, retailers need to place considerable emphasis on the allocation of space in their stores. They must use as much of their facilities as possible and determine the amount of space and its placement for each product category. Sometimes, retailers decide to drop merchandise lines altogether because they occupy too much store space in relation to their sales and profit. That is why J.C. Penney dropped its home electronics, hard sporting goods, and photographic equipment in all stores.[13]

These are just some of the tactics being used to increase the productivity of store space. Many retailers have vertical displays, which occupy less room than horizontal displays; they may hang displays on store walls or from ceilings. Formerly free space is now devoted to vending machines and small point-of-sale displays; product displays are also being located in front of stores. Open doorways, mirrored walls, and vaulted ceilings give small, cramped stores the appearance of being larger. Retailers allocate 75–80 per cent of their total floor space to selling; the balance is used for storage, rest rooms, and so on. Scrambled merchandising (involving high-profit, high-turnover items) is occupying more square feet in a wider range of stores and more space in mail-order catalogs than ever before. By staying open longer hours, retailers are also better using their space.[14]

Utilization of Personnel

From an operations perspective, the efficient utilization of retail personnel is important for several reasons. First, labor costs are high. As an example, in supermarket chains, the average part-time clerk is paid about $5 an hour, the average full-time clerk over $6 an hour, and the average meat cutter about $10 an hour; the latter two also receive fringe benefits. At full-line discount stores, personnel costs account for one-half of all operating expenses.[15]

Second, high employee turnover leads to increased recruitment, training, and supervision costs. Third, poor personnel may not have good selling skills, mistreat customers, misring sales transactions, and make other costly errors. Fourth, productivity gains in technology have taken place much more rapidly than those in labor; yet many retailers are quite labor-intensive.

Fifth, labor deployment decisions are often complex and subject to unanticipated fluctuations in customer demand. For instance, while retailers know that they should increase sales personnel during peak sales periods and reduce them during slow periods, they may still be over- or understaffed if the weather changes, competitors run special sales, suppliers increase their advertising, and so on.

Finally, unionization places restrictions on retailers that have unionized employees. In these cases, working conditions, compensation, job tasks, overtime rates, performance measurement, termination procedures, seniority rights, promotion criteria, and other factors are generally specified in written contracts. Not only must retailers abide by the terms of these contracts, but their flexibility in utilizing the labor force may be affected.

These are among the tactics that retailers may use to maximize personnel productivity:[16]

❑ Hiring process—Careful screening of potential employees before they are offered jobs by the retailer can reduce employee turnover and lead to better performance.

❑ Workload forecasts—For each season, week, day, and time period, the retailer can determine the number and type of personnel needed. As an example, a drugstore may have one pharmacist, one cashier, and one stockperson in the store from 2 to 5 P.M. on Wednesdays and add a pharmacist and a cashier from 5 P.M. to 7:30 P.M. (to accommodate people shopping after work). When developing workload forecasts, the retailer must balance its personnel costs against the possibilities of lost sales if customer waiting time is excessive. It is important that a firm be both efficient (cost-oriented) and effective (service-oriented).

❑ Job standardization and cross-training—With job standardization, the retailer makes sure that the tasks of personnel with similar positions in different departments, such as cashiers and stockpersons in clothing and candy departments, are relatively uniform. With cross-training, personnel learn tasks associated with more than one job, such as cashier, stockperson, gift wrapper, and customer complaints handler. Through job standardization and cross-training, a firm can increase its personnel flexibility and minimize the total number of employees needed at any given time. For example, if one department is slow, a cashier could be assigned to another that is busy; and a salesperson for appliances could also process transactions, help set up displays, and handle customer complaints. Cross-training can also reduce employee boredom.

❑ Employee performance standards—Each retail employee should have clear performance standards and be accountable for attaining them. Cashiers can be judged on the basis of transaction speed and misrings; buyers can be judged on the basis of department sales, the need for markdowns, and so on; and senior executives can be judged on the basis of the firm's reaching sales and profit goals. Personnel are usually more productive when they work toward specific goals.

❑ Compensation—Financial compensation, promotions, and recognition should be provided for good performance. They serve to better motivate employees. For example, a cashier will be motivated to reduce misrings if he or she knows there is a bonus for keeping mistakes under a certain percentage of all transactions processed.

❑ Self-service—Personnel costs as a percentage of sales can be reduced significantly if the retailer uses self-service facilities (thus cutting down on the need for personnel). However, two points should be taken into account. First, self-service requires better in-store displays, well-known brands, ample assortments on the selling floor, and goods/services with simple features. Second, by reducing or eliminating sales personnel, some customers may feel that they are receiving inadequate service; and there is no cross-selling (whereby customers are encouraged to buy goods they had not been thinking about).

❑ Length of employment—Long-term employment should be encouraged. As a rule, full-time employees who have been with a company for a long time are more productive than those who are part-time and/or who have worked for the firm for a short time. The former are often more knowledgeable, are more anxious to see their company succeed, require less supervision, are popular with their customers, can be promoted to higher-level positions, and are more likely to accept and adapt to the special environment of retailing. In many cases, the high level of productivity associated with full-time, long-term employees far outweighs their relatively high compensation.

Store Maintenance

Store maintenance includes all the activities involved in managing the retailer's physical facilities. These are just some of the facilities that must be managed as productively as possible: exterior—parking lot, points of entry/exit, outside signs and display windows, and common areas adjacent to a store (e.g., sidewalk); interior—windows, walls, flooring, climate control, lighting, displays and signs, store fixtures, and ceilings. Selected store maintenance decisions are shown in Figure 10-2.

The quality of store maintenance affects the consumer's perceptions of the retailer, the life span of facilities, and operating expenses. Consumers do not like to patronize stores that are unsanitary, decaying, or otherwise poorly maintained. Furthermore, continuous and thorough maintenance could enable a firm to use its current facilities for an extended period before having to invest in new ones. For instance, in full-line discount stores, heating, ventilation, and air-conditioning equipment last an average of fifteen years; lighting fixtures an average of twelve years; and flooring an average of thirteen years. But store maintenance can also be costly. During a typical year, a 90,000 square-foot full-line discount store would spend about $25,000 on flooring maintenance alone.[17]

Because of the rapid rise in energy costs during the 1970s and early 1980s, energy management has become a major consideration in store maintenance for more retailers. For firms with special needs such as supermarkets and florists, energy management is especially critical. An average supermarket outlet operated by a chain retailer has annual energy costs of nearly $100,000.[18] These are some of the ways in which retailers are better managing their energy resources:

❑ By using good insulation materials when constructing and renovating their stores, retailers are obtaining long-run monthly savings in energy bills.

❑ Interior temperature levels are carefully adjusted during nonselling hours; in the summer, air-conditioning is reduced for off-hours, and in the winter, heating is lowered for off-hours.

❑ Computerized systems closely monitor temperature levels and can be programmed by store department and to fractions of a degree.

❑ By substituting high-efficiency light bulbs for regular ones, retailers are reducing energy costs significantly. As an illustration, Sloan's Supermarkets

- What should be the responsibility of the retailer for maintaining outside facilities? For example, does a lease agreement make the retailer or the property owner responsible for snow removal in the parking lot?

- Should store maintenance activities be performed by the retailer's own personnel or by outside specialists? Will that decision differ by type of facility (e.g., air conditioning versus flooring) and by type of service (e.g., maintenance versus repairs)?

- What repairs should be classified as emergencies? How promptly should nonemergency repairs be made?

- How frequently is store maintenance required for each type of facility (e.g., daily vacuuming of floors versus weekly or monthly washing of exterior windows)? How often should special maintenance activities be undertaken (e.g., waxing floors and restriping the spaces in a parking lot)?

- How should store maintenance vary by season and by time of day (e.g., when a store is open versus when it is closed)?

- How long should existing facilities be maintained before acquiring new ones? What schedule should be followed?

- What performance standards should be set for each element of store maintenance? Do these standards balance costs against a desired level of maintenance?

FIGURE 10-2
Selected Store Maintenance Decisions

has lowered energy consumption for lighting by 20 per cent by substituting high-efficiency 60-watt fluorescent bulbs for traditional 75-watt bulbs (with little effect on illumination).[19]

Inventory Management

Through **inventory management,** a retailer seeks to acquire and maintain a proper assortment of merchandise while keeping ordering, shipping, handling, and other related costs in check. From an operations vantage point, inventory management has three interrelated phases: retailer to supplier, supplier to retailer, and retailer to consumer. See Figure 10-3.

First, a firm places orders with its suppliers based on sales forecasts and actual customer behavior. Both the number of items and the variety of them (such as assorted colors, sizes, and materials) are requested in ordering. Order size and frequency depend on quantity discounts and various inventory costs. Second, the supplier fills orders for its retailers and sends merchandise to warehouses or directly to stores. Third, the retailer receives merchandise, makes it available for sale (e.g., by removing items from their shipping cartons, marking prices on goods, and placing goods on the selling floor), and completes transactions with consumers. Some transactions are not complete until merchandise is delivered to the customer. The cycle starts anew when a retailer places another order.

These are some of the factors retailers should consider in inventory management:

❑ What are the trade-offs between delivery times from suppliers and shipping costs?

❑ How can the handling of merchandise received from different suppliers be coordinated?

❑ How much inventory should be on the selling floor versus in a warehouse or storage area?

❑ How often should inventory be moved from nonselling to selling areas of the store?

❑ What inventory functions can be performed during nonstore hours rather than while the store is open?

❑ What support is expected from suppliers in storing merchandise and/or setting up displays?

❑ What level of in-store merchandise breakage is acceptable?

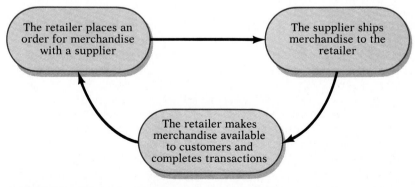

FIGURE 10-3
The Phases of Inventory Management

❑ Which items require delivery to customers? How should this be accomplished (e.g., timing and responsibility)?

To improve their inventory management performance, a number of retailers have begun using just-in-time (JIT) inventory planning, which until recently was utilized almost exclusively by manufacturers in dealing with their suppliers. With **just-in-time inventory planning,** a retailer reduces the amount of inventory it keeps on hand by ordering more frequently and in lower quantity. This allows inventory costs to be reduced, minimizes the space required for product storage, and enables the retailer to better match its orders with market conditions. However, a JIT system requires that retailers have close (nonadversarial) relations with suppliers, coordinate shipments, monitor inventory levels carefully (to avoid running out of stock), and use computerized inventory systems to communicate with suppliers. Among the retailers using JIT systems for at least some of their merchandise are K mart, Carter Hawley Hale, Ross Stores, Sears, J.C. Penney, and Wal-Mart.[20]

Merchandising decisions are discussed thoroughly in Chapters 11 and 12.

Store Security

Since 1.4 per cent of overall retail sales (more than $20 billion annually) are lost as a result of employee theft, customer shoplifting, and vendor theft (due mostly to short shipping), some type of store security program aimed at minimizing these losses is necessary for all retailers. Figure 10-4 shows the percentage

---

RETAILING IN ACTION

An Inventory System for Retailers That's "Just in Time"?

Auto Shack, based in Memphis, Tennessee, operates nearly four hundred retail automobile-parts stores in fifteen states. The firm has three main objectives: "to offer merchandise at a discount price, to have top-quality either through private-branded merchandise or leading names in auto parts, and to provide service that will always save the sale by keeping the customer from going to a competitor." Therefore, since the chain handles 29,000 different parts, JIT inventory planning has arrived "just in time."

Each Auto Shack store carries a portion of the 29,000 items that the company sells in order to maximize its stock turnover, minimize its inventory investment, be flexible in its offerings, and maintain its merchandise freshness. To accommodate customer requests for parts that are not in stock at a particular outlet, Auto Shack has a three-pronged JIT strategy. First, through a computerized linkup among all stores, it is determined if a nearby outlet has the requested item. Second, if the part is not available from a local outlet, Auto Shack's Express Parts automated warehouse in Memphis (which stocks all 29,000 parts) could ship the item via overnight air transportation. Third, Auto Shack could have a part shipped overnight directly from a supplier to the requesting store.

By utilizing a seven-day per week national air delivery system, including Sundays and holidays, Auto Shack can satisfy virtually every request, from a set of spark plugs to an automobile engine. It views the cost of emergency shipments as secondary in importance; its key motivation is "to save the sale." The goal is to enhance service, "which is increasingly the most important element in any company's competitive strategy."

Source: Kenneth B. Ackerman, "Just-in-Time, Right for Retail," *New York Times* (January 17, 1988), Section 3, p. 2.

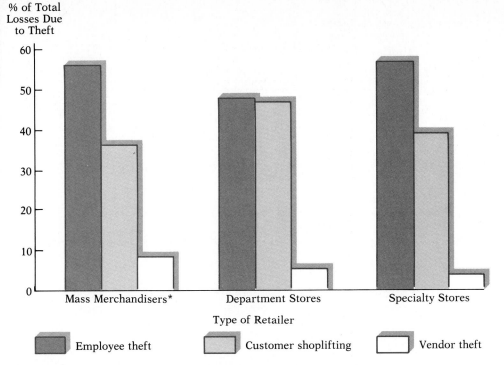

% of Total Losses Due to Theft

Employee theft   Customer shoplifting   Vendor theft

*Includes discount, general merchandise, drug, and variety chains with multiple departments, central checkouts, and limited selling staffs.

FIGURE 10-4
Retailers' Losses Due to Theft by Category and Store Type
Source: Adapted by the authors from *An Ounce of Prevention* (New York: Arthur Young and the National Mass Retailing Institute, 1987).

of losses by type of theft for mass merchandisers, department stores, and specialty stores.

To reduce losses due to theft, three key points should be incorporated into retailers' operating plans. First, loss prevention should be taken into consideration when stores are built and designed. For example, the placement of store entrances, dressing rooms, delivery areas, and so on should be planned from a security standpoint. Second, a combination of security measures should be utilized, such as employee background checks, in-store guards, electronic security equipment, and merchandise tags. Third, retailers need to communicate the importance of loss prevention to employees, customers, and vendors, as well as the actions they are willing to take to reduce losses (such as firing employees).

These are among the activities retailers are engaging in to reduce losses due to thefts:[21]

❑ Electronic product tags, security guards, cameras, point-of-sale computers, employee surveillance, and burglar alarms are each being used by various retailers as primary security systems. See Table 10-7. Storefront protection devices are also quite popular. See Figure 10-5.

❑ With regard to merchandise tags, a large number of general merchandise retailers are utilizing plastic tags which are clipped to items and must be

TABLE 10-7
The Primary Security Systems Used by Selected Retailers

Security System	% of Retailers Using as Primary System						
	All Stores	Discount Stores	Drugstores	Supermarkets	Department Stores	Home Centers	Apparel Specialty Stores
Electronic merchandise tags	42	40	53	33	43	27	53
Guards	22	27	20	27	33	17	10
Cameras	21	10	27	50	27	3	10
Employee surveillance	13	13	10	13	NR*	33	10
Point-of-sale software	12	10	10	10	23	13	7
Burglar alarms	4	3	3	3	NR*	7	7
Do not use a security system	4	3	3	NR*	3	10	7

*NR is not reported.

Source: Adapted by the authors from "Employers Take Firm Stand Against Shrinkage," *Chain Store Age Executive* (July 1986), p. 50. Reprinted by permission. Copyright Lebhar-Friedman, Inc., 425 Park Avenue, N.Y., N.Y., 10022.

removed mechanically. Supermarkets are experimenting with paper labels which are adhered to goods and desensitized by electronic scanning equipment. In both cases, a failure to have an item processed by a cashier will result in an alarm's going off. See Figure 10-6.

❑ Many firms are including honesty testing in employee hiring. For example, Kay-Bee Toy and Hobby Shops, a large chain, administers a 45-minute honesty test to each new worker. While the test costs $10 or more per employee, it has reduced losses by over 25 per cent.

❑ Employee training programs on the impact of losses and incentives for reducing them are being used by more retailers. Neiman-Marcus shows employees a film containing interviews with convicted shoplifters in prison to demonstrate the seriousness of the problem. Bloomingdale's awards $1,250 to $2,500 to employees who report thefts by their co-workers. In 1986, Marshall Field paid $114,000 to more than 700 employees who reported employee theft or customer shoplifting.

❑ Many retailers are now more likely to fire employees and prosecute those involved. Courts are imposing stiffer penalties; and in a number of areas, store detectives are now empowered by local police to make arrests.

Figure 10-7 presents a detailed list of the tactics that retailers can use to combat employee and shopper theft, by far the leading causes of losses.

When developing and implementing a store security plan, a retailer must assess the impact of such a plan on employee morale, shopper comfort, and vendor relations. For example, at J.C. Penney, there are no rewards for employees to report co-workers involved in theft: "We want employees to pay attention to selling—not have them watching each other or wondering if someone's looking over their shoulder."[22] Likewise, by setting overly strict rules for fitting rooms (such as severely limiting the number of garments that may be brought in at one time) and/or placing chains on expensive furs and suede coats, the retailer may cause some customers to try on and buy less clothing.

Insurance

In retail operations, the purchase of insurance (which covers a firm in case of losses due to fire, customer lawsuits regarding on-premises accidents, and so on)

A COMPLETE RANGE OF HANG TAGS AND STIKKERS TO PROTECT MORE KINDS OF MERCHANDISE.

THE STIKKER™

The pressure-sensitive STIKKER can protect a wide range of items. Ordered either pre-printed with a simulated bar code or sales message, or plain, the STIKKER offers low-cost, low-profile, disposable protection. And the STIKKER can be automatically deactivated at the point of sale.

THE HARD TAG

Primarily used for higher priced merchandise, the Hard Tag is incredibly strong and durable. Easily attached by hand, the Hard Tag

features a unique locking system which makes it nearly impossible for shoplifters to remove. Yet it is easily detached at the point of sale for reuse on other merchandise.

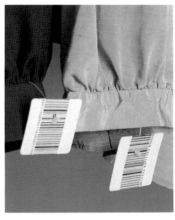

THE FLEX TAG

Designed with a simulated UPC code, the Flex Tag is a lightweight and economical alternative to other reusable tags. It attaches easily to any merchandise with a simple plastic fastener, and removes just as easily at the point of sale.

THE DESIGNER™ TAG

Checkpoint's Designer Tag offers custom printing on a high-quality, reusable EAS tag. Printed

with your logo or message in up to three colors and encased in clear plastic, Designer Tags are an attractive alternative to the Hard Tag. They are easily removed at the register for reuse.

CHEKLINK™ TAGS

Labor-free, disposable CHEK-LINK tags offer the ultimate in efficient, effective protection for every type of merchandise. Virtually identical to standard price tags, CHEKLINK tags can be custom imprinted on standard equipment from every major manufacturer. Applied exactly like your present price tags, they can be deactivated automatically at the point of sale.

Check|**point**®
SYSTEMS INC.

550 Grove Road • PO Box 188
Thorofare, NJ 08086
(609) 848-1800 • TELEX: 84-5396

© COPYRIGHT 1987 CHECKPOINT SYSTEMS, INC.

Store security is a necessary part of operations management, because over $20 billion of retail merchandise is lost each year due to some type of theft. Checkpoint Systems offers a variety of security measures for retailers, including those shown here.

Photo courtesy of Checkpoint Systems.

Federated Department Stores, now a subsidiary of Campeau Corporation, has a sophisticated regional data center in Atlanta. This center facilitates communications among various divisions and coordinates merchandising efforts.

Photo courtesy of Federated Department Stores.

Wetterau, a full-service food wholesaler, provides a computer assisted design system for its affiliated retailers. This system allows the retailers to graphically portray and modify store interiors and exteriors before making actual decisions.

Photo courtesy of Wetterau.

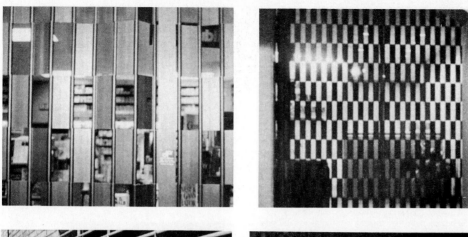

FIGURE 10-5
Protective Storefronts
Reprinted by permission of Dynaflair Corporation.

Checkpoint's AFFORDABLE I

Here's how it works

Each Checkpoint detection tag contains an electronic circuit that can be detected by the sensing screens at the doorway. If a tag passes through the system, the screens will sense the presence of the tag and alert you. During normal operation, tags are either removed at the time of purchase by a special Checkpoint detacher or passed around the system by the cashier.

The AFFORDABLE I system uses standard electrical power and can be installed in just minutes. Its radio frequency technology is perfectly safe for all kinds of merchandise—even sensitive videotapes and computer disks.

Checkpoint tags are designed to be used with all types of merchandise.

■ Hard tags with a unique locking system for most merchandise.

■ Universal flex tags for sheer or fragile items.

■ Paper tags for a variety of merchandise requiring pressure-sensitive tag application.

Hard tag

Universal flex tag

Paper tag

Point-of-sale detector

AFFORDABLE I Accessories

■ Point-of-sale detector—A discreet counter unit that helps save time by verifying the presence of a tag on merchandise.

■ Portable verifier—A hand-held unit that verifies the presence of a tag hidden in a pocket, purse, or under clothing.

■ Detacher—A specially-designed unit that easily removes the hard tag and the flex tag from merchandise.

Portable verifier

Detacher

FIGURE 10-6
Merchandise Tagging to Reduce Losses Due to Theft
Reprinted by permission of Checkpoint Systems.

must also be carefully planned. Among the types of insurance purchased by retailers are workers' compensation, public liability, product liability, property, and directors' and officers' liability. During 1986, industrywide, a typical retailer spent $0.51 on its overall annual insurance package for every $100 of sales.[23] This means that a chain with $25 million in sales would have spent $127,500 on insurance.

Insurance decisions are important for several reasons. First, between 1983 and 1986, insurance costs rose by 50 per cent. Second, insurers have been reducing the scope of coverage. Many now require higher deductibles before paying claims and/or will not provide coverage on all aspects of operations (such as the professional liability of pharmacists). Third, there are fewer insurance carriers servicing retailers today than a decade ago; this limits the choices of retailers.

As a result, a number of retailers have embarked on costly programs aimed at

A. Employee Theft

- Using polygraph tests, voice stress analysis, and psychological tests as employee screening devices.
- Developing a system of locking up trash to prevent merchandise from being thrown out and then retrieved.
- Verifying through use of undercover personnel whether all sales are rung up.
- Utilizing cameras, mirrors.
- Implementing central control of all exterior doors to monitor opening and closing.
- Properly identifying deliverypeople.
- Verifying receipts and goods taken out.
- Sealing all trucks after they are loaded with goods.
- Inspecting worker packages, tool boxes, lunch boxes.
- Dividing responsibilities (e.g., having one employee record sales; another making deposits).
- Vigorously investigating all known losses.
- Firing offenders immediately.

B. Shopper Theft While Store Is Open

- Using in–store detectives or uniformed guards.
- Prosecuting all individuals charged with theft.
- Using electronic article surveillance wafers, electromagnets, or stick–ons for high–value and theft–prone goods.
- Developing comprehensive employee training programs.
- Providing employee bonuses based upon overall reduction in shortages or based on value of recovered merchandise.
- Inspecting all packages brought into store.
- Utilizing self–closing/self–locking showcases for high–value items such as jewelry.
- Chaining down expensive samples, such as high–fidelity equipment, to fixtures.
- Placing goods with high value/small size in locked showcases.
- Attaching expensive clothing together.
- Alternating the direction of hangers on clothing near doors.
- Limiting the dollar value and quantity of merchandise displayed near exits.
- Limiting the number of entrances and exits to the store.
- Utilizing cameras and mirrors to increase visibility, especially in low–traffic areas.
- Using two–way mirrors where appropriate.

C. Employee/Shopper Theft While Store Is Closed

- Conducting thorough check of the building at night to make sure no one is left in store.
- Locking all exits, even fire exits, at night.
- Utilizing ultrasonic/infrared detectors, burglar alarm traps, or guards with dogs when store is closed.
- Placing valuables in safe.
- Using shatterproof glass and/or iron gates on display windows to prevent break–ins.
- Making sure exterior lighting is adquate when store is closed.
- Periodically testing burglar alarms.

FIGURE 10-7
Ways Retailers Can Deter Employee and Shopper Theft

lessening their vulnerability to employee and customer claims due to dangerous or unsafe conditions and at holding down insurance premiums:

> They entail installing no-slip floors and rubber mats at entrances; training fixture designers to design risk-free fixtures; conducting frequent elevator and escalator maintenance checks; conducting fire drills; designing and constructing fire resistant stores, warehouses, and distribution centers; building separate structures to warehouse aerosols; implementing employee training programs. The list is as long as a retailer—or its insurance company—wants to make it.[24]

Credit Management

Credit management involves the policies and practices retailers follow in receiving payments from their customers.[25] These are the major operations decisions that must be made:

❑ What form of payment is acceptable? A retailer may accept cash only; cash and personal checks; cash and credit card(s); or all of these.

❑ Who administers the credit plan? The firm can have its own credit system and/or accept major credit cards (such as Visa, MasterCard, American Express, and Discover).

❑ What are customer eligibility requirements to make a check or credit purchase? For a check purchase, identification such as a driver's license might be sufficient. For a credit purchase, a new customer would have to satisfy requirements regarding age, employment, annual income, and so on; and an existing customer would be evaluated in terms of his or her outstanding balance and credit limit. A minimum purchase amount may also be specified before a credit transaction is allowed.

❑ What credit terms will be used? A retailer using its own plan needs to determine when interest charges will begin, what the rate of interest would be, and minimum monthly payments.

❑ How will late payments or nonpayments be handled? Some retailers that have their own credit plans rely on outside collection agencies to follow up on past-due accounts.

In credit management, the retailer generally needs to balance the ability of credit to generate additional revenues against the cost of processing credit payments. The latter can include screening, transactions, and collections costs as well as bad debts. If the firm completes all credit functions itself, it will incur these costs; if outside credit arrangements (e.g., Visa) are used, the firm covers the costs via its payments to the credit organization.

Regardless of the payment plan adopted, it is imperative that the retailer clearly communicate all policies to both employees and customers. Credit is discussed further in Chapter 14 in the section on customer services.

Computerization

Through some form of computerization, many retailers are improving their operations productivity; and with the falling prices of computer systems and related software, the number of retailers using computers to assist them in operations will continue to increase greatly in the future. These are just a few of the ways in which some retailers are using computers in operations:[26]

❑ To schedule personnel.

❑ To coordinate inventory orders and handling.

❑ To reduce checkout time and cashier misrings.
❑ To communicate with suppliers.
❑ To obtain current information.
❑ To generate and maintain mailing lists.
❑ To allocate shelf space and advertising expenditures.
❑ To analyze performance.

Following are two examples of how retailers are utilizing computers in their operations.

Revco is a leading drugstore chain with nine regional distribution centers, six of which use a sophisticated computer software package to manage personnel and inventory (the other facilities need to be remodeled or rebuilt before the software could be properly used). At its computerized distribution centers, Revco uses the Exeter Warehouse Management System (WMS), which "automates the planning, control, and management of warehouse operations. It directs the flow of merchandise through the warehouse and provides data on the amount of labor necessary to conduct warehouse operations."[27] Figure 10-8 shows the distribution center activities managed by WMS.

Discus Music World is a Montreal-based chain that uses a computerized point-of-sale system; all important sales data (such as item number, price, and day and time of transaction) are automatically transmitted to the firm's distribution center. Since Discus' average outlet is only 1,500 square feet and carries 12,000 to 15,000 items, such a system has dramatically enhanced store productivity:

In our opinion, it is impossible to exist in the record industry without some sort of computerized point-of-sale system. For the consumer, having this system in place means that you have the right product at the right time. You can also have better information on exactly what the consumer wants and stock certain products accordingly.

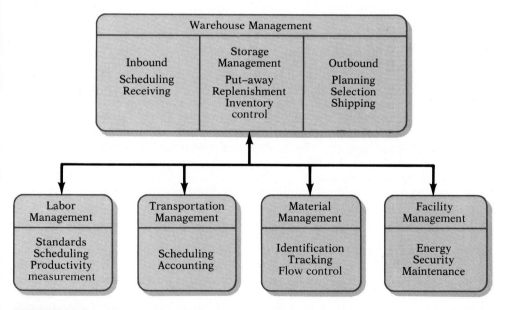

FIGURE 10-8
Revco Distribution Center Activities Controlled by Exeter's
Warehouse Management System
Source: Exeter, "Strategy for Distribution Automation (SDA)," *Chain Store Age Executive* (March 1986), p. 52. Reprinted by permission.

In the record business, there are 25,000 to 30,000 catalog items—there may be even more. This means that tracking our inventory is critical so that we don't have too much of the wrong thing in stock and also have a better idea of what items our customers are more interested in.[28]

Crisis Management

Sometimes, despite their best intentions, retailers may be faced with crisis situations that need to be managed as smoothly as possible. Crises may be brought on by such occurrences as an in-store fire or broken water pipe, bad weather breaking the store's front window, a car accident in the parking lot, a burglary, an illness by the owner, unexpectedly high or low consumer demand for a good or service, a sudden increase in a supplier's prices, or other factors.

While crises cannot always be anticipated, and some adverse effects may take place regardless of a retailer's efforts, some general principles should be followed in developing operations management plans. First, the retailer should establish contingency plans for as many different types of crisis situations as possible; that is why insurance is purchased. For example, what steps should be followed if there is an in-store fire or a parking-lot accident? Second, essential information should be communicated to all affected parties, such as the fire or police department, employees, customers, the media, and so on, when a crisis occurs. Third, there should be cooperation and not conflict among the involved parties. Fourth, responses should be as quick as feasible; indecisiveness may worsen the situation. Fifth, the chain of command for decisions should be clear and the decision maker given adequate authority to act.

As one expert noted, "Unless we have a means of dealing with crises when they hit, all the dollars and energies spent on operating a retail business can either be quickly wiped out or reduced. We've got to be prepared for whatever comes down the road."[29]

SUMMARY

Operations management involves efficiently and effectively implementing the tasks and policies necessary to satisfy the retailer's customers, employees, and management. This chapter divides operations management into two parts: financial dynamics and specific aspects of operations.

The major financial concepts related to operations management are asset management, budgeting, and resource allocation. Each retailer has various assets and liabilities that it must manage. Assets are any items owned by a retailer that have a monetary value. Liabilities are any financial obligations that are incurred in running a business. The retailer's net worth, also known as owner's equity, is computed as assets minus liabilities. A balance sheet itemizes a retailer's assets, liabilities, and net worth at a specific point in time.

The results of asset management may be measured through return on assets (ROA) and return on net worth (RONW). Return on assets is a ratio based on a retailer's net sales, net profit, and total assets. It enables a firm to evaluate the ratio of net sales to assets (asset turnover) and the ratio of

net profit to net sales (profit margin). Return on net worth is a ratio based on a retailer's net profit, total assets, and net worth. It allows a firm to assess ROA and the ratio of total assets to net worth (financial leverage). The strategic profit model incorporates asset turnover, profit margin, and financial leverage.

Budgeting outlines a retailer's planned expenditures for a given time period based on its expected performance; costs are linked to satisfying goals. There are six preliminary decisions. First, responsibility is defined. Top-down budgeting places decisions in the hands of upper managers, who communicate them down the line. Bottom-up budgeting requires that lower-level executives present financial requests, which are assembled and then coordinated in an overall company budget. Second, the time frame is specified. Third, the frequency of budget planning is set. Fourth, cost categories are established. Fifth, the level of detail is ascertained. Sixth, the amount of flexibility is determined.

Then, the ongoing budgeting process proceeds: goals, performance standards, planned expenditures, actual expenditures, monitoring results, and adjustments. With zero-based budgeting, each new budget is started from scratch; with incremental budgeting, current and past budgets serve as guides. In all budgeting decisions, the impact of cash flow, which relates the amount and timing of revenues received with the amount and timing of expenditures made, must be considered.

In resource allocation, the magnitude of costs and productivity need to be examined. Costs can be divided into capital and operating categories; the amount of both must be regularly reviewed. Opportunity costs involve forgoing possible benefits that may occur if a retailer invests in an opportunity other than the one chosen. Productivity is the efficiency with which a retail strategy is carried out; the goal is to maximize sales and profits while keeping costs in check.

There are many specific aspects of operations management, each requiring complex and ongoing decisions and implementation by the retailer. Store format, size, and space allocation considerations include the use of prototype stores, the size of stores,

and the allocation of space in the stores. Personnel utilization activities that could improve productivity range from workload forecasts to job standardization and cross-training. Store maintenance encompasses all activities involved in managing a retailer's physical facilities; it affects customer perceptions, the life span of facilities, and operating costs.

Through inventory management, a retailer seeks to acquire and maintain a proper assortment of merchandise while keeping ordering, shipping, handling, and other related costs in rein. Just-in-time inventory planning, which relies on frequent and small orders, is growing in usage. Store security is necessary to prevent employee, customer, and vendor theft. Insurance covers the retailer against losses arising from fire, customer lawsuits, and so on. Credit management pertains to the policies and practices retailers follow in receiving payments from their customers. Through computerization, many retailers are improving their operations productivity. Crisis management is necessary to handle unexpected situations as smoothly as possible.

QUESTIONS FOR DISCUSSION

1. Describe the relationship of assets, liabilities, and net worth for a retailer. How is a balance sheet useful in examining these items?
2. A retailer has net sales of $300,000, net profit of $23,000, total assets of $400,000, and a net worth of $150,000.
   a. Calculate asset turnover, profit margin, and return on assets (ROA).
   b. Compute financial leverage and return on net worth (RONW).
   c. Evaluate the financial performance of this retailer.
3. Under what circumstances would you recommend top-down budgeting rather than bottom-up budgeting?
4. What is zero-based budgeting? Why do most retailers utilize incremental budgeting, despite its limitations?
5. How could a seasonal retailer improve its cash-flow situation during periods when it must buy goods for future selling periods?
6. What factors should retailers consider when assessing opportunity costs?
7. What are several ways that each of these retailers could improve productivity?
   a. Restaurant
   b. Convenience store

   c. Retail catalog showroom
8. Comment on the pros and cons of prototype stores. For which kinds of retailers are they most desirable?
9. Present three performance standards for each of these retail positions:
   a. Store manager
   b. Cashier
   c. Salesperson
   d. Deliveryperson
10. Could a small retailer use a just-in-time inventory system? Why or why not?
11. Would you offer a reward to retail employees who report theft on the part of co-workers? Explain your answer.
12. A mom-and-pop store does not accept credit cards because of the costs involved. However, it does accept personal checks. Evaluate this strategy. What conditions should the store have for cashing checks?
13. What are the potential problems that may result if a retailer relies on its computer to implement too many actions (such as employee scheduling or inventory reordering) automatically?
14. Outline a contingency plan a retailer could have in case an in-store fire occurs.

1. Stephen Bennett, "Gromer: An Independent Innovator," *Progressive Grocer* (November 1987), pp. 73–74.

2. See James McNeill Stancill, "When Is There Cash in Cash Flow?" *Harvard Business Review*, Vol. 65 (March–April 1987), pp. 38–49.

3. Computed by the authors from "Annual Decision-Makers' Digest," *Chain Store Age Executive* (July 1987), pp. 36–70.

4. "54th Annual Report of the Grocery Industry," *Progressive Grocer* (April 1987), p. 35; and David P. Schulz, "'86: Better FOR Some," *Stores* (November 1987), pp. 92–94.

5. "K mart to Close Regional Office," *Discount Store News* (August 10, 1987), pp. 3, 90; and "Sears Plans to Close Its 4 Regional Offices in Cost-Cutting Move," *Wall Street Journal* (April 15, 1986), p. 2.

6. "Dollar General Realigns Operations Management Approach," *Discount Store News* (March 30, 1987), p. 3.

7. "Best Repositions Core Biz in Bid to Cure Stagflation," *Discount Store News* (January 5, 1987), pp. 1, 53.

8. "Togetherness May Keep CAM Costs Down," *Chain Store Age Executive* (May 1987), pp. 56–60.

9. *Toys "R" Us 1987 Annual Report.*

10. "Assembly-Line Chinese Food," *New York Times* (January 1, 1985), pp. D1, D22.

11. "Silo Uses New Image to Build National Chain," *Chain Store Age Executive* (July 1987), pp. 94–96.

12. "Woolworth Express: On Fast Growth Track," *Chain Store Age Executive* (January 1988), pp. 146–148; "Lazarus: Embarking on a Small Store Strategy," *Chain Store Age Executive* (March 1987), pp. 98–99; and "Annual Decision-Makers' Digest," pp. 36–37.

13. "Penney to Drop 3 Store Lines," *New York Times* (October 29, 1987), p. D4.

14. See Holly Klokis, "Space Exploration: With Retail Rents in the Stratosphere, the Challenge Is to Use Every Inch," *Chain Store Age Executive* (March 1986), pp. 13–16; and Iris Rosenberg, "Nonfoods in Supermarkets," *Stores* (March 1987), pp. 58–62.

15. "54th Annual Report of the Grocery Industry," p. 36; and *Operating Results of Self-Service Discount Department Stores, 1985–86* (New York: National Mass Retailing Institute, 1986).

16. See David W. Cunningham, "Change Old-Time Attitudes to Improve People Productivity," *Discount Store News* (December 14, 1987), pp. 203, 205; Steve Weinstein, "Costs: Trying to Hold the Line," *Progressive Grocer* (January 1987), pp. 23–28; and William R. Darden, Ronald D. Hampton, and Earl W. Boatwright, "Investigating Retail Employee Turnover: An Application of Survival Analysis," *Journal of Retailing*, Vol. 63 (Spring 1987), pp. 69–88.

17. "Physical Supports Census," *Chain Store Age Executive* (July 1987), pp. 39–70.

18. "54th Annual Report of the Grocery Industry," p. 34.

19. Mark Harris, "Evaluate Lighting Systems as a Marketing Device, Not Overhead," *Marketing News* (October 26, 1984), p. 1.

20. See Jules Abend, "UPC + QR = JIT Inventory Replenishment," *Stores* (May 1987), pp. 44–54.

21. "Employers Take Firm Stand Against Shrinkage," *Chain Store Age Executive* (July 1986), pp. 50–52; "Prehire Tests Cut Chain's Theft by 28%," *Chain Store Age Executive* (June 1983), p. 25; Jules Abend, "Back to Basics," *Stores* (June 1983), p. 54; Jules Abend, "Employee Theft," *Stores* (June 1986), pp. 57–62; David J. Solomon, "Hotlines and Hefty Rewards: Retailers Step Up Efforts to Curb Employee Theft," *Wall Street Journal* (September 17, 1987), p. 37; Gary Taylor, "What's New in Shoplifting Prevention," *New York Times* (September 13, 1987), Section 3, p. 19; and "PCs Take a Byte out of Retail Crime," *Chain Store Age Executive* (August 1987), pp. 94, 98.

22. Solomon, "Hotlines and Hefty Rewards: Retailers Step Up Efforts to Curb Employee Theft," p. 37.

23. Holly Klokis, "A Bad Break for Retailers," *Chain Store Age Executive* (June 1986), pp. 14–16.

24. Ibid., p. 16.

25. See Jules Abend, "Turmoil in Credit: What's Next?" *Stores* (April 1987), pp. 86–96.

26. See "Computer Solves Labor Scheduling Mess," *Chain Store Age Executive* (September 1986), pp. 148–152; "ComputerLand Counts on Its New Forms," *Chain Store Age Executive* (September 1987), pp. 106–108; David Wessel, "Computer Finds a Role in Buying and Selling, Reshaping Businesses," *Wall Street Journal* (March 18, 1987), pp. 1, 10; Ronald Tanner, "Computerization: The Future Is Now," *Progressive Grocer* (January 1987), pp. 40–44; Erik Sandberg-Diment, "A Weapon for Grocery-Shelf Wars," *New York Times* (August 2, 1987), Section 3, p. 12; and Joe Agnew, "In-Store Software System Is Designed for Mass-Market Product Promotion," *Marketing News* (October 23, 1987), p. 10.

27. "Everything's Up-to-Date in Kansas Facility," *Chain Store Age Executive* (March 1986), pp. 50–52.

28. "Discus Tunes Up Tracking Process," *Chain Store Age Executive* (April 1987), pp. 82, 87.

29. "Warning to Mall Managers: Plan Ahead," *Chain Store Age Executive* (May 1987), pp. 64–70.

Case 1

Starr Movie: Conducting an Energy Audit

Starr Movie is a duplex movie theater in Ann Arbor, Michigan. It allows patrons to choose between different movies playing in its two screening rooms, which have 250 seats each. Like many large movie theaters built in the 1950s, Starr Movie was converted to duplex status in the 1970s because of the increased popularity of television and the difficulty of filling up the theater's 500 seats with one movie attraction.

TABLE 1
Utility Usage and Conservation Report Prepared for Starr Movie Theater
by Ken Marr, Professional Engineer (Highlights)

Building:

❑ Fiberglass insulation in attic is insufficient. There is no insulation under the ground floor of the theater. This results in the loss of air-conditioning in the summer and heat in the winter.

Electrical:

❑ Incandescent bulbs should be changed to fluorescent ones wherever possible. Recommended locations include the lobby, bathrooms, and the ticket booth area.

❑ In some cases, incandescent bulb wattage consumption can be reduced by using smaller-wattage bulbs and by reducing the number of bulbs used. Targeted areas include part of the basement and the projection room entrance area.

❑ Outside lights should be connected to a timer. This will prevent maintenance personnel from forgetting to turn off parking-lot lights one-half hour after the last show ends.

❑ Outside lights in the parking area and alongside the building can be changed to a more efficient sodium variety. These bulbs give more light per watt of energy usage than traditional spotlights.

Heating and Air-Conditioning:

❑ The heating-system efficiency level is 67 per cent. The system needs to be tuned up. A low-cost tune-up should raise the efficiency level to 80–85 per cent. The heating-system efficiency should be checked annually by the fuel oil contractor at no expense to the theater owner. Adjustments to increase efficiency should be made at no cost.

❑ An automatic thermostat controlled by a clock could turn on the heating and cooling system prior to the first movie and reduce lighting considerably after the last movie.

❑ Air-conditioning filters need replacement. Semiclogged filters reduce the efficiency and overload the system's capacity.

❑ Hot water temperature in all faucets is too hot. Besides possibly severely burning someone, the temperature should be reduced to 120 degrees as an energy-saving procedure.

Water:

❑ Consumption can be lowered by reducing the water levels in toilet tanks.

❑ All faucets in public rest rooms should be of the automatic variety. This will prevent water from being left running after someone leaves the rest room.

Today, movie theaters face other problems because of the rising use of videocassette recorders, patronage of videocassette rental retailers, cable television, and various state laws restricting children under the age of seventeen from attending a movie theater without a parent or guardian.

In response to the uncertainty surrounding the firm's ability to maintain its current customer attendance in the future, Alice Starr (the owner and manager of Starr Movie) has begun to pay more attention to cost control. Personal computer-based programs now allow Starr to easily determine weekly costs as a percentage of revenues and to compare present costs with expenditures in similar weeks during prior years. Trade association literature is also paying much more attention to cost control than before.

Of the expenses studied, Alice Starr is most interested in utility costs: electricity, fuel oil, and water. Starr's review of utilities is based on several factors:

❑ In total, these expenses represent a large proportion of the theater's controllable operating costs; Starr owns the building. In contrast, expenses such as property taxes are not controllable since they are set by municipalities, and labor costs are difficult to reduce because of minimum personnel needs (even during slow periods).

❑ An analysis of utility expenses fits well with the concept of zero-based budgeting, which would require Starr to justify costs on an annual basis.

❑ She is well aware of the need for conserving utility consumption from a social responsibility perspective, and from her own behavior as a consumer.

❏ She assumes that there are good opportunities for cost savings because of the large number of energy conservation products available, the age of the building (which was constructed at a time when there was little or no concern about energy costs or conservation), and the uneven pattern of movie theater usage.

Accordingly, Alice hired Ken Marr, a civil engineer, to inspect her property from the perspective of utility usage and potential cost savings. He compiled a report divided into these classifications: building, electrical, heating/air-conditioning, and water. An abstract of this report is contained in Table 1.

From conversations with the engineer, Starr noted three key points. One, energy conservation measures should be based on a plan. The steps with the greatest efficiency improvement should be performed first. For example, improving the heating efficiency level could result in a 13–18 per cent reduction in heating costs; depending on the nature of the adjustments, the investment could range from $0 to $600. Timers for outside lighting (estimated cost $400), sodium outside-lighting fixtures (estimated cost $2,500), and an automatic thermostat (estimated cost $250) also have high expense-reduction-to-investment ratios. Marr estimates that these expenditures will have a five-year payoff based upon current energy costs.

Two, the engineer is concerned that Starr Movie's fuel oil provider has not commented on the burner's efficiency and that a tune-up is overdue by at least one full year. An automatic thermostat should also have been suggested by the fuel oil provider.

Three, while polite, Marr mentioned that the final responsibility for inefficient energy usage was with Starr, who should have had a checklist for energy conservation. Also, theater personnel need to be trained in reducing energy waste. For example, Ken noted that for a recent popular movie, with a long waiting line, three lobby entrance doors were constantly open while people were purchasing tickets. Ushers should be trained to close those doors. Maintenance staff should be trained to turn off all interior lights after they clean the facility. As Ken Marr said, "You can't set up timers for everything."

QUESTIONS

1. What factors could explain Starr Movie's not being involved in energy conservation until now?
2. How could Alice Starr use zero-based budgeting in controlling her theater's energy costs? Are there any disadvantages to such an approach?

3. Evaluate Ken Marr's report.
4. Develop a two-year plan for energy conservation by Starr Movie in terms of equipment, employees, service providers, and Starr's management.

Case 2

Electronic City: Controlling Employee Theft*

Electronic City is a three-store chain selling high-fidelity equipment, videocassette recorders, video cameras, telephone-answering machines, televisions, and related accessories. Employee theft has been substantial only in the past year, since the firm expanded from two to three locations. Until then, trusted family members and long-time employees had always been present at each location to carefully monitor customer and employee activity. However, with the opening of the third outlet, at the same time store hours were lengthened at each location, a large number of new employees were hired. Many of the new employees are part-timers.

Two years ago, merchandise shortages were 1 per cent of total net sales. Now, they are averaging 2.7 per cent of sales. Shortages at the new location are 4.0 per cent of sales, a high level considering that Electronic City's net profit margins have typically ranged between 3.0 and 3.7 per cent of sales.

*The material in this case is drawn from Gary Taylor, "What's New in Shoplifting Prevention," *New York Times* (September 13, 1987), Section 3, p. 19; and David J. Solomon, "Hotlines and Hefty Rewards: Retailers Step Up Efforts to Curb Employee Theft," *Wall Street Journal* (September 17, 1987), p. 37.

John and Joanne Wyse, the chain's owners, realize that it is especially vulnerable to employee theft. Items such as portable cassette players, telephone-answering machines, and high-fidelity accessories have high value relative to their size. These items can be easily resold. The rapid turnover among part-time personnel also makes control of employee theft especially difficult.

In reading trade publications relating to employee theft, the Wyses found some interesting information:

❑ In general, employee theft accounts for almost 70 per cent of retailers' losses due to all kinds of crime.

❑ On average, three out of four retail employees know at least one colleague who has stolen or is stealing.

❑ A University of Florida sociologist believes that the increase in employee theft may be due to the rise in young workers (because of Sunday hours and longer store hours during the week). The younger work force may be less committed to retailing than their predecessors.

❑ Other experts attribute the increase in employee theft to an overall decline in morality.

❑ A study by Arthur Young & Co. found that almost 40 per cent of employee thefts occur at the point of sale. Other places where the most thefts occur are on the sales floor, in the stock and receiving areas, and in the trash collection area.

The Wyses have read with great interest about how stores such as Alexander's and Marshall Field are seeking to control employee theft. Alexander's, a New York-based retailer, offers a $1,000 reward to each employee who informs store management that a fellow employee is stealing company merchandise (double its previous reward); employees also receive a year of tickets in the New York State lottery. Workers receive the full amount of the reward regardless of the value of the merchandise recovered. Marshall Field offers a $500 reward to each employee who reports a theft by a co-worker and $100 for alerting store detectives about customer shoplifting. Security personnel give out rewards to all levels of employees from stockroom workers to top management. Besides the reduction in employee theft and the savings due to the recovery of merchandise, Marshall Field has been able to reduce its security personnel as a result of this program.

While such programs have been successful at other stores, the Wyses have some concern about their applicability in their environment. They feel that a reward-based program may lead to poor morale (particularly among long-time employees who feel they should be trusted), that many employees would not tell on a fellow worker because of fear of reprisals, and that a program could lead to a diversion from selling activities.

In addition to a reward-based security program, the Wyses are considering using new employee screening procedures, emphasizing ethics in employee training, full prosecution of offenders, and central surveillance by video cameras.

QUESTIONS

1. Is controlling merchandise theft more difficult at the employee or customer level? Explain your answer.
2. Evaluate each method of employee theft control being considered by the Wyses.

3. Should the Wyses concentrate their theft control efforts at the problem store or develop a chain-wide approach to this problem? Why?
4. Recommend a plan for the Wyses to reduce employee theft.

Part Five Comprehensive Case

The Great Atlantic & Pacific Tea Company (A&P): An Organizational and Operations Restructuring*

Company Background and History

A&P was founded in 1859 as the Great American Tea Company. The firm began by purchasing tea directly from clipper ships at "cargo prices" and found customers eager to buy the tea at 50 per cent discounts from the regular prices at that time. The corporate name was later changed to the Great Atlantic & Pacific Tea Company (A&P) to mark the establishment of the transcontinental railroad and to separate the firm's retail store and mail-order operations.

For many years, A&P was considered an industry innovator. It was the first retailer to develop a dealer brand (for its tea blend and its Eight O'Clock coffee products in the 1860s). A&P was the leader in giving premiums to encourage customer loyalty and repurchases (in the 1870s). It was among the first retailers to sell prepackaged meats (in the 1920s). The company was the first food retailer to sponsor a radio program (1924). By 1936, A&P had 5,600 supermarkets, and it was the number one U.S. supermarket chain in terms of sales through 1972.

However, during the 1960s and into the 1970s, many problems began to emerge:

❏ Over the ten-year period from 1961 to 1970, A&P's share of the grocery business declined from 10 per cent to 6 per cent, and profits decreased from $57.5 million to $50 million. In 1975, the company lost over $157 million.

❏ Among the nation's five largest supermarket chains, only A&P failed to achieve large growth during the 1960s and 1970s.

❏ Between 1965 and 1980, A&P had six different chief executives. This resulted in little planning continuity.

❏ The firm overlooked suburban growth and had too many small inner-city stores.

❏ Most A&P stores did not stock highly profitable non-food items and they did not encourage one-stop shopping.

❏ The company did not respond to consumer demand for national brands. This was partly due to A&P's extensive ownership of manufacturing facilities.

❏ A&P had very high labor costs. Seniority plans, high wage rates, and the lack of flexibility regarding its unionized employees' performing other tasks (such as the inability to have checkout personnel unload merchandise from trucks when store traffic was slow) put A&P at a significant disadvantage with competing supermarket chains and nonunionized independent supermarkets.

In 1979, Tenglemann, a privately held West German grocery store company, acquired a major interest in A&P. Tenglemann installed a new management team, headed by James Wood, in 1980. To lure Wood away from his chief executive position at Grand Union, Tenglemann offered him about 1.8 million shares of A&P stock for $4 per share less than the market rate at that time. A&P pays Wood an annual salary of $660,000 plus 1 per cent of pre-tax profits. In 1986, he earned $4.3 million (including stock options). His current contract expires in 1990.

Wood has had a large role in transforming A&P and restoring it to profitability. During the late 1970s, competitors called A&P the "worst run supermarket chain in the business." As of 1980, it had no cash and was on the threshold of bankruptcy. But by 1982, A&P had once again begun to show a profit and was on the way to a steady recovery that led industry observers to comment that the chain's performance represented the "most well-documented turnaround story in the supermarket business."

These are among the major actions undertaken by Wood to revitalize A&P:

❏ Loss-generating and surplus assets have been sold, resulting in a $1 billion development fund. These monies and operating profits have been and are being used to renovate 75 per cent of existing stores, to build over one hundred new ones, and to add about four hundred other stores through acquisitions.

❏ Stores in unprofitable territories have been closed. In 1974, the chain operated 3,468 stores; in 1986, it had 1,200 stores (up from a low of 1,001 stores in 1984).

❏ The company's organization structure has been drastically changed through the purchase and integration of such companies as Kohl's, Dominion Stores (Can-

*The material in this case is drawn from Richard DeSanta, "Formats: Growing Apart, Coming Together," *Progressive Grocer* (January 1987), pp. 33–34 ff.; *The Great Atlantic & Pacific Tea Company, Inc. Annual Report 1986;* Ralph King, Jr., "Food Distributors," *Forbes* (January 11, 1988), p. 131; Holly Klokis, "A&P's Wood: Still Intrigued by the Challenge," *Chain Store Age Executive* (June 1987), pp. 19–20 ff.; Caroline E. Mayer, "A&P Getting A New Name," *Washington Post* (November 6, 1986), p. B9; Michael Sansolo, "A New West Side Story," *Progressive Grocer* (July 1987), pp. 30 ff.; Bill Saporito, "Just How Good Is the Great A&P?" *Fortune* (March 16, 1987), pp. 92–93; Lenore Skenazy, "A Trip to the Aisles," *Advertising Age* (June 8, 1987), p. 54; and Alix M. Freedman, "A&P to Sell a Private-Label Food Line to Compete Against Top-Shelf Brands," *Wall Street Journal* (June 2, 1988), p. 28.

ada), Shopwell, and Waldbaum. A&P now uses a multiformat strategy.

❑ In labor relations, A&P has extended its "quality of work life" concept to nearly one-quarter of its U.S. stores. Under this concept, employee participation is encouraged, and employees are rewarded for achieving labor savings and sales goals.

❑ The firm has overhauled its operations management procedures. It now more actively manages its costs and is beginning to centralize operations.

Current Strategy

There are several important components of A&P's current strategy. They include store organization, labor relations, and operations.

Store Organization

The store organization strategy of A&P is complex because of its recent acquisition policy and the large number of formats that it operates. A&P has been the most aggressive of the major food chains in expanding by acquiring existing chains rather than building new units. Between 1980 and 1986, A&P acquired 347 outlets from seven chains. See Table 1. Although these acquisitions cost A&P over $500 million, they also accounted for more than $3 billion of A&P's $7.4 billion in revenues during 1986.

To accommodate the acquisitions, A&P has reorganized itself on the basis of store format. While some of the acquired firms, such as Pantry Pride and Eagle Stores, have been consolidated into other A&P divisions, many of the firms listed in Table 1 have been allowed to retain a lot of autonomy. In A&P's new structure, there are five distinct store formats, with strategies differentiated accordingly. On the corporate planning level, the five formats are integrated by James Wood and his management team.

A&P's store formats, which are operated under twelve trade names, are shown in Figure 1 and described here:

❑ Gourmet stores—They sell exotic fruits, vegetables, imported provisions, and fresh fish. This format is located in affluent downtown and suburban areas.

❑ Conventional supermarkets—They are located in middle-class markets.

TABLE 1
Recent Acquisitions by A&P

Date	Chain	Number of Units
1980	Stop & Shop	11
1983	Kohl's	19
1984	Pantry Pride	20
	Eagle Stores	11
1985	Dominion Stores	93
1986	Shopwell/Food Emporium	53
	Waldbaum/Food Mart	140
		347

❑ Superstores—There are two formats: price-oriented (promotional) and full-service (upscale). Both formats are larger and offer more product lines than conventional supermarkets.

❑ Superwarehouse stores—They have a very strong price/promotional approach to merchandising and utilize warehouse-type fixtures and displays. They are located at secondary sites.

A&P uses its multiformat strategy with different types of stores—and even different trade names—in the same market areas. For example, in the New York metropolitan area, A&P operates four different formats (gourmet stores, conventional supermarkets, promotional superstores, and upscale superstores) and six trade names (Food Emporium, Waldbaum, Shopwell, A&P, Sav-A-Center, and A&P Futurestore). The format(s) chosen for a particular community depends on that area's population characteristics and needs.

Wood believes that A&P's acquired units need a degree of autonomy for them to continue to capitalize on their consumer loyalties:

> There's no way you can take a group of stores and just integrate them to get the maximum efficiencies without losing the benefit of the franchise they obviously have in the market. When you do take a company . . . you really have to understand that to some extent it will always be operated as a separate subsidiary of A&P Holding Co., as I call it.

Labor Relations

Labor costs are the largest single component of a supermarket's operating costs; they commonly account for 70 per cent of total operating costs. In the past, A&P's labor costs averaged 13 per cent of sales. They were about 11 per cent for major competitors. A&P's Philadelphia stores had labor costs that were 15 per cent of sales. This severely affected A&P's profitability. Each time A&P closed a store, its labor costs rose, since veteran workers (at high wage rates) transferred to other outlets and few entry-level workers (hired at lower wages) were being employed.

The situation in Philadelphia became intolerable in 1981, and A&P closed eighty-three area stores after failing to win union concessions. Several months later, A&P (minus eighty-three stores) and the union (with 1,500 fewer members) negotiated an unprecedented arrangement. These are the important elements of that arrangement:

❑ A&P agreed to start a new 50-unit free-standing chain, Super Fresh, in Philadelphia (using existing outlets).

❑ Initial wages for Super Fresh employees were set 20 per cent below those at competing supermarkets.

❑ If labor costs are 11 per cent or less of sales, employees earn 0.5 per cent of sales as a bonus. Employees are eligible for a 1.0 per cent bonus if labor costs are 10 per cent or less of sales, and a 1.5 per cent bonus if labor costs are 9.5 per cent or less of sales.

❑ Each Super Fresh store's books are open to union officers.

❑ Regularly scheduled bimonthly meetings are held to solicit employee suggestions. For example, in-store

341

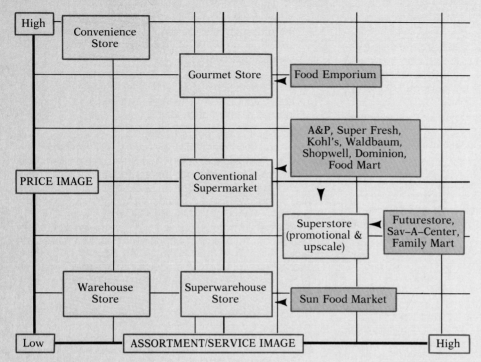

High

Convenience Store

Gourmet Store ◄ Food Emporium

A&P, Super Fresh, Kohl's, Waldbaum, Shopwell, Dominion, Food Mart

PRICE IMAGE

Conventional Supermarket ◄

▼

Superstore (promotional & upscale) ◄ Futurestore, Sav–A–Center, Family Mart

Warehouse Store

Superwarehouse Store ◄ Sun Food Market

Low   ASSORTMENT/SERVICE IMAGE   High

Note: This figure was developed by A&P to depict the diversity of strategies in food retailing. A&P does not operate convenience or traditional warehouse stores.

FIGURE 1
A&P's Store Formats and Trade Name Groupings
Source: Holly Klokis, "A&P's Wood: Still Intrigued By the Challenge," *Chain Store Age Executive* (June 1987), p. 23. Reprinted by permission.

personnel could suggest modifications in the express checkout system.

❑ Work rules are relaxed (as to what tasks each employee can perform). This gives A&P greater flexibility.

❑ Each store is more adaptable to its community's needs and can now buy goods from outside suppliers. During the summer, Super Fresh stores can buy corn and tomatoes locally; in the past, they had to rely totally on headquarters' purchasing.

❑ Seniority privileges are restricted to an employee's home store. If an outlet fails, its employees cannot bump more junior workers at successful stores. This also means that employees of successful stores do not have to fear being bumped.

The approach with Super Fresh has been quite a success. Prior to adopting the practices just noted, the average store had $120,000 in sales per week. Under the Super Fresh model (using the same people in the same outlets), the average store now has $220,000 in weekly sales. Since establishing Super Fresh, A&P's market share in Pennsylvania, New Jersey, and Delaware has doubled. Over the years, $10 million in bonuses have been paid to Super Fresh employees.

A&P has been broadening its use of these human relations concepts as a result of its positive experience with

Super Fresh: part of the risk of poor store performance should be shared by workers; employees should be encouraged to participate in decision making; and employees should be rewarded for achieving specified goals. A&P's "quality of work life" program is now in effect at nearly one-quarter of its U.S. stores (including Kohl's Wisconsin stores in 1983; A&P Baton Rouge in 1985; and Super Fresh Richmond, Baltimore, and Washington, D.C., in 1986). Under the plan the company's labor costs have been reduced to 11 per cent of sales (versus 12 per cent as the current industry average).

Operations

A&P's operations strategy is geared to reducing its costs while maintaining a satisfactory level of customer service. Yet, the firm is careful not to use price increases to cover operations cost inefficiencies. To Wood, the industry's favorite maxim, that higher prices will solve all cost-related problems, is overstated. He believes that

it's ceased to be a price business. For instance, everybody in the New York market trades at the same price, within 1 per cent. But the guy who's got the best lever on his economics, on his costs, is the one who wins at the end of the game.

While giving its store divisions considerable merchandis-

342

ing autonomy, A&P has also been paying close attention to opportunities to reduce costs by centralizing operations. In Canada, A&P consolidated its warehousing facilities after it acquired Dominion. In New York, the company expects to achieve purchasing, distribution, and administrative cost savings because of shared personnel and facilities among A&P, Food Emporium, and Waldbaum.

However, some critics feel that although centralization may lower costs, it may also blur some of the distinctions among the firm's formats and trade names. For example, A&P has planned that its Futurestore upscale superstore outlets offer better quality and higher-priced groceries than either conventional A&P supermarkets or Sav-A-Center promotional superstores. In reality, the products and prices at these outlets are very similar (even when these stores are located very close to one another).

A&P is investing heavily in technology that will further reduce costs and give it access to important data. Cash-control systems and information systems are being centralized as a means of decreasing costs, utilizing specialists, and developing comparable data categories to be used throughout the company. The information systems relay employee attendance records, labor schedules, warehouse bills, payroll data, ordering data, and other facts on a store-to-headquarters basis. In addition, A&P is investing in store-checkout scanning equipment to speed transaction time, note important inventory data by item, and ensure shelf/product/checkout price uniformity.

Some operating procedures are now standardized. For example, in A&P's Futurestores, planograms are used extensively. These are detailed blueprints showing exactly which items go where on each shelf. Such planograms might show that three shelf facings of Bayer aspirin should be located next to three shelf facings of Anacin on the third shelf. A&P sends out a shelf management supervisor to ensure that stores adhere to plans.

Recent Financial Performance

Table 2 shows selected financial data for A&P from 1982 to 1986. The firm had substantial increases in net profit as a percentage of sales and sales per store over this period. However, sales per square foot in 1986 were only 16 per cent higher than in 1982, and sales per employee were actually 18 per cent lower in 1986 than in 1982.

The need for A&P's continuing productivity improvements is apparent when comparing A&P's recent financial performance with other major retail food chains. See Table 3. A&P's average return on equity for the five-year period 1982 to 1987 was 10.0 per cent, the lowest figure for any leading firm. Yet, A&P's annual sales growth between 1986 and 1987 was the highest among the retailers shown in the table.

A&P has also been below the industry average for such performance measures as sales per square foot, sales per store per week, store size, inventory turnover, and pre-tax profit margins.

TABLE 2
Selected Financial Data for A&P, 1982–1986

	1986*	1985	1984	1983	1982
Financial Measures:					
Net sales (000s)	$7,834,859	$6,615,422	$5,878,286	$5,222,013	$4,607,817
Net income after taxes (000s)	$95,010	$88,290	$215,779	$47,551[†]	$31,211
Number of employees	81,500	60,000	53,000	53,000	40,000
Number of stores (at year end)	1,200	1,045	1,001	1,022	1,016
Total store area (000s of sq. feet)	32,609	27,648	25,313	23,276	22,601
Financial Ratios:					
Net profit as a percentage of sales	1.2	1.3	3.7	0.9	0.6
Sales per employee	$94,319[††]	$110,257	$110,911	$98,528	$115,195
Sales per store	$6,405,859[††]	$6,330,547	$5,872,396	$5,109,602	$4,535,253
Sales per sq. foot	$236[††]	$239	$232	$224	$204

*Reflects 53 weeks. All other yearly periods are 52 weeks.

[†]Cannot be directly compared to other years because of the high level of an extraordinary credit to income.

[††]Adjusted because of 53-week reporting period, to an annualized 52-week basis.

Source: The Great Atlantic & Pacific Tea Company, Inc. Annual Report 1986.

TABLE 3
Selected Financial Data for Major Supermarkets

Supermarket Chain	Return on Equity Rank, 1982–87	Average Return on Equity, 1982–87 (%)	Return on Equity, 1987 (%)	Net Profit Margin, 1987 (%)	Average Annual Sales Growth, 1982–87 (%)	Sales Growth, 1986–87 (%)
American Stores	1	25.9	13.7	1.1	17.6	1.3
Lucky Stores	2	20.9	91.8	4.2	0.1	−1.6
Albertson's	3	20.5	18.5	2.0	9.0	8.5
Winn-Dixie	4	19.3	15.8	1.3	5.5	5.6
Stop & Shop	5	17.1	8.5	0.9	13.4	7.2
Kroger	6	12.8	14.9	0.9	9.7	3.7
A&P	7	10.0	11.9	1.0	7.0	32.9
Median performance		19.3	14.9	1.1	9.0	5.6

Source: Ralph King, Jr., "Food Distributors," *Forbes* (January 11, 1988), p. 131. Reprinted by permission. © Forbes, Inc., 1988.

QUESTIONS

1. Evaluate A&P's decision to organize itself into five store formats with twelve trade names. Refer to Figure 1 in your answer.
2. Draw and explain an organization chart for A&P.
3. What are the pros and cons of A&P's expanding the human resource management plans that have worked so well with Super Fresh to other stores in the chain?
4. Explain the ramifications of James Wood's statement that "the guy who's got the best lever on his economics,

on his costs, is the one who wins at the end of the game."
5. How can purchasing, distribution, and administrative cost savings be obtained while maintaining the store format and trade name identity of each store type?
6. Should A&P use prototype stores? Why or why not?
7. Evaluate the data in Tables 2 and 3. How can A&P improve its financial performance?

PART SIX

Merchandise Management and Pricing

❑ *In Part Six, two elements of the retail strategy mix are presented. Merchandise management consists of the buying, handling, and financial aspects of merchandising. Pricing decisions are crucial because of their impact on the financial aspects of merchandise management and their interaction with other retailing elements.*

❑ *Chapter 11 deals with buying and handling merchandise. Each stage in the buying and handling process is described: organization, merchandise plans, information about customer demand, merchandise sources, evaluation methods, negotiations, concluding the purchase, merchandise handling, reordering, and re-evaluation.*

❑ *Chapter 12 concentrates on financial merchandise management. First, the cost and retail methods of accounting are introduced. Next, the merchandise forecasting and budgeting process is presented. Then, unit control systems are discussed. The last part of the chapter integrates dollar and unit financial inventory controls.*

❑ *Chapter 13 covers pricing. The outside factors affecting decisions are discussed: consumers, government, suppliers, and competitors. A framework for developing a price strategy is described: objectives, broad policy, basic strategy, implementation, and adjustments.*

Chapter 11

Buying and Handling Merchandise

❑ **Chapter Objectives** ❑

1 To examine the major aspects of nonfinancial merchandise planning and management

2 To explain the merchandise buying and handling process and each of its elements: organization, merchandise plans, information about customer demand, merchandise sources, evaluation methods, negotiations, concluding the purchase, merchandise handling, reordering, and re-evaluation

3 To discuss what merchandise a retailer should carry, how much to stock, when to stock items, and where to store items

4 To consider the ongoing nature of merchandise buying and handling

Two contrasting approaches to merchandise assortment planning are being practiced by chain-store retailers. With the first, all the stores in a chain carry the same basic product lines, and the number of items in any merchandise category stocked by an individual outlet depends on its size and the needs of the consumers in its market area. In this strategy, retailers can run blanket ads covering their stores and present a common "look" for customers.

For instance, at Philadelphia-based Strawbridge & Clothier stores, this philosophy is followed:

When you're a tightly focused, narrow geographic chain, there are only perceived differences in store needs as you go from unit to unit. Unless you have an unbelievably discerning eye, you wouldn't be able to

see a difference among our stores in assortments and presentation. However, some stores can sell higher levels of merchandise; others are stronger in more moderate price points.

With the second approach, all the stores in a chain do not carry the same product lines; the merchandise mix at each store may vary. In this strategy, retailers try to preserve an overall image but feel it is inappropriate to handle limited assortments in smaller stores; they would rather drop a product line completely in those outlets.

Elder-Beerman, a chain based in Dayton, Ohio, adheres to this second philosophy:

We would rather eliminate lines or departments than miniaturize them in branches. We look more for departmental content, rather than a representation of all lines and all departments. If we are going to be in the business, we are going to have complete selections.[1]

Determining the product assortment at branch stores is just one of the many merchandise buying and handling decisions that retailers have to make.

Overview

Developing and implementing a merchandise plan is a primary component of a retail strategy. To be successful, a retailer must have the proper assortments of goods and services when they are in demand and must sell them in a manner consistent with the overall strategy.

Merchandising is defined as:

The planning and supervision involved in marketing particular goods and/or services at the places, times, and prices and in quantities which will best serve to realize the marketing objectives of the business.[2]

In this chapter, the buying and handling aspects of merchandise planning and management are discussed. The financial side of merchandising is described in Chapter 12. Retail pricing is presented in Chapter 13. Planning for a service retailer is examined in Chapter 17.

The Merchandise Buying and Handling Process

Figure 11-1 shows the stages involved in an integrated merchandise buying and handling process. It is essential that each of the stages be utilized in merchandising. In addition, a systematic approach should be followed.

Establishing a Formal or Informal Buying Organization

The first step in the merchandise buying and handling process is establishing a buying organization. Merchandising cannot be conducted in a thorough, systematic manner unless the buying organization is well defined. This organization specifies who is responsible for merchandise decisions, the activities of these people, authority to make decisions, and the relationship of merchandising to overall retail operations. Figure 11-2 highlights the attributes of buying organizations.

A **formal buying organization** exists when merchandising is viewed as a distinct retail task and a separate department is set up. All merchandising operations (Figure 11-1, Steps 2 through 10) are under the control of this department. A formal organization usually occurs among large retailers and involves distinct buying personnel. In an **informal buying organization,** merchandising is not viewed as a distinct task. Existing personnel handle merchandising and other retail functions. Responsibility and authority are not always clear-cut. Informal buying organizations generally occur in smaller retailers.

The major advantages of a formal buying organization are well-defined responsibilities and authority and the use of full-time, specialized merchandisers. The major disadvantage is the cost of operation. The important advantages of an informal buying organization are low costs and flexibility. The important disadvantages are less defined responsibilities and authority, and the de-emphasis on merchandise planning.

Both structures exist in great numbers. It is not crucial that a retailer use a formal buying organization. However, it is crucial that the retailer realize the role of merchandising and ensure that responsibility, activities, authority, and the interrelationship with store operations are systematically defined and enacted.

Multiunit retailers must also determine whether to create a centralized buying organization or a decentralized one. In a **centralized buying organization,** all

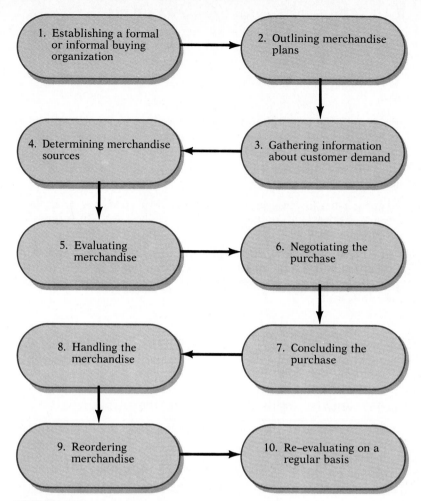

FIGURE 11-1
The Merchandise Buying and Handling Process

purchase decisions emanate from one office. For example, a chain may have fourteen stores, with all merchandise decisions made in the headquarters store. In a **decentralized buying organization,** purchase decisions are made locally or regionally. As an example, a chain with eight stores may allow each outlet to select its own merchandise, or a chain with twelve stores may divide the branches into geographic territories (four per territory) and have regional decisions made by the headquarters store in each territory.

Among the advantages of a centralized buying organization are integration of effort, strict controls, consistent image, nearness to top management, staff support, and discounts through volume purchases. Among the possible disadvantages of centralized buying are inflexibility, time delays, poor morale at local stores, and excessive uniformity.

Decentralized buying offers these advantages: adaptability to local market conditions, quick order process, and improved morale because branches have autonomy. The potential disadvantages are disjointed planning, inconsistent image, limited management controls, little staff support, and loss of volume discounts.

Many chains have combined the benefits of both systems. A centralized buying organization is used, but local store managers are given substantial power to

Factor	Attributes
LEVEL OF FORMALITY	
Formal	Well–defined responsibilities and authority, use of full–time specialists; costly
Informal	Low costs, flexible; less–defined responsibilities and authority, de–emphasis on merchandise planning
DEGREE OF CENTRALIZATION	
Centralized	Integrated effort, strict controls, consistent image, nearness to management, staff support, volume discounts; inflexible, time delays, poor morale at branch stores, excessive uniformity
Decentralized	Adaptable, quick, improved morale; disjointed planning, inconsistent image, limited controls and staff support, loss of volume discounts
BREADTH	
General	Better for small retailers or few goods/services
Specialized	Improved knowledge, well–defined responsibility; high costs, extra personnel
SOURCE OF PERSONNEL	
Internal	Staffed by the retailer's personnel, who make all merchandise decisions
External	Outside personnel hired (usually at a fee), used by small retailers or those far from supply sources
Resident buying office	Located in important merchandise centers, staffed by internal or external personnel
Cooperative buying	Independent retailers involved with shared purchases
PHILOSOPHY	
Merchandising	All stages in the buying and selling of goods and services, smooth flow of command through an integrated effort, buyer's expertise used in selling, clear responsibility and authority, proper displays, reduced costs, closeness to consumer
Buying	Separation of buying and selling functions, recognizes dissimilar skills required for each function, higher morale of in–store personnel, selling not treated as subordinate, greater closeness to consumers, specialization, buyers not required to be good supervisors
STAFFING	
Buyer	Aggressive, travel–oriented, customer–oriented, creative
Sales manager	Planner and supervisor, detail–oriented, customer–oriented
Merchandising buyer	Attributes of buyer and sales manager

FIGURE 11-2
The Attributes of Buying Organizations

revise merchandise orders or place their own orders (if substantiated). At K mart, there is a director of centralized merchandise systems planning, and individual store managers have input:

The store managers are our eyes and ears; but the initial decision making comes from headquarters. At the store level, decisions are made based on the relationship of the store to its own retail environment. We want to incorporate those insights into the overall corporate thrust.[3]

A choice must be made between a general buying organization and a specialized buying organization. In the general buying organization, one or several people buy all of a retailer's merchandise. For example, the owner of a small hardware store may buy all merchandise for his or her store. With a specialized buying organization, each buyer is responsible for a product category. As an example, a department store could have separate buyers for girls', juniors', and women's clothes.

The general approach is better when the retailer is small or there are few different goods/services involved. The specialized approach is better when the retailer is large or many goods/services are handled. With specialization, knowledge is improved and responsibility well defined; however, costs are higher and extra personnel are usually required.

A retailer can choose between an inside buying organization and an outside one. An **inside buying organization** is staffed by a retailer's own personnel. All merchandise decisions are made by permanent employees of the firm. With an **outside buying organization,** a company or personnel external to the retailer are hired, usually on a fee basis.

An outside organization is most often used by small or medium-sized retailers or by those that are far from their sources of supply. In these cases, it is cheaper and more efficient for the retailers to hire an outside buyer than to use company personnel. An outside organization has clout in dealing with suppliers (because of the volume of purchases), usually services noncompeting retailers, offers marketing research expertise, and sometimes sponsors private-label merchandise. Outside buying organizations may be paid by retailers who subscribe to their services, or by manufacturers, which give commissions. Sometimes, individual retailers decide to set up their own internal organizations if they believe their outside group is dealing with direct competitors or the retailers find that they can buy merchandise more efficiently on their own.

Resident buying offices are used to allow retailers to keep in close touch with the market. These offices operate in important merchandise centers (sources of supply) and provide valuable information and contacts. A resident buying office can be an inside or outside organization. There are about four hundred outside resident buying offices in the United States (three-quarters of them are in New York City). These offices serve several thousand retailers.

Smaller, independent retailers are now using cooperative buying to a greater degree than ever before (in an attempt to compete successfully with bigger chains). Under **cooperative buying,** a group of independent retailers gets together to make large purchases from a supplier. Volume discounts are then achieved. Cooperative buying is most popular among food and hardware retailers. In some cases, the retailers initiate the cooperative; in others, the wholesaler or manufacturer may initiate the cooperative as an attempt to cut costs.

Another decision involves the retailer's determination of whether the buying organization is to be concerned with merchandising or buying. As stated at the beginning of the chapter, merchandising includes all the steps in the buying and selling of goods and services, such as purchases, pricing, storage, display, and delivery. Buying includes only the purchasing of products and not the sale of them. Many retailers consider merchandising the key to their success, and buyers (or merchandise managers) are involved with buying and selling. Other retailers consider their buyers highly skilled specialists who should not be active in the selling function. This activity is undertaken by skilled selling specialists.

The advantages of a merchandising philosophy are that a smooth flow of command is caused by an integrated effort; the expertise of the buyer is used in selling; responsibility and authority are clear (the buyer does not blame sales personnel for poor sales efforts, and vice versa); the buyer ensures that the merchandise is properly displayed; costs are reduced (few staff specialists); and the buyer is close to the consumer through his or her interaction with the sales function.

The advantages of separate buying and selling functions are that similar skills are not required for each function; the morale of in-store personnel increases as authority is granted; selling is not treated as a subordinate function; salespeople are closer to customers than buyers; specialists can develop in each area; and buyers may not be good supervisors because of their time away from the store and differences in the management of buying and selling personnel.

Both approaches are used, and the advantages of merchandising or buying are still open to debate. An individual retailer must evaluate which procedure is better for carrying out its overall strategy.

The last decision in this stage of buying and handling merchandise centers on the staffing of the buying organization. What positions must be filled, and what qualifications should the retailer require? Retailers who take a merchandising perspective are most concerned with hiring good buyers. Retailers who take a buying and selling perspective are concerned with hiring both buyers and sales managers.

Many large retailers hire college graduates whom they place in extensive training programs and promote internally to positions as buyers and sales managers. A buyer must be aggressive to be successful in bargaining sessions with suppliers. A buyer must also make extensive use of buying plans (detailed shopping lists that completely outline purchases) and may have to travel to major marketplaces. A sales manager must be a good planner and supervisor. A merchandising buyer must possess the attributes of each.

More and more retailers are realizing that the most important qualification for good buying personnel is the ability to relate to customers and anticipate their future needs. To an extent, buyers are involved with each of the remaining activities described in the balance of this chapter and many of those detailed in Chapter 12.

Outlining Merchandise Plans

Merchandise planning centers on four basic decisions: what merchandise to stock, how much merchandise to stock, when to stock merchandise, and where to store merchandise.

What Merchandise Is Stocked

First, a retailer must determine what quality of merchandise to carry. Should it carry top-line, expensive items and sell to upper-class customers? Or should it sell middle-of-the-line, moderately priced items and cater to middle-class customers? Or should it sell bottom-line, inexpensive items and attract lower-class customers? Or should the retailer try to draw more than one market segment by offering a variety in quality, such as middle- and top-line merchandise for middle- and upper-class shoppers? The firm must also decide whether to carry promotional merchandise (low-priced closeout items or special buys that are used to generate store traffic).

In considering the quality of merchandise to be carried, the retailer should evaluate several factors: the desired target market(s), competition, store image, store location, stock turnover, profitability, national versus private brands, customer services that must be offered, the type of personnel needed, the perceived goods/service benefits, and constrained decision making. Table 11-1 shows how each of these factors affects the planning of merchandise quality.

TABLE 11-1

The Factors to Be Considered in the Planning of Merchandise Quality

Factor	Relevance for Merchandise Quality Planning
Target market	Quality must be matched to the wishes of the desired target market.
Competition	A retailer can choose to sell similar quality (follow competition) or different quality (carry different merchandise and appeal to a different market than competitors).
Store image	The quality of merchandise is directly related to the image customers have of the store.
Store location	A location affects store image and the number of competitors, which, in turn, relate to quality.
Stock turnover	High quality and high prices usually yield a lower turnover than low quality and low prices.
Profitability	High-quality merchandise generally brings higher profit per unit than low-quality merchandise; however, turnover may cause total profits to be higher for low-quality merchandise.
National versus private brands	For many consumers, national (manufacturer) brands connote higher quality than private (dealer) brands.
Customer services to be offered	High-quality merchandise requires personal selling, alterations, delivery, and so on. Low-quality merchandise may not.
Personnel	Skilled, knowledgeable personnel are necessary for quality merchandise. Limited personnel are needed for low-quality merchandise.
Perceived goods/ service benefits	Low-quality merchandise attracts customers who desire functional product benefits (e.g., warmth, comfort). High-quality merchandise attracts customers who desire extended product benefits (e.g., status, services, style).
Constrained decision making	a. Franchise or chain operators have limited or no control over product quality. They either buy directly from the franchisor (chain) or must abide by quality standards. b. Independent retailers who buy from a few large wholesalers will be limited to the range of quality offered by the wholesalers.

For example, Highland Superstores is a chain with more than fifty consumer electronics–major home-appliance stores in Michigan, Ohio, Indiana, Illinois, Texas, and Louisiana which believes that

Today, in addition to low pricing, shoppers want appealing stores, a broad assortment of quality merchandise, and salespeople who know their products and are interested in helping customers make informed decisions. In addition, they want service after the sale.[4]

It has a very consistent merchandising strategy which is consist with that belief:

❑ Only leading brands such as GE, Litton, Magnavox, Maytag, Panasonic, Sony, Technics, Whirlpool, and Zenith are carried.

❑ Each store contains an extensive assortment and full inventory.

❑ There is a thirty-day "no questions" return policy for customers.

❑ Stores are clean, neat, bright, and well stocked.

❑ Sales personnel are knowledgeable and helpful.

❑ Very competitive prices are offered, along with a lifetime low-price guarantee.

❑ Middle-income and upscale customers are sought.

Highland is so successful that its annual sales have quadrupled since 1983.

The second major decision a retailer makes concerning what merchandise to handle involves determining how innovative (new) it should be. Several factors should be examined before the retailer plans the level of innovativeness: the target market, goods/service growth potential, fashion trends and theories (where applicable), store image, competition, customer segmentation, responsiveness to consumers, investment costs, profitability, risk, constrained decision making, and dropping of old goods/services. These factors are summarized in Table 11-2.

An innovative retailer, one that carries new goods and services and plans for upcoming trends, faces a great opportunity (being the first in the market) and a great risk (possibly misreading customer interests and being stuck with large inventories). By evaluating each of the factors in Table 11-2 and developing a thorough plan for handling new goods and services, a retailer should be able to capitalize on its opportunities and reduce its risks.

These are illustrations of innovative merchandising strategies by retailers:

❑ Sears is selling popularly priced and colorful sportswear, nightwear, shoes, and accessories under the McKids brand name, under an exclusive licensing arrangement with McDonald's. Its redesigned Kids Store departments now feature storybook trees, castles, fun mirrors, giant posters, videoscreens, and sugar-free gumball machines.[5]

❑ Carson Pirie Scott's State Street department store in Chicago has pioneered a stationery department known as Arcadia. It carries "funky stationery, way-out greeting cards, trendy gifts, goofy games, and hundreds of items that emanate just one message—fun." Arcadia is decorated in bold colors, plays rock music and rock music videos, and offers fresh baked cookies, soft yogurt, and fresh-squeezed orange juice.[6] See Figure 11-3.

❑ In 1987–1988, Wendy's introduced a new all-you-can-eat self-service SuperBar in many of its restaurants. The fifty-item SuperBar has fresh pasta dishes, hot Mexican entrees, a variety of toppings for baked potatoes, and

TABLE 11-2
The Factors to Be Considered in Planning Merchandise Innovativeness

Factor	Relevance to Innovativeness Planning
Target market	Evaluate whether the target market is conservative or progressive.
Goods/service growth potential	Consider each new offering on the basis of rapidity of initial sales, maximum sales potential per time period, and length of sales life.
Fashion trends and theories	Understand the "trickle-down" and "trickle-across" theories, if selling fashion merchandise.
Store image	The kinds of goods/services a retailer carries are influenced by its image. The level of innovativeness should be consistent with this image.
Competition	Lead or follow competition in the selection of new goods/services.
Customer segmentation	Customers can be segmented by dividing merchandise into established-product displays and new-product displays.
Responsiveness to consumers	New offerings should be handled when they are requested by the target market.
Amount of investment	These types of investment are possible for each new good/service: product costs, new fixtures, and additional personnel (or additional training for old personnel).
Profitability	Each new offering should be assessed for potential profits (on the good/service and additions to the profits of the overall retailer).
Risk	The major risks are damages to image, investment costs, and opportunity costs.
Constrained decision making	Franchise and chain operators may be restricted in the new goods/services they can purchase.
Dropping old goods/services	Old goods/services should be deleted when sales and/or profits are low.

Tell Me, Why Should My Store Carry Your Merchandise?

Today, there is a proliferation of suppliers and potential suppliers calling on retailers, making the merchandise-buying process difficult for both parties. Nowhere is this situation more complex than in selling products to supermarket chain buyers. Here is why.

A typical supermarket chain-store buyer listens to twelve sales presentations on new items each week, in addition to holding discussions with vendors regarding existing products. The average new-product presentation lasts about twenty minutes, which means that a buyer could spend four hours (or more) weekly just listening to these proposals. In response to a survey, on an A to F grading scale, 41 per cent of the buyers would give the sales pitches a C; only 3 per cent would give a grade of A. As one buyer noted, "Most presentations are poorly planned."

Just under half of the supermarket chains encourage suppliers to make sales presentations at individual stores; one-third do not allow such calls. Many larger chains have buying committees that review new product ideas; these committees consist of three to ten or more buyers. In most cases, membership on the buying committee rotates among the chain's buyers, since it usually meets weekly. On average, a buying committee reviews 2,500 new items per year.

In deciding whether or not to carry new products, the buyers place the greatest emphasis on introductory terms, such as ad allowances; the amount of consumer advertising conducted by the supplier; the supplier's use of coupons to stimulate consumers; the features of the product; and the supplier's reputation and track record. Of every ten new products described to supermarket chain buyers, about three or four are accepted. Once on the selling floor, they are generally given six months or less to prove themselves. About half the time that new products are purchased by a chain, other items are discontinued.

Source: Based on material in "The Pot Is Bigger, But It's the Same Game," *Progressive Grocer* (November 1987), pp. 53–68.

a full range of salad items. The price per customer is $2.99 to $3.59. The SuperBar is intended to compete against McDonald's and Burger King's more traditional offerings.[7] See Figure 11-4.

The retailer should evaluate the growth potential for each new good or service. Three elements of growth are of special interest: rapidity of initial sales, maximum sales potential per period, and length of sales life. How fast will the good or service generate sales? What are the most sales (dollars and units) that can be achieved in a season or a year? Over what time period will the good or service continue to sell?

A useful tool for assessing the potential of a new good or service is the **product life cycle,** which shows the expected behavior of a good or service over its life. The traditional product life cycle has four stages: introduction, growth, maturity, and decline. Figure 11-5 shows the shape of the traditional cycle and describes each of the stages. An understanding of this tool is quite helpful in strategy planning.

During the introductory stage of the cycle, the retailer should anticipate a limited target market, consisting of high-income and innovative consumers. The good or service will probably be supplied in one basic version, not a choice of alternatives. The manufacturer (supplier) may limit the distribution of the product to "finer" stores. However, convenience items such as food and houseware products are normally mass-distributed. Items that are initially distributed selectively generally utilize a skimming (high) price strategy. Merchandise that is mass-distributed typically uses penetration (low) pricing to encourage faster ac-

FIGURE 11-3
The Excitement of Arcadia

Reprinted by permission of
Carson Pirie Scott.

ceptance by consumers. In either case, introductory promotion must be explanatory, geared to informing hesitant consumers. At this stage, there is only one or very few possible suppliers.

As innovative consumers buy a new good or service and recommend it to their friends, sales increase rapidly and the product life cycle enters the growth stage. The target market expands to include middle-income consumers who are somewhat more innovative than the average. Variations of the basic offering appear; width and depth of assortment expand. The number of retailers carrying the product increases. Price discounting is not widely employed, but a wide variety of retailers offer a large range of prices, customer services, and quality. Retail promotion is more persuasive and is aimed at acquainting consumers with product availability and extended services. There is an increasing number of suppliers.

In the maturity stage of the life cycle, good or service sales reach their maximum. The largest portion of the target market is reached during this period. Lower-, middle-, and upper-class consumers select from a very wide variety of offerings and options. All types of retailers (discount to upscale) carry the good or service in some form. Although prestige retailers continue to emphasize brand names and customer services, other retailers enter into active price competition. Price is prominently mentioned in promotional activities. For both retailers and their suppliers, the maturity stage is the most competitive.

A good or service would then enter the decline stage, usually brought on by two factors: the target market shrinks (saturation and product obsolescence), and price cutting minimizes profit margins. In the decline stage, the target market becomes the lowest-income consumer and laggards. The variety of the offering is cut back (to reduce the retailer's space allotted to these items). Many retailers drop the good or service for profit and image reasons. Low prices are offered, and promotion is reduced and geared to price. There are fewer suppliers, as many turn to other goods and services.

It should be noted that not all new goods and services conform to the life cycle

FIGURE 11-4
Wendy's New SuperBar

displayed in Figure 11-5 and just detailed. Some derivatives of the traditional product life cycle are shown in Figure 11-6. In a boom sales pattern, sales rise quickly and maintain a high level for a long period of time. Many cosmetics, pharmaceutical products, and rental services can be placed in this category.

A fad curve occurs when a good or service generates a lot of sales, but only for a short time. The retailer must be careful not to overorder because of enthusiasm over high sales. Often, toys and games are shortlived fads, such as Pound Puppies and the Clue video game. An extended fad is like a fad, except that residual sales continue for a long period at a fraction of earlier sales. Clothing with designer insignias is an example of a product that can be classified as an extended fad.

A seasonal or fashion curve results when a good or service sells well during nonconsecutive time periods. Seasonal items, such as camping equipment and air-conditioner servicing, have good sales during one season each year. Usually, the strongest sales of seasonal goods and services occur during the same season each year, and retail planning is relatively simple. A fashion product is much less predictable. Sales of products like bow ties or miniskirts are often sizable

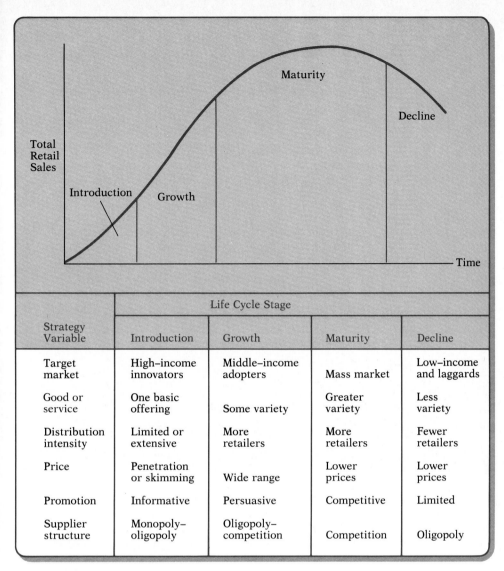

Strategy Variable	Life Cycle Stage			
	Introduction	Growth	Maturity	Decline
Target market	High–income innovators	Middle–income adopters	Mass market	Low–income and laggards
Good or service	One basic offering	Some variety	Greater variety	Less variety
Distribution intensity	Limited or extensive	More retailers	More retailers	Fewer retailers
Price	Penetration or skimming	Wide range	Lower prices	Lower prices
Promotion	Informative	Persuasive	Competitive	Limited
Supplier structure	Monopoly–oligopoly	Oligopoly–competition	Competition	Oligopoly

FIGURE 11-5
The Traditional Product Life Cycle

for a number of years, become unpopular for a number of years, and then become popular again. For these products, retail planning is harder.

A nostalgia or revival curve happens when a seemingly obsolete good or service is revived. An innovative retailer will recognize the potential in this area and merchandise accordingly. For example, direct marketers frequently use television commercials to sell records, cassettes, and compact discs emphasizing music or artists who were previously successful. They also heavily promote "greatest hits" recordings featuring a combination of artists.

A bust product life cycle is one in which a good or service is not successful at all (unlike a fad), and the retailer loses money and, sometimes, status. This occurred with McDonald's McRib sandwiches; despite its strong push, the product never did well and was removed from the market. Sometimes, retailers have

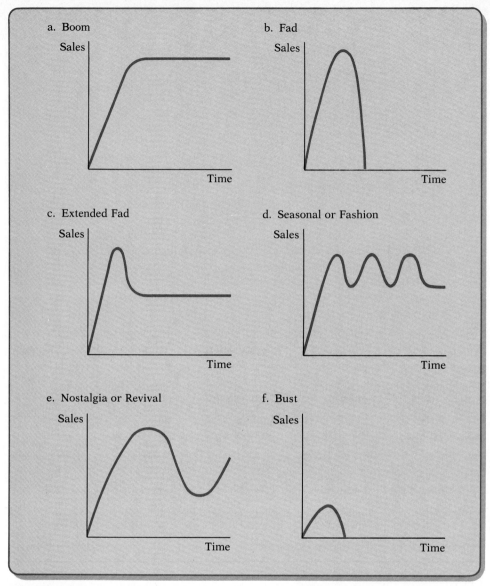

FIGURE 11-6
Selected Product Life Cycles

to slash prices drastically to sell a huge amount of excess inventory. This took place with the IBM PCjr and the Coleco Adam computers.

The retailer that sells fashion merchandise must be familiar with fashion trends and theories. Fashion trends may be divided into both vertical and horizontal categories; fashions may go through one or a combination of these trends. A vertical trend occurs when a fashion is first accepted by an upscale market segment and undergoes changes in its basic form before it is sold to the general public. The **trickle-down theory** states that a fashion is passed from the upper to the lower social classes, through three vertical stages: distinctive (original designs, designer dress shops, custom-made, worn by high society); emulation (modification of original designs, finer department stores, alterations, worn by the middle class); and economic emulation (simple copy of original, discount and bargain stores, mass-produced, mass-marketed). Under this theory, Paris has often been considered the fashion capital of the world.

In recent years, the importance of horizontal fashion trends has also been recognized. A horizontal trend occurs when a fashion is accepted by the general public while retaining its basic form. According to the **trickle-across theory,** within any social class there are innovative customers who act as opinion leaders. Fashion must be accepted by these leaders, who then convince other members of the same social class (who are more conservative) to buy the item. Merchandise is sold across the class and not from one class down to another.

By understanding both theories and determining which one is more appropriate for a specific fashion, the retailer is better able to predict fashion successes and the types of customers fashions will appeal to during each stage of the product life cycle. Figure 11-7 contains a checklist for predicting fashion adoption.

In planning innovativeness, the retailer's emphasis is too often on new-product additions. Equally important are the decisions involved in dropping existing goods or services. Because of limited resources and shelf space, some items have to be dropped when others are added. Instead of intuitively removing old offerings, the retailer should use structured guidelines:

1. Select items for possible elimination on the basis of declining sales, prices, and profits; the appearance of substitutes; the loss of usefulness; and excessive demands on executives' time.

2. Gather and analyze information about these items, including profits, financial considerations, employee relations, and marketing factors.

3. Consider nondeletion strategies such as cutting costs, revising marketing efforts, adjusting prices, and cooperating with other retailers.

4. After a deletion decision is made, consider timing, parts and servicing, inventory, and holdover demand.[8]

		Yes	No
1.	Does the fashion satisfy a consumer need?	___	___
2.	Is the fashion compatible with emerging consumer life–styles?	___	___
3.	Is the fashion oriented toward the mass market? Toward a market segment?	___ ___	___ ___
4.	Is the fashion radically new?	___	___
5.	Are the reputations of the designer(s) and the retailers carrying the fashion good?	___	___
6.	Are several designers marketing some version of the fashion?	___	___
7.	Is the price range for the fashion appropriate for the target market?	___	___
8.	Will extensive advertising be used?	___	___
9.	Will the fashion change over time?	___	___
10.	Will consumers view the fashion as a long–term trend?	___	___

FIGURE 11-7
A Checklist for Predicting Fashion Adoption

As an illustration, Montgomery Ward recently stopped selling hunting equipment, skates, hardware, cabinets, and flooring and lessened its emphasis on paint, lawn mowers, tillers, grills, lawn furniture, garbage disposals, and ceiling fans. At that time, only about 6 per cent of total company sales were in these products. In their place, Montgomery Ward now carries more of its better-selling merchandise, such as automotive goods, appliances, apparel, and home furnishings.[9]

How Much Merchandise Is Stocked

After a retailer decides what merchandise to carry, it must determine how much merchandise to stock.[10] Width and depth of assortment should be planned. With how many goods/service categories should the firm be involved, and how many varieties should be stocked in any category? As described in Chapter 4, product assortment can range from wide and deep (a department store) to narrow and shallow (a box store). Some of the advantages and disadvantages of each type of assortment strategy are shown in Table 11-3.

Assortment strategies vary widely, as these two examples show. Kentucky Fried Chicken emphasizes "We do chicken right" and specializes in chicken and related

TABLE 11-3
Retail Assortment Strategies

Advantages	Disadvantages
Wide and Deep (many goods/service categories and a large assortment within each category)	
Broad market	High inventory investment
Full stocking of items	General image
High level of traffic	Many items have low turnover
Customer loyalty	Obsolete merchandise
One-stop shopping	
No disappointed customers	
Wide and Shallow (many goods/service categories and a limited assortment in each category)	
Broad market	Limited variety
High level of traffic	Disappointed customers
Emphasis on convenience customers	Weak image
Less costly than wide and deep	Many items have low turnover
One-stop shopping	Reduced loyalty
Narrow and Deep (few goods/service categories and a large assortment in each category)	
Specialist image	Limited variety
Good customer choice in the category(ies)	Limited market
Specialized personnel	Limited traffic
Customer loyalty	
No disappointed customers	
Less costly than wide and deep	
Narrow and Shallow (few goods/service categories and a limited assortment in each category)	
Aimed at convenience customers	Limited variety and traffic
Least costly	Disappointed customers
High turnover of items	Weak image
	Reduced loyalty

Because of newer technology, merchandise handling can be made more efficient than ever before. Wetterau offers an on-line, computer-based WICS system for its retail customers. With this system, buyers have access to valuable data which helps them manage inventory and make investment buying decisions. WICS can track the location of every item in a warehouse and automatically rotate stock to ensure freshness. It can also analyze each item and every vendor on a daily basis, thus decreasing the lead time needed for reordering and reducing the needed level of warehouse inventory.

By using portable price scanners (which rely on the Universal Product Code) and small personal computers, retailers now have the ability and flexibility to closely monitor merchandise at any location and to complete physical inventories. As a result, merchandise can be easily allocated to various departments and/or branch stores and proper assortments can be maintained.

Photos courtesy of Wetterau.

Items placed on conveyer belt

Tray tips to proper packing station

Merchandise conveyed to packing department

Packer assembles individual customer orders

To efficiently and effectively handle the merchandise sold via its catalog operations, J.C. Penney utilizes an elaborate and systematic process to fill customer orders with merchandise maintained in stock in the warehouse. Without such a detailed handling procedure, J.C. Penney would not be able to keep up with customer orders or be able to control distribution costs adequately.

Photos courtesy of J.C. Penney.

products. Tandy (Radio Shack) sells products in several categories: radios, phonographs, and video; citizen band radios, walkie-talkies, scanners, and public address systems; audio equipment, tape recorders, and related accessories; electronic parts, batteries, test equipment, and related items; toys, antennas, security devices, timers, and calculators; telephones, intercoms, and pagers; and microcomputers, software, and peripheral equipment.

Several factors should be considered in planning how much merchandise (width and depth of assortment) to carry. Sales should be evaluated. If goods/ service variety is increased, will overall sales go up? Will overall profits rise? Carrying ten varieties of cat food will not necessarily yield greater sales or profits than stocking four varieties. The retailer should also look at the investment costs that occur with a large variety.

Space requirements should be examined in planning. How much space is required for each good or service category? How much space is available? Because available selling space is limited, it should be allocated to those goods and services generating the greatest customer traffic and sales. Turnover should also be considered in the assigning of shelf space.

A careful distinction should be made between scrambled merchandising, complementary goods and services, and substitute goods and services. With scrambled merchandising, the retailer adds unrelated items to generate greater customer traffic and improve profit margins (e.g., a florist adding greeting cards). Handling complementary goods/services enables the retailer to sell basic items and related offerings (e.g., stereo and records, automobile and tires, lawn care service and tree spraying). Both scrambled merchandising and the stocking of complementary goods/services are intended to raise sales. However, the handling of many substitute goods or services (e.g., competing brands of toothpaste) may shift sales from one brand to another but have little impact on a retailer's overall sales.

For some retailers, particularly supermarkets, the proliferation of substitute products has created a difficult problem: how to offer consumers an adequate choice without tying up too much investment and floor space in one product category. At Ralphs' supermarkets, a California-based chain, shelves are stocked with a dozen or more varieties of green peas, chicken noodle soup, and frozen pizza.[11]

In some instances, a retailer may have no choice about stocking a full product line. The manufacturer may insist that the retailer carry the entire line or else the product will not be distributed through the retailer at all. However, more and more, retailers are standing up to manufacturers, and in many cases, retailers stock their own brands next to the manufacturers' brands. As retail chains grow larger, this phenomenon increases. When retailers and manufacturers compete for the shelf space allocated to various brands and for control over the location of displays, this is known as the **battle of the brands.**

A retailer needs to consider the appropriate mix of manufacturer (national), dealer (private), and generic brands that should be carried. **Manufacturer brands** are produced and controlled by manufacturers. These brands are usually well known, are supported by manufacturer advertising, are somewhat presold to consumers, require limited retailer investment, and represent maximum product quality to consumers. Manufacturer brands dominate retail sales for most product categories.

Dealer brands contain names designated by wholesalers or retailers, are more profitable to retailers, are better controlled by retailers, cannot be sold by competing retailers, are less expensive for consumers, and lead to retailer (rather than manufacturer) loyalty. However, with most private-label merchandise, retailers must line up suppliers, arrange for physical distribution and warehousing, sponsor advertising, create in-store displays, and absorb losses from unsold items. Retailers' interest in the sales of their own brands can be shown through the following examples:

❑ In the leading 100 U.S. department store chains, private-label merchandise accounts for 47 per cent of men's sweater sales, 37 per cent of men's woven-sport-shirt sales, 29 per cent of men's dress shirt sales, and 27 per cent of men's knit shirt sales.[12]

❑ Carter Hawley Hale sells more than a dozen different dealer brands in its various store divisions.[13]

❑ At the Lucky Stores' supermarket chain, dealer brands represent about one-fifth of total food sales. Lucky carries dealer brands when they are of good quality, can be sold at low prices, yield good profit margins, and require a moderate advertising effort.[14]

As one expert has noted:

Private label usage and sales have been rising at a pace higher than retail sales in general in recent years. In a stiffening, competitive climate, it's easy to see why. The private label—whether it's the retailer's own creation or a confined label by a branded producer—is viewed as one of the most potent weapons to achieve better margin, to offset the over-distribution of branded and designer names, and, in general, a good way to stand out for reasons of exclusivity.[15]

Generics are unbranded, no-frills goods stocked by some retailers. These items usually receive secondary shelf locations, obtain little or no advertising support, are sometimes of less overall quality than other brands, are stocked in limited assortments, and have plain packages. Generics are controlled by retailers and are priced well below other brands. In U.S. supermarkets carrying them, generics have stabilized at about 2 per cent of food sales. However, in the prescription drug industry, where the product quality of manufacturer brands and generics is virtually identical, generics' share of retail sales has almost doubled in the last decade to over 20 per cent.[16]

There are several other considerations that take on added importance if a retailer moves toward a wider and deeper merchandising strategy:

❑ Risks, merchandise investments, and damages and obsolescence may increase.

❑ Personnel may be spread too thinly, sometimes over dissimilar goods and services.

❑ The positive and negative ramifications of scrambled merchandising may occur.

❑ Inventory control procedures may become much more difficult. Merchandise turnover probably will slow down.

Merchandise assortment planning should be conducted with the use of a basic stock list (for staples), a model stock plan (for items such as fashion merchandise), and a never-out list (for best-sellers). Staple merchandise consists of the regular items carried by a retailer. To a supermarket, staples are milk, bread, canned soup, facial tissues, and so on. To a department store, staples include such items as luggage, cameras, housewares, glassware, and china. Because these items have relatively stable sales (sometimes seasonal) and the basic nature of the merchandise does not change drastically, a retailer can clearly specify the requirements for each of these items. A **basic stock list** specifies the inventory level, color, brand, style category, size, package, and so on for every staple item carried by the retailer.

Assortment planning for fashion merchandise, furniture, and other nonstandardized items is more difficult than for staples because of variations in demand, changes in styles, and the number of sizes and colors that must be carried. With these items, merchandise planning involves two stages. First, product lines, styles, designs, and colors are selected. Second, a **model stock plan** is used to order specific items, such as the number of green, red, and blue pullover sweaters of a certain design by size. With a model stock plan, many items of popular sizes and colors are ordered; nonetheless, small amounts of less popular sizes and colors are ordered to fill out the assortment. For example, a specialty store may stock one Size 18 dress and six Size 10 dresses for each style carried.

Never-out lists are utilized when a retailer plans the stock levels for best-sellers. Items that account for large sales volume are stocked in a manner to ensure that they are always available. Items are added to and deleted from this list as their popularity and their importance to the store vary. For example, when a new Stephen King or Robert Ludlum book is released, bookstores order a large quantity to be sure that they can meet anticipated sales. After the book disappears from newspaper best-seller lists, smaller quantities are maintained.

For virtually all types of retailers, it is usually a good strategy to use a combination of a basic stock list, a model stock plan, and never-out lists. In many cases, these lists may overlap.

When Merchandise Is Stocked

Next, a retailer should ascertain when each type of merchandise would be stocked. For new goods and services, the retailer must decide when they would first be displayed and sold. For established goods and services, the retailer must plan the regular merchandise flow during the year.

To order merchandise properly, the retailer should forecast sales during the year and take into account various other factors: peak seasons, order time, delivery time, routine versus special orders, stock turnover, discounts, and the efficiency of inventory procedures.

As mentioned earlier in the chapter, some goods and services have peak seasons during the year. For these items (e.g., winter coats and boat rentals), a retailer should plan large inventories during the peak periods and less for the off-season. Because some customers like to shop during the off-season, the retailer should not eliminate the items.

A retailer should plan merchandise purchases based on order time and delivery time. How long does it take the retailer to process a merchandise order? After the order is sent to the supplier, how long does it take to receive delivery of the merchandise? By adding these two time periods together, the retailer can get a good idea of the lead time necessary to restock its shelves. For example, if it takes a retailer seven days to process an order and the supplier an additional fourteen days to deliver merchandise, the retailer should begin to order new merchandise at least twenty-one days before the old inventory runs out.

Planning differs for routine versus special orders. A routine order involves the restocking of staples and other regularly sold items. Deliveries are received weekly, monthly, and so on. Accordingly planning and problems are minimized. A special order involves the purchase of merchandise that is not sold regularly. This order involves a lot of planning and close cooperation between retailer and supplier. A special delivery date is usually arranged. Custom furniture is an example of this type of product.

Stock turnover (how quickly merchandise sells) greatly influences how often items must be ordered. Convenience items like milk and bread (which are also highly perishable) have a high turnover rate and must be restocked quite often. Shopping items like refrigerators and color televisions have a lower turnover rate and may be restocked less often.

In deciding when and how often to purchase merchandise, a retailer should consider quantity discounts. Large purchases may result in lower per unit costs.

Also, the use of efficient inventory procedures, such as computerization linked to the Universal Product Code (UPC), would decrease costs and order times while increasing merchandise productivity.

Where Merchandise Is Stored

The last basic merchandise planning decision involves where products are handled. A single-unit retailer usually must determine how much merchandise to place on the selling floor, how much to place in the stockroom, and the use of a warehouse. A multiunit retailer must also allocate merchandise among stores.

Many chain retailers use warehouses as central distribution centers. Merchandise is shipped from the supplier to the warehouses. Products are then allotted and shipped to individual outlets. Some retailers do not use central warehouses. Instead, products are shipped directly to each store. The advantages of central warehousing include reduced transportation and handling costs, the mechanized processing of goods, improved security, the efficient marking of merchandise, the ease of returns, and the smooth flow of merchandise. The major disadvantages of central warehousing are excessive centralized control and potential order-processing delays.

In allocating merchandise among its outlets, a retailer should consider the target market. Products should be carried by a branch store only if the tastes and the needs of the customers served by that branch are satisfied. The more geographically dispersed a retailer is, the more important it is to pinpoint the differences in store product assortments.

Store size should also be considered in allotting products among branch stores. When the target markets are similar, the allotment should be based on sales. If Store A has sales of $1 million and Store B has sales of $2 million, Store B should receive twice as many items as A. Refinements must be made when the target markets are different. Woolworth learned this after placing the wrong items in some of its stores:

> Oh let's say a lady's skirt was selling well in the larger stores where we carried eight different varieties. The theory was take the two best-selling skirts and put them in the smaller stores. Well, it doesn't work that way. There are different customer profiles. Different traffic patterns.[17]

Gathering Information About Consumer Demand

After overall merchandising plans are established, information about the target market is needed. The retailer should gather information about consumer demand before purchasing or repurchasing any merchandise.

The marketing research process, as related to retailing, was detailed in Chapter 6. A good merchandising plan depends on the retailer's ability to generate a relatively accurate sales forecast. After all, the most important merchandising functions performed by a retailer are the anticipation and the satisfaction of customer demand.

In gathering data for merchandising decisions, the retailer has several important sources of information. The most valuable source is the consumer. By researching the target market's demographics, life-styles, and stated purchase plans, a retailer is able to study consumer demand directly.

Other sources of information can be used when direct consumer data are unavailable or insufficient. Suppliers (manufacturers and/or wholesalers) usually do their own sales forecasts and marketing research (e.g., test marketing). They also know how much outside promotional support a retailer will get, and this has an important impact on sales. When closing a deal with the retailer, a supplier may present charts and graphs, showing sales forecasts and promotional support. However, the retailer should remember one significant point: it is the retailer who has direct access to the target market and its needs.

Retail personnel can provide information about consumer demand. Sales and display personnel have direct contact with customers and can pass their observations along to management. The retailer can maintain a **want book** or a **want slip** system. These are tools for recording consumer requests on unstocked or out-of-stock merchandise. The want book is used in smaller stores, and want slips are requests for specific items that are used in larger stores. These tools are very helpful to a retailer's buyers.

Personnel should be encouraged to offer feedback and should not be shut off from making comments based on interaction with consumers. Outside of the customer, a retailer's sales personnel may provide the most useful information for merchandising decisions. Buying personnel learn a lot about consumer demand by visiting suppliers, talking with sales personnel, and observing customer behavior. Usually, buyers are responsible for complete sales forecasts and merchandise plans; then, top management combines the forecasts and plans of individual buyers to obtain overall company projections.

Competitors are another source of information. A conservative retailer may not stock an item until the competition does so. Therefore, comparison shoppers (who look at goods and service assortments and prices of competitors) may be employed. In addition, trade publications report on trends in each area of retailing and provide a legal way of gathering information from competitors. See Figure 11-8 for an example of a competition shopping report.

Other sources may offer useful pieces of information: government sources can show unemployment, inflation, and product safety data; independent news sources conduct their own consumer polls and do investigative reporting; and commercial data can be purchased.

Information should be considered from several of these sources. One type of data is usually insufficient. Whatever the amount of information acquired, the retailer should feel comfortable that it will enable the retailer to make as accurate a decision as possible. For routine merchandising decisions (e.g., milk and bread), limited information may be sufficient. On the other hand, new-car sales can fluctuate widely and require extensive data for sales forecasts.

Determining Merchandise Sources

The next step in merchandise buying and handling is to determine the sources of merchandise. Three major sources exist: company-owned; outside, regularly used; and outside, new.

With the company-owned supplier, a large retailer owns a manufacturing and/or wholesaling facility. The company-owned supplier handles whatever merchandise the retailer requests.

An outside, regularly used supplier is one that is not owned by the retailer but is used regularly by that retailer. The retailer knows the quality of the goods and services and the reliability of the supplier through experience.

An outside, new supplier is one that is not owned by the retailer and has not been dealt with before by that retailer. Therefore, the retailer may be unfamiliar with the quality of the merchandise and the reliability of this supplier. The basic types of outside suppliers (regularly used and new) are shown in Figure 11-9.

These two examples show the complexity involved with choosing suppliers. Sears purchases merchandise from nearly 10,000 suppliers in the United States alone; this means constantly evaluating potential vendors and the performance of existing suppliers. The annual Southern Furniture Market in High Point, North Carolina, is the world's largest wholesale furniture fair. The fair lasts nine days, takes place in ninety locations, involves 1,300 showrooms, draws 40,000 people

COMPETITION SHOPPING REPORT

Store # _____   Date _____

Dept. # _____

Qualified Competition Shopped:

1. _____
2. _____

Our Style No.	Mfr. Model or Style	Description	Our Price	1st Compet. Price	2nd Compet. Price	Store's Recom. Price	Buyer's Recom. Price

Item Seen at Our Competitor's Store which We Should Carry:					
Manufacturer	Mfr. Model or Style	Description	Reg. or List Price	Sale Price	Buyer's Comments

Signature of Shopper   _Store Manager_

FIGURE 11-8
A Competition Shopping Report

(over half of whom are retail buyers), and results in purchases of several hundred million dollars.[18]

In selecting merchandise sources, a retailer should consider several criteria:[19]

❑ Reliability—Will the supplier fulfill all promises?

❑ Price-quality—Who provides the best merchandise at the lowest price?

❑ Order-processing time—How fast will a delivery be made?

❑ Exclusive rights—Will the supplier give exclusive selling rights?

❑ Functions provided—Will the supplier provide shipping, storing, and other functions, if needed?

Source	Characteristics
1. Manufacturer	Physically produces goods, may provide shipping and credit.
2. Full–Service Merchant Wholesaler a. General Merchandise b. Specialty Merchandise c. Rack Jobber	Buys goods from manufacturers, performs many services for retailer (shipping, storing, credit, information, etc.). Carries a very wide assortment. Carries a very deep assortment. Brings and sets up own displays, usually deals with nonfood items in supermarkets and other stores, paid in cash after merchandise is sold, convenient for store.
3. Limited–Service Merchant Wholesaler a. Drop Shipper b. Mail Order c. Cash–and–Carry	Same as full service, except that fewer retailer services are provided and costs are lower. Buys and sells via the telephone (never physically touches merchandise), major task is connecting buyer and seller. Catalog sales to small retailers. Store where small retailers buy and take merchandise.
4. Agents and Brokers	Do not take title to goods (ownership remains with manufacturer), provide a variety of functions for a fee or commission. Included are auction companies, salespeople, and selling agents.

FIGURE 11-9
Outside Sources of Supply

❑ Information—Will the supplier pass along any important goods/service information?

❑ Ethics—Will the supplier fulfill all verbal promises?

❑ Guarantee—Does the supplier stand behind its offerings?

❑ Credit—Can a credit purchase be made?

❑ Long-run relations—Will the supplier be available over an extended period of time?

❑ Reorders—Can the supplier fill reorders?

❑ Markup—Will markup (price margins) be adequate?

❑ Innovativeness—Is the supplier's line innovative or conservative?

❑ Local advertising—Does the supplier advertise in local media?

❑ Risk—How much risk is involved in dealing with the supplier?

❑ Investment—How large are total investment costs?

Evaluating Merchandise

Whatever source is chosen, the retailer should develop a procedure for evaluating the merchandise that is under consideration for purchase. Should each individual unit be examined, or can an item be bought by description?

Three types of evaluation are possible: inspection, sampling, and description. The choice of technique depends on the cost of an item and its regularity of purchase. Inspection occurs when each individual unit is examined before purchase and after delivery. Jewelry and art are two examples of expensive, one-time purchases where the retailer would carefully inspect every item.

Sampling takes place when a large quantity of breakable, perishable, or expensive items is regularly purchased. It becomes inefficient to inspect each piece of merchandise in this situation. Therefore, items are sampled for quality and condition. For example, a retailer purchasing several hundred tomatoes or bananas would not inspect each tomato or banana. Instead, a number of units (a sample) would be examined. The entire selection would be purchased if the sample is satisfactory. An unsatisfactory sample might cause a whole shipment to be rejected. Sampling also occurs on receipt of the merchandise.

Description buying takes place when a retailer purchases standardized, unbreakable merchandise. The items are not inspected or sampled; they are ordered in quantity from a verbal or pictorial description. For example, an office supply retailer can order paper clips, pads, typing paper, and so on from a catalog or order form. When an order is received, only a count of items is conducted.

Negotiating the Purchase

After the merchandise sources have been chosen and the method of evaluating merchandise has been conducted, the retailer has to negotiate the purchase and its terms. A new or special order will usually result in a **negotiated contract.** In this case, the retailer and the supplier carefully negotiate all aspects of the purchase. On the other hand, a regular order or reorder usually results in a **uniform contract.** In this instance, terms are standard or have already been agreed on, and the order is handled in a routine manner.

Many purchase terms must be specified, whether a negotiated or a uniform contract is involved, including

❑ Date of delivery.

❑ Quantity purchased.

❑ Price.

❑ Discounts.

❑ Form of delivery.

❑ Point of transfer of title.

The date of delivery and the quantity purchased should be clearly stated. A retailer can cancel the order if either provision is not carried out. The selling price and the stipulations for discounts are also important. In many cases, the selling price will be discounted for early payments (e.g., "2/10/net 30" means that a 2 per cent discount will be given if the full bill is paid in ten days; the full bill is due in thirty days), trade activities (such as setting up displays), and quantity purchases. Stipulations are necessary for the form of delivery (water, air, truck, rail, and so on) and the party responsible for shipping charges (e.g., FOB factory—free on board—means that a supplier places merchandise with the shipper, but the retailer pays the freight). Last, the point of transfer of title—when ownership changes from supplier to buyer—should be indicated in the contract.

Concluding the Purchase

For many medium-sized and large retailers, purchases are concluded automatically. Computers are used to complete and process orders, and each purchase is fed into the computer's data file. Smaller retailers usually conclude their purchases manually. Orders are written up and processed manually, and purchases are added to the store's book inventory in the same manner.

Multiunit retailers must determine whether to use central, regional, or local approval to conclude purchases: Should central or regional management have the final okay in a purchase, or should the local manager have the final input? The issue was discussed in detail in the buying organization part of this chapter. Advantages and disadvantages accrue to each approval technique.

As mentioned in the previous section, **transfer of title** should be carefully specified with the supplier. Several alternatives are possible:

1. The buyer takes title immediately upon purchase.
2. The buyer assumes ownership after the merchandise is loaded onto the mode of transportation.
3. The buyer takes title when a shipment is received.

RETAILING IN ACTION

Is Haggar's Merchandise Ordering System HOT?

In recent years, foreign apparel manufacturers have had rapidly growing sales. Today, imported merchandise represents about 42 per cent of the apparel sales of retailers in the United States. To improve their competitive position, several American manufacturers (such as Haggar) are developing and enacting better systems for processing merchandise orders from their retailers.

Haggar's system is called Haggar Order Transmission (HOT) and is intended to serve as an industry standard. Via computer hookups, it transmits information from the retailer to the manufacturer to the textile supplier and back to the manufacturer. It monitors participating retailers' inventory levels and reorders automatically when inventory on hand reaches a certain amount:

HOT eliminates the risk of buying foreign-made goods by keeping track of what's selling so that re-

tailers can restock quickly, and customers are more likely to find the merchandise they want when they want it.

Tracking consumer purchases and reordering from apparel and textile manufacturers that are set up to give quick response make it possible for retailers to keep better-rounded stocks and significantly improve their profit and return on investment.

In contrast,

It takes at least eight months for foreign goods to be styled, purchased, made, and shipped to the retailer.

Belk Stores, a 300-unit chain with headquarters in Charlotte, North Carolina, is among the retailers using HOT. Thus far, it has benefited with large sales gains and a reduction in inventory levels (and the related merchandise investment that is necessary).

Source: Based on material in "Haggar Develops HOT Idea to Sew Up Apparel Market," *Marketing News* (February 27, 1987), p. 7.

4. The buyer does not take title until the end of a billing cycle, when the supplier receives payment.

5. The retailer accepts merchandise on consignment and does not own the items. The supplier is paid after merchandise is sold.

It is important that a retailer understand the differences among these alternatives, because its responsibilities and rights differ in each case.

Consignment or **memorandum purchases** are made when the supplier is in a relatively weak position and wants to get the retailer to carry merchandise. In both instances, the retailer does not pay for items until they are sold and has the right to return merchandise. With a consignment deal, the retailer runs no risk because title is not taken; the supplier owns the merchandise until it is sold. With a memorandum deal, risk is still low, but the retailer takes title on delivery and is responsible for damages.

Handling the Merchandise

During this phase, a retailer is concerned with the physical handling of merchandise, which involves various functions: receiving merchandise, marking prices, setting up displays, determining on-floor quantities and assortments, completing customer transactions, arranging for customer delivery or pickup, processing returns and damaged goods, monitoring pilferage, and controlling merchandise. See the color photo portfolio following page 360.

First, items are usually shipped from a supplier to warehouses, for storage and dispersement, or directly to a retailer's store(s). For example, chain supermarkets receive almost 80 per cent of their merchandise through warehouses (operated by themselves or their wholesalers) and a little over one-fifth via deliveries directly from vendors. On the other hand, rather than rely on deliveries from suppliers, Loehmann's (an off-price retailer of high-quality women's apparel) picks up merchandise from its manufacturers, ships items to its own central warehouse, and then delivers them to its stores—all within forty-eight hours.[20] Figure 11-10 illustrates merchandise handling at 7-Eleven.

Next, prices and inventory information are marked on merchandise. Supermarkets estimate that price marking on individual items costs them an amount equal to their annual profits, and they look forward to the time when shelf prices will be sufficient.

Price marking can be conducted in several ways. Small retailers often hand-post prices. Many larger retailers rely on UPC information on packages. Others rely on batch tags, which usually have price and inventory data that are computer- and human-readable; Kimball Systems makes a variety of product tags that contain this information. The Dennison Manufacturing Company produces a system for receiving, marking, and routing merchandise to sales floors. The more information that labels or tags possess, the more efficient the inventory control system. For example, Figure 11-11 shows the Pathfinder printer developed by Monarch Marking Systems. This hand-held device can print UPC-based or OCR-A labels. It can also be connected to a store's computer system.

Store displays and on-floor quantities and assortments depend on the type of store and merchandise involved. Supermarkets usually utilize rack displays and place most inventory on the sales floor. Department stores have all kinds of interior displays and place a lot of inventory in the back room, off the sales floor. Displays and on-floor merchandising are discussed more fully in Chapter 14.

Merchandise handling is not completed until the customer purchases and receives it from the retailer. This involves order taking, credit or cash transactions, packaging, and delivery or pickup. Automation has improved retailer performance in each of these areas.

A procedure for processing returns and damaged goods must also be devel-

FIGURE 11-10
Merchandise Handling at 7-Eleven
Five highly automated centers comprise the most extensive distribution system in retailing, enabling
7-Eleven to respond quickly to customer needs. Reprinted by permission of Southland Corporation.

oped. In particular, a retailer needs to determine who is responsible for customer
returns (the supplier or the retailer) and under what provisions damaged goods
would be accepted for refund (such as the length of time under which a warranty
is honored).

FIGURE 11-11
The Monarch Pathfinder®
Labeler: A Portable
Marking System
The Pathfinder label printer is
fully portable and electronically
controlled. It can produce both
bar codes and human-readable
information. Through this printer,
a store can monitor inventory
movement from receipt of goods
through inventory to sale. Photo
courtesy of Monarch Marking
Systems, Inc., a subsidiary of
Pitney Bowes, Inc.

As detailed in Chapter 10, monitoring and reducing inventory losses due to theft is an aspect of merchandise handling that has rapidly grown in importance. More retailers are taking aggressive actions in dealing with this problem than before, because of the high costs of merchandise theft.

Merchandise control includes evaluating sales, profits, turnover, theft, seasonality, costs, and so on for each goods/service category and item carried by a retailer.[21] Control is generally achieved by developing and maintaining book (perpetual) inventory data, and then periodically conducting a physical inventory count to check the accuracy of the book figures. The latter usually must be adusted to reflect damaged goods, pilferage, and customer returns. An in-depth discussion of this topic appears in the next chapter.

Reordering Merchandise

A plan for reordering merchandise must be developed and implemented for those items that are purchased more than once. Four factors are most important in devising such a plan: order and deliver time, inventory turnover, financial outlays, and inventory versus ordering costs.

Order and delivery time need to be determined. How long would it take for a retailer to process an order and a supplier to fulfill and deliver that order? It is possible that delivery time could be so lengthy that a retailer must reorder while a full inventory still exists. On the other hand, overnight delivery may be available for some items.

The turnover rate for each type of merchandise needs to be calculated. How long would it take for a retailer to sell out its inventory? A fast-selling product allows a retailer to have two choices: order a surplus of items and spread out reorder periods, or keep a low inventory and order frequently (short order periods). A slow-selling item may enable a retailer to reduce its initial inventory level and spread out the reorder period.

The financial outlays that must be made under various purchase plans need to be considered. A large order, which would provide a discount, may involve a large cash outlay. However, a small order, although more expensive per item, would result in lower total costs at any one time (because less inventory is maintained).

Finally, inventory holding versus ordering costs must be measured. The advantages of maintaining a large inventory are customer satisfaction, quantity discounts in purchases, low per item transportation charges, and ease of control and handling. The disadvantages are high investment costs; the greater possibility of obsolescence, deterioration, and damages; storage costs; insurance costs; and opportunity costs. The advantages of placing many orders and keeping a low inventory are low investment, low opportunity costs, low storage costs, and limited damages and obsolescence. The disadvantages are more disappointed customers, higher per unit costs, time delays, partial shipments, service charges, and complex control and handling. Retailers normally try to trade off these two costs by maintaining a large enough inventory to satisfy customers while not keeping a high surplus inventory. Just-in-time inventory planning is aimed at reducing both inventory and ordering costs through closer retailer–supplier relationships.

Re-Evaluating on a Regular Basis

Once a well-integrated merchandise buying and handling plan is established, the retailer should not ignore this process. Re-evaluation should take place on a regular basis. Management should review the buying organization (Step 1 in Figure 11-1), and that organization should review the buying and handling process (Steps 2 through 9). The overall procedure, as well as the handling of individual goods and services, should be constantly monitored.

SUMMARY

A key element in a successful retail strategy is developing and implementing a merchandise plan. Merchandising includes all the activities involved in the buying and selling of goods and services by a retailer.

A merchandise buying and handling plan is an integrated, systematic procedure for acquiring and processing merchandise. Ten steps are involved: (1) establishing a formal or informal buying organization; (2) outlining merchandise plans; (3) gathering information about consumer demand; (4) determining merchandise sources; (5) evaluating merchandise; (6) negotiating the purchase; (7) concluding the purchase; (8) handling the merchandise; (9) reordering merchandise; and (10) re-evaluating on a regular basis.

Buying-organization decisions include the level of formality, degree of centralization, amount of specialization, inside-outside, cooperative efforts, merchandising versus buying, and staffing. Buying includes only the purchasing of goods and services and not the sale of them, whereas merchandising entails both activities. Some retailers separate the buying and selling functions.

Merchandise plans involve four basic decisions. First, in determining what items to handle, a retailer must decide on the quality of merchandise (bottom, top, or middle) to stock and how innovative (progressive or conservative) to be. The product life cycle is a useful tool for projecting the sales of a product over its lifetime and the types of customers who purchase during different time periods.

Second, how much merchandise is stocked is a decision involving width and depth of assortment. A product assortment can range from wide and deep to narrow and shallow. When planning an assortment, many factors should be examined: sales, prof-its, investment costs, space requirements, turnover, complementary and substitute products, manufacturer insistence, and the brand mix.

A third decision required is when merchandise is to be stocked. An accurate sales forecast is necessary for efficient planning. Among the points to be considered are peak seasons, order time, delivery time, routine versus special orders, turnover, discounts, and the efficiency of inventory procedures.

A fourth decision must be made concerning where merchandise is stored. The retailer must determine whether to use warehouses or to have items shipped directly to its store(s). Merchandise also has to be allocated among store branches.

Information from customers, sources of supply, personnel, competitors, and others must be collected to help the retailer forecast and adapt to demand.

A retailer must choose among sources of supply: company-owned; outside, regularly used; and outside, new. Inspection, sampling, and/or description techniques of merchandise evaluation must be planned.

The terms of the purchase have to be negotiated in their entirety, and the purchase must be concluded (automatic-manual, management approval, and transfer of title).

Merchandise handling must be outlined, including receiving, marking, displays, on-floor assortments, customer transactions, delivery or pickup, returns and damaged goods, monitoring inventory theft, and control.

Reorder procedures are necessary and depend on order and delivery time, turnover, outlay, and efficiency.

Finally, the overall merchandising procedure and specific goods and services are regularly reviewed.

QUESTIONS FOR DISCUSSION

1. Describe the merchandise buying and handling process.
2. What are the advantages and disadvantages of decentralized buying?
3. Under what circumstances could a retailer carry a wide range of merchandise quality without hurting its image? When should the quality of merchandise carried be quite narrow?
4. How innovative should each of these retailers be in planning its merchandise? Explain your answers.
   a. Variety store
   b. Sporting-goods store
   c. Small grocer

d. Mail-order computer firm
5. How should a toy retailer use the product life cycle concept?
6. If you were a franchise operator, how would you feel about enforcing constrained decision making with regard to merchandise planning?
7. Why are many retailers hesitant to drop old goods and services?
8. Give several examples of retailers that would fit into each of these merchandise assortment plans.
   a. Narrow-deep
   b. Wide-deep
   c. Wide-shallow
9. How could a college store use a basic stock list, a model stock plan, and never-out lists?
10. What problems may occur if a retailer mistimes purchases?

11. What types of information should a specialty store gather before adding a new brand of perfume?
12. Cite the advantages and disadvantages associated with these merchandise sources for a small art store. How would your answers differ for a large art store chain?
    a. Company-owned
    b. Outside, regularly used
    c. Outside, new
13. Develop a checklist a retailer could use in negotiating purchase terms with its suppliers.
14. Which is more difficult, merchandise planning for a superstore or a children's clothing store? Explain your answer.

NOTES

1. Carole Sloan, "Merchandising the Branches," *Stores* (January 1988), pp. 71–74.

2. Ralph S. Alexander (Chairman), *Marketing Definitions: A Glossary of Marketing Terms* (Chicago: American Marketing Association, 1960), p. 17.

3. "K mart Creates Purchasing Post to Establish Central Reordering," *Discount Store News* (March 2, 1987), p. 66.

4. *Highland Superstores 1987 Annual Report.*

5. "McDonald's, Sears Introduce Clothes for Small Fries," *Marketing News* (September 11, 1987), p. 28.

6. Shirley Cayer, "Arcadia: Hot and on a Roll (Out)," *Stores* (May 1986), pp. 98, 100.

7. Richard Koenig, "Wendy's to Expand Test of 'SuperBar' to Most of Its 1,120 Owned Restaurants," *Wall Street Journal* (October 13, 1987), p. 38; and Scott Hume, "Wendy's Looks for Salad Days," *Advertising Age* (October 19, 1987), p. 102.

8. Adapted from the classic article by Ralph S. Alexander, "The Death and Burial of 'Sick' Products," *Journal of Marketing*, Vol. 28 (April 1964), pp. 1–7.

9. Steve Weiner, "Mobil's Ward Unit Will Stop Selling Some Merchandise," *Wall Street Journal* (March 26, 1986), p. 39.

10. For a good discussion, see Edgar A. Pessemier, *Retail Assortments—Some Theoretical and Applied Problems* (Cambridge, Mass.: Marketing Science Institute, 1980).

11. Betsy Morris, "Food Items Proliferate, Making Grocery Aisles a Corporate Battlefield," *Wall Street Journal* (April 17, 1984), pp. 1, 5.

12. "In Men's Wear, How Big Is PL?" *Stores* (April 1987), p. 23.

13. Hank Gilman, "Retailers Bet Their Designer Wear Can Lure You Past Calvin Klein," *Wall Street Journal* (February 1, 1985), p. 25.

14. *Lucky Stores Corporate Profile*, p. 14.

15. Isadore Barmash, "Private Label: Flux," *Stores* (April 1987), p. 18.

16. Julie Franz, "Ten Years May Be Generic Lifetime," *Advertising Age* (March 23, 1987), p. 76; Pamela G. Hollie, "Generic Drugs in Bigger Role," *New York Times* (July 23, 1984), pp. D1, D5; and "The Big Lie About Generic Drugs," *Consumer Reports* (August 1987), pp. 480–485.

17. Geoffrey Smith, "We're Moving! We're Alive!" *Forbes* (November 21, 1983), pp. 66 ff.

18. *Sears, Roebuck and Company Form 10K*, for the fiscal year ended December 31, 1983, p. 4; and James A. Revson, "The Furniture Connoisseurs Go to Market," *Newsday* (October 15, 1984), At Home Section, pp. 12–13.

19. See "Evaluating Suppliers," *Small Business Report* (December 1986), pp. 44–48.

20. "53rd Annual Report of the Grocery Industry," *Progressive Grocer* (April 1986), p. 26: and *1983 Associated Dry Goods Corporation Annual Report*, p. 10.

21. See William E. Moss and Daniel C. Seeley, "Inventory Management Crucial to Good Customer Service," *Discount Store News* (November 9, 1987), pp. 51, 57.

Consolidated Stores: How a Closeout Retailer Buys Merchandise*

Consolidated Stores, based in Columbus, Ohio, operates well over two hundred Odd Lots stores. (Note: This chain is not affiliated with Revco's Odd Lot or with Job Lot Trading). All of Consolidated's Odd Lots stores are located in small to medium-sized cities. About 95 per cent of Odd Lots' merchandise is purchased by the chain as one-time closeouts. The remaining 5 per cent of Odd Lots' goods are health and beauty aids, tools, and paints.

While Consolidated sends two to three truckloads of goods to each store every other day, the merchandise sent on one Saturday is rarely the same as that sent on the following Saturday. Sources of closeout merchandise include distributors that are loaded with goods, manufacturers' overstocks, and items liquidated as a result of distributor and manufacturer bankruptcies.

Closeout buying is complex, but it is critical to the success of Consolidated. The complexity in buying is due to the discontinuous nature of much of closeout buying. Even though some manufacturers and distributors may not be overloaded with goods on a regular basis, Odd Lots needs to maintain a constant stream of merchandise for distribution and stocking in its stores; this means buying from many different sources. Also, for merchandise purchased as one-time closeouts and sold at deep discount prices, past sales trends are usually both unavailable and inappropriate. Nonetheless, when effectively conducted, closeout buying can provide much excitement for the consumer, generate store opportunities for impulse sales, and result in loyal shoppers visiting Odd Lots stores several times per month (a greater frequency than for more traditional retailers).

Even though its merchandise offerings are discontinuous, Consolidated has a structured buying plan. Management feels that such a plan is necessary for Odd Lots' positioning to

TABLE 1
Consolidated's Odd Lots Merchandising Policies

❑ About 95 per cent of the merchandise carried is purchased strictly as one-time closeouts; the remaining 5 per cent is health and beauty aids (shampoo, toothpaste, mouthwash, cosmetics, etc.).

❑ Since Consolidated purchases most of its merchandise on a closeout basis, there is no or little merchandise continuity. Goods cannot usually be restocked.

❑ Eighty per cent of Odd Lots' sales are in durable goods.

❑ Consolidated prefers to purchase well-known manufacturers' brands. Consumers are more able to determine actual savings and are more inclined to accept guarantees as applicable to these brands. The brands also require less selling effort than private-label merchandise.

❑ Consolidated needs to buy items at about 50 per cent of what they will be priced at in its stores to enable it to maintain a gross margin of between 40 and 42 per cent because of markdowns and unsaleable goods). It needs to price these goods so low that they will be clearly recognized as bargains to retail customers and purchased on an impulse basis.

❑ In contrast to traditional hard goods retailers, which have a large percentage of their business in the fourth quarter of the year, Consolidated's breakdown of sales is first quarter, 20 per cent; second quarter, 25 per cent; third quarter, 25 per cent; and fourth quarter, 30 per cent.

❑ Individual store managers have little say about what merchandise will be ordered for their outlets. On the other hand, they have considerable latitude in terms of where items are displayed.

❑ Consolidated agrees not to advertise certain branded items, and even to remove labels, as a condition of buying merchandise. The firm realizes the importance of its manufacturers' maintaining long-term relationships with their traditional retailers and does not want to negatively affect these relationships. Consolidated's small-town locations are also unlikely to affect manufacturers' more important department and specialty store customers.

*The material in this case is drawn from "Consolidated Ups Share of Close-Out Market," *Chain Store Age Executive* (April 1987), pp. 94–100.

be clear to customers, buyers, store managers, and potential sellers of merchandise; that it ensures the appropriateness of merchandise (in terms of quality, innovativeness, and brands) which is carried; and that it matches the goods available for sale with seasonal patterns. Consolidated's merchandising policies are shown in Table 1.

Consolidated intends to double its Odd Lots outlets in the next two years. It believes that its opportunities for securing closeout merchandise will expand as the number of its stores grows. Furthermore, the firm's wholesale liquidation division helps provide sources of merchandise and supplies for expansion. For example, Consolidated has never bought new store fixtures, and its wholesale liquidation division is able to supply Odd Lots with enough fixtures for 100 of its store openings.

QUESTIONS

1. What kind of retail assortment strategy should Odd Lots seek to maintain? What are the advantages and disadvantages of this strategy?
2. How does buying for a closeout retailer such as Odd Lots differ from buying for a traditional discount store featuring hard goods? Explain.

3. What other sources of goods are appropriate for a closeout retailer such as Odd Lots? Evaluate these sources.
4. Evaluate the policies identified in Table 1.

Case 2

Competitech: How Order-Processing Operations Affect Sales*

Brenda Johnson, Vice-President of Marketing, is confronted with a major problem. Her company, Competitech, a retailer of computer supplies, has recently started to feature a toll-free 800 number in all of its advertisements, direct mail pieces, and catalogs. The public has been responding very well to this easy-to-use, economical method of ordering products. Response rate reports indicate that sales should be up by 12–15 per cent. Actual sales, however, are just about the same as before Competitech started using telemarketing. In studying the report, Johnson has found that her three telemarketing service representatives have received approximately 4,000 calls during the last twenty working days. Brenda Johnson is pleased to note that about fifty per cent of the callers had never previously purchased anything from Competitech. Nonetheless, the fact that the "telephone has been ringing but the cash register has not" is cause for deep concern.

To review the matter further, Brenda has called a meeting of the managers of the telemarketing operation, the shipping and inventory management group, the mail-order department, and customer service. The goal of the meeting is to determine where and how business is being lost. The group of managers is to devote most of its attention to the steps of order processing as depicted in Figure 1 and described below.

The telemarketing personnel, when they receive a call for a computer part or a software package, record the customer's name, address, product identification information, and credit card information, and then they ask the caller where he or she saw a Competitech advertisement or other promotional information. This last bit of information is considered vital by Johnson to learn which media are stimulating the most responses. At the end of a workday, the telemarketers pass all of their orders over to the mail-order department, where that day's orders are combined. The orders are then forwarded to the shipping and inventory management department, which verifies credit worthiness (if the order needs it); and then order pickers fill each request and prepare the products for shipment.

If the requested merchandise is out of stock, a written notice of the shortage and the customer's name and address are presented to the customer service group. Customer service sends a letter apologizing for the temporary delay in completing the order and indicates when Competitech anticipates that the back-order product can be shipped.

The telemarketing group is beginning to receive calls from customers stating that they do not want to wait for back orders and therefore wish to cancel their requests. In some situ-

*This case was prepared and written by Professor John I. Coppett and Professor William A. Staples, University of Houston–Clear Lake, Houston, Texas.

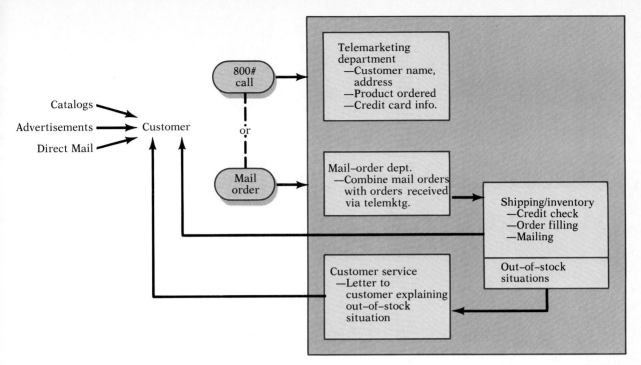

FIGURE 1
Order-Processing Operations

ations, customers have said angrily that if they had known about this delay they would never have done business with Competitech.

Johnson realizes that Competitech not only is losing an opportunity to capitalize on new business but, even worse, is alienating some customers.

QUESTIONS

1. Evaluate the order-processing system shown in Figure 1.
2. How would you alleviate the difficulties being experienced by Competitech?
3. How would order processing and inventory management differ for in-store sales versus telemarketing or mail-order transactions?
4. How could telemarketing be used to more efficiently support the customer services function?

Chapter 12

Financial Merchandise Management

□ **Chapter Objectives** □

1 To describe the major aspects of financial merchandise planning and management
2 To explain the cost and retail methods of accounting
3 To study the merchandise forecasting and budgeting process
4 To examine alternative methods of inventory unit control
5 To integrate dollar and unit merchandising control concepts

Clover Stores is a Philadelphia-based discount chain with twenty-one outlets that has recently begun using the FlowRIGHT merchandise management system developed by Garr Consulting Group (a subsidiary of Touche Ross, a Big Eight accounting company). This system enables Clover to determine when and how much merchandise it must order so that its stores have specific items in stock 90–95 per cent of the time.

With FlowRIGHT, a retailer's

entire merchandise planning process, from initial development of the sales budget to the final execution of each element, is integrated into one. The objective is to improve overall performance of assets as measured by net profits, sales, gross margins, stock turns, and inventory management and distribution costs. The FlowRIGHT process coordinates merchandise planning, inventory management, distribution, store operations, systems support, and organization.

This is how FlowRIGHT works at Clover. First,

individual items of merchandise are identified by sku (stock-keeping unit) number. Then, the shipping performance of the vendors associated with the items is assessed. Next, Clover's buyers make sales forecasts by season for each item. Last, the data are fed into a computer and analyzed. From this process, Clover learns how much lead time is needed to place orders with various vendors and the amount of merchandise to order at one time. It also determines the inventory levels by sku number for each store and whether vendors should send goods to a distribution center or directly to its stores: "You have to have this information, or else you have things stacked over each other in the distribution center. The goal is to get the merchandise to the ultimate consumer as quickly, efficiently, and economically as possible."[1]

Dollar and unit inventory control are key elements of a retailer's financial merchandise plan.

A **financial merchandise plan** specifies exactly which products (goods and services) are purchased, when products are purchased, and how many products are purchased. Both dollar and unit controls are employed in a merchandise plan.

Dollar control refers to the planning and monitoring of the total inventory investment a retailer makes during a stated time period. **Unit control** relates to the quantities of merchandise handled during a stated time period. Dollar controls usually precede unit controls, as a retailer must plan its total dollar investment before making assortment decisions.

Establishing a financial merchandise plan offers several advantages for a retailer:

❏ It controls the amount and value of inventory in each department or store unit during a given period of time. Stock is balanced, and fewer markdowns may be necessary.

❏ It stipulates the amount of merchandise (in terms of investment) that a buyer can purchase during a given period of time. This gives the buyer direction.

❏ It allows the buyer to balance the total inventory investment against planned and actual sales. This improves the return on investment.

❏ It helps determine the retailer's space requirements by estimating beginning-of-month and end-of-month inventory levels.

❏ It can be used to evaluate the performance of buyers. Stock reductions (due to sales and shortages), purchases, markups, and gross margins may be used as performance standards.

❏ It enables the buyer to determine the level of stock shortages, giving an estimate of bookkeeping errors and pilferage.

❏ It can classify slow-moving items, thus allowing increased sales efforts or markdowns to be made.

❏ It helps maintain a proper balance between inventory level and out-of-stock conditions.

This chapter divides financial planning into four main sections: methods of accounting, merchandise forecasting and budgeting, unit control systems, and financial inventory control.

Overview

Retail inventory accounting systems can be complex, since they involve a great number of data. A retailer's dollar control system must provide information such as the sales and purchases made by the retailer during a budget period, the value of beginning and ending inventory, the extent of markups and markdowns, and merchandise shortages.

Table 12-1 shows a profit-and-loss statement for Handy Hardware Store for the period from January 1, 1988, through June 30, 1988. The sales amount is from the store's total receipts during this time period. Beginning inventory is calculated by a count of the merchandise in stock on January 1, 1988, which is recorded at cost. Purchases (at cost) and transportation charges (costs incurred in shipping merchandise from the supplier to the retailer) are derived by adding the invoice slips for all merchandise bought by the store during this time period.

Together, beginning inventory, purchases, and transportation charges equal the cost of **merchandise available for sale.** Since Handy Hardware does a physical inventory every six months, ending inventory is determined by a count of the merchandise in stock on June 30, 1988, which is recorded at cost (Handy codes each item so costs can be derived for each item in stock). The **cost of goods sold** equals the cost of merchandise available for sale minus the value of

Inventory Valuation: The Cost and Retail Methods of Accounting

TABLE 12-1
Handy Hardware Store Profit-and-Loss Statement,
January 1, 1988–June 30, 1988

Sales		$208,730
Less cost of goods sold:		
Beginning inventory (at cost)	$ 22,310	
Purchases (at cost)	144,700	
Transportation charges	1,300	
Merchandise available for sale	$168,310	
Ending inventory (at cost)	45,250	
Cost of goods sold		123,060
Gross profit		$ 85,670
Less operating expenses:		
Salaries	$ 35,000	
Advertising	12,500	
Rental	8,000	
Other	13,000	
Total operating expenses		68,500
Net profit before tax		$ 17,170

ending inventory. Sales less cost of goods sold yields **gross profit**, while **net profit** is gross profit minus retail operating expenses.

Retailers typically have substantially different information needs from manufacturers. Retail assortments are larger; costs cannot be printed on cartons unless coded (because of customer inspection). Stock shortages are greater; sales are more frequent; and retailers require monthly, not quarterly, profit data.

Two inventory accounting systems are available to a retailer: the cost and retail methods of accounting. The cost accounting system values merchandise at cost plus in-bound transportation charges. The retail accounting system values merchandise at current retail prices.

The cost and retail inventory methods are described and analyzed here on the basis of the frequency with which merchandise information is received, difficulties in completing a physical inventory, difficulties in maintaining records, the ease of settling insurance claims (in case of inventory damage), the extent to which stock shortages can be calculated, and the complexities of the systems.

The Cost Method

In the **cost method of accounting**, the cost to the retailer of each item is recorded on an accounting sheet or is coded on a price tag or merchandise container. When a physical inventory is conducted, the costs of each item must be ascertained, the quantity of each item in stock counted, and the total inventory value at cost calculated.

One method of coding the cost of merchandise is to use a ten-letter equivalency system, such as M = 0, N = 1, O = 2, P = 3, Q = 4, R = 5, S = 6, T = 7, U = 8, and V = 9. An item coded with the letters *STOP* would have a cost value of $67.23. This technique is useful as an accounting tool and also for retailers who allow price bargaining by customers (profit per item is easy to calculate).

The cost method can be used when a retailer computes physical or book inventories. A physical inventory involves an actual count of merchandise, whereas a book inventory depends on bookkeeping entries.

A Physical Inventory System Using the Cost Method
With this system, ending inventory is determined by an actual count of the merchandise remaining in stock at the close of a sales period; ending inventory

is recorded at cost. A retailer cannot calulate gross profit until after ending inventory is valued. Thus, a retailer using the cost method and relying on a **physical inventory system** can determine its gross profit only as often as it conducts a complete physical inventory. Because most retailers undertake physical inventories just once or twice a year, strict reliance on the physical method would impose severe limitations on the retailer's merchandise planning.

By using only the physical inventory method, a retailer could also be prevented from calculating inventory shortages (resulting from pilferage, unrecorded breakage, and so on) because the ending inventory is determined by adding the costs of all items in stock. What the ending inventory level should be is not computed.

A Book Inventory System Using the Cost Method

A **book inventory system** (commonly called a **perpetual inventory system**) avoids the problem of infrequent financial statements by keeping a running total of the value of all inventory on hand at cost at a given time. Therefore, end-of-month inventory values can be computed without a physical inventory, and frequent financial statements can be developed. In addition, a book inventory allows a retailer to see the level of shortages by comparing projected inventory values with actual inventory values via a physical inventory.

A retailer maintains a perpetual system by regularly recording purchases and adding them to the existing inventory value; sales are then subtracted to arrive at the new current inventory value (all at cost). Table 12-2 shows a book (perpetual) inventory system for Handy Hardware for the period from July 1, 1988, to December 31, 1988. Note that the ending inventory in Table 12-1 becomes the beginning inventory in Table 12-2.

Table 12-2 assumes that merchandise costs are relatively constant and that monthly sales at cost are easily computed. However, suppose that merchandise costs rise. How, then, would inventory be valued? Two methods of costing inventory are **FIFO** (first-in–first-out) and **LIFO** (last-in–first-out).

With the FIFO method, it is logically assumed that old merchandise is sold first and that new items remain in inventory. Under the LIFO method, it is assumed that new merchandise is sold first and that old stock remains in inventory. FIFO matches inventory value with the current cost structure, while LIFO matches current sales with the current cost structure. During periods of rising inventory values, LIFO offers retailers a tax advantage. According to a study by the accounting firm of Peat, Marwick, Mitchell & Co., the vast majority of large retailers use the LIFO method.[2]

In Figure 12-1, the FIFO and LIFO methods of inventory valuation are illus-

TABLE 12-2
Handy Hardware Store Perpetual Inventory System,
July 1, 1988–December 31, 1988*

Date	Beginning-of-Month Inventory (at Cost)	+	Net Monthly Purchases (at Cost)	–	Monthly Sales (at Cost)	=	End-of-Month Inventory (at Cost)
7/1/88	$45,250		$ 20,000		$ 31,200		$ 34,050
8/1/88	34,050		14,000		19,200		28,850
9/1/88	28,850		13,800		14,400		28,250
10/1/88	28,250		22,000		14,400		35,850
11/1/88	35,850		25,200		20,400		40,650
12/1/88	40,650		7,950		30,600		18,000
		Total	$102,950		$130,200		(as of 12/31/88)

*Transportation charges are not included in computing inventory value in this table.

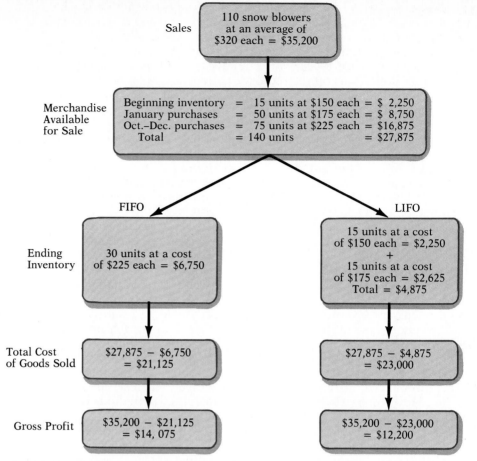

FIGURE 12-1
Applying FIFO and LIFO Inventory Methods to Handy Hardware,
January 1, 1988–December 31, 1988

trated for Handy Hardware's snow blowers for the period January 1, 1988, to December 31, 1988; the store carries only one model of snow blower. Handy has determined that it sold 110 snow blowers in 1988 at an average retail price of $320. Handy knows that it started 1988 with a beginning inventory of 15 snow blowers, which it purchased for $150 each. During January 1988, it bought 50 snow blowers at $175 each; from October to December 1988, Handy bought another 75 snow blowers for $225 apiece. Since Handy sold 110 snow blowers in 1988, as of the close of business on December 31, it had 30 units remaining in inventory.

Using the FIFO method, Handy would assume that its beginning inventory and initial purchases were sold first. The 30 snow blowers remaining in inventory would be valued at $225 each, resulting in a total cost of goods sold of $21,125 and gross profit of $14,075. Using the LIFO method, Handy would assume that the most recently purchased items were sold first and that the remaining inventory would consist of beginning goods and early purchases. Fifteen of the snow blowers remaining in inventory would be valued at $150 each and 15 at $175 apiece, resulting in a total cost of goods sold of $23,000 and gross profit of $12,200. Accordingly, the FIFO method presents a more accurate picture of the cost of goods sold and ending inventory. The LIFO method indicates a lower profit, which would lead to the payment of lower taxes, but the value of ending inventory would be understated.

The retail method of inventory, which combines FIFO and LIFO concepts, is explained later in this chapter. A fuller discussion of FIFO and LIFO may be found in any basic accounting text.

Disadvantages of Cost-Based Inventory Systems

Cost-based physical and perpetual systems have significant disadvantages. First, both require a retailer to assign costs to each item in stock (and to each item sold). Therefore, during periods when merchandise costs are changing, cost-based inventory valuation systems are most useful only for retailers that have low inventory turnover, limited variety and assortments, and high average prices. Examples of retailers with these characteristics are car dealers, furriers, furniture stores, and large-appliance dealers.

Second, neither cost-based method provides for adjusting inventory values to reflect style changes, end-of-season markdowns, or sudden surges of demand (which may increase prices). Thus, the ending value of inventory, based on the cost of the merchandise, may not reflect its actual worth. This discrepancy would be particularly troublesome when the ending inventory valuation is used in calculating required insurance coverage or filing insurance claims for losses.

Despite these disadvantages, retailers that make the products they sell—such as bakeries, restaurants, and furniture workrooms—often keep records on a cost basis. A department store with these operations (or others involving manufacturing) would use the cost method for them and the retail method for other departments.

The Retail Method

With the **retail method of accounting,** closing inventory value is determined by calculating the average relationship between the cost and retail value of merchandise available for sale during the period. While the retail method overcomes the disadvantages of the cost method, it requires a detailed bookkeeping system. The complexity of the retail method is due to the fact that inventory is valued in retail dollars and must be converted to cost for a retailer to compute gross margin (gross profit).

There are three basic steps in computing an ending inventory value, using the retail method:

1. Calculating the cost complement.
2. Calculating deductions from retail value.
3. Converting retail inventory value to cost.

Calculating the Cost Complement

In the retail method, the value of beginning inventory, net purchases, additional markups, and transportation charges are all included. The value of beginning inventory and net purchase amounts (purchases less returns) are recorded at both cost and retail levels. Additional markups represent the extra revenues received by a retailer because of increases in its selling prices during the period covered, due to inflation or unexpected demand. Transportation charges are the retailer's costs for shipping the merchandise it purchases from suppliers to the retailer. Table 12-3 shows the total merchandise available for sale at cost and at retail for Handy Hardware for the period from July 1, 1988 to December 31, 1988, using cost data from Table 12-2.

TABLE 12-3

Handy Hardware Store, Calculating Merchandise Available for Sale at Cost and at Retail, July 1, 1988–December 31, 1988

	At Cost	At Retail
Beginning inventory	$ 45,250	$ 69,600
Net purchases	102,950	170,263
Additional markups	—	8,200
Transportation charges	1,746	—
Total merchandise available for sale	$149,946	$248,063

Based on the data in Table 12-3, the average relationship of cost to retail value for all merchandise available for sale by Handy Hardware during the six-month period can be calculated. This concept is called the **cost complement**:

$$\text{Cost complement} = \frac{\text{Total cost valuation}}{\text{Total retail valuation}}$$

$$= \frac{\$149,946}{\$248,063}$$

$$= 0.6045$$

Because the cost complement is 0.6045, or 60.45 per cent, an average of 60.45 cents of every retail sales dollar is comprised of Handy Hardware's merchandise cost.

Calculating Deductions from Retail Value

The retail valuation process must reflect any deductions from the total merchandise available for sale. In addition to sales to customers, deductions would include any markdowns (such as special sales, reduced prices on discontinued merchandise, and reduced prices on end-of-season and shopworn merchandise), employee discounts, and stock shortages (due to pilferage, unrecorded breakage, and so on). While sales, markdowns, and employee discounts can be recorded throughout an accounting period, a physical inventory is necessary to compute stock shortages.

From Table 12-3, it is known that Handy Hardware had a retail value of merchandise available for sale of $248,063 during the period from July 1, 1988, to December 31, 1988. This amount was reduced by sales of $211,270 and recorded markdowns and employee discounts of $7,017. The ending book value of inventory at retail as of December 31, 1988, was $29,776. See Table 12-4.

Actual **stock shortages** are simple to compute from a physical inventory using the retail method. The retail book value of ending inventory is compared to the actual physical ending inventory value. If the book value is greater than the

TABLE 12-4

Handy Hardware Store, Computing Ending Retail Book Value, as of December 31, 1988

Merchandise available for sale (at retail)		$248,063
Less deductions:		
Sales	$211,270	
Markdowns	5,817	
Employee discounts	1,200	
Total deductions		218,287
Ending retail book value of inventory		$ 29,776

TABLE 12-5

Handy Hardware Store, Computing Stock Shortages and Adjusting Retail Book Value, as of December 31, 1988

Ending retail book value of inventory	$29,776
Physical inventory (at retail)	28,235
Stock shortages (at retail)	1,541
Adjusted ending retail book value of inventory	$28,235

physical ending inventory, shortages exist. Table 12-5 shows the results of a physical inventory by the Handy Hardware Store. Shortages of $1,541 (at retail) are revealed, and the book value is adjusted accordingly. While Handy recognizes that the shortages are due to pilferage (by customers and/or employees), book-keeping errors (not recording markdowns, employee discounts, and breakage), and overshipments not billed to customers, it cannot determine the proportion of the shortages caused by each of these factors.

In rare instances, a physical inventory may reveal **stock overages,** which represent the excess of physical ending inventory value over book value. Overages may be due to errors in conducting a physical inventory or in maintaining a book inventory. If overages occur, the ending retail book value of inventory must be adjusted upward.

Since a retailer must undertake a physical inventory to compute shortages (overages), and a physical inventory is taken only once or twice a year, shortages (overages) are often estimated for monthly merchandise budgets.

Converting Retail Inventory Value to Cost

Next, the retailer must convert the adjusted retail book value of ending inventory to cost in order to compute dollar gross margin (gross profit). The ending inventory at cost equals the adjusted ending retail book value multiplied by the cost complement. In the case of Handy Hardware, this would be:

$$\text{Ending inventory (at cost)} = \text{Adjusted ending retail book value} \times \text{Cost complement}$$

$$= \$28,235 \times .6045$$

$$= \$17,068$$

This equation does not yield the exact ending inventory at cost for Handy Hardware but approximates the value based on the average relationship between cost and retail selling price for all merchandise available for sale.

The adjusted ending inventory at cost can then be used to find gross profit. See Table 12-6. For Handy Hardware, the July 1, 1988, to December 31, 1988, cost of goods sold was $132,878, resulting in gross profit of $78,392. By deducting operating expenses of $69,500, Handy would see that net profit before tax for that six-month period was $8,892.

Advantages of the Retail Method

In comparing the cost and the retail accounting methods, several strengths of the retail method are evident:

1. The retail method is easy to use when taking a physical inventory. Therefore, the chances of error in the valuation of merchandise are reduced because the physical inventory is recorded at retail value and costs do not have to be decoded.

2. Because the task of taking a physical inventory is simplified, these inventories can be completed more frequently. This frequency enables the retailer

TABLE 12-6

Handy Hardware Store Profit-and-Loss Statement, July 1, 1988–December 31, 1988

Sales		$211,270
Less cost of goods sold:		
Total merchandise available for sale (at cost)	$149,946	
Adjusted ending inventory (at cost)*	17,068	
Cost of goods sold		132,878†
Gross profit		$ 78,392
Less operating expenses:		
Salaries	$35,000	
Advertising	12,500	
Rental	8,000	
Other	14,000	
Total operating expenses		69,500
Net profit before tax		$ 8,892

*Adjusted ending inventory (at cost) = Adjusted retail book value × Cost complement = $28,235 × .6045 = $17,068

†Cost of goods sold = Monthly sales (at cost) + Transportation charges + Stock shortages (at cost) = $130,200 + $1,746 + $932 = $132,878

to be more aware of slow-moving items and stock shortages and to take appropriate corrective actions.

3. The physical inventory method at cost requires a physical inventory for the preparation of a profit-and-loss statement. In contrast, the retail method allows a retailer to prepare a profit-and-loss statement on the basis of book inventory figures. These figures can be adjusted to account for stock shortages between physical inventory periods. Because frequent statements are necessary if a firm is to examine profit trends by department, a book inventory system is superior to a physical system at cost.

4. A complete record of ending book values is extremely important in determining the appropriate level of insurance coverage and in settling insurance claims. The retail book method gives a firm an estimate of inventory value throughout the year. Because physical inventories are usually taken when merchandise levels are low, the book value at retail allows companies to plan insurance coverage during peak periods and shows the values of the goods on hand (in case of a claim adjustment). The retail method is accepted in insurance claims.

Limitations of the Retail Method

The greatest limitation of the retail method is the bookkeeping burden of recording price changes. The ending book inventory figures can be correctly computed only if the following are accurately noted: purchases, transportation charges, markups, markdowns, employee discounts, transfers from other departments or stores, returns, and sales. Although store personnel are freed from the burden of taking many physical inventories, the ending book value at retail may be a meaningless figure unless these required data are precisely recorded. With computerization, this potential problem is reduced.

A second limitation of the retail method is that the cost complement is an average figure based upon the total cost of merchandise available for sale and its total retail value. Therefore it is possible that the resultant ending inventory value only approximates the true cost of the merchandise on hand. This is especially true if fast-selling merchandise has different markups from slow-selling merchandise and/or if there are wide variations among the markups of goods within a single department.

Familiarity with the retail and cost methods of inventory is essential for understanding the financial merchandise-planning material described in the balance of this chapter.

Dollar control involves the process of planning and controlling the total inventory investment during a specified time period. Figure 12-2 illustrates the dollar control process. As can be seen, the process is broken down into six successive stages: designating control units, forecasting sales, inventory-level planning, retail-reduction planning, planning purchases, and profit-margin planning.

It is important that the sequential nature of this process be followed. A change in any one stage affects all the stages after it. For example, if a company using the retail method underestimates its markdowns by $20,000 during a monthly period, it must revise planned purchases (up $20,000) and planned profit margins to reflect the markdowns.

Merchandise Forecasting and Budgeting: Dollar Control

Designating Control Units

Merchandise forecasting and budgeting require the selection of **control units;** these are the merchandise categories for which data are gathered. It is important that control unit classifications be narrow enough to isolate opportunities and problems with specific lines of merchandise. A retailer wishing to control merchandise within departments must separately record data relating to dollar allotments for each category.

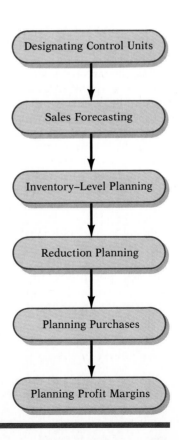

FIGURE 12-2
The Merchandise Forecasting and Budgeting Process: Dollar Control

387

As an example, knowing that total markdowns in a department are 20 per cent above last year's level is less valuable than knowing the specific merchandise lines in which large markdowns are taken. It should be noted that a retailer can broaden its control system by summarizing the categories that comprise a department. However, a broad category cannot be broken down into components. Therefore, it is better to err on the side of too much information than too little.

It is also helpful to select control units that are consistent with other company data and trade association data, wherever possible. Intracompany comparisons are meaningful only when the classification method is stable over time. A classification system that shifts over time because of fashions or fads does not allow comparisons between time periods. External comparisons can be made if control systems are similar (e.g., company versus trade associations).

Inventory may be categorized on the basis of departments, classifications within a department, standard merchandise classifications, and price line classifications.

Adequate information may be obtained by specifying departmental categories. Thus, even a small specialty shop selling ladies' sportswear should acquire data on a departmental basis for buying, inventory control, and markdown decisions. The broadest practical division of control is the department unit, in that this unit allows the retailer to evaluate the performance of each general merchandise grouping or buyer.

Classification merchandising divides each department into related types of merchandise. For example, a houseware department needs data not only on overall performance but also on the performance of electric appliances—food preparation, electric appliances—fans, knives—gourmet, knives—regular, kitchen gadgets, and so on in order to plan merchandise activities.

About twenty years ago, the National Retail Merchants Association (NRMA) developed a **Standard Merchandise Classification,** useful for a wide range of retailers and products. The NRMA Financial Executives Division annually publishes *Merchandising and Operating Results of Department and Specialty Stores* using its classification system. In addition, tailor-made standard merchandise classifications are also popular for different retailer types. For example, published yearly is *Progressive Grocer*'s "Supermarket Sales Manual," which relies on standard merchandise classifications appropriate to that industry.

Price line classifications involve the analysis of retail sales, inventories, and purchases by retail price category. This analysis has special utility when different prices of the same product type are offered to different customers (e.g., $20 power tools for do-it-yourselfers and $135 power tools for contractors). Retailers with wide assortments are frequently involved with price line control. As a case in point, a men's clothing department, for merchandise budgeting purposes, may want to differentiate between sports jackets selling in the $79–$99 price range and those selling in the $139–$179 price range. Such diverse categories of sports jackets are usually sold to different customers or to the same customers for different purposes.

After the appropriate dollar control unit is determined, all transactions—such as sales, purchases, transfers, markdowns, and employee discounts—must be recorded under the proper classification number. For instance, if house paint is Department 25 and brushes are 25-1, all transactions must carry these category designations.

Sales Forecasting

Companywide and departmentwide sales of larger retailers are often forecast by the use of statistical techniques such as trend analysis, time series analysis, and multiple-regression analysis. A discussion of these techniques is beyond the

How Have Zayre's Sales Forecasts Been Off the Mark?

In fiscal 1988, Zayre Corporation's discount department store division had a $14-million operating loss, after recording a $130-million operating profit in 1987. This result was largely due to ineffective merchandising decisions that could be traced to poor sales forecasts. In some cases, it was too optimistic; in others, it greatly underestimated customer demand. Both of these errors had negative effects on sales.

Zayre's nearly four hundred stores featured many goods that were not desired by consumers, such as women's dresses that were out of fashion:

In the women's department we took a tremendous beating. We were fully stocked, but sales were disappointing. What didn't sell? I wouldn't know where to begin.

To attract customers to its higher-priced, higher-profit merchandise, Zayre's ran special sales on everyday goods such as disposable diapers and paper towels to increase customer traffic. But this did not work: "We practically gave these items away. Yet, it didn't help boost overall sales as we would have liked."

At the same time it was having trouble selling its less popular merchandise, Zayre's stores ran out of its best-selling staples: "In the all-important Christmas selling season, we got hurt. We were out of basics, like men's dress shirts, underwear, brand-name toothpaste, aspirin."

Zayre's misfortunes bear out this retail merchandising adage: You've got to have the right goods in the right place at the right time in the right quantity.

Source: Based on material in Joseph Pereira, "Zayre's Major Task Is to Re-Store Itself," *Wall Street Journal* (March 11, 1988), p. 6.

scope of this text. It should be noted that few small retailers use those procedures; they rely more on "guesstimates," projections based on past experience.

Sales forecasting for classifications within departments, for standard merchandise classifications, and for price line classifications generally relies on more qualitative techniques, even for larger firms. One way of forecasting sales for these narrower categories is first to project sales on a companywide basis and then to judgmentally break down the overall figure into component classifications, based on external and internal company factors.

Perhaps the most important element of any budgetary process is an accurate sales forecast. An incorrect estimate of future sales throws off the entire process, because of its effect on the other steps in budgeting. A sales forecast must carefully incorporate external variables that affect sales, internal store factors that can influence sales, and seasonal trends.

External factors affecting future sales include population size, changes in disposable income, changes in the age distribution of the population, mobility of the population, the number and size of competitors, the economy, and changes in the life-style of the target market.

Internal store factors impacting on future sales include additions and deletions of merchandise lines, changes in promotion and credit policies, changes in the hours of business, the opening of new stores, and the remodeling of existing stores. Seasonal variations must also be taken into account in developing a sales forecast. For example, yearly toy sales should not be estimated from December sales alone.

A retailer can estimate future sales by examining past trends and projecting future growth (based on external and internal factors). Table 12-7 shows such a forecast for Handy Hardware. However, the forecast should be regarded only as

TABLE 12-7
Handy Hardware Store, A Simple Sales Forecast by Product Control Unit

Product Control Units	Actual Sales 1988	Projected Growth/ Decline (%)	Sales Forecast 1989
Lawn mowers/snow blowers	$100,000	+10.0	$110,000
Paint and supplies	64,000	+ 3.0	65,920
Hardware supplies	54,000	+ 8.0	58,320
Plumbing supplies	44,000	− 4.0	42,240
Power tools	44,000	+ 6.0	46,640
Garden supplies/chemicals	34,000	+ 4.0	35,360
Housewares	24,000	− 6.0	22,560
Electrical supplies	20,000	+ 4.0	20,800
Ladders	18,000	+ 6.0	19,080
Hand tools	18,000	+ 9.0	19,620
Total year	$420,000	+ 4.9	$440,540

an estimate, subject to revisions. The merchandise plan should be a flexible buying tool.

The firm should be aware that some factors are difficult to incorporate into a sales forecast, such as merchandise shortages, major shifts in consumer purchasing habits, strikes by store personnel, economic factors affecting the earnings of customers, and the enactment of new government legislation.

After an annual sales forecast is made, it is broken down into planning periods (such as quarterly or monthly). In retailing, monthly sales forecasts are usually required. To acquire these more specific estimates, a retailer should use a **monthly sales index,** which it calculates by dividing each month's actual sales by average monthly sales and multiplying the results by 100.

For example, Table 12-8 shows actual monthly sales and monthly sales-index calculations for Handy Hardware in 1988. The data reveal that the store is highly seasonal, with peaks occurring during the late spring and early summer (for lawn mowers, garden supplies, house paint and supplies, and so on) and during the Christmas season (for lighting fixtures, snow blowers, and gifts).

TABLE 12-8
Handy Hardware Store, 1988 Sales by Month

Month	Actual Sales	Monthly Sales Index*
January	$ 23,400	67
February	20,432	58
March	24,000	69
April	32,800	94
May	56,098	160
June	52,000	148
July	52,180	149
August	31,400	90
September	23,452	67
October	23,400	67
November	33,442	96
December	47,396	135
Total yearly sales	$420,000	
Average monthly sales	$ 35,000	
Average monthly index		100

*Monthly sales index = (Monthly sales/Average monthly sales) × 100

TABLE 12-9
Handy Hardware Store, 1989 Sales Forecast by Month

Month	Actual Sales 1988	Monthly Sales Index	Monthly Sales Forecast 1989*
January	$ 23,400	67	$36,712 × .67 = $ 24,597
February	20,432	58	36,712 × .58 = 21,293
March	24,000	69	36,712 × .69 = 25,331
April	32,800	94	36,712 × .94 = 34,509
May	56,098	160	36,712 × 1.60 = 58,739
June	52,000	148	36,712 × 1.48 = 54,334
July	52,180	149	36,712 × 1.49 = 54,701
August	31,400	90	36,712 × .90 = 33,041
September	23,452	67	36,712 × .67 = 24,597
October	23,400	67	36,712 × .67 = 24,597
November	33,442	96	36,712 × .96 = 35,244
December	47,396	135	36,712 × 1.35 = 49,561
Total sales	$420,000		Total sales forecast $440,540†
Average monthly sales	$ 35,000		Average monthly forecast $ 36,712

*Monthly sales forecast = Average monthly forecast × (Monthly index/100). In this equation, the monthly income is computed as a fraction of 1.00 rather than 100.
†There is a small rounding error.

In Table 12-8, the average monthly sales for the year are $35,000 ($420,000/ 12). As the table indicates, the monthly sales index for January is 67 [($23,400/ $35,000) × 100]; other monthly indexes are calculated similarly. The sales indexes show the percentage deviations of each month's sales from average monthly sales. Therefore, the May index of 160 means that sales in May are 60 per cent higher than average monthly sales. The October index of 67 means that sales in October are 33 per cent below the average.

Once monthly sales indexes are determined, a retailer can forecast monthly sales, based on a yearly sales estimate. Table 12-9 demonstrates how Handy Hardware's monthly sales can be forecast if next year's (1989's) average monthly sales are expected to be $36,712. May sales are projected to be $58,739 ($36,712 × 1.60). October sales would be $24,597 ($36,712 × 0.67).

Inventory-Level Planning

After a retailer forecasts sales for a specified time period, it must plan the inventory levels for that period. Inventory must be sufficient to meet sales expectations, allowing a margin for error. Among the techniques used to plan inventory requirements are the basic stock method, the percentage variation method, the weeks' supply method, and the stock-to-sales ratio method.

The **basic stock method** dictates that a retailer carry more items in stock than are expected to be sold during a specified time period. In the basic stock plan, a retail buyer purchases an amount equal to planned sales plus a basic stock:

Basic stock = Average monthly stock at retail − Average monthly sales

Beginning-of-month planned inventory level (at retail) = Planned monthly sales + Basic stock

For example, if Handy Hardware with an average monthly sales forecast of $36,712 wants to have extra stock on hand equal to 10 per cent of 1989 average monthly sales (or $3,671) and expects January 1989 sales to be $24,597:

Basic stock $= (\$36,712 \times 1.10) - \$36,712$

$= \$40,383 - \$36,712 = \$3,671$

Beginning-of-January
planned inventory level $= \$24,597 + \$3,671 = \$28,268$
(at retail)

The basic stock method gives a retailer a cushion in case sales are higher than anticipated, merchandise shipments are delayed, and customers want to select from a variety of items. This method is best when inventory turnover is low or sales are erratic throughout the year.

The **percentage variation method** is recommended when stock turnover is more than six times a year or relatively stable, since it results in planned monthly inventories that are closer to the monthly average than other techniques. With this method, the actual stock on hand during any month varies from average planned monthly stock by only half of the month's variation from average estimated monthly sales:

Beginning-of-month   Planned average monthly stock at retail
planned inventory level $= \times \frac{1}{2}$ [1 + (Estimated monthly sales/
(at retail)   Estimated average monthly sales)]

If Handy Hardware plans average monthly stock of $40,383 and November sales are estimated as 4 per cent less than average monthly sales of $36,712, the store's planned inventory level at the beginning of November 1989 would be:

Beginning-of-November
planned inventory level $= \$40,383 \times \frac{1}{2}$ [1 + ($\$35,244/\$36,712$)]
(at retail)

$= \$40,383 \times \frac{1}{2} \ (1.96) = \$39,575$

However, for Handy Hardware, the percentage variation method is not a good one for it to use because of its variable sales. With that method, Handy would plan a beginning-of-December inventory level of $47,450 (based on average stock of $40,383), less than it expects to sell.

The **weeks' supply method** involves planning sales on a weekly basis, so that stock on hand is equal to several weeks' anticipated sales. This method assumes that the inventory carried is in direct proportion to sales. Accordingly, too much merchandise may be stocked in peak selling periods (when turnover is high) and too little during slow selling periods:

Beginning-of-month
planned inventory level $=$ Average weekly sales $\times$ Number of
(at retail)   weeks to be stocked

If Handy Hardware forecasts average weekly sales of $5,478.54 during the period from January 1, 1989, through March 31, 1989, and it wants to stock 13 weeks of merchandise (based on expected turnover in the first part of 1989), beginning inventory would be $71,221:

Beginning-of-January
planned inventory level $= \$5,478.54 \times 13 = \$71,221$
(at retail)

The **stock-to-sales ratio** assumes that a retailer wants to maintain a specified ratio of goods-on-hand to sales. A stock-to-sales ratio of 1.3 means that if Handy

Hardware plans sales of $34,509 in April 1989, it should have $44,862 worth of merchandise available during the month. Like the weeks' supply method, the stock-to-sales ratio tends to adjust inventory levels more drastically than changes in sales require.

Industrywide stock-to-sales ratios are available from sources such as *Merchandising and Operating Results of Department and Specialty Stores* (New York: National Retail Merchants Association, annual), *Industry Norms and Key Business Ratios* (New York: Dun & Bradstreet, annual), and *Annual Statement Studies* (Philadelphia: Robert Morris Associates). Thus, a retailer can compare its ratios with other firms'.

Reduction Planning

Retail reductions include markdowns, employee and other discounts, and stock shortages. They represent the difference between beginning inventory plus purchases during the period and sales plus ending inventory. It is essential that a firm estimate and plan reductions, not just wait for them to occur:

$$\text{Planned reductions} = \begin{array}{l}(\text{Beginning inventory} + \text{Planned purchases}) \\ - (\text{Planned sales} + \text{ending inventory})\end{array}$$

In addition to forecasting sales, a retailer should project the level of markdowns (reductions in price to stimulate merchandise sales), employee and other discounts (reductions in price given to employees, senior citizens, clergy, and others), and stock shortages (caused by pilferage, breakage, and bookkeeping errors) over the budget period.

Reduction planning for a retailer involves two specific factors: determining the total reductions for the budget period and distributing these reductions by month. A retailer should study the following in planning total reductions for the budget period:

❑ Past experience with reductions.
❑ Markdown data for similar retailers.
❑ Changes in company policies.
❑ Carryover of merchandise from one budget period to another.
❑ Price trends.
❑ Stock shortages.

Past experience is a good starting point in reduction planning. This information can be compared with that of similar firms. A retailer having more markdowns than competitors should investigate and correct this situation by adjusting buying practices and price levels or training sales personnel better. The *Merchandising and Operating Results of Department and Specialty Stores,* shows retail reduction data for department and specialty stores of various sizes. In 1986 for department stores having annual sales of over $5 million, markdowns were 19.3 per cent of sales. Specialty stores with annual sales over $1 million had markdowns of 15.0 per cent of sales.[3]

In evaluating past reductions, a retailer must consider its company policies. Changes in policy during a budget period often affect the quantity and timing of markdowns. For instance, a retailer's expanding its assortment of seasonal and fashion merchandise would probably lead to an increase in markdowns.

Merchandise carryover, price trends, and stock shortages also affect merchandise planning. When items such as gloves and antifreeze are held in stock during off-seasons, markdowns are usually not needed to clean out inventory. In other cases, the carryover of fad merchandise merely postpones reductions. Price trends of product categories influence retail reductions. For example, many microwave ovens are now available for under $200, down substantially from introductory prices. This means that high-priced microwave ovens would have to be marked down accordingly. On the other hand, inflation (leading to higher costs) might make large purchases by retailers more attractive.

Stock-shortage planning means projecting reductions due to employee, customer, and vendor theft; breakage; and bookkeeping mistakes. At the end of an accounting period, actual stock shortages would be determined by taking a physical inventory and comparing the closing book inventory value at retail with the physical inventory value at retail. If a firm has total stock shortages amounting to less than 2 per cent of its annual sales, it is usually considered to be doing well. Generally, about one-quarter of all stock shortages in retailing are the result of clerical and handling errors.[4] Figure 12-3 contains a checklist that retailers could use to reduce shortages from these errors. Suggestions for decreasing shortages arising from theft were discussed in Chapter 10.

After total reductions are determined, they must be planned by month because reductions as a percentage of sales are not the same during each month. For example, stock shortages may be much higher during busy periods, when stores are more crowded and transactions happen more quickly.

Answer yes or no to each of the following questions. A no answer to any question means corrective measures must be taken.
Buying
1. Is the exact quantity of merchandise purchased always specified in the contract?
2. Are purchase quantities recorded by size, color, model, etc.?
3. Are special purchase terms clearly noted?
4. Are returns to the vendor recorded properly?
Marking
5. Are retail prices clearly marked on merchandise?
6. Are the prices marked on merchandise checked for correctness?
7. Are markdowns and additional markups recorded by item number and quantity?
8. Does a cashier check with a manager if a price is not marked on an item?
9. Are the prices shown on display shelves checked for consistency with those marked on the items themselves?
10. Are old price tags removed when an item's price is changed?
Handling
11. After receipt, are purchase quantities checked against contract specifications?
12. Is merchandise handled in a systematic manner?
13. Are goods separated by merchandise classification?
14. Are all handling operations monitored properly (e.g., receiving, storing, distribution)?
15. Is enough merchandise kept on the selling floor (to reduce excessive handling)?
16. Are items sold in bulk (such as produce, sugar, candy) measured accurately?
17. Are damaged, soiled, returned, or other special goods handled separately?

FIGURE 12-3
A Checklist to Reduce Inventory Shortages Due to Clerical and Handling Errors

Selling	
18.	Do sales personnel know correct prices or have easy access to them?
19.	Are markdowns, additional markups, etc., communicated to sales personnel?
20.	Are misrings by cashiers made on a very small percentage of sales?
21.	Are special terms noted on sales receipts?
22.	Do sales personnel confirm that all items are rung up by cashiers?
23.	Are employee discounts noted?
24.	Is the addition on sales receipts done mechanically or double checked if computed by hand?
25.	Are sales receipts numbered and later checked for missing invoices?
Inventory Planning	
26.	Is a physical inventory conducted at least annually?
27.	Is a book inventory maintained throughout the year?
28.	Are the differences between physical inventory counts and book inventory always accounted for?
29.	Are sales and inventory records reviewed regularly?
Accounting	
30.	Are permanent records on all transactions kept?
31.	Are both retail and cost data maintained?
32.	Are all types of records monitored for accuracy?
33.	Are inventory shortages compared with industry averages to determine acceptability of performance?

FIGURE 12-3
(Continued)

Planning Purchases

The formula for calculating planned purchases for a period is

$$\text{Planned purchases (at retail)} = \begin{array}{l} \text{Planned sales for the month} + \text{Planned} \\ \text{reductions for the month} + \text{Planned} \\ \text{end-of-month stock} - \text{Beginning-of-month stock} \end{array}$$

If Handy Hardware projects June 1989 sales to be \$54,334 and planned reductions to be 5 per cent of sales, plans ending inventory at retail to be \$36,000, and has a beginning inventory at retail of \$40,000, planned purchases would be

$$\text{Planned purchases (at retail)} = \$54,334 + \$2,717 + \$36,000 - \$40,000$$

$$= \$53,051$$

Since Handy Hardware expects merchandise costs to be about 60 per cent of retail selling price, it is planning to purchase \$31,831 of goods at cost in June 1989:

$$\text{Planned purchases (at cost)} = \begin{array}{l} \text{Planned purchases at retail} \\ \times \text{ Merchandise costs as a} \\ \text{percentage of selling price} \end{array}$$

$$= \$53,051 \times 0.60 = \$31,831$$

Open-to-buy is the difference between planned purchases and purchase commitments made by a buyer for a given time period, often a month. Open-to-buy is the amount the buyer has left to spend for that month, and it is reduced each time a purchase is made. At the beginning of a month, a retailer's planned purchases and open-to-buy would be equal if no purchases have been committed prior to the start of that month. Open-to-buy is recorded at cost.

As an illustration of open-to-buy, Handy Hardware's buyer has already made purchase commitments for June 1989 valued in the amount of $27,500 at retail. Handy's open-to-buy at retail for June is $25,551:

$$\begin{array}{ll} \text{Open-to-buy} \\ \text{(at retail)} \end{array} = \begin{array}{l} \text{Planned purchases for the month} \\ - \text{ Purchase commitments for that month} \end{array}$$

$$= \$53,051 - \$27,500 = \$25,551$$

To calculate the open-to-buy at cost, $25,551 is multiplied by Handy Hardware's merchandise costs as a percentage of selling price:

$$\begin{array}{ll} \text{Open-to-buy} \\ \text{(at cost)} \end{array} = \begin{array}{l} \text{Open-to-buy at retail} \\ \times \text{ Merchandise costs as a} \\ \text{percentage of selling price} \end{array}$$

$$= \$25,551 \times 0.60 = \$15,331$$

The open-to-buy concept has two significant strengths. First, it assures the retailer that a specified relationship between stock on hand and planned sales is maintained, which avoids overbuying and underbuying. Second, it shows a retailer how to adjust merchandise purchases to reflect changes in sales, markdowns, and so on. For instance, if Handy Hardware revises its June sales estimate to $60,000, it will automatically increase planned purchases and open-to-buy by $5,666 at retail and $3,400 at cost.

From a strategic perspective it is usually advisable for a retailer to leave itself with at least a small open-to-buy figure for as long as possible. This would allow the firm to take advantage of special deals, to purchase new models, and to fill in merchandise that sells out. Sometimes the open-to-buy limit must be exceeded because of underestimates of demand (low sales forecasts).

Planning Profit Margins

When developing a merchandise budget, the retailer is quite interested in profitability and must consider its sales level, retail expenses, profit goal, and retail reductions in pricing merchandise:

$$\begin{array}{ll} \text{Required initial} \\ \text{markup percentage} \end{array} = \frac{\text{Retail expenses} + \text{Profit} + \text{Reductions}}{\text{Net sales} + \text{Reductions}}$$

The required markup figure is an overall company average; individual items may be priced according to demand and other factors, as long as the company average is maintained. A more complete discussion of markup is contained in the next chapter. The concept of initial markup is introduced at this point for continuity in the description of merchandise budgeting.

As an example of markup planning, Handy Hardware has an overall 1989 sales forecast of $440,540 and expects annual operating expenses to be $145,000. Reductions are anticipated to be $22,000. The profit goal is $30,000. Therefore, the required initial markup is 42.6 per cent:

$$\begin{array}{ll} \text{Required initial} \\ \text{markup percentage} \end{array} = \frac{\$145,000 + \$30,000 + \$22,000}{\$440,540 + \$22,000} = 42.6\%$$

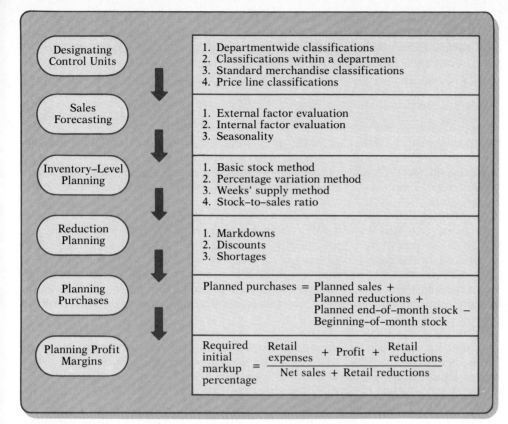

FIGURE 12-4
The Merchandise Forecasting and Budgeting Process: Dollar Control

Required initial markup percentage
(all factors expressed as a
percentage of net sales)
$$= \frac{32.9\% + 6.8\% + 5.0\%}{100.0\% + 5.0\%} = 42.6\%$$

Figure 12-4 summarizes the merchandise forecasting and budgeting process. It expands on Figure 12-2 by including the bases for each decision stage.

Unit Control Systems

Unit control systems deal with quantities of merchandise in units rather than in dollars. Information typically contained in unit control systems includes

❑ The identification of items that are selling well and those that are selling poorly.

❑ A focus on opportunities and problem areas for buyers in terms of price, color, style, size, and so on.

❑ The computation (where a perpetual inventory system is used) of the quantity of goods on hand. This minimizes overstocking and understocking.

❑ An indication of the age of the inventory, highlighting those items that are candidates for markdowns or special promotions.

❑ A determination of the optimal time to reorder merchandise.

❑ An examination of experiences with alternative sources (vendors) when problems arise.

❑ The level of inventory and sales for each item in each store branch. This improves the flow of goods transfer between branches and alerts sales personnel as to which branches have desired products. Also, less stock can be maintained in each store, reducing costs.

Physical Inventory Systems

A physical-inventory unit-control system is similar to a physical-inventory dollar-control system. Whereas the dollar control system is concerned with the dollar value of inventory, the unit control system examines the number of units by item classification. In the unit control system, someone within the retail firm is assigned the responsibility for monitoring inventory levels of merchandise, either by visual inspection or by actual count.

An example of a **visual inspection system** is the use of stock cards in the houseware and hardware displays of many discount, department, variety, and hardware stores. Merchandise is placed on pegboard displays, with each item numbered on the back of its package on a stock card. Minimum stock quantities are clearly noted on the item, and sales personnel are responsible for reordering when the items reach minimum inventory levels. In this type of visual inspection system, accuracy occurs only if merchandise is placed in numerical order on the displays.

Although a visual system is easy to maintain and inexpensive, it has two shortcomings. First, it does not provide information on the rate of sales of individual items. Second, minimum stock quantities may be arbitrarily defined and not drawn from in-depth analysis.

The other physical inventory system, actual counting, relies on tabulating the number of units on hand at regular intervals. A **stock-counting system** records inventory on hand, purchases, sales volume, and shortages during specified periods. For example:

	Number of Items, for the Period 12/1/88–12/31/88
Beginning inventory, December 1, 1988	200
Total purchases for period	150
Total units available for sale	350
Closing inventory, December 31, 1988	120
Sales and shortages for period	230

A stock-counting system requires more clerical work than a visual system, but it enables a retailer to obtain sales data for given periods and stock-to-sales relationships as of the time of each count. A physical system is not as sophisticated as a perpetual inventory system, and its use is more justified with low-value items having predictable sales rates.

Perpetual Inventory Systems

Perpetual (book) inventory systems can be maintained manually, can use merchandise tags that are processed by computers, or can rely on point-of-sale devices such as optical scanning equipment. Technological advances have greatly improved retailers' abilities to develop strong perpetual inventory systems and to utilize computers.

A **perpetual inventory unit system** keeps a running total of the number of units handled by a retailer by adjusting for sales, returns, transfers to other departments or stores, receipt of merchandise shipments, and so on. All additions and subtractions from beginning inventory are recorded.

A manual system requires employees to gather information by examining sales checks, merchandise receipts, transfer requests, and other merchandise documents. This information is then coded and tabulated.

A merchandise-tagging system relies on preprinted tags attached to each item in stock. These tags include data on department, classification, vendor, style number, date of receipt, color, and material. When an item is sold, one copy of the merchandise tag is removed and sent to a tabulating facility, where the coded information is analyzed by computer. Because preprinted merchandise tags are processed in batches, they can be used by small and medium-sized retailers (which subscribe to independent service bureaus) and by branches of chains (with data being processed at a central location).

Point-of-sale systems, developed and sold by companies such as IBM and NCR, feed information from merchandise tags or product labels directly into in-store computer terminals for immediate data processing. As discussed in Chapter 6, the Universal Product Code (UPC) has become the dominant industrywide computer classification format for coding information onto merchandise. Many point-of-sale systems utilize an optical scanner, which transfers information from merchandise to an in-store computer via a wand or a stationary device that interacts with a sensitized strip on the merchandise. Figure 12-5 shows how a UPC-based scanner system works.

Computer-based systems are quicker, more accurate, and of higher quality than manual systems. And because of the availability of personal computers, computerized checkout equipment, and service bureaus, costs are reasonable for smaller retailers.

A retailer does not have to use a perpetual system for all of its inventory. Many firms combine perpetual and physical systems. Key items, accounting for a large proportion of sales, would be controlled through a perpetual system, and other items would be controlled through a physical inventory system. In this way, attention would be properly placed on the retailer's most important products.

Financial Inventory Control: Integrating Dollar and Unit Concepts

Until this point, dollar and unit control concepts have been discussed as separate entities. However, in practice, dollar and unit controls are directly linked. For example, the decision on how many units to buy at a given time affects and is affected by dollar investment, inventory turnover, quantity discounts, warehousing and insurance costs, and so on.

Three aspects of financial inventory control are described in this section: stock turnover and gross margin return on investment, when to reorder, and how much to reorder.

Stock Turnover and Gross Margin Return on Investment

Stock turnover represents the number of times during a specific period, usually one year, that the average inventory on hand is sold. A high level of stock turnover has several virtues. Inventory investments are productive on a per dollar basis. Merchandise on the shelves is fresh. Losses due to changes in styles and fashion are reduced. Costs associated with maintaining inventory—such as interest, insurance, breakage, and warehousing—are lessened.

Stock turnover can be calculated in units or in dollars (at retail or at cost):

$$\text{Annual rate of stock turnover (in units)} = \frac{\text{Number of units sold during year}}{\text{Average inventory on hand (in units)}}$$

When the checker passes an item with the UPC symbol over a scanning device, the symbol is read by a low–energy laser.

The UPC symbol is found on many supermarket products and looks like this.

Each product has its own unique identification number. For example, the first five digits, 11146, represent the manufacturer, Giant in this case. The second five digits represent the specific items; 01345 identifies 24 ounce iced tea mix.

Note that the price is not in the symbol. The symbol identifies the product, not the price.

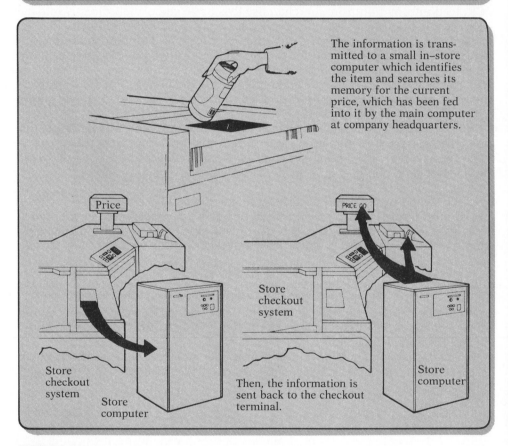

The information is transmitted to a small in–store computer which identifies the item and searches its memory for the current price, which has been fed into it by the main computer at company headquarters.

Price

Store checkout system

Store computer

Store checkout system

Then, the information is sent back to the checkout terminal.

PRICE .00

Store checkout system

Store computer

FIGURE 12-5
How Does a UPC-Based Scanner System Work?
Courtesy Giant Food Inc.

$$\text{Annual rate of stock turnover (in retail dollars)} = \frac{\text{Net yearly sales}}{\text{Average inventory on hand (at retail)}}$$

$$\text{Annual rate of stock turnover (at cost)} = \frac{\text{Cost of goods sold during the year}}{\text{Average inventory on hand (at cost)}}$$

The choice of a stock turnover formula depends on the retailer's accounting system.

The computation of stock turnover needs to reflect the average inventory level for the entire time period covered in the analysis. Computations will be incorrect if the true average inventory is not used, as occurs when a retailer mistakenly uses the inventory level of a peak or slow month as the yearly average.

Table 12-10 shows stock turnover rates for a variety of retailers. Gasoline service stations and grocery stores have very high turnover rates. These firms must rely on high sales volume for their success. Jewelry, shoe, clothing, and hardware stores have very low turnover rates. They must rely on large profit margins for each item they sell and must maintain a sizable assortment for their customers.

A retailer can increase stock turnover through a number of different strategies, such as reducing assortment, eliminating slow-selling items, maintaining minimal inventory for slow-sellers, buying in an efficient and timely manner, and utilizing reliable distributors.

Despite the advantages of high stock turnover, there are instances in which it can adversely affect profits. First, purchasing items in small amounts could increase merchandise costs because quantity discounts may be lost and transportation charges may rise. Second, since a high turnover rate could be due to low width and/or depth of assortment, some customer sales may be lost. Third, high stock turnover could result in low profits if prices must be reduced in order to move inventory quickly. A retailer's return on investment is composed of both turnover and profit per unit.

TABLE 12-10
Annual Median Stock Turnover Rates for Selected Retail Institutions (1987–1988)

Type of Retailer	Annual Median Stock Turnover Rate
Auto and home supply stores	5.9 times
Department stores	4.7
Family clothing stores	3.5
Furniture stores	4.8
Gasoline service stations	28.1
Grocery stores	15.8
Hardware stores	3.5
Household appliance stores	5.6
Jewelry stores	2.4
Lumber and other building materials dealers	6.2
Men's and boys' clothing stores	3.4
New and used-car dealers	6.5
Shoe stores	3.3
Women's accessory and specialty stores	3.9

Source: 1987–1988 Industry Norms and Key Business Ratios (New York: Dun & Bradstreet Credit Services, 1987).

How Can a Small Retail Chain Manage Ten Thousand CD Titles?

Compact Disc Warehouse is a small, but growing, California-based chain of CD-only stores. In 1987, it had seven stores (six of which were franchised) and annual sales of $1.5 million. By the end of 1988, it intended to have over twenty outlets. Since a typical Compact Disc Warehouse store occupies only 2,500 square feet and carries ten thousand CD titles, good financial merchandise management is critical.

Accordingly, Compact Disc Warehouse has developed a distinctive merchandising strategy:

Ours isn't the supermarket approach. It's a more personalized approach, with a better selection, but not as deep as a Tower or a Wherehouse [two large competitors]. We don't carry 200 of every title. The dollar commitment that's required for CD is considerably more than it is for inventory in LP. In order to cover your bases in CDs you have to control inventory and monitor everything. You can't carry too many of anything; it's too many dollars.

Unlike the traditional music store, our inventory is completely computerized. We know daily what we have and don't have. The traditional stores, there's a cycle they go through that involves a physical check of what is there and not there.

Compact Disc Warehouse's perpetual inventory control system (along with weekly or, if necessary, daily reordering) allows its stores to keep an average total inventory level of only twelve thousand CDs for the ten thousand titles they carry. This increases stock turnover, reduces the investment in inventory, and improves cash flow and gross margin return on investment.

Source: Based on material in "Compact Disc Warehouse Ups Growth Tempo," *Chain Store Age Executive* (March 1988), pp. 116–120.

Gross margin return on investment (GMROI) shows the relationship between total dollar operating profits and the average investment in inventory by combining profitability and sales-to-stock measures:

$$\text{Gross margin return on investment (GMROI)} = \frac{\text{Gross margin in dollars}}{\text{Net sales}} \times \frac{\text{Net sales}}{\text{Average inventory at cost}}$$

$$= \frac{\text{Gross margin in dollars}}{\text{Average inventory at cost}}$$

In this formula, gross margin in dollars (total dollar operating profits) is defined as net sales minus the cost of goods sold. Gross margin in dollars divided by net sales is the gross margin percentage. Net sales divided by average inventory at cost provides a sales-to-stock ratio. [Note: This ratio may be converted to stock turnover by multiplying by (100 − Gross margin percentage)/100.]

GMROI is a useful concept for several reasons:

❑ It shows how different retail institutions can prosper despite different gross margins and sales-to-stock ratios. For example, a conventional supermarket may have a gross margin percentage of 20 and a sales-to-stock ratio of 22, resulting in a GMROI of 440 per cent (20% × 22). A department store may have a gross margin percentage of 44 and a sales-to-stock ratio of 10, resulting in a GMROI of 440 per cent (44% × 10). The GMROIs of the two stores are the same because of the trade-off between profitability per item and turnover.

❑ It is a good indicator of a manager's performance, since it focuses on factors controlled by that person. Interdepartmental comparisons can also be made.

❑ It is simple to plan and understand, and data collection is easy.

❑ The retailer can determine if GMROI performance is consistent with other company goals, such as company image and cash flow.

Some retailing analysts have suggested that the basic GMROI formula shown in this section be expanded to include accounts receivable, accounts payable, and inventory carrying costs.[5]

When to Reorder

One means of controlling inventory investment is to establish stock levels at which new orders must be placed. These stock levels are called **reorder points.** The determination of reorder points depends on three factors: order lead time, usage rate, and safety stock. **Order lead time** is the time span from the date an order is placed by a retailer to the date merchandise is ready for sale (received, price-marked, and put on the selling floor). The **usage rate** refers to average sales per day, in units, of merchandise. **Safety stock** is the extra inventory kept on hand to protect against out-of-stock conditions due to unexpected demand and delays in delivery. Safety stock is planned in accordance with a retailer's policy toward running out of merchandise (service level).

This is the formula for when to reorder if a retailer does not plan to carry safety stock, believing that customer demand is stable and that orders are promptly filled by suppliers:

Reorder point = Usage rate × Lead time

Thus, if Handy Hardware sells ten paint brushes a day and needs eight days to order, receive, and display merchandise, it would have a reorder point of eighty paint brushes. This means that it would reorder the brushes once inventory on hand reaches eighty. By the time the new order is completed (eight days later), stock on hand will be zero, and the new stock will replenish the inventory.

This strategy would be correct only if Handy Hardware has a perfectly steady customer demand of ten paint brushes per day and it takes exactly eight days for all stages in the ordering process to be completed. However, this does not normally occur. For example, should consumers buy fifteen brushes per day during a given month, Handy would run out of merchandise in 5⅓ days and be without brushes for 2⅔ days. Similarly, should an order take ten days to process, Handy would have no paint brushes for two full days, despite correctly estimating demand. Figure 12-6 graphically demonstrates how these stockouts may occur if safety stock is not planned.

When a retailer plans to incorporate safety stock into its planning, the reorder formula becomes:

Reorder point = (Usage rate × Lead time) + Safety stock

As a rule, companies should include safety stock in their merchandise planning, because demand is rarely constant from day to day or week to week and deliveries from suppliers can be delayed.

Suppose Handy Hardware decides to plan a safety stock of 30 per cent for paint brushes; then its reorder point is

Reorder point = (10 × 8) + 30%(80) = 80 + 24 = 104

In this case, Handy still expects to sell an average of ten paint brushes per day and receive orders in an average of eight days. However, a safety stock of twenty-

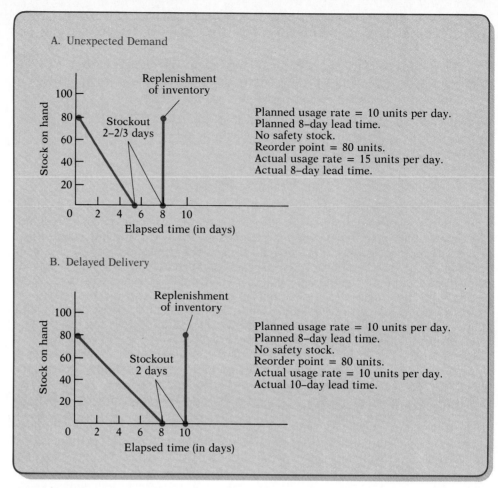

A. Unexpected Demand

Planned usage rate = 10 units per day.
Planned 8-day lead time.
No safety stock.
Reorder point = 80 units.
Actual usage rate = 15 units per day.
Actual 8-day lead time.

B. Delayed Delivery

Planned usage rate = 10 units per day.
Planned 8-day lead time.
No safety stock.
Reorder point = 80 units.
Actual usage rate = 10 units per day.
Actual 10-day lead time.

FIGURE 12-6
How Stockouts May Occur

four extra brushes is kept on hand to protect against unexpected demand or a late shipment.

For retailers that deal with staples (products with small sales variations throughout the year or their primary selling season), a procedure is available for estimating safety stock. This procedure is based on the Poisson probability distribution and is shown in Table 12-11. As an example, if Handy Hardware estimates its basic reorder point to be 80 for paint brushes during the spring and summer, it would plan a safety stock of 9 to have an 80 per cent probability of not running out of stock; 14 to have a 95 per cent probability of not running out of stock; and 21 to have a 99 per cent probability of not running out of stock. Therefore, Handy Hardware would take a 20 per cent chance of being out of stock by planning a reorder point of 89 (including safety stock).

Table 12-11 shows that the level of safety stock required is proportionately greater for low-turnover items than for high-turnover items. For instance, at the 99 per cent level, safety stock for a retailer having an estimated basic reorder point of 40 is 37.5 per cent (15/40) of that reorder point. At the same level, safety stock for a retailer having an estimated basic reorder point of 400 is 11.5 per cent (46/400) of that reorder point.

By combining a perpetual inventory system and reorder point calculations, a

TABLE 12-11
Safety Stock Levels Required to Obtain Various Probabilities of Not Running Out of Staples

Estimated Basic Reorder Point	Retail Stock Policy Chance of Not Running Out of Stock (%)	Safety Stock Needed to Achieve Stock Policy	Required Reorder Point*
25	99	$2.3\sqrt{\text{Estimated reorder point}}$ $= 2.3\sqrt{25} = 12$	37
40	99	$2.3\sqrt{40} = 15$	55
80	99	$2.3\sqrt{80} = 21$	101
100	99	$2.3\sqrt{100} = 23$	123
200	99	$2.3\sqrt{200} = 33$	233
400	99	$2.3\sqrt{400} = 46$	446
25	95	$1.6\sqrt{\text{Estimated reorder point}}$ $= 1.6\sqrt{25} = 8$	33
40	95	$1.6\sqrt{40} = 10$	50
80	95	$1.6\sqrt{80} = 14$	94
100	95	$1.6\sqrt{100} = 16$	116
200	95	$1.6\sqrt{200} = 23$	223
400	95	$1.6\sqrt{400} = 32$	432
25	80	$\sqrt{\text{Estimated reorder point}}$ $= \sqrt{25} = 5$	30
40	80	$\sqrt{40} = 6$	46
80	80	$\sqrt{80} = 9$	89
100	80	$\sqrt{100} = 10$	110
200	80	$\sqrt{200} = 14$	214
400	80	$\sqrt{400} = 20$	420

*Required reorder point = Estimated basic reorder point + Safety stock

merchandise ordering procedure can be programmed into a computer and reorders can take place automatically when stock-on-hand reaches the reorder point. This is referred to as an **automatic reordering system.** However, intervention by a store manager or buyer must be possible, especially in cases where monthly sales fluctuate greatly.

How Much to Reorder

The decision about how much to order affects how often a retailer must order merchandise. A firm that places large orders generally reduces ordering costs but increases inventory-holding costs. A firm that places small orders often minimizes inventory-holding costs while maximizing ordering costs (unless a just-in-time inventory system is utilized).

The **economic order quantity (EOQ)** is the order quantity that minimizes the total costs of processing orders and holding inventory. Order-processing costs include computer time, order forms, labor, and handling new merchandise. Holding costs include warehousing, inventory investment, insurance, taxes, depreciation, deterioration, and pilferage. EOQ can be utilized by both large and small firms.[6]

As can be seen in Figure 12-7, order-processing costs drop as order quantity goes up because fewer orders are needed to purchase the same total annual quantity, and inventory-holding costs increase as order quantity goes up because

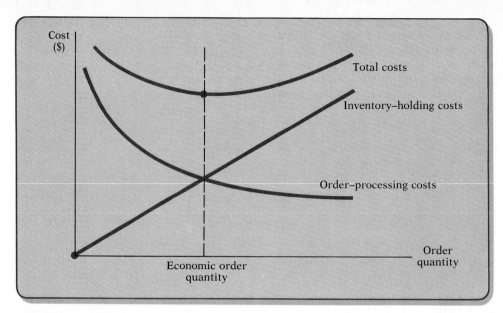

FIGURE 12-7
Economic Order Quantity

more units must be maintained in inventory and they are kept for longer periods. The two costs are summed into a total cost curve.

Mathematically, the economic order quantity (EOQ) is

$$EOQ = \sqrt{\frac{2DS}{IC}}$$

where

EOQ = order quantity (in units)
 D = annual demand (in units)
 S = costs to place an order (in dollars)
 I = percentage of annual carrying cost to unit cost
 C = unit cost of an item (in dollars)

For example, Handy Hardware estimates that it can sell 200 power tool sets per year. These sets cost $90 each. Breakage, insurance, tied-up capital, and pilferage equal 10 per cent of the costs of the sets (or $9 each). Order costs are $15 per order. The economic order quantity is

$$EOQ = \sqrt{\frac{2(200)(\$15)}{(0.10)(\$90)}} = \sqrt{\frac{\$6,000}{\$9}} = 26$$

The EOQ formula must often be modified to take into account changes in demand, quantity discounts, variable ordering costs, and variable holding costs.

SUMMARY

Financial merchandise planning stipulates which products are purchased, when products are purchased, and how many products are purchased. Dollar control involves planning and monitoring the to-

tal inventory investment made during a given time period, while unit control relates to the quantities of merchandise handled during that period. Financial planning encompasses methods of accounting, merchandise forecasting and budgeting, unit control systems, and financial inventory control.

The two accounting techniques available to retailers are the cost and retail methods of inventory valuation. Physical and book (perpetual) procedures are possible with each. Physical inventory valuation requires the actual counting of merchandise at prescribed intervals. Book inventory valuation relies on accurate bookkeeping and a smooth flow of data.

The cost method obligates a retailer to maintain careful records for each item purchased or code its cost on the package. This is necessary to determine the exact value of ending inventory at cost. Many retailers use the LIFO method of accounting to approximate that value, since merchandise costs often rise during a budget period. With the retail method, closing inventory value is determined by calculating the average relationship between the cost and retail value of merchandise available for sale during the period. While the retail method more accurately reflects market conditions, it is also more complex.

Merchandise forecasting and budgeting is a dollar control system that consists of six stages: designating control units, sales forecasting, inventory-level planning, planning retail reductions, planning purchases, and profit-margin planning. Adjustments at any stage of the process would require that all later stages be modified accordingly.

Control units are the merchandise categories for which data are gathered. They must be narrow enough to isolate problems and opportunities with specific lines of merchandise. Sales forecasting may be the most important stage in the merchandising and budgeting process, because its accuracy affects so many other stages. Through inventory-level planning, a firm sets merchandise levels for specified periods. Popular techniques of inventory-level planning are the basic stock, percentage variation,

weeks' supply, and stock-to-sales methods. Retail reduction planning estimates reductions due to markdowns, discounts, and stock shortages. Planned purchases are based on expected sales, reductions, ending inventory, and beginning inventory. Profit margins are related to a retailer's planned sales, expenses, profit goal, and reductions.

A unit control system deals with physical units of merchandise. Key unit control information includes the identification of best-sellers and poor sellers, the quantity of goods on hand, inventory age, reorder time, and so on. A physical-inventory unit-control system may use visual inspection or a stock-counting procedure. A perpetual inventory unit system keeps a running total of the number of units handled by a retailer, adjusting for sales, returns, transfers, new merchandise received, and so on. A perpetual system can be maintained manually, via merchandise tags processed by computers, or via point-of-sale devices.

Financial inventory control integrates dollar and unit control concepts. Three financial controls are stock turnover and gross margin return on investment, when to reorder, and how much to reorder. Stock turnover represents the number of times during a specified period that the average inventory on hand is sold. Gross margin return on investment shows the relationship between total dollar operating profits and average investment. A reorder point calculation would include the retailer's usage rate, order lead time, and safety stock. The economic order quantity aids a retailer in choosing how large an order to place, based on both ordering and inventory costs.

Throughout the chapter, a number of important merchandising equations are introduced and illustrated.

QUESTIONS FOR DISCUSSION

1. What kind of retailers can best use a perpetual inventory system that involves the cost method?
2. Since the FIFO method of costing inventory seems more logical than the LIFO method, because it assumes that the first merchandise purchased is the first merchandise sold, why do many more retailers use LIFO?
3. Explain the cost complement concept in the retail method.
4. Differentiate between the basic stock method and the stock-to-sales method of merchandise planning.
5. Present two situations in which it would be advisable to carry over merchandise from one

budget period to another, instead of taking a markdown.
6. What are the disadvantages of a high stock turnover?
7. How does an automatic reordering system work? What are its shortcomings?
8. Why is the formula for the economic order quantity shown in this chapter an oversimplification?
9. A retailer has yearly sales of $900,000. Inventory on January 1 is $360,000 (at cost). During the year, $800,000 of merchandise (at cost) is purchased. The ending inventory is $425,000 (at cost). Operating costs are $125,000. Calculate

the cost of goods sold and net profit, and set up a profit-and-loss statement. There are no retail reductions in this problem.

10. A retailer has a beginning monthly inventory valued at $30,000 at retail and $19,000 at cost. Net purchases during the month are $70,000 at retail and $40,000 at cost. Transportation charges are $2,000. Sales are $65,000. Markdowns and discounts equal $14,000. A physical inventory at the end of the month shows merchandise valued at $18,500 (at retail) on hand. Calculate the following.

    a. Total merchandise available for sale—at cost and at retail
    b. Cost complement
    c. Ending retail book value of inventory
    d. Stock shortages
    e. Adjusted ending retail book value
    f. Gross profit

11. The monthly sales of a full-line discount store are listed here. Calculate the monthly sales indexes. What do they mean?

January	$ 40,000	July	$ 50,000
February	45,000	August	70,000
March	45,000	September	80,000
April	60,000	October	80,000
May	60,000	November	80,000
June	60,000	December	110,000

12. If the planned average monthly stock for the discount store in Question 11 is $100,000, how much inventory should be planned for July if the retailer uses the percentage variation method? Comment on this retailer's choice of the percentage variation method.

13. The discount store in Questions 11 and 12 knows that its cost complement for all merchandise purchased last year was 0.66; it projects this figure to remain constant. For the current year, it expects to begin and end December with an inventory valued at $35,000 at retail and estimates reductions for December to be $6,000. The company has already made purchase commitments for December worth $60,000. What is the open-to-buy at cost for December?

14. A retailer sells an average of ten standard touch-tone telephones per day and desires a safety stock of twenty phones. If it takes fourteen days for an order to be placed and received by the retailer, what is its reorder point? Explain your answer.

NOTES

1. "Clover, Zellers Go With the FlowRIGHT System," *Chain Store Age Executive* (July 1987), pp. 98, 101.

2. "Lifo Survey Shows Its Here to Stay," *Chain Store Age Executive* (January 1984), pp. 32–33. See also Kenneth E. Christensen and Paul W. Wilson, *LIFO for Retailers: A Business, Financial and Tax Guide* (New York: Wiley, 1986).

3. David P. Schulz, " '86: Better FOR Some," *Stores* (November 1987), pp. 92–94.

4. Jack L. Hayes, "Retailers Shift from Preventing Losses to Arresting Thieves," *Discount Store News* (May 11, 1987), p. 162.

5. See Ray R. Serpkenci and Robert L. Lusch, "New Model Offers Retailers a Realistic Estimate of Gross Margin Return from Merchandise Lines," *Marketing News* (February 18, 1983), p. 6; Charles A. Ingene and Michael Levy, "GMROI: A New View of Planning and Measuring Merchandising Performance," in Bruce J. Walker et al. (Editors), *An Assessment of Marketing Thought & Practice* (Chicago: American Marketing Association, 1982), pp. 216–219; and Michael Levy and Charles A. Ingene, "Residual Income Analysis: A Method of Inventory Investment Allocation and Evaluation," *Journal of Marketing*, Vol. 48 (Summer 1984), pp. 93–104.

6. See Larry H. Beard, Al L. Hartgraves, and Fred A. Jacobs, "Managing Inventories in a Small Business," *Business*, Vol. 33 (April–June 1983), pp. 45–49.

Magnum Stores: Reversing a Downward Sales Trend in Junior Sportswear*

Liz Collins has just been appointed as Department Manager/Buyer of Junior Sportswear for Magnum Stores. The previous manager of this department was recently fired (just after her first annual performance review) because of poor sales and profit performance. In Liz's initial meeting with her immediate supervisor, Jane Bennett, the Divisional Merchandise Manager, commented:

> Your appointment to this position is a significant opportunity and promotion. Junior Sportswear is one of the most important departments to our company in terms of sales, profits, and customer traffic generated. While the previous manager was viewed as hard-working and enthusiastic, sales and profit performance had declined. I want you to spend the next two weeks in the headquarters store's Junior Sportswear department observing sales patterns, speaking to sales personnel, and reviewing financial data. Let's meet in three weeks to discuss your analysis of the problem areas and your initial comments about financial merchandise planning in this department.

For the next two weeks, Collins spoke with salespeople in her new department, carefully reviewed the department's merchandise forecasting and budgeting process, and visited the Junior sportswear departments of two competing retailers (with a good reputation in the area).

At that point, Collins concluded that:

❑ The department sales staff appeared to be well motivated and to work well together. A few of the better salespeople commented to Liz, "It seems that we sell out of the 'hot new fashions' quickly, and that regular customers increasingly leave without making a purchase."

❑ In comparing sales data for the past twelve months with those from the prior year (for corresponding months), Liz found that the department had failed to meet the previous year's monthly sales levels for each of the last eight months. Liz realizes that the previous department manager/buyer was responsible for buying decisions in this eight-month period.

❑ Markdowns in the department have averaged 14 per cent of sales for the last year; two years ago, they were 20 per cent of sales. National Retail Merchants Association data for markdowns for all women's apparel indicates that about 24 per cent is an industry average figure.

❑ Stock turnover has increased significantly over the past year:

	Stock Turnover	
Season	Last Year	This Year
Spring	2.3	3.0
Fall	2.5	4.0

❑ Collins also evaluated retail sales, inventories, and purchases by retail price category over the past two years. She found that the number of price lines per subclassification of merchandise (such as long-sleeved solid-color cotton sweaters) had been reduced from three to four as of two years ago to one or two price lines now. In addition, the dollar range between the lowest and highest prices in these subclassifications had narrowed significantly during this period. See Table 1 for pricing data on classic-styled sweaters sold in the spring.

❑ Liz found that there had been no significant difference in the quantity of advertising or in the scheduled sales promotion activities over the past two years.

*This case was prepared and written by John L. Roman, Director of Stores, Rochester Institute of Technology.

TABLE 1
Pricing Data for Classic-Styled Sweaters

Sweater Description	Prices Two Years Ago	Prices Now
Cotton, solid color, crew neck, long sleeves. Available in red, navy, and ivory.	$55, 47, 38, 30	$60, 52
Cotton, stripes with reverse stitching, crew neck, long sleeves. Available in navy/white, yellow/white, and jade/white.	$47, 35, 22	$50, 43
Ramie/cotton, padded shoulders, short turned-back sleeves. Available in red, navy, and white.	$62, 48, 35	$70, 62
Updated wool, buttons on shoulder, oversized, ribbed crew neck, long sleeves. Available in red, navy, and white.	$72, 57, 45	$77, 64
Wool, jacquard pattern, shoulder pads, ribbed trim, long sleeves. Available in blue/yellow and green/pink.	$64, 58, 42	$70, 62

QUESTIONS

1. Comment on the salespeople's statement: "It seems that we sell out of the 'hot new fashions' quickly, and that regular customers increasingly leave without making a purchase."

2. Examine the relationship among the decrease in markdowns, the increase in stock turnover, and the reduction in price lines stocked. Use numbers in your analysis.

3. If markdowns have been reduced and stock turnover has risen over the past year, do you think gross margin return on investment has increased, decreased, or remained the same? Explain your answer.

4. What specific actions should Liz recommend to reverse the decline in sales? Explain your answer.

Case 2

Fit for Life: Analyzing a Financial Merchandising Plan

Fit for Life is a moderate-sized sporting-goods store located in a regional shopping mall in a suburb of Pittsburgh. The store has been open since 1981 and offers a broad assortment of warm-up suits, athletic shoes (for tennis, jogging, skiing, etc.), athletic equipment (tennis rackets, skis, baseball gloves, etc.), and accessories (socks, T-shirts, wristbands, etc.). It stresses a full-service, personal approach and sets prices accordingly. Fit for Life is well respected in the community, and consumers particularly like the advice provided by its experienced sales force.

The store has a clear merchandising plan:

❑ It concentrates on seven key sports and maintains a good product depth in these categories: baseball, basketball, football, golf, jogging (running), skiing, and tennis. Fit for Life does not carry bowling, physical fitness, and other equipment, nor does it offer bicycles or bicycle accessories.

❑ Prices are similar to those in department stores and 20 per cent higher than in discount stores.

❑ Inventory is limited to national brands that are heavily advertised by manufacturers. Private-label brands are not stocked.

❑ All merchandise is coded with date of purchase and cost information that cannot be read by consumers.

❑ A physical inventory is conducted once very two months. A book inventory is maintained using the LIFO method. Fit for Life does not use the retail method of inventory.

❑ Sales forecasts are made annually by sports category; the forecasts are broken down by month.

❏ Regular prices are maintained throughout the year. A special clearance sale is conducted once a year (in February); then the prices of all merchandise are reduced by 30 per cent.

❏ Merchandise is reordered when stock levels for an item are low: safety stock is not kept.

Recently, the manager of Fit for Life completed an analysis of the firm's merchandising plan. He focused on financial measures and compared Fit for Life with average industry data found in a variety of sources. See Table 1.

TABLE 1
Selected Financial Data

Factor	Fit for Life	Sporting-Goods Stores— Industry Average
Annual net sales	$500,000	$350,000
Annual sales per square foot	$135	$150
Markdowns, discounts, and stock shortages (% of sales)	9.0	7.5
Initial markup percentage	39.44	36.7
Gross margin percentage (maintained markup)	34.0	32.0
GMROI (%)	155	165
Net profit before taxes (% of sales)	7.0	4.5
Stock turnover (times per year)	3.0	3.5

QUESTIONS

1. Evaluate Fit for Life's merchandising plan.
2. What conclusions can be reached from Table 1?
3. What other financial merchandising factors discussed in this chapter should Fit for Life consider? Why?
4. Offer several suggestions for Fit for Life to improve its financial merchandising plan.

Chapter 13

Pricing in Retailing

☐ **Chapter**
Objectives ☐

1 To describe the role of pricing in a retail strategy

2 To examine the impact of consumers; government; manufacturers, wholesalers, and other suppliers; and current and potential competitors on pricing decisions

3 To present a framework for developing a retail price strategy: objectives, broad policy, basic strategy, implementation, and adjustments

4 To show that pricing decisions must be made in an integrated and adaptive manner

While overall consumer electronics sales increased by 20 per cent or more annually in the early and mid-1980s, as one electronics product after another (such as phone-answering machines, videocassette recorders, stereo televisions, and compact disc players) caught on with the buying public, annual sales are expected to grow by only 5–7 per cent over the next several years. This low sales growth is occurring at a time when the top ten retail electronics chains have increased their store space by more than 25 per cent.

To stimulate sales in a marketplace saturated with retailers, companies are using one of two different strategies: price competition and nonprice competition. With price competition, consumer electronics stores seek customers by offering lower prices than competitors. In nonprice competition, retailers stress attributes other than price.

A price competition approach requires that participating retailers accept reduced profit margins and has resulted in price wars in several markets. For example, at some large consumer electronics stores, nineteen-inch color televisions that cost retailers $180 are sold for as little as $189; and the profit on a $500 videocassette recorder may be as little as $25. One analyst has criticized the industry for too heavy a reliance on price advertising: "If two companies advertise price every second day, it does not take long for consumers to believe that the only critical variable in their purchase decision should be price." The emphasis on price competition can be seen from these advertising slogans: "Everyday Lowest Prices Guaranteed" (Federated Group); "Nobody Beats the Wiz"; and "Crazy Eddie Cannot Be Undersold."

Efforts at nonprice competition have been

largely based on offering extra customer services, a pleasant shopping environment, salesperson expertise, product guarantees (providing replacements for products that cannot be satisfactorily repaired within a given time period), the sale of extended service plans, and training salespeople to sell such profitable accessories as compact disc cleaners and television stands. Extended service plans and accessories can have profit margins that are two to four times as profitable as the basic product.[1]

Overview

A retailer must price goods and services in a manner that achieves profitability for the firm and satisfies customers, while adapting to a variety of constraints.

Pricing is a crucial strategic variable for a retailer because of its direct relationship with a firm's objectives and its interaction with other retailing-mix elements. A retailer's pricing strategy must be consistent with its overall sales, profit, and return-on-investment objectives. For example, a retailer interested in an early recovery of a cash investment, because of expansion plans, might enact a mass-marketing strategy. This approach utilizes low prices.

The interaction of price with other retail elements can be shown through the following illustration. Tie Town is a tie shop whose two partners have developed a broad strategy consisting of

❏ A target market of price-conscious men.
❏ Selling inexpensive ties in the $7 to $10 range.
❏ A limited range of merchandise quality.
❏ Self-service.
❏ A downtown location.
❏ A deep assortment.
❏ Quantity purchases at discount.
❏ An image of efficiency and variety.

This chapter divides retail pricing into two major sections: factors affecting price strategy and developing a price strategy.

Factors Affecting Retail Price Strategy

Before detailing how a retail price strategy is developed, it is necessary to discuss the factors that affect price decision making. Consumers, government, manufacturers and wholesalers, and competitors each have an impact on the pricing strategy of a retailer, as shown in Figure 13-1. In some cases, these factors have only a minor effect; in other cases, the factors severely restrict a retailer's options in setting prices.

The Consumer and Retail Pricing

A retailer must understand the relationship between price and consumers' purchases and perceptions. Two economic principles explain this relationship: the law of demand and the price elasticity of demand.

The **law of demand** states that consumers usually purchase more units at low prices than at high prices. The **price elasticity of demand** relates to the sensitivity of buyers to price changes in terms of the quantities they will purchase. If relatively small percentage changes in price result in substantial percentage changes in the number of units purchased, then price elasticity is high. This occurs when the urgency of a purchase is low or acceptable substitutes exist. However, when large percentage changes in price have small percentage changes in the number of units purchased, demand is considered inelastic. This occurs when the urgency

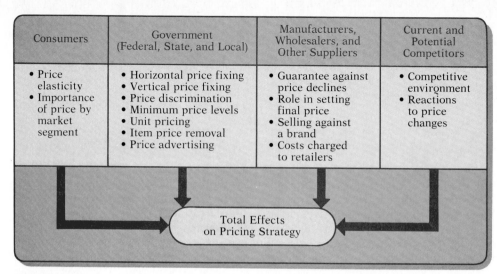

FIGURE 13-1
Factors Affecting Retail Price Strategy

of purchase is high or there are no acceptable substitutes (as takes place with store loyalty). Unitary elasticity occurs in cases where percentage changes in price are directly offset by percentage changes in quantity.

Price elasticity is computed by dividing the percentage change in quantity demanded by the percentage change in the price charged:

$$\text{Elasticity} = \frac{\dfrac{\text{Quantity 1} - \text{Quantity 2}}{\text{Quantity 1} + \text{Quantity 2}}}{\dfrac{\text{Price 1} - \text{Price 2}}{\text{Price 1} + \text{Price 2}}}$$

Because the law of demand shows that quantities purchased decline as prices go up, elasticity is usually a negative number.

Table 13-1 shows the calculation of price elasticity for a 1,000-seat movie theater (the elasticities are converted to positive numbers). The table demonstrates that the quantity demanded (tickets sold) declines at every price level from $3.00 to $6.00; fewer customers patronize the theater at $6.00 than at $3.00. Demand is inelastic from $3.00 to $4.50; total ticket receipts increase because the percentage change in price is greater than the percentage change in tickets sold. Demand is unitary from $4.50 to $5.00; total ticket receipts are constant because the percentage change in tickets sold exactly offsets the percentage change in price. Demand is elastic from $5.00 to $6.00; total receipts decline because the percentage change in tickets sold is greater than the percentage change in price.

For this example, total ticket receipts are highest at $4.50 or at $5.00. But what about the total revenues for the theater? If patrons spend an average of $2.00 each at the concession stand, the best price would be $4.50 (total overall revenues of $5,525). The movie theater is interested only in the total revenues generated, because its operating costs would be the same whether there are 850 or 765 patrons. Other retailers would evaluate profit as well as sales from serving additional customers.

In retailing, computing price elasticity is often difficult for two reasons. First, as in the case of the movie theater, demand for individual events or items may be hard to predict. One week the theater may attract 1,000 patrons to a movie,

TABLE 13-1
A Movie Theater's Elasticity of Demand

Price	Tickets Sold (Saturday Night)	Total Ticket Receipts	Elasticity of Demand*
$3.00	1,000	$3,000	$E = \dfrac{\dfrac{1,000 - 950}{1,000 + 950}}{\dfrac{\$3.00 - \$3.50}{\$3.00 + \$3.50}} = 0.33$
3.50	950	3,325	
			$E = \quad 0.41$
4.00	900	3,600	
			$E = \quad 0.49$
4.50	850	3,825	
			$E = \quad 1.00$
5.00	765	3,825	
			$E = \quad 1.71$
5.50	650	3,575	
			$E = \quad 3.00$
6.00	500	3,000	

*Expressed as a positive number.

and the following week it may attract 400 patrons to a different movie. Second, retailers such as supermarkets and department stores sell thousands of items and could not possibly compute elasticities for each one. Accordingly, many retailers rely on average markup pricing, competition, tradition, and industry-wide data as indicators of price elasticity.

Consumer sensitivity to price varies by market segment. On the basis of a classic study, retailers can divide consumers into four categories, depending on their shopping orientation:

1. Economic—interested primarily in shopping for values and extremely sensitive to price, quality, and goods/service assortment.
2. Personalizing—shops where he or she is known, strong personal attachment with retail personnel and the firm itself.
3. Ethical—willing to sacrifice lower prices and a better goods/service assortment with larger retailers or chains to help the smaller firm stay in business.
4. Apathetic—shops only because he or she must, wants to finish as quickly as possible, and places emphasis on convenience.[2]

The Government and Retail Pricing

When examining the impact of government on planning a pricing strategy, it must be remembered that three levels of government exist: federal, state, and local. Although many of the key laws are federal, these laws apply only to interstate commerce. Therefore a retailer that operates exclusively within the boundaries of one state may not be restricted by federal legislation.

Legislation focuses on seven major areas: horizontal price fixing, vertical price fixing, price discrimination, minimum price levels, unit pricing, item price removal, and price advertising.

Horizontal Price Fixing

Horizontal price fixing involves an agreement among manufacturers, among wholesalers, or among retailers to set certain prices. Such agreements are illegal according to the Sherman Antitrust Act and the Federal Trade Commission Act, regardless of how "reasonable" the resultant prices may be. It is also illegal for retailers to reach agreements with one another regarding the use of coupons, rebates, or other price-oriented tactics.

These are two examples of horizontal price fixing and the legal ramifications:

❑ The managers of three supermarkets (First National, Fisher Foods, and Stop & Shop) met weekly in parking lots late at night and jointly decided what "specials" each would offer and at what prices. These managers knew their actions were not legal and worked hard to keep them secret. As a result, the supermarkets were fined a total of $1.7 million, and four executives were fined $100,000 each. The executives also received suspended jail sentences and were placed on five years' probation.[3]

❑ Four supermarket chains (Waldbaum, Supermarkets General-Pathmark, King Kullen, and LAMM) had an agreement that limited the use of double and triple coupons. With such coupons, the retailers would match or exceed the coupon value offered by the manufacturer with store discounts. However, it was charged that the chains conspired to stop double- and triple-couponing during certain periods. The chains were ordered to pay fines totaling $830,000.[4]

Vertical Price Fixing

Vertical price fixing occurs when manufacturers or wholesalers are able to control the retail prices of their goods and services. Until 1976, this practice was allowed because of the belief that manufacturers and wholesalers had the right to protect the reputations of their brands and that these reputations could be diluted through indiscriminant price cutting by retailers. In addition, vertical price fixing was viewed as providing **fair trade** protection for smaller and full-service retailers in competition with discounters. Manufacturers enforced fair trade legislation by setting uniform retail prices for their items and then refusing to sell to those retailers utilizing price cutting or by seeking legal intervention.

Fair trade laws were criticized by consumer groups and many manufacturers, wholesalers, and retailers as being anticompetitive, keeping prices artificially high, and allowing inefficient retailers to stay in business. As a result, the Consumer Goods Pricing Act, which terminated the interstate use of fair trade practices and resale price maintenance, was enacted. At present, retailers cannot be required to adhere to list prices developed by manufacturers and wholesalers.

Today, manufacturers and wholesalers can legally control retail prices only through one of these methods: they can own retail facilities; they can use consignment selling, whereby the supplier owns items until they are sold and assumes costs normally associated with the retailer; they can carefully screen retailers; they can set realistic list prices; they can preprint prices on products (which retailers do not have to utilize); and they can establish regular prices that are accepted by consumers (such as 25 cents for a newspaper).[5]

Nonetheless, many discount retailing executives believe that the Federal Trade Commission and the Department of Justice have not adequately protected their right to compete on the basis of retail prices. From 1981 to 1988, neither agency brought one enforcement action to curb vertical price fixing, even though various discount retailers contended that they had been denied access to merchandise lines and that consumers had been forced to pay higher prices as a result.[6]

In response to the criticism, the Federal Trade Commission chairman stated that the FTC's position on vertical price fixing reflects mainstream antitrust theory. Under the "rule-of-reason" interpretation, a retailer denied certain brands because of its discount pricing strategy would have to prove not only that a conspiracy had taken place (between a supplier and other retailers in the selling area) to keep it from getting merchandise, but that the conspiracy had had the effect of reducing competition in the marketplace.

Not satisfied with the FTC's view, forty-seven of the nation's fifty state attorneys general recently filed legal documents in support of enforcement of the current laws which protect retailers and consumers from the adverse effects of vertical price fixing.[7]

Price Discrimination

The **Robinson-Patman Act** prohibits manufacturers and wholesalers from discriminating in price or sales terms when dealing with individual retailers if these retailers are purchasing products of "like quality" and the effect of such discrimination would be to injure competition. The intent of the Robinson-Patman Act is to prevent large retailers from using their power to obtain discounts that are not justified by the cost savings achieved through sizable orders. It is feared that, without the Robinson-Patman Act, smaller retailers could be driven out of business because of noncompetitive final prices due to significantly higher merchandise costs.

There are exceptions to the Robinson-Patman Act, which allow justifiable price discrimination when

- ❑ Products are physically different.
- ❑ The retailers paying different prices are not competitors.
- ❑ Competition is not injured.
- ❑ Price differences are due to differences in the supplier's costs.
- ❑ Market conditions change.
    - a. Manufacturing costs and so on increase or decrease.
    - b. Competing suppliers change their prices.

Discounts are not illegal, as long as a supplier follows the preceding rules, makes discounts available to competitive retailers on an equal basis, and offers discounts that are sufficiently graduated so that small (as well as large) retailers can qualify. Discounts for cumulative purchases (total orders during the year) and for multistore purchases by chains are extremely difficult to justify.

For example, the Federal Trade Commission recently ordered Max Factor to make its promotional allowances (a form of price discounting) available on a proportionately equal basis to all retailers that sell its cosmetics and beauty aids. Max Factor was also required to provide alternative discount arrangements for small retailers for whom its basic promotional discount plans are unsuitable.[8]

Although the Robinson-Patman Act seems to restrict sellers more than buyers, retailers do have specific liabilities under Section 2(F) of the Act, which states:

> It shall be unlawful for any person engaged in commerce, in the course of such commerce, knowingly to induce or receive a discrimination in price which is prohibited in this section.

From a strategic perspective, a retail buyer must attempt to receive the lowest prices charged to any competitor of its class; yet, it must also be careful not to bargain so hard that the discounts received cannot be justified by one of the acceptable exceptions.[9]

Minimum-Price Laws

Several states have **minimum-price laws** that prevent retailers from selling merchandise for less than the cost of the product plus a fixed percentage that covers overhead. Merchandise costs are defined in various ways; typically, they are the acquisition or replacement costs, whichever are lower.[10]

Minimum-price laws are intended to protect small retailers from predatory pricing by larger competitors. In **predatory pricing**, big retailers attempt to destroy competition by selling goods and services at extremely low prices, which cause small retailers to go out of business.

Loss leaders, items priced below cost to attract customers to a retailer, are restricted by minimum-price laws. Retailers such as supermarkets frequently use loss leaders to increase overall sales and profits under the assumption that consumers will buy more than one item once drawn into a store.[11] Since loss leaders are usually consumer-oriented, minimum-price laws are rarely applied in these cases.

In addition to general laws, a number of states have acts that set minimum prices for specific products. For instance, in New Jersey and Connecticut, state laws require that the retail price of liquor be not less than the wholesale cost (including taxes and delivery charges).[12]

In recent years, the FTC has been advising states to be less strict with their minimum-price laws:

> Predatory pricing is difficult to accomplish and is therefore quite rare. Firms will rarely engage in genuine below-cost pricing, since they typically know they cannot count on a later period of monopoly power during which they can raise prices above their costs and recoup their earlier losses.[13]

According to this argument, predatory pricing would be effective only if a firm selling merchandise at or below cost could be assured that no new competitors would enter a market area after existing competition is reduced.

Unit Pricing

The proliferation of different-sized product packages has led to **unit-pricing** legislation in many states. The aim of such legislation is to enable final consumers to compare prices of products that come in many sizes (e.g., small, medium, and large).

Food stores are most affected by unit price regulations, and in many cases, these stores are required to express both the total price of an item and its price per unit of measure. For example, a 6.5-ounce can of tuna fish priced at 89 cents would also have a shelf label showing that this represents $2.19 per pound. Through unit pricing, a consumer could determine that a 12-ounce can of soda selling for 30 cents (2.5 cents per ounce) is actually more expensive than a 67.6-ounce—two-liter—bottle of soda selling for $1.19 (1.76 cents per ounce).

Unit-pricing laws are intended to give basic information to consumers who feel price is an important decision factor and to provide added data for those customers who consider brand-name or other strategic variables as most important. Although early research studies questioned the effectiveness of unit pricing, later findings have indicated that it is advantageous for retailers as well as consumers.[14]

Not all retailers must comply with unit pricing. Generally, there are exemptions for retailers with low-volume sales or for those operating only one outlet. In addition, grocery items are much more heavily regulated than nongrocery items.

The costs of unit pricing to affected retailers include calculating per unit prices, printing product labels, printing shelf labels, and maintaining computer records. These costs are influenced by the way prices are adhered to goods (manually versus machine), the number of items in a store subject to unit pricing, the frequency of price changes, sales volume, and the number of stores in a chain. A number of supermarket chains have reported that the costs of unit pricing are not excessive, whereas smaller food stores report that the costs are quite high.

Unit pricing is an advantageous strategy for consumer-oriented retailers to follow, even when not required by law. As an illustration, Giant Food has found that its unit-pricing system more than pays for itself through decreased price-marking errors, better inventory control, and improved space management.

Item Price Removal

The expansion of computerized checkout systems has led many retailers, particularly supermarkets, to advocate **item price removal.** With item price removal, prices are marked only on shelves or signs and not on individual items. This practice is banned in several states and local communities.

Supermarkets assert that item price removal would significantly reduce their labor costs and enable them to offer lower prices to consumers. Opponents argue that item price removal would lead to more checkout errors against consumers and make it virtually impossible for consumers to verify prices as they are rung up.

Giant Food practices item price removal in its supermarkets, and there have been little consumer resistance and considerable cost savings. Giant carefully maintains accurate, highly visible shelf prices and gives items free to consumers if the prices processed by its electronic cash registers (equipped with scanners) are higher than those posted on shelves.

Price Advertising

The Federal Trade Commission has guidelines with regard to advertising retail prices. These guidelines deal with advertising price reductions, advertising retail prices in relation to competitors' prices, and bait-and-switch advertising.

In general, FTC guidelines state that a retailer cannot claim or imply that a price has been reduced from some former level (such as a manufacturer's list or suggested list price) unless the former price was an actual, bona fide one at which the retailer offered a good or service to the public on a regular basis during a reasonably substantial, recent period of time.

When a retailer claims that its prices are lower than those offered by other firms, FTC guidelines state that it must make certain that the price comparisons

---

RETAILING IN ACTION

Does Your Advertising Refer to "Real Market Prices"?

When advertising sale or discount prices, FTC guidelines specify that references must be to "real market prices," not to manufacturers' list prices or other inflated reference values. These guidelines are often applied by attorneys general in individual states.

Recently, the attorney general's office in North Carolina has been particularly active in policing deceptive pricing ads. As an assistant attorney general in that state's consumer affairs division remarked:

> From my perspective, the best way to protect the consumer is to have really good competition. To the extent they [retailers] start throwing out phony information, that hurts honest merchants and consumers.

In 1987, three retailers agreed to out-of-court settlements with the North Carolina attorney general's office. Without admitting guilt, these retailers paid investigative and legal fees and stopped their questionable price-advertising practices. Rhodes, an Atlanta-based furniture chain with outlets in North Carolina, paid the state a $10,000 fee and ceased advertising reference prices that were based on merchandise's "value to the public." It now advertises reference prices at which merchandise has had a "substantial number of sales" or at which goods have been offered "for a substantial period, a minimum of 30 days."

The Helig-Meyers Furniture chain of Richmond, North Carolina, paid $70,000 in its settlement. It was accused of citing high competitors' prices in its ads without verifying or substantiating that the high prices to which it referred were actually charged by competitors. McNeill Jewelers, a North Carolina store, paid $3,000. It was accused of using manufacturers' suggested list prices rather than its own original prices when advertising sales. Both firms have changed their advertising.

Source: Based on material in "Attorney General's Office Investigates Advertising Claims," *Marketing News* (February 29, 1988), p. 16.

pertain to competitive retailers selling large quantities in the same trading area. For example, because of alleged improprieties in this regard, Kroger reached an agreement with the FTC that it would not advertise itself as the "price leader." The agreement was in effect from 1981 to 1984.[15]

Bait advertising, or **bait-and-switch advertising,** is an illegal practice whereby a retailer lures a customer by advertising goods and services at exceptionally low prices; then, once the customer contacts the retailer (by entering a store or calling a toll-free 800 number), he or she is told that the good/service of interest is out of stock or of inferior quality. A retail salesperson attempts to convince the customer to purchase a better, more expensive substitute that is available. In bait advertising, the retailer has no intention of selling the advertised item.

As an illustration, over the years, a number of automobile dealers have been accused of bait-and-switch practices. These dealers advertise models in "stripped-down" versions at very low prices. Customers place deposits on these models and agree to accept delivery six to eight weeks later. Then, when only higher-priced models equipped with factory-installed options are received by the dealers, their customers are given the choice of refunds (after several weeks of waiting for a car) or purchasing the models that have arrived at the dealers' prices. Many consumers buy the higher-priced autos to avoid going through the process again.

Manufacturers, Wholesalers, and Other Suppliers— and Retail Pricing

Manufacturers, wholesalers, and other suppliers have an impact on the retailer's pricing strategy. In cases where suppliers are unknown or products are new, retailers seek price guarantees to ensure that inventory values and profits will be maintained. **Price guarantees** protect retailers against price declines. For example, a new manufacturer sells a retailer radios that have a final selling price of $20. The manufacturer guarantees this price to the retailer; if a retailer is unable to sell the radios at this price, the manufacturer pays the difference. Should the retailer have to sell the radios at $15, the manufacturer would give a rebate of $5 per radio. The relative power of the retailer and its suppliers determines whether a guarantee is provided.*

As indicated earlier in the chapter, there are often conflicts between manufacturers and other suppliers and their retailers in setting final prices, since each would like some level of input and control. Typically, a manufacturer wants to achieve and retain a certain image and to allow all retailers, even those that are relatively inefficient, to earn profits. In contrast, most retailers would rather set prices based upon their own image, objectives, and so on.

A manufacturer can control prices by utilizing an exclusive distribution system and refusing to sell to price-cutting retailers. A strong manufacturer can even operate its own retail facilities. A retailer can gain control by being important to its manufacturers as a customer, by threatening to stop carrying manufacturer lines, and by selling private brands.

In many instances, manufacturers derive the selling prices to their retailers by estimating final retail prices and then subtracting the required retailer and wholesaler profit margins from these figures. For example, in the men's haberdashery industry, the common retail markup (gross profit) is 50 per cent of the final selling price. Accordingly, a man's shirt that retails at $18 can be sold to the retailer for no more than $9. If a wholesaler is involved in the transaction, the manufacturer's price to the wholesaler must be substantially less than $9.

---

*Another type of price guarantee is one where the supplier guarantees a retailer that no other retailer will buy merchandise for a lower price. If anyone does, the retailer would get a rebate.

Sometimes, retailers carry manufacturer brands and place high prices on them. When they do this, rival brands (such as private-label merchandise) can be sold more easily. This is called **selling against the brand** and is disliked by manufacturers because sales of their brands are likely to decline.

A retailer has suppliers other than manufacturers and wholesalers. These include employees, store fixtures manufacturers, landlords, and outside agents (e.g., advertising firms). Each of these suppliers has an impact on price because of their costs to the retailer.

The impact of manufacturers, wholesalers, and other suppliers on retail pricing strategies can be seen from these two examples:

❑ Leading Edge, a personal computer importer, has a reputation of being aggressive in its relations with retailers. Some retailers have complained that while Leading Edge demands cash payments from them when they buy merchandise, the firm is frequently late in shipping its computers and behind in payments for warranty work done by retailers. According to one major retailer, relations with Leading Edge have become so poor "that retailers are saying, I don't care how much the customer wants Leading Edge. I'm switching to another suitable machine."[16]

❑ The greeting-card industry is dominated by three large manufacturers: Hallmark (40 per cent market share), American Greetings (35 per cent market share), and Gibson (11 per cent market share). To keep their major retailer accounts and attract new ones, all of these card makers have been increasing their discounts to retailers and providing such special concessions as the installation of new greeting-card racks in stores (the average cost of these racks for a typical drugstore would be $10,000). As an American Greetings executive commented, "We pay the chains to keep our cards there."[17]

Competition and Retail Pricing

The degree of control a firm has over prices often depends on the competitive environment in which it operates. In a market-pricing situation, there is a lot of competition, and consumers can seek out the lowest prices. Retailers price similarly to each other and have little control over price. Supermarkets, fast-food firms, and gas stations are all in highly competitive industries and generally sell similar goods and services; therefore, retailers in these categories utilize **market pricing.** Demand for these retailers is weak enough so that a number of customers would switch to a competitor if prices are raised.

With **administered pricing,** retailers seek consumer patronage on the basis of distinctive retailing mixes. If strong differentiation from competitors can be achieved, a retailer can have control over the prices it charges. This occurs when consumers consider image, assortment, personal service, and so on more important than price and will pay above-average prices for goods and services when shopping with desirable retailers (under the assumption that less desirable retailers do not offer as good an image, assortment, personal service, and so on). Department stores, fashion clothing stores, and upscale restaurants are among those that work hard to create distinct offerings and have some control over their prices.

Because most price-oriented strategies can be easily copied in a short time, the reaction of competition is predictable if the leading firm is successful. Therefore, a retailer should view price strategy from a short-run as well as a long-run perspective.

In some cases, competitive reactions to price changes result in **price wars** whereby various retailers continually lower prices below regular amounts and sometimes below merchandise costs to attract consumers. Price wars frequently result in low profits, losses, or even bankruptcy for competitors. These are two examples of recent price wars:

❑ In Buffalo, four major supermarket chains (Wegmans, Bells, Super Duper, and Tops Friendly Markets) have been engaged in a price war to improve or maintain their market share. Wegmens, whose market share is far below those of Bells and Tops (the market leader), started the war when it lowered prices, increased print ad spending, and began a television-based campaign which touted itself as the "Best in Buffalo." In response, the other firms have all stepped up their price advertising. For instance, Bells, with a 30 per cent market share, calls its stores the "low-price champions"; and Super Duper promotes the "real story on food costs."[18]

❑ Since deregulation about a decade ago, the U.S. airline industry has undergone a number of major price wars. Today, Continental Airlines, as part of the country's largest airline system (Texas Air), has the lowest cost structure in the industry; this gives it substantial pricing clout. Said the chairman of American Airlines, "whoever has the lowest costs can set the prices." In 1987, Continental introduced MaxSaver fares, priced up to 80 per cent less than full coach prices. To remain competitive, every major airline introduced their own MaxSaver plans, which continue to the present. These low fares have significantly constrained overall industry revenues.[19]

Developing a Retail Price Strategy

The development of a retail price strategy is broken down into five components (objectives, policy, strategy, implementation, and adjustments) as depicted in Figure 13-2. First, it is important to note that all aspects of the process are affected by the external factors already discussed. Second, like any other strategic activity, pricing begins with a clear statement of objectives and ends with an adaptive or corrective mechanism. Third, pricing policies must be integrated with the firm's total retail mix. This occurs in the second step of price planning. Fourth, price planning is complex because of the often erratic nature of demand and the number of items carried by many retailers.

Retail Objectives and Pricing

A retailer's pricing strategy must be consistent with and reflect overall objectives. As discussed in Chapter 2, financial retail objectives can be stated in terms of sales and profits. In addition to these broad objectives, a retailer needs to develop more specific pricing objectives to avoid such potential problems as confusing consumers by having too many prices, spending too much time in bargaining with customers, having to use frequent sales to stimulate customer traffic, having inadequate profit margins, placing too much emphasis on price in the strategy mix, and so on.

Overall Objectives and Pricing

A sales goal is usually stated in terms of dollar revenues and/or unit volume. An example of a sales goal and a resultant pricing strategy is a car dealer's desire to capture large dollar revenues by setting low prices and selling a high unit volume. This strategy is called **market penetration.** A penetration strategy is proper when customers are highly sensitive to price, low prices discourage actual and potential competition, and total retail costs do not increase as much as sales volume increases.

A profit-in-dollars objective is sought when a retailer concentrates on total profits or profits per unit. With a **market skimming** strategy, the retailer charges premium prices and attracts those customers who are less concerned with price than with service, assortment, and status. Although this approach typically does

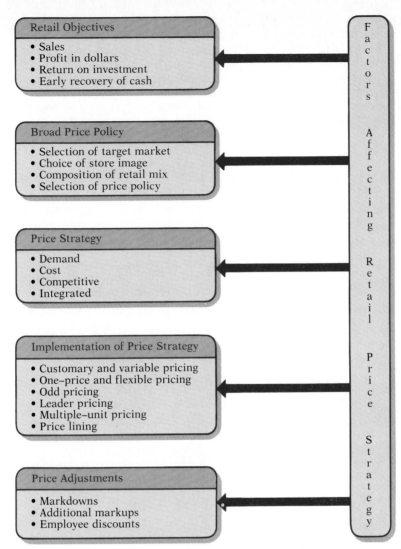

FIGURE 13-2
A Framework for Developing a Retail Price Strategy

not maximize sales, it does achieve high profits per unit. This strategy is appropriate when the market segment that a retailer defines as its target market is insensitive to price, new competitors will not enter the market, and additional sales will greatly increase total retail costs.

Return on investment and early recovery of cash are two other profit-based objectives. A return-on-investment goal is sought when a retailer stipulates that profits must be a certain percentage of its investment, such as profits' being 20 per cent of inventory investment. Early recovery of cash is a goal set by retailers that may be short on cash, wish to expand, or be uncertain about the future. A market skimming strategy is often used by retailers with return on investment or early recovery of cash as an objective.

Tie Town, the tie shop mentioned at the beginning of this chapter, offers a good illustration of a retailer interested in sales, profit, and return-on-investment goals. Tie Town sells inexpensive ties (avoiding competition with department and haberdashery stores), uses a single selling price for all ties (to be set for the next year from within the range of $7 to $10), minimizes operating costs, maximizes self-service, and carries a large variety to generate traffic.

Table 13-2 contains data gathered by Tie Town pertaining to demand, costs, profit, and return on inventory investment at various prices between $7 and $10. It must select the most appropriate price within that range. Table 13-3 shows the methods used to arrive at the figures in Table 13-2.

From Table 13-2, several conclusions concerning the best price for Tie Town can be drawn:

❑ A sales objective would lead the company to a selling price of $8. At that price, total sales are highest ($400,000).

❑ A dollar profit objective would lead the firm to a selling price of $9. At that price, total profits are highest ($66,000).

❑ A return-on-investment objective would also lead the store to a selling price of $8. At that price, return on inventory investment is 159 per cent.

❑ Although a large quantity can be sold at $7, that selling price would lead to the lowest profit ($27,800).

❑ Although a selling price of $10 would yield the highest profit per unit and as a percentage of sales, total dollar profits are not maximized at this price.

❑ High inventory turnover would not necessarily lead to high profits.

As a result, Tie Town's partners have decided that a price of $9 would enable them to earn the highest dollar profits, while also generating good profit per unit and profit as a percentage of sales.

TABLE 13-2
Tie Town: Demand, Costs, Profit, and Return on Investment*

Selling Price (in $)	Quantity Demanded (in units)	Total Sales Revenue (in $)	Average Cost of Merchandise† (in $)	Total Cost of Merchandise (in $)	Total Nonmerchandise Costs‡ (in $)	Total Costs (in $)
7.00	57,000	399,000	5.60	319,200	52,000	371,200
8.00	50,000	400,000	5.85	292,500	47,000	339,500
9.00	40,000	360,000	6.25	250,000	44,000	294,000
10.00	30,000	300,000	6.75	202,500	40,000	242,500

Selling Price (in $)	Average Total Costs (in $)	Total Profit (in $)	Profit/Unit (in $)	Markup at Retail (in %)	Profit/Sales (in %)	Average Inventory on Hand (in units)
7.00	6.51	27,800	0.49	20	7	6,000
8.00	6.79	60,500	1.21	27	15	6,500
9.00	7.35	66,000	1.65	31	18	7,000
10.00	8.08	57,500	1.92	33	19	8,000

Selling Price (in $)	Inventory Turnover (units)	Average Investment in Inventory at Cost (in $)	Inventory Turnover (in $)	Return on Investment (in %)
7.00	9.5	33,600	9.5	83
8.00	7.7	38,025	7.7	159
9.00	5.7	43,750	5.7	151
10.00	3.8	54,000	3.8	106

*Numbers have been rounded off.

†Reflects quantity discounts.

‡Includes all retail operating expenses.

Ralphs is a California-based supermarket chain with about 130 outlets. Since 1986, it has opened a number of Ralphs Giant superstores, which occupy 70,000 square feet and carry more than 30,000 items each. Ralphs Giant stores satisfy customer needs by using everyday minimum pricing and by offering a clean, well-marked store presentation of warehouse-priced packaged goods. A large assortment of high-quality produce, bakery, meat, and seafood are also featured in exciting and dramatic perishable departments.

Photos courtesy of Federated Department Stores.

When displaying prices and promoting sales, retailers must be sure that they present prices in a manner consistent with their overall store image. Shown here are examples of the way prices are displayed in four discount-oriented retail outlets: K mart, Sterling Heights, Michigan (1); Target Stores, Sacramento, California (2); Best Buy, Kansas City, Missouri (3); and ShopKo, Spokane, Washington (4).

Photos courtesy of *Discount Store News.*

(1)

(2)

(3)

(4)

TABLE 13-3
Derivation of Tie Town Data

425

Pricing in Retailing

Column in Table 13-2	Source of Information or Method of Computation
Selling price	Trade data, comparison shopping, experience
Quantity demanded (in units) at each price level	Consumer surveys, trade data, experience
Total sales revenue	Selling price × Quantity demanded
Average cost of merchandise	Contacts with suppliers, quantity discount structure, estimates of order sizes
Total cost of merchandise	Average cost of merchandise × Quantity demanded
Total nonmerchandise costs	Experience, trade data, estimation of individual retail operating expenses
Total costs	Total cost of merchandise + Total nonmerchandise costs
Average total costs	Total costs ÷ Quantity demanded
Total profit	Total sales revenue − Total costs
Profit per unit	Total profit ÷ Quantity demanded
Markup (at retail)	(Selling price − Average cost of merchandise) ÷ Selling price
Profit as a percentage of sales	Total profit ÷ Total sales revenue
Average inventory on hand (in units)	Trade data, merchandise turnover data, experience
Inventory turnover (in units)	Quantity demanded ÷ Average inventory on hand (in units)
Average investment in inventory (at cost)	Average cost of merchandise × Average inventory on hand (in units)
Inventory turnover (in $)	Total cost of merchandise ÷ Average investment in inventory (at cost)
Return on inventory investment	Total profit ÷ Average investment in inventory (at cost)

Specific Pricing Objectives

Figure 13-3 provides a list of specific pricing objectives other than sales and profits. Although a number of pricing objectives are enumerated in this figure, each retailer must determine the relative importance of the various goals in its particular situation and plan accordingly. It should be noted that some of the goals in this figure may not be compatible with one another, such as not encouraging customers to be overly price-conscious versus "we will not be undersold."

Broad Price Policy

A broad price policy enables a retailer to generate a coordinated series of actions, a consistent image (especially important for chain and franchise units), and a strategy that incorporates short- and long-run considerations (where the retailer balances immediate and long-term goals). The color photo portfolio following page 424 illustrates this concept. A useful technique for planning a broad price policy is the **multistage approach.**

This approach divides the major elements of pricing into six successive steps, with each step placing limits on those that follow: selecting a target market, choosing a store image, outlining the retail strategy mix, selecting a broad price policy, selecting a price strategy, and choosing specific prices.[20] The first four steps concentrate on the evolution of a broad policy; the last two steps center on specific price decisions and their implementation (which are discussed later in this chapter).

The starting point in developing any price policy is the selection of a target market. Once the market is selected, an appropriate store image is created that

1. To maintain a proper image.
2. To not encourage customers to become overly price–conscious.
3. To be perceived as fair by all parties (including suppliers, employees, and customers).
4. To be consistent in setting prices.
5. To increase customer traffic in slow periods.
6. To clear out seasonal merchandise.
7. To match competitors' prices without starting a price war.
8. To promote a "we–will–not–be–undersold" philosophy.
9. To be regarded as the price leader in the market area by consumers.
10. To provide ample customer service.
11. To minimize the chance of government actions relating to price advertising and antitrust matters.
12. To discourage potential competitors from entering the marketplace.
13. To create and maintain customer interest.
14. To encourage repeat business.

FIGURE 13-3
Specific Pricing Objectives

would establish the relevant associations in the minds of the target market. Thus, the selection of a target market limits the retailer's choice of a store image. In composing its retail strategy mix, the firm must assign a role to price, such as appealing to customers via extensive price cutting or generating store traffic through convenience, quality of service, and so on, rather than price.

Next, a retailer determines its broad price policy, which translates price decisions into an integrated framework. For example, a company must decide whether prices should be established for individual items, interrelated for a group of goods and services, or based on an extensive use of special sales.

These are some of the price policies from which a retailer could choose:

❑ No competitors will have lower prices; no competitors will have higher prices; or prices will be consistent with competitors'.

❑ All items will be priced independently, depending on the demand for each; or the prices for all items will be interrelated to maintain an image and ensure proper markups.

❑ Price leadership will be exerted; no other firm will adjust prices earlier; or competitors will be price leaders and set prices first.

❑ Prices will be constant throughout the year or season; or prices will change if merchandise costs change.

Price Strategy

A price strategy can be either demand, cost, or competitive in orientation. In demand-oriented pricing, the retailer sets prices based on consumer desires. It determines the range of prices acceptable to the target market. The top of this range is called the demand ceiling, the maximum consumers will pay for a good or service.

Cost-oriented pricing sets a price floor, the minimum price acceptable to a retailer so that it can obtain a specified profit goal. Usually, the retailer computes merchandise and retail operating costs and adds a profit margin to these figures.

With competition-oriented pricing, a retailer sets prices in accordance with competitors'. In this technique, the price levels of key competitors and how they affect the retailer's sales are studied.

All three approaches should be considered when setting a price strategy. They do not operate independently of one another. Figures 13-4 and 13-5 show distinctive price-oriented advertisements.

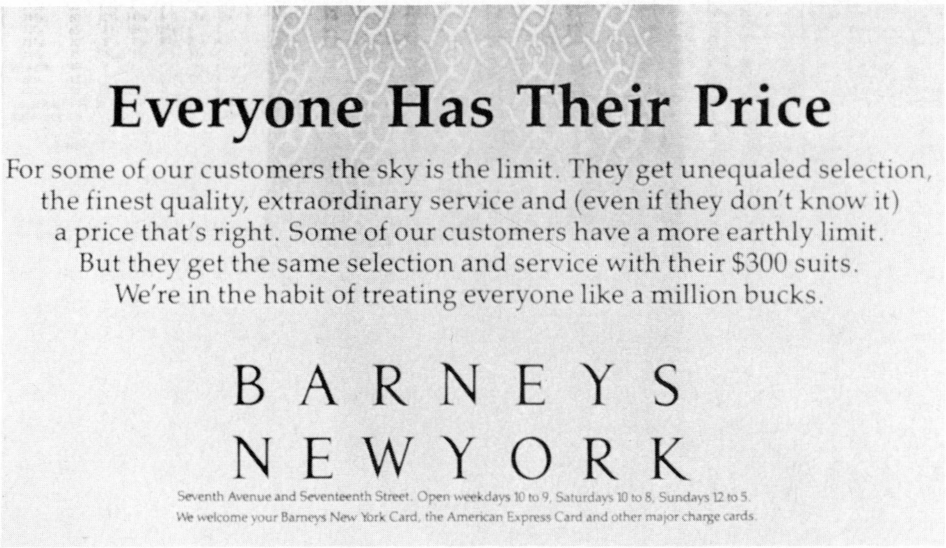

Everyone Has Their Price

For some of our customers the sky is the limit. They get unequaled selection,
the finest quality, extraordinary service and (even if they don't know it)
a price that's right. Some of our customers have a more earthly limit.
But they get the same selection and service with their $300 suits.
We're in the habit of treating everyone like a million bucks.

B A R N E Y S
N E W Y O R K

Seventh Avenue and Seventeenth Street. Open weekdays 10 to 9, Saturdays 10 to 8, Sundays 12 to 5.
We welcome your Barneys New York Card, the American Express Card and other major charge cards.

FIGURE 13-4
A Barneys Clothing Advertisement
Reprinted by permission of Barneys New York.

Demand-Oriented Pricing

Demand-oriented pricing is often used by retailers whose goals are listed in terms of sales or market share. It seeks to estimate the quantities customers would demand at various price levels and concentrates on the prices associated with stated sales goals. Whereas a cost-oriented pricing strategy examines costs, a demand-oriented approach looks at demand irrespective of costs.

When using a demand-oriented approach, it is necessary to understand the psychological implications of pricing. The term **psychological pricing** refers to the consumers' perceptions of retail prices. Two aspects of psychological pricing are the price–quality association and prestige pricing.

The **price–quality association** is a concept stating that many consumers believe that high prices connote high quality and that low prices connote low quality. This is particularly true in cases where goods/service quality is difficult to judge on bases other than price, buyers perceive large differences in quality among brands, buyers have little experience or confidence in judging quality (as in the case of a new product), and brand names are an insignificant factor in product choice.

Although a number of studies have documented the price–quality relationship, research indicates that when other quality cues, such as product features and a well-known brand name, are introduced, these factors may be more important than price in a person's judgment of overall product quality.

Prestige pricing is drawn from the price–quality association. In **prestige pricing,** it is assumed that consumers do not buy goods and services at prices that are considered too low. Consumers actually set price floors and may not purchase certain items if they are priced below these floors. Their feeling is that too low a price would mean that quality and status are also low. In addition, some consumers use prestige pricing in the selection of retail stores and do not shop at stores that have prices that are too low. For example, Saks Fifth Avenue and Neiman-Marcus do not generally carry the least expensive versions of items because their customers may perceive them to be inferior.

It should be noted that prestige pricing does not apply to all customers. That

FIGURE 13-5
A This End Up Furniture Advertisement
Reprinted by permission.

is why the target market must be defined before the retailer reaches this stage. Some customers may be economizers and may always shop for bargains. For these consumers, neither aspect of psychological pricing–price–quality and prestige–may be applicable.

Cost-Oriented Pricing

The **cost-oriented approach,** markup pricing, is the most widely practiced retail-pricing technique. In the cost-oriented method, a retailer sets prices by adding per-unit merchandise costs, retail operating expenses, and desired profits. The difference between merchandise costs and selling price is the retailer's **markup.** For example, a retailer buys a desk for $200 and wants to sell it for $300. The extra $100 is needed for retail operating expenses and profit. The markup is 33⅓ per cent on retail price, or 50 per cent on cost.

The markup percentage depends upon many factors, such as a product's traditional markup, the manufacturer's suggested list price, inventory turnover, the competition, rent and other overhead costs, the extent to which a product must be altered or serviced, and the selling effort required.

Would You Pay $14,000 for a Child-Size Ferrari Testarossa?

Some upscale retailers really seem to test the upper limits of prestige pricing. After all, how much would you pay for a child-sized Ferrari Testarossa? While most of us would not even consider such an object, F.A.O. Schwarz, probably the world's most expensive toy store, has been selling the miniature Ferrari for $14,000:

> The people that are going to buy extraordinarily special things for their children have a very high level of discretionary income. Parents will always spend with wild abandon and love on their children.

Geary's, a crystal and china shop in Beverly Hills, California, sells sets of Faberge crystal eggs covered with rubies and silver at $14,000 per set. Bloomingdale's carries $10,000 hand-cut crystal ornaments. Hammacher Schlemmer, a chain that sells unusual items, offers a $450 two-way radio helmet for skiers. Neiman-Marcus sells a day at a circus for $5,000. The customer gets to invite up to twenty-five friends, act as ringmaster, and ride an elephant. Animal Manors of New York sells dog and cat houses at prices ranging from $1,500 to $10,000 apiece.

Yet, despite these "outrageous" prices, as Geary's president says, "business has never been better." Adds a retailing expert, "Americans will probably never lose their fascination with unusual [status-filled] gadgets and gifts." All of the upscale retailers noted above recognize that there is a market segment of affluent consumers who are willing to pay dearly for exciting and unique merchandise. They also realize that this segment is rather small.

Source: Based on material in Kathleen A. Hughes, "This Christmas, the Luxury Gift Counter Includes a $425 Dinosaur and $14,000 Eggs," *Wall Street Journal* (December 24, 1987), p. 9.

Although markups can be computed on the basis of retail selling price or cost, they are typically calculated in terms of retail selling price. There are several reasons for this. First, retail expenses, markdowns, and profits are always stated as a percentage of sales. Therefore, when markups are expressed as a percentage of sales, these percentages are quite meaningful. Second, manufacturers quote their selling prices and trade discounts to retailers as percentage reductions from retail list prices. Third, retail selling-price information is more readily available than cost information. Fourth, profitability statistics appear to be smaller if expressed on the basis of retail price instead of cost; this can be useful when dealing with the government, employees, and consumers.

Markup percentages are calculated as

$$\text{Markup percentage (at retail)} = \frac{\text{Retail selling price} - \text{Merchandise cost}}{\text{Retail selling price}}$$

$$\text{Markup percentage (at cost)} = \frac{\text{Retail selling price} - \text{Merchandise cost}}{\text{Merchandise cost}}$$

As shown in these equations, the difference is in the denominator used. In both formulas, merchandise cost is the per unit invoice and freight cost to the retailer, less per unit trade or quantity discounts.[21]

Table 13-4 contains markups at retail and at cost for a wide range of percentages. As the markup increases, the disparity between retail and cost percentages grows. For example, a watch retailer buys a watch for $20 and is undecided as to whether to sell it for $25, $40, or $80. In evaluating markup, it is determined

TABLE 13-4
Markup Equivalents

Percentage at Retail	Percentage at Cost
5.0	5.3
10.0	11.1
15.0	17.6
20.0	25.0
25.0	33.3
30.0	42.9
35.0	53.8
40.0	66.7
45.0	81.8
50.0	100.0
60.0	150.0
75.0	300.0
80.0	400.0
90.0	900.0

that the $25 price yields a markup of 20 per cent (at retail) or 25 per cent (at cost), the $40 price yields a markup of 50 per cent (at retail) or 100 per cent (at cost), and the $80 price yields a markup of 75 per cent (at retail) or 300 per cent (at cost).

The markup concept has various applications in pricing and purchase planning. The following illustrations of markups detail the usefulness of the concept:

❏ A discount clothing store can purchase a shipment of men's jeans at $10 each and wants to obtain a 40 per cent markup at retail. What retail price should the store charge to achieve this markup?

$$\frac{\text{Markup percentage}}{\text{(at retail)}} = \frac{\text{Retail selling price} - \text{Merchandise cost}}{\text{Retail selling price}}$$

$$0.40 = \frac{\text{Retail selling price} - \$10.00}{\text{Retail selling price}}$$

$$0.40 \,(\text{Retail selling price}) = \text{Retail selling price} - \$10.00$$

$$0.60 \,(\text{Retail selling price}) = \$10.00$$

$$\text{Retail selling price} = \$16.67$$

The retailer should charge $16.67 to achieve the 40 per cent markup at retail.*

❏ A stationery store desires a minimum 30 per cent markup at retail for legal-sized envelopes. If the retailer feels that the envelopes should retail at 59 cents per box, what is the maximum price the retailer can pay for the envelopes?

---

*One may also calculate selling price by transposing the markup formula into

$$\text{Retail selling price} = \frac{\text{Merchandise cost}}{1 - \text{Markup}}$$

$$\text{Retail selling price} = \frac{\$10.00}{1 - 0.4} = \frac{\$10.00}{0.6} = \$16.67$$

$$\text{Markup percentage (at retail)} = \frac{\text{Retail selling price} - \text{Merchandise cost}}{\text{Retail selling price}}$$

$$0.30 = \frac{\$0.59 - \text{Merchandise cost}}{\$0.59}$$

$$\$0.59 - \text{Merchandise cost} = (0.30)(\$0.59)$$
$$\$0.59 - \text{Merchandise cost} = \$0.177$$
$$\text{Merchandise cost} = \$0.59 - \$0.177$$
$$\text{Merchandise cost} = \$0.413$$

To achieve at least a 30 per cent markup, the retailer cannot pay more than 41.3 cents per box of legal-sized envelopes.*

❏ A bicycle store has been offered a closeout purchase on an imported line of bicycles. The per-unit cost of each bicycle is $80, and the bikes should retail for $120 each. What markup at retail will the store obtain?

$$\text{Markup percentage (at retail)} = \frac{\text{Retail selling price} - \text{Merchandise cost}}{\text{Retail selling price}}$$

$$\text{Markup percentage} = \frac{\$120.00 - \$80.00}{\$120.00}$$

$$\text{Markup percentage} = \frac{\$40.00}{\$120.00}$$

$$\text{Markup percentage} = 33.3$$

The store will receive a markup of 33.3 per cent on these bikes.

Markup may also be determined by examining planned retail operating expenses, profits, and net sales:

$$\text{Markup percentage (at retail)} = \frac{\text{Planned retail operating expenses} + \text{Planned profits}}{\text{Planned net sales}}$$

As an example, a florist estimates retail operating expenses (rent, salaries, electricity, cleaning, bookkeeping, and so on) to be $45,000 per year. The desired profit is $35,000 per year, including the owner's salary. Net sales are forecast to be $200,000. The planned markup is

$$\text{Markup percentage (at retail)} = \frac{\$45,000 + \$35,000}{\$200,000} = 40$$

Because flowers cost the florist an average of $8.00 a dozen, the retailer's selling price per dozen is

$$\text{Retail selling price} = \frac{\text{Merchandise cost}}{1 - \text{Markup}}$$

$$\text{Retail selling price} = \frac{\$8.00}{1 - 0.40} = \$13.33$$

---

*One may also compute merchandise cost by transposing the markup formula into

Merchandise cost = (Retail selling price) (1 − Markup)
Merchandise cost = ($0.59) (1 − 0.3) = ($0.59) (0.7) = $0.413

The florist will need to sell approximately 15,000 dozen flowers at $13.33 per dozen to achieve sales and profit goals. In order to achieve goals, all flowers must be sold at the $13.33 price.

Because it is highly unusual for a retailer to be able to sell all items in stock at their original prices, it is necessary to compute initial markup, maintained markup, and gross margin. **Initial markup** is based on the original retail value assigned to merchandise less the costs of the merchandise. **Maintained markup** is based on the actual prices received for merchandise sold during a time period less merchandise cost. Because maintained markups are related to actual prices received, it is difficult to estimate them in advance. The difference between initial and maintained markups is that the latter reflect adjustments from original retail values caused by markdowns, added markups, shortages, and discounts.

The initial markup percentage depends on planned retail operating expenses and profits plus planned reductions:

$$\text{Initial markup percentage (at retail)} = \frac{\begin{array}{c}\text{Planned retail operating expenses}\\ + \text{ Planned profit}\\ + \text{ Planned retail reductions}\end{array}}{\begin{array}{c}\text{Planned net sales } +\\ \text{Planned retail reductions}\end{array}}$$

If retail reductions are zero, the markup is equal to retail operating expenses plus profit, which results in the markup formula explained earlier in this section.

To return to the florist example, suppose that the retailer projects that retail reductions will be 20 per cent of estimated sales, or $40,000. The initial markup will have to be

$$\text{Initial markup percentage (at retail)} = \frac{\$45,000 + \$35,000 + \$40,000}{\$200,000 + \$40,000} = 50$$

and the original selling price will be

$$\text{Retail selling price} = \frac{\text{Merchandise cost}}{1 - \text{Markup}} = \frac{\$8.00}{1 - 0.50} = \$16.00$$

This means that the original retail value of 15,000 dozen flowers will be about $240,000. Retail reductions of $40,000 will result in net sales of $200,000. Therefore, the retailer must begin selling flowers at $16.00 per dozen if the objective is to have an average selling price of $13.33 per dozen and a maintained markup of 40 per cent.*

Maintained markup percentages can be viewed as

$$\text{Maintained markup percentage (at retail)} = \frac{\text{Actual retail operating expenses } + \text{ Actual profit}}{\text{Actual net sales}}$$

or

$$\text{Maintained markup percentage (at retail)} = \frac{\text{Average selling price } - \text{ Merchandise cost}}{\text{Average selling price}}$$

---

*There are small rounding errors in these calculations.

Gross margin is the difference between net sales and the total cost of goods sold. The total cost figure, as opposed to the gross cost figure, adjusts for cash discounts and additional expenses:

Gross margin (in $) = Net sales − Total cost of goods

For the florist, gross margin (which is the dollar equivalent of maintained markup) is $200,000 − $120,000 = $80,000. The total costs are merchandise cost times the number of units purchased.

Although a retailer must set an overall company markup goal, the markups for categories of merchandise or even individual products may differ. In fact, markups may vary significantly. In department stores, maintained markup as a percentage of sales ranged from 31.5 per cent for recreation items to 36.7 per cent for home furnishings to 46.2 per cent for female accessories in 1985.[22]

The utilization of a **variable markup policy** achieves three major purposes. First, variable markups recognize that costs associated with separate goods/ service categories may fluctuate widely. Some items require extensive alterations (such as clothing) or installation (such as carpeting). Even within a product line like women's clothing, expensive fashion items require greater end-of-year mark-downs than inexpensive items. Therefore, the more expensive line would receive a higher initial markup.

Second, variable markups allow for differences in product investments. For instance, in a large appliance department where the retailer orders regularly from a wholesaler, lower markups would be required than in a fine jewelry department, where the retailer would have to maintain a complete stock of merchandise.

Third, a variable policy accounts for differences in selling efforts and merchandising skills. The selling of a food processor may necessitate substantial sales effort, whereas a blender may involve significantly less effort and skill.

One emerging technique for planning variable markups is called **direct product profitability (DPP),** which is growing in popularity among supermarkets, discount stores, and other retailers. With DPP, a retailer determines the profitability of each category or unit of merchandise by computing adjusted per-unit gross margin and assigning direct product costs for expense categories such as warehousing, transportation, handling, and selling. In this way, the appropriate markup for each category or item could be set. The major problem with DPP is the complexity and difficulty of allocating costs accurately.[23]

Figure 13-6 shows how DPP works. In this example, each of two items has a retail selling price of $20. With Item A, the retailer has a merchandise cost of $12. Its per-unit gross margin is $8. However, because the firm receives a $1 per-unit allowance (rebate) for setting up a special display for Item A, its adjusted gross margin is $9. Total direct retail costs for Item A are estimated at $5. Therefore, the direct product profit for Item A is $4, or 20 per cent of sales.

With Item B, the retailer has a merchandise cost of $10. Its per-unit gross margin is $10; and there are no special discounts or allowances. Since Item B requires a greater selling effort, its total direct retail costs are $6. And, its direct profit is $4, or 20 per cent of sales. To attain the same direct profit per unit, Item A has a markup of 40 per cent (per-unit gross margin/selling price) and Item B has a markup of 50 per cent.

For many reasons, cost-oriented (markup) pricing is very popular among retailers. It is fairly simple, especially as a retailer can apply a standard markup for a category of products much more easily than it can estimate demand at various price levels; the retailer also can adjust prices according to changes in demand or it can segment a market. Markup pricing has an inherent sense of equity in that the retailer earns a fair profit. In addition, when all retailers adhere to similar markups, price competition is significantly reduced. Last, markup pric-

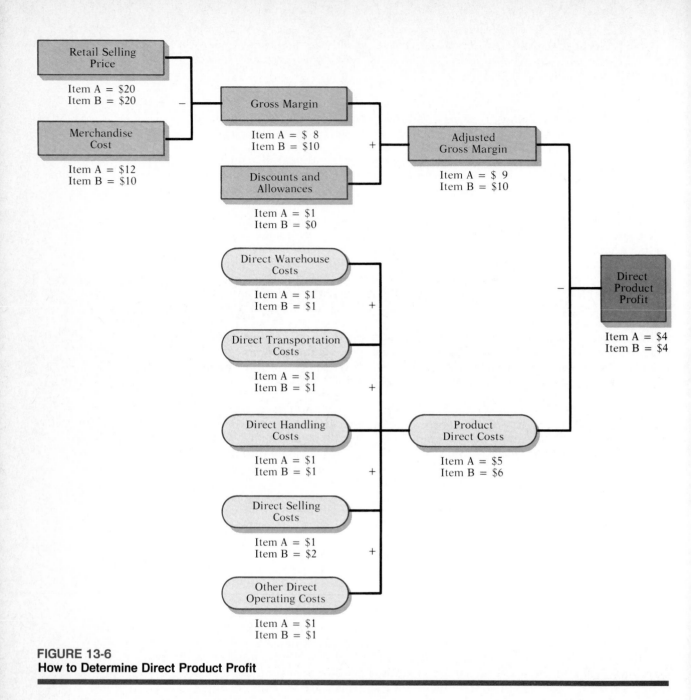

FIGURE 13-6
How to Determine Direct Product Profit

ing is quite efficient if it takes into account competition, seasonal factors, and difficulties in selling specific merchandise categories.

Competition-Oriented Pricing

With a **competition-oriented pricing** approach, a retailer uses competitors' prices as a guide, rather than demand or cost considerations. A competition-oriented firm would not alter its prices to react to changes in demand or costs unless competitors alter their prices. Similarly, a competition-oriented retailer would alter its prices when competitors do, even if demand or cost factors remain the same.

434

A competition-oriented retailer can price below the market, at the market, or above the market. Table 13-5 outlines the conditions that would influence a retailer's choice of one of these levels. It is clear from this table that pricing strategy must be integrated with the overall retail strategy mix. For example, a retailer with a strong location, superior customer service, good product assortment, favorable image, and exclusive brands could set prices above those of competitors. On the other hand, above-market pricing would not be appropriate for a retailer that has an inconvenient location, relies on self-service, concentrates on best-sellers, is a fashion follower, and stresses private-label merchandise.

Competition-oriented pricing is utilized for several reasons. It is relatively simple; there are no calculations of demand curves or concern with price elasticity. The ongoing market price is assumed to be fair for both the consumer and the retailer. Pricing at the market level does not disrupt competition and therefore does not usually lead to retaliation.

Integration of Approaches to Price Strategy

The three approaches for setting a retail price strategy should be integrated, so that demand, cost, and competition are all taken into account. To accomplish this, a retailer should answer questions such as these before a price strategy is enacted:

❑ If I reduce a price, will sales increase greatly? (Demand orientation)

❑ Should I charge different prices for a product, based on negotiations with customers, seasonality, and so on? (Demand orientation)

❑ Will a given price level allow me to attain the traditional markup? (Cost orientation)

❑ What price level is necessary for a product that requires special costs in purchasing, selling, or delivery? (Cost orientation)

❑ What price levels are competitors setting? (Competitive orientation)

❑ Can I charge higher prices than competitors because of my reputation and image? (Competitive orientation)

By no means is this list complete, but it should give some idea as to how a retailer can apply demand, cost, and competitive orientations to pricing.

TABLE 13-5
Competition-Oriented Pricing Alternatives

Retail Mix Variable	Alternative Price Strategies		
	Pricing Below the Market	Pricing At the Market	Pricing Above the Market
Location	Poor, inconvenient site	Close to competitors, no locational advantage	Absence of strong competitors, convenient to consumers
Customer service	Self-service, little product knowledge on part of salespeople, no displays	Moderate assistance by sales personnel	High levels of personal selling, delivery, exchanges, etc.
Product assortment	Concentration on best-sellers	Medium assortment	Large assortment
Atmosphere	Inexpensive fixtures, little or no carpeting or paneling, racks for merchandise	Moderate atmosphere	Attractive, pleasant decor with many displays
Role of fashion in assortment	Fashion follower, conservative	Concentration on accepted best-sellers	Fashion leader
Special services	Cash and carry	Not available or extra charge to customers	Included in price
Merchandise lines carried	Private labels, name-brand closeouts, small manufacturers	Name brands	Exclusive name brands

Implementation of Price Strategy

The implementation of a price strategy involves a wide variety of separate but interrelated specific decisions in addition to those broad concepts discussed previously. A checklist of selected decisions is shown in Figure 13-7. In this section, many of the specifics of pricing strategy are detailed.

Customary and Variable Pricing

Customary pricing occurs when a retailer sets prices for goods and services and seeks to maintain them over an extended period of time. Prices are not altered during this time period. Examples of goods and services with customary prices are newspapers, candy, mass transit, telephone booths, pinball machines, cigarettes, vending-machine items, and foods on restaurant menus. In each of these cases, a retailer would seek to establish customary prices and have consumers take them for granted.

However, in many instances, a retailer cannot or should not use customary pricing. The retailer cannot maintain constant prices if its costs are rising. The retailer should not maintain constant prices if customer demand varies. Under **variable pricing,** the retailer alters prices to coincide with fluctuations in costs or consumer demand.

Cost fluctuations can be seasonal or trend. Seasonal fluctuations affect retailers that sell items whose production is limited to certain times during the year. For example, prices in supermarkets and floral shops vary during the year because of the seasonal nature of many agricultural and floral products. When items are scarce, their costs to the retailer go up. Trend fluctuations, which are common to almost all retailers today, refer to the constant upward (or downward) spiral of costs to the retailer. As costs increase, the retailer must raise prices permanently (unlike seasonal fluctuations, which cause temporary changes).

Demand fluctuations can be place- or time-based. Place fluctuations exist for retailers who sell seat locations, such as concert theaters and athletic stadiums. Different prices can be charged for different seat locations; tickets close to the stage or the field command higher prices. If variable pricing is not followed, seat location is based on first come, first served. Time fluctuations occur when consumer demand differs by hour, day, or season. For example, demand for a movie theater is greater on Saturday than on Wednesday; demand for an airline is greater during December than during February. Accordingly prices should be lower during periods of low demand.

---

1. How important is price stability? How long should prices be maintained?
2. Should prices change if costs and/or customer demand vary?
3. Should the same prices be charged of all customers buying under the same conditions?
4. Should customer bargaining be permitted?
5. Should odd pricing (e.g., $5.99) be used?
6. Should leader pricing be utilized to draw customer traffic? If yes, should leader prices be above, at, or below costs?
7. Should consumers be offered discounts for purchasing in quantity?
8. Should price lining be used to provide a price range and price points within that range?
9. Should pricing practices vary by department or product line?

FIGURE 13-7
A Checklist of Selected Specific Pricing Decisions

It is possible to combine customary and variable pricing. For instance, a theater can charge $2 every Wednesday night and $5 every Saturday. An airline can lower prices by 20 per cent during off-seasons.

One-Price Policy and Flexible Pricing

Under a **one-price policy,** a retailer charges the same price for all customers who seek to purchase an item under similar conditions. A one-price policy may be used in conjunction with customary pricing or variable pricing. In the latter case, all customers interested in a particular section of seats or arriving at the same time would pay the same price.

The one-price policy was begun by John Wanamaker, who was the first major merchant to mark prices clearly on each item in stock. This marking system did away with price bargaining, found favor with consumers, and was quickly copied by others. Throughout the United States, one-price policies are the rule for most retailers, and bargaining over price is usually not permitted.

In contrast, **flexible pricing** allows consumers to bargain over selling price, and those consumers who are good at bargaining obtain lower prices than those who are not. Jewelry stores, automobile dealers, house painters, flea markets, health spas, and appliance stores are examples of retailers that use flexible pricing. Retailers using flexible pricing do not clearly post their bottom-line prices; consumers must have prior knowledge in order to bargain successfully.[24]

A one-price policy speeds up transactions, reduces labor costs, and permits self-service, catalogs, and vending-machine sales. Flexible pricing requires high initial prices and qualified sales personnel.

Odd Pricing

An **odd-pricing strategy** occurs when retail prices are set at levels below even dollar values, such as $0.49, $4.95, and $199.00. The assumption is that consumers feel that these prices represent bargains or that the amounts are beneath consumers' price ceilings. For example, realtors hope that consumers who set a price ceiling of under $100,000 will be attracted to houses selling for $99,500. From this perspective, odd pricing is a form of psychological pricing (which was discussed earlier in the chapter).

Originally, odd prices were imposed to force sales clerks to give change on each purchase, thus preventing the clerks from pocketing receipts without ringing up sales. Now odd prices are accepted as part of the American system of retailing and are used more for psychological reasons.

Odd prices that are 1 cent or 2 cents below the next highest even price (e.g., $0.29, $0.99, $2.98) are most common up to the $4.00 level. Beyond that point and up to $50.00, 5-cent reductions from the highest even price (e.g., $19.95, $49.95) are more usual. For higher-priced merchandise, odd endings are in dollars (e.g., $399; $4,995). As an example, a nationwide study of restaurant newspaper ads found that advertised prices ended with '5' or '9' 88 per cent of the time, with '5' used 68 per cent of the time.[25]

Despite the widespread use of odd pricing in retailing, there has been little research on its psychological effects.

Leader Pricing

In **leader pricing,** a retailer advertises and sells key items in its goods/service assortment at less than the usual profit margins. The objective of leader pricing is to increase customer contacts with the retailer in the hope of selling regularly priced goods and services in addition to the specially priced items. Leader pricing is different from bait-and-switch, in which the sale items are not sold.

Leader pricing often involves frequently purchased, nationally branded, high-turnover goods and services, because it is easy for customers to detect low prices and they generate high customer traffic. There are two kinds of leader pricing: loss leaders and sales at lower than regular prices (but higher than costs). As described earlier in the chapter, loss leaders are regulated on a statewide basis under minimum-price laws.

In many drugstores, the best-selling item in terms of dollar sales is film. To stimulate consumer traffic, drugstores price film at low markups, sometimes close to cost, and advertise the special prices. Film is an excellent item for leader pricing, because consumers know a good value and are likely to add a shopping trip to make a purchase.

Multiple-Unit Pricing

Multiple-unit pricing is a strategy whereby a retailer offers its customers discounts for buying in quantity. For example, by selling items at two for $0.78 or six for $2.19, a retailer would attempt to sell more products than at $0.40 each.

There are two reasons for utilizing multiple-unit pricing. First, the retailer seeks to have customers increase their total purchases of an item. However, if customers buy multiple units and stockpile them, instead of consuming more, the sales of the retailer would not increase. Second, multiple-unit pricing could enable a retailer to clear out slow-moving and end-of-season merchandise.

Price Lining

Instead of stocking merchandise at all different price levels, retailers usually employ **price lining** and sell merchandise at a limited range of prices, with each price representing a distinct level of quality. With price lining, retailers first determine the price floors and ceilings for their offerings. Then they set a limited number of prices (price points) within the range. For example, department stores typically carry good, better, and best versions of merchandise consistent with their overall price policy and set individual prices accordingly.

Price lining benefits both consumers and retailers. For the consumer, price lining minimizes confusion in shopping. If a price range for personalized stationery is $6 to $12 and the price points are $6, $9, and $12, the consumer would know that distinct product qualities exist. However, should the retailer have prices of $6, $7, $8, $9, $10, $11, and $12, the consumer could be confused about product qualities and differences.

For the retailer, price lining greatly aids the merchandise buying and handling process. A retail buyer would seek out only suppliers that carry products at appropriate prices; and he or she can use final selling price as a starting point in negotiations with suppliers. The retailer would automatically disregard products that do not fit within the price line and thereby reduce inventory investment. Also, stock turnover would be greatly increased by limiting the models carried.

Four difficulties do exist with price lining. First, depending on the specific price points selected, a price-lining strategy may have gaps between prices that are perceived as too large by the consumer. Thus, a mother shopping for a graduation gift for her son might find a $100 typewriter to be too inexpensive and a $220 typewriter to be too expensive. Second, inflation makes it difficult to maintain price points and the price range. When costs rise, retailers can either eliminate lower prices or reduce markups. Third, markdowns or special sales may disrupt the balance in a price line, unless all items in the line are reduced proportionally. Fourth, price lines must be coordinated for complementary product categories, such as blazers, skirts, and shoes.

Price Adjustments

Price adjustments allow retailers to use price as an adaptive mechanism. Markdowns and additional markups may be necessary in adapting to factors

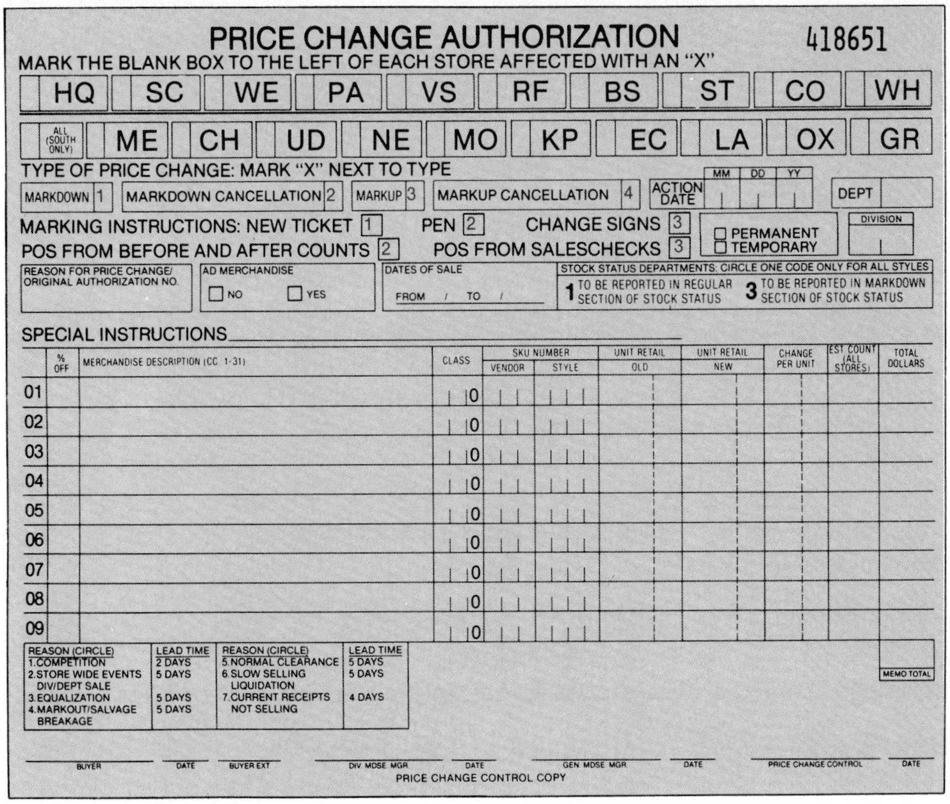
PRICE CHANGE AUTHORIZATION 418651
MARK THE BLANK BOX TO THE LEFT OF EACH STORE AFFECTED WITH AN "X"
HQ SC WE PA VS RF BS ST CO WH
ALL (SOUTH ONLY) ME CH UD NE MO KP EC LA OX GR
TYPE OF PRICE CHANGE: MARK "X" NEXT TO TYPE
MARKDOWN 1 MARKDOWN CANCELLATION 2 MARKUP 3 MARKUP CANCELLATION 4 ACTION DATE MM DD YY DEPT
MARKING INSTRUCTIONS: NEW TICKET 1 PEN 2 CHANGE SIGNS 3 PERMANENT TEMPORARY DIVISION
POS FROM BEFORE AND AFTER COUNTS 2 POS FROM SALESCHECKS 3
REASON FOR PRICE CHANGE/ ORIGINAL AUTHORIZATION NO.
AD MERCHANDISE NO YES
DATES OF SALE FROM / TO /
STOCK STATUS DEPARTMENTS: CIRCLE ONE CODE ONLY FOR ALL STYLES
1 TO BE REPORTED IN REGULAR SECTION OF STOCK STATUS
3 TO BE REPORTED IN MARKDOWN SECTION OF STOCK STATUS
SPECIAL INSTRUCTIONS

	% OFF	MERCHANDISE DESCRIPTION (CC 1-31)	CLASS	SKU NUMBER VENDOR	SKU NUMBER STYLE	UNIT RETAIL OLD	UNIT RETAIL NEW	CHANGE PER UNIT	EST COUNT (ALL STORES)	TOTAL DOLLARS
01			0							
02			0							
03			0							
04			0							
05			0							
06			0							
07			0							
08			0							
09			0							

REASON (CIRCLE)	LEAD TIME	REASON (CIRCLE)	LEAD TIME
1.COMPETITION	2 DAYS	5.NORMAL CLEARANCE	5 DAYS
2.STORE WIDE EVENTS DIV/DEPT SALE	5 DAYS	6.SLOW SELLING LIQUIDATION	5 DAYS
3.EQUALIZATION	5 DAYS	7.CURRENT RECEIPTS NOT SELLING	4 DAYS
4.MARKOUT/SALVAGE BREAKAGE	5 DAYS		

MEMO TOTAL
BUYER DATE BUYER EXT DIV. MDSE MGR DATE GEN MDSE MGR DATE PRICE CHANGE CONTROL DATE
PRICE CHANGE CONTROL COPY

FIGURE 13-8
A Price Change Authorization Form

such as competition, seasonality, style preferences, and pilferage. Figure 13-8 shows a price-change authorization form.

A **markdown** from the original retail price of an item may be used to meet the lower price of another retailer, to adapt to errors in overstocking fashions, to clear out shopworn merchandise, to deplete assortments of odds and ends, and to increase customer traffic. **Additional markups** are increases in retail prices after and in addition to original markups that are used when demand is unexpectedly high or when costs are rising.

A third type of price adjustment, discounts to employees, is mentioned here because such discounts may influence the computation of markdowns and additional markups. Also, although employee discounts are not an adaptive mechanism, they affect employee morale. Some retailers give employee discounts on all merchandise and also let employees buy sale merchandise before it is made available to the general public.

Computing Markdowns and Additional Markups

Markdowns and additional markups can be calculated in dollars (total dollar markdown or markup) or percentages. Two ways of calculating a markdown are the markdown percentage and the off-retail percentage. The **markdown percentage** is computed as

$$\text{Markdown percentage} = \frac{\text{Total dollar markdown}}{\text{Net sales (in \$)}}$$

A difficulty with this formula is that additional markups and employee discounts must be included in net sales (along with dollar markdowns). Furthermore, this formula does not enable a retailer to determine the percentage of items that are marked down as compared to those sold at the original price.

A complementary measure is the **off-retail markdown percentage:**

$$\text{Off-retail markdown percentage} = \frac{\text{Original price} - \text{New price}}{\text{Original price}}$$

With this formula, the percentage of markdown for each item can be computed, as well as the percentage of items marked down.

For example, a gas barbecue grill sells for $100 at the beginning of the summer and is reduced to $70 at the end of the summer. The off-retail markdown is 30 per cent [($100 − $70)/$100]. If 100 grills are sold at the original price and 20 are sold at the sale price, the percentage of items marked down is 17 per cent, and the total dollar markdown is $600.

Additional markup percentages and **additions to retail percentages** are computed as

$$\frac{\text{Additional markup}}{\text{percentage}} = \frac{\text{Total dollar additional markups}}{\text{Net sales (in \$)}}$$

$$\frac{\text{Addition to retail}}{\text{percentage}} = \frac{\text{New price} - \text{Original price}}{\text{Original price}}$$

Retailers should be aware that price adjustments affect their markups per unit, and that significantly more customers would have to be attracted at reduced prices to attain total gross profits equal to those at higher prices.[26] The impact of a markdown or an additional markup on total gross profits may be ascertained through this formula:

$$\begin{matrix}\text{Unit sales required to} \\ \text{earn the same total} \\ \text{gross profit with a} \\ \text{price adjustment}\end{matrix} = \frac{\text{Original markup (\%)}}{\begin{matrix}\text{Original markup (\%)} \\ +/- \text{ Price change (\%)}\end{matrix}} \times \begin{matrix}\text{Expected unit} \\ \text{sales at} \\ \text{original price}\end{matrix}$$

For example, at a specialty store, a Sony Walkman with a cost of $50 has an original retail price of $100, a markup of 50 per cent. The firm expects to sell 500 of these units over the next year; this would lead to a total gross profit of $25,000 ($50 × 500). How many units would the retailer have to sell if it reduced the price to $85 or raised it to $110 and still earn a $25,000 gross profit? This is how it would compute the answer:*

$$\begin{matrix}\text{Unit sales required} \\ \text{(at \$85)}\end{matrix} = \frac{50\%}{50\% - 15\%} \times 500 = 1.43 \times 500 = 714$$

$$\begin{matrix}\text{Unit sales required} \\ \text{(at \$110)}\end{matrix} = \frac{50\%}{50\% + 10\%} \times 500 = 0.83 \times 500 = 417$$

The retailer's judgment regarding price adjustments would be affected by its operating expenses at various sales volumes and customer price elasticity.

Markdown Control

Markdown control evaluates the number of markdowns, their proportion of sales, and their causes. It must be such that reductions can be evaluated and buying plans altered in later periods to reflect markdowns. A good technique for evaluating the causes of markdowns is to have a buyer record the reasons for

---

*There are small rounding errors in these calculations.

1. Adhere to a buying plan in terms of the quantities to be ordered, and the timing of receipt of merchandise. Do not buy too much merchandise to secure an additional quantity discount or promotional allowance. Learn to say "no" to vendors' salespeople.

2. Be an important customer. Limit the number of vendors with which you deal. Bargain for the right to exchange slow–selling merchandise during the season, if necessary.

3. Evaluate the reasons for slow–selling merchandise. Can additional displays or sales incentives quicken the sales pace?

4. Carefully study the impact of special purchases on the sale of traditional merchandise.

5. Be careful in size selection. It may be wise to risk being out of stock, for example, in very small and very large sizes versus having to take drastic markdowns.

6. Maintain a perpetual inventory of large–ticket items to avoid large markdowns.

7. Limit spoilage by properly caring for and displaying perishable or breakable goods, and by using appropriate packaging and containers.

8. Monitor layaway payments. Beware of an item being held back for a long period of time and then not being wanted by a customer. Request partial prepayments to hold a layaway item.

9. Make sure that salespeople are properly motivated and trained.

10. Staple merchandise can generally be carried over to next year. The carrying costs must be weighed against the size of the necessary markdown, potential increases in price next year, shelf space occupied, shipping costs, etc.

FIGURE 13-9
Ten Ways to Control Markdowns
Source: Adapted by the authors from William Burston, *A Checklist of 38 Ways of Controlling Markdowns* (New York: National Retail Merchants Association, n.d.).

each markdown he or she uses and to examine these reasons on a regular basis. Examples of buyer notations are "end of season," "to match the price of a competitor," "worn merchandise," and "obsolete style."

Markdown control enables a retailer to monitor its policies, such as the way merchandise is stored and late acceptance of fashion shipments. In addition, careful planning may allow a retailer to avoid some markdowns by increasing advertising, training and compensating employees better, shipping goods more efficiently among branch units, and returning items to vendors. Figure 13-9 shows ten ways to control markdowns.

The need for markdown control should not be interpreted as meaning that all markdowns can be minimized or eliminated. In fact, too low a markdown percentage may indicate that a store buyer has not assumed enough risk in purchasing goods.

Timing Markdowns

Although there is some disagreement among retailers as to the best timing sequence for markdowns, much can be said about the benefits of implementing an early markdown policy. First, this policy offers merchandise at reduced prices when demand is still fairly active. Second, an early markdown policy requires lower markdowns to sell products than markdowns late in the selling season. Third, early markdowns free selling space for new merchandise. Fourth, a retailer's cash flow position can be improved.

The main advantage of a late markdown policy is that a retailer has every opportunity to sell merchandise at original prices. However, the advantages cited for an early policy are disadvantages under a late markdown policy.

Retailers can also use a staggered markdown policy, where prices are marked down throughout the selling season. A staggered markdown policy for reducing prices throughout the selling season often involves an **automatic markdown plan.** In such a plan, the amount and timing of markdowns are controlled by the length of time merchandise remains in stock. For example, Filene's Basement applies markdowns under this timetable:

Length of Time in Stock	Percentage Markdown (from Original Price)
12 selling days	25
18 selling days	50
24 selling days	75
30 selling days	Given to charity

Such a plan ensures fresh stock and early markdowns.

A storewide clearance, usually conducted once or twice a year, is another way of timing markdowns. Often a storewide clearance takes place after peak selling periods like Christmas and the Fourth of July. The objective is to clean out merchandise before taking a physical inventory and beginning the next season. The advantages of a storewide clearance over an automatic (staggered) markdown policy are that a longer period is provided for selling merchandise at original prices; frequent markdowns can destroy a consumer's confidence in a retailer's regular pricing policy: "Why buy now, when it will be on sale next week?" And an automatic policy may encourage a steady stream of bargain hunters who are not potential customers for the firm's regular merchandise, while clearance sales limit bargain hunting to once or twice a year.

Retailers should be concerned about too frequent a use of markdowns. In the past, some major department stores would introduce merchandise at high prices and then mark down prices on many items by as much as 60 per cent to increase store traffic and improve inventory turnover. This caused customers to wait for price reductions and treat initial prices with skepticism. Today, a number of these stores have lower initial markup percentages, run fewer sales, and apply fewer markdowns than before.[27]

SUMMARY

Pricing is important to a retailer because of its interrelationship with overall objectives and the other components of the retail strategy mix. Before developing a price strategy, the retailer must study the factors that affect pricing. These include consumers, government, manufacturers, wholesalers, other suppliers, and competitors. In some instances, these factors have only a minor effect on a retailer's pricing discretion; in others, they severely limit pricing options.

With regard to consumers, retailers should be familiar with the law of demand and the price elasticity of demand. Government restrictions deal with horizontal and vertical price fixing, price discrimination, minimum prices, unit pricing, item price removal, and price advertising. Manufacturers, wholesalers, and other suppliers may be required to provide price guarantees (if they are in a position of weakness). Each channel member desires some control over pricing. The competitive environment may foster market pricing, which could lead to price wars, or administered pricing.

The framework for planning retail prices consists of five stages: objectives, broad price policy, price strategy, implementation of price strategy, and price adjustments.

Retail pricing objectives are chosen from among sales, dollar profits, return on investment, and/or early recovery of cash. After the objectives are chosen, broad policy is set. A coordinated series of actions is outlined, consistent with the firm's image and oriented to the short and long run. In setting policy, a retailer would use the multistage approach to pricing.

A price strategy integrates demand, cost, and competitive concepts. Each of these orientations must be understood separately and jointly. Psychological pricing, markup, gross margin, direct product profitability, and pricing below, at, or above the market are key aspects of strategy planning.

When implementing a price strategy, retailers can use several specific tools to supplement the broad base of strategy. Retailers should be familiar with and know when to use customary and variable pricing, one-price policies and flexible pricing, odd pricing, leader pricing, multiple-unit pricing, and price lining.

Price adjustments may be necessary for a retailer to adapt to a variety of internal and external conditions. Adjustments include markdowns, additional markups, and employee discounts. It is important that adjustments be controlled by a budget, that the causes of markdowns be noted, and that future company buying reflect earlier errors or adaptations.

QUESTIONS FOR DISCUSSION

1. Why is it important for retailers to understand the concept of price elasticity even if they cannot compute it?
2. Comment on each of the following from the perspective of a small retailer.
   a. Horizontal price fixing
   b. Vertical price fixing
   c. Price discrimination
   d. Minimum-price law
   e. Item price removal
3. Why do retailers sometimes sell against the brand?
4. Give an example of a price strategy that integrates demand, cost, and competitive criteria.
5. Explain why markups are usually computed as a percentage of selling price rather than of cost.
6. A floor tile retailer wants to receive a 35 per cent markup (at retail) for all merchandise. If one style of tile retails for $5 per tile, what is the maximum that the retailer would be willing to pay for a tile?
7. A car dealer purchases CB radios for $30 each and desires a 30 per cent markup (at retail). What retail price should be charged?
8. A photo store charges $7.00 to process a roll of slides; its cost is $5.20. What is the markup percentage (at cost and at retail)?
9. A retailer has planned operating expenses of $100,000, a profit goal of $40,000, and planned reductions of $20,000 and expects annual sales to be $575,000. Compute the initial markup percentage.
10. At the end of the year, the retailer in Question 9 determines that actual operating expenses are $110,000, actual profit is $30,000, and actual sales are $600,000. What is the maintained markup percentage? Explain the difference in your answers to Questions 9 and 10.
11. What are the advantages and disadvantages of the direct product profitability concept?
12. How would price lining differ for a discount store and a specialty shop?
13. What is the difference between markdown percentage and off-retail percentage?
14. A retailer buys merchandise for $25. At an original retail price of $40, it expects to sell 1,000 units.
   a. If the price is marked down to $35, how many units must the retailer sell to earn the same total gross profit that it would attain with a price of $40?
   b. If the price is marked up to $45, how many units must the retailer sell to earn the same total gross profit that it would attain with a price of $40?

NOTES

1. Jeffrey A. Tannenbaum, "Slumping Electronics Sales May Drive Some Dealers Out of Business," *Wall Street Journal* (May 17, 1988), p. 10; Mary J. Pitzer, "Electronic 'Superstores' May Have Blown a Fuse," *Business Week* (June 8, 1987), pp. 90, 94; and Bill Saporito, "Discounters in the Dump," *Fortune* (August 3, 1987), pp. 103–114.

2. Gregory P. Stone, "City Shoppers and Urban Identification: Observation on the Social Psychology of City Life," *American Journal of Sociology*, Vol. 60 (July 1954), pp. 36–45.

3. Michael A. Duggan, "United States v. First National Supermarkets," *Journal of Marketing*, Vol. 47 (Fall 1983), pp. 127–128.

4. "Four Supermarket Concerns Are Fined Total of $830,000," *Wall Street Journal* (November 27, 1984), p. 64.

5. Joel R. Evans and Barry Berman, *Marketing*, Third Edition (New York: Macmillan, 1987), p. 514.

6. Ken Rankin, "Discount Retailing: Fate Lies in Proof of RPM," *Discount Store News* (February 15, 1988), p. 6.

7. Ken Rankin, "End in Sight to Slack Antitrust Enforcement," *Discount Store News* (January 18, 1988), p. 6.

8. "FTC Orders Max Factor to Halt Discrimination in Its Pricing," *Advertising Age* (November 24, 1986), p. 3; and C. Burk Tower, "In Re Max Factor & Co.," *Journal of Marketing*, Vol. 51 (July 1987), p. 117.

9. See James C. Johnson and Kenneth C. Schneider, "The Robinson-Patman Act: Potential Pitfalls for Retailers," *Business*, Vol. 34 (January–March 1984), pp. 34–42.

10. See Willard F. Mueller and Thomas W. Paterson, "Effectiveness of State Sales-Below-Cost Laws: Evidence from the Grocery Trade," *Journal of Retailing*, Vol. 62 (Summer 1986), pp. 166–185.

11. See Rockney G. Walters and Heikki J. Rinne, "An Empirical Investigation into the Impact of Price Promotions on Retail Store Performance," *Journal of Retailing*, Vol. 62 (Fall 1986), pp. 237–266.

12. Joseph P. Fried, "Court Upsets New York's Minimum Liquor Pricing," *New York Times* (June 12, 1984), p. B4.

13. FTC Scores Below-Cost Selling Law," *Discount Store News* (January 18, 1988), p. 2.

14. See David A. Aaker and Gary T. Ford, "Unit Pricing Ten Years Later: A Replication," *Journal of Marketing*, Vol. 47 (Winter 1983), pp. 118–122.

15. Louis W. Stern and Thomas L. Eovaldi, *Legal Aspects of Marketing Strategy* (Englewood Cliffs, N.J.: Prentice-Hall, 1984), p. 394.

16. Bob Davis, "To Sell PCs on Price, Leading Edge Presses Suppliers and Dealers," *Wall Street Journal* (April 10, 1986), pp. 1, 12.

17. Gregory Stricharchuk, "Card Makers' Tough Tactics Belie Sweet Verse as Competition Rises," *Wall Street Journal* (December 24, 1987), p. 9.

18. Judith A. Biltekoff, "Grocers Check Out Ad Blitz, Price Cuts," *Advertising Age* (October 26, 1987), p. 82.

19. Jo Ellen Davis, James E. Ellis, and Chuck Hawkins, "Continental: Full Planes May Not Mean Full Coffers," *Business Week* (March 16, 1987), p. 37.

20. Alfred R. Oxenfeldt, "Multi-Stage Approach to Pricing," *Harvard Business Review*, Vol. 38 (July–August 1960), pp. 125–133.

21. Markup calculations are explained in depth in Marvin A. Jolson, "Markup Calculations—Still a Fuzzy Area?" *Journal of Retailing*, Vol. 49 (Winter 1973–1974), pp. 77–80 ff.; and Marvin A. Jolson, "A Diagrammatic Model for Merchandising Calculations," *Journal of Retailing*, Vol. 51 (Summer 1975), pp. 3–9 ff.

22. "New Data in New MOR," *Stores* (February 1987), p. 44.

23. See Rhonda Razzano, "DPP: Merchandising Decision-Maker," *Chain Store Age Executive* (May 1986), pp. 169–170; and John R. Phipps and Randy L. Allen, "Retailers Profit Through Measuring DPP on Individual Items," *Discount Store News* (June 23, 1986), p. 18.

24. See Kenneth R. Evans and Richard F. Beltramini, "A Theoretical Model of Consumer Negotiated Pricing: An Orientation Perspective," *Journal of Marketing*, Vol. 51 (April 1987), pp. 58–73.

25. "Penny Pricing Facing Pinch from Nickel Discounts: Restaurant Study," *Marketing News* (April 11, 1986), p. 14.

26. See Charles W. Kyd, "Pricing for Profit," *Inc.* (April 1987), pp. 119–120 ff.

27. Isadore Barmash, "Trying to Sell Without Sales," *New York Times* (May 3, 1987), p. 15.

Case 1

Southern Institute of Technology: A College Store's Pricing Strategy

Southern Institute of Technology is a four-year university located in the Southeast. Its college store sells new and used texts, stationery and related products, signature goods (sweat shirts, T-shirts, hats, and so on, with the school's name and emblem), newspapers and magazines, candy and gum, gift items and greeting cards, small appliances, and dormitory products (such as health and beauty aids, food items, and laundry supplies) to current students, their families, university personnel, and alumni.

Jack Barnes, the store manager, is in the process of evaluating the profitability of the overall store and its various departments. Of special interest is the store's pricing strategy. Jack is under pressure from the university's controller to generate improved profits, while still serving the needs of customers. For example, the store must carry products used by dormitory students even though they have low inventory turnover.

Barnes is aware of several factors that affect the store's profitability and sales:

❑ The profit margins on new texts are quite low relative to operating costs. While the store prices new texts using a 22 per cent markup at retail, its costs of doing business are about 24 per cent of net sales. The store must also pay freight in (on text purchases) and freight out (on text returns due to overordering). It is common for the store to overorder texts, since professors do not want them to be out of stock. Freight costs can average 2–4 per cent of net sales for new texts.

- While the initial profit margins on used texts are 40 per cent at retail, Jack really does not feel that these texts are all that profitable. Considerable time is spent by store employees in purchasing used texts and determining their quality (different prices are established for excellent, good, and fair quality). The store also has problems in being "stuck" with an old edition or with having to transport texts to a wholesaler when faculty decide to no longer assign a current title.

- Even though signature goods have been priced at a full 50 per cent markup at retail, the store has had large problems with size assortments. The store's buyer assumed that these goods are staples and purchased them in a standard size distribution; he did not foresee the current appeal of oversized clothing. Even 100-pound students want extra-large sizes. As a result, the store has had to take large unplanned markdowns. Much older merchandise remains unsold.

- Dormitory items must be stocked to accommodate students, but many of these items are slow-moving. It is hard to get students into the bookstore to purchase health and beauty aids or small appliances, even with special sales. Many students report purchasing these items at neighboring supermarkets or on trips home. They believe that the college store has above-average prices and does not have a sufficient selection.

Table 1 contains data on planned versus actual sales, markups, operating expenses, and profit for the most recent year. Jack Barnes wants to review these data carefully in planning his pricing strategy for the coming year, and in deciding whether to add a personal computer line.

Southern's engineering and business schools plan to require entering freshmen to purchase IBM or compatible computers within the next two academic years. This policy will affect three hundred new students per year. Although the personal computer business represents a significant opportunity (units can be sold for more than $1,000 each if fully configured with a graphics board, a monitor, and a printer), Barnes has two major concerns. One, he estimates that there will be a 10–15 per cent markup if the store stocks computer units and handles warranty shipments for students. This may not be enough to compensate the store for the space and inventory risk. Personal computer prices typically drop 15–20 per cent per year, and a new configuration may also render a peripheral (such as a graphics board) obsolete. Two, many students will be able to get better prices through mail-order merchants. These merchants do not charge sales tax to out-of-state purchasers.

TABLE 1
Southern Institute of Technology's College Store, Planned Versus Actual Pricing and Profit Data (for the most recent academic year)

	Total	New Texts	Used Texts	Signature Goods	Health & Beauty Aids	Other
Planned Data						
Net sales	$1,085,000	$600,000	$300,000	$70,000	$15,000	$100,000
Cost of goods sold	764,600	469,700	182,600	42,100	10,600	59,600
Initial markup at retail	334,250	132,000	120,000	35,000	5,250	42,000
Retail reductions	13,850	1,700	2,600	7,100	850	1,600
Operating expenses*	260,400	144,000	72,000	16,800	3,600	24,000
Net profit	60,000	(13,700)	45,400	11,100	800	16,400
Actual Data						
Net sales	$1,088,000	$630,000	$270,000	$50,000	$10,000	$128,000
Cost of goods sold	770,100	487,800	180,400	27,100	7,000	67,800
Maintained markup at retail	317,900	142,200	89,600	22,900	3,000	60,200
Operating expenses*	280,000	162,132	69,485	12,868	2,574	32,941
Net profit	37,900	(19,932)	20,115	10,032	426	27,259

*Allocated on the basis of percentage of overall sales.

QUESTIONS

1. Describe why the college store did not reach the planned goals identified in Table 1.
2. Using the data in Table 1, compute the initial and maintained markup percentages for the total store and each product category. Explain the differences.

3. Recommend a pricing strategy to improve the store's performance.
4. If the store decides to carry personal computers, what pricing strategy should it use?

Case 2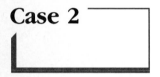

Nixon-Blade: Attacking Selling Practices in the Discount Appliance Industry*

Before studying this case, complete the brief questionnaire that follows. In fact, you will benefit greatly if you take out a sheet of paper *right now* and write down your answer to each question. Use the following hypothetical information to answer the questions:

> You visit a typical discount appliance store in order to consider the purchase of an advertised 19-inch TV set which has been priced at $228. After demonstrating the advertised set, the salesperson points out that it does not have the "color lock" feature. This means you may be required to readjust the color controls every time you switch channels. The salesperson indicates that if this would be an inconvenience to you, an alternative would be another well-known set that *has* color lock but is priced at $299. The salesperson then demonstrates the higher-priced set.

Questionnaire:

1. Do you think this is a normal practice for an appliance salesperson?
2. How often have you had an experience similar to that just cited?
3. How did you feel about the practice described? If you have not had such an experience, how do you think you would react if you did experience such a situation?
4. How did you feel (or would you feel) about the salesperson's mention of the limitation (or missing feature) of the advertised item?
   ____ I was pleased (or would be pleased) to receive the information.
   ____ I was not pleased (or would not be pleased) to receive the information (even though it was probably correct) since it gave the salesperson an opportunity to sell a higher-priced item.
   ____ I was not pleased (or would not be pleased) since the information was probably false and was given to me so that the salesperson could try to sell me a higher-priced version of the product.
   ____ The information had (or would have had) no effect on me one way or another.
   ____ Other (please insert) _____.
5. If the salesperson had not mentioned the limitation of the advertised product and I had purchased the item:
   ____ I would not be concerned even after noticing the limitation.
   ____ Upon noticing the limitation, I would have been concerned and would have felt that the salesperson had withheld important information.
   ____ Upon noticing the limitation, I would have been concerned, but I would not have entertained the thought that the salesperson had acted improperly.
   ____ Other (please insert) _____.

*This case was prepared and written by Professor Marvin A. Jolson, University of Maryland.

6. Do you think the salesperson was correct in suggesting a higher-priced item that did not have the cited limitation?

_____ Yes, I would be willing to see a suggested product that did not have the limitation. It is my decision whether the added benefit is worth the additional money.

_____ Absolutely not! The salesperson should not suggest a higher-priced item regardless of how many limitations are associated with the advertised product. Only the customer should make that suggestion.

_____ I have no opinion either way.

After you have completed the questionnaire, go ahead and read the case.

Nixon-Blade, Inc. (NBI), is a specialty retailer of home entertainment and consumer electronic products and household appliances. The company operates forty-one stores in a large midwestern state and offers high-quality, nationally recognized merchandise at discount prices. The firm was founded in 1943 by Bertram Blade and his family and has grown in sales volume and profits each year, as shown by the following table for the years 1984 through 1988:

	1984	1985	1986	1987	1988
Sales (000s)	$51,672	$59,782	$79,630	$107,515	$134,980
Earnings before income taxes (000s)	$976	$1,196	$1,831	$2,483	$5,736

Although Bert Blade is not a sophisticated retailer, he has developed a high level of "street smarts" over the years. Accordingly, NBI has positioned itself as the dominant home-entertainment consumer electronic and appliance retailer in its market areas by offering a broad selection of products at very attractive prices. The company reinforces its competitive pricing policy by offering a limited price-protection pledge on every purchase. If, within thirty days of a purchase, the same model is sold or advertised by any local retailer regularly stocking the item at a price below that paid by the purchaser, the consumer may request and receive a refund of the price differential plus 10 per cent. If NBI undersells itself within seven days of a purchase, a refund of the price differential is also available.

The company uses extensive newspaper and selected radio and television advertising to promote its broad selection of products and to stress its competitive pricing. All of the company's newspaper advertisements are designed by NBI's personnel. This permits daily changes in ad copy to introduce new products or to match price and promotional competition in the local market.

The company conducts audio and video expositions annually. These shows are held in large exhibition areas separate from NBI store locations and provide unique opportunities to sell newer and more sophisticated models and products. These shows are augmented with substantial advertising to increase attendance at these events.

In November 1988, the attorney general of the state initiated civil proceedings against the company and its principals. The complaint alleged that the company had violated certain consumer protection, advertising, pricing, and personal selling statutes. The complaint sought civil penalties, restitution to injured customers, reimbursement for the cost of the lawsuit, and to enjoin NBI from future violations.

The primary claims seemed to focus on bait-and-switch tactics and were set forth as follows:

❑ NBI regularly offered appliances to consumers by widespread advertising. Defendants did not intend to sell many of the advertised items, nor did they have a sufficient number of the advertised items in stock to meet reasonably expected public demand.

❑ NBI sales personnel made little or no effort to sell many advertised appliances. Instead NBI advertised these low-priced name-brand appliances in order to attract consumers to stores where salespeople could "step up" shoppers to nonadvertised higher-margin products.

❑ Defendants used a method of compensating their salespeople in such a way that they were encouraged to dissuade the sale of lower-priced advertised items.

❑ In order to earn the substantially higher commissions paid on nonadvertised items, NBI sales personnel disparaged or made false statements about the advertised items and then attempted to sell higher-priced versions of the products.

The firm vehemently denied any bait-and-switch tactics. It admitted that commission rates were generally higher for higher-margin products and was able to offer evidence that many sales organizations (including nonretailers) used the same procedure to encourage salespeople to sell slower-moving items in the product line. Moreover, the company contended that advertised price leaders were not expected to have the same features as higher-priced product versions.

As a major defense mechanism, NBI's law firm authorized a study of a random sample of the company's customers. The research was built around the same hypothetical statement that you read earlier except that it specifically referred to a Nixon-Blade experience:

> You visit a Nixon-Blade store in order to consider the purchase of an advertised 19-inch TV which has been priced at $228. After demonstrating the advertised set, the salesperson points out that it does not have the "color lock" feature. This means you may be required to readjust the color controls every time you switch channels. The salesperson indicates that if this would be an inconvenience to you, an alternative would be another well-known set that *has* color lock but is priced at $299. The salesperson then demonstrates the higher-priced set.

The responses of NBI's customers to the same six questions that you answered are shown in Table 1.

TABLE 1
Customer Answers to NBI's Survey

(1) Do you think this is a normal practice for retail salespeople?

	Frequency	Percentage
Yes	208	58.4
No	92	25.8
Not sure	56	15.8
	356	100.0

(2) How often have you had an experience at Nixon-Blade which was similar to the above case?

	Frequency	Percentage
Never	34	9.6
Once or twice	158	44.4
A few times	126	35.4
Very often	38	10.6
	356	100.0

(3) When this happened, I felt . . .

	Frequency	Percentage
Positive answer	112	31.5
Negative answer	232	65.2
Can't classify	12	3.3
	356	100.0

(4) How did you feel (or would you feel) about the salesperson's mention of the limitation (or missing feature) of the advertised item?

	Frequency	Percentage
Pleased	187	52.5
Not pleased/true inform.	67	18.8
Not pleased/false inform.	47	13.2
No effect	55	15.5
	356	100.0

(5) If the salesperson had not mentioned the limitation of the advertised product and I had purchased the item:

	Frequency	Percentage
Not concerned	73	20.5
Withheld inform.	128	36.0
Not improper	97	27.2
Other	58	16.3
	356	100.0

(6) Do you think that the salesperson was correct in suggesting a higher-priced item that did not have the cited limitation?

	Frequency	Percentage
Yes	243	68.3
No	90	25.3
No opinion	23	6.4
	356	100.0

QUESTIONS

1. Considering the research findings and other evidence, do you think that Nixon-Blade is guilty of bait-and-switch tactics? Explain your answer.
2. Can you justify the firm's strategy of advertising price leaders that have limitations in comparison to product alternatives that are priced higher?
3. Can you justify the firm's strategy of coordinating commission rates with each product's gross margin?
4. If you were a neutral researcher and wished to gather evidence to further support or reject the bait-and-switch claim, what would you do?
5. Do you think that Nixon-Blade should change any of its advertising, pricing, personal selling, or other strategies? Explain your answer.

Sears, Roebuck & Co.: Buying, Handling, and Pricing Merchandise at the Nation's Largest Retailer*

Introduction

Sears, Roebuck & Co. can now be viewed as a diversified family of businesses: Sears Merchandising Group, Dean Witter Financial Services Group, Allstate Insurance Group, and the Coldwell Banker Real Estate Group. See Table 1 for a description of each of these businesses.

TABLE 1
Sears, Roebuck & Co.:
A Diversified Family of Businesses

> **Sears Merchandising Group**
> This group is involved with the buying and selling of a broad assortment of goods and services through retail stores and catalogs. There are separate domestic and international operations. A large credit department initiates and manages customer accounts.
>
> **Dean Witter Financial Services Group***
> This group provides financial services to individuals and institutional clients as well as deposit and lending programs (where the law permits) for customers. It is also responsible for the Discover credit card.
>
> **Allstate Insurance Group***
> This group provides personal and business property and casualty insurance, as well as group life and health insurance.
>
> **Coldwell Banker Real Estate Group***
> This group offers commercial and residential real-estate brokerage and related services. It also develops, owns, and manages real estate.
>
> *Together, Dean Witter, Allstate, and Coldwell Banker comprise the Sears Financial Network with offices in many Sears retail stores and other sites.

Yet, despite Sears' diversification, the Merchandising Group remains at the core of the firm because of its size, percentage of overall company sales, impact on other divisions, and Sears' continuing belief in the central nature of retailing to its mission. After all, Sears, Roebuck is the nation's largest retailer. According to one report, one out of every ten Americans has worked at Sears at one time, and eight of ten Americans shop at its stores each year. Forty million households have a Sears charge card; and 70 per cent of them actively use that credit card.

The Merchandising Group accounts for 61 per cent of Sears' total sales and 81 per cent of company profit. It is also very important to Dean Witter, Allstate, and Coldwell Banker, since many financial services, insurance, and real-estate outlets are located in traditional Sears stores. Thus, these units are dependent on Sears' retailing prowess in generating customers.

In a recent annual report, Sears' top management reiterated the firm's commitment to retailing:

> Sears remains a company built on the belief that taking care of the customer is the cardinal rule of success. Our diversification simply creates new channels and opens up opportunities to put that principle into practice.

Nonetheless, a number of industry observers have recently criticized Sears' merchandising operations because of slow growth; and they believe that Sears has lacked a clear customer and product focus. For example, Sears' retail sales have been growing at half the industry rate. In response, the company has attempted to revitalize its stores by upgrading several of its merchandise lines. But this has alienated many of its traditional blue-collar customers. Furthermore, the newly renovated and upgraded stores have not yet caught on with the white-collar segment, Sears' new target market. Last, there is some concern that the shift from an emphasis on durables to one featuring nondurables has

---

*The material in this case is drawn from Steven Greenhouse and Scott Kilman, "Sears to Bring Back Goldstein in Bid to Establish a Specialty-Store Presence," *Wall Street Journal* (February 9, 1987), p. 10; Michael Oneal, "Can Sears Get Sexier But Keep the Common Touch?" *Business Week* (July 6, 1987), pp. 93–95; Michael Oneal, "How Three Master Merchants Fell from Grace," *Business Week* (March 16, 1987), pp. 38–40; Bill Saporito, "Are IBM and Sears Crazy? Or Canny?" *Fortune* (September 28, 1987), pp. 76–80; *Sears, Roebuck & Co. 1986 Annual Report;* Barry Stavo, "Minding the Store," *Forbes* (April 7, 1986), pp. 31–32; "Where Sears Has Stumbled," *New York Times* (June 5, 1986), pp. D1, D8; Steve Weiner and Scott Kilman, "Sears' Retailing Lines Have Grim Long-Run Prospects," *Wall Street Journal* (November 18, 1986), p. 6; "McKids: Sears' Bid for Mac-Millions," *Women's Wear Daily* (July 1987), p. 31; Laurie Freeman, "Mac Creatures Help Sears with McKids," *Advertising Age* (July 27, 1987), p. 64; Cyndee Miller, "Sears Gets Merchandising Rights to Disney Characters," *Marketing News* (December 18, 1987), p. 1; Francine Schwadel, "Sears Expected to Reorganize Buying Staff," *Wall Street Journal* (February 29, 1988), p. 26; Julia Flynn Siler, "Sears Group to Undergo Revamping," *New York Times* (March 3, 1988), pp. D1, D12; Julia Flynn Siler, "Sears to Bolster Merchandising Group," *New York Times* (April 20, 1988), p. D6; and Francine Schwadel, "Sears Will Introduce New Clothing Lines to Woo Women," *Wall Street Journal* (April 7, 1988), p. 35.

not been well received. This is partly a result of Sears' strong reputation with durable goods such as major appliances and its weaker reputation with nondurables such as fashion clothing, and partly because Sears' traditional durable-goods customers have different demographics from its new fashion customers.

This case concentrates on a number of the opportunities and threats facing the Sears Merchandising Group with regard to the buying, handling, and pricing of the goods it carries.

Merchandise Buying

In 1988, Sears decided to implement a three-year plan to restructure its Merchandising Group to decentralize the buying process:

> We are competing in many diverse businesses, each with its own unique environment. Yet, we have been essentially using one organizational format to compete in all of these businesses. But, you don't buy junior apparel the way you buy toasters. The changes will result in a company that is better structured to maintain its position as America's premier retailer.

Sears' buying strategies differ significantly for durable goods versus nondurable goods. Furthermore, within its nondurable goods lines, Sears uses distinct strategies for adult versus childrens' clothing. In general, the distinctions relate to buying relationships with vendors, brand names used, and the importance of image.

Durable Goods

Durable goods include such items as hardware, refrigerators, paint, and tools. For years, more than 60 per cent of Sears' retail sales have come from durable goods. The company buys or obtains a large part of this merchandise from manufacturers in which it has an equity interest. For example, Sears owns a large proportion of the common stock of De Soto (its manufacturer of paints).

Many durables are sold under Sears' private label brands, such as Kenmore, Sears, Eager 1, Craftsman, and DieHard. Its private-label policy has given Sears considerable channel control in dealing with its suppliers and has reduced price competition at the retail level (since consumers cannot easily compare the prices of Sears' brands with those of the brands carried by other retailers). In several cases, Sears has high market shares for its durable goods. For example, its brands have a 37 per cent market share for automobile replacement batteries, 22 per cent for paint, and 39 per cent for clothes dryers.

Frequently, Sears' relationships with its durable goods vendors have been long-term. The manufacturers benefit from lower-cost financing, Sears' market research and production expertise, and large orders. Sears benefits from long-run involvement in quality control efforts, lower costs, and greater coordination between manufacturing and selling.

The reliance on private-label durable goods did present some difficulties when consumers desiring brand names such as Kitchen Aid or Sony could not find them at Sears.

As a result, for the first time, Sears began carrying manufacturer brands of home appliances and consumer electronics in 1988.

Nondurable Goods for Adults

Nondurable goods include such items as clothing, beauty aids, and home furnishings. In many of its nondurable goods lines, Sears is now placing greater emphasis on higher-priced products. This program is especially important to Sears since its nondurable goods generally have profit margins that are 20 per cent above the margins of the durable goods it sells. Thus, by generating an extra 2 per cent of Merchandising Group sales from nondurable goods, Sears could increase its overall profit by about $100 million per year. To facilitate its shift from a retailer dominated by durable goods sales to one with a greater balance between durable and nondurable products, Sears has established a new buying organization and is engaged in a comprehensive store renovation program called "The Store of the Future."

For the first time in its history, Sears is using external fashion consultants to help its fashion buyers. Sears is also paying more attention to regional sensitivity to fashion. For example, it has opened buying offices in Los Angeles and Miami. In addition, it is using marketing research to determine merchandise selections for certain market areas based on results in test stores. Because of test store results in Arizona and Kansas, these market areas are placing more emphasis on women's casual apparel and bath linens, respectively.

The Store of the Future program involves renovating over six hundred of Sears' large retail stores by the end of 1989. The redesigned stores feature more aisles, recessed ceilings, more merchandise at eye level, and a greater accent on apparel and home furnishings. Nondurable goods departments are differentiated by color, with burgundy in the women's clothing department, green in the men's clothing department, and blue in the children's department. In some of the chain's jeans sections, neon signs and rock music have been added.

In its Stores of the Future, Sears has incorporated boutique areas aimed at younger, more style-conscious customers. For example, men's clothing in two hundred stores is being arranged in six distinct selling departments. Three of these departments cater their merchandise offerings to Sears' traditional, older customers. Three other new departments seek to compete aggressively with such retailers as Eddie Bauer and The Gap. These new departments are Trader Bay, a sportswear shop for young men; a jeans shop featuring Levi's and Lee brands; and Fieldmaster, a shop for outdoor wear. At these stores, a new boutique (Changes) for young women that features imported cotton apparel is also being added.

Sears has developed its own private labels, such as Cheryl Tiegs, Arnold Palmer, Evonne Goolagong, and Diane von Furstenberg for ladies' and men's clothing, household furnishings, and sporting apparel. It now also sells manufacturer brands in these categories. Today, the private labels and manufacturer brands have a greater fashion orientation than in previous years.

Despite the efforts just noted, Sears has had some difficulties with its new fashion strategy aimed at adults:

- After they were remodeled, Sears' Stores of the Future originally dropped the lowest-priced products in some of their merchandise lines to entice more women shoppers and slightly more affluent customers. However, these stores have had to reintroduce the lower price points since not enough fashion customers have been attracted.
- In particular, Sears has had trouble selling higher-priced apparel to both teenagers and career women, despite the use of the Cheryl Tiegs brand.
- While the chief executive of the Merchandising Group has publicly stated that the firm will consider adding more apparel brand names if there are voids in Sears' product assortment, the company has been reluctant to place too much attention on manufacturer brand names. For example, even though it has not been successful with teenagers and wants to develop an upscale image, Sears has not stocked such popular brands aimed at this market as Esprit.
- Sears must be cautious in its image change. In the late 1970s, the firm also tried to aim its apparel merchandise at upscale shoppers. This attempt was unsuccessful. Too many changes in apparel merchandising may create confusion and a blurred identity. In its current strategy, Sears must walk a fine line by drawing new customers without turning off current ones.

Nondurable Goods for Children

Sears' infants' and children's wear departments have been among Sears' most profitable. In recent years, however, its market share in this category has begun to slip because of increased competition from children's specialty retailers such as Kids "R" Us (owned by Toys "R" Us) and Children's Place (owned by Federated Department Stores).

For over twenty years, Sears' children's clothing has featured its Winnie-the-Pooh brand, and over the last ten years, this brand has produced more than $1 billion in sales for the firm. But whereas in the past the Winnie-the-Pooh name was used on activewear, sportswear, and dressy apparel, Sears now plans to use the brand only on dressy separates and coordinates. It also plans to update the fashion emphasis, broaden the mix at the top end of the price structure, and use other licensed brand-name designations. For example, Sears intends to have the following sales distribution by brand for its infant and toddler line: Winnie the Pooh, 35 per cent; McKids (a new brand), 25 per cent; and other Sears and national brands (including clothing using the names of Disney characters), 40 per cent.

The McKids brand, licensed from McDonald's, is exclusive to Sears, and Sears hopes that its clothing will capitalize on the instant recognition of the McDonald's name. The familiar "golden arches" logo appears on all McKids labels, but only about 15 per cent of the clothes have the McDonald's logo or trade characters on the outside. The McKids line initially supplemented the Pooh brand in sportswear (such as jerseys, sweaters, sweatshirts, and T-shirts), sleepwear, and accessories (such as hats, girls' jewelry, gloves, belts, and sunglasses). Sears expects the McKids brand to eventually account for 50 per cent of the volume in girls' clothing sized 4 to 6X, and for 65 per cent of boys' clothing sized 4 to 7.

The McKids line is being housed in separate boutiques, with space taken from the existing children's clothing department. The McKids boutiques have electronic games, fun mirrors, life-sized cutouts of "Mayor McCheese" and the "Hamburglar," and other attractions for children.

Merchandise Handling

Sears has had some problems with its distribution system, which has been criticized as being too costly. In recent years, distribution costs have been as high as 8 per cent of sales, compared to costs of 2–3 per cent of sales at K mart and Wal-Mart. Although part of Sears' additional costs may have been due to its large catalog operations (which account for 17 per cent of total Merchandising Group sales) and its product mix (which is heavy on major appliances that are expensive to ship and deliver), its distribution system is outmoded in many ways. For example, Sears has many inefficient multistory warehouses and often uses old-fashioned labor-intensive equipment.

Accordingly, Sears wants to reduce its distribution costs by the equivalent of 2 per cent of sales. As part of its cost reduction strategy, Sears is closing five of its twelve distribution centers. The affected facilities employ about 5,500 of Sears' 18,500 distribution center workers and are located in Chicago, Boston, Atlanta, Memphis, and Minneapolis. Of the remaining seven distribution centers, the ones in Columbus, Ohio; Dallas, Texas; Greensboro, North Carolina; Jacksonville, Florida; and Kansas City, Kansas, are being upgraded. Sears is studying whether to renovate or relocate the centers in Los Angeles and Philadelphia.

Sears also acknowledges that its distribution response time needs improvement. On average, it has taken eighteen weeks for goods to get to individual stores after a Sears buyer has ordered them from a supplier. The company estimates that it could save $43 million a year if it could reduce delivery time by a single day. Much of the saving would be from reducing inventory levels, since improved delivery times would lower inventory carrying costs and convert some storage space to selling space. At present, only about 55 per cent of Sears' floor space in its large stores located in shopping malls is devoted to selling versus nearly 80 per cent of the space at K mart outlets and at many department stores. One way response time can be improved is by encouraging suppliers to ship directly to stores rather than to Sears' distribution centers.

Pricing

Sears pioneered the concept of price lining, whereby goods are sold in "good," "better," and "best" categories with each representing a distinct level of quality. Price lining allows Sears to manage product assortments, increase inventory turnover, and facilitate salesperson effort (since clear product differences exist). While this strategy was originally most important in catalog sales, today it is particularly critical in store departments with a high percentage of self-service sales.

Yet, Sears' overall pricing strategy and recent practices, such as phasing out and then bringing back low price lines in Stores of the Future, have caused confusion and not been overly effective. Many analysts have been critical of Sears' pricing policies, as these two comments indicate:

> You can take a store like Sears, and I can tell you a dozen places to get products more efficiently, at a better selection, or a lower price.

> Sears' basic problem is they still try to be all things to all people in one store. But the future is either being a mass merchant with low prices, or a specialty store with higher-priced goods.

There are various reasons for Sears' current pricing difficulties. First, because of its focus on private-label goods, Sears has been somewhat insulated from competition. Now that it is carrying more manufacturer brands and appealing to more fashion-conscious consumers, Sears must be aware of competitors' prices and be responsive to the marketplace. Second, unlike K mart, Sears does not stock gray market items (imported goods purchased by a retailer through unauthorized distribution channels) such as Seiko watches. Meanwhile, K mart has increased its price-cutting image by stocking gray-market merchandise. Third, Sears is a high-cost merchant. For example, its selling and administrative costs are 29 per cent of sales versus 24 per cent at K mart and 18 per cent at Wal-Mart. See Table 2. Thus, these retailers can easily undercut Sears.

TABLE 2
Selected Financial Data for Sears' Domestic Retailing Operations, 1984–1986*

$ millions	1986	1985	1984
Merchandise sales and services	$22,091.5	21,549.7	21,670.6
Cost of sales, buying, and occupancy expense	$14,918.1	14,533.5	14,283.1
Ratio to sales	67.5%	67.4%	65.9%
Selling and administrative expense	$ 6,335.3	6,296.3	6,240.7
Ratio to sales	28.7%	29.2%	28.8%
Operating income	$ 820.6	693.7	1,113.0
Ratio to sales	3.7%	3.2%	5.1%
Merchandising income	$ 457.9	446.8	655.5
Ratio to sales	2.1%	2.1%	3.0%
Net sales per square foot (dollars)	$ 342	335	337
Merchandise inventories—LIFO basis	$ 3,481.1	3,589.5	4,024.9
Merchandise inventories—FIFO basis	$ 4,092.0	4,034.6	4,412.0
Merchandise on order at Dec. 31	$ 3,606.6	3,594.6	3,932.2

*Excluding the credit department.

Source: Sears, Roebuck & Co. 1986 Annual Report.

QUESTIONS

1. Evaluate and compare Sears' merchandise buying strategies for durable and nondurable goods.
2. Develop a proper assortment strategy for major appliances in terms of width and depth. Explain your answer.
3. Evaluate Sears' current emphasis on fashion merchandising.
4. Comment on Sears' decision to close five of its twelve distribution centers.
5. Present several suggestions for Sears to reduce its distribution costs and delivery times while maintaining a superior level of customer service.
6. Should Sears be the lowest-priced retailer for the branded goods it sells? Explain your answer.
7. Describe the relationship among Sears' merchandise buying, handling, and pricing strategies. Refer to the data in Table 2 in your answer.

PART SEVEN

Communicating with the Customer

❑ In Part Seven, the elements involved in a retailer's communicating with its customers are discussed. First, the role of store image and how it is developed and maintained are covered. Then, various aspects of promotional strategy are detailed.

❑ Chapter 14 shows the importance of communications for a retailer. The significance of store image in the communications effort and the components of store image are explained. The creation of an image depends heavily on the atmosphere that the store develops, including its exterior, general interior, layout, and displays. The impact of customer services on store image and the value of community relations are also studied.

❑ Chapter 15 focuses on promotional strategy, specifically how a retailer can inform, persuade, and remind its target market. The first part of the chapter deals with the four basic types of retail promotion: advertising, publicity, personal selling, and sales promotion. The second part describes the steps in a promotional strategy: objectives, budget, mix of forms, implementation of mix, and review and revision of the plan.

Chapter 14

Establishing and Maintaining a Store Image

Nordstrom has some of the most loyal customers in all of retailing, largely because of the outstanding store image it projects, based on superior customer service. This is why:

At many department stores these days, the customer isn't always right. In fact, the customer is barely tolerated. But Nordstrom Inc., a Seattle-based apparel, shoe, and soft-goods retailer since 1901, has become legendary for its good service. Sales clerks gift-wrap packages for no extra charge and drop off orders at customers' homes. Piano players serenade shoppers year-round. In Alaska, Nordstrom has been known to warm up cars while drivers spend a few more minutes shopping. There's even the story—which the company doesn't deny—about a customer getting money back on a tire. Since Nordstrom doesn't sell tires, it was a testament to the store's no-questions-asked return policy.

Nordstrom offers this customer service in attractive, fully stocked stores that sell good-quality merchandise at prices "comparable to other upscale retailers." As a result, Nordstrom has the highest sales per square foot of any department store chain in the United States, and total company revenues have risen at least 25 per cent annually since 1984.

Unlike a large number of other retailers, Nordstrom places great emphasis on its sales clerks, calling them the "most important employees." Every senior executive of the firm began his or her career in retail sales. Recent college graduates start on the selling floor and earn commissions above their base salaries; they also participate in a profit-sharing program. They are reviewed regularly; and good sales personnel are promoted to management-level positions. Most department

Exterior storefronts communicate with customers via their marquees, entrances, windows, lighting, and construction materials. They help attract consumers to the stores and create and maintain images for the retailers. These storefronts greatly contribute to retailers' positioning in the marketplace.

Photos courtesy of Dillard's, Longs Drugs, and K mart.

(1)

(2)

(3)

(4)

For retailers that locate in enclosed shopping centers, interior storefronts are generally more important than exterior storefronts in communicating with consumers. These retailers seek to present distinctive, yet appropriate, interior storefronts to set the proper shopping mood as well as to stand out among the many stores in their malls. The stores represented here are Campus Connections at the Rochester Institute of Technology (1); Etage, a beauty products and fashion accessories outlet (2); Kay Jewelers (3); and Hobby Center Toys (4).

Photos courtesy of the Rochester Institute of Technology Communications Department, the Brown Group, Kay Jewelers, and *Discount Store News*.

Store interiors have a great impact on customer perceptions of retailers, patrons' shopping moods, the length of time spent in stores, the extent of impulse purchases, and other factors. Well-planned interiors can facilitate shopping and generate a sense of excitement. Shown here are interior displays from Best Buy (1); Petries (2); Finders Keepers (3); and Hills Department Stores (4).

Photos courtesy of *Discount Store News* (1, 3, and 4) and American Marazzi Tile, Inc., Dallas, Texas (2).

(2)

(3)

Shopping Bag

Appleseed's

Three forms of promotion are under the complete control of retailers and they are represented here: advertising at Toys "R" Us (1); personal selling at Jack Somers Shoes, a family shoe-store division of the Brown Group (2); and sales promotion at Appleseed's, a ladies' clothing chain (3). These elements of promotion, along with pub-licity, can inform, persuade, and/or remind the target market about any aspect of a retailer or its strategy.

Photos courtesy of Toys "R" Us, the Brown Group, and Selame Design.

(1)

stores pay their new sales personnel only a straight salary and generally do not view sales positions as part of the career path for executives. Accordingly, Nordstrom personnel are highly motivated to satisfy their customers. As one of its salespersons commented, "Nordstrom tells me to do whatever I need to make you happy. Period."

Competitors have been trying to adopt some elements of Nordstrom's customer-service approach in order to enhance their own store images, but as a Marshall Field's executive vice-president noted, upgrading service "doesn't come cheap, and it is an ongoing process requiring constant reinforcement."[1]

Overview

Communicating with customers is necessary for a firm to convey its philosophy of business, objectives, and strategy. Every retailer has information about itself to present to customers, and this information must be interpreted by the target market as intended if sales are to be made. A variety of physical and symbolic cues can be used by a retailer in communicating with its customers. See the color photo portfolio following page 456.

In this chapter, the establishment of a store image is described. The use of atmosphere, storefronts, store layouts, displays, customer services, and community relations are enumerated, as they relate to communicating with customers. Chapter 15 concentrates on the typical promotional tools available to retailers in reaching their customers: advertising, publicity, personal selling, and sales promotion.

The Significance of Store Image

To be successful, a retailer must create and maintain a distinctive, clear, and consistent image. Once established, this image permeates all goods and service offerings. In the consumer's mind, a retailer is placed in a niche relative to competitors based on its perceived image. It is extremely difficult to break out of this niche once it is firmly implanted in consumers' minds. **Store image** can be defined as

the way in which the store is defined in the shopper's mind, partly by its functional qualities and partly by an aura of psychological attributes.[2]

not simply someone's impersonal observations of a store's characteristics. Thus I consider image a combination of factual and emotional material. The customer reacts to the store's characteristics, as he views them, in an emotional way.[3]

a subjective phenomenon that results from the acquisition of knowledge about the store as it is perceived relative to other stores and in accordance with the consumer's unique cognitive framework.[4]

Common to these definitions are the concepts that image is comprised of functional (physical) and emotional attributes, that these attributes are organized into perceptual frameworks by shoppers, and that the frameworks determine shoppers' expectations about a retailer's overall policies and practices.

Components of Store Image

There are numerous factors that contribute to a store image, and it is the totality of these factors that determines an overall image. In different settings, it has been stated that store image is composed of

❏ Quality, price, and assortment.[5]
❏ Fashionability, salesmanship, outside attractiveness, and advertising.[6]
❏ Clientele mix, institutional maturity, merchandise offerings, locational convenience, shopping pleasure, transaction convenience, promotional emphasis, integrity, and image strength and clarity.[7]

457

From these lists, the following is offered as a detailed summary of the components of a store's image:

1. Characteristics of the target market.
2. Store positioning.
3. Store location.
4. Merchandise assortment.
5. Level of prices.
6. Physical attributes of the store (atmosphere).
7. Availability of credit and other services.
8. Civic responsibility.
9. Mass advertising and publicity.
10. Type and extent of personal selling.
11. Sales promotions.

Items 1 through 5 and their relation to image have been examined in earlier chapters in the text. Items 6 through 11 are the focal points for the discussion involving communications with the consumer in this and the next chapter. Figure 14-1 contains a detailed breakdown of all the elements of store image (incorporating Items 1 through 11).*

The Dynamics of Creating and Maintaining a Store Image

Creating and maintaining a store image is a multistep, ongoing process for retailers, as these examples show. Bloomingdale's prides itself on an image as "the country's trendiest department store." To preserve this image, it must constantly introduce merchandise before competitors and display it in an exciting manner. When adding new merchandise, Bloomingdale's evaluates the items themselves, saleability, freshness, innovativeness, uniqueness, and customer appeal. Its new store in Boca Raton was cited by *Chain Store Age Executive* magazine as the best designed luxury department store in 1987:

> In creating this store, the major objective was to insure that the store reflect its Florida location while bringing the image of a high-fashion New York City department store at the same time.[8]

Recently, Fidelity Prescriptions, a Dayton, Ohio, drugstore, spent $75,000 in remodeling its physical facilities. As a result, Fidelity successfully achieved its major goals: "to develop and solidify a progressive, consistent image; to distinguish and balance the three store areas [prescriptions, home health care, and over-the-counter]; to communicate its array of customer services; and to devise a flexible design that could be adapted to any space."[9]

Toddy's is an upscale supermarket in Englewood, Colorado, that has two-tone mauve and burgundy carpeting on the floor, brass lighting fixtures, and stained-glass skylights:

> Our average customer is upper-end with an income of more than $40,000 a year. We are trying to offer her the best value of things in the store. This includes the decor, comfort, variety of product, and service. This does not mean that these shoppers are not price-conscious. They are, so we still have to drive the message home to them that we are price competitive.[10]

In 1985, when John Hacala became president of Spencer Gifts retail division (with over five hundred stores in a number of states), he "looked at the stores

---

*See Figures 6-3 to 6-6 for examples of how to measure store image.

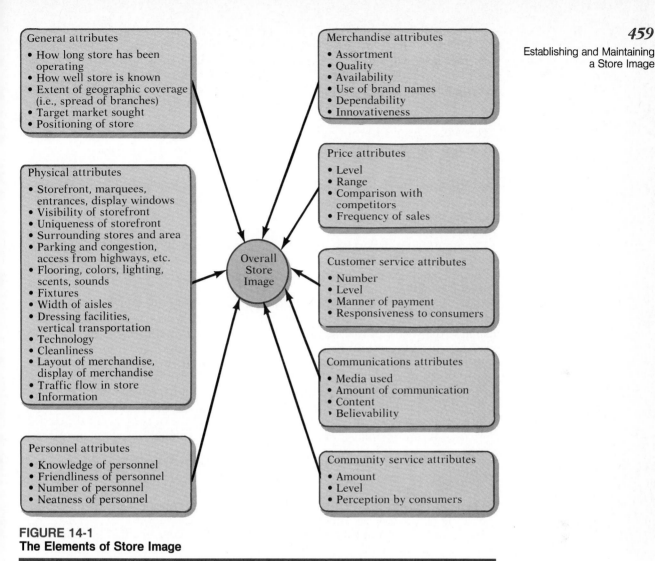

General attributes
- How long store has been operating
- How well store is known
- Extent of geographic coverage (i.e., spread of branches)
- Target market sought
- Positioning of store

Physical attributes
- Storefront, marquees, entrances, display windows
- Visibility of storefront
- Uniqueness of storefront
- Surrounding stores and area
- Parking and congestion, access from highways, etc.
- Flooring, colors, lighting, scents, sounds
- Fixtures
- Width of aisles
- Dressing facilities, vertical transportation
- Technology
- Cleanliness
- Layout of merchandise, display of merchandise
- Traffic flow in store
- Information

Personnel attributes
- Knowledge of personnel
- Friendliness of personnel
- Number of personnel
- Neatness of personnel

Merchandise attributes
- Assortment
- Quality
- Availability
- Use of brand names
- Dependability
- Innovativeness

Price attributes
- Level
- Range
- Comparison with competitors
- Frequency of sales

Customer service attributes
- Number
- Level
- Manner of payment
- Responsiveness to consumers

Communications attributes
- Media used
- Amount of communication
- Content
- Believability

Community service attributes
- Amount
- Level
- Perception by consumers

Overall Store Image

FIGURE 14-1
The Elements of Store Image

and found them confusing. I wanted them cleaned up and brought into the 1980s." He also had problems in seeing what the division's merchandise thrust was, since it carried many unrelated items. Today, Spencer Gifts is

> a marketing-driven specialty store business operating in major shopping centers nationwide. We sell primarily unusual fun-oriented, impulse merchandise that entertains, amuses, or adorns, presented in an attractive, theatrical atmosphere. We cater to customers of all ages with contemporary, fun-loving, trend-oriented life-styles. We will be the first to present new trends and fads with the objective of maximizing their profitability.[11]

Of particular concern to chain retailers and franchisors is maintaining a consistent image among all branches and units. However, despite the best planning, a number of factors may vary widely and have an effect on image. These factors include management and employee performance, consumer profiles, competitors, convenience in reaching the store, parking, safety, the ease of finding merchandise, and the quality of the surrounding area.

Sometimes, retailers with good images receive negative publicity. This must be countered in order for the company to maintain its desired image. A few years ago, McDonald's had problems with a promotion it was using, called "Glasses to Go." On the outside of these glasses were lead-paint decals. An uproar arose when the lead content was disclosed, and although it was not proven harmful (the decals were on the outside of the glasses), parents were quite alarmed. But McDonald's voluntarily removed the glasses from its stores and thereby blunted the negative publicity. Because of its quick actions, McDonald's sales did not suffer.

There have been several research studies on store image. Retailers should look at these studies as they develop and maintain their own store images.[12]

Atmosphere

The creation of an image depends heavily on the atmosphere that the store develops. **Atmosphere** refers to the physical characteristics of the store that are used to develop an image and to draw customers. It is a major component of image.

The sights, sounds, smells, and so on of a store contribute greatly to the image that is projected to consumers. It is important that atmosphere be understood as the psychological feeling a customer gets when visiting a store, or as the personality of the store.

Many consumers form impressions of a store before entering (because of its location, storefront, and so on) or just after entering (because of the merchandise displays, the width of aisles, and so on). These customers may judge the store prior to closely examining merchandise and prices. One study on store atmosphere found that it influences the customer's enjoyment of the shopping experience, the time spent browsing and examining the store's offerings, the willingness to converse with store personnel, the tendency to spend more money than originally planned, and the likelihood of future patronage.[13]

Atmosphere can be divided into several elements: exterior, general interior, store layout, and displays. Figure 14-2 contains a detailed breakdown of these elements.

Exterior

The exterior characteristics of a store have a strong impact on its image and should be planned accordingly.

The **storefront** is the total physical exterior of the store itself. It includes marquees, entrances, windows, lighting, and construction materials. Through the storefront, a retailer can present a conservative, progressive, lavish, discount, or other image to the consumer. A retailer should not underestimate the importance of the storefront as a major determinant of image, particularly for new customers. When passing through an unfamiliar business district or shopping center, consumers often judge a store by its exterior.

There are various alternatives that a retailer could consider when planning its basic storefront. These are a few of them:

❑ A modular structure—It is a one-piece rectangle or square that sometimes attaches several stores.

❑ A prefabricated (prefab) structure—It utilizes a store frame that is built in a factory and assembled at the store site.

❑ A prototype store—It is used by franchisors and chains. Because a consistent image is sought, uniform storefronts are constructed.

❑ A recessed storefront—In this case, the store is one of many at its location. To lure customers, the storefront is recessed from the level of other stores. Customers have to walk in a number of feet to examine the storefront.

❑ A unique building design—For example, round structures are quite distinctive.

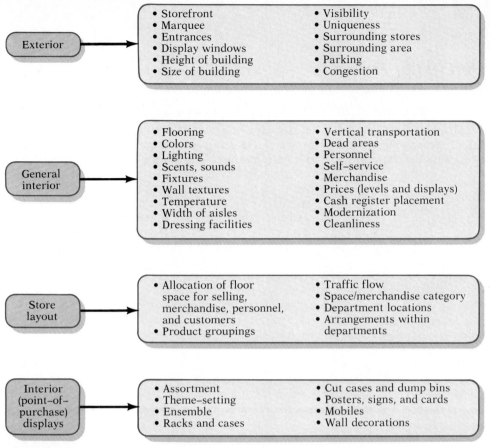

FIGURE 14-2
The Elements of Atmosphere

In addition to the actual storefront, atmosphere can be created by trees, fountains, and benches placed in front of the store. These enhance the consumer's feelings about shopping and about the store by establishing a relaxed environment.

A **marquee** is a sign that is used to display the store's name. The marquee can be painted or a neon light, printed or script, and alone or mixed with a slogan (trademark) and other information. To be effective, the marquee should stand out and attract attention. Image is influenced because a marquee can be gaudy and flashy or subdued and subtle. Probably the most widely known marquee in the world is the McDonald's golden arch, which some communities consider an environmental eyesore.

The entrances to the store should be designed carefully; and three major decisions must be made. First, the number of entrances is determined. Many smaller stores have only one entrance. Larger department stores may have four to eight or more entrances. A store hoping to draw vehicular and pedestrian traffic should have at least two entrances (one in the front of the store to lure pedestrians, another in the rear of the store adjacent to the parking lot). Because front and back entrances serve different purposes, they should be designed separately. One factor limiting the number of entrances is the problem of pilferage. Some urban stores have closed off entrances to reduce the size of their security forces.

Butt, How Can Store Design Foster a Proper Atmosphere?

H.E. Butt is a San Antonio, Texas-based supermarket chain with over 150 outlets. It recently opened a 68,000-square-foot prototype store in Austin, Texas, incorporating this design philosophy:

> The ultimate goal is to highlight the products. With the elements of store design, you don't want to startle the customer and make her forget the reason she is in the store in the first place. Let's face it, the real reason the interior is there is to display the merchandise.

Accordingly, the exterior of the building must also be considered carefully to

> make sure that when the shopper walks in, she doesn't feel like she has entered the twilight zone. A lot of people make the mistake of concentrating only on the inside.

Although this philosophy may appear rather conservative, it is really intended to keep the proper focus on store design: it is there to help sell merchandise. The design of Butt's new Austin outlet is really quite progressive and exciting. At the store, the exterior has a 24-foot-high curved wall which "undulates." There are six 10-foot-high openings that lead shoppers into a courtyard: "The customer feels as if she has bypassed the hustle and bustle of the walk areas and the parking lot. The courtyard serves as a transition." Inside the store, very high ceilings are used, so that there is not a "bowling alley effect." To cover the empty areas caused by the high ceilings, the store has space frames featuring different color panels, each designating a separate department.

Source: Based on material in "Design Sets the Stage for Products," *Chain Store Age Executive* (February 1988), pp. 13–14.

Second, the type of entrance is chosen from among many options. The doorway is selected: revolving; electric, self-opening; regular, push-pull; or climate-controlled open entry. The climate-controlled entry is an open entrance with a curtain of warm or cold air, set at the same temperature as inside the store. This entry makes the store inviting, reduces pedestrian traffic congestion, and enables customers to see inside the store. The entrance flooring is picked: cement, tile, or carpeting. Lighting is ascertained: traditional or fluorescent, white or colors, and/or flashing or constant.

Third, the walkways are considered. A wide, lavish walkway creates a very different image and mood from a narrow, constrained one. In the construction of the storefront, ample room must be provided for the walkways. Large window displays may be very attractive, but customers would be unhappy if there is not sufficient space for a comfortable entry into the store.

Display windows serve two main purposes: to identify the store and its offerings, and to induce customers to enter. They give a wide variety of information about a store. By showing a representative merchandise offering, a store can create an overall image. By showing fashion or seasonal goods, a store can show that it is contemporary. By showing sale items, a store can lure price-conscious consumers. By showing eye-catching displays that have little to do with its merchandise offering, a store can attract the attention of pedestrians. By showing public service messages (e.g., a window display for the Jerry Lewis Telethon), the store can show its concern for the community.

Considerable planning is necessary to develop good display windows. Therefore, more and more, larger stores are employing specialists to set up their displays properly. Window decisions include number, size, shape, color, theme, and changes per year. Some stores, particularly in shopping centers, do not use display windows for the side of the building that faces the parking lot; they have solid building exteriors. These stores feel that vehicular patrons are not lured by expensive outside display windows; but those retailers do invest in display windows for their storefronts that are inside malls.

The height and the size of the exterior building also contribute to a store's image. The height of a building can be disguised or nondisguised. Disguised building height occurs when part of the store is beneath ground level. As a result, the building is not so intimidating to consumers who are turned off by a large, impersonal structure. Nondisguised building height is when the entire store can be seen by pedestrians (all floors are at ground level or higher). This is most often true of small stores. The overall size of a building cannot really be disguised; the target market should be researched for a correlation of store size and patronage. An intimate boutique image cannot be generated with a block-long building. Neither can a department store image be linked to a quarter-block site.

Few retailers are able to succeed without good exterior visibility for their stores and/or shopping centers. This means that pedestrian and/or vehicular traffic can clearly see the storefront or marquee. For this reason, a store located behind a bus stop has poor visibility for vehicular traffic and pedestrians across the street. Many retailers that operate near highways must use billboards for visibility because drivers quickly pass by.

Visibility is developed through a combination of exterior characteristics. The objective is to make the store appear unique, to make it stand out somehow, and to catch the consumer's eye. A distinctive store design, an elaborate marquee, recessed open-air entrances, decorative windows, and different building height and building size are one grouping of storefront features that can attract consumers through uniqueness. In the process, a store image would be fostered.

Uniqueness, although it provides excellent visibility, may not be without its problems. An example is Macy's in Elmhurst, Queens, New York, which is a "store-in-the-round." The department store, located on a square city block, is round-shaped. Parking is provided on each level of the store, making the walking distances of customers very short. The problems with the store-in-the-round are that a rectangular store provides greater floor space on a lot of the same size; convenient on-floor parking may minimize customer shopping on other floors; added entrances increase chances for pilferage; customers dislike inclined and circular driving; and architectural costs are higher for unique buildings.

When the retailer is planning a store's exterior, the surrounding stores and the surrounding area should be examined. Each contributes to a store's image, regardless of the retailer's distinctive storefront and building. The surrounding stores present an image to consumers. The image may be progressive, conservative, high-price, personal-service, and so on. This overall area image rubs off on the individual retailer because consumers tend to have a general image of a shopping center or a business district. Therefore, the individual storefront should be distinctive but not contradictory to the image of the area chosen by a retailer to do business.

The surrounding area includes the demographics and the life-styles of people living near the store. Store image is affected by the type of neighborhood in which it is located. An unfavorable atmosphere exists if vandalism and crime are high, the people living near the store are not part of the target market, and the area is rundown.

Parking facilities can add to or detract from a store's atmosphere. Plentiful, free, nearby parking (with large parking spaces) creates a much more positive atmosphere than scarce, costly, distant parking (with tiny parking spaces). Countless potential shoppers may never enter the store if they drive around looking for on-street parking spaces, and not finding them, they go elsewhere or return home disgruntled. Other customers may run in and out of the store so that they can complete their shopping before the parking meters expire. In assessing parking facilities, retailers should also be aware that some customers may have a limit to the distance they will walk from a parking space to the most distant stores, and many customers dislike multilevel garages (because of discomfort in driving or a concern for safety).

Allied with the parking problem is that of congestion. A store's atmosphere would be diminished if its parking lot, sidewalks, and/or entrances are jammed. Consumers who feel crushed in the crowd generally spend less time shopping and are in poorer moods than those who feel comfortable.

General Interior

Once a customer is inside a store, there are numerous elements that affect his or her perception of it. The general interior elements of atmosphere are described here and shown in Figure 14-2.

Flooring can be made of cement, wood, linoleum, carpet, earth, and so on. A plush, thick carpet creates one kind of image, and a cement floor causes another.[14] Because customers use cues to develop their store perceptions, the materials used in floors are important. As an example, a high-quality shoe store would use thick carpeting; a discount, self-service store often uses linoleum.

Colors and lighting affect the store's image.[15] Bright, vibrant colors contribute to a different atmosphere than light pastels or plain white walls. Lighting can be direct or indirect, white or colors, constant or flashing. For instance, a jeans boutique could use bright colors and bright, flashing lights to establish one atmosphere, and a maternity dress shop could utilize pastel colors and indirect lighting to foster a different atmosphere. Recently, Golub Corp. began redesigning the interiors of its Price Chopper supermarkets and superstores (located in the Northeast). It replaced the hunter green and yellow colors used in the stores, which after a period of time "tend to look drab and dirty," with white, red, aluminum, and charcoal gray; and neon lights were featured more prominently.[16]

Scents and sounds can be used to influence the customer's mood. A pet store wants the natural scents and sounds of its animals to woo customers. A cosmetics store hopes that its array of perfume scents will result in sales. A record store plays its top-sellers. A beauty salon plays soft music or rock, depending on its target market. A restaurant uses the scents from the kitchen to increase customers' appetites. Slow-tempo music in supermarkets encourages consumers to move more slowly (and purchase more) than fast-tempo music, which speeds behavior.[17] In each case, a favorable atmosphere is sought.

Store fixtures should be planned not only on the basis of their utility but also because of their aesthetics. Pipes, plumbing, vents, beams, doors, storage rooms, and display racks and tables should be considered in the interior decorating. A store seeking a high-price, high-quality image should disguise and decorate those fixtures. A store seeking a low-price, low-quality image should leave the fixtures exposed. Because the latter choice is inexpensive, it reinforces the desired image.

Wall textures can enhance or diminish a store's image. Prestigious stores often use fancy, raised wallpaper. Department stores are more likely to use flat wallpaper, while discount stores could have barren walls. Prestige stores might also have elaborate chandeliers, while discount stores would have simple lighting fixtures.

The customer's mood is affected by the temperature of the store and its manner of achieving it. A customer would be uncomfortable if there is insufficient heat in the winter and coolness in the summer. This can hasten his or her trip through the store. In another vein, the store's image is influenced by the use of central air-conditioning, unit air-conditioning, fans, or open windows.

The width of the aisles has an impact on store image. Wide, uncrowded aisles create a better atmosphere than narrow, crowded aisles. Customers shop longer and spend more when they are not pushed and shoved while walking or looking at merchandise. In Boston, Filene's basement has many items at bargain prices; however, overcrowding keeps some customers away.

Dressing facilities may be elaborate, plain, or nonexistent. A prestige store may have carpeted, private dressing facilities. An average-quality store may have linoleum-floored, semiprivate facilities. A discount store may have small stalls or no dressing facilities at all. For some apparel customers, dressing facilities (and their maintenance) are a major factor in store selection. Atmosphere and type of dressing facility are closely intertwined.

Multilevel stores must have some form of vertical transportation. The choices are elevator, escalator, and/or stairs. Larger stores may have a combination of all three. Traditionally, the operator-run elevator has appeared in finer stores, and stairs have appeared in discount stores. Today, escalators are quite popular and are gaining in stature. They provide consumers with a quiet ride and a panoramic view of the store. Finer stores decorate their escalators with fountains, shrubs, and trees. The placement and design of vertical transportation determine its contribution to atmosphere. Stairs remain important for discount and smaller stores.

Light fixtures, wood or metal beams, doors, rest rooms, dressing facilities, vertical transportation, and so on cause dead areas for the retailer. **Dead areas** are awkward spaces where normal displays cannot be set up. In some instances, it is not possible for these areas to be used profitably or attractively. However, in general, retailers are learning to utilize their dead areas better. For example, mirrors can be attached to exit doors. Vending machines can be located near rest rooms. Advertisements can be placed in dressing rooms.

The most creative use of a dead area involves the escalator. For a long time, retailers considered it an ugly fixture in the middle of the store. Now, it is viewed differently. The escalator enables the consumer to view the whole floor of the store, and sales of impulse items go up when placed at the entrance or exit of the escalator. In addition, most retailers build their escalators so that customers must get off at each floor and pass by attractive displays.

The number, manner, and appearance of store personnel reflect a store's atmosphere. Polite, well-groomed, knowledgeable personnel generate a positive atmosphere. Ill-mannered, poorly groomed, unknowing personnel engender a negative one. In general, research findings show that customers like to deal with personnel having demographics similar to their own; therefore, store personnel should resemble the target market as closely as possible. The store that uses self-service minimizes its personnel and creates a discount, impersonal image. A store cannot develop a prestige image if it is set up for self-service.

The merchandise that a retailer sells influences its image. Top-of-the-line merchandise yields one kind of image, and bottom-of-the-line merchandise yields another. The mood of the customer is affected accordingly.

Store prices contribute to image in two ways. First, price levels yield a perception of store image in the consumer's mind. Second, the way that prices are displayed is a vital part of atmosphere. Prestige stores have few or no price displays and rely upon hidden price tags. Sales are de-emphasized. Discount stores accentuate price displays and show prices in large numbers. The placement of cash registers is associated with the type of price displays a store uses. A prestige store places its cash registers in inconspicuous areas such as behind posts or in employee rooms. Discount stores locate their cash registers centrally and have large signs to point them out.

The technology of the store and the modernization of its building and fixtures also have an impact on image. A store that employs current technology, such as computerized cash registers and automated inventory-movement procedures, impresses customers with its efficiency and speed of operations. A store that uses slower, older techniques can have long lines and impatient customers. A store with a modernized building (new storefront, marquee, and so on) and new fixtures (lights, floors, walls, and so on) fosters a more favorable atmosphere than one with older facilities.

In general, these observations can be made about modernizing a store:

❏ Renovations are easier, faster, and less costly than constructing or opening new stores.

❏ Improving store appearance, updating facilities, expansion, and the need to reallocate space are the main reasons for remodeling.

❏ It results in strong sales and profit increases after completion.

❏ Almost all stores are kept open during a renovation.

Last, but certainly not least, a retailer must have a plan for maintaining store cleanliness. No matter how impressive a store's exterior and interior may be, an unkempt store will be received negatively by customers. As one store manager remarked about cleanliness:

> I think it's the most important thing in a store. It sets the tone. Housekeeping is many things; keeping showcases clean; keeping bases clean where they are rapped by the vacuum cleaner. Everybody thinks of a store as the place where the merchandise is. But are your toilet facilities taken care of properly? Are the trash baskets empty? It's not merely going through with a vacuum cleaner. It's the cleaning of the doors, of the countertops, of dust on top of seven foot units.[18]

Store Layout

Next, the specifics of store layout are planned and set up.

Allocation of Floor Space

Each store has a total square footage of floor space available and must allocate it among selling, merchandise, personnel, and customers. **Selling space** is the area set aside for displays of merchandise, interactions between sales personnel and customers, demonstrations, and so on. A retailer such as a supermarket or other self-service business usually has selling space as a large portion of total store space.

Merchandise space is the area where nondisplayed items are kept in stock or inventory. A shoe store is a good example of a retailer whose merchandise space takes up a large percentage of total store space.

Store personnel often require space for changing clothes, lunch and coffee breaks, and rest room facilities. Retailers may try to minimize **personnel space** by insisting on off-the-job clothes changing and other tactics. Because floor space is so valuable, that part allotted to personnel is strictly controlled. However, when planning personnel space, a retailer should consider employee morale and personal appearance.

Customers also require space, and such space contributes greatly to a store's image. **Customer space** can include a lounge, benches and/or chairs, dressing facilities, rest room facilities, a restaurant, vertical transportation, smoking areas, a nursery, parking, and wide aisles. Low-image retailers generally skimp on or omit most of these areas; retailers with consumer-oriented images provide their customers with adequate amounts of space for many or all of these factors.

A retailer cannot go further in its store-layout planning until floor space is properly allocated among selling, merchandise, personnel, and customers. Without that allocation, the firm would have no conception of the space available for displays, signs, rest rooms, and so on.

Classification of Store Offerings

A store's offerings are then classified into product groupings. Four types of groupings and combinations of them can be employed: functional, purchase motivation, market segment, and storability. With **functional product groupings,** a store's merchandise is categorized and displayed by common end uses. For example, a men's clothing store might carry these functional groups: shirt, tie, cuff links, and tie pins; shoes, laces, and shoe polish; T-shirts, undershorts, and socks; suits; and sports jackets and slacks.

Purchase-motivation product groupings appeal to the consumer's urge to buy a product and the amount of time he or she is willing to spend in shopping. A committed customer with time to shop will visit the upper floors and extremities of a store; an uninterested customer with little time to spend will gravitate to displays on the first floor, near the exit. A retailer can capitalize on this fact by grouping its products by purchase motivation. Examine the first floor of any department store. The items located there are impulse products and other quick purchases. On the third floor of the department store are items that encourage and require more thoughtful shopping.

Market-segment product groupings can be used. In this instance, all products appealing to a given target market are grouped together. Some examples are a clothing store's dividing its products into juniors', misses', and ladies' clothing categories; a record store's separating its merchandise into rock, jazz, classical, rhythm and blues, country and western, gospel, and popular music sections; an art gallery's placing its paintings in different price groups; and a toy store's setting up distinct display areas for children and adult games.

For products requiring special handling, **storability product groupings** may be employed. A supermarket has freezer, refrigerator, and room-temperature sections. A florist keeps some flowers in a refrigerator and others at room temperature. The same is true for a bakery or a fruit store.

Progressive retailers often use a combination of product groupings and plan their store layouts accordingly. In addition to the considerations just covered, provisions must be made for minimizing shoplifting and pilferage. This means positioning product groups away from corners and doors.

Determination of a Traffic-Flow Pattern

The traffic-flow pattern of the store is determined next. There are two basic traffic-flow alternatives available to a retailer: straight (gridiron) and curving (free-flow). A **straight traffic flow** means that displays and aisles are constructed in a rectangular or gridiron pattern, as shown in Figure 14-3. A **curving traffic flow** means that displays and aisles are constructed in a free-flowing pattern, as shown in Figure 14-4.

A straight traffic pattern is most often used by food retailers, discount stores, hardware stores, and other convenience-oriented stores (such as stationery outlets). This layout has several advantages:

❑ An austere, efficient atmosphere is created.

❑ Customers can shop quickly; regular customers particularly desire clearly marked, distinct aisles and develop a routine pattern through the store.

❑ All available floor space is utilized.

❑ Inventory control and security are simplified.

❑ Self-service is possible, thereby reducing labor costs.

The disadvantages of the gridiron are an impersonal atmosphere, limited browsing by customers, and rushed shopping behavior.

A curving traffic pattern is most often used by boutiques, department stores, clothing stores, and other shopping-oriented stores. There are several benefits from this approach:

❑ A friendly atmosphere is present.

❑ Shoppers do not feel rushed and will browse around.

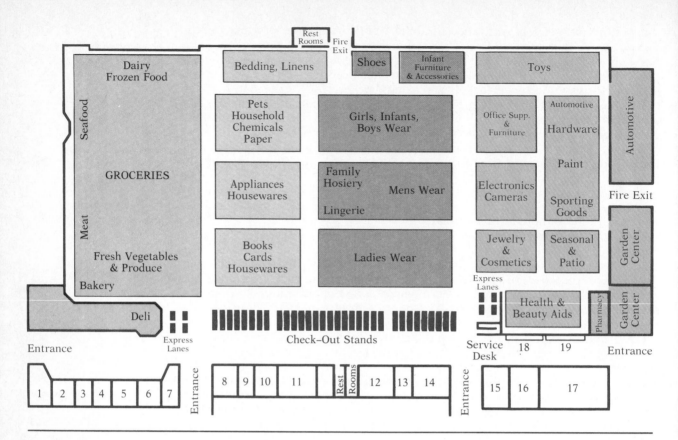

Legend for Freestanding Food & Services

1. Anthony's Pizza 'N Pasta
2. Aspen Creamery
3. One Smart Cookie
4. Corn Dog 7
5. TCBY (The Country's Best Yogurt)
6. Flyer's Express
7. Taco Bueno

8. Children's Play Area
9. Office
10. Ace Cash Express
11. Grand Bank
12. Pictureland Portrait Studio
13. One–Hour Photo Processing

14. Value Eyecare
15. General Nutrition Center
16. Cost Cutters Hair Salon
17. Fliks Video
18. Cole Key
19. Heel Quik

FIGURE 14-3
How Hypermart USA in Garland, Texas, Uses a Straight (Gridiron) Traffic Flow
Source: Hypermarket USA. Reprinted by permission.

❑ Customers are encouraged to walk through the store in any direction or pattern they desire.

❑ Impulse or unplanned purchases are increased.

The disadvantages of a free-flow pattern are potential customer confusion, wasted floor space, difficulties in inventory control and security, high labor-intensiveness, and the encouragement of loitering. In addition, free-flow displays are often more expensive than standardized gridiron displays.

Determination of Space Needs

The space for each product category is then ascertained. Selling as well as nonselling space must be considered in any calculations.

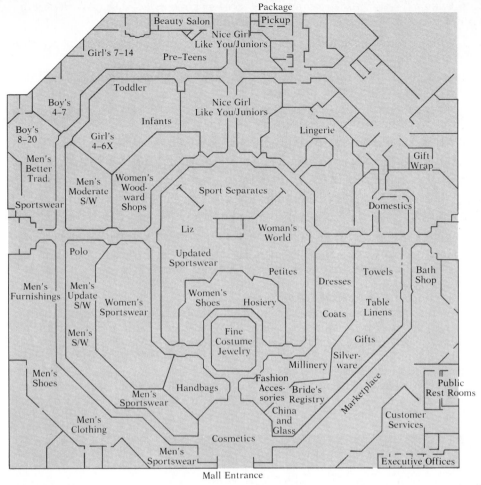

FIGURE 14-4
How Hudson's Department Store in East Lansing, Michigan, Uses a
Curving (Free-Flow) Traffic Flow
Reprinted by permission.

Two approaches are possible: the model stock method or the space-productivity ratio. Under the **model stock approach,** a retailer tabulates the amount of floor space necessary to carry and display a proper assortment of merchandise. Clothing stores and shoe stores are examples of retailers that use the model stock method. With the **sales-productivity ratio,** a retailer assigns floor space on the basis of sales or profit per foot. Highly profitable product categories receive large chunks of space; marginally profitable categories receive less space. Food stores and bookstores are examples of retailers that use space-productivity ratios in planning floor space.

Mapping Out In-Store Locations

Department locations are mapped out at this point. For multilevel stores, this procedure includes assigning departments to floors and laying out the individual floors. What product categories should be placed on each floor? What should the layout of each floor be? The single-level store is concerned with only the second issue. Generally speaking, these questions have to be considered:

❑ Which products should be placed in the basement, on the first floor, on the second floor, and so on?

❑ On a given floor, how should the groupings be placed in relation to doors, vertical transportation, and so on?

❑ Where should impulse or unplanned product categories be located in relation to categories that consumers preplan to buy?

❑ Where should convenience products be situated?

❑ How should associated product categories be aligned? See Figure 14-5.

❑ Where should seasonal and off-season products be placed?

❑ Where should space-consuming categories such as furniture be located?

❑ How close should product displays and stored inventory be to each other?

❑ What travel patterns do consumers follow once they enter the store?

❑ How can consumer lines be avoided near the cash register, and how can the overall appearance of store crowding be averted?

Arrangement of Individual Products

Individual products are then arranged within departments; a number of criteria may be used in positioning them. The most profitable items and brands would receive favorable locations where consumer traffic is heavy. Products may also be arranged by package size, price, color, brand, level of personal service required, and/or customer interest.

End-aisle display positions, eye-level positions, and checkout-counter positions are most likely to increase sales for individual items. Continuity of locations is

FIGURE 14-5
A K mart Department Location Display
This elevated department sign indicates that consumers may find related products in one Homecare Center in K mart stores.
Reprinted by permission of
Discount Store News.

also important; shifts in store layout may decrease sales. The least desirable display position is knee or ankle level, because consumers do not like to bend down.

Individual retailers should conduct their own research and experiments to measure the effects of different product positions on sales. It must also be remembered that the objectives of the manufacturer and the retailer are often quite dissimilar. The manufacturer wants the sales of its brand to be maximized and therefore pushes for eye-level, full-shelf, end-aisle locations. On the other hand, the retailer is more interested in maximizing total store sales and profit, regardless of the brand.

Retailers that utilize self-service have special considerations. The gridiron layout is normally used to minimize customer confusion. Similarly, aisles, displays, and merchandise must be clearly marked. A large selling space, with on-floor assortments, is necessary. Cash registers must be plentiful and accessible. It is difficult to sell complex and/or expensive items through self-service.

Interior (Point-of-Purchase) Displays

After the store layout is fully detailed, a retailer devises interior displays. These **point-of-purchase displays** provide consumers with information, add to store atmosphere, and serve a substantial promotional role.[19] In this section, several types and forms of displays are described. Most retailers use combinations of several or all of these kinds of displays.

An **assortment display** is one in which a retailer exhibits a wide range of merchandise for the customer. With an open assortment, the customer is encouraged to feel and/or try on a number of products. Pocketbooks, greeting cards, magazines, and gloves are the kinds of products for which retailers use open assortments. Recently, a number of supermarkets have returned to a practice that they had all but abandoned: selling items such as candy in open, bulk displays. See Figure 14-6. With a closed assortment, the customer is encouraged to look at a variety of merchandise but not touch it or try it on. Shirts, games, and records are prepackaged items that the customer is not allowed to open before buying.

A **theme-setting display** positions a product offering in a thematic environment or setting. A theme enables a retailer to generate a specific atmosphere or mood. Retailers often change their displays to reflect seasons or special events; some have their employees dress to fit the occasion. All or part of a store may be adapted to a theme, such as Washington's Birthday, Columbus Day, Valentine's Day, Independence Day, Lunch with a Star, or some other concept. Each special theme is enacted to attract customers' attention and make shopping more enjoyable (and not a chore).

Ensemble displays have become very popular in recent years. Instead of grouping and displaying merchandise in separate categories (e.g., shoe department, sock department, pants department, shirt department, sports jacket department), complete ensembles are displayed. For example, a mannequin could be dressed in a matching combination of shoes, socks, pants, shirt, and sports jacket, and these items would be readily available in one department or adjacent departments. Customers are pleased with the ease of a purchase and like being able to envision an entire outfit.

Rack displays are heavily used by clothing retailers, houseware retailers, and others. These racks have a primarily functional use: to neatly hang or present the products. The major problems are cluttering and customers' returning items to the wrong place (e.g., disrupting the proper size sequence). Current technology allows retailers to use sliding, disconnecting, contracting, lightweight, attractive rack displays. **Case displays** are employed to exhibit heavier, bulkier items than

FIGURE 14-6
A Bulk Display in a Supermarket
Reprinted by permission of Winn-Dixie.

racks hold. Records, books, prepackaged goods, and sweaters are typically contained in case displays. See Figure 14-7.

Cut cases are inexpensive displays, in which merchandise is left in its original cartons. Supermarkets and discount houses frequently set up cut-case displays. These cases do not create a warm atmosphere. Neither do **dump bins,** which are cases that house piles of sale clothing, marked-down books, and so on. Instead of neat, precise displays, dump bins contain open assortments of roughly handled items. The advantages of cut cases and dump bins are reduced display costs and a low-price image.

Posters, signs, and cards can be used to dress up all types of displays, including cut cases and dump bins. These tools provide information about in-store product locations and stimulate customers to shop. **Mobiles,** a type of hanging display with parts that move, especially in response to air currents, serve the same purpose—but are more appealing to the eye and stand out. Wall decorations also enhance a store's atmosphere and add to displays. Wall decorations are particularly useful with thematic displays and ensemble displays.

FIGURE 14-7
Combining Rack and Case Displays
Reprinted by permission of Montgomery Ward, Inc.

The number and variety of customer services that a retailer provides have a strong impact on and contribute to the image that is created. To use customer services successfully, a retailer should first outline an overall service strategy and then plan individual services.[20] Figure 14-8 shows one way that a retailer may view customer services.

Customer Services

Developing a Customer Services Strategy

In developing a customer services strategy, a retailer has to make decisions involving the range, level, choice, price, measurement, and retention of its services.

What services are primary and ancillary for the retailer? **Primary customer**

Cost of Offering Service

	High	Low
High Value of Service to Customer **Low**	*Patronage builders-* High–cost activities that are the primary factors behind customer loyalties. Examples: transaction speed, credit, gift registry	*Patronage solidifiers-* The "low–cost little things" that increase loyalty. Examples: courtesy (referring to the customer by name and saying thank you), suggestion selling.
	Disappointers- Expensive activities that do no real good. Examples: weekday deliveries for two–earner families, home economists	*Basics-* Low–cost activities that are "naturally expected." They don't build patronage, but their absence could reduce patronage. Examples: free parking, in–store directories

FIGURE 14-8
Classifying Customer Services
Source: Adapted by the authors from Albert D. Bates, "Rethinking the Service Offer," *Retail Issues Letter* (December 1986), p. 3. Reprinted by permission.

services are those that are considered basic ingredients in the retail offering and must be provided. Examples are credit for a furniture retailer, new car preparation for an automobile dealer, and a liberal return policy for a gift shop. These services form an essential part of the retail strategy mix, and a firm could not stay in business without them.

Ancillary customer services are extra ingredients that add to the retail offering. A retailer could adequately cater to a target market without these services. Examples are home delivery for a supermarket, an extra warranty for an automobile dealer, gift wrapping for a toy dealer, and credit for a discounter.

It is vital that a retailer determine which customer services are primary and which are ancillary for its particular situation. Primary services for one retailer, such as delivery, may be ancillary for another. Remember that primary services have to be provided; ancillary services enhance a retailer's competitive advantage but are not required. See Figure 14-9.

What level of customer services is necessary to complement the store's image? A prestige store would define more services as primary than a discount store, because consumers expect a prestige store to supply a wide range of services as part of the store's basic retail offering. This is not true of the discount store. In addition, the performance of services would be different. As an example, the customers of a prestige store may expect elaborate gift-wrapping facilities, valet parking, a restaurant, and a ladies' room attendant, whereas the customers of a discount store may expect cardboard gift boxes, self-service parking, a lunch counter, and an unattended ladies' room. In these instances, the generic services are the same; however, the level of the services is quite dissimilar.

Should a choice of customer services be furnished? Some retailers allow customers to choose among levels of service; others provide one level of service. For

FIGURE 14-9
Using Ancillary Services to Enhance a Retailer's Competitive Advantage
In the past, when supermarket personnel loaded groceries into a customer's car, this was considered a primary service. But today, because of greater emphasis on self-service and controlling labor costs, many supermarkets do not offer this service. One exception is Fry's, an Arizona chain that offers this ancillary service to maintain customer loyalty. Also note that Fry's is involved in community relations via Special Olympics announcements on its shopping bags. Reprinted by permission of Kroger.

instance, a store may honor several credit cards or only its own. Trade-ins may be allowed on some items or all. Television warranties may have optional extensions or fixed lengths. A retailer may offer one-month, three-month, and six-month payment plans or may insist on a one-month payment period.

Should customer services be free? Two factors are causing a number of retailers to charge for customer services: rapidly increasing costs and consumer behavior. Delivery, gift wrapping, and other services are labor-intensive, and their costs are steadily rising. Also, it has been found that customers are more likely to remain at home for a delivery or a service call if a fee is imposed. Without a fee, retailers may have to deliver an item two or three times to find someone at home. In settling on a free or fee customer-service strategy, a retailer must determine which services are primary (these are usually free) and which are ancillary (these could be provided for a fee). Furthermore, competitors and profit margins should be watched closely, and the target market should be surveyed. When setting customer service fees, a retailer must also decide whether its objective is to break even or to make a profit on the services.

How can a retailer measure the benefits of providing customer services against their costs? The purpose of customer services is to attract and retain consumers, thus maximizing company sales and profits. This means that ancillary services should not be offered unless they increase sales and profits. Unfortunately, little investigation of the benefit–cost ratios of various services has been undertaken. Therefore, a retailer should plan ancillary services on the basis of its experience, competitors' actions, and customer comments; and when the costs of providing these services increase, higher prices should be passed on to the consumer.

How can customer services be terminated? Once a retailer establishes an image, consumers are likely to react negatively to any reduction of services. None-

How Can an Independent Retailer and Its Customers Win-Win?

Robert Hall TV & Appliance, an independent retailer in Riverside, California, has been in business for thirty years. During that time, it has faced heavy competition from other local stores as well as from large chains such as Circuit City. Yet, Robert Hall remains in a strong position and generates annual sales of more than $3 million.

Robert Hall's success is due to its focused store image, a good sales force, a "win-win" pricing philosophy, and innovative customer services. Its focused image stems from three factors. First, "all things equal, people prefer to shop at an independent." Second, Robert Hall concentrates on a few leading brands such as Magic Chef, Speed Queen, and Kitchen Aid. As a result, it is one of the top Magic Chef retailers in southern California. Third, it has de-emphasized its relatively unprofitable consumer electronics line.

Its sales force consists of three well-trained people, who are polite to customers and very knowledgeable. The win-win pricing philosophy encourages negotiation with patrons, so that they "receive good values that meet their needs while allowing Robert Hall to hold acceptable margins."

Robert Hall's customer service program includes these elements:

❑ A rent-to-own option. This enables customers who cannot initially afford to buy major appliances to rent them and apply their rent payments toward purchases, if they so desire.

❑ A choice of appliance color at no extra charge.

❑ Free delivery.

❑ A special relationship with a local repair firm. "If something breaks, we'll get it fixed."

❑ A liberal exchange policy.

Source: Based on material in Elliot King, "This Feisty Independent Isn't Afraid of Power Retailers," *Dealerscope Merchandising* (August 1987), pp. 67–68.

---

theless, inefficient and costly ancillary services might have to be discontinued. When dropping customer services, a retailer's best strategy is to be forthright and explain why the services are being terminated and how the customer will benefit through low prices and so on. Many times, a retailer may choose a middle ground, charging for previously free services and allowing the customers who want the services to continue to receive them.

Planning Individual Services

After a broad customer-service strategy is outlined, individual services are planned. For example, a large department store might offer all of these customer services: gift wrapping, layaway plans, pay telephones, bridal registry, car parking, restaurant, women's beauty salon, credit, carpet installation, dressing rooms, clothing alterations, customer rest rooms and sitting areas, baby strollers available, home delivery, fur storage, and others. The range of customer services described in this section is shown in Table 14-1.

Today, most retailers allow their customers to make credit purchases. The last major holdouts, supermarkets and discount stores, now usually accept personal checks with proper identification. Whereas smaller and medium-sized retailers rely on bank cards and companies such as American Express to process purchases made on credit, larger retailers generally have their own credit systems and credit cards. In greater numbers, larger retailers have also begun to accept outside credit cards in addition to their own.

TABLE 14-1
Typical Customer Services

Credit
Delivery
Alterations and installations
Packaging (gift wrapping)
Complaints and returns handling
Gift certificates
Trade-ins
Trial purchases
Special sales for regular customers
Extended store hours
Mail and telephone orders
Miscellaneous

❑ Bridal registry	❑ Rest rooms
❑ Interior designers	❑ Restaurant
❑ Personal shoppers	❑ Baby-sitting
❑ Ticket outlets	❑ Fitting rooms
❑ Parking	❑ Beauty salon
❑ Water fountains	❑ Fur storage
❑ Pay telephones	❑ Shopping bags
❑ Baby strollers	❑ Information

The role of credit in retail purchases can be seen through the following:[21]

❑ Visa, MasterCard, American Express, Carte Blanche, Diners Club, and Discover (a new credit-card service of Sears) are just some of the national credit cards accepted by various retailers.

❑ Well over half of department store and specialty store purchases are made on credit.

❑ Consumer use of credit cards increases with the amount of the purchase. While only 5 per cent use credit cards for purchases of $50 or less, 34 per cent use credit cards for purchases above $250.

❑ Together, Sears and J.C. Penney have more than sixty-five million holders of their credit cards.

❑ Computerization has eased the credit process and made it more efficient, thus encouraging more retailers to accept some form of credit system.

Retailer-generated credit cards have four advantages. The retailer saves the 3–6 per cent of sales fee that it would have to pay for outside card sales. The customer is encouraged to shop with a given retailer because its card would usually not be accepted elsewhere. Contact can be maintained with customers, and information learned about them. An attractive card design contributes to overall store image. There are also disadvantages to retailer credit cards: start-up costs are high, the retailer must worry about unpaid bills and slow cash flow, credit checks and follow-up tasks must be performed, and customers without the retailer's card may be discouraged from making purchases.

Bank and other commercial credit cards enable small and medium-sized retailers to offer credit, generate increased business for all types of retailers, appeal to tourists and mobile consumers, provide advertising support from the sponsor, reduce bad debts, eliminate startup costs for the retailer, and provide information. However, these cards do charge a service fee for each transaction (based on the purchase amount) and do not engender store loyalty.

As noted, both types of credit cards enhance the retailer's information capabilities. They provide data on credit sales (such as the size of the average transaction and the merchandise purchased), customer demographics (such as place of residence and income), and branch store performance (such as credit versus cash sales by product category).

All bank credit cards and most retailer credit cards are based on revolving accounts. With a **revolving credit account,** a customer charges items and is billed monthly on the basis of the outstanding cumulative balance. An **option credit account** is a form of revolving account; no interest is assessed if the consumer pays the bill in full when it is due. See Table 14-2, Example 1. However, should the customer make a partial payment, he or she will be assessed interest monthly on the unpaid amount. See Table 14-2, Examples 2 and 3.

The customer receives a credit limit with a revolving account, and his or her total balance cannot exceed this limit. Because of the high costs of money during the early 1980s, many states have allowed retailer and bank credit cards to raise

TABLE 14-2
Credit Payment Plans

Example 1: Revolving Account
(no interest paid)

Purchases in June	$100.00	
End-of-month bill		$100.00
Payment		$100.00
Balance due		$ 0.00

Example 2: Revolving Account
(interest paid)

Purchases in June	$100.00	
End-of-month bill		$100.00
Payment		$ 50.00
Balance due		$ 50.00
Purchases in July	$ 0.00	
Balance from June	$ 50.00	
One month's interest	$ .75	
(at 1½% per month)		
Total end-of-month bill		$ 50.75
Payment		$ 50.75
Balance due		$ 0.00

Example 3: Revolving Account
(interest paid)

Purchases in June	$400.00	
End-of-month bill		$400.00
Payment		$100.00
Balance due		$300.00
Purchases in July	$400.00	
Balance from June	$300.00	
Interest on balance	$ 4.50	
Total end-of-month bill		$704.50
Payment		$200.00
Balance due		$504.50
Purchases in August	$ 0.00	
Balance from July	$504.50	
Interest on balance	$ 7.57	
Total end-of-month bill		$512.07
Payment		$512.07
Balance due		$ 0.00

their interest rates, some up to 2 or more per cent per month (an annual rate of 24 per cent or more) on unpaid balances.

Some retailers use **open credit accounts.** In this arrangement, a consumer must pay his or her bill in full when it comes due. Partial, revolving payments are not permitted. A consumer operating with an open account is also given a credit limit.

Under a **monthly payment credit account,** the consumer pays for a purchase in equal monthly installments. Interest is usually charged. As an illustration, a consumer buys a $300 camera and pays for it over twelve months. Equal monthly payments of $27.50 ($25 principal and $2.50 interest) yield a total cost of $330 for the camera. The true interest rate is 18.46 per cent on the average monthly balance.*

Deferred billing enables regular charge customers to buy merchandise and not pay for it for several months, with no interest charge. Deferred billing may be used as a Christmas or other seasonal promotional tool. Customers would be encouraged to buy in November and December and not pay until March.

A **layaway plan** allows any customer to give the retailer a deposit to hold a product. When the customer completes payment, he or she takes home the item. In the meantime, the consumer does not have to worry about the store's running out of stock.

COD (collect on delivery) lets a customer have a product delivered to him or her before paying for it. Payment in full must be made when the merchandise is received. Direct marketers often use COD.

It should be apparent that retailers have wide flexibility in choosing a credit strategy. The one that best fits a firm's image, customers, and needs should be selected. While the trend toward credit-card usage continues, some retailers (such as a number of gas stations) have moved in the opposite direction and terminated credit-card transactions to reduce costs and prices. In the proper setting (e.g., off-price chains), discounts for cash payments also seem feasible.

A retailer has three considerations in setting up delivery service: the method of transportation, ownership versus rental of equipment, and timing. The method of transportation can be car, van, truck, train, boat, mail, or plane. The costs and appropriateness of these methods depend on the merchandise involved.

Large retailers often find it economical to own their own delivery vehicles. Ownership also enables retailers to advertise their company names, have control over delivery time, and have company employees handle deliveries. Small retailers may operate out of their own cars. However, many small, moderate-sized, and even large retailers use United Parcel Service or utilize commercial truckers, when consumers reside away from the delivery area, transportation is used sporadically, and shipments are not efficient (because less than full truckloads would be shipped).

Last, the timing of deliveries must be planned. A retailer must decide how quickly orders are to be processed and how often deliveries are to be made to different geographic areas. For example, will customers in a Baton Rouge, Louisiana, suburb receive deliveries daily, once a week, or monthly?

For some retailers, alterations and installations are primary services and would be treated accordingly, although more of these firms now charge fees. Many discount stores have discontinued giving alterations of clothing and installations of heavy appliances on both a free and a fee basis. These stores have concluded that the services are too ancillary to their business and not worth the expense. Other retailers offer only basic alterations: shortening pants, taking in the waist, and lengthening the jacket sleeves. They do not adjust jacket shoulders or width

*The computation for this is ($30 interest)/[(½) ($300 initial principal + $25 last month principal)] = ($30)/[(½)($325)] = ($30)/($162.50) = 18.46 per cent.

and so on. Appliance retailers may hook up a washing machine but not do plumbing work. Some clothing-store chains have set up centralized alteration systems to reduce costs.

Packaging as well as complaints and returns handling can be centrally located or decentralized. Centralized packaging counters and complaints and returns departments have several advantages: they may be located in otherwise dead spaces; the main selling areas are not cluttered; specialized personnel can be used; and a common store policy is implemented. The advantages of decentralized facilities are that consumers are not inconvenienced; customers are kept in the selling area, where a salesperson may resolve any problems or offer different merchandise; and extra personnel are not required. In either case, a clearly established store policy regarding the handling of complaints and returns must be stated. The axiom "The customer is always right" should be followed whenever possible. Unfortunately, customers are often not convinced this policy is used.

Gift certificates encourage new and existing customers to shop with a retailer. Many retailers require that gift certificates be spent and not redeemed for cash. As a result, customers come into contact with the store's atmosphere while shopping. Trade-ins induce new and regular customers to patronize a retailer. Customers get a feeling of a bargain and an accommodation. Trial purchases enable shoppers to try out products before purchases become final, thereby reducing risks. If customers like the merchandise, it is kept and paid for; should customers dislike the merchandise, it is simply returned. Trial purchases are often allowed by mail-order retailers.

Increasingly, stores are offering special services to regular customers. Special sales, not open to the general public, are run to increase customer loyalty. Extended hours, such as evenings and weekends, are provided. This policy extends in-store shopping time and decreases rushing. Mail and telephone orders placed by regular customers are handled for convenience. All of these tactics give a firm an atmosphere of warmth for its most important customers.

Other useful customer services, some of them discussed previously, include bridal registry, interior designers, personal shoppers, ticket outlets, free (or low-cost) and plentiful parking, pay telephones, baby strollers, in-store water fountains, rest rooms, a restaurant, baby-sitting, fitting rooms, beauty salon, fur storage, shopping bags, and in-store information. The latter should not be underestimated; confused customers are less likely to be satisfied and/or to complete their shopping trips. A retailer's willingness to offer some or all of these services indicates to its customers its concern for them and is a strong contributor to image.

In particular, retailers need to be attentive to consumer needs and consider the impact of excessive self-service. As these marketing consultants point out, in general, customers do not have a high opinion of sales service:[22]

> You can hardly find anyone to wait on you, or if you do, they usually know less about what you want to buy than you do (Maxwell Sroge).

> Americans have developed an utter contempt for the retail clerk. When the choice is between bad service and no service, the American will always choose no service (Leo J. Shapiro).

However, some retailers are doing an excellent job in this area. Palais Royal, a Houston-based fashion specialty-store chain, is one of them:

> When our store directors go around to the stores, they do an atmosphere test: are the salespeople smiling, are they greeting people? We tell our sales staff: "Look at customers from a standpoint of their being guests in your home. You're there as the host or hostess, so treat them accordingly." I believe our people do, and, obviously, our customers do, too.[23]

The manner in which retailers relate to the communities around them also has an impact on store image. Companies can enhance their images by actions such as:[24]

Community Relations

❏ Making sure that their stores are barrier-free for disabled shoppers.

❏ Showing a concern for ecology, such as clean streets.

❏ Supporting charities.

❏ Participating in antidrug programs.

❏ Employing area residents.

❏ Running special sales for senior citizens and other groups.

❏ Sponsoring little league and other youth activities.

❏ Cooperating with neighborhood planning groups.

For example, McDonald's sponsors Ronald McDonald Houses, where terminally ill children and their families can live. Hills Department Stores, K mart, and Wal-Mart are among the numerous retailers participating in some type of "Just Say No" antidrug program.

SUMMARY

Customer communications are necessary for a retailer to convey its philosophy of business, objectives, and strategy. Creating and maintaining the proper store image, the way a retailer is perceived by its customers, is an essential aspect of the retail strategy mix. Store image comprises both functional and emotional attributes; and it requires a multistep, ongoing process.

A retailer's image depends heavily on the atmosphere that a store projects. Atmosphere is defined as the physical attributes of the store utilized to develop an image and is composed of the exterior, general interior, store layout, and displays.

The exterior of a store is planned in terms of its storefront, marquee, entrances, display windows, building height and size, visibility, uniqueness, surrounding stores and area, parking, and congestion. The exterior sets a mood or tone before a prospective customer even enters a store.

The general interior of a store incorporates flooring, colors, lighting, scents, sounds, fixtures, wall textures, temperature, width of aisles, dressing facilities, vertical transportation, dead areas, personnel, self-service, merchandise, price displays, cash register placements, technology, modernization, and cleanliness. The interior of an upscale retailer would be far different from that of a discounter, a reflection of the store image desired as well as the costs of doing business.

In laying out a store's interior, six steps are fol- lowed. Floor space is allocated among selling, merchandise, personnel, and customers; and adequate space must be provided for each, based on the firm's overall strategy. Product groupings are determined; they could be based on function, purchase motivation, market segment, and/or storability. Traffic flows are planned, using a straight or a curving pattern. The space per product is calculated through a model stock approach or sales–productivity ratio. Departments are located. Individual products are arranged within departments.

Interior (point-of-purchase) displays provide consumers with information, add to store atmosphere, and have a promotional role. Interior display possibilities include assortment, theme, ensemble, racks and cases, cut cases and dump bins, posters, mobiles, and wall decorations.

The customer services that a retailer offers affect its image. When a firm outlines its customer services strategy, several decisions must be made: What services are primary and ancillary? What level is necessary to complement the store's image? Should a variety be presented? Should fees be charged? How can service effectiveness be measured? How can unprofitable services be terminated? Customer services include credit, delivery, alterations, installations, packaging, returns, gift certificates, trade-ins, and so on.

When determining a credit strategy, a retailer must choose which of these tactics to utilize: re-

481

volving account, option account, open account, monthly payment account, deferred billing, layaway plan, and COD.

Customers are apt to react favorably to retailers that show community interest and involvement in such activities as establishing stores that are barrier-free for disabled persons, supporting charities, and running special sales for senior citizens.

QUESTIONS FOR DISCUSSION

1. Why is it sometimes difficult for a retailer to convey its image to consumers?
2. How could a restaurant project an upscale store image? How could a major appliance retailer project such an image?
3. Define the concept of *atmosphere*. How does this differ from that of *store image?*
4. Which aspects of a store's exterior are controllable? Which are uncontrollable?
5. How would the following be different for a prestige and a discount store?
   a. Flooring
   b. Lighting
   c. Fixtures
   d. Width of aisles
   e. Dressing facilities
   f. Vertical transportation
   g. Personnel
   h. Level of self-service
   i. Placement of cash registers
6. What are the disadvantages of self-service?
7. What are meant by selling, merchandise, personnel, and customer space?
8. Develop a purchase-motivation product grouping for a wine store.
9. What type of traffic-flow pattern should a convenience store use? Why?
10. Which stores should not use a free-flowing layout? Explain your answer.
11. Why would a retailer use a model stock approach rather than a sales–productivity ratio when determining space needs? What are the limitations of the model stock approach?
12. For each of these services, give an example of a retailer that would consider them primary and a retailer that would consider them ancillary.
    a. Delivery
    b. Credit
    c. Alterations
    d. Packaging
    e. Gift certificates
    f. Trade-ins
    g. Mail order
13. Distinguish among revolving, open, and monthly credit accounts. What are the pros and cons of each?
14. What kinds of complaints do you have about the retailers with whom you deal? How do the retailers usually react to them?
15. Why should a retailer contribute to a charity or pay to sponsor a little-league team?

NOTES

1. Joan O'C. Hamilton and Amy Dunkin, "Why Rivals Are Quaking as Nordstrom Heads East," *Business Week* (June 15, 1987), pp. 99, 100.
2. Pierre Martineau, "The Personality of the Retail Store," *Harvard Business Review*, Vol. 36 (January–February 1958), p. 47.
3. Alfred R. Oxenfeldt, "Developing a Favorable Price-Quality Image," *Journal of Retailing*, Vol. 50 (Winter 1974–1975), p. 9.
4. Elizabeth C. Hirschman, "Retail Research and Theory" in Ben N. Enis and Kenneth J. Roering (Editors), *Review of Marketing* (Chicago: American Marketing Association, 1981), p. 119.
5. Don L. James, Richard M. Durand, and Robert A. Dreves, "The Use of a Multi-Attribute Attitude Model in a Store Image Study," *Journal of Retailing*, Vol. 52 (Summer 1976), p. 30.

6. Ronald B. Marks, "Operationalizing the Concept of Store Image," *Journal of Retailing*, Vol. 52 (Fall 1976), p. 44.
7. Edgar A. Pessemier, "Store Image and Positioning," *Journal of Retailing*, Vol. 56 (Spring 1980), pp. 96–97.
8. "Top Honors for Top Designs," *Chain Store Age Executive* (March 1988), p. 65.
9. Ibid., p. 84.
10. "Hot Toddy's Cures the Supermarket Blahs," *Chain Store Age Executive* (August 1987), pp. 68–72.
11. "Spencer Gifts' Plan Yields 'Concept' Selling," *Chain Store Age Executive* (March 1987), pp. 87–88.
12. See Jacob Jacoby and David Mazursky, "Linking Brand and Retailer Images—Do the Potential Risks Outweigh the Potential Benefits?" *Journal of Retailing*, Vol. 60 (Summer 1984), pp. 105–122; David Mazursky and Jacob Jacoby, "Exploring the Development of Store Images,"

Journal of Retailing, Vol. 62 (Summer 1986), pp. 145–165; Linda L. Golden, Gerald Albaum, and Mary Zimmer, "The Numerical Comparative Scale: An Economical Format for Retail Image Measurement," *Journal of Retailing*, Vol. 63 (Winter 1987), pp. 393–410; and Bob T. W. Wu and Susan M. Petroshius, "The Halo Effect in Store Image Measurement," *Journal of the Academy of Marketing Science*, Vol. 15 (Fall 1987), pp. 44–51.

13. Robert J. Donovan and John R. Rossiter, "Store Atmosphere: An Environmental Psychology Approach," *Journal of Retailing*, Vol. 58 (Spring 1982), pp. 34–57.

14. See "Flooring Functions as a Funnel as Well as a Fashion Feature," *Chain Store Age Executive* (February 1985), p. 30; and "Shiny Floors Can Reflect Badly on Retailers' Safety Record," *Chain Store Age Executive* (February 1985), pp. 35, 38.

15. See Joseph A. Bellizzi, Ayn E. Crowley, and Ronald W. Hasty, "The Effects of Color in Store Design," *Journal of Retailing*, Vol. 59 (Spring 1983), pp. 21–45; and "Resourceful Lighting Can Transform a Store into Theater," *Chain Store Age Executive* (February 1985), p. 32.

16. Stephen Bennett, "The Right Combination for Price Chopper," *Progressive Grocer* (October 1987), pp. 45–50.

17. Ronald E. Milliman, "Using Background Music to Affect the Behavior of Supermarket Shoppers," *Journal of Marketing*, Vol. 46 (Summer 1982), pp. 86–91.

18. Jules Abend, "Neat and Clean," *Stores* (November 1983), p. 15.

19. See John A. Quelch and Kristina Cannon-Bonventre, "Better Marketing at the Point of Purchase," *Harvard Business Review*, Vol. 61 (November–December 1983), pp. 162–169; and Joe Agnew, "P-O-P Displays Are Becoming a Matter of Consumer Convenience," *Marketing News* (October 9, 1987), pp. 14, 16.

20. See, for example, Bernie Whalen, "Retail Customer Service: Marketing's Last Frontier," *Marketing News* (March 15, 1985), pp. 10, 18; Albert D. Bates and Jamie G. Didion, "Special Services Can Personalize Retail Environment," *Marketing News* (April 12, 1985), p. 13; Sandra L. Schmidt and Jerome B. Kernan, "The Many Meanings (and Implications) of 'Satisfaction Guaranteed,'" *Journal of Retailing*, Vol. 61 (Winter 1985), pp. 89–108; Chip R. Bell and Ron E. Zemke, "Service Breakdown: The Road to Recovery," *Management Review* (October 1987), pp. 32–35; and Laura A. Liswood, "Once You've Got 'Em, Never Let 'Em Go," *Sales & Marketing Management* (November 1987), pp. 73–77.

21. See Laurie Freeman and Kate Fitzgerald, "Sears May Hold Winning Card," *Advertising Age* (January 18, 1988), p. 12; Jeff Bailey, "Sears Is Discovering Discover Credit Card Isn't Hitting Pay Dirt," *Wall Street Journal* (February 20, 1988), pp. 1, 12; Jules Abend, "Marketing Speeds Up!" *Stores* (February 1987), pp. 25–33; Payment Systems Education Association, "Purchase Plans," *Wall Street Journal* (November 23, 1987), p. 29; and David Schulz, "Counting the Cards," *Stores* (October 1987), pp. 42–47.

22. Steve Weiner, "Find It Yourself," *Wall Street Journal* (March 16, 1981), p. 1.

23. "Staying Ahead of the Chimes," *Chain Store Age Executive* (February 1988), pp. 31–32.

24. See Yvonne Duffy, "Remove the Barriers for Disabled Shoppers," *Progressive Grocer* (May 1987), p. 205; "Discounters Participate in 'Just Say No' to Drugs Campaign," *Discount Store News* (October 12, 1987), p. 30; and Joe Agnew, "Local Involvement Helps Franchisees 'Dechain the Chain,'" *Marketing News* (November 21, 1986), pp. 1, 30.

Units: Using an Unusual Form of Merchandise Presentation*

Case 1

Units is a chain with over twenty women's specialty clothing stores that sells about forty different items, all made of a jersey material. Unlike traditional clothing, merchandise sold by Units is generally one-size-fits-all (with the exception of petite sizes). Units' clothing can be worn in a variety of different ways and with different outfits. For example, the same jersey fabric can be worn either as a sash around the waist or as a turban. Most items are priced in the $20 to $30 range. The chain's clothing is available in six basic colors year-round, in addition to seasonal colors.

Units has been a very successful chain. While it does not disclose financial data, its estimated annual sales are about $17 million. Since the size of a typical Units outlet is between 750 and 800 square feet, the firm has average sales per square foot of more than $950. This makes Units one of the top performing retailers (on the basis of sales per square foot) in each shopping center where it is located.

The long-run potential for Units has been seen by J.C. Penney, which recently acquired

*The material in this case is drawn from "Units Retail Concept Hits Target Squarely," *Chain Store Age Executive* (November 1987), p. 226.

40 per cent of its common stock. Two Penney executives currently sit on Units' board of directors. However, according to Penney's director of specialty retailing:

> We have no goal to put Units in our stores. Instead, I believe that the concept works in a specialty store environment because of the degree of service required. I don't think it would work in a department store environment.

Units has developed a clear store image as a result of its unusual method of merchandise presentation. It uses distinctive packaging, a unique storefront, and high levels of sales support.

Each item of clothing at Units is packaged in a self-sealing plastic bag. Every bag includes complete instructions on how individual items can be worn with different outfits. When customers try on but do not purchase merchandise, they place that item in a store hamper. Then, Units' employees fold and put the merchandise back into the proper plastic bag before returning it to the selling floor, where it is displayed in the appropriate white cube. The see-through bag allows goods to be arranged in a color-coordinated manner. This is visually striking when seen by customers either from within the store or from a shopping-center mall entrance.

The storefront has a mirrored look. Prospective customers can look into the store and see white cubes with coordinated colors in sealed bags. These cubes are stacked from floor to ceiling. However, potential customers often cannot tell what merchandise is featured inside. In some cases, customers' curiosity causes them to walk into a store to determine what is actually being sold. Thus, the front-area arrangement of clothing generates excitement for customers both in the store and in the mall. The high interior visibility is also important, because Units' salespeople (who are called stylists) are situated at the front of each store.

Units relies upon a high degree of sales support. Stylists help patrons choose the desired "look" and aid in assembling an outfit. An important job of the stylists is to reassure customers that they will be able to reproduce the same look with Units' clothing when they return to their homes.

Despite the store image and the sales generated by its unique approach, Units' management has had some difficulties with its overall concept:

❑ The packaging is so neat that many consumers resist opening it.

❑ Since the firm has no descriptive information on the storefront and the white cubes with color-coordinated merchandise contain many different goods, a relatively low degree of consumer recognition exists for the chain. Some consumers think the chain sells wallpaper; other guess it is a linen/sheet store.

❑ A high degree of sales support is required to get many customers to walk into the store, to try on outfits, and to reinforce the fashion lessons learned in the store in an at-home environment. Obtaining, training, and keeping stylists is an ongoing and difficult process.

QUESTIONS

1. Evaluate Units' method of merchandise presentation.
2. Could Units operate successfully as leased departments in J.C. Penney stores? Explain your answer.
3. Develop a total store atmosphere plan for Units based on the elements shown in Figure 14-2.
4. What customer services are primary for Units? Which ancillary customer services should it offer? Explain your answer.

Case 2

The Furniture Center: Evaluating Store Services

Nancy Sands has owned and operated the Furniture Center for four years. The store itself has been open since 1963. Nancy bought the store in 1985 from Arnold Dirk, when Dirk decided to retire.

Except for renovating the exterior and the interior of the store, Sands has operated the Furniture Center in the same manner as Arnold Dirk did. High-quality living-room, dining-room, and bedroom furniture is sold. The furniture is well constructed but is not made to order. Prices are high, consistent with the store's image and the quality of the furniture. The Center advertises every Sunday in the local newspaper. A number of free services are provided: delivery, assembly, credit, trade-ins, and trial purchases. Extended store hours are maintained.

The Furniture Center is located in a strip that is off a main highway in suburban Kansas City. Other stores in the strip are a men's clothing store, a women's clothing store, a stereo store, and a gift shop. Each of these stores caters to the same type of upper-middle-class market as the Furniture Center, and they all utilize similar retail strategies. The Furniture Center is the middle store in the strip, between the women's clothing store and the gift shop.

The Furniture Center is in a two-story building; on the first floor are the dining-room displays and individual living-room pieces, such as sofas and armchairs. On the second floor are coordinated living-room and bedroom sets. A wide variety of styles is available.

Nancy Sands employs a number of salespeople, who are very knowledgeable, courteous, and patient. The salespeople are also trained not to be pushy but to be helpful assistants. No part-time workers are employed.

The atmosphere of the store is one of quiet dignity. The exterior is simple and contains no window displays. Inside, soft music is played and sections of the store are decorated to match the types and styles of the furniture. Cash registers are hidden, and an operator-controlled elevator transports customers between floors.

Business at the Furniture Center has never been better, and future prospects appear bright. The only area Nancy Sands feels that she must evaluate is customer services. The costs of administering these services have increased steadily, and Sands has decided to review them on an individual basis:

Delivery. The delivery of furniture is essential. Furniture is heavy and bulky, and customers cannot be expected to take it home with them. The problem is that many customers are not at home when the deliveries are made, and the furniture must be redelivered. Charging for delivery might overcome this problem.

Assembly. All tables, chairs, and so on are assembled after they are delivered. Customers dislike assembling furniture themselves. The average assembly takes one hour and costs the Furniture Center $30.

Credit. Furniture is expensive. Few customers are prepared to pay in cash or by check. Therefore credit (like delivery) is essential. The Furniture Center accepts MasterCard and Visa, as well as its own FC card. The costs of MasterCard and Visa are much greater than the costs of the FC card, and only the latter promotes store loyalty.

Trade-ins. The Furniture Center encourages trade-ins as long as the furniture is well constructed and in good condition. This merchandise is displayed in the basement (after refurbishing) and sells for 50 per cent less than the store's regular prices. Basement sales show a very small profit.

Trial purchases. A unique service of the Furniture Center is the trial purchase. A customer is allowed to purchase furniture, keep it for one week, and if dissatisfied, exchange it for other merchandise. The returned merchandise is displayed in the basement and sells for 10 per cent less than the store's regular prices.

Extended store hours. The Furniture Center is open from noon to 10 P.M., Monday through Friday, and Saturday from 10 A.M. to 7 P.M. These long hours require extra full-time personnel because salespeople work forty hours per week.

Other services. Special sales are held for regular customers, mail and telephone orders are accepted, and free parking is available.

QUESTIONS

1a. Which of the services offered by the Furniture Center are primary and which are ancillary? Explain your answer.

b. Would your answers to (a) be the same for all kinds of furniture stores? Why or why not?

2a. Should the Furniture Center charge customers separately for its services, pass the costs along in the form of higher prices, or absorb the costs of the services? Explain your answer.

b. Would your answer to (a) be the same for all kinds of furniture stores? Why or why not?

3. Determine if any services should be deleted.

4. Is the firm's image a consistent one? Why? How can it be made more consistent?

Chapter 15

Promotional Strategy

□ **Chapter**
Objectives □

1 To examine retail promotion, specifically how a retailer can inform, persuade, and remind its target market

2 To study the elements of retail promotion: advertising, publicity, personal selling, and sales promotion

3 To explain the strategic aspects of retail promotion: objectives, budget, mix of forms, implementation of mix, and review and revision of the plan

In late 1987, Zayre, a 375-store discount chain, began testing a "frequent-buyer" sales-promotion program (known as Frequent Z) in 51 outlets in four markets: Cleveland, Memphis, Greensboro/Winston-Salem (North Carolina), and Tampa/St. Petersburg. The Frequent Z program was extended nationally in mid-1988. The goal of this sales promotion is to attract non-Zayre shoppers and to increase patronage by current Zayre shoppers.

With the Frequent Z program, buyers are given points for all purchases at Zayre; each dollar purchase rewards customers with 100 points, which are redeemable by mail for gifts from a thirty-page Frequent Z catalog. The catalog contains over one-hundred gifts, including sailboats, grandfather clocks, and vacations to Disney World and Hawaii.

The Frequent Z program is a combination of an airline frequent-flyer program, meant to increase loyalty and patronage among consumers, and a trading-stamp promotion, in which purchases are rewarded by gifts from a catalog. Zayre's program is patterned after the one developed by Zellers, a 210-store Canadian discount chain. Unlike Zellers, which offers frequent customers gift merchandise that it has purchased itself, Zayre uses an outside firm to supply and ship gifts.

Zayre is using a "There's Just No Point Shopping Anywhere Else!" theme in ads as well as in-store promotions to communicate its Frequent Z plan. Membership cards, information brochures, and catalogs are available at Zayre's customer-service departments. All new participants are given 3,000 free bonus points (equivalent to a $30 purchase). Once a customer becomes a member, each subsequent purchase is noted in his or her account. Computer software designed by Zayre automatically accumulates all of a member's points and displays them on his or her latest sales receipt. Group membership for schools, families, and clubs is allowable.[1]

The long-run success of the Frequent Z program will depend on how well it is administered and marketed. Also, like all forms of promotion, the Frequent Z program will need to be monitored and fine-tuned, as necessary.

Overview

Retail promotion is broadly defined as any communication by a retailer that informs, persuades, and/or reminds the target market about any aspect of that retailer. This chapter deals with the development of a retail promotional strategy. In the first part of the chapter, the elements of promotion (advertising, publicity, personal selling, and sales promotion) are detailed. The second part centers on the strategic aspects of promotion: objectives, budget, mix of forms, implementation of mix, and review and revision of the plan.

Elements of the Retail Promotional Mix

Advertising, publicity, personal selling, and sales promotion are the four elements of promotion. Each is discussed here in terms of objectives, advantages and disadvantages, and basic forms. Although these elements are described individually, a good promotional plan normally integrates them—based on the overall strategy of the retailer. A movie theater would concentrate more on advertising and sales promotion (point-of-purchase displays to prompt food and beverage sales) and would have less emphasis on personal selling and publicity. An upscale independent specialty store would stress personal selling, with less emphasis on advertising, publicity, and personal selling.

Retailers spend significant sums on their promotion efforts. For example, in a typical department store, about 3.1 per cent of sales is spent on advertising, 7.0 per cent on personal selling, and 4.1 per cent on sales promotion.[2] In addition, most department-store chains employ internal or external public relations offices to generate favorable publicity and respond to media requests for information.

Advertising

Advertising is "any paid form of nonpersonal presentation and promotion of ideas, goods, and services by an identified sponsor."[3] Three aspects of this definition merit further clarification:

1. Paid form—This distinguishes advertising from publicity, for which no payment is made by the retailer for the time or space used to convey a message.
2. Nonpersonal presentation—In advertising, a standard message is delivered to the entire audience, and it cannot be adapted to individual customers. Mass media rather than personal contacts are used.
3. Identified sponsor—Advertising clearly divulges the name of the sponsor, unlike publicity.

In 1986, Sears, the largest U.S. retailer, also had the highest dollar expenditures for advertising: $1.005 billion, 2.3 per cent of overall company sales. By comparison, many other retailers had much higher advertising-as-a-percentage-of-sales ratios, despite lower dollar expenditures; these included McDonald's (4.8 per cent of systemwide sales) and Zale, a large jewelry store chain (9.8 per cent).[4] Table 15-1 shows 1986 advertising-to-sales ratios for a number of retailing categories.

Differences Between Retailer and Manufacturer Advertising Strategies

Although the definition given applies to all advertising, it is important to examine some of the key differences between retailer and manufacturer advertising

TABLE 15-1
Selected Advertising-to-Sales Ratios, 1986, by Type of Retailer

Type of Retailer	Advertising Dollars as Percentage of Sales*	Advertising Dollars as Percentage of Margin†
Apparel and accessories stores	2.4	6.1
Auto dealers and gas stations	3.2	11.7
Auto repair and service stations	2.7	4.1
Computer stores	2.9	12.0
Convenience stores	0.4	1.7
Department stores	3.1	13.5
Drug and proprietary stores	1.5	5.4
Eating places	3.8	17.6
Fuel and ice dealers	0.6	3.6
Furniture stores	5.8	12.9
Grocery stores	1.5	6.2
Hotels/motels	3.5	12.9
Household appliance stores	3.8	12.6
Insurance firms	0.5	1.9
Jewelry stores	5.1	10.1
Mail-order firms	14.5	38.5
Photofinishing labs	1.9	4.6
Radio, television, and music stores	4.9	15.1
Retail catalog showrooms	3.5	16.6
Shoe stores	1.8	4.6
Toy, amusement, and sporting-goods stores	12.5	27.2
Variety stores	2.3	8.6

* Advertising dollars as a percentage of sales = Advertising expenditures/Net company sales

† Advertising dollars as a percentage of margin = Advertising expenditures/(Net company sales − Cost of goods sold)

Source: Pansophic Systems, "Advertising-to-Sales Ratios, 1986," *Advertising Age* (October 12, 1987), p. 50. Reprinted by permission. Copyright Crain Communications Inc.

strategies. First, retailers usually have more geographically concentrated target markets than manufacturers. This means that a retailer can better adapt to local needs, habits, and preferences than can a manufacturer. However, a retailer typically is not able to utilize national media as readily as a manufacturer. For example, only large retail chains and franchises can advertise on national television programs. An exception is direct marketing, because trading areas for these firms are geographically dispersed.

Second, retail advertising emphasizes immediacy. Individual items are placed for sale and advertised during specific, short time periods. Immediate purchases are sought. On the other hand, a manufacturer is often concerned with developing a favorable attitude toward a product or the company and not with short-run sales increases.

Third, retailers generally stress price in advertisements, whereas manufacturers usually emphasize several attributes of a product. In addition, many retailers display a number of different products in one advertisement, whereas manufacturers tend to minimize the number of products mentioned in one advertisement.

Fourth, media charges are often lower for retailers than for manufacturers. Because of this factor and the desire of many manufacturers and wholesalers for wide distribution, the costs of retail advertising are sometimes shared by a manufacturer or wholesaler and a retailer. Two or more retailers may also share costs. This is known as **cooperative advertising**.

Objectives

Retail advertising is based on a wide number of specific objectives, including

❑ Short-term sales increases.

❑ Increases in store traffic.

❑ Developing and/or reinforcing a store image. See Figure 15-1.

❑ Informing customers about goods and services and/or store attributes.

❑ Easing the job for sales personnel.

❑ Developing demand for private brands.

A retailer selects one or more of these objectives and bases advertising efforts on it (them).

FIGURE 15-1
Using Advertising to Project an Upscale Image
D&L is a Connecticut-based department store chain that communicates an upscale image in its ads.
Reprinted by permission of Selame Design.

Advantages and Disadvantages

The major advantages of advertising are that

1. A large audience is attracted. Also, for print media, circulation is supplemented by the passing of a copy from one reader to another.
2. The costs per viewer or reader or listener are low.
3. A large number of alternative media are available. Therefore, a retailer can match a medium to the target market.
4. The retailer has control over message content, graphics, times, and size (or length), so that a standardized message in a chosen format can be delivered to the entire audience.
5. In print media, a message can be studied and restudied by the target market.
6. Editorial content (a television show, a news story, and so on) often surrounds an advertisement. This may increase its credibility or the probability that it will be read.
7. Because a customer can become aware of a retailer and its goods and services before shopping, self-service or reduced-service operations are possible.

The major disadvantages of advertising are that

1. Because a message is standardized, it is inflexible. The retailer is unable to focus on the needs of individual customers.

Why Feature a "Spokespig" in Supermarket Advertisements?

Piggly Wiggly is a forty-year-old supermarket chain with about one hundred franchised outlets in South Carolina and Georgia. It has been quite successful in its market areas, despite intense competition and an annual advertising budget of only $75,000. Over the years, Piggly Wiggly has become known for its "warm and humorous approach to commercials," many featuring some form of pig image:

> When consumers who live in any of Piggly Wiggly's prime market areas are driving down the road and see a billboard featuring a pig, chances are very good that they recognize it immediately as an advertisement for that regional supermarket. The pig image is so well established that nothing more is needed for identification.

The firm's most offbeat campaign is the current one using a company "spokespig" in television commercials. The spokespig is a human wearing a $1,000 pig mask and dressed in a business suit who extolls the virtues of Piggly Wiggly and its everyday low prices, freshness, and so on, in a humorous manner via a series of ads: "Our executive is a spokesperson for Piggly Wiggly and the only difference between him and Lee Iacocca is that our actor looks like a pig. In addition, he says funny things about the supermarket chain."

Why does Piggly Wiggly use a "spokespig," rather than a traditional corporate spokesperson such as Lee Iacocca? First, many competitors use their executives in ads; therefore, a traditional approach would not get much consumer attention. Second, Piggly Wiggly is capitalizing on its well-known company image. Third, this type of campaign helps a limited budget maximize its impact. Fourth, Piggly Wiggly can combine humor and information in its messages.

Source: Based on material in "Piggly Wiggly Spots Bring Home the Bacon," *Chain Store Age Executive* (December 1987), pp. 40, 42.

2. Some types of advertising require high levels of investment. This may eliminate the access of small retailers to certain media (e.g., television).

3. Many media appeal to large geographic areas, and for retailers, waste occurs. For instance, a small supermarket chain may find that only 40 per cent of a newspaper's readers reside within its trading area.

4. Some media require an extremely long lead time for the placing of advertisements. This reduces a retailer's ability to advertise fad items or to react to some current-events themes.

5. Some media have a high throwaway rate. For instance, circulars and mail advertisements are often thrown away without being read.

6. Advertisements must be brief. For example, a thirty-second television commercial or a one-eighth-of-a-page newspaper advertisement cannot contain much information.

These are broad conclusions about the entire field of advertising. Generalities have been made. The pros and cons for specific media are described in the following section.

Media

A retailer can choose from among newspapers, telephone directories, direct mail, radio, television, transit, outdoor, magazines, and flyers/circulars. A summary of the attributes of these media appears in Table 15-2.

According to a recent survey of major department store, supermarket, home center, drugstore, discount store, and apparel-specialty chain retailers, these chains were expected to spend a companywide average of $7.2 million on advertising media in 1988. Print media (such as newspapers, magazines, and telephone directories) accounted for 61.9 per cent of expenditures, followed by direct mail (15.4 per cent), television (12.9 per cent), radio (8.8 per cent), and outdoor (1.0 per cent).[5]

Newspapers can be classified as dailies, weeklies, and shoppers. Among retailers, the newspaper is the most preferred medium, having the advantages of market coverage, reasonable costs, flexibility, longevity, graphics, and editorial association (ads next to columns or articles). Disadvantages are waste (circulation to a wider geographic area than that containing the target market), the black-and-white format, and an appeal to fewer senses than television. To maintain their dominant position with retailers, many newspapers have redesigned their graphics, and some have begun running a limited number of color ads. Free-distribution shopper newspapers (also known as "penny savers") that are delivered to all consumer households in a geographic area are growing strongly, sometimes at the expense of other types of newspapers.

Telephone directories (the White and Yellow Pages) are important advertising media. In the White Pages, the retailer receives a free alphabetical listing along with all other telephone subscribers, commercial and noncommercial. The major advantage of the White over the Yellow Pages is that a customer who is familiar with the retailer's name is not distracted by seeing competitors' names. The major disadvantage, as contrasted with the Yellow Pages, is the alphabetical rather than type-of-business listing. For example, a customer unfamiliar with repair services in his or her area will usually look in the Yellow Pages under "Repair" and choose a firm that is listed.

In the Yellow Pages, a retailer pays for an alphabetical listing (and a larger display ad, if desired) within its business category. The overwhelming majority of retailers advertise in the Yellow Pages. The advantages are widespread customer usage and long life (one year or more). The disadvantages are limited flexibility and long lead time for new ads. As a result of the breakup of AT&T,

TABLE 15-2
Advertising Media Comparison Chart

Medium	Market Coverage	Sample Time/ Space Costs*	Particular Suitability	Major Advantage	Major Disadvantage
Daily newspaper	Single community or entire metro area; zoned editions sometimes available.	$0.25–$2.50+ per agate line, depending on audience size.	All general retailers.	Wide circulation.	Nonselective audience.
Weekly newspaper	Single community usually; sometimes a metro area.	$0.35–$1.25+ per agate line, depending on audience size.	Retailers that service a strictly local market.	Local identification.	Limited readership.
Shopper	Most households in a single community; chain shoppers can cover a metro area.	$25–$750+ per one-quarter-page black-and-white ad.	Neighborhood retailers and service businesses.	Consumer orientation.	A giveaway and not always read.
Telephone directories	Geographic area or occupational field served by the directory.	$35–$150+ per half column per month, depending on audience size.	Services, retailers of brand-name items, highly specialized retailers.	Users are in the market for goods or services.	Limited to active shoppers.
Direct mail	Controlled by the advertiser.	$0.35 and up per person, depending on audience size and message characteristics.	New and expanding businesses; those using coupon returns or catalogs.	Personalized approach to an audience of good prospects.	High CPM (cost per thousand).
Radio	Definable market area surrounding the station's location.	$50–$500+ for a 60-second commercial.	Businesses catering to identifiable groups: teens, commuters, housewives.	Market selectivity, wide market coverage.	Must be bought consistently to be of value.

retailers now have many Yellow Pages companies vying for their business—at lower rates.

Direct mail is the medium whereby a retailer sends customers catalogs or advertisements via the U.S. mail. Some of its advantages are controlled costs, a targeted audience, a tailor-made format, quick feedback, and potential tie-ins (for example, a retailer with its own credit card can send advertisements with the monthly billing statements). Computer advances have greatly improved the efficiency of direct-mail advertising. Some disadvantages of direct mail are a low response rate, a high throwaway rate ("junk mail"), and obsolete mailing lists (addressees may have moved).

Radio is utilized by a variety of retailers. Its major advantages are short lead time, importance as a medium for car drivers and riders, market segmentation, and wide reach. Major disadvantages are no visual impact, a need for brevity, a need for repetition, and waste. The use of radio by retailers has gone up in recent years.

Television, although increasing in importance because of the rise of national and regional retailers, is far behind newspapers in retail advertising expenditures.[6] Advantages of television are video messages (impact), a large market,

TABLE 15-2
(Continued)

Medium	Market Coverage	Sample Time/ Space Costs*	Particular Suitability	Major Advantage	Major Disadvantage
Television	Definable market area surrounding the station's location.	$100–$350,000+ for a 30-second commercial, depending on audience size.	Sellers of goods or services with wide appeal.	Dramatic impact, wide market coverage.	High cost of time and production.
Transit	Urban or metro community served by transit system; may be limited to a few transit routes.	$50–$15,000 per month, depending on number of placements and audience size.	Businesses along transit routes, especially those appealing to wage earners.	Repetition and length of exposure.	Limited audience.
Outdoor	Entire metro area or single neighborhood.	$200–$10,000 per month, depending on audience and sign size.	Amusement, tourist businesses, brand-name retailers.	Dominant size, frequency of exposure.	Clutter of many signs reduces effectiveness of each one.
Local magazine	Entire metro area or region; zoned editions sometimes available.	$275–$750+ per one-sixth-page black-and-white ad.	Restaurants, entertainment, specialty shops, mail-order businesses.	Delivery of a loyal, special-interest audience.	Limited audience.
Flyers/Circulars	Single neighborhood.	$0.10+ per flyer plus distribution costs.	Restaurants, dry cleaners, service stations, and other neighborhood retailers.	Caters to specific audience.	Not always read.

*Agate line—the column inch of a newspaper (1 inch deep by 2 inches wide) contains fourteen agate lines.

Source: Adapted by the authors from "Advertising Small Business" (Bank of America NT & SA, 1982). Reprinted by permission. © *Small Business Reporter* 1982.

creativity, and program affiliation (for regular sponsors). Disadvantages of television are high minimum costs, waste, need for brevity, a need for repetition, and limited availability of time slots for nonregular sponsors.

Transit advertising is utilized by retailers in urban areas that have mass-transit systems. Advertisements are displayed on buses and in subway cars and taxis. Transit ads have the advantages of a captive audience, a mass market, a high level of repetitiveness, and a geographically defined market. Disadvantages include a lack of availability in smaller cities, restricted travel paths, and graffiti. In addition to the transit advertising already mentioned, retailers often advertise on their delivery trucks.

Outdoor or billboard advertising is sometimes used by retailers. Posters and signs may be displayed in public places, on buildings, and alongside highways. Advantages are high exposure, economy, and informativeness. Disadvantages are limited information, clutter, high-speed travel (missing the message), and some legislation banning outdoor ads.

Magazines are growing in importance because of three factors: the increase in national and regional retailers, the creation of regional and local editions, and use by mail-order retailers. Advantages of magazines are tailoring to a specific market, editorial association, longevity of a single message, and color. Among the disadvantages are long lead time, costs, and waste.

Flyers/circulars are an important advertising medium. Single-page (flyers) or multiple-page (circulars) ads are distributed in parking lots or door to door. Advantages include low costs, flexibility, speed, and a targeted audience. Disadvantages are the high level of throwaways, poor quality of paper, and clutter. Flyers are good for smaller retailers, while circulars are used by larger ones.

Types

Advertisements can be classified by content and by manner of payment. See Figure 15-2. An ad may be pioneering, competitive, reminder, or institutional in nature. A **pioneer advertisement** has awareness as its objective and provides information (usually about a new retailer or location). A **competitive advertisement** has persuasion as its objective. A **reminder advertisement** is geared to the loyal customer and emphasizes the attributes that have made the retailer successful. An **institutional advertisement** strives to keep the retailer's name before the public without emphasizing merchandise sales.[7] Public service messages (such as sponsorship of a telethon or a little-league team) are institutional in nature.

When using advertisements, a retailer may pay its own way and/or seek cooperative ventures. For the retailer that pays its own way, the major advantages are control and flexibility. The major disadvantages are the costs and efforts required. A cooperative venture is one where two or more parties share the costs and the decision making. It is estimated that about $10 billion is spent annually on cooperative advertising, most through vertical agreements. Newspapers are much preferred over any other medium for cooperative ads.

In a **vertical cooperative-advertising agreement,** a manufacturer and a retailer

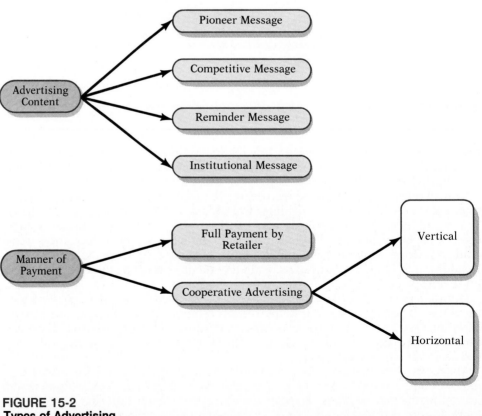

FIGURE 15-2
Types of Advertising

or a wholesaler and a retailer share an advertisement. The duties and responsibilities of each party are usually specified contractually. Retailers are not reimbursed until after advertisements are run and invoices are provided to the manufacturer or the wholesaler.* The advantages of a vertical agreement are reduced costs, assistance in the preparation of advertisements, greater coverage of the market, and less expenditure of the retailer's time. Disadvantages include less control, flexibility, and distinctiveness. Some retailers have been concerned about the requirements they must satisfy to be eligible for supplier support and the emphasis on the supplier's name in ads. Manufacturers and other suppliers are responding to this by being more flexible and understanding of retailers' concerns. For example, in the American Express cooperative program, restaurants can choose from among twenty-nine border designs and forty copy blocks (which feature fourteen styles of cuisine). Restaurants can also insert their own logos and additional copy.[8]

Under a **horizontal cooperative-advertising agreement,** two or more retailers (usually small) share an advertisement. The advantages and disadvantages are similar to those in a vertical agreement. A further benefit is the increased bargaining power of retailers in dealing with the media.

When planning a cooperative advertising strategy, a retailer should consider these questions:

❏ What advertising qualifies, in terms of merchandise and special requirements?
❏ What percentage is paid by each party?
❏ When can advertisements be run?
❏ What media can be used?
❏ Are there special provisions regarding message content?
❏ What documentation is required for reimbursement?
❏ How does each party benefit?
❏ Do cooperative advertisements obscure the image of the individual retailer?[9]

Publicity

Publicity is the

nonpersonal stimulation of demand for a good, service, or business unit by planting commercially significant news about it in a published medium or obtaining favorable presentation of it upon radio, television, or stage that is not paid for by the sponsor.[10]

The basic distinction between advertising and publicity is the nonpaid nature of the latter. Because of this difference, publicity messages are not controllable. For example, a story about a new store opening may not appear at all, may appear after the fact, or may not appear in the form that is desired.[11] On the other hand, publicity is usually considered more credible and important than an advertisement. Accordingly, advertising and publicity should be viewed as complements and not as substitutes for each other. In many cases, publicity may precede advertising.

Objectives
Retail publicity seeks to accomplish one or more of these objectives:

❏ To increase awareness of the retailer and its goods and services.

---

*Vertical cooperative advertising is regulated by the Robinson-Patman Act. Manufacturers and other suppliers must offer similar arrangements to all retailers on a proportional basis.

❑ To maintain or improve a company's image.

❑ To show the retailer as a contributor to the quality of life.

❑ To demonstrate innovativeness.

❑ To present a favorable message in a highly believable manner.

❑ To minimize total promotion costs.

Advantages and Disadvantages

The major advantages of publicity are that

1. An image can be presented or enhanced.
2. An objective source presents the message for the retailer, providing credibility (e.g., a good review of a restaurant).
3. There are no costs for the message time or space.
4. A mass audience is addressed.
5. Carryover effects are possible (e.g., if a store is perceived as community-oriented, the merchandise it carries would be viewed as good).
6. People pay more attention to news stories than to clearly identified advertisements.

The major disadvantages of publicity are that

1. There is no control over the message, its timing, its placement, and its coverage by a given medium.
2. It is difficult to plan in advance and is more suitable in short-run rather than long-run planning.
3. Although there are no media costs, there are often costs for a public relations staff, planning activities, and the activities themselves (e.g., parades and store openings).

Types

Community services, such as donations and special sales, are sometimes reported in the media. Parades are sponsored on holidays; Macy's Thanksgiving Day Parade receives tremendous media coverage. The sales of new goods and services may be featured in the media, as local news programs and others show new items and mention where they are sold. The opening of a new store may receive media coverage if the store location or design is particularly newsworthy. Television and newspaper reporters visit restaurants and other retailers and rate their performance and quality.

Each of these forms of publicity enhances a retailer's image and provides the other advantages already mentioned. However, there may be difficulties. For example, Macy's parade, although it receives free television time, is not inexpensive. The publicity for McDonald's muscular dystrophy contributions is free, but the costs of the donation run into seven figures. In addition, how long do people remember the contribution, which is a once-a-year occurrence?

In the case of a store opening, the media may describe the location in less than glowing terms, may criticize the store's effects on the environment, and so on. The retailer has no control over the message. Also, the media may not cover this or any other publicity event.

Finally, some publicity events can be planned in advance (parades, donations), but others cannot (the appearance of a newspaper reporter, interest by a local television station, and so on). Publicity must be viewed as a component of the promotion mix, not as the whole mix.

Personal selling involves an "oral presentation in a conversation with one or more prospective purchasers for the purpose of making sales."[12]

Objectives

Among the objectives of personal selling are to

❑ Persuade the customer to consummate a purchase, because he or she often enters a store after acquiring some information through advertising.

❑ Create awareness of direct-to-home sales products.

❑ Feed back information to the retailer.

❑ Provide adequate levels of service.

❑ Improve and maintain customer satisfaction.

Advantages and Disadvantages

The major advantages of personal selling are related to the nature of personal contact:

1. Immediate feedback is provided.
2. A salesperson is able to adapt his or her message to the needs of the individual customer.
3. A salesperson can be flexible in analyzing alternative solutions to a customer's needs.
4. The attention span of the customer is high.
5. In many cases, there is little or no waste; most people who walk into a store are potential customers.
6. Customers respond more often to personal selling than to advertisements.

The major disadvantages of personal selling are that

1. Only a small audience is reached at a given time.
2. The costs of interacting with each customer may be high.
3. Customers are not lured into a store through personal selling.
4. Self-service may be discouraged.

Types

Most types of retail selling can be categorized as either order taking or order getting. An **order-taking** position is one in which the salesperson is involved in routine clerical and sales functions, such as setting up displays, placing inventory on the shelves, filling reorders, answering simple questions, and ringing up the sale. This type of selling most often occurs in stores that have a strong mix of self-service with some personnel on the floor.

Order-getting personnel are more involved in informing and persuading customers. These are the true "sales" employees. Order getters usually sell higher-priced or complex items, such as real estate, automobiles, personal computers, and refrigerators. On the average, they are more skilled and better paid than order takers.

In some instances, a manufacturer may help finance the personal selling function by providing **PMs** (defined as promotional money, push money, or prize money) for retail salespeople who sell the manufacturer's brand. PMs are in addition to the compensation received from the retailer. Many retailers are concerned about this practice because it encourages their sales personnel to be loyal to the manufacturer, and salespersons may be less responsive to actual customer desires (if customers desire brands not yielding PMs).

Functions

Sales personnel may be responsible for all or many of these functions: greeting customers, determining customer wants, showing merchandise, giving a sales presentation, demonstrating goods and/or services, answering objections, and closing the sale. See Figure 15-3.

Upon entering a store or a department within the store (or being contacted at home), a customer would be greeted by a salesperson. Typical in-store greetings are

"Hello, may I help you?"

"Good morning [afternoon]. If you need any help please call upon me."

"Hi, is there anything in particular you are looking for?"

With any greeting, the salesperson seeks to put the customer at ease and build a rapport.

Next, the salesperson would determine what the customer wants:

❑ Is the customer just looking, or is there a specific good or service in mind?

❑ For what purpose is the item to be used (gift or personal)?

❑ Does the customer have a price range in mind?

❑ What other information can the customer provide that would be helpful to the salesperson?

From the perspective of the retailing concept, a salesperson could not be successful without first ascertaining the consumer's wants.

At this point, the salesperson may show or present merchandise. Based on a determination of customer wants, the salesperson would select the good or service that is most likely to be satisfactory and show it to the customer. The salesperson may decide to trade up (show a more expensive version) or present a substitute (particularly if the retailer does not carry or is out of the requested item).

Now the salesperson would make a sales presentation to influence the customer to buy a good or service. Two kinds of presentations are most common: the **canned sales presentation** and the **need-satisfaction approach**. The canned sales presentation is a memorized, repetitive speech given to all customers in-

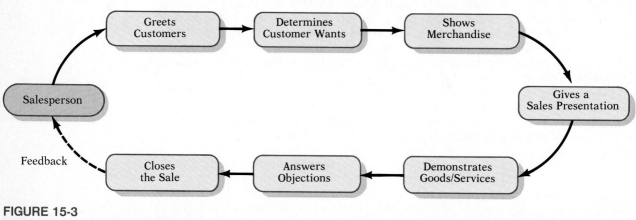

FIGURE 15-3
Typical Personal Selling Functions

terested in a particular item. The need-satisfaction approach is based upon the principle that each customer has a different set of wants and that the sales presentation should be geared to the demands of the individual customer. This approach is being utilized more and more in retailing.

During the sales presentation, a demonstration may be helpful. The demonstration would show the customer the actual utility of an item and allow customer participation. Demonstrations are often used to sell stereos, automobiles, televisions, health club memberships, dishwashers, videogames, and watches.

A customer may raise questions during a sales presentation, and the salesperson must answer these objections. After the questions are answered, the salesperson closes the sale. This involves getting the customer to conclude his or her purchase. Typical closing lines are

"Will you take it with you or have it delivered?"

"Cash or charge?"

"Would you like this gift-wrapped?"

"Have you decided on the color, red or blue?"

In order for the personal selling function to be completed effectively, sales personnel must be enthusiastic, knowledgeable about the retailer and its offerings, interested in their consumers, and able to communicate effectively. For example, a new six-thousand-square-foot Liz Claiborne boutique at Jordan Marsh in Boston has twelve salespeople, double the number typically found in a department that size. These personnel are provided by Claiborne, which also has a staff of consultants who travel throughout the United States training retail salespeople on how to best sell the company's clothing and interact with customers. These efforts are having a dramatic effect on sales. As one observer noted: "If a shopper walks away empty-handed, it's not for lack of service."[13]

Table 15-3 contains a selected list of how retail sales can be lost through poor personal selling, and how to correct these problems.

TABLE 15-3
Selected Reasons That Retail Sales Are Lost

❑ *Poor qualification of the customer:* Information should be obtained from the customer that enables a salesperson to tailor his or her presentation to the prospective buyer.

❑ *Salesperson does not demonstrate the good or service:* A good sales presentation should be built around the item shown in use; then, benefits can be easily visualized.

❑ *Failure to put feeling into presentation:* The salesperson should be sincere and consumer-oriented in his or her presentation.

❑ *Poor knowledge:* The salesperson should know the major advantages and disadvantages of his or her goods and services, as well as those of competitors, and be able to answer questions.

❑ *Arguing with a customer:* A good salesperson should avoid arguments in handling customer objections, even if the customer is completely wrong.

❑ *No suggestion selling:* A salesperson should attempt to sell related items (such as service contracts, product supplies, and installation) along with the basic product.

❑ *Giving up too early:* If an attempt at closing a sale is unsuccessful, it should be tried again.

❑ *Inflexibility:* A salesperson should be flexible in analyzing alternative solutions to a customer's needs, as well as in altering his or her message to the requirements of the individual consumer.

❑ *Poor follow-up:* A salesperson should be sure that the order is correctly written, that merchandise arrives at the agreed-on time, and that the customer is satisfied.

Sales Promotion

Sales promotion consists of

those marketing activities, other than personal selling, advertising, and publicity, that stimulate consumer purchasing and dealer effectiveness, such as displays, shows and exhibitions, demonstrations, and various nonrecurrent selling efforts not in the ordinary routine.[14]

Objectives
Sales promotion objectives include

❑ Increasing short-run sales.

❑ Maintaining customer loyalty.

❑ Emphasizing novelty.

❑ Supplementing other promotion tools.

Advantages and Disadvantages
The major advantages of sales promotion are that

1. It has eye-catching appeal.
2. The themes and tools can be distinctive.
3. The consumer may receive something of value, such as coupons, stamps, or calendars.
4. It helps draw customer traffic and maintain store loyalty.
5. Impulse purchases are increased.
6. Customers can have fun, particularly with contests and demonstrations.

The major disadvantages of sales promotion are that

1. It may be difficult to terminate special promotions without adverse customer reactions.
2. The retailer's image may be hurt if low-status promotions are used.
3. Sometimes frivolous selling points are emphasized, as opposed to goods/service assortment and prices.
4. Many sales promotions are short-run.
5. It should only be used as a supplement to other promotional forms.

Types
Figure 15-4 contains a listing of the major types of sales promotions. Point-of-purchase promotion consists of in-store displays, which are designed to increase sales. The effect of point-of-purchase displays on store image was discussed in Chapter 14. From a promotional perspective, point-of-purchase displays may remind customers, stimulate impulse behavior, allow self-service to be used, and reduce promotion costs because of manufacturers' supplying these displays. See Figure 15-5. The long-run effects of point-of-purchase promotions must be carefully studied. It may be that total sales do not rise; customers may stockpile when displays are used and purchase less when they are not.

Following are several examples of the widespread use and value of point-of-purchase displays:

❑ Actmedia, a promotional firm, provides ads that appear on shopping carts in half of all U.S. supermarkets.[15]

❑ The Point-of-Purchase Advertising Institute (POPAI) estimated that manufacturers and retailers spent almost $11 billion on in-store displays in 1986.

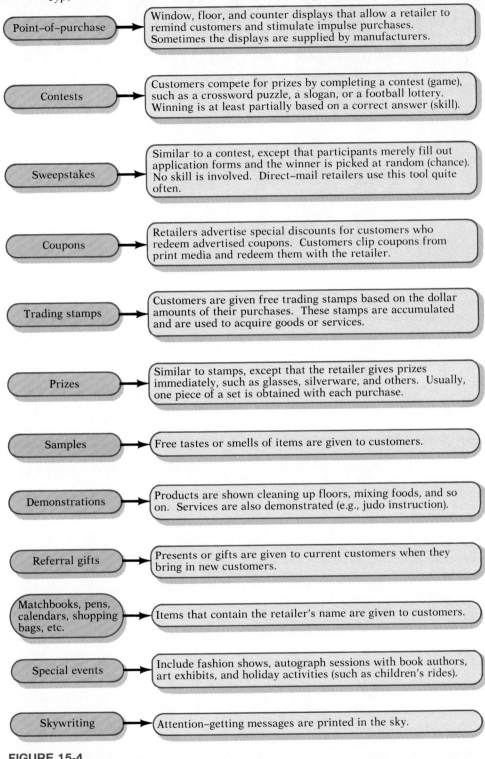

Type	Description
Point-of-purchase	Window, floor, and counter displays that allow a retailer to remind customers and stimulate impulse purchases. Sometimes the displays are supplied by manufacturers.
Contests	Customers compete for prizes by completing a contest (game), such as a crossword puzzle, a slogan, or a football lottery. Winning is at least partially based on a correct answer (skill).
Sweepstakes	Similar to a contest, except that participants merely fill out application forms and the winner is picked at random (chance). No skill is involved. Direct-mail retailers use this tool quite often.
Coupons	Retailers advertise special discounts for customers who redeem advertised coupons. Customers clip coupons from print media and redeem them with the retailer.
Trading stamps	Customers are given free trading stamps based on the dollar amounts of their purchases. These stamps are accumulated and are used to acquire goods or services.
Prizes	Similar to stamps, except that the retailer gives prizes immediately, such as glasses, silverware, and others. Usually, one piece of a set is obtained with each purchase.
Samples	Free tastes or smells of items are given to customers.
Demonstrations	Products are shown cleaning up floors, mixing foods, and so on. Services are also demonstrated (e.g., judo instruction).
Referral gifts	Presents or gifts are given to current customers when they bring in new customers.
Matchbooks, pens, calendars, shopping bags, etc.	Items that contain the retailer's name are given to customers.
Special events	Include fashion shows, autograph sessions with book authors, art exhibits, and holiday activities (such as children's rides).
Skywriting	Attention-getting messages are printed in the sky.

FIGURE 15-4
Types of Sales Promotion

FIGURE 15-5
Child World's Point-of-Purchase Displays
Reprinted by permission.

RETAILING IN ACTION

At K Mart, What Happens When the Blue Light Flashes?

The hoopla began in 1965, when Earle Bartell, a young assistant manager at a K mart store in Michigan, noticed that customers had trouble locating goods on sale. So Mr. Bartell put a police light on a pipe, attached it to a 12-volt car battery, and put the whole contraption on a shopping cart, which he wheeled to sales areas. Since then, K mart Corp. has institutionalized its spur-of-the-moment sales, bringing to its stores excitement and customers.

Today, K mart shoppers know that a flashing blue light at an in-store display is a type of sales promotion that represents an unannounced sale that will last only five to fifteen minutes and involves a limited supply of merchandise. Individual K mart store managers decide how frequently to run blue-light specials and which items are involved. While the typical store runs about two specials an hour, some outlets offer up to thirty blue-light specials a day, and customers "cruise the aisles for hours in hopes of snaring unexpected bargains."

K mart does have one strict rule with its blue-light specials:

The blue light always flashes above goods that are inexpensive and that can be bought on impulse. A sudden special on washing machines, for example, would probably sell few machines and would certainly disappoint blue-light regulars.

Despite the long-run popularity of blue-light specials, K mart is faced with two key decisions. First, what level of specials is desirable to minimize in-store loitering and customer emphasis on bargain hunting? Second, what role should the specials have as K mart continues to upgrade its company image and tries to attract more upscale shoppers?

Source: Based on material in Melinda Grenier Guiles, "Attention, Shoppers: Stop That Browsing and Get Aggressive," *Wall Street Journal* (June 16, 1987), pp. 1, 21.

It also believes that up to two-thirds of all purchasing decisions are made at the point of purchase.[16]

❏ In 1987, major department store, supermarket, home center, drugstore, discount store, and apparel-specialty retail chains spent almost $400,000 each on point-of-purchase displays.[17]

❏ Over seventy-five grocery store chains in thirty-three states have Information Systems kiosks in place. Information Systems displays consist of computerized kiosks that direct shoppers to the proper aisles for selected products, dispense cents-off coupons, and provide recipes. Among the participating manufacturers are Coca-Cola, Pepsi Cola, Lever Brothers, Frito-Lay, and General Foods.[18]

Contests and sweepstakes are similar in nature; they seek to attract and retain customers through participation in events that can lead to substantial prizes. A contest requires a customer to demonstrate some skill in return for a reward. A sweepstakes requires only participation, with the lucky winner chosen at random. The disadvantages of contests and sweepstakes are their costs, customer reliance on these tools as the reason for continued retailer patronage, the effort required of consumers, and entries by nonshoppers.[19] Together, manufacturers and retailers spend about $250 million each year on contests and sweepstakes.[20]

Coupons are used to offer discounts in the selling prices of dealer and manufacturer brands. During 1986, over 200 billion coupons were distributed, with grocery products accounting for 79 per cent of all coupons. Free-standing inserts in Sunday newspapers represented about 66 per cent of total coupons distributed. Coupons via daily newspaper, direct mail, in or on packages, regular magazines, Sunday newspaper magazines, and in-store machine dispensers made up the balance. Consumers saved $2.8 billion through coupons, while retailers received $586 million for handling redeemed coupons. The average face value of a grocery coupon reached $0.30 in 1986.[21]

There are four important advantages of coupons. First, in many cases, manufacturers pay for the advertising and the redemption of coupons. Second, coupons are very helpful to an ongoing advertising campaign and increase store traffic. One recent study found that coupons were redeemed at least once in a six-month period by 88 per cent of the households surveyed. Twenty per cent of the households were responsible for more than one-half of all redemptions; this heavy-usage group redeemed an average of eight coupons per week.[22] Third, the use of coupons increases the consumer's perception that a retailer offers good value. Fourth, the effectiveness of advertisements can be measured by counting redeemed coupons.

The disadvantages of coupons include their effect on the retailer's image, consumers shopping only when coupons are available, low redemption rates, the clutter of coupons (largely due to the expanding number of coupons distributed), retailer and consumer fraud, and handling costs. For example, only about 4 per cent of all coupons are redeemed by consumers, because of the large number of them that are received by each American household.

Trading stamps were very popular in the 1950s and 1960s; however, they have had a significant decline since the late 1960s. From a peak of over $800 million in trading-stamp volume during 1969, the industry bottomed out at less than $300 million in 1975. During 1986, stamp volume was about $400 million. Only 8 per cent of U.S. supermarkets now offer trading stamps; and there are just three national trading-stamp companies: S&H, Quality Stamp, and Gold Bond.[23]

The advantages of trading stamps are store loyalty (customers can accumulate stamps only through patronage at one or a few stores), the "free" nature of stamps to many consumers, and a competitive edge for a retailer that is similar to others. On the other hand, a number of consumers realize that stamps are not free and therefore would rather shop at lower-priced, nonstamp stores. In addition, profit margins may be small if retailers offering trading stamps try to price competitively with firms not offering stamps.

Prizes are similar in concept to stamps, but instead of stamps, prizes are given. Prize giveaways are most effective when sets of glasses, silverware, dishes, place mats, and so on are distributed one at a time to shoppers. These encourage store loyalty. The problems are the costs of the prizes, the difficulty of termination, and the impact on image.

As a supplement to personal selling, free samples (e.g., a taste of a cake, a smell of perfume) and/or demonstrations (e.g., cooking lessons) may be used. These are effective because the customer becomes involved, and impulse purchases increase. Loitering and costs may be problems.

Referral gifts are used to encourage existing customers to bring in new customers. Direct marketers, such as book and record clubs, often use this tool. It is a technique that has no important shortcomings and recognizes the value of friends in influencing purchasing decisions.

Items such as matchbooks, pens, calendars, and shopping bags are sometimes given to customers. They differ from prizes in that they advertise the retailer's name and are usually not part of a set. These items should be used as supplements. Their advantage is longevity. There is no real disadvantage.

Retailers may use special events to foster consumer enthusiasm. The special events can range from elaborate grand openings to fashion shows to art exhibits. For example, the grand opening of Jersey City's Newport Centre featured two world records (the greatest number of people—7,500—to participate in a ribbon-cutting ceremony and the cutting of the longest continuous ribbon—12,000 feet—in history), a sweepstakes with 100,000 prizes, and a Vietnam veterans' color guard.[24] In general, when a special event is planned, the potential increase in consumer awareness and store traffic needs to be weighed against that event's costs.

Skywriting can be used by restaurants, hotels, and others as an attention getter. It may help in creating awareness or reminding customers. However, the retailer's image can be affected, and costs can be high.

Planning a Retail Promotional Strategy

In order to communicate successfully with its customers, a retailer should carefully plan its overall promotional strategy. A systematic five-step approach to an overall promotion plan is depicted in Figure 15-6 and explained in the following sections.

Determining Promotional Objectives

Broad promotional objectives include increasing sales, stimulating impulse and reminder buying, increasing store traffic, producing leads for sales personnel, developing and reinforcing a retailer's image, informing customers about goods and service attributes, popularizing a new store location, capitalizing on manufacturer support, offering customer service and improving customer relations, and maintaining customer loyalty.

In developing a promotional strategy, a retailer must determine which of these objectives are most important. It is necessary for the retailer to state its goals clearly in order to give direction to the selection of promotional types, media, and messages.

Objectives must be stated as specifically as possible. As an example, increasing company sales is not a specific enough goal. However, increasing sales by 20 per cent is directional, quantitative, and measurable. With such an objective, a retailer would be able to develop a thorough promotional plan and evaluate its success.

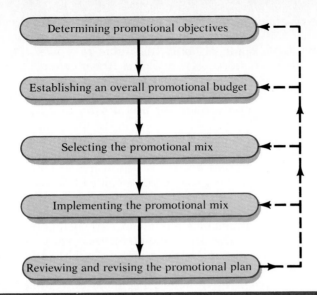

FIGURE 15-6
Planning a Retail
Promotional Strategy

Establishing an Overall Promotional Budget

There are several procedures available for ascertaining the size of the promotion budget. Five alternative budgeting techniques are discussed in this section.

The **all-you-can-afford method** is probably the weakest of the budgeting techniques. In this procedure, a retailer first allocates funds for every element of the retail strategy mix except promotion. Whatever funds are left over are placed in a promotional budget. The shortcomings of this method are that little importance is placed on promotion as a crucial retail strategy-mix variable; expenditures are not linked to objectives; and if no funds are left over, there is no promotion budget. This method is used predominantly by small, conservative retailers.

The **incremental method** of promotion budgeting relies on previous budgets in the allocation of funds. A percentage is either added to or subtracted from this year's budget to determine next year's budget. For instance, if this year's promotion budget is $10,000, next year's budget would be calculated by adding or subtracting a percentage to or from that amount. A 10 per cent increase means that next year's budget would be $11,000. This technique is useful for a small retailer. A reference point is used. The budget is adjusted based on the retailer's feelings about past successes and future trends. It is an easy method to calculate. However, important disadvantages do exist. The size of the budget is rarely tied to specific objectives. Intuition or "gut feelings" are used. Evaluation is also difficult.

The **competitive parity method** has utility for small and large retailers. In this procedure, a retailer's budget is raised or lowered according to the actions of competitors. For example, if the leading retailer in an area raises its promotion budget by 8 per cent, competitors in the area could follow suit. The advantages of competitive parity are that it utilizes a point of comparison and is market-oriented and conservative. The disadvantages are that it is a following, not a leading, philosophy; it may be difficult to obtain data; and there is an assumption that competing firms are similar (in terms of years in business, size, target market, type of location, merchandise, prices, and so on). The last point is particularly important: competing retailers might really need quite different promotional budgets.

With the **percentage-of-sales technique**, a retailer bases its promotion budget on sales revenue. In the first year, the retailer would develop a promotion-to-sales ratio. During succeeding years, the ratio of promotion dollars to sales dollars remains constant, although the value may vary. For example, a retailer decides that promotion costs should be 10 per cent of sales. First-year sales are estimated at $100,000, and a $10,000 promotion budget is planned. Second-year sales are estimated at $140,000, and a $14,000 promotion budget is planned. The benefits of this procedure are the use of sales as a base, adaptability, and the correlation of promotion with sales. Shortcomings are that there is no relation to objectives (e.g., for an established retailer, an increase in sales may not require an increase in promotion); promotion is utilized not as a leader of sales, but a follower; and promotion decreases during poor sales periods when increases might be beneficial. This technique provides too many promotional funds in periods of high sales and too few funds in periods of low sales.

The **objective-and-task method** is probably the best of the budgeting techniques. Under this procedure, a retailer clearly defines its promotional objectives and then determines the size of the budget necessary to satisfy these objectives. For example, a retailer may decide that it would like to have 70 per cent of the people in its trading area know the firm's name by the end of a one-month promotion campaign, up from 50 per cent currently (objective). It then calculates what tasks and costs are required to achieve this objective:

Objective	Task	Cost
1. Gain awareness of housewives.	Use eight quarter-page ads in four successive Sunday editions of two local newspapers.	$8,000
2. Gain awareness of motorists.	Use forty 30-second radio commercials during prime time on local radio stations, at $125 each.	
3. Gain awareness of pedestrians.	Give away shopping bags—5,000 bags at $0.50 each.	5,000
		2,500
	Total budget	$15,500

The advantages of the objective-and-task technique are that objectives are clearly stated; expenditures are related to the completion of goal-oriented tasks; it is adaptable; and success (or failure) can be evaluated. The major shortcoming is the complexity in setting goals and specific tasks, especially for small retailers.

In selecting a method for planning its promotion budget, a retailer should weigh the strengths and weaknesses of each technique in relation to its individual requirements and constraints.

Table 15-4 shows the advertising expenditures of selected small retailers, expressed as a percentage of sales. These expenditures vary from 0.5 per cent of sales for some auto supply stores to 3.0 per cent of sales for some apparel stores, beauty salons, and restaurants.

Selecting the Promotional Mix

After the budget is determined, a retailer must determine its promotional mix: the combination of advertising, publicity, personal selling, and sales promotion. A firm with a relatively small budget may rely on in-store displays, flyers, targeted direct mail, and publicity to generate customer traffic, whereas a firm with a large promotion budget may rely heavily on newspaper and television advertising.

The type of retailer often affects the choice of promotional mix. For example, Table 15-4 shows that coin-operated laundries emphasize Yellow Page directo-

TABLE 15-4

Advertising as Practiced by Selected Small Retailers

Type of Retailer	Average Ad Budget (% of Sales)	Favorite Media	Other Media	Special Considerations	Promotional Opportunities
Apparel store	2.5–3.0	Weekly or suburban newspapers; direct mail.	Radio; Yellow Pages; exterior signs.	Cooperative advertising available from manufacturers.	Fashion shows for community organizations or charities.
Auto supply store	0.5–2.0	Local newspapers; Yellow Pages.	Point-of-purchase displays; exterior signs.	Cooperative advertising available from manufacturers.	For specialty stores, direct mail is a popular medium.
Bar and/or cocktail lounge	1.0–2.0	Yellow Pages; local newspapers (entertainment section).	Tourist publications; radio; specialties; exterior signs.	Manufacturers do all product advertising.	Unusual drinks at "happy hour" rates; hosting postevent parties.
Bookstore	1.5–1.7	Newspapers; shoppers; Yellow Pages; local magazines.	Radio; exterior signs.	Cooperative advertising available from publisher.	Autograph parties.
Coin-op laundry	0.6–2.0	Yellow Pages; flyers distributed in area; local.	Direct mail; exterior signs.	—	Coupons in newspaper ads for "free trial."
Gift store	1.5–2.5	Weekly newspapers; Yellow Pages.	Radio; direct mail; consumer magazines; exterior signs.	—	Open houses; in-store demonstrations of products such as cookware.
Hair-grooming/beauty salon	2.5–3.0	Yellow Pages.	Newspapers; name credits for styles in feature articles; exterior signs.	Word-of-mouth advertising is very important to a salon's success.	Styling for community fashion shows; conducting free beauty clinics and demonstrations.
Health food store	1.1–2.8	Local newspapers; shoppers; college newspapers.	Direct mail; point-of-purchase displays; exterior signs.	—	Educational displays and services.
Restaurant	0.8–3.0	Newspapers; radio; Yellow Pages; transit; outdoor.	Local entertainment guides or tourist publications; theater programs; TV for chain or franchise restaurants; exterior signs.	Word-of-mouth advertising is relied upon heavily by independently owned restaurants.	"Free" advertising in critics' columns; specialities; birthday cakes or parties for customers.

Source: Adapted by the authors from "Advertising Small Business" (Bank of America NT & SA, 1982), p. 16. Reprinted with permission. © *Small Business Reporter* 1982.

ries, whereas health food stores emphasize local newspapers as well as point-of-purchase displays. Figure 15-7 shows the usage of selected promotional forms by supermarkets. Newspapers and flyers/circulars are used most often in advertising. Continuity programs (such as coupons, point-of-sale promotions, trading stamps, and so on), theme sales, and bonus coupons are the sales promotion techniques used most.

Frequently, retailers use a variety of promotional forms that reinforce one another. For example, one study concluded that a combination of media advertising and point-of-purchase displays is more effective in getting across a message than one form alone.[25]

When reacting to promotion, a consumer generally goes through a series of steps called the **hierarchy of effects**, leading from awareness to purchase. The

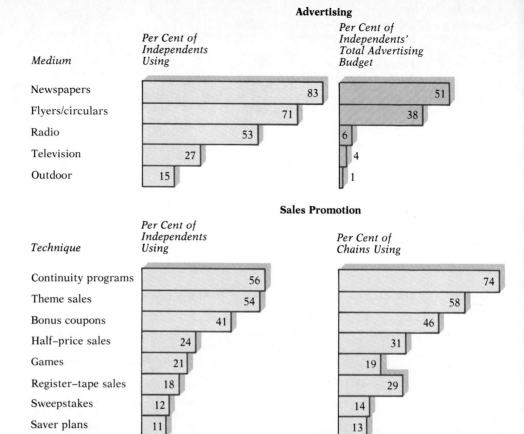

FIGURE 15-7
The Usage of Selected Promotional Tools by Supermarkets
Source: "54th Annual Report of the Grocery Industry," *Progressive Grocer* (April 1987), p. 29; and Richard De Santa, "Advertising: A Balancing Act," *Progressive Grocer* (June 1987), p. 90. Reprinted by permission.

steps are awareness, knowledge, liking, preference, conviction, and purchase.[26] Different promotional mixes are required during each step; these are cited in Figure 15-8. As a rule, advertising and publicity are most effective in developing awareness, and personal selling is most effective in changing attitudes and stimulating desires. This is especially true for expensive and complex goods or services.

Implementing the Promotional Mix

Implementation of a promotional mix involves choosing which specific media to use (Newspaper A versus Newspaper B), the timing of promotion, the content of messages, the makeup of the sales force, specific sales-promotion tools, and the responsibility for coordination.

Media Decisions

The choice of specific media is based on a wide variety of elements, including overall costs, efficiency (cost to reach a member of the target market), lead time,

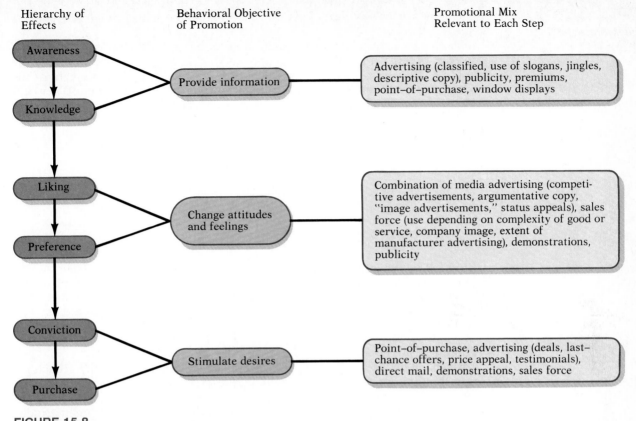

Hierarchy of Effects	Behavioral Objective of Promotion	Promotional Mix Relevant to Each Step

Awareness → Knowledge → **Provide information** → Advertising (classified, use of slogans, jingles, descriptive copy), publicity, premiums, point–of–purchase, window displays

Liking → Preference → **Change attitudes and feelings** → Combination of media advertising (competitive advertisements, argumentative copy, "image advertisements," status appeals), sales force (use depending on complexity of good or service, company image, extent of manufacturer advertising), demonstrations, publicity

Conviction → Purchase → **Stimulate desires** → Point–of–purchase, advertising (deals, last–chance offers, price appeal, testimonials), direct mail, demonstrations, sales force

FIGURE 15-8
Promotion and the Hierarchy of Effects
Source: Adapted by the authors from Robert Lavidge and Gary A. Steiner, "A Model for Predictive Measurements of Advertising Effectiveness," *Journal of Marketing,* Vol. 25 (October 1961), p. 61. Reprinted with permission of the American Marketing Association.

and editorial content. Overall costs are important because the extensive use of an expensive medium may preclude the implementation of a balanced promotional mix. In addition, a retailer may not be able to repeat a message in a costly medium, and advertisements are rarely effective when shown only once.

The efficiency of a medium relates to the cost of reaching a given number of target customers. Newspaper efficiency is measured by the milline rate, which reflects both the cost per **agate line** (there are fourteen agate lines to an inch of space, one column wide) and the newspaper's circulation:

$$\text{Milline rate (newspaper efficiency)} = \frac{\text{Cost per agate line} \times 1,000,000}{\text{Circulation}}$$

The **milline rate** represents the cost to a retailer of one agate line per million circulation. A newspaper with a circulation of 400,000 and an agate-line rate of $5.50 has a milline rate of $13.75.

Magazine efficiency is based on cost per thousand (rather than a milline rate):

$$\text{Cost per thousand (magazine efficiency)} = \frac{\text{Cost per page} \times 1,000}{\text{Circulation}}$$

509

A magazine with a circulation of two million and a per-page rate of $23,000 has a cost per thousand of $11.50.

In both of these calculations, total circulation is used to obtain efficiency. However, because a retailer usually appeals to a limited target market, only the relevant portion of circulation should be considered. Thus, if 70 per cent of the magazine's readers are target customers for a retailer (and the other 30 per cent live outside the firm's trading area), the real cost per thousand is

$$\text{Cost per thousand} \atop \text{(target market)} = \frac{\text{Cost per page} \times 1,000}{\text{Circulation} \times \dfrac{\text{Target market}}{\text{Circulation}}}$$

$$= \frac{\$23,000 \times 1,000}{2,000,000 \times 0.70}$$

$$= \frac{\$23,000,000}{1,400,000} = \$16.43$$

Different media require different lead times. For instance, a newspaper advertisement can be placed shortly before publication, whereas a magazine advertisement sometimes must be placed months in advance. In addition, the retailer must decide what editorial content it wants to be near its advertisements (e.g., sports story, comics, personal care column, or feature story).

Timing of the Promotional Mix

Advertising decisions involve the concepts of reach and frequency. **Reach** refers to the number of distinct people who are exposed to a retailer's ads during a specified time period. **Frequency** measures the average number of times each person who is reached is exposed to company ads during a given time period.

A retailer can advertise extensively or intensively. **Extensive coverage** means that ads reach many people but with relatively low frequency. **Intensive coverage** means that ads are placed in selected media and repeated frequently. Repetition is important, particularly for a retailer seeking to develop an image or selling new goods or services.

In implementing its promotional mix, a retailer must consider peak seasons and whether to mass or distribute efforts. When peak seasons occur, all of the elements of the mix are usually utilized; during slow periods, promotional efforts are usually reduced. A **massed advertising effort** is used by retailers, such as Avon, that promote mostly during one or two seasons. A **distributed advertising effort** is employed by retailers, such as McDonald's, that promote constantly throughout the year.

Peak advertising is practiced by supermarkets, the majority of which use Wednesday as the day when major weekly newspaper ads are placed. This placement takes advantage of the fact that a heavy proportion of consumers conduct their major shopping trip on Thursday, Friday, or Saturday.

Sales-force size can vary by time (morning versus evening), day (weekdays versus weekends), and month (December versus January). Sales promotions also vary in their timing. Store openings and holidays are especially good times for sales promotions. See Figure 15-9.

Content of Messages

Whether written or spoken, personally or impersonally delivered, message content is important. In advertising, themes, wording, headlines, use of color, size, layout, and placement must be decided on. Publicity releases need to be written. In personal selling, the greeting, the sales presentation, the demonstration, and the closing need to be enacted. In sales promotion, the firm's message must be composed and placed on the promotional device.

FIGURE 15-9
A Valentine's Day Promotion
Reprinted by permission of
the Rochester Institute of
Technology Communications
Department.

To a large extent, the characteristics of the promotional form influence the message. A shopping bag often contains no more than a retailer's name; a billboard (seen at fifty-five miles per hour) is good for a visual effect but can hold limited written material; and a salesperson may be able to maintain a customer's attention for a while, thus expanding the content of the message that is conveyed. For example, several shopping centers are now using a glossy magazine format to communicate a community-oriented image, introduce new stores to consumers, and promote the merchandise available at stores in the center.[27]

In advertising, distinctiveness can be an aid to a retailer because of the proliferation of messages. For example, cluttered advertisements displaying many products may suggest a discounter's orientation, while fine pencil drawings and selective product displays may suggest a specialty store orientation.

Recently, more retailers have become involved in **comparative advertising**, whereby messages compare their offerings with those of competitors. Comparative advertising is used to help position a retailer in relation to competitors, increase awareness of the retailer, maximize the efficiency of a limited budget, and provide credibility. However, comparative ads provide visibility for competitors, may confuse consumers, and may lead to legal action by competitors. Some fast-food and off-price retailers are among those now utilizing comparative advertising.

Makeup of Sales Force

Qualifications for sales personnel are detailed, and personnel are recruited, selected, trained, compensated, supervised, and controlled. Personnel are also classified (order takers versus order getters) and assigned to the appropriate departments. An in-depth discussion regarding the personal sales force was provided in Chapter 10.

Sales Promotion Tools

The specific sales-promotion tools are chosen from among those cited in Figure 15-4. The combination of sales promotion tools depends on short-run (and changing) objectives and the other components of the promotion mix. Wherever possible, cooperative ventures with manufacturers or other suppliers would be sought, and tools inconsistent with the retailer's image would not be used.

Responsibility for Coordination

Regardless of a firm's size or organizational form, someone within the retail organization must have authority over and responsibility for the promotion function. Larger retailers normally assign this job to a vice-president of promotion, who is in charge of display personnel, works with the firm's advertising agency, supervises the retailer's own advertising department (if there is one), and supplies branch stores with necessary supplementary (in-store) materials. Personal selling is usually under the jurisdiction of the store manager in a large retail setting.

A recent study of major department store, supermarket, home center, drugstore, discount store, and apparel-specialty chain retailers found that 84 per cent of these companies had their own in-house advertising departments, with an average staff of seventeen people. Only 14 per cent of the firms used an outside advertising agency, although the drugstore and apparel chains were slightly more likely to utilize an outside agency.[28]

For a promotional strategy to be successful, its components have to be coordinated with other elements of the retail mix. As an example, sales personnel must be informed of a special sale and must know product characteristics; sales items must be received, marked, and properly displayed; and bookkeeping entries must be made.

Often, a shopping center or a shopping district runs a theme promotion, such as "back-to-school," and someone has to be charged with the responsibility of coordinating the activities of all the stores participating in the event. Figure 15-10 shows an annual promotion schedule for Eaton Centre, a leading Toronto, Canada, shopping center (note that this schedule begins in November, in time for the crucial Christmas selling season).

Reviewing and Revising the Promotional Plan

An analysis of the success of a promotion plan depends on the objectives sought, and analysis is simplified if promotional objectives are clearly stated in advance (as suggested in this chapter). Revisions would be made for promotional tools not achieving their preset goals.

Table 15-5 lists a number of research approaches for testing the effectiveness of a promotional effort. Although difficulties may sometimes exist in reviewing promotion (e.g., increased sales may be due to a variety of factors, not just promotion), it is still necessary for a retailer to systematically study and adjust the promotional mix.

Week of Monday	NOV				DEC					JAN			
	29	5	12	19	26	3	10	17	24	31	7	14	21
Television: 30's (52 Weeks)	X	X	X	X	X	X	X	X	X	X	X	X	X
Subway Door Cards (200)	X	X	X	X	X	X	X	X	X	X	X	X	X
Queen Street Sign	X	X	X	X	X	X	X	X	X	X	X	X	X
Information Centres	X	X	X	X	X	X	X	X	X	X	X	X	X
Newspaper													
Star (SUN) B&W			X			X							
(M-F) B+1 Color									X				
(M-F) B+1 Color												X	
Sun (SUN) B+W			X			X							
(M-F) B+1 Color									X				
(M-F) B+1 Color												X	
Magazines													
Toronto Life Fashion 4 Color													
Toronto Life 4 Color	X												
Key to Toronto 4 Color													
Transit Shelters													
Special Events and Promotions	X	X		X	X	X			X			X	X

Week of Monday	FEB				MAR					APR				MAY			
	28	4	11	18	25	4	11	18	25	1	8	15	22	29	6	13	20
Television: 30's (52 Weeks)	X	X	X	X	X	X	X	X	X	X	X	X	X	X	X	X	X
Subway Door Cards (200)	X	X	X	X	X	X	X	X	X	X	X	X	X	X	X	X	X
Queen Street Sign	X	X	X	X	X	X	X	X	X	X	X	X	X	X	X	X	X
Information Centres	X	X	X	X	X	X	X	X	X	X	X	X	X	X	X	X	X
Newspaper																	
Star (SUN) B&W		X					X								X		
(M-F) B+1 Color																	
(M-F) B+1 Color																	
Sun (SUN) B+W		X					X								X		
(M-F) B+1 Color																	
(M-F) B+1 Color																	
Magazines																	
Toronto Life Fashion 4 Color								X					X				
Toronto Life 4 Color			X													X	
Key to Toronto 4 Color															X		
Transit Shelters																	
Special Events and Promotions	X	X	X				X	X							X	X	

Week of Monday	JUNE					JULY				AUG				SEPT					OCT			
	27	3	10	17	24	1	8	15	22	29	5	12	19	26	2	9	16	23	30	7	14	21
Television: 30's (52 Weeks)	X	X	X	X	X	X	X	X	X	X	X	X	X	X	X	X	X	X	X	X	X	X
Subway Door Cards (200)	X	X	X	X	X	X	X	X	X	X	X	X	X	X	X	X	X	X	X	X	X	X
Queen Street Sign	X	X	X	X	X	X	X	X	X	X	X	X	X	X	X	X	X	X	X	X	X	X
Information Centres	X	X	X	X	X	X	X	X	X	X	X	X	X	X	X	X	X	X	X	X	X	X
Newspaper																						
Star (SUN) B&W			X										X				X			X		
(M-F) B+1 Color											X											
(M-F) B+1 Color								X														
Sun (SUN) B+W			X										X				X			X		
(M-F) B+1 Color											X											
(M-F) B+1 Color								X														
Magazines																						
Toronto Life Fashion 4 Color											X											
Toronto Life 4 Color			X				X									X				X		
Key to Toronto 4 Color		X				X																
Transit Shelters		X	X	X	X	X	X	X	X													
Special Events and Promotions			X						X		X						X		X		X	X

My City. My Centre.
The Eaton Centre

FIGURE 15-10
An Eaton Centre Annual Promotion Schedule
Courtesy Eaton Centre, Toronto, Canada.

TABLE 15-5
Measuring Promotional Effectiveness

Behaviorally Oriented Promotion Objectives	Examples of Retail Promotion Objectives	Research Approaches for Evaluating Promotion Effectiveness
Cognitive: the realm of thoughts; promotion designed to provide information and facts.	Inform current customers about new credit plans; acquaint potential customers with new offerings.	Study company and product offering awareness before and after promotion; evaluate extent of promotion readership by number of people and degree of readership.
Affective: the realm of emotions; promotion designed to change attitudes and feelings.	Develop and reinforce high-fashion image; maintain customer loyalty.	Study image via semantic differential, projective techniques, rank-order preference for stores, and rating scales before and after promotion.
Conative: the realm of motives; promotion designed to stimulate or direct desires.	Increase store traffic; produce leads for salespeople; increase sales over last year; reduce customer returns from last year.	Evaluate sales performance and number of inquiries; study customers' intentions to buy before and after promotion; study customer trading areas and average purchases; study coupon redemption.

Source: Adapted by the authors from Robert Lavidge and Gary A. Steiner, "A Model for Predictive Measurement of Advertising Effectiveness," *Journal of Marketing*, Vol. 25 (October 1961), p. 61. Reprinted with permission of the American Marketing Association.

SUMMARY

Retail promotion involves informing, persuading, and/or reminding customers through advertising, publicity, personal selling, and sales promotion. Advertising is nonpersonal and has the advantages of a large audience, low costs per person, many alternative media, and so on. The disadvantages of advertising include an inflexible message, high absolute costs, and a wasted portion of audience. The major advertising media are newspapers, telephone directories, direct mail, radio, television, transit, outdoor, magazines, and flyers/circulars. Of particular importance are cooperative ads, for which the retailer shares the costs and message with manufacturers, wholesalers, or other retailers.

Publicity is nonpersonal, nonpaid communication. Advantages include enhancing image, objective source, and no costs for message. Disadvantages include its short-run nature, the lack of control over messages, and actual costs. Types of publicity are community service, parades, new-product introductions, store openings, and media visits (e.g., gourmet reporter).

Personal selling involves personal contact with customers and is important for persuasion and in closing sales. Some advantages are personalization, flexibility, and immediate feedback. Some disadvantages are small audience, high costs per customer, and inability to lure customers into the store. Order-taking (routine) and/or order-getting (creative) selling personnel can be employed. Sales functions include greeting the customer, determining wants, showing merchandise, making a sales presentation, demonstrating merchandise, answering objections, and closing the sale.

Sales promotion is a supplement to advertising and personal selling. Among the advantages are that it is eye-catching, unique, and valuable to the customer. Among the disadvantages are that it is difficult to terminate, may have a negative effect on image, and may rely on frivolous selling points. Examples of sales promotion are point-of-purchase displays, contests, sweepstakes, coupons, trading stamps, prizes, samples, demonstrations, referral gifts, matchbooks, pens, calendars, shopping bags, special events, and skywriting.

Planning a retail promotional strategy consists of five steps: determining promotion objectives, establishing a promotion budget, selecting the promotion mix, implementing the mix, and reviewing and revising the promotion plan. First, objectives need to be stated in specific and measurable terms. Second, an overall promotion budget is set on the basis of a technique from among the all-you-can-afford, incremental, competitive-parity, percentage-of-sales, and objective-and-task methods.

Third, the promotional mix is outlined, based on the size of the budget, the type of retailing, the coverage of the media, and the stage in the hierarchy-of-effects model. Fourth, the promotional mix is implemented. Included are decisions involving specific

513

media, timing of promotion, content of messages, makeup of the sales force, specific sales promotion tools, and responsibility for coordination. Last, the retailer systematically reviews and revises the promotional plan, consistent with its preset objectives.

QUESTIONS FOR DISCUSSION

1. Are there any retailers that should not use advertising? Explain your answer.
2. How would an advertising plan for a small retailer differ from that of a large retail chain?
3. How do manufacturers' and retailers' cooperative advertising goals overlap? How do they differ?
4. How should a retailer react to negative publicity?
5. Develop a plan for a small retailer to generate positive publicity for its store.
6. Give three examples of order takers and order getters. Under which circumstances should each type of salesperson be used?
7. How do advertising and personal selling complement each other for a retailer?
8. Are there any retailers that should not use sales promotion? Explain your answer.
9. Develop sales promotions for each of the following.
   a. A new amusement park in a major metropolitan area
   b. An existing restaurant now open on Sunday for the first time
   c. An existing wallpaper retailer
   d. A new warehouse store in a moderate-sized suburb
10. Which method of promotional budgeting should a small retailer use? Why? A large retailer? Why?
11. Explain the hierarchy-of-effects model from a retail perspective. Apply your answer to a new beauty salon.
12. Describe the difference between frequency and reach in retail advertising. Which is more important? Why?
13. Develop a checklist for coordinating a promotional plan.
14. For each of these promotional objectives, explain how to evaluate promotional effectiveness.
    a. Increase customer traffic by 10 per cent
    b. Develop an innovative image
    c. Maintain customer loyalty

NOTES

1. Donald Longo, "Zayre Attempts to Zap Rivals with Frequent Z Gift Program," *Discount Store News* (October 26, 1987), pp. 1, 29; Janet Meyers, "Zayre Will Target Frequent Buyers in Bonus Program," *Advertising Age* (October 19, 1987), pp. 3, 132; "Zayre Gives Points to Frequent Buyers," *Chain Store Age Executive* (December 1987), pp. 18, 21; and "Zayre Launches 'Frequent Z' to Make Points with Shoppers," *Marketing News* (November 20, 1987), p. 1.
2. Computed by the authors from David P. Schulz, "'86 Better FOR Some," *Stores* (November 1987), pp. 92–94.
3. Ralph S. Alexander (Chairman), *Marketing Definitions: A Glossary of Marketing Terms* (Chicago: American Marketing Association, 1960), p. 9.
4. "100 Leading Advertisers by Primary Business," *Advertising Age* (September 24, 1987), p. 162.
5. "New Store Competition Drives Ad Budgets," *Chain Store Age Executive* (December 1987), p. 17.
6. See "New Store Competition Drives Ad Budgets," pp. 16–17; "TV Spending Propels Ad Budgets to New Highs," *Discount Store News* (May 11, 1987), p. 115; and "Piggly Wiggly Spots Bring Home the Bacon," *Chain Store Age Executive* (December 1987), pp. 40, 42.
7. See Erin M. Sullivan, "Advertising an Image," *Progressive Grocer* (November 1986), pp. 19–20; and Rhonda Razzano, "Wave of Ad Campaigns Freshens Publix Image," *Chain Store Age Executive* (April 1987), pp. 66–67.
8. "Restaurants Offered Co-Op Ad Program," *Marketing News* (January 30, 1987), p. 23.
9. See Paul Edwards, "Levi, Boston Retailer Join in Catalog Effort," *Advertising Age* (November 24, 1986), p. 58; Larry Rothstein, "Building Dealer Relations with Co-Op," *Sales & Marketing Management* (February 3, 1986), pp. 59 ff.; and "Ernst In-Store Billboards Show Name Brands," *Chain Store Age Executive* (December 1987), p. 46.
10. Alexander, *Marketing Definitions: A Glossary of Marketing Terms*, p. 19.
11. See Frank Di Costanzo, "What the Press Thinks of Press Releases," *Public Relations Quarterly* (Winter 1986–1987), pp. 22–24.
12. Alexander, *Marketing Definitions: A Glossary of Marketing Terms*, p. 18.
13. Ann Hagedorn, "Apparel Makers Play Bigger Part on Sales Floor," *Wall Street Journal* (March 2, 1988), p. 31.
14. Alexander, *Marketing Definitions: A Glossary of Marketing Terms*, p. 20.
15. Russell Mitchell, "An Upstart Is Upsetting Actme-

dia's Shopping Carts," *Business Week* (September 7, 1987), pp. 28–29.

16. Laurie Freeman and Judann Dagnoli, "Point-of-Purchase Rush Is On," *Advertising Age* (February 8, 1988), p. 47.

17. "New Store Competition Drives Ad Budgets," p. 17.

18. Freeman and Dagnoli, "Point-of-Purchase Rush Is On," p. 47.

19. Scott Hume, "Coupons Score with Consumers," *Advertising Age* (February 15, 1988), p. 40.

20. Mary Kuntz, "Taking a Chance on Sweepstakes," *Newsday* (June 21, 1987), p. 76.

21. "1987 Nielsen Review of Retail Grocery Store Trends." *Progressive Grocer 1987 Nielsen Review* (September 1987), pp. 16–17.

22. Steve Kingsbury, "Study Provides Overview of Who's Redeeming Coupons and Why," *Marketing News* (January 2, 1987), p. 56.

23. Ann E. La Forge, "What's New in Trading Stamps," *New York Times* (August 16, 1987), Section 3, p. 19.

24. "Guinness Puts Newport Centre's Opening Day in Its Record Book," *Chain Store Age Executive* (December 1987), p. 25.

25. "Display Effectiveness: An Evaluation," *Nielsen Researcher* (Number 2, 1983), p. 8.

26. Robert Lavidge and Gary A. Steiner, "A Model for Predictive Measurements of Advertising Effectiveness," *Journal of Marketing,* Vol. 25 (October 1961), pp. 59–62.

27. Holly Klokis, "Center Advertising: Upgrading the Tab," *Chain Store Age Executive* (May 1987), pp. 78, 80; and Len Strazewski, "Magazine Fashioned for Malls," *Advertising Age* (June 1, 1987), p. 28.

28. "New Store Competition Drives Ad Budgets," p. 17.

Banana Republic: A Distinctive Promotional Strategy*

Case 1

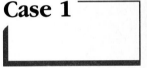

Banana Republic began in 1977 as a catalog retailer to "offer the kind of clothing that consumers liked and could not find: intelligently designed, comfortable, natural-fabric garments for dedicated travelers and other independent souls who don't step to the march of fashion." At its inception, much of the clothing sold by Banana Republic was military surplus, often of defunct political regimes. Today, Banana Republic has garments manufactured to its own specifications and from its own fabrics.

Throughout its growth, until recently, the firm (which now also operates about one-hundred retail outlets) carefully maintained a safari, expedition, and outback image. For example, Banana Republic maintained a toll-free climate-service desk to give its customers advice on weather conditions anywhere in the world. The retailer also sold travel books and maps. Its mail-order catalogs entertained readers with reviews from notable travelers from many fields. The firm viewed its catalog as the official chronicle of "our imaginary republic."

The Spring 1988 mail-order catalog featured items such as a pigskin Australian schoolbag, a snap-brim jungle hat, a women's 100 per cent sarong skirt, a leather flight jacket, and rubber rain boots. Customer interest in the catalog was generated by handwritten copy and printed descriptions and histories alongside items, and through comments by celebrities. Most of the merchandise consisted of adaptations of original concepts (for example, a women's Aztec belt that was a "sturdy union of fine English bridle leather and Aztec-influenced metalwork with contrasting top-stitching") that were made exclusively for Banana Republic. Consistent with its catalogs, Banana Republic stores presented an exotic jungle and expedition image. Some outlets even had a jeep as part of their storefront display.

Banana Republic is aware that one of the potential threats of its store expansion is that these stores could depress catalog sales. Accordingly, its goal has been to achieve greater overall company sales by having direct marketing and in-store efforts complement one another. Thus, catalogs are used to sell merchandise to customers who prefer shopping by mail or who do not live near a retail store, make consumers aware of Banana Republic stores, help store customers preshop, show how outfits can be assembled, and make potential store shoppers familiar with store policies. Likewise, store displays are linked to catalogs. For example, store merchandise is often displayed with the appropriate catalog page appearing next to it. Table 1 contains a listing of some of the principles of catalog design and presentation used by Banana Republic.

*This case was prepared and written by Professor Elaine Sherman, Hofstra University.

515

TABLE 1

Banana Republic's Principles of Catalog Design and Presentation

- ❏ All clothing is hand-sketched. This gives the catalog a noncommercial, almost highbrow image.
- ❏ Product features are highlighted in a handwritten style instead of type.
- ❏ Each item is accompanied by a short story of the history, ideal uses, and wearability of the garment.
- ❏ Ensembles are shown to increase multiple purchases. Readers are referred to other pages for related clothing.
- ❏ A brown border around the catalog's pages gives it a distinctive look.
- ❏ Quotations and endorsements by celebrities are sprinkled through the catalog.
- ❏ A toll-free phone number is listed (in handwritten style) throughout the catalog.
- ❏ Color choices of fabrics are shown. The drawings show the texture of these fabrics.
- ❏ No human models appear in the catalog.
- ❏ An order form, preprinted with the respondent's name and address, is included with each mailed catalog.

In a typical year, Banana Republic mails over three million catalogs during each selling season. The mailing list comprises persons in Banana Republic's customer files, those who have made inquiries, and names purchased from 117 different rental lists. In developing a mailing, Banana Republic is careful to maintain an even split between males and females, since it does not want to be identified with either a male or a female image. Each time a new catalog is mailed, the firm suspends all other print advertising for a period of three weeks.

About 20 per cent of the catalogs are sent to customers in areas where the firm already has stores. In areas where a new store is opening, copies of the current catalog are inserted in local newspapers two weeks after the store's opening date. These catalogs have special covers that announce the new store. Several thousand catalogs with stickered store-opening announcements are also created for street distribution in locations near new stores.

Banana Republic's budget for three million catalogs for creative services, catalog production and printing costs, list rentals, mailing and postage, list maintenance, and in-store and on-street distribution equals almost $1.5 million (about 40–45 cents per catalog).

In 1988, the Gap (Banana Republic's parent firm) decided to slow Banana Republic's store expansion plans and revamp its image and merchandise offerings. Banana Republic's popularity had fallen because safari-type clothing was a "tired look that needs to be refreshed." In the stores, theme park fixtures were to be replaced by more subdued displays, and the safari and exhibition departments were to be dropped. While clothing such as khaki slacks and simple cotton dresses would continue to dominate the merchandise offering, more upscale European-style casual clothing was to be added.

QUESTIONS

1. What should Banana Republic's promotional goals be?
2. Present a promotional mix plan for Banana Republic. Include advertising, publicity, personal selling, and sales promotion in your answer.
   a. Develop the plan using Banana Republic's original image and merchandise offering.
   b. How would you revise the plan to reflect the firm's new image and merchandise offering?
3. Evaluate Banana Republic's use of catalogs and stores as complementary promotional tools. What are its risks with this approach?
4. What budgeting technique should Banana Republic use with its mail-order catalogs? Why?

Hartwick Clothes: Maintaining Effective Personal Selling in an Upscale Men's Clothing Store*

Hartwick Clothes is a retail chain operated by a vertically integrated clothing manufacturer that features fine men's apparel. Hartwick suits sell for $270 to $790, sports jackets sell for $235 to $650, and outerwear prices are as high as $1,200 for a suede jacket.

Hartwick's retail strategy is based on a consistent high-quality philosophy. To Hartwick, this means that high-quality salesmanship is as important as high-quality tailoring, fabrics, and alterations. Its salespeople have been with the firm for an average of twelve years. In general, Hartwick sees the salesperson's role as properly communicating with and servicing customers in the store; maintaining a list of key customer accounts; knowing the names, clothing sizes, and color and style preferences of important customers; and telephoning regular customers when a new selection of clothing arrives.

Its best salespeople are motivated to call adjacent Hartwick stores so that their most important clients can get a larger selection of garments to choose among when these clients make an appointment to see their salesperson. The salespeople also know how to sell their clients accessories, such as ties, shirts, and slacks, to coordinate with new sports jackets or suits. See Table 1 for a statement of Hartwick's selling philosophy.

TABLE 1
Hartwick's Philosophy for Effective Salesmanship

❑ All sales personnel should be honest in appraising the style, color, and fit of a garment. Hartwick wants its customers to be satisfied.

❑ When meeting a new client, a salesperson should explain the long-term relationship sought by Hartwick. The client's height and weight, and color, style, and texture preferences should be determined and noted in the salesperson's log. The client's desired price range for various garments should also be recorded. All other company policies, such as free lifetime alterations, should be described.

❑ A salesperson should try to schedule appointments with loyal customers. In this way, undivided attention is given to individual clients, the salesperson can assemble selections in advance of an appointment, and the customer can allocate adequate time for an in-store visit.

❑ The salesperson should be aware of the opportunities available through cross-selling. For example, a sports jacket purchase should lead to the purchase of slacks. Suit buyers should be encouraged to look at ties and shirts. The client should be reminded that the best time to purchase an accessory is when the garment is in the store, so that he can see how it actually looks.

❑ A salesperson should stay with the customer throughout the in-store experience. It is important to verify the need for alterations, and to remind the customer of the date when his garments will be ready. Nonetheless, the client should be allowed to browse throughout the store, if he so desires. The salesperson should be available at his request.

❑ A Hartwick salesperson's job is not complete when the sale is made. Salespeople are expected to be present when the customer returns to pick up the altered garments to verify the fit. This is another opportunity to ensure client satisfaction and to suggest other items (in a subtle way).

❑ Clients should be encouraged to trade up to better-quality garments as they go through their career cycles.

❑ Regular clients should be contacted in advance of special sales to alert them to the opportunity to purchase Hartwick garments, with free alterations, at 10–50 per cent off usual prices. This gives the salesperson another reason to contact customers.

*This case was prepared and written by John L. Roman, Director of Stores, Rochester Institute of Technology.

Hartwick trains its salespeople to be honest with their clients. They are encouraged to tell a client which garment looks better (instead of trying to sell him two garments or the more expensive of the two), to apprise customers of upcoming sales, and to properly judge the quality of alterations. Hartwick further believes that a good salesperson should allow a client to browse, as impulse sales may be stimulated.

Henry Holmes, the manager of Hartwick's Philadelphia store, now faces a difficult task. A new salesperson that Henry hired two months ago, Bill Rice, has been creating quite a bit of discord among Hartwick's current salespeople and some very important customers. Yet, since joining the company, Rice (a former real-estate broker) has had the highest sales volume of any salesperson in Holmes' memory.

These are the causes of Holmes' dilemma:

❑ The other salespeople resent Bill's "working" their customers. Some are even afraid to go to the back office or to call home for fear that Bill will steal their customers as they enter the store.

❑ Bill does not believe that he needs to undertake such essential selling tasks as gathering the styles and colors most preferred by clients from the factory or other stores; to him, this is too time-consuming and may mean waiting to complete a sale. Instead, he tries to "sell" customers on the styles and colors available in the store. He has been known to sell a customer a larger size of a garment and have it altered for free rather than have the customer leave the store without buying anything. Bill feels that the person may not come back when the right-size item is received by the store.

❑ Many customers resent Bill's pushy attitude. While they understand that salespeople have a commission component as part of their earnings, they resent being pressured. In addition, customers often prefer to browse without being bothered. Bill, in contrast, believes that he can stimulate many impulse sales through his assertiveness.

❑ Customers really appreciate salespeople's saying that an item does not fit well, or that a color or style is not right for them. But many feel that Bill will not tell them the truth.

Henry Holmes sees Bill Rice as an "unpolished jewel." However, he knows that he cannot leave the situation unchanged.

QUESTIONS

1. Evaluate Hartwick's philosophy of selling as outlined in Table 1. How would you improve this philosophy?
2. Develop a selling philosophy for a discount men's clothing store selling suits for $119, sports jackets for $79, and outerwear for $79 to $179. The clothing store makes nominal alterations (such as cuffs on slacks) for free.
3. Should Hartwick sales personnel use the canned sales presentation or need-satisfaction approach in dealing with customers? Why? Would your answer be the same for a discount clothing store? Why?
4. What should Henry Holmes do about Bill Rice? Explain your answer.

Harry's Pharmacy: Rethinking Its Store Image and Promotional Strategy*

Introduction

Harry's Pharmacy is a twenty-five-year-old independent drugstore in suburban New Jersey. The store is situated in a string location about 1,000 feet from a popular neighborhood shopping center. Other retailers in the string location are an Italian restaurant, a delicatessen, and a ladies' sportswear shop. The tenants in the neighborhood shopping center include a major chain-supermarket outlet, a butcher shop, a florist, and a stationery store.

While Harry's Pharmacy has been moderately successful, its owner, Harry Walters, is seriously concerned about the planned opening of a new pharmacy department in the shopping center's supermarket. Walters views the supermarket as an especially aggressive competitor and fears if he does not revise his store's image and promotional strategy that Harry's Pharmacy may become unprofitable.

In thinking about various strategy alternatives, Harry has reviewed his store's current image and promotional strategy, analyzed the characteristics of the trading area, studied the performance of the pharmacy departments in two nearby outlets of the supermarket chain, and developed three possible new image and promotional strategies to consider.

Harry's Current Store Image and Promotional Strategy

While Harry Walters has conducted limited formal research concerning his store's image, he feels that he has a solid understanding of the image and the promotional dynamics of his business. Walters reads industry publications, keeps in touch with current customers, and even calls former prescription customers to find out why they no longer use his pharmacy. During the past six months, he has enclosed a questionnaire with monthly customer bills to determine the customers' perceptions of the store's image, merchandise selection, and service. Harry feels confident that he can objectively appraise his image and promotional strategy relative to the supermarket chain and more traditional competitors.

Among the positive store-image attributes of Harry's Pharmacy are its personal service, excellent location, and free delivery. Personal service is perhaps Harry's most important perceived advantage. He will dispense prescriptions based on phone calls from physicians, so that patients have their medicine ready when they arrive at the pharmacy from a doctor's office. Walters readily keeps the store open late at night or comes in early in the morning in the event of emergencies. Harry lives in the same community as his store, posts an emergency phone number on his front window (for customer use), and does not have an unlisted home phone number.

Harry is also trusted by his customers to recommend over-the-counter drugs for such common ailments as sore throats, dandruff, and headaches. Often, chain competitors hire recent pharmacy-school graduates and have significant turnover among their pharmacists. Therefore, customers in those stores are not able to develop a relationship of trust with the pharmacists employed there.

The pharmacy is located on a main road with clear visibility. Parking is plentiful. Community residents are mostly middle-class professionals who can afford impulse purchases, such as small gift items and quality health and beauty aids. Since Harry's Pharmacy has been at the same site since opening in the early 1960s, it has had a loyal customer following, and long-time residents have been extremely loyal. Until now, Harry has benefited by being so near to the supermarket outlet, since consumers often combine supermarket and drugstore shopping on one trip. But the supermarket's new pharmacy may turn this locational advantage into a disadvantage.

Harry's Pharmacy employs several clean-cut and neatly groomed high school students as deliverypersons. The drugstore will deliver prescription medicine to a customer's home with no service charge and no minimum order amount. This service is especially important when a customer or his or her relative is not feeling well enough to drive, the customer is a nondriver, or a parent must remain at home with a sick child. Harry provides free delivery for telephone orders not involving prescriptions if the purchase amount is at least $10.

*The material in this case is drawn from "Customer Service Is the Best Medicine," *Chain Store Age Executive* (December 1987), pp. 50 ff.; "Drug Retailing," *Standard & Poor's Industry Surveys* (January 22, 1987), pp. R87–R94; N. R. Kleinfeld, "Pills—and Peas—at the Pharmacy," *New York Times* (May 31, 1987), p. F4; "New Store Competition Drives Ad Budgets," *Chain Store Age Executive* (December 1987), pp. 16–17; *1986 Nielsen Review of Retail Drug Store Trends* (Northbrook, Ill.: Nielsen Marketing Research), 1986; Janice Suczewski, "Build Strong Store Reputation Through Customers' Perceptions," *Discount Store News* (July 6, 1987), p. 29; "Deep Discount Drug Store Waters Run Still," *Chain Store Age Executive* (March 1988), pp. 102–108; and "F&M Distributors Aims at 100," *Chain Store Age Executive* (March 1988), pp. 109–110.

Walters is also aware of his pharmacy's image weaknesses. These include being perceived as a high-priced store, having a cluttered store interior, and having a lack of excitement in merchandise. Harry feels that his store is perceived by many as having high prices, despite a fair pricing strategy. He attributes this to some potential customers' believing that chain stores have low prices (because of their buying economies and their heavy use of price advertising for items such as perfume, housewares, and paper goods). Harry further feels that his not charging for delivery may be incorrectly viewed by customers as evidence of high markups. Yet, he is convinced that his prices are within 5 per cent of those at chain stores for all prescription drugs by the same manufacturer.

The pharmacy has a cluttered appearance. Its fixtures are about twenty-five years old; the store is not really amenable to self-service; and displays of merchandise are not overly appealing. While Harry knows where all merchandise is located, it may be ten feet above a counter, on the floor, or in the stockroom. Harry acknowledges that some merchandise may be somewhat dusty.

Harry readily admits that his drugstore's nonprescription merchandise lacks a sense of excitement. Unlike many other pharmacies, Harry's does not have a distinctive line of cosmetics, does not have a cosmetician, does not sell gourmet chocolates, and offers only a limited selection of toys (generally aimed at children under three years old). Walters defends his merchandise offerings based upon his view that he is running a pharmacy/health and beauty-aid store. Harry takes great pride in the fact that he stocks the broadest selection of prescription drugs possible, so that he is prepared for relatively rare illnesses.

With regard to promotional strategy, Harry Walters has been quite conservative:

❑ The annual advertising budget has never been more than 1 per cent of sales. Harry has a quarter-page listing in the Yellow Pages and runs a weekly advice column in the local newspaper. He does not advertise via the regular newspaper, flyers, radio, and so on.

❑ In a low-key way, Harry's Pharmacy receives publicity by sponsoring a girl's softball team and a boy's basketball team. Harry also makes appearances at civic group functions to talk about physical fitness.

❑ There are one full-time and four part-time workers who function as sales clerks and cashiers. They are paid a straight salary, are encouraged to be polite, and never sell the customer a product which would be ineffective or inappropriate for that customer. Harry is a stickler for honesty at all times.

❑ Harry uses some sales promotions, such as giving free sugarless lollipops to children and running special in-store sales.

Walters has never really had promotional objectives, certainly not specific ones. His promotion budget has relied on the all-you-can-afford approach; after looking at all other expenses, Harry sets aside an amount for promotion. He has also never thought about advertising in other media or the timing and content of messages throughout the year. Promotion efforts have been implemented in a rather haphazard fashion, with little coordination. Harry realizes this has to change.

Characteristics of the Trading Area

Harry Walters feels that any evaluation of store image and promotional strategy needs to include the shifting demographic characteristics of the residents within his pharmacy's trading area as well as competitive developments.
 According to Walters:

> The area surrounding my store is definitely getting more affluent. This can be seen in the automobiles driven by customers (Mercedes and BMWs have replaced many Fords and Buicks), the doubling of house prices over the past four years, and the increase in the economic base of the region (based on the number of new office-building complexes).

Along with the rising economic wealth of the community, Harry has been observing a change in the age distribution of the population. When he first opened his pharmacy, most of the families were headed by people in their thirties. Now three distinct household age groups are important: households headed by new homeowners in their thirties (they typically have young children who require such items as baby formulas, vitamin and fluoride supplements, and disposable diapers), households headed by people in their forties (whose teenage children are large purchasers of cosmetics), and households headed by people in their sixties (who make up a large proportion of Harry's prescription business). Each year, the proportion of households headed by individuals aged sixty and over is being reduced, as many of these people retire and move to warmer climates.

Walters has noticed that competition both for health and beauty aids and for prescription drugs has markedly increased. In greater numbers, supermarkets and other mass merchandisers, for example, are selling such items as shampoo, lipstick, disposable diapers, toothpaste, over-the-counter medicines, and vitamin supplements as part of their scrambled merchandising and one-stop-shopping philosophy. One discount retailer in Harry's trading area operates a store with used fixtures and self-service; it sells only closeout merchandise (bought from manufacturers that are overstocked). While that retailer has no continuity in merchandise offerings, it can outprice Harry by as much as 50 per cent on the same brand of merchandise.

Walters is very concerned about increased competition from physicians, who are beginning to sell pharmaceutical products (the Pharmaceutical Corporation of America estimates that doctors can make $15,000 to $20,000 a year in extra income by selling drugs directly to their patients); from health maintenance organizations (HMOs) that have on-premises pharmacies; and from mail-order pharmacies that appeal to consumers who are price-conscious and convenience-oriented, and who must use a given drug over an extended time period.

The Supermarket Chain's Drugstore Image and Promotional Strategy

The supermarket outlet in the neighborhood shopping center near Harry's Pharmacy has been open six years. It occupies a total of 30,000 square feet. In planning the new pharmacy department, the supermarket has decided to cut down on several existing departments in order to give the pharmacy 2,300 square feet of space (not counting the store space already devoted to items such as shampoo, gifts, and disposable diapers). Like Harry's Pharmacy, the supermarket location has high vehicular traffic, excellent visibility, and good parking availability.

After studying the supermarket chain's overall performance and analyzing two of its pharmacy departments in nearby stores, Walters has reached these conclusions:

❏ The supermarket chain has been in business for twenty-three years. It has a reputation for clean, well-staffed stores with good assortments and fair prices. It has a superior reputation for cleanliness and freshness.

❏ The chain operates pharmacy departments in over sixty stores. The average annual sales volume per pharmacy department is over $700,000 per store. Harry's yearly revenues are about $650,000.

❏ The number of pharmacy departments operated by the supermarket chain gives it considerable buying power as well as the ability to use broadcast and daily-newspaper media in advertising. The chain spends over $15 million annually on television commercials, newspaper ads, and weekly circulars. It regularly offers store coupons and runs a sweepstakes once a year. While only about 1–2 per cent of advertising actually features pharmacy department items, every ad for the chain stimulates consumer interest in the store.

❏ The chain emphasizes everyday low prices. For example, the pharmacy departments accept union and pension reimbursement plans in full payment on prescriptions; they rebate the typical $1.50 to $2.50 deductible to the customer. When entering a particularly competitive market, the chain gives customers a $10 discount for each long-term prescription assigned to its store from a neighboring pharmacy. In contrast, Harry typically charges prescription customers his wholesale cost plus a $4 fee. If the prescription amount exceeds $15, an additional 10 per cent markup is applied (based in part on the expense of Walters' stocking costly drugs). Harry does not rebate the deductible for customers using insurance plans nor offer special discounts to attract new patrons.

❏ The pharmacists employed in the two departments visited by Harry appear to be in their early twenties. While they are friendly, Walters believes that they do not project themselves as trusted sources of health-related information.

❏ The nonfood departments in supermarket outlets generate a lot of customer traffic. For instance, the video rental department has a wide selection of current videos, and the book department stocks the top-ten best-sellers and has a large selection of paperbacks.

The combination of one-stop shopping, the large selection of merchandise, low prices, heavy advertising, and high-traffic departments (such as videos and books) has

Harry concerned about what will happen once the supermarket outlet, which is virtually across the street from his store, introduces its pharmacy department.

Potential Store Image and Promotional Strategies for Harry's

Harry Walters is convinced that some revisions in his store image and promotional strategy are necessary if he is to be competitive in the future. Harry intends to continue to capitalize on his pharmacy's important strengths (personal service, excellent location, and free delivery), while reducing major weaknesses (perceived high prices, cluttered store interior, and unexciting merchandise). Walters understands that he must develop some kind of consistent promotion strategy, based on defined goals.

Harry has developed three possible strategies to enhance his store image and promotional efforts. He is now deciding whether to enact any or all of these strategies. While each approach involves a significant departure from the manner in which Harry has conducted his store, he is not contemplating any strategy in which the pharmaceutical business is not central to the firm. Harry's philosophy of business, expertise, personal interests, and customer following are all keyed to his running a pharmacy. Furthermore, prescriptions currently account for 45 per cent of his sales and 60 per cent of gross profits.

Various industrywide trends also favor Harry's staying with pharmaceuticals as the central thrust of a store-image and promotional campaign. One, some states have begun allowing pharmacists to prescribe selected drugs (such as remedies for colds and fluoride products). Two, Harry believes that substantial opportunities will exist for selling over-the-counter medicines as more prescription drugs (such as Dimetapp, a cough remedy) change to over-the-counter status. Three, new drug remedies for ulcers, arthritis, and baldness may significantly increase pharmaceutical sales. Four, the national increase in the proportion of the population that is over age sixty raises opportunities for prescription drug sales.

Harry requires that any promotional plan be limited to 3 per cent of sales in the long run; this would triple the amount he has been allocating. Walters realizes that he may have to spend 4–5 per cent of sales on promotion efforts in the short run (the first six months after the new plan is enacted) to develop and reinforce a modified image. However, he wants to control his expenses as much as possible.

The three strategies that Harry is seriously considering involve hiring a full-time cosmetician, adding and promoting seasonal merchandise, and carrying discounted general merchandise. For Harry to select one (or more) of these approaches, he must be certain that it will update his store's image, will be pleasing to existing customers, will draw new customer traffic, and will increase impulse purchases. A good strategy will successfully compete with the supermarket outlet and others.

With the first strategy, Harry would upgrade the image of his cosmetics department by installing attractive mirrored and chrome fixtures and hiring a full-time cosmetician. Harry would then carry a few high-quality cosmetic lines that are not stocked by nearby competitors. The cosmetician and the new product lines would be advertised in the leading newspaper, and in-store demonstrations would take place on a regular basis (such as every Wednesday morning and Friday evening). This strategy would help Harry differentiate his store from other pharmacies, reduce the store's cluttered look, and improve profitability.

A research study conducted by A.C. Nielsen indicates that only 29 per cent of large independent drugstores employ cosmeticians. Yet, independent drugstores with cosmeticians average 147 per cent greater sales for eye makeup, face makeup and creams, and lotions than those without cosmeticians. Furthermore, the use of a cosmetician has increased inventory turnover in these product categories by 32 per cent.

Other advantages of the first strategy would be the appeal to upscale females, the attraction of the pharmacy's convenient location for shoppers who otherwise would have to go to a department store for their cosmetics, the sizable markup when selling these goods at list prices (which would yield a 35–40 per cent profit margin—the same as prescriptions), the potential for reorders, the ease of home delivery, and the exclusivity of merchandise lines (which are not carried by discounters or chain drugstores without cosmeticians).

Under the second strategy, Walters would hire a buyer/merchandiser who would be responsible for developing a department for seasonal merchandise. Events could be sponsored throughout the year and tied to major holidays and seasonal themes. In this plan, the buyer would greatly expand such merchandise categories as greeting cards, chocolate (exclusive brands), watches and costume jewelry, small appliances, toys, and school supplies. A seasonal promotional calendar and an ongoing series of special events would be planned and implemented. Table 1 shows a sample calendar.

Free-standing inserts would be placed in the local newspaper once a month (every other week for the initial six months). Each insert would have a message from Harry Walters on the top one-half page and advertising for seasonal goods on the other page and a half. Harry's messages would be on topics such as the company's free delivery and emergency delivery services, its pricing philosophy, and the importance of a customer's knowing his or her pharmacist.

The advantages of the second strategy would be the new customer traffic generated, the concentration on upscale customers of both genders, the sale of high-profit-margin items, an expanding customer base, trading up gift-item customers (beyond customary chocolates and similar goods), and the use of sincere messages from Harry.

TABLE 1
A Sample Promotional Calendar for Seasonal Merchandise

Month	Emphasis in Advertising and Sales Promotion
January	Snow-related supplies, winter auto accessories
February	Snow-related supplies, winter auto accessories; Valentine's Day gifts, chocolates, cards
March	St. Patrick's Day gifts, chocolates, cards
April	Chocolates, cards, small appliances
May	Mother's Day gifts, chocolates, cards; sunglasses, beach supplies, barbecue supplies
June	Father's Day gifts, cards; suntan lotion, sunglasses, beach supplies, barbecue accessories
July	Suntan lotion, sunglasses, beach supplies, barbecue accessories
August	Same as July plus back-to-school supplies
September	Back-to-school supplies
October	Same as September plus Halloween and Thanksgiving promotions
November	Christmas gifts
December	Same as November plus New Year's promotion

The third strategy would be based on Harry Walters' joining a buying/marketing group for discounted general merchandise. These groups limit membership to noncompeting pharmacies and seek to purchase closeout merchandise, special offers from overstocked manufacturers, and goods with special rebate incentives. Advertising flyers would be prepared by the buying/marketing firm; these flyers are distributed with local weekly newspapers on a monthly basis. The name of the pharmacy and its address, phone number(s), and store hours are individualized to accommodate each member. Past discounted purchases have included hair dryers, Seiko watches, deodorant, paper plates, and beach chairs. These items had retail prices that were one-third to one-half of the customary amounts, while still allowing the pharmacies to have markups of 15–20 per cent.

The advantages of the third strategy would be cooperative promotion on a regular basis, an association with low-priced merchandise that may reduce customer perceptions of Harry's prices, less need to renovate the store, and freedom from some buying and promotion responsibilities.

QUESTIONS

1. Evaluate the store image of Harry's Pharmacy. Make broad recommendations for its exterior, general interior, layout, and displays.
2. Develop a plan for Harry Walters to allocate floor space, classify store offerings, determine space needs, and map out locations for his store's merchandise.
3. Assess Walters' customer service strategy.
4. Comment on Harry's current and proposed promotional efforts.

5. Which of the three promotional strategies under consideration should Harry select? Why? Could he utilize all three approaches? Explain your answer.

6. Analyze the promotional calendar in Table 1.

7. Present an integrated promotional plan for Harry's Pharmacy, including objectives, budget, and promotional mix.

PART EIGHT

Planning for the Future

☐ *In Part Eight, three aspects of retailing that are crucial in anticipating, planning for, and responding to the future are detailed.*

☐ *Chapter 16 ties together the elements of a retail strategy that have been described throughout the text. The chapter examines planning and opportunity analysis, performance measures, productivity, and the uses of new technology. The value of industrywide data comparisons is studied. Strategic control via the retail audit is covered.*

☐ *Chapter 17 focuses on how firms offering rented-goods, owned-goods, and nongoods services can develop and enact good strategies, as well as prepare for the future. These retailers must address the intangibility of service offerings, the inseparability of services from their providers, the perishability of services, and the variability of service performance.*

☐ *Chapter 18 looks at the dynamic, changing environment with which retailers must cope. To attain and maintain long-run success, retailers must understand how their environment is expected to change in the future and react accordingly. In this chapter, consumer demographic and life-style trends are projected. The impact of consumerism is forecast. The expected technology available to retailers and emerging retail institutions are noted. The evolving international environment of retailing is considered.*

Chapter 16

Integrating and Controlling the Retail Strategy

□ **Chapter Objectives** □

1 To demonstrate the importance of integrating a retail strategy

2 To examine four key factors in the development and enactment of an integrated retail strategy: planning and opportunity analysis, performance measures, productivity, and the uses of new technology

3 To show how industrywide data can be used in strategy planning and analysis

4 To explain the principles of a retail audit, its utility in controlling a retail strategy, and the difference between horizontal and vertical audits

5 To provide examples of audit forms

Mrs. Fields' Cookies is a chain of more than 700 stores in thirty-seven states and several foreign countries that is run by Debbi and Randy Fields. These stores are all company-owned (none are franchised) and sell homemade-style cookies, brownies, and frozen snacks. Because Mrs. Fields' Cookies has so many geographically dispersed outlets, one of the chain's real challenges is to integrate and control its retail strategy to ensure consistency and superior performance at each outlet.

Mrs. Fields' Cookies uses a Tandy computer system, which links in-store personal computers with the corporate data base in Park City, Utah, and also allows store managers to communicate with their sales managers and their regional operations directors. The firm has developed its own computer software, which does an excellent job of integrating efforts and monitoring results.

At the beginning of a day, every store manager uses the Day Planner program in his or her personal computer to project that day's sales based on prior periods. The program provides hourly projections by product, and it takes into account day of the week and type of day (e.g., normal versus holiday). It tells the manager how many customers will be needed and what they must buy to reach the day's sales goal, when to bake products, and how to act if sales are less than expected.

The computer system also accomplishes the following:

□ Debbi Fields can directly "talk" to her store managers and offer suggestions.

□ Store personnel needs can be scheduled two weeks in advance, based on sales forecasts.

□ It facilitates the interviewing process for new

employees. There is an interviewing software program that suggests questions for the store manager to ask. The answers are then keyed into the computer, which scores applicants on the basis of the traits of successful and unsuccessful past employees.

❑ Payroll and employee records are kept in the computer and can easily be called up for analysis.

❑ A store maintenance software program helps the manager diagnose problems and suggests possible solutions (such as how to repair a mixer).

As Randy Fields says, "MIS in this company has always had to serve two masters. First, control. Rapid growth without control equals disaster. We needed to keep improving control over our stores. And second, information that leads to control also leads to better decision making. To the extent that the information is then provided to the store and field-management level, the decisions that are made there are better, and they are more easily made. That has been our consistent vision."[1]

Overview

Throughout the text, a variety of individual factors pertaining to the development of retail strategies have been examined. This chapter focuses on integrating and controlling retail strategy. Accordingly, the chapter ties together the material detailed previously, shows why it is necessary for retailers to plan and enact coordinated strategies, and describes how to assess success or failure.

Integrating the Retail Strategy

It is vital that a retailer view strategy planning as an integrated and ongoing process and not as a fragmented and one-time-only concept. As Figure 16-1 shows, Kay Jewelers understands this well. One of the major goals of this text has been to explain the interrelationships between the various stages of strategy and the need to operate in an integrated format. Figure 16-2, reproduced from Chapter 2, shows the overall development of a retail strategy and how the steps are interconnected and integrated. Figure 16-3 highlights the integrated strategy of Swiss Colony, a retailer of gift foods and related merchandise.

In particular, four fundamental factors need to be considered in developing and enacting any integrated retail strategy: planning procedures and opportunity analysis, performance measures, productivity, and the uses of new technology. These factors are discussed next.

Planning Procedures and Opportunity Analysis

Planning procedures can be optimized by following a series of coordinated activities. First, senior management outlines the general direction and goals of the firm. Next, written guidelines are provided to middle- and lower-level managers. Then, these managers get input from all types of internal and external sources. Fourth, middle- and lower-level managers are encouraged to offer new ideas at an early stage of planning. Fifth, top-down (generated by upper management) and bottom-up or horizontal (generated by middle- and lower-level management) plans are combined. Finally, specific plans are presented, including checkpoints and dates.[2] By following these activities, planning is made systematic and information is acquired from all types of relevant sources.

Opportunities need to be systematically examined in terms of their impact on overall strategy, and not in an isolated manner. For example, Woolworth variety stores now emphasize merchandise in which Woolworth can excel, such as health and beauty aids, candy, handbags, stationery, notions, children's wear, and hosiery. More ego-sensitive merchandise classifications (such as shoes and women's apparel) have been scaled down or eliminated.

When evaluating new opportunities, retailers should develop some form of **sales opportunity grid**, which rates the promise of new goods, services, and/or

At Kay Jewelers, the beauty of fine jewelry is combined with the business of merchandising. The "Kay Exclusive" jewelry design process profiled here shows the special Kay Jewelers approach to every aspect of merchandising, from initial design to final sale.

1. Merchandise Positioning.
Kay Jewelers buyers strive to anticipate consumers' desires. Our buyer notes that diamond and precious gem combinations are increasingly sought after, and suggests a necklace and earring set.

2. Design Proposal.
A designer is given the parameters: a pear-shaped sapphire and round diamond combination in a necklace and earrings. More than a dozen preliminary sketches are assessed by the buyer and top management.

3. Preliminary Casting.
Designs selected for execution are carved in wax, a mold is made, and the jewelry is casted by artisans. With input from management, fine-tuning decisions are made about weight, polishing, angles, etc.

4. Test Marketing.
Kay Jewelers executives agree on a test market. Past experience shows that test marketing as few as 25 pieces over just six weeks can yield very accurate estimates, used to project chainwide distribution and sales figures.

5. Manufacturing.
Kay's purchasing agents buy gems and precious metals strictly for projected need and do not maintain substantial inventories of raw materials vulnerable to wide fluctations in market value. Kay realizes cost efficiencies by subcontracting jewelry manufacture to outside goldsmiths.

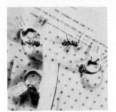

6. Quality Control.
Inspectors examine each item for gold content, quality of finish, gold and diamond weights, and proper setting. The items are scrutinized again in the store before they are put into inventory.

7. Retail Showcasing.
When the new merchandise arrives in the stores, the excitement among store personnel guarantees that it will be featured prominently in displays.

8. Advertising/Promotion
The public hears about the "Kay Exclusive Line" through advertising in print and on the radio. It is emphasized that these pieces are Company designs, meet high standards of quality, and are backed by Kay's warranties.

9. Warranty.
The new design carries our lifetime guarantee, the most extensive in the business, of a trade-in allowance at least 25% greater than the original purchase price after five years. Customers also are protected from the loss of a diamond from its setting.

10. Inventory Control.
Kay Jewelers salespeople tally all purchases on in-store point-of-sale terminals. Within 24 hours, a printout of sales results by specific item allows us to make accurate reordering and forecasting decisions.

This "Kay Exclusive" item. (pictured at right). a diamond and sapphire earring and necklace set. illustrates the step-by-step process through which fashion trends are transformed into new designs and increased sales.

FIGURE 16-1
Kay Jewelers' 'Facets of a Sale'
Reprinted by permission.

store outlets across a variety of criteria.[3] In this way, opportunities may be evaluated on the basis of the integrated strategies the retailers would follow if the opportunities are pursued.

Table 16-1 shows a sales opportunity grid for a large supermarket that wants to select one brand of salad dressing from among two alternatives. The supermarket's manager has specified the integrated strategy that would be followed for each brand; Brand A is established, whereas Brand B is new. Because of its newness, the manager believes initial sales of Brand B would be lower, but total first year sales would be similar. The brands would be priced the same and

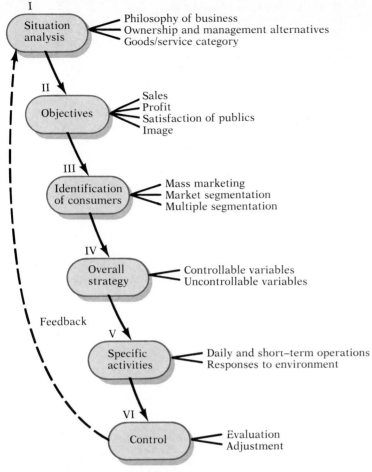

I

Situation analysis
— Philosophy of business
— Ownership and management alternatives
— Goods/service category

II

Objectives
— Sales
— Profit
— Satisfaction of publics
— Image

III

Identification of consumers
— Mass marketing
— Market segmentation
— Multiple segmentation

IV

Overall strategy
— Controllable variables
— Uncontrollable variables

Feedback

V

Specific activities
— Daily and short–term operations
— Responses to environment

VI

Control
— Evaluation
— Adjustment

FIGURE 16-2
Elements of a Retail Strategy

occupy identical floor space. Brand B would require more display costs but would offer the store a larger markup. Brand B would return a greater total gross profit ($781 to $613) and net profit ($271 to $193) than Brand A by the end of the first year. On the basis of the overall grid depicted in Table 16-1, the store manager would choose Brand B. However, if the supermarket is more concerned about immediate profit, Brand A might be chosen instead, because it is expected to take B much longer to be accepted by consumers.

Performance Measures

By determining the relevant measures of performance and setting standards (goals) for each of them, a retailer can better develop and integrate its strategy. Among the **performance measures** frequently used by retailers are total sales revenues, sales revenue by goods/service category, gross margins in dollars and percentages, sales per square foot, gross margin return on investment, inventory turnover, markdown percentages, employee turnover, financial ratios, and profitability.

Retailers of varying sizes and in different goods or service lines can acquire a lot of industrywide data for firms such as themselves from secondary data

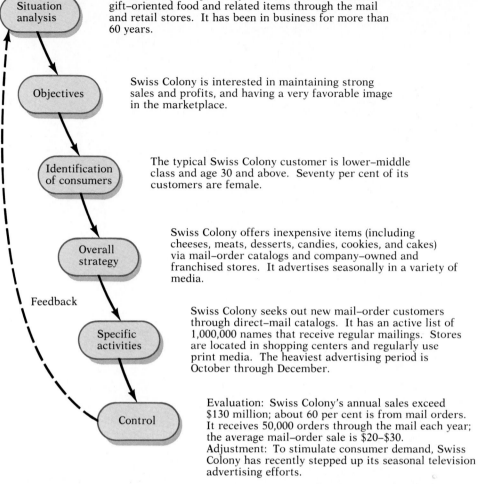

Swiss Colony is a privately owned retailer that sells gift–oriented food and related items through the mail and retail stores. It has been in business for more than 60 years.

Swiss Colony is interested in maintaining strong sales and profits, and having a very favorable image in the marketplace.

The typical Swiss Colony customer is lower–middle class and age 30 and above. Seventy per cent of its customers are female.

Swiss Colony offers inexpensive items (including cheeses, meats, desserts, candies, cookies, and cakes) via mail–order catalogs and company–owned and franchised stores. It advertises seasonally in a variety of media.

Swiss Colony seeks out new mail–order customers through direct–mail catalogs. It has an active list of 1,000,000 names that receive regular mailings. Stores are located in shopping centers and regularly use print media. The heaviest advertising period is October through December.

Evaluation: Swiss Colony's annual sales exceed $130 million; about 60 per cent is from mail orders. It receives 50,000 orders through the mail each year; the average mail–order sale is $20–$30.
Adjustment: To stimulate consumer demand, Swiss Colony has recently stepped up its seasonal television advertising efforts.

FIGURE 16-3
The Integrated Retail Strategy of Swiss Colony
Source: Compiled by the authors from "Leading Food Company Profiles," *Direct Marketing* (June 1987), p. 81.

sources such as *Progressive Grocer, Stores, Discount Store News, Chain Store Age,* Dun & Bradstreet, the National Retail Merchants Association, and Robert Morris Associates. This information enables retailers to use industry norms to set company standards. Tables 16-2 through 16-6 contain a wide range of industry performance data for a number of retail categories and provide a large amount of information that could be used by individual retailers to set their own performance standards.

Tables 16-2 and 16-3 present industry performance data for supermarkets. Table 16-2 shows sales and gross margins for each product category in a supermarket. For example, in a typical supermarket, perishable items account for the largest percentage of overall store sales and dollar gross margin. Sales are lowest for syrups, dried fruits, and desserts and toppings and highest for meat, dairy, and produce. The gross margin for baby foods is only 9.3 per cent of their sales, while it is 35.5 per cent of sales for general merchandise. Although general merchandise accounts for just 4.5 per cent of store sales, it contributes 6.6 per cent of overall store dollar gross margin.

TABLE 16-1
A Supermarket's Sales Opportunity Grid for Two Brands of Salad Dressing

	Brand	
Criteria	A (established)	B (new)
Retail price	$1.29/bottle	$1.29/bottle
Floor space needed	8 square feet	8 square feet
Display costs	$10.00/month	$20.00/month for 6 mos.
		$10.00/month thereafter
Operating costs	$0.12/unit	$0.12/unit
Markup	19%	22%
Sales estimate		
During first month		
Units	250	50
Dollars	$323	$65
During first six months		
Units	1,400	500
Dollars	$1,806	$645
During first year		
Units	2,500	2,750
Dollars	$3,225	$3,548
Gross profit estimate*		
During first month	$ 61	$ 14
During first six months	$343	$142
During first year	$613	$781
Net profit estimate†		
During first month	$ 21	−$ 12
During first six months	$115	−$ 38
During first year	$193	$271

*Gross profit estimate = Sales estimate − [(1.00 − Markup percentage) × (Sales estimate)]
Example: Brand A gross profit estimate during first six months = $1,806 − [(1.00 − 0.19) × ($1,806)] =
$1,806 − [(0.81) × ($1,806)] = $343

†Net profit estimate = Gross profit estimate − (Display costs + Operating costs)
Example: Brand A net profit estimate during first six months = $343 − ($60 + $168) = $115

Table 16-3 provides many industry performance statistics for independent supermarkets, classified by store size. In this way, industrywide performance can be compared for small, medium, and large independent supermarkets. From the table, it is clear that large supermarkets are significantly more efficient than smaller ones. Several measures support this, for example, sales per employee, sales per square foot of selling space, average customer transaction size, and inventory turnover. Smaller supermarkets must keep this in mind when designing their strategies and setting performance standards. These standards should realistically reflect the impact of store size on results.

Table 16-4 provides industry performance data for department stores with annual sales of $2 million and above. Here are just a few of the conclusions that can be reached by studying this table: sales per square foot are highest for cosmetics and drugs and lowest for home furnishings; the level of selling salaries is highest for shoes and lowest for female apparel; the level of advertising varies little by product category; stock shortages are highest for female apparel and recreation items; female apparel yields by far the highest gross margin return on inventory investment; annual turnover for furnishings and shoes is low; and cosmetics and drugs are rarely marked down. Individual retailers should set their own performance standards for each category of merchandise they carry, based on the special characteristics of the product category.

TABLE 16-2
Supermarket Sales by Product Category, 1986*

Product Category	Dollar Sales (mil.)	% of Store Sales	Dollar Gross Margin (mil.)	% of Store Gross Margin	Gross Margin Percentage†
Baby foods	1,193.76	0.54	111.32	0.21	9.3
Baking needs	4,015.76	1.83	848.60	1.60	21.1
Beer and wine	6,599.99	3.01	1,527.43	2.89	23.1
Breakfast foods	4,829.66	2.20	936.49	1.77	19.4
Candy and gum	2,610.88	1.19	824.04	1.56	31.6
Coffee	3,968.60	1.81	583.80	1.10	14.7
Cookies and crackers	4,609.27	2.10	1,107.98	2.10	24.0
Desserts and toppings	582.65	0.27	142.11	0.27	24.4
Diet and low-calorie foods	905.66	0.41	239.96	0.45	26.5
Dressings	1,431.38	0.65	290.19	0.55	20.3
Dried fruits	458.66	0.21	135.50	0.26	29.5
Dried vegetables	713.53	0.33	186.49	0.35	26.1
Fish	1,784.51	0.81	360.22	0.68	20.2
Fruit	1,128.57	0.51	266.68	0.50	23.6
Juice	2,929.66	1.33	623.38	1.18	21.3
Meat and specialty foods	1,243.80	0.57	308.46	0.58	24.8
Nuts	830.60	0.38	244.91	0.46	29.5
Pasta products	1,175.44	0.54	299.26	0.57	25.5
Pickles and olives	849.45	0.39	245.46	0.46	28.9
Sauces	2,079.60	0.95	498.36	0.94	24.0
Snacks	3,271.88	1.49	956.59	1.81	29.2
Soft drinks and mixes	8,483.84	3.87	2,339.13	4.42	27.6
Soup	1,668.16	0.76	356.53	0.67	21.4
Spices and extracts	774.22	0.35	269.77	0.51	34.8
Spreads	1,059.36	0.48	226.52	0.43	21.4
Syrups	445.36	0.20	102.17	0.19	22.9
Tea	735.81	0.34	168.05	0.32	22.8
Vegetables	2,476.51	1.13	602.23	1.14	24.3
Total grocery food	**62,856.57**	**28.63**	**14,801.63**	**27.99**	**23.5**
Household supplies	7,780.22	3.54	1,715.40	3.24	22.0
Paper, plastic, film, and foil	8,305.00	3.78	1,473.58	2.79	17.7
Pet foods	4,485.72	2.04	955.67	1.81	21.3
Tobacco products	7,749.95	3.53	1,067.58	2.02	13.8
Total grocery nonfoods	**28,320.89**	**12.90**	**5,212.23**	**9.86**	**18.4**
Bakery foods	7,585.89	3.46	1,555.11	2.94	20.5
Dairy products	20,665.49	9.41	4,724.65	8.94	22.9
Delicatessen	5,163.25	2.35	1,432.78	2.71	27.7
Frozen foods	13,903.28	6.33	3,811.14	7.21	27.4
Ice cream	2,283.61	1.04	698.78	1.32	30.6
Meat	36,994.74	16.85	7,509.92	14.20	20.3
Produce	19,449.63	8.86	6,301.68	11.92	32.4
Total perishables	**106,045.89**	**48.32**	**26,034.06**	**49.24**	**24.5**
General merchandise	**9,827.37**	**4.48**	**3,488.72**	**6.60**	**35.5**
Health and beauty aids	**8,679.67**	**3.95**	**2,222.00**	**4.20**	**25.6**
Unclassified††	**3,769.61**	**1.72**	**1,115.80**	**2.11**	**29.6**
Total supermarket	**219,500.00**	**100.00**	**52,874.44**	**100.00**	**24.1**

*There are small rounding errors in the table.

†Does not take into consideration in-store promotions, markdowns, deals, or allowances.

††Includes goods and services such as pharmacy, fresh fish, catering, sit-down eating, bakery, seasonal merchandise, liquor, and money orders.

Source: "Supermarket Sales by Category," *Progressive Grocer* (July 1987), p. 46. Reprinted by permission.

TABLE 16-3
Selected Performance Data for Independent Supermarkets, 1986

Performance Measure	Annual Store Sales		
	$2–4 million	$6–8 million	$12+ million
Weekly sales/checkout	$13,315	$19,973	$31,320
Weekly sales/employee	$ 2,819	$ 3,362	$ 4,007
Sales/employee hour	$ 70.94	$ 84.23	$100.29
Store sales/hour	$ 625	$ 1,279	$ 2,723
Weekly sales/square foot of selling area	$ 5.61	$ 7.59	$ 11.59
Average selling area (square feet)	10,257	17,892	30,132
Average total store area (square feet)	13,497	23,486	40,724
Average number of items stocked	9,083	13,984	19,544
Average inventory value (thousands)	$ 194	$ 383	$ 735
Number of weekly transactions	5,858	9,791	17,077
Average customer transaction size	9.84	$ 13.88	$ 20.29
Annual inventory turnover	12.8	15.3	20.8
Number of checkouts	4.4	6.8	11.2
Number of full-time employees	13.2	23.8	47.2
Number of part-time employees	14.3	32.3	86.5
Hours open per week (median)	90	97	117
Percentage open on Sunday	87	93	91
Percentage open 24 hours	7	17	45

Source: "54th Annual Report of the Grocery Industry," *Progressive Grocer* (April 1987), pp. 20–21. Reprinted by permission.

TABLE 16-4
Selected 1986 Performance Data for Department Stores with Annual Sales of $2 Million and Above

Performance Measures	Product Category						
	Shoes	Female Apparel	Men's & Boys' Apparel	Children's Apparel	Home Furnishings	Recreation	Cosmetics and Drugs
Net sales as % of total store	4.4	35.0	15.3	5.6	14.9	3.3	6.2
Annual net sales per square foot	$178.50	$129.00	$141.00	$96.00	$74.00	$106.00	$241.00
Selling salaries as % of category's sales	9.7	5.9	6.5	8.4	8.2	8.7	8.0
Buying salaries as % of category's sales	NA*	2.0	1.7	3.5	2.0	3.6	2.4
Advertising as % of category's sales	3.0	2.4	2.8	2.8	3.2	2.7	2.6
Stock shortages as % of category's sales	1.0	2.7	2.1	1.8	1.5	2.6	0.8
Gross margin as % of category's sales	41.2	43.5	41.5	41.4	37.1	32.8	39.0
Gross margin return per dollar of inventory investment (GMROI)	1.60	3.10	2.20	2.40	1.20	1.20	1.50
Stock turnover (times per year)	1.9	3.4	2.6	2.7	1.8	2.0	2.1
Markdowns as % of category's sales	23.9	26.3	21.3	22.2	14.4	12.8	1.7

*NA means data not available.

Source: "New MOR: New Data," *Stores* (January 1988), p. 123. From *MOR Merchandising and Operating Results of Department and Specialty Stores in 1986.* Copyright National Retail Merchants Association. Reprinted by permission.

Table 16-5 displays performance statistics for fifteen leading full-line discount stores. An analysis of this table reveals the following: Sales per store vary dramatically; while Meijer's annual per-store sales are over $26.4 million, Dollar General and Family Dollar have annual per-store sales of only $422,000 and $441,000, respectively. Yearly sales per square foot range from $63 for Family Dollar to $179 for Target. Nonetheless, Family Dollar has very respectable pretax earnings as a percentage of sales of 6.4. What this all means is that full-line discount stores can succeed under many different approaches with regard to per-store sales and store size. Other factors not represented in Table 16-5, such as gross margins and customer loyalty, must also be taken into account when setting performance standards as a full-line discounter.

Table 16-6 presents median key business ratios for a number of retailer categories. Each of the ratios in this table has a strong impact on the short- and long-run performance of retailers. The definitions of these ratios are as follows:

❑ Quick ratio—cash plus accounts receivable divided by total current liabilities, those due within one year. This ratio establishes the retailer's liquidity. A ratio greater than 1 to 1 means the firm is liquid and therefore easily able to cover short-term liabilities.

❑ Current ratio—total current assets (including cash, accounts receivable, inventories, and marketable securities) divided by total current liabilities. A ratio of 2 to 1 or more is considered good.

❑ Collection period—accounts receivable divided by net sales and then multiplied by 365. This ratio measures the quality of accounts receivable (the amounts due, but not yet paid by customers). In general, when most sales are on credit, any collection period more than one-third over normal selling

TABLE 16-5
Selected 1986 Performance Data for 15 Leading Full-Line Discount Store Chains*

Discount Chain	1986 Sales (millions)	Number of Stores (as of 12/31/86)	Estimated 1986 Sales/Store	Average Store Size (square ft.)	1986 Sales/ Square Foot	1986 Pre-tax Earnings (millions)†	Pre-tax Earnings as % of 1986 Company Sales†
K mart	$22,107	2,204	$10,030,000	60,000	$167	$1,311	5.9
Wal-Mart	10,200	980	10,408,000	65,000	160	846	8.3
Target	4,355	246	17,703,000	99,000	179	311	7.1
Zayre	3,046	362	8,414,000	53,000	159	130	4.3
Bradlees	1,900	162	11,728,000	NA‡	NA‡	57	3.0
Ames	1,888	321	5,882,000	51,000	115	54	2.9
Caldor	1,411	114	12,377,000	94,000	132	75	5.3
Meijer	1,400	53	26,415,000	NA‡	NA‡	NA‡	NA‡
Hills	1,343	136	9,875,000	65,000	152	94	7.0
Rose's	1,199	222	5,401,000	37,000	146	24	2.0
Venture	1,100	65	16,923,000	107,000	158	80	7.3
Fred Meyer	1,074	93	11,548,000	99,000	117	23	2.1
Gold Circle	969	76	12,750,000	109,000	117	32	3.3
Dollar General	565	1,339	422,000	6,000	70	4	0.7
Family Dollar	488	1,107	441,000	7,000	63	31	6.4

*Based on general merchandise sales only.

†Includes interest expenses, corporate expenses, and other unusual items.

‡NA means data not available.

Source: Computed by the authors from "Discount Industry Annual Report," *Discount Store News* (July 20, 1987), pp. 27–28. Reprinted by permission. Copyright Lebhar-Friedman, Inc., 425 Park Avenue, N.Y., N.Y., 10022.

TABLE 16-6
Median Key Business Ratios for Selected Retailer Categories, 1987

Line of Business	Quick Ratio (times)	Current Ratio (times)	Collection Period (days)	Assets to Net Sales (%)	Accounts Payable to Net Sales (%)	Return on Net Sales (%)	Return on Net Worth (%)
Lumber and other building materials dealers	1.0	2.5	34.2	40.7	5.1	2.6	10.8
Hardware stores	0.8	3.6	18.3	52.2	4.9	3.2	10.0
Department stores	1.2	3.3	32.9	50.5	4.5	1.6	6.1
Grocery stores	0.6	2.3	2.9	19.1	2.3	1.6	15.7
Car dealers (new and used)	0.2	1.3	6.6	24.2	0.9	1.5	18.8
Auto and home supply stores	0.9	2.4	24.1	40.6	6.6	2.7	11.1
Gasoline service stations	1.0	2.3	7.3	20.1	2.1	2.4	15.9
Men's and boys' clothing stores	0.8	3.4	14.6	50.8	5.6	4.2	12.8
Women's ready-to-wear stores	0.9	3.4	14.6	45.7	4.8	5.3	15.9
Family clothing stores	0.9	4.0	15.0	54.6	4.4	4.5	11.6
Shoe stores	0.4	3.0	6.2	48.1	6.5	4.6	13.4
Furniture stores	1.0	2.9	31.4	49.4	5.0	3.6	11.1
Radio and television stores	0.6	2.0	10.2	35.9	4.3	3.9	20.5
Eating places	0.7	1.2	5.5	34.0	2.7	3.6	15.1
Sporting-goods and bicycle stores	0.5	2.9	8.0	43.8	5.9	4.5	16.4
Drug and proprietary stores	0.9	3.0	15.0	30.9	4.6	3.5	17.7
Jewelry stores	0.8	3.3	23.7	69.4	7.7	5.5	13.1
Hobby, toy, and game shops	0.5	2.9	4.8	43.6	4.5	4.2	16.9
Gift and novelty shops	0.8	3.7	6.2	50.5	4.0	5.4	17.6
Sewing, needlework, and piece-goods stores	0.5	4.1	4.8	52.8	5.2	4.5	13.4
Mail-order houses	0.9	2.3	15.7	35.7	5.0	4.7	19.3
Vending-machine operators	0.5	1.4	4.8	37.1	3.4	3.5	14.9
Direct-selling companies	1.1	2.1	22.5	32.9	3.5	5.7	29.3
Florists	1.1	2.2	23.4	34.0	3.8	4.5	18.7
Newsstands	0.8	2.4	15.7	29.2	5.6	3.6	13.7

Source: 1987–88 Industry Norms and Key Business Ratios (New York: Dun & Bradstreet, 1987), pp. 145–160. Reprinted by permission.

terms (e.g., 40.0 for 30-day credit arrangements) indicates slow-turning accounts receivable.

❑ Assets to net sales—total assets divided by annual net sales. This ratio links sales and the total investment needed to generate those sales. An excessively low number may indicate financial difficulty. A high number may indicate that the firm's policies are too conservative.

❑ Accounts payable to net sales—accounts payable divided by annual net sales. This compares how a retailer pays suppliers relative to volume transacted. A figure larger than the industry average may indicate that the retailer relies on suppliers to finance operations.

❑ Return on net sales (profit margin)—net dollar profit after taxes divided by annual net sales. This measures profitability per dollar of sales.

❑ Return on net worth—net dollar profit after taxes divided by net worth. This ratio is used to examine the ability of management to achieve an adequate return on the capital invested. Generally, 10 per cent is regarded as a desirable objective.[4]

From Table 16-6, a hardware store manager or owner would learn that the industry average is an extremely poor quick ratio of 0.8; liquid assets are less than current liabilities. The current ratio of 3.6 is quite good, mostly because of the value of inventory on hand. The collection period of 18.3 days is moderate, considering that many small purchases are paid for by cash. Assets to net sales are strong, 52.2 per cent, another indicator of the value of inventory. Accounts payable of 4.9 per cent of sales is good. The return on net sales of 3.2 per cent is a low-to-middle figure for retailing. The return on net worth percentage of 10.0 is barely acceptable. In sum, on average, hardware stores require inventory and other investments and yield a low-to-medium profit.

Productivity

As noted in Chapter 10, productivity refers to the efficiency with which a retail strategy is carried out; and it is in any retailer's interest to reach sales and profit goals while keeping control over costs. The most productive retail strategies are those that are well integrated in terms of the target market, retailer location and operations, merchandising, pricing, and communications efforts.

The retailer must be careful when enacting its strategy. On the one hand, it does not want to incur unnecessarily high expenses. For example, a firm would not want to have eight salespeople working at the same time if four of them could satisfactorily handle all customers. Likewise, it would not want to pay a high rent for a location in a new regional shopping center if its customers would be willing to travel a few miles further to a less expensive site. On the other hand, a retailer would not want to lose customers because there are insufficient sales personnel to handle the rush of shoppers during peak hours. Furthermore, it would not want to be in a low-rent location if this would result in a significant decline in customer traffic.

This means that often neither the least expensive retail strategy nor the most expensive retail strategy would be the most productive retail strategy, since the former approach might not adequately service customers and the latter approach might be wasteful. The most productive approach would be one which implements a specific integrated retail strategy (e.g., a full-service jewelry store) as efficiently as possible. As a result, a productive strategy for an upscale retailer would be far different from that for a discounter. For instance, an upscale retailer would not succeed with self-service operations, and it would be unnecessary (and inefficient) for a discounter to have a large sales staff.

Prange's, a department store chain with outlets in Wisconsin, Illinois, and Michigan, is an example of a retailer with a well-integrated and productive strategy. Its key target market consists of married women, aged twenty-five to forty-four, with children and an annual household income of $30,000:

> She is conservative and very family-oriented. If she works, it's not to drive a Cadillac or take a yearly trip to Bermuda. It's to drive an Oldsmobile and maybe take a vacation every ten years. Our customer works to improve the life-style of her family. That's whom we merchandise to and that's how we market our stores.

Prange's does not try to be all things to all customers. Its stores are positioned to "meet the needs of customers and stay within these boundaries." It does not "try to lead or change the customer." This focus enables it to be more productive:

> We recognize that there are certain core businesses that we must own in our market-place. To these we not only assign the best available talent, but give priority physical location, make an inventory statement, and provide a content assortment and a price so superior to the competition that it takes them a minimum of one year to catch up. We recognize that our markets are very active and casual, rather than being formal and sophisticated. So in our markets, if we own the misses' sportswear business, we're going to basically own a woman's wardrobe. And we've always had a very high penetration in this business.[5]

How Do You Rejuvenate a "Plain-Jane" Retailer?

For many years, Carter Hawley Hale (CHH), the parent company of the Broadway, Emporium Capwell, Thalhimers, and Weinstock's department store chains, has had a reputation as a "plain-Jane" retailer. Even Philip Hawley, the firm's chief executive, once remarked that "department stores have been charging customers more and giving them less. That is not a sure-fire formula for success." This was brought on by overexpansion, poor cost control, and a reduction in key customer services.

To turn around Carter Hawley Hale, whose earnings dropped from $69 million in 1979 to $4 million in 1986, the firm has embarked on an aggressive, well-integrated strategy. CHH is hiring better salespeople and using an intensive training program for them (based on that used by Neiman-Marcus, once a division of Carter Hawley Hale). It has spent $90 million to hire more salespeople and to convert its salesperson compensation system from straight salary to commission; salespeople now receive 6 per cent of sales. This has increased employee motivation and pro-

ductivity, and reduced absenteeism on busy days.

The merchandising focus has been sharpened. There is greater emphasis on mid-priced brands, private-label items, and women's and men's wear. "The game is really to have less of what customers don't want and more of what they do want—it's that simple." As a result, markdowns are used to move slow-sellers and keep merchandise current. At the same time, CHH hopes to minimize the need for sales by setting more realistic beginning-of-season prices.

CHH has implemented a basic stock system to reduce out-of-stock situations. Today, its stores run out of stock half as often as typical department stores, and because the system can reorder items automatically, company buyers can devote more time to fashion merchandising and less to tracking down inventory.

Nonetheless, CHH still needs to remodel many stores and generate more excitement for customers before its strategy can be fully successful. Says Philip Hawley, "If it's a ten-mile journey, then we're four miles down the road."

Source: Based on material in Bill Saporito, "Makeover for a Plain-Jane Retailer," *Fortune* (April 11, 1988), pp. 68–71.

Uses of New Technology

Throughout the text, new retail technology, such as computerized retail information systems, has been described. New technology is also discussed in Chapter 18. In this section, examples of how retailers are using technology in integrating their strategies are presented.

Day & Palin IGA is a small Illinois supermarket chain that has implemented a new computer-based program to control labor, advertising, and merchandising costs as well to make department managers more knowledgeable. The chain acquired an IBM PC, an Epson printer, and relevant software programs for about $4,000. Then all types of data were keyed into the system and reviewed regularly. Said one executive, "We found out things about our sales, our merchandising abilities, our staff potential—and about our competitors—that we never knew before." As a result, Day & Palin IGA has increased its gross margins by over 1 per cent (a very large amount for a supermarket).[6]

Walgreens operates over 1,300 pharmacies throughout the United States. It considers itself "the industry leader in technology." Walgreens is utilizing several technological advances in planning, implementing, and monitoring its retail strategy mix:

❑ Intercom—This is a computer system that links all outlets in the chain. It enables a customer to go into any Walgreens pharmacy across the nation

537

and have his or her records accessed by that pharmacy. Prescription transfers between Walgreens outlets can be made automatically.

❑ WIN (Walgreens Information Network)—This system aids individual pharmacies and Walgreens' senior executives in cash and inventory management, credit card transactions, price changes, managing employee payrolls, and so on. WIN will be installed in all stores by the early 1990s and will connect stores, offices, and distribution centers.

❑ Scanning—By 1990, Walgreens expects to have point-of-purchase scanners in every store. These will yield faster and more accurate checkout service, payroll savings, better sales and inventory data, and so on.

❑ Inventory management study—Walgreens is now engaged in a "major, multiyear systems development effort. The ultimate goals are to improve in-stock conditions for better customer service, and to substantially increase inventory turnover."[7]

The Hechinger chain of home centers for do-it-yourselfers (billed as "the world's most unusual lumber yards") has more than seventy stores in Washington, D.C., Virginia, Pennsylvania, North Carolina, Ohio, Maryland, South Carolina, and other states. It has been quite active in applying new technology to further integrate its strategy:

Our computerized distribution system, developed in-house, is the most sophisticated in the industry. Designed to ship to our stores no less than twice a week, it maximizes the amount shipped on each truck with the use of a computerized merchandise cubing support system. In addition to expediting delivery of advertised goods to our stores, our system of strong centralized distribution allows us to handle seasonal and imported goods, as well as bulk quantities.

Besides supporting the distribution center, our state-of-the-art management information systems play a crucial role in all of our operations. Last year we made several key improvements to the system, including a new credit authorization system that speeds up checkouts, an automatic markdown system that eliminates the need for a physical count of sale merchandise before and after the sale, a computer-aided design system

TABLE 16-7
How Retailers Use Point-of-Sales (POS) Systems

Factors	Percentage Using a POS System to Acquire Information			
	Discounters/ Mass Mechandisers	Department Stores	Specialty Stores: Durable Goods	Specialty Stores: Nondurable Goods
Markdowns	52	60	55	57
Receipts	28	22	50	38
Purchases	20	16	34	16
Physical inventory	36	24	42	20
Price changes	24	44	58	36
Price look-up	48	26	58	16
Merchandise data capture	92	77	61	76
Special-order printing	8	4	21	3
Inquiry for stock availability in warehouse or other stores	20	7	26	5
Automatic ordering and customer delivery	12	4	16	2
Merchandise trade-ins	16	11	26	17
Merchandise exchanges	36	56	42	54
Merchandise credits and refunds	72	66	55	66

Source: "NRMA's New POS Study," *Stores* (April 1987), p. 68. Copyright National Retail Merchants Association. Reprinted by permission.

used by our real estate and store operations people, and an expansion of our data processing capacity through new hardware.[8]

Table 16-7 shows how discount/mass merchandise, department store, and durable goods and nondurable goods specialty-store chains are using computerized point-of-sales systems to better coordinate strategy.

Control: Using the Retail Audit

After a retail strategy has been developed and put into action, it must be continuously evaluated, and necessary adjustments must be made. An important evaluation tool is the **retail audit,** which may be defined as

> a systematic, critical, and unbiased review and appraisal of the basic objectives and policies of the retail function, and of the organization, methods, procedures, and personnel employed to implement those policies and to achieve those objectives. Clearly, not every evaluation of retail personnel, organization, or methods is a retail audit; at best, most such evaluations can be regarded as parts of an audit.[9]

and

> an independent examination of the entire retailing effort of a company, or some specific retailing activity, covering objectives, strategy, implementation, and organization, for the triple purpose of determining what is being done, appraising what is being done, and recommending what should be done in the future.[10]

An audit includes an investigation of a retailer's objectives, strategy, implementation, and organization. First, the objectives of the firm are ascertained and then evaluated for clarity, consistency, and appropriateness. Second, the firm's strategy and its methods for deriving it are examined and assessed. Third, how well the strategy has been implemented and actually received by customers is considered. Fourth, the retail organizational structure is analyzed; lines of command, types of organization charts, and so on are the kinds of information gathered in this phase.

A good retail audit incorporates four elements. It is conducted on a regular, periodic basis; comprehensive; systematic; and enacted in an open-minded, unbiased manner.[11]

Undertaking an Audit

Several steps should be completed in undertaking a retail audit:

1. Determining who does the audit.
2. Determining when and how often the audit is conducted.
3. Determining areas to be audited.
4. Developing audit form(s).
5. Conducting the audit.
6. Reporting to management.

See Figure 16-4 for a description of the retail audit process.

Determining Who Does the Audit

When a retail audit is conducted, one or a combination of three parties can be utilized: company specialists, company department managers, and outside auditors. The advantages and disadvantages of each are noted here.

Company specialists are internal personnel whose prime responsibility is the retail audit. The advantages of this source include auditing expertise, thoroughness, the level of knowledge about the retailer, and the ongoing nature (no time lags). Disadvantages include the costs (very expensive for small retailers, which do not need full-time auditors) and the limited independence of these auditors.

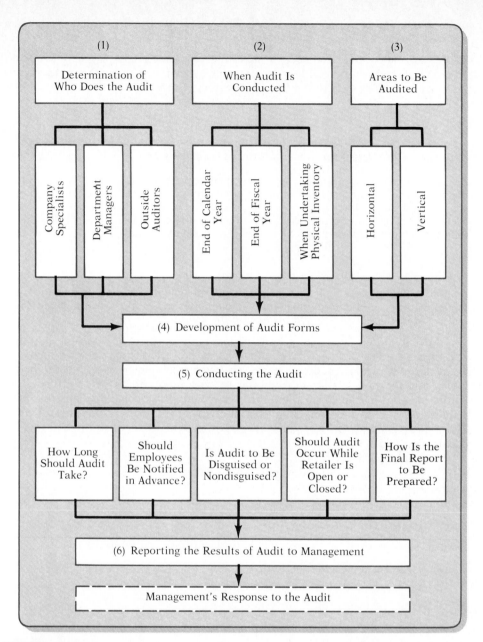

FIGURE 16-4
The Retail Audit Process

Company department managers are internal personnel whose prime responsibility is operations management, but they are also asked to participate in the retail audit. Advantages of this source are that they are inexpensive, are knowledgeable about the firm, and have a complete understanding of departmental operations. Disadvantages include the time away from the primary job, a lack of objectivity, time pressure, and the complexity of conducting companywide audits.

Outside auditors are people who are not permanent employees of the retailer but who work as consultants (usually for fees). Advantages include their broad experience, objectivity, and thoroughness. Disadvantages include the high costs per day or hour (however, for small retailers, it may be cheaper to hire expensive, per diem consultants than to employ full-time auditors; the opposite is usually true for larger firms), the time lags while the consultants gain familiarity, the failure of some retailers to use outside specialists on a continuous basis, and the reluctance of some employees to cooperate with outsiders.

Determining When and How Often the Audit Is Conducted

Logical times for conducting an audit are at the end of the calendar year, at the end of the company's annual reporting year (fiscal year), or at the time of a complete physical inventory. Each of these times is appropriate for evaluating a retailer's operations during the previous period.

An audit must be enacted at least annually, although some retailers desire more frequent analysis. It is important that the same period(s), such as January–December, be analyzed each year if meaningful comparisons, projections, and adjustments are to be made.

Determining Areas to Be Audited

A good retail audit encompasses more than financial analysis and would regularly examine various aspects of a firm's strategy and operations. In addition, an audit can be used during successful and unsuccessful periods to identify strengths and weaknesses.

There are two basic types of retail audits—horizontal and vertical:

The horizontal audit examines all of the elements that go into the retailing whole, with particular emphasis upon the relative importance of these elements and the "mix" between them. It is often referred to as a "retailing mix" audit. The vertical audit singles out certain functional elements of the retail operations and subjects them to thorough searching study and evaluation.[12]

A **horizontal audit** is an analysis of the overall performance of a retailer, from its philosophy of business to objectives to customer satisfacton to the basic retail strategy mix and its implementation. A **vertical audit** is an in-depth analysis of a firm's performance in one area of its retail operations, such as the credit function, customer service, merchandise assortment, or interior displays. The two audits should be used in conjunction with one another because the horizontal audit often reveals areas that need further investigation.

Developing Audit Forms

In order to be systematic and thorough, the retailer should utilize detailed audit forms. These **audit forms** list the areas to be examined and the exact information required in evaluating each area. Audit forms usually resemble questionnaires, and they are completed by the auditor.

Without audit forms, the analysis becomes haphazard and subjective, and it is not standardized. Important questions may be omitted or poorly worded. The biases of the auditor may show through. And most significantly, questions may differ from one audit period to another, which could limit comparisons over time.

Examples of audit forms are presented later in the chapter.

Conducting the Audit

After the auditor is selected, the timing of the audit is determined, the areas to be analyzed are chosen, and the audit forms are constructed, the audit itself is undertaken.

Management should specify in advance how long the audit will take and conform to this timetable. Prior notification of employees depends on management's

Vertical Auditing: Can Advertising Effectiveness Be Measured?

During a one-month period, a retailer spends $5,000 on advertising and generates sales volume of $100,000. Question: Has this advertising been effective? Answer: It depends on the retailer's goals and past performance. These would be examined in a vertical audit of the firm's advertising efforts.

If the retailer's goal is to increase customer awareness of its name, to enhance its image as an industry innovator, or to promote the opening of a new store, then the sales volume for the month would not provide the information needed to measure ad effectiveness. The firm would have to study the level of customer awareness (or the company's image) before and after the ad campaign or the number of consumers visiting the new store during the first month.

If the retailer's goal is to reach a certain sales level, then it could compare the current sales volume with that in prior periods or determine if the desired advertising-to-sales ratio has been achieved. For example, if the retailer wants its ad expenditures to be no more than 3 per cent of sales, then it would not be satisfied.

Some retailers, such as R.H. Macy, use PON (plus over norm) calculations when deciding whether or not to increase advertising expenditures. These firms ask themselves what additional sales volume will be generated by raising their budgets: "They look at the whole picture. If they spend X amount of dollars to do Y amount of business, how much advertising does it take to increase that business?"

The success of annual events, such as January white sales or seasonal sweater sales, is often the easiest to measure:

We have last year's sales and profits and share of market, and we can compare. We take a look at what we're advertising. Sweaters, for instance. We count the number of sweaters we've sold. If we sold 25,000 sweaters at $20 each, we realized $500,000. We know the profit margin, and how many dollars we spent on advertising and promotion to achieve that goal.

Source: Based on material in "Ad Effectiveness: Can It Be Calculated?" *Chain Store Age Executive* (September 1987), pp. 64–68.

perception of two factors: the need to compile some information in advance to increase efficiency and save time versus the desire to present a true picture and not a distorted one (which may occur if too much prior notification is given).

A **disguised audit** is one in which a retailer's employees are not aware that an audit is taking place. This is useful if the auditor is investigating an area like personal selling and wishes to act out the role of a customer to elicit employee responses. A **nondisguised audit** is one in which a retailer's employees are aware that an audit is being conducted. This technique is desirable when employees are asked specific operational questions and help in gathering data for the auditor.

The decision as to whether to perform an audit when the firm is open or closed depends on the type of information required. Some audits should be conducted while the retailer is open, such as analyses of the adequacy of the parking lot, in-store customer traffic patterns, the adequacy of vertical transportation, and customer relations. Other audits should be completed while the retailer is closed, such as analyses of the condition of fixtures, inventory levels and turnover, financial statements, and employee records.

It must be determined what format the audit report will take. The report can be formal or informal, brief or long, oral or written, and a statement of findings or a statement of findings plus recommendations. A report has a much greater chance of acceptance if it is presented in the format desired by management.

Reporting Audit Findings and Recommendations to Management

The last step in an audit is the presentation of findings and recommendations to management. It is the responsibility of management, not the auditor, to determine what adjustments (if any) to implement. It is essential that the proper company executives read the audit report thoroughly, consider each point made in the report, and make the necessary changes in strategy.

It is important that management regard the report seriously and react accordingly. A serious mistake would be made if the report is downgraded or only lip service is paid to the findings. A firm's long-term success is predicated on its evaluating the present and adapting to the future. No matter how well an audit is performed, it is a worthless exercise if not taken seriously by management.

Responding to an Audit

After management has studied the findings of an audit, appropriate actions should be taken. Areas of strength should be continued and areas of weakness revised. All actions must be consistent with the retail strategy and recorded and stored in the retail information system. For example, at Younkers (a Des Moines, Iowa, department store chain):

> Every department in every store comes under automatic review once a year; but also whenever our ongoing renovation program calls for any substantial floor-space revamp. In recent years such renovations have seen our elimination of white goods, fabrics, and notions from all stores; and the space reduction or elimination of art needlework, drapery, and records in some. These have generally, but not with store-by-store uniformity, been replaced with food departments, wine bars, life-style furniture, computers, and wrapit-mailit-sendit stations.[13]

Problems in Conducting a Retail Audit

There are several potential problems that may occur when conducting a retail audit; a retailer should be aware of them:

- ❑ The audit may be costly to undertake.
- ❑ The audit may be quite time-consuming.
- ❑ Performance standards may be inaccurate.
- ❑ Employees may feel threatened and not cooperate as much as desired.
- ❑ Incorrect data may be collected.
- ❑ Management may not be responsive to the findings.

At the present time, many retailers do not understand or perform systematic retail audits. As retailing moves through the 1980s and into the 1990s, this will have to change if companies are to analyze themselves properly and plan correctly for the future.

Illustrations of Retail Audit Forms

In this section, a management audit form for retailers and a retailing performance checklist are presented. Each of these forms demonstrates how small and large retailers can inexpensively, yet efficiently, conduct retail audits.

An auditor would complete one of these forms in a systematic, periodic manner and then discuss the findings with management. The examples described are both horizontal audits. A vertical audit consists of an in-depth analysis of any one area contained in these forms.

Answer Yes or No to Each Question

A Look at Yourself and Your Ability to Grow

_____ 1. Do you keep abreast of changes in your field by subscribing to leading trade and general business publications?

_____ 2. Do you plan for a profit (your net income) above a reasonable salary for yourself as manager?

_____ 3. Are you an active member of a trade association?

Customer Relations

_____ 4. Do you purposely cater to selected groups of customers rather than to all groups?

_____ 5. Do you have a clear picture of the store image you seek to implant in the minds of your customers?

_____ 6. Do you evaluate your own performance by asking customers about their likes and dislikes and by shopping competitors to compare their assortments, prices, and promotion methods with your own?

Personnel Management and Supervision

_____ 7. Do employees in your firm know to whom they each report?

_____ 8. Do you delegate as much authority as you can to those immediately responsible to you, freeing yourself from unnecessary operating details?

_____ 9. Do you seek your employees' opinions of stock assortments, choice of new merchandise, layout, displays, and special promotions?

_____ 10. Do you apply the concept of "management by objectives," that is, do you set work goals for yourself and for each employee for the month or season ahead and at the end of each period check the actual performance against these goals?

Merchandise Inventory Control

_____ 11. Do you keep sales, inventory, and purchase records by types of merchandise within your departments?

_____ 12. Do you control your purchases in dollars by means of an open-to-buy system?

_____ 13. For staple and reorder items, do you prepare a checklist (never-out list) that you frequently check against the actual assortment on hand?

_____ 14. Do you make certain that best-sellers are reordered promptly and in sufficient volume and that slow-sellers are processed swiftly for clearance?

_____ 15. Are you taking adequate safeguards to reduce shoplifting and pilferage in your store?

Budgetary Control and Productivity

_____ 16. In controlling your operations, do you frequently compare actual results with the budget projections you have made; and do you then adjust your merchandising, promotion, and expense plans as indicated by deviation from these projections?

_____ 17. Do you study industry data and compare the results of your operation with them?

_____ 18. Do you think in terms of ratios and per cents, rather than exclusively in dollars-and-cents?

_____ 19. Do you use a variety of measures of performance, such as:

    _____ a. Net profit as a per cent of your net worth?

    _____ b. Stockturn (ratio of your sales to the value of your average inventory)?

    _____ c. Gross profit margin per dollar of cost investment in merchandise (dollars of gross margin divided by your average inventory at cost)?

    _____ d. Sales per square foot of space (net sales divided by total number of square feet of space)?

    _____ e. Selling cost per cent for each salesperson (remuneration of the salesperson divided by that person's sales)?

FIGURE 16-5
A Management Audit Form for Retailers
Source: This table is adapted from John W. Wingate and Elmer O. Schaller, _Management Audit for Small Retailers_ (Washington, D.C.: Small Business Administration, Small Business Management Series No. 31, Third Edition, 1977).

Buying

_____ 20. Are you continually searching the market for the most suitable merchandise, prices, and services rather than relying too much on established sources?

_____ 21. When reordering new items that have shown volume potential, do you make it a point to order a sufficient number?

_____ 22. Do you keep up assortments through important selling seasons, such as Christmas and Easter, in spite of the probability of markdowns on the remainders?

_____ 23. For goods having a short selling season (such as straw hats), do you predetermine the following dates: (a) when first orders are to be placed, (b) when retail stocks are to be complete, (c) extent of peak selling period, (d) start of clearance, and (e) final cleanup?

_____ 24. Do you take advantage of all available discounts—trade, quantity, seasonal, and cash—and do you include them on your written orders?

Pricing

_____ 25. Do you figure markup as a percentage of retail selling price rather than as a percentage of costs?

_____ 26. Do you set price lines or price zones?

_____ 27. Do the prices you set provide adequate markups within the limits of competition?

_____ 28. In retail pricing of new items and in evaluating their cost quotations, are you guided by what you think the typical customer will consider good value?

_____ 29. Before you mark down goods for clearance, do you consider alternate supplementary ways of moving them—such as special displays, repackaging, or including them in a deal?

Advertising and Sales Promotion

_____ 30. Do you advertise consistently in at least one appropriate medium: newspapers, direct mail, handbills, local television, or radio?

_____ 31. Does each of your ads specifically "sell" your firm in addition to the merchandise advertised?

_____ 32. Do you regularly and systematically familiarize your salespeople with your plans for advertised merchandise and promotions?

_____ 33. Do you consult your suppliers about dealer aids helpful to the promotion of their merchandise in your store?

_____ 34. Do you use "co–op ads" with other merchants in your community?

_____ 35. Do you conduct a continuing effort to obtain free publicity in the local press or broadcast media?

Display

_____ 36. Are your window displays planned to attract attention, develop interest, create desire, and prompt a customer to enter your store for a closer inspection?

_____ 37. Do you give as much attention to your interior displays as to your windows?

Equipment and Layout

_____ 38. Are goods that the customers may not be specifically looking for but are likely to buy on sight (impulse merchandise) displayed near your store entrances and at other points that have heavy traffic?

_____ 39. Are your cash registers well located?

_____ 40. Are nonselling and office activities kept out of valuable selling space?

_____ 41. Do you receive, check, and mark incoming goods at central points rather than on the selling floor?

FIGURE 16-5
(Continued)

A Management Audit Form for Retailers

The Small Business Administration has published a booklet entitled *Management Audit for Small Retailers* (Small Business Management Series No. 31, Third Edition), by John W. Wingate and Elmer O. Schaller. This booklet, although written for small retailers, provides a series of questions and discussions that

Cash and Finance

_____ 42. Does someone other than the cashier or bookkeeper open all mail and prepare a record of receipts that will be checked against deposits?

_____ 43. Do you deposit all of each day's cash receipts in the bank without delay.?

_____ 44. Do you calculate your cash flow regularly (monthly, for example) and take steps to provide enough cash for each period's needs?

_____ 45. Have you established, in advance, a line of credit at your bank, not only to meet seasonal requirements but also to permit borrowing at any time for emergency needs?

Credit

_____ 46. Do you have a credit policy?

_____ 47. Are your bad–debt losses comparable with those of other similar retailers?

_____ 48. Periodically, do you review your accounts to determine their status?

Insurance

_____ 49. Is your company's insurance handled by a conscientious and knowledgeable agent?

_____ 50. Have you updated your insurance needs to assure adequate protection for buildings, equipment, merchandise, and other assets, as well as for public liability?

Accounting Records

_____ 51. Do you have your books balanced and accounts summarized each month?

_____ 52. Do you use a modern point–of–sale register for sales transactions and modern equipment to record accounts receivable?

_____ 53. Do you keep data on sales, purchases, inventory, and direct expenses for different types of merchandise in your store?

Taxes and Legal Obligations

_____ 54. To be sure you are not overpaying your taxes, do you retain a tax accountant to review your accounting records and prepare your more complicated tax returns?

_____ 55. Do you retain a good lawyer to confer with on day–to–day problems that have legal implications?

Planning for Growth

_____ 56. Over the past few years, have you done very much long–range planning for growth?

_____ 57. When you find that change is called for, do you act decisively and creatively?

_____ 58. Do you make most of your changes after thoughtful analysis rather than as reactions to crises?

_____ 59. Are you grooming someone to succeed you as manager in the not too distant future?

FIGURE 16-5
(Continued)

are applicable to all retailers; in it, the components of a retail audit are comprehensively detailed.*

Figure 16-5 contains selected questions from each of the sixteen areas covered in the _Management Audit for Small Retailers_. "Yes" is the desired answer to every question in Figure 16-5. For those questions answered in the negative, a retailer would need to determine the causes for these responses and adjust strategy accordingly. Figure 16-5 should be viewed as a single, overall horizontal audit, not as fragmented pieces.

A Retailing Performance Checklist

Figure 16-6 shows another type of audit form, a retailing performance checklist, which is used to evaluate overall strategy performance. Included are each of

*In addition to the information presented here, _Management Audit for Small Retailers_ discusses each point of the audit in great detail and lists a number of sources of further information.

Rate your firm's performance for each of the following criteria on a scale of 1 to 5, with 1 being excellent and 5 being poor.

I. Development of strategy
   1. Adherence to the philosophy of business _____
   2. Clear objectives _____
   3. Consistent objectives and image _____
   4. Well–defined goods and/or service offerings _____
   5. Well–defined and ongoing budget _____
   6. Proper use of research _____
   7. Thorough short–run planning _____
   8. Thorough long–run planning _____
   9. Reactions to external environment _____
   10. Well–established evaluation criteria _____
   11. Adjustments in strategy _____

II. The consumer
   1. Well–defined target market _____
   2. Consistency with image _____
   3. Size of target market _____
   4. Knowledge of consumer needs _____
   5. Demographic trends for target market _____

III. Store location
   1. Consistency with image _____
   2. Size of trading area _____
   3. Popularity of trading area _____
   4. Access to vehicular traffic _____
   5. Access to mass transportation _____
   6. Parking facilities _____
   7. Composition of existing stores _____
   8. Affinity with existing stores _____
   9. Turnover of stores _____
   10. Visibility of store _____
   11. Condition of building _____
   12. Terms of occupancy _____
   13. Store hours _____
   14. Store facilities _____
   15. Maintenance of facilities _____

IV. Human resource management
   1. Clarity of retail organization _____
   2. Appropriateness of retail organization _____
   3. Adaptability of retail organization _____
   4. Employee recruitment _____
   5. Employee selection _____
   6. Employee training _____
   7. Employee compensation _____
   8. Employee supervision _____
   9. Employee motivation _____
   10. Opportunities for advancement _____

FIGURE 16-6
A Retailing Performance Checklist

the components of a retail strategy. The checklist, which is a horizontal audit, can be used by small and large retailers alike.

The purpose of the checklist is to pinpoint a retailer's areas of strength and weakness, so that strategy can be adjusted accordingly. Unlike the yes-no answers in Figure 16-5, the checklist enables the retailer to rate performance in each area. This provides more in-depth information. A total score is not computed. Because all items are not equally important, a simple summation would not present a meaningful score.

V. Operations management
1. Return on assets
2. Return on net worth
3. Appropriateness of budgeting style _____
4. Cash flow _____
5. Store size _____
6. Space allocation _____
7. Employee turnover _____
8. Store maintenance _____
9. Inventory management
10. Store security
11. Use of insurance _____
12. Credit management _____
13. Level of computerization _____
14. Crisis management _____

VI. Merchandising
1. Buying organization
2. Appropriateness of merchandise quality _____
3. Level of innovativeness _____
4. Width of assortment _____
5. Depth of assortment _____
6. Availability of manufacturer brands _____
7. Availability of private brands _____
8. Knowledge of merchandise sources _____
9. Caliber of merchandise sources _____
10. Purchase terms _____
11. Reordering procedures _____
12. Use of dollar control systems _____
13. Use of unit control systems _____
14. Inventory valuation procedures _____
15. Accuracy of records _____
16. Merchandise forecasting and budgeting process _____
17. Stock turnover _____
18. Gross margin return on investment _____

VII. Pricing
1. Consistency with other retail strategy mix factors _____
2. Awareness of consumer sensitivity to price _____
3. Awareness of and compliance with government restrictions _____
4. Relations with suppliers _____
5. Competitive pricing environment _____
6. Use of multistage approach to pricing _____
7. Use of demand–, cost–, and competition–based pricing techniques _____
8. Adaptability _____
9. Use of price lining _____
10. Level of markdowns _____

VIII. Communications
1. Appropriateness of store image _____
2. Customer perception of store image _____
3. Storefront(s) _____
4. Cleanliness of store _____
5. Traffic flow _____
6. Width of aisles _____
7. Use of dead space _____
8. Displays _____
9. Customer service _____
10. Amount of promotion _____
11. Quality of promotion _____
12. Diversity of promotion _____
13. Amount of personal selling _____
14. Quality of sales force _____
15. Uses of publicity _____
16. Uses of sales promotion _____

FIGURE 16-6
(Continued)

SUMMARY

This chapter shows why it is necessary for retailers to plan and enact coordinated strategies, and describes how to assess success or failure. Retail strategy must be viewed as an ongoing, integrated process of interrelated steps.

The development and enactment of an integrated retail strategy must take into account planning procedures and opportunity analysis, performance measures, productivity, and the uses of new technology. Planning procedures can be optimized by following a series of specified activities. Opportunities need to be examined in terms of their impact on overall strategy, and not in an isolated manner. The sales opportunity grid is a good tool for comparing various strategic options.

By determining the relevant measures of performance and setting standards for them, a retailer can better develop and integrate strategy. Such measures include total sales revenues, sales revenue by goods/service category, gross margins in dollars and percentages, sales per square foot, gross margin return on investment, inventory turnover, markdown percentages, employee turnover, financial ratios, and profitability.

To maximize productivity, retailers need to make the implementation of their strategies as efficient as possible. However, efficiency does not necessarily mean having the lowest possible expenditures on operations (since this may lead to customer dissatisfaction), but keying expenditures to the performance standards required by a retailer's chosen strategy mix and niche in the market (e.g., upscale versus discount). By using new technology, retailers are often able to better integrate strategies and raise their performance.

A strategy needs to be regularly monitored, evaluated, and fine-tuned or revised. The retail audit is one technique that can accomplish this control function; it is a systematic, critical, and unbiased review and appraisal. With an audit, a retailer's objectives, strategy, implementation, and organization could each be investigated.

A retail audit consists of six steps: determining who does the audit (company specialists, company department managers, and/or outside auditors); determining when and how often it is conducted; determining areas to be audited (horizontal or vertical auditing); developing audit forms; conducting the audit; and reporting results and recommendations to management. After the appropriate executives read the audit report, the necessary revisions in strategy should be made.

Among the problems of auditing may be the costs, the time commitment, the possibility of inaccurate performance standards, poor cooperation from some employees, the collection of incorrect data, and an unresponsive management. A number of retailers do not utilize the audit. They may have problems in evaluating their positions and planning for the future.

Two examples of audit forms have been presented in the chapter: a management audit for retailers and a retailing performance checklist.

QUESTIONS FOR DISCUSSION

1. Why is it so important for a retailer to view its strategy as an integrated and ongoing process?
2. Present an integrated strategy for Swiss Colony to increase sales by 10 per cent annually for each of the next three years. Refer to Figure 16-3 in your answer.
3. Develop a sales opportunity grid for a convenience store planning to add women's cosmetics to its product line.
4. Cite five performance measures commonly used by retailers, and explain what could be learned by studying each.
5. Assess the performance of the shoe product category in department stores. Refer to Table 16-4 in your answer. What would you recommend to improve shoe performance?
6. Evaluate each of the key business ratios shown for hobby, toy, and game shops in Table 16-6. In general, how would you rate the performance of this type of retailer?
7. Comment on this statement: "Often neither the least expensive retail strategy nor the most expensive retail strategy would be the most productive retail strategy." Does this mean that warehouse stores should upgrade their strategies? Explain your answer.
8. How could the use of new technology be harmful in a retailer's efforts to better integrate its strategy?
9. Distinguish between horizontal and vertical retail audits. Develop a vertical audit form for a retailer selling lamps for the home.
10. Why must a good retail audit be periodic, comprehensive, systematic, and independent?

11. Distinguish among the following auditors. Under what circumstances would each be preferred?
   a. Outside auditors
   b. Company specialists
   c. Company department managers
12. Under what circumstances should a disguised audit be used?
13. How should management respond to the findings of an audit? What may happen if the findings are ignored?
14. Why do many retailers not conduct any form of retail audit? Are these reasons valid? Explain your answer.

NOTES

1. Tom Richman, "Mrs. Fields' Secret Ingredient," *Inc.* (October 1987), pp. 65–72; and "Mrs. Fields Automates the Way the Cookie Sells," *Chain Store Age Executive* (April 1988), pp. 73–76.

2. Stanley F. Stasch and Patricia Lanktree, "Can Your Marketing Planning Be Improved?" *Journal of Marketing*, Vol. 44 (Summer 1980), pp. 88–89. See also "CEOs Give Mixed Reviews to Staffs," *Chain Store Age, General Merchandise Trends* (January 1985), pp. 20, 23.

3. See "Developing a Sales Opportunity Grid," *Nielsen Researcher* (Number 1, 1980), pp. 10–11.

4. *1987–88 Industry Norms and Key Business Ratios* (New York: Dun & Bradstreet, 1987), pp. v–vi.

5. "Pragmatic Prange's," *Stores* (October 1987), pp. 55–59.

6. Robert E. O'Neill, "SLAM Adds 1.4 Points to Gross Profit," *Progressive Grocer* (February 1985), pp. 55–59.

7. *Walgreens Annual Report 1986*, pp. 9–10.

8. *Hechinger Company Annual Report 1987*, p. 13.

9. Adapted from A. Schuchman, "The Marketing Audit: Its Nature, Purpose, and Problems," *Analyzing and Improving Marketing Performance* (New York: American Management Association, 1959), p. 13; and Alfred R. Oxenfeldt, *Executive Action in Marketing* (Belmont, Calif.: Wadsworth, 1966), p. 746.

10. Adapted from Philip Kotler, *Marketing Management: Analysis, Planning, and Control*, Sixth Edition (Englewood Cliffs, N.J.: Prentice-Hall, 1988), p. 747.

11. Ibid.

12. Adapted from Richard D. Crisp, "Auditing the Functional Elements of a Marketing Operation," *Analyzing and Improving Marketing Performance* (New York: American Management Association, 1959), pp. 16–17.

13. Lewis A. Spalding, "Down and Out?" *Stores* (February 1984), p. 13.

Case 1

Venture Stores: Improving Productivity Through Smaller Outlets*

Venture Stores is a sixty-five-unit full-line discount-store chain that is a division of May Department Stores Company. All of Venture's outlets are in seven midwestern states, with the greatest concentration in the Chicago area. As of 1990, the firm plans to be operating ninety stores.

Venture's total sales were $1.1 billion in 1986, an increase of 12.5 per cent from 1985; its per-store sales were $16.9 million in 1986, an 8.8 per cent increase from 1985. Pre-tax earnings were $80 million in 1986, a $22 million or 37.9 per cent increase from 1985. As a result, Venture's pre-tax earnings rose from 5.8 per cent of sales in 1985 to 7.3 per cent of sales in 1986; and sales per square foot went from $131 in 1983 to $148 in 1985 to $158 in 1986. Although performance on these key criteria has been high, Venture executives are aware that Target, an upscale full-line discount-store-chain division of Dayton Hudson, had sales per square foot of $179 in 1986, and that Venture's average store size has been considerably larger than most other full-line discount-store chains.

To further improve its productivity, Venture has begun to experiment with a smaller, high-profile prototype store. The new store occupies 65,000 square feet. Five years ago, Venture's standard store size was 116,000 square feet; at that point, the prototype store size was reduced to 100,000, then to 90,000, and next to 80,000 square feet.

*The material in this case is drawn from Richard C. Halverson, "Venture Slices Store Size to Raise Productivity," *Discount Store News* (July 20, 1987), pp. 1, 173; and *The May Department Stores Annual Report 1986*.

550

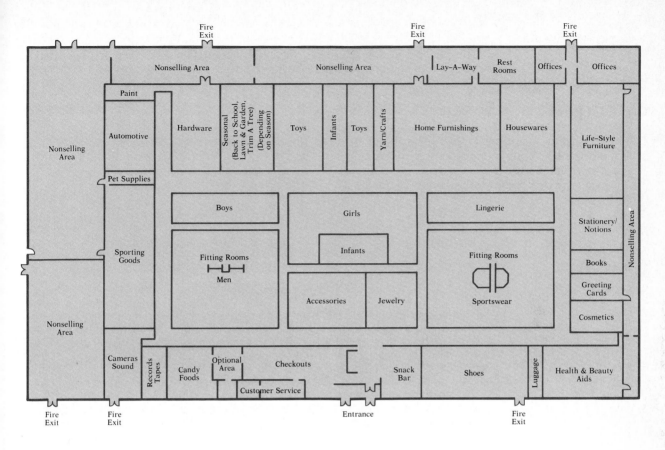

FIGURE 1
Venture's 65,000-Square-Foot Prototype Store in Oklahoma City
Source: Discount Store News. Reprinted by permission.

By operating smaller stores, Venture intends to improve sales per square foot, to lower such operating costs as rent and utilities, and to be better able to compete in smaller market areas. Figure 1 contains a scale drawing of Venture's new prototype store.

Venture is using this strategy in its 65,000-square-foot prototype store:

❏ Although the same merchandise assortment is being kept, the total volume of goods stocked in the store has been reduced. This requires more frequent restocking schedules, or else out-of-stock situations may develop.

❏ Back-area storage space is being reduced.

❏ Displays are more visual and occupy more of the selling space than in other Venture stores. Gondola displays are 84 inches high, compared to 54 to 66 inches high in other outlets; this uses space quite efficiently.

❏ Many goods are stocked on the selling floor, above the new 84-inch displays.

❏ The same number of employees (three hundred) as in 80,000-square-foot Venture stores is being used.

❏ Checkout stands feature automated check approval to speed customer transaction time and to reduce the length of lines.

❏ A customer service desk cashes customers' personal checks (up to a $25 limit) to further speed up transactions. All checks are insured by Telecheck to reduce bad-check losses.

551

❑ The register system includes automatic sale-price look-up, which is activated when a cashier enters the item's inventory code.

As another productivity measure, by the end of 1988, Venture planned to have computerized scanning equipment installed in all of its stores.

QUESTIONS

1. Evaluate Venture Stores' recent performance.
2. What are the pros and cons of Venture's reducing the size of its stores?
3. Evaluate the prototype store's layout as depicted in Figure 1.

4. Develop a ten-item checklist that could be used to determine if Venture is applying an integrated retail strategy.

Case 2

Davey Distributors, Inc.: Evaluating a Catalog Showroom Strategy*

Jed Turner was puzzled. He had been working as a consultant on the Davey Distributors' case for over five weeks now, and he had not come up with many answers. Jed had been assigned to the case by Josh Lawson, senior partner of his employer, Walsh, Lawson, and DuVal, which had recently been hired by the bankruptcy court that was handling the Davey Distributors' Chapter XI proceedings. The court wanted Walsh, Lawson, and DuVal to evaluate the problems with Davey Distributors and come up with a plan of action to put the company back on its feet again.

Davey Distributors, Inc., had been a fairly small but successful wholesale distributor of camera equipment and consumer electronic merchandise for over twenty years. Like many wholesalers, Davey entered the catalog showroom business after this type of firm showed great success in the late 1970s and early 1980s.

Opening the catalog showroom seemed straightforward, and the concept had a lot of appeal to consumers. Davey management was able to develop catalogs with relative ease because there were several companies that printed catalogs. A store simply affiliated with a catalog printer, stocked the merchandise in the catalog, and sold the items at the prices listed in the catalog. Customers were mailed or given large, full-color catalogs picturing all of the merchandise carried in the store. The catalogs also contained the manufacturer's suggested list price and the showroom's actual selling price (usually in code).

Davey management realized that although its prices in certain categories were really low (for example, cameras and small appliances were sold at just above cost), profits in other categories (such as gifts and jewelry) were quite high. Thus, the weighted average of all merchandise sold would give the store an overall gross margin of over 30 per cent, enough to make a handsome profit.

Customers liked catalog showrooms, because they were able to preshop at home, then walk into the store and fill out a form that indicated what merchandise was wanted. The form was handed to a store clerk, who got the merchandise from the in-store warehouse (which utilized 10,000 of the store's 15,000 square feet) and brought it out to the customer. In addition to the convenience of the catalog, customers paid prices significantly below the regular prices of even the local discount stores.

Davey Distributors quickly leased five locations, hired a staff of buyers to handle the merchandise not carried by the company up to that point, and borrowed from its bank to invest in fixtures and inventory. It was projected that each store would do a $1.8-million volume the first year, and that the five stores together would almost double Davey's volume. Profits were projected at $100,000 per store before taxes.

However, volume averaged only $1.4 million the first year. Losses averaged $40,000 per store. Accordingly, Davey used some newspaper advertising in addition to the catalog during the second year. Business seemed to improve, but new competition kept volume down to

*This case was prepared and written by Dr. Franklin Rubenstein, retail management consultant.

$1.6 million per store. By the fourth year, increased advertising and cost cutting had brought volume up to $1.8 million per store. Yet, losses were bigger than ever. Finally, a week before Christmas, creditors seized Davey's assets and forced the company into bankruptcy.

Jed Turner's in-depth research revealed that the showrooms' gross margin for the first year was only 25 per cent and had decreased subsequently to 23 per cent, 22 per cent, and 21 per cent by the final year. At the same time, advertising expenses had increased, and payroll expenses had remained constant as a percentage of sales. Jed discovered that the mix of merchandise sold was a major reason behind the low gross margins.

High-priced items did not sell as well as expected. For example, jewelry sales were 40 per cent below projections during the first year, and gifts were 35 per cent below first-year expectations. On the other hand, camera sales met initial projections and later exceeded forecasts after this item was advertised. The resultant average gross margin could not cover the expense structure, which was only slightly higher than the industry average. Although several catalog chains shared the problem of excessively high sales of low-priced items, many of these chains were quite successful.

Davey's management gave the impression that the strategy they had followed had been forced on them by competition and the necessity to build sales volume. Turner was not convinced that these conclusions were correct, and he had to come up with sound ideas that would drastically improve the gross margins of the stores. Otherwise, the store leases would be disavowed, and Davey's would be limited to its original wholesale business.

QUESTIONS

1. Describe the auditing process used in this case.
2. Was the court correct in selecting an outside consultant to conduct the analysis? Explain your answer.
3. Comment on Jed Turner's conclusions. Offer recommendations.
4. What further information is necessary?
5. Create an audit form that can be utilized by Jed Turner.

Chapter 17

Planning by a Service Retailer

As part of its multimedia entertainment empire, Walt Disney Co. owns and operates two leading retail service businesses: Disney World in Lake Buena Vista, Florida, and Disneyland in Anaheim, California. Annual attendance at Disney World is more than twenty-two million people; Disneyland attracts over twelve million people each year. According to the International Association of Amusement Parks and Attractions, Disney World and Disneyland are the top two amusement parks in the United States; and together, their annual attendance is greater than that of the next eight amusement parks combined. In 1987, its amusement park division (which has parks around the world) accounted for 62 per cent of Walt Disney Co.'s revenues and 71 per cent of its operating income.

Walt Disney Co. works very hard to ensure the highest possible level of customer satisfaction with, and repeat visits to, its amusement parks. It sets high service standards and seeks consistency in reaching them. The company realizes that its parks' offerings are largely intangible; the goal is to leave customers with a good feeling. For example, virtually all the employees who interact with the public (such as those dressed in Snow White and Mickey Mouse costumes) must first complete Tradition I, a day-long course on the company's history and central values. Tradition I covers such concepts as the need to be neatly groomed and "unfailingly cheerful." The company reinforces its consumer service orientation by using catchy terms to describe employees, the property, and customers: employees are "cast members"; the property is the "set"; and customers are "guests." Because Disneyland is over thirty years old, Walt Disney Co. continually renovates its property and provides new attractions to retain guest enthusiasm. And to keep attendance at the

15-year-old Disney World increasing, the firm recently added four new hotels; Norway, the eleventh nation at Epcot Center (part of Disney World) opened in 1988; and a fifty-acre park with a water-wave machine, called Typhoon Lagoon, is planned for Orlando.

Michael Eisner, Disney Co.'s current chairman, and his three sons are frequent visitors to the parks and are always on the lookout for improvements. As an illustration, after his sons complained that Disneyland's hot dogs were inferior, Eisner decided to build a whole new restaurant devoted to various kinds of hot dogs.

Walt Disney Co. is also very much concerned about the cleanliness of its amusement parks. To maintain its high standards, the firm does not sell chewing gum in the parks; and it is persistent and consistent in its care of facilities. According to one industry expert, "the remarkable cleanliness of the parks is merely a matter of a lot of people trying to do cleanliness better. Disney is a thousand people dreaming up a thousand 'no gum ideas'!"[1]

Service retailers of all types and sizes can benefit by applying Disney's philosophy: Satisfy the customer by doing a lot of little things well.

Overview

Service retailing in the United States is increasing steadily and represents a very large portion of overall retail trade. Consumers now spend just over half of their after-tax income on services such as travel, recreation, credit, product rentals and repairs, personal care, education, medicine, and shelter.

Although the total revenues generated by service retailing are difficult to estimate, because key government data do not separate retail services from business services, the dimensions of service retailing can be seen from these examples:

❏ Each year, Americans spend over $80 billion to maintain and repair their cars; $21 billion to repair their televisions, lawnmowers, and air conditioners; and $80 billion to renovate and repair their kitchens, bathrooms, and recreation rooms.[2]

❏ Until reversed by a U.S. Supreme Court decision in 1977, state bar associations banned all advertising by attorneys. Since that Supreme Court ruling, attorney advertising has risen dramatically. For example, in 1978, lawyers spent $900,000 on television advertising; during 1987, they spent $56 million on television advertising. Large law firms offering low prices are the leading advertisers in this area. Together, Jacoby & Meyers, Hyatt Legal Services, and Injury Helpline spend about $15 million per year on television advertising.[3]

❏ During the past twenty years, the prices of services have risen about 80 per cent more than the prices of goods (excluding food and energy). Because of technological advances, automation has reduced labor costs in manufacturing; however, many services remain very labor-intensive as a result of their personal nature. As one expert has commented, "goods have become cheap and services expensive."[4]

As defined in Chapter 4, there are three general categories of service retailing: rented goods, owned goods, and nongoods. With rented-goods services, consumers lease physical products for a specified period of time. With owned-goods services, consumers have physical products that they own repaired or altered. With nongoods services, consumers receive the personal expertise of the service provider; physical products are not involved.

The growth of service retailing and the differences in strategic planning for a service retailer and a goods retailer make this a part of retailing that should be thoroughly examined. In the future, the service sector will continue to expand in importance. Opportunities will be plentiful for those who know how to react to them.

Strategy Concepts Applied to Service Retailing

The unique aspects of services, which influence a retail strategy, are that (1) the intangible nature of many services makes a consumer's choice of competitive offerings more difficult than with goods; (2) the service provider and his or her services are sometimes inseparable (thus localizing marketing efforts and giving consumers a more limited choice of alternatives); (3) the perishability of most services prevents storage and increases risks; and (4) the human nature of many services makes them more variable.

The intangible (and possibly abstract) nature of services would make it harder for a firm to outline a clear consumer-oriented strategy, particularly as many retailers (e.g., carpenters, repairpersons, and landscapers) start businesses on the basis of their product expertise. The inseparability of the service provider and his or her services means that the owner-operator is often indispensable and that good customer relations are necessary. Perishability presents a risk that in many instances cannot be overcome. For example, the revenues from an un-rented hotel room are forever lost. Variability means that service quality may differ for each shopping experience, store, or service provider. See Figure 17-1.

Figure 17-2 shows a system for classifying service retailers; an individual company should precisely identify the combination of attributes in this figure that it

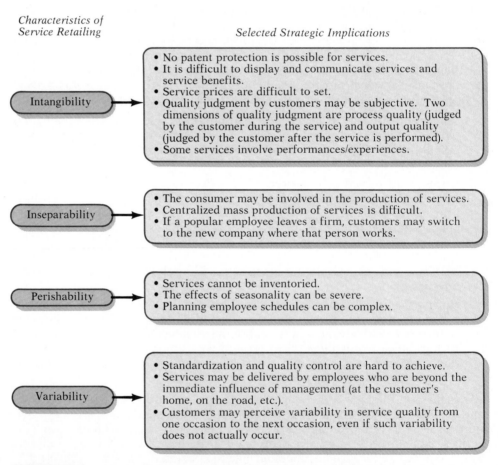

Characteristics of Service Retailing

Selected Strategic Implications

Intangibility
- No patent protection is possible for services.
- It is difficult to display and communicate services and service benefits.
- Service prices are difficult to set.
- Quality judgment by customers may be subjective. Two dimensions of quality judgment are process quality (judged by the customer during the service) and output quality (judged by the customer after the service is performed).
- Some services involve performances/experiences.

Inseparability
- The consumer may be involved in the production of services.
- Centralized mass production of services is difficult.
- If a popular employee leaves a firm, customers may switch to the new company where that person works.

Perishability
- Services cannot be inventoried.
- The effects of seasonality can be severe.
- Planning employee schedules can be complex.

Variability
- Standardization and quality control are hard to achieve.
- Services may be delivered by employees who are beyond the immediate influence of management (at the customer's home, on the road, etc.).
- Customers may perceive variability in service quality from one occasion to the next occasion, even if such variability does not actually occur.

FIGURE 17-1
Characteristics of Service Retailing That Differentiate It from Goods Retailing and Their Strategic Implications
Source: Adapted by the authors from Valarie A. Zeithaml, A. Parasuraman, and Leonard L. Berry, "Problems and Strategies in Service Marketing," *Journal of Marketing,* Vol. 49 (Spring 1985), p. 35. Reprinted by permission of the American Marketing Association.

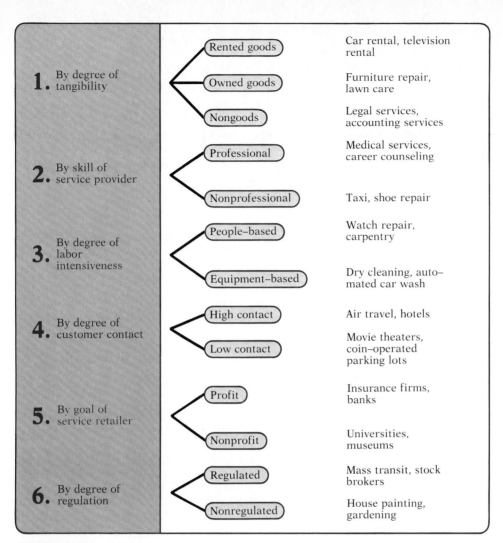

FIGURE 17-2
A Classification System for Service Retailers
Source: Adapted from Joel R. Evans and Barry Berman, *Principles of Marketing,* Second Edition
(New York: Macmillan, 1988), p.448. Reprinted by permission.

possesses (or wants to possess) and act accordingly. Typically, a service retailer is described in terms of each of the categories depicted in Figure 17-2. For example, a car-rental firm may be classified as rented goods (degree of tangibility), nonprofessional (skill of service provider), equipment-based (degree of labor intensiveness), low contact (degree of customer contact), profit-oriented (goal), and relatively nonregulated (degree of regulation). However, this classification system is subject to change. When a problem occurs (such as a rental vehicle's not functioning properly, or a promised car's being unavailable), a low-contact car-rental firm would become a high-contact firm.[5]

Although service-oriented retailing is quite different from goods-oriented retailing, strategy planning should be conducted by use of the same overall procedure:

1. The situation is analyzed, including a definition of the service category.

2. The objectives of the firm are enumerated and ranked.

3. Consumer characteristics and needs are identified.
4. The overall strategy is outlined.
5. The strategy is implemented.
6. The strategy is regularly re-evaluated and adjusted.

In particular, service retailers must understand their business, set clear objectives, efficiently select service opportunities, cater to consumer needs, be cost-effective, plan for competition, present a distinctive offering, determine how to set prices, and communicate with their customers. Table 17-1 points out how companies can plan for the differences between service and goods retailing.

Situation Analysis

When developing a service strategy, a retailer must determine whether rented-goods, owned-goods, or nongoods services are involved, because planning is different for each type of service. Then the service category must be more narrowly defined, as the following illustrations show:

❑ Is a retailer interested in opening a barber shop and giving haircuts? Or should a men's personal-care salon be opened, with such services as hair cutting, manicures, facial massages, hair coloring, and facial-care advice?

❑ Is a retailer going to operate an upscale resort hotel? Or should a discount motel chain be started?

❑ A new college is opening. Should it offer classes and majors in liberal arts and sciences, education, medicine, law, and/or business administration?

❑ A dry cleaner is undecided: Should the focus be on consumer dry-cleaning or commercial dry-cleaning? One or the other must be chosen, since the owner believes the two services cannot be combined efficiently.

These illustrations indicate the range of options available to a prospective service retailer and demonstrate the necessity of defining the service category.

A retailer should decide on a service category before making any other strategic decisions. Too narrow a definition of the service category runs the risk of attracting a small target market and ignoring related services that may be vital to customer satisfaction. For example, a retailer that repairs typewriters may receive a lot of requests from existing customers to repair their printing calculators. If the firm defines its offering too narrowly (and decides not to repair calculators), it misses out on an opportunity to expand sales and it takes a chance of losing the typewriter-repair business from these customers. On the other hand, too broad a definition of the service category (e.g., equipment repair) could result in a nonspecialist image and may require a larger operation and greater investment than desired.

In determining the service category, personal abilities, financial resources, and time resources should be matched to the requirements of the business. The personal abilities required of a service-oriented retailer are usually quite different from those of a goods-oriented retailer:

❑ In service retailing, the major value provided to the customer is some type of service, not a physical product.

❑ Many specific skills may be required, and these skills may not be transferable from one type of service to another. For example, a television repairperson, a beautician, and an accountant cannot easily change positions or transfer skills. An appliance retailer, a cosmetics retailer, and a toy retailer (all goods-oriented firms) would have a much easier time in changing and transferring their skills to another area.

TABLE 17-1
Special Managerial Considerations for Service Retailers in Seven Key Strategic Areas

Service Retailing as Compared with Goods Retailing	Managerial Adjustments Needed by Service Retailers
a. *Measuring performance*	
Capital expenditures vary widely for different services.	Return on net worth may not be the most important measurement of the value of a service to the retailer.
Small or no inventories are required to offer services.	Turnover, markdown controls, and other goods-related controls are not as appropriate.
Higher labor costs exist for services.	Profit after labor costs replaces the gross margin of goods retailing.
Some services support the sale of goods.	Sales-supporting services should be evaluated differently from revenue-producing services.
Cost accounting is more important.	Job-specific records will be required to assess the profitability of each sale.
b. *Store organization*	
More specialized supervision is needed.	Separate management for service areas will be required.
More specific search for service employees is needed.	Nontraditional sources for identification of employees must be used.
Lower employee turnover is needed.	Frequent salary and performance reviews must be carried out.
Higher pay for skilled craftspeople than for merchandising personnel is needed.	Pay levels will need to be adjusted upward over periods of longevity for service employees.
c. *Service production*	
More involvement in manufacturing the service is necessary.	Production skills will need to be obtained by supervisors.
More emphasis on quality control is needed.	Supervisors must be able to assess the quality of a service performed for a customer.
There is more need to monitor consumer satisfaction.	Prior customers should be researched to measure their satisfaction with the service.
There is more need to refine scheduling of employees.	Maximizing the service employees' time requires matching consumer purchasing with the employees' ability to produce the service.
Quality must be consistent among all outlets.	Standards for consistency of the service must be established and continually evaluated; central training may be required for workers in multiple-branch operations.
d. *Pricing*	
Services vary in cost; therefore, pricing is more difficult.	Prices may be quoted within a range instead of an exact figure before the purchase.
There is more difficulty in price competition or promotion based on price.	Services should be promoted on the basis of criteria other than price.
e. *Promotion*	
Value is more difficult for consumers to determine.	Consumers need to be convinced of value through personal selling.
It is difficult to display services within a store.	In-store signing or a service center is required to notify customers of services availability.
Visual presentation is more important.	Photographs of before-and-after may be possible with some services. Testimonials may be possible with other services.
Cross-selling with goods is important.	A quota or bonus for goods salespersons who suggest services will lead to increased service selling.
It is more difficult to advertise in catalogs.	Conditions for the sale and away-from-the-store performance must be specified.
f. *Complaints*	
It is more difficult to return a service.	Policies must be established on adjusting the service purchased with a dissatisfied customer.
A customer is more sensitive about services involving a person (rather than a good).	Specific guarantees and policies about adjustments must be established; new types of insurance must be added to cover liabilities.
g. *Controls*	
There is a greater opportunity to steal customers.	Employee assurance of loyalty must be established. Protection of store loyalty must be obtained.

Source: J. Patrick Kelly and William R. George, "Strategic Management Issues for the Retailing of Services," *Journal of Retailing,* Vol. 58 (Summer 1982), pp. 40–42. Reprinted by permission.

Is the Time Right for Drive-Through Video-Rental Kiosks?

In May 1987, after more than a year of careful planning, Todd LeRoy and Michael Atkinson opened their first two Video's 1st video-rental kiosks in Albany, New York. By the end of 1988, they hoped to have a national franchised chain with 100 outlets. The firm's long-term growth (and survival) will depend on how well consumers react to its unique strategy. Are consumers interested in drive-through video-rental kiosks featuring a limited selection of current best-sellers?

During their preliminary research, LeRoy and Atkinson learned that a typical video-rental retailer occupies about 2,100 square feet of space and stocks nearly 3,500 videocassettes (representing about 2,400 individual titles). On an average day, that video-rental retailer rents only 5 per cent of all the cassettes in its inventory; and it is often unable to fill requests for popular new releases because it has few copies of each title.

From this research, LeRoy and Atkinson concluded that Video's 1st could carve out a niche in a very competitive market by doing the following: setting up stores with total inventories of 300 videocassettes spread among the most popular 30 new releases, utilizing 48-square-foot drive-through kiosks (to reduce operating costs and emphasize customer convenience), employing one full-time worker and four part-time workers per store (compared with four full-time and four part-time workers in more traditional stores), and selling used tapes at discount prices. Because of the focus on customer convenience, Video's 1st's rental prices are about $1 higher than the industry average. Franchisees make an initial investment of approximately $87,700 per outlet, including the cost of the kiosk, initial inventory, a grand opening, and training. Royalty and advertising fees are 8 per cent of sales.

Industry experts are quite skeptical about Video's 1st's prospects. They believe the market is saturated, question whether consumers will actually pay more for drive-through convenience, wonder how the kiosks will handle customer traffic on a busy Saturday afternoon, think the franchise fees are too high, and feel that LeRoy and Atkinson have substantially underestimated the complexity of setting up a national franchise.

What do you think? Would you invest in Video's 1st?

Source: Based on material in Tom Richman, "Drive-In Movies," *Inc.* (February 1988), pp. 42–49.

❑

❑ Many service retailers must possess licenses or certification in order to operate their businesses. Barbers, real-estate brokers, medical personnel, attorneys, plumbers, and others must pass examinations in their chosen fields.

❑ A service retailer really needs to enjoy his or her profession and have an aptitude for it. Because of the close personal contact with customers, these elements are essential and difficult to fake.

The financial resources necessary for a service-oriented retailer may differ significantly from those of a goods-oriented retailer. The major ongoing cost for many service retailers is labor. Whereas the opening of a service station demands a high capital investment, the compensation for mechanics is the largest ongoing cost of doing business. For a goods retailer, the major ongoing investment is inventory.

Therefore, many service retailers can operate on lower overall investments and require less yearly revenue than goods retailers. A new service station can function with one gas attendant and one skilled mechanic. A tax preparation firm can succeed with one accountant. A watch repair business needs only one repairperson. In each case, the owner may be the only skilled laborer. Accordingly, costs can be held down. In contrast, a goods retailer must have an adequate assortment and supply of inventory, which may impose financial obligations, require storage facilities, and be costly.*

It must be pointed out that some service retailing requires not only an initial capital investment but also other ongoing nonlabor costs. For instance, an amusement park, a car wash, and a laundromat all have expensive electrical and maintenance costs.

In selecting a service category, it is crucial that all costs be calculated. The owner's labor should not be viewed as cost-free because he or she could earn wages as someone else's employee (and the owner needs a steady income to maintain a given life-style).

The time resources of the prospective retailer should be weighed in terms of the time requirements of alternative business opportunities. Some businesses, like a self-service laundromat or a movie theater, require low time investments. Other businesses, like house painting or a travel agency, require large time investments because personal service is the key to profitability. More service retailers fall into the high-time-investment than the low-time-investment category.

Setting Objectives

In addition to the sales, profit, and image objectives sought by goods-oriented retailers, service-oriented retailers should set other objectives because of their unique characteristics. These include increasing service tangibility, matching demand and supply, standardizing services, and making services more efficient.[6]

Service tangibility can be increased by stressing service-provider reliability, promoting a continuous slogan (e.g., at Delta Airlines, "we love to fly and it shows"), describing specific service accomplishments (such as an automobile tune-up's improving gasoline consumption by one mile per gallon), and offering warranties. H&R Block has promoted a program that guarantees the tax refunds computed by its preparers. In 1988, Block also had a multimillion-dollar loan program, whereby it prepaid refunds to its customers, using the tax refunds as collateral.

Demand and supply can be better matched by marketing similar services to market segments having different demand patterns, marketing new services having demand patterns that are countercyclical from existing services, marketing new services that complement existing services, marketing "extras" during nonpeak times, and marketing new services not subject to existing capacity constraints (e.g., a restaurant's starting a catering service).[7]

Standardizing services reduces variability, makes it easier to set prices, and improves efficiency. Services can be standardized by clearly defining each of the tasks involved, determining the minimum and maximum time necessary to complete each task, selecting the best order for tasks to be completed in, and specifying the optimum time and quality of the entire service. Standardization has been successfully applied to such retailers as quick-auto-service providers (oil change, tune-up, and muffler repair firms), legal services (for wills, house closings, and so on), and emergency-medical-treatment centers.[8] When these services are standardized, there is often a trade-off: more consistent quality and convenience in exchange for less of a personal touch.

An important tool in standardizing labor-intensive services is a **service blueprint,** which systematically lists all the functions to be performed and the average time required for each function to be completed.[9] Figure 17-3 contains a service blueprint for a quick-oil-change firm's employees to follow. The blueprint iden-

*This distinction between service and goods retailing may not be as great as expected, because manufacturers and wholesalers may allow their goods-oriented retailers to receive inventory on consignment or may offer low-interest credit terms.

**Expected average
time per activity**

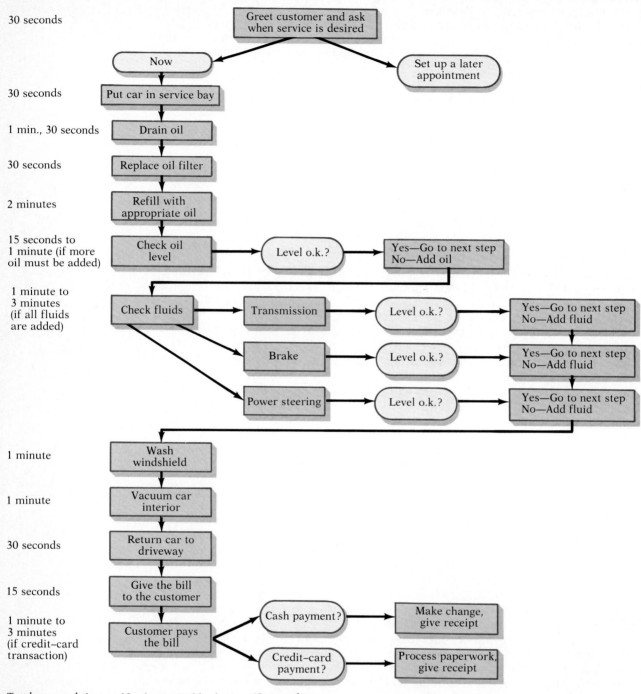

30 seconds

30 seconds

1 min., 30 seconds

30 seconds

2 minutes

15 seconds to
1 minute (if more
oil must be added)

1 minute to
3 minutes
(if all fluids
are added)

1 minute

1 minute

30 seconds

15 seconds

1 minute to
3 minutes
(if credit–card
transaction)

Greet customer and ask
when service is desired

Now

Set up a later
appointment

Put car in service bay

Drain oil

Replace oil filter

Refill with
appropriate oil

Check oil
level

Level o.k.?

Yes—Go to next step
No—Add oil

Check fluids

Transmission

Level o.k.?

Yes—Go to next step
No—Add fluid

Brake

Level o.k.?

Yes—Go to next step
No—Add fluid

Power steering

Level o.k.?

Yes—Go to next step
No—Add fluid

Wash
windshield

Vacuum car
interior

Return car to
driveway

Give the bill
to the customer

Customer pays
the bill

Cash payment?

Make change,
give receipt

Credit–card
payment?

Process paperwork,
give receipt

Total expected time = 10 minutes to 14 minutes, 45 seconds.

FIGURE 17-3
A Service Blueprint for a Quick-Oil-Change Firm's Employees

tifies employee and customer activities (in sequence), as well as expected average performance times for each activity. Among the advantages of a service blueprint are that it helps standardize services (within a location and between locations), isolates places where the service is weak or prone to failure (for example, do employees actually check the transmission, brake, and power-steering fluid levels in one minute?), develops a plan which can be evaluated for completeness (for example, should the customer be offered options for oil grades?), evaluates personnel needs (for example, should one employee change the oil and another wash the windshield?), and helps recommend productivity improvements (for example, should the customer or an employee drive the car into and out of the service bay?).

In addition to standardized services, retailers may be able to make services more efficient by automating them, thereby substituting machinery for labor. For instance, attorneys are increasingly using computerized word-processing for common paragraphs in wills and house closings. This results in more consistent quality, time savings, and neater, more error-free, documents.[10] Among the service retailers that have automated most are car washes, banks, bowling alleys, long-distance telephone services, and hotels.

Defining and Examining the Target Market

The target market must be defined and examined, and the consumer and the service offering carefully matched. Consumer demographics, life-styles, and decision making should all be studied. In this way, the retailer can develop a strategy in a logical and consistent manner. To illustrate with an earlier example, a barber shop would attract customers who are more conservative, less affluent, less mobile, and more convenience-oriented than those drawn to a personal-care salon.

Service retailers can use segmentation and/or mass marketing approaches. These examples show the variety of target market alternatives available to service firms:

❏ Moto Photo, a one-hour film-processing chain, targets heavy film users; this group includes expectant and new parents, and travelers. To stimulate business, Moto gives expectant parents a free baby book; it gives new parents a free teddy bear when they bring in a roll of film for processing; and it gives travelers free diaries to log their vacations.[11]

❏ Barnett Bank, based in Jacksonville, Florida, aims its efforts at retirees. This segment holds an estimated three-quarters of all funds on deposit in Florida. Its "Senior Partners" program offers free checking, special checks and a checkbook cover, accidental death insurance, and a 10 per cent discount on the first transaction with Barnett's brokerage department. Free photocopy services and help with medical and insurance forms are also provided at almost all Barnett branches. To qualify for the program, customers must be at least fifty-five years old and keep both a checking account and a money-market (or certificate-of-deposit) account at the bank. Barnett has dominated the Florida market by blanketing it with branches and by giving such high attention to services for senior citizens. It even has a branch in a life-care center.[12]

❏ Decades ago, Club Med started out by marketing all-inclusive prepaid vacations to young single adults; now more than one-half of the club's clientele are married. The average annual income for Club Med vacationers is $54,000, and more than 20 per cent earn over $80,000 per year. Yet, Club Med's long-standing image as a singles' resort has been hard to shake. According to the firm's president, "We have gone through a gradual evolution [from young singles to baby boomers] and what we need to do now is not so much change our image as erase the misconceptions—to better explain."[13]

❑ To attract and satisfy a mass market, General Motors has developed a national "Mr. Goodwrench" service program with its automobile dealers. The program requires participating dealers to satisfy ten specific quality standards. In return, General Motors sponsors mass advertising and encourages standardized performance among dealers.[14]

Outlining Overall Strategy

In planning the overall strategy for operating a service business, the full range of controllable factors (store location and operations, service offering, pricing, and store image and promotion) and uncontrollable factors (consumer, competition, technology, economic conditions, seasonality, and legal restrictions) must be examined.[15] Figure 17-4 contains a list of the special considerations and problems facing service retailers in each of these areas. They are detailed in the sections that follow.

Controllable Factors: Store Location and Operations

The store location and operations aspect of strategy must be thoroughly outlined. The importance of store location to service retailers varies greatly. In some service categories, such as television repairs, house painting, and lawn care, the service may be "delivered" to the appropriate site. The retailer's location becomes the client's home or office, and the actual office of the retailer is relatively unimportant. Many service clients might never even see the retailer's office; they maintain contact by telephone or by personal visits from the retailer, and customer convenience is optimized. In these instances, the retailer incurs travel expenses, but it also has low (or no) rent and does not have to maintain store facilities, set up store displays, and so on.

Other service retailers are visited on "specific-intent" shopping trips. Although the customer is concerned about the convenience of a location, he or she usually does not select a skilled practitioner such as a doctor or a lawyer on the basis of location. It is common for doctors and attorneys to locate their offices in their homes or near hospitals or court buildings, respectively.

For some service retailers that are visited by customers, location is quite important. Car washes, travel agencies, and airline reservation offices are examples of retailers that must be concerned about the convenience of their locations. In fact, car-rental agencies pay premium rents to be situated in airports. For example, the rent at airports for the "Big Four" agencies (Hertz, Avis, National, and Budget) is generally about 10 per cent of their locally generated sales—in addition to fees for desk space and parking. Airports situated in some popular tourist areas derive up to 30 per cent of their revenues from the Big Four car agencies. Smaller car-rental agencies avoid the high rent by locating nearby and driving customers to and from the airport; thus, these firms can compete on the basis of low prices.[16]

The store size and level of investment are considerably lower for many service-oriented retailers than they are for goods-oriented retailers. A small store can often be utilized, because little or no room is needed for displaying merchandise. As an example, a travel agency may have twelve salespeople and book several million dollars in trips; yet it may fit into a store with less than five hundred square feet. The investment factor relates to the absence of inventory, as discussed in the previous section. In addition, telephone business can further reduce the importance of store size and fixtures for service retailers.

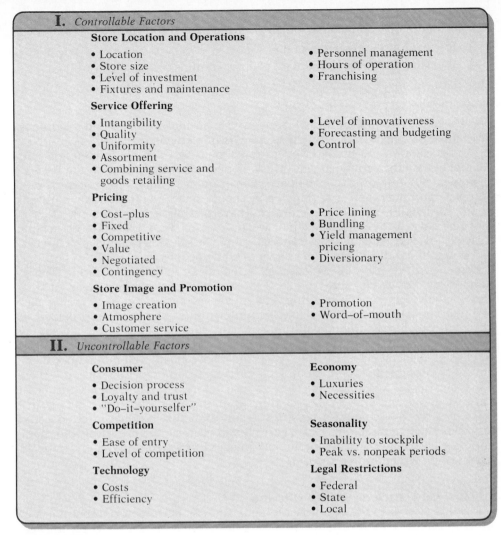

I. *Controllable Factors*

Store Location and Operations

- Location
- Store size
- Level of investment
- Fixtures and maintenance

- Personnel management
- Hours of operation
- Franchising

Service Offering

- Intangibility
- Quality
- Uniformity
- Assortment
- Combining service and goods retailing

- Level of innovativeness
- Forecasting and budgeting
- Control

Pricing

- Cost–plus
- Fixed
- Competitive
- Value
- Negotiated
- Contingency

- Price lining
- Bundling
- Yield management pricing
- Diversionary

Store Image and Promotion

- Image creation
- Atmosphere
- Customer service

- Promotion
- Word–of–mouth

II. *Uncontrollable Factors*

Consumer

- Decision process
- Loyalty and trust
- "Do–it–yourselfer"

Economy

- Luxuries
- Necessities

Competition

- Ease of entry
- Level of competition

Seasonality

- Inability to stockpile
- Peak vs. nonpeak periods

Technology

- Costs
- Efficiency

Legal Restrictions

- Federal
- State
- Local

FIGURE 17-4
Special Strategy Considerations and Problems Faced by a Service Retailer

Some fixtures and maintenance are more important for many service-oriented retailers than they are for goods-oriented retailers. Because the sale of tangible, branded goods (which can be compared among different stores) is not the major focus of service retailing, the customer may base part of his or her opinion of a retailer on its visible store fixtures and appearance. To use the travel agency example again, the desks, carpeting, light fixtures, typewriters, and so on would be used by the customer in developing an image of the retailer—even though these items are not part of the promotion mix.

Some aspects of personnel management can be difficult and frustrating for a service retailer:

❏ When should the firm be staffed? Are there peak business hours?

❏ How can customer waiting time be minimized?

❏ What should permanent employees do during the time when no customers appear?

❑ How can employee performance be measured? How should the performance of technical personnel with high customer contact be evaluated?

❑ How can productivity be increased?

❑ How should employees be paid (salary, commission, and so on)?

❑ If an employee quits or is fired, will customers follow him or her to another company?

Because of the personal nature of many service businesses, these and other questions must be considered before a strategy is implemented.[17]

The decision on the hours of operation should be made in conjunction with personnel management decisions. These hours must be planned on the basis of customer, not employee, convenience. For example, a shoe repair store should be open mornings, and a savings bank should have evening and/or Saturday hours. Although a shoe repair store can have one worker to open the store in the morning just to receive broken or worn shoes, as the work will be done later, a savings bank must plan to have enough employees during evening and/or weekend hours to handle all customer services while people wait.

Franchised services are expanding.[18] Dentahealth, Fantastic Sam's, Thrifty Rent-A-Car, Jazzercize, and Century 21 Real Estate are some examples of franchises involved in service retailing. The greatest potential problem facing each of these companies involves a lack of uniformity in the services provided by different franchisees. Dentahealth must ensure that its dentists provide similar services at similar prices. Fantastic Sam's must provide consistent hair-cutting services at all locales. Thrifty Rent-A-Car must have clean, well-maintained economy cars available for rental at all locations. Jazzercise must be sure that there are professional, knowledgeable fitness instructors at each studio. Century 21 must weed out unethical brokers and insist on certain performance standards.

If any unit in a franchise fails, the whole franchise would suffer. Because service is such an intangible, extra care should be given to generating and maintaining a clear and consistent company image. Employee training and supervision take on added importance.

Controllable Factors: Service Offering

A goods-oriented retailer, carrying items such as perfume or automobiles or televisions, has tangible products to offer. The merchandise can be seen, smelled, touched, heard, and, in some cases, tasted. A service retailer that handles rentals and/or repair services deals with tangible products, but the service it provides is still intangible. Nonetheless, a nongoods service retailer, such as an accountant, has the greatest level of intangibility to overcome in marketing its services to consumers, since the services offered often cannot be seen, smelled, touched, heard, or tasted.

For example, an airline rents seats on its planes to passengers; yet the quality of the service it offers depends on such intangibles as customers' perceptions of several factors: flight attendant courtesy, the cleanliness of the aircraft, the smoothness of the flight, the company's record for on-time flights, and the efficiency of baggage handling. As one airline president remarked, "We have 50,000 moments of truth out there every day."[19]

This is how one service retailer, a travel agency, might deal with the intangibility of its offering. The agency could emphasize the expertise of its agents and the types of travel arrangements it handles. Employees would be trained so that they are aware of all available vacation packages, and their options, and they are able to design customized trips. The agency would have good relationships with popular airlines and hotels to provide one-stop shopping for customers. To present its service offering as tangibly as possible to customers, the agency could utilize computer terminals in acquiring airline and other information and in processing orders (to demonstrate knowledge and efficiency), place certificates on office walls (that indicate the training received by employees, the awards recognizing the firm's fine past performance, and testimonials from satisfied clients), have a large assortment of colorful and descriptive brochures (to show sightseeing opportunities, hotel accommodations, and so on), and market specific vacation packages (with the name of the hotel and airline, all package components, and preprinted prices).

Like the goods-oriented retailer, the service-oriented retailer must consider the quality of its offering. Airlines are always competing on the basis of "no frills" versus "extra service," trying to satisfy different market segments. For instance, many students look for no-frills flights, whereas businesspeople are often more concerned about the time of departure and direct flights, and tourists desire inflight services.

Quality may also be difficult for a service retailer to plan because of the different customer perceptions of the same service. As an example, a tax preparation service may be purchased because the consumer desires accurate mathematical computation, an opportunity for financial savings, advice, convenience, or freedom from responsibility. Different market segments could be lured by each of these perceived benefits. Figure 17-5 shows ten factors that consumers may use in determining the quality of a service.

When a service retailer selects its level of service quality, the target market, competition, the firm's image, store location, turnover, profitability, national versus private brands, the services to be offered, personnel, perceived customer benefits, and constrained decision making should each be considered. An additional factor (of greater importance than to a goods-oriented retailer), the uniformity of the offering provided by the same service firm, must be thoroughly planned.

The customer is interested in receiving the same service each time a particular retailer is patronized. For example, employees' appearance, skills, attitude, and performance must be consistent. Customer loyalty is predicated on uniform service. If a person eats at a restaurant where it usually takes one hour to complete dinner, this person would probably be very dissatisfied with a visit taking two hours to finish dinner (because of slow service). On the other hand, when a restaurant normally has two-hour service, its regular customers would not be unhappy with the length of the meal.

Service assortment needs to be determined. Width and depth of assortment, although different from that of a goods-oriented retailer, must be planned. Two illustrations will demonstrate this point. The width of assortment for a car-rental agency may consist of cars, trucks, vans, and camper-trailers. The depth of assortment consists of the various models within any line (e.g., cars) and the range of services (e.g., daily, weekly, and monthly rentals; automatic and manual transmissions; air-conditioned and non-air-conditioned). In Florida, many car-rental agencies concentrate on one product line (cars) and offer small economy cars only. This is a narrow-shallow service assortment that has proved very popular with the budget-oriented vacationer.

Sports arenas must also make assortment decisions involving the events they will exhibit. Madison Square Garden in New York, owned by Gulf & Western, utilizes a wide-deep strategy. The assortment is wide because all types of sports and nonsports events are exhibited, including basketball and hockey games, tennis tournaments, boxing and wrestling matches, rodeos, circuses, dog shows, the Ice Capades, political conventions, rock concerts, and trade shows. There is depth of assortment because numerous basketball teams, hockey teams, tennis stars, and others play there. In addition, tickets are priced over a wide range and are available on a daily, seasonal (one sport), and all-events basis.

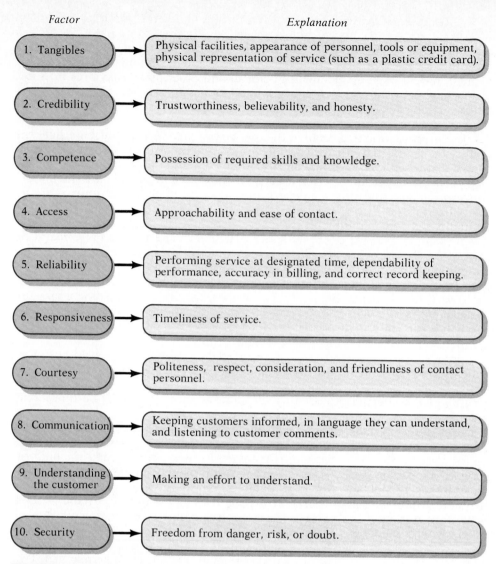

Factor	Explanation
1. Tangibles	Physical facilities, appearance of personnel, tools or equipment, physical representation of service (such as a plastic credit card).
2. Credibility	Trustworthiness, believability, and honesty.
3. Competence	Possession of required skills and knowledge.
4. Access	Approachability and ease of contact.
5. Reliability	Performing service at designated time, dependability of performance, accuracy in billing, and correct record keeping.
6. Responsiveness	Timeliness of service.
7. Courtesy	Politeness, respect, consideration, and friendliness of contact personnel.
8. Communication	Keeping customers informed, in language they can understand, and listening to customer comments.
9. Understanding the customer	Making an effort to understand.
10. Security	Freedom from danger, risk, or doubt.

FIGURE 17-5
Ten Factors Consumers Use to Determine Service Quality
Source: Adapted by the authors from A. Parasuraman, Valarie A. Zeithaml, and Leonard L. Berry, "A Conceptual Model of Service Quality and Its Implications for Future Research," *Journal of Marketing*, Vol. 49 (Fall 1985), pp. 45–46. Reprinted by permission of the American Marketing Association.

Every service retailer, small or large, must define the limits of the offering in terms of the width and the depth of assortment. This decision is not restricted to goods-oriented retailers.

Because of the growth of service retailing, many traditional retailers are now combining service and goods retailing. Among the traditional retailers operating a retail service in the same stores where they sell merchandise are the following:

❑ Sears owns and operates insurance, real-estate, stock-brokerage, and other services.

❑ 7-Eleven outlets rent videocassettes.

- Many department stores own and operate restaurant facilities.
- Many larger supermarkets sell film processing and contain automatic banking windows.

Other traditional goods-oriented retailers lease sections of their stores to service operators, such as banks, opticians, beauty parlors, jewelry appraisers, and professionals, such as dentists and lawyers. In some instances, traditional retailers have working arrangements with finance companies (automobile dealers) and repairpeople (television appliance stores) and receive commissions for performing the sales function for them.

A retailer that combines goods and services into one offering must follow a consistent strategy. The goods and services should complement each other, be a logical extension for the retailer, and not adversely affect the firm's image. The combinations just cited follow these guidelines. Combination goods/service retailing will continue to grow rapidly in the future.

Planning for innovation by a service-oriented retailer is significantly different from that in goods-oriented retailing and is sometimes unpredictable. A rented-goods retailer must anticipate which models or styles will be popular. For example, which movies will be the most desirable videocassettes to be rented during the next twelve months? Which car models will customers prefer to rent?

A service retailer that handles repairs and improvements must deal with two types of innovation planning. First, techniques for repairing or improving new merchandise must be learned. There is normally sufficient time to prepare for new items (e.g., large-screen rear-projection televisions) because these goods often have factory warranties for ninety days up to one year or longer. Second, new techniques must be developed and marketed for servicing existing items (e.g., a new way to paint a car or treat the lawn). Customers must be sold on the technique, which may require overcoming resistance to the new method.

A nongoods-service retailer has the toughest job in planning new services because it deals with the most intangibles. For example, an accountant has to determine which financial planning services to offer clients. A university must decide which courses and programs to add and which to delete.

Forecasting and budgeting are central to any retailer's plans; but these tasks take on greater importance for a service retailer, because of the perishability of its services and the need to carefully plan employee schedules. Daily, weekly, monthly, and yearly sales must be forecast as accurately (and realistically) as possible. For established retailers, past sales data often provide good estimates for the future, when combined with an analysis of competition, the target market, and the economy. Strong customer loyalty means that repeat sales can be predicted. The new retailer must look at demographics and so on but will rely essentially on estimates (usually keyed to the hours of work expected by the owner-operator) that are subject to large errors. The budget must be constructed on the basis of projected sales and the level of service quality to be offered, and it must allow for an acceptable profit margin.

A specified control mechanism is necessary in the evaluation and revision of the service retailer's strategy. As compared to a goods-oriented retailer, a service-oriented retailer has one area simplified and another magnified. Inventory control, including pilferage, is simple for nongoods retailers. For repair and rental retailers, the complexity of inventory is usually less than for goods-oriented retailers, although the rental retailer is sometimes confronted with sloppy or malicious customers. However, service-oriented retailers may be hard-pressed to measure productivity. After all, a fast worker may be a haphazard, incomplete, or messy worker. To overcome this difficulty, performance standards must be set, and equally important, service employees must be compared with one another on their overall performances.

Controllable Factors: Pricing

In setting prices, a service retailer has several alternative methods to consider: cost-plus pricing, fixed pricing, competitive pricing, value pricing, negotiated pricing, contingency pricing, price lining, price bundling, yield management pricing, and diversionary pricing. Many of these methods may be combined.

Cost-plus pricing occurs when a retailer uses the cost of a service as the basis for price. The firm adds the cost to a desired profit margin to arrive at the selling price. This is straightforward for some service retailers, such as coin-operated laundromats. Comtech, a New York laundromat chain, estimates that 60 per cent of its revenue covers leases; 17 per cent goes to repairs, service, and collections; 10 per cent goes to new washing and drying machines; 5 per cent covers operating expenses; and 8 per cent is profit.[20]

However, for many service retailers, service costs may be hard to determine. For instance, how does a self-employed repairperson determine labor costs? The simplest way is to find out the wages earned by a comparable repairperson working as an employee. But in addition to labor costs, materials, rent, taxes, and so on must be included in the calculation.

Cost-plus pricing has many disadvantages. It is not market-oriented; the price consumers are willing to pay for a service is not ascertained. Idle time is seldom included in this technique. Total per-sale costs are difficult to compute. Cost cutting is rarely pursued actively.

Fixed pricing exists in situations where the government or professional organizations have control and retailers must conform to the stated price structure. In some cities, parking-lot rates are fixed by law. Congress sets the rates for postage stamps. Train and bus prices must, in most cases, be government-approved.

Fixed pricing produces mixed results. Advantages are the elimination of price wars, the protection of small firms, and consumer protection. Disadvantages are the lack of retailer control over an important marketing factor, inflexibility, and complacency.

Competitive pricing is a marketing-oriented strategy. In this instance, a service retailer sets its prices on the basis of the prices charged by competitors. If a neighborhood theater charges $3 per ticket for a movie that has been in circulation for six months, a theater showing first-run movies can charge $4 to $6. Similarly, two hotels with comparable facilities and locations, catering to the same market, should have similar prices. Competitive pricing is the simplest, and probably the most effective, method for pricing services (because costs can usually be adjusted to accommodate the price). As always, pricing must be consistent with the overall retail strategy.

The use of competitive pricing is easy, responsive to the marketplace, and adaptive to the environment. It is a conservative strategy because a retailer goes along with its competitors. In addition, a retailer might incorrectly assume that its costs, image to consumers, and service offering are the same as those of competitors.

With **value pricing**, prices are set on the basis of fair value for both the service provider and the consumer. For value pricing to be effective, service retailers must be in a strong competitive situation and have relative control over prices. Value pricing is common for service professionals such as doctors and lawyers. They set fees based upon the value of their time and the services performed.

Negotiated pricing occurs when a retailer works out pricing arrangements with individual customers, because a unique or complex service is desired and a one-time price must be negotiated. Unlike cost-plus, fixed, or competitive pricing (whereby each consumer pays the same price for a standard service), each consumer may be charged a different price under negotiated pricing (depending on the nature of the unique service). For example, a moving company charges different fees, depending on the distance of the move, who packs the breakable furniture, the use of stairs versus an elevator, access to highways, and the weight of furniture such as a piano.

Under negotiated pricing, a retailer can be very responsive to each consumer and develop tailor-made proposals. It is critical that negotiated prices be competitive with those of other service retailers and include a thorough cost analysis. This technique can also be quite time-consuming and expensive (because an estimate must usually be given to the consumer). Negotiated pricing is inefficient for standardized, recurrent services.

Contingency pricing is an arrangement whereby the retailer does not receive payment from the customer until after the service is performed and payment is contingent on the service's being satisfactory. A real-estate broker earns his or her fee only when a house purchaser (who is ready, willing, and able to purchase a house) is presented to the home seller. Several brokers may show a house to prospective buyers, but only the broker who actually sells the house earns a commission. Many lawyers work on a contingency basis. They receive a percentage of the settlement if the client wins and nothing if the client loses.

In some areas, such as real estate, law, and lawn care, consumers prefer contingency payments because they want to be assured that the service will be satisfactorily performed. This pricing technique presents some risks to the retailer because considerable time and effort may be spent without payment. A real-estate broker may show a house twenty-five times, may not sell it, and therefore is not paid.

A **price-lining strategy** is used by service retailers that provide a wide selection of services. A line of prices is matched to the services. A travel agent handling European vacations can use price lining by creating several packages over a price range. Vacations to Spain, France, and Italy may be priced from $1,500 to $5,000 per person. At each package price, a different combination of travel features is offered (from no frills to top-of-the-line). A country club can use price lining by creating different types of membership: golf, tennis, and pool; golf and pool; golf only; tennis and pool; tennis only; and pool only. Each membership, from pool to all three activities, is priced differently.

Price lining, as a supplement to one of the other pricing methods already mentioned, enables a retailer to expand its target market and to create a differentiated service offering. The latter point is very important because many consumers relate price to quality. Therefore, price lining helps a retailer to foster a diversified service image.

A service retailer may offer bundled and/or unbundled prices to its customers. With a **bundled pricing** strategy, a retailer provides a number of services for one basic price. For example, a $30 air-conditioner tune-up could include in-home servicing, vacuuming the unit, replacing the air filter, unclogging all tubing, lubricating the unit, and checking air circulation. This approach helps standardize the service offering and makes bookkeeping simpler. However, it is not responsive to different customer needs.

As an alternative to bundled pricing, many service retailers use **unbundled pricing**, whereby they charge separate prices for each service provided. For example, a television-rental retailer could charge separate prices for the television rental, home delivery of the television set, and a monthly service contract. This approach enables a service retailer to more closely link its prices with actual costs, to present consumers with alternative service options, and to perform only those services specifically requested. Unbundled pricing may be harder to manage and may result in consumers' buying fewer services than they would purchase under bundled pricing. When a retailer offers both bundled and unbundled pricing, it is engaged in a form of price lining.

In **yield management pricing,** a service retailer determines the combination of prices that yield the highest level of revenues for a given time period. This approach is widely used in the airline industry, because a crucial decision by an airline involves how many tickets should be sold as first-class, full-coach, inter-mediate-discount, and deep-discount on each of its flights. With yield manage-ment pricing, an airline would offer fewer discount tickets for flights during peak periods than for ones in nonpeak times. The airline has two goals: to try to fill as many seats as possible on every flight and to sell as many full-fare tickets as it can ("You don't want to sell a seat to a guy for $79 when he's willing to pay $400"). Although yield management pricing is efficient and consumer-oriented, it is too complex for many small service retailers and often requires sophisticated computer software.[21]

Diversionary pricing is a practice used by deceptive service retailers. In this case, a low price is stated for one or a few services (which are emphasized in promotion) to give the illusion that all of the retailer's prices are low. However, the prices of services that are not advertised are higher than the average. The intention is to attract the consumer to the low-priced service and then entice him or her to purchase the high-priced ones as well. A service station may pro-mote an inexpensive tune-up to give the impression that all prices are low and then have high prices on repairs.

Because price and image are so closely related for a service retailer, it is im-perative that a thoughtful, cohesive pricing strategy be implemented. The tech-niques described in this section provide good insights into the alternatives avail-able. The major difficulties lie in assessing market demand and determining service costs.

Controllable Factors: Store Image and Promotion

Proper image creation is crucial to a service retailer's success. People patronize a retailer because a unique and desirable image is created and reinforced. Every restaurant presents an image, whether it be clean and efficient, rustic, romantic, or a gourmet's delight. Each movie theater presents an image by virtue of its prices, selection of movies, cleanliness, parking, and waiting lines. Dry cleaners develop their images through the quality of cleaning, speed, and prices.

The most important element in a service retailer's image is the customer's perception of how well the basic service is performed. A clear image can be relatively easily established by a rental retailer because tangible goods are in-volved; the consumer perceives a well-defined offering, which can be compared with that of other retailers. A repair or nongoods retailer may find it more difficult to carve out a distinct place in the market because of the intangibility of its offering (which makes it hard for people to comparison shop). To succeed, a repair or nongoods retailer must generate an image based on a stated set of criteria (keyed to the factors cited in Figure 17-5), which are communicated to customers.

In the creation of an image, the proper atmosphere must be established. A clean and efficient restaurant image is aided by waxed floors, regularly washed windows, functional booths and tables, and counter service. A rustic image is fostered by early-American furniture, lanterns, wooden fixtures, and pioneer at-tire for the waiters and waitresses. The romantic restaurant has secluded booths, candlelight, and soft background music. The gourmet's delight has the local newspaper critic's comments in the window, a lavish dessert display near the front door, and freshly cooked meals.

A movie theater affects its image by having extra cashiers on busy nights, separating smokers and nonsmokers (or not permitting smoking at all), cleaning popcorn and other debris from floors, and projecting a clear picture and sound. A dry cleaner can influence store image by providing an easy-opening front door, having a clean countertop, displaying prices and cleaning data, and arranging clean clothes neatly on hangers.

An important part of atmosphere is store design. This includes the storefront, the store layout, and the displays. The design must be constructed in a manner that is consistent with and adds to the service retailer's image and atmosphere. For example, one consumer survey found that the major factor (after quality of care) in attracting and retaining dental patients was the reception area. Cleanliness, lighting, roominess, and reading materials all contribute to patient perceptions.[22]

The level of customer service has a strong impact on image. Personal care, parking, delivery, credit, and telephone sales are some of the supplemental customer services for a service retailer to consider. A self-service laundromat is perceived much differently from a laundry service that picks up, cleans, and returns clothes. A restaurant that has metered, on-street parking is viewed as distinct from a restaurant that has valet parking. A university that provides deferred tuition has an image unlike one that insists on full payment before the semester begins. A taxi service that operates via the telephone is not the same as one that requires the patron to stand in the middle of a crowded street and wave.

At many banks, several customer services once provided free to all customers are now given free only to the most affluent customers. The banks charge fees for "excessive" withdrawals from savings accounts, cashing social-security checks, using live tellers, and balancing checkbooks. They believe that the charges are necessary for them to survive in today's highly competitive environment; in effect, these banks are now using unbundled pricing for customer services.

Some service retailers are rarely involved in extensive mass promotion. Seldom do barber shops, dry cleaners, repair retailers, house painters, laundromats, taxis, parking lots, or interior decorators advertise in any media other than Yellow Pages or local newspapers. They tend to be small and localized and rely on loyal customers and/or convenient locations. Other service retailers do rely heavily on promotion. These include hotels, motels, health spas, insurance companies, banks, and travel agents. These retailers are usually larger and have a wider geographic market. In addition, multiple outlets are common.

Until the late 1970s, many professional associations did not allow their members to advertise. However, the courts and the Federal Trade Commission have ruled that attorneys, doctors, pharmacists, optometrists, opticians, accountants, and others may advertise. Today, when advertising, these professionals are expected to exhibit high standards of ethics and concern for clients, explain when services should be sought, outline the attributes clients should consider when evaluating professionals, describe how clients can communicate with professionals, and state what they themselves can realistically provide to clients.[23]

With the exception of self-service businesses, all types of service retailers stress personal selling in their promotion mix. A barber, a dry-cleaning attendant, a repairperson, a painter, a taxi driver, and a parking-lot attendant all provide an important selling function as well as their primary service. So do hotel and motel personnel, health spa employees, insurance agents, bank tellers, and travel agents. Again, it must be mentioned that it is often personal attention that wins customers for service retailers.

Sometimes, service retailers supplement their communication effort with sales promotions. A credit-card company may offer a free month's trial for a new credit-card protection program. An airline may offer extra discounts for frequent passengers. A cruise ship may run coupon offers in newspapers. Premiums or prizes may be given by banks, insurance companies, movie theaters, and car-rental firms.

As a result of its good performance, a service retailer hopes to attain positive word-of-mouth communication. This occurs when a satisfied customer tells his or her friends to use that retailer, and this builds into a chain of customers. No service retailer can succeed if it is receiving extensive negative word-of-mouth communication (for example, "The hotel advertised that everything was included

How Are Ski Resorts Giving Business a Lift?

Since 1980, 25 per cent of all U.S. ski resorts have gone out of business as industry growth has slowed. And the remaining six hundred resorts have become more aggressive in attracting and retaining their customers:

Ski buffs in several major cities can now catch scheduled flights into once-isolated ski resorts such as Jackson Hole, Crested Butte, and Aspen. It's just one of the latest ski-resort gimmicks. In the flat $1.5 billion skiing market, resorts are trying everything from balloon rides to fireworks to lure skiers—and even nonskiers. They're building fancy restaurants, shops, tanning salons, skating rinks, and spas. They're offering a blizzard of bargain packages and discount tickets.

Here are some of the specific tactics being used: Diamond Peak (California) is running diamond and gold jewelry sweepstakes. Keystone (Colorado) offers snowmobile rides, tennis, and free car rentals with some of its package vacations. Killington (Vermont) has wine tastings, fireworks, and racquetball. Stratton (Vermont) pro-

vides flower-arranging, nutrition, and financial-planning classes. Vail (Colorado) has "Adventure Mountains" for children, complete with teepees, forts, and bear caves; it also operates hot-air balloon rides. Remarked one ski-resort marketing manager, "It used to be enough to ski your brains out. Now people want a more rounded experience."

Despite these efforts, ski resorts are still facing some difficulties. They must be sure not to alienate their hard-core customers who are interested in skiing, not promotional events or activities. To get airlines to schedule direct flights, some of the resorts have made expensive guarantees; if flights are not full, the resorts make payments to the airlines. In 1987, Jackson Hole (Wyoming) lost $450,000 on its direct-flight program. Then, there's always the potential problem of warm weather and not enough snow. As one resort president stated, "You have to be out of your mind to be in the ski business."

Source: Based on material in Mark Ivey, Corie Brown, and Alice Z. Cuneo, "Hi, I'm Goofy. Come Ski with Me," *Business Week* (February 15, 1988), pp. 58, 60.

in the price. Yet it cost me twenty dollars to play golf"). Such comments would cause the retailer to lose substantial potential business.

A service-oriented retailer, much more than its goods-oriented counterpart, must have positive word-of-mouth to attract new customers and retain the ones. For example, health-care professionals credit word-of-mouth with generating 63 per cent of all new patients. Noted one marketing expert, "Advertising can only bring a person into an office once. If you are incompetent, don't treat patients properly, or overcharge, you're not going to get any repeat business. Word-of-mouth is still the most important source of new patients."[24]

Uncontrollable Factors: The Consumer

A service retailer must understand and respond to its consumers, who go through some form of decision process in selecting and purchasing services. The manner in which consumers use the process depends on the cost of the service, the newness of the service, the recurrence of the purchase, and so on. Because of the intangible nature of many services, it is imperative that each element in the decision process be studied: stimulus, problem awareness, information search, evaluation of alternatives, purchase, and postpurchase behavior. In addition, the relation of purchase behavior to consumer demographics and lifestyles should be studied.

The successful service retailer relies upon the continued patronage and trust of customers, since many customers exhibit high levels of loyalty once they have selected a barber, a dentist, a doctor, a plumber, an accountant, a service station, or other service provider. This loyalty is usually much greater than for a goods-oriented retailer, because customers can easily switch among retailers selling the same merchandise. It is not as easy to switch among repair or nongoods retailers; satisfaction with these service retailers is based upon a total offering that is hard to compare. In addition, loyal customers have a trust with their current service provider that is sometimes impossible for a competitor to break.

Once a service retailer is established, business should be good as long as a consumer orientation is maintained. In this situation, a new barber, dentist, doctor, plumber, accountant, or service station would find it extremely difficult to break into the market.

One type of customer is generally beyond the reach of some service retailers: the do-it-yourselfer. The number of do-it-yourselfers is growing, as both service costs and leisure time increase. The do-it-yourselfer does his or her own tune-ups, paints his or her house, landscapes the lawn, plans his or her own vacation, and/or sets up his or her own darkroom for developing film. Goods-oriented discount retailers do very well by selling supplies to do-it-yourselfers. However, service retailers suffer because the major service (labor) is undertaken by the customer himself or herself. Market segmentation becomes desirable, and perhaps even necessary, to avoid the do-it-yourself segment or to serve it by offering very low prices for basic services.

Uncontrollable Factors: Competition

The ease of entry into service retailing differs for rentals from repairs and nongoods. A rental retailer must often invest a large amount in the item to be rented, such as an automobile or an apartment. This investment limits entry into the market. On the other hand, a repair or nongoods retailer usually relies on labor (often his or her own) and tools, which minimizes investment costs. In this case, entry into the marketplace is easy. An exception occurs when extensive education and licensing provisions restrict entry.

Where easy entry exists, the level of competition will be high. In particular, small businesses will crop up, and they can be profitable if they appeal to specific target markets. Numerous small travel agencies, restaurants, and film processors flourish. Where entry is difficult, the level of competition is low. There are few bowling alleys, amusement parks, and country clubs operating in any geographic area.

When a service retailer chooses a location, the amount of existing and potential competition should be measured. The site selected should have sufficient traffic and growth potential to accommodate that service retailer. For instance, a location with one profitable car wash may become a site with two unprofitable car washes if a second retailer opens and shares business with the first. And a car wash cannot easily be moved once it is constructed.

Uncontrollable Factors: Technology

A service retailer has a wide variety of technological options available in operating a business. A hotel could use an expensive computerized reservation system or older, less costly manual reservation procedures. A taxi service could feature old Yellow Cabs or new Chevrolet Celebrities. A car wash could clean vehicles by hand or via large machines. A gardener could use a hand mower and cutting shears or elaborate automatic tools. An airline could fly 707s, 727s, 737s, 747s, 757s, 767s, and/or SSTs.

A business that relies on older technology must provide superior personal service and rely on a loyal customer following. A firm that depends on newer methods can eventually lower costs and do a more efficient and consistent job, which, in turn, results in an improved image and lower prices than those of competitors. A modern reservation system eliminates duplication, provides accurate information, and aids in strategy planning. A new, more compact taxi gets good gas mileage and is inexpensive to maintain. An automatic car wash has the capacity to clean and wax one hundred or more cars per hour and leaves the cars sparkling. A gardener with automatic tools handles twice as many customers and does a consistent job. A 767 jet allows an airline to schedule large, fuel-efficient flights, which cut down on expenses.

Uncontrollable Factors: The Economy

A service retailer should consider the effect of the economy on business. Because a number of services can be classified as luxuries, they are likely to be affected by economic conditions. When the economy is poor, air travel, overseas vacations, restaurants, and others are adversely influenced. Laundromats, beauty salons, dry cleaners, and others are less affected because for many consumers they are more necessities than they are luxuries.

In adapting to uncertain economic conditions, a service retailer can reduce sales fluctuations by offering a variety of services and de-emphasizing the luxury aspects of the services. It is important that business conditions be anticipated and included in strategy planning.

Uncontrollable Factors: Seasonality

Some service retailers are faced with seasonal demand for their services. Country clubs are most popular in the late spring, the summer, and the early fall. Many hotels are busiest on weekends and holidays. Landscapers work most often in the fall and spring. Local buses and trains are most crowded during the morning and evening commuter rush hours.

The greatest problem for these service retailers is their inability to stockpile resources. If a country club has the capacity to accommodate 500 people, it cannot admit 750 people on Friday because there were only 250 on Thursday. Similarly, a hotel cannot fill 1,000 rooms with 6,000 holiday visitors, even though during midweek, half the rooms were empty. A landscaper cannot handle two customers at the same time during the spring to make up for idle time in the winter. Buses and trains cannot sell 20,000 tickets for 5,000 seats during the rush hour to make up for the lack of passengers during the rest of the day.

Service businesses must be oriented toward satisfying peak demand periods. Employees must be deployed accordingly, and long-range planning must be based on realistic forecasting (including peak and nonpeak periods). Special services and offers can be used to attract customers during nonpeak times. Country clubs can introduce indoor activities. Hotels can offer low prices and additional services (such as the free use of a golf cart or free drinks at a show) for midweek patrons. Landscapers can offer snow removal and other winter services. Buses and trains can offer fare discounts and tie-ins with restaurants and theaters for off-hour riders.

Uncontrollable Factors: Legal Restrictions

All service retailers should be familiar with the federal, state, and local restrictions under which they must operate. On the federal level, various agencies, such as the Federal Aviation Administration and the Federal Deposit Insurance Corporation, oversee service retailers. In addition, many national self-governing bodies set guidelines for their members. These groups include the American Bar Association, the American Medical Association, and the American Institute of Certified Public Accountants.

In recent years, the federal government has actively pursued a policy of deregulating transportation, banking, communications, and other service industries. This has greatly increased the flexibility of firms in developing and carrying out their strategies. It has also led to a greater use of marketing practices, such as consumer research.

On the state level, these are some illustrations of the legal restrictions facing service retailers: insurance companies and their rates are approved; licensing exams are administered and qualifications set for various professionals; utility rates are approved; trade schools are certified; and advertising messages may be limited. For instance, in Iowa and New Jersey, lawyers are not allowed to use music, lyrics, or animation in ads (on the grounds that clients could be misled). Most state bar associations do not allow law firms to use movie stars, famous athletes, or even former clients as spokespersons.[25]

At the local level, a retailer must be aware of zoning, operating, and other laws. Each municipality has different limitations, and this factor should be considered when a firm is selecting a store location.

Implementing a Service Strategy

After a general strategy is outlined, the service retailer must put it into action. The tactics followed must conform to the company's overall strategy, and an integrated plan must be carried out. In addition, the strategy should be fine-tuned whenever necessary. The following are a variety of examples involving the implementation of service strategies.

Retail strategies used by service professionals vary greatly. On the one hand, there are many doctors, lawyers, dentists, and other professionals who do not believe in retailing tactics or utilize them. They do not accept the fact that they are service retailers, think that activities such as advertising are demeaning, deplore competitive tactics, and do not understand all the elements in strategic retail-planning. These professionals believe that their services and skills market themselves.

On the other hand, there are a growing number of service professionals who are quite involved in retail strategies in response to growing competition. For example, the number of dentists in the United States has increased by two-thirds over the past twenty-five years. Yet, during the same period, because of better prevention measures (such as fluoride toothpaste and fluoridated water), the number of cavities has dropped significantly. Studies now show that 37 per cent of children between the ages of five and seven have no cavities at all. Many dentists are reacting to this situation by adopting such marketing practices as twenty-four-hour emergency services, in-home services (for realigning slipped dentures, etc.), free initial examinations, and increased attention to atmosphere and location.[26]

Hyatt Legal Services is the largest chain of legal clinics in the United States. The firm has almost two hundred offices and a staff of more than 630 attorneys. Initially, Hyatt emphasized low fees in its promotion efforts (such as $20 for an initial half-hour consultation and $75 for a simple will). Currently, it is concentrating on the marketing of its new LawPlan prepaid legal services. For $10 per month, LawPlan clients receive unlimited consultations and preparation of wills for members and their spouses. Hyatt plans to increase its revenues by handling additional services for members, including divorce actions and personal bankruptcies.[27]

Rented-goods retailing has expanded as the costs of purchasing merchandise have risen sharply. Annually, U.S. consumers spend $8–$10 billion renting appliances, tools, household goods, and television sets. For example, retailers involved in television rentals emphasize product currency, no large initial payments, repair service, consumer mobility, delivery and installation, loaner sets, and trade-ins. Some firms provide ownership at the end of the rental agreement. Although consumers make no large initial payment, total rental costs are usually greater than outright purchases. Typically, a retailer must rent a set for two years before a profit is returned to the firm.

The household-goods moving industry is undergoing significant changes because of deregulation. Prior to the Household Goods Transportation Act of 1980, interstate shippers were limited to hauling used household goods at rates controlled by federal regulators. Now, carriers can ship a wide range of goods, offer various services, and control the prices they charge. As the president of Allied Van Lines noted:

> We didn't pay a whole lot of attention to what the customer wanted before. Our services were pretty well governed by what the Interstate Commerce Commission would let us do. Now we're out battling for customers like everyone else in the competitive environment. There's more emphasis on sales and market training, guarantees, and other consumer attractions. We certainly have hiked our media advertising and our marketing research as a result of deregulation.[28]

Private storefront postal services rent mailboxes, receive and forward letters and packages, and pack boxes for consumers. At a time when the U.S. Postal Service has cut back on post office hours and some of the services provided, these private retailers are thriving. They offer customers longer hours of opera-

	True	False
1. Marketing accounting services means selling accounting services.	___	___
2. Concentration on servicing clients' needs is the best marketing plan to follow.	___	___
3. Individual offices and sectors (auditing, tax, management advisory services, etc.) within the firm mainly concern themselves with expanding firm's services in their respective areas of responsibility.	___	___
4. Professional staff are hired on the basis of technical competence only.	___	___
5. Developing new business is not important enough to put a senior officer in charge with firmwide responsibility.	___	___
6. Marketing of accounting services means advertising accounting services.	___	___
7. Most of the top officers of the firm have not attended a marketing seminar within the past two years.	___	___
8. We do not have a written list of target customers for business expansion.	___	___
9. Marketing, for an accounting firm, is inconsistent with professionalism.	___	___
10. We do not have a written business expansion plan.	___	___
11. It is best to hold business development meetings outside regular business hours so they won't interfere with ongoing operations.	___	___
12. Less than 10 per cent of total company time is spent on planning and preparing for business development.	___	___

Interpretation key

9–12 falses: Truly marketing–oriented
5–8 falses: Somewhat marketing–oriented
0–4 falses: Not at all marketing–oriented

FIGURE 17-6
A Quiz for Assessing a CPA Firm's Marketing Orientation
Source: John G. Keane, "How Accounting Firms Can Use Marketing Concept, Techniques to Develop Their Practices," *Marketing News* (March 6, 1981), p.12. Reprinted by permission of the American Marketing Association.

tion, quicker service, flexibility, and assistance with mailing problems. Some even have telex and facsimile machines and offer telephone-answering, word-processing, and photocopying services. Because of the level of service, these firms have prices far above those charged by the Postal Service. For example, the Postal Service charges about $22 per year for a small mailbox at a post office; private firms charge $10 to $25 per month (but many allow twenty-four-hour access to the boxes). Nationwide, there are about 3,500 storefront postal services generating annual revenues of more than $350 million.[29]

Re-Evaluating the Service Strategy

Once a service strategy is in full operation, it should be continuously monitored. For example, Figure 17-6 contains an audit form that CPAs (certified public accountants) can use to evaluate their level of marketing orientation. This audit form could be utilized by virtually all types of service retailers.

Both the overall strategy and the individual components of it, as well as their implementation, should be re-evaluated on a regular basis and adjustments made when necessary. In this way, a service retailer can quickly and accurately adapt to changes in the uncontrollable environment (consumers, competition, technology, economy, seasonality, and legal restrictions). The retail audit, described in Chapter 16, is as useful a tool for a service-oriented retailer as for a goods-oriented retailer.

SUMMARY

Service retailing now represents a sizable share of total retail sales and will continue to expand in the future. Service retailing can be divided into three broad categories: rentals, repairs and improvements, and nongoods. In each category, the customer receives a service but does not obtain ownership of a physical product. Service retailers can be classified in terms of their tangibility, service provider skill, labor intensiveness, customer contact, goals, and the degree of regulation.

Strategy planning and implementation are the cornerstones of a profitable retail service business. Although the overall principles of strategy are the same whether service-oriented or goods-oriented retailing is involved, there are some major differences. These differences exist because of the intangibility, inseparability, perishability, and variability associated with many services.

When conducting a situation analysis, the service category must be well defined. Personal abilities, financial resources, and time resources should be weighed in the selection of a service category. Next objectives are set to reflect service tangibility, demand and supply, standardization, and the efficiency of services. Then the target market is specified and described.

The overall strategy is outlined, consistent with the service category and target market. In planning the general strategy, the retailer must consider various controllable factors. Store location and operations factors include location, store size, the level of investment, fixtures and maintenance, personnel management, hours, and type of ownership. Service-offering factors include intangibility, quality, uniformity, assortment, combinations of goods and services, innovativeness, forecasting and budgeting, and control. Pricing techniques include cost-plus pricing, fixed pricing, competitive pricing, value pricing, negotiated pricing, contingency pricing, price lining, price bundling, yield management pricing, and diversionary pricing. Image and promotion factors include image creation, atmosphere, customer services, promotion, and word-of-mouth.

Uncontrollable factors must also be analyzed while a service retailer is developing an overall strategy. The consumer, competition, technology, the economy, seasonality, and legal restrictions should each be investigated. The strategy should adapt to these variables.

After a service-retailing strategy is carefully outlined, it must be implemented as prescribed. The strategy is then regularly monitored and adjusted as necessary.

QUESTIONS FOR DISCUSSION

1. What are the unique aspects of service retailing? Give an example of each.
2. It has often been stated that service retailers are not consumer-oriented. Why do you think this comment has been made? Is it accurate?
3. Should medical, accounting, and other services be considered a part of retailing? Why or why not?
4. In what kinds of service retailing are personal skills important? In what kinds are they unimportant?
5. For each of the following, name several alternative market segments to which they can appeal.
   a. Dance studio
   b. Stock broker
   c. Restaurant
   d. Accountant
   e. Amusement park
   f. Lawn service
6. What reasons can you give for the growth of franchised services?
7. Give several advantages and disadvantages of combining service and goods retailing in the same store facilities.
8. Why is personnel management difficult in service retailing?
9. Present an example of each type of pricing:
   a. Cost-plus
   b. Fixed
   c. Competitive
   d. Value
   e. Negotiated
   f. Contingency
   g. Bundled
   h. Diversionary
10. Explain the concept of atmosphere from a service-retailer perspective.
11. Explain the importance of word-of-mouth to a service retailer.
12. Does the consumer use the decision process differently for services than for goods? Explain your answer.
13. What alternative strategies can service retailers use to deal with the do-it-yourselfer?
14. Describe the difficulties in evaluating a service-retailing strategy.

NOTES

1. Becky Aikman, "Bringing Back That Disney Magic," *Newsday* (April 19, 1987), pp. 68 ff.; Ronald Grover and Gail DeGeorge, "Theme Parks: The Slugfest Is No Fantasy," *Business Week* (March 23, 1987), p. 38; and Ronald Grover, Mark N. Vamos, and Todd Mason, "Disney's Magic," *Business Week* (March 9, 1987), pp. 62–65.

2. Jeffrey A. Trachtenberg, "Shake, Rattle, and Clank," *Forbes* (July 14, 1986), pp. 71–74.

3. Stephen Lebaton, "Propriety on Trial in Legal Ads," *New York Times* (March 21, 1988), pp. D1, D10.

4. Joan Berger, "In the Service Sector Nothing Is 'Free' Anymore," *Business Week* (June 8, 1987), p. 144.

5. For other methods of classifying services, see Christopher H. Lovelock, "Classifying Services to Gain Strategic Marketing Insights," *Journal of Marketing*, Vol. 47 (Summer 1983), pp. 9–20; and Roger W. Schwenner, "How Can Service Businesses Survive and Prosper?" *Sloan Management Review*, Vol. 27 (Spring 1986), pp. 21–31.

6. See Valarie A. Zeithaml, A. Parasuraman, and Leonard L. Berry, "Problems and Strategies in Services Marketing," *Journal of Marketing*, Vol. 49 (Spring 1985), pp. 33–46.

7. Leonard L. Berry, A. Parasuraman, and Valarie A. Zeithaml, "Synchronizing Demand and Supply in Service Businesses," *Business*, Vol. 34 (October–December 1984), pp. 35–36.

8. " 'Standardized' Services Run Gamut from Mufflers to Wills," *Marketing News* (April 10, 1987), pp. 17, 43.

9. Karl Albrecht and Ron Zemke, *Service America! Doing Business in the New Economy* (Homewood, Ill.: Dow Jones–Irwin, 1985), pp. 86–92; Ernest J. McCormick, *Job Analysis: Methods and Applications* (New York: AMACOM, 1979); and G. Lynn Shostack, "Designing Services That Deliver," *Harvard Business Review*, Vol. 62 (January–February 1984), pp. 133–139.

10. Gregory Stricharchuk, "Law Office in Cleveland Goes Electronic: Computers Track Cases, Offer Motions," *Wall Street Journal* (October 9, 1987), p. 27.

11. "Extra Services Provide Niche for Film Processor," *Marketing News* (March 13, 1987), p. 26.

12. Roberta Reynes, "Seniority System Paying Dividends," *Advertising Age* (August 3, 1987), pp. S-8–S-9; and Thomas E. Ricks, "Attentive to Service, Barnett Banks Grow Fast, Keep Profits Up," *Wall Street Journal* (April 3, 1987), pp. 1, 12.

13. Amy Dunkin, John Rossant, and Gail DeGeorge, "How Club Med Wants an Antidote for Competition," *Business Week* (November 2, 1987), pp. 120–121.

14. Raymond Serafin, "Mr. Goodwrench Bets 'Hands' on Aftermarket," *Advertising Age* (November 4, 1985), p. 45.

15. See A. J. Magrath, "When Marketing Services, 4Ps Are Not Enough," *Business Horizons*, Vol. 29 (May–June 1986), pp. 44–50.

16. James E. Ellis, "Small Fry Start Nipping at the Whales of Auto Rental," *Business Week* (August 31, 1987), p. 81.

17. See Carol Surprenant and Michael R. Solomon, "Predictability and Personalization in the Service Encounter," *Journal of Marketing*, Vol. 51 (April 1987), pp. 86–96.

18. See James C. Cross and Bruce J. Walker, "Service Marketing and Franchising: A Practical Business Marriage," *Business Horizons*, Vol. 30 (November–December 1987), pp. 50–58.

19. Jan Carlzon, "We Fly People, Not Planes," *Across the Board* (June 1987), pp. 16–17 ff.

20. "A Growing Operator of Laundry Rooms," *New York Times* (January 3, 1984), p. D1.

21. Eric Schmitt, "The Art of Devising Air Fares," *New York Times* (March 4, 1987), pp. D1–D2; Kenneth Labich, "Winners in the Air Wars," *Fortune* (May 11, 1987), pp. 68–79; and Paulette Thomas, "Computers Permit Airlines to Use Scalpel to Cut Fares," *Wall Street Journal* (February 2, 1987), p. 25.

22. Randall E. Wade, "Study Suggests 10 Critical Areas for Dentists' Attention," *Marketing News* (December 9, 1983), p. 8.

23. Paul N. Bloom, "Effective Marketing for Professional Services," *Harvard Business Review*, Vol. 62 (September–October 1984), pp. 102–110.

24. "Experience Belies Healthcare Professionals' Ad Fear," *Marketing News* (June 8, 1984), p. 1.

25. "Propriety on Trial in Lawyer's Ads," pp. D1, D10.

26. Paul Duke, Jr., and Albert Karr, "Dentists Step Up Services and Marketing as Competition Increases in Crowded Field," *Wall Street Journal* (November 20, 1986), p. 31.

27. Patricia Belley Gray, "Hyatt Legal Services' Fast Growth Leaves Trail of Management Woes," *Wall Street Journal* (May 6, 1987), p. 33.

28. Kevin Higgins, "Movers Grope for Marketing Orientation," *Marketing News* (May 11, 1984), p. 1.

29. "Storefront Postal Services Thriving," *New York Times* (March 22, 1988), pp. D1, D9.

Minit Lube: Standardizing a Retail Service Business*

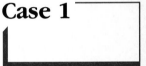

Case 1

Minit Lube, a division of the Quaker State Corporation, offers consumers a no-frills oil change for about $20, including a new oil filter. Minit Lube is a profitable retail service business, as well as a mechanism for selling Quaker State oil. In terms of market share, Minit Lube is now the second leading firm in the quick-oil-change industry. As of 1987, the company had 210 stores, about 40 per cent of which were franchised.

The quick-oil-change industry's origins can be traced to the oil embargo against the United States in 1973. Since that time, about one-half of U.S. service stations have gone out of business. This has led to a shortage of service stations to handle necessary car oil changes, while at the same time opening up convenient locations for quick-oil-change centers. Furthermore, since 1973, the average age of autos driven in the United States has risen from four to almost eight years; and consumers view regular oil changes as vital to prolonging the lives of their older cars.

There are currently about 3,000 quick-oil-change centers throughout the United States, and they account for 15 per cent of all purchased oil changes (many do-it-yourselfers perform their own oil changes). By 1990, there are expected to be as many as 6,000 outlets. Besides Minit Lube, the leading firms in the quick-oil-change business are Jiffy Lube (the industry leader with 670 franchised locations as of 1987), Valvoline (the Number 3 firm in terms of market share), Exxon, Texaco, and Avis. Minit Lube is so important to Quaker State that the company invested $75 million in Minit Lube during 1987 alone; this amount exceeded Quaker's capital spending for all projects in any previous year. And the president of Pennzoil (the major supplier for Jiffy Lube) has called the quick-oil-change business "the second great revolution in motor-oil marketing."

Most quick oil-change patrons are twenty-five to forty-nine years old and have above-average income and education. According to the vice-president of marketing for Minit Lube, "They're busy, they're working hard, they want to spend time with their families, they don't have time to do it themselves, and they don't have the inclination."

Minit Lube uses a strategy similar to that adopted by most of its competitors. Typically, up to three employees work on a car simultaneously. One drains the old oil. A second adds the new oil and checks and tops off other vehicle fluids (such as transmission, differential,

---

*The material in this case is drawn from " 'Standardized Services' Run Gamut from Mufflers to Wills," *Marketing News* (April 10, 1987), p. 17; and Caleb Solomon, "Changes Happening in Retail Motor Oil Business," *Wall Street Journal* (September 9, 1987), p. 6.

brake, power-steering, battery, and windshield fluids). A third worker vacuums the car interior, cleans the windshield, and properly inflates the tires. Although the advertised service price is about $20, the average sale is higher because air filters are not included in the basic price. Another employee usually processes payments. The advertised turnaround time is ten minutes; this time is based on when a car starts being serviced.

These are among the advantages of quick-oil-change centers over new-car dealers or local service stations:

❑ Frequently, quick-oil-change patrons can drive their cars into the centers without scheduling appointments or having to wait several hours for the car to be serviced. Extended automobile warranties and large-scale recalls have made scheduling routine maintenance at new-car dealers particularly difficult.

❑ The centers charge about the same prices as the traditional local service station, but considerably less than new-car dealers.

❑ Usually, neither new-car dealers nor local service stations check tire pressure, vacuum the car interior, or top off all fluids.

On the other hand, quick-oil-change centers have some disadvantages when compared with new-car dealers and local service stations:

❑ The advertised ten-minute turnaround time refers only to the time the service takes. On weekends, customers may have to wait in line in their cars for as much as one hour.

❑ Many people like a mechanic to visually inspect their vehicles at regular intervals; they view oil changes as the appropriate times for such inspections.

❑ Many people have social relationships with their mechanics. It is difficult for quick-oil-change centers to break such bonds; these centers rotate employees and are perceived as impersonal. This is summed up in this comment: "I wouldn't give a Minit Lube oil attendant a Christmas present."

❑ Service personnel at new-car dealers and local service stations are acknowledged as experts; quick-oil-change personnel are seen as hourly employees.

In some respects, the strategies of quick-oil-change centers resemble those of fast-food franchises. First, prior to locating an outlet, potential sites are usually studied in terms of the size of the surrounding population, traffic patterns, income levels, and the number of registered cars. Many times, quick-oil-change centers and fast-food franchises even compete for the same sites. Second, both quick-oil-change centers and fast-food outlets emphasize cleanliness. Third, both attempt to standardize their services via employee training and superior equipment. Their goal is to achieve a uniform level of service quality regardless of where the services are performed. Fourth, the market for both types of services is becoming increasingly saturated. Competition is rising faster than the market is growing.

QUESTIONS

1. Rate Minit Lube with regard to service intangibility, inseparability, perishability, and variability.
2. Evaluate Minit Lube's strategy on the basis of the seven special considerations cited in Table 17-1.
3. Although 40 per cent of Minit Lube centers are franchised (the others are owned and operated by Quaker State), all Jiffy Lube outlets are franchised. Comment on this.
4. How can Minit Lube differentiate itself from other quick-oil-change centers?

Larry Clark: A House Painter Rethinks His Service Strategy

Larry Clark is a thirty-four-year-old house painter, in business for himself. Larry has had his own business for eleven years and has done reasonably well. Larry can measure his success by several factors: most of his work comes from recommendations; he often has a backlog of work that can be up to three months long; and he has a high percentage of repeat business.

Until recently, Clark had been content to use a one-person service strategy. He knows there are several advantages to this strategy. People trust him in their homes (often both spouses work) and give him their keys without hesitation. Clark's customers know the quality of his work and his neatness. Although different painters may use the same paint, the quality of the job is largely related to how well surfaces are prepared (e.g., using mildew remover, plaster, and wood filler) and actually painted. Larry has a reputation for leaving a house and its surroundings at least as clean as when he started. He is personally responsible for all work and has total control over his business.

However, several developments have forced Larry Clark to rethink his one-person service strategy:

❑ His earnings have not kept up with inflation. See Table 1.

❑ When he is in demand, accounts backlog too long.

❑ The number of accounts has not grown in several years. Although Clark works 200 days per year, he would like to work 225 days (but not with the same hours per day he is keeping as a single worker).

❑ To keep his customers, Larry has maintained prices that are 20–30 per cent lower than those of larger competitors.

❑ He is unable to handle big jobs. Many newer homes, and homes whose exteriors have cedar, require special preparation, such as sanding. These jobs are difficult for one person to do. Clark has chosen not to take on major jobs for fear of losing several smaller ones.

❑ He is beginning to tire of the long hours he keeps. Larry generally arrives at the paint store at 8:00 A.M., paints from 9:00 A.M. to 5:00 P.M., and goes on estimates from 7:00 P.M. to 9:00 P.M. And since he does not have any employees, Clark must continually interrupt his work to go for additional supplies.

❑ Customers sometimes resent Larry's being at their homes for as long as one week to paint the exterior. By comparison, competitors with five to seven painters can finish a large house in as little as one day.

TABLE 1
Larry Clark, House Painter: An Eleven-Year Record

Year	Revenue	Total Paint Costs	Other Costs*	Net Income†	Number of Customers	Days Worked	Interior Jobs	Exterior Jobs‡
1988	$43,300	$8,000	$7,900	$27,400	60	200	20	40
1987	41,100	7,800	7,000	26,300	64	200	28	36
1986	39,900	7,500	6,600	25,800	57	200	18	39
1985	37,940	7,200	6,400	24,340	62	200	34	28
1984	35,010	7,000	6,000	22,010	63	200	35	28
1983	32,840	6,100	5,500	21,240	59	200	31	28
1982	31,400	5,700	5,400	20,300	57	190	31	26
1981	29,600	5,100	5,300	19,200	51	170	25	26
1980	27,710	5,000	4,800	17,910	46	130	25	21
1979	23,340	4,110	4,100	15,130	38	100	25	13
1978	20,220	4,080	4,000	12,140	27	80	17	10

*Such as trucking, bookkeeping, insurance, equipment, advertising, and an answering service.

†Before taxes.

‡Exterior jobs take longer but pay better than interior jobs.

TABLE 2

Strategy Changes Under Consideration by Larry Clark

1. A contract form could be developed. Until now, Clark has relied on verbal agreements. The contract form would provide starting and completion dates, specify the brand of paint to be used, state the type of surface preparation to be conducted, provide a written three-year guarantee against peeling, and cite the price of the job and the payment terms.

2. Homeowners who allow Clark to place a sign on their property (for a thirty-day period) stating that all painting work has been done by Larry Clark could receive a 5 per cent discount.

3. Only customers within a five-mile radius of Larry's home could be serviced. To date, Clark has agreed to paint customers' homes as far as thirty-five miles away. He realizes that he has not been reimbursed for travel time. In addition, he often has trouble finding a paint store to purchase supplies at when he travels to an unfamiliar area.

4. Bargaining over price could be eliminated. Larry has permitted loyal customers to cut $50 to $100 off the price he quotes.

5. All clients could be called a week after painting is finished to determine their satisfaction and recommend potential new accounts. For each recommendation, Clark could give the existing customer a small thank-you gift.

Right now, Larry Clark is undecided as to how he should proceed. These are among the options he is considering: hiring one or two full-time painters; hiring two to four part-time painters to work with him on major jobs; or hiring a full-time helper who would go to the paint store each morning, set up ladders, put down and pick up drop cloths, replenish supplies, and do other necessary nonpainting tasks. In addition, Clark is also contemplating whether to seek out more interior jobs (which are less likely to be canceled or delayed because of the weather, and less likely to have callbacks because of peeling paint) and whether to advertise his services more heavily. Larry is also giving thought to the other strategy changes listed in Table 2.

QUESTIONS

1. Comment on the data in Table 1.
2. Evaluate Larry Clark's current strategy in terms of location and operations, the service offering, pricing, and image and promotion.
3. Evaluate the strategy options under considera-tion by Larry Clark. Which should he adopt? Which should he avoid? Explain your answer.
4. What other suggestions would you make to Larry Clark?

As a result of continuing technological advances, even the smallest retailers will be able to computerize their operations, thus making them more efficient and more responsive to consumers. Shown here is a portable computer system that better enables video-cassette stores to manage their inventories.

Photo courtesy of Wetterau.

Radio Shack is one of a growing number of retail chains that will be using rationalized retailing to control costs and standardize operations among branches. With rationalized retailing, there are a heavy reliance on centralized decision making and detailed procedures for each phase of business. In the future, most of Radio Shack's outlets will feature the same Technology Store design depicted above.

Photo courtesy of Radio Shack, a division of Tandy Corporation, Fort Worth, Texas.

Many U.S. retailers will be increasing their international efforts to capitalize on the sizable opportunities in various foreign markets. Most of McDonald's sales growth will come from international sales. Shown here are McDonald's outlets in North Sydney, Australia (1) and Paris (2). The latter has a piano player entertaining patrons on the second floor. Hartmarx has licensing agreements for its clothing in 12 countries. It provides retailing, merchandising, and marketing expertise, such as the point-of-sale display presented on this page (3), in exchange for a minimum guarantee and royalty payments.

Photos courtesy of McDonald's and Hartmarx.

(1)

(2)

(3)

Chapter 18

The Changing Environment of Retailing

1 To examine demographic, life-style, consumerism, and regulatory trends and consider the impact of these factors on retailing

2 To consider the effects of technological developments

3 To discuss the potential responses of retail institutions to environmental trends

4 To analyze the international dimension of retailing

❑ **Chapter Objectives** ❑

After several years of development and testing, and an investment of about $40 million, J.C. Penney introduced its Telaction video-ordering system in early 1988 by making it available to 4,000 Chicago-area cable television subscribers. During 1988, J.C. Penney was expected to spend another $40 million to market Telaction, as it moved toward a goal of having more than 100,000 Chicago-area Telaction subscribers by the end of the year. In the long run, Penney wants Telaction to be a nationwide electronic shopping network.

This is how Telaction works. In neighborhoods where cable subscribers are wired to Telaction's "black box," a customer turns on his or her television set and turns to the Telaction cable channel. Next, he or she dials the local telephone number displayed on the television screen. Then, from a menu that appears on the television screen, the customer selects the goods/service category and retailer in which he or she is interested by entering a code number into a touch-tone telephone:

> If, for example, a female customer is interested in buying a winter coat, she can electronically enter any store hooked into the system that carries coats, view still photos of the coats available on the system, take close-up looks at the styling and color details and get the price, fabric content, and other information. When she selects a coat, she can purchase it via phone using her credit card number.

J.C. Penney is working very hard to make sure that Telaction is desirable and easy to use. The system offers goods and services from about forty retailers, including Penney, Marshall Field's, Sears, Neiman-Marcus, Spiegel, Dayton Hudson, Zale, Johnston & Murphy, and Abercrombie & Fitch.

Nash-Finch's grocery-shopping service provides home delivery (for a $3.50 surcharge). Holiday Condominiums shows time-sharing condominium apartments around the world (for vacationers). Express Music shows excerpts of compact discs, tapes, and albums. Ticketron shows ticket locations for various entertainment and sporting events.

Unlike other systems, Telaction does not require a consumer to use a personal computer or purchase a costly computer modem. With Telaction, the customer needs only to be a cable subscriber (who is hooked into Telaction) and to have access to a touch-tone telephone. All information requests and ordering procedures are completed via digital entries into the telephone. The television screen provides any necessary instructions. There are no monthly membership fees.

Penney realizes that Telaction will take time to be widely accepted by consumers; and it knows that technological glitches may occur from time to time. But Penney also understands that it must be responsive to a changing environment which will offer significant opportunities for nonstore retailing.[1]

Overview

In order to attain and maintain long-run success, a retailer must anticipate and plan for the future. A firm needs to spot and react to trends early enough to satisfy the target market and stay ahead of competitors, yet not so early that the target market is unready for changes or that false trends are perceived. A late response to trends would mean that a retailer might miss profitable opportunities but minimize its risks.

Strategic planning for the future must take into account the nature of important factors in terms of their certainty of occurrence and magnitude of change, their effect on the retailer's business, and the time required for the retailer to react properly. Demographics, life-styles, consumerism, the regulatory environment, new technology, institutional changes, and internationalization are among the factors that will affect the long-run success of retailers. Several of these factors are illustrated in the color photo portfolio following page 584.

Environmental factors vary with regard to their certainty of occurrence. For example, population size can be forecast more accurately than average household income because the former relies on birth rates and death rates (which can be estimated with relative precision), whereas the latter depends on the unemployment rate, labor productivity, the level of inflation, the amount of imports, and so on (which are difficult to predict). When forecasts are accurate, future planning is simplified; for uncertain forecasts, retailers are forced to be more hesitant in their adaptation strategies.

A retailer must plan greater modifications in its strategy if a factor's magnitude of change is large. For instance, a retailer of appliances may have to develop significant changes in its strategy to adjust to the large long-term increase in working women. Hardware and other retailers must react to the rise in do-it-yourselfers.

The time required for a retailer to adapt to change depends on the strategic element undergoing change. Merchandising-strategy shifts—for example, the stocking of an unexpectedly popular fad item—are much more quickly consummated than adjustments in a firm's overall locational, pricing, or promotional strategy. In addition, a new store can more readily adapt to trends than existing stores that have established images, ongoing leases, space limitations, and so on.

Although other years are noted, this chapter emphasizes the anticipated changes in the environment of retailing between now and 2000. Trends in demographics, life-styles, consumerism, the regulatory environment, technology, retail institutions, and the international environment of business are each discussed and related to retail strategy.

The period of the present to 2000 is emphasized because

❑ Relatively short forecasts are more accurate than longer ones.
❑ This time period is lengthy enough for one to develop long-range retail plans and react to forecast changes.
❑ Much research is available.

U.S. trends involving population size and age distribution, the number of households, population mobility, the location of population, working women, and income are detailed in this section. Individually, each of these demographic factors has a great impact on retailing; collectively, they dominate a retailer's planning for the future.

Demographic Trends[2]

Population Size and Age Distribution

Figure 18-1 shows the growth in U.S. population size by age from 1980 to 2000. Although the rate of population growth will be less than 1 per cent per year from 1980 to the year 2000, the United States will add about 40 million people during this period. The median age of the population will rise from thirty years to thirty-six years.

	Year			Age Group
	1980	1990	2000	
	11.3	12.7	13.0	65+
	9.5	8.4	8.9	55–64
	10.0	10.2	13.9	45–54
	11.4	15.2	16.3	35–44
Percentage by Age Group	16.5	17.4	13.6	25–34
	13.3	10.3	9.2	18–24
	7.1	5.2	5.7	14–17
	13.6	12.9	12.8	5–13
	7.2	7.7	6.6	Under 5 years
Total Population	228 million	250 million	268 million	
Median Age	30	33	36	

FIGURE 18-1
U.S. Population by Age, 1980–2000*
*Totals may not equal exactly 100.0 per cent because of rounding errors.
Source: U.S. Bureau of the Census, *Current Population Reports*, Series P-25.

When studying U.S. population size and age trends, retailers also need to be aware of these factors:

❑ The average life span of males will expand from 70 years for those born in 1980 to 73 years for those born in 2000. The corresponding figures for females are 77.5 and 80.5.

❑ The average annual number of births will range from 3.5 million to 3.9 million (compared with about 4 million annually during the 1960s). However, more of these will involve firstborns, requiring parents to spend several thousand dollars in "tooling-up" costs for items such as baby furniture, clothing, and supplies.

❑ Couples will continue to get married at later ages than previously. In 1970, men were 22 years old at first marriage while women were 20. Today, men are about 26 and women about 23 at first marriage; and they are waiting longer to have children.

❑ The fastest-growing age segments will be 35 to 44, 45 to 54, and 65 and over. The under-35 segments will fall from a total of 57.7 per cent of the population in 1980 to 47.9 per cent in 2000.

Retailers must recognize that while younger markets will always represent large segments of the population, their relative importance is declining; and retailers should respond accordingly. For example, the eating, shopping, recreational, and other patterns of younger people are far different from those of their older counterparts. In addition, the approximately one-fifth of the population ages fifty-five and older controls one-third of all personal household income in the United States.

Number of Households

Despite the slow rate of overall U.S. population growth, the number of households is forecast to rise significantly by the year 2000. From a definitional perspective, a **household** is comprised of a person or a group of persons occupying a dwelling unit, whether related or unrelated. In contrast, a **family** consists of two or more people residing together who are related.

There were almost 81 million households in 1980. This figure is expected to rise to 95 million in 1990 and 106 million by 2000. At the same time, the average size of a U.S. household will drop from about 2.8 in 1980 to about 2.5 in 2000. The percentage of single-person households should go from 23 per cent in 1980 to 25 per cent in 1990 and to 28 per cent in 2000.

The decrease in the size of households is based on three major trends: the larger number of older people who live apart from their grown children, the high divorce rate, and the later age at first marriage.

Older people will increasingly live apart from their grown children. In the late 1940s, 55 per cent of those over age sixty-five were heads of households; by 1980, this figure had grown to 65 per cent, and the percentage will continue to increase. Part of the growth is due to the number of widows. Well over half of women aged sixty-five and over are widows. Forty per cent of all single-person households involve senior citizens.

Not only the number but also the rate of divorces has increased greatly. Between 1970 and 1980, the number of divorces rose by two-thirds, before stabilizing. The high number of divorces is expected to continue, while the rate per 1,000 marriages declines slightly.

Because many young adults are getting married at a later age, because of the desire to finish their education, advance in their careers, and so on, they are likely to live in smaller households. This is most true for persons who wait until their thirties to be married for the first time; as of 1985, about 21 per cent of men and 14 per cent of women aged thirty to thirty-four had never married (more than double the percentages in 1970). Furthermore, about 10–12 per cent of all adults will never marry. On the other hand, to combat the high costs of living, an increasing number of adults under the age of twenty-five are living at home longer.

These household trends will have two key implications for retailers. First, more decisions will be made by individuals functioning as both buyers and consumers; there will be more purchasing for self-use. Second, because each separate household requires furniture, housewares, and so on, there will be opportunities for retailers in these areas.

Population Mobility

Each year, about one-sixth of all Americans move, and this percentage is expected to continue. The rate of mobility will vary widely by age group; it will be highest among households headed by adults under the age of thirty-five. People will continue to move in increased numbers to South Atlantic, Southwest, Mountain, and Pacific states.

These are several retail implications of high mobility:

❑ Well-known chains and franchises will prosper.

❑ National brands will sell well among mobile persons.

❑ Purchase levels, particularly of clothing and home-related goods and services, will be high because many people discard items when moving to new environments (particularly if there are changes in climate or long-distance moves).

❑ Rentals become important.

❑ Shopping centers will be focal points for purchases.

❑ Use of a unified, nationwide credit system will ease purchase transactions.

❑ Large-scale advertising will be helpful in generating and maintaining a retailer's image.

Location of the Population

During the last decade, the number of people living in suburban communities has increased by over 18 per cent, or almost twice as much as the total U.S. population has grown. Over the same time period, the number of people living in big cities has remained almost constant. A similar trend is foreseen through 2000.

The average earnings of suburban families are higher than the average earnings of city families. It is estimated that the suburbs account for well over two-thirds of all personal income in metropolitan areas and an even higher proportion of discretionary income.

The growth of suburban markets has important implications for retailers:

❑ Firms may have to shift to suburban sites or add branch stores.

❑ Warehouses may have to be relocated to be near suburban store locations.

❑ Retail opportunities will exist relating to suburban home ownership and life-styles for items such as lawn care, snow blowers, do-it-yourself projects, and home freezers.

❑ Planned shopping centers will maintain their strength.

❑ It may be appropriate for chain stores to re-examine their use of central-city buying offices.

Working Women

At present, about 54 per cent of all U.S. adult women are in the labor force; and the trend for more women to work outside the home is projected to continue. From 1970 to 2000, the number of women in the labor force will almost double and will account for more than 47 per cent of the total adult working population by the year 2000.

In addition, the profile of the working woman is changing. Traditionally, the working woman was young and unmarried (including divorced and separated) or her husband was unable to provide for the family. Now, the working woman is likely to be married (60 per cent of all working women) and somewhat older (median age of thirty-six years) and to have one or more children under the age of six in the home (54 per cent of those mothers). The factor most directly related to female employment is the level of education. The higher the education achieved, the greater the probability of a woman's working.

The increase in the number of females combining the roles of working woman, wife, and/or mother has these implications for retailers:

❑ Working women are apt to spend large amounts for major appliances and household equipment, especially when they are time-saving.

❑ Working women are more independent in their purchases, as they seek individualism and personal identity.

❑ Working women are prone to use their leisure time for pleasure. This has a strong influence on the market for ready-made clothing, sporting goods, and car-rental agencies.

❑ Working women may be unable to shop during regular retail hours. This is meaningful for mail-order retailers and twenty-four-hour retailers.

❑ Working women have less time to prepare meals. Growing in importance are prepared foods, convenience foods, and fast-food restaurants. Some forecasters are predicting limited growth in supermarket sales.

❑ Working women require that services (e.g., repairs) be offered during evenings and weekends.

❑ Working women increase family affluence, thus expanding the purchase of luxury goods and services.

❑ Working women will be more responsive to advertising placed in evening time periods, particularly on television.

Income

After a decade of almost no **real income** growth during the 1970s and early 1980s, whereby household income after adjusting for inflation did not increase, the period from the mid-1980s to the year 2000 is forecast to provide solid real-income rises (averaging 1–3 per cent per year). Figure 18-2 shows the anticipated trends in real household income between 1985 and 1995 based on age of head of household, assuming a 2 per cent annual increase in household income. By 1995, 45 per cent of all U.S. households will have annual incomes of $25,000 and over; and the number of households with incomes of $50,000 and over will triple between 1980 and 1995.[3]

The higher incomes suggest broadened markets for luxury goods and services. It can also be anticipated that the demand for quality and specialty merchandise, better customer services, and wider assortments will increase. At the same time, retailers need to consider the effect of unemployment, inflation, and resource shortages on consumer spending patterns and to plan accordingly.

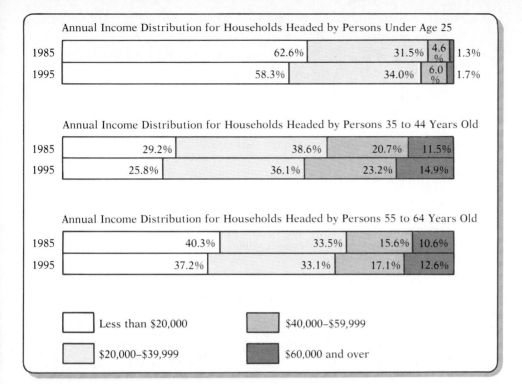

FIGURE 18-2
Household Income by Age of Head of Household, 1985 and 1995*
*Income expressed in 1985 dollars.
Source: Computed by the authors from data appearing in several issues of *American Demographics*.

In addition to analyzing demographic trends, it is necessary for a retailer to study the life-style trends of its target market. As explained in Chapter 5, life-styles are the ways in which individual consumers and families (households) live and spend time and money. The life-style trends with regard to gender roles, consumer sophistication, the poverty of time, leisure activities, and self-fulfillment are examined next. These life-style trends must be interpreted by retailers and interrelated with demographic trends.

Life-Style Trends

Gender Roles

The increasing number of working women, who may work an average of sixty to seventy hours (or more) each week between job and home responsibilities, is altering life-styles significantly.

In comparison to women who have not worked, working women tend to be more[4]

❑ Appearance-conscious (concerned with fashion and dress).

❑ Interested in maintaining a youthful posture.

❑ Confident and individualistic.

❑ Adept at dealing with the external world.

❑ Concerned with the convenience and ease of performing household duties.

❑ Cosmopolitan in taste and knowledgeable and demanding as consumers.

❑ Interested in leisure and travel.

❑ Concerned with improving themselves and their educational background.

❑ Interested in equal rights.

❑ Indifferent to small price differences among stores or merchandise.

❑ Uninterested in leisurely shopping trips.

As a result of the trend toward more working women, the life-styles of American males are also changing. Large numbers of men now take care of children, take out the garbage, wash the dishes, cook for the family, vacuum the house, shop for food, do the laundry, and clean the bathroom. There are four groups of husbands: progressives, who are young, affluent, and well educated; traditionalists, who are older and less educated; ambivalents, who possess average demographics and have internal conflicts over old and new values; and all talk/no action, who possess average demographics, except for greater youthfulness.[5]

The future will see still more changes in women's roles and conflicts over them. Furthermore, the authority and duties of husbands and wives will be shared with greater frequency than before.[6] Retailers need to understand and adapt to these trends.

Consumer Sophistication and Confidence

Consumer life-styles will reflect increased levels of education. For example, as of 1980 almost one-third of all Americans twenty-five years of age and older had completed at least one year of college. This figure is expected to be over 40 per cent by the year 2000; and about one-quarter will have four-year degrees by that time. For younger adults, education levels are and will be even higher.

Thus, the emerging consumer will be more knowledgeable and cosmopolitan; more cognizant of national and worldwide trends in tastes, styles, and goods and services; and more sophisticated. Furthermore, nonconforming behavior will be more widely accepted because increased education will create the self-assurance that shoppers need to reduce their need for conformity, while providing an appreciation of available choices. The confident shopper depends less on brands and labels and is more willing to experiment, but the more educated consumer also insists on detailed information about goods and services.

As an example, supermarket customers are becoming much more demanding. They want "delicate and interesting blends of spices" but not a lot of sodium or monosodium glutamate. Growing numbers of consumers "perceive foods that are loaded with additives, salt, sugar, and fat as not good for them. They want foods that make them feel healthy."[7]

As two analysts have commented:

Education changes career expectations, social attitudes, and consumer behavior. Once consumers start thinking, they change. They begin to ask questions, and businesses have to provide satisfactory answers.[8]

Consumers will exhibit a sharply stronger demand for quality in goods and services. Retailers will be forced to use all means at their disposal to satisfy quality requirements: careful merchandise buying, visual assurances, service, store layout, amenities, and reliable follow-through on the promised benefits of patronage.[9]

Poverty of Time

For some consumer households, the increased number of working women, the desire for personal fulfillment, the longer distances between the location of work and home, and the greater number of people working at second jobs contribute to the concept of **poverty of time.** According to this concept, greater affluence may actually result in less rather than more free time, because the alternatives competing for consumers' time will rise significantly. Therefore, many customers are likely to place a high value on goods and services that minimize time expenditures.

Retailers can respond to the poverty-of-time concept through a variety of activities:

❏ Describing, labeling, and identifying merchandise more clearly in advertising and displays. Popular brands also facilitate customer shopping.

❏ Carrying prepackaged merchandise, which can be selected through self-service. For example, selected items can be pre-gift-wrapped, so that they can be easily selected and purchased immediately.

❏ Setting up specialized departments by goods/service category within the store. For instance, retailers can place all cookware and dinnerware items in one specific department, instead of scattering them throughout the store.

❏ Maintaining adequate inventory to avoid running out of stock.

❏ Increasing the number of branch stores to limit customer travel time.

❏ Maintaining longer hours of operation, including evening and weekend openings.

❏ Adding on-floor sales personnel.

❏ Reducing checkout time.

❏ Using direct-marketing techniques, such as mail-order and telephone selling. There will be considerable opportunities for retailers engaged in direct marketing.

Leisure Activities

While a greater proportion of days and time is spent away from the primary job, many Americans are now involved in second jobs, and they and others may seek leisure-oriented activities, rather than shopping-oriented activities, on days off (as discussed under "Poverty of Time"). As a result, people are spending blocks of time on passive entertainment (e.g., television) and/or active recreation (e.g., tennis).

It is necessary for retailers to determine whether customers have a poverty of time or excess leisure time and how much of their leisure time consumers are willing to spend in shopping. A number of consumers are attracted to stores and shopping centers that cater to one-stop shopping.

In addition, retailers need to assess the sales opportunities presented by consumer participation in various leisure activities and plan accordingly. For example, one of the most heavily researched consumer segments is the generation of "baby boomers" born between 1946 and 1964. Overall, there are nearly eighty million baby boomers, representing a large and increasingly affluent consumer group. Table 18-1 contrasts the activities of baby boomers and non-baby-boomers, based on the results of a survey of two thousand adults aged eighteen to sixty-five.[10]

Self-Fulfillment

Of growing importance is the concept of **self-fulfillment,** whereby

consumer behavior is becoming more individualistic and less defined by reference to easily identified social groups. Americans are piecing together "component life-styles" for themselves, choosing goods and services that best express their growing sense of uniqueness. A consumer may own a BMW but fill it with self-service gasoline. Buy

TABLE 18-1
The Leisure Activities of U.S. Adults (Percentages)

Leisure Activity	Baby Boomers	Non-Baby-Boomers	Leisure Activity	Baby Boomers	Non-Baby-Boomers
Belong to a health club	17	8	Eating out	68	67
			Hobbies (outside home)	30	17
Currently participate in exercise			Work-related education	22	14
classes	18	9	Non-work-related education	16	9
			Gambling	11	9
Engage in on a regular basis:			Volunteer work	12	19
Walking (or climbing stairs)	56	56			
Swimming	46	23	At home:		
Dancing (e.g., aerobic, disco,			Listening to radio	78	66
ballroom)	39	18	Playing stereo/records	71	46
Baseball/softball	30	7	Watching television	80	85
Camping	31	20	Entertaining friends	59	56
Fishing	29	26	Reading	63	65
Regular bicycling	29	11	Garden and lawn work	49	61
Boating	19	13	Home improvements	46	48
Jogging (running)	26	10	Repair work on automobile	33	25
Football	18	4	Entertaining relatives	44	55
Hiking	17	10	Hobbies (at home)	36	32
Basketball	18	3	Playing videogames	25	8
Calisthenics (home or gym)	23	13	Caring/baby-sitting for		
Hunting	14	10	children	25	19
Tennis	19	5	Using a home computer	4	4
Racquetball	12	3			
Skiing	14	3	Number of:		
Stationary bicycling	9	5	Books read in past year		
			(median)	5.2	4.3
Attending events:			Hours radio listened to per		
Movies	66	35	week (median)	11.1	7.3
Sporting events	36	29			
Concerts	33	16	Hours television watched per		
Plays	18	19	week (median):		
			Noncable	10.4	11.5
Other Activities:			Cable (nonpay)	0.4	0.4
Attending parties/social			Pay cable	0.3	0.3
gatherings	66	49			

Source: Barbara I. Brown, "How the Baby Boom Lives," *American Demographics* (May 1984), pp. 36–37. Reprinted by permission.

take-out fast food for lunch but good wine for dinner. Own sophisticated photographic equipment and low-priced home stereo equipment. Shop for socks at K mart and suits or dresses at Brooks Brothers.[11]

These are some of the ways in which different consumers may seek to fulfill themselves:

❑ By emphasizing physical health, fitness, and exercise.

❑ By searching for meaningful careers.

❑ By emphasizing or de-emphasizing material possessions and status symbols.

❑ By becoming more or less interested in romanticism.

❑ By turning to or away from life-style simplicity.

❑ By trying for self-improvement.

❑ By attaining individuality ("Do your own thing").

594

When reacting to consumer desires for self-fulfillment, retailers need to understand the motivations of their target markets, and they must present an appropriate value orientation:

> Value has many meanings. It is situational because it depends on the needs and perceptions of the customer. For example, assuming a fair price, white-collar consumers are most likely to shop department stores, specialty stores, and off-price retailers because *quality* and *fashion* dominate their perceptions of value. By contrast, blue-collar customers are more likely to shop mass merchandisers, discount stores, lower-priced specialty stores, and possibly off-price stores for the same kinds of goods because *price* tempers their perceptions of quality and price.

> Today's best retailers match the value perceptions of their customers. Value is as important for retailers as it is for consumers.[12]

Consumer interest in self-fulfillment will continue to expand in the future.

Consumerism is defined as the

> activities of government, business, and independent organizations that are designed to protect individuals from practices that infringe upon their rights as consumers.[13]

and as

> a social force within the environment designed to aid and protect the consumer by exerting legal, moral, and economic pressure on business.[14]

Both definitions focus on the fact that consumers have rights and that these rights should be protected by government, business, and independent organizations. As enunciated by President Kennedy in 1962, consumers have the right to safety (protection against hazardous goods and services), the right to be informed (protection against fraudulent, deceptive, misleading, and incomplete information, advertising, and labeling), the right to choose (access to a variety of goods, services, and retailers), and the right to be heard (consumer feedback, both positive and negative, to the firm and to government agencies).

There are a number of reasons that retailers need to avoid deceptive or potentially harmful business practices, and that they should do all they can to understand and protect consumer rights:

❑ Since retailing is so competitive, consumers will be more likely to patronize firms that are perceived as "customer-oriented" and not to shop with those perceived as "greedy."

❑ Consumers are becoming more knowledgeable, selective, and affluent than those of the past, and this trend will continue. Therefore, retailers must offer fair value, provide detailed information, and be prepared to handle questions and complaints.

❑ Consumers are becoming more price-conscious. The popularity of off-price retailing is also heightening consumer awareness of prices.

❑ Large retailers are sometimes perceived as indifferent to consumers. They may not provide enough personal attention for shoppers or may have inadequate control over employees (resulting in poor practices and a lack of uniformity from one branch outlet to the next).

❑ The use of self-service is increasing, and it can cause confusion and frustration for consumers.

❑ The rise in new technology is unsettling to many consumers, who must learn new shopping behavior (e.g., automatic teller machines).

❑ Because retailers are in direct contact with consumers, they are frequently blamed for and asked to resolve problems actually caused by manufacturers

Consumerism and the Regulatory Environment

(such as defective products and unclear operating instructions). Retailers need to be able to balance the interests of their suppliers and their customers. In addition, retailers can pass along safety, information, and other recommendations to their suppliers.

Accordingly, several retailers have developed and implemented programs to protect consumer rights without waiting for government or consumer pressure to do so. Following are examples of these actions.

J.C. Penney adopted the "Penney Idea" in 1913 and still adheres to its seven basic concepts:

> To serve the public, as nearly as we can, to its complete satisfaction; to expect for the service we render a fair remuneration and not all the profit the traffic will bear; to do all in our power to pack the customer's dollar full of value, quality, and satisfaction; to continue to train ourselves and our associates so that the service we give will be more and more intelligently performed; to improve constantly the human factor in our business; to reward men and women in our organization through participation in what the business produces; and to test our every policy, method, and act in this way—"Does it square with what is right and just?"[15]

During the 1970s, Giant Food hired Esther Peterson (formerly President Johnson's special consumer-affairs assistant) at a rank equivalent to vice-president. The firm then developed a consumer's bill of rights, based on President Kennedy's, which it follows today:

1. Right to safety—Giant's product safety standards, such as age-labeling toys, go far beyond those required by government agencies.
2. Right to be informed—Giant has a detailed labeling system and utilizes unit pricing, open dating, and nutritional labeling.
3. Right to choose—Consumers who want to purchase harmful or hazardous products can do so (e.g., cigarettes, foods with additives).
4. Right to be heard—A continuing dialogue with reputable consumer groups has been established.
5. Rights to redress—A money-back guarantee policy on all products is used.
6. Right to service—Customers should expect and receive good in-store service.[16]

A number of retailers have voluntarily enacted product-testing programs. Products are tested for value, quality, misrepresentation of contents, and durability before they are placed on sale. Some of the retailers involved in product testing are Sears, J.C. Penney, A&P, Macy's, Target Stores, Montgomery Ward, and Giant Food. See Figure 18-3. Among the other consumerism programs undertaken by retailers are providing consumer education, setting clear procedures for handling customer complaints, reviewing advertising-message clarity, and training company personnel on how to interact properly with customers.

Consumer-oriented programs should not be limited to large retail chains; small retailers can also be involved. For example, Ideal Super Foods is an independent supermarket in Laramie, Wyoming, a city with a population of thirty-five thousand and Safeway and Albertson's outlets. The supermarket has a full-time, in-store home economist and uses a consumer panel. Each year, Ideal conducts educational programs through its panel that involve learning about and responding to community concerns.[17]

After considerable government legislation in the 1960s and 1970s to protect consumer rights, consumerism is now in a period of maturity. And major new federal consumer legislation is not expected in the near future. Congress is more interested in self-regulation by companies; and federal agencies are encouraging greater voluntary actions on the part of business. In addition, because so many firms have done a good job in responding to consumer issues, the American

Target's Responsibility

At Target, toys are an important part of our business. We want the toys you buy to meet Target's and the U.S. Government's high standards of quality, value, and safety. Therefore, we abide by all U.S. Consumer Product Safety Regulations. Target also utilizes an independent testing agency. They test samples of all toys we sell to help ensure your child's safe play.

All toys sold at Target are tested to be certain they are free from these dangers:

 Sharp edges

Toys of brittle plastic or glass can be broken to expose cutting edges. Poorly made metal or wood toys may have sharp edges.

 Small parts

Tiny toys and toys with removable parts can be swallowed or lodged in child's windpipe, ears, or nose.

 Loud noises

Noise making guns and other toys can produce sounds at noise levels that can damage hearing.

 Sharp points

Broken toys can expose dangerous points. Stuffed toys can have barbed eyes or wired limbs than can cut.

 Propelled objects

Projectiles and similar flying toys can injure eyes in particular. Arrows or darts should have protective soft tips.

 Electrical shock

Electrically operated toys that are improperly constructed can shock or cause burns. Electric toys must meet mandatory safety requirements.

 Wrong toys for the wrong age

Toys that may be safe for older children can be dangerous when played with by little ones.

FIGURE 18-3
Voluntary Product Testing at Target Stores
Courtesy Target Stores.

public will be more concerned with employment, resource shortages, inflation, the international trade deficit of the United States, and industrial productivity than with consumerism in the future. Finally, consumer groups will be consolidating the gains made during the 1960s and 1970s rather than emphasizing new issues.

Deregulation of industries is expected to continue well into the 1990s. In particular, banks, communications companies, professions, transportation firms, and insurance companies will operate in more competitive environments. Laws affecting retail practices such as pricing, merchandise assortment, and store hours will also continue to be loosened in the future.

To succeed in this deregulated environment, retailers will need to be innovative, responsive to consumer needs, flexible, and responsible. Strategies resulting in deceptive practices, price wars, or defamatory criticism of competitors will probably be ineffective. They will motivate consumers to select the most efficient and reputable retailers.

For example, the American Telemarketing Association (ATA) recently established a voluntary code of ethics that member firms are "strongly encouraged" to follow:

- ❏ Consumers should receive calls that are presented efficiently, courteously, and professionally.
- ❏ The caller should clearly identify the company he or she represents as well as his or her name at the beginning of each telephone conversation.
- ❏ Abusive language or rudeness should never be used.
- ❏ The caller should be responsive to the time constraints of consumers.
- ❏ All offers should have recognized value and be fulfilled according to stated terms.
- ❏ Repeated calls for the same goods or service offering should not be made to the same consumer.
- ❏ Telephone presentations to potential new customers should be introduced by a person, not a computer.
- ❏ All equipment should be carefully monitored to be sure of proper operation.
- ❏ Firms must comply with all federal, state, and local regulations.[18]

Technology

Over the next several years, many technological advances that impact on retailers will continue. The emerging technology most affecting retailers will center on electronic banking, video-ordering systems, and computerization of operations.

Electronic Banking

Electronic banking involves the use of automatic teller machines (ATMs) and the instant processing of retail purchases. It provides centralized record keeping and allows customers to complete transactions twenty-four hours a day seven days a week at a variety of bank and nonbank locations (such as supermarkets and hotel lobbies).[19] In addition to bank transactions (deposits, withdrawals, and transfers), electronic banking will increasingly be used in retailing; the purchase price of a good or service would be automatically deducted from a customer's bank account and entered into a retailer's account without cash changing hands by using an appropriate computer terminal.

At present, there are over seventy thousand ATMs in use in the United States, a number that is expected to keep rising in the future. They are located in banks, shopping centers, department stores, and airports; on college campuses; and at a host of other sites. For example, virtually all eight thousand 7-Eleven stores have ATMs; this will enable customers to make both cash and credit payments for purchases. There are about 175 regional and 8 national ATM networks. These networks allow consumers to make transactions at ATMs outside their local area; for instance, the Cirrus network allows transactions to be made at more than 19,000 ATMs nationwide.[20]

In the future, more banks and other retailers (especially those that have previously accepted only cash or check payments, such as supermarkets) will rely on **debit-only transfer systems,** where purchase prices are immediately deducted from consumer bank accounts. Retailer costs are reduced substantially when debit rather than credit transactions are used. The debiting process is quite different from that used with traditional credit cards, which rely on end-of-month billings (with no interest charges if payments are made promptly). With debit cards, delayed billing carries interest charges from the day of the purchase. However, there has been and will continue to be resistance to debit transactions by many consumers who like the delayed-payment benefit of traditional credit cards.[21]

Does Randall's Have Its Pulse on Debit Cards?

Randall's is a forty-store supermarket chain based in Houston that recently spent $1 million to purchase 800 point-of-sale terminals, buy a host computer, and develop related software that would enable its stores to accommodate debit-card transactions and more effectively process check transactions. The terminals are mounted alongside and connected to Randall's cash registers (which also utilize scanning technology). Each time, a debit-card or check transaction is involved, the customer's plastic card is inserted into and cleared by a terminal. At present, only 17 per cent of Randall's revenues are generated through cash exchanges, a very low figure for a supermarket.

Randall's system accepts debit cards that are issued through the Pulse ATM network, which involves hundreds of banks in Texas, Louisiana, New Mexico, and Oklahoma. The retailer pays a small monthly fee to its bank (Texas Commerce) and 2 cents for every debit transaction that is completed. When a customer's debit card is placed in a Randall's point-of-sale terminal, a transaction is concluded in about five seconds (including the deduction's being made from the customer's bank account).

Consumers can make purchases via check if they possess a Randall's check-cashing card. Randall's computer accepts or rejects a check on the basis of the customer's past payment history. On an annual basis, Randall's new system saves it about $1 million by reducing the number of bad checks it handles.

Randall's computerized system is improving its record-keeping ability and enabling it to give detailed receipts to shoppers. For example, Randall's knows exactly what percentage of its transactions and what percentage of its revenues come from cash, check, and debit-card payments.

Because many customers are still hesitant to use debit cards, in an average month, Randall's may have three thousand debit-card transactions compared with more than one million check transactions. To address this, Randall's is running television ads and using other types of promotion to educate consumers as to the benefits of debit transactions. As Randall's executive vice-president of finance and administration noted, "Right now I'm getting more out of the check-cashing than electronic funds transfer. But it's going to turn around, I guarantee. We're dealing with good technology."

Source: Based on material in Stephen Bennett, "Draw Your Debit Card, Pardner," *Progressive Grocer* (January 1988), pp. 61–64.

Some retailing experts believe the importance of individual-retailer credit cards and accounts will be lessened by the year 2000 because of the implementation of a centralized, nationwide credit and banking system (dominated by firms such as Visa and MasterCard). Nonetheless, many retailers will continue to emphasize their own credit cards, because they feel that they will lose their identities if their individual credit cards are used less frequently by customers.

These are some of the ramifications associated with the projected long-term growth in electronic banking:

❑ Consumers must be educated as to how to use electronic banking and the benefits of doing so.

❑ More retailers will have to accept national credit (debit) cards in addition to or rather than their own.

❑ Retail operating expenses will be reduced. Collection, bad debts, and so on will not be retailer problems.

❑ Customer loyalty will be reduced because credit (debit) cards will be accepted by a number of retailers and not just by those originally issuing the cards.

FIGURE 18-4
Using a Debit Card to Make a Vending Machine Purchase
Reprinted by permission of Debitek, Inc.

❑ Financial transactions (e.g., check deposits and cash withdrawals) will occur in more nonbank settings, such as supermarkets and department stores.

❑ The need for bank personnel will be decreased.

❑ Financial services will be available twenty-four hours per day, seven days a week.

❑ Vending machines will be able to process transactions very easily because of their acceptance of debit cards. See Figure 18-4.

Video-Ordering Systems

A substantial number of retailers believe that the spread of video-ordering systems will have a revolutionary effect on their sales and promotional methods. **Video-ordering systems** enable retailers to efficiently, conveniently, and promptly present information, receive orders, and process transactions with customers. Such systems may be oriented toward in-store and/or in-home shopping.

With an in-store video-ordering system, a consumer orders merchandise by entering data into a self-prompting computerized video-display monitor; most times, product information and photos are also available via the video display. The order is processed by the computer, and the consumer goes to a checkout area, where he or she picks up and pays for merchandise. For example, at Service Merchandise's 300+ retail catalog showrooms in the United States, consumers can place their orders via "Silent Sam," an in-store video-ordering system.

An in-home video-ordering system may rely on one of three basic formats: television programming, videotex programming, and merchandise catalogs. In a television-based system, the consumer watches special programming that appears on commercial or cable television and places an order through a toll-free 800 telephone number. The Home Shopping Network, which operates the Home Shopping Club, is by far the largest retailer involved in direct marketing via television with annual sales of $1 billion.[22]

In a videotex-based system, an in-home consumer uses a personal computer to view graphic or pictorial representations of goods and services with accompanying text descriptions and ordering procedures. Then, the consumer orders by entering a product code number into the computer keyboard, indicating the quantity desired. Information is exchanged between the consumer and the retailer via a computer modem linked to the consumer's telephone. The retailer's computer records and interprets the order, schedules delivery, and posts transactions. To date, videotex-based systems have not generated the consumer usage anticipated, mostly because of the relatively low number of U.S. households that have personal computers with modems. However, Sears has great confidence that videotex will succeed over the next decade. Together with IBM, Sears has invested $250 million to develop a videotex system named Prodigy. This system was planned for introduction during summer 1988.[23]

With a merchandise video catalog, the retailer usually reproduces its printed shopping catalog on a videocassette or videodisc and sends the catalog to appropriate customers. Then, in-home shoppers watch the catalog on their television sets (via their VCRs or videodisc players) and telephone orders to the retailer.

Many retailers are expected to intensify their use of video-ordering systems for several reasons:

❑ Inventory needs can be lowered (with direct marketing, merchandise can be obtained as customer orders come in).
❑ Investment costs can be reduced (e.g., less need for an expensive store location or displays if sales due to direct marketing increase).
❑ Fewer personnel are needed.
❑ The geographic trading area can be expanded.
❑ Efforts can be targeted to specific groups.
❑ Customers can place orders twenty-four hours per day, seven days a week.

Despite the long-run potential of video-ordering systems, retailers should keep these points in mind:

❑ Many consumers will not be interested in in-home video shopping, preferring to go to stores.
❑ Expensive, complex items do not readily lend themselves to video shopping.
❑ Without personal selling, consumers may not trade up to higher-priced models or add options.
❑ Attractive in-store displays are usually more likely to generate impulse purchases.
❑ Image is difficult to portray through graphic or pictorial representations.

Computerization of Operations

There will continue to be more and more retailers computerizing their operations, as a result of improving technology, interest in productivity, and the affordability of new computer networks. In this section, computerized checkouts and electronic point-of-sale systems, computer software, and applications of computer utilization by retailers are discussed.

Computerized checkouts, used by many types of retailers (both large and small), enable these firms to efficiently process transactions and maintain strict control over inventory. As noted in Chapter 6, retailers will increasingly rely on Universal Product Code–based systems, whereby cashiers manually ring up sales or pass items over or past optical scanners. Then computerized checkout registers instantly record and display sales, customers are given detailed receipts, and all inventory information is stored in the computer's memory bank.

Computerized checkouts lower costs by reducing transaction time, employee training, misrings, and the need for price markings on merchandise. In addition, retailers can increase their efficiency because of better inventory control, reduced spoilage, and improved ordering. They also enable retailers to obtain a list of data on an item-by-item basis. This aids in determining store layout and merchandise plans, assists in establishing the amount of shelf space per item, and allows inventory to be replenished automatically.

There are two potential problems facing retailers that use computerized checkouts. First, Universal Product Code–based systems will not reach peak efficiency until all manufacturers attach UPC labels to their merchandise; otherwise, retailers must incur heavy labeling costs. Second, because UPC labels are unreadable by humans, several states have enacted laws making price labels on individual packages mandatory; other states are considering legislation in this area. This lessens the labor savings of retailers that would like to post only shelf prices, rather than enter prices on all individual items.

Many retailers are and will be expanding beyond computerized checkouts to **electronic point-of-sale systems,** which verify check and charge transactions, provide instantaneous sales reports, monitor and change prices, send intra- and interstore messages, evaluate personnel and profitability, and store information. In most cases, point-of-sale systems would be used in conjunction with a firm's retail information system.[24]

A variety of computer software firms are developing packages tailored for retailers' use, as these examples show:[25]

❑ MTS (Minding the Store) software automates merchandise ordering, receiving, and pricing and aids in merchandise planning, distribution, and open-to-buy calculations for small to medium-sized retailers.

❑ FSMA (Food Service Management Applications) software is used by restaurants to control food and inventory costs, process payrolls, and maintain accounting records.

❑ SIM (Store Item Management) software enables retailers to reorder merchandise, forecast sales, allocate inventory, control store deliveries, and so on.

Each of the preceding software packages costs about $1,000 to $1,200 and may be operated via a personal computer. The National Retail Merchants Association has also published a directory listing several hundred such packages.

Here are illustrations of how retailers themselves are devising uses for their computers in order to improve operations:

❑ Valu Foods, a Baltimore-based fourteen-store supermarket chain, has its own "home-grown" computer software programs and an eight-person data-processing department. It uses an integrated approach for its electronic scanners, automated reordering, inventory control, computerized pharmacy system, direct store delivery, warehouse management, and item tracking: "Our philosophy has been that if the big chains save by doing their own warehousing, why shouldn't we do it? If they cut costs by writing their own software, and integrating as many systems as possible for greater efficiency, then why can't we? It's a matter of doing what you have to do to gain the expertise, and moving according to a plan."[26]

❏ Capital Marine Supply in Baton Rouge, Louisiana, utilizes a Honeywell minicomputer-based system, which Capital has tailored to its own needs: "The core of the system is the inventory master file which permits you to see a current status report of any given item you have in your inventory. It tells you such things as the product's location, receipts to date, usages to date, current average cost, the retail valuation, markup, retail price, and currently owned quantities."[27]

❏ Mervyn's, a full-line discount-store chain operated by Dayton Hudson, has been experimenting with technology whereby a computerized robot answers customers' telephone inquiries regarding their credit accounts: "It combines artificial intelligence, a natural language interface, and advanced voice technology in a telephone inquiry and data entry system. The system can be 'trained' to answer the telephone in a human voice and to accept instructions entered by a caller using a touch-tone telephone."[28]

❏ Figure 18-5 shows Giant Foods' (a leading supermarket chain) in-store computer software that provides considerable information for its pharmacists and better service for its customers.

Computers can either stand alone (the "intelligent" type) or be integrated with an in-store minicomputer. In both systems, keyboards, printers, scanners, wands, and screens can be utilized as needed by the retailer.

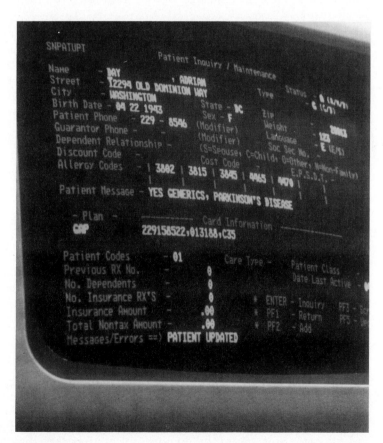

FIGURE 18-5
Giant Foods' PROFILE System
PROFILE helps the health care team of the Giant pharmacist and the patient's doctor guard the customer against potentially harmful drug interactions. Reprinted by permission.

Retail Institutions

The changes in demographics, life-styles, consumerism, the regulatory environment, and technology will undoubtedly have an impact on the nature of retail institutions. In addition, many retailers believe that profit margins will continue shrinking, as a result of intense competition and high costs. This shrinkage will put pressure on retailers to tighten internal cost controls and to promote higher margin goods and services while eliminating unprofitable items. Also, many retailers recognize that strategies must be modified as their retail institutions evolve over time. Complacency is not desirable, as May Department Stores (one of the leading retailers in the United States) recently acknowledged in its mission statement:

> Our performance in the past has been good, but it has not been excellent. We all recognize the performance gaps that must be closed. Only in certain areas—and limited ones—is the May Company "excellent" in the common use of the word. We will need major improvements in virtually all areas of financial performance—to levels that have never been attained by us in the past.
>
> Strategically, we have been making progress. But the challenges are clear to all of us, in the areas of productivity, merchandising, customer service, pricing, sales promotion, and—most important—organizational development. The May Company's mission is aggressive—but achievable.[29]

Accordingly, the skills of retailing executives will be critical to their firms' long-run success. This is illustrated by the findings of a study involving U.S. food retailers:

❑ The 1990s manager "will oversee a store with more customers, higher sales volume, greater product diversity, and more capital investment. Managing this store will involve less of a hands-on approach with more attention given to delegation and management by exception."

❑ New responsibilities will include "building and maintaining a strong sense of the company's values and beliefs in store personnel, using automated information systems to develop plans and monitor results, and adapting the store's merchandise and services to its local customer base."

❑ In 1990, 42 per cent of potential supermarket managers will be recruited from college into a training program and rapidly moved from assistant to store manager, compared with 6 per cent in 1983. There will be much more analytical training and emphasis on teaching leadership skills.

❑ Better defined and attainable career paths will be needed, along with financial incentives. Authority will be more decentralized down to the store level.[30]

Retail institutions will respond to the changing environment through nonstore retailing, risk minimization, mass merchandising, positioned retailing, diversification and mergers, and adaptation strategies.

Nonstore Retailing

As indicated in Chapter 4, nonstore retailing, with sales exceeding $200 billion in 1986, represents a major dimension of retailing. With the rapidly improving technology of video equipment, described earlier in this chapter, nonstore retailing promises to undergo large expansion in the 1990s.

Nonstore retailing will enable firms to reduce personnel staff and costs, locate at less costly sites, maintain low inventories, and appeal to specific target audiences. The new technology in telephones, financial-services equipment, personal computer-based software, order-processing equipment, and truck routing, as well as video equipment, will allow firms to reduce costs per transaction, speed up deliveries, and appeal to wider geographic markets. Two examples of the advances in nonstore retailing follow.

Comp-U-Card is an in-home shopping service that was begun in 1973. Today, Comp-U-Card has three million members who pay an annual fee of $39 to utilize the company's data bank; its annual revenues are more than $150 million. The data bank contains product specifications and prices on more than 250,000 products and hundreds of brands. Shoppers buying through Comp-U-Card receive discounts of 10–50 per cent over prices in typical retail stores. The company earns an average commission of 7 per cent on these sales. With the present system, subscribers receive information through direct mailings, telephone calls to Comp-U-Card, and/or data transmitted to their personal computers (with no graphics displayed); they then order merchandise via the telephone or through their computers, using a modem. As of now, fewer than 100,000 customers use their personal computers to shop with Comp-U-Card.[31]

Unlike Comp-U-Card, CompuServe (a Columbus, Ohio–based division of H&R Block), offers totally computerized in-home shopping and related services to its 400,000 members. It

> features more than 400 services, including news, sports, and weather; stock and mutual fund quotes; corporate and individual electronic mail; interactive games; and access to dozens of professional and hobbyist special-interest groups that range from computer programming to gourmet cooking.

> The Electronic Mall, added to CompuServe in 1985, offers goods and services from more than 90 retailers and direct marketers, including American Express Co., Brooks Brothers, Pepperidge Farm, New York's Metropolitan Museum of Art, and Walden-Books.

> Shoppers use computers to review price and product information and place orders by following on-screen instructions. The orders then are sent by electronic mail to the companies, which ship products directly to the consumers.[32]

Risk-Minimization Retailing

With **risk-minimization retailing,** firms strive to hold down both their initial investment costs and the costs of operations.[33] In the future, a risk-minimization approach will be utilized by many retailers because of the rising number of discounters, the need to control complicated chain or franchise operations, higher land and construction costs, the volatility of the economic environment, and the interest in maximizing productivity.

Risk-minimization retailing can be accomplished through a combination of retail strategy-mix components:

❑ By emphasizing secondary locations, freestanding units, locations in older strip centers and by occupying abandoned supermarkets or discount-department-store sites (second-use locations).

❑ By moving to smaller towns where building restrictions are less stringent, labor costs are lower, and construction and operating costs are reduced.

❑ By using inexpensive construction materials, such as exposed rafters, bare cinder-block walls, and concrete floors.

❑ By using plain fixtures and lower-cost displays.

❑ By buying used equipment.

❑ By joining cooperative buying and advertising groups.

❑ By encouraging manufacturers to finance inventories.

Currently, a number of firms have some type of risk-minimization strategy in their small-town stores. These include Dollar General (discount variety stores),

Bi-Lo (food stores), Pamada (discount department stores), Kentucky Fried Chicken, and Wal-Mart.

In conjunction with risk minimization, some retailers are also turning to **rationalized retailing** programs that involve a high degree of centralized management control combined with rigorous operating procedures for each phase of business.[34] Each aspect of a company's operations would be performed in a virtually identical manner in every store outlet. Rigid control and standardization make this technique an easy one to implement and manage. In addition, a firm can add a significant number of units in a relatively short time period.

Radio Shack (part of the Tandy Corporation) and Toys "R" Us are examples of firms applying rationalized retailing. Each operates stores that are similar in size, the number of items carried, store layout, merchandising, and sales approaches to others in that chain.

In the future, the use of rationalized retailing will increase and lead to more centralized management, sophisticated supplier-evaluation programs, and formalized, computerized buying plans. Prototype stores will be particularly popular.

Mass Merchandising

Mass merchandising involves retailers' presenting a discount image, handling several merchandise lines, and having ten thousand square feet or more of floor space. Today, there are over ten thousand traditional mass-merchandising outlets (discount stores, combination stores, superstores, and warehouse outlets). Retailers with forty or more outlets own well over 80 per cent of all stores in this category.[35]

Because mass merchants have relatively low operating costs, achieve economies in operations, and appeal to price-conscious consumers, their continuing popularity is forecast. The sales for traditional mass merchandisers are expected to remain relatively level, while the sales of newer forms (e.g., factory outlet malls, flea markets, and membership stores) rise more substantially:

> No matter what you call it, offering the right merchandise and with the right value is what counts. That's the name of the game.[36]

Positioned Retailing

An opposite approach to mass merchandising is **positioned retailing,** which consists of identifying a target market segment and developing a unique retail offering, designed to meet that segment's needs. The retailer positions the store for one specific segment and not the mass market. Positioning creates a high level of loyalty and shields a retailer from more conventional competitors.[37]

A good example of positioned retailing is the strategy followed by The Limited, Inc., a successful apparel chain. Each of its divisions appeals to a distinct market segment, such as: The Limited, clothes for fashion-conscious women aged twenty to forty; Limited Express, trendy clothing for women fifteen to twenty-five years of age; Lane Bryant, Roaman's, and Sizes Unlimited, catering to full-sized women; Lerner, a budget apparel chain for young women; Henri Bendel, offering expensive clothing for high-fashion shoppers; and Victoria's Secret and Brylane's, oriented to mail-order customers.[38] Figure 18-6 shows a typical storefront for an outlet of The Limited.

Positioned retailing will have a large impact in the future. It will lead many firms to stress nonprice competition and encourage more specialized focusing by firms with broad target markets (such as department and discount stores), and it may force manufacturers to use multiple market-segmentation programs to meet the requirements of retailers with different market positions. The growth

FIGURE 18-6
Positioned Retailing by The Limited, Inc.
This is an outlet of The Limited, geared to fashion-conscious women from ages 20 to 40, that is
located in the Georgetown Park Mall, Washington, D.C. Reprinted by permission of Georgetown Park
Mall.

of boutiques, specialty stores, and compartmentalized department stores is expected to continue. And the department store concept of one-stop shopping may be changed to that of the one-stop shopping center.

Recently, several department-store chains have begun to place emphasis on positioned retailing, as these two illustrations show: Montgomery Ward has been experimenting with new Electronic Avenue appliance and consumer electronics stores, Home Ideas home-furnishings stores, Auto Express auto parts and service stores, and Gold 'N Gems jewelry stores.[39] Sears is now operating a woman's apparel chain (Pinstripes Petites) and a chain of optical stores (Eye Care Centers of America).[40]

Diversification and Mergers

In order to sustain or enhance sales growth, larger retailers will often turn to diversification and mergers.

With diversification, retailers become active in businesses outside their normal operations. Diversification is an advanced form of scrambled merchandising, whereby distinctly new goods and/or service categories are added. For example, by the early 1980s, K mart believed that it had reached a saturation point with its traditional full-line discount stores; therefore, in order to thrive in the long run, the company decided to diversify (a strategy that it still follows). In 1984, K mart acquired WaldenBooks and Builders Square (formerly Home Centers of America). In 1985, it purchased Pay Less (a large discount-drugstore chain) and

In Retailing, Who Has the Power?

What do The Limited, Inc., May Department Stores, Toys "R" Us, and Wal-Mart (four very different kinds of retailers) have in common? All of these firms are considered "power retailers," because of their size, clout, and operating efficiency. And in the future, many industry experts predict that such power retailers will be even more dominant than they are now:

These power retailers are fast and focused. Their merchandise is well-selected and plentiful. Customers go out of their way to shop at power retailers' stores because they know they'll find what they want with a minimum of hassles. Charles Lazarus of Toys "R" Us and Leslie H. Wexner of The Limited, Inc., have shown that power retailing works in specialty formats. Sam M. Walton has applied it to his Wal-Mart discount stores. Now David C. Farrell of May is showing that power retailing can bring a new nimbleness even to the clay-footed giants of retailing—old-line department stores.

Power retailing means following a clear, consistent, and comprehensive strategy. Target customer groups are defined and their needs identified and addressed. There is constant attention to the marketplace ("Wal-Mart's Walton may be the richest man in the country, but he remains a tireless floor-stalker who frequently patrols stores to observe merchandise displays and talk to customers"). Since trends are spotted early, power retailers can order early and in quantity. They emphasize "power assortments" that overwhelm lesser competitors. These firms have invested and are investing heavily in technological advances, particularly those involving information systems and inventory control. Power retailers are often flexible, creative, and willing to take risks (such as The Limited, Inc.'s, beginning to sell men's clothing). However, management policies tend to be centralized and standardized; some critics believe this may be the major weakness of power retailing: "The key to surviving in the 1990s will be using power systems to usher in new ideas, not to prop up old ones."

Source: Based on material in Amy Dunkin, Michael Oneal, and Stephen Phillips, "Power Retailers," *Business Week* (December 21, 1987), pp. 86–92.

began to expand the financial services offered in selected K mart stores (by experimenting with banks in Indiana stores, real-estate services in Michigan and Wisconsin stores, and consumer loan centers in Chicago outlets). In 1988, it acquired controlling interest in Makro warehouse-club stores and planned to open its first hypermarket outlet in Atlanta.[41]

Mergers involve the combination of independently owned retailers. Diversification mergers take place between retailers of different types, such as the one between K mart and WaldenBooks. Specialization mergers take place between similar types of retailers, such as two local banks. By merging, retailers hope to maximize resources, enlarge their customer base, limit weaknesses, and gain competitive advantages. The merger trend is expected to continue at its current intense pace.

Adaptation Strategies

In response to the dynamic environment of the 1990s, many retailers will develop adaptation strategies. One of the most important challenges for retailers will be to get consumers to perceive them as **destination stores** rather than convenience stores:

The challenge—and opportunity—is the creation of destination stores. These are units whose merchandise selection and presentation, pricing, or other unique features act as a magnet for customers and distinguish them from their counterparts, patronized primarily because of convenience. Today, most stores in the United States are in the convenience category, but those that are not demonstrate the pulling power of a unique franchise. Bloomingdale's flagship unit in New York is an outstanding destination store. Customers shop Bloomingdale's because of the exciting atmosphere created through the attractive merchandise, appealing visual displays, and special fairs. The branches throughout the country generate the same kind of excitement.

At the other end of the spectrum, wholesale clubs, such as BJ's, Sam's, PACE, and Costco also are destination stores. In this case, price is the most persuasive argument for shopping in a warehouse outlet. The retailers that will prosper in the future are those that can define and project a destination store image.[42]

Illustrations of adaptation strategies follow.

Tasca Lincoln-Mercury in Seekonk, Massachusetts, is one of the leading Lincoln-Mercury dealers in the United States. In 1987, this single dealership sold 3,517 cars, resulting in revenues of $53 million. Yet, "its cramped showroom-garage is 17 years old. The salesmen look like sharks. The mechanics are scruffy. And Seekonk, an old farm town just over the state line from East Providence, Rhode Island, is hardly a go-go growth area." So, how has Tasca become so successful? It has adapted to its environment and developed a tremendous consumer following because of its customer service. Tasca delivers vehicles in sparkling clean condition, schedules and keeps service appointments, has valet parking when customers pick up their vehicles, has salespeople make follow-up calls after sales are made, and gives monthly bonuses to sales and service personnel who score highest in customer satisfaction surveys.[43]

Allison's Place is a Los Angeles–based apparel chain that sells all its merchandise for one price ($7, as of 1988). Between 1985 and the end of 1987, the chain grew from 27 company-owned stores to 200 company-owned stores and 80 franchised outlets; annual sales reached $40 million. However, because of its rapid expansion, the company has had to adapt its strategy. It is using training coordinators and regional training centers to improve employee skills, enhancing store appearance via new interior designs and displays, increasing average store size from 1,400 to 2,400 square feet, and conducting more marketing research with customers than in the past.[44]

To maintain its position as one of the largest supermarket chains in the United States, Safeway has embarked on an aggressive strategy. The firm is "going up-scale" through its Bon Appetit stores, which feature gourmet foods, a large selection of fine wine, choice meats, exotic produce items, and sizable floral departments. It has eliminated 500 of its traditional supermarkets not fitting into its long-run plans. On the other hand, it has invested heavily to remodel 700 stores, to install scanning equipment in over 80 per cent of its outlets, and to add service departments (e.g., delis, bakeries, and pharmacies) in many of its stores. Safeway also more carefully monitors consumer desires, and then expands or contracts the shelf space allocated to merchandise categories. And the advertising of private-label goods is now less than before: "Private labels don't attract new customers. National brands are better vehicles for this."[45]

The International Environment of Retailing

The international environment of retailing encompasses both U.S. firms operating in foreign markets and foreign retailers operating in U.S. markets. In the future, more retailers will become international in scope, continuing the strong recent trend in this direction. When embarking on an international retailing strategy, companies should consider the factors shown in Figure 18-7.

Opportunities and Risks in International Retailing

There are wide-ranging opportunities and risks in international retailing. International retailing opportunities may exist for several reasons. One, foreign

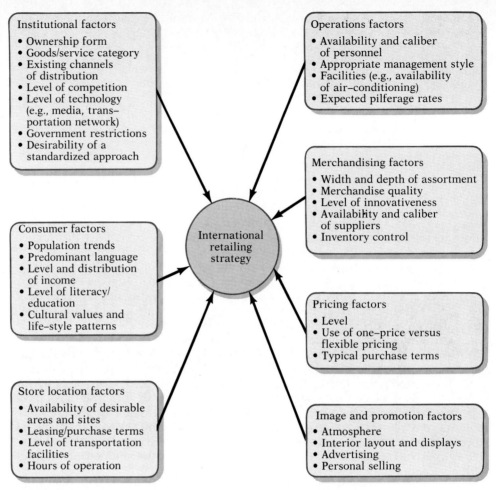

FIGURE 18-7
Key Factors to Consider When Engaging in International Retailing

markets may represent better growth opportunities (e.g., because of population trends). Two, domestic markets may be saturated or stagnant. Three, the retailer may be able to offer goods, services, or technology not yet available in foreign markets. Four, competition may be less in foreign markets. Five, foreign markets may be used to supplement, not replace, domestic sales. Six, there may be tax or investment advantages in foreign markets.

International retailing risks may also exist for several reasons. One, there may be cultural differences between domestic and foreign markets. Two, management styles may not be easily adaptable. Three, foreign governments may place heavy restrictions on operations. Four, personal income may be poorly distributed among consumers in foreign markets. Five, distribution systems may be inadequate (e.g., poor roads, lack of refrigeration, and a weak mail system).

In developing international strategies, retailers must pay particular attention to the concept of **standardization.** Can the strategy followed in the domestic market be standardized and directly applied to foreign markets, or do personnel, the physical structure of outlets, advertising, product lines, and other factors have to be adapted to local conditions and needs? For example, a study of retail pricing behavior found that 63 per cent of the stores in India permitted bargaining, compared with 11.9 per cent in Brazil and 3.4 per cent in the People's

Republic of China.[46] And as Table 18-2 shows, direct marketers must take several major differences into account when planning mail-order sales in Europe rather than in the United States.

TABLE 18-2
European Versus U.S. Mail Order: Major Differences

❏ Media:
    ❏ Limited media availability:
        ❏ Limited customer-list rentals.
        ❏ Limited TV channel and commercial time availability.
❏ Regulatory:
    ❏ Tighter regulation of promotional claims, copy content, competitive comparisons.
    ❏ Tighter product-safety-approval requirements.
❏ Delivery Systems:
    ❏ Generally higher postal rates.
    ❏ Variability in postal rates (60:1 ratio between United Kingdom and Austria).
❏ Payment Systems:
    ❏ Low credit-card penetration.
    ❏ Variability in payment-systems sophistication between countries.
❏ Business Organization:
    ❏ Mail-order holding companies rather than financial or consumer-product conglomerates with mail-order holdings.
❏ Catalog Operations:
    ❏ Catalog operations are often agent-based, with agents for the catalog company distributing catalogs, aggregating and paying for their customers' orders after deducting their commission, and assuming responsibility for collecting from their customers (most common in United Kingdom and West Germany).
❏ Sales Concentration:
    ❏ Lesser development of specialty mail order and greater concentration of sales by catalog general merchandisers.
❏ Market Fragmentation:
    ❏ Marketing expansion internationally in Europe from national market bases hindered by:
        ❏ Differences in population structure, life-style, fashion trends.
        ❏ Differences in sizes standardization.
        ❏ Differences in legal and technical regulations.
        ❏ Differences in taxes.
        ❏ Differences in post office regulations.
        ❏ Differences in credit-sales legal regulations.
        ❏ Existing custom formalities.
        ❏ Possible changes in currency parities during duration of fixed-price offers.
        ❏ Obstacles in merchandise return across national frontiers.
        ❏ Obstacles in providing aftersales customer service across national frontiers.
❏ Merchandising:
    ❏ Lower proportion of high-end items.
    ❏ Product quality consciousness.
❏ Graphics:
    ❏ Color fidelity essential in catalog merchandising.

Source: Arnold L. Fishman, *1987 Guide to Mail Order Sales* (Lincolnshire, Ill.: Marketing Logistics Inc., June 1988), pp. viii–7. Reprinted by permission.

These are illustrations of how retailing is conducted by domestic retailers in three foreign countries (e.g., Japanese retailers in Japan): Japan, Spain, and the People's Republic of China.

Japanese retailers are advanced in designing their stores but are behind U.S. retailers when it comes to operating controls and private branding. Said one Japanese management consultant, "We are just emerging from the stage where U.S. chains were in the 1930s. While we have already overtaken American retailers in terms of presentation, we have not yet learned other things, such as labor scheduling, for example. We are also behind U.S. retailers when it comes to the merchandise we sell."[47]

Until recently, Spain was a country dominated by small mom-and-pop stores; there were very few large retail outlets. But, this arrangement is slowly changing. In 1985, the government enacted legislation that "liberalized" store hours, thus encouraging large stores to open evenings and on Sundays. A government official stated that "Spain had three times as many small shops per capita as other countries in Western Europe and that many should close down."[48]

In the People's Republic of China, most retailing is state-owned; a small amount of free-market retailing is allowed:

> In the major cities of China, the state system uses large department stores and supermarkets to distribute goods, supplemented by some neighborhood shops offering convenience items. There are, in addition, some stores that specialize in specific kinds of merchandise such as bicycles or fruits and vegetables. Service is impersonal, no credit is extended, and prices are uniform across stores. There is no bargaining. The channel is short, since goods go directly from manufacturers to wholesalers to retailer. In a sense, the state system is managed much like a single chain of stores with uniform prices, policies, merchandise, and displays.
>
> Free-market retailing is still an addition or supplement to the state system, rather than a substitute for it. Moreover, free-market retailing has not yet penetrated uniformly across China. Because change is not proceeding at a uniform rate in all geographic areas or in all industries, it is a stronger force in some areas than in others.[49]

U.S. Retailers and Foreign Markets

Many U.S. retailers are looking for sales and profit growth by expanding into foreign markets. Following are examples of U.S. retailers with high involvement in foreign markets.

Many of the leading mail-order retailers in the world are based in the United States. These include American Express, Avon, Citibank, Franklin Mint, K-Tel, Reader's Digest, and Time, Inc. These firms are efficient and have a clear handle on their customers and distribution methods. Nonetheless, as of now, total worldwide mail-order sales (for both U.S. and foreign companies) outside the United States are only a fraction of those in the United States. This means there is great growth potential in foreign markets.[50]

Southland Corporation introduced the convenience store to Japan through its 7-Eleven stores in 1972. It offered operators of Japanese outlets inventory, financing, low-cost loans, partial payments for electricity, and name recognition. From 15 Japanese stores in 1975, 7-Eleven reached 2,000 outlets by the mid-1980s; the leading competitor has fewer than 1,000 stores. Its Japanese stores are very profitable for Southland, which also operates 7-Eleven outlets in such countries as Mexico, Sweden, Hong Kong, Taiwan, Australia, and Canada.[51]

In late 1987, Kentucky Fried Chicken (KFC) became the first retailer to open a fast-food outlet in China. In the near future, the five-hundred-person capacity store is expected to become the highest volume restaurant in the entire KFC chain, because of the number of people working and living near it. The outlet is open longer hours than Chinese restaurants (which are usually closed from 2:00

P.M. to 5:00 P.M.) and serves chicken (imported from West Germany or bred from West German stock in China), soda (PepsiCo is Kentucky Fried Chicken's parent company), and side dishes such as mashed potatoes, cole slaw, and rolls. The same recipes and ingredients are used as in KFC stores around the world. One problem which Kentucky Fried Chicken must overcome is in generating more frequent customer visits; in China, a $40-per-month salary is considered good— but a complete dinner at KFC costs $1.85. KFC was also planning to have twenty-five restaurants in South Korea in time for the 1988 Summer Olympics.[52]

Esprit de Corps is a San Francisco–based clothing manufacturer and retailer. Yet, its future growth depends on its sales outside the United States, which already account for 60 per cent of the firm's $800 million in annual revenues. Esprit does business in twenty-five countries, with the greatest emphasis on France, Italy, Great Britain, Australia, Hong Kong, Mexico, New Zealand, and West Germany. In most overseas markets, its major competitor is the Italian-based Bennetton.[53]

Foreign Retailers and the U.S. Market

A large number of foreign retailers have entered the United States in order to appeal to the world's most affluent mass market. Here are three examples.

IKEA is a Swedish-based home-furnishings retailer with operations in about twenty countries; in 1985, IKEA opened its first U.S. store in Plymouth Meeting, Pennsylvania. A second store has since opened in Woodbridge, Virginia. IKEA features durable, stylish ready-to-assemble furniture at "rock-bottom prices," such as armchairs for $60 to $100 and couches for $250 to $600. Its stores are large; the one in Plymouth Meeting is 160,000 square feet and has a playroom for children and other customer amenities. IKEA places emphasis on its annual furniture catalog, which has both photographs and descriptions of its merchandise. In 1988, it expected to distribute 1.2 million U.S. catalogs. The company generates annual revenues of $80 million dollars from just the two stores it now has in the United States.[54]

Carrefour is a French-based retailer with over $9 billion in yearly sales. It was Carrefour that invented the hypermarket concept in Europe during the 1960s. In late 1987, Carrefour opened its first U.S. hypermarket in Philadelphia; it planned to open a second hypermarket in Brookhaven, New York, in 1989. The company projects that its 330,000-square-foot Philadelphia store will account for $80 to $100 million in annual sales by 1990:

> The Philadelphia hypermarket is the latest version of Carrefour's prototype format. As such, it's a marriage of a conventional discount store and supermarket, featuring a broad assortment of commodity general merchandise—soft goods like men's slacks and jeans and ladies' tops and bottoms and basic hard lines—and food in a simple, no-frills self-service environment.

> We don't want to stress price as it's only one element. We want to promote the hyper-market concept of one-stop easy shopping, name brands, our own bakery and deli-catessen, wide aisles, and lots of parking space.[55]

Harrods of London is one of the most well-known department stores in the world. It occupies 675,000 square feet of selling space (spread over five floors) and has 230 departments: "Customers can buy almost anything at Harrods." To stimulate business from U.S. shoppers, without opening any branch stores in the United States, Harrods uses direct-marketing efforts. It advertises merchandise in the *New York Times*, complete with a twenty-four-hour toll-free 800 telephone number for ordering. It also sends out forty thousand catalogs (at about $3 each) to consumers in the United States, who can order by telephone or by mail.[56]

TABLE 18-3

Selected Acquisitions of U.S. Retailers by Foreign Firms Over the Past Decade

U.S. Retailer	Principal Business	Foreign Acquirer	Country of Acquirer
Allied Stores	General merchandise	Campeau	Canada
Alterman Foods	Supermarkets	Delhaize-Le Leon	Belgium
Bonwit Teller	General merchandise	Hooker Corp.	Australia
Brooks Brothers	Apparel	Marks & Spencer	Great Britain
Federated Department Stores	Diversified	Campeau	Canada
Fed-Mart	General merchandise	Hugo Mann	West Germany
Great Atlantic & Pacific (A&P)	Supermarkets	Tengelmann	West Germany
Hardee's	Restaurants	Imasco	Canada
Herman's	Sporting goods	Dee Corp.	Great Britain
International House of Pancakes (IHOP)	Restaurants	Wienerwald	Switzerland
Parisian	General merchandise	Hooker Corp.	Australia
Talbots	Apparel	Jusco Ltd.	Japan
Tiffany	Jewelry, fine objects, giftware	Merchant Navy Officer's Pension Fund	Great Britain
Ups 'n Downs	Sportswear	Tootal	Great Britain
Zale	Jewelry	PS Associates	Netherlands

In addition to extending their traditional businesses into the United States, a number of foreign companies have been acquiring major ownership interests in American retailers. Some of the key acquisitions made by foreign firms over the past decade are shown in Table 18-3.

As with U.S. retailers operating in foreign markets, foreign firms operating in the U.S. market need to be careful in their approach:

> What similarities, if any, are there between operating a U.S. retail company and one in a foreign market? How many of the same systems and operating methods can be utilized by the two different entities?[57]

Foreign companies seeking to create a retail presence here require American expertise in such key areas as selecting store locations, training sales staffs, and product presentation. Equally critical is tracking consumer trends and developing a marketing strategy, because buying habits in the U.S. are different than those elsewhere.[58]

SUMMARY

Various environmental factors will have a strong impact on the abilities of retailers to attain and maintain long-run success. Far-sighted retailers must study demographic, life-style, consumerism, regulatory, technological, and institutional trends and adapt their retail strategy mixes to these trends.

U.S. population forecasts show a low growth rate, a population increase of forty million people between 1980 and 2000, and the importance of first-born babies, later first marriages, and older consumer groups. Other important U.S. demographic trends involve the growing number of households (because of increases in one-person households),

relatively high population mobility, the steady movement of the population to suburban communities, the rising number of working women, and the rising number of higher-income families.

Life-style trends will include different and expanding roles for women and increased consumer sophistication and confidence. Some consumers will experience a poverty of time and will seek convenience in shopping; other consumers will have greater amounts of leisure time and will purchase more entertainment and recreation goods and services. In addition, consumers will be increasingly concerned with self-fulfillment.

Consumerism activities (those practices designed to protect consumer rights) have reached a level of maturity. Consumer groups will consolidate the gains they have made to ensure the consumer rights of safety, information, choice, and participation. Many retailers have already implemented voluntary plans to aid consumers. Government will also stress self-regulation and a deregulated environment.

The major technological trends affecting retailers will focus on electronic banking (credit and/or debit transactions through some form of automatic teller machines, including in-store sales registers), video-ordering systems (consumers' ordering goods and services in a store or from their homes after seeing them listed or described on video-display monitors, television programs, personal computer monitors, or VCRs or videodisc players), and computerization of operations (through computerized checkouts, electronic point-of-sale systems, and other applications).

Many retail institutional changes will occur because of the evolving environment. Nonstore retailing will continue to grow. More firms will engage in risk-minimization retailing, whereby they strive to hold down their initial investment costs as well as their operating costs. One risk-minimization approach is rationalized retailing, through which a high degree of centralized management control is combined with rigorous operating procedures for each phase of business. Both mass merchandising and positioned retailing, two opposite strategies, are expected to be popular in the future, as some firms capitalize on the bigness of their stores, while others concentrate on pinpointing smaller market segments. Large firms will often turn to diversification and mergers to sustain or enhance their sales growth.

International retailing, encompassing both U.S. firms in foreign markets and foreign firms in U.S. markets, will continue to rise in the future. When entering a foreign market, a retailer must consider institutional, consumer, store location, operations, merchandising, pricing, and image and promotion factors. Opportunities and risks need to be evaluated, as well as the applicability of standardization. The retailer must decide how much of its domestic strategy must be modified to address foreign needs and legal requirements.

QUESTIONS FOR DISCUSSION

1. Comment on this statement: "Strategic planning for the future must take into account the nature of important factors in terms of their certainty of occurrence and magnitude of change, their effect on the retailer's business, and the time required for the retailer to react properly."
2. What impact will the changes in the number of households and household size have on retailers?
3. If you operated a store in a central business district, how would you react to the statistics showing population movement to the suburbs?
4. How should a home-improvement retailer modify its strategy in response to the changing gender roles of U.S. males and females? What elements of its strategy should not be modified? Explain your answer.
5. How will consumer sophistication and confidence affect retailers? Will they affect all types of retailers? Explain your answer.
6. Will deregulation succeed? Why or why not? Take both a consumer's and retailer's perspective.
7. What are the pros and cons of debit-only transfer systems? As a retailer, how would you promote such a system?
8. Will the time come when most consumer purchases are made through some form of video-ordering system? Explain your answer.
9. Distinguish between computerized checkouts and electronic point-of-sale systems. Which would be more useful in the long run? Why?
10. What types of nonstore retailing will *not* grow in the future? Why?
11. Describe the advantages and disadvantages of rationalized retailing. What kind of retailer should *not* use it? Explain your answer.
12. Differentiate between mass merchandising and positioned retailing. Why would a retailer such as Sears decide to engage in both?
13. How could a standardized strategy on the part of a U.S. retailer fail when introduced into Canada, a country with many similarities to the United States?
14. What are the opportunities and risks facing a U.S. retailer that enters the People's Republic of China?
15. Why do you think that so many foreign-based firms have acquired U.S. retailers?

1. Ann Hagedorn, "Penney's 'TV Mall' Makes Its Late, Humbled Debut," *Wall Street Journal* (February 16, 1988), p. 6; Joanne Cleaver, "Penney's Comes Home with TV Shopping Entry," *Crain's New York Business* (October 19, 1987), p. 27; and Rick Gallagher, "Telaction: Is It Ready for Prime Time?" *Chain Store Age Executive* (July 1988), pp. 16–19.

2. Unless otherwise indicated, the data in this section are drawn from U.S. Bureau of the Census, *Current Population Reports* and *Census of Population*. For a good review article, see "Information on Demographics and Psychographics Serves as Guidepost to Help Retailers Prepare for Turn of the Century," *Chain Store Age Executive* (May 1987), pp. 19–25.

3. William Lazer, "How Rising Affluence Will Reshape Markets," *American Demographics* (February 1984), pp. 17–21. See also "Household Income," *Wall Street Journal* (August 25, 1987), p. 41.

4. John Smallwood, William Lazer, et al., *A Report on Consumer Environments and Life Styles of the Seventies* (Benton Harbor, Mich.: Whirlpool Corporation, 1971), pp. 18–31; Alladi Venkatesh, "Changing Roles of Women—A Life-Style Analysis," *Journal of Consumer Research*, Vol. 7 (September 1980), pp. 189–197; Barbara A. Price, "What the Baby Boom Believes," *American Demographics* (May 1984), pp. 31–33; Joan Kron, "Clothes-Shopping Habits Changing As Men Seek Style, Women Service," *Wall Street Journal* (December 21, 1984), pp. 21, 28; and Scott Kilman, "Retailers Change Their Stores and Goods, Looking to Cash in on New Buying Habits," *Wall Street Journal* (September 8, 1986), p. 29.

5. "Large Numbers of Husbands Buy Household Products, Do Housework," *Marketing News* (October 3, 1980), pp. 1, 3.

6. For example, see Ronald D. Michman, "The Male Queue at the Checkout Counter," *Business Horizons*, Vol. 29 (May–June 1986), pp. 51–55; and Priscilla Donegan, "The Myth of the Male Shopper," *Progressive Grocer* (May 1986), pp. 36–42.

7. R. Gordon McGovern, "The Consumer Revolution in the Supermarket," *Journal of Business Strategy*, Vol. 5 (Fall 1984), pp. 93–95.

8. "The Year 2000: A Demographic Profile of Consumer Market," *Marketing News* (May 25, 1984), Section 1, p. 10.

9. "Retail Trend to Affect Quality of Goods, In-Store Service," *Marketing News* (February 15, 1988), p. 18.

10. See also Barbara Everitt Bryant, "Built for Excitement," *American Demographics* (March 1987), pp. 39–42.

11. "31 Major Trends Shaping the Future of American Business," *The Public Pulse*, Vol. 2, No. 1 (1988), p. 1.

12. Max L. Densmore and Sylvia Kaufman, "How Leading Retailers Stay on Top," *Business*, Vol. 35 (April–June 1985), pp. 28–35.

13. George S. Day and David A. Aaker, "A Guide to Consumerism," *Journal of Marketing*, Vol. 34 (July 1970), p. 12.

14. David W. Cravens and Gerald E. Hills, "Consumerism: A Perspective for Business," *Business Horizons*, Vol. 13 (August 1970), p. 24.

15. J.C. Penney.

16. Giant Food.

17. Mary Johnson, "The New Consumer Advocate: Supermarkets," *Progressive Grocer* (January 1983), pp. 83–88.

18. "Telemarketing Association Adopts Nine-Point Code of Ethics, Standards," *Marketing News* (October 9, 1987), p. 23.

19. Joel R. Evans and Barry Berman, *Marketing*, Third Edition (New York: Macmillan, 1987), pp. 722–723.

20. Kate Fitzgerald, "ATM Network Plans Big Sweep," *Advertising Age* (May 9, 1988), p. 44.

21. See Jules Abend, "Debit Cards? Enthusiasm Is Slightly Underwhelming," *Stores* (February 1988), pp. 82–83.

22. See Sydney P. Freedberg, "Home-Shopping Shakeout Forces Survivors to Find Fresh Approach," *Wall Street Journal* (November 4, 1987), p. 39; and Diane Schneidman, "Better Goods, Entertainment," *Marketing News* (February 1, 1988), pp. 1–2.

23. Bill Saporito, "Are IBM and Sears Crazy? Or Canny?" *Fortune* (September 28, 1987), pp. 74–79; and Andrew Pollack, "Videotex: The I.B.M.-Sears Venture Is Ready," *New York Times* (April 12, 1988), p. D27. See also W. Wayne Talarzyk, "Videotex: Are We Having Fun Yet?" (Columbus, Ohio: Ohio State University, June 1987), Working Paper Series 87–72.

24. See Gary Robins, "Better Service, POS = Faster Shopper Checkout," *Stores* (February 1988), pp. 71–75; and Rick Gallagher, "POS Technology: Scanners 'R' Us," *Chain Store Age Executive* (March 1988), pp. 95–96.

25. "Software for Retailers Covers All the Bases," *Chain Store Age Executive* (February 1985), pp. 62–71; and "Roster of Retail-Oriented Programs Increases," *Chain Store Age Executive* (August 1984), pp. 71–75. See also Richard Gibson, "Electronic Price Labels Tested in Supermarkets," *Wall Street Journal* (March 31, 1988), p. 25.

26. "Home-Grown Software: Not Just for the Big Guys," *Progressive Grocer* (October 1987), pp. 95–98.

27. "Keeping Inventory in Tow at Capital Marine Supply," *Chain Store Age Executive* (November 1984), pp. 66, 68.

28. "Thrift Drug Keeps in Touch," *Chain Store Age Executive* (June 1987), pp. 58, 60.

29. "Excellence in Retailing," a statement of mission for the May Department Stores Company, n.d.

30. "Manager Challenges for 1985 and Beyond," *Progressive Grocer* (January 1985), pp. 22, 24.

31. Russell Mitchell, "How Comp-U-Card Hooks Home Shoppers," *Business Week* (May 18, 1987), pp. 73–74.

32. Len Strazewski, "Computerized Service Sets Shoppers Hacking," *Advertising Age* (February 22, 1988), p. 62.

33. Albert D. Bates, "The Troubled Future of Retailing," *Business Horizons*, Vol. 19 (August 1976), pp. 22–28.

34. Ibid.

35. "A Look at Mass Merchandisers," *Nielsen Researcher* (Number 1, 1982), pp. 16–23; and H. R. Jones, "Mass Merchandisers: A Maturing Retail Concept," *Nielsen Researcher* (Number 3, 1984), pp. 14–20.

36. "Whatever the Name, Value Is the Game," *Chain Store Age Executive* (February 1985), p. 47.

37. See Leonard L. Berry, "Retail Positioning Strategies for the 1980s," *Business Horizons*, Vol. 25 (November–December 1982), pp. 45–50.

38. *The Limited, Inc. 1986 Annual Report.*

39. "Department Stores 'Specialize' in Competitive Maneuvers," *Marketing News* (February 15, 1988), p. 14.

40. Francine Schwadel, "Sears Plans to Buy Chain of Stores in Specialty Line," *Wall Street Journal* (December 16, 1987), p. 11.

41. Doron P. Levin, "K mart to Buy Pay Less for $500 Million," *Wall Street Journal* (January 15, 1985), p. 7; "K mart Says 31 Stores Will Offer a Range of Financial Services," *Wall Street Journal* (January 22, 1985), p. 42; Patrica Strnad, "K mart Pares Unprofitable Units," *Advertising Age* (April 13, 1987), p. 22; and "K mart Acquires 51% of Warehouse-Club Stores' Operator," *Wall Street Journal* (March 7, 1988), p. 22.

42. Walter Loeb, "Retailers with Destination Store Image Will Prosper in '90s," *Discount Store News* (May 11, 1987), pp. 171–172.

43. Thomas Moore, "Would You Buy a Car from This Man?" *Fortune* (April 11, 1988), pp. 72–74.

44. "Allison's Place Slows Growth to Sharpen Image," *Discount Store News* (November 23, 1987), pp. 13–14.

45. Steve Weinstein, "The New Safeway," *Progressive Grocer* (November 1987), pp. 21–28.

46. Laurence Jacobs, Reginald Worthley, and Charles Keown, "Perceived Buyer Satisfaction and Selling Pressure Versus Pricing Policy: A Comparative Study of Retailers in Ten Developing Countries," *Journal of Business Research*, Vol. 12 (March 1984), pp. 63–74.

47. Jacquelyn Bivins, "Japan: Land of Contradictions," *Chain Store Age Executive* (March 1988), pp. 14–18.

48. Paul Delaney, "Shoppers in Spain Now Staying Mainly at the Mall," *New York Times* (August 13, 1987), p. A4.

49. Heidi Vernon-Wortzel and Lawrence H. Wortzel, "The Emergence of Free Market Retailing in the People's Republic of China," *California Management Review*, Vol. 29 (Spring 1987), pp. 59–76.

50. Arnold Fishman, "1986 International Mail Order Guide," *Direct Marketing* (August 1987), pp. 168–169.

51. Susan Chira, "7-Eleven Stores Find Favor with Japanese," *New York Times* (December 24, 1984), pp. 33, 36; Valerie Mackie and Coleen Garaghty, "Southland Bid for Worldwide 7-11 Growth," *Advertising Age* (November 21, 1983), pp. 42, 44; and *Southland Corporation 1986 Annual Report.*

52. Lynne Curry, "Chinese Gobble Kentucky Fried Chicken," *Advertising Age* (November 9, 1987), p. 57.

53. Pat Sloan, "Retailers Take on the World," *Advertising Age* (October 26, 1987), p. 76.

54. Bill Kelley, "The New Wave from Europe," *Sales & Marketing Management* (November 1987), pp. 45–51; and Jack Burton, "Furniture Chain Has Global View," *Advertising Age* (October 26, 1987), p. 58.

55. Arthur Markowitz, "Carrefour Opens U.S. Hypermarket; Maintains True to European to Roots," *Discount Store News* (February 15, 1988), pp. 1, 100.

56. Nitin Sanghavi, "Harrods Reaches Out with Its Plush Touch," *Direct Marketing* (April 1987), pp. 43–49.

57. "Foreign Firms Invest in U.S. Retail Chains," *Chain Store Age Executive* (September 1987), p. 58.

58. "Foreign Retailers Recruit U.S. Talent," *Marketing News* (March 13, 1987), p. 12. See also Mark Maremont, "Marks & Spencer Pays a Premium for Pinstripes," *Business Week* (April 18, 1988), p. 67.

Kroger: Linking Technological Advances and Self-Service*

Case 1

Kroger is one of the leading supermarket chains in the United States, with annual sales now approaching $20 billion. Despite its success, Kroger has been quite concerned about how long its customers must wait in line at the checkout counter. Consumer surveys have consistently shown that many consumers are more negative toward waiting in line than toward any other supermarket attribute. This compounds the difficulty of scheduling checkout personnel: in busy periods additional checkout personnel are required; yet, these personnel are not always available. Industrywide, the shrinking teenage population in the United States (this group makes up the largest age category for checkout personnel) has made it difficult to secure and retain appropriate employees. And if a supermarket seeks to have existing personnel skip lunch or break time to accommodate customers waiting in line, it can cause morale problems and a higher level of personnel turnover.

In an effort to reduce customer waiting time, as well as to alleviate some difficulties with checkout personnel, Kroger has begun an experiment with a "scan-your-own" checkout system in one of its Atlanta, Georgia, supermarkets. In that Atlanta store, seven standard checkout lanes have been replaced with seven CheckRobot ACM 1000 systems (self-service

*The material in this case is drawn from "The Ultimate in Self-Service: Scan Your Own," *Chain Store Age Executive* (June 1987), pp. 53–54; and "DIY Promos Via Video POS," *Chain Store Age Executive* (April 1988), pp. 76, 78.

scanners) and four payment stations. Some of the lanes are cashier-operated; others are totally self-service. This is the first full-store test of this new technology.

The CheckRobot ACM 1000 automatic-checkout machine incorporates a flat-top scanner, a touch-sensitive video-display monitor, a conveyor belt, and a sensing mechanism (which is used for security purposes). The system works in the following manner. The consumer scans each item in his or her shopping basket (the prices for the last five scanned items are displayed on a monitor) and then places it on a conveyor belt which is scanner activated. Groceries move down the conveyor belt to a bagging area, where a Kroger bagger is positioned. After all the items have been scanned, the consumer takes the receipt to a payment station and pays the amount due.

The CheckRobot ACM 1000 system offers several attractive features:

❑ The monitor screen is touch-sensitive, has a subtotal button, and can voice prices. If an item does not scan, the consumer can press the UPC code numbers into the video monitor.

❑ If a consumer uses coupons, he or she presses a coupon button alongside the price designation on the monitor. This helps verify that a couponed product has actually been purchased. The CheckRobot machine will be able to handle coupon scanning when this is available.

❑ A security feature keeps the consumer from running an item through the conveyor belt without its first being scanned. CheckRobot also has a feature which prohibits the consumer from placing one item on the scanner and another item on the conveyor belt. The system checks the dimensions of products placed on the conveyor belt with those of the scanned goods. Items with improper dimensions are returned to the consumer (the conveyor belt automatically reverses direction).

❑ If an item is scanned and not placed on the conveyor belt (the consumer may change his or her mind or may not have enough money), the price purchase is automatically voided from the receipt.

❑ Two bagging areas per machine allow one consumer to start scanning as another customer's order is being packed.

Kroger feels that "scan-your-own" technology will enable it to use more checkout lanes with fewer personnel, thus reducing waiting times. The CheckRobot system will also help reduce labor expenses. In addition, consumers will be better able to note prices as they are scanned.

So far, the reaction at the customer level has been mixed. Although Kroger's official policy is that self-service scanning will never be imposed on consumers and that "scanning your own" is a free choice of customers, it is obvious that Kroger can motivate consumers to use the do-it-yourself method by holding down the number of checkout personnel, thereby "motivating" consumers who do not want to wait in line to use self-service scanning. Accordingly, some consumers fear that Kroger may eventually do away with a large proportion of its checkout personnel. In response, Kroger states that it is more concerned with checkout speed and that labor savings are a supplemental benefit. Kroger compares consumer fears and confusion regarding CheckRobot with early consumer reactions to UPC scanning.

QUESTIONS

1. What demographic and life-style trends of consumers will help determine the success or failure of CheckRobot ACM 1000?

2. Will do-it-yourself supermarket checkouts be accepted by consumers more or less quickly than debit-only transfer systems? Explain your answer.

3. Would you view the CheckRobot ACM 1000 system as risk-minimization retailing? Why or why not?

4. Should Kroger introduce CheckRobot ACM 1000 into all of its stores? Explain your answer.

Toys "R" Us: Pursuing A Global Retail Strategy*

Toys "R" Us is the largest toy retailer in the United States with well over three hundred stores and annual sales exceeding $2 billion. Since 1984, the firm has been aggressively opening stores in foreign markets, while continuing its U.S. expansion. Its early global efforts focused on Canada, Great Britain, Singapore, and Hong Kong. More recently, Toys "R" Us has opened stores in West Germany, France, Italy, and Japan. Its ambitious international retailing plans are based on the fact that the international toy market is twice as large as the U.S. toy market. Although Toys "R" Us still has considerable room to grow in the United States (it does not have stores in many major U.S. markets), it is concerned about the long-term prospects and the relative degree of market saturation in the United States.

In international operations, Toys "R" Us uses a similar strategy to the one it employs in the United States:

❏ The company generally expands in one market area at a time. It seeks to have adequate distribution facilities to service its stores and to be able to advertise efficiently.

❏ It builds market strength through internal expansion. It does not grow through mergers or acquisitions. Yet, mergers or acquisitions could quicken Toys "R" Us' pace of growth in foreign markets, because initial consumer recognition of the firm's name is rather low.

❏ Its foreign stores are almost identical to its U.S. stores. Toys "R" Us uses freestanding-style buildings and suburban locations for both U.S. and foreign operations. All Toys "R" Us outlets carry eighteen thousand to twenty thousand items per store; 80 per cent of the merchandise sold internationally is the same as that sold in the United States. Neither U.S. nor foreign Toys "R" Us stores place a lot of emphasis on sales; they feature everyday competitive prices.

❏ Infant-care items are heavily discounted in both its U.S. and its foreign stores. The company assumes that first-time mothers who are attracted will remain as steady customers throughout their toy-purchasing life cycle.

Although Toys "R" Us does not compare profit and sales performance between its domestic and international operations in financial statements, market analysts assume that many Toys "R" Us foreign operations are too new to be profitable. However, long-run sales and profit expectations are high. For example, the customer traffic at its Great Britain stores is among the highest of that at all Toys "R" Us locations in the world. Traditional competitors are carefully monitoring the success of Toys "R" Us in foreign markets.

Of all the foreign markets in which Toys "R" Us operates, West Germany presents some of the greatest challenges. There are tight government regulations with which it must cope; for the most part, these regulations are much more demanding than those in the United States. In West Germany, Toys "R" Us must particularly deal with zoning requirements and the power of labor unions. It also needs to carefully assess West German demographic trends.

A 1977 West German law restricts any retailer from building a store larger than fifteen thousand square feet in areas outside the core of any German city (France has a similar restriction). The official reasons for this regulation are that the government wants to protect West Germany's small independent retailers in suburban areas from large chain stores and that it wants to encourage city construction and growth. In practice, this restriction makes it difficult for retailers such as Toys "R" Us to find large urban locations for their units (to build large stores, they would often have to purchase adjoining properties from multiple owners).

The labor unions in West Germany are quite powerful. An employee's work week is restricted to 38.5 hours. In addition, stores are limited to this schedule of hours: 7 A.M. to 6:30 P.M. Monday to Friday, and 7 A.M. to 2 P.M. Saturday. No Sunday hours are permitted. According to a retailing consultant,

> In my view, the biggest disadvantage to German retailers is the working hours. Initially, the limitations were meant to protect the workers, but now, shopping motives have changed and so has daily life. More women are working and have less time in the afternoon to shop. Now the labor unions are opposing any change toward less stringent opening hours.

*The material in this case is drawn from Mark Maremont, Dori Jones Yang, and Amy Dunkin, "Toys 'R' Us Goes Overseas—And Finds That Toys 'R' Them Too," *Business Week* (January 26, 1987), pp. 71–72; Rhonda Razzano, "Deutschland in Dutch," *Chain Store Age Executive* (April 1987), pp. 13–20 ff.; and Subrata N. Chakravarty, "Will Toys 'Be' Great?" *Forbes* (February 22, 1988), pp. 37–39.

In contrast, in the United States, Toys "R" Us stores are ⌐
10 P.M. Monday through Saturday, and Sunday from 12 noon to ⌐
law.

Toys "R" Us must be very careful in its future planning for West Germany, b⌐
expected decline in the population. There are now about sixty-one million West G⌐
the population is forecast to fall to forty-eight million as of the year 2030. Yet, although ⌐
West German population will be getting smaller and older, the high per capita disposable
income will increase further as average family size shrinks. Thus, West German families may
become more prone to purchase expensive toys for their children and grandchildren.

QUESTIONS

1. Which factors should Toys "R" Us place the greatest emphasis on when determining which foreign markets to enter next?
2. What are the advantages and disadvantages of Toys "R" Us' strategy of simultaneously pursuing domestic and foreign growth?
3. Comment on Toys "R" Us' use of standardization in its international efforts.
4. Develop a ten-year plan for Toys "R" Us to pursue in West Germany. Note: The first Toys "R" Us outlet opened in West Germany during 1987.

Part Eight Comprehensive Case

Tom Borch Traditional Clothier: Integrating, Evaluating, and Controlling a Retail Strategy*

Introduction

Steve and Dawn Carlton were at a turning point in the late fall of 1988. Sales volume for their store, Tom Borch Traditional Clothier, was erratic, cash flow was poor, and profits were not looking good. However, plans had been made for better merchandise and financial controls for 1989, and new promotions envisioned. Would this be enough to warrant continued efforts to maintain the business, possibly with additional bank loans and/or injections from the Carltons' personal resources? Steve Carlton was particularly concerned that they were falling behind planned sales. If sales were not strong through the fall, Dawn Carlton was afraid they would have to consider closing up their store.

History of the Business

Tom Borch Traditional Clothier was located in Bowling Green, Ohio, a small college community in the north-central part of the state. Steve Carlton, the owner, opened his business August 15, 1986. His parents had recently died, leaving him two farms in south-central Ohio. He was not interested in farming, having spent several years in retailing following his graduation from Kent State University in 1977. He was able to lease the farms and wanted to use the proceeds to finance the opening of his own business. After investigating various areas, Carlton settled on Bowling Green as a location.

Carlton wanted to open a traditional menswear store owing to his expertise in the field: he had spent six years buying menswear for L.L. Bean and two years managing a menswear store in Maine. Bowling Green had only three men's specialty clothing stores at the time. A fourth successful men's traditional store had recently closed because the building in which it was located had to be razed.

Steve Carlton leased a freestanding building on Dover Street, one block off Main Street, the main thoroughfare of Bowling Green. At the time, this was the best location and building he could find, although he had heard that businesses off Main Street often suffered from lack of visibility because of low student pedestrian traffic. Tom Borch's custom fixturing and furnishings were in the country gentry manner. Clothing and accessories were traditional and of very good quality. More as an afterthought, Steve added some women's clothing to his stock, which he was able to get through his menswear suppliers. Upon opening, about 85 per cent of the merchandise was for men and 15 per cent for women.

At first, business was slow and most of the traffic was female. Within a short time, Steve Carlton knew that he needed to find a place on Main Street and change his merchandise split to favor women. By August 1987, Carlton was able to negotiate an agreement to get out of his lease and secure a spot on Main Street. He moved into the lower level of a newly constructed brick building between a new restaurant and a camera–art–card store. The building had three levels; all were open to the street with outside stairways connecting them. The interiors were long and narrow, about eighteen feet by fifty-five feet. There was a gift store on the second level and a quick print shop on the third level. A three-year lease at $1,000 a month was negotiated for this space. Fifty per cent of stock was devoted to women's apparel. Sales began to improve dramatically.

Carlton was married in the spring of 1988. His wife, Dawn, was formerly a buyer at Symphony, an exclusive Toledo women's specialty store, and also had experience in computer hardware and software sales. Her expertise proved to be a great asset for the business. She became full-time manager of Tom Borch's in August 1988.

During the spring of 1988, the Carltons made the decision to go entirely into women's wear with the beginning of the fall 1988 season. Thus, they could offer a better selection to the women who continued to make up the vast majority of their business. The fall season sales got off to a slow start in August and continued to be soft in September and October, producing a sales volume decline from the same months in the previous year.

Merchandising Strategy

Target Market

Bowling Green is located thirty-five miles south of Toledo, Ohio. Its permanent residents number about nine thousand and the student population of Bowling Green State University's residential campus is a little over fifteen thousand. Bowling Green merchants have typically targeted their merchandise offerings primarily to the student population, with permanent Bowling Green residents as a secondary market. There has been some success in drawing summer visitor traffic from the nearby Maumee State Park, but June, July, and early August are usually still slow selling periods.

A September 1988 survey of Bowling Green residents' buying habits revealed that of the 570 students surveyed, 11.7 per cent had made their last purchase of women's

*This case was prepared and written by Professors Pat Gifford and Jack Gifford, Miami University, Oxford, Ohio.

clothing in uptown Bowling Green, and 6.2 per cent had made their last purchase of men's clothing in uptown Bowling Green. Of the 559 permanent residents surveyed, 17.8 per cent had made their last purchase of women's clothing in Bowling Green, while 12.3 per cent had made their last purchase of men's clothing in Bowling Green. A large proportion of the students bought at home before they came to school, while a majority of the Bowling Green residents shopped in Toledo or at Maumee shopping malls.

The Carltons had identified their target market over time through conversations with other local merchants and observations of customers in their store.

Market Centers

There were two major shopping areas in Bowling Green, the "uptown" area and the Southgate Mall. The "uptown" area was adjacent to the main entrance of Bowling Green University. It was six blocks long with the vast majority of businesses facing Main Street, the main east–west thoroughfare, or on the side streets, extending one block north or south of Main Street. The primary north–south thoroughfare, Phillip Street, was three blocks from campus and tended to be an invisible barrier for student pedestrian traffic. Bowling Green merchants who expected to primarily cater to student pedestrian traffic felt that it was necessary to locate within the three blocks of Main Street closest to campus. Businesses in the uptown area included fast-food restaurants, restaurant/bars; bookstores; stationery and art-supply stores; drugstores; florists; movie theaters; gift shops; copying services; ice cream shops; services such as banks, insurance, travel agencies; and two gas stations. In terms of apparel, Lee's Bookstore carried some junior women's and men's clothing. Hudson's College Shop (a division of Minneapolis-based Dayton Hudson) retailed junior and women's fashions and accessories; the Nutmeg was one of the chain of traditional women's apparel; David Brood's Shoes sold men's and women's shoes; and finally, there was the Carltons' Tom Borch Traditional Clothier.

The Southgate Mall was generally service-oriented. A Kroger's superstore replaced a smaller Kroger's at the location in the summer of 1983. There were also a Super-X drugstore, a K Mart, a J.C. Penney catalog store, a card store, beauty shops, a fabric store, two dentists' offices, a Radio Shack, and miscellaneous small convenience stores. The mall was a mile and a quarter from the main business district and two miles from the center of campus.

Sales Volume

The fiscal year for Tom Borch's accounting records ran from August 15, 1986 to June 30, 1987, and July 1, 1987 to June 30, 1988. Although these periods were not exactly the same in length, they were used for purposes of comparison. The beginning of the second fiscal year roughly coincided with the opening of the store on Main Street; thus, the two sets of fiscal data prove valuable in comparing the success of the two locations, especially in terms of sales volume. Sales for Tom Borch rose dramatically from 1987 to 1988. See Table 1. Both higher traffic and a year's worth of experience in the Bowling Green market enabled the Carltons to better assess the needs of their customers and make

the necessary adjustments to inventory. The Carltons also cultivated customers from Toledo and other surrounding areas, which may have contributed a small amount to the increased volume.

Sales volume was closely tied to the academic year and holidays.

Cost Structures

Steve Carlton conceded to being a person who worked on hunches and "gut feelings" concerning the store and believed that he had been lucky with the business to this point. He was, however, beginning to see the need for closer control over the financial and merchandising aspects of the business. The financial accounting procedures were performed by an accountant on retainer by the corporation. Carlton relied on him for advice and assistance, but communication was difficult as both were very busy. No specific goals were set in terms of the cost structures. The accountant was simply to suggest cost-saving measures and keep taxes at a minimum. Table 2 provides income statements for fiscal 1987 and 1988.

The Carltons hoped to increase their profits for 1989. They also wanted to draw $20,000 in salaries from the business ($10,000 over last year), which would add to their current expenses. The projected income statement is included in Table 2.

Financing

Tom Borch was owned by the Carltons as a corporation under Subchapter S of the Internal Revenue Code. The corporation had limited liability, limited stockholders, and shareholders (Steve and Dawn) were taxed as individuals.

The firm's balance sheets as of June 30, 1987, and June 30, 1988, are shown in Table 3. Total assets for Tom Borch included cash on hand, accounts receivable—trade, inventory, prepaid expenses (the first year only), furniture and fixtures, leasehold improvements, and an auto. Tom Borch had no formal store charge, under most circumstances. A few preferred customers deferred half of the purchase price for two weeks and then paid the remainder biweekly. These instances were few and did not show up as accounts receivable on the balance sheets from either year. Stockholders' equity (net worth), which included common stock, retained earnings, and profit (loss), was not sufficient to cover the investment requirements during the first year. Therefore, Steve Carlton had to contribute to the business from his personal funds in the form of an officer's loan (note payable).

The Carltons had made it a practice to pay for all merchandise they purchased within the discount period (usually ten days from the receipt of invoice) in order to get a reduction in the cost of merchandise. This reduction was usually 8 per cent. The ability to pay these bills required adequate cash flow. When current sales did not adequately cover business needs, the Carltons dipped into their personal assets to pay the bills. In mid-September of 1988, the Carltons were in a temporary cash bind both for the business and personally and decided to borrow money from the bank in order to pay business bills within the discount period

TABLE 1
Tom Borch Traditional Clothier, Monthly Credit and Cash Clothing Sales

	Fiscal 1987 Sales*	Fiscal 1988 Sales†	% Change 1987–1988‡	Preliminary Fiscal 1989 Sales	% Change 1988–1989
JULY					
Credit	—	$ 586	N/A	$ 364	−37.9
Cash	—	6,882	N/A	10,127	47.2
Total	—	$ 7,468	N/A	$10,491	40.5
AUGUST					
Credit	$ 455	$ 881	93.6	$ 734	−16.7
Cash	1,972	17,424	783.6	14,968	−14.1
Total	$ 2,427	$18,305	654.2	$15,702	−14.2
SEPTEMBER					
Credit	$ 299	$ 581	94.3	$ 1,226	111.0
Cash	6,538	18,840	188.2	9,490	−49.6
Total	$ 6,837	$19,421	184.1	$10,716	−44.8
OCTOBER					
Credit	$ 315	$ 1,469	366.3	Not Available	
Cash	12,018	21,653	80.2		
Total	$12,333	$23,122	87.5		
NOVEMBER					
Credit	$ 834	$ 900	7.9	Not Available	
Cash	8,460	20,304	140.0		
Total	$ 9,294	$21,204	128.1		
DECEMBER					
Credit	$ 1,418	$ 2,121	49.6	Not Available	
Cash	16,004	21,333	33.3		
Total	$17,422	$23,454	34.6		
JANUARY					
Credit	$ 593	$ 120	−79.8	Not Available	
Cash	10,295	21,790	111.7		
Total	$10,888	$21,910	101.2		
FEBRUARY					
Credit	$ 1,449	$ 440	−69.6	Not Available	
Cash	15,878	15,113	−4.8		
Total	$17,327	$15,553	−10.2		
MARCH					
Credit	$ 134	$ 476	255.2	Not Available	
Cash	5,836	8,506	45.8		
Total	$ 5,970	$ 8,982	50.5		
APRIL					
Credit	$ 1,168	$ 455	−61.0	Not Available	
Cash	12,374	16,033	29.6		
Total	$13,542	$16,488	21.8		
MAY					
Credit	$ 1,684	$ 457	−72.9	Not Available	
Cash	8,816	10,633	20.6		
Total	$10,500	$11,090	5.6		
JUNE					
Credit	$ 486	$ 278	−42.8	Not Available	
Cash	2,991	6,636	121.9		
Total	$ 3,477	$ 6,914	98.8		
Yearly Total	$110,017	$193,911	76.3	Not Available	

*August 15, 1986-June 30, 1987
†July 1, 1987-June 30, 1988
‡N/A is not applicable.

TABLE 2
Tom Borch Traditional Clothier, Income Statements

	Fiscal 1987	Fiscal 1988	Projected Fiscal 1989
INCOME			
Clothing sales	$110,017	$193,911	$220,000
Alterations	680	3	0
Miscellaneous	326	4,891	9,000
Returns & allowances	(2,467)	(2,610)	(3,000)
TOTAL INCOME	$108,556	$196,195	$226,000
Less **COST OF GOODS SOLD**	$ 81,251	$131,386	$142,083
GROSS PROFIT	$ 27,305	$ 64,809	$ 83,917
SELLING & ADMIN. EXPENSES			
Officers' salaries	$ 1,849	$ 10,000	$ 20,000
Office salaries	$ 9,334	11,055	12,000
Cleaning and sanitation	67	125	125
Telephone	1,474	1,701	1,800
Utilities	1,968	1,450	1,500
Insurance	1,917	1,838	2,000
Travel & entertainment	0	0	0
Office supplies & postage	462	521	650
Legal & accounting	762	1,371	900
Advertising	4,096	1,118	1,500
Dues & subscriptions	1,142	733	750
Bad debts	0	0	0
Auto & travel expenses	205	63	100
Depreciation	975	2,888	3,500
License fees	13	0	0
Employee welfare	0	0	0
Interest	0	0	330
Miscellaneous	1,098	1,557	1,975
Employment insurance	230	539	540
Workman's compensation	0	0	0
Payroll taxes	3,104	2,259	2,300
Personal property taxes	0	410	450
City income taxes	0	0	0
Real-estate taxes	0	0	0
Supplies	1,123	670	700
Freight	480	195	200
Rent	9,634	11,952	13,000
Bank charges	11	0	0
Repairs	112	0	0
Refunds	281	499	650
Discounts allowed	28	120	150
Contract labor	2,683	6,082	800
Less **TOTAL S & A EXPENSES**	$ 43,048	$ 57,146	$ 65,920
NET PROFIT OR LOSS	$ (15,743)	$ 7,663	$ 17,997

and take care of a personal financial need. Their track record was such that they had no difficulty getting a two-year loan, which totalled $11,200, $8,000 of which was for the business. Interest on the loan was 11 per cent plus 2 per cent variable at the first of each month.

Merchandise

Tom Borch was conceived of as a fine, traditional apparel store, targeted toward college students and townspeople who had discriminating taste in quality clothing at a reason-

TABLE 3
Tom Borch Traditional Clothier, Balance Sheets

	As of June 30, 1987	As of June 30, 1988		As of June 30, 1987	As of June 30, 1988
Assets			**Liabilities**		
Current:			Current:		
Cash in bank	$ 3,616	$ 2,137	Accounts payable—trade	$ 1,028	$ 0
Accounts receivable—trade	1,501	1,688	Accrued payroll taxes	313	505
Inventory	47,089	48,077	Accrued sales tax	817	294
Prepaid expenses	2,110	0	Notes payable—bank	8,887	3,132
Total	$54,316	$51,902	Estimated Federal income taxes	0	0
			Total	$11,045	$3,931
Fixed (present value):			Fixed:		
Furniture & fixtures	$ 851	$ 9656	Notes payable—officers	$62,600	$65,264
Less: accum. depn.	(85)	(1,005)			
Leasehold improvements	3,173	3,173	Total liabilities	$73,645	$69,195
Less: accum. depn.	(317)	(634)			
Auto	8,531	8,531			
Less: accum. depn.	(375)	(2,025)	**Net worth**		
Total	$11,778	$17,696	Value of common stock	$8,192	$8,483
Total assets	$66,094	$69,598	Annual profit or loss	(15,743)	7,663
			Retained earnings	0	(15,743)
			Total net worth	$(7,551)	$ 403
			Liabilities + net worth	$66,094	$69,598

able price. The interior of the store was designed to create a casual but tasteful atmosphere, an appropriate backdrop for the merchandise. The original women's line included slacks, shirts, sweaters, a few suits, skirts, and outerwear jackets. Featured brands were Thomson, David Brooks, Robert Scott, Aston, and Sero. Belts and canvas bags rounded out the store. Later, some dresses and nightgowns by Lanz were added to the women's line.

As the first months of operation passed and Steve Carlton found that he had more female customers than he had anticipated, he began to increase the proportion of women's clothing and tried a few dresses and more sweaters and pants. He found that the market for traditional men's clothing was not as great as he had earlier thought. He guessed that male students were interested only in jeans and T-shirts and that the taste level and price of his merchandise weren't matched to the needs of the majority of professors on moderate budgets with practical clothing in mind.

Most of the brands carried by Tom Borch during the first year and a half were available at better department stores and often at lower prices than Steve Carlton could afford to sell his merchandise. After the fall season of 1987, Carlton took a hard look at the store and its direction for the future. By this time, he had moved to the new location, sales had

picked up, and the business seemed to be better. But there were still things that needed to change.

Tom Borch was by now selling women's wear quite well with 60–65 per cent of its stock in female apparel. But the men's business was doing poorly. There was direct competition for much of the women's wear from the Nutmeg Shop, located down the street. That store carried many of the same brands of sweaters, pants, and skirts as Tom Borch and had a broader selection and, sometimes, lower prices. The Bowling Green Nutmeg was one of fifteen stores and had buying power that Tom Borch did not have as a single unit. To remedy this, Tom Borch joined a resident buying office in New York in March 1988 and was hoping to reap the benefits of experts in the market.

Over the first few months of 1988, the Carltons made their decision to go entirely into women's wear, to drop many of the common styles and brands that they had been using, and to try to forge a new, more unique merchandise line for Tom Borch. The new strategy was initiated with the fall 1988 line. Dawn Carlton, the store manager since late summer of 1988, and then buyer for the store, planned to develop this more unique, sophisticated merchandise look for the spring and beyond. She found that the college students bought their everyday sweaters and corduroys at other stores but were coming to Tom Borch for "special" clothes, and that Bowling Green women were beginning to look at Tom Borch for "something different." Many parents who visited their children at college were delighted to find Tom Borch and frequently bought for themselves as well as their daughters. Merchandise available in the fall included the categories previously carried with the addition of raincoats, a few more one- and two-piece dresses, and more accessories—ties, belts, purses, briefcases, umbrellas, and a limited line of jewelry. Generally there was a broader range of all merchandise. New brands were Boston Trader, Jason Younger, Needleworks, Scotland Yard, Numa, British Khaki, and several two- or three-of-a-kind sweaters and sweater dresses. For spring 1989, Dawn Carlton again sought the unusual and ordered many interesting fabrications in styles with a new twist.

Merchandise Control

During the first two years of operation, Steve Carlton did all the buying for the store. He visited the New York apparel market twice a year, once for his fall line and once for his spring line. He also made some interim orders from sales representatives who visited the store and a few by phone through the buying office. Carlton did not use a formal buying plan when he went to market. He normally had some idea of what he wanted, worked the market to see what was offered, and ordered what he concluded to be the appropriate merchandise. He did not attempt to control for the cost or the specific units of merchandise purchased.

Dawn Carlton, from her previous experience in retail buying, was aware of the need for greater controls and was in the process of setting up procedures for inventory control in the store. She also attempted a more organized method of planning her spring purchases during her market trip for spring 1989. The Carltons had never taken a physical inventory. They did not know why their accountant had never asked for one for tax purposes and assumed that he had used book inventories to derive data for income statements and balance sheets.

Pricing

The Carltons generally priced merchandise with a 50 per cent initial markup, assuming that this would cover expenses and provide some profit. Virtually all the merchandise in the store was priced at what would be considered the upper end of "moderate" or the low end of "better." Steve Carlton estimated that annual reductions were 27 per cent of net sales.

Promotion

The Carltons changed their promotional emphasis over the two years of operations and drastically reduced their advertising costs from 1987 to 1988. They reduced expensive newspaper advertising in local university and community newspapers, which was not effective. They decided to focus on such things as gift certificates for new sorority pledges; sponsorship of various college activities, including style shows; ads in selected playbills and game programs; and only occasional newspaper advertising. Tom Borch did not advertise on the radio. Dawn Carlton also did some direct mailing for special store events. In addition, she tried to reach customers outside the immediate Bowling Green area, by hosting Sunday brunches in the store. She was considering fashion shows, direct mailing, and perhaps special events directed at women in Bowling Green and nearby towns.

The Carltons took great pride in their store and the Bowling Green community. They were members of the Chamber of Commerce and the Bowling Green Retail Merchants Association. They made special efforts to generate goodwill in their store, with other businesses, and with the community in general.

QUESTIONS

1. How well have the Carltons integrated the merchandise assortment, pricing, promotion, financial, and control elements of their retail strategy mix? Explain your answer.
2. Evaluate Tom Borch Traditional Clothier's performance on the basis of the data in Tables 1, 2, and 3.
3. How could the Carltons benefit from a periodic retail audit?
4. What methods of data collection and control should the Carltons use in order to improve their store's performance?
5. Are the projections in Table 2 realistic? Why or why not?
6. What environmental trends should the Carltons study and address as they plan for the future?
7. What specific recommendations would you make to the Carltons?

Appendix A

Careers in Retailing

A person looking for a career in retailing has two broad possibilities: owning a business or working for an employer. One alternative does not preclude the other. Many retailers open their own outlets after getting experience as employees. A person can also choose franchising, which has elements of both entrepreneurship and managerial assistance. Franchising was discussed in Chapter 3.

Owning a Business

Owning a retail establishment is quite popular, and many opportunities exist. About 79 per cent of all retail outlets are sole proprietorships. In addition, many of today's retail giants started out as independents. J.C. Penney, R.H. Macy, K mart, Filene's, Toys "R" Us, McDonald's, and Sears are examples of this phenomenon. The founders of Wal-Mart, The Limited, Petrie Stores, Weis Markets, Lands' End, and Mrs. Fields' Cookies are profiled in Table 1.

Too often, people overlook the possibility of owning a retail business. In a number of cases, initial investments can be quite modest (several thousand dollars). For example, mail-order, vending-machine, direct-to-home selling, and many service retailers require relatively low initial investments. In addition, financing may be available from banks, manufacturers, store-fixture firms, and equipment companies. Chapter 2 contained an in-depth discussion of starting and operating a retail business.

Opportunities as a Retail Employee

Retailing is a significant source of employment. As noted in Chapter 1, about eighteen million people were employed by traditional retailers in the United States during 1987. This does not include millions of other people working for service firms such as banks, insurance companies, and airlines. By any measure, more people are employed in retailing than in any other industry. For example, retailing employs some 5.5 million people in the general merchandise sector alone (which includes department and specialty stores selling apparel, home furnishings, books, sporting goods, and other leisure items).[1]

According to research conducted by a consulting firm using the *Forbes* magazine data base, retailers accounted for the greatest growth in employment between 1981 and 1986 among the large firms that were studied. Of the 40 firms

TABLE 1
Profiles of Leading Retail Entrepreneurs

Sam Walton	He opened his first retail store shortly after World War II; his first Wal-Mart discount department store was opened in 1962. Now, Wal-Mart has over 1,100 stores and annual sales volume in excess of $12 billion. Sam Walton is "the richest man in America" and is estimated to have a personal worth of more than $8.5 billion.
Leslie Wexner	He borrowed $5,000 from an aunt to start a ladies' clothing store in the early 1960s. Now his firm, The Limited, Inc., has almost 3,000 stores (including The Limited, Limited Express, Victoria's Secret, Lerner Shops, and Henri Bendel) and annual sales of over $3 billion. Wexner's personal worth is estimated to be well over $2 billion.
Milton Petrie	He started in retailing as a $10-per-week department-store clerk in Indianapolis. Today, Petrie Stores' medium-priced clothing chain with a teen emphasis has over 1,500 stores and annual sales of $1.2 billion. Petrie's personal worth is estimated to be more than $1.3 billion.
Sigfried Weis and Robert Weis	The Weis cousins began by operating a cash-and-carry grocery store about 75 years ago. Now, they now have 117 supermarkets in Pennsylvania, West Virginia, and Maryland. Sigfried Weis' personal wealth is estimated to be over $620 million; Robert's is over $510 million.
Gary Comer	He founded Lands' End, a mail-order retailer. Prior to that, Comer was an advertising copywriter for Young & Rubicam. Lands' End became a publicly held corporation in 1986. Comer's personal wealth is now estimated at over $350 million.
Debbi Fields and Randy Fields	In 1977, at age twenty, Debbi Fields opened a small cookie store in Palo Alto, California. Today, there are more than 700 company-owned Mrs. Fields' Cookies stores, with outlets in thirty-seven states and Australia, Canada, Great Britain, Hong Kong, and Japan. The personal wealth of Debbi Fields and her husband, Randi, is estimated at between $50 and $100 million.

Source: Based on material in "The Forbes Four Hundred Billionaires," *Forbes* (October 26, 1987) pp. 114 ff.; Joan Bergman, "The Saga of Sam Walton," *Stores* (January 1988), pp. 129–130 ff.; and "Mrs. Fields Automates the Way the Cookie Sells," *Chain Store Age Executive* (April 1988), pp. 73–76.

with the highest employment gains, 19 were retailers. Of the 10 firms with the highest employment gains, 5 were retailers; Table 2 shows selected data for these retailers.

Retail career opportunities are plentiful because of the number of new retail stores opening each year and the labor-intensive nature of retailing. Nationally, thousands of new outlets open every year in the United States.[2] Furthermore, certain segments of retailing are growing at particularly rapid rates. For example, direct-marketing sales (by home, phone, and mail) are rising about 15 per cent per year, twice the rate of sales growth in many traditional retail stores.[3]

The increases in retail employment due to new store openings and the sales growth of retail formats (such as mail order) also mean that there are significant opportunities for personal advancement for talented retail personnel.

The following sections describe selected retailing positions, career paths, and compensation ranges for retail positions.

Types of Positions in Retailing

Employment in retailing is not confined to buying and merchandising. Career opportunities with retail firms encompass such areas as advertising, public relations, credit analysis, marketing research, warehouse management, data

TABLE 2
The Five Retail Firms with the Largest Increases in Employment from 1981 to 1986

Firm	1981 Employees (thousands)	1986 Employees (thousands)	Employee Increase, 1981–1986 (thousands)	Employee Increase, 1981–1986 (percentage)
Wal-Mart	34.5	122.5	88.0	255.1
Sears	395.0	475.7	80.7	20.4
The Limited, Inc.	5.0	38.4	33.4	668.0
McDonald's	126.9	159.0	32.1	25.3
Zayre	32.0	60.0	28.0	87.5

Source: Jonathan Clements, "The Turbulent Job Market," *Forbes* (July 13, 1987), p. 116.

processing, personnel management, auditing, accounting, and real estate. See Figure 1 for a listing and description of a variety of positions in retailing. From this figure, one can see the diversity of employment opportunities available. It should be noted that some of the more specialized positions may be available only in large retail firms.

To a certain extent, the type of position a person seeks should be matched with the type of retailer likely to have such a position. For example, chain stores and franchises have real-estate divisions. Department stores and chain stores have large personnel departments. Mail-order houses and retail catalog showrooms have large advertising production departments. If one is interested in travel, a buying position or a job with a retailer having geographically dispersed operations should be sought.

Career Paths in Retailing

For new college graduates, the executive training programs of larger retailers offer good learning experiences and the potential for substantial advancement. These retailers often offer careers in merchandising and nonmerchandising areas.

Here is how a new college graduate could progress through a career path at a typical department store: He or she usually begins with a training program (which may last from three months to a full year or more), designed to train him or her to run a merchandise department. The training program often involves on-the-job and classroom experiences. On-the-job training usually includes handling merchandise records, reordering stock, planning displays, and supervising salespeople. Classroom activities normally include learning how to evaluate vendors, analyze computer reports, forecast fashion trends, and administer store policy.

At the completion of the initial training program, the employee is designated as assistant department manager or assistant buyer. An assistant department manager or assistant buyer works under the direction of a department manager or buyer and analyzes sales, assists in purchasing goods, handles reorders, and assists in displays. The assistant department manager supervises personnel and learns store operations, whereas the assistant buyer is more involved in purchasing decisions than operations. Depending on store philosophy, either type of assistant may follow the same type of career path, or the assistant department manager may progress up the store management ladder and the assistant buyer up the buying ladder.

The responsibilities and duties of an assistant depend on the department manager's (buyer's) willingness to delegate and teach. They also depend on the au-

Job Title	Description
Accountant (internal)	Records and summarizes the retailer's transactions. Verifies reports. Provides financial information, budgets, forecasts, and comparison reports.
Advertising manager	Develops and implements a retailer's advertising program. Determines media, copy, and message frequency. Recommends advertising budget and choice of advertising agency.
Assistant buyer	Works under the direction of a buyer, usually in a specific product category. Assists in sales analysis, handling reorders, purchasing goods, and setting up displays.
Assistant department manager	Works under the supervision of a department manager. Assists in managing personnel, controlling inventory, and other store operations.
Assistant store manager	Helps in implementing merchandising strategy and policies; interviews, hires, and trains sales personnel; takes inventory; orders necessary supplies.
Auditor (internal)	Analyzes data, interprets reports, verifies accuracy of data, and monitors adherence to the retailer's regular policies and practices.
Buyer	Develops and controls sales and profit projections for a product category (generally for all stores in a chain); plans proper merchandise assortment, styling, sizes, and quantities; negotiates with and evaluates vendors; and supervises in-store displays.
Catalog manager	Selects merchandise for inclusion in catalogs, works with vendors, orders catalogs, and monitors order fulfillment (particularly, timely shipments).
Commercial artist	Creates illustrations, layouts, and types of print to be used in the retailer's advertisements and catalogs as well as on private-label packages.
Credit manager	Supervises the retailer's credit process, including credit eligibility, credit terms, late payment fees, and consumer credit complaints.
Data-processing manager	Oversees day-to-day operations of the retailer's computer facility. Generates appropriate accounting, credit, financial, inventory, and sales reports. Recommends computer hardware and software for the retailer.
Department manager	Responsible for a department's merchandise displays, analyzing merchandise flow, and the training and direction of the sales staff. Assists buyers in selecting merchandise for branch stores.
District store manager	Responsible for management personnel, sales generation, merchandise presentation, expense control, and customer services in all stores in district.
Divisional merchandise manager	Plans, manages, and integrates buying for an entire merchandise division (composed of several departments).
Fashion coordinator	Directs buyers in evaluating fashion trends. Orchestrates fashion shows.
Fashion director	Responsible for developing and maintaining a retailer's overall fashion perspective.
Franchisee	Purchases a business from a franchisor. Benefits by common format, joint advertising, and trouble shooting of franchisor. Operates under constraints set by franchisor.

FIGURE 1
Selected Positions in Retailing

tonomy given to the manager (buyer) to design and implement strategies. In a situation where the manager (buyer) has the authority to make decisions, the assistant will usually be given greater responsibility. When a retailer operates under a centralized management philosophy, the manager (buyer) is limited in

Job Title	Description
Franchisor	Develops a successful business format and reputation, then licenses the right to utilize this format and name to independent businesspeople. Oversees franchises, maintains operating standards, and receives royalty fees.
Group manager	Manages a number of department managers in different merchandise classifications. Trains, supervises, and evaluates these department managers.
Management trainee	First position for most college graduates entering retailing. Involves company orientation, classroom and on–the–job training, and close contact with buyers and group managers. Leads to department manager or assistant buyer.
Marketing research director	Acquires and analyzes relevant and timely information that assists executives in making important decisions. Heavily involved in research methodology and data collection.
Merchandise administrator	Coordinates and evaluates the work of buyers in several related merchandise classifications (in a division).
Merchandise analyst	Plans and evaluates merchandise allocation to stores to ensure merchandise is delivered at right time, in proper quantities, and in right assortments. Develops assortment and variety strategies based on trends and past performance history. Monitors reorder systems.
Merchandise manager	Coordinates the selling efforts among different departments (merchandise categories). Acts as liaison between store managers and buyers. Similar to group manager, however there are expanded merchandise responsibilities.
Operations manager	Responsible for receiving, checking, marking, and delivering merchandise; customer service; workroom operations; personnel; and maintenance of the physical plant of the retailer.
Personnel manager	Develops a personnel policy. Analyzes long–run personnel needs. Recruits, selects, and trains personnel. Works on compensation scales and supervision rules.
Public relations director	Keeps the public aware of the retailer's positive accomplishments. Measures public attitudes. Seeks to maintain a favorable image of the company.
Real–estate director	Evaluates retail sites. Negotiates lease or purchase terms. Works with builders on major construction projects.
Salesperson	Assists customers in making appropriate choices. Handles minor complaints. Stocks some merchandise and sets up some displays. Notes understocked items. May also serve as a cashier.
Sales promotion manager	Plans and enacts special sales, themes, and sales promotion tools (such as contests).
Security supervisor	Responsible for minimizing pilferage among store personnel and customers. Recommends security systems and procedures. Supervises the retailer's security personnel.
Senior vice–president for merchandising	Responsible for developing and evaluating all merchandise categories' performance. Has direct accountability for growth and profit.
Store manager	Oversees all store personnel and operations in a particular outlet. Coordinates activities with other units in a chain. Responsible for customer service; implements merchandising and human resource policies.
Warehouser	Stores and moves goods within a retailer's warehouse. Maintains inventory records and rotates stock.

FIGURE 1
(Continued)

his or her responsibilities, as is the assistant. Furthermore, the assistant will gain more experience if he or she is located in a store near a wholesale market center and can make trips to the market to buy merchandise.

The next step in the department store career path is to department manager or buyer. This position can be viewed as entrepreneurial, the running of a business. The manager or buyer selects merchandise, develops a promotional campaign, decides which merchandise to reorder, oversees departmental personnel, and supervises record keeping. In some stores, manager and buyer are synonymous terms. In others, the distinction is as explained above for an assistant. Generally, an assistant is considered for promotion to manager or buyer after two years.

Large department stores have additional levels of personnel to plan, supervise, and control merchandise departments. On the store management side, there can be group managers, store managers, vice-presidents of branches, and so on. On the buying side, there can be divisional managers, vice-presidents of merchandising, and so on.

In many retail firms, advancement is clearly indicated by specific career paths. This enables employees to monitor their performance, to know what their next career step is, and to progress in a systematic, clear manner. Selected career paths at Abraham & Straus (a department store chain), J.C. Penney, Osco (a drugstore chain), and Giant Food are shown in Figures 2 through 5. At each

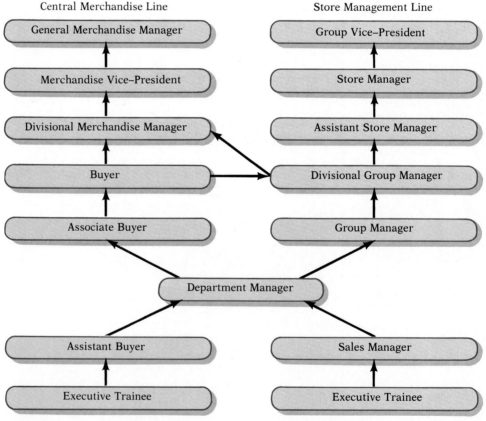

FIGURE 2
A Career Path at Abraham & Straus
Source: Rate Yourself as a Retail Executive (New York: Abraham & Straus), p. 9. Reprinted by permission.

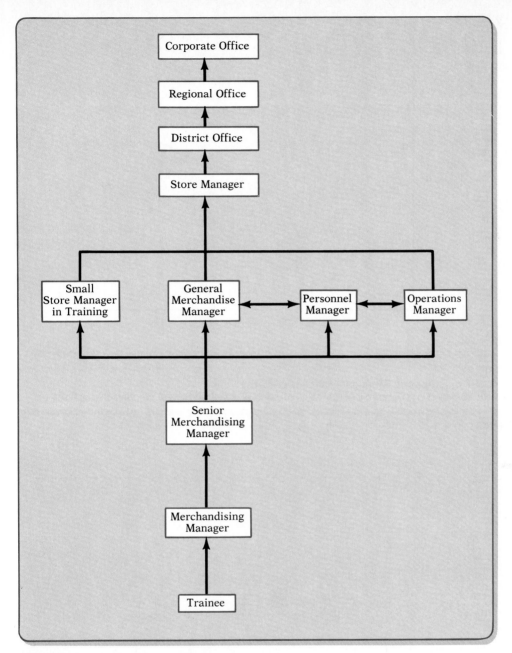

FIGURE 3
A Merchandising Career Path at J.C. Penney
Source: J.C. Penney Stores. Reprinted by permission.

succeeding step on these career ladders, a manager gains additional responsibility and authority.

Many times in retailing, individuals are given significant responsibility and authority at early stages in their careers. For example, nearly half of all U.S. variety-store managers are between twenty and thirty. The typical computer-store manager is thirty-four years old and has been in retailing an average of six years (with about half of those years as a manager).[4] A number of top retail executives

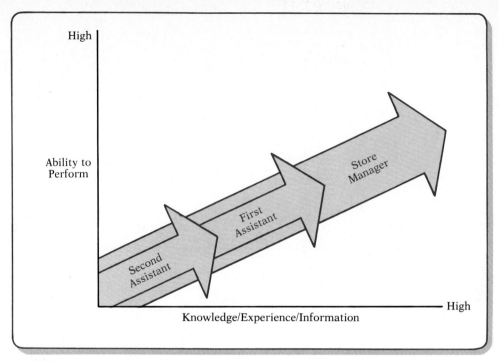

FIGURE 4
An Osco Drugstore Management Career Path
Source: Osco Drug Career Opportunities (a division of American Stores). Reprinted by permission.

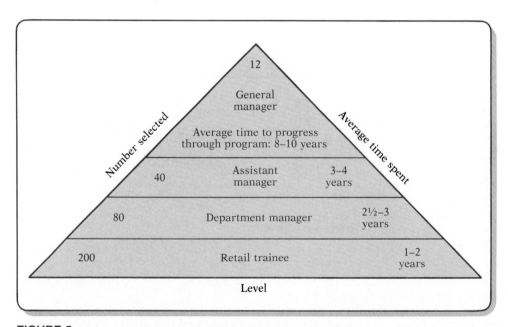

FIGURE 5
A Career Development Program at Giant Food
Source: Giant Career Development Program: Steps to Future Success. Reprinted by permission.

TABLE 3
Typical Compensation Ranges for Personnel in Selected Retailing Positions

Position	Compensation Range
Store management trainee	$ 16,000–$ 22,500+
Assistant buyer	$ 16,000–$ 25,000+
Store manager—specialty store, home center, drugstore	$ 16,000–$ 50,000+
Store manager—discount store, national chain, department store	$ 22,000–$ 80,000+
Warehouse director	$ 22,000–$ 80,000+
Buyer—specialty store, home center, drugstore, department store	$ 22,000–$ 40,000+
Buyer—discount store	$ 27,000–$ 50,000+
Buyer—national chain	$ 30,000–$ 70,000+
Security director	$ 30,000–$ 70,000+
Senior human resources executive	$ 30,000–$ 140,000+
Divisional merchandise manager	$ 40,000–$ 85,000+
Senior advertising executive	$ 40,000–$ 100,000+
Operations director	$ 45,000–$ 80,000+
Senior real-estate executive	$ 45,000–$ 120,000+
General merchandise manager—drugstore, home center	$ 45,000–$ 80,000+
General merchandise manager—specialty store, department store	$ 52,000–$ 95,000+
General merchandise manager—discount store, national chain	$ 60,000–$ 125,000+
Senior financial executive	$ 60,000–$ 175,000+
Senior merchandising executive	$ 75,000–$ 250,000+
President	$150,000–$ 400,000+
Chairman of the board	$150,000–$4,000,000+

Source: Adapted by the authors from "Major Chain Chairmen Average $420,120 Pay," *Discount Store News* (December 8, 1986), p. 7; "Retail Pay: Surprisingly Better," *Career Paths* (January 1988), pp. 8–9, 11; and "Sure the Hours Are Long, But . . . ," *Career Paths* (January 1987), pp. 6–8.

are also fairly young. The president of McDonald's international operations (a division accounting for over one-fifth of McDonald's pre-tax profits in 1986) was forty-three at the time of his appointment to that position.[5] The chief executive officer of Supermarkets General's Pathmark division was forty-seven at the time of his appointment to that position.[6]

Compensation Ranges in Retailing

Table 3 lists compensation ranges for personnel in a number of retailing positions. Table 4 shows the total compensation for the ten highest paid chief executives in retailing during 1986.

The search for career opportunities in retailing, interview preparation, and the evaluation of the retail career options available to you are important steps in getting your first professional position in retailing. It is essential that you devote sufficient time to these steps so that your job hunt progresses as quickly and as smoothly as possible.

This section offers some pointers to assist you in obtaining a rewarding first position as a retail professional.

Searching for Career Opportunities in Retailing

Various sources should be consulted in the search for appropriate career opportunities. These sources should include your school's placement office, career directories (such as the one contained in Appendix B of this text), the placement services of your local American Marketing Association chapter, classified adver-

Getting Your First Position as a Retail Professional

TABLE 4
The Compensation Levels of the Ten Highest Paid
U.S. Retailing Chief Executives, 1986

Company of Chief Executive	Total 1986 Compensation of Chief Executive*
The Great Atlantic & Pacific Tea Company	$4,279,000
Giant Food	3,436,000
K mart	3,104,000
Toys "R" Us	3,020,000
F.W. Woolworth	2,216,000
Sears	2,097,000
Kroger	1,919,000
May Department Stores	1,640,000
Stop & Shop	1,520,000
Wickes Companies	1,503,000

*Includes salary, bonus, stock gains, and other payments (from long-term compensation plans, thrift-plan contributions, and so on).

Source: "What the Boss Makes," Forbes (June 15, 1987), pp. 162–173 ff.

tisements in your local newspapers, and networking (with professors, friends, neighbors, and family members).

These are some hints to keep in mind when searching for career opportunities in retailing:

❑ Do not "place all of your eggs in one basket." Do not rely too heavily on a friend or relative to get you a position. Remember that in most cases, a friend or relative may be able to get you an interview, but not a guaranteed job offer.

❑ Treat your career search in a serious and systematic manner. Plan in advance and do not wait until the recruiting season at your school has started to generate a list of potential retail employers.

❑ Utilize directories that list retail organizations in your search. Appropriate publications include *Fairchild's Manual of Retail Stores;* the American Marketing Association membership directory; the College Placement Council's annual manual; the annual *Peterson's Business & Management Jobs;* and the directories of major professional associations (such as the National Retail Merchants Association and the International Council of Shopping Centers).

❑ Rely on the law of large numbers. When sending out resumes to companies, realize that you may have to write to at least ten to twenty retailers in order to secure just two to four interviews.

❑ Make sure that your resumé and accompanying cover letter highlight your distinctive qualities. These may include school honors, officer status in an important organization,, appropriate work experience, special computer expertise, and the proportion of your college tuition that you paid for yourself. Figure 6 shows a sample resumé that is geared to an entry-level position in retailing.

❑ Show your resumé to least one of your professors for his or her reaction. Be receptive to the constructive comments made by your professor(s). Remember, their goal is to help you get the best possible first job.

Preparing for the Interview

The initial and subsequent interviews for a retail position, which may last for twenty to thirty minutes or longer, play a large role in determining whether you

Sample Resumé

Jennifer Marcus
17 Hart Drive
West Hartford, Connecticut 06117
203–200–7416

EMPLOYMENT OBJECTIVE: Assistant Buyer Position, Formal Training
Program Desired

EDUCATION:
Bachelor of Business Administration, June 1988
Hofstra University   Hempstead, New York 11550
Major: Marketing   Class Rank: Top 10%

SCHOLARSHIPS
AND AWARDS:
Hofstra University Distinguished Scholar Academic Award
Member, Beta Gamma Sigma, National Business Honor Society

EXTRACURRICULAR
ACTIVITIES:
Vice-President, American Marketing Association,
Fall 1986–Spring 1988; Hofstra Collegiate Chapter
Responsible for recruitment of members, planning of
student career conference, and budget preparation and control.

Member, American Marketing Association; New York and
National Chapters.

COMPUTER
SKILLS:
Working knowledge of Lotus 1–2–3.

WORK
EXPERIENCE:

January 1985–
Present
Sales Clerk, Fashion World, 200 Main Street,
Hempstead, New York
20 hours per week
Responsibilities include selling women's clothing,
setting up displays, and checking inventory in high fashion
ladies' specialty store.

July 1983–
September 1984
Cashier, Thrifty Drug Stores,
Green Acres Shopping Center, Valley Stream, New York
Responsibilities included setting up inventory and displays, and
selling cameras, film, and radios.

Paid half of tuition expenses by working 20 hours per week
while attending college.

PERSONAL:
Willing to relocate.

REFERENCES:
Will be furnished upon request.

FIGURE 6

are offered a job by a company. For that reason, it is necessary that you properly prepare for all interviews.

Here are some hints in preparing for a retail position interview:

❏ Adequately research the company. Be aware of its goods/service category, current size, overall retail strategy, competitive developments, and so on.

❏ Anticipate these kinds of questions and plan out general responses in advance: "Tell me about yourself." "Why are you interested in a career in retailing?" "Why do you want a job with this company?" "What are your major strengths?" "What are your major weaknesses?" "What do you want to be doing five years from now?" "Are you willing to relocate?" "Which college courses did you like most?" "Which courses did you like least?" "What would your previous employers say about you?"[7] In your preinterview preparation, role-play your answers to these questions with a parent, a friend, or a professor. Listen to their critical comments.

❑ Prepare for each interview as if it is the most important one you will be having. Otherwise, you may not be properly prepared for an interview when the position involved turns out to be more desirable than you had originally thought. Also keep in mind, that you represent both your college and yourself at every interview you go on.

❑ Be prepared to ask your own pertinent questions when asked during the interview. Such questions should relate to career paths, training programs, and opportunities for advancement.

❑ Dress appropriately and be well groomed.

❑ Verify the date and place of the interview. Be prompt.

❑ Have a pen and pad available to record key information after the interview has been completed.

❑ Write a note to the interviewer within a week after the interview to thank him or her for spending time with you and to express a continuing interest in the company.

Evaluating Retail Career Opportunities

Often, graduating students place too much emphasis on initial salary or the image of a retailer (in terms of fashion emphasis or target market) when evaluating retail career opportunities. Yet, many other factors should be considered.

These are several key questions to address when deciding what career opportunity to pursue. The questions should be linked to the attributes of each of the specific job offers that you may receive:

❑ What tasks do you enjoy performing?

❑ What are your strengths and weaknesses?

❑ What are your short-run and long-run goals?

❑ Do you want to work for a small, medium, or large retailer?

❑ Does the opportunity offer a clearly defined career path?

❑ Does the opportunity include a rigorous training program?

❑ Does the opportunity provide an attainable reward structure?

❑ Does the opportunity involve relocation?

❑ Will each promotion along the career path result in greater responsibility and authority?

❑ Is the compensation level fair?

❑ Can an exceptional employee gain faster recognition and rewards than an average employee?

❑ If ownership of a retail firm is your long-term goal, which opportunity will provide the best preparation?

NOTES

1. "Retailing: A Fast-Paced, Diverse Industry," *Career Paths* (January 1986), p. 5.

2. "Retail Pay: Surprisingly Better," *Career Paths* (January 1988), pp. 8, 11.

3. Elizabeth M. Fowler, "Jobs Grow in Direct Marketing," *New York Times* (June 30, 1987), p. D23.

4. "Sure the Hours Are Long, But . . . ," *Career Paths* (January 1987), p. 6.

5. Robert Johnson, "Wide Horizons for McDonald's Cantalupo," *Wall Street Journal* (April 27, 1987), p. 29.

6. Alix M. Freedman, "A Penny Pincher in a $1.8 Billion Buyout," *Wall Street Journal* (April 29, 1987), p. 36.

7. See James E. Challenger, "10 Tough Questions," *Business Week Careers* (April–May 1988), pp. 24–25.

Appendix B

Selected Firms Seeking College Graduates for Retail-Related Positions

Abraham & Straus
420 Fulton Street
Brooklyn, NY 11202
Subsidiary of Campeau Corporation
13,000 employees
Department store chain
East, South, Midwest

Albertson's
250 Parkcenter Boulevard
P.O. Box 20
Boise, ID 83726
40,000 employees
Supermarket chain
West

Alexander's
731 Lexington Avenue, Department CG
New York, NY 10020
Discount department store chain
New York, New Jersey, Connecticut

Allied Stores
1114 Avenue of the Americas
New York, NY 10036
62,000 employees
Subsidiary of Campeau Corporation
National department store group

Allied Stores of Pennsylvania-Ohio
326 Market Street
Harrisburg, PA 17105
1,440 employees
Subsidiary of Campeau Corporation
Department store chain
Pennsylvania, Ohio

B. Altman & Co.
361 5th Avenue
New York, NY 10016
5,000 employees
Department store chain
East, Southeast

American Stores Co.
P.O. Box 27447
709 East South Temple
Salt Lake City, UT 84127
129,000 employees
Supermarket and drugstore chains
East and West Coasts

Ames Department Stores
2418 Main Street
Rocky Hill, CT 06067
25,000 employees
Discount department store chain
East

ARA Holding Company
ARA Tower Building Center, 1101MK
Philadelphia, PA 19107
115,000 employees
Vending and food services firm
South, Southeast

Associated Dry Goods
417 5th Avenue
New York, NY 10016
Subsidiary of May Department Stores
60,000 employees
Specialty clothing and discount store
  chains
U.S.

Associated Merchandising Corp.
1440 Broadway
New York, NY 10018
860 employees
Affiliated with 30 department stores
Retail service organization
Northeast

Banana Republic
1 Harrison Street
San Francisco, CA 94107
Subsidiary of The Gap
Specialty travel clothing
U.S.

Best Products
P.O. Box 26303
Richmond, VA 23260
21,000 employees
Retail catalog showrooms
U.S.

Bloomingdale's
1000 Third Avenue
New York, NY 10022
Subsidiary of Campeau Corporation
13,000 employees
Department store chain
U.S.

The Bon
3rd and Pine Streets
Seattle, WA 98101
Subsidiary of Campeau Corporation
7,500 employees
Department store chain
California, Pacific Northwest

Bonwit Teller
1120 Avenue of the Americas
New York, NY 10036
Subsidiary of Allied Stores East Inc.
2,500 employees
Fashion specialty chain
Mid-Atlantic

The Broadway—Southern California
3880 North Misson Road
Los Angeles, CA 90031
Subsidiary of Carter Hawley Hale
16,500 employees
Department store chain
West, Southern California

Buffums Department Stores
301 Long Beach Boulevard
Los Angeles, CA 90802
Subsidiary of AAM Inc.
2,000 employees
Department store chain
Southern California

Bullock's
800 South Hope Street
Los Angeles, CA 90014
Subsidiary of R.H. Macy
9,000 employees
Department store chain
West Coast, Southwest

Burdine's
22 East Flagler Street
Miami, FL 33132
Subsidiary of Campeau Corporation
10,000 employees
Department store chain
Florida

Burger King
7360 North Kendall Drive
Miami, FL 33156
Subsidiary of Pillsbury Co.
1,700 employees
Fast-food franchisor
U.S.

Cain-Sloan Co.
5th Avenue and Church Street
Nashville, TN 37219
1,300 employees
Department store chain
Southeast

Canadian Tire Corp.
2180 Yonge Street
P.O. Box 770, Station K
Toronto, Ontario, Canada
M4P 2V8
2,500 employees
Hardware, sports equipment, auto
    products retail chain
Canada

Carson Pirie Scott & Co.
36 South Wabash Avenue
Chicago, IL 60603
25,000 employees
Department store chain
Midwest

Carter Hawley Hale
550 South Flower Street
Los Angeles, CA 90071
52,000 employees
Department store chains
Eastern and Western U.S.

Circle K
P.O. Box 20230
Phoenix, AZ 85040
20,000 employees
Supermarkets, convenience stores
U.S.

County Seat Stores
Box 1442
Minneapolis, MN 55440
Subsidiary of Super Valu Stores
Retail apparel chain
Mideast, Midwest

CVS/Pharmacy
1 CVS Drive, Department MG
Woonsocket, RI 02895
Pharmacy chain
U.S.

Davidson's Golden Rule
601 Nicollet Mall
Minneapolis, MN 55402
Subsidiary of Allied Central Stores
2,700 employees
Department store chain
Midwest

Dayton Hudson Corp.
777 Nicollet Mall
Minneapolis, MN 55402
126,000 employees
Department store, discount store, and
    electronics store chains
U.S.

Dey Brothers & Co.
401 South Salina Street
Syracuse, NY 13201
Subsidiary of Campeau Corporation
1,060 employees
Department store chain
Northern New York

Dillard Department Stores
P.O. Box 486
Little Rock, AK 72201
18,500 employees
Department store chain
South

Walt Disney Co.
500 Buena Vista Street
Burbank, CA 91521
32,000 employees
Leisure, recreation, entertainment
U.S.

Dollar General Corp.
427 Beech Street
Scottsville, KY 42164
2,000 employees
Retail and wholesale general-merchandise
    chain
Southeast

Dun & Bradstreet
299 Park Avenue
New York, NY 10171
58,000 employees
Information advisory services
U.S.

Jack Eckerd Corp.
8333 Bryan Dairy Road
P.O. Box 4689
Clearwater, FL 33518
25,100 employees
Drugstore chain
East, Southeast

Edison Brothers Shoe Stores
501 North Broadway
P.O. Box 14020
St. Louis, MO 63178
20,000 employees
Women's shoe-store chain
U.S.

Emporium-Capwell
835 Market Street
San Francisco, CA 94103
Subsidiary of Carter Hawley Hale
10,000 employees
Department store chain
West Coast

Famous-Barr Co.
601 Olive Street
St. Louis, MO 63101
Subsidiary of May Department Stores
8,000 employees
Department store chain
Midwest

Federated Department Stores
7 West 7th Street
Cincinnati, OH 45202
Subsidiary of Campeau Corporation
133,000 employees
Department store, discount store, and
    supermarket chains
U.S.

Filene's
426 Washington Street
Boston, MA 02101
Subsidiary of May Department Stores
7,400 employees
Fashion specialty chain
Northeast

First National Supermarkets
17000 Rockside Road
Maple Heights, OH 44137
Subsidiary of FNS Holding Co. Inc.
15,000 employees
Retail grocery chain
East

Fisher Foods, Inc.
5300 Richmond Road
Bedford Heights, OH 44146
15,000 employees
Supermarket chain
Midwest

Foley's
1110 Main Street
Houston, TX 77001
Subsidiary of May Department Stores
8,000 employees
Department store chain
Southwest

Food Lion
P.O. Box 1330
Salisbury, NC 28144
21,000 employees
Supermarket chain
Southeast

G. Fox and Co.
611 Olive Street
St. Louis, MO 63101
Subsidiary of May Department Stores
4,000 employees
Department store chain
New England, East

The Gap Stores Inc.
P.O. Box 60
900 Cherry Avenue
San Bruno, CA 94066
11,500 employees
Specialty store chain
U.S.

GENDIS, Inc.
General Distributors of Canada Ltd.
1370 Sony Place
Winnipeg, Manitoba, Canada
R3C 3C3
6,000 employees
Junior department and family-clothing
    store chains
Canada

Genesco Inc.
230 Genesco Park
Nashville, TN 37202
16,000 employees
Manufacturer, wholesaler, and retailer of
    shoes and specialty store operator
U.S.

Genovese Drug Stores
80 Marcus Drive
Melville, NY 11747
1,800 employees
Retail drug chain
East

Giant Food Inc.
6300 Sheriff Road
Landover, MD 20785
20,000 employees
Retail food, general merchandising, and
    pharmacy chains
Maryland, Virginia, Washington, D.C.

Gold Circle Stores
6121 Huntley Road
Worthington, OH 43085
Subsidiary of Campeau Corporation
6,500 employees
Discount store chain
East, Midwest, West Coast

Goldsmith's
123 South Main Street
Memphis, TN 38143
Subsidiary of Campeau Corporation
3,000 employees
Department store chain
Mid-South

Grand Union
100 Broadway
Elmwood Park, NJ 07407
Subsidiary of Cavenham U.S.A.
31,000 employees
Supermarket chain
East, Puerto Rico, Virgin Islands

The Great Atlantic & Pacific Tea Company
Box 418
2 Paragon Drive
Montvale, NJ 07645
Subsidiary of Tengelmann
81,500 employees
Supermarket chain
South, Central, Eastern U.S., and Canada

Hahne's
609 Broad Street
Newark, NJ 07101
Department store chain
New Jersey

Hecht Co.
611 Olive Street
St. Louis, MO 63101
Subsidiary of May Department Stores
11,000 employees
Department store chain
East, Mid-Atlantic, Southeast

Hennessy's Department Stores
140 South 24th Street, West
Billings, MT 59102
Subsidiary of Mercantile Stores
500 employees
Department store chain
Montana

Hills Department Stores
3010 Green Garden Road
Aliquippa, PA 15001
Discount department store chain
Mid-Atlantic

Hilton Hotels
9336 Civic Center Drive
Beverly Hills, CA 90210
34,500 employees
Hotel chain
U.S.

Holiday Corp.
3742 Lamar Avenue
Memphis, TN 38118
44,000 employees
Hotel chain and franchisor
U.S.

Host International
34th Street and Pico Boulevard
Santa Monica, CA 90406
Subsidiary of Marriott Corporation
13,100 employees
Quick-service and sit-down restaurant
    facilities
Michigan, Ohio

Hudson's Bay Company
Hudson's Bay House
77 Main Street
Winnipeg, Manitoba, Canada
R3C 2R1
43,000 employees
Department store chain
Canada

IBM
Old Orchard Road
Armonk, NY 10504
350,000 employees
Computer manufacturer
U.S.

IHOP Corp.
6837 Lankershim Boulevard
North Hollywood, CA 91605
1,500 employees
Coffee shop chain
U.S. and Canada

Jay Jacobs
1530 5th Avenue
Seattle, WA 98101
Fashion specialty store chain
Northwest

Jewel Food Stores
1955 West North Avenue
Melrose Park, IL 60160
Subsidiary of American Stores
37,000 employees
Supermarket, self-service drug, and
   department store chains
U.S.

Jordan Marsh—Florida
1501 Biscayne Boulevard
Miami, FL 33132
Subsidiary of Campeau Corporation
4,700 employees
Department store chain
Southeast

Jordan Marsh—New England
450 Washington Street
Boston, MA 02111
Subsidiary of Campeau Corporation
10,000 employees
Department store chain
Northeast

Joslin's
934 16th Street
Denver, CO 80202
Subsidiary of Mercantile Stores
Retail clothing chain
West

K mart
3100 West Big Beaver
Troy, MI 48084
320,000 employees
Discount department store chain
U.S., Puerto Rico, Canada

Kaufman's
400 5th Avenue
Pittsburgh, PA 15219
Subsidiary of May Department Stores
5,000 employees
Department store chain
Midwest

Kids Mart
P.O. Box 8020
City of Industry, CA 91748
Children's sportswear specialty-store chain
West

Kroger Co.
1014 Vine Street
Cincinnati, OH 45201
174,000 employees
Food and drug chain
Midwest, South, Southeast, Southwest

Lazarus
Seventh and Race Streets
Columbus, OH 45202
Subsidiary of Campeau Corporation
8,000 employees
Department store chain
Midwest

Lerner Shops
460 West 33rd Street
New York, NY 10001
Subsidiary of The Limited, Inc.
Women's apparel chain
East

Levitz Furniture Corp.
6111 Broken Sound Parkway
Boca Raton, FL 33169
Subsidiary of LFC Holding Corporation
4,600 employees
Furniture and home-furnishings chain
U.S.

The Limited, Inc.
1 Limited Parkway
P.O. Box 16528
Columbus, OH 43216
38,500 employees
Women's fashion apparel chain
U.S.

Loblaws Companies Limited
22 St. Clair Avenue East
Toronto, Ontario, Canada
M4T 2S3
10,000 employees
Retail food chain
Canada, Minnesota, New York

Loehmann's
2500 Halsey Street
Bronx, NY 10475
Women's fashion apparel chain

Longs Drug Stores
P.O. Box 5222
Walnut Creek, CA 94596
Drugstore chain
12,000 employees
West

Lord and Taylor
424 5th Avenue
New York, NY 10018
Subsidiary of May Department Stores
7,000 employees
Specialty chain
East, Midwest, Southeast

Lowe's Companies
Box 111
North Wikesboro, NC 28656
15,000 employees
Home care centers
South

Lucky Stores
6300 Clark Avenue
P.O. Box BB
Dublin, CA 94568
54,000 employees
Supermarket chain
U.S.

Maas Brothers
P.O. Box 311
Tampa, FL 33602
Subsidiary of Campeau Corporation
5,500 employees
Department store chain
Southeast

Macy's Atlanta
180 Peachtree Street, NW
Atlanta, GA 30303
Subsidiary of R.H. Macy
4,000 employees
Department store chain

Macy's California
Stockton and O'Farrell Streets
San Francisco, CA 94119
Subsidary of R.H. Macy
Department store chain

Macy's New Jersey
131 Market Street
Newark, NJ 07101
Subsidiary of R.H. Macy
3,000 employees
Department store chain

Macy's New York
151 West 34th Street
New York, NY 10001
Subsidiary of R.H. Macy
55,000 employees
Department store chain

I. Magnin
135 Stockton Street
San Francisco, CA 94108
Subsidiary of R.H. Macy
3,500 employees
Specialty store chain
U.S.

Marks & Spencer Canada
3770 Nashua Drive
Mississauga, Ontario, Canada
L4T 3R1
4,000 employees
Department store chain
Canada

D&F May
16th at Tremont Street
Denver, CO 80202
Subsidiary of May Department Stores
3,000 employees
Department store chain
Southwest

May Co.—Cleveland
158 Euclid Avenue
Cleveland, OH 44114
Subsidiary of May Department Stores
4,000 employees
Department store chain
Midwest, North

May Department Stores Co.
611 Olive Street
St. Louis, MO 63101
152,000 employees
Department store chain
U.S.
  221

McDonald's
One McDonald's Plaza
Oak Brook, IL 60521
159,000 employees
Fast-food franchise and restaurant chain
U.S.

Melville Corporation
3000 Westchester Avenue
Harrison, NY 10528
81,000 employees
Shoe manufacturer and retail chain
U.S.

Mercantile Stores Co.
128 West 31st Street
New York, NY 10001
22,000 employees
Department store chain
Midwest, Northwest, Southeast, Northeast

Merry-Go-Round Enterprises
1220 East Joppa Road
Towson, MD 21204
2,000 employees
Specialty clothing chain
U.S.

Fred Meyer
3800 22nd Avenue
Portland, OR 97209
13,000 employees
Supermarket chain
Northwest

Montgomery Ward
1 Montgomery Ward Plaza
Chicago, IL 60671
56,000 employees
Department and discount store chain
U.S.

Morrison Inc.
P.O. Box 160266
Mobile, AL 36625
15,000 employees
Cafeteria, motel, and food-service-facility
  chain
South, Southeast

Morse Shoe Inc.
555 Turnpike Street
Canton, MA 02021
Retail shoe chain
U.S.

G.C. Murphy Co.
531 5th Avenue
McKeesport, PA 15132
16,000 employees
Subsidiary of Ames Department Stores
Variety store chain
East, Midwest, South, and Southwest

Nash Finch Co.
3381 Gorham Avenue
St. Louis Park, MN 55246
7,000 employees
Retail and wholesale food distributor
Midwest, West

National Convenience Stores Inc.
100 Waugh Drive
Houston, TX 77006
5,200 employees
Convenience store chain
West, Midwest, Southeast

NCR
World Headquarters
1700 South Patterson Boulevard
Dayton, OH 45479
62,000 employees
Manufacturer of electronic business
  equipment systems
U.S.

Neiman-Marcus
Main and Ervay Streets
Dallas, TX 75201
8,000 employees
Specialty store chain
U.S.

A.C. Nielsen
Nielsen Plaza
Northbrook, IL 60062
Subsidiary of Dun & Bradstreet
23,000 employees
Market research services
U.S.

O'Neil's
226 South Main Street
Akron, OH 44308
Subsidiary of May Department Stores
2,800 employees
Department store chain
Midwest

Osco Drug
1818 Swift Drive
Oak Brook, IL 60521
Subsidiary of American Stores
10,500 employees
General merchandise, drug, and
  department store chain
Midwest, Northwest, New England

The Oshawa Group Limited
302 The East Mall
Islington, Ontario, Canada
M9B 6B8
12,700 employees
Department store and drugstore chains
Canada

P&C Food Markets
State Fair Boulevard
P.O. Box 4965
Syracuse, NY 13221
4,500 employees
Supermarket chain, franchisor
Northeast

Peebles
1 Peebles Street
South Hills, VA 23970-5001
Junior department store chain
Southeast

J.C. Penney
P.O. Box 659000
Dallas, TX 75265
176,000 employees
Department store and mail-order chains
U.S., Puerto Rico

Petrie Stores
70 Enterprise Avenue
Secaucus, NJ 07094
16,000 employees
Specialty apparel chain
U.S.

Pizza Hut
9111 East Douglas
Wichita, KS 67207
Subsidiary of PepsiCo
27,000 employees
Fast-food chain
U.S.

H.C. Prange Co.
2314 Memorial Drive
Sheboygan, WI 53081
6,000 employees
Department, discount, and specialty store
  chains
Midwest

Price Company
P.O. Box 85466
San Diego, CA 92138
Discount store chain
7,300 employees
U.S.

Rapid-American Corporation
888 7th Avenue
New York, NY 10106
40,000 employees
Conglomerate with retail store chains
U.S.

Reitman's (Canada) Limited
250 Sauve Street West
Montreal, Quebec, Canada
H3L 1Z2
3,000 employees
Women's and misses' apparel chain
Canada

Revco Drug Stores
1925 Centerprice Parkway
Twinsburg, OH 44087
Drugstore chain
Midwest

Rich's
45 Broad Street
Atlanta, GA 30302
Subsidiary of Campeau Corporation
8,000 employees
Department store chain
Midwest, Southeast

Richman Gordman Stores
12100 West Center Road
Omaha, NE 68144
2,500 employees
Department store chain
Midwest

Rite Aid
P.O. Box 3165
Harrisburg, PA 17105
17,000 employees
Drugstore chain
Mid-Atlantic

Rose's Stores
P.H. Rose Building
Henderson, NC 27536
11,000 employees
Variety store chain
East, Southeast

Safeway Stores
Fourth and Jackson Streets
Oakland, CA 94660
172,500 employees
Supermarket chain
U.S.

Sanger Harris
303 North Akard
Dallas, TX 75201
Subsidiary of Campeau Corporation
10,000 employees
Department store chain
Midwest, South

Sav-On Drugs
1500 South Anaheim Boulevard
Anaheim, CA 92805
Subsidiary of American Stores
7,000 employees
Drugstore chain
West

Sears, Roebuck & Co.
Sears Tower
Chicago, IL 60684
485,500 employees
Department store and mail-order chain
U.S.

Service Merchandise Co.
P.O. Box 24600
2968 Foster Creighton Drive
Nashville, TN 37202
25,000 employees
Catalog showroom chain
Midwest, Southeast, West, East

Sherwin-Williams
101 Prospect Avenue
Cleveland, OH 44115
13,000 employees
Manufacturer and retailer of paints and
    related products
U.S.

Shoe Corporation of America
35 North Fourth Street
Columbus, OH 43215
4,000 employees
Retail shoe stores and leased departments

Sigmor
3643 East Commerce Street
San Antonio, TX 78220
Subsidiary of Diamond Shamrock
    Corporation
5,200 employees
Gasoline and auto products chain

Skaggs Companies
1500 South Anaheim Road
Anaheim, CA 92800
11,000 employees
Drugstore chain
Southwest, Midwest, West

Southland Corporation
2828 North Haskell Avenue
P.O. Box 719
Dallas, TX 75221
67,000 employees
Convenience-food-store chain and
    franchisor
U.S.

Steinberg Inc.
Alexis-Nihon Plaza
1500 Atwater Avenue
Montreal, Quebec, Canada
H3Z 1Y3
25,700 employees
Retail food market and self-service
    department store chains
Canada

Stern's
Route 4, Bergen Mall
Paramus, NJ 07652
Subsidiary of Campeau Corporation
5,700 employees
Department store chain
New York, New Jersey, Connecticut

Stewart Dry Goods Company
501 South 4th Street
Louisville, KY 40202
Subsidiary of May Department Stores
Department store chain
East, Midwest, South

Stop & Shop Companies
P.O. Box 369
Boston, MA 02101
46,000 employees
Supermarket chain and discount
    department store chain
Northeast

Strawbridge and Clothier
Market East at 8th Street
Philadelphia, PA 19105
12,000 employees
Department store chain
Mid-Atlantic, New England

Stride Rite Corporation
5 Cambridge Center
Cambridge, MA 02142
Footwear manufacturer and retailer
U.S.

Super Valu
P.O. Box 990
Minneapolis, MN 55440
27,000 employees
Food wholesaler
Midwest, South

Supermarkets General
200 Milik Street
Carteret, NJ 07008
53,000 employees
Supermarket, drugstore, and home center
    chains
Northeast

Tandy Corporation/Radio Shack
1800 One Tandy Center
Forth Worth, TX 76102
36,000 employees
Manufacturer and retailer of electronics
Nationwide

Target Stores
33 South 6th Street
P.O. Box 1392
Minneapolis, MN 55440-1392
Subsidiary of Dayton Hudson
Upscale discounter
U.S.

Thrifty Corp.
3434 Wilshire Boulevard
Los Angeles, CA 90010
5,200 employees
Retail drugstores
West

Tiffany
727 5th Avenue
New York, NY 10022
Fine jewelry and accessories chain
U.S.

Toys "R" Us
395 West Passaic Street
Rochelle Park, NJ 07662
28,600 employees
Retail toy and clothing chain
U.S.

United States Shoe
1 Eastwood Drive
Cincinnati, OH 45227
35,000 employees
Specialty chains
U.S.

Ups 'N Downs Stores
107 Phoenix Avenue
Enfield, CT 06082
Subsidiary of U.S. Shoe Corporation
1,500 employees
Apparel specialty chain
East

Urban Decision Systems
P.O. Box 25953
2032 Armcost Avenue
Los Angeles, CA 90025
Retail site-selection consultant

Venture Stores
615 Northwest Plaza
St. Ann, MO 63074
Subsidiary of May Department Stores
12,000 employees
Discount retail chain
Midwest

Volume Shoe Corporation
3231 East 6th Street
Topeka, KS 66607
Subsidiary of May Department Stores
6,000 employees
Family shoe store chain
34 states

Waldbaum
Hemlock Street and Boulevard Avenue
Central Islip, NY 11722
Subsidiary of The Great Atlantic & Pacific
  Tea Company
11,000 employees
Supermarket chain
New York, Connecticut, Massachusetts

Walgreen
200 Wilmot Road
Deerfield, IL 60015
40,000 employees
Restaurant and drugstore chain
U.S.

Wal-Mart Stores
702 Southwest 8th Street
P.O. Box 116
Bentonville, AR 72712
141,000 employees
Discount department store chain
South, Midwest

John Wanamaker
13th and Market Streets
Philadelphia, PA 19101
Department store chain
New York, Pennsylvania

Weis Markets
1000 South Second Street
Sudbury, PA 17801
13,000 employees
Supermarket chain
Pennsylvania, West Virginia, Maryland

Wendy's International
P.O. Box 256
Dublin, OH 43017
49,000 employees
Fast-food franchise and restaurant chain
25,000 employees
U.S.

Western Auto
2107 Grand Avenue
Kansas City, MO 64108
10,000 employees
Retailer and wholesaler of durable goods
U.S.

Wetterau
8920 Pershall Road
Hazelwood, MO 63042
11,000 employees
Food distributor

Wickes Companies
3340 Ocean Park Boulevard
Santa Monica, CA 90405
51,000 employees
Retail lumber and building-supplies chain
U.S.

Wiebolt Stores
1 North State Street
Chicago, IL 60602
4,900 employees
Department store chain
Midwest

Winn-Dixie Stores
5050 Edgewood Court
P.O. Box B
Jacksonville, FL 32203
77,000 employees
Supermarket chain

Woodward and Lothrop
1025 F Street N.W.
Washington, D.C. 20004
8,000 employees
Department store chain
Washington, D.C.; Maryland; Virginia

F.W. Woolworth
Woolworth Building
New York, NY 10279
121,000 employees
Variety and specialty store chains
U.S.

Zale Corporation
901 West Walnut Hill Lane
Irving, TX 75038-1003
19,000 employees
Jewelry store chain
U.S.

Zayre Corporation
30 Speen Street
Framingham, MA 01701
64,000 employees
Discount department store and specialty
  store chains
Northeast, Southeast, Midwest

Appendix C

Glossary

Addition to Retail Percentage Measures a price rise as a percentage of original price:

$$\text{Addition to retail percentage} = \frac{\text{New price} - \text{Original price}}{\text{Original price}}$$

Additional Markup An increase in retail price after and in addition to original markup, used when demand is unexpectedly high or when costs are rising.

Additional Markup Percentage The addition of a further markup to the original markup as a per cent of net sales:

$$\text{Additional markup percentage} = \frac{\text{Total additional dollar markup (in \$)}}{\text{Net sales (in \$)}}$$

Administered Pricing Occurs when retailers seek consumer patronage on the basis of distinctive retailing mixes. If strong differentiation can be achieved, a retailer can have control over the prices it charges.

Advertising Any paid form of nonpersonal presentation of ideas, goods, and services by an identified sponsor.

Affinity Occurs when various retailers are attracted to the same location in order to complement, blend, and cooperate with one another and each benefits from the others' presence.

Agate Line Used in newspaper advertising; there are 14 agate lines to an inch of space, one column wide.

All-You-Can-Afford Promotional Budgeting Occurs when a retailer first allocates for every element of the retail strategy mix except promotion. Any funds left over are placed into a promotional budget.

Analog Model A computer site-selection model in which potential sales are estimated on the basis of competi-

tion, market share, and the size and density of the primary trading area.

Ancillary Customer Services Those services that add to the retail offering. They do not have to be provided.

Application Blank Provides data on an applicant's education, experience, health, reasons for leaving previous jobs, organizational memberships, hobbies, and references.

Asset Any item a retailer owns that has a monetary value.

Assortment Display An interior display in which a wide range of merchandise is exhibited. It may be open or closed.

Atmosphere The physical characteristics of a store that are used to develop an image and to draw customers.

Attitudes (Opinions) The positive, neutral, or negative feelings that a person has about the economy, politics, goods, services, institutions, and so on.

Audit Form Lists the areas to be examined and the exact information required in evaluating each area.

Automatic Markdown Plan Controls the amount and timing of markdowns on the basis of the length of time merchandise remains in stock.

Automatic Reordering System Orders merchandise when a predetermined minimum quantity of goods in stock is reached. An automatic reorder can be generated by a computer on the basis of a perpetual inventory system and reorder point calculations.

BPI See Buying Power Index.

Bait Advertising An illegal practice whereby a retailer lures a customer by advertising goods and services at exceptionally low prices. Once the customer contacts the retailer, he or she is told that the good or service is out of stock or is of inferior quality and higher-priced goods or services are offered. In bait advertising, the retailer has no intention of selling the advertised low-priced item.

Bait-and-Switch Advertising See Bait Advertising.

Balance Sheet Itemizes a retailer's assets, liabilities, and net worth at a specific point in time; it is based on the principle that assets equal liabilities plus net worth.

Balanced Tenancy Occurs when the types and number of stores in a shopping area are related to the overall needs of the surrounding population. Common in shopping centers.

Basic Stock List The planned composition of staple merchandise that specifies the inventory level, color, brand, style category, size, package, and so on for every staple item carried by the retailer.

Basic Stock Method An inventory-level planning tool wherein the retail buyer purchases an amount equal to planned sales plus a basic stock.

Basic stock = Average monthly stock at retail
             − Average monthly sales

Battle of the Brands When retailers and manufacturers compete for the shelf space allocated to various brands and for control over the location of displays.

Book Inventory System Keeps a running total of all inventory on hand at cost at a given time. A perpetual system is maintained by regularly recording purchases and adding them to the inventory value, then subtracting existing sales to arrive at the new current inventory value (all at cost).

Bottom-Up Budgeting Requires that lower-level executives develop budget requests for their departments; these requests are then assembled, and an overall companywide budget is developed. Varied perspectives are included in the budget-setting process, managers are held accountable for their own decisions, and employee morale is enhanced.

Box (Limited-Line) Store A food-based discounter that focuses on a small selection of items, restricted hours of operation, few services, and limited national brands.

Bundled Pricing Involves a retailer providing a number of services for one basic price.

Buying Club Straddles the line between wholesaling and retailing. Appeals to price-conscious customers who are required to be members in order to be able to shop there.

Buying Power Index (BPI) A measure of a geographic area's market characteristics, expressed as:

0.5 (the area's per cent of U.S. effective buying income)

+0.3 (the area's per cent of U.S. retail sales)

+0.2 (the area's per cent of the U.S. population)

CBD See Central Business District.

COD (Collect on Delivery) Lets a customer have a product delivered to him or her before paying for it.

Canned Sales Presentation A memorized, repetitive speech given to all customers interested in a particular item.

Case Display Employed to exhibit heavier, bulkier items than racks hold.

Cash Flow Relates the amount and timing of revenues received to the amount and timing of expenditures during a specific time period.

Central Business District (CBD) The hub of retailing in a city. It is the largest shopping area in a city and exists in that part of a town or city that has the greatest concentration of office buildings and retail stores.

Centralized Buying Organization Occurs when a retailer has all purchase decisions emanating from one office.

Chain Multiple retail units under common ownership that engage in some level of centralized (or coordinated) purchasing and decision making.

Channel Control One member of a channel able to dominate the decisions made in the channel through some power that it possesses.

Channel of Distribution Comprises all of the businesses and people involved in the physical movement and transfer of goods and services from producer to consumer.

Class Consciousness The extent to which social status is desired and pursued.

Classification Merchandising Divides each department into related types of merchandise for data-reporting purposes for dollar control.

Cognitive Dissonance Doubt that occurs after a purchase is made, which can be alleviated by money-back guarantees, prompt service calls, and realistic sales presentations and advertising campaigns.

Collect on Delivery See COD.

Combination Store Combines supermarket and general merchandise sales in one facility, with general merchandise accounting for 30 to 40 per cent of total sales.

Commercial Cue A message that is sponsored by a retailer, manufacturer, wholesaler, or some other seller.

Community Shopping Center A planned shopping area that sells both convenience and shopping items to city and suburban dwellers. This center has a variety store and/or a small department store in addition to the outlets found in the neighborhood center. Twenty thousand to one hundred thousand people who live within 20 minutes of the center are serviced by this type of retail arrangement.

Company Department Manager Auditor Internal personnel whose prime responsibility is operations management, but who is asked to participate in the retail audit.

Company Specialist Auditor Internal personnel whose prime responsibility is the retail audit.

Comparative Advertising Message that compares a retailer's offerings with those of competitors.

Compensation Includes direct monetary payments (such as salary, commission, and bonus) and indirect payments (such as paid vacations, health and insurance benefits, and a retirement plan).

Competitive Advantage The distinct competency of a retailer relative to its competitors.

Competitive Advertisement Has persuasion as its objective.

Competitive-Oriented Pricing A pricing approach in which a retailer uses competitors' prices as guides rather than demand or cost considerations.

Competitive Parity Method of Promotional Budgeting Technique whereby a retailer's budget is raised or lowered according to the actions of competitors.

Computerized Checkout Enables retailers to efficiently process transactions and maintain strict control over inventory. In a UPC-based system, cashiers manually ring up sales or pass items over or past optical scanners. The computerized checkout instantly records and displays sales, customers are given detailed sales receipts, and all inventory information is stored in the computer's memory bank.

Conglomerchant See Diversified Retailer.

Consignment Purchase Items not paid for by retailer until they are sold. The retailer can return unsold merchandise. Title is not taken by the retailer until the final sale is completed.

Constrained Decision Making Excludes franchisees from or limits their involvement in the strategic planning process.

Consumer Behavior The process whereby individuals decide whether, what, when, where, how, and from whom to purchase goods and services.

Consumer Cooperative A retail establishment that is owned by its consumers. A group of consumers invest, receive stock certificates, elect officers, manage the operations, and share the profits or savings that accrue.

Consumer Decision Process The stages a consumer goes through in purchasing a good or service: stimulus, problem awareness, information search, evaluation of alternatives, purchase, and postpurchase behavior. Demographics and life-style affect this decision process.

Consumerism Involves the activities of government, business, and independent organizations that are designed to protect individuals from practices that infringe upon their rights as consumers.

Contingency Pricing An arrangement whereby the retailer does not receive payment from the customer until after a service is performed. Payment is contingent on the service's being satisfactory.

Control Units Merchandise categories for which data are gathered.

Controllable Variables Those aspects of business that the retailer can directly affect, such as store hours and sales personnel. See Uncontrollable Variables.

Convenience Store A food store that is well located, is open long hours, and carries a moderate number of items. This type of retailer is small, has average to above-average prices, and average customer services.

Conventional Supermarket A departmentalized food store that emphasizes a wide range of food and related products, with limited sales of general merchandise.

Cooperative Advertising Occurs when a manufacturer or wholesaler and a retailer, or two or more retailers, share advertising costs.

Cooperative Buying Procedure used when a group of independent retailers get together to make large purchases from a single supplier.

Corporation A retail firm that is formally incorporated under state law. It is a legal entity apart from individual stockholders.

Cost Complement The average relationship of cost to retail value for all merchandise available for sale during a given time period.

Cost Method of Accounting Requires the retailer's cost of every item to be recorded on an accounting sheet or coded on a price tag or merchandise container. When a physical inventory is conducted, the cost of each item must be ascertained, the quantity of each item in stock is counted, and the total inventory value at cost is calculated.

Cost of Goods Sold Equals the cost of merchandise available for sale minus the value of ending inventory.

Cost-Oriented Pricing A technique where a retailer sets prices by adding per-unit merchandise costs, retail operating expenses, and desired profits.

Cost-Plus Pricing Calculates price by adding a profit margin to merchandise or service cost.

Culture A group of people sharing a distinctive heritage. It affects the importance of family, work, education, and other concepts by passing on a series of beliefs, norms, and customs.

Curving Traffic Flow Presents aisles and displays in a free-flowing pattern.

Customary Pricing A pricing strategy in which a retailer sets prices for goods or services and seeks to maintain them over an extended period of time.

Customer Space Area for shoppers to lounge, try on clothing, eat, park, and so on.

Cut Case An inexpensive display, in which merchandise is left in its original cartons.

Data Analysis Stage in the research process whereby secondary and primary data are related to the defined problem.

Dead Areas Awkward spaces where normal displays cannot be set up.

Dealer Brand Contains a name designated by a wholesaler or the retailer. It is more profitable to retailers, better controlled by retailers, cannot be sold by competing retailers, is less expensive for customers, and can lead to retailer (rather than manufacturer) loyalty.

Debit-Only Transfer System A computerized system in which purchase prices are immediately deducted from consumer bank accounts. Interest is charged to the consumer's account from the day of the purchase.

Decentralized Buying Organization Allows purchase decisions to be made locally or regionally.

Deferred Billing Enables regular charge customers to buy merchandise and not pay for it for several months, with no interest charge.

Demand-Oriented Pricing A pricing approach that estimates the quantities customers would demand at various price levels and concentrates on the price associated with the stated sales goals.

Demographics Easily identifiable and measurable population statistics, such as age and income.

Department Store A large retail business unit that handles an extensive assortment (width and depth) of goods and services and is organized into separate departments for purposes of buying, promotion, customer service, and control.

Destination Store   A retail unit where the merchandise, selection, presentation, pricing, or other unique features act as a magnet for customers.

Direct Marketing   A form of retailing in which a customer is first exposed to a good or service through a nonpersonal medium and then orders by mail or telephone.

Direct Product Profitability   Calculated when a retailer determines the profitability of each category or unit of merchandise it sells by computing adjusted per-unit gross margin and assigning direct product costs for expense categories such as warehousing, transportation, handling, and selling.

Direct-to-Home Selling   Involves both personal contact with consumers in their homes and telephone solicitations that are initiated by the seller.

Disguised Retail Audit   Retail employees not aware that an audit is taking place.

Disguised Survey   Respondents not told the real purposes of a research study.

Distributed Advertising Effort   Involves advertising continuously throughout the year.

Diversified Retailer   A multiline merchandising firm under central ownership.

Diversionary Pricing   A practice used by deceptive retailers. A low price is stated for one or a few goods or services (emphasized in promotion) to give the illusion that all of a retailer's prices are low.

Dollar Control   The planning and monitoring of the total inventory investment a retailer makes during a stated time period.

Dual Vertical Marketing System   Involves firms engaged in more than one type of distribution system. This enables those firms to appeal to different consumers, increase sales volume, share some of their costs, and maintain a good degree of control over their strategy.

Dump Bin   A case display that houses piles of sale clothing, marked down books, and so on.

EOQ   See Economic Order Quantity.

Economic Base   Refers to an area's industrial and commercial structure, the companies and industries that residents depend on to earn a living.

Economic Order Quantity   The order quantity that minimizes the total costs of processing orders and holding inventory:

$$EOQ = \sqrt{\frac{2DS}{IC}}$$

where

EOQ = Economic order quantity, in units
D = Annual demand, in units
S = Costs to place an order
I = Percentage of annual carrying cost to unit cost
C = Unit cost of an item

Elasticity of Demand   See Price Elasticity of Demand.

Electronic Banking   Involves the use of automatic teller machines (ATMs) and the instant processing of retail purchases.

Electronic Point-of-Sale System   Verifies check and charge transactions, provides instantaneous sales reports, monitors and changes prices, sends intra- and interstore messages, evaluates personnel and profitability, and stores information.

Ensemble Display   Interior display in which coordinated merchandise is grouped and displayed together.

Equal Store Organization   Centralizes the buying function. The main store and branches become sales units with equal organization status.

Evaluation of Alternatives   Stage in the decision process where the consumer selects one good or service to purchase from a list of alternatives.

Exclusive Distribution   Takes place when suppliers enter into agreements with retailers that designate the latter as the only companies in specified geographic areas allowed to carry certain brands and/or product lines.

Experiment   A type of research whereby one or more factors are manipulated under controlled conditions.

Extended Decision Making   Occurs when a consumer makes full use of the decision process, usually for expensive, complex goods or services.

Extensive Advertising Coverage   An approach whereby advertising reaches many people but with relatively low frequency.

FIFO   A method of costing inventory which assumes that old inventory is old first while new items remain in inventory.

Factory Outlet   A manufacturer-owned store that sells manufacturer's closeouts, canceled orders, discontinued merchandise, and irregulars.

Fair Trade   Protects smaller and full-service retailers against discounters by requiring uniform retail prices. Fair trade is now banned.

Family   Consists of two or more people residing together who are related.

Family Life Cycle   Describes how a typical family evolves from bachelorhood to children to solitary retirement.

Feedback   Signals or cues as to the success or failure of a part of a retail strategy.

Financial Merchandise Plan   Specifies exactly which products (goods and services) are purchased, when products are purchased, and how many products are purchased.

Financial Resources   Funds needed for a retailer to operate. They must cover both business and personal living expenses.

Fixed Pricing   Occurs in situations where the government or a professional organization controls prices and retailers must conform to the stated price structure.

Flat Organization   An organization with a large number of subordinates reporting to one supervisor.

Flea Market   Has many retail vendors that offer a range of goods at discount prices in plain surroundings. Many flea markets are located at nontraditional sites not normally associated with retailing.

Flexible Pricing A pricing strategy that allows consumers to bargain over selling prices; those consumers who are good at bargaining obtain lower prices than those who are not.

Formal Buying Organization Views the merchandise buying function as a distinct retail task; a separate department is set up.

Franchising A contractual arrangement between a franchisor (a manufacturer, wholesaler, or service sponsor) and a retail franchisee, which allows the franchisee to conduct a given form of business under an established name and according to a given pattern of business.

Free-Flow Traffic See Curving Traffic Flow.

Frequency Refers to the average number of times each person who is reached is exposed to company ads during a given time period.

Fringe Trading Area Includes the customers not found in primary and secondary trading areas. These are the most widely dispersed customers.

Full-Line Discount Store A type of department store characterized by (1) a broad merchandise assortment; (2) relatively low operating costs; (3) relatively inexpensive building, equipment, and fixtures; (4) low-rent location; (5) emphasis on self-service; (6) frequent use of leased departments; and (7) everyday low prices.

Fully Integrated Vertical Marketing System Exists when a single firm performs all production and distribution functions without the aid of any other firm.

Functional-Oriented Job Classification Divides jobs among functional areas such as sales promotion, buying, and store operations so that expert knowledge is utilized.

Functional Product Grouping Categorizes and displays a store's merchandise by common end uses.

GMROI See Gross Margin Return on Investment.

Generic An unbranded, no-frills good stocked by some retailers. It usually receives secondary shelf space locations, obtains little or no advertising support, is sometimes of lower overall quality than other brands, is stocked in limited assortments, and has plain packages.

Geographic-Oriented Job Classification Divides jobs by area so that personnel in multiunit stores are adapted to local conditions.

Goal-Oriented Job Description Enumerates a position's functions, the relationship of a job to overall goals, the interdependence of positions, and information flows.

Goods Retailing Focuses on the sale of tangible (physical) products.

Graduated Lease Calls for precise rent increases over a specified period of time.

Gravity Model A computer site-selection model based on the theory that consumers gravitate to stores that are closer and more attractive than competitors.

Gridiron Traffic Flow See Straight Traffic Flow.

Gross Margin The difference between net sales and the total cost of goods sold. Also known as Gross Profit.

Gross Margin Return on Investment (GMROI) Shows the relationship between total dollar operating profits and the average investment in inventory by combining profitability and sales-to-stock measures:

$$\text{GMROI} = \frac{\text{Gross margin in dollars}}{\text{Net sales}}$$

$$\times \frac{\text{Net sales}}{\text{Average inventory at cost}}$$

$$= \frac{\text{Gross margin in dollars}}{\text{Average inventory at cost}}$$

Gross Profit See Gross Margin.

Herzberg's Theory Specifies that factors involved in producing job satisfaction and motivation (satisfiers) are distinct from those that lead to job dissatisfaction (dissatisfiers).

Hierarchy of Authority Outlines the job relationships within a company by describing the reporting relationships among employees (from the lowest level to the store manager to the board of directors). Coordination and control are provided through this hierarchy.

Hierarchy of Effects Steps a consumer goes through from awareness to purchase, in reacting to promotion. These steps include awareness, knowledge, liking, preference, conviction, and purchase.

Horizontal Cooperative-Advertising Agreement Enables two or more retailers (usually small) to share an advertisement.

Horizontal Price Fixing Involves an agreement among manufacturers, among wholesalers, or among retailers to set certain prices. Such agreements are illegal according to the Sherman Antitrust Act and the Federal Trade Commission Act, regardless of how reasonable the resultant prices may be.

Horizontal Retail Audit An analysis of the overall performance of a retailer, from its philosophy of business to customer satisfaction to the basic retail strategy mix and its implementation.

Household A person or a group of persons occupying a dwelling unit, whether related or not.

Huff's Law Outlines trading areas on the basis of the product assortment carried at various shopping locations, travel time from the customer's home to alternative shopping locations, and the sensitivity of the kind of shopping to travel time. Huff's law is expressed as:

$$P_{ij} = \frac{\dfrac{S_j}{(T_{ij})^\lambda}}{\sum_{j=1}^{n} \dfrac{S_j}{(T_{ij})^\lambda}}$$

where

P_{ij} = Probability of a consumer's traveling from home i to shopping location j

S_j = Square footage of selling space in shopping location j devoted to a particular product category

651

Tij = Travel time from consumer's home i to shopping location j

λ = A parameter used to estimate the effect of travel time on different kinds of shopping trips

n = Number of different shopping locations

Human Resource Management Personnel management in a manner consistent with a retailer's organization structure and strategy mix.

Human Resource Management Process Consists of several interrelated personnel activities: recruitment, selection, training, compensation, and supervision. The goals of this process are to obtain, develop, and retain employees.

Hypermarket A special type of combination store that integrates an economy supermarket with a discount department store.

Image How a retailer is perceived by consumers and others.

Implementation Stage in the research process during which recommendations are put into practice.

Importance of Purchase Affects the amount of time which the consumer will spend in making a decision and the range of alternatives considered.

Impulse Purchases Occur when consumers purchase products and/or brands that they had not planned on buying before entering a store or reading a mail-order catalog.

Incremental Budgeting Process whereby a firm uses current and past budgets as guides and adds or subtracts from these budgets to arrive at the coming period's expenditures.

Incremental Method of Promotional Budgeting Technique by which a percentage is either added to or subtracted from this year's promotion budget to determine next year's budget.

Independent A retailer that owns only one retail unit.

Independent Vertical Marketing System Consists of three levels of independently owned businesses: manufacturer, wholesaler, and retailer. It is the leading form of vertical marketing system.

Index of Saturation A general ratio of store saturation combining the number of customers, retail expenditures, and size of retail facilities for a specific good or service category in a trading area. This is expressed as:

$$\text{Index of saturation} = \frac{Ci \times REi}{RFi}$$

where

Ci = Number of customers in area i for the good (service)

REi = Dollar expenditures per customer in area i for the good (service)

RFi = Total square feet in area i allocated to the good (service)

Informal Buying Organization Does not view merchandising as a distinct retail function; existing personnel handle merchandising and other retail functions.

Information Search When a customer determines the alternative goods or services that will solve the problem at hand and then determines the characteristics of each alternative. Search may be internal or external.

Initial Markup (at Retail) The difference between the original retail value and merchandise cost for an item, expressed as a percentage of the original retail price. This may be expressed as:

Initial markup percentage (at retail) =

$$\frac{\substack{\text{Planned retail operating expenses} \\ + \text{ Planned profit } + \text{ Planned retail reductions}}}{\text{Planned net sales } + \text{ Planned retail reductions}}$$

Inside Buying Organization Staffed by the retailer's own personnel.

Institutional Advertisement Strives to keep the retailer's name before the public without emphasizing merchandise sales.

Intensive Advertising Coverage Occurs when ads are placed in selected media and repeated frequently.

Intensive Distribution Takes place when suppliers sell through as many retailers as possible. This arrangement usually maximizes suppliers' sales; and it enables retailers to offer many different brands and product versions.

Inventory Management Involves a retailer seeking to acquire and maintain a proper assortment of merchandise while keeping ordering, shipping, handling, and other related costs in check.

Inventory Shrinkage Comprised of customer shoplifting, employee theft, and inventory errors.

Isolated Store A freestanding retail outlet located on either a highway or a side street. There are no adjacent retailers with which this type of store shares traffic.

Item Price Removal Practice whereby prices are marked only on shelves or signs and not on individual items. This practice is banned in several states and local communities.

Job Analysis The gathering of information about employee job functions and requirements: duties, responsibilities, aptitudes, interests, education, experience, and physical condition.

Job Description Contains each position's title, supervisory relationships, committee responsibilities, and ongoing functions.

Just-in-Time Inventory Planning Encourages a retailer to reduce the amount of inventory it keeps on hand by ordering more frequently and in lower quantity.

LIFO A method of costing inventory which assumes that new stock is sold first while old stock remains in inventory.

Law of Demand States that consumers usually purchase more units at low prices than at high prices.

Layaway Plan Allows any customer to give the retailer a deposit to hold a product. When the customer completes payment, he or she takes home the item.

Leader Pricing Occurs when a retailer advertises and sells key items in its goods/services assortment at less than their usual profit margins. The objective of leader pricing is to increase customer contacts with the retailer in the hope of selling regularly priced goods and services in addition to the specially priced items.

Leased Department A department in a retail store, usually a department, discount, or specialty store, that is rented to an outside party.

Liability Any financial obligation that a retailer incurs in operating a business.

Life-Style The way in which an individual consumer or family (household) lives and spends time and money.

Limited Decision Making Occurs when a consumer uses each step in the purchase process but does not need to spend a great deal of time in each of the steps.

Limited-Line Store See Box Store.

Loss Leader Item priced below cost to attract customer traffic into the store. Loss leaders are restricted by state minimum-price laws.

Maintained Markup (at Retail) The difference between actual net sales and the cost of goods sold, expressed as a percentage:

Maintained markup (at retail) =

$$\frac{\text{Actual retail operating expenses} + \text{Actual profit}}{\text{Actual net sales}}$$

or

$$\frac{\text{Average selling price} - \text{Merchandise cost}}{\text{Average selling price}}$$

Maintenance Increase Recoupment A lease provision providing for increases in rent if the property owner's taxes, heating bills, insurance, and expenses go beyond a certain point.

Manufacturer Brand Produced and controlled by the manufacturer. It is usually well known, is supported by advertising, is somewhat presold to consumers, requires limited retailer investment, and represents quality to consumers.

Mapping A technique to determine the trading area of a store by charting the distances consumers are likely to travel to get to the store, the population density of the geographic area surrounding the store, and the travel patterns and times from various locations. A map is drawn showing these factors.

Markdown A reduction from retail selling price to meet the lower price of another retailer, to adapt to errors in overstocking fashions, to clear out shopworn merchandise, to deplete assortments of odds and ends, and to increase customer traffic.

Markdown Control Evaluates the number of markdowns, their proportion of sales, and their causes.

Markdown Percentage Total dollar markdown expressed as a percentage of net sales (in dollars):

$$\text{Markdown percentage} = \frac{\text{Total dollar markdown}}{\text{Net sales}}$$

Market Penetration A pricing strategy in which a retailer seeks to capture a large sales volume by setting low prices and selling a high unit volume.

Market Pricing Occurs in a competitive environment characterized by retailers pricing similarly to each other. In market pricing, retailers have little control over price. Demand for the retailer is weak enough so that a number of customers will switch to a competitor if prices are raised.

Market Segment Product Grouping Places all products appealing to a given target market together.

Market Segmentation Selling goods or services to a specific group of consumers.

Market Skimming A pricing strategy wherein a retailer charges premium prices and attracts those customers who are less concerned with price than with service, assortment, and status.

Marketing Research in Retailing The systematic collection and analysis of information relating to any part of a retailing strategy.

Markup The difference between retail selling price and merchandise cost.

Markup Percentage (at Cost) The difference between retail price and merchandise cost expressed as a percentage of merchandise cost:

Markup percentage (at cost) =

$$\frac{\text{Retail selling price} - \text{Merchandise cost}}{\text{Merchandise cost}}$$

Markup Percentage (at Retail) The difference between retail price and merchandise cost expressed as a percentage of retail price:

Markup percentage (at retail) =

$$\frac{\text{Retail selling price} - \text{Merchandise cost}}{\text{Retail selling price}}$$

Marquee A sign that is used to display the store's name and/or logo.

Mass Marketing Selling goods or services to a broad spectrum of consumers.

Mass Merchandising Involves retailers presenting a discount image, handling several merchandise lines, and having 10,000 square feet or more of floor space.

Massed Advertising Effort Concentrates advertising during peak periods, usually during one or two seasons.

Mazur Plan Divides all retail activities into four functional areas: merchandising, publicity, store management, and accounting and control.

Memorandum Purchase Items not paid for by retailer until they are sold. The retailer can return unsold merchandise. However, the retailer takes title on delivery and is responsible for damages.

Merchandise Available for Sale Equals beginning inventory, purchases, and transportation charges.

Merchandise Space Area where nondisplayed items are kept in stock or inventory.

Merchandising The planning and supervision involved in marketing particular goods or services at the places, times, and prices and in the quantities that will best serve to realize the marketing objectives of the business.

Milline Rate Represents the cost to a retailer of one agate line of advertising per million circulation:

$$\text{Milline rate} = \frac{\text{Cost per agate line} \times 1{,}000{,}000}{\text{Circulation}}$$

Minimum Price Laws State regulations preventing retailers from selling merchandise for less than the cost of the product plus a fixed percentage, which covers overhead. These laws restrict loss leaders and predatory pricing.

Mobile A type of hanging display with parts that move, especially in response to air currents.

Model Stock Approach Method of tabulating the amount of floor space necessary to carry and display a proper assortment of merchandise.

Model Stock Plan The planned composition of fashion goods, which reflects the mix of merchandise available based on expected sales. The model stock plan indicates product lines, colors, and size distributions.

Monthly Payment Credit Account Requires the customer to pay for a purchase in equal monthly installments. Interest is usually charged.

Monthly Sales Index A measure of sales seasonality that is calculated by dividing each month's sales by average monthly sales and multiplying the result by 100.

Mother Hen Organization All branch stores operated from headquarters. This plan works well when there are few branches and where the buying preferences of branch customers are similar to those of the main store's customers.

Motivation The drive within people to attain goals.

Motives A person's reasons for behavior.

Multidimensional Scaling A statistical technique that allows attitudinal data to be collected for several attributes in a manner that yields a single overall rating of a retailer.

Multiple Segmentation Selling goods or services to two or more distinct consumer groups, with different approaches for each group.

Multiple-Unit Pricing A policy whereby a retailer offers customers discounts for buying in quantity.

Multistage Approach A technique that divides the major elements of pricing into six successive steps with each step placing limits on those that follow: selecting a target market, choosing a store image, outlining the retail strategy mix, selecting a broad price policy, selecting a price strategy, and choosing specific prices.

NBD See Neighborhood Business District.

National Brand See Manufacturer Brand.

Need-Satisfaction Approach Sales technique based on the principle that each customer has a different set of wants and that the sales presentation should be geared to the demands of the individual customer.

Negotiated Contract Requires that the retailer and the supplier carefully negotiate all aspects of the purchase.

Negotiated Pricing Occurs when the retailer works out pricing arrangements with individual customers.

Neighborhood Business District (NBD) Satisfies the convenience shopping needs of a neighborhood. This district contains either a supermarket or a variety store and is located on the major street(s) of a residential area.

Neighborhood Shopping Center A planned shopping area that sells mostly convenience items. The largest store is a supermarket and/or drugstore. This center type caters to 3,000 to 50,000 people who live within 15 minutes' driving time (usually less than 10 minutes).

Net Lease Mandates that all maintenance expenses such as heat, insurance, and interior repair are to be paid by the retailer, which is responsible for the quality of these items.

Net Profit Equals gross profit minus retail operating expenses.

Net Worth Computed as a retailer's assets minus its liabilities.

Never-Out List Key items or best-sellers that are separately listed (from a basic stock list and model stock plan) and separately planned and controlled. These items account for large sales volume and are stocked in a manner so that they are always available.

Nondisguised Audit An audit of which a retailer's employees are aware.

Nondisguised Survey Respondents told the real purposes of a research study.

Nongoods Services That area of service retailing in which intangible personal services (rather than goods) are offered to consumers as experiential possessions.

Nonstore Retailing Utilizes strategy mixes that are not store-based to reach consumers and complete transactions. Nonstore retailing is conducted through vending machines, direct-to-home selling, and direct marketing.

Objective-and-Task Method of Promotional Budgeting Technique by which a retailer clearly defines its promotional objectives and then determines the size of the budget necessary to satisfy these objectives.

Objectives The goals, long run and short run, that a retailer hopes to attain. Types of goals are sales, profit, satisfaction of publics, and image.

Observation A form of research whereby present consumer behavior or the results of past consumer behavior are observed and recorded. Observation can be human or mechanical.

Odd Pricing A pricing strategy in which retail prices are set at levels below even-dollar values, such as $0.49, $4.95, and $199.

Off-Price Chain Features brand-name apparel, footwear, linens, fabrics, and housewares and sells them at low prices in an austere, limited-service environment.

Off-Retail Markdown Percentage The markdown for each item or category of items as a percentage of original retail price:

$$\text{Off-retail markdown percentage} = \frac{\text{Original Price} - \text{New Price}}{\text{Original price}}$$

One-Hundred Per Cent Location The optimum site for a particular store. A location classified in this manner for one retailer may be less than optimal for another retailer.

One-Price Policy A pricing strategy wherein the retailer charges the same price for all customers who seek to purchase an item under similar conditions.

Open Credit Account Requires the customer to pay his or her bill in full when it comes due.

Open-to-Buy The amount a buyer has left to spend at any point in a month. It is the difference between a month's planned purchases and purchase commitments made by a buyer for a given time period.

Operations Management Involves efficiently and effectively implementing the tasks and policies necessary to satisfy the firm's customers, employees, and management (and stockholders, if a publicly owned company).

Opinions See Attitudes.

Opportunity Costs Involve forgoing the possible benefits that may occur if the retailer makes expenditures in an opportunity other than the one it chooses.

Optical Character Recognition (OCR-A) An industrywide classification system for coding information onto merchandise. This technology enables retailers to instantaneously record information on a product's model number, size, color, and so on, when an item is sold; and to transmit the data to a computer that monitors unit sales. OCR-A is readable by both machines and humans.

Option Credit Account A form of revolving account that allows partial payments. No interest is assessed if the consumer pays the bill in full when it is due.

Order-Getting Sales Personnel Those involved with informing and persuading customers. They are creative salespeople.

Order Lead Time The time span from the date an order is placed by the retailer to the date merchandise is ready for sale (received, price marked, and put on the selling floor).

Order-Taking Sales Personnel Involved with routine clerical and sales functions such as setting up displays, placing inventory on the shelves, filling reorders, answering simple questions, and ringing up the sale.

Organization Chart Graphically displays the hierarchical relationships within the firm.

Outshopping When a customer goes out of his or her hometown to shop.

Outside Auditor A consultant to a retailer who performs a retail audit.

Outside Buying Organization A company or person external to the retailer that is hired to fulfill the buying function, usually on a fee basis.

Overstored Area Has so many stores selling a specified good or service that some retailers are unable to earn an adequate profit.

Owned-Goods Services That area of service retailing in which goods owned by customers are repaired, improved, or maintained.

PMs Manufacturer's payments to retail sales personnel for selling specific brands. PMs are in addition to the compensation received from the retailer.

Parasite A store that does not generate its own traffic and that has no trading area of its own.

Partially Vertically Integrated Marketing System Involves two independently owned businesses along a channel that perform all production and marketing functions without the aid of a third. For example, a manufacturer and retailer may complete transactions and shipping, storing, and other distribution functions without an independently owned wholesaler.

Partnership An unincorporated retail firm owned by two or more persons, each of whom has a financial interest.

Perceived Risk The level of risk that a consumer believes exists regarding the purchase of a specific good or service from a specific retailer, whether or not that belief is factually correct.

Percentage Lease Stipulates that rent is related to a retailer's sales or profits.

Percentage-of-Sales Method of Promotional Budgeting Technique whereby a retailer keys its promotion budget to sales revenue.

Percentage Variation Method An inventory-level planning method wherein the actual stock on hand during any month varies from average planned monthly stock by only half of the month's variation from average estimated monthly sales. Under this method:

Beginning-of-month
planned inventory level (at retail) =

Planned average monthly stock at retail

$$\times \frac{1}{2}\left(1 + \frac{\text{Estimated monthly sales}}{\text{Estimated average monthly sales}}\right)$$

Performance Measures Include total sales revenue by goods/service category, gross margins in dollars and percentages, sales per square foot, gross margin return on investment, inventory turnover, markdown percentages, employee turnover, financial ratios, and profitability.

Perpetual Inventory System Keeps a running total of the number of units handled by adjusting for sales, returns, transfers to other departments or stores, and receipt of merchandise shipments. This system can be maintained manually, by using a merchandise-tagging system that is processed by computers, or by using point-of-sale information tools such as optical scanning devices.

Personal Abilities The aptitude, education, and experience necessary for success in different types of retailing.

Personal Selling An oral presentation in a conversation with one or more prospective purchasers for the purpose of making sales.

Personality The sum total of an individual's traits which make that individual unique.

Personnel Space Area required for employees for changing clothes, lunch and coffee breaks, and restroom facilities.

Philosophy of Business The retailer's understanding of its role in the business system; it is reflected in the firm's attitudes toward consumers, employees, competitors, government, and others.

Physical Drive Stimulation resulting from the senses being affected.

Physical Inventory System Involves an actual counting of merchandise. A retailer using the cost method of inventory valuation and relying on a physical inventory system can determine its gross profits only as often as it conducts a physical inventory.

Pioneer Advertisement Has awareness as its objective and provides information (usually about a new retailer or location).

Planned Shopping Center A group of store buildings centrally owned or managed, based on balanced tenancy, and surrounded by parking facilities.

Point of Indifference The geographic breaking point between two cities or communities, so that the trading area of each can be determined. At the point of indifference, consumers would be indifferent to shopping at either area.

Point-of-Purchase Display An interior display that provides consumers with information, adds to store atmosphere, and serves a substantial promotion role.

Point-of-Sale Perpetual Inventory System A system that feeds information from merchandise tags or product labels directly into computers for immediate data processing. Many point-of-sale systems utilize optical scanners, which transfer information to a computer via a wand or stationary device that interacts with a sensitized strip on the merchandise; in others, merchandise classification data must be manually entered at the time of sale.

Positioned Retailing A retail strategy that consists of identifying a target market segment and then developing a unique retail offering, designed to meet that segment's needs.

Postpurchase Behavior Further purchases and/or re-evaluation based on a purchase.

Poverty of Time Occurs when greater affluence results in less rather than more free time, because the alternatives competing for consumers' time rise significantly.

Predatory Pricing Involves large retailers that attempt to destroy competition by selling goods at extremely low prices, which cause small retailers to go out of business. Predatory pricing is restricted by federal and state laws.

Prestige Pricing Assumes that consumers will not buy goods and services at prices that are considered too low.

Pretraining An indoctrination on the history and policies of the retailer and a job orientation on hours, compensation, chain of command, and job duties.

Price Adjustments Allow retailers to use price as an adaptive mechanism by taking additional markups and additional markdowns. Also included are employee discounts.

Price Elasticity of Demand Relates to the sensitivity of buyers to price changes, in terms of the quantities they will purchase:

$$\text{Elasticity} = \frac{\dfrac{\text{Quantity 1} - \text{Quantity 2}}{\text{Quantity 1} + \text{Quantity 2}}}{\dfrac{\text{Price 1} - \text{Price 2}}{\text{Price 1} + \text{Price 2}}}$$

Price Guarantee Protects retailers stocking merchandise against price declines. In the event a retailer cannot sell an item at a given price, the manufacturer or wholesaler pays the retailer the difference between the planned retail and the actual retail selling price.

Price Line Classification A dollar-control classification system that analyzes sales, inventories, and purchases by retail price category.

Price Lining Practice whereby retailers set a limited range of prices at which merchandise is sold, with each price representing a distinct level of quality.

Price-Quality Association The concept that many consumers believe that high prices connote high quality and low prices connote low quality.

Price War Situation in which competitive reactions to price changes result in retailers continually lowering prices below regular levels and sometimes below merchandise costs to attract consumers.

Primary Customer Services Those that are considered as basic ingredients in the retail offering and must be provided.

Primary Data Information collected to solve the specific problem under investigation. Primary data can be gathered internally or externally through surveys, observations, experiments, and simulations.

Primary Trading Area Encompasses 50 to 70 per cent of a store's customers. It is the geographic area closest to the store and possesses the highest density of customers to population and per capita sales.

Private Brand See Dealer Brand.

Prize Money See PMs.

Problem Awareness Stage in the decision process where the consumer recognizes that the good or service under consideration may solve a problem of shortage or unfulfilled desire.

Problem Definition Step in the marketing research process that involves a clear statement of the topic to be examined.

Product-Oriented Job Classification Divides jobs on a goods or service basis.

Product Life Cycle Shows the expected behavior of a good or service over its life. The traditional product life cycle has four stages: introduction, growth, maturity, and decline.

Productivity The efficiency with which a retail strategy is carried out.

Profitability Profits expressed in dollars or as a per cent of sales during a designated time period, usually a year.

Promotional Money See PMs.

Prototype Store Occurs with an operations strategy that requires various outlets in a chain to conform to relatively uniform construction, layout, and operating standards.

Psychological Pricing Involves consumers' perceptions of retail prices.

Publicity Involves the nonpersonal stimulation of demand for a good, service, or business unit by planting commercially significant news about it in a published medium or obtaining favorable presentation of it on radio, television, or stage that is not paid for by the sponsor.

Purchase Act   The exchange of money or a promise to pay for ownership or use of a good or service. Purchase variables include the place of purchase, terms, and availability of merchandise.

Purchase Motivation Product Grouping   Categorizes and displays merchandise according to the customer's urge to buy a product and the amount of time he or she is willing to spend in shopping.

Push Money   See PMs.

Rack Display   Interior display that neatly hangs and presents products.

Rationalized Retailing   A retail strategy involving a high degree of centralized management control combined with rigorous operating procedures for each phase of business.

Reach   Refers to the number of distinct people who are exposed to a retailer's ads during a specified time period.

Real Income   Income level after adjusting for inflation.

Recognition of Shortage   Occurs when a consumer realizes that a good or service needs to be repurchased.

Recognition of Unfulfilled Desire   Occurs when a customer becomes aware that a good or service never purchased before is desirable.

Recommendations   Stage in the research process during which the alternative approach to best solve a problem is presented.

Recruitment   The activity whereby a retailer generates a list of job applicants.

Reference Group   One that influences a person's thoughts and/or behavior. There are aspirational, membership, and dissociative reference groups.

Regional Shopping Center   A planned shopping location that sells predominantly shopping goods to a geographically dispersed market. This center type has at least one or two large department stores and as many as 100 small retailers. The market for the regional center is over 100,000 people who live within 30 minutes' driving time from the center.

Regression Model   A computer site-selection model in which sales are estimated based on a series of mathematical equations that show an association between sales and a variety of independent variables at each location under consideration.

Reilly's Law of Retail Gravitation   A means of trading area delineation that establishes a point of indifference between two cities or communities so that the trading area of each can be determined. The law may be expressed algebraically as

$$Dab = \frac{d}{1 + \sqrt{\dfrac{Pb}{Pa}}}$$

where

Dab = Limit of city A's trading area, measured in miles along the road to city

d = Distance in miles along a major roadway between cities A and B

Pa = Population of city A

Pb = Population of city B

Reminder Advertisement   Geared to the loyal customer; emphasizes the attributes that have made the retailer successful.

Rented-Goods Services   That area of service retailing in which consumers lease and use goods for specified periods of time.

Reorder Point   The stock level at which a new order is placed:

Reorder point = (Usage rate × Lead time)
+ Safety stock

Resident Buying Office   An inside or outside buying office that is located in an important merchandise center (source of supply) and provides valuable information and contacts.

Retail Audit   A systematic, critical, and unbiased review and appraisal of the basic objectives and policies of the retail function and of the organization, methods, procedures, and personnel employed to implement those policies and to achieve those objectives.

Retail Balance   The mix of stores within a district or shopping center.

Retail Catalog Showroom   A retail operation where the consumer selects merchandise from a catalog and shops at a warehouse store. Usually all the goods are stored out of the shopper's reach.

Retail Conglomerate   See Diversified Retailer.

Retail Information System   Anticipates the information needs of retail managers; collects, organizes, and stores relevant data on a continuous basis; and directs the flow of information to the proper retail decision makers.

Retail Institution   Refers to the basic format or structure of a business. Retail institutions can be classified by ownership, store-based retail strategy mix, nonstore-based retail strategy mix, and service versus goods retail strategy mix.

Retail Life Cycle   Theory which assumes that retail institutions, like goods and services, pass through four identifiable stages: innovation, accelerated development, maturity, and decline.

Retail Method of Accounting   A procedure wherein the closing inventory value is determined by computing the average relationship between the cost and retail value of all merchandise available for sale during the period.

Retail Organization   How a firm structures and assigns tasks (functions), policies, resources, authority, responsibilities, and rewards in order to efficiently and effectively satisfy the needs of its target market, employees, and management.

Retail Promotion   Any communication by a retailer that informs, persuades, and/or reminds the target market about any aspect of that retailer.

Retail Reductions   Include markdowns, employee discounts, and stock shortages.

Retail Strategy   The overall plan that guides the firm. It has an influence on the retailer's business activities and its response to market forces, such as competition or the economy.

Retailing   Encompasses those business activities involved in the sale of goods and services to consumers for their personal, family, or household use.

Retailing Concept   Bases planning on these elements: customer orientation, coordinated effort, and goal orientation.

Return on Assets   A ratio based on a retailer's net sales, net profit, and total assets:

$$\frac{\text{Return}}{\text{on assets}} = \frac{\text{Net sales}}{\text{Total assets}} \times \frac{\text{Net profit}}{\text{Net sales}} = \frac{\text{Net profit}}{\text{Total assets}}$$

Return on Net Worth   A ratio based on a retailer's net profit, total assets, and net worth:

$$\frac{\text{Return on}}{\text{net worth}} = \frac{\text{Net profit}}{\text{Total assets}} \times \frac{\text{Total assets}}{\text{Net worth}} = \frac{\text{Net profit}}{\text{Net worth}}$$

Revolving Credit Account   Allows a customer to charge items and be billed at the end of the month on the basis of the outstanding cumulative balance.

Risk-Minimization Retailing   A strategy that reduces both initial investment costs and the costs of operations.

Robinson-Patman Act   Prohibits manufacturers and wholesalers from discrimination in price or terms of sale among retailers purchasing products of "like quality" if the effect of such discrimination is to injure competition.

Routine Decision Making   Occurs when a consumer buys out of habit and skips steps in the purchase process.

SBD   See Secondary Business District.

Safety Stock   The extra inventory kept on hand to protect against out-of-stock conditions because of unexpected demand or delays in delivery.

Sale-Leaseback   The practice of retailers building new stores and selling them to real-estate investors who then lease the buildings back to the retailers on a long-term basis.

Sales Objectives   Those concerned with the sales volume of a retailer, such as growth, stability, and/or market share.

Sales Opportunity Grid   Rates the promise of new goods, services, and/or store outlets across a variety of criteria.

Sales-Productivity Ratio   Method for assigning floor space on the basis of sales or profit per foot.

Sales Promotion   Those marketing activities, other than personal selling, advertising, and publicity, that stimulate consumer purchasing and dealer effectiveness, such as displays, shows and exhibitions, demonstrations, and various nonrecurring selling efforts not in the ordinary routine.

Satisfaction of Publics   An objective to satisfy stockholders, consumers, suppliers, employees, and/or the government.

Saturated Area   A geographic area having just enough retail facilities to satisfy the needs of its population for a specified good or service.

Scrambled Merchandising   Occurs when a retailer adds goods and services that are unrelated to each other and to the firm's original business.

Secondary Business District (SBD)   A shopping area in a city or town that is usually bounded by the intersection of two major streets. A secondary business district has at least a junior department store, a variety store, and several small service shops.

Secondary Data   Data that have already been gathered for purposes other than solving the current problem under investigation. Internal secondary data are obtainable within the company. External secondary data are collected from sources outside the firm.

Secondary Trading Area   A geographic area containing an additional 20 to 25 per cent of a store's customers beyond those in the primary trading area.

Selective Distribution   Takes place when suppliers sell through a moderate number of retailers. This allows suppliers to have higher sales than possible in exclusive distribution and lets retailers carry some competing brands.

Self-Fulfillment   A life-style concept whereby people express their growing sense of uniqueness by purchasing goods and services.

Selling Against the Brand   The practice of retailers carrying manufacturer brands and placing very high prices on them so that rival brands (such as private-label retailer merchandise) can be sold more easily.

Selling Space   Area set aside for displays of merchandise, interactions between sales personnel and customers, demonstrations, and so on.

Semantic Differential   A disguised or nondisguised survey technique, whereby a respondent is asked to rate one or more retailers on several criteria by commenting on a list of bipolar adjectives.

Separate Store Organization   Treats each branch as a separate store with its own buying responsibilities. In this system, customer needs are quickly identified, but duplication of effort by main store and branch managers is possible.

Service Blueprint   Systematically lists all the service functions to be performed and the average time required for each function to be completed.

Service Retailing   Involves transactions between companies or individuals and final consumers in which the goal is other than the transfer of ownership of a tangible commodity.

Simulation   A type of experiment that creates a complex model to resemble a real process or system, in which a researcher runs the model in the hope of learning something about the real system.

Situation Analysis   The objective evaluation of the opportunities and potential problems facing a prospective or existing retailer.

Social Class System   An informal ranking of people in a culture, based on income, occupation, education, dwelling, and so on.

Social Cue   A signal communicated through talking with friends, fellow employees, etc. It is interpersonal and noncommercial.

Social Performance   Refers to how well a person carries out his or her roles as a worker, citizen, parent, consumer, and so on.

Sole Proprietorship   An unincorporated retail firm owned by one person.

Sorting Process   Involves the retailer's collecting an assortment of goods and services from various suppliers and offering them to final consumers.

Specialty Store A retailer that concentrates on selling one goods or service line, such as apparel and its accessories, toys, furniture, or muffler repair.

Standard Merchandise Classification A standardized dollar control product classification system developed by the National Retail Merchants Association. The use of this system enables retailers to compare their performance to that of others.

Standardization A strategy of directly applying a domestic market retail strategy to foreign markets.

Stimulus A cue (social or commercial) or a drive (physical) meant to motivate or arouse a person to act.

Stock-Counting System A unit control system that determines the number of units on hand at regular intervals by recording inventory on hand, purchases, sales volume, and shortages during a specified time period.

Stock Overage The amount by which a physical inventory value exceeds the book inventory figures. This generally occurs when there are errors in conducting a physical inventory or in maintaining a book inventory.

Stock Shortage The amount by which a retail book inventory figure exceeds a physical ending inventory. Stock shortages are the result of such factors as pilferage, bookkeeping errors, unrecorded breakage, etc.

Stock-to-Sales Ratio An inventory-level planning method that assumes a retailer wants to maintain a specified ratio of goods on hand to sales.

Stock Turnover Represents the number of times during a specified period, usually one year, that the average inventory on hand is sold. Stock turnover can be calculated in units or in dollars (at retail or at cost):

Annual rate of stock turnover (in units) =

$$\frac{\text{Number of units sold during year}}{\text{Average inventory on hand (in units)}}$$

Annual rate of stock turnover (in retail dollars) =

$$\frac{\text{Net yearly sales (in retail dollars)}}{\text{Average inventory on hand (in retail dollars)}}$$

Annual rate of stock turnover (at cost) =

$$\frac{\text{Cost of goods sold during the year}}{\text{Average inventory on hand (at cost)}}$$

Storability Product Grouping Classifies and displays products requiring special handling and storage together.

Store Image The way in which a store is defined in a shopper's mind, partly by its functional qualities and partly by an aura of psychological attributes.

Store Loyalty Exists when a consumer regularly patronizes a retailer that he or she knows, likes, and trusts.

Store Maintenance Includes all the activities involved in managing the retailer's physical facilities.

Store Positioning Enables a retailer to determine how consumers perceive the company (its image) relative to its retail category and its competitors.

Storefront The total physical exterior of the store itself, including marquees, entrances, windows, lighting, and construction materials.

Straight Lease Requires the retailer to pay a fixed amount per month over the life of the lease. It is the simplest, most straightforward type of lease.

Straight Traffic Flow Presents displays and aisles in a rectangular or gridiron pattern.

Strategic Approach Concentrates on planning for and adapting to a complex, changing environment.

Strategic Profit Model Involves the planning of a retailer's strategy based on both return on assets (which focuses on asset turnover and profit margin) and return on net worth (which focuses on financial leverage):

Strategic profit model =

Asset turnover × Profit margin
× Financial leverage =
Return on net worth

Strategy Mix Composed of location, operating procedures, goods/services offered, pricing tactics, and promotion methods.

String A group of stores, usually with similar or compatible product lines, that has located along a street or highway.

Supermarket A self-service food store with grocery, meat, and produce departments, and minimum annual sales of $2 million. Includes conventional supermarkets, combination stores, superstores, box (limited-line) stores, and warehouse stores.

Superstore A food-based retailer that is larger and more diversified than a conventional supermarket but usually smaller and less diversified than a combination store.

Supervision The manner of providing a job environment that encourages accomplishment.

Survey A research technique whereby information is systematically gathered from respondents by communicating with them. A survey can be conducted in person, over the telephone, or via the mail.

Tactics Actions involving the daily and short-run operations of a retailer.

Tall Organization An organization with several levels of supervision. This leads to close supervision and fewer employees reporting to each manager.

Target Market The consumer group that a retailer tries to satisfy.

Terms of Occupancy Include ownership or leasing terms, operations and maintenance costs, taxes, zoning restrictions, and voluntary regulations.

Theme-Setting Display Interior display where the product offering is positioned in a thematic environment or setting.

Theory X A traditional view of motivation assuming that personnel must be closely supervised and controlled.

Theory Y A more modern view of motivation that assumes personnel can use self-management and can be delegated authority.

Theory Z An emerging view that assumes employees can

be given a more participatory role in defining their jobs and share some decision making with management.

Time Demands The time a retailer needs to spend operating a business. They vary by goods or service category, by consumer demand and needs, and by the owner's/manager's ability to automate operations or delegate activities to others.

Time Utilization Refers to the types of activities in which a consumer is involved and the amount of time allocated to them.

Top-Down Budgeting Places decisions in the hands of upper management. These decisions are then communicated down the line to succeeding levels of managers. Top managers centrally direct and control budgets.

Trading Area The geographic area from which a store draws its customers.

Trading Area Overlap Occurs when the trading areas of stores in different locations encroach upon one another. In the overlap area, the same customers are served by both stores.

Training Programs Used to teach new (and old) personnel how best to perform their jobs or how to improve themselves.

Transfer of Title When ownership changes from supplier to buyer.

Trickle-Across Theory States that within any social class there are innovative consumers who act as opinion leaders.

Trickle-Down Theory States that a fashion is passed from the upper to the lower social classes through three vertical stages: distinctive, emulation, and economic emulation.

UPC See Universal Product Code.

Unbundled Pricing Involves a retailer charging a separate price for each service provided.

Uncontrollable Variables Those aspects of business to which the retailer must adapt (such as laws, the economy, and competition). See Controllable Variables.

Understored Area A geographic area having too few stores selling a specified good or service to satisfy the needs of its population.

Uniform Contract Involves terms that are standard or have already been agreed on, and the order is handled in a routine manner.

Unit Control Relates to the quantities of merchandise handled during a stated time period.

Unit Pricing Practice required by various states, whereby certain sized food retailers must express price both in terms of the total price of an item and the price per unit of measure.

Universal Product Code (UPC) An industrywide classification for coding information onto merchandise through a series of thick and thin vertical lines. This technology enables retailers to instantaneously record information on a product's model number, size, color, and so on, when an item is sold; and transmits the data to a computer that monitors unit sales. The UPC is not readable by humans.

Unplanned Business District A retail location where two or more stores are situated together or in close proximity; this proximity is not the result of prior planning.

Usage Rate Average sales per day, in units, of merchandise.

Value Pricing Occurs when prices are set on the basis of fair value for both the service provider and the consumer.

Variable Markup Policy A strategy whereby the markups for separate goods/service categories may differ.

Variable Pricing A pricing strategy wherein a retailer alters prices to coincide with fluctuations in cost or consumer demand.

Variety Store A retail establishment selling a wide assortment of inexpensive and popularly priced goods and services such as stationery, gift items, toys, housewares, confectionary items, and shoe repair.

Vending Machine A retail format that involves the coin-operated dispensing of goods and services. The vending machine eliminates the use of sales personnel, and allows for around-the-clock sales.

Vertical Cooperative-Advertising Agreement Enables a manufacturer or a wholesaler and a retailer to share an advertisement.

Vertical Marketing System Consists of all the levels of independently owned businesses along a channel of distribution. Goods and services are normally distributed through one of three types of vertical marketing system: independent, partially integrated, and fully integrated.

Vertical Price Fixing Occurs when manufacturers or wholesalers are able to control the retail prices of their goods and services. All interstate fair trade regulations were terminated by the Consumer Goods Pricing Act.

Vertical Retail Audit An in-depth analysis of a firm's performance in one area of its retail operations.

Video-Ordering System Can be in-store or in-home based. In an in-store system, a customer orders merchandise by entering data into a self-prompting computerized video-display monitor. The order is processed by the computer; then the consumer goes to a checkout area where he or she picks up and pays for the merchandise. An in-home video-ordering system can rely on television programming, videotex programming, or video merchandising catalogs.

Visibility A site's ability to be seen by pedestrian and vehicular traffic.

Visual Inspection System A unit control system that uses stock cards to monitor inventory levels.

Want Book A notebook in which store employees record items desired by customers but unstocked or out of stock.

Want Slip A slip on which store employees record requested merchandise that are unstocked or out of stock.

Warehouse Membership Club See Buying Club.

Warehouse Store A discount retailer that offers a moderate number of food items in a no-frills setting.

Weeks' Supply Method An inventory-level planning method wherein stock on hand is equal to several weeks' anticipated sales. This method assumes that stock carried is in direct proportion to sales. Under this method:

Beginning-of-month planned inventory level (at retail) = Average weekly sales × Number of weeks to be stocked

Weighted Application Blank   A form whereby criteria that best correlate with job success (which can be measured by longer tenure, higher sales volume, and less absenteeism) are given more weight than others. After a weighted score has been totaled for each application blank, a minimum score can be determined to use as a cutoff point for hiring.

Wheel of Retailing   Theory stating that retail innovators first appear as low-price operators with a low cost structure and low profit-margin requirements. Over time, the innovators upgrade the merchandise they carry and improve store facilities and customer services. As these innovators become mature, they become vulnerable to new discount retailers with lower cost structures.

Yield Management Pricing   Used when a service retailer determines the combination of prices that yield the highest level of revenues for a given time period.

Zero-Based Budgeting   Practice followed when a firm starts each budget period from scratch and outlines the expenditures that would be necessary to reach the company's goals during that period. All expenses must be justified each time a budget is devised.

Name Index

Subject Index

Selected Operating Results for Specialty Stores and Department Stores, 1986

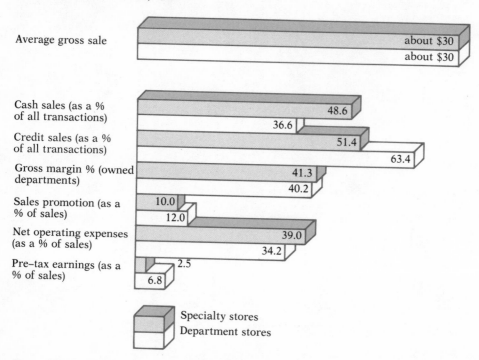

	Specialty stores	Department stores
Average gross sale	about $30	about $30
Cash sales (as a % of all transactions)	48.6	36.6
Credit sales (as a % of all transactions)	51.4	63.4
Gross margin % (owned departments)	41.3	40.2
Sales promotion (as a % of sales)	10.0	12.0
Net operating expenses (as a % of sales)	39.0	34.2
Pre-tax earnings (as a % of sales)	2.5	6.8

Source: "'86: Better FOR Some," *Stores* (November 1987), pp. 92–94; and authors' estimates. Copyright National Retail Merchants Association 1987. Reprinted by permission.

Selected Performance Data for Full-Line Discount Stores, 1986

Product Category	Percentage of Industry Sales	Annual Sales Per Square Foot ($)	Percentage Gross Margin
Ladies' wear	19.0	195	31.3
Housewares	13.7	189	24.8
Men's/boys' wear	11.0	144	34.2
Hardware and paint	8.1	188	32.7
Consumer electronics	7.6	338	17.2
Health and beauty aids	7.1	227	19.3
Automotives	6.6	283	25.2
Toys	5.5	221	27.2
Sporting goods	4.8	197	28.5
Domestics	4.5	145	35.0

Source: "Full–Line Discount Store Productivity," *Discount Store News* (July 20, 1987), p. 22. Reprinted by permission. Copyright Lebhar–Friedman, Inc., 425 Park Avenue, N.Y., N.Y. 10022.